Countries, Peoples & Cultures

Eastern Europe

Countries, Peoples & Cultures

Eastern Europe

First Edition

Volume 4

Editor

Michael Shally-Jensen, PhD

SALEM PRESS
A Division of EBSCO Information Services, Inc.
Ipswich, Massachusetts

Grey House
Publishing

947
Ea13c

Publisher's Cataloging-In-Publication Data
(Prepared by The Donohue Group, Inc.)

Eastern Europe / editor, Michael Shally-Jensen, PhD. – First edition.

pages : illustrations ; cm. – (Countries, peoples & cultures ; v. 4)

Includes bibliographical references and index.
ISBN: 978-1-61925-794-8 (v. 4)
ISBN: 978-1-61925-800-6 (set)

1. Europe, Eastern – History. 2. Europe, Eastern – Economic conditions. 3. Europe, Eastern – Social life and customs. 4. Europe, Eastern – Religion. I. Shally-Jensen, Michael. II. Series: Countries, peoples & cultures ; v. 4.

DJK38 .E27 2015
947

First Printing
PRINTED IN CANADA

Contents

Publisher's Note

Countries, Peoples & Cultures: Eastern Europe is the fourth volume of a new 9-volume series from Salem Press. *Countries, Peoples & Cultures* offers valuable insight into the social, cultural, economic, historical and religious practices and beliefs of nearly every country around the globe.

Following the extensive introduction that summarizes this politically and physically complex part of the world, this volume provides 20-page profiles of the 25 countries that make up eastern Europe. Each includes colorful maps—one highlighting the country's location in the world, and one with its major cities and natural landmarks—and a country flag, plus 10 categories of information: General Information; Environment & Geography; Customs & Courtesies; Lifestyle; Cultural History; Culture; Society; Social Development; Government; and Economy. Each profile also includes full color photographs, valuable tables of information including fun "Do You Know?" facts, and a comprehensive Bibliography.

Each country profile combines must-have statistics, such as population, language, size, climate, and currency, with the flavor and feel of the land. You'll read about favorite foods, arts & entertainment, youth culture, women's rights, health care, and tourism, for a comprehensive picture of the country, its people, and their culture.

Appendix One: World Governments, focuses on 21 types of governments found around the world today, from Commonwealth and Communism to Treaty System and Failed State. Each government profile includes its Guiding Premise, Structure, Citizen's Role, and modern-day examples.

Appendix Two: World Religions, focuses on 10 of the world's major religions from African religious traditions to Sikhism. Each religion profile includes number of adherents, basic tenets, major figures and holy sites, and major rites and celebrations.

The nine volumes of *Countries, Peoples & Cultures* are: *Central & South America; Central, South & Southeast Asia; Western Europe; Eastern Europe; Middle East & North Africa; East & Southern Africa; West & Central Africa; North America & the Caribbean; and East Asia & the Pacific.*

Introduction

Eastern Europe is as much a political and historical entity as it is a geographical one. It is an area in which relatively few of the major physical features, such as mountains and rivers, have played a major role in establishing boundaries that separate peoples, cultures, and nations. In part because of this fact, a variety of conflicting definitions of the region and its limits exist. Most scholars agree that Eastern Europe undoubtedly includes the countries of Poland, the Czech Republic, Slovakia, Hungary, Romania, Bulgaria, Albania, and the countries of the former Yugoslavia (Slovenia, Croatia, Bosnia and Herzegovina, Macedonia, Montenegro, Serbia, and Kosovo). But things get a little tentative after that. Many would broaden the definition to include additional countries of the Soviet-era Eastern bloc—namely, Estonia, Latvia, and Lithuania (the Baltic states), in the north, and Belarus, Ukraine, and Moldova, in the east. Moreover, if one accepts this eastern extension and wishes to take account, as well, of the boundary running along the crests of the Ural and Caucasus mountains and the shores of the Caspian Sea, then Eastern Europe would include Russia itself—or, at least, the western portion of Russia. This is the approach taken here. We cast a wide net over the region and include all of the above, along with the border states (Georgia, Armenia, and Azerbaijan) of the Caucasus region.

Geography and Language

The map of Eastern Europe presents a number of notable physical features. To the north is the great North European Plain skirting the southern and eastern edges of the Baltic Sea. This plain is open to both east and west and ranges from 250 to 350 miles inland from the shore. Its southern limit gives way to the Carpathian Mountains, a large, winding chain that traverses much of the central portion of Eastern Europe. To the west

of the Carpathians lies the great Danube River valley, which runs first north-south and then eastward to the base of the Carpathians and out to the Black Sea. Other prominent rivers in the region include the Vistula (in Poland), the Oder (Czech Republic and Poland), the Dnieper (Belarus and Ukraine), and the Don and Volga (both in Russia). In the south, finally, lies the Balkan Peninsula, a rugged, semi-mountainous region situated between the Danube valley, the Adriatic Sea, and the Black Sea. The countries there lie amid the Dinaric Alps, in the west, and the Balkan and Rhodope ranges, in the east. In general, the climate of Eastern Europe is continental, with cold snowy winters and warm humid summers. Temperatures decline toward the north and east, while precipitation decreases toward the south and east. However, an incredible array of local microclimates exists, from the almost Mediterranean southern Adriatic coast to the high Alpine conditions of the Carpathian peaks, with virtually everything in between.

The region is marked by the predominance of Slavic languages, but with notable exceptions. The migration of the Slavs from inside modern-day Russia from the 6th to the 10th century spread the language broadly westward and southward throughout central and eastern Europe. Three main branches developed: West Slavic, which produced modern Polish, Czech, and Slovak; East Slavic, which produced modern Russian, Belorussian, and Ukrainian; and South Slavic, which produced Slovene, Serbo-Croat, Macedonian, and Bulgarian. Romanian and Moldovan, meanwhile, are Romance languages ultimately hailing from Latin, while Hungarian is a Finno-Ugric language distantly related to Finnish and Estonian but with a marked admixture of elements from other European languages. Lithuanian and Latvian are both Baltic languages yet are not mutually intelligible. Albanian, finally, is a separate language deriving from a separate language branch (Albanian). Thus, just as Eastern Europe is physically diverse, so too is it diverse with respect to its people.

Modern History

Throughout its history, Eastern Europe, by virtue of its position, has been buffeted by every people, religion, philosophy, and political current flowing between the open vista of Eurasia on the one hand and the bounded peninsula of Western Europe on the other. It has always been relatively fragmented culturally, despite the imposition of overarching political or religious schemes atop this diversity at various times in the past. Its countries were all communist states between the end of World War II and the collapse of communism beginning in 1989. Russia, as the home of the Union of Soviet Socialist Republics (USSR), was long the nerve center of what was once the second greatest military and industrial power in the world; yet each country cultivated its own homespun version of communism, as well, and in varying degrees of intensity.

The Russian Revolution of 1917 laid the groundwork for an extension of communism to some of the nations of the old Russian Empire (e.g., Belarus, Ukraine, the Caucasus). Under Josef Stalin from the mid-1920s, the fledgling states of the USSR underwent a brutal form of industrialization where entire populations were forcefully relocated and required to produce food and goods for the Soviet conglomerate. By the time of the onset of World War II, the Soviet Union had made impressive gains, albeit at the expense of millions of human lives. At first a nonaggression pact with Hitler was put in place, but in 1941 the USSR was forced to defend itself against a Nazi invasion. The invasion, in fact, marked the beginning of the end of the German Reich and its visions of a thousand-year reign. During the siege of Leningrad (Saint Petersburg), and at battles in Stalingrad (Volgograd), Moscow, and elsewhere, the German army, once an unstoppable force, hit the immovable object of Soviet defenses and ultimately yielded its lead in the war. Meanwhile, the Russians themselves were devastated during the long confrontation.

In 1945 Stalin, Churchill, and Roosevelt met at Yalta (southern Crimea), formally ending the war and hammering out a template of postwar Europe that divided the continent into various "spheres of influence" between the East and the West. In subsequent years the Soviet Union declared its purposes in no uncertain terms: the Baltic states of Estonia, Latvia, and Lithuania were made Soviet republics within the USSR, while Poland, Czechoslovakia, Hungary, Romania, and Bulgaria were folded into the Soviet sphere of influence. Yugoslavia and Albania became communist states of their own accord, leaving them less subject to Moscow's will.

For most of the rest of the 20th century, the Eastern bloc countries maintained communist governments that denied their citizens freedom of speech, freedom of travel, and freedom of assembly. (The constraints were somewhat less onerous in Yugoslavia and Albania.) In many respects, the individual states became pawns in the Cold War with the West. Their leaders imposed harsh penalties for political opposition or any contacts with the West, seeking to stifle outside influences. A 1956 uprising in Budapest and a 1968 attempt at loosening communism in Czechoslovakia were suppressed by means of Soviet tanks. Meanwhile, countries such as Hungary and Romania, which had been moderately well off before the creation of centralized economies under communism, became poorer and less hospitable. Throughout the 1970s and early 1980s, economic stagnation held sway in most of Eastern Europe, even as Soviet armies operated on Cold War fronts across the globe and East European athletes made headlines for their record-breaking performances. The Russian space and nuclear programs, too, seemed to suggest the workings of high-achieving, well-ordered nation.

Under the stimulus of Soviet leader Mikhail Gorbachev, beginning in 1985 economic goals were shifted from heavy industry to areas such as computers, automation, new materials, and new technologies. In this way the bloc was to overcome the backwardness that had become increasingly evident both internally and externally.

Gorbachev's dual policies of *glasnost* (openness) and *perestroika* (restructuring) brought some new vitality to the system, but immediately there was a counter-reaction from the old guard (who had benefitted from the old ways). The Communist Party was soon in tatters, as the crimes and misdemeanors of its leaders came to be widely disseminated and the horrors of the past revealed in terrible detail. By 1989 the oppositional Solidarity movement in Poland was gaining ground, as were movements in Czechoslovakia, Hungary, and East Germany. When the Berlin Wall came down that year, it marked the end of an era. Subsequent revolutions took place in Romania, Lithuania, Yugoslavia, and elsewhere—including, in 1991, the Soviet Union itself. A great period of instability and experimentation ensued, as defunct states and former controlled economies became transformed into something resembling democratic nations with capitalist economies. In Russia, entire industries were taken over by quasi-autonomous "oligarchs"—potent capitalist operators, usually with muscle behind them. In the former Yugoslavia, the break up was even more traumatic, as age-old ethnic hostilities erupted into gruesome sectional wars and genocidal mass killings. Still today, twenty years after the fact, animosities linger. More recently, Ukraine, after throwing off its Soviet shackles, saw the return of a pro-Russian government, its ouster in a popular uprising, and the onset of armed hostilities with Russia over Crimea and Ukraine's eastern provinces. Thus, as "free" as Eastern Europe is today, it remains forever tied to its past.

Culturally, despite these upheavals, Eastern Europe remains a rich depository in all areas—literature, art, music, dance, film, philosophy, folk traditions, and more. In recent years, it has begun to exceed all expectations and now features a thriving tourism industry and significant advances in science and technology along with increasingly robust economies, many of them tied to the European Union. Indeed, the old East-West division has started to succumb to a new differential based on globalization and forward thinking. Much of Eastern Europe is now "Europe East," even as conflicts with Russia, the easternmost contingent and historic power center, persist.

Michael Shally-Jensen, PhD

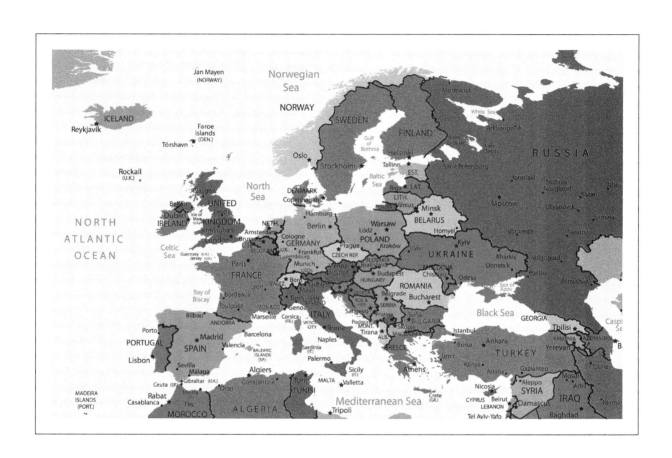

Eastern Europe

Skanderbeg Square, Tirana, Albania

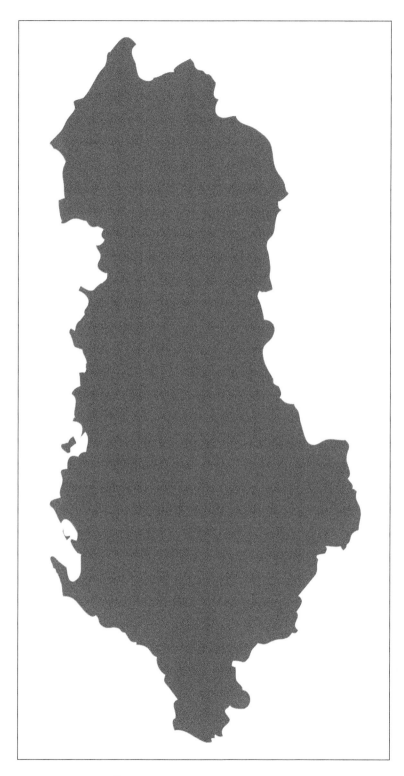

ALBANIA

Introduction

The Republic of Albania (Republika e Shqipërisë) is in southeastern Europe on the Balkan Peninsula. Emerging in the 1990s from 46 years under a government considered the most repressive in the Communist Bloc, Albania has struggled toward democracy, economic stability, and recognition as a partner in the European community. Its assets include rich mineral resources, beautiful seacoasts, and a high literacy rate.

The nation is particularly known for its folk arts, which are rich and varied. Albania, almost uniquely, retains an oral epic tradition, and in the rural north, a single performer will sing narratives from the past, usually of heroes battling the Turks. Folk dances vary from region to region, and southern dances often incorporate polyphonic music, an ancient and still living tradition. Painting and architecture in Albania embody both Eastern and Western, ancient and modern artistic traditions in astonishing variety.

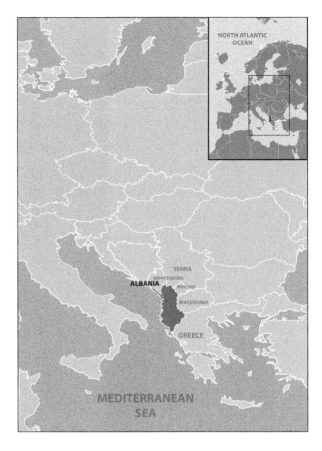

GENERAL INFORMATION

Official Language: Albanian
Population: 2,893,005 (2015 estimate)
Currency: Albanian lek
Coins: One hundred qindarka equal one lek, although coins are no longer issued in qindarka. Coins are issued in denominations of 5, 10, 20, 50, and 100 lekë.
Land Area: 27,398 square kilometers (10,578 square miles)
Water Area: 1,350 square kilometer (521 square miles)

National Anthem: "Himni i Flamurit" ("Hymn to the Flag")
Capital: Tirana
Time Zone: GMT +2
Flag Description: The Albanian flag is solid red with a black two-headed eagle emblazoned in the center. The historic nature of the flag harkens back to the country's independence in the fifteenth century, when the double-headed eagle acted as the seal of Gjergj Kastrioti Skanderbeg, the Dragon of Albania, who led the revolt against the Ottoman Empire.

Population

Albania's ethnic demographic statistics are out of date, with the latest official records dating back to 1989. At that time, ethnic Albanians made up 95 percent of the population. The other five percent include Greeks, Vlachs, Roma (gypsies), Serbs, Macedonians, and Bulgarians. In the past 20 years, some argue that the number of Greek

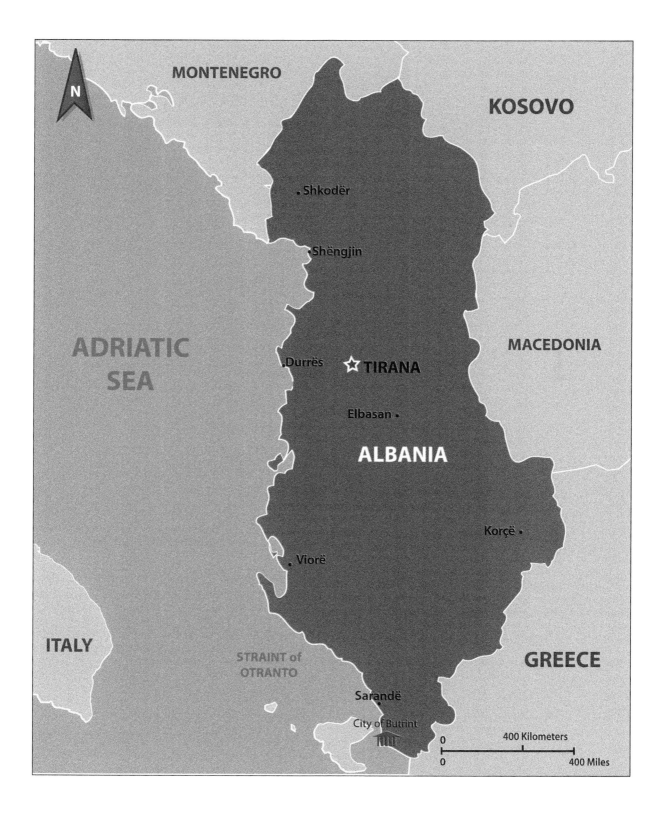

Principal Cities by Population (2011):

- Tirana (536,998)
- Durrës (199,073)
- Lushnjë (143,276)
- Fier (125,353)
- Elbasan (116,971)
- Vlorë (104,827)
- Shkodër (96,328)
- Korçë (88,358)
- Berat (64,497)

immigrants has increased, with estimates ranging from one percent to 12 percent of the population.

Most Albanians live in political and educational centers, ports, and industrial cities: the capital Tirana (or Tiranë), for instance; the port of Durrës; industrial Elbasan; Korça (or Korçë), the carpet center; and Shkodra (or Shkodër), where major rivers and highways cross. In contrast, rural areas, particularly the mountains, are sparsely populated.

Tirana is Albania's most populous city. It has also experienced some of the fastest population growth of any European city since the last decade of the 20th century. Within 10 years of the fall of Albania's communist regime, in fact, Tirana's population had doubled; the exodus of many of its inhabitants was offset by a crush of economic refugees from other parts of Albania.

Languages

The Albanian language taught in schools since 1909 is derived from the Tosk dialect. Although Albanian is an ancient Indo-European language, probably predating Greek, like most languages it has been modified by assimilating vocabulary from other peoples: first classical Greek, then Latin, then Turkish.

Before 1909, Albania's poets and other writers composed in their separate dialects or in Greek or Italian, transcribing their work using different alphabets: the Roman, Cyrillic, and Arabic. As the 20th century began, Albanian nationalists realized that without a common language and alphabet, a unified nation would

not be possible. Accordingly, Albanian statesmen and intellectuals met and adopted a thirty-six-letter, Roman-based alphabet and an official Albanian language.

Native People & Ethnic Groups

Albanians believe themselves descended from the earliest Aryan peoples in Europe. Their ancestors, the Illyrians, settled the land in prehistoric times. The earliest known king of Illyria, Hyllus, died in 1225 BCE. The Illyria of Hyllus and his successors comprised not only Albania, but also Dalmatia, Croatia, Bosnia and Herzegovina, Montenegro, and much of present-day Serbia. Its capital was Shkodra (Scutari), still a major Albanian city.

Religions

Albania's religious institutions, like its language, have been affected by political movements. In 1967, the communist government, declaring Albania the world's first official atheist nation, ordered that all mosques and churches be closed. Since 1990, private religious practice has been permitted and religious identification has recently been taken up again by Albanian citizens. The 2011 census revealed that 56.7 percent of religious Albanians are Sunni Muslims, 2.09 percent are Bektashi Order, 10.03 percent are Catholics, 6.75 percent are Orthodox Christians, and 2.5 percent are atheists. Albania is, therefore, the only European nation with a Muslim majority.

The Albanian Orthodox church, though similar to Greek and Eastern Orthodox Christian churches, is independent, and has been since its founding in 1922. Since 1990, several Protestant churches have established footholds in Albanian cities, and their membership is growing.

Climate

The coastal climate is Mediterranean, with hot, dry summers, especially along the Adriatic. In contrast, Albania's mountains can be cold and difficult. Heavy snowfall in February 2012, for example, isolated mountain communities, and NATO's Euro-Atlantic Disaster Response

Coordination Centre (EADRCC) provided aerial delivery of food and other necessities. Melting snowpack in December 2010 caused heavy flooding and mass evacuations, while prompting assistance from both NATO and neighboring countries. Still, in the capital, the average daytime temperature during the winter is around 7° Celsius (45° Fahrenheit), while its summertime counterpart averages around 28° Celsius (82° Fahrenheit). Albania, like Greece to its south, is subject to earthquakes, and, at times, tsunamis have ravaged coastal towns.

ENVIRONMENT & GEOGRAPHY

Topography

Albania is bordered on the south by Greece and the Ionian Sea, on the east by Serbia and Montenegro, on the north and east by Macedonia, and on the west by the Adriatic Sea. Although it is a small country, Albania offers dramatic environmental contrasts. Along the Adriatic Sea, the "Albanian Riviera" is a low-lying coastline of broad, sandy beaches and extensive lagoons. The coast along the Ionian Sea rises in steep cliffs from smaller, rockier beaches of fine white sand.

Large lakes, including Lake Ohrid, the deepest on the Balkan Peninsula at 294 meters (931 feet), extend along Albania's borders with Yugoslavia, Macedonia, and Greece. This is limestone country, and caves abound. In the interior and north rise high mountains, the Alpet, or Albanian Alps. Mount Korab, near the Macedonian border, is Albania's highest, at 2,764 meters (9,067 feet).

Plants & Animals

Pine woods border Albania's Adriatic beaches, and olive, fig, and citrus groves flourish near both coasts. The Ionian coast from Vlorë to Saranda is called, for its vegetation, "the Riviera of flowers." In contrast, the mountains in the interior and north are heavily forested with conifer, oak, and beech groves. Forests cover over 36 percent of Albania's land.

Among the animals native to the forests are wolves, wild boars, brown bears, chamois and roe deer, the lynx, two kinds of wildcat, foxes, jackals, weasels, and pine martens. Albania's lakes provide nesting for water birds, notably the endangered Dalmatian pelican. The Karavasta Lagoon (now Divjakë-Karavasta National Park) is its westernmost nesting site.

To preserve Albania's beauty and the diversity of its plant and animal life, the country has established six national forests, 24 nature reserves, and 2,000 national monuments. Unfortunately, available funding is insufficient to preserve these sites and to reverse the environmental pollution that threatens them.

Dangers range from hunting and woodcutting within the reserves (illegal but common) to widespread pollution of waterways. As standard practice, raw sewage is pumped untreated into Albania's rivers. Increasingly, this sewage contains chemicals leaked from deteriorating factories built 25 or 30 years ago by communist benefactors. Albania's government is environmentally sensitive; it is party to most international treaties and initiatives dealing with the environment. However, it lacks the funds to follow through.

CUSTOMS & COURTESIES

Greetings

In Albania, the general greeting habit is a handshake. When greeting each other for the first time, a man and a woman may also typically shake hands. Family members or acquaintances might kiss each other on the cheek when greeting. They also may address each other as "Zoti" ("Mr.") or "Zonja" ("Mrs."), followed by the surname. Albanians make direct, steady eye contact when greeting. Eye contact is also especially important when having a conversation. Albanians believe that steady eye contact is a sign of sincerity.

Personal space is either minimal or about arm's length and depends on the familiarity of the persons involved. It is customary for Albanians who know each other to stand or sit close to each

Traditional Albanian peasant costume.

other when talking. For lesser known acquaintances, Albanians tend to allow more personal space when meeting and conversing. Among friends, it is customary for Albanians to frequently grab the other's hand and hold it while talking. They also often touch friends' arms when talking, though they are more reserved with new acquaintances. Men typically do not enter a woman's personal space; such practices are thought to be inconsiderate and too forward.

Albanians address professional people with their title when greeting them, followed by the person's surname. When attending a business meeting, Albanians greet first those who are considered most important, such as business and political leaders. In fact, if such a person enters a meeting, other attendees stand in respect.

Gestures & Etiquette

Albanians are generally very expressive and not at all reserved with gestures. They use their arms and hands frequently. For example, Albanians call a person to them by extending an arm and gesturing with their fingers to come forward.

Contrary to many gestures in other countries, the gesture of shaking the head from side to side means "yes," and nodding up and down means "no." Albanians will also let a person know whether he or she does not want something offered to eat or drink by wagging the index finger and making a slight noise to suggest "no thank you."

Albanians are known to spend long hours talking with friends and family at home and in cafés, and view time as flexible whether for business or social activities. When talking, Albanians tend to be indirect when discussing issues that they consider deeply emotional. However, when discussing more superficial topics, they can be very direct and respect directness in others. They hold their family in high regard and in conversation will convey the family in the best terms possible. Albanians also talk about politics quite openly and can be very engaged when hearing about the politics in foreign countries. To that end, Albanians are especially welcoming to and curious about foreigners, as their country was closed to visitors during the Soviet era.

Eating/Meals

Though Albanian cuisine has varied little over the centuries—meat is eaten at the midday and evening meal, and includes pork, beef, chicken, lamb, and fish—the typical Albanian meal differs from the rural mountainous areas to cities and urban centers. Flat corn bread is a main staple in farming and mountain communities, which have experienced famine. Traditionally, the host breaks the bread before any other food is brought to the table, and each of the day's meals generally resembles the others. In urban areas, all food arrives at the lunch or dinner table at the same time. Raki, which is a clear, anise-flavored brandy, is traditionally served first as an appetizer. In late afternoon, Albanians enjoy strong coffee or tea, which often accompanies sweet pastries and fruit.

Breakfast is generally light, with bread and yogurt or jam, and coffee or tea. The main meal is lunch, during which Albanians often eat a small serving of meat (either lamb, pork, beef) or fish, bread, and a vegetable, such as a salad of fresh cucumbers, tomatoes, olives, and green peppers. Albanians also enjoy rice pilaf and potatoes, and a thick yogurt sauce with garlic is used for dipping bread. A savory pastry called byrek, which is phyllo dough containing a cheese, meat, or vegetable filling, is also popular. Beer, wine, or liquor might accompany lunch, depending on the occasion, and Albanians love strong coffee. Dinner is a smaller variation of the midday meal and is typically eaten later in the evening.

When dining at a restaurant, it is customary in Albania for a host to pay for a guest's meal. It is then protocol for the guest to repay the favor another time. When business meetings end well or with an important agreement, then colleagues often celebrate by going out for dinner immediately afterward.

Visiting

Albanians spend ample time visiting with friends and family at home, as hospitality is extremely important to them. In fact, it is common for people to drop by unexpectedly, and they are traditionally welcomed with open arms. Their concept of hospitality, known as mikpritja, includes valuing guests as sacred visitors, and Albanians use the greeting "Mirë se vini" (meaning "welcome") to convey this general notion.

Albanians prefer visitors to arrive a few minutes late, as punctuality is not typically of great importance. In fact, Albanians prefer a looser adherence to time than in many European countries. If a situation calls for a gift (such as an invitation to dinner), an Albanian will not open it in front of the giver, but in private after her or she has left. Otherwise, gifts are not common for adults, and it is more customary to bring a small gift for the host's children. Hosts traditionally offer visitors a glass of raki, as well as coffee and sweets. It is considered rude to refuse such offers, especially in the host's home. They might also offer a pair of slippers or plastic sandals to wear inside the home, as they do not customarily wear shoes inside.

When invited to a traditional meal at an Albanian's home, visitors might expect to find a large number of dishes offered, potentially more than twenty or thirty, of various sizes and types. It is polite to try each, but to not consume a typical full portion.

LIFESTYLE

Family

The traditional Albanian family is patriarchal and comprised of extended family members. Should the father die, the family is left in the care of a son. In the highland rural areas, the father has the responsibility to help the children earn a livelihood. He also divides the property among the sons, as daughters and wives traditionally do not own property in rural Albania. Rural Albanian families are also usually larger than urban families, with three or four children as opposed to one or two.

Overall, women take care of domestic responsibilities and child rearing (this may also include caring for livestock and producing dairy products in rural Albania). It is not unusual for adult children to live at home and care for aging parents in rural or urban areas. Additionally, while rural families still tend to choose their children's spouses, urban youth choose their own. Communist rule sought to end the male-dominated traditions of the clan system prevalent throughout Albania before World War II, and more women now work outside of the home, increasingly in cities.

Housing

The traditional rural home still has a ground floor for animals, and the family lives upstairs, where they cook by fire in a fireplace. There is often a loom for making use of spun goats' and sheep's wool, from which they make their own carpets and clothing. (Urban homes might have additional space for entertaining, but they do not have a place to keep animals inside.) Contemporary rural homes are mostly built with rock or stone, have one or two rooms, and a hearth for cooking; many lack running water. Urban apartments also are small and typically constructed of concrete and brick. They often lack central heating, and up to four families share bathrooms and kitchens. Similar to many rural homes, some urban houses and apartments still lack running water.

A great deal of Albania's housing was destroyed during World War II. Under communist rule, the government built more than 232,000 houses and almost 165,000 apartments to accommodate the growing, post-war, urban population. After communist rule, Albania privatized most of its public housing.

Food

The Mediterranean diet, which includes Greek, Turkish, and Italian elements, has heavily influenced Albanian cuisine. Generally, dairy is a main staple in the Albanian diet. Yogurt is combined with garlic and eaten as a dip for bread, much as it is in Greece. Yogurt can sometimes also be included in baba ghanoush, a Middle Eastern dish that consists primarily of roasted eggplant, garlic, tahini (pureed sesame seeds), lemon, and olive oil. Sour cream also figures heavily in traditional Albanian dishes that often include lamb, such as tavë kosi, and Greek feta cheeses are popular. Albanians traditionally eat some form of bread and fruit—either whole or in a jam—at every meal. The savory pastry of meat, cheese, or greens—called byrek—is a common Turkish specialty, and fruits include figs, grapes, and oranges. Figs might also be dried for the dessert hoshaf me fiq të thatë, which includes milk, sugar, and cinnamon.

Though Albanian cuisine includes an abundance of fresh vegetables, such as cucumbers, peppers, onions, and potatoes, the food can be heavy, especially in rural areas. Lamb and mutton are baked or used as the basis of many stews and rice pilaf (and even byrek), and boiled bean soups might also include meat. Kidney and liver are considered delicacies in Albania. Tavë dheu Tiranëse is a traditional specialty that is made with pieces of liver and kidney, yogurt, tomato sauce, and garlic and baked in an earthenware casserole dish. These foods are all common at the beginning of the 21st century, as ingredients

are local, and Albanians place a high value on their traditional cuisine.

Life's Milestones

The centuries-old Kanuni i Lekë Dukagjinit, or Kanun, is a set of civil, criminal, and family laws that many Albanians continue to follow. The Kanun dates from about the fifteenth century CE and describes traditional familial, marital, and religious obligations. The responsibility that Albanians have to uphold honor, called besa, and blood relationships is stronger than other obligations and dominates family life and the larger community. Because of the need to uphold honor and the family, blood feuds, called gjaks, have been common occurrences in Albania's history. They continue to some degree in the early 21st century. The ultimate goal of the family, according to the Kanun, is to marry and have children so as to increase the size of the family.

In a patriarchal society such as Albania's, the birth of a son is considered a sign of good fortune for the extended family. The hardships and wars that Albanians have faced throughout the centuries have, at times, created declining male populations. Traditional northern populations would shoot rifles into the air after a son was born. Showing respect for the dead at a funeral is also important in Albanian culture. Though there are limited numbers of funeral parlors, especially in rural areas, the dead are often placed at home for the wake for about two or three days before they are buried.

CULTURAL HISTORY

Art

During the medieval era, when the region of modern Albania was administered and influenced by the Byzantine Empire (330–1453 BCE), religious art was widespread. This included ornate mosaics in churches, such as in Tirana, Dyrrachion, and near Durrës, and richly-colored icon painting. By the end of the 15th century, Albanian art became influenced by Italian art, particularly Italian-influenced painted icons from the Renaissance era. Much of this work can still be seen in churches and on cave walls. These icons became a popular form of public folk art, which continued until the early 20th century. The Ottoman Empire's Arab influence and Orientalism (imitation of Asian or Eastern culture) led to the creation of ornate mosaics and murals. This trend dominated the country's art forms until independence in 1912. Once liberated, artists turned toward national symbols and icons, such as the Albanian national hero Gjergi Kastrioti Skanderbeg (1405–1468).

After World War II, communist control eliminated artistic expression and promoted socialist realism and the elevation of the worker in artistic representations. The Albanian Art School opened after the war, in 1946. The country's first national art gallery opened in 1954, assisting artists who depicted socialist subjects and landscapes. After the collapse of the Soviet Union, Albanian artists gained an international perspective, implementing impressionistic and expressionistic techniques. However, the fine arts of Albania have largely concentrated on realism, as a majority of modern subjects are realistic portrayals and scenes.

Architecture

Albania has a long history, having been a part of both the Greek and Roman Empires. Butrint, in the south of the country near Saranda (or Sarandë) and close to the border with Greece, was an ancient center of trade inhabited by the Chaonians, an ancient Greek tribe, dating back to between the 10th and eighth centuries BCE. Archeological efforts in the early 21st century revealed remains of both Hellenistic (Greek) and Roman artifacts and ruins. It has since been named as a World Heritage Site.

Architecture in the country has taken on regional forms that are tied somewhat to the religious affiliation of its people as well as their location, with wooded regions featuring wooden construction and coastal buildings made of clay or adobe. In the south, where the Muslim population settled, Islamic and Turkish architectural forms dominate. Traditional forms include the

Byzantine structure favored by the Ottomans, which features a square formation topped with a dome and a three-domed portico, and a more distinctly Balkan structure, which is rectangular and wooden. Several older mosques include the Berat Congregational Mosque (built in 1380) and the Iljaz Mirahori Mosque (1494). In the north of the country stand examples of the European influence on architecture. The Hapsburg Empire initiated an Austrian influence on architecture that lasted through the early 20th century.

Typical urban structures are constructed of stone, can reach five stories, and have both internal and external staircases. The lower story may have, at one time, housed animals and contained a cistern. Living quarters were above, with additional stories added to accommodate growing families. Some homes feature hand-painted wooden interiors.

Much of the country's historic architecture was destroyed during the country's communist past, but cities such as Gjirokastër and Berat stand as living examples of the country's ancient past. Under the communists, more austere, functional buildings were constructed throughout the country, with function driving design rather than cultural and historic forms. The communists ushered in an anti-urbanization policy, which fit the then-agricultural society, but did not evolve with the country's post-communist growth. For example, in the late 20th century, more than 500,000 illegal buildings were constructed in Tirana—without connection to basic needs, such as water, sewer, electricity, etc.

Drama

After the end of communist rule, Albanian cinema went through a transformation that included the development of independent films. Though the economy struggled for stability, 21st century films have included the works of young directors, as well as older directors who were active during the Soviet era. Contemporary Albanian films examine life during and after communist rule as well as the mix of traditional and global cultures young Albanians confront. The films *Parullat* (*Slogans*, 2001) by director Gjergj Xhuvani

(1963–) and *Tirana, année zero* (*Tirana, Year Zero,* 2001) by Fatmir Koçi (1959–) have won international acclaim. *Parullat* focuses on communist Albania, when slogans were used as blatant government propaganda. Told as a love story, *Tirana* is about young Albanians' search for work in other countries after the fall of communism. In 2003, the Albanian National Center of Cinematography began hosting the annual Tirana International Film Festival (TIFF), which shows Albanian and international films and aims to create a strong independent film culture in the Balkans. In 2014, over 5,400 films were submitted for consideration, and in 2015, the Albania Art Institute, the Albanian National Center of Cinematography, and the Albanian Ministry of Culture expanded TIFF to focus specifically on documentary filmmaking with a new annual festival, DocuTIFF.

Music

Invasions over the centuries influenced Albania's rich music traditions, which vary between the north and the south, between rural and urban. Rural Albanian folk music was patriotic and celebrated themes such as courage and loyalty. An individual typically sang songs of epic poetry in the north. There, songs about feuds and honor conveyed a heroic narrative that often included fighting the Turkish peoples. The lahuta, which is a single-stringed fiddle, accompanied the singing and is the most common instrument of Albanian folk music. In the south, where the Tosk dialect is spoken, more people joined in singing, which was polyphonic. They played a number of instruments, including clarinets, violins, and llautës, which are a type of lute. Northern Albanian folk music remains popular in the country's highlands.

Ottoman music's modal scales combined with Albania's northern folk music to form urban "art song" music between the two World Wars. Greek modal music also influenced southern urban music during this same time. However, after independence, efforts to purge Albanian music of Turkish influences steered the music in nationalist and lyrical directions. After World War II, folk music regained popularity, with the addition of

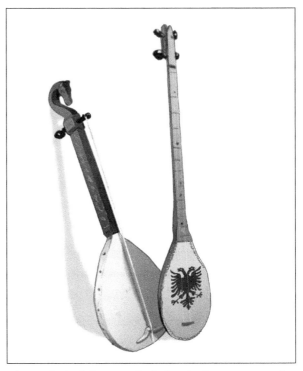

These plucked, long-necked chordophones are used in Albanian folk music.

the sharki, similar to a lute, and the two-stringed wooden instrument called the çiftelia.

During the communist era, music tended toward socialist themes. However, during Albania's post-communist era, folk music again flourished, especially with the help of the Berat music festival. During the latter part of the 20th century, Bosnian, Romani, Western European, and American music influenced Albanian music.

Dance

As with other art forms, the history of folk dance varies according to the many different ethnic influences throughout the country. Albanian folk dance typically evokes the themes of honor, bravery, and loyalty through its movements. In northern Albania, the shota dance was traditionally performed by Albanians in Kosovo to honor famed resistance fighter Shote Galica (1895– 1927), who fought the Serbian government. Today, it is danced at Albanian weddings.

The traditional, national dance is the Cham Albanian though it is also danced in Greece. (Cham Albanians are Albanians from Greece). While traditionally performed by men, women now join in the slow, graceful movements. Dancers join hands, bending their elbows up at a 90-degree angle, while one dancer is supported while kicking his or her legs high into the air. The traditional dance of Osman Taka also features dancers holding hands. However, in this dance, the lead dancer performs a few steps and then falls to his knees. Then, arching his back, he allows dancers step onto his stomach, one by one.

The Turkish Halay dance, imported from Anatolia during the Ottoman Empire's reign, features a line of male and female dancers holding their neighbors' pinky fingers. Musicians accompany the dancers with the zurna and davul. The zurna is a double-reed wind instrument, whose end resembles a trumpet, and the davul is a bass drum.

Literature

Albania's rich and varied literary history begins with the first known work in the Albanian language—the *Meshari* (*Prayer Book*, 1555) by the Catholic cleric Gjon Buzuku. The book is a compilation of the main parts of the Catholic liturgy (public worship and ritual) for Albanians to read in their own language. In addition to religious texts, Albanian literature during the Middle Ages included humanistic and Renaissance ideas. Pjetër Bogdani (1630–1689) wrote *Cuneus Prophetarum* (*The Band of Prophets*, 1685), the first considerable work of Albanian prose. It included literary theory, astronomy, physics, and history, as well as philosophy and theology. During this time, printing presses in Albania helped spread knowledge and information in the Albanian language.

Nineteenth-century romanticism took hold in Albania, most notably in the poetry of Naim Frashëri (1846–1900) and Jeronim de Rada (1814–1903). Between the two world wars, Albanian authors wrote realist works; following World War II, authors wrote novels and short stories. Communist rule in Albania strongly favored socialist realism, but a few courageous Albanians challenged this norm, such as novelist and poet Ismail Kadare (1936–). Kadare, who has been a candidate for the Nobel Prize in Literature, has been published in more than 40 countries. His writing has often been critical of those in power in Albania. In the dystopic novel *The Palace of Dreams* (1981), Kadare depicted the government's manipulative control of the people in a way that pointed to oppression exerted by Albania's authoritarian ruler at the time, Enver Hoxha (1908–1985).

CULTURE

Arts & Entertainment

Albania's economy floundered during the country's post-communist transformation into a global culture. During the last decade of the 20th century, arts funding was virtually nonexistent. However, 21st century painters, film directors, writers, and musicians have been exploring the country's communist past and conflicts while exploring the existence of Albania in a global culture.

Modern Albanian painting still emphasizes socialist realism as far as its portrayal of realistic people and scenes, often capturing the daily challenges Albanians face. However, in some artistic works, the influence of impressionism and post-impressionism remains strong. Artist Alush Shima's (1942–) application of bright primary colors to paint still lifes and seaside landscapes are reminiscent of the French painter Paul Cézanne (1839–1906). Contemporary Albanian painter Toni Milaqi (1974–) studied engraving, which is evident in many of his paintings that feature bright acrylic colors, bold lines, and near-graphic detail. The influence of expressionism is also evident in his style, which includes social critiques of political and religious institutions, as well as war and violence. Another contemporary artist, Genc Mulliqi (1966–), is a sculptor, whose large ceramic heads are part of his exploration of Albanian identity and the need to belong.

Contemporary Albanian writers and poets are also confronting their country's recent history. Arian Leka's (1966–) collection of poems, *Strabizëm* (*Strabismus*, 2004) deals with pain and loss. Brikena Smajli's (1970–) poems and recent novel, *Përditë ndërtoj shtëpi me ashkla* (*Every Day I Build a House with Splinters*, 2006), center on women's emerging role in post-communist and patriarchal Albania. She is among the first generation of women publishing literature in a democratic Albania. Novelist Ornela Vorpsi (1968–), whose book is *Le pays où l'on ne meurt jamais* (*The Country Where No One Ever Dies*, 2003), fled Albania for Italy at 22 years of age. The novel features a young girl growing up in Albania and facing the challenges that late-20th-century Albanians were forced to confront under communist rule.

Albanian musicians, too, are expressing recent history in their work. The 2003 release by Albanian composer Aleksandër Peçi (1951–), called "Albanian Lament," folds in the traditional Albanian dirge with recent tragedies, such as the sinking of an Albanian refugee ship in 1997. Peçi mixes emotional singing with modern, electronic instruments that have only recently been used in Albanian music. A substantial effort has also contributed to the cataloging and storing of traditional folk, classical, and contemporary music in Albania. Muslim, Christian, and Jewish music has also been included in this effort, undertaken by the International Society for Contemporary Music (ISCM). The ISCM continues to preserve rare music manuscripts and scores. The Network of the Documentation and Communication Centre for Regional Music (DCCRM) has published numerous Albanian scores and compositions in an effort to spread knowledge of Albanian music.

Cultural Sites & Landmarks

The many cultural sites and landmarks of Albania are a testament to the region's long history. Ancient buildings that date back to the Illyrians (ancient inhabitants of the Balkan region) dot Albania's landscape. In turn, the Greeks and Romans left traces of their culture and architecture. The architecture of the Byzantine Empire is seen in the country's church cupolas and monasteries. The Ottomans built numerous fortresses and mosques, many of which have been refurbished. This varied and rich history was recognized by the United Nations Educational, Scientific and Cultural Organization (UNESCO) when it designated three sites in Albania as World Heritage Sites: the ancient city of Butrint, and the historic centers of the towns of Berat and Gjirokastër.

The ancient seaside city of Butrint was designated as a World Heritage Site in 1992. The earliest archaeological findings in Butrint date to somewhere between the 10th and eighth centuries BCE. First flourishing as an ancient Greek city, Butrint became a Roman protectorate and later fell under the rule of Byzantium. Ruins that remain from the Greek era include walls of an acropolis (early citadels), while parts of a theater and a bath date from the Roman era. Parts of a Byzantine baptistery and a palace are also preserved. The area is now the Butrint National Park. Near Butrint, Greek ruins are also found in the southern Albanian seaside city of Saranda. The remains of a fourth-century Greek theater and temples, and a fifth-century Christian basilica and Jewish synagogue are all found in this Albanian city.

The Soviet Union demolished most of Albania's older architecture between World War II and 1990. However, much of the architecture that survived has distinct Balkan and Ottoman influences. The Ottoman Turks built hundreds of Muslim mosques, many of which have been restored. These mosques have domes, whereas the Balkan mosques are rectangular with painted wood ceilings.

The historic towns of Berat and Gjirokastër, both of which are well-preserved Ottoman towns, have been recognized as World Heritage Sites. The homes of Berat sit on river terraces around a citadel and are built from timber and plaster. They are known for their unique whitewash exterior and numerous large windows. The houses of Gjirokastër are built on the side of a mountain and feature roofs covered with stones. An

18th-century castle sits above the fortress town that overlooks the Drino River and is the site of the National Albanian Folk Festival.

Castles and fortresses nestled in the mountains are common throughout Albania. The medieval town of Krujë has a restored medieval castle and bazaar. The castle of Rozafa, built in the fourth century BCE, rises on a hill overlooking the large ancient city of Shkodër. The city itself sits next to Lake Shkodër, which is the largest freshwater lake in the Balkans. Farther south is Korçë, at the foot of Morava Mountain, an important center of trade during the 18th century and home to numerous museums.

Libraries & Museums

The National History Museum, in Tirana, documents Albanian history from prehistoric times through communist era. Special exhibits are dedicated to the thousands imprisoned, tortured, and killed during the reign of Enver Hoxha, who ruled Albania with an iron fist from 1944 until his death in 1985. An enormous, gold-leaf-encrusted statue of Hoxha that once adorned the front of the museum was removed in 1991 as the dictator's cult of personality began to crumble.

Other key Tirana museums include the Tirana Archeological Museum, which contains artifacts ranging from prehistoric times through the early Middle Ages and the Museum of Natural Sciences, which focuses on the geology, mineralogy, and flora and fauna of the greater Tirana area. Museums in Korçë include the Museum of Medieval Art, which showcases traditional Albanian art, the Museum of Education, and the Archaeological Museum. The National Art Gallery includes works of Albanian and European artists from the 13th century through the present.

Holidays

November 28 is Independence and Liberation Day, Albania's great public holiday. On this date in 1912, nationalist delegates in Vlorë declared Albanian independence from the Ottoman Empire and established a provisional government. On this date in 1998, Albanians by

referendum approved their constitution. Other public holidays are New Year's Day (January 1), the Christian Christmas and Easter Monday, and the Muslim Ramadan and Bajram.

Albanians celebrate two unique holidays each March: Teachers' Day (March 7), which commemorates the 1846 opening of the first school to teach in the Albanian language, and Women's Day (March 8), a day honoring women that is celebrated in all of the Baltic nations.

Youth Culture

Education has held special importance in 20th-century Albania. Albanian youth are guaranteed the right to free education through the secondary level, which is compulsory. Compulsory education from grades one through nine is most often followed by secondary education, after which students must pass an exam to graduate. To pursue higher education, Albanians must take an entrance examination. There are currently more than seven public universities in the country and a number of private universities. Under communist rule, Albania's literacy rate dramatically increased. According to UNICEF, in 2012, the country's total adult literacy stood at 96.8 percent.

Because of economic turmoil following Soviet rule, Albania lacks cultural spaces for youth. Cinemas exist in urban areas, but teenagers must still be fairly self-reliant when socializing. Many Albanian youth socialize in cafés or bars, or watch television. Sports such as European football (soccer) and volleyball are also popular. Though mobile phones are becoming increasingly more common, they are still somewhat expensive for many Albanian youths.

Popular music in Albania can sometimes be heard live, but youth more frequently listen to the radio or CDs. Albanians can now easily download music from the Internet, making music from other countries, as well as Albania, accessible. Those who have access to computers either at home or in cybercafés are increasingly joining social networking sites (SNS) to interact with friends.

SOCIETY

Transportation

Albania's transportation system under the control of the Soviet Union, up to the early 1990s, was extremely limited and in serious disrepair. Roadways were mostly full of holes and rocks, and the railways were dangerously broken down. Albanians were also restricted in their travel and could not own automobiles. When the government allowed the private ownership of vehicles in 1991, Albanians began importing used vehicles from around Europe.

At the turn of the 21st century, however, a large number of road-construction projects were underway. New roads link the major cities, and one four-lane highway runs between the capital of Tirana and Durrës, Albania's second largest city. The Durrës-Priština Highway, also known as the Rrëshen-Kalimash dual carriageway, was completed in 2013, connects Albania and Kosovo with Serbia, includes a six-kilometer tunnel, and cost one billion euros to construct. In 2015, Albania also finished its contribution to the Adriatic-Ionian highway, connecting Montenegro with Greece. Traffic moves on the right side of the road in Albania.

Transportation Infrastructure

The railroad system is limited; though there are a few railway lines in the country, passengers have historically not used them. Their current state of disrepair requires substantial investment to make them a viable alternative to automobile or airline travel. Albania's one international airport, in Tirana, has been remodeled and is used by 14 airlines that fly to 29 destinations. It has the capacity for more than one million passengers annually. A second, civilian airport opened in Kukës in 2008. Highways and roads are poorly maintained, and gasoline stations are sparse between cities. Of Albania's 18,000 kilometers of roadway, only 7,020 kilometers are paved.

Media & Communications

As with all of the other industries in Albania, the media and communications were under strict communist control between 1945 and 1990. Operators were required to assist callers, and by 1990, the phones and wiring were obsolete. By 2009, the phone system was still overloaded and in poor repair, but large numbers of urban Albanians had begun using mobile phones. As of 2012, 3.5 million cellular lines were in use.

Even after becoming democratic, the business interests, politicians, and media interests exert strong control of the media, and the US organization Freedom House has ranked the country "partly free" in terms of the press. State-controlled radio and television stations are meeting competition from the private sector and residents can access both Italian and Greek broadcasts. Radio Televizioni Shqiptar (RTSH) is Albania's public broadcaster. The largest broadcast audience tunes into privately-owned TV Klan. In 2008, there were three cable networks. The country has over 150 newspapers, more than twenty of which are dailies, such as the major socialist newspaper *Zëri i Popullit,* the Democratic Party daily *Rilindja Demokratike*, and private dailies such as *Koha Jonë* and *Shekulli.*

As Albania has been slow to receive the latest technological advancements in communication, there are only a handful of Internet service providers (ISPs) in the country. However, computers are becoming more common in urban areas, and there are over 10,000 local Internet hosts. As of 2010, there were approximately 1.3 million Internet users in Albania, representing about 44 percent of the population.

SOCIAL DEVELOPMENT

Standard of Living

Albania ranked 95th on the 2012 United Nations Human Development Index (HDI), which measures quality of life indicators.

Water Consumption

According to UNICEF (the United Nations International Children's Emergency Fund), 94.7 percent of the Albanian population has access to clean water, with urban populations at 95.5 percent and rural populations at 93.7 by 2011 estimates. Additionally, the access to improved sanitation stands at 93.9 percent, with rural populations at 93 percent and urban populations at 94.7 percent.

Education

Approximately 96.8 percent of Albanians over age nine can read and write. Education for any citizen is free, and for children six to 14, compulsory. They attend an eight-grade primary school divided into two, four-grade segments. Upon successful completion, they receive a leaving certificate. Many proceed to college-preparatory secondary schools called middle schools. If they prefer, students may attend pre-vocational and/or vocational schools.

To enter a university, students must pass entrance examinations. There are numerous public and private universities in Albania, as well as several post-graduate programs. Tirana is home to the University of Tirana, the Polytechnic University of Tirana, and a medical school.

The system of universal public education was first developed during Albania's communist epoch and was subsidized by other communist countries. Albania has reorganized its educational system, but lacks funds to support it. Often, rural educational administrators lack training, and opportunities for professional enrichment do not exist.

Women's Rights

Under Article 18 of Albania's constitution, women are considered equal and cannot be discriminated against. But the lack of enforcement of the law has often left women vulnerable to discrimination. Albanian society, as a whole, generally evades the issue. Albania's Ministry of Labor, Social Affairs, and Equal Opportunities has been charged with promoting gender equality in the country and has consented to the Convention on the Elimination of All Forms of Violence against Women (CEDAW). However, the ministry has admitted that much work needs to be done in gender equality, and as of early 2009, legislation concerning gender equality had yet to be ratified. Women are also underrepresented politically.

Albanian women also suffer domestic violence, which has increased in the last two decades after Albania's economy followed free market principles and women grew increasingly dependent on their husbands for support. The crime is not sufficiently reported, investigated, or prosecuted, and the victims either have difficulty identifying domestic violence or fear repercussions. The government is attempting to resolve these problems. In 2007, the National Strategy on Gender Equality and Domestic Violence was created. To help families identify violence, the government also developed the Law on Measures against Violence in Family Relations that same year. The UN has also been tasked to assist social services to deal with domestic violence, which is considered a serious crime under Article 88 of the criminal code. Numerous laws are also in place to punish crimes of sexual assault against minors and adults, including spousal rape. However, it has been reported that many spouses rarely report such crimes and that government officials often fail to consider this specific form of violence a crime.

Albania continues to warrant international monitoring because it has failed to eliminate human trafficking, specifically of women and young girls. Albania is considered a source country for trafficking, and women and children are exploited sexually and used for forced labor. Though the country is no longer considered a major country of transit, women and girls are trafficked to neighboring countries, such as Kosovo, Macedonia, Italy, and Greece. They are then moved to other Western European countries. Nearly half of the victims are children, many of whom end up in Greece as forced labor. The government has also failed to provide evidence of the prosecution of those complicit in the crime, nor is it sufficiently tracking victims.

In early 2008, Albania was one of 14 states that signed on the Council of Europe Convention on Action against Trafficking in Human Beings. The convention aims to identify and protect the victims who are often treated as criminals. Trafficking decreased sharply in 2007, when 13 cases were reported and 10 men were convicted of trafficking either women or children. However, enforcement of the crime remains the weakest link in the agenda to halt the practice of human trafficking.

Health Care

In theory, all health and medical care in Albania is free. All new mothers are entitled to six-months of maternity leave at 85 percent of their salaries. In practice, the change from communism to a free-market economy has limited available health care outside the cities. Excellent physicians are available, but they function with little or none of the technical equipment and supplies that health care workers in developed countries consider essential.

Nevertheless, Albanians are comparatively healthy. Their neonatal mortality rate is low: only 8 deaths for every 1,000 live births, while infant mortality rates are also relatively low, with 15 deaths for every 1,000 children. The average life expectancy is almost seventy-eight years, seventy-five years for men, and over eighty years for women.

GOVERNMENT

Structure

Albania is an emerging democracy with a constitution established in 1998 by popular referendum. All citizens aged 18 years or older may vote. Of the many political parties, the Socialist Party predominates. The largest minority party, the Democratic Party, competes by creating a coalition with smaller factions.

The national government has three branches. The legislative branch consists of the unicameral, 140-seat People's Assembly, the members of which are elected to four-year terms. The executive branch, following the European model, includes a chief of state, the president, elected to five-year-terms by the People's Assembly; and a head of government, the prime minister. The prime minister proposes a Council of Ministers who are then nominated by the president and approved by the Assembly.

Political Parties

Two parties dominate Albanian politics—the Democratic Party of Albania (PD) and the Socialist Party of Albania (PS). In the June 2013 parliamentary elections, the PS, leading the Alliance for European Albania coalition, dominated, taking almost 58 percent of the vote and eighty-three seats. The PD, leading the Alliance for Employment, Prosperity and Integration, took over 39 percent of the vote and fifty-seven seats. The Socialist Movement for Integration (LSI), a PS splinter group founded in 2004, took slightly over 10 percent of the vote, attaining twelve seats.

Local Government

Albania is divided into 12 administrative divisions called qarke (counties). Each qarke, with its headquarters in a regional city, is responsible for local needs and law enforcement.

Judicial System

The judicial branch consists of a Constitutional Court and a Supreme Court whose chair is elected by the People's Assembly to a four-year term. There are many district courts and courts of appeals. Albanian citizens are subject to the jurisdiction of the International Criminal Court.

Taxation

Critics have characterized the Albanian taxation system as "arbitrary and inconsistent." As of January 2014, the government has begun levying taxes on corporations at 15 percent, up from 10 percent in previous years. Also in 2014, three income tax brackets were instituted: workers making up to 30,000 are not taxed; earnings of 30,000–130,000 are taxed at 13 percent; and income of 130,000 or above is taxed at 23 percent. Capital gains, inheritance, and property taxes are also levied. Large corporations have claimed that they are disproportionately penalized by the Albanian tax system, as their smaller competitors have found ways around the tax system, avoiding payment.

Armed Forces

The Albanian Armed Forces (AAF) consists of an army, navy, and air force. Compulsory military service was abolished in 2010. By that same year, the government had planned on maintaining a professional force totaling 14,500 troops. The Albanian Armed Forces joined NATO in 2009, and have been active in missions in the Mediterranean region.

Foreign Policy

Having been admitted to the North Atlantic Treaty Organization (NATO) as a full member in 2009, Albania has revealed its desire to become involved in the international community and has applied to become a member of the European Union (EU). The country also seeks better ties with neighboring countries and the United States. It holds membership in the Organization for Security and Cooperation in Europe (OSCE), the World Trade Organization (WTO), and the United Nations (UN). In 2006, Albania signed the Stabilization and Association Agreement (SAA) with the EU, the first step in joining the EU. The goal aligned with this first step is to develop legal reforms and decrease organized crime and corruption in the country, which has been problematic since the fall of communism.

Albania has a strong relationship with the Republic of Montenegro, and it is working closely with the Republic of Macedonia and Italy to halt the trafficking of people, arms, and drugs across all of their borders. These problems have created serious challenges for Albania's potential EU membership. Albanians in Macedonia still face discrimination in employment, education, and

political representation. As in the past, occasional tensions continue to arise with Greece because of the treatment of ethnic Greeks in Albania and ethnic Albanians in Greece. A mass emigration of Albanians occurred during the early 1990s, when large numbers fled to Greece and Italy for work. Many Albanian workers in Greece still have yet to receive legal papers for work. Likewise, tensions with Italy increased rapidly during the emigration, as the situation presented Italy with a humanitarian crisis. However, Italy responded by providing some economic relief to Albania to avert further emigration.

Ethnic tensions among Albanian extremists in Kosovo and Macedonia have been a serious problem in the past. However, Albania has recently been more diligent in arresting and prosecuting those who are accused of inciting ethnic hatred in those neighboring countries. Tensions with Serbia have arisen because of the Albanian majority in Kosovo, which called for independence from Serbia in early 2008. Albania has recognized Kosovo's independence.

Serious tensions have arisen between Serbia and Albania, which stems from the 1999 Kosovo war. Serbia has repeatedly made serious allegations that hundreds of Serbs were abducted into Albania and murdered for the purpose of taking their organs. Though Albania has repeatedly denied these humanitarian crimes were committed by Albanians on Albanian soil, the UN, OSCE, and the Council of Europe investigated the matter.

Albania has been intent on developing strong ties with the US. In efforts to strengthen new ties with the U.Ss, Albania signed the treaty on the Prevention of Weapons of Mass Destruction as well as a supplementary agreement to the NATO Partnership for Peace, among other agreements. The U.S. has also provided millions of dollars in food aid and support for building the country's democratic institutions, including rule of law.

Human Rights Profile

International human rights law insists that states respect civil and political rights and also promote an individual's economic, social, and cultural rights. The United Nations Universal Declaration on Human Rights (UDHR) is recognized as the standard for international human rights. Its authors sought the counsel of the world's great thinkers, philosophers, and religious leaders and were careful to create a document that reflects the core values shared by every world culture. (To read this document or view the articles relating to cultural human rights, go to http://www.udhr.org/UDHR/default.htm.).

Albania is a parliamentary democracy that gives the people the capacity, by direct popular vote, to change the country's government. The constitution guarantees freedom of expression, religion, and the press. Albanians also have the right to information but have limited rights under certain conditions, such as for failure to comply with the courts or when illegally entering the country.

In late 2008, Albania was one of 66 countries to sign a UDHR document that includes equal rights for all human beings, regardless of sexual orientation and gender identity. This agreement further extends the UDHR Article 7, which states that all are equal before the law. As such, Albania has also agreed not to arrest, torture or deprive of any economic, cultural, or social rights any individuals. However, Amnesty International (AI) has reported that Albania's police force has repeatedly used violence and torture against prisoners during investigations. In late 2008, the organization called on the country's justice system to invoke Article 86 of Albania's criminal code for penalizing torturers.

Orphans in Albania, as the result of war, have faced a serious lack of protection and adequate housing, which results in their being denied sufficient protections and the possibilities of employment. As one of Europe's poorest countries, serious shortages of urban housing exist throughout Albania's cities. Even though Albanian law stipulates such protections as housing for orphaned children, the law is rarely followed.

Large numbers of trafficked organs remains a serious problem in Albania. After the 1998–1999 Kosovo War, approximately 400 Serbs and women from Albania, Kosovo, and Russia turned up missing, allegedly abducted or transferred across the border from Kosovo to Albania. The captors allegedly removed the internal organs from a large number of these victims, resulting in their deaths. In late 2008, one of Albania's top prosecutors rejected a request from Serbia to investigate these claims that a former UN war crimes prosecutor made earlier in 2008. In April 2014, the EU publicized plans to establish a tribunal, at an estimated cost of $170 million, to investigate allegations against former Albanian rebels.

Migration

Albania's migration rate was estimated at –5 migrants per 1,000 residents in 2012, meaning that it continues to lose citizens. The migration rate has largely been attributed to the lagging economic growth.

ECONOMY

Overview of the Economy

Although natural resources abound, Albania's economy is one of the poorest among European states. In 2015, Albania's estimated gross domestic product (GDP) was the equivalent of $32.26 billion U.S. dollars. The average per capita GDP was approximately $4,659 USD. Approximately 15 percent of the GDP comes from Albanians employed abroad who send earnings home (remittances). In 2012, the annual inflation rate was 2 percent. According to the US Central Intelligence Agency (CIA), the agricultural sector employs more than half of the working population (54.6 percent), but accounts for only 18.4 percent of the GDP.

Albania's major trading partner is Italy, with Greece, Turkey, the European Union countries, Bulgaria and the former Yugoslavian nations engaged in substantial trade.

Some trade revenue eludes official accounting. Albanian drug traffickers are increasingly active, receiving cannabis, hashish (compressed and purified cannabis), cocaine, and other illegal drugs from southwest Asia and South America and redistributing them in Western Europe. These groups are branching into illicit money laundering, arms dealing, and transporting of undocumented aliens. Albania's difficulty in controlling these groups has slowed its progress in establishing ties to the European Union.

Tirana's economy drives the Albanian national economy. The capital's manufacturing sector turns out perfumes and cosmetic products, chemicals, concrete, asphalt, lumber, metal goods, textiles, clothing, footwear, tobacco products, processed foods, pharmaceuticals, electronics, basic metals, and farming equipment. Foreign investment has spurred a considerable expansion of Tirana's industrial base. Legal trade and foreign investment in Albania overall, however, has been handicapped by the country's weak infrastructure.

Industry

Approximately 15 percent of Albania's work force is employed in legitimate industries, which include timber, hydropower, food processing, textiles and clothing, mining, oil, cement, and chemicals. Most of these industries were developed by the former communist government and are now struggling an open-market economy.

Albania faces severe energy shortages. The government is working to solve this problem through increased imports, although this is increasing Albania's already considerable trade deficit. Albania now exports textiles, footwear, asphalt, metals, metal ores, and crude oil, as well as agricultural products.

Labor

With a labor force of 1.28 million workers, Albania's unemployment rate in 2014 was officially 13.3 percent, unofficially as high as 30 percent. As of December 2014, the majority of the Albanian work force—over 65 percent—is employed in the services sector.

Energy/Power/Natural Resources

Albania's resources include timber, fish, and soil. Natural gas is found in southwest Albania. Many of Albania's resources were exploited under the communist government, which used loans and grants from the Soviet bloc, then from communist China. As industrial activity expanded, so did industrial pollution.

In 2008, Albania signed a €160 million concession agreement with the Austrian firms Verbund and EVN, both major hydroelectric producers, to build the two-phase Ashta Hydropower Plant in Shkodër on the Drin River (different from the abovementioned Drino River, as the Drin empties into the Adriatic). While the state-run Albanian electric company must initially purchase from Verbund and EVN the power created at Ashta, ownership of the plant reverts to the Albanian government within 35 years. In 2010, the Albanian government also began seeking a partnership with the intent to begin construction of a nuclear power plant. Both Croatia and Italy have expressed interest, as their own countries have banned the construction of nuclear power plants in the near future. Despite these steps towards cleaner, more reliable energy production, an antiquated grid system and recurring equipment theft can cause rolling blackouts throughout the country.

Fishing

Albania boasts a coastline of 362 kilometers on the Adriatic and Ionian seas. Trawlers predominate and fishing is concentrated in the port cities of Durrës, Vlorë, Shëngjin, and Sarandë. As of November 2013, Albania boasted 552 fishing vessels. Domestic production in 2012 was approximately 6.6 tons—about 4.4 tons from capture and 2.2 tons from aquaculture.

Forestry

Albania has about 29 percent forest cover, comprised of mostly broad-leaved trees (evergreen oak and beech). While all forests are government-owned, this has not stopped the harvesting of stock, which is in decline. A government forestry project has sought international aid assistance. Threats include deforestation, soil erosion, and pollution.

Mining/Metals

Albania is the world's fourth largest producer of chrome and also mines iron, nickel, salt, bauxite (an aluminum ore), coal, and petroleum; copper is mined near Shkodër. Since 2007, production increases have been noted for crude and rolled steel, ferrochromium, asphalt and bitumen, coke, natural gas, and crude oil. According to the International Monetary Fund, the mineral extraction industry accounted for about 10 percent of industrial production and one percent of Albania's GDP in 2010.

Agriculture

Just over 18 percent of Albania's workers are employed in agriculture, providing just under a quarter of the nation's GDP. Major crops are wheat and corn, potatoes and vegetables, sugar beets, wine grapes, and meat and dairy products. Albania's farmers could do more, but antiquated farm equipment makes competition with Western European countries difficult. Droughts are another frequent problem, only partially solved by irrigation: in a 2007 report released by the World Bank, 1,030 square kilometers were irrigated. Generally, farms in Albania are small, independent, and largely unprofitable.

Animal Husbandry

Albania, because of a shortage of fodder during the communist regime, is rebuilding its livestock sector. In spite of this, livestock accounts for more than half of the agricultural industry value, including cattle, sheep, goats, and pigs. The challenge of bringing livestock up to European Union standards is in development.

Tourism

While the tourism industry in Albania is underdeveloped, the country has seen an increase in the beginning of the 21st century, with visitors largely coming from across Europe. The country ranked ninetieth in a list of 133 countries. Growth in this industry is hindered by the lagging infrastructure. In 2013, the tourism industry accounted for 41,000 jobs and contributed 4.8 percent towards the country's GDP.

The country boasts warm beaches, rugged mountains, caves, diversity of climate and wildlife, dramatic history, ancient cities and archeological sites, exotic architecture, plentiful museums, unique folk traditions, and an active artistic community.

By Kathryn Bundy, Ann Parrish, &
Beverly Ballaro

DO YOU KNOW?

- Roman emperors Gaius, Claudius Gothicus, Aurelian, Probus, Diocletian, and Constantine the Great were all of Illyrian (Albanian) origin.

- The Albanian flag, a black double eagle on a red banner, is adapted from the Byzantine seal of Skanderbeg (1405–1468), the national hero who freed Albania from Turkish rule and kept it free for twenty-five years. Skanderbeg's heroic life inspired poems by Ronsard and Longfellow and an opera by Vivaldi.

Bibliography

_____. *Social Currents in Eastern Europe: The Sources and Consequences of the Great Transformation.* Second ed. Durham, NC: Duke UP, 2012.

Abrahams, Fred C. *Modern Albania: From Dictatorship to Democracy in Europe.* New York: NYU Press, 2015.

Albanian Constitution. Transl. Kathleen Imholz, Esq., Krenar Loloçi, Esq., & AACCAPP. *Institute for Policy & Legal Studies*, 1999. http://www.ipls.org/services/kusht/contents.html

Clarissa de Waal. *Albania Today: A Portrait of a Country in Transition.* London, England: I.B. Tauris, 2014.

Gillian Gloyer. *Albania: Bradt Travel Guides*. Fifth ed. Bucks, England: Bradt Travel Guides, 2015.

Hermine G. DeSoto., Hermine G., Sabine Beddies, & Ilir Gedeshi. *Roma and Egyptians in Albania: From Social Exclusion to Social Inclusion*. Washington, DC: World Bank Publications, 2005.

Kim Burton. "The Eagle Has Landed." *World Music, Vol. 1: Africa, Europe and the Middle East*. Ed. Simon Broughton & Mark Ellingham. London, England: Rough Guides Ltd., 2000.

Mark Pittaway, Mark. *The Fluid Borders of Europe*. Milton Keynes, England: Open University Worldwide, 2003.

Miranda Vickers. *The Albanians: A Modern History*. London, England: I.B. Tauris, 2011.

Paulin Kola, Paulin. *In Search of Greater Albania*. London, England: Hurst & Co, 2003.

Robert C. Ostergren. & John G. Rice. *The Europeans: A Geography of People, Culture, and Environment*. New York, New York: The Guilford Press, 2004.

Sabrina P. Ramet. *Eastern Europe: Politics, Culture, and Society Since 1939*. Bloomington, Indiana: Indiana UP, 1999.

Susan E. Pritchett Post. *Women in Modern Albania: Firsthand Accounts of Culture and Conditions from Over 200 Interviews*. Jefferson, North Carolina: McFarland and Company, 1998.

Abrahams, Fred C. *Modern Albania: From Dictatorship to Democracy in Europe*. New York: NYU Press, 2015.

Albanian Constitution. Transl. Kathleen Imholz, Esq., Krenar Loloçi, Esq., & AACCAPP. Institute for Policy & Legal Studies, 1999. http://www.ipls.org/services/kusht/contents.html.

Burton, Kim. "The Eagle Has Landed." *World Music, Vol. 1: Africa, Europe and the Middle East*. Ed. Simon Broughton & Mark Ellingham. London, England: Rough Guides Ltd., 2000.

DeSoto, Hermine G., Sabine Beddies, & Ilir Gedeshi. *Roma and Egyptians in Albania: From Social Exclusion to Social Inclusion*. Washington, DC: World Bank Publications, 2005.

de Waal, Clarissa. *Albania Today: A Portrait of a Country in Transition*. London, England: I.B. Tauris, 2014.

Gloyer, Gillian. *Albania: Bradt Travel Guides*. Fifth ed. Bucks, England: Bradt Travel Guides, 2015.

Kola, Paulin. *In Search of Greater Albania*. London, England: Hurst & Co, 2003.

Ostergren, Robert C. & John G. Rice. *The Europeans: A Geography of People, Culture, and Environment*. New York, New York: The Guilford Press, 2004.

Pittaway, Mark. *The Fluid Borders of Europe*. Milton Keynes, England: Open University Worldwide, 2003.

Pritchett Post, Susan E. *Women in Modern Albania: Firsthand Accounts of Culture and Conditions from Over 200 Interviews*. Jefferson, North Carolina: McFarland and Company, 1998.

Ramet, Sabrina P. *Eastern Europe: Politics, Culture, and Society Since 1939*. Bloomington, Indiana: Indiana UP, 1999.

_____. *Social Currents in Eastern Europe: The Sources and Consequences of the Great Transformation*. Second ed. Durham, NC: Duke UP, 2012.

Vickers, Miranda. *The Albanians: A Modern History*. London, England: I.B. Tauris, 2011.

Works Cited

"Albania." *Culture Crossing Guide*. Culture Crossing, 2014. http://guide.culturecrossing.net/basics_business_student.php?id=2

"Albania." *Encyclopedia Britannica*. Encyclopædia Britannica, Inc., 2015. http://www.britannica.com/place/Albania

"Albania." *Eurofish International Organisation*. Eurofish.dk, 2015. http://www.eurofish.dk/index.php?option=com_content&view=article&id=110%3Aalbania&catid=37&Itemid=27

"Albania." *Amnesty International Report 2014/2015*. Amnesty International, 2015. https://www.amnesty.org/en/countries/europe-and-central-asia/albania/

Albania Art Institute. Home page. Albania Art Institute, 2005. http://www.albaniaartinstitute.org/

"Albania Facts and Culture." *CountryReports*. CountryReports, 2015. http://www.countryreports.org/country/Albania.htm.

Albanian Center for Human Rights. ACHR, Tirana, n.d. http://www.achr.org/en/index.html.

Albanian Constitution. Transl. Kathleen Imholz, Esq., Krenar Loloçi, Esq., & AACCAPP. Institute for Policy & Legal Studies, 1999. http://www.ipls.org/services/kusht/contents.html.

"Albanian Food." *Food Culture and Tradition of the World*. Food-links.com, 2015. http://www.food-links.com/countries/albanian/foods-albania.php. Food-Links

"Albanian Report." *International Society for Contemporary Music*. ISCM, 2015. http://www.iscm.org/catalogue/annualreports/memberreports/2004iscm-albanian-section

Stefan Capaliku. "Albania/Historical perspective: cultural policies and instruments." *Compendium: Cultural Policies and Trends in Europe*. Council of Europe/ERICarts, 18 Jan. 2011. http://www.culturalpolicies.net/web/albania.php

"Albania." *The World Fact Book*. Central Intelligence Agency, n.d. https://www.cia.gov/library/publications/the-world-factbook/geos/al.html

Elsie, Robert. "Modern Authors from Albania." *AlbanianLiterature.net*. Robert Elsie, n.d. http://www.albanianliterature.com/en/authors_modern1.html

"Mineral Resources and Mining Activity in Albania." *AEA News*. Albania Energy Association, 17 May 2015.

http://aea-al.org/mineral-resources-and-mining-activity-in-albania/

"New Exhibition at the Stephen Lawrence Gallery: *Communication in between...* by Genc Mulliqi." *News & Events*. University of Greenwich, 2007. http://www.gre.ac.uk/news?a=57036

"Population of Albania." *INSTAT*. Instituti I Statistikave, 2012. http://www.instat.gov.al/en/publications/press-releases/press-release-population-of-albania-1-january-2015.aspx

"Serbs Seek Info from Albania on Organ Trafficking." *Reuters*. Thomson Reuters, 23 Feb. 2009. http://www.reuters.com/article/latestCrisis/idUSLN435679

Tirana International Film Festival. *Albania Art Institute*, 20 Jun. 2015. http://tiranafilmfest.com/

"U.S. Relations with Albania." U.S. Department of State. 11 Mar. 2015. Web. http://www.state.gov/r/pa/ei/bgn/3235.htm

"Violence Against Women in Albania." *Stop Violence Against Women*. The Advocates for Human Rights, 2010. Web. http://www.stopvaw.org/Albania.html

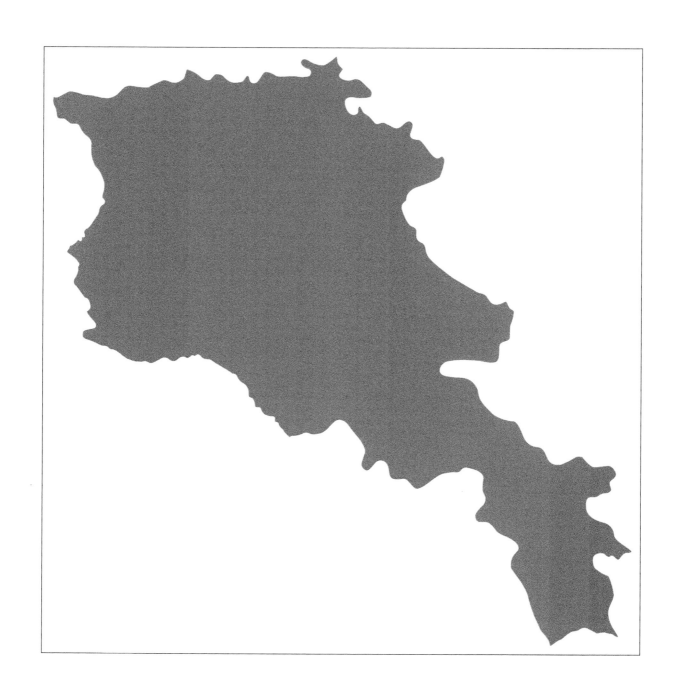

ARMENIA

Introduction

The Republic of Armenia (Hayastani Hanrapetut'yun) is a landlocked country on the Asian continent. It is bordered on the east by Azerbaijan; on the south by Iran and the Azerbaijani exclave, Nakhchivan Autonomous Republic; on the north by Georgia; and on the west by Turkey.

Its citizens, known as Armenians, take pride in the ancient heritage of their country. Armenia's borders have changed many times. The country was once much larger, stretching from the Black Sea to the Caspian. Since then, it has been attacked and occupied by Parthians, Romans, Mongols, Arabs, Egyptians, Persians, Turks, and Russians.

Today, Armenia is independent, but it is still haunted by its 20th-century history. Armenians hold Turkey responsible for the 1915 genocide in which 1.5 million Armenians died. In addition, hundreds of thousands were forced to emigrate. In 1920, Armenia became part of the Soviet Union after being annexed by Russian in 1829. Armenia was at war with Azerbaijan from 1988–1994. The conflict shattered Armenia's economy and created territorial and human rights issues, many of which remain unresolved.

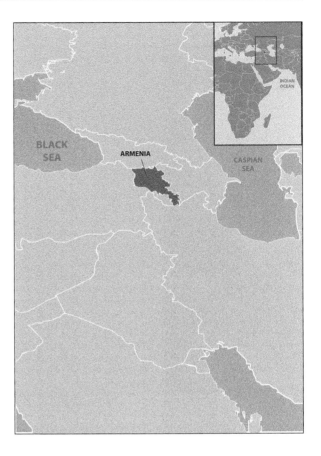

GENERAL INFORMATION

Official Language: Armenian (Ashkharabar and Grabar)
Population: 3,018,854 (2014 estimate)

Currency: Dram
Coins: One hundred luma equal one dram. Coins are issued in 10, 20, 50, 100, 200, and 500 dram.
Land Area: 29,743 square kilometers (11,484 square miles)
Water Area: 1,540 square kilometers (595 square miles)
National Anthem: 'Mer Hayrenik' ('My Fatherland')
Capital: Yerevan
Time Zone: GMT +4
Flag Description: The Armenian flag is a horizontal tricolor of red (top), blue (center), and orange (bottom). The red of the flag stands for the blood shed for the country; the blue represents the sky; and the orange (apricot) symbolizes the country's fertile landscape.

Population

The majority of the population (just over 98 percent) is comprised of ethnic Armenians. There

Principal Cities by Population (2015):

- Yerevan (1,071,500)
- Gyumri (119,000)
- Vanadzor (83,400)
- Vagharshapat (46,800)
- Abovyan (44,300)
- Kapan (42,800)
- Hrazdan (41,700)

are small minorities of Russians, Yezidi Kurds, and Azeri, most of whom fled the country during the conflict with Azerbaijan.

An earthquake in 1988 devastated Armenia, killing 25,000 people. As farms and villages were destroyed, leaving thousands homeless, hundreds of survivors moved to larger cities or left the country altogether. As of 2014, almost 63 percent of the population lives in urban areas.

Yerevan is home to about 1.6 million people, most of whom are ethnic Armenians. A small proportion of the population is made up of Russians and Kurds. A densely populated city, recent estimates suggest that there are 4,754 people per square kilometer (12,310 people per square mile). The estimated 2014 population growth rate was very low, however: –0.13 percent.

Languages

Armenian was originally a separate branch of the Indo-European language family. Through centuries of commerce and conflict, the language assimilated a rich vocabulary from other branches, such as Indo-Iranian, Greek, and Latin, and also from Semitic languages. It remained an oral language until, in the early fourth century, Bishop Mesrop Mashtots developed a 36-letter alphabet for use in translating the Bible. This written language, called Grabar or Classical Armenian, became the language of Armenian literature and scholarship through the 19th century, and remains the ritual language of the Armenian Apostolic Church.

Spoken Armenian, however, evolved differently, shaped by varying Byzantine, Ottoman, Iranian, and Russian influences. Called

Ashkharhabar, it is spoken by Armenians worldwide and has become the language of modern Armenian literature.

Native People & Ethnic Groups

The Armenian people have inhabited the Caucasus since prehistoric times. Their legendary beginnings, based on the Bible, tell of Haik, a descendent of Noah who settled below Mount Ararat and whose name is the source of 'Hayastan' ('land of Haik'). 'Armenia,' the name given the country by the Persians, honors Aram, a legendary descendent of Haik, and the ancestor of all ethnic Armenians.

The Yezidi Kurds, the only other significant ethnic group remaining in Armenia, live in the western mountains in villages made up of stone houses. Sheep herding is their chief occupation. Ethnic Armenians often call them Yezidis, theorizing that they are not Kurds but a separate tribe. The Yezidi Kurds deny this, believing that only religion distinguishes them from other Kurds and that all Kurds practiced Yezidi before being forcibly converted to Islam.

Religions

Armenia declared itself a Christian country 1,700 years ago, well before Rome did. Nearly 95 percent of the population belongs to the Armenian Apostolic Church, which is similar in ritual to the Coptic and Syrian Christian Churches. The remainder of the population belongs to other Christian denominations, and Yezidi Kurds adhere to Yezidi, a form of Zoroastrianism, a religion older than Christianity. Until the early 1990s, many other Kurds, ethnic Azeris, Iranians, and Georgians lived in Armenia and practiced Islam. They have nearly all fled and have been replaced by ethnic Armenians (Christians) who fled Azerbaijan.

Climate

Winters are frigid in Armenia. Summers, while hot in the valleys, are cool on the plateau. There is little rainfall, however, and frequent droughts, so crops rely on irrigation using water drawn from Lake Sevan and from the Arax River.

Yerevan experiences cold winters and hot summers. Between November and February, temperatures hover between –10° and –5° Celsius (14° and 23° Fahrenheit). The sun makes short appearances during the winter months. In the spring and summer months, temperatures average between 22° and 36°Celsius (72° and 97° Fahrenheit), although temperatures as high as 40° Celsius (104° Fahrenheit) are not uncommon. The city receives about 26 millimeters (1 inch) of precipitation per month on average, leaving Yerevan and the surrounding areas arid.

Armenia is subject to severe earthquakes. Its most catastrophic earthquake in modern times occurred in 1988, centering in Spitak. It killed 25,000 people and left hundreds of thousands homeless, with thousands more injured and disabled.

ENVIRONMENT & GEOGRAPHY

Topography
Armenia lies south of the Caucasus Mountains on a wooded plateau varied by mountainous outcroppings and fast-flowing rivers. The highest peak, Mount Aragats, reaches 4,090 meters (13,420 feet) above sea level. Its lowest point, on the Debed River, is still 400 meters (1,312 feet) above the sea. Landlocked Armenia's largest body of water is Lake Sevan, which lies 1,900 meters (6,200 feet) above sea level and has a last-recorded area of 940 square kilometers (550 square miles), down from 1,236 square kilometers (363 square miles) recorded in 2002.

At the eastern boundary of the Ararat Plain, just 50 kilometers (31 miles) north of the towering, snow-capped Mount Ararat, lies the small city of Yerevan. The city is located on the banks of the Getar and Hrazdan Rivers. Yerevan sits on a plateau at 989.4 meters (3,246.1 feet) above sea level and is situated in the eastern portion of land-locked Armenia.

Yerevan has an area of 223 square kilometers (86 square miles). The city is broken into 13 different districts, but is autonomous from the country's other provinces.

Plants & Animals
Apricots and peaches originated in Armenia. They grow well there, as do grapes, pears, and most other fruits of temperate and sub-tropical zones. In fact, 3,500 species of vascular plants grow in Armenia, with an average density of more than 100 species per square kilometer, almost a world record.

Armenia is particularly rich in native and rare species and is prized by botanists as a potential genetic resource, a site where long-domesticated plants (wheat, for instance) still grow wild. The Erebuni Reserve, established in 1981 with the specific goal of wild grain preservation, contains many such uncultivated cereal plants.

Armenia's variety of landscape accounts for the diversity of plant life found there. Climbing from the lowest point one encounters deserts, semi-deserts, mountain steppes, forest land, and sub-alpine, then alpine meadows.

Armenia's 500 animal species are also varied. Its protected reserves harbor rare bezoar goats, wild boars, panthers, gray bears, porcupines, and the Caucasian wood grouse. Situated on a major crossway, the country hosts countless migratory fowl each season.

CUSTOMS & COURTESIES

Greeting
A vast majority of Armenians speak both Armenian and Russian. The most common greeting in Armenian is simply 'Barev' ('Hello'), with 'Barev dzez' the more formal construction. Armenian men generally greet each other with a handshake. If the two men know each other well, they might follow the handshake with a kiss on the cheek. Women most often give each other a hug and a kiss on the cheek. Traditionally, women wait for men to offer a handshake, and men and women only exchange a kiss and a hug if they are close friends or family.

Gestures & Etiquette
Armenians are friendly and courteous people. It is considered customary to look another in the

eye when speaking and to call one's attention by politely raising the hand. Gesturing with a fist, with the thumb between the forefinger and middle finger, is considered extremely offensive.

Armenians tend to stand or sit close together when speaking. Unfamiliar people generally keep about an arm's length between them, while friends and family are generally closer. Touching while conversing is rare between men and women, but common between friends and family members of the same sex.

Eating/Meals

Most Armenians begin the day with a light breakfast and have an afternoon snack or lunch. Armenians enjoy taking afternoon coffee breaks accompanied by sweet Armenian biscuits called katahs. Dinner comes late in the day and is usually the most important and largest meal.

Breakfast traditionally involves a combination of scrambled eggs, bread, cheese, honey, jam, cheese, butter, yogurt, and tea or coffee. Armenians usually serve an appetizer before dinner and dessert afterward. Dinners include a salad of raw and cooked vegetables, a soup, and a main course based on meat or fish. Armenians often end a meal with a thick, slightly sweet coffee called haikakan surch.

Armenians tend to begin most meals with a toast, and refusing to toast can be considered an insult. Meals are a time for families and friends to gather, and dinners can often go on for a long time.

Visiting

Armenians enjoy socializing and gathering with friends and family. They value guests and traditionally go to great lengths to make people feel welcome. Food is important in Armenia, and guests are almost always offered something to eat and drink. It is important to try any food or drink that is offered. Armenians like to give a small gift, such as a jar of fruit preserves or a photo, to a new friend or acquaintance.

When visiting churches, people are expected to buy and light candles. It is also considered proper to exit a church by walking out

backwards. Women who plan to participate in a church service are traditionally expected to wear a headscarf.

LIFESTYLE

Family

Armenians value family and life is traditionally centered on family connections and the household. Families are patriarchal, and the wife often moves in with her husband and her husband's family. The eldest woman on the husband's side of the family tends to run the household, and women gain more authority within the home once they have children. In rural areas, large extended families often share a home.

In urban areas, nuclear families (a married couple and their children) are common. However, this smaller nuclear family maintains close ties to their relatives. The average urban couple has two or three children, while rural families tend to have more children. Many rural and mountain families are isolated during the winter and depend on and interact with one another as a result.

Housing

More than half the population of Armenia is urban, with many city-dwellers residing in apartment buildings. Many of these apartment-style complexes were built during the Soviet era and are more functional than aesthetic. In addition, many older homes and buildings have been destroyed by earthquakes. New construction efforts have been underway since the 1990s, and both singular residences and apartment buildings are being built in and around urban areas. The government is also working with international aid organizations to provide better housing for thousands of homeless and displaced citizens and refugees, many of which live in hostels and converted nonresidential buildings.

In rural villages, single-family houses are the norm and are traditionally within walking distance to farmland, orchards, or vineyards. Village housing is mostly made from wood and stone, and many such homes lack indoor plumbing and electricity. Residents instead rely on outhouses and wood-burning stoves and furnaces.

Food

Armenian cuisine blends European and Asian influences, but most closely resembles Mediterranean and Middle Eastern culinary traditions. In general, Armenians consume a well-balanced diet that consists of a variety of fruits and vegetables, grains, and livestock. Meats, such as lamb and pork, often served as kebabs, are common, as are, to a lesser extent, chicken and beef. Dolma is a popular dish in which minced lamb is cooked with a rice pilaf and rolled into grape or cabbage leaves or stuffed into tomato, pepper, or eggplant skins. Armenians also eat fish, mostly whitefish and trout. Popular fruits include watermelons, peaches, plums, pears, apples, cherries, and apricots. Walnuts and pistachios are preferred nuts.

The main grain is bulghur, a type of wheat cooked with soups and meat or vegetable dishes. Bread is generally served with every meal and includes lavash, a thin, flat bread that is often served rolled around meat, cheese, and vegetables. Lavash may be served with any number of dishes, or it can be used to create ksurdgin, which is a type of dumpling made with a beef stew-like filling. The perennial herb sorrel is often braided into strands, sautéed with garlic and other spices, and then cut and served.

Madzoon (or matzoon), a fermented milk product much like yogurt, is common, and most Armenians drink fruit nectars, mineral water, and coffee or tea. (Armenia has more than 700 natural springs and mineral water deposits.) Spicy tea, for example, is often served with meals, and Yerevan, the capital, is also known for its brandy. For dessert, Armenians enjoy fresh fruit, cheese, and sometimes pastries. Pakhlava, a treat made from honey and nuts similar to bakhlava, is a popular dessert. Sugar cookies called shakarishee are also common.

Life's Milestones

More than 92 percent of Armenians follow Armenian Orthodox Christianity, and a minority follows Yazidism and other branches of Christianity, Islam, or Judaism. Accordingly, many of life's milestones are observed within the constructs and sacraments of the Christian faith. Baptism and Holy Communion are widespread rites of passage for infants and youth, respectively, and marriage is considered one of the most significant milestones. Most Armenians tend to marry early—as young as sixteen for girls in rural areas. Some families still arrange marriages, but this tradition is waning.

One common Armenian tradition, called hadik, has its roots in ancient pagan beliefs. Families celebrate agra hadig when a baby's first tooth emerges. During agra hadig, the infant's head is covered with a veil and foods such as grains, raisins, and nuts are spooned over his or her head. Family members arrange objects representing different professions, such as a pen for a writer, in a circle around the baby. The veil is then removed and the first object that the infant grabs indicates what path the child will follow in life.

CULTURAL HISTORY

Art

Armenian art, in terms of style and subject matter, has historically reflected both European and Asian as well as Christian and Islamic influences. Traditional Armenian folk arts include metalwork, ceramics, embroidery and weaving, jewelry-making, and stone and wood carving.

Most Armenian art has its roots in the Christian faith. During the fourth century, artists began painting and sculpting religious icons, especially within churches. Religious artistic influence is also visible in the crafting of sacred objects and the illumination of sacred texts. In fact, Armenians became known worldwide for their skills at manuscript illumination, and many of these manuscripts are preserved in the Matenadaran in Yerevan, which houses more than 17,000 ancient manuscripts.

Armenia is also well known for its monumental khatchkars, scattered across the landscape. Khatchkars, meaning 'cross stones,' were erected from the ninth through the 11th centuries. More than 4,000 of these huge stone slabs, etched with religious symbols and intricate designs, can be found at monasteries and churches throughout the country. Some were raised as tomb markers, others as memorials to mark important battles and other events. Many Armenians believe that the khatchkars ward off danger and provide protection.

The 19th century brought a distinct Russian influence to Armenian art. Armenian painting shifted toward social realism (the state-sanctioned style of Soviet rule) and away from iconography, symbolism, and design. Hakob Hovnatanyan (1806–1881) began painting portraits in a style that combined realism with manuscript illumination. His successor, Hovhannes (Ivan) Aivasovsky (1817–1900) was known for his seascapes, and Eghishe Tatevosian (1870–1936) became known for his painted landscapes. Today, the National Gallery of Art in Yerevan displays many sculptures, paintings, and other artwork dating back to the 17th century, and other examples of Armenian art can be found in indoor and outdoor public spaces throughout the country.

Architecture

Armenian architecture is a curious and remarkable blend of the ancient and modern. The first permanent settlements in Armenia were built with wood and stone and consisted of homes, temples, and fortified complexes. One prominent example is the Erebuni Fortress, one of the oldest archaeological sites in Armenia. Built in 782 BCE by King Argishti I of the Urartu, an Iron Age kingdom, the fortress is triangular in shape and made from stone slabs and adobe. The monumental architecture of both the Greeks and Romans followed, including religious and palatial structures. One notable example is the Temple of the Sun at the village of Garni, which, unlike other Greco-Roman temples, was constructed from basalt. Many temples were replaced by churches following the advent of Christianity. (Armenia was the first state to adopt Christianity as the official religion.)

Much of the historic architecture preserved in Armenia derives from the country's medieval period, and includes numerous fortresses, churches, and monasteries. These structures were largely made from stone, such as volcanic tuff and basalt. (Volcanic tuff has a hard sponge-like appearance and is often brown in color.) The first Armenian churches were basilicas, built in circular form with large cupolas and domes. From the outside, they had a polygonal shape, with domed or conical roofs. This style later gave way to the cruciform—or cross-shaped—construction most often found in modern Armenia. Cruciform churches retained the cupola and dome, but gained extra rooms and a bell tower. Saint Hripsimé Church and Noravank Monastery provide impressive examples of medieval church architecture, as do the monastery ensembles of Haghartsin and Goshavank, near Dilijan.

Islamic rule and Armenia's role as a major thoroughfare for ancient caravans along the Silk Road between Europe and Asia were also influential in the development of Armenia's architecture. The Arabs and Ottoman Turks built numerous palaces, mosques (many of which were later destroyed), and caravanserais, which were inns that provided shelter to caravans and their goods and animals. These caravanserais (or khans) were mostly made from stone, with some wood. One particular caravanserai, the Orbelian's Caravanserai (formerly known as the Selim Caravanserai), was built in 1332 and remains the best-preserved example in Armenia. Made from basalt, its pillared main hall included two side naves for travelers and a large central nave for their animals. The flat-tiled roof had numerous openings for lighting and ventilation.

Armenian architecture shifted under Soviet rule. The architecture of Soviet Armenia was represented by Soviet architecture, which was functional in design and often consisted of monuments to social realism and its principles. For example, simple structures, such as bus stops, were designed in a monumental way to extol the virtues of Soviet public transportation. Soviet rule also produced collective farms, large apartment blocks, and office buildings made from basalt, tuff, and other stone. Many of these structures had a monolithic but flat appearance, with little painting or adornment. With the collapse of the Soviet Union, Armenians have attempted to reclaim the landscape of their country. Many Soviet buildings have been demolished, replaced by modern architecture incorporating steel and glass.

Music & Dance

Armenia has a long tradition of folk and classical music. Much of Armenia's folk traditions developed as a means of celebration, for weddings, harvests, and other events. During the Middle Ages, minstrels also traveled, performing non-religious music and singing of love, legend, daily life, and the countryside around them. Called ashugh, these poets and musicians made an art of turning love poetry into song.

Armenian musicians also developed distinct classical forms of music during medieval times and combined their styles with Russian and other influences in the 19th and 20th centuries. The earliest forms of classical music were liturgical, or religious, in nature. More than 1,000 medieval Christian hymns, meant to be sung without instrumental accompaniment, have been preserved. In the 19th century, the priest Komitas Vardapet

The duduk is an ancient, double-reed woodwind flute made of apricot wood indigenous to Armenia.

(1869–1935) journeyed across Armenia, writing down the songs he heard in each village. Before this, most folk songs were transmitted orally. He is often regarded as the founder of modern Armenian classical music.

Following the Russian conquest, Armenian classical music assumed Russian and European flavors. Russian composers incorporated traditional Armenian sounds with their own forms, and Armenian composers, such as Aram Khachaturian (1903–1978), mixed Russian and European sound into their music. Khachaturian, who composed his body of work during the Soviet era, is the most recognized Armenian classical musician and composer. He wrote not only orchestral symphonies, but also ballets and choral music.

Many old folk dances involved individuals dancing in pairs, one facing the other. Men often had had quicker, more complicated footwork, while women moved slowly and gracefully, making flowing gestures with their arms and wrists. Other traditional dances involved groups of people dancing in lines, shoulder to shoulder, or in circles, linked by hands or fingers. Locally-made instruments provided musical accompaniment for most dances. Such instruments included a double-reed instrument called the duduk (Armenian oboe); a three-stringed sort of violin called the kamāncha; two varieties of lute, the tar and the oud; a lap harp called the kanun; and metal or wooden drums called the dumbek and the dahol. In 2005, the United Nations Educational, Scientific, and Cultural Organization (UNESCO) proclaimed the duduk and its traditional music as one of the Masterpieces of the Oral and Intangible Heritage of Humanity.

Literature & Drama

While Armenia's rich oral tradition dates back thousands of years, the culture's written tradition can be traced to Greek rule. In the fourth century BCE, the Greeks introduced their literature and drama and several amphitheaters were constructed. Then, in the fourth century CE, Armenia became a Christian nation, and many remnants of pagan traditions, including Greek and Roman plays and literature, were prohibited. The Armenians began to develop their own literary tradition, focusing on sacred texts. Armenian drama and theater did not reemerge until the 18th century.

In the fifth century, the monk Mesrop Mashtots (360–440) developed the first Armenian alphabet. He used it to translate religious materials and to compose original sharakans, or short poems that were chanted during church services. That same century, Movses Khorenatsi (c. 410–490s), or Moses of Chorene, authored the epic *History of Armenia,* and Eznik Koghbatsi, or Yeznik of Kolb, wrote *Refutation of the Sects.* An anonymous cleric continued Khorenatsi's history in the late fifth century with *The Epic Histories,* which emphasized the religious devotion and national pride of Armenian historical figures.

The late medieval period saw an increase in secular writing. Translations of ancient Greek and Roman texts appeared, and love poetry reemerged, having been neglected since the time of Greek and Roman literature. Nerses Shnorhali (or Nerses IV the Gracious, 1100–1173) became known for his poem *Lament on the Fall of Edessa*, as well as for his hymns. In the 13th century, the poet Constantine of Erznka wrote about love, beauty, and nature. Bards (poet minstrels) began traveling and performing lyric tales and love poems in the 15th and 16th centuries.

In the 18th and 19th centuries, Armenia drama reappeared. The Russians introduced European drama, and Armenians began to develop their own realistic dramatic style. In 1865, *Khatabala* by Armenian dramatist Gabriel Sundukian (1825–1912) was the first Armenian play performed in the first regular theater in Yerevan. Armenian theater then spread, and new theaters opened in other towns and cities, performing Russian and western European plays, as well as Armenian.

Armenian novelists also produced more work in the 19th century. Hakob Melik Hakobian (1835–1888) known by his pen name Raffi, began authoring works such as *Khentâ* (*The Fool*, 1881) and *Jalaleddin* (1878) late in the century. Hovhannes Tumanian (1869–1923) translated

works by prominent European authors, such as Lord Byron (1788–1824) and Johann Wolfgang von Goethe (1749–1832), and composed his own epic poetry and fables. As with the other arts, the Soviet government restricted Armenian literature and drama in the 20th century. Still, many authors and playwrights sought to preserve their culture and resist Soviet domination by composing works with nationalist and anti-Soviet themes. Soviet rulers often responded by exiling, arresting, and even killing Armenian authors, including Yeghishe Charents (1897–1937) and Vahan Totovents (1893–1938).

CULTURE

Arts & Entertainment

Contemporary arts in Armenia are rooted in the nation's rich cultural heritage. Armenians continue to produce handmade jewelry, embroidery, metalwork, ceramics, woodwork, stone carving, and manuscript illumination. Armenian artists are also noted for contemporary painting and sculpture, including frescoes. In fact, Armenia is often referred to as an outdoor museum because of the many ancient and modern sculptures that adorn its countryside and cityscapes. The fine arts continue to be a focal point of youth education as well. The Children's Art Gallery in Yerevan, opened in 1970, displays artwork produced by Armenian youth, and the National Center for Aesthetics enrolls thousands of children each year.

Music and dance in Armenia derive from the region's folk roots, as well as from Russian and European influences in later centuries. Such traditional music includes church hymns, classical choral and orchestral music, opera, and folk songs. Today, modern troubadours and street performers are commonplace and contemporary Armenian music has acquired international sounds and influences from popular jazz and rock styles out of the United States and other Western countries. Refined styles such as opera, ballet, and musical theater also continue to be popular art forms. The Armenian Opera in Yerevan holds several performances throughout the year, and several orchestras and dance companies tour Armenia on a regular basis.

As with the other arts, literature and drama were largely restricted under Soviet rule (socialist realism was the only state-sanctioned art style). Since Armenia gained independence in 1991, the nation's authors, playwrights, and actors have been working to reclaim their art. Many contemporary writers have focused on translating old Armenian works into English, while others have been developing their own writing. However, funding for publishing has been limited in the past two decades.

Theater and film remains popular in Armenia, and several dramatic theaters operate in Yerevan and Gyumri. The Yerevan State Institute of Theatre and Cinematography sponsors many contemporary theater programs, including the Armenian Hamazgayin Theatre. Armenia's historic film industry nearly died out as a result of war, but has undergone a revival. Hayfilm, founded in 1923, flourished under Soviet control. It is being rescued by Armenian American entrepreneurs who plan to create production facilities for foreign film companies as well as Armenian filmmakers. In addition, most towns and cities have movie theaters, which play Armenian, Russian, and American movies. Armenians participate in international competitions for wrestling, judo, boxing, weightlifting, tennis, and chess.

Cultural Sites & Landmarks

UNESCO recognizes three sites in Armenia as World Heritage Sites. These are the monasteries of Haghpat and Sanahin, the cathedral and churches of Echmiatsin and the archaeological site of Zvartnots, and the monastery of Geghard and the upper Azat Valley. Each of these sites was chosen for its cultural and historical significance.

The two Byzantine monasteries of Haghpat and Sanahin are located in the Debed Canyon of northern Armenia and date back to the 10th century. Both monastery complexes include churches, libraries, scriptoria (place for writing), and other chambers and structures. Khatchkars

adorn the grounds of both. The site at Haghpat also includes later medieval chapels and a free-standing bell tower built in the 13th century. Each complex is a testament to Armenian religious architecture, with a central domed cupola topping cylindrical structures marked by interior pillars. The monks at Sanahin were known for their skilled manuscript illumination.

The oldest church in Armenia stands at Echmiadzin. Built in the fourth century by Gregory the Illuminator (c. 257–c. 331), patron saint of the Armenian Apostolic Church, it was the seat of the Armenian Church. In 480, a new church, Echmiadzin Cathedral, was built on the site. The cathedral took the form of a domed cruciform church, a style that became a hallmark of Armenian religious architecture. The seventh-century Churches of Saint Gayane and Saint Hripsimé are also located at Echmiadzin, as is the archaeological site of Zvartnots. Built in the seventh century, Zvartnots Cathedral was destroyed by a 10th-century earthquake. Ruins of the foundation were uncovered in the early 20th century, along with the ruins of the Katholikos's palace and winery. Ruins dating back another 1,000 years were also revealed.

The Geghard Monastery, also founded by Gregory the Illuminator, was carved into the cliffs of the Geghama Mountains. Originally called Ayrivank, its name meant 'Monastery of the Cave.' It later came to be called Geghardavank, meaning 'Monastery of the Spear,' because the spear that wounded Jesus Christ had allegedly been carried to the monastery. The vast complex includes several caves and chapels, as well as living quarters and other structures, many of which were built directly into the cliffs. The main church, Katoghike, was built in 1215. The site includes many khatchkars as well as ornamental carvings, and some of the designs reveal traces of Arabic influence.

Another four sites are being considered for addition to the World Heritage Sites list: the archaeological site at Dvin, the basilica and archaeological site at Yererouk, the monasteries of Tatev and Tatevi, and the monastery of Noravank and the upper Amaghou Valley. Other notable landmarks include the archaeological sites found at Gyumri. Yerevan offers not only ancient fortresses and churches, but also many more modern museums and galleries. The Blue Mosque, the Genocide Memorial, Victory Park, Republic Square, and the singing fountains near the Hotel Armenia all reflect different periods in Armenia's past. Remarkable natural landmarks include Jermuk Nature Preserve, Devil's Bridge, Lake Sevan and Sevan National Park, and Mount Aragats. On Mount Aragats, the Byurakan Astrophysical Observatory offers insight into Soviet-era scientific explorations.

Though Yerevan predates Rome, most of the structures that would indicate its historic significance were destroyed before or during Soviet rule. The characteristic churches and other buildings that existed in Yerevan were torn down by the Soviet Union and replaced with utilitarian structures. However, the remains of the original eighth-century fortress can still be found, and other ancient vestiges of Yerevan's history have also been discovered.

The Opera House is among the most popular attractions in Yerevan. A neoclassical, colosseum-like structure, the Opera House was built in the 20th century in an effort to revitalize the city. The Armenian Genocide of 1915 is also memorialized throughout the city. Among the most famous of these memorials is the Tsitsernakaberd (Swallow Castle). The Tsitsernakaberd includes a long, steep white stairway and a flame. There are over twenty other memorials to victims of the genocide.

Libraries & Museums

Yerevan is home to numerous museums. Among these, the Mesrop Mashtots Institute of Ancient Manuscripts (or Matenadaran) safeguards thousands of ancient scrolls and documents. There are roughly 17,000 Armenian manuscripts at the institute alone. The State History Museum (or National History Museum), and the Museum of Yerevan, detail the city's role in Armenia's history. Other museums of note in the capital include the Armenian Craft Museum, Contemporary Art Museum, Genocide Museum, and the Middle East Museum.

The National Library of Armenia, in Yerevan, dates back to the early 19th century and serves as Armenia's legal depository; as of January 1, 2012, it houses a collection of approximately 6.8 million items and books, including a collection of rare books (the first printed books in Armenia) dating back to the 16th century. Other libraries of note in the capital include the Yerevan State University Library, the Yerevan City Central Library, and the State Engineering University Library.

Holidays

Armenia's national holiday is Independence Day, also called Referendum Day (September 21), celebrating the 1991 separation from the Soviet Union. Other holidays include Armenian Genocide Memorial Day (April 24), Republic Day (May 28), and Christmas Day (January 6). Constitution Day (July 5) celebrates the adoption of the present Constitution in 1995.

Youth Culture

Armenians generally value their children and early youth culture traditionally centers on the family. Children are expected to assist with household chores and younger siblings as they grow older, and deference to elders is an important practice. In rural areas, children are also traditionally expected to learn the family business or trade. Football (soccer) is the preferred sport, but athletic recreations, such as boxing, gymnastics, tennis, and hiking, are also popular. Swimming is likewise a favored activity, and during the summer, public fountains are open for water play. Children also enjoy playing the nation's most popular board game, nard, which is Persian for backgammon. In general, Western-style culture, including music and fashion trends, is popular among older Armenian youth.

Young Armenians enjoy a high level of literacy and access to education. Education is free and compulsory from the ages of six to sixteen. After primary school, secondary education may be vocationally-based, and examinations are required in order to graduate to the next level. Often, graduation is a milestone event marked by a celebration, including singing and dancing, as well as poetry reciting and the performance of plays. In Yerevan, on the last day of school, students amass in Republic Square for a public celebration called the Night of the Last Bell. Higher education encompasses university learning or technical or vocational studies. Most colleges and universities specialize in certain fields, such as teaching, medicine, and engineering, and several institutions focus on athletic and performing arts fields. In fact, the Academy of Television and Radio was considered the first of its kind in a former Soviet republic.

Since the collapse of Soviet rule, funding for education and other children's programs has declined, while access to health care and other services has also been an issue. In addition, school buildings and materials have deteriorated and agrarian and domestic obligations often take precedence over school attendance in rural areas. Though children under the age of sixteen are not legally permitted to work, many assist with the family business or sell wares at local markets. UNICEF (United Nations Children's Fund) has reported that between 2002 and 2005, Armenia's dropout rate grew from 1,531 to 7,630, with an expected annual increase of 250 percent.

SOCIETY

Transportation
Armenia is a landlocked nation that relies primarily on overland travel. Buses and trains—Armenian Railway is the national rail operator—are the most common modes of public transportation and most urban buses run on electrical cables. Minibuses (called marshotni or marshrutkas), taxis, and trolleys are also common in urban areas. There is also a metro (subway) system in Yerevan. In addition, the use of horse-drawn carts is not uncommon in rural areas. Traffic moves on the right-hand side of the road.

Transportation Infrastructure
Armenia has two international airports, one at Yerevan (Zvartnots International Airport) and the other at Gyumri (Shirak Airport). Armenian Airlines, opened in 1993, is the national carrier. Armenia relies on neighboring countries such as Georgia for shipping imports and exports (the nearest seaport is Poti, in Georgia). As of 2014, the length of roadways measured only 7,700 kilometers (4,784 miles) and 845 kilometers (521 miles) of railway. Armenia is considered an important transportation link in the Europe-Caucasus-Asia corridor, and efforts have been made to expand and improve roads, railways, and bridges since the 1990s.

Media & Communications
Armenia offers more than a dozen print newspapers, and more than a dozen radios stations broadcast local and regional programs, but television is the leading medium. The state-run Public TV of Armenia is one of two public networks and operates many stations that provide national coverage. Armenia TV is the national commercial station. The number of private television and cable stations has increased in recent years, numbering more than 48 as of 2014. Media access, including telecommunications and radio or TV broadcasts, is limited in rural regions, and the government has been working to increase access since the 1990s.

By the early 21st century, Armenia had nearly 300,000 telephone landlines, many of which were old and unreliable, and cell phone use has been increasing rapidly. As of June 2014, Armenia had 3.3 million cell plan subscribers, distributed among three companies: Viva, which boasts 2.1 million and offers 4G coverage; Beeline, which has 0.7 million and offers only 2G and 3G service; and Orange, which has 0.5 million and only 2G and 3G. Some Armenians still rely on call centers, which are often available in post offices, and most towns and cities also have Internet cafés. As of 2014, Armenia had nearly 1.4 million Internet users, representing roughly 47 percent of the population. A few of Armenia's Internet providers are Russian, and for that reason, the official Russian telecommunications watchdog, Roskomnadzor, places filters that sometime block completely free access to the Web for some Armenian users.

SOCIAL DEVELOPMENT

Standard of Living

Armenia ranked eighty-seventh out of 195 countries on the 2012 United Nations Human Development Index, which measures quality of life and standard of living indicators.

Water Consumption

According to 2012 statistics from the World Bank, nearly 100 percent of the Armenian population had access to improved sources of drinking water. The United States Agency for International Development (USAID) reported that, in fiscal year 2014, the country spent $0.7 million to maintain and upgrade these supply and sanitation systems, which are regulated by the Water Code of the Republic of Armenia. Five privately-operated water supply and sewerage companies are currently in operation.

Education

Like most peoples of the former Soviet Union, Armenians are highly literate—the literacy rate among adults is near 99 percent. Although Armenia's public schools remain free and, in theory, compulsory through grade 10, state expenditure on education fell during the war with Azerbaijan, and it remains low. UNICEF reports that only 77 percent of primary school teachers are professionally trained, and teachers, on the whole, make only 68 percent of the average national wage, a fact that forces many to supplement their income with other work.

In 1995, when over 70 percent of Armenians were unemployed, more than 20,000 school-age children received no schooling. Parents could not afford food and transportation to school, nor school supplies. Since then, circumstances have markedly improved. UNICEF reported in 2008 that 98.8 percent of Armenian children transition into secondary school, although chronic absenteeism is a serious problem in the upper grades and dropout numbers have steadily increased since 2002.

Armenia currently has many private schools at all levels, often supported by charitable groups outside Armenia. Although tuition-based, these can be more affordable for poor families than free public schools are, as some private schools provide supplies, transportation, and even free breakfasts.

Having completed two years of high school, students may continue in specialized and technical secondary education, and then to college for a four-year bachelor's degree. Graduate degrees include the two-year 'magistracy' (or master's degree) followed by the 'aspirantura,' a two-year program which culminates in a Candidate in Science degree. Students wishing doctoral degrees enroll in an 'Academy of Science,' taking no courses but doing independent research, which they must defend before a Highest Attestation Commission.

Women's Rights

Despite constitutional guarantees of equal rights and high levels of education and literacy, many Armenian women continue to suffer from discrimination, harassment, and violence. Women are still expected to adhere to traditional gender expectations and Armenian society remains largely patriarchal, with men dominating business and government and directing family life.

Violence against women in Armenia remains a pressing issue that has drawn international attention. No laws prohibit domestic violence or spousal abuse and incidents of abuse and violence are generally underreported. Though rape and spousal rape is illegal, many women also hesitate to report these abuses. In all instances, women fear that the legal system will neither protect them nor punish their abuser or rapist. Many women are also reluctant to expose violence in the family to public view. Since 1997, the Women's Rights Center, an Armenian non-governmental organization (NGO), has been working to report violations of women's rights and to increase protections for women. In 2007, the Women's Rights Center, reported that nearly 40 percent of Armenian women had suffered some form of physical abuse.

Human trafficking for the purpose of sexual exploitation remains a problem for women in Armenia. According to a 2008 report, Armenia is considered a source country for women who are forced into sex slavery, with countries such as Turkey and the United Arab Emirates (UAE) as primary destinations. While human trafficking is prohibited, few traffickers are arrested and convicted, with many serving lenient sentences. It is also reported that Armenian women are trafficked to neighboring countries such as Turkey and Russia for forced labor purposes. In addition, prostitution continues to be legal.

Although women are guaranteed equal status and opportunities under the law, many Armenian women still report suffering discrimination and harassment in the workplace. In fact, there is no law that directly prohibits sexual harassment. Reports also indicate that women are generally kept in lower-status and lower-paying jobs and they earn lower wages than their male counterparts do. In addition, the proportion of women in the national assembly and the government has declined since Soviet rule ended in 1991. In 2014, women held just 14 of 131 National Assembly seats, although this figure has been rising due in part to a quota law passed in 2005 that requires political parties to name women as 15 percent of their nominees.

Armenia has implemented several other initiatives in the early 21st century to address women's rights and their roles in society. In 2007, the Anti-Human Trafficking on Air Act was enacted, which requires airlines to notify passengers about human trafficking. In 2004, the government adopted both the Action Plan for Prevention of Trafficking in Persons from the Republic of Armenia for 2004–2006 (though considered inefficient by some agencies) and the 2004–2010 Republic of Armenia National Action Plan (NAP) on Improving the Status of Women and Enhancing Their Role in Society. However, international monitoring agencies, such as Amnesty International (AI), continue to contend the violence against women is ingrained and widespread, asserting in a 2008 report that domestic violence continues to be perceived as a 'private matter,' and that one in four women are abused by family members.

Health Care

Under the Soviet system, Armenia's government provided free health care for its citizens. The Armenian government pays only five percent of health care costs, or approximately $10 (USD) per capita on health care annually.

In rural areas, hospitals and clinics are dilapidated and often unheated. Basic drugs and supplies are lacking. Nurses and physicians are poorly paid. Moreover, those educated under the Soviet system often rely on drugs and methods long rejected by Western medical practitioners.

Armenians suffer from high rates of cardiovascular disease, cancer, stroke, and mental illness. Contagious diseases such as tuberculosis and sexually-transmitted diseases, including HIV, are spreading. Approximately 80 percent of children receive no medical care. A 2003 sample survey of rural families found that nearly half did not seek health care for sick family members, due to the cost.

Charitable agencies and private interests outside Armenia supply many needs, creating mobile clinics to visit remote communities, supplying wheelchairs for the disabled, and cooperating with hospitals and medical personnel to supply necessary equipment and medical supplies. Western universities, such as Canada's McGill University, have established alliances with Armenian institutions of higher learning for sharing experience and technology.

GOVERNMENT

Structure

Armenia is a republic with a government modeled on that of European parliamentary democracies. It consists of three branches: legislative, executive, and judicial. The legislative branch is unicameral, consisting of a National Assembly of 131 members elected to four-year terms.

The executive branch includes a president elected by popular vote to a five-year term, a prime minister appointed by the president, and a Council of Ministers named by the prime minister. Should the General Assembly reject their program, the prime minister and Council of Ministers must resign. The judicial branch consists of a Constitutional Court and a Court of Cassation (Appeals).

Political Parties

Armenians support many political parties, none of which holds an overwhelming majority. Assembly members frequently switch parties, declare themselves independent, or initiate new parties. Still, several parties currently steer Armenian politics. The Republican Party of Armenia, a center-right party, presently exerts the most power. In the 2012 parliamentary elections, they garnered almost 52.7 percent of the vote and took sixty-nine seats in the assembly. The conservative Prosperous Armenia Party took 28.2 percent of the vote and thirty-seven seats. The Armenian National Congress, a centrist party promoting market liberalism, received 5.3 percent of the vote and gained seven seats. Other parties of note are the centrist Rule of Law Party, the socialist-oriented Armenian Revolutionary Federation, and the liberal Heritage Party.

Local Government

There are 10 marzer (provinces) responsible for local administration and an additional administrative unit for the city of Yerevan, which is led by a directly elected mayor. Decentralization has been a goal of the central government, which, since passage of the Law on Local Self-Government in 2002, has tried to establish local governance through appointed governors and staff. The second tier of local government includes more than 914 communities, each led by a Council of Elders. Decentralization has been hampered by economic constraints, which have limited the actions of these local administrations, as they depend on the central government for revenues.

Judicial System

The structure of the Armenian system of justice is three-tiered, with courts of first instance, courts of appeal, and courts of cassation (the equivalent of a Supreme Court).

Taxation

The government of Armenia levies corporate, personal income, social security, pension, value-added, excise, land, and property taxes. Tax rates are low, and include a top corporate rate of 20 percent and a top personal income tax rate of 20 percent as well.

Armed Forces

The Armenian Armed Forces consist of an army, air force, and border guard (which mostly monitor the borders of Georgia and Azerbaijan). Conscription is instituted and consists of a two-year military service obligation. The minimum military age is eighteen. Armenian troops have served in peacekeeping and support missions in both Kosovo and Iraq (though only non-combat troops were deployed to the latter). Armenia has also provided support to Armenians in the contested Nagorno-Karabakh area. In 2010, while facing a shortage of army personnel, the Armenian government reduced the number of post-graduate spots in academia that offered exemption from military service, a move that was criticized as a method to increase the military's ranks. As of 2015, Armenia has 70 troops stationed in Kosovo, 33 in Lebanon, and 130 in Afghanistan for peacekeeping operations.

Foreign Policy

Armenia's primary foreign policy goals involve the development of foreign trade and investment, European integration, and stability in the region. In 1991, Armenia and the neighboring republics of Georgia and Azerbaijan won their independence from the collapsed Soviet Union. All three countries immediately sought to stabilize themselves politically and economically and focus was quickly centered on gaining international recognition and aid. In 1991, Armenia joined the Commonwealth of Independent States (CIS), a body meant to bring together former Soviet republics in mutual cooperation and support. The following year, Armenia joined the United Nations (UN). Armenia has since become a member of 40 international and regional bodies, including the Council of Europe, the

Organization for Security and Co-operation in Europe (OSCE). It is also a member of NATO's Partnership for Peace, the North Atlantic Cooperation Council, the Organization of the Black Sea Economic Cooperation (BSEC), the International Monetary Fund (IMF), the World Bank, and the World Trade Organization (WTO).

As Armenia continues to transition to a democratic state and free market economy, it continues to be the recipient of a substantial amount of foreign aid, including a substantial March 2009 loan—$540 million (USD)—from the IMF and an agreement of partnership and cooperation with the European Union (EU), implemented in 1999. In 2006, Armenia signed a treaty with the Millennium Challenge Corporation (MCC), a U.S. governmental organization. Under the compact, the Armenian government has pledged to meet certain goals in policy and government reform. In return, the United States will increase its economic aid and investment in the nation by as much as $235 million (USD). In addition, dozens of U.S.-based corporations are conducting business in Armenia, and Armenia in turn hopes to increase foreign business investment as well as international tourism. Armenia is also economically tied to Russia and Georgia and relies on support from the Armenian Diaspora, concentrated mainly in the US and France.

Since achieving independence, Armenia has been involved in a conflict with Azerbaijan over the province of Nagorno-Karabakh. Located in western Azerbaijan, the province has a majority population of ethnic Armenians and declared its intentions to separate from Azerbaijan. Armenia supported the province's move, leading to a conflict with Azerbaijan and Turkey, which supported Azerbaijan's rule of Nagorno-Karabakh. Tens of thousands of Armenians fled Azerbaijan due to violence, and Turkey and Azerbaijan closed their respective borders. Efforts to resolve the dispute have so far failed, but negotiations are ongoing. The Minsk Group—co-chaired by the United States, Russia, and France—and the Organization for Security and Co-operation in Europe (OSCE) has increased peacemaking efforts in the region.

Armenia's relations with Turkey also have remained strained due to Turkey's refusal to recognize as genocide the killing of hundreds of thousands of Armenians during World War I. As of 2015, only 27 countries officially recognize the events as genocide, and the passage of a resolution recognizing the Armenian Genocide has been a matter of debate in several countries, including the U.S. The governments of Turkey, Azerbaijan, and Pakistan officially deny its occurrence.

Human Rights Profile

International human rights law insists that states respect civil and political rights and promote an individual's economic, social, and cultural rights. The United Nations Universal Declaration on Human Rights (UDHR) is recognized as the standard for international human rights. Its authors sought the counsel of the world's great thinkers, philosophers, and religious leaders and were careful to create a document that reflects the core values shared by every world culture. (To read this document or view the articles relating to cultural human rights, go to http://www.ohchr.org/EN/UDHR/Pages/Introduction.aspx.).

In 1995, Armenia adopted a new constitution and established a representative democracy with an elected president and parliament and an independent judiciary. The constitution protects civil and human rights, including the freedoms of speech, assembly, religion, and the press. In addition, all citizens aged eighteen and over are guaranteed the right to vote. Despite this structure, a number of human rights issues have surfaced in recent years. Both the U.S. Department of State and several international monitoring agencies reported serious problems with restrictions of civil liberties and violations of human rights in 2007 and 2008 in Armenia. These included incidents of election fraud and voter intimidation, government corruption, discrimination, and human trafficking.

Outside observers particularly reported serious problems with the presidential election in February 2008. According to a report by the U.S. Department of State, the election had been geared in favor of the government candidate, ballot boxes had been stuffed, voters intimidated, votes bought, and government funds misused. Furthermore, following the election, when thousands of citizens protested the results, the government used force to end the protests, resulting in ten deaths and allegations of police abuse, including arbitrary arrests and detentions. Fraud issues arose again with the parliamentary elections of 2012, when 5,000 Armenian National Congress members marched to protest alleged vote-buying and other violations and ultimately appealed to the Constitutional Court to annul the election results.

The government has also been found to limit freedom of the press, speech, and assembly. For example, the government has used force to quell political demonstrations, and the news media was repeatedly restricted in its coverage. Journalists, reporters, and photographers were also subject to harassment, violence, and arrest at various times. In 2014, the Committee to Protect Freedom of Expression, an Armenian non-governmental organization, reported that seven physical attacks against journalists occurred between January and September. As a result, self-censorship has become a common practice to avoid government interference. Outside observers also repeatedly reported discrimination against women, religious and ethnic minority groups, and persons with disabilities, particularly in regards to employment, housing, and access to health care and education. Human trafficking in Armenia has also extended to men, who are forced into labor in other countries.

Migration

In 2012, Armenia's net migration rate was –5 migrants per 1,000 residents, according to the World Bank. The country's negative migration rate has been a concern in the early 21st century, and some politicians have tied it to the Nagorno-Karabakh conflict, which they claim should be resolved in order to turn the tide of Armenian migration.

ECONOMY

Overview of the Economy

Under the Soviet Union, Armenia imported raw goods and energy from other Soviet states and returned them as finished manufactured products. Following independence and severe economic depression in the 1990s, Armenia is recovering, supported by the International Monetary Fund and private investment. The inflation rate has been stabilized; small and medium-sized businesses have been privatized, and the Metsamor Nuclear Power Plant supplies energy, though at a risk.

Yerevan's economy has grown substantially since the turn of the 21st century. International corporations, such as IBM and Proctor & Gamble, have offices in Yerevan. Additionally, trade with Iran continues to fuel the economy. Yerevan is also the home of several of the country's major universities; however, many of the skilled, trained graduates of the city's educational establishments immigrate to other countries.

Industry

Industries in Armenia include the manufacture of machine tools and instruments, electric motors, trucks, tires, shoes, clothing, and jewelry. Microelectronics and software development are growing in importance. As of April 2012, the diamond processing industry engaged between 3,000 and 4,000 people, down from the 8,000 employed before the field's 2004 recession.

Armenia's major exports include cut diamonds, metal goods (machinery, copper ore, scrap metal), vegetables and fruits (especially grapes), and livestock. The country imports uncut diamonds, petroleum, natural gas, food, and tobacco. Major trading partners are Russia, Bulgaria, Belgium, the United States, and Iran. In 2014, Armenia exported approximately $1.75 billion USD in goods and imported $4.02 billion USD. The country's estimated gross domestic product (GDP) in 2014 was $7,400 (USD) per capita.

Labor

In 2014, Armenia's labor force numbered an estimated 1.48 million, while the unemployment rate was approximately 7.1 percent that same year. The majority of the labor force—an estimated 44.2 percent—works in agriculture, while industry accounts for 16.8 percent, and the services sector accounts for 39 percent. Due to the global economic crisis, unemployment rose sharply in Armenia in 2009 and has continued to rise: as of 2013, the unemployment rate has climbed to 15.9 percent, while 35.8 percent of Armenians live below the poverty line.

Energy/Power/Natural Resources

Armenia's mineral resources consist of small quantities of gold, copper, molybdenum, zinc, and alumina ores. During the 1990s, an energy blockade imposed on Armenia forced families to rely on wood fuel. As a result, once-forested areas are now barren slopes subject to erosion.

Hydropower and nuclear power are the nation's only non-imported sources of energy. Use of Lake Sevan for hydropower has threatened the supply of local drinking water. The once-abandoned Soviet-era Metsamor Nuclear Power Plant has been reinstated, although it is located on land that is subject to earthquakes.

Fishing

As a landlocked country, Armenia's fishing industry is limited to fresh water lakes and rivers. Lake Sevan, for example, is home to a rare fish called the Sevan Trout, a salmonid brown trout. It has suffered from overfishing and from competition posed by other invasive fish species introduced during the Soviet era. However, because of conservation efforts and commercial fishing prohibitions begun in the late 1970s, two of the Sevan Trout's four varieties are returning. Fish farming has also increased in response to commercial fishing bans. Export markets in Russia for Armenian fish products opened up in the early 21st century, while the development of similar European markets are dependent on the country's ability to meet EU safety standards.

Forestry

Less than 10 percent of the land area of Armenia is covered by forest, making it one of the 70 countries designated as low forest-covered countries. The result of the continued efforts of timber companies is that much more threatening to the country's environment. The government has increased its regulation of the industry, but more needs to be done in terms of reforestation. In 1994, the Armenian Tree Project (ATP) was established to help rectify this problem, and, as of 2015, they have planted over 4.5 million trees at 900 sites throughout Armenia as well as practiced forest-management techniques to foster new and established growth. However, the struggle is ongoing, as livestock grazing and logging activity have severely damaged or destroyed 35 percent of ATP's efforts.

Mining/Metals

Armenia's mineral resources include gold, silver, lead, zinc, copper, molybdenum, and iron-ore, as well as salt, gypsum, zeolite, diatomaceous earth, limestone, granite, and basalt. Mining alone made up over half the country's exports in 2011.

Agriculture

In 1990, Armenia became the first post-Soviet republic to privatize its farmland, dividing large, mechanized communes into three-acre family farms. In the new economy, complicated by an economic blockade, good seed, fertilizer, water rights, and appropriate farm machinery were difficult to obtain. Cattle were slaughtered for lack of feed, and fruit trees and vines were uprooted.

Now, however, farms are being combined for efficiency, although farmers' cooperatives are still nonexistent. The major food crops are wine grapes and citrus fruit, grown in the sub-tropical Aras River Valley. Other important crops include sugar beets, potatoes; wheat, barley, cotton, and tobacco. Still, a great deal of arable soil is polluted from use of the toxic pesticide DDT.

Animal Husbandry

Armenia exports both cattle and sheep. In 2013, according to the Armenian Ministry of Agriculture, an estimated 150,000–180,000 Armenian sheep were exported to Iran and several Arab countries. Pigs, poultry, and goats are also bred. September 2013 estimates indicated that meat production climbed to 74,600 tonnes (82 tons), and milk production increased overall by 17,000 tonnes (18.7 tons), with increases expected to continue.

Tourism

Tourism in Armenia is a healthy and growing part of the economy. Approximately 843,330 tourists visited the country in 2012 and this number continues to increase annually. Tourists in Armenia spend an average of $650 (USD) per day.

Ethnic Armenians visiting the homeland account for 70 percent of all visitors. Others come for the country's famous spas at mineral springs. Eager to increase these numbers, the Department of Tourism cites the need to expand the airport in Yerevan, to repair roads, and to fund the restoration and protection of museums and historic monuments.

Tourism has also contributed to Yerevan's economic recovery, as many eco-tourists include Yerevan on their itineraries. However, heritage tourism dominates the industry. Heritage tourists are made up of the descendants of Armenians displaced by the forced resettlement carried out by the Ottoman Empire in the early 20th century. As with the rest of the country, members of the Armenian diaspora make up the bulk of the tourists who visit Yerevan every year.

Four of Armenia's historic monuments are listed by the United Nations Educational, Scientific, and Cultural Organization (UNESCO) as World Heritage sites. Among the oldest centers of Christianity, they are all accessible from Yerevan and include the Haghpat monastic complex, Etchmiadzin Cathedral (the first church of the Armenian Apostolic religion and the country's first cathedral), the ruins of Zvartnots (built where Christianity was introduced), Geghard Monastery (carved from rocks and caves), and the monastic complex of Noravank.

By Christina Dendy, Ann Parrish, &
Amanda Wilding

DO YOU KNOW?

- Varazdat Arshakuni, King of Armenia, entered the 291st Olympic Games in 385 CE and won the championship in boxing.
- One of the 13 districts of Yerevan is named Bangladesh.

Bibliography

Arra S. Avakian. *Armenia: A Journey Through History.* Fresno, California: The Electric Press, 2008.

Michael Bobelian. *Children of Armenia: A Forgotten Genocide and the Century-long Struggle for Justice.* New York: Simon & Schuster, 2012.

Thomas De Waal, *Black Garden: Armenia and Azerbaijan Through Peace and War.* Tenth ed. New York: NYU Press, 2013.

Vasily Grossman. *An Armenian Sketchbook.* Transl. Robert Chandler & Elizabeth Chandler. New York: New York Review Books Classics, 2013.

Martin Hintz. *Armenia: Enchantment of the World.* New York: Children's Press, 2004.

Diedre Holding. *Armenia with Nagorno Karabagh.* Bucks, England: Bradt Travel Guides, 2014.

Lucine Kasbarian. *Armenia: A Rugged Land, an Enduring People.* Parsippany, New Jersey: Dillon Press, 1998.

David Kherdian. *The Road from Home: The Story of an Armenian Girl.* New York: Harper Trophy, 1995.

Thomas Streissguth. *The Transcaucasus.* San Diego: Lucent Books, 2001.

Gabriella Uluhogian, Boghos Levon Zekiyan, & Vartan Karapetian. *Armenia: Imprints of a Civilization.* New York: Skira, 2012.

Works Cited

"Armenia Tree Project—Greening Armenia Since 1994." *Armenia Tree Project*. Armenia Tree Project, 2015. Web. http://www.armeniatree.org/.

"Armenia." *Culture Crossing Guide*. Culture Crossing, 2014. Web. http://guide.culturecrossing.net/basics_business_student.php?id=11.

National Statistical Service of the Republic of Armenia (NSSRA). *Statistical Indicators*. NSSRA & World Bank, 3 Apr. 2015. Web. http://www.armstat.am/en/.

"Armenia" *Amnesty International Report 2014/15*. Amnesty International, 2015. https://www.amnesty.org/en/countries/europe-and-central-asia/armenia/.

"Armenia—Housing." Nations Encyclopedia. *Nations Encyclopedia*. Advameg, Inc., 2015. Web. http://www.nationsencyclopedia.com/Europe/Armenia-HOUSING.html.

"Country Reports on Human Rights Practices for 2013: Armenia." *Bureau of Democracy, Human Rights and Labor*. U.S. Department of State, 2013. Web. http://www.state.gov/j/drl/rls/hrrpt/humanrightsreport/index.htm#wrapper.

"U.S. Relations with Armenia—Fact Sheet." *Bureau of European and Eurasian Affairs*. U.S. Department of State, 20 Mar. 2015. http://www.state.gov/r/pa/ei/bgn/5275.htm.

"World Heritage Sites in Armenia." *World Heritage Site*. WHS, 2015. Web. http://worldheritagesite.org/countries/armenia.html.

Nicole Itano, "Quota Law Puts More Women in Armenian Election." *WeNews*. Women's eNews Inc., 10 May 2007. Web. http://womensenews.org/story/the-world/070510/quota-law-puts-more-women-armenias-election.

Sima A. Aprahamien, "Armenia." *Countries and Their Cultures*. Advameg, Inc., 2015. Web. http://www.everyculture.com/A-Bo/Armenia.html.

UNESCO. "Armenia." *World Heritage Convention*. UNESCO, 2015. Web. http://whc.unesco.org/en/statesparties/am.

Mosque in Baku, Azerbaijan

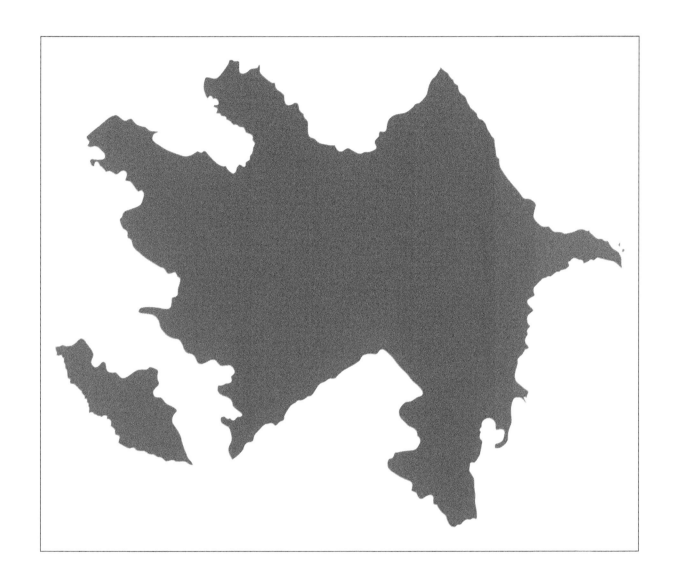

AZERBAIJAN

Introduction

The Republic of Azerbaijan is a small Transcaucasian republic on the Caspian Sea, bordered by Armenia, Georgia, Iran, and Russia. Historically, the region has long been at the center of power struggles between stronger neighbors, as well as the Greeks and Romans. Most recently, Russia dominated Azerbaijan's affairs until it gained independence in 1991.

Like other former Soviet republics, Azerbaijan became involved in post-independence conflicts that have slowed serious social and economic reforms. Significant oil reserves give the country great potential for future growth and stability, but the industry will require further development and careful management if it is to benefit a broad section of the population.

Azerbaijan's rich cultural traditions reached their pinnacle during the medieval era, in literature, science, music, architecture, and decorative arts. Miniatures, calligraphy, 9,494,600[the country is most famous for its carpets. The tradition of carpet weaving continues to this day.

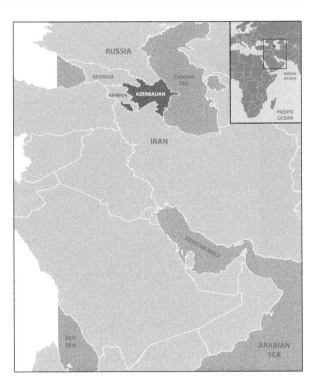

GENERAL INFORMATION

Official Language: Azeri (also known as Azerbaijani Turkish)
Population: 9,494,600 (2014 estimate)
Currency: Azerbaijani manat

Coins: The Azerbaijani manat is subdivided into 100 qəpik. Coins are available in denominations of 1, 3, 5, 10, 20, and 50 qəpik.
Land Area: 86,600 square kilometers (33,436 square miles)
Water Area: 500 square kilometers (193 square miles)
National Anthem: "Azərbaycan Marşı" ("March of Azerbaijan")
Capital: Baku
Time Zone: GMT +5
Flag Description: The flag of Azerbaijan features three horizontal bands, one blue (top), one red (middle), and one green (bottom). In the center of the flag is a white crescent moon, which is a symbol of Islam, and an eight-pointed star, which signifies the Turkic people.

Population

Azerbaijan's average population density is 109 persons per square kilometer (282 per square mile). The population is concentrated in valleys and irrigated lowlands, including the Absheron Peninsula, the most densely populated region.

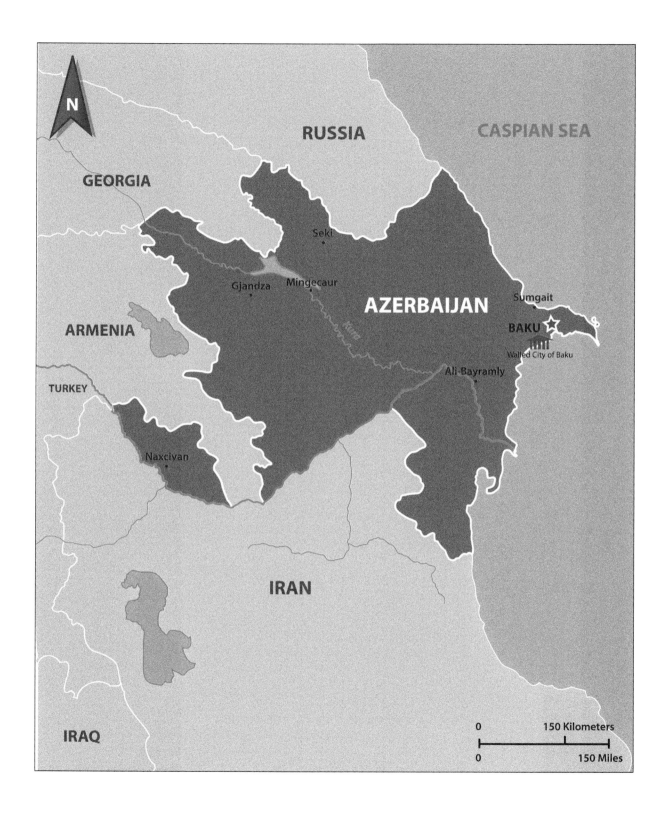

Principal Cities by Population (2014):

- Baku/Baki (2,181,800)
- Ganja/Gəncə (1,054,962)
- Sumgait/Sumqayit (333,700)
- Mingəçevir/Mingachevir (99,775)
- Shirvan/Şirvan (81,200)
- Qaraçuxur (77,619)
- Naxçivan/Nakhchivan (74,500)
- Bakixanov (70,923)
- Sheki/Şəki (63,700)
- Yevlax/Yevlakh (59,036)

Approximately 48 percent of the population lives in rural areas. Baku, with a population of almost 2.2 million, is the largest city. Sumgait, also on the Absheron Peninsula and Ganja are the other major urban centers.

The Turkic Azeris comprise almost 92 percent of the population. Dagestanis, an ethnic group concentrated in southern Russia along the border with Azerbaijan, make up 2.2 percent of the population, while Russians constitute 1.3 percent and Armenians make up 1.3 percent. The Russian population has decreased since the fall of the Soviet Union, and nearly all Armenians are concentrated in the Nagorno-Karabakh region, which has proclaimed its independence and been the focus of fierce fighting between Armenia and Azerbaijan.

Azerbaijan's population has shown a slight growth trend in the 21st century. The growth rate was estimated at 1.3 percent in 2013. As of 2014, 53 percent of the population lives in urban areas.

Languages

Azeri is spoken by 90 percent of the population. An Altaic language, it is related to Turkish and other Central Asian languages. It has made a full conversion from the Cyrillic alphabet and is once again written in a modified Latin alphabet. Minority languages include Russian and Armenian.

Native People & Ethnic Groups

Russians, the most recent ethnic group to arrive in Azerbaijan, began colonizing the region in the early 18th century. Under this yoke, native Azerbaijanis suffered for most of the next 200 years, especially during the Soviet era, when attempts were made to demolish their history and culture and replace it with pro-Russia, Marxist propaganda. In the early 21st century, Turkic Azeris make up approximately 90 percent of the population.

In 1988, ethnic tensions between Azerbaijan and Armenia over the predominantly Armenian Nagorno-Karabakh region flared up. A cease-fire was declared in 1993, though the status of this region remains unresolved. Casualties from the conflict numbered near 20,000, and more than one million people were made refugees. Armenians are one of the largest minority groups in the country, behind Russians and Dagestanis.

Religions

Approximately 96 percent of the population professes belief in Islam, a religion that is no longer proscribed by the government. Many Azerbaijanis, however, do not practice their religion. Shia Muslims comprise the largest sect. Russians and Armenians practice their respective forms of Orthodox Christianity.

Climate

The steppe, the lowlands, the coastal regions, and the mountains give Azerbaijan several distinct climatic zones. On the eastern and central steppe, summers are long and hot, rainfall is low—sometimes reaching only 200–350 mm (8–13 inches) annually—and the region is prone to drought. In the lowlands of the southeast, a subtropical climate prevails. This region receives the most rainfall, between 1,600 and 1,800 millimeters (63–71 inches) a year; it is arid in the summers and very humid in the winters. Along the Caspian Sea, the climate is mild year round. The coldest temperatures occur in the northern mountains, where snowfall is heavy during the winter.

Average temperatures for spring and summer fall between 20° and 30° Celsius (70° and 80° Fahrenheit) and between 5° and 10° Celsius (40° and 50° Fahrenheit) in the fall and winter.

ENVIRONMENT & GEOGRAPHY

Topography

Azerbaijan has two separate areas, with a stretch of Armenia dividing them: the main portion and the autonomous republic of Naxçivan.

Half of Azerbaijan's terrain is low coastal land and low rolling steppe, while the rest is mountainous. The Caspian Sea forms the eastern coast, parts of which dip well below sea level. The coast's most distinctive feature is the Absheron Peninsula, where the capital is located. The central portion of the country and the southeast are also lowlands.

In general, Azerbaijan is surrounded by mountains. The Greater Caucasus stretch along part of the northeastern border and continue southeast to the Absheron Peninsula. Mount Bazardüzü, the country's highest peak at 4,466 meters (14,652 feet), rises from this range. Along part of the border with Armenia rises the Lesser Caucasus. In the southeast, bordering Iran, are the Talish Mountains.

Several large rivers have their source in the Caucasus and cross Azerbaijan's central lowlands and eventually empty into the Caspian Sea. The Kura and Aras are the most significant rivers. The damming of the Kura has formed the country's largest body of water, the Mingachevir (or Mingəçevir) Reservoir, measuring 605 square kilometers (234 square miles). Like the rivers themselves, water released from the reservoir along the Upper Karabakh Canal is vital for the irrigation of the lowlands.

Plants & Animals

Both the mountains and the southeast lowlands support tree growth, which covers only 11.3 percent (or 2,313 acres) of the country's total area. Species include pine, beech, and oak.

Wild boar, deer, and bear inhabit the mountain forests. In the dry lowlands, reptiles such as snakes and lizards are common. Among the larger animals are hyenas and gazelles.

The coast of the Caspian Sea is an important migratory corridor for an array of birds, though the pollution in this area has harmed their populations. For the same reason, the Caspian seal is listed as vulnerable, and populations of sturgeon have decreased.

CUSTOMS & COURTESIES

Greetings

Most Azerbaijanis speak Azerbaijani, also called Azeri, a language similar to Turkish. Many also speak Russian as a result of more than a century of Russian and Soviet rule. The most common greeting in Azeri is "Salaam," which translates as both "peace" and "hello." Another common phrase is "sağ ol" ("Be well"). Familiar people use each other's first names, while unfamiliar people address each other by their first names followed by "hanum" for women and "bey" for men.

Generally, the Azerbaijani are a hospitable and welcoming people. Men customarily greet one another by shaking hands, and close male friends may embrace and exchange alternate kisses on the cheek. Women do not usually shake hands, unless meeting someone for the first time, and instead prefer to embrace and kiss each other on the left cheek. A man typically waits until a woman offers her hand in greeting and then shakes it lightly. It is important to note that, in Muslim culture, only the right hand is used for greeting; this is because the left hand is traditionally associated with the cleansing of the body and is considered impure.

Gestures & Etiquette

Azerbaijanis are direct people, and it is considered polite to maintain direct eye contact during greetings and conversations. People tend to point or gesture with the entire hand rather than just with a finger, which is considered rude. Holding the hand palm up and shaking it back and forth indicates a question. Offensive gestures include putting one's thumb and forefinger together in a circle (as in the American gesture for "okay"); putting one's thumb between the forefinger and middle finger in a fist; and slapping one's palm on a closed fist. It is also rude for a person to cross one's legs in a way that shows the sole of the foot.

Azerbaijanis are less strict about social conventions and taboos than people in other Muslim countries are. However, men and women generally do not touch one another unless they are close friends and family. Friends and family also stand close together when talking and may even keep a hand on each other's arm or back. Men and women who are close friends often walk arm in arm. Women do not have to cover their hair, and casual dress is permitted, though shorts are frowned upon outside of recreational activity.

Eating/Meals

Meals are an important time in Azerbaijani homes, and dinners, especially with family and friends, are often long. Azerbaijanis adhere to several traditional eating customs. For example, they are mindful of keeping their elbows off the table; their hands, however, remain above the table and within sight. Azerbaijanis also use only their right hand to pass food, as the left hand is considered unclean. They also eat in the continental style: fork held in the left hand and the knife held in the right. Traditionally, bread is sacred and the sharing of bread is considered a sign of friendship.

Visiting

Hospitality is important in Azerbaijan. Hosts try to make guests feel welcome, and guests are expected to be respectful. Guests should arrive early, as punctuality is considered important. Customarily, visitors remove their shoes, and some hosts will offer their guests slippers. At meals, guests stand until being invited to sit at the table. The hostess will often serve the meal, beginning with elder members of the family, then guests, and then the children; guests should not serve themselves.

It is polite to bring a gift as a small token of appreciation when visiting, especially if invited for a meal. Common gifts include flowers, fruit, or pastries for the hostess. Azerbaijanis typically refrain from giving alcohol as a gift, as Islam prohibits drinking alcohol. Gifts should always

be offered three times, as it is common for people to refuse a gift twice before accepting it. Flowers given as gifts should always come in bouquets of odd numbers; even numbers of flower are traditionally reserved for funerals. Azerbaijanis often offer guests tea, and it is impolite to refuse.

Because Azerbaijan is a Muslim state, there are certain rules of etiquette when visiting religious sites, such as a mosque. Customarily, people are expected to remove their shoes before entering a mosque. Women should also be sure to cover their hair and shoulders. Women traveling alone are uncommon, and they generally avoid dining in any male-dominated restaurants, teahouses, or cafés.

LIFESTYLE

Family

Family is highly valued in Azerbaijani culture, and daily life, both urban and rural, continues to revolve around family obligations and connections. The importance of child bearing remains strong, and it is still considered unusual, even unorthodox, for a couple in Azerbaijan to remain childless. Close familial ties are customary among extended family members, and it is considered a relative's responsibility to help another find work, conduct business, or advance politically.

Although Azerbaijani women appear to have a great deal of freedom, society, and family life is still patriarchal. Women do not socialize and gather in the same restaurants, teahouses, or other places as men. Women are also expected to take care of the house and provide meals. In many cases, women are expected to serve food as soon as their husbands return home.

Housing

During the heavily industrialized and Soviet-dominated decades of the 20th century, the population in Azerbaijan shifted from rural to urban. The Soviets introduced new construction methods, such as block-style apartments, and modernized utilities, such as sanitation and heat. The Soviets also expanded technologies, such as telecommunications during the mid- to late 20th century.

After Soviet rule, farms that were run collectively were returned to private ownership, and most home and property ownership in Azerbaijan is now private. More than half of the current housing in Azerbaijan was built after 1981, though many of the dwellings need renovations and improvements. Many urban residents live in apartment buildings as opposed to houses, and extended families often share homes, especially in rural areas. The Azerbaijani government has been working to provide more and better housing, especially in and near cities.

In the early 21st century, the overall population number of Azerbaijan is split nearly evenly between the rural and urban populations. A small number of the population continues to live in isolation in mountainous regions. Azerbaijan still has thousands of refugees and displaced persons who require housing as a result of the conflict with Armenia over Nagorno-Karabakh. Most of them currently live in temporary refugee camps where shelter and services are inadequate and overburdened.

Food

Most Azerbaijanis maintain a diverse and healthy diet. The varying climate zones within the country make it possible to grow many varieties of fruits, vegetables, and grains, such as wheat and barley. Azerbaijanis also raise a great deal of livestock and include dairy products, such as yogurt, in their diet. Lamb is the preferred meat, and bread is a revered staple. Their abundant natural springs make mineral water the most popular beverage, though Azerbaijanis also like to drink tea.

Azerbaijanis cook with many herbs and spices, giving the cuisine a rich flavor. A steamed rice dish called pilau is one of the most popular dishes. It is usually served with chicken or lamb and dried fruit. Kebabs are another common main dish. Azerbaijanis tend to cook vegetable and meat kebabs separately rather than mixing meat and vegetables on the same skewer. People also enjoy dolma, a dish made from minced lamb, rice, mint, fennel, and cinnamon rolled

in cabbage or grape leaves. Hot and cold soups and stews, such as piti (stew containing mutton and vegetables), dovga (soup containing yogurt, herbs, and rice), and dushbara (little meat dumplings), are also popular.

Years of Russian influence also left an impression on Azerbaijani cuisine. Common Russian dishes such as goulash and borscht are still served in Azerbaijan. Russian salad made of beans, potatoes, carrots, pickled beets, and cabbage, is served with most meals. Russians also introduced fast-food snack bars, called yemakxanos, where quickly made foods such as pirozhki and blinchiki are served. Pirozhki are a ravioli-like pasta dough stuffed with potatoes, rice, meat, or fruit. Blinchiki are pancakes wrapped around meat or cheese. These snack bars also serve wider selections of Azerbaijani foods. Baklava has long been the traditional dessert of Azerbaijan, and the Russians introduced varieties of cakes and ice cream to the country.

Life's Milestones

Most Azeri are Shia Muslim—an estimated 85 percent—and follow Muslim customs and rituals. In Muslim society, two important rituals take place after birth: adhan and aqiqah. During adhan, the new infant is bathed and the adhan, or the call to worship, is whispered in the baby's right ear. The iqamah, or the command to rise and worship, is then whispered in the baby's left ear. This ritual commits the child to the Muslim faith. Within a week of the birth, the aqiqah, or naming ceremony, occurs. The father reads from the Koran (or Qur'an, Islam's holy book) and announces the name of the child. Male babies are also generally circumcised, a ritual called khitan.

General milestones for all Azerbaijanis include graduation and marriage. Azerbaijanis typically marry in their twenties, and siblings are expected to marry in order from oldest to youngest; unmarried children live with their families until they marry. Traditionally, married couples are expected to have their first child within a year of marriage. Married couples tend to live with the husband's family until they are able to maintain their own household.

CULTURAL HISTORY

Art

Art in Azerbaijan dates back to prehistoric times, when ancient petroglyphs (rock carvings) were etched into the caves of Gobustan. These simple drawings depict scenes of hunting and fighting; wild animals, such as horses and deer; and objects, such as tools, weapons, and reed boats. More than 6,000 etchings adorn the caves and rocks. The site also features remains of inhabited caves and burials. In 2007, the United Nations Educational, Scientific, and Cultural Organization (UNESCO) designated the Rock Art and Ancient Cultural Landscape of Gobustan as a World Heritage Site.

Azerbaijan is renowned for its traditional art, including handicrafts such as embroidery, ceramics, metalwork, and sculpture. The influence of Islam, which emerged in the seventh century, was significant in the development of both art and architecture in Azerbaijan. This influence led to a focus on geometric and abstract design, evident in the highly colorful and detailed Azerbaijani textile art. Because Islam forbids the representation of the human form in art, Azeri artists refrained from painting or depicting people and instead focused on stylized lettering, such as calligraphy, and natural subjects, such as birds and flowers.

During the 20th century, modern styles, such as realism, were introduced in Azerbaijani art, including portraiture. Artists such as Bahruz Kangarli (1892–1922), considered Azerbaijan's most prolific painter, began painting people, landscapes, and other subjects using Russian and European techniques. Though he created more than 2,000 works of art, he is best known for his series of refugee paintings, in which he painted portraits of Azerbaijani refugees who fled Armenia during 1919 and 1920.

Architecture

Like many Eurasian countries, Azerbaijan's architecture is a rich blend of fragmented prehistoric remnants, such as megalith monuments; military medieval architecture, such as fortresses and other defensive constructions; and Islamic architecture, such as mausoleums, madrassas, and mosques. The country's architectural heritage also reflects traces of Greco-Roman architecture, as well as European styles such as Gothic and baroque architecture, brought to Azerbaijan in the 19th and 20th centuries under Russian rule. Russia would further influence Azerbaijani architecture when the country adopted Soviet-style architecture, which emphasized nationalism and functionality.

Azerbaijan's architecture is perhaps best witnessed in the cities of Nakhchivan and Baku. Nakhchivan is one of the oldest known cities in Azerbaijan and contains examples of ancient, medieval, and modern architecture. The oldest remaining ruin is the stone fortress of Gyaur-Kala, believed to have been built around 2000 BCE. The city is also known for its remarkable examples of medieval Turkish architecture, including mausoleums and mosques, as well as two stone arch bridges, the Khudaferin Bridges, which span the Aras (or Araks) River to connect Azerbaijan and Iran.

The capital of Baku contains the most extensive selection of medieval architecture in the country. Established as early as the seventh century, Baku's old town includes the ruins of an 11th-century walled fortress, as well as of Turkish caravanserai (inns) and bathhouses built by the Ottomans in the 15th century. Two particularly famous landmarks are the oval-shaped Maiden Tower, built in the 12th century, and the Palace of the Shirvanshahs, built in the 15th century. The latter represents a school of architecture characterized by arches, cupolas, and Islamic ornamental carvings.

Russian conquest in the 19th century and Soviet rule in the 20th century also changed the face of Azerbaijan's architecture. The Russians introduced Gothic and Baroque styles from Europe, while industrialization and the discovery of oil funded impressive building projects, such as lavish mansions and corporate and civic structures that blended Arabic and European styles. Following communist rule, Azerbaijan adopted

Soviet architecture, a so-called "nationalistic" style that incorporated national elements, such as inner courtyards, arches, and fountains. This style, known for its functional block-style apartment buildings, focused less on aesthetics than traditional Azerbaijani structures.

Drama

Like its national music, Azerbaijani dance is rooted in folk traditions. People dance to celebrate and mark special occasions. Many dances were performed strictly by men or by women, while an entire group performed others. The lesginka (or lezginka), a popular medieval dance, involves a man and a woman dancing alternate steps in order to attract each other. The yalli (or halay) is the oldest folk dance, dating back to ancient times.

Music

Folk music in Azerbaijan dates back to the centuries-old tradition of the ashik (or aşıq), or travelling minstrels. These performers roamed the countryside, travelling from village to village, performing songs and poems at weddings and other public events. While they often sang without instrumentation, ashiks were also associated with a number of traditional instruments. These include stringed instruments, such as the saz and kobyz, and wind instruments, such as the balaban. The folk songs they typically performed told of work, love, and beauty, and recounted history and legend. Some songs were satirical or humorous, while others were written for special occasions. Ashiks also competed in special contests, improvising their lyrics and music.

The national music of Azerbaijan is as mugham. This genre of music is customarily performed in cycles and is based on lyrical poetry. The music is expressive and improvisational in a way similar to jazz music. Traditionally, mugham is performed by a trio of musicians and features the classic instrumentation of the ghaval (Azerbaijani frame drum), tar (lute), and kamancheh (or kamānche) (fiddle). In 2003, UNESCO proclaimed this traditional music form as a Masterpiece of the Oral and Intangible Heritage of Humanity for the music's reflection of different periods and influences, namely Persian and Turkic. Singers and musicians still compete in mugham competitions today.

Literature

Azerbaijani literature has its roots in oral traditions. These early stories included creation myths, historical accounts of daily life, and folklore, including pre-Islamic epic poems or ballads known as dastans. The Azerbaijani folk tradition also includes a wide body of proverbs and sayings. Most of these folk tales and traditions were not written down for thousands of years. One of the most notable epics is *The Book of Dede Korkut*, which details early nomadic life in Central Asia while relating the heroic tale of Dede Korkut. Considered the most famous tale of the Oghuz Turks, the epic story was preserved through storytelling until possibly written down in the 15th century.

The first written text in Azerbaijan is attributed to Zoroaster, an ancient Iranian prophet and poet who lived in the first century BCE and founded Zoroastrianism, a religious faith that began in ancient Persia. He is believed to have written a collection of sacred texts known as the Avesta. His ideas proposed a dualist universe in which equal forces of good and evil competed, and his teachings had a significant influence on humankind.

Azerbaijani literature flourished during the middle and late medieval period, during which poetry was the dominant form. From the 11th through the 18th centuries, poets composed lyrical, romantic, and epic poetry and prose in the Azerbaijani, Persian, and Turkish languages. One particular poet celebrated in the cultural heritage of Azerbaijan is Nezami Ganjavi (1141–1209). He penned long narrative poems involving history and nationalism and using rhyming couplets. Other celebrated poets include Gatran Tabrizi (1012–1088); Afzaladdin Khagani, known by the pen name Khāqānī (c.1120–c.1199); and Sheykh Mahmud Shabistari (1288–1340), who composed poems with religious and mystical themes. The fifteenth-century poet Fuzûlî, the pen name of Muhammad bin Suleyman (c. 1483–1556), wrote great poems of love and religious devotion as well as philosophical prose.

Nineteenth-century Azerbaijani literature is characterized by the influence of Russian and European styles. More Azerbaijani authors began writing educational and humanist texts, as well as satires critical of social and political conditions. Azerbaijani playwrights also introduced satires and philosophy into their works. The 20th century saw a brief period of Azerbaijani nationalist writing between 1918 and 1920, when the Azerbaijan Democratic Republic was declared. This was followed by Soviet rule, during which Soviet officials worked to stamp out Azerbaijani literary and artistic expression. Many poets, novelists, playwrights, and visual artists were imprisoned or killed, while others fled the country. Still, artists of the 20th century sought to hold onto their cultural heritage and resisted Soviet oppression. Writers during this period include Suleyman Rustam (1906–1989), considered the creator of Azerbaijan Soviet poetry; poet, playwright, and novelist Mammed Said Ordubadi (1872–1950); and the playwright Huseyn Javid (1882–1941), who introduced the form of tragic theater to Azerbaijan.

CULTURE

Arts & Entertainment

Azerbaijan has a long and diverse tradition in the arts. Though many artists were restricted and persecuted during Soviet rule in the 20th century, Azerbaijanis have been reclaiming and restoring their artistic culture since achieving independence in 1991. Government funding for art has been limited by economic hardship. Many artists continue to earn a living and practice their skills independently. This includes Azerbaijan's well-regarded artisans who specialize in ceramics, metalwork, pottery, and other traditional crafts for which Azerbaijan is known. The Kurdish and Talysh cultural groups are particularly known for their hand-woven rugs and carpets. Many of these contemporary crafts continue to display the same ornate varieties of Islamic art, including geometric design and symbolism.

The collapse of the Soviet Union resulted in a strong resurgence in Azerbaijani literature. Azerbaijan poets, writers, and playwrights suffered the most persecution under Soviet rule. In 2004, President Ilham Aliyev (1961–) declared a mass publication effort of classical Azerbaijani literature, as well as the start of the Azerbaijani National Encyclopedia. The nation also has about 10,000 libraries, as well as the Azerbaijan Literature Museum. Poetry remains a major form of literary expression in Azerbaijan. Theater groups have also been incredibly active since Azerbaijan declared its independence. The Azerbaijan State National Academic Drama Theatre has staged numerous performances in the past two decades, and twenty-six state theaters are in operation throughout the country. In Baku, the Puppet Theatre and the Musical Comedy Theatre are especially popular.

Traditional folk music and dance are still performed regularly in Azerbaijan at special occasions and public events. Professional troupes of folk musicians and dancers continue to tour the country, and refined art forms, such as the opera and ballet, continue to be attended. Azerbaijan has a State Symphonic Orchestra, State Chamber Orchestra, and a State Choir and hosts several international music festivals and concerts, such as the Baku Jazz Festival and the Mugham (or Shusha) Festival in Shaki. In addition, a new, more upbeat variety of mugham, called meyxana, has become popular, though more traditional forms of mugham and Western styles, such as jazz, are still common. Modern Azerbaijani musicians have also combined this musical form with hip-hop to create a new genre of Azeri rap.

Cultural Sites & Landmarks

In addition to the Gobustan Rock Art Cultural Landscape, Azerbaijan is home to one other UNESCO World Heritage Site: the Walled City of Baku with Shirvanshahs' Palace and Maiden Tower. The city was recognized for its diverse blend of cultures, including Zoroastrian, Persian, Arabic, Ottoman, and Russian. The old town center contains the remarkable remnants of Baku's rich and ancient architecture, ranging from fortresses, churches, and mosques, to mausoleums and mansions. The city is particularly famous for its 12th-century walls and the landmarks of the 12th-century Maiden Tower (Giz Galasi) and the 15th-century Shirvanshahs' Palace. Within the walls of the palace is the Divankhana complex, a stone pavilion carved with intricate mosaics and Kufic (Arabic calligraphy) inscriptions. The mausoleum and temple mosque are both considered to be unique examples of Persian architecture and carry many inscriptions celebrating the Shirvanshah dynasty. In 1939, archaeologists uncovered the sprawling palace bathhouses, which were constructed underground and include an astounding 26 rooms.

Azerbaijan is home to numerous other historic and cultural sites that have been nominated for World Heritage status, including the fire temple and museum at Surakhany and the 18th-century Khan's Palace at Sheki. The fire temple at Surakhany (or Suraxanı) was built in an important region for Zoroastrianism and was a significant center of worship and pilgrimage for fire-worshippers. The temple was built in the 17th century over a natural gas vent that reportedly fed seven eternally burning fires. Khan's Palace was built as a summer residence in the city of Sheki, once a thriving center for silk production. At the time of its construction, the palace was considered a rare architectural feat. A small fortification, it has two stories and numerous drawings and patterns etched into its walls. There are several other architectural monuments surrounding the site. Other sites recommended for cultural preservation include defensive constructions along the Caspian Sea and the 12th-century mausoleum at Nakhinchevan.

Azerbaijan has many natural features worthy of special recognition, several of which have also been recommended for World Heritage status. These include the Hyrkan State Reservation in southern Azerbaijan, an ancient flora and fauna deposit containing thousands of ancient animal bones and plant remains. The Lok-Batan mud cone near Baku first erupted in 1864 and has erupted at least twenty times since. Overall, Azerbaijan has four national parks, 14 nature reserves, and 20 restricted natural habitats, as well as more than 200 lakes.

Libraries & Museums

The most significant collections of art and artifacts are found at the State Museum of Shirvan-Shakh, which highlights the country's royal history, and the Nizami Museum of Azerbaijani Literature, founded in 1939. The open-air Petroglyph Museum at Gobustan presents Neolithic rock carvings. The Baku-based Azerbaijan Carpet Museum, established in 1967, features a collection of carpets ranging from the 17th through the 20th centuries, as well as collections of ancient jewelry, ceramics, and other artifacts.

The Mirza Fatali Akhundov National Library of Azerbaijan, located in Baku and named for the Azerbaijani writer and philosopher, was founded in 1922 and houses over 5 million resources, including books, manuscripts, maps, magazines, newspapers, dissertations, and other printed materials.

Holidays

Azerbaijanis celebrate a host of patriotic holidays. Among them are Martyrs' Day (January 20), Republic Day (May 28), Constitution Day (November 12), and Azeri Solidarity Day (December 31). Independence Day, celebrated on October 18, marks Azerbaijan's independence from the Soviet Union.

The most commonly celebrated Islamic holidays are Ramadan; Eid al-Fitr, which concludes Ramadan and involves feasting and gift giving; and Kurban Bayrami (also known as Eid al-Adha), a day on which Abraham's obedience to God is commemorated with the slaughter of animals and large feasts. Nowruz, an Islamic festival with pagan roots, welcomes spring and a new year. It lasts several days in the third week of March and includes musical performances and dances, sporting events, and family feasts.

Youth Culture

Soviet rule instilled a strong educational foundation in Azerbaijan, providing more children with greater access to schools. As a result, the literacy rate and the cultural importance placed on education both increased. Though funding has been more restricted since independence, Azerbaijan has continued to invest in public education for its youth.

In 2012, Azerbaijan began celebrating "Knowledge Day," the first day of the academic year, usually in September. Moreover, in 2011, over 60 schools were renovated in Baku alone, and in 2012, 81 were renovated. According to President Ilham Aliyev's official website, in the previous decade, 2,200 primary and secondary schools were either newly constructed or refurbished throughout Azerbaijan. Additionally, there are 36 state-run universities and 15 private universities in Azerbaijan.

Most Azerbaijani children attend elementary and secondary school for 10 years, with attendance compulsory for at least eight years. However, in rural areas, children, especially girls, are sometimes pulled from school to help with family businesses and farms. Many secondary schools focus on vocational training to prepare youth for work in the industrial sector. More and more Azerbaijani youth are also learning English.

Family is the center of social life in Azerbaijan. When they are not in school, youth are often gathered with family members or friends, and are expected to assist with domestic and agrarian responsibilities, or work for the family business. Social recreation for older youth is much more expanded in urban areas, such as the capital of Baku, which offers a number of venues for young people. Young adults tend to prefer socializing at teahouses.

Football (soccer) is the most popular sport in Azerbaijan. Youth engage in local pickup games and participate in school, community, and national teams and clubs. Young people also enjoy playing chaugan, an outdoor sport similar to both golf and polo, and competing at gyulash, a traditional form of wrestling. Swimming, fishing, and hiking are popular outdoor activities, and Azerbaijani youth play chess and nard (or backgammon), considered the nation's two most popular games. A common game among girls is the traditional Seven Beauties, in which they compete in crocheting stockings.

SOCIETY

Transportation

In urban areas, buses, taxis, and the metro (subway) are the most popular modes of public transportation. Minibuses, called marshrutkas, are also common and, along with buses, connect cities to smaller towns and villages. Few people travel by bicycle because of the rocky and difficult terrain. Two highways cross the province of Nagorno-Karabakh, but the landscape, marked by numerous canyons, makes direct overland travel difficult. Traffic moves on the right-hand side of the road.

Transportation Infrastructure

Under Soviet rule, the government expanded Azerbaijan's infrastructure, including the construction of roads and a public rail network. However, this infrastructure was not maintained, and the nation has since worked to expand and improve highways and secondary roads, the railroad, and public transportation lines.

Baku is the hub of air travel and shipping. An international airport operates out of the capital, and a few domestic flights connect Baku and other cities. The port offers freight and passenger transport, as well as ferry service across the Caspian Sea. Work is progressing on the 826 kilometer (513 mile) Baku-Tbilisi-Kars Railroad that connects Georgia, Azerbaijan, and Armenia to Europe via Turkey. In addition to facilitating human travel, this line will also allow Azerbaijan to more easily export its petroleum products to trade partner Turkey. In 2009, Azerbaijan Railways also signed an agreement with the Islamic Republic of Iran Railways and Russian Railways to begin building a linking railroad.

Media & Communications

Television is the dominant medium in Azerbaijan. There are currently forty-seven channels, four of which are state-owned. The largest television and radio broadcasting company in Azerbaijan is the state television and radio network, Azerbaijan Television and Radio Broadcasting (AzTV). ANS Television was the first privately owned television network opened in Azerbaijan after the collapse of the Soviet Union. It is considered the least biased or government-controlled programmer. However, the Azerbaijani government in the past has shut it down, and its current level of independence is debated. Greater access to cable and satellite television has enabled Azerbaijanis to view international stations. Similarly, Azerbaijan has nine AM radio stations, seventeen FM stations, and one shortwave station. All are under the watch of Azerbaijan's Ministry of Communications and Information Technologies.

Azerbaijan has a wide selection of print media, ranging from the government-run daily, *Azarbaycan*, to English- and Russian- language papers such as *Baku Sun*, *AzerNEWS*, and *Zerkalo*. Most independent Azerbaijani media outlets are closely monitored or even steered by the government, which has come under fire from international monitoring agencies for limiting freedom of the press. In May 2009, the Institute for Reporters' Freedom and Safety (IRFS) set up a twenty-four hour hotline to assist journalists and media outlets in need. However, according to the Committee to Protect Journalists (CPJ), as of December 2014, there were nine imprisoned reporters in Azerbaijan.

Internet cafés are common in Baku and other urban areas. Moreover, as of 2013, the International Telecommunications Union reported that 58.7 percent of the population regularly uses the Internet. That same year, government restrictions imposed on the press were extended to online dissenters: Azerbaijan's criminal defamation laws now apply to any disparaging online content, especially government-related postings. The penalty for such activity includes large fines, community service, and up to three years in prison.

Since the turn of the 21st century, Azerbaijan has been updating telephone landlines and simplifying access, removing old Soviet codes. Most people use mobile phones, and call centers, available in most post offices, are used to place international and domestic calls.

SOCIAL DEVELOPMENT

Standard of Living

Azerbaijan ranked 86th out of 195 countries on the 2012 United Nations Human Development Index, which measures quality of life and standard of living indicators.

In 2014, life expectancy at birth was an estimated sixty-nine years for males and seventy-five years for females. In addition, while nearly 50 percent of the country's population lived below the poverty line in 2001, the World Bank reports that, in 2013, only 5.3 percent of the population did.

Water Consumption

According to the United Nations, approximately three-quarters of the country's population have access to improved water sources; however, in rural areas, access to water and sanitation facilities is much more limited. For example, only 29.3 percent of the rural populace has access to piped water systems. Still, in urban areas, outdated infrastructure can also make providing an uninterrupted, clean water supply challenging. For example, in 2010, water rationing was instituted in 87 percent of households in Azerbaijan's capital, Baku, whose Soviet-built water and sanitation systems were not designed to accommodate such rapid population growth. Water could only be provided to affected households between four and seven hours each day. An hour outside Baku, in Siyazan, running water only became available in 2015 through a World Bank-funded reservoir and pumping-station project. Previously, water was delivered by tanker truck to Siyazan residents and was then stored in open rain barrels.

Education

After independence, Azerbaijan's educational system was put under considerable strain, with educational materials and teachers becoming scarce and few funds available to change the structure put in place by the Soviets. However, with this decline, the curriculum was revised, making Azeri the language of instruction. Marxist-Leninist ideology was revised out, while religious instruction was once again included. The high literacy rate, a legacy of the Soviet era, stands at 99.9 percent (100 percent for men and 99.8 percent for women).

Education is free and compulsory through the ninth grade. At that point, students can choose to attend secondary schools, vocational schools, or professional lyceums, which combine a general education with technical training. Approximately 94.6 percent of female students who begin primary school complete it, compared to 96.4 percent of male students (2012).

Education at the university level is also free to those students who pass the National Entrance Examination. Institutions of higher education are largely situated in the capital. The oldest and most prestigious university is Baku State University. Other institutions include the Azerbaijan Technical University and the Azerbaijan State Petroleum Academy.

Women's Rights

Azerbaijan is considered a liberal Muslim-majority nation. Azerbaijani women have access to high levels of education and are granted the same constitutional rights as men. However, women continue to face challenges, including societal discrimination, sexual harassment, and domestic abuse and violence. Azerbaijan also remains a patriarchal society; men continue to dominate business, politics, and direct family life, while women are still expected to maintain their traditional secondary or subordinate role in the home.

Domestic violence in Azerbaijan remains a serious issue. There are no laws prohibiting spousal abuse or spousal rape, and incidents of abuse and violence are generally underreported due to social stigma. Rape is prohibited

and carries a minimum sentence of 15 years, but also goes frequently underreported because of fear and shame. The government provides little or no support for abuse victims. The Institute for Peace and Democracy (IPD), a humanitarian organization under the Azerbaijan Council of Transcaucasus Women's Dialogue for Peace and Democracy, operates a women's crisis center in Baku that provides medical and legal help. Numerous other NGOs (non-governmental organization) are also active in the country.

Human trafficking and sexual exploitation remain a problem for both women and children in Azerbaijan, and for that reason, the country remains on the US Department of State's Tier 2 Watch List. Azerbaijan is considered a source and transit country for human trafficking, particularly for the purposes of sexual exploitation and forced labor. It is estimated that women constitute 90 percent of victims and are generally underprivileged or displaced females, aged twenty to thirty-eight. According to government estimates, crimes related to human trafficking increased by over 50 percent in 2008, and because of this, in 2014, Azerbaijan moved to align its own trafficking law with international law. However, corruption, underreporting, failure to investigate claims, and significantly low levels of victim support continues to hamper official rectification efforts. Pimping and owning a brothel are now illegal and punishable by imprisonment. However, prostitution itself, while currently unlawful, is punishable only by small monetary fine. High levels of prostitution are still reported in Baku.

Women also generally suffer from societal discrimination in Azerbaijan. The law does not prohibit sexual harassment, and Azerbaijani women report suffering both discrimination and harassment in the workplace. Reports also show that women are generally kept in lower status and lower paying jobs. Women are also underrepresented politically. As of May 2015, only nineteen women (15.6 percent) serve in the National Assembly and only one woman, Hijran Huseynova, holds a cabinet-level government position. Many of these discriminations are culturally ingrained. For example, boys are given the priority in education in rural areas, while girls are kept home to assist with domestic tasks. In addition, many husbands vote on behalf of their wives and other female relatives.

Health Care

Azerbaijan's health care system, already inadequate in comparison to other Soviet republics, declined further following independence. The government has failed to meet its policy of universal health care, and there have been shortages of medicine and equipment. Health care practitioners are poorly paid, and most patients have to pay for their medical services.

The government is now focused on improving pre-natal and post-natal care in order to reduce the country's high infant mortality rate, which stands at 31 in 1,000 live births. Advances are indeed being made, since UNICEF reports that the 1990 infant mortality rate was 74 in 1,000. Azerbaijan's government is also intent on making the healthcare system cost-effective and introducing an insurance program. Environmental clean-up projects, which could reduce the incidence of illnesses and birth defects, have received little funding.

GOVERNMENT

Structure

Since independence in 1991, democratic reform has been lackluster, and both internal and regional conflicts have occurred. Though the current government has presided over a period of stability, it is dominated by former Soviet leaders, and international observers have pronounced elections as being neither free nor fair.

Azerbaijan is a republic as set out in the 1991 constitution. A president is head of state, and a prime minister is head of government. The president is elected to a five-year term by popular vote and is responsible for appointing the prime minister as well as the Council of Ministers, both of which the legislature must approve.

The legislature is a unicameral body called the National Assembly (Milli Mejlis). It consists of 125 members, all but five of whom are elected by popular vote to five-year terms. The remaining seats are assigned proportionally according to votes per party. Azerbaijan and Armenia have not made progress regarding the status of Nagorno-Karabakh, which has proclaimed its independence, but which neither country recognizes.

Political Parties

Major political parties include the Azerbaijan Popular Front, the Civic Solidarity Party, the Motherland Party, the Musavat Party, the Liberal Party of Azerbaijan, and the Social Democratic Party of Azerbaijan. Opposition parties are often fractious and tend to form new coalitions frequently.

In the 2010 National Assembly elections, which were marred by allegations of media suppression, President Ilham Aliyev's ruling New Azerbaijan Party won 72 of 125 seats. During the 2005 elections, a coalition, termed Azadliq (Freedom), was formed by established groups opposing Aliyev, including the Democratic Party, the Popular Front Party, and the Musavat Party. This coalition won six seats in the 2005 election. However, in 2010—for the first time in history—no candidate from any of these parties was elected. Largely, independent candidates took the remaining 53 seats.

Local Government

Administratively, Azerbaijan is divided into nine regions, 59 districts, 11 cities, and Naxçivan, an autonomous republic that complies with the governmental framework of the country. Local governance occurs at the municipal level, and direct elections decide local officials. Local governments are responsible for the imposing and collection of taxes, designing local budgets, and regional and localized economic development, among other programs and areas.

Judicial System

The judicial branch consists of the Supreme Court, the Constitutional Court, and the Economic Court. Justices are nominated by the president and approved by the National Assembly.

Taxation

In 2015, the top income tax rate in Azerbaijan is 35 percent, while the top corporate tax rate is 20 percent. Other taxes levied include property tax and value-added taxes (VAT). Sales tax currently stands at 18 percent.

Armed Forces

The Azerbaijani Armed Forces consists of a land force, an air defense force, and a naval force, and men between the ages of 18 and 35 are considered eligible for service. In 2012, the government spent almost $3.1 billion (USD) on military expenditures, which is 4.6 percent of the country's GDP. The armed forces remain active in the Nagorno-Karabakh conflict and 2014 was considered the worst year on record, with 72 deaths reported.

Foreign Policy

Azerbaijan maintains peaceful relations with many nations, though a number of them have criticized the state of human rights in the country. The nation is a member of numerous international bodies, including the Council of Europe, the Organization for Security and Co-operation in Europe (OSCE), the Euro-Atlantic Partnership, and the European Bank for Reconstruction and Development (EBRD) and Islamic Development Bank (IDB). It is also a member of the International Monetary Fund (IMF) and the World Bank, and receives a large amount of assistance from both. As a member of the North Atlantic Treaty Organization's (NATO) Partnership for Peace, Azerbaijan contributed troops to the U.S.-led invasions of Afghanistan and Iraq. In 2008, Azerbaijan pulled out its troops in Iraq, but its troops in Afghanistan remained.

Azerbaijan's main foreign policy objectives include growing foreign trade, investment, and maintaining regional security and economic stability. To that end, Azerbaijan joined the Commonwealth of Independent States (CIS) in 1991, an organization meant to bring together former Soviet republics in mutual cooperation and support, both politically and economically. The following year, Azerbaijan joined

the UN. The country also signed a Partnership and Cooperation Agreement (PCA) with the European Union (EU) in 1996, and became part of the EU's European Neighborhood Policy (ENP) in 2004. Azerbaijan also has a bilateral trade agreement with the United States, and received millions of dollars in U.S. assistance in 2007.

Resolving the conflict in the province of Nagorno-Karabakh and the dispute with Armenia over the province's status is a primary focus of Azerbaijan's foreign relations. After the dissolution of the Soviet Union, conflict erupted between Azerbaijan and the province of Nagorno-Karabakh., which has a majority population of ethnic Armenians. The province declared it wanted to separate from Azerbaijan, and Armenia quickly moved to support self-determination for the province. Turkey, with which Azerbaijan remained close, also became involved on the side of Azerbaijan. Violence erupted, and tens of thousands of Armenians fled Azerbaijan. Turkey and Azerbaijan responded to Armenia's support for the province by closing its borders.

Efforts to resolve the dispute have so far failed, but negotiations are ongoing. The OSCE Minsk Group, led by the U.S., Russia, and France, has increased its peace-building efforts in the region, and a truce was reached in 2008. Azerbaijan continues to maintain close relations with Turkey, which Azerbaijan considers a strategic link to the West, and maintains key economic ties to Georgia, Russia, and Iran.

Human Rights Profile

International human rights law insists that states respect civil and political rights, and promote an individual's economic, social, and cultural rights. The United Nations (UN) Universal Declaration of Human Rights (UDHR) is recognized as the standard for international human rights. Its authors sought the counsel of the world's great thinkers, philosophers, and religious leaders and were careful to create a document that reflects the core values shared by every world culture. (To read this document or view the articles relating to cultural human rights, go to http://www.ohchr. org/EN/UDHR/Pages/Introduction.aspx.).

Azerbaijan continues to be criticized internationally for its poor human rights record. International monitoring agencies, such as Amnesty International (AI) and Human Rights Watch, as well as the US Department of State, have reported serious violations and restrictions of human rights since 2006. These include the detainment of political prisoners and government corruption, the restriction of free speech and press, arbitrary arrest and detention, poor prison conditions, societal discrimination, and human trafficking. In April 2009, a coalition of nongovernmental organizations (NGOs) questioned Azerbaijan's candidacy in the May 2009 elections to the UN Human Rights Council (HRC). The country was first elected to the council in 2006, during which time the coalition alleged human rights had deteriorated.

Azerbaijan became a presidential republic in 1995 when it adopted a new constitution. The constitution guaranteed universal civil and human rights and established an elected presidency and legislature, as well as an independent judiciary. In practice, however, elections fraud has been observed, and outside observers found serious problems with the elections in 2005, 2008, and 2010. Reports of corruption and fraud include tampering with vote counts, restrictions on political participation and freedom of the press, and restrictions on the observers themselves. In addition, state security forces arrested many members of the political opposition, and some reported suffering violence and torture by authorities.

The government has also been criticized for restricting the freedoms of assembly, press, and speech, as well as the right to organizational protest. In particular, journalists, photographers, and observers have suffered persecution and arrest, and publications and human rights organizations have been penalized for publishing material critical of the government. In 2009, the Azerbaijani government banned international radio broadcasts, such as those by British Broadcasting Corporation (BBC), Voice of America, and

Radio Free Europe/Radio Liberty. Human Rights Watch reports that, since 2013, there have been fifty cases of unfounded criminal charges being filed against journalists, political activists, and government critics.

Corruption at all levels and in all branches of government was reported. The judiciary has been criticized as merely a functioning arm of the executive, and arbitrary fines were levied repeatedly. The World Bank concluded that bribery of public officials was a serious problem in Azerbaijan; select members of law enforcement received extravagant pay raises, while others continued to be underpaid. The country has also been roundly criticized for its harsh prison conditions. Prisons suffered from overcrowding and poor nutrition, sanitation, and medical practices, and many prisoners reported suffering abuse and torture.

Azerbaijan also continues to suffer from widespread societal discrimination. International monitoring agencies have repeatedly reported discrimination against women, religious and ethnic minority groups, and persons with disabilities. Some religious minorities faced registration requirements and were subject to harassment, while unfair treatment in employment and access to housing, health care, and education continue to be challenges for women and some ethnicities. Disabled children were institutionalized, under questionable care in some instances, and laws do not yet require equal access to public facilities for persons with disabilities. International organizations and the U.S. Department of State also reported human trafficking among men, women, and children.

ECONOMY

Overview of the Economy

Azerbaijan's economy has been steadily growing since the mid-1990s. Decades of economic mismanagement, followed by a costly conflict with Armenia, have impeded reforms. However, high oil prices as well as further development of the oil industry have contributed to the positive trend. In 2014, Azerbaijan's per capita gross domestic product (GDP) was an estimated $17,900 USD.

Industry

Industry accounts for just over 61 percent of the GDP, but only employs 12 percent of the labor force (2014 estimate). Offshore oil drilling and oil refining dominate the sector. Guneshli (Günəşli), Chirag (Çıraq), Azeri, and Kepez are the four major oilfields located in the Caspian Sea. Foreign investment, new pipelines, and agreements with neighboring countries for the flow of oil to various ports have encouraged the expansion of the industry. Natural gas production is less developed, but also important, and expanding its production will offset the country's reliance on oil revenues.

Other portions of the industrial sector include food processing, textiles, metallurgy, and the generation of hydroelectricity. The capital of Baku remains a major center for Azerbaijani carpets, which are prized around the world for their intricate design and high quality. Other industries in the capital include the production of machine tools, petrochemicals, commercial fishing, and electronics. The United Nations Development Program (UNDP) recently boosted the relatively small tourism industry.

Labor

The labor force is estimated at 4.8 million, and the unemployment rate is 4.9 percent. Just over 49 percent of the labor force works in the services sector, while 38.3 percent is engaged in agricultural work, and 12 percent are in industry.

Energy/Power/Natural Resources

Azerbaijan has modest mineral deposits, including zinc, iron ore, aluminum, copper, lead, cobalt, bauxite, molybdenum, and limestone. Enormous offshore oil and natural gas reserves are the most important resources, though neither has yet been exploited to its fullest potential.

As in many former Soviet republics, Azerbaijan has troubling environmental problems

that arose from an emphasis on production at any cost. Among the worst affected areas are the Absheron Peninsula and the waters of the Caspian Sea. Oil spills, untreated sewage, DDT, and chemical fertilizers have all contributed to the degradation of the land and sea, including animal populations. Moreover, the air of industrial cities, especially Baku, is subject to severe pollution from the oil industry.

Fishing

The capital of Baku, a large port city, has a commercial fishing fleet that harvests beluga and sturgeon for the sale of black caviar (the Caspian Sea is considered the source of the world's finest caviar). However, depletion of sturgeon stocks from over-fishing has seriously jeopardized the future of the fishing industry.

Forestry

Roughly, 11 percent of Azerbaijan is forested. Common tree species include pine, juniper, oak, pistachio, and goyrush. Illegal harvesting of trees has been a problem in the past, but has diminished in the early 21st century. The government owns much of the forested land.

Mining/Metals

Commonly mined minerals include alumina, aluminum, iron ore, and steel. The mining industry is relatively small; however, in the early 21st century, the sector is growing, particularly in regard to aluminum and iron ore.

Agriculture

Agriculture occupies 38.3 percent of the labor force, but it only accounts for 5.7 percent of the GDP (2014 estimate). Nearly 23 percent of the land is arable, according to 2014 World Bank figures, and most of this land requires irrigation. Azerbaijan's distinct climatic diversity means that it can produce a wide range of crops.

Grapes, cotton, and tobacco, followed by citrus fruits and vegetables, have the highest yield, accounting for half of the country's overall production. Silk, nuts, grains, and tea are also produced. Child labor has been a chronic problem in Azerbaijan's agricultural sector, particularly in cotton, tea, and tobacco production. According to UNESCO, in 2012, of the 4.5 percent (7,034) of working children ages seven to fourteen, 92 percent of them were engaged in agricultural tasks.

Animal Husbandry

Cattle, goats, pigs, and sheep are the most common livestock. The livestock industry is growing in the early 21st century. In fact, livestock production increased 5 percent from the year 2008 to 2009. In 2014, President Ilham Aliyev signed an executive order to allocate 15 million manat from the Azerbaijani budget to expand the number of artificial insemination centers, where specially-trained technicians work. Begun in 2011, such centers have dramatically lowered the cost of cattle and significantly increased the production of milk.

Tourism

Azerbaijan's formerly state-run tourism industry is showing promise after the setbacks it experienced in the early 1990s because of the country's violent conflict with neighboring Armenia. Since the ceasefire, the annual number of visitors has risen steadily. According to Azerbaijan's State Statistical Committee, the country hosted over 2.3 million foreign visitors in 2014, while an estimated 6.5 million people arrived inside the country's borders in 2014.

The country boasts outstanding cultural attractions. These include the old quarter of Baku, medieval castles, palaces, and mosques. The Ateshgah Temple, where fire burns from natural gas deposits emitted from the ground, has been an important religious site for 2,000 years. Natural attractions include the Caucasus Mountains, medicinal spas based around hot springs, and a great range of animal and bird life.

Christina Dendy, Michael Aliprandini, &
Jeffrey Bowman

DO YOU KNOW?

- Chess Grandmaster and Russian political dissident Garry Kasparov, the highest-rated player in the history of chess, was born in Baku in 1963. He is of Armenian-Jewish descent.

- The name Baku comes from an old Persian word meaning "City of God" and is thought to refer to the fire worship practices of Zoroastrianism. The prophet Zoroaster, around whom the religion of Zoroastrianism was formed, was born in Azerbaijan in the seventh century BCE.

Bibliography

David C. King. David C. *Azerbaijan.* New York: Benchmark Books, 2006. Cultures of the World Ser.

John Noble, John, Michael Kohn, & Danielle Systermans. *Georgia, Armenia & Azerbaijan.* Fourth ed. Oakland, CA: Lonely Planet, 2012.

Lerner Geography Department, ed. *Azerbaijan: Then & Now.* Minneapolis: Lerner Publications Company, 1993.

Nikki Kazimova, Nikki. *Azerbaijan—Culture Smart!: The Essential Guide to Customs & Culture.* London: Kuperard, 2011.

Suha Bolukbasi, Suha. *Azerbaijan: A Political History.* London: I. B. Tauris, 2013.

Tahir Amiraslanov & Leyla Rahmanova. *The Azerbaijani Kitchen: A Cookbook.* London: Saqi Books, 2014.

Thomas De Waal, Thomas. *Black Garden: Armenia and Azerbaijan Through Peace and War.* Tenth ed. New York: NYU Press, 2013.

Works Cited

_____. "Ancient literature of Azerbaijan." Ministry of Culture and Tourism of Azerbaijan Republic, 2015. Web. http://mct.gov.az/service/lang/en/page/98/sid/21/nid/116/.

_____. "Azerbaijani literature of the New Period." Ministry of Culture and Tourism of Azerbaijan Republic, 2015. Web. http://mct.gov.az/service/lang/en/page/98/sid/21/nid/148/.

_____. "Literature in the XIX–XX centuries." Ministry of Culture and Tourism of Azerbaijan Republic, 2015.

Web. http://mct.gov.az/service/lang/en/page/98/sid/21/nid/146/.

_____. "Medieval literature of Azerbaijan." Ministry of Culture and Tourism of Azerbaijan Republic, 2015. Web. http://mct.gov.az/service/lang/en/page/98/sid/21/nid/145/.

_____. "The literature of the Soviet period." Ministry of Culture and Tourism of Azerbaijan Republic, 2015. Web. http://mct.gov.az/service/lang/en/page/98/sid/21/nid/147/.

"About Folklore." Ministry of Culture & Tourism Republic of Azerbaijan. Ministry of Culture

"Art Gallery." *Azerbaijan International.* Azerbaijan International, 1999. http://azgallery.org/.

"Azerbaijan International." Azerbaijan International Magazine, n.d. Web. http://www.azer.com/

"Azerbaijan." *Country Reports on Human Rights Practices for 2013.* Bureau of Democracy, Human Rights and Labor, U.S. Department of State, 2013. Web. http://www.state.gov/j/drl/rls/hrrpt/humanrightsreport/index.htm?year=2013&dlid=220255#wrapper.

"Azerbaijan." UNESCO. *UNESCO World Heritage Convention*, 2015. Web. http://whc.unesco.org/en/statesparties/az.

"Azerbaijan—Housing." *Encyclopedia of the Nations.* Advameg, Inc. http://www.nationsencyclopedia.com/Asia-and-Oceania/Azerbaijan-HOUSING.html.

"Azerbaijan—Language, Culture, Customs and Etiquette." *Kwintessential.co.uk.* Kwintessential, 2014. Web. http://www.kwintessential.co.uk/resources/global-etiquette/azerbaijan.html.

"Bureau of European and Eurasian Affairs Fact Sheet." *U.S. Relations with Azerbaijan.* Bureau of European and Eurasian Affairs, U.S. Department of State, 18 Feb. 2015. Web. http://www.state.gov/r/pa/ei/bgn/2909.htm.

"Development of architecture from ancient times till the adoption of Islam." *Azerbaijan.* Heydar Aliyev Foundation, n.d. Web. http://www.azerbaijan.az/_Culture/_Architecture/_architecture_e.html.

"Ganja—true Azerbaijani flavor." *Advantour.com.* Advantour, 2015. Web. http://www.advantour.com/azerbaijan/ganja.htm.

"Ilham Aliyev attended the opening of school No 18 in the Yasamal district of Baku after reconstruction on 'Knowledge Day.'" *Official Website of the President of the Republic of Azerbaijan.* Press Service of the President of the Republic of Azerbaijan, 2012. Web. http://en.president.az/articles/6212.

"In Azerbaijan: The Life-Changing Impact of Water." *TheWorldBank.org.* The World Bank Group. 16 Feb. 2015. Web. http://www.worldbank.org/en/results/2015/02/16/in-azerbaijan-the-life-changing-impact-of-water.

"Nakhchivan region." Oriental Express Central Asia. *OrexCA.com.* Oriental Express Central Asia, 2015. Web. http://azerbaijan.orexca.com/eng/info/regions/nakhchivan.html.

"Nakhichevan, Azerbaijan." *Advantour.com.* Advantour, 2015. Web. http://www.advantour.com/azerbaijan/nakhichevan.htm.

"Ordubad, Azerbaijan." *Advantour.com.* Advantour, 2015. Web. http://www.advantour.com/azerbaijan/ordubad.htm.

"The Azeri Language and Literature." *Azerbaijan International.* Azerbaijan International Magazine, 17 Nov. 2008. Web. http://azeri.org.

"Two-thousand-year old Gabala—the most ancient city of Azerbaijan." *Advantour.* Avantour, 2015. Web. http://www.advantour.com/azerbaijan/gabala.htm.

"Uzeyir Hajibeyov." *Hajibeyov.com.* Azerbaijan International Magazine, 18 Apr. 2005. Web. http://hajibeyov.com/.

"World Heritage Sites in Azerbaijan." *World Heritage Site.* WHS, 2015. http://worldheritagesite.org/countries/azerbaijan.html.

Abbasov, Shahin. "Azerbaijan: Energy Rich and Water Poor … For Now." http://mct.gov.az/service/lang/en/page/98/nid/127/.

Daisy Sindelar, Daisy. "Azerbaijan Bans RFE/RL, Other Foreign Radio From Airwaves." Radio Free Europe/Radio Liberty, 30 Dec. 2008. Web. http://www.rferl.org/content/Azerbaijan_Bans_RFERL_Other_Foreign_Radio/1364986.html.

Eurasianet.org. The Open Society Institute, 4 Oct. 2010. Web. http://www.eurasianet.org/node/62079.

Ilham Aliyev, Ilham. "The Soviet Period of Architecture in Azerbaijan." *Azerbaijan International* 6.4 (Winter 1998): 46–47. http://www.azer.com/aiweb/categories/magazine/64_folder/64_articles/64_useynov.html.

Pirouz Khanlou, Pirouz. "Baku's Architecture: A Fusion of East and West." *Azerbaijan International,* (Winter 1994) 2.4: 20–23. Web. http://www.azer.com/aiweb/categories/magazine/24_folder/24_articles/24_architecture.html.

Republic of Azerbaijan Ministry of Foreign Affairs. *Nakhchivan Autonomous Republic: Culture. Republic of Azerbaijan Ministry of Foreign Affairs*, n.d. Web. http://dmfa.nakhchivan.az/page.php?lang=eng&page=000105.

State Statistical Committee of the Republic of Azerbaijan. *Statistical Database.* AzSTAT, 2015. Web. http://www.stat.gov.az/menu/13/indexen.php.

Ziyadkhan Aliyev, Ziyadkhan. "Bahruz Kangarli (1892–1922)." *Azerbaijan International* (Summer 1999) 7.2: 26. http://www.azer.com/aiweb/categories/magazine/72_folder/72-articles/72_kangarli.html.

BELARUS

Introduction

The Republic of Belarus is a small country located in Eastern Europe. It is bordered to the east by Russia, to the south by Ukraine, to the west by Poland, and to the north by Lithuania and Latvia. Belarus was a member of the Soviet Union until 1991, when it declared itself an independent republic. The country is a member of the Commonwealth of Independent States (CIS), a consortium of former Soviet nations. Minsk, the capital of Belarus, is also the administrative center for the CIS.

GENERAL INFORMATION

Official Language: Belarusian, Russian
Population: 9,608,058 million (2014 estimate)
Currency: Belarusian ruble
Coins: Belarus currency does not include coins. The Belarusian ruble is only available in paper denominations.
Land Area: 207,600 square kilometers (80,154 square miles)
Water Area: 4,700 square kilometers (1,814 square miles)
National Anthem: "Dziaržaŭny himn Respubliki Biełaruś" ("State Anthem of the Republic of Belarus," or, unofficially, "My Belarusy")
Capital: Minsk
Time Zone: GMT +3
Flag Description: The flag of Belarus features two broad horizontal stripes of red and green. The upper red stripe is larger (two-thirds the entire height of the flag) than the lower green stripe (one third of the entire flag height). The flag features a traditional Belarusian red-on-white border pattern on the hoist (left) side. The red of the flag symbolizes the country's past and the green stands for the forests and hope. The red and white border pattern resembles a rushnyk, or towel woven with ancient cryptograms and used in ceremonies.

Population

Belarus has a homogeneous Caucasian population. More than three-quarters of the population is made up of ethnic Belarusians, who typically have fair skin, blond hair, and blue eyes. The largest minority groups in Belarus are Russians, Poles, and Ukrainians. Although there is little ethnic tension between these ethnic groups, other minorities have experienced discrimination.

Two-thirds of Belarusians live in urban areas. The most densely populated area is Minsk, the

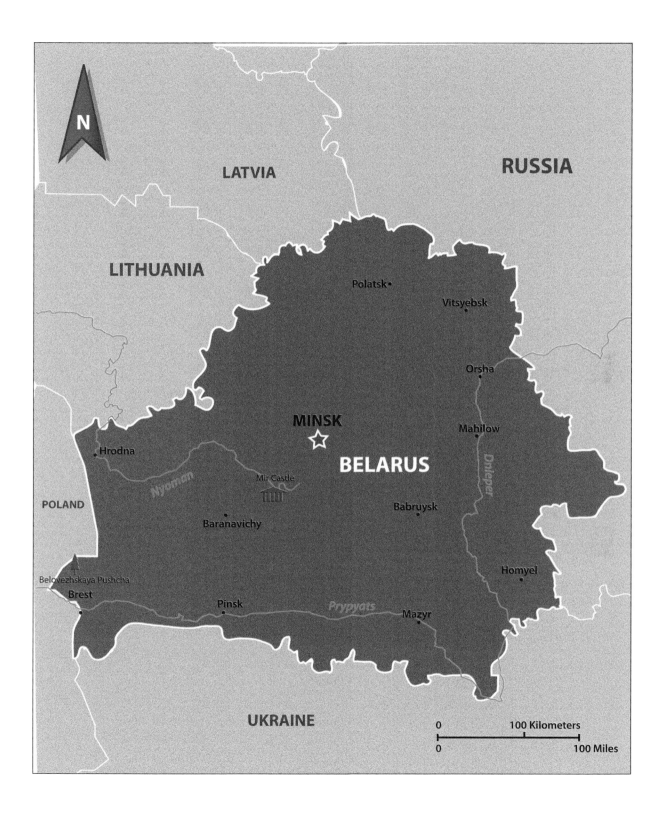

Principal Cities by Population (2014):

- Minsk (1,921,807)
- Gomel (526,872)
- Vitebsk (363,061)
- Mogilev (360,918)
- Hrodno/Grodno (356,557)
- Brest (309,764)
- Babruysk (215,092)
- Barysaw/Barysaŭ (180,100)
- Baranovici/Baranovichi (170,286)
- Pinsk (136,096)

centrally located capital and largest city. Other major cities include Gomel, Mogilev, Vitebsk, Hrodno, and Brest.

Most Belarusians living outside of urban centers are farmers. Rural dwellings are typically small wooden houses. Many Belarusian families work with other families on collective farms.

Languages

Although Belarusian and Russian are both considered official languages, most citizens speak Russian (around 70 percent of the population). The two languages are verbally similar and are both written in the Cyrillic alphabet. Some rural inhabitants employ the hybrid pidgin language known as Trasyanka or Trasianka, a Belarusian–Russian mixed language.

Native People & Ethnic Groups

There is evidence that people have lived in the area now known as Belarus since the Stone Age. Eastern Slavic tribes inhabited and settled the area during the ninth and 10th centuries. Belarus' modern population is descended from the Slavs. Belarus is one of the few European countries whose native population is also its majority modern population.

Religions

Most of the population of Belarus identifies as Eastern Orthodox (80 percent); other religious affiliations include Roman Catholic, Protestant, Jewish, and Muslim.

Climate

Belarus has a damp continental climate, typical of Eastern European nations. Winters are cold, with temperatures averaging –6° Celsius (21° Fahrenheit). Summer temperatures average 18° Celsius (64° Fahrenheit). Average annual rainfall is 60 to 70 centimeters (24 to 28 inches). Belarus does not typically experience natural disasters other than occasional harsh winter storms.

ENVIRONMENT & GEOGRAPHY

Topography

Belarus is a relatively flat country. Forests cover 39 percent of it, and most of the southern land is covered by the Pinsk (or Pripet) Marshes. The Pinsk Marshes make up the largest marshland in Europe. Another significant marshland, the Polesye (or Polesia), is also located in the southern region of Belarus. The highest point in the country is atop Dzyarzhynskaya Hara, at 345 meters (1,131 feet).

There are over 11,000 glacial lakes in Belarus, all of which are so small that the total water area of the country is negligible. The country's principal rivers are the Western Dvina, Neman, the Pripyat, and the Dnieper. Other rivers include the Berezina, the Sozh, and the Bug.

Minsk, the capital, is located roughly in the center of Belarus, on the banks of the Svisloch and the Nyamiha rivers, both of which link the Baltic and Black Seas. Because of its location, Minsk has been an important trading route since ancient times. The city lies among the hills of the Belarusian Ridge, with a total area of about 207,600 square kilometers (80,155 square miles). Specifically, the city is on the southeastern slope of the Minsk Hills, about 280 meters (920 feet) above sea level. While the western end of the city is almost entirely in the hills, Minsk expanded to include the plains of the southeast during the 20th century.

Plants & Animals

Much of Belarus' wildlife may be found in the country's marshes. The Pinsk Marshes have been affected by nuclear radiation from the Chernobyl accident (on the border of Belarus and Ukraine) more than any area in Eastern Europe. Belarus, in fact, suffered 70 percent of the fallout from that disaster and one quarter of its land was contaminated by radiation. Fish, such as carp and catfish, have shown high levels of plutonium radiation poisoning. Many small mammals living in the marshes, including beavers, hares, minks, and squirrels, have been affected as well.

The forests in the northern areas of Belarus have not been severely endangered by plutonium radiation. Varieties of trees found in Belarus' forests include oak, elm, white beech, birch, fir, pine, and spruce.

There are many wildlife preserves and national parks in Belarus. Among them are the Berezinsky Biosphere Reserve, the Braslav Lakes National Park, and the Narachanski National Park. Animals such as elk, deer, raccoon dogs (or tanuki), brown bears, wolves, eastern hedgehogs, and foxes are typically found in these areas.

The Belovezhskaya Pushcha National Park, a nature preserve on the border between Belarus and Poland, is home to a number of Belarus' endangered animal species, including a rare breed of European bison, the zubr. The zubr is the largest land mammal in all of Europe.

Common birds in Belarusian forests include woodpeckers, forest grouses, hazel grouses, common crossbills, crested tits, red-backed shrikes, white-tailed eagles, hawfinches, black redstarts, and goshawks.

CUSTOMS & COURTESIES

Greetings

Brief embraces are common between friends and family. In an informal introduction, Belarusians shake hands, maintain direct eye contact, and offer their last names to strangers. When a Belarusian woman greets another woman who is a good friend, it is quite common to see them offer three alternating kisses on the cheek (starting with the left). There are two types of greetings, one formal and the other informal. When meeting someone for the first time, or when showing additional respect, one should say "Zdrastvuichi" ("Wishing you good health"). In a less formal situation, one would simply say "Privjet" ("Hi").

Unless they are family and friends, Belarusians generally use honorific titles followed by a last name. Education commands high respect and status in Belarusian culture, and the title "professor" is used more broadly than in other cultures. Doctors of science as well as schoolteachers at levels higher than elementary or basic school are customarily addressed as such. Belarusians are generally not openly expressive with their gestures or emotions.

Gestures & Etiquette

Belarusians believe it is important to maintain eye contact when speaking, although in a non-business situation, a lot of eye contact from a man to a woman may be interpreted as forward and flirtatious. Belarusians are sometimes quite direct when requesting something. For example, a Belarusian will formulate passing the salt as a command rather than as a question. Although Belarusians have a sense of personal space equivalent to Western culture, there are various circumstances where less personal space is accepted. For instance, when Belarusians are packed onto mass transportation, such as trains or buses, they do not complain about the lack of space.

Belarusians do not speak loudly. For example, it is considered bad manners to laugh loudly in public or even converse loudly. Also, one should not wear an overcoat indoors, and one should use the cloakroom at concerts and restaurants rather than keeping one's coat. At concerts, stadiums, or sporting events, one should be aware that whistling does not mean enthusiastic approval. On the contrary, whistling is the equivalent of jeering or booing. Also, Belarusians do not give gifts for a newborn until after the child is born, as it is considered bad luck to give a gift sooner.

Table manners in Belarus are continental: the fork is held in the left hand, while the knife is held in the right hand when eating. During meals, the oldest or most honored guest is served first, and no guest should begin eating until the host has invited everyone to start. It is also considered impolite to rest one's elbows on the table, although one's hands should be visible at all times. In Belarus, guests are urged to have additional helpings, indicated by leaving a small amount of food on the plate. Etiquette also dictates that men should pour drinks for women seated next to them and that no one retires from the table until the host invites everyone to do so.

Eating/Meals

Belarusians typically eat a quick and light breakfast and have larger meals for lunch and dinner. Breakfast is often a few pieces of bread with honey, jam, or cheese and is usually accompanied with Turkish-style coffee. Belarusians have a relatively late lunch, usually consisting of a bowl of soup, a salad (during growing season), and then the main course. Belarusians eat dinner later in the evening, and it is typically the largest meal of the day.

Belarus observes many traditional holidays, and there are special dishes that accompany nearly every holiday. For example, Belarusians traditionally put hay on the table at Christmas. A tablecloth is then put over the hay, upon which twelve dishes are placed to represent the number of apostles who were at the Last Supper with Jesus. The most common foods served for Christmas are porridge with ground poppy-seeds, sweet soups (known as kissel, which are made of cranberries, currants, or other berries thickened with cornstarch, potato starch, or arrowroot), and buns. The main dishes are usually mushroom dishes and fish dishes, which are the most traditional part of Christmas dinner. Also, regardless of the occasion, Belarusian men refrain from setting the table, as it is still considered a woman's job.

Visiting

By tradition, Belarusians are known for their hospitality. Belarusian guests understand it is an honor to be invited to another Belarusian's home. The Belarusian host considers a visit as an important event alongside various traditions that are observed. Belarusians typically stock the dining room table with snacks and drinks, and guests are not surprised by a table loaded with items such as pickles, tomatoes, meat, cheese, bread, cakes, and alcoholic drinks. (The liquor is quite often a home-brewed distillation of plums or other fruits).

When invited to a Belarusian's house, it is customary to dress in semiformal attire, as this indicates respect for the hosts. It is also customary to be punctual and remove one's shoes before entering, and it is not uncommon for the host to offer house shoes, sandals, or slippers. The guest should also offer to help with preparations or cleaning up afterward. When visiting, the guest traditionally brings a bouquet of flowers (with an odd number of flowers) or a box of chocolates. If invited to a Belarusian's home for lunch or dinner, the guest may bring an appropriate small gift.

LIFESTYLE

Family

Until the last century, households in Belarus were based on zadruga, or extended kinship relations. The traditional zadruga consisted of a father and all his sons living on a mutual piece of farmland. Each married son would construct and live in his own cottage, while the entire extended family worked together. Although there are some families still living under this arrangement in the most rural parts of Belarus, this family structure has largely changed to the more urban lifestyle of nuclear families.

Housing has been difficult to obtain for newly married couples in recent years, and many young couples reside with one of the spouse's parents for the first few years, until they obtain separate housing. Belarusians also customarily remain living near where their parents and grandparents are buried, so that they can regularly visit the graveyard. In fact, it is not uncommon to have picnics at the gravesites of their deceased relatives. This tradition has been a problem since the Chernobyl nuclear power plant catastrophe of 1986. Belarusians who lived in the highly contaminated areas have been restricted from visiting their relatives' gravesites except for one day each year, when they are allowed to return to the gravesites to maintain them.

Housing

World War II caused the destruction of about 75 percent of all urban housing and left Belarusians living in temporary huts until new housing could be constructed. The new housing was built under the communist regime and is consequently similar to other Soviet Union housing projects. These are typically low quality, prefabricated multistory boxes with very little space or aesthetic appeal. The housing shortage, already prevalent under communism, was made worse by the Chernobyl nuclear reactor disaster in 1986. Though the disaster occurred in the Ukraine, Chernobyl is very near the southern border of Belarus. Winds spread over 70 percent of the radiation fallout throughout the Belarusian countryside, making 20 percent of the land completely uninhabitable. Many villages and small towns throughout the countryside became ghost towns, and about 15 percent of the entire Belarusian population was forced to relocate to cities further north. Thus, many rural Belarusians were forced into cities that were already facing severe housing shortages.

After Belarus became an independent state in 1991, the new nation's economy remained largely as it was under communism. The government still uses five-year central planning as it did when it was part of the Soviet Union. Consequently, the process of building is extremely bureaucratic and corrupt, with high fees and lengthy permit processes. For this reason and because of restricted laws on private ownership, individuals' investment in new real estate projects has not occurred since the fall of the Soviet Union. Minsk and every other large city is surrounded by Soviet-era apartment buildings, and the majority of urban Belarusians

live in these housing projects—including most of the Belarusians who were displaced by the Chernobyl disaster. According to World Bank data, in 2014, 76 percent of all Belarusians live in urban areas.

Food

The most commonly prepared foods in Belarus are bread, potatoes, cabbage, and pork. Also, various types of patties and pies are quite common. Because food used to be cooked on hot clay stoves for hours, many of today's traditional Belarusian dishes are either slowly baked or stewed. Although various cabbage dishes are a basic part of Belarusian cuisine, potatoes are actually the most-consumed vegetable in Belarus. Potatoes became the main vegetable from the 18th century, when peasants began growing them. Since that time, the Belarusians have developed about 200 different recipes using potatoes. For example, draniki is a potato pancake made from grated potatoes; babka is grated potatoes with meat, onions, and eggs; and kliotskas are a kind of potato dumpling with meat. Pork is the most-consumed meat, although beefsteak and poultry are also common. Additionally, freshwater fish, such as perch and crayfish, are quite plentiful in Belarus and are served in most restaurants. Many of these dishes are served with either potatoes or cabbage.

Traditional Belarusian dishes include borscht, which is a thick soup made with beets and served hot with sour cream. Mochanka is another thick soup that is mixed with lard and accompanied by hot pancakes. Mushrooms are a most important ingredient in many Belarusian dishes and are used in many sauces. Some national mushroom dishes are mushrooms served in sour cream, mushroom and barley soup, or pork cutlets covered with mushroom sauce. Garlic is also frequently used in Belarusian cooking, as is caraway. A national drink known as kvas is quite popular, and is traditionally made from black or rye bread, sugar, yeast, water, and a fruit, most often raisins. Despite being a fermented beverage, it has a very low alcohol content and is considered an excellent source of vitamin B.

Life's Milestones

Many traditional ceremonies in Belarus mark life's milestones, such as baptisms, funerals, or other occasions, and all include the use of hand-embroidered towels, which are central symbolic objects in the ceremonies. In traditional weddings, for example, a hand-embroidered towel is tied around the bride's hand, and she drags it behind her on the ground as she walks to the wedding altar. The towel represents the pathway that her girlfriends will follow to get married. The couple then stands on this "padnozhnik" towel ("under foot" towel) during the wedding ceremony. The towel symbolically represents the path of entering a new family structure.

Funerals also use these towels in various ways. Traditionally, the Belarusian funeral is a ritual that assists the passing of the dead into the next world. A towel is hung behind a window of the deceased's house, so that their soul could take the path to another world. The towel is hung in the house for an additional six weeks after the funeral. Also, when lowering the coffin into the grave, long towels or linen are used to symbolize the way to the afterworld.

CULTURAL HISTORY

Art

Belarusian painting and sculpting developed out of Eastern Europe's long history of religious icon painting. In the 20th century, artists such as sculptor Ossip Zadkine (1890–1967) and painter Kazimir Malevich (1879–1935) helped initiate the abstract movement. Other prominent artists include Pinchus Kremegne (1890–1981), a sculptor and painter who flourished in Paris, France; painter and sculptor Jazep Drazdovich (1888–1954), whose work is considered reflective of nationalism; and Chaïm Soutine (1893–1943), an expressionist painter whose best-known work focuses on animal carcasses. In May 2013, Soutine's work *Le petit pâtissier* sold for $18 million USD at Christie's auction in New York, setting a new world record for the artist's work.

Belarusian artist Marc Chagall (1887–1985), who worked in several mediums, is considered a pioneer of modern art. Combining native themes with the avant-garde, Chagall became one of the 20th century's most successful and renowned artists. His work is consistently described as both poetic and unorthodox. In May 2013, in the same New York auction that brought the record amount for Soutine's work, a Chagall painting, *Les trois acrobats*, sold for $13,003,750 million (USD), a testament to the artist's international appeal and growing legacy. Many Belarusian artists including Chagall, Kremegne, Soutine, and Zadkine immigrated to France.

Traditional Belarusian arts include weaving, box making, and other folk arts. Traditional Belarusian folk clothing, an important part of the country's performing arts heritage, is usually made from wool or flax and decorated with multicolored silk threads.

Architecture

Slavic and Lithuanian tribes settled in current-day Belarus from the late sixth to the early eighth century CE. Over the next few centuries, most of the earliest Belarusian cities developed along the banks of rivers and lakes in the north and northwestern area of the country. To defend against invaders, these cities were built with fortified structures, such as castles and fortresses. In the High Middle Ages (1000–1299 CE), when the first period of urbanization occurred in Europe, the number of Belarusian towns increased rapidly. During this period, Belarusians settled the swampy southern region, and southern cities were strengthened as the earliest regional trade centers.

One of the oldest stone buildings in Belarus, St. Sophia Cathedral, was built in the northern city of Polotsk during the Kingdom (or Duchy) of Polotsk, which existed from the ninth through the 13th centuries. Prince Vseslav Briacheslavich (c. 1030–1101) built the cathedral originally using a mixture of Romanesque and Byzantine architectural styles. However, St. Sophia Cathedral has been through many renovations, and little remains of its architectural beginnings. Today, the church has the appearance of the Baroque style of Vilnius (the capital of Lithuania) that was popular in the 1700s. After the Polotsk kingdom fragmented, the Grand Duchy of Lithuania claimed control over Belarus.

At its height in the 15th century, the Grand Duchy of Lithuania was the largest kingdom in Europe. It covered the territory of present-day Lithuania, Belarus, Ukraine, and parts of Poland and Russia. Although this period is considered a golden age for Belarus, there were, nevertheless, various wars and invasions that significantly disrupted the economic and cultural development of Belarusian cities. Consequently, Belarusian architecture developed sporadically and did not see a period of major growth until around the late 18th century. Also, for obvious practical reasons, Belarusian architecture always incorporated defensive architecture, including in its churches. Most of Belorussia's military fortifications were built between the 13th and the 17th centuries and were built in the Gothic and Renaissance styles. (Belorussia is the historical region that corresponds to modern-day Belarus.) Many Baroque churches were constructed from the 16th through the 18th centuries.

During the Belarusian Baroque period, sacral architecture was predominant. Afterward, classical architecture using Rococo (a French style that evolved from Baroque) mixed with Baroque became widespread, especially among large estates or palaces. However, continuous wars, particularly World War II, destroyed many architectural gems and caused extensive damage to the major cities of Belorussia. Many major cities, such as the capital of Minsk, mostly have the appearance of post-World War II, Stalinist architecture that originated from the Soviet Union. This style of architecture is functional in nature, often includes socialist monuments, and is characterized by a lack of aesthetics.

Drama

The Orthodox Christian and Catholic Churches developed religious and mystical rituals over the centuries. However, religion does not seem to have strongly influenced the development of theater in Belarus. Rather, the most influential development very early in Belarusian history was that of the "skomorokhi" tradition, first mentioned in a chronicle from 1068. Skomorokhi were wandering minstrels whom the folk of Belorussia quite enjoyed and admired. Generally, they were entertainers who could play musical instruments and sing ballads and other songs. They also performed comical theatrics that were sometimes bitingly satirical toward the powers of church and state. Some of the oldest paintings show these jesters with bears, suggesting they were also animal trainers.

Skomorokhi were quite direct and irreverent, which tended to make them popular—and even legendary—among common folk, but unpopular with the clergy and the elite. In fact, extant church sermons from the 11th and 12th centuries warn the people that skomorokhi are evil sinners. They were persecuted by organized religion for propagating paganism and heresy, much like sorcerers and soothsayers. However, the common people enjoyed skomorokhi entertainment, so a primitive folk theater became rooted in the skomorokhi tradition. Traveling minstrels did not actually start theaters or theater troupes, but the spirit of theater as entertainment and art can certainly be traced back to the skomorokhi. One of the oldest traditions in Belarusian theater is puppet theater, and in some ways, this may have been like skomorokhi on strings. Puppet theater has been a central influence in shaping Belarusian theatrical traditions.

Music & Dance

Belarusians have a rich folk music tradition that dates back several centuries, even reaching back to pagan roots. Religion became one of the main influences on the Belarusian musical tradition. Some 12th-century Orthodox hymns, unique to Belarus, have survived, indicating that Orthodox Christianity was important in early Belarusian society and in forming a music tradition. From the 16th century forward, the religious influence strengthened such that church and folk music had obvious connections.

However, folk songs are fundamentally rooted in pagan traditions that predate Christianity. The most ancient Belarusian folk songs, which are still popular today, celebrate seasonal changes and are connected to rituals and superstitions that have passed into contemporary Belarusian folk culture. Also, Belarusian folk dances go back to pagan times and are today distinct styles found in six ethnographic regions.

Prior to the dissolution of the Soviet Union, folk arts were strongly encouraged and supported by the communist government. As in all Soviet republics, many towns had a cultural center where folk music and dance performances were regularly held. Since 1991, the Belarusian government has largely cut off funding of these cultural centers, and many have ceased operations, which has caused a decline in the popularity of folk art.

Literature

The earliest kingdom in Belarus had Byzantium traditions at its heart. This foundation meant Orthodox Christianity became the common religion early in the nation's history, helping to foster an interest in education and writing. Orthodoxy, therefore, set the initial direction and tone for Belarus's literary tradition, with the earliest Belarusian literary works being 11th-century sermons and hymns. For many centuries, religious writings were the only literary works in Belorussia. In the 12th century, the Orthodox Church recognized Cyril of Turaw (1130–1182) for the prolific sermons and hymns he wrote.

Shortly after the invention of the printing press, Francysk Skaryna of Polatsk (1490–1551) became the first publisher in Belarus. As might be expected, the first book in Belarusian was the Bible. Skaryna translated the Bible into Belarusian—along with his extensive notes about biblical chapters—and began printing the work in Prague in 1517. Skaryna's biblical work was the first book to be printed in Eastern Europe. The next advance in Belarusian literature also came out of Polatsk (also Polotsk). In the 17th century, a monk named Simeon Polatski (Symeon of Polotsk, 1629–1680) introduced the verbose

Baroque literary styles to Moscow. He lived in Moscow from 1663 until his death and did much to contribute to a literary scene in Russia. He introduced syllabic poetry and the basic concept of metered verse. He also wrote satires as well as other literary works.

By the beginning of the 19th century, modern Belarusian literature became focused on the question of national identity. Belarusian linguist Yefim Karskiy (1861–1931) authored the seven-volume work *Belarusians*, which created a new perception of Belarusian as a language. Karskiy demonstrated that the Russian and the Old Belarusian languages were separate developments. He argued that Belarusian was a distinct language and that Belarusians were a separate nationality. His work spread in Belarusian academia and to the common folk. This caused a great majority of Belarusians to believe, for the first time and upon a scientific basis, that they really should be considered an independent nation. Karskiy's seminal linguistic work coincided with Belarusian national movements in the late 1800s. Belarus experienced an unprecedented surge of national sentiment, including among the mainstream working class and peasants. These movements, in turn, added momentum to the rapid growth of a separate Belarusian literature and press.

The work of the earliest modern Belarusian poet and playwright, Vincent Dunin-Marcinkievič (1808–1884), is a good example of the transition from a nationally mixed literature to a fully separate Belarusian literature. Dunin-Marcinkievič came from a noble family of the Polish-Lithuanian Commonwealth, and he wrote works in both the Polish language and contemporary Belarusian. In 1855, Dunin-Marcinkievič authored the first poem that was written entirely in contemporary Belarusian, and he translated various works from Polish into literary Belarusian masterpieces. The next generation of writers created the high point of Belarusian classic literature. Belarusian nationalist writers, such as Yanka Kupala (1882–1942), Yakub Kolas (1882–1956), and Maksim Bahdanovič (1891–1917), all contributed significantly to a new, distinctly Belarusian literature. Also, during this same time, the newspaper *Nasha Niva* promoted Belarusian identity and culture. From this period forward, many excellent Belarusian poets, dramatists, and novelists have added to the national literary heritage.

CULTURE

Arts & Entertainment

The contemporary arts in Belarus have become an important medium of dissent, though some journalists and writers have paid dearly for their opposition with the post-Soviet Belarusian government. Belarusian film has also become an important new medium for political dissent. The Belarusian Ministry of Culture has consistently suppressed such opposition, as can be seen in several cases where filmmakers released unflattering films or documentaries about the Belarusian government. Jury Chaščavacki (1948–) released a 1996 documentary titled *Obyknovennyj Prezident* (*The Usual President*). The documentary won the Berlin International Film Festival Peace Prize in 1997 as well as the European Parliament's Sakharov Prize for Freedom of Thought. However, the movie was highly critical of Belarusian President Alexander Lukashenko (1954–), and the government began harassing the director of the film (both of the director's legs were broken by unknown assailants). When a Belarusian cable TV station attempted to debut this same documentary in Belarus, the Belarusian secret police (KGB) arrested the manager of the station and confiscated the film; it has never been aired in Belarus.

Another example of artistic suppression occurred when director Viktor Dashuk released the documentary *Long Knives Night* (1999). The film documented the difficult and dangerous lives of political dissidents who oppose President Lukashenko. Belarusian secret police demanded that Dashuk hand over the videotape of his film, after which the film was banned from release in Belarus. Dashuk made a second, secretly-filmed documentary, *Reporting from a Rabbit Hole*

(2002), a film about the many political opposition members who have mysteriously gone missing in Belarus. This film also has been banned in Belarus. Thus, the arts in contemporary Belarus have, in recent years, become an important instrument of political opposition. Some of these documentary projects have been supported, or even largely financed, by democratic European states, such as Sweden in Dashuk's case. Consequently, the Belarusian government has recently enacted legislation aimed at preventing international funding for various artistic projects, magazines, and other media.

Soccer, track and field, and volleyball are the most popular sports in Belarus.

Cultural Sites & Landmarks

Belarus has three cultural properties and one natural property inscribed on the United Nations Educational, Scientific and Cultural Organization (UNESCO) World Heritage List. The first building to be inscribed, in 2000, was the Mir Castle Complex. Construction began on Mir Castle near the end of the 15th century, when Gothic architecture was popular. However, the castle was renovated and expanded over the next several centuries, so that it has obvious influences of Renaissance and Baroque architectural styles as well. The castle was abandoned and neglected for about a century, but restoration began at the end of the 19th century. At that time, the castle was further expanded and the surrounding area was landscaped into a beautiful park. It is an excellent example of a European castle that blends Gothic, Renaissance, and Baroque architectural styles. These styles themselves serve as the physical embodiment of the various political and cultural struggles that occurred over several centuries of Belarusian history.

The second building on the UNESCO World Heritage List, inscribed in 2005, is the Architectural, Residential and Cultural Complex of the Radziwill Family at Nesvizh, in central Belarus. The Radziwill noble family built the estate in the 16th century and maintained it until the outbreak of World War II. The Radziwill dynasty supported scientists and artists over several centuries, and for that reason, the town of Nesvizh became an important cultural center in Belarus. The estate also contains the Church of Corpus Christi, which was built with a cross-cupola basilica that influenced the architecture of Central Europe. Altogether, the estate has ten interconnected buildings that were designed as an architectural whole to surround a central courtyard.

The Struve Geodetic Arc was inscribed on the UNESCO World Heritage List in 2000. The Struve Arc represents a point in an extensive survey—over 2,820 kilometers (1,752 miles)—that runs through ten countries. The astronomer Friedrich Georg Wilhelm Struve (1793–1864) carried out the survey from 1816 to 1855, and this survey represented the first accurate measuring of a long segment of a meridian. The Struve Geodetic Arc represents an early international scientific collaboration that advanced human knowledge.

Belarus's only natural area on the World Heritage List is the Belovezhskaya Pushcha/ Białowieża Forest, inscribed in 1979. The Belovezhskaya Pushcha Forest is an immense forest range that is home to rare European animals, such as the wolf, the lynx, and the otter. Also, about 800 European Bison now inhabit the park, which covers the watershed between the Baltic and Black Seas.

Libraries & Museum

As of 2014, there were 14 major museums in Belarus. Museums located in the capital of Minsk include the National Museum of Culture and History of Belarus, which contains the country's largest archaeological collection and which was reorganized as the national museum in 1991; the Belarusian National Arts Museum, the largest museum in the county, containing iconography dating back to the fifteenth century; the Belarusian State Museum of the Great Patriotic War, which is concentrated on World War II; and Maksim Bahdanovič's Literary Museum, dedicated to the famous writer. In Vitebsk is the Marc Chagall Museum, which features more than 300 of Chagall's etchings, lithographs, relief prints,

and aquatints and provides visitors with an opportunity to see Chagall's childhood home.

Founded in 1922, the National Library of Belarus is located in Minsk and acts as the nation's legal depository and copyright library. It also has the world's third largest collection of Russian-language books. The national library's new building, opened in 2006 and designed by architects Mihail Vinogradov (Belarusian) and Viktor Kramarenko (Ukrainian), is architecturally progressive with its rhombicuboctahedron shape. In 2010, the national library entered into a cooperative agreement with the Boris Yeltsin Presidential Library of Russia. That same year, the library established a similar agreement with the national library of Turkey.

Holidays

Most of Belarus' national holidays are days that commemorate war-related events. November 2 is Dzyady, or Remembrance Day, which honors the memory of those who died in the world wars. Constitution Day, which celebrates the anniversary of the adoption of Belarus' post-Soviet constitution, is observed on March 15.

Other official holidays include Victory Day (May 9) and October Revolution Day (November 7). Many Eastern Orthodox holidays are observed throughout the year as well, including Orthodox Christmas, which falls on January 7.

Although Belarus' birth as an independent republic came on August 25, 1991, Independence Day is celebrated on July 3. On this day in 1944, Minsk was liberated from German troops at the end of World War II.

Youth Culture

Most Belarusian youth are characterized as being either apolitical or strongly engaged in political activism against the Lukashenko regime. There has been a consistently low voter turnout among youth during Belarusian elections, which indicates a lack of respect or belief in political authorities and politics in general. However, political opposition is largely a youth movement, and there is a relatively high youth turnout for political protests. The Belarusian regime has increased its pressure on politically active youth through the illegal arrests and detention of youth activists and subsequent criminal prosecution.

The authorities also use the country's educational institutions to silence political activism. For example, the government has been accused of placing pressure on students through threats of expulsion, while schools that support student protests are shut down or otherwise persecuted. Before 2014, the Internet had been the only source of information the Belarusian government had not managed to control. Since Belarusian youth are technologically savvier than previous generations, the Internet had become the strongest political tool among Belarusian youth. However, the December 2014 amendments to existing Belarusian media laws have put a significant damper on this form of political activism and made it increasingly perilous to speak out online.

SOCIETY

Transportation

Transportation in the capital of Minsk is well developed. The city has two subway lines, and trolleybuses and trams operate efficiently at frequent intervals. The transportation costs are inexpensive, and the majority of Minsk inhabitants use the subway system. Also, many bus routes run throughout the larger metropolitan area. Traffic moves on the right-hand side of the road in Belarus.

Transportation Infrastructure

Belarus has an efficient railway network with major interregional railways networking throughout the country and, according to Belarus' official website, reaching an average of 2,100 in-country destinations. The main routes run from east to west, with end destinations to Berlin, Warsaw, and Moscow; north to south, with end destinations to St. Petersburg and Kiev (Ukraine); and northwest to southeast, with end destinations to major cities in the Baltic countries

and Ukraine. The Belarusian road system is not nearly as developed as the railway system. Minsk has one major east-west trunk road running through it, but the other roads are inferior. Minsk has good air connections for international flights, though most Belarusians use the railway system rather than domestic flights. Rivers are much used as transportation routes for cargo, and there are ten ports at cities located along the rivers Dnepr, Berezina, Sozh, Pripyat, Zapadnaya Dvina, Neman, and Mukhavets, as well as the Dnepr-Bug canal.

Media & Communications

Belarusian television is controlled by the Belarusian government. The government operates the First National Channel (Belarus-1), as well as the entertainment network called Lad (Harmony) and the TV satellite station Belarus-TV. As for other broadcast stations, Belarus has Nationwide TV (ONT), which is a joint venture with Russia's Channel One (the Belarusian government holds a majority stake). STV is locally broadcast in Minsk and is also state-run. Belsat, based in Poland, is the only broadcast station not controlled by the Belarusian government and is broadcast by satellite and the Internet. Belarusian radio is also state-controlled, though a few stations from beyond the Belarusian border are broadcast into Belarus. Radio Baltic Waves, which is backed by the European Union (EU), broadcasts into Belarus from its base in Lithuania, and Radio Racyja broadcasts from Poland.

The printed press in Belarus is similar to the electronic media, in that state control is tight. Various parts of Belarusian government entirely own the four main newspapers in Belarus. There is a business daily that is privately owned, though it has run into severe problems for criticizing the Lukashenko government and exposing corruption. The second privately-owned newspaper that is critical of the Belarusian government is an opposition daily, and it has also faced court battles on grounds of defamation for its critical views. The newspaper has also been banned from the state-controlled newspaper distribution system, thus restricting its national circulation.

Through its company Beltelcom, the Belarusian government is a monopolistic landline telephone service provider. Unlike the other former Soviet Union countries, Belarus has yet to significantly modernize its telecommunications infrastructure. Fixed line services to Belarusians have slowly increased, though the rural areas are still sparsely supplied with landlines. Wireless telephone networks have compensated for the slow growth of landline infrastructure, and well over half of all Belarusians use cellular phones. In 2014, from a total population of about 9.6 million Belarusians, 3,974 million had landlines while 10.3 million had cell phones. As of December 2013, there were an estimated 5,204,685 Internet users, representing just over 54 percent of the population.

SOCIAL DEVELOPMENT

Standard of Living
Belarus ranked 53rd out of 195 countries on the 2012 United Nations Human Development Index, which measures quality of life and standard of living indicators.

Water Consumption
According to UNICEF (United Nations International Children's Emergency Fund), Belarus enjoys almost 100 percent access to improved drinking water; urban areas are at 99.8 percent, and rural areas are at 99.4 percent. In terms of improved access to sanitation, the country's average is 93 percent, broken down into 91 percent access in urban areas and 97 percent access in rural areas.

Education
Belarus has high levels of school attendance and one of the highest literacy rates in the world. More than 99 percent of adult Belarusians are literate, many in more than one language.

Belarusian children between ages six and fifteen are required to attend free public schools. Secondary school attendance levels are also high, and many students continue their education at the university level. There are six academies, six institutes, three colleges, and 32 universities in Belarus, the largest of which is Belarusian State University in Minsk.

Women's Rights
Gender roles in Belarus have remained rigidly traditional. Families are patriarchal, with males the main financial supporter and women expected to care for the children and maintain the household. This marginalization is pervasive in society at large. Despite the fact that Belarusian law enforces gender equality, women are still discriminated against, especially in the workforce. For example, women generally earn less than male counterparts. In addition, though women may advance to middle management positions, they have significantly less opportunity to advance to the highest ranks. Also, women report that company employers practice discriminatory hiring and usually consider whether a woman has children. This situation has been slowly changing since the late 1990s, and some Belarusian women have gained more access to high-profile jobs in both business and government. However, Belarusian women are still the least-protected group in the job market. Many Belarusian women do not consider their rights and interests in terms of women's issues, and this, in turn, exacerbates gender inequality. In fact, many Belarusians, both men and women, consider lower status for women in society as socially correct.

Domestic violence against women and spousal rape continue to be major problems in Belarus. In particular, there are no laws prohibiting spousal rape, and numerous rapes go unreported due to social stigma and the fact that blame is often associated with victims. Sexual harassment also continues to be prevalent, and prostitution, though illegal, is not considered a criminal offense. Belarus has also been targeted by non-governmental organizations (NGOs) and other human rights groups for human trafficking. Belarus is considered a source and transit country for the purposes of forced labor and sexual exploitation.

Several feminist initiatives have come to the forefront in the last decade. In the late 1990s, several Belarusian women's organizations were formed, although these organizations tend to be politically affiliated. For example, social-democratic women belong to one women's group, while women of a different political viewpoint belong to other women's groups. In 2015, the Ministry of Justice in Belarus had fourteen registered women's organizations. There has also been some important international cooperation with women's groups in Belarus. The Belarusian government has been cooperating in the implementation of projects for women organized by the World Health Organization (WHO) and the United Nations Development Programme (UNDP). Also, through cooperation with the United Nations Children's Fund (UNICEF), a comprehensive analysis of the situation facing Belarus' women and children was made into a lengthy and informative UN report. The Belarusian government has cooperated in establishing a Regional UNICEF Office in Belarus.

Health Care

Belarusians are generally healthy, with an estimated average life expectancy in 2014 of seventy-eight years for women and sixty-six years for men. Fallout from the 1986 reactor meltdown at the Chernobyl site in Ukraine has caused health problems in Belarus, and approximately one-quarter of the country's land remains uninhabitable. The most common health problem related to exposure to nuclear radioactivity is thyroid cancer among Belarusian children.

Under Soviet control, Belarus had an established, effective health care system. Since the Soviet Union disbanded in 1991, the system has been problematic. Antibiotics, vaccinations, and anesthetics have often been in short supply. However, Belarus' government has implemented significant reforms and changed their purchasing model for pharmaceuticals. According to the World Health Organization (WHO), Belarus now ranks fifty-third among 190 nations for health-care accessibility and efficacy. That's up from a ranking of 72 in 2000.

GOVERNMENT

Structure

Since becoming independent, Belarus has constructed a democratic government with a constitution, president, prime minister, and a bicameral legislature. The legislature consists of a 110-member House of Representatives, and a sixty-four member Council of the Republic.

Despite the fact that Belarus' government appears to be a democratic republic, it is, in fact, a dictatorship. The president is extremely powerful. Among his duties are the appointment of the prime minister, justices, and members of the legislature. The president is given lifetime immunity to prosecution and may remain a member of the presidential cabinet after his presidency ends. The prime minister's main duty is to head the Council of Ministers.

Western nations, including the United States, have accused Belarus' dictatorial government of violating human rights. Offenses committed by the government include suppressing media sources, limiting public access to information, and arresting citizens expressing dissent.

Political Parties

Politics in Belarus is not based on a party system; rather, it is comprised of those supportive of the Lukashenko presidency and those opposed. Of the 110 members of the House of Representatives, 105 of those seats are held by "non-partisans," or members of organizations, such as labor unions or civic or public organizations. Of the remaining five members, three are members of the Communist Party of Belarus, one is a member of the Republican Party of Labor and Justice, and one is a member of the Agrarian Party of Belarus. All three of these parties are supportive of Lukashenko, and he is also supported by the Belarusian Socialist Sporting Party.

Opposition parties have coalesced under opposition umbrella groups. One of those coalitions is the United Democratic Forces of Belarus, which includes the United Civil Party of Belarus, the United Civic Party, the Belarusian United Left Party "A Just World," and other parties.

Another opposition coalition is the Belarusian Independence Bloc, which includes eight parties, such as the Partyja BPF (Belarusian People's Front Party) and Belarusian Christian Democracy. Opposition parties have not gained any seats in the 2004, 2008, or 2012 parliamentary elections.

Local Government

There are six provinces or oblasts in Belarus, in which voters elect members to local councils. Councils of Deputies are directly elected and operate on three levels, primary (villages and towns), basic (towns and regions), and oblasts. The provinces/oblasts are Minsk, Vitebsk, Mogilev, Grodno, Gomel, and Brest. Issues handled on a local level include health, education, social welfare, trade, and transport.

Judicial System

Courts in Belarus are divided into the general courts, economic courts, and the Constitutional Court. General courts address civil, criminal, and administrative matters. Military, regional, town, and Minsk's city courts are general courts, as is the Supreme Court. The economic courts include the Minsk Economic Court, regional economic courts, and the Supreme Economic Court. The Constitutional Court, established by Article 116 of Belarus' constitution, addresses matters related to legislation and statutes and is comprised of twelve judges, six appointed by the president and six by the Council of the Republic.

Taxation

The government of Belarus levies corporate, excise, personal income, and a value-added tax (or VAT, similar to a consumption tax). There is a 12 percent withholding tax for companies not registered within, but doing business in Belarus, and the top corporate rate, based on an aggregate of profits, is 26.3 percent. However, to encourage Belarus-based entrepreneurial efforts, there is a low, 8 percent tax rate for small businesses. Income tax rates are low, approximately 3 percent, with the top tax rate a flat 12 percent.

Armed Forces

The Belarus armed forces consist of an army and air force (including air defense). The country established an integrated air defense system with Russia, and the armed forces of both nations have conducted large-scale integrated training exercises. In 2014, there were an estimated 62,000 active personnel and 289,500 reserves.

Foreign Policy

Belarus became an independent state in 1991, but of all the former Soviet Republics, Belarus has been the least independent from the policies and economics of Russia. Belarus and Russia were the founding members of the Commonwealth of Independent States (CIS), which was a new agreement for cooperation and confederation that replaced the former Soviet Union arrangement. In the early 1990s, the two countries negotiated another agreement for creating a monetary union. In April 1996, the two countries signed the Treaty on Forming a Community. That agreement more clearly promoted the coordination of the two countries' foreign and economic policies. This led to the establishment of a Russia-Belarus parliamentary assembly (though this assembly holds little political power, and the two countries are still quite independent of each other). At the end of 1999, the two countries signed a treaty on a two-state union aimed at creating greater political and economic integration. However, Alexander Lukashenko has consolidated his own power over Belarus through authoritarian use of law, justice, and enforcement branches of his administration.

Since achieving independence, and while under the presidency of Lukashenko, Belarus has had strained relations with the EU and Western capitalist countries. This is partly because Lukashenko has created economic policies that have isolated Belarus. In 1995, Lukashenko implemented policies that allowed the government to take over the Belarusian free market. Lukashenko created new methods for government control over market prices and currency exchange rates, and he expanded government power over the management of private enterprises. Since 2005, the government has also re-nationalized a number of private companies and has used various legal tools to subjugate private businesses. For example, the government uses unpredictable and sudden changes in business regulations (used retroactively) and conducts numerous harsh inspections and arrests of "disruptive" businessmen. These various controls over the Belarusian free market have discouraged foreign investment and isolated the country from Western market integration. In 2005, the United States government called Belarus the last remaining "outpost of tyranny" in Europe. The EU has even banned President Lukashenko and a number of Belarusian ministers and officials from entering EU member countries. Additionally, Lukashenko's assets were frozen in EU and U.S. banks.

However, since late 2008, tensions between Lukashenko and the West seem to have eased, and foreign relations have slightly improved. There are several reasons for this. First, Belarus has had some severe disagreements with Russia, particularly over energy supplies and taxation of oil. Belarus is dependent on Russia's oil supply, and this has caused tensions to increase since they are not one union. Lukashenko also refused to take a sharp stand with Russia over the 2008 conflict in Georgia, wherein Russia attacked Georgia over the South Ossetia region. In July 2009, Russia banned Belarus' dairy products, citing Belarus' inability to comply with new regulations. Russia soon followed with a $231 million USD gas bill for product Belarus used. Relations between the EU and Russia have likewise become severely strained over the Georgia conflict, so Lukashenko's decision to remain uncommitted to Russia's position has placed him closer to the EU's position.

One last reason for thawed relations between Lukashenko and the West is Lukashenko's decision to release what were clearly political prisoners from Belarusian prisons. In the past, several strong opposition politicians in Belarus have disappeared or were imprisoned, but in late 2008, Lukashenko released several opposition activists. As of 2009, Belarusian authorities had released the last three political prisoners, and the EU had lifted its ban on Lukashenko from entering EU countries. However, following Belarus' 2010 presidential election, with its mass arrests and protester imprisonments, the EU's denunciations of Belarus' human rights violations and subsequent punitive sanctions caused relations to again deteriorate.

Human Rights Profile

International human rights law insists that states respect civil and political rights and also promote an individual's economic, social, and cultural rights. The United Nations Universal Declaration on Human Rights (UDHR) is recognized as the standard for international human rights. (To read this document or view the articles relating to cultural human rights, go to http://www.ohchr.org/EN/UDHR/Pages/Introduction.aspx).

The right to freedom of speech and expression continues to be a major concern in Belarus, both in terms of press freedom and individual expression. Human rights and media watch groups have been highly critical of the Belarusian authorities for suppressing individual freedom of speech, for hampering (if not altogether shutting down) the independent press, and for denying all opposition voices access to the state-owned media. The state-run media is nearly the only media that the majority of Belarusians have access to, so controlling the state media largely controls all public discussion. In both 2014 and 2015, the organization Reporters Without Borders ranked Belarus 157th out of 180 countries in its worldwide press freedom index. This is down from the country's 154th ranking in 2010.

Lukashenko passed a media law in the summer of 2008 that raises serious questions about whether a free press is possible in Belarus. The new law gives the government additional control over any media that is backed by organizations such as the EU or other governments such as Lithuania, Sweden, or other democratic European states. Media watch groups have claimed that the 2008 media law is extremely restrictive, particularly with its new restrictions on foreign funding for the media and government ability to censor the Internet. TV is the main source of news for Belarusians, and all main broadcast channels are already state-controlled. And while government-controlled newspapers receive large subsidies and other financial advantages, opposition print media often face prosecution or other government tactics intended to cease or limit their circulation. Freedom of religion and gay rights have also been areas of concern.

In December 2014, the Belarusian parliament adopted and Lukashenko signed amendments to the existing media law, which extends restrictions placed on traditional journalists and news outlets to all online content. The Committee to Protect Journalists, a freedom-of-press watchdog organization, expressed concern over the vague wording of these amendments.

Another problem in Belarus's human rights record is its suppression of political opposition leaders. Not only are opposition protestors routinely arrested and charged with various crimes, human rights organizations have reported that the Belarusian government actively creates many obstacles to the investigation of alleged human rights violations. The Belarusian government used methods of espionage to follow written correspondence and telephone conversations of international human rights representatives. In addition, members of the Belarusian Helsinki Committee, a non-profit, non-governmental, human rights organization, were arrested when observing a political demonstration, and human rights monitors have been physically attacked and threatened for trying to gather information on political opposition court trials. Human rights monitors are harassed for pursuing internal cases and are sometimes even arrested during fact-finding missions in Belarus.

In November 2006, a referendum of questionable legitimacy significantly revised the original Belarusian constitution. The new constitution has greatly expanded presidential powers, while at the same time, greatly diminishing the powers of the national parliament. Since that time, President Lukashenko has increased his control over Belarusian government and society.

ECONOMY

Overview of the Economy
Since the Soviet Union disbanded, Belarus has experienced economic hardship. Inflation and unemployment have both risen significantly, despite growth in the industrial and agricultural sectors. Because Belarus has not been an independent nation for very long, there is room for growth in trade, tourism, and the service industries. The per capita GDP was estimated at $16,100 (USD) in 2013.

Industry
Manufacturing accounts for 46.2 percent of Belarus' GDP. Farm machinery and equipment, cement, steel, televisions, radios, refrigerators, motorcycles, bicycles, and computers are among the primary manufactured goods. The service industry is not as important to the industrial sector as manufacturing. Yet, in 2013, the service sector did account for 44.7 percent of the GDP. Most service sector jobs are in the fields of communications, transportation, construction, and information technology.

Belarus' major trading partners are Russia, the destination for over 40 percent of the Belarus's export volume and half its imports; Ukraine; and Kazakhstan. Belarus also trades with more than 180 other countries, including Great Britain, Netherlands, Germany, Latvia, Lithuania, Italy, Poland, Australia, New Zealand, Canada, and the United States. Exports include oil, potash, nitrogen fertilizers, machinery, mineral products, chemicals, metals, and textiles.

Labor
The labor force in Belarus numbered 4,489,746 people in 2013. Forty-five percent of the population finds work in the service sector, 46 percent finds work in industry, and nine percent works in the agricultural sector. As of 2014, the National Statistical Committee of the Republic of Belarus reported that unemployment stands at 0.50 percent, unchanged from 2013. It is important to note is that there is no official index of

unemployed workers, and underemployment remains widespread issue.)

Energy/Power/Natural Resources

The forests of Belarus provide important resources in the forms of lumber, plywood, paper, and wood for furniture, all of which are valuable exports. Oil, coal, and natural gas exist in small amounts, but Belarus' more significant mineral resources are limestone, granite, marl, chalk, sand, gravel, rock salts, and potassium. One of the most valuable natural resources in Belarus is peat, which is abundant in the soil and can be used as a fuel source.

Fishing

Commercial fishing in Belarus, a landlocked nation, once occurred largely in the country's rivers; as of the early 21st century, the Gomel region had accounted for 70 percent of all river fish caught in the country. However, since 2010, state-run pond farms, overseen by the Ministry of Agriculture and Food, have begun to provide Belarus with just over 87 percent of its total fish production. The primary commercial species has traditionally been the carp bream, whose production volume topped off at just over 79 percent in 2010. In that same year, the state began work on complexes to facilitate the industrial rearing of trout, sturgeon, and catfish populations. The European Union and Russia are the two largest importers of Belarusian fish products, with amounts reaching 737.5 tons in 2011 alone.

Forestry

About 42 percent of Belarus is covered by forest. Most of the country's stock is made up of conifers, primarily pine. Birch, alder, and oak are also prominent deciduous woods. Roundwoods and pulpwood production are major exports for the country. In 2011, commercial forestry contributed $575,000,000 (USD) to the Belarusian economy and employed 113,000 people, according to Global Forest Watch.

However, the Chernobyl disaster had a substantial effect on Belarus' forests, since they ultimately absorbed discharged radioactivity. These forests cannot be cleared away, as trees mitigate radiation's overall impact.

Mining/Metals

Belarus' largest mining and mineral exports are fertilizers and steel. As of 2014, the country also mines small deposits of iron ore, nonferrous metal ores, dolomite, potash, rock salt, phosphorites, refractory clay, and sand, along with titanium, copper ore, industrial diamonds, lead, mercury, bauxite, nickel, and vanadium.

Agriculture

Although industry employs the majority of the workforce, agriculture is a substantial part of Belarus' economy as well, accounting for roughly 9.2 percent of the GDP. However, the effects of the 1986 Chernobyl nuclear accident are still being felt by Belarusian farmers, who are unable to use contaminated land to grow crops.

Potatoes are the country's most important agricultural product, and Belarus is the world's eighth largest potato producer. Other vital crops include rye, barley, sugar beets, fruits, and vegetables. Livestock and dairy farming are also important to the agricultural sector.

At one time, Belarusian farms were state-run collectives. Now, however, many farms have been privatized and sold to foreign investors, who have enhanced production capacity and harvesting processes.

Animal Husbandry

Livestock traditionally bred in Belarus include cattle, sheep, goats, horses, and pigs. The country's central region is where pigs are traditionally bred, while the northern and southern regions are home to the majority of cattle farms.

Tourism

The tourism industry in Belarus generates moderate revenue, but is inhibited by the difficulty of traveling in Eastern Europe. Belarus boasts many national sites associated with its culture and history. Minsk contains most of the nation's prominent tourist attractions, including Independence Square. Other popular tourist sites in Minsk include the State Museum of Folk Architecture and Rural Lifestyle, Mir Castle, and the National Academic Bolshoi Opera and Ballet Theater.

Tourists often visit Minsk to view the modern city's architecture, which reflects its Soviet heritage. The city was entirely destroyed during World War II and was rebuilt under the orders of Soviet leader Josef Stalin.

Sinclair Nicholas, Richard Means, & Alex K. Rich

DO YOU KNOW?

- Minsk has been an important part of European trade routes since the prehistoric era, and some historians believe that the city's name comes from the Slavic word "miena," which means barter. Another possible origin for the city's name has to do with an ancient legend about a giant, named Menesk or Mine, who lived by the river.

Bibliography

"Lukashenka at bay." *The Economist*. The Economist Newspaper Limited, 2 Sept. 2010. Web. http://www.economist.com/node/17632929. http://www.bbc.com/news/world-europe-17941131.

Aleksandar Pilecki. "Justice Serves the State of Belarus." *New Presence: The Prague Journal of Central European Affairs* 10.2 (Summer 2008): 19. *EBSCO Academic Search Complete*. Web.

Alexander Bely. *The Belarusian Cookbook*. New York: Hippocrene Books, 2009.

Andrew Wilson, *Belarus: The Last European Dictatorship*. New Haven, CT: Yale UP, 2012.

Anne Coombes. *Belarus—Culture Smart!: The Essential Guide to Customs & Culture*. London, UK: Kuperard, 2011.

BBC News Services. "Country profile: Belarus." *BBC News*. BBC, 10 Feb. 2015.

"Belarus: The Official Website of the Republic of Belarus." *BelTA News Agency*, 2015. http://www.belarus.by/en.

"Europe: Belarus." *The World Factbook*. Central Intelligence Agency, 11 Jun. 2015. Web. https://www.cia.gov/library/publications/the-world-factbook/geos/bo.html.

Nigel Roberts. *Belarus*. Bucks, England: Bradt Travel Guides, 2015.

Stewart Parker. *The Last Soviet Republic: Alexander Lukashenko's Belarus*. Bloomington, IN: Trafford Publishing, 2007.

Works Cited

Balazs Jarabik, Balazs & Alastair Rabagliati. "The Minsk Maneuver." *Transitions Online* (21 Jul. 2008): 7. *EBSCO Academic Search Complete*. Web.

"Belarus adopts restrictive media law amendments, blocks websites." *CPJ.org*. Committee to Protect Journalists, 23 Dec. 2014. Web. https://cpj.org/2014/12/belarus-adopts-restrictive-media-law-amendments-bl.php.

"Belarus." UNESCO. *UNESCO.org*. United Nations Organization for Education, Science, and Culture, 2015. http://portal.unesco.org/geography/en/ev.php-URL_ID=2441&URL_DO=DO_TOPIC&URL_SECTION=201.html.

"Belarusian Architecture." *World Architecture Community Website*. Virtual Guide to Belarus, 2004. http://www.belarusguide.com/culture1/visual_arts/Architecture.html.

Castle, Stephen & Michael Schwirtz. 'EU suspends visa ban on Belarussian leader." *New York Times*. (31 Oct. 2008). Web.

"Foreign Trade in Goods." Ministry of Foreign Affairs of the Republic of Belarus. *Foreign Trade of Belarus*. Ministry of Foreign Affairs of the Republic of Belarus, 15 Mar. 2015. http://mfa.gov.by/en/foreign_trade/.

Grigory Ioffe, "Lukashenka: Last Defender of Belarusian Statehood." http://www.nytimes.com/2008/10/13/world/europe/13iht-belarus.4.16917158.html?_r=0.

Iurii Godin, "Russia and Belorussia: Ten Years of Integration Incompatibility." *Russian Politics & Law* 46.2 (1 Mar. 2008): 17–23. *EBSCO Academic Search Complete*. Web. http://www.tandfonline.com/doi/abs/10.2753/RUP1061-1940460202?journalCode=mrup20

"Transitions Online." (3 Nov. 2008): 2. *EBSCO Academic Search Complete*. Web. http://www.belarusguide.com/culture1/visual_arts/Belarusian_rushnik.htm.

Vol'ha Labacheuskaia, Vol'ha. "Belarusian Ruchnik: Belarusian Traditional Ornamental Towel." *Belarusguide.com*. Trans. A.L. Vasil'eva. Virtual Guide to Belarus, 2004.

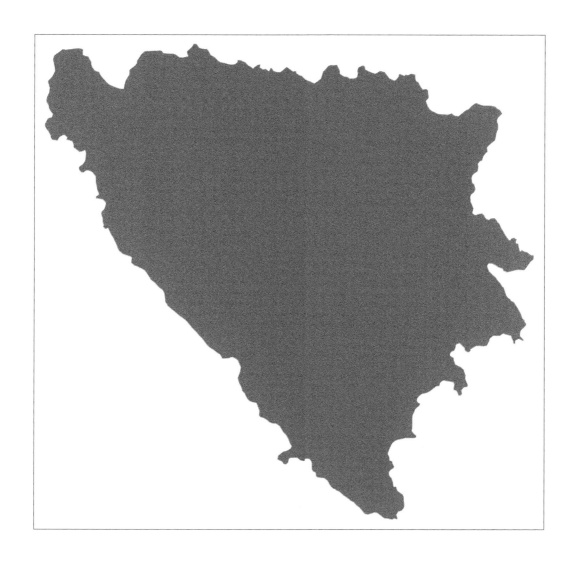

BOSNIA &
HERZEGOVINA

Introduction

Bosnia and Herzegovina is a federal republic in southeast Europe, bordered by Croatia to the north and west, Montenegro to the southeast, and Serbia to the west. Long a crossroads between East and West, its culture and multi-ethnic character is the result of a stream of migrants and invaders.

From the end of the Second World War until it declared its independence in the early 1990s, Bosnia and Herzegovina was one of six republics of the Yugoslav Federation. The dissolution of this communist republic led to a brutal civil war that lasted until 1995. The country remains divided along ethnic and religious lines, and is, in part, supervised by an international force charged with maintaining order.

From February 4–8, 2014, anti-government protests—nicknamed "Bosnian Spring" and paralleling similar demonstrations occurring in the Middle East—were waged in response to mass unemployment and political stagnancy, which has prevailed since the end of the civil war in 1995. By February 8, the protests largely concluded. During the riots, four of Bosnia's ten canton (region) prime ministers were forced to resign their positions.

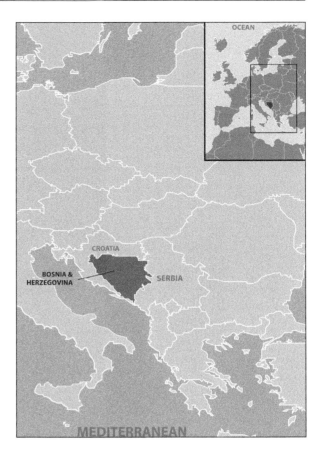

GENERAL INFORMATION

Official Language: Bosnian, Croatian, Serbian
Population: 3,871,643 (2014 estimate)
Currency: Bosnia and Herzegovina convertible mark (or marka)

Coins: The Bosnia and Herzegovina convertible mark is subdivided into 100 fenings (or feninga). Coins are available in denominations of 5, 10, 20, and 50 feninga, and 1, 2, and 5 marka.
Land Area: 51,197 square kilometers (19,767 square miles)
Water Area: 10 square kilometers (3 square miles)
National Anthem: Državna himna Bosne i Hercegovine ("National Anthem of Bosnia and Herzegovina")
Capital: Sarajevo
Time Zone: GMT +1
Flag Description: The flag of Bosnia and Herzegovina is solid blue, with a line of white stars (seven whole and two half) crossing the flag diagonally, from the upper hoist (left) to the lower right side. The stars form a border along the longest side of a yellow isosceles triangle. The three points of the triangle represent the Bosniaks, Serbs, and Croats who live in the

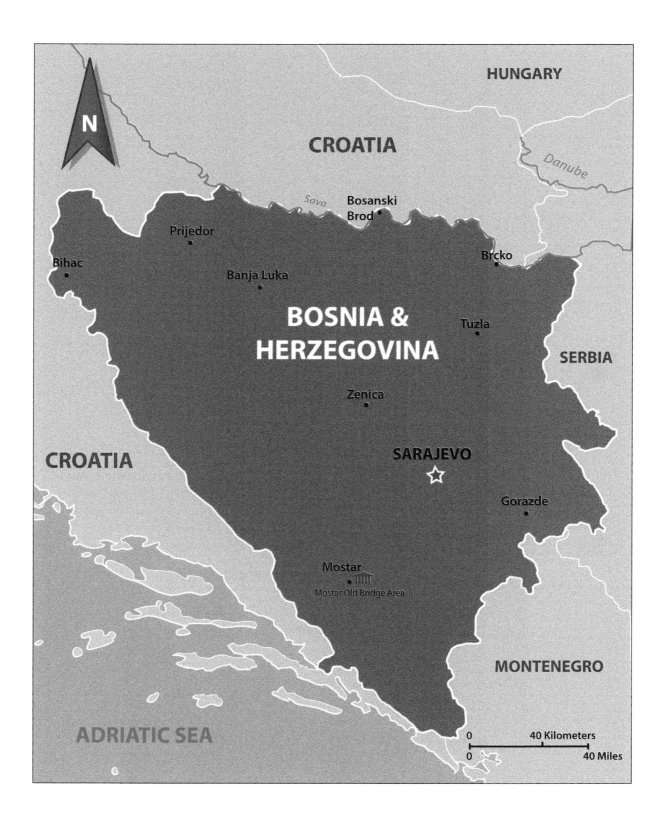

Principal Cities by Population (2013 census):

- Sarajevo (297,416)
- Banja Luka (199,191)
- Tuzla (80,570)
- Zenica (73,751)
- Mostar (65,286)
- Bijeljina (45,291)
- Brčko (43,859)
- Bihać (43,007)
- Prijedor (32,342)
- Trebinje (25,589)

country. The stars represent Europe, hence the reason they look as if they extend beyond the flag, and the colors were chosen to represent peace and neutrality.

Population

Bosnia and Herzegovina has a growing population that suffered setbacks in the early 1990s, with an estimated 100,000 killed during the civil war and as many as 300,000 displaced. Population density is 194 per square mile.

The population consists of Bosniaks (Muslim Serbs), Croats, and Serbians, all of whom belong to the larger South Slav ethnic category. When Bosnia was part of the Yugoslav Federation, the three groups lived in neighboring enclaves. Since the end of the civil war, the population has lived in separated administrative zones: Bosniaks and Croats in the Federation of Bosnia and Herzegovina, which comprises 51 percent of the country's total territory, and the Serb Republic, which comprises the rest of the territory.

Approximately 48 percent of the population is Bosniak, 32.7 percent is Serbian, and 14.6 percent is Croat. Jews and Roma each account for a small percentage of the total.

An estimated 39.6 percent of the population lives in urban areas. Sarajevo is the largest city. The other large cities are Banja Luka, the capital of the Serb Republic; Brčko; Mostar; Tuzla; and Bihać. Before the civil war, the cities often had multi-ethnic composition. Now, however,

their nearly homogenous populations are dictated by the part of the country in which they are located.

Languages

Bosnian, Croatian, and Serbian are all variants of Serbo-Croat, a South Slavic language. Croatian is rendered exclusively in a modified Latin script, while Bosnian and Serbian are rendered in both Cyrillic and Latin. While Cyrillic is the official alphabet of Serbia's government, the media and Internet sources increasingly employ the Latin script. The issue of language has become confused, with interpretation of the linguistic differences deriving from one's political perspective.

Native People & Ethnic Groups

The three main ethnic subgroups in Bosnia and Herzegovina all have long histories in the region. When the country was part of the larger Yugoslav framework, a common South Slav identity was stressed. With the dissolution of that framework, however, the identity also dissolved, and each group asserted its interests. Croats and Bosniaks formed an alliance, backed by Croatia, while the Serbs were backed by Serbia. The ensuing hostilities devastated the country's infrastructure and led to great loss of life, particularly among the Bosniaks and Serbs.

Bosnian Roma, who have had small communities in the region for centuries, also experienced extensive hardship during the civil war. Targets of racial violence, many of them fled abroad and now exist in political limbo, with neither the right of return nor political asylum in their host countries.

There is also a small population of Jews whose history in the area dates back to their expulsion from Spain in the 15th century and their resettlement by invitation of the Ottoman government.

Religions

The area now known as Bosnia and Herzegovina was once noteworthy for its religious tolerance and predominantly secular character. The hostilities that fueled the civil war seriously harmed the notion of tolerance and inspired an assertion of religious identity. In general, the Bosniaks have been Sunni Muslim (40 percent) since the 15th century, the Serbs are Serbian Orthodox (31 percent), and the Croatians are Roman Catholic (15 percent). There are also small groups of Protestants and Jews.

Climate

The climate of Bosnia and Herzegovina is a mixture of the Mediterranean and the continental. In the south and along the western border, the weather is moderated by winds from the Adriatic Sea, giving the area mild, wet winters and warm summers. Further inland, the continental temperature prevails. In the flat, lower regions, winters are cold and summers warm.

Snow occurs at the higher elevations, where winters are long and summers brief. Temperatures for Sarajevo average –1° Celsius (30° Fahrenheit) in January and 20° Celsius (68° Fahrenheit) in July, which is typical for continental areas at lower elevations.

The entire country is prone to powerful earthquakes such as the one that devastated the northern city of Banja Luka in 1969. On average, however, earthquakes of lesser magnitude, usually ranging from 3.9 to 4.5, are not infrequent, with a dozen such quakes occurring between mid-2014 and mid-2015 alone.

ENVIRONMENT & GEOGRAPHY

Topography

Bosnia and Herzegovina generally has a mountainous terrain. It is landlocked except for a 20-kilometer (13-mile) strip of coastline along the Adriatic Sea. The interior of the country has flat, fertile areas.

Mountains and valleys dominate the landscape along the border with Croatia and in the southern portion of the country. Mount Maglić, near the border with Serbia, is the highest point (2,386 meters/7,828 feet). This range is part of the Dinaric Alps and is composed mainly of a limestone, dolomite, and gypsum strata called karst, which forms many caves and valleys. Karst accounts for nearly 35 percent of the country's terrain.

The Sava and the Bosna, from which the country takes half of its name, are important rivers, both flowing north. The Sava supports several ports along its course and feeds the northern Sava Plain. The Neretva River flows into Croatia and drains into the Adriatic Sea. The Miljacka, a tributary of the Bosna, flows through Sarajevo.

Sarajevo lies in the center of Bosnia and Herzegovina, at the foot of Mount Trebević in the forests of the Miljacka River Valley. The city is surrounded by five mountains. Because of the city's relative seclusion, outsiders tend to treat Sarajevo as a hidden gem. The city proper is in the center of the valley and has relatively level terrain. The suburbs are situated on the small hills at the bases of the mountains, which are popular skiing and hiking destinations.

Plants & Animals

Bosnia and Herzegovina has two vegetation zones: the Euro-Siberian and the Mediterranean. Just under half of the country is forested, some of it with primeval growth. Tree species include beech, pine, evergreen, oak, spruce, and chestnut. The mountains are also lush with flowering plants, with an estimated 3,700 distinct species growing in the country. The karst regions support typical Mediterranean shrubs as well as many wild flowers.

The forests, inhabited by deer, chamois (a species of goat-antelope), gray bears, wolves, and wildcats, are especially rich in wildlife. Hawks, vultures, and eagles are common birds. There are seventy endangered or threatened species in the country, with ten species of mammals, ten species of birds, seven species of crustaceans, and thirty species of fish among them.

CUSTOMS & COURTESIES

Greetings

Polite forms of greeting in Bosnia include "Dobrodošli" ("Welcome"), "Dobro jutro"

("Good morning"), and "Döbar dân " ("Good day"). Among themselves, younger people will often use the less formal "Zdrävo" ("Hello") or "Šta ima" ("What's up?"). People often follow the initial greeting by asking "Kako si" ("How are you?").

A firm handshake, with direct eye contact, is the usual greeting between strangers and acquaintances and in business situations. Bosnian Serbs will typically state their surname as they shake hands, and a man will wait for a woman to offer her hand before shaking it. It is not uncommon for Bosnians to offer their wrist instead of their hand if their hands are wet or dirty. Close friends and family members often kiss each other's cheeks in greeting. Croats and Bosniaks (the term Bosnian Muslims prefer) give one kiss on each cheek. Serbs kiss each other three times, alternating cheeks.

People are generally introduced using their professional or courtesy title and their surname. For the most part, only good friends or family members use someone's first name. Inquiring of someone's name is the equivalent of asking their ethnicity, and this is generally considered disrespectful in postwar Bosnia.

Gestures & Etiquette

Like many European languages, Bosnian has both a formal and an informal form of "you." A Bosnian will use the formal mode to address anyone to whom he owes respect as a result of age or status. The formal mode is also used between acquaintances, even if they have known each other for many years. Adults always use the informal mode when speaking with children.

The Serbian three-fingered salute, or tri prsta, is made by raising the thumb, index finger, and middle finger (as if signaling three). During the Bosnian War, Serbian soldiers often flashed the salute during military operations in response to the "V" gesture used by Croats and Bosniaks. The tri prsta is an ethnically-charged gesture in post-war Bosnia and Herzegovina. It is often seen in Serbian-dominated areas, but is considered rude in those parts of the country dominated by Croats or Bosniaks.

Bosnians gesture for someone to "come here" with the palm facing him and the fingers folded down. Motioning "come" with the palm up or by curling the index finger is used only to call animals.

Traditional Muslim ideas concerning modest behavior for women influence behavior in Bosnian culture as a whole. It is common to see couples of the same sex walking hand in hand or arm in arm, but public displays of affection between members of the opposite sex are rare. Even casual physical contact and direct eye contact between men and women is limited, especially in Muslim-dominated areas. As in other Muslims countries, both worshipers and non-Muslim visitors remove their shoes before entering a mosque, and women cover their heads.

Eating/Meals

Bosnians and Herzegovians generally eat three meals per day. Breakfast is usually light and might include rolls, butter, jam, and perhaps a little ham or soft white cheese, with coffee, tea, or hot chocolate to drink. Bosnians typically eat their main meal of the day at home in the late afternoon or at the end of the workday. Dinner is typically eaten later in the evening and tends to be light, often just fruit, bread, and cheese. Freshly baked bread generally accompanies every meal.

Bosanska kafa, or Bosnian coffee, plays an important role in Bosnian social life. Known elsewhere as Turkish coffee, each cup is brewed individually by boiling finely ground coffee and water together in a special metal pot with a long handle. The final result is a very strong coffee, complete with coffee grounds, that is served in tiny cups. The coffee is usually served with a cube of sugar on the saucer, which many people dip into the coffee and eat instead of adding to the cup. Sweets are often served with coffee, including ratluk (or rahat lokum), a sweet jellied candy that is known in the West as Turkish Delight.

Other popular beverages include himber, a thick juice. One special type of himber is made from rose petals and sugar. Bosnians often drink kefir, a thin yogurt drink, instead of milk. Strong brandies made from plums, pears, apples, or grapes are popular and often made at home; slivovitz (plum brandy) is found in Croatian areas, while loza (grape brandy) is more popular with Serbs. Alcoholic beverages have been prohibited in some Muslim-controlled areas.

Visiting

Much of the social life in Bosnia and Herzegovina takes place in public. Traditional coffee houses (kafane) and more modern bars (kafici) are popular places for Serbs to entertain their friends. In warm weather, the main street in many towns is closed to traffic in the evenings so that people can stroll along it after dinner, meeting friends and neighbors. This common activity is called korzo (promenade) after the word for a pedestrian street.

Bosnians consider it perfectly polite to visit someone without calling ahead. As a rule, even an informal or unannounced guest will be given coffee and a sweet, often followed by the offer of a cigarette. It is generally considered rude not to accept. Many Bosnians remove their shoes on entering their homes and ask their guests to do the same. They often provide an assortment of slippers for guests to wear.

Bosnians generally bring a small wrapped gift when they are invited to someone's home. Chocolates, pastries, and flowers are common choices, though Bosnians are careful that the bouquet doesn't total thirteen flowers or include an even number of blossoms, since both are considered to be bad luck. Such gifts are presented to the host with both hands. They are often put aside to be opened later.

LIFESTYLE

Family

The traditional family unit in Bosnia was the zadruga, an extended family that included a man, his adult sons, and their families, all living together in a single house or cluster of houses. Land was owned in common, and the work was shared. During the communist period, opportunities to work abroad or in the city took men away from rural communities and made sons less dependent on their fathers. As a result, the zadruga became less common, though the extended family remained important. When a couple and their children lived alone, family members often lived nearby, and students who moved to the city to work or study often lived with relatives.

The extended family structure, and the support system that it provides, remains an ideal in postwar Bosnia. The wars with Serbia and Croatia in the 1990s forced many families to change their living arrangements. The extreme shortage of housing caused many relations to once again live together as large, extended families. At the same time, thousands of men were killed in the civil wars, and many women were left as the head of single-parent households, often without the support of other family members.

Housing

Bosnia suffers from a serious housing shortage as a result of the Bosnian War. Many buildings were damaged, especially in Sarajevo, and thousands of people were displaced from their homes. In fact, it is common for divorced couples to continue as a cohabiting couple, since alternative housing is unavailable.

Traditional houses in rural Bosnia were built of wood and natural materials, such as interwoven branches and twigs, and featured steep, tent-shaped roofs covered in wooden shingles. Inside, the central room was built around an open hearth. Muslim homes had separate quarters for men and women. Housing in the older areas of Bosnian cities includes many Ottoman-style townhouses. These are typically two stories tall and built around an interior courtyard or garden. The second stories have large windows with wooden grills and are cantilevered, or extended outward, over the street. The interiors of these houses are commonly finished with elaborately-carved wooden furniture, staircases, screens, and paneling. Housing in newer areas is mostly high-rise apartment buildings dating from the communist period of rapid reconstruction, which followed the destruction caused by World War II.

Food

Bosnian cuisine is a combination of Eastern European, Turkish, and Mediterranean flavors. Traditionally, beef and lamb, grilled or stewed, are the center of the Bosnian diet. Due to the large Islamic population, pork plays a smaller role in the Bosnian diet than in other Eastern European countries. One of the most common meat dishes is ćevapčići, spicy grilled sausages made from a mixture of ground meats that are grilled over an open charcoal fire. They are traditionally served on somun, flat bread similar to pita, with onions and pavlaka, a soured heavy cream similar to Mexican crema. Other popular Bosnian meat dishes include Bosanski lonac, a slow-cooked stew of meat and vegetables; kapama, which is stewed lamb shanks with onions; and bamija, a beef and okra stew.

Vegetables are not often served alone, but are often used in dishes with meat. A number of traditional dishes are made of vegetable, such as cabbage, eggplant, zucchini, or peppers stuffed with meat. The most common salad is one that appears in all the countries of the former Ottoman Empire, made from chopped peppers, onions, and tomatoes. Phyllo dough (made with flour, water, and oil) is used to make a variety of popular dishes and the popular dessert, baklava. Meat, spinach, and cheese stuffed pies are traditionally served topped with pavlaka.

Life's Milestones

Bosnia is made up of three major ethnic groups who practice three different religions. Historically, Bosniaks are Muslim, Serbs are Orthodox, and Croats are Roman Catholic. Rituals associated with birth, marriage, and death vary with ethnicity and religion. As of the early 21st century, an estimated 40 percent of the population is Muslim.

Godparents (kumovi) play an important role in the baptism of children for both Croats and Serbs and are actively involved in the lives of their godchildren. Godparents often become valuable members of the family. Bosnian Muslims practice the rite of circumcision. The ceremonial operation is generally performed when a boy is three years old, following a feast.

All three groups tend to have civil marriages followed by a religious wedding service and festive celebration. In the city, families tend to hold weddings in a restaurant or their home. Rural weddings are often more elaborate and may include several days of festivities. Traditionally, the parents of a Muslim bride give the couple a special carpet with the wedding date and the new couple's initials woven into it.

Bosnian Serbs hold elaborate graveside funeral feasts. Similar feasts are held forty days after the funeral, as well as at the six month and one-year marks. The gravestone, which typically includes photographs and an inscription, is placed on the grave at the one-year anniversary.

CULTURAL HISTORY

Art

The medieval kingdom of Bosnia produced one unique art form: the monumental tombstones known as stećci (stećak is the noun's singular form). Roughly 60,000 examples remain, mostly located in modern Bosnia and Herzegovina. Created from the 12th through the 15th centuries, stećci are medieval tombstones of the Bogomil form of Christianity. This faith predominated in the medieval kingdom of Bosnia prior to Ottoman conquest (when many Bosnians converted to Islam). Seen as a heresy by both the Roman Catholic and the Orthodox churches, Bogomilism, founded in the 10th century, is a dualist religious sect, which teaches that God created the human soul and Satan created the human body.

Very little is known about the stećci graveyards. Some of the house-shaped monuments are inscribed in Cyrillic script, and many are decorated with elaborate carvings. Some of these carvings are abstract patterns, including spirals, arcades, rosettes, vine and leaf patterns, and the sun and moon symbols that were important to

Bogomil iconography. Others are more representational, including processions of deer, dancing, and hunt scenes. The best-known design is the recurring image of a man with his right hand raised.

The stećci were the central element in an exhibition of medieval Bosnian art that opened in Paris in 1950. During the following decade, they have provided inspiration for a wide variety of Bosnian arts, including poetry, painting, sculpture, documentary films, and music.

Other Bosnian artists of note include painter Gabrijel Jurkic (1886–1974); painter, illustrator, graphic and fiber artist Mersad Berber (1940–); painter and scenic designer Nesim Tahirovic (1941–); installation artist Braco Dimitrijevic (1948–); and Paris-based, Bosnian-born painter Darmin Veletanlic (1962–).

In late December 2011, eighty-six Sarajevo artists signed a petition and delivered it to the Bosnian government, demanding a contemporary art museum be built in the country's capital. Italian architect Renzo Piano promised to work *pro bono* on the building, which would house work by 160 international artists, who contributed pieces between 1992 and 2003 specifically for a Sarajevo art museum. The collection, called *Ars Aevi* (an anagram of Sarajevo) is Latin for 'Art of the Epoch.' The museum opened on December 19, 2014.

Architecture

The architecture of Bosnia and Herzegovina (also spelled Bosnia-Hercegovina) during the medieval period consisted of military fortresses and clustered houses or villages of simple design, made with natural materials. The majority of modern towns and cities were developed under the Ottoman Empire, which arrived in the region in the late 15th century. As a result, Bosnian cities contained some of the finest examples of Ottoman architecture. These included the 16th-century Stari Most (Old Bridge) in Mostar, the Ferhat Pasha Mosque in Banja Luka (which was destroyed by Serbian nationalists in 1993), and the great covered market in Sarajevo. Two Ottoman stone bridges, the Stari Most and the

Mehmed Paša Sokolović Bridge in Višegrad, were designated as World Heritage Sites by the United Nations Educational, Scientific and Cultural Organization (UNESCO) for their beauty and architectural daring.

After Bosnia fell under Austro-Hungarian rule in 1878, many public buildings were constructed in the European style, known as Moorish revival architecture, which the Hapsburg government promoted as appropriate for a European Islamic culture. The town hall in Sarajevo, now the National Library, is a notable example of this style of architecture, which features pointed arches and decorative ornamentation. After World War II, when Bosnia and Herzegovina came under communist control, homogeneity and industrialization would influence architectural design. For example, block apartment housing projects favored functionality over aesthetics, and concrete was a dominant construction material.

Music

Bosnia and Herzegovina has two thriving folk music traditions: sevdalinka (or sevdah) and izvorna bosanska muzika (Bosnian root music). Sevdalinka ("love songs") derives from the Turkish word for passion. It developed in the multicultural world of Bosnian cities through the combination of Islamic, Eastern European, and Sephardic elements. (The Sephardim were Jews of Spain and Portugal during the Middle Ages.) Sung at a slow to moderate tempo and marked by elaborate harmonies, sevdalinka are mostly melancholy in tone, with lyrics that speak of hopeless love in all its forms. Traditionally, the songs were performed by women, either a cappella or accompanied by the saz, a Turkish plucked string instrument similar to the lute. Modern sevdalinka ensembles typically include an accordion, a violin, a type of oboe called a zurna, and guitar.

Izvorna bosanka musika is a very old form of Balkan music that was adapted to modern instruments around World War II. Traditionally, izvorna utilizes two voices singing in such close harmony that it sounds dissonant to the Western ear. Today it is generally performed by a small group of two singers, two violins, and a šargija, the village equivalent of the Turkish saz. It can range in style from a traditional folk sound to punk.

Literature

Under Ottoman rule, Bosnian literature was divided between an urban-based literary tradition and an oral folk tradition. The largely Muslim urban elite wrote both prose and poetry that was more Ottoman than Bosnian, using the Islamic literary languages of Persian, Arabic, and Turkish. In the mid-17th century, Muslim Bosnians created aljamiado literature, which was written in the Bosnian vernacular using Arabic script. This practice continued into the 20th century. The dominant form of the oral tradition was epic poetry. Epic ballads were created by all three major ethnic groups in Bosnia: Muslim, Croat, and Serb. For the most part, these narrative poems deal with heroic tales and warfare.

Under Austro-Hungarian rule at the end of the 19th century, fundamental changes took place in the intellectual and artistic life of Bosnia and Herzegovina. Educated in the European rather than the Ottoman tradition, a new generation of Bosnian writers used the characters and themes of the oral tradition to feed a new Southern Slav nationalism. At first a defense of cultural identity, nationalism became a search for independence that ended with the assassination of Archduke Franz Ferdinand of Austria (1863–1914) at Sarajevo in 1914, starting World War I.

The two most important writers to emerge in Bosnia in the 20th century were Serbian novelist Ivo Andrić (1892–1975) and Bosniak poet Mak Dizdar (1917–1971). Andrić won the 1961 Nobel Prize in Literature, becoming the first Yugoslavian to win a Nobel Prize. He is perhaps most famous for *The Bridge on the Drina* (1945), a depiction of four centuries of Bosnian history told by interweaving stories, historical events, and folk tales connected to a famous Ottoman bridge in the medieval city of Višegrad. (The bridge is believed to be the Mehmed Paša Sokolović Bridge, a World Heritage Site.) Andrić donated his prize money to buy books for the new system of Bosnian public libraries that was developed in the 1960s. Dizdar's most important collection of poetry is *Stone Sleeper,* which was originally published in 1966 and substantially revised shortly before his death. The work uses imagery and epitaphs drawn from the medieval stećci to explore Bosnian national identity. The portraits of both authors appear on Bosnian currency.

During the communist era, Sarajevo enjoyed a far less restrictive atmosphere than the Yugoslavian capital of Belgrade. The city was home to some of the most important publishing houses in Eastern Europe and was also an important center for film and theater.

Drama

Two internationally-famous film directors come from Bosnia. Serbian director Emir Kusturica (1954–) directs films that are known for their surrealism and absurdist humor. He is best known for *Time of the Gypsies (*1988), a film about Serbia's Roma; the controversial *Underground* (1995), a black-comedy history of Yugoslavia stretching from beginning of World War II through the wars of the 1990s; and *Black Cat, White Cat* (1998), which won the Venice Film Festival's Silver Lion for best direction. Both *Time of the Gypsies* and *Underground* also won awards at the prestigious Cannes Film Festival. Born to a Muslim family, Kusturica chose to identify himself as a Serbian rather than a Bosnian during the Bosnian wars. He moved to Belgrade in 1992 and converted to the Orthodox faith in 2005. Bosniak director Danis Tanović (1969–) is best known for *No Man's Land* (2001), a documentary about the Bosnian civil war that won forty-two international film awards, including the Academy Award for Best Foreign Film in 2001.

The Bosnian film industry also produced one of Yugoslavia's most successful world music artists, Goran Bregović (1950–). Famous in the former Yugoslavia as the founder of the popular rock band Bijelo Dugme (White Button), Bregović is best known internationally as a film composer. He began working with Kusturica in 1978, producing the scores for *Arizona Dream*

(1993), *Underground,* and the song "Ederlez" for *Time of the Gypsies.* He has also worked with Turkish diva Sezen Aksu (1954–) on the pan-Balkan recording *Weddings and Funerals* (*Düğün ve Cenaze*) and with Greek folk singer George Dalaras (1949–).

CULTURE

Arts & Entertainment
Under siege for the majority of the civil war, Sarajevo's arts communities remained active, holding concerts, theatrical performances, and art exhibitions in the city's burned-out buildings. The Sarajevo War Theatre (SARTR) gave some 2,000 performances over the course of the war, many of works inspired by the writings of Dizdar. After the war, the Sarajevan government recognized the group for its special role in the defense of the city. *Art Monthly* magazine reported that at least twenty-five exhibitions of visual arts were held during the siege. The Obala Art Center organized events called "war cinema," screening new movies smuggled in from abroad.

In addition to events designed to support wartime morale, Sarajevo's artists also produced work designed to inform the outside world, largely unaware of the realities of the war. Popular musicians of all types recorded songs that broadcasted Bosnia's suffering to the world in a tiny recording studio in the basement of RTV Sarajevo. Members of the award-winning design group, TRIO Sarajevo, stayed in Sarajevo during the war, often working for food and cigarettes. They are best known for creating a series of postcards in which they digitally altered famous images from film and advertising to comment on the city's plight.

Many significant works of literature were born from the Bosnian war and the ethnic conflict that defined it. Bosniak poet and publisher Damir Uzunović (1965–) published a series of short stories about life in the trenches based on his experiences as a soldier in the war. Poet and screenwriter Abdulah Sidran (1944–) wrote the script for the Ademir Kenović (1950–)

film *Perfect Circle* (1997), which uses the war as a background. It is also considered the first Bosnian feature film since Bosnia became a sovereign state in 1992. Other important works to come out of the war include novelist and playwright Zlatko Topčić's (1955–) *Kulin* (1994); Nermina Kurspahić's (1956–) *Disappearance of the Blue Riders* (1994); poet Semezdin Mehmedinović's (1960–) collection *Sarajevo Blues* (1992); and the novelistic work of writer and sculptor Nedžad Ibrišimović (1940–2011).

Possibly the most important writer in the generation that came to prominence following the war is Aleksandar Hemon (1964–). In the United States on a journalist exchange program when the war broke out, he stayed in Chicago and worked odd jobs while he learned to write in English. His collection of short stories, *The Question of Bruno* (2000), is set in both Chicago and Sarajevo. Two other acclaimed novels, *Nowhere Man* (2002) and *The Lazarus Project* (2008), further cemented his reputation, with the latter becoming a finalist for the 2008 National Book Award. Hemon was named a Guggenheim Fellow in 2003 and received a MacArthur "Genius Grant" in 2004.

Basketball and football (soccer) are the country's most popular sports, and professional athletic events draw wide and strong support from the populace. Skiing on the country's mountain slopes is popular during winter.

Cultural Sites & Landmarks
Provincial Ottoman governor Gazi Hüsrev Bey (1480–1541) ordered the construction of many of the buildings in Old Sarajevo. One of the most important is the Gazi Hüsrev-beg Mosque. The mosque was built in 1531 by the most famous of the Ottoman architects, Mimar Sinan (1489–1588). It is considered one of the finest examples of Ottoman architecture and consists of a large central dome surrounded by smaller half-domes, slender minarets, and a colonnaded courtyard. It was originally part of an extensive complex that included a Koranic school, soup kitchen, hospital, library, bazaar, and public baths. Damaged in

the Bosnian War (1992–1995) by Serbian shelling, the mosque was rebuilt in 1994 with the help of foreign aid, primarily from Saudi Arabia. The initial restoration left out much of the interior decoration for which the mosque was famous. A more complete restoration of the interior was begun in 2000.

The city of Mostar (literally, "bridge keeper") is named for the Stari Most (Old Bridge) over the Neretva River. The Old Bridge was built in 1566 to replace a wooden suspension bridge that was no longer adequate for the booming river town. At the time of its construction, the bridge was the largest single-span stone arch bridge in the world and widely considered the most beautiful of the Ottoman stone bridges. A symbol of Bosnia's multicultural unity, the bridge was targeted by Croatian artillery during the Bosnian War in 1993. Its destruction became one of the most vivid images of the ethnic conflict that caused the war. An international consortium restored the Old Bridge to its original design in 2004, using bridge stones recovered from the river and new stones hand cut from the original quarry. The Old Bridge area, with its Turkish houses and pre-Ottoman and Ottoman architecture, was listed as a World Heritage Site by UNESCO in 2005.

The remote village of Medjugorje in Herzegovina became one of the largest Catholic pilgrimage sites in the world in 1981, when six young Herzegovian Croats reported that they had seen the Virgin Mary. Since that time, they have reported almost daily appearances of the religious apparitions. The Vatican has not yet affirmed the reported appearances and miracles, but has launched an ongoing official investigation. Thousands of pilgrims visit the site each year, transforming the small mountain village into a cultural and religious destination and phenomenon.

Sarajevo, the capital, is also home to its share of cultural sites and landmarks. The Siege of Sarajevo—lasting from 1992 until 1996 and considered the longest siege in modern warfare—damaged much of the infrastructure. A substantial amount of damage was fixed by 2004. The city is home to a wealth of museums, as well as the Sarajevo Film Festival, the premier cinematic event in the Balkans. One striking landmark is the Sarajevo Tunnel, dug with picks, shovels, and wheelbarrows by Bosnians—paid with a pack of cigarettes per day of work—when the city was cut off by Serbian troops during the Bosnian War. The 1.5-meter (5 feet) wide tunnel traveled 793 meters (2,600 feet) under the Sarajevo airport to the United Nations (UN) neutral zone. For 1,450 days, the tunnel was used to move supplies and people in and out of the city and is credited with saving Sarajevo during its long siege. Most of the tunnel collapsed after the war, but there is a museum in the portion that is still open.

Libraries & Museums

The National Museum is home to many of Bosnia and Herzegovina's historical artifacts, while the Museum of the Revolution is dedicated to the country's recent history. There is also a Jewish museum in Sarajevo, and the capital's Orthodox Church is also home to a museum.

The National Library (officially the National and University Library of Bosnia and Herzegovina, or NUBBiH) is another important landmark. Ravaged and burned during the war, the library is rebuilding and replacing the innumerable important documents that were lost.

Holidays

Bosnians celebrate many Muslim, Catholic, and Orthodox holidays. Secular holidays include Independence Day, which commemorates the country's split from Yugoslavia (March 1), and National Day (November 25).

Youth Culture

The civil war of 1992–1995 had a tremendous impact on the lives of young people in Bosnia and Herzegovina. Children were a prime target for snipers, especially in Sarajevo, and schools were subject to mortar attacks. As a result, many children were left with no access to education. The destruction of the Bosnian economy continues to be an enormous burden. In 2013, the unemployment rate for youth was 60.4 percent, up from 57.2 percent in 2010. Many leave school as early as possible, entering the job market at the age of fifteen or sixteen.

Many Bosnian young people are part of the international youth culture. However, a sizeable number of young people from all three major ethnic groups have increasingly rejected internationalism in favor of their ethnic and religious cultural heritage.

SOCIETY

Transportation

Car ownership is a luxury in Bosnia and Herzegovina, with less than 100,000 cars in a population of slightly less than 4 million. Most urban areas have local rail, bus, and tram services. Taxis are available in larger towns and intercity bus lines are available throughout the country. Traffic moves on the right-hand side of the road.

The capital of Sarajevo was the first European city to construct a full-time electric tram network, which is still operational.

Transportation Infrastructure

Travel within Bosnia is difficult. Much of the transportation system in Bosnia and Herzegovina was destroyed during the civil wars. Restoration has been slow even with help from international aid programs. A large portion of the road network is in poor condition, though the risk posed by abandoned landmines has been reduced and most remaining mine areas are clearly marked. In addition, 80 percent of the railway system was badly damaged, and international rail service was not restored until July 2007. Rail connections were not restored between the two autonomous entities until 2008. Furthermore, sections of the River Sava remain unnavigable because they are blocked with damaged bridges, silt, and debris, and none of the river's inland ports are in full working condition. As of 2013, only seven of the country's twenty-four airports had paved runways.

Media & Communications

The most important media in Bosnia and Herzegovina are the three public broadcasting networks: one run by the central government and the other two controlled by Bosnia's independent entities, which are second-tier governmental units within Bosnia, set by the 1995 Dayton Accords. The centrally-controlled public broadcaster, Radio and Television of Bosnia and Herzegovina (BHRT), operates the nationwide BHTV1 and BH Radio 1 networks. It is the only Bosnian broadcasting company to be a member of the European Broadcasting Union. By contrast, Radio-Television of the Federation of Bosnia and Herzegovina (RTVBiH) broadcasts to only one of the two Bosnian entities: the Federation of Bosnia and Herzegovina. RTVBiH runs radio and television broadcasting services from its Sarajevo headquarters and produces Serbian- and Croatian-language broadcasts. Finally, Radio Televizija Republike Srpske (RTRS) serves Bosnia's other political entity, the Republika Srpska, from its Banja Luka headquarters. There are also more than 200 local commercial radio and television stations, but a weak advertising market has limited their development. Bosnia's Communications Regulatory Agency ultimately oversees all television and radio media.

There are approximately ten daily newspapers in Bosnia, with only three having national distribution. Of these, *Oslobođenje* and *Dnevni Avaz* are both based in Sarajevo, and *Nezavisne Novine* is based in Banja Luka in the Serbian Republic.

Bosnia and Herzegovina's telecommunication system was almost totally destroyed during the civil war. Communications systems have been substantially rebuilt, with the help of international aid. Three state-owned companies run telephone networks in different parts of the country. The number of both fixed lines and mobile phones are growing; as of 2012, almost 99 percent of the population had a mobile phone—with 3.4 million active subscriptions. Exactly 70 percent have 3G and 4G coverage. An estimated 57 percent of the population has Internet access as of 2012.

SOCIAL DEVELOPMENT

Standard of Living

Bosnia and Herzegovina ranked eighty-sixth out of 190 countries on the 2012 United Nations Human Development Index, which measures quality of life and standard of living indicators.

Life expectancy at birth is seventy-three years for males and seventy-nine years for females (2014 estimate).

Water Consumption

According to UNICEF (United Nations International Children's Emergency Fund), 98.8 percent of the population in Bosnia Herzegovina has access to improved drinking water—99.7 percent in urban areas and 98 percent in rural areas. Ninety-six percent of the overall population has access to improved sanitation, with urban areas measuring 99.7 percent and rural areas measuring 92.1 percent.

Education

The civil war devastated Bosnia and Herzegovina's educational system, which had been well developed. An estimated 70 percent of schools were destroyed, damaged, or used for military purposes, and educators were often drafted into military service.

Since then a great degree of normalcy has returned, though not to pre-war levels. Children between the ages of six and fifteen receive free, compulsory education. Many of them continue on to secondary school, which is likewise free. There are numerous institutes of higher learning throughout the country, including five universities. These are located in Sarajevo, Tuzla, Banja Luka, and Mostar. Mostar University is now two universities, one for Bosnian Croats, the other an Islamic university.

According to UNICEF, the literacy of Bosnia's entire population measured 98 percent in 2012, with young men and young women—ages fifteen to twenty-four—equally literate at 99.7 percent.

Women's Rights

Bosnia and Herzegovina has a long tradition of patriarchy, based on both Islamic and Eastern European cultural norms. The traditional division of labor left women responsible for housework, children, and agriculture. Women were raised to be subservient to men, and daughters were valued less than sons. The position of women in Bosnia improved under the communist regime. Women received the right to vote, to divorce, and to inherit property. Mandatory elementary education raised literacy rates and benefits, such as paid pregnancy leave and a system of state-run day care, made work outside the home possible.

The status of women in Bosnia and Herzegovina was severely damaged as a result of the civil wars of 1992–95. War crimes against women were common and soldiers used rape and torture as psychological weapons. Many women survived the trauma of rape only to suffer the further trauma of pregnancy resulting from rape and the stigma of raising a child fathered by an enemy soldier. After the war, women were the hardest hit by the destruction of the Bosnian economy. An unprecedented number of Bosnian women whose husbands had been killed in the war headed single-parent households. Even women who were judges, doctors, or professors in the former Yugoslavia often held low-paying jobs or were unemployed. In addition, a boom in the sex trade paralleled the fall in women's economic status after the war. International agencies reported large scale trafficking in women and underage girls as well as a rise in incidents of debt bondage and physical abuse.

According to Bosnian labor law, women have the same rights in the workplace as men. In practice, however, gender discrimination and sexual harassment are widespread. A 2013 US Department of State report found that many job advertisements included discriminatory criteria for women, such as requirements related to physical appearance and age. Thirty-five percent of Bosnian women are employed outside the home and the average salary for women is 20 to 50 percent lower than that of their male counterparts.

Among Bosnian women, there is still 29.9 percent unemployment, and many women find their ability to work outside the home is limited by their dependence on immediate family members for childcare assistance. Unable to find work outside the home, a growing number are taking advantage of micro-loan programs sponsored by international agencies. They are also using traditional skills, such as weaving and knitting, to run home-based businesses that produce and market textiles and crafts.

Traditional family attitudes also limit the status of women in Bosnia and Herzegovina, especially in rural areas. Even though women have the right to inherit property, rural women often give their share of the property to their brothers. Domestic abuse is also a common problem. Nongovernmental organizations (NGOs) estimated in 2008 that one of every three Bosnian women is a victim of domestic abuse, and that only one instance in ten is reported. Adult literacy rates suggest that access to education is another area of discrimination despite mandatory education laws; only 96 percent of Bosnian women are able to read, although the 99.7 literacy rate in Bosnian women between fifteen and twenty-four suggests that the situation is improving.

In 2003, the government passed laws designed to give women the right to equal representation in public and private institutions. The government also set up a Gender Equality Agency to monitor the implementation of the new laws and inform women of their legal rights.

More recently, between October 2011 and March 2015, USAID initiated the Political Processes Program in Bosnia and Herzegovina, putting $3.7 million USD into a program that would enhance Bosnia's political system, increase governmental accountability, and raise the number of women participating in the Bosnian political process. In collaboration with the Women's Democracy Network, a three-year curriculum was offered to women, training them to develop effective political communication, media relations, and platform development, among other vital skills.

Health Care

The country's health care system underwent similar stresses and breakdown because of the civil war. Moreover, it was forced to deal with war-related injuries and large numbers of internally displaced people.

Before the war, the government extended free and universal health care. Today, health care is decentralized, with each of the 10 cantons tasked with organizing and financing the system, which is plagued by underfunding, inadequate provision management, poorly-motivated staff, outdated equipment, and population-distribution imbalances.

GOVERNMENT

Structure

A new constitution was adopted as part of the 1995 Dayton Accords, which formally brought the civil war to a close. It asserts that the country is composed of the Federation of Bosnia and Herzegovina and the Serb Republic. Each of these entities exercises wide powers over their respective areas, whereas the central government manages international affairs. The current arrangement has not proven very effective, but attempts to unite the three ethnic groups into a more coordinated coalition have failed.

Bosnia's executive branch is overseen by a three-member joint presidency. Each of the country's ethnic groups—Bosnian, Croatian, and Serbian—elects a president by popular vote to four-year terms, and the presidency rotates between them every eight months. The presidents are responsible for nominating two prime ministers (one Bosniak, one Serb) and a deputy prime minister (a Croat) as well as the Council of Ministers, selected for a similar balance. Together the presidents make decisions, which the legislature drafts into law.

The bicameral legislature consists of the House of Peoples and the House of Representatives. Each ethnic group is represented by five members in the House of Peoples (five Bosniaks, five Serbs, and five Croats); the forty-two directly elected members of the House of Representatives are likewise proportional (twenty-eight seats for Federation of Bosnia and Herzegovina and fourteen seats for Republika Srpska). Members of both houses serve four-year terms. In addition to its legal duties, the legislature approves the ministerial selections.

Political Parties

Parties are generally linked to ethnic groups, as are the offices to which various candidates are elected. In the 2014 general elections, sixty-five parties, twenty-four independent candidates, and twenty-four coalitions participated in the election, with an estimated 3.2 million eligible voters. There were ten Bosniak, four Croat, and three Serbian candidates for the three-member presidency.

The Bosniak Party of Democratic Action (SDA) candidate, Bakir Izetbegović, won a second presidential term in Bosnia and Herzegovina with 305,715 votes. Milorad Dodik, leader of the Serb-dominated Alliance of Independent Social Democrats since 1996, won 255,156 votes to become the president of Republika Srpska. Mladen Bosić, leader of the Serb Democratic Party since 2006, won the second vice presidency position with 211,603.

Of the forty-two seat House of Representatives, twenty-eight hail from the Federation of Bosnia and Herzegovina and fourteen from Republika Srpska. As of the 2014 elections, The Party of Democratic Action holds ten seats; the Serbian-dominated Alliance of Independent Social Democrats holds six; the Democratic Front and the Serbian Democratic Party each have five seats, while the Alliance for a Better Future and the Croatian Democratic Union each hold four. Finally, the Social Democratic Party holds three seats.

Local Government

Local government in Bosnia and Herzegovina is complex and multi-layered. First, the country is divided into two separate governing entities: the Federation of Bosnia and Herzegovina and the Republika Srpska. The Federation is divided up unto ten cantons, with their own governments; cantons are further divided into seventy-four municipalities, with their own directly-elected local governments. Within the Republika Srpska, local administration is divided into sixty-three municipalities, again, with directly-elected officials. Municipalities in Bosnia and Herzegovina are responsible for such things as utilities, education, and social services.

Judicial System

The only court with powers that extend over the entire country is the Constitutional Court. It is comprised of two members from each ethnic group plus three members appointed by the European Court of Human Rights. They are responsible for solving disputes between the two entities and for interpreting the constitution. Each entity has its own court system for internal judicial operations. In fact, there are four systems in the country, the state system, and separate systems for the Federation of Bosnia and Herzegovina, the Republika Srpska, and the Brcko District. Judicial reform is an outstanding and unresolved issue.

Taxation

The government of Bosnia and Herzegovina levies value-added, corporate income, personal income, property, social security, and excise taxes. The highest income tax rate is 10 percent, while the top corporate rate is also 10 percent.

Armed Forces

The Armed Forces of Bosnia and Herzegovina consist of an Air Force and Aircraft Defence division and an army branch, the Bosnian Ground Forces. The armed forces were unified in 2005, formed from the Bosniak-Croat Army of the Federation of Bosnia and Herzegovina and the Bosnian Serb Army of Republika Srpska, with full integration occurring in 2006. Conscription was abolished in 2006, and the minimum age for voluntary service is eighteen. In 2009, the armed forces contributed a limited number of officers to Afghanistan as part of the NATO-led

International Security Assistance Force (ISAF). As of 2015, the country boasted 14,725 active personnel and 7,000 reserves; eighty-five are deployed in Iraq, forty-five in Afghanistan, and five in the Congo. Military expenditures represent 1.1 percent of the country's GDP.

Foreign Policy

Bosnia and Herzegovina declared independence from the former Yugoslavia in 1992, following a referendum that was boycotted by the region's ethnic Serbs. The country suffered three years of devastating civil war, as Bosnian Serbs and Croats, with military support from Serbia and Croatia, fought to partition the region along ethnic lines. The Muslim Bosniaks, the only Bosnian ethnic group with no outside "homeland," suffered expulsion and massacre at the hands of the Serbs in the name of ethnic cleansing. At the urging of the United States, the North Atlantic Treaty Organization (NATO) intervened in 1995, bombing Serbian positions in Bosnia in August and September. The modern state of Bosnia and Herzegovina was formed as part of the Dayton Peace Accords of 1995.

The country is made up of a central government and two-semi-autonomous entities: the Federation of Bosnia and Herzegovina (FBiH), which is mostly populated by Croats and Bosniaks, and the Republic of Serbia, which is dominated by Serbs. International peacekeeping forces, led first by NATO and later by the European Union (EU), have been stationed in the country since 1995 to supervise implementation of the Dayton Accords and promote stability. In October 2007, the EU's mission in Bosnia was changed from peacekeeping to civil policing and the troop levels were reduced from 7,000 to less than 2,500. The Office of the High Representative (OHR), which is staffed by diplomats from the countries involved in negotiating the accords, was created to oversee implementation of the civilian aspects of the Dayton Accords.

In addition to funding economic development and humanitarian programs, a number of international organizations, including the World Bank, the US Agency for International Development (USAID), and the EU, have provided financial aid for dealing with the ongoing danger of landmines and other such anti-personnel devices left behind after the 1992–1995 war. Activities funded by international donors include mine awareness training, minefield marking, and demining. Relationships with other republics of the former Yugoslavia have been relatively stable since the Dayton Peace Accords was signed. However, minor territorial disputes with both Serbia and Croatia are unresolved, and more than 13,000 people who went missing during the Bosnian war are still unaccounted for.

Bosnia and Herzegovina is a founding member of the Mediterranean Union and a member of the UN, the Central European Free Trade Agreement (CEFTA), the World Bank, the International Monetary Fund (IMF), the Organization for Security and Cooperation in Europe (OSCE), the Council of Europe, and NATO's Partnership for Peace. In April 2010, NATO delivered a Membership Action Plan, the final step towards NATO membership. In May 2014, NATO's secretary general Anders Fogh Rasmussen met with seated president Bakir Izetbegović in Sarajevo to discuss NATO's continued support of Bosnia and Herzegovina's membership application.

Membership in the EU is a major political objective for Bosnia and Herzegovina. The EU signed a Stabilization and Association agreement with Bosnia in June 2008. And in July 2012, the EU offered strategy whereby the country could gain candidacy status. The proposed EU plan called for alterations to Bosnia's constitution and the tackling of urgent environmental protection issues. However, in 2013, these goals had not yet been met and the application was, therefore, deferred.

Human Rights Profile

International human rights law insists that states respect civil and political rights and also promote an individual's economic, social, and cultural rights. The United Nations Universal Declaration on Human Rights is recognized as the standard for international human rights. Its authors sought the counsel of the world's great thinkers, philosophers, and religious leaders and were careful to create a document that reflects the core values shared by every world culture. (To read this document or view the articles relating to cultural human rights, go to: http://www.ohchr.org/EN/ UDHR/Pages/Introduction.aspx.)

During the communist regime, Bosnia was often held up as an example of multicultural unity. After the country declared its independence in 1992, ethnic unity dissolved into hostilities and a general repudiation of the principal of equal rights defined in Article 2 of the UDHR. The civil wars of 1992–95 were based on the violent expression of ethnic differences, resulting in the forced displacement of ethnic communities and atrocities committed in the name of ethnic cleansing. In an attempt to bring warring ethnic factions together, the Dayton Peace Accords designed the government of Bosnia and Herzegovina to ensure an equal division of power between the three major ethnic groups: Bosniaks, Serbs, and Croats. The law calls for proportional representation of the three major ethnic groups in the government and the military. Despite constitutional efforts to ensure shared power, ethnic tensions linger and violent demonstrations of ethnic hatred are common. Moreover, constitutional protections have not been extended to cover minority groups in the country. The Roma population, in particular, suffers from routine discrimination in education, employment, and access to government services.

The government of Bosnia and Herzegovina generally recognizes the right to freedom of religion, as defined in Article 18 of the UHDR. There is no state religion and no regulation of religious communities by the government. Nonetheless, there is a close association between politics and religion within Bosnia. The three major ethnic groups in Bosnia tend to define themselves in terms of religion: Bosniaks are Muslim, Serbs are Orthodox, and Croats are Roman Catholic. Consequently, religious buildings and leaders become the targets of attacks in times of ethnic conflict, and political leaders often use religion in their appeals to the electorate during elections.

The press was an official mouthpiece of the government in communist Yugoslavia. In independent Bosnia and Herzegovina, the freedom of opinion and expression called for in Article 19 of the UHDR is under continuous pressure from the state government and ethnically-based political parties in both FBiH and the Republic of Serbia. Tactics for controlling the press range from threatening loss of advertising revenue to physical assaults on reporters. In March 2012, the Center for Humane Politics reported that the prime minister of Republika Srpska paid media outlets several million in Bosnian currency for positive coverage. The multinational watchdog organization Freedom House rated Bosnia and Herzegovina "partly free" and awarded it a score of 49 in its 2013 Freedom of the Press rankings; for reference, a score of 100 was awarded to the worst offenders.

ECONOMY

Overview of the Economy

Bosnia and Herzegovina's economy was shattered by the end of the war. The industrial sector and infrastructure was severely damaged, inflation was out of control, and unemployment figures were staggering. Since then, the situation has improved significantly and the gross domestic product (GDP) increases annually, due in part to the billions of dollars the country has received in international aid. The country's economy continues to transition from post-conflict conditions to a privatized economy.

The country's economic progress has been threatened by the global economic crisis, which particularly hit countries on the rise in the early 21st century. According to the CIA's *World Factbook*, the country's 2014 per capita GDP was an estimated $9,800 USD, with a thriving underground economy. The labor force is estimated at just 1.47 million in 2013. Despite the progress, the industrial production growth rate stands at 1.2 percent (2014); unemployment was at 44.3 percent (2013), and poverty levels were still high, with 18.6 percent of the population below the poverty line.

Industry

Industry accounts for 29.8 percent of the GDP. Before the war, much of Yugoslavia's heavy industry was concentrated in the republic of Bosnia and Herzegovina. The sector included oil refineries, arms factories, manufacturing, and metallurgy. These industries were largely ruined during the war and are functioning at low production levels. They are, moreover, concentrated within the Muslim-Croat area of the country, putting Bosnian Serbs at a disadvantage.

Sarajevo's major manufacturing industries include metalwork and carpet making, crafts that have survived since the city's earliest days. Tobacco, textiles, and shoes are among Sarajevo's other important industries. Construction is also important, both as an industry itself and as a consumer of Sarajevo's manufacturing industry.

Labor

As of 2013, Bosnia and Herzegovina has a labor force numbering 1.47 million people. The unemployment rate is 44.3 percent. Among the labor force, 51.3 percent work in the services sector, almost 30 percent work in the manufacturing and industry sector, and nearly 19 percent are employed in agriculture.

Energy/Power/Natural Resources

Significant portions of the country are heavily wooded, much of the interior has dark, fertile soil, and the rivers yield some hydropower. Inadequate sanitation, air pollution from the industrial sector, and deforestation are all environmental problems which the country is currently facing. Not only did the war extensively damage the infrastructure, it left an estimated 3 million unexploded landmines planted across the country, in both populated and unpopulated areas. In September 2013, there were still approximately 28,699 unexploded landmines throughout the country. With the help of nongovernmental organizations and NATO units, the

country aims to have located and disposed of all remaining landmines by 2019.

Forestry

Bosnia and Herzegovina is 53 percent covered by forests. There are three types of forestation: temperate continental forests to the north, temperate mountain forests in the country's middle, and subtropical forests to the country's south. Deciduous trees dominate the landscape, such as beech (40 percent), oak (20 percent), and fruit trees. Spruce, fir, Scotch and European pine (20 percent) are found at higher elevations. The state controls 80 percent of forests, and the timber industry is largely undeveloped. However, concerns about deforestation persist, and as of December 2013, The World Bank has been assisting the country in working to put a sustainable forest and landscape management protocol in place.

Mining/Metals

Bosnia has large deposits of metals and minerals. Silver, manganese, zinc, copper, lead, nickel, iron ore, chromium, bauxite, coal, gypsum, and salt are all present. In 2008, the mining industry reported that the value of mining and quarrying production increased in value due to increased value of commodities. Increases were seen in the production of pig iron, zinc, lead, bauxite, and crude steel. In 2012, bauxite, zinc, and iron were the principal minerals mined, while increases were seen in revenue from mineral fuels, such as brown coal, coke, and lignite.

Agriculture

In 2014, agriculture accounted for an estimated 8 percent of the GDP; the most fertile land lies within Serb areas. Products include wheat, corn, fruits, vegetables, and livestock.

Animal Husbandry

The war was detrimental to the country's livestock, which was reduced by 70 percent of its pre-war level. Cattle, dairy cows, pigs, sheep, and goats are the most commonly raised animals. Between 2013 and 2016, the Czech Development

Agency, using foreign aid money, is working with the government of Bosnia Herzegovina to develop an effective beef cattle breeding system, geared specifically to the needs of small-to-medium farmers. The ultimate goal is to set up breeding centers, implement standard breeding methods, and increase the country's overall self-sufficiency.

Tourism

Bosnia and Herzegovina has been struggling to shed its war-torn image and encourage tourists to return. It has been a slow process, hampered by a seriously damaged infrastructure, landmines, erratic services, and some hostility towards the West in the Serbian portion of the country. In 2013, approximately 844,189 tourists visited the country, and 58.6 percent of these tourists came from foreign countries, primarily Croatia, Serbia, Poland, Slovenia, and Italy. Most visitors went to Sarajevo, Mostar, and the mountain ranges, which offer winter skiing and summer hiking.

Despite its previous difficulties, the country has enormous potential to develop as a tourist center, as evidenced by the recent re-opening of the bridge in the city of Mostar, which had been destroyed by shelling during the war. The World Tourism Organization estimates that Bosnia and Herzegovina will have the world's third highest tourism growth rate between 1995 and 2020.

The country also offers several alternative forms of tourism. Many tourists, for example, are interested in the effects of a disastrous civil war and the amount of reconstruction that has occurred. Others visit the village of Međugorje in southwest Bosnia and Herzegovina, an important place of pilgrimage for Catholics who believe that the Virgin Mary makes regular appearances there.

The medieval gravestones, called stećci, are another draw. An estimated 60,000 are scattered across the country, many of them decorated with floral motifs and various human and animal figures.

By Pamela D. Toler, Michael Aliprandini,
& Alex K. Rich

DO YOU KNOW?

• World War I began in Sarajevo on June 28, 1914, when a Bosnian Serb, named Gavrilo Princip, assassinated Archduke Francis Ferdinand and his wife.

Bibliography

Andric, Ivo. *The Bridge on the Drina.* Trans. Lovett F. Edwards. Chicago: University of Chicago Press, 1977.

Cataldi, Anna. *Letters from Sarajevo.* Trans. Avril Bardoni. Rockport, MA: Element Press, 1993.

Clancy, Tim. *Bradt Travel Guides: Bosnia and Herzegovina.* Fourth ed. Bucks, UK: Bradt Travel Guides, 2014.

Dina, Lordanova. *Cinema of Flames: Balkan Film, Culture, and the Media.* London: British Film Institute, 2001.

Donia, Robert J. *Sarajevo: A Biography.* Ann Arbor: University of Michigan Press, 2006.

Filipovic, Zlata. *Zlata's Diary: A Child's Life in Sarajevo.* New York: Viking, 1994.

Gjelton, Tom. *Sarajevo Daily: A City and Its Newspaper Under Siege.* Harper Perennial, 1995.

Horn, Steve. *Pictures Without Borders: Bosnia Revisited.* Stockport, UK: Dewi Lewis Publishing & The Bosnian Institute, 2005.

Lovrenovic, Ivan. *Bosnia: A Cultural History.* New York: New York University Press, 2001.

Malcolm, Noel. *Bosnia, A Short History.* New York: New York University Press, 1994.

Sudetic, Chuck. *Blood and Vengeance: One Family's Story of the War in Bosnia.* New York: W.W. North & Co, 1998.

Trebincevic, Kenan & Susan Shapiro. *The Bosnia List: A Memoir of War, Exile, and Return.* New York: Penguin, 2014.

Works Cited

Advocates for Human Rights, The. "Violence Against Women in Bosnia & Herzegovina." *Stop Violence Against Women*. The Advocates for Human Rights, April 2014. Web. http://www.stopvaw.org/bosnia_and_herzegovina.

Amnesty International. *Bosnia and Herzegovina: Amnesty International Report 2014/15*. Amnesty International, 2014. Web. https://www.amnesty.org/en/countries/europe-and-central-asia/bosnia-and-herzegovina/.

BBC. "Country Profile—Bosnia-Herzegovina" *BBC News*. BBC, 2015. Web. http://www.bbc.com/news/world-europe-17211415.

Bosnia and Herzegovina: The Heart-shaped Land. Tourism Association of Feberation of BiH, 2005. Web. http://www.bhtourism.ba/eng/default.wbsp.

Bosnian Institute. London, n.d. Web. http://www.bosnia.org.uk/default.cfm.

Broughton, Simon, Mark Ellingham, David Muddyman, & Richard Trillo, eds. *World Music: The Rough Guide*. London: Rough Guides, Ltd., 1994.

Central Intelligence Agency. "Bosnia and Herzegovina" *The World Factbook*. CIA, 2015. Web. https://www.cia.gov/library/publications/the-world-factbook/geos/bk.html.

Czech Development Agency. *Development of a System for Breeding Beef Cattle in Bosnia and Herzegovina*. Czech Development Agency, 2013. http://www.czda.cz/czda/en_126/en_130/en_652.htm?lang=en.

Denny, Walter B. & Joel Martin Halpern. *The Thin Veneer: The Peoples of Bosnia and their Disappearing Cultural Heritage*. Amherst, MA: University of Massachusetts at Amherst, 1997.

Dodds, Jerrilyn D. "Hearts and Stones" *Saudi Aramco World*. (September/October 1998). 49.5: 2–9.

Government of the Federation of Bosnia and Herzegovina. *Constituting of the Government of the Federation of Bosnia And Herzegovina*. Government of Federation of Bosnia and Herzegovina, 2010. Web. http://www.fbihvlada.gov.ba/english/index.php.

Hirsch, Michelle Lent. "Conflict Profiles: Bosnia." *Women Under Siege*. The Women's Media Center, 8 Feb. 2012. http://www.womenundersiegeproject.org/conflicts/profile/bosnia.

Milivojevic, JoAnn. *Bosnia and Herzegovina*. New York: Children's Press, 2004.

Moranjak-Bamburać, Nirman. *Bosnien-Herzegovina: Interkultureller Synkretismus*. Vienna: Gesellschaft zur Förderung slawistischer Studien, 2001. Wiener Slawisticher Alamanach Ser.

Nidel, Richard. World Music: The Basics. New York & London: Routledge Taylor and Francis Group, 2005.

"Recent Earthquake Near Federation of Bosnia and Herzegovina, Bosnia and Herzegovina" *Earthquake Track*. Earthquake Track, 2015. http://earthquaketrack.com/p/bosnia-and-herzegovina/federation-of-bosnia-and-herzegovina/recent.

Saracevic, Javorka. *Architecture of Bosnia and Herzegovina*. Javorka Saracevic, 2001. Web. http://research.the-bac.edu/bosnia/.

Saric, Velma & Elizabeth D. Herman. "Why Bosnia Has the World's Highest Youth Umemployment Rate." *GlobalPost*. GlobalPost International News, 9 Oct. 2014. http://www.globalpost.com/dispatch/news/regions/europe/141008/bosnia-youth-unemployment-rate.

Slipicevic, Osman & Adisa Malicbegovic. "Public and Private Sector in the Health Care System of the Federation Bosnia and Herzegovina: Policy and Strategy." *Mater Sociomed* (2012) 24.1: 54–57. National Center for Biotechnology Information, U. S. National Library of Medicine, 2012. Web. http://www.ncbi.nlm.nih.gov/pmc/articles/PMC3633389/.

Turner, Barry, ed. *Statesman's Yearbook Online*. New York: Palgrave, 2008. www.statesmansyearbook.com.

UNESCO. *World Heritage Center*. UNESCO, 2015. Web. http://whc.unesco.org/en/statesparties/ba.

United Nations. *United Nations in Bosnia and Herzegovina*. United Nations, 2008. Web. http://www.unhcr.ba/updateoct08/United_Nations_in_Bosnia_and_Herzegovina.pdf.

US Department of State. "U.S. Relations with Bosnia and Herzegovina." *Bureau of European and Eurasian Affairs: Fact Sheet*. US Department of State, 21 Jan. 2015. Web. http://www.state.gov/r/pa/ei/bgn/2868.htm.

World Bank. *Bosnia and Herzegovina—Sustainable Forest and Landscape Management Project*. World Bank Group, 2013. Web. http://documents.worldbank.org/curated/en/2013/12/18741506/bosnia-herzegovina-sustainable-forest-landscape-management-project.

Rose Picking Festival in Bulgaria

BULGARIA

Introduction

The Republic of Bulgaria is situated on the Balkan Peninsula in southeastern Europe. It is bounded on the east by the Black Sea, on the south by Turkey and Greece, on the southwest by Macedonia, on the west by Serbia, and on the north by Romania.

Once one of the most successful satellite states of the Soviet Union, the collapse of communist rule in Eastern Europe in the 1980s and 1990s ushered Bulgaria into a new era of democratic government and free-market economics. Part of the North Atlantic Treaty Organization (NATO) since 2004, Bulgaria joined the European Union in 2007.

In March 2015, as part of Operation Atlantic Resolve, Bulgaria and fellow UN member, the United States, performed bilateral drills at Bulgaria's Nevo Solo training range. The U.S. has also invested $30 million (USD) in Bulgaria's military infrastructure, so that it will be prepared to respond to a crisis, like that faced by Ukraine in 2014 during Russia's armed annexation of Crimea in March 2014.

GENERAL INFORMATION

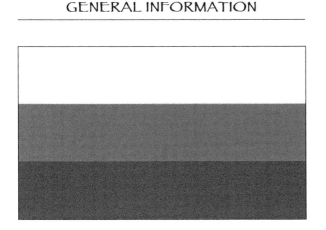

Official Language: Bulgarian
Population: 6,924,716 (2014 estimate)
Currency: Bulgarian lev
Coins: The Bulgarian lev is divided in 100 stotinki. Coins are available in denominations of 1, 2, 5, 10, 20, and 50 stotinki, and 1 lev.

Land Area: 108,489 square kilometers (41,887 square miles)
Water Area: 2,390 square kilometers (922 square miles)
National Anthem: "Mila Rodino" ("Dear Motherland")
Capital: Sofia
Time Zone: GMT +2
Flag Description: The Bulgarian flag features a tricolor design with equal, horizontal bands of white (top), green (middle), and red (bottom). The red and white are Pan-Slavic colors, and the green stands for freedom.

Population

The majority of Bulgaria's population is descended from the Bulgars, a tribe from central Asia, who conquered the indigenous Slavic farmers and adopted their language. This majority accounts for 76.9 percent of the population.

Principal Cities by Population (2014):

- Sofia (1,296,714)
- Plovdiv (382,737)
- Varna (364,537)
- Burgas (219,606)
- Stara Zagora (149,137)
- Ruse (147,001)
- Sliven (144,150)
- Pleven (106, 954)
- Šumen (115,700)
- Dobrič (110,150)

Turks account for eight percent of the population, 4.4 percent are Romani, and the remaining 0.7 percent includes Macedonians, Armenians, Russians, Tatars, and Circassians.

As of 2014, the capital of Sofia was home to approximately—and unofficially—almost 1.3 million people, or more than a sixth of the total Bulgarian population. The country's population growth rate, as of 2014, stood at –0.83, a figure attributed to a high death rate and migration. Bulgaria's growth rate is the lowest in European Union, and, in 2014, the country lost almost three people to migration for every 1,000 citizens.

Languages

Bulgarian is the official and predominant language, with many older Bulgarians also speaking Russian (younger citizens are learning English). Most of the minority population groups live in self-contained communities and speak their own languages, with Turks and Roma having the largest numbers of minority language speakers. Bulgaria, like Russia, uses the Cyrillic alphabet.

Native People & Ethnic Groups

Although the Romani, often known as gypsies, are traditionally nomadic, many are now settled permanently in enclaves within Bulgaria's major cities. Sofia contains several such enclaves, the largest containing more than 20,000 Romani. Overall, in 2013, there were an estimated 430,000 Romani living within Bulgaria, and their population is expected to continue growing.

The capital is also home to a very small Jewish community. Spanish Jews forced into exile first arrived in Sofia in the 15th century and went on to play a vital role in the capital's social and economic fabric. By the end of the 19th century, they made up as much as 20 percent of Sofia's total population. Although not subjected to genocide on the scale witnessed in other European countries during World War II, the vast majority of Sofia's Jewish community chose to move to Israel in the postwar period.

Religions

Of religious Bulgarians, 59.4 percent are Eastern Orthodox and 7.8 percent are Muslim. Roman Catholics, Protestants, Armenian Apostolic Orthodox, and Jews account for 1.7 percent. Those not professing their religious identity are at 27.4 percent, and 3.7 percent are expressly unaffiliated with any religious practice.

Bulgarian Christianity dates from 865, when Tsar Boris I accepted the teachings of a Byzantine monk. By 870, the Bulgarian church was independent, with its own Patriarch.

Most of Bulgaria's Turks are Muslims and live in the southeast of the country, near the Turkish border. Until recently, they have participated little in Bulgarian public life. They were represented for the first time in national government after the 2001 national election.

Climate

Bulgaria has two distinct climate zones, separated by the Balkan Mountains. To the south, the climate is Mediterranean with hot, dry summers. The temperate north has four seasons, with warm summers and cold winters when heavy snowfalls can disrupt transportation and electrical power.

In Sofia, the average temperature in January is around 2° Celsius (29° Fahrenheit), but can drop below −15° Celsius (5° Fahrenheit); in July, temperatures reach 21° Celsius (69° Fahrenheit). The average annual rainfall there is 58 centimeters (22.8 inches). Although the city sits in a valley, its relatively high altitude of around 550 meters (1,804 feet) above sea level makes the summers in the capital less oppressive than in other regions of the country.

Landslides and earthquakes are natural hazards threatening Bulgaria's mountain landscapes. Still more threatening are industrial hazards: raw sewage, detergents, and heavy metals polluting the rivers; heavy metals and industrial waste polluting the soil; air pollution and acid rain damaging forests; and actual deforestation. Bulgaria is, however, a party to most international agreements to safeguard the environment.

ENVIRONMENT & GEOGRAPHY

Topography

The Danube River forms the border between Bulgaria and Romania. Its tributaries include the Ogosta, Iskar, Òsam, Yàntra, and Lom. Two rivers, the Provadiya and Kamchiya, flow to the Black Sea; the Maritsa, Struma, and Mesta (also called the Nestos) rivers flow south to the Aegean.

The Stara Planina (Balkan Mountains), between the Danube and the Maritsa, cross Bulgaria from east to west. In the south are the Rhodope Mountains. South of Sofia, the Rila Mountains include Mount Musala, which is Bulgaria's highest peak at 2,925 meters (9,596 feet).

Sofia is located in western Bulgaria and is surrounded by mountains, the tallest of which is Mount Vitosha, whose highest peak reaches a height of 2,292 meters (7,520 feet). Several rivers flow through the capital, the two most prominent of which are the Vladayska and the Iskar.

Plants & Animals

Bulgaria is home to 3,567 species of plants. Of these, 105 date from the ice age or earlier, 56 are protected under international law and 92 under Bulgarian law. There are 750 medicinal plant species growing in Bulgaria, and over 250 mushroom species. The country ranks fifth in Europe in plant diversity.

Beech, oak, and pine trees are plentiful. In the mountains, coniferous forests open onto high mountain meadows, home to many rare species of plants. Bulgaria's three national parks, 11 nature parks, and 54 nature reserves protect most of these habitats. Management of these areas falls under the purview of Bulgaria's Ministry of Environment and Water.

These parks and reserves also protect more than 4,000 invertebrate animal species and over 300 vertebrate species. Included among these are many large mammals, such as the Balkan chamois (a goat-like antelope), the brown bear, the red deer, and the wolf, along with 25 species of smaller mammals. Bulgaria has 25 species of bats, the second largest number in Europe. All are protected under Bulgarian and international law.

The Danube wetlands harbor several rare species of Nymphea (a waterlily) and several threatened bird species, such as pygmy cormorants, night herons, squacco herons, purple herons, ferruginous ducks, spoonbills, corncrakes, aquatic warblers, and white-tailed eagles. Herons, egrets, cormorants, and ibises breed there, and about twenty more species rest there on their migrations.

Black Sea wetlands are diverse, providing freshwater, brackish, salty, and hyper-salty habitats, where 260 rare and endangered plant and animal species have been recorded, including the Etruscan shrew and a rare otter (Lutra lutra), which has been on the International Union for Conservation of Nature and Natural Resources' Red List of threatened species since 2004. Stopovers for migratory birds, the Black Sea wetlands provide breeding ground for ibises, spoonbills, and five species of heron. Tufted ducks, white-headed ducks, great white egrets, and Dalmatian pelicans make these wetlands their winter home.

CUSTOMS & COURTESIES

Greetings

Greetings among non-family members are typically reserved in Bulgaria. A firm handshake while making eye contact is the most common form of greeting. It may be accompanied by "Dobre utro" ("Good morning"), "Dobre den" ("Good day"), "Dobre vecher" ("Good evening"), or the more informal "Zdraveite" ("Hello"). Close female friends may kiss each other on the cheek. In business situations, handshakes are typically offered upon greeting and parting. More intimate greetings, such as embraces or kisses, are usually reserved only for family members or close friends. When saying goodbye, "Dovijdane" ("Until I see you") and "Dochuvane" ("Until I hear from you") are common phrases.

Gestures & Etiquette

In Bulgaria, the gesture for "no" is the nodding of the head, while shaking the head means "yes." The nod begins with the head briefly rising up and then down and is sometimes accompanied by shaking the finger or clicking the tongue. When shaking "yes," the head moves from side to side instead of turning the face from right to left as is the custom in many other cultures.

It is polite to address people by their honorific titles, such as "Gospodin" ("Mr.") or "Gospozha" ("Mrs."). Generally, first names are used only by close friends or family members, and formal titles remain appropriate until a first-name basis is initiated. Making eye contact when conversing or shaking hands is also very important, since it is thought to convey one's sincerity. Additionally, Bulgarians tend to stand close together and may speak emphatically while conversing.

Flowers are a standard gift in Bulgaria. However, it is customary to give an odd number of flowers (most are only sold in odd-numbered bouquets) because even-numbered bouquets are reserved for funerals. Likewise, chrysanthemums, lilies, and gladiolas should be avoided since they are associated with mourning. If giving presents to a newborn child, the number of presents should be odd as well.

Eating/Meals

Bulgarians typically eat three meals per day. Breakfast is usually informal and consists of a bread or pastry, such as banitsa, or boza, a thick, fermented drink with a low alcohol content that is usually made from millet, wheat, or rye. Lunch is eaten at midday and usually consists of light fare, possibly a soup or salad followed by meat with cooked vegetables and bread. Dinner is served in the evening and mainly consists of several hot meat and vegetable dishes, accompanied by a salad and bread. Stewed fruits are also popular for dessert.

Traditionally, Bulgarian meals are often very protracted affairs, especially during holidays and celebrations. During family meals, it is common for a communal bowl of salad or other appetizers to be placed in the center of the table, with guests eating directly out of the bowl. Different foods may also be accompanied by different types of alcohol in a traditional Bulgarian household. For example, vodka or rakia (plum or grape brandy) is served with salads, beer is served with potatoes or cheese, and wine is served with sausages.

Holiday meals also follow specific traditions. For instance, in the Eastern Orthodox tradition, no animal products can be eaten on Christmas Eve, and so the meal is often entirely vegan, featuring dishes such as stuffed cabbage leaves. The number of dishes must be odd as well. The Christmas Eve meal is also traditionally eaten on the floor as a symbol of the nativity. Superstition holds that after Christmas dinner, the remnants of the meal should be left on the table through the night for spirits to feast on. In addition, baked dishes like banitsa (pastry) are often stuffed with small charms or little pieces of paper on which the word "luck" or other good wishes are written.

Visiting

Paying visits is a common form of Bulgarian courtesy. When invited to someone's house, it is polite to bring an inexpensive, but thoughtful gift, such as alcohol or flowers. In most Bulgarian homes, it is customary to remove one's shoes at the door to avoid dirtying the floor, and many hosts will offer their guests slippers to wear. Visiting and gift-giving are also both reciprocal; for example, if a Bulgarian were to receive a gift of food on a platter, that platter would be returned to the gift giver a few days later freshly topped with food.

At meals, guests may be invited to partake of the food first. However, because of the Bulgarian custom of respect for the elderly, guests often decline, asking the most senior person at the table to begin instead. It is also considered impolite to begin eating until the host has invited the guests to start. Additionally, it is customary to always keep a little food on one's plate when finished, and the same holds true for drinking. Although meals tend to be long, friendly, and noisy affairs, basic table manners, such as keeping one's elbows off the table and one's hands in view, are appreciated.

LIFESTYLE

Family

Families in Bulgaria are close. The traditional family structure was the zadruga, an extended network of blood relatives headed by a patriarch. During the move for Bulgarian independence from the Ottoman Empire in the mid-1800s, these familial institutions began breaking up, particularly as new ideas about women's rights were introduced. However, patriarchal structures and arranged marriages continued to be common until the 1960s.

Today, nuclear families are more common in Bulgarian cities, and multi-generational households remain common in rural areas. Young people may live with their parents until they marry, and a young married couple may even continue to live with one set of parents until they

are financially independent. In urban areas, it is becoming more common for young couples to cohabit without marrying. Grandparents also often live with the family so that they may assist with childrearing, particularly as both parents are increasingly entering the workforce. Dependency on a two-parent income has grown in recent years, though housework is still considered the responsibility of women.

Since the elderly are shown great respect, grandparents, especially grandmothers, are central figures in any family. Family and social gatherings tend to be ordered hierarchically by age: older members will be greeted first, served first during meals, and offered the choicest parts of the food. In addition, elder members will be expected to make important family decisions.

Housing

In urban areas, most Bulgarians live in housing blocks. In smaller towns, detached single-family homes are common. Many are two-story dwellings with protruding basements, so that the first floor is elevated and reached by steps. Light-colored stucco walls with red tile roofs are common in the countryside. In some towns, traditional Bulgarian Revival architecture can still be seen, which is characterized by brightly-painted manor houses with ornate wooden carvings on the gate and ceiling.

Homegrown produce continues to provide a staple part of the diet of many Bulgarians. As such, small gardens or orchards are common in the more temperate parts of the country. A typical garden includes a grape arbor (for making homemade rakia), plum, apricot, pear, peach, and/or apple trees, blackberry or strawberry patches, and rows of tomatoes, beans, peppers, cucumbers, and onions. Very few residences have air conditioning, so outdoor living space is also common, often in the form of picnic tables under the shade of the grape arbor. In the countryside, many families still maintain their agrarian roots by owning livestock, such as goats, sheep, or cows. Typically, these animals are sent to pasture in the mountains or fields around the town during the day and are kept in pens near the house during the night.

Food

Due to its central location, long history, and varied geography, Bulgarian cuisine is quite diverse. It has been influenced over the centuries by several different cultures, most notably Balkan, Turkish, Greek, Middle Eastern, Mediterranean, and even Italian culinary traditions. One staple of Bulgarian cuisine is salad, an indispensable part of every meal. Salads made of chopped, shredded, or mashed vegetables (like carrots or kohlrabi) mixed with vinegar, salt, parsley, and sunflower oil are popular. Since sunflowers are a major crop in Bulgaria, sunflower oil is the most common kind of oil used. One particularly popular national dish is shopka salad, which includes chopped tomatoes, cucumbers, onions, and red peppers topped with cheese.

Bulgarian milk products are renowned throughout the region, and include yogurt and sirene, a crumbly cheese made of brined sheep's or cow's milk that is much like feta. Yogurt is often used to make cold soups such as tarator, which is a mix of yogurt, grated cucumbers, dill, walnuts, and garlic. Banitsa is a flaky, circular pastry popular at breakfast and as an accompaniment to meals. It is composed of coils of very thin filo (phyllo) dough filled with egg and sirene, which are then wound around each other to form a wheel shape that is baked. Sometimes spinach or pumpkin is also included.

A common Bulgarian dish is sarmi, little rolls of rice, ground meat, onion, and spices wrapped in grape or pickled cabbage leaves and boiled in a clay pot. Sarmi are traditionally eaten during cold weather, especially on Christmas Eve, and are often served with yogurt. A popular national drink is rakia, home-brewed fruit wine, usually made from plums or grapes and having a high alcohol content. Rakia traditionally accompanies most meals, especially during celebrations.

Life's Milestones

Bulgarian wedding traditions are very complex. Before the wedding, the bride and groom both undergo a "coming of age" ritual—the man's face is shaved and the woman's hair is braided. Long ago, marriages occurred at a very young age, which typically meant the act of marriage represented a man's first shave and a woman's first braid. In addition to these symbolic acts, another tradition involved the approval of the groom, who has to "prove" himself worthy by either fighting male relatives of the bride or answering riddles. Bread is also central to the Bulgarian tradition of marriage, and breads with symbols and designs wishing future luck and happiness were specially baked. In addition, after the wedding ceremony, the bride and groom will each seize one end of a loaf of bread and pull. Tradition states that whoever has the biggest half will be the boss in their marriage.

Traditions surrounding the birth of a new baby include not visiting the baby, unless specifically invited, until forty days have passed, which is meant to give the mother and child time to bond. Also, well-wishers should only bring the baby and its new parents an odd number of gifts. On birthdays, it is common for the person celebrating to treat their friends and guests to candy, pastries, and other treats.

CULTURAL HISTORY

Art

Much of Bulgaria's unique art originated in the early Bulgarian church. Bulgaria is famous for its centuries-old tradition of beautifully detailed fresco painting. Commonly found on the walls of tombs and monasteries throughout the country, these murals are characterized by their deep coloring and depictions of religious or historical themes. Many of these ancient frescoes are noted for the technical skill and attention to detail they display. The frescoes adorning the Boyana Church in Sofia, which were painted by an unknown artist around 1259, are often regarded as a precursor to the focus on life and realism that characterized the Italian Renaissance several centuries later.

One of the best-known figures in Bulgarian medieval fresco art is Zahari Zograf (1810–1853), a primary figure of the Bulgarian national revival period (or Bulgarian Renaissance). This period lasted from the 18th to the late 19th century. Although primarily a painter of church murals and icons, Zograf is considered the founder of Bulgarian secular art due to his incorporation of elements of daily life into his paintings. His work can be found in churches and monasteries throughout Bulgaria, such as the Rila Monastery and the Troyan Monastery, as well as in Mount Athos, an autonomous monastic state in Greece. A controversial issue surrounding Zograf's work was that he occasionally included a portrait of himself in his murals.

Architecture

Bulgaria's rich and complex architectural history is perhaps best reflected above all in the capital's renowned religious architecture. Sofia's most emblematic landmark is the enormous, neo-Byzantine St. Alexander Nevsky Cathedral, which was built in the period around the turn of the 20th century to commemorate the Russian forces who helped expel the Ottoman Empire from Bulgaria during the 1878 Russian-Turkish war.

The Nevsky Cathedral's sparkling gold and copper domes top an interior famed for its elaborate stained glass windows, marble carvings, mosaic designs, and, especially, the intricate murals painted by dozens of Russian and Bulgarian artists. The church also houses, in an underground crypt, a museum with a large collection of Bulgarian Orthodox icons and murals, some of which date to the 9th century.

The 4th-century Church of St. George, now a museum, is considered Sofia's oldest preserved building, which has served, at different points in its long history, as a Roman temple, a Turkish mosque, and a Christian church. The Russian Church, also known as the Church of St. Nicholas the Miracle-Maker, which is Russian Orthodox and located in central Sofia, has five small gold-plated, onion-like domes.

Bulgaria's rich residential architecture is evident by the many neighborhoods of 18th- and 19th-century homes found in cities such as Plovdiv, Nesebar, Lovech, Tryavna, Gabrovo, and others. These homes are characterized by their two to three stories, of which the basement is used for storage, and the ground floor (usually made of stone) was traditionally used to house livestock; the living quarters above, often projecting over the ground floor using wooden beams, were slightly larger. Grander 18th- and 19th-century homes in Bulgaria took several forms, with exterior styles that included elaborately-painted facades, bowed overhangs, large verandahs, and numerous windows. The interiors were as elaborate, with carved ceilings, murals, and European details.

The communist era brought the grandeur of earlier architecture to a halt, and larger industrial-sized housing complexes became the norm. The end of communism in 1989 has ushered in a new era for Bulgarian architects, who seek to honor the country's architectural heritage, while using modern techniques and materials.

Drama

Bulgaria faced centuries of repression that impeded the country's literary and dramatic development. Falling under the control of the Ottoman Empire from the 14th to the 19th centuries, the first Bulgarian literary achievement was a history of its people, written by a Bulgarian Orthodox monk in 1762. Drama and theater did not develop until the 19th century, when a full-length play was staged. Early Bulgarian theatrical efforts in the late 19th century initially served as vehicles of propaganda (as printed material was dangerous) for those seeking liberation from the Turks. These early dramas often depicted tales from Bulgaria's medieval period as a means of bolstering national pride, as well as melodramatic tales of Bulgarian repression. Early playwrights include Dobri Voynikov (1833–1878), Iliya Bluskov (1839–1913), and Vasil Drumev (known as Kliment of Tarnovo, c. 1841–1901). Some critics have credited the best of these early efforts to Drumev, who wrote the historical play

Ivanko ubietšut na Asenia I (*Ivanko the Assassin of Asen I*, 1872) and was cofounder of the Bulgarian Literature Society in 1869.

Author and poet Ivan Minchoff Vazoff (1850–1921) produced some plays in the 1880s and 1890s, and his greatest accomplishment in the theater is thought to be *Khushove* (1894), a tale of impoverished revolutionaries. In 1907, the National Theatre in Sofia opened its doors, with Vozov producing a great number of its dramas, mostly historical tales, and for this reason, the theater's official name is The Ivan Vazov National Theatre. Early 20th-century modernists began to influence theatrical productions. Social critics such as Anton Strashimirov (1872–1937) began writing plays about life in the country, social and family dynamics, and later, the corruption of political figures. Playwright Petko Todorov (1879–1916) wrote plays that harken back to the country's folklore and then began to write plays concerned with social justice, such as *Purvite* (*The First*, 1912). A contemporary, Peyo Yavorov (1878–1914), is said to have written what some characterize as Bulgaria's greatest play, *V polite na Vitosha* (*In the Foothills of Vitosha*, 1911), a tragedy in the style of Chekov or Ibsen that ends with the hero killing himself minutes before the heroine perishes from being hit by a streetcar. He followed this play with several domestic dramas that ended tragically. This was Bulgarian drama's golden age, which would end with the First World War.

While some plays were produced between the wars, many are no longer available. Stefan L. Kostov (1879–1939) produced comedies in the 1920s and Yordan Yovkov (1880–1937) continued the production of comedies in the 1930s. Psychological dramas were also part of the dramatic landscape of the 1930s, but the period is not acknowledged for its dramatic heights. Communism, which took hold in 1944, threw development of theater in Bulgaria off, and it wasn't until the 1990s that Bulgarian drama regained its footing.

Modern theater in Bulgaria takes many forms. Sfumato Theatre, an experimental theatrical form that addresses complex ethical issues, has been produced by playwrights such as Konstantin Iliev (1937–). Other post-communism and postmodern playwrights include Bojan Papazow (1943–) Georgi Gospodinov (1968–), Plamen Dojnov (1969–), and Georgi Tenev (1969–). Directors have a strong influence in modern Bulgarian theater, as they use new techniques to tell traditional tales.

Music

According to legend, Bulgarians can trace their musical roots back to the Greek mythological figure of Orpheus, the "father of songs." Orpheus was born in Thrace, whose ancient boundaries encompassed part of present-day Bulgaria, and Bulgarians take this musical ancestry very seriously. Bulgarian folk music has much in common with the folk music of the Balkan region, and many of its influences derive from traditional Turkish instruments. Common instruments in Bulgaria include the gaida, a bagpipe made of goatskin; the gadulka, similar to the violin; the tambura, a lute-like instrument; and the tarambuka, a clay goblet-shaped drum.

Women, who would sing while dancing, working in the fields, or sewing at work-parties (called sedenka) often performed traditional Bulgarian vocal music. Bulgarian music is known for its complex rhythms of quick and slow beats and is often played with an accent on the first beat. Today, folk music groups, such as the female vocal choir Le Mystère des Voix Bulgares (The Mystery of Bulgarian Voices), draw on traditional choral styles of complex singing patterns and throat trills (quick alternation between adjacent notes) to delight audiences.

A more refined music culture surfaced in Bulgaria toward the end of the 19th century after the country's liberation from the Ottoman Empire. Operas during this period became especially popular, building on the literature of the national revival period and inspired by touring opera companies from Europe. Notable composers during this period include Georgi Atanassov (1882–1931), whose operas draw on Bulgarian folk music and explore the intersection of everyday life with the fantastical and historical.

One of the most influential Bulgarian composers is Pancho Haralanov Vladigerov (1899–1978), who composed many pieces for the piano as well as other orchestral instruments. He helped found the Bulgarian Contemporary Music Society in 1933, which became the Union of Bulgarian Composers in 1954. The union still functions as a central promoter of Bulgarian music today. Vladigerov was among the first composers to successfully fuse traditional folk music with classical styles and arranged many folk songs for voice, piano, and orchestra. His best-known work is "Bulgarian Rhapsody," or "Vardar," a patriotic song considered the emblem of Bulgarian composition. Another famous Bulgarian singer is Valya Balkanska (1942–), from the Rhodope Mountains in Bulgaria. One of her signature songs, "Izlel e Delyo Haydutin," is one of the musical pieces included on the golden phonograph record (called the Voyager Golden Record) that was included in two Voyager spacecrafts sent into space in 1977.

During the mid-20th century, the Communist Party of Bulgaria adapted Bulgarian folk music to suit its ideological needs. This state-sponsored style of music was called obrabotka narodna muzika ("arranged folk music"). Its purpose was to create a unified national "folk music" that expressed the pure nature of Bulgarian culture and identity. However, in so doing, the government ignored or discouraged the musical styles of different regional groups, particularly of Bulgaria's ethnic Turkish or Roma minorities (which the Communist Party felt contributed nothing to Bulgarian culture). In the party's attempt to create a homogenous Bulgaria, ethnically Turkish or Roma Bulgarians were also forced to change their names to more Slavic-sounding ones and to give up vestiges of their culture. Because of this politicization, folk music developed a negative connotation for many Bulgarians, and new types of music were sought, paving the way for the increasing popularity of genres such as rock and roll. In fact, rock music sung in Bulgarian became a popular way to make political statements, as did wedding music (svadbarska muzika). This style combines Roma, Turkish, Serbian, and other Balkan music forms.

Dance

Dancing has long been a central form of entertainment in Bulgarian society. The horo is the most common Bulgarian dance, variations of which can be found across the Balkans. There are many different types of the horo, ranging in difficulty from simple to complex. Traditionally performed at weddings, graduations, and other celebrations, the horo features several lines of people holding hands and dancing in a series of steps in a circle. Each type of music generally has a different horo that accompanies it, and most Bulgarians learn all the different types of dances at a young age. Horo musicians and singers are also often pop icons, and Bulgarian television stations regularly feature horo performances.

One unusual form of Bulgarian dance is the Nestinarstvo, or fire dancing, which is indigenous to the Strandzha region of southeastern Bulgaria. During the Nestinarstvo, a prophet and healer called a nestinar dances over red-hot embers to the music of drums and bagpipes. The nestinar enters a trance, which prevents of the burning sensation of the embers and offers prophecies about the future. Fusing pagan and Christian traditions, the Nestinarstvo is usually performed at saint's day celebrations, particularly those which take place during "St. Constantine's Month" in May and June. These celebrations are called panagyrs.

Literature

Bulgarian is considered the first Slavic language to have a written form. It was first written down in the 9th century using the Glagolitic alphabet. This was later modified to become the Cyrillic alphabet, which underwent various changes until it was streamlined in the 1870s. The Cyrillic alphabet is still used today in Bulgaria, Russia, Ukraine, and Serbia.

Early literature was primarily religious in nature, although Bulgarian writers also stressed independence from Byzantium, the rulers of the region from 1018 through 1185.

Bulgarian literature flourished from the 12th through the 14th centuries under the Second Bulgarian Empire (1185–1422). Writers from this period include members of the influential Tarnovo Literary School. Their texts became the models for Orthodox churches throughout the region.

After the empire fell to the Ottomans in 1386, literary production in Bulgaria declined. The little that remained was primarily religious, including the first printed book in the mid-17th century. In 1741, Hristofor Zhefarovich published a book of engravings and quatrains called *Stemmatographia*, which is often considered the first example of Bulgarian secular poetry.

The movement for Bulgarian independence, often referred to as the "national awakening," is said to have begun as early as 1762. Paisius of Hilendar (1722–1773), a clergyman, scholar, and forefather of Bulgarian nationalism, wrote *Istoriya Slavyanobolgarskaya* (*Slavonic-Bulgarian History*). The book was first copied by hand and finally printed in 1844, by which time copies had travelled around the country. One central figure in the national revivalist period was Georgi Stoykov Rakovski (1821–1867). His work *Gorski Patnik* (*A Traveler in the Woods*, 1857) is considered one of the first Bulgarian literary poems. Major themes in this and other works of the period are the desire to fight for freedom and to take revenge on the oppressive Ottoman Turks.

One of the most influential revolutionary activists and poets of this period was Hristo Botev (1848–1876), who is regarded as a national hero. His poems range from the romantic to the revolutionary, and relate the struggles of the poor and downtrodden and the freedom against oppression. Dobri Voynikov (1833–1878) is considered the father of modern Bulgarian theatre, whose patriotic plays made him a central figure in the National Revolution. He influenced later playwrights and authors, such as Ivan Vazov (1850–1921), whose celebrated novel *Under the Yoke* (1888) depicts the oppression of Bulgarians under Ottoman rule.

CULTURE

Arts & Entertainment

With the transition from communism to capitalism following independence in 1989, new questions about Bulgarian national identity began to emerge. One response to communist ideology of a unified, purely Bulgarian folk music was the new music form called chalga. Also called ethnopop or popfolk, chalga is a highly innovative blend of several styles of music, including traditional Bulgarian music, popular music from Serbia, Turkey, Greece, and Macedonia, Balkan Romani music, Western hip-hop, and Afro-Cuban music. Chalga music has been praised for its distinctive musical voice and political content, and has focused on issues such as new-found freedom, shifting values, capitalism, and materialism. It is sometimes characterized as aggressive and satirical. Since many performers of chalga are Romani artists, chalga has been seen as a reaction or threat to communist conceptions of Bulgarian musical identity, particularly since the music is sometimes linked to class division.

In addition to music, Bulgarians have made a significant impact both at home and abroad in the fields of art and literature. One of the most renowned contemporary artists of Bulgarian descent is Christo (1935–), part of the artist duo Christo and Jeanne-Claude (1935–2009). The two are famous for their outdoor art installation projects, which included wrapping the Pont Neuf Bridge in Paris in textured brown fabric (1985), putting up 3,000 yellow and blue umbrellas simultaneously in California and Japan (1991), and constructing a walkway of orange flags called *The Gates* in New York's Central Park (2005). Bulgarian novelist Elias Canetti (1905–1994) received the Nobel Prize in Literature in 1981. His works span a number of subjects and genres, such as the novel *Die Blendung* (*Blinding*, also titled *Auto-da-Fé*, 1935) and the study of crowd psychology, *Masse und Macht* (*Crowds and Power*, 1960).

Bulgarians enjoy the outdoor sports for which their country is especially suited, including skiing, fishing, hiking, and tennis. Soccer is a popular team sport. Sofia has two important professional soccer teams, Levski and CSKA. Bulgaria's national soccer team's best finish at a World Cup was a fourth-place finish in 1994.

In the Olympic Games and other world competitions, Bulgaria's most successful sports records are in rhythmic gymnastics. Their team consistently ranks high, and has won the world championship ten times. Bulgarians also perform well in weightlifting, boxing, wrestling, badminton, and the decathlon.

Cultural Sites & Landmarks

Bulgaria is home to a wealth of cultural sites and landmarks, including nine World Heritage Sites as designated by the United Nations Educational, Scientific, and Cultural Organization (UNESCO). These include the Boyana Church; the Rock-hewn Churches of Ivanovo; the Thracian Tomb of Kazanlak; the Rila Monastery; and the Srebarna Nature Reserve. The capital of Sofia, often referred to as Bulgaria's cultural center, is also known for its architectural and historic heritage.

Murals and frescoes play a key role in Bulgaria's artistic history. The Boyana Church, located just outside Sofia, is one of Bulgaria's original World Heritage Sites. Constructed between the 10th and 11th centuries, the church's gold and blue frescoes date back to 1259. The paintings portray scenes from the life of Saint Nicholas and also feature full-length portraits of Bulgarian royalty and the church's patrons. More murals can be seen in the Rock-hewn Churches of Ivanovo, a cluster of churches and monasteries built into caves on the side of the cliffs of the Rusenski Lom, a river in northeastern Bulgaria. Monks inhabited the site from the 1320s until the 17th century. Most of the murals inside the caves were painted in the 13th and 14th centuries and are considered good examples of medieval Bulgarian art.

One of the oldest sites is the Thracian Tomb of Kazanlak, a beehive-shaped burial chamber dating back to the 4th century BCE. The murals of the tomb are considered the only extant example of Hellenistic art that has been preserved in exactly the same state in which it was executed. Although the tomb is not open to the public, a replica is located close by. The murals feature scenes of battles and a ceremonial feast of farewell for the dead dignitary whom the tomb honors.

One of the most awe-inspiring sites in Bulgaria is the Rila Monastery, which was designated as a World Heritage Site in 1983. The monastery's original buildings date from the late 10th century, but the central church was reconstructed 1837 after a fire ravaged many of the buildings in 1833. It is located in the Rila Mountains on a legendary site where it is believed a wise hermit known as Saint John of Rila lived in a cave and preached to his followers during the late 10th century. The Rila Monastery is considered one the most beautiful monasteries in Europe, famed for its brilliant frescoes and grand architecture, which includes arches, cupolas (dome-like structures), domes, and stone engravings.

In addition to historical sites, Bulgaria also has several nature reserves and parks, renowned for their beauty. The Srebarna Nature Reserve is a wetland area that is home to 180 species of bird, and the Pirin National Park, which includes the Pirin Mountains, contains a wealth of biological diversity. Both were designated as World Heritage Sites for their diverse landscapes and rare species. The Seven Rila Lakes form a stunning natural landmark. From the air, the seven glacial lakes make a series of footsteps up the Rila Mountains. The names of the lakes were inspired by their distinctive shapes, such as Babreka ("The Kidney"), Salzata ("The Tear"), and Okoto ("The Eye").

Libraries & Museums

Sofia features many excellent museums, the most noteworthy of which include the National Art Gallery, which contains thousands of works by the most renowned Bulgarian painters and sculptors of the 19th and 20th centuries, and the National History Museum, which highlights Bulgarian history from its origins to the present. The Earth and Man National Museum houses mineralogical collections that contain more than more than 20,000 samples from all over globe, representing 40 percent of all known, naturally-occurring minerals. The National Archaeological Museum features exhibits of Thracian, Greek, and Roman artifacts and treasures. The National Ethnographic Museum displays Bulgarian folk costumes, jewelry, crafts, and traditional musical instruments from the 17th to the 20th centuries.

The SS. Cyril and Methodius National Library are Bulgaria's national library and legal depository. It is located in Sofia and was established in 1878. The library's rare collection contains 30,000 volumes written in Old Church Slavonic, the first literary Slavic language, as well as more than 1,700 original codices dated as far back as the 11th century. As of 2015, the national library's collection totals approximately 7,753,188.

As of 2015, there were four major science libraries, like the Central Library at the Bulgarian Academy of Sciences in Sofia; fourteen university libraries scattered throughout the country; and eight major public libraries, of which SS. Cyril and Methodius National Library is one.

Holidays

Bulgarians allocate two days each year to celebrate Christmas and the New Year. Other holidays include Liberation Day (March 3), commemorating the day in 1878 when Bulgaria became self-governing within the Ottoman Empire, and Cyrillic Alphabet Day (May 24), also known as the Day of Bulgarian Culture.

Many Bulgarians celebrate February 3 as Day of St. Trifon Zarezan, when grape growers prune their vines and, to assure a good harvest, sprinkle them with wine. This ceremony dates from the pre-Christian cult of the god of wine, Dionysus. On March 1, Bulgarians exchange martenitsi, red and white tasseled threads. These are worn to celebrate spring and to assure health and happiness in the coming year.

Youth Culture

Bulgarian youth, like many young people, are granted more freedom as they progress from adolescence and focus much of their leisure time socializing. Western European and American cultural influences are particularly strong, and Bulgarian youth are usually very interested in learning about other languages and cultures. Dating is common, and as young people mature, cohabitation is becoming more common and culturally accepted, particularly in urban areas.

Similar to other youth cultures, Bulgarian youth are becoming increasingly technology-savvy. In 2008, an estimated 85 percent of Bulgarian youths owned a cellular phone, and approximately 40 percent owned or had access to home computers. An alarming trend, however, is the high rate of smoking among Bulgarian youth, particularly among adolescents. In a 2000 survey, 51 percent of adolescent female respondents reported smoking, as did 48 percent of male respondents in the same age group. In 2014, the numbers dropped somewhat, with only 18 percent of females, ages 15 to 19, and 20 percent of males the same age smoking. However, the numbers climb radically as Bulgarian youth enter their twenties, with 52 percent of males 20 to 24 and 43 percent of females the same age taking up the habit. The rates of other risky behavior has also been increasing and has been attributed to the confusion many Bulgarian youth experience arising from conflicting messages in society. The family-based, homogenous, egalitarian society of traditional and communist Bulgaria is set against the influx, via the media, of Western concepts, such as individualism, freedom, and personal independence.

SOCIETY

Transportation

Traffic in Bulgaria travels on the right side of the road. Driving in Bulgaria can be dangerous. Mixed transportation on the road, such as Soviet-era cars, horse-drawn carts, and herds of livestock, increases the chance of accidents, and roads are often poorly maintained.

The most common way to travel in Bulgaria is by train or bus. Trains are operated by the

Bulgarian Railway Company (BDZ) and are relatively inexpensive. Express trains and local trains are both available, but not all railways are connected, meaning passengers may have to change trains several times to get to their destination. In July 2012, the Plovdiv–Dimitrovgrad high-speed line was completed and modernization of several other lines, like the Plovdiv-Sofia; Sofia-Pernik-Radomir; and Vidin-Sofia are part of the European Union's "Priority Axis I."

Another option for travelling between small cities is marshrutki, small buses that can hold between ten and twenty people. Many private bus companies offer air-conditioned bus service, and public buses, which are less comfortable but cheaper, also travel between cities. Many of the larger cities may have more than one bus station, and many stations will have different ticket vendors offering various prices for different buses.

Transportation Infrastructure

Bulgaria has focused on improving its transportation infrastructure in the early 21st century. In particular, the country was identified as being located on four Pan-European transportation corridors (three of which are overland), designated as vital to Europe's overall transportation infrastructure. As such, the country has received World Bank and European Union funding and loans to improve roadways, rail and water utilities, border crossing points, and port infrastructure (EU funds were suspended at one point due to alleged corruption). The Trans-European Motorway (TEM), a joint project with other European Union member nations, connects Sofia with Istanbul, the capital of Turkey. As of 2010, many roadways remain unfinished.

Bulgaria has four international airports: Sofia International Airport (Sofia-Vrazhdebna Airport), Burgas International Airport (Sarafovo Airport), Plovdiv International Airport, and Varna International Airport.

Media & Communications

Bulgaria has nine newspapers, most of which are tabloid format. The business-orientated *Dnevnik* includes English-language pages, and the most widely-circulated paper is *Dneven Trud*. This paper put out its first issue in 1936, which makes it one of the oldest Bulgarian papers in continuous publication. The German newspaper *Westdeutsche Allgemeine Zeitung* (WAZ) and its parent company, WAZ-Mediengruppe, own the two major daily newspapers, *Dneven Trud,* and *24-Chasa*. Bulgarian National Radio and Bulgarian National Television are both state-owned, but frequently criticize the government. The main television station—and the first to be privately owned—is BTV, a national station operated by the Balkan News Corporation, which is in turn owned by the global media conglomerate News Corporation.

Alarmingly, in 2014, the non-governmental organization Reporters Without Borders issued their annual Freedom of the Press Index, which ranked Bulgaria 100 out of 180 countries, the lowest rating of all EU members. Although freedom of the press is protected by the constitution, fear of retaliation for negative coverage leads some journalists to practice self-censorship, particularly when covering stories involving corruption. Reports of intimidation, coercion, and assault of journalists at the hands of political figures, police, and individuals are not uncommon, and attacks on journalists occasionally go unpunished. Reports have also surfaced of Sofia's government using EU funds to compensate media outlets for positive coverage.

As of 2013, there were approximately 3,589,347 Internet users, an estimated 51 percent of the population. The Internet is not restricted by the government.

SOCIAL DEVELOPMENT

Standard of Living

Bulgaria ranked 58th out of 190 countries on the 2012 United Nations Human Development Index, which measures quality of life and standard of living indicators.

Water Consumption

According to UNICEF (United Nations International Children's Emergency Fund), improved access to clean water in Bulgaria stands at 99.5 percent—99.7 percent for those in cities and 99 percent for those in rural areas. Access to improved sanitation is at 100 percent in the country—100 percent for urban areas and 100 percent for rural areas.

Education

Almost 99 percent of Bulgarians over the age of fifteen are literate. Before 1989, when the country was part of the Soviet bloc, Bulgaria placed high priority on education, which was free. Research was prioritized, Bulgarian students excelled in international science and mathematics competitions, and their futures were guaranteed. After the Soviet breakup, however, budgets for education were slashed. Schools went without heat, shifting to half-sessions in winter or closing altogether on the coldest days.

Although Bulgarian education is still beset by difficulties, the school curriculum is demanding. Students must take three science courses each year for four years, and approximately 80 percent of Bulgarian students choose to study English as a foreign language.

Secondary schools are often specialized, with courses lasting from three to five years. Some are technical, and others emphasize languages. Like the secondary schools, universities in Bulgaria set their own admissions policies, placing their own weight of importance on achievement in secondary school and on independent test results. However, some have called for an overhaul of university curricula, which they have characterized as outdated.

As part of the European Union's educational strategy, Europe 2020, a study of the Bulgarian educational system finds that while educational practices within schools yield results, keeping students in school is becoming more of a challenge. Bulgaria's National Statistical Institute finds that 93 percent of seven- to 10-year-olds attended school during 2009–2010, but that attendance rates fell for students between the ages of 11 and f14, with only 82 percent attending school.

In 2010, the government was preparing goals related to early dropout rates and the number of students earning advanced degrees. According to the 2012 Programme for International Student Assessment, administered by the Organisation for Economic Co-operation and Development (OECD), standardized test scores place Bulgarian students 45th in the world in science, 47th in mathematics, and 51st in reading.

Women's Rights

Traditional Bulgarian society was strictly patriarchal and marriages were typically arranged. Women left their families and clans when they married and were not expected to have much contact with them afterward. Under Soviet rule, women were ostensibly equal with men and worked outside the home with their male counterparts. However, they still bore the brunt of most housework and child rearing. Today, this is still commonly the case. As of 2012, an estimated 47.8 percent of women in Bulgaria were employed. In terms of political representation, as of 2014, there were 59 women in the Bulgarian National Assembly, which represents 24.6 percent.

One of the largest challenges facing women in Bulgaria today is sexual exploitation. In 2007, aid groups estimated that around 10,000 women a year are trafficked from Bulgaria to other countries in the EU, where they are often forced into prostitution and sexual slavery. Many women are enticed to leave Bulgaria with promises of better work or marriage prospects. The mental, emotional, and physical tolls of sexual slavery are severe. Although rehabilitation programs, such as La Strada-Bulgaria and the Animus Association, exist to help victims, stigmas against prostitutes, as well as emotional distress, can prevent rescued victims from smoothly reentering society. The Bulgarian government has taken steps to try to combat human trafficking. However, the U.S. Department of State criticized Bulgaria's National Anti-Trafficking Commission in 2007 for being understaffed and for relying extensively on non-governmental and international organizations for the funding and implementation of public awareness campaigns.

The Bulgarian constitution guarantees the same rights to all citizens regardless of gender, but in practice, this is not always the case. For instance, in 2007, women earned an average of 17 percent less than their male counterparts. In order to enter the EU in 2007, Bulgaria committed to making improvements in this area. The Law on the Protection against Discrimination was put into effect in 2004, and the Ministry of Labor and Social Policy established a Gender Equality Department in 2005. Also, the Bill on Equal Opportunities for Women and Men was presented in 2006, although, as of 2015, it has not been adopted. Bulgaria ratified the United Nations Convention on the Elimination of All Forms of Discrimination against Women (CEDAW) in 2006. In 2008, the Stop Violence against Women Program of the U.S.-based Advocates for Human Rights found that, in general, Bulgarian women were not well informed about the option of bringing complaints against gender discrimination to court.

Domestic violence is also an issue for women, and the U.S. Department of State estimates that one in four women have been subject to domestic physical or verbal abuse in Bulgaria. The Act on Protection against Domestic Violence was adopted in 2005, which gave a legal definition of domestic violence and provides protections measures for the victim. However, services are provided mainly by NGOs (non-governmental organizations), like the Alliance for Protection against Domestic Violence; as of 2006, these included two shelters, two crisis centers, and 16 telephone hotlines. Many organizations, such as the Open Society Institute, deem these resources insufficient. Although rape is a criminal offense, sexual assault is not explicitly mentioned in the criminal code, nor is spousal rape. The ECtHR (European Court of Human Rights) found that rape cases in Bulgaria are not effectively prosecuted. In 2013, of 196 cases filed, only 69 were prosecuted. NGOs like the Bulgarian Gender Research Foundation have been established to promote awareness of these issues and work for social justice and gender equality. In March 2013, in order to raise awareness about domestic violence and sexual assault, several NGOs organized Bulgaria's first "Walk a Mile in Her Shoes" event in Sofia.

Health Care

Bulgaria's health system faced a crisis following the collapse of the Soviet Union. In recent years, the system has been reorganized. For administration purposes, Bulgaria is divided into 28 Regional Health Centers and 262 municipalities, each largely responsible for its own health care needs. Crucial to this plan are Bulgaria's General Practitioners (GP); anyone seeking treatment must register as a patient with a GP. While a financial crisis in the 1990s forced Bulgaria to seek free medicines and technical supplies from the West and to rely on help from such groups as Doctors without Borders, the crisis is largely over, and Bulgarian health workers, having learned from foreign initiatives, are increasingly taking charge.

The 1998 Health Finance Act created a National Health Insurance Fund (NHIF), which is linked to a compulsory payroll tax of eight percent. Central and local government budgets cover those who cannot afford or otherwise contribute to the healthcare system, such as pensioners, students, the unemployed, and the poor. Physicians and centers contract with the NHIF for by-patient funding, or alternately, they can provide private services on a fee-for-procedure basis. Alongside 21st-century medical practice, there remains a traditional reliance on the healing properties of salt and mineral springs and of certain muds. Bulgaria has well-established spas near Sofia, Plovdiv, and Melnik.

GOVERNMENT

Structure

Bulgaria is a constitutional democracy with a government comprised of three branches. All citizens 18 years of age and over can vote.

The executive branch includes a president and vice-president, elected together by popular vote to five-year terms. The head of government (prime minister) is called the chairman, since he or she chairs the Council of Ministers (cabinet). The chairman is nominated by the president and approved by the National Assembly. The chairperson nominates the Council of Ministers and some deputy prime ministers, all of whom must be approved by the National Assembly. The legislative branch consists of a unicameral National Assembly. Elected by popular vote, its 240 members serve four-year terms.

Political Parties

Parliamentary democracies often have a large number of political parties, which have a tendency to shift in terms of political platform and their alliance with other parties sharing common interests. Often, parliamentary systems are ruled by coalitions of two or more parties that unite to form a majority coalition.

Bulgaria has many political parties, and coalitions are common. In the 2014 parliamentary elections, which determined the forty-third National Assembly members, 84 of the 240 seats (or one-third) were won by the conservative, center-right party, GERB, founded in 2006 and led by Boyko Borisov, who became Bulgaria's prime minister. Thirty-nine seats went to the left-wing, democratic-socialist party the Coalition for Bulgaria, led by Mihail Mikov. Thirty-six seats were taken by the center-left Movement for Rights and Freedoms, a party interested primarily in Turkish minority interests and led by Lyutvi Mestan. Twenty-three seats were taken by center-right Reformist Bloc; 19 seats by the right-wing Patriotic Front; 15 by the populist Bulgaria without Censorship party; 11 by the far-right Attack Party; and 11 by the center-left Bulgarian Socialist Party.

Local Government

Bulgaria is divided into 28 provinces, each governed from a provincial seat by means of a provincial governor, who is appointed by Bulgaria's centralized Council of Ministers. These provinces are then divided into 264 municipalities. Each municipality is, in turn, governed by a mayor, elected to four-year terms, and an elected municipality council. These municipal governments are responsible for public safety, budgets, planning and development, environmental policy, education, and culture.

Judicial System

The judicial system, based on Roman law, includes the Supreme Administrative Court, the Supreme Court of Cassation, a Constitutional Court, and a Supreme Judicial Council. The Supreme Judicial Council consists of 25 members, and appoints the justices, prosecutors, and investigative magistrates in the judicial system.

Taxation

The government of Bulgaria levies income, value-added, corporate, capital gains, property, transfer, and inheritance taxes, among others. The country has relatively low tax rates and since in 2008, the government abolished the progressive taxation system in favor of a flat tax rate of 10 percent for both the corporate and income tax. There is no non-taxable income level, and taxes on income made worldwide must be paid in Bulgaria if a person lives there for six months or longer.

Armed Forces

The Bulgarian armed forces consist of a land force, air force, and navy. Conscription was abolished in 2008, and 18 is the minimum age for service. The number of active personnel in 2010 was 34,975 and reserve numbers were 302,500. These numbers are likely to climb, as the U.S. has begun to help Bulgaria enhance and upgrade its military infrastructure in the wake of the 2014 Ukrainian annexation by Russia, an event that has come to be known as the Crimean Crisis. As of March 2015, in preparation for potential conflicts with Russia, Bulgaria began performing bilateral drills with U.S. troops as part of Operation Atlantic Resolve.

Foreign Policy

Since achieving independence in the late 20th century, Bulgaria's foreign policy has focused on fostering relations with the Balkan region and Western Europe. In 2004, Bulgaria joined the North Atlantic Treaty Organization (NATO) and, as a member of the UN, served as a non-permanent member of the UN Security Council (UNSC) from 2002–03. Bulgaria also joined the Central European Free Trade Agreement (CEFTA) in 1998 and developed free trade agreements (FTA) with Turkey, Macedonia, Croatia, Lithuania, Estonia, Israel, Albania, and Latvia. Bulgaria joined the EU in 2007.

Bulgaria's relations with its neighbors tend to be friendly and pragmatic, with joint energy projects such as gas and oil pipelines serving as central points of cooperation. Bulgaria, Russia, and Greece signed an agreement in 2008 for the construction of an oil pipeline which will run from the seaport Alexandroupoli in Greece to Burgas in Bulgaria. However, due to the constraints of the weakening economic environment of the early 21st century, construction was delayed. In the spring of 2008, Bulgaria hosted the Southeast Europe Cooperation Process (SEECP), a program it helped launch in 1996 with the intention of promoting judicial cooperation, regional stability, and economic relations among its members.

Following the fall of communism in Bulgaria in 1989, relations between Bulgaria and the U.S. have been good, with Bulgaria maintaining a pro-Western stance. From 1990–2007, Bulgaria was a recipient of the U.S. Support for East European Democracies Act (SEED), which provided Bulgaria with over $600 million (USD) to support the development of democratic and free market institutions. (Upon its entry into the EU in 2007, Bulgaria graduated from the SEED program.) In 2006, Bulgaria signed a defense agreement with the U.S. to allow for the use of Bulgarian military bases and training camps by the U.S. army. Bulgaria also sent several hundred troops to aid coalition forces in Iraq, which were withdrawn at the end of 2008. It has also sent troops to work with international forces in Afghanistan, Bosnia and Herzegovina, and Kosovo. This partnership continues in 2015, with Bulgaria's contribution to Operation Atlantic Resolve, in which 12 U.S. Air Force A-10 Thunderbolt II aircrafts and around 200 aviators from the 354th Expeditionary Fighter Squadron deployed to Bulgaria's Graf Ignatievo Air Base and conducted drills to ensure the country's preparedness in light of the Crimean Crisis and Russia's forced annexation of Ukraine.

Bulgaria officially became part of the EU on January 1, 2007. Certain elements of Bulgarian law, notably those dealing with corruption, organized crime, and judicial reform, were deemed unsatisfactory by the EU at the time of admission. Therefore, the European Commission reviews Bulgaria's progress on these issues twice a year. The most recent detailed report was issued on 28 January 2015. It concluded that Bulgaria is committed to judicial reform and improving its fight against corruption and organized crime. Improvements to the penal procedures were noted, but the EU expressed concern that too few cases make their way through the court system. The 2015 European Commission report also indicated that some retrogression had occurred since the last report, particularly in relation to organized crime and administrative corruption, and additional work would have to be done to bring Bulgaria up to the standard of other member countries.

Human Rights Profile

International human rights law insists that states respect civil and political rights and promote an individual's economic, social, and cultural rights. The United Nations Universal Declaration on Human Rights (UDHR) is recognized as the standard for international human rights. Its authors sought the counsel of the world's great thinkers, philosophers, and religious leaders and were careful to create a document that reflects the core values shared by every world culture. (To read this document or view the articles relating to cultural human rights, click here: http://www.ohchr.org/EN/UDHR/Pages/Introduction.aspx.)

Since achieving independence, Bulgaria has drastically improved its human rights record. The National Plan for Protection against Discrimination (NPAD) was approved by the Bulgarian government in January 2008 and covers all areas of discrimination, including gender, ethnicity, and sexual orientation. However, ethnic discrimination is still a problem in Bulgaria, particularly with regards to the Roma and Turkish minorities, which, as of 2014, constituted an estimated 4.4 percent and 8.8 percent of the population, respectively. According to Amnesty International's (AI) 2013 report, Roma people continue to face discrimination in acquiring housing, education, employment, and healthcare. They were also subject to arbitrary eviction from their homes. Asylum-seekers, refugees, and migrants are also viewed with suspicion and subject to detention for months or even years before deportation.

In January 2013, the European Court of Human Rights ruled that, in Shahanov v. Bulgaria, an inmate imprisoned at Varna had been subjected to debasement due to inadequate sanitation facilities. And in the same month, in the Stanev v. Bulgaria case, the European High Court of Human Rights ruled that the country had violated six rules Article of the European Convention on Human Rights when forcing a man to live in a psychiatric institution since 2002.

In 2006, the NGO International Helsinki Federation for Human Rights expressed concern about the rise in anti-minority rhetoric and hate speech, particularly at the instigation of the right-wing Ataka (Attack) Party. In each of the 2005, 2009, and 2013 parliamentary elections, Ataka was the fourth strongest party, winning 23 of 240 total seats in 2013.

Mentally disabled people are also discriminated against with frequency. If a person is deemed mentally incompetent, regardless of the skills they may possess, they are often deprived of legal rights and placed under guardianship. Those with disabilities are typically placed in a residential institution where they run a high risk of ill-treatment. According to the Hungarian-based Mental Disabilities Advocacy Center, this process infringes on the basic rights of the mentally handicapped, such as the rights to marry, own property, work, or take legal action. Bulgaria has signed the UN Convention on the Rights of Persons with Disabilities. However, the January 2013 Stanev v. Bulgaria case noted above indicates that more work must be done to improve conditions.

Bulgaria's police force has been criticized by Amnesty International and the European Court of Human Rights (ECtHR) for the use of excessive force and ill-treatment against detainees, particularly against those of Romani descent, or based on sexual orientation. Additionally, in a review by the European Commission in February 2009, Bulgaria's judiciary was found to still not meet the EU's expectations in terms of judicial independence, autonomy, and transparency. The judiciary has been accused of corruption and a lack of checks and balances, although the EU praised Bulgaria in February 2008 for working to improve the judicial system. Yet, the EU and journalists have noted that as of 2015, Bulgaria has done very little to curb organized crime or inhibit high-level corruption. There is very little protection for prosecution witnesses, and, according to the independent online newspaper *EUObserver*, an anti-corruption official was dismissed for "trading in influence" in late 2014.

Freedom of religion is protected by the constitution, although it designates Eastern Orthodox Christianity as Bulgaria's traditional religion. The ECtHR determined in February 2009 that a decision by the Bulgarian government to take sides in a dispute involving a split in the Bulgarian Orthodox Church violated the government's responsibility to remain neutral in matters of religion. Freedom of speech is also protected by the constitution. However, in 2014, the non-governmental organization Reporters without Borders issued their annual Freedom of the Press Index, which ranked Bulgaria 100 out of 180 countries, the lowest rating of all EU members. Journalists have reported being threatened and harassed while pursuing articles dealing with issues such as corruption. Therefore, self-censorship is prevalent.

Although public education is mandatory for children until the age of 16, this requirement has not been strictly enforced, particularly with regards to the Roma community. The U.S. Department of State reported that, in 2006, nearly 10 percent of Roma children had never been to school, and 30 percent attended mostly segregated schools. NGOs have reported that institutions for children, such as those with disabilities or from indigent or abusive families, often have poor living conditions.

ECONOMY

Overview of the Economy

The global economic downturn of 2009 hurt Bulgaria's economy significantly, diminishing Bulgaria's GDP by 5.5 percent. The economy continues to struggle, with 11 percent unemployment in 2014 and nearly 22 percent of citizens living below the poverty line. However, inflation is markedly improved at –0.6 percent, and the per capita GDP has climbed to $17,100 (USD), indicating a broader financial upswing. Nevertheless, corruption in public administration, along with organized crime, is cited as major contributors to the country's slow economic recovery.

Sofia is Bulgaria's premier economic center. Most major Bulgarian businesses have their corporate headquarters in the capital and an increasing number of multinational companies are establishing offices in the city as well. Sofia is also home to Bulgaria's national bank, stock exchange, and other key financial services institutions.

Industry

Bulgaria's industrial production growth rate was 3.5 percent in 2014. Major industries include food processing, brewing and winemaking, leather goods manufacturing, and petrochemical manufacturing. Other manufacturing activity includes forklift trucks, concrete, and electronics; metals, chemicals, coke, refined petroleum and nuclear energy; and tobacco. The country produces 10 percent of the world's hydraulic machinery.

Sofia's large industrial base also turns out chemicals, rubber goods, metal products, electronics, printed materials, processed foods, textile, clothing, and shoes at more than 800 manufacturing plants. The city is also a major distribution center for the agricultural and dairy products produced by the regions surrounding the city.

The nation's exports consist largely of clothing and footwear, iron and steel, machinery and equipment, and foodstuffs. Bulgaria imports fuel (almost 100% of it from Russia in 2014), minerals and raw materials, machinery and equipment, metals and ores, chemicals and plastics, food, and textiles. Its major trading partners are Italy, Germany, Greece, Turkey, Russia, France, and the United States.

Organized crime cartels, with the help of corrupt customs officials, have used Bulgaria as an outlet for drug trafficking. The central government is cooperating with agents from Britain and other countries to combat drug trafficking.

Labor

Bulgaria has a labor force is 2.513 million. Of these workers, 35.2 percent work in industry, 7.1 percent in agriculture, and 57.7 percent in service occupations (2014 estimates).

Energy/Power/Natural Resources

Bulgaria has small underground deposits of oil and lignite coal, iron ore, copper, manganese, lead, zinc, polymetallic ores, gypsum, and salt. It has a good supply of timber, and 40 percent of the country's land is arable. There are numerous mineral and hot springs throughout Bulgaria.

Fishing

Commercial fishing in Bulgaria is largely based on the Danube River and in the Black Sea, which alone boasted 2,332 registered commercial fishing vessels. Sprattus, a tiny, oily fish similar to sardines, is a primary commercial catch for the Bulgarian fishing industry. However, aquaculture has increased in the 21st century, with rainbow trout representing 36.6 percent of Bulgaria's freshwater fish farming and common carp representing 29.5 percent.

Forestry

The state owns about 76 percent of the nation's forests. The wood processing and furniture industry contributes about 2.5 percent towards the nation's GDP.

Mining/Metals

Bulgaria's mining industry contributed 4 percent to the industrial portion of the nation's GDP in 2014. The country's natural resources include ferrous and non-ferrous metals, coal, clay, gypsum, rock salt, copper, gold, iron, steel, lead, silver, and zinc. A general decrease in mining activity was evident during the global economic crisis that began in 2008 and peaked in 2009. However, rising global prices in gold, lead, and copper facilitated a recovery in the mining industry in 2010.

Agriculture

Bulgaria's favored status in the Soviet Union won its farmers permission to work small plots of land for themselves. This contributed to the state's prosperity in the past, and has eased its transition to an independent economy. Today, the nation's farms produce vegetables and fruits (particularly grapes for wine), sugar beets and sunflowers, and cereal grains such as wheat and barley. Approximately 8,000 square kilometers (3,089 square miles) of land is irrigated.

Animal Husbandry

Livestock include cows, pigs, and poultry, with sheep on the hillsides. In the early 21st century, Bulgaria was working to restructure and upgrade its livestock sector in anticipation of EU accession.

Tourism

Tourism has recently passed agriculture as the nation's most lucrative business. Bulgaria has a well-established (and, so far, affordable) tourist infrastructure of skiing and fishing lodges, beach resorts, and health spas. History enthusiasts can explore Roman and Byzantine ruins and medieval Christian architecture and frescoes. The government has invested substantial resources into the restoration of Sofia's historic attractions and tourist infrastructure in the hopes of drawing a broad base of visitors from throughout the EU and beyond.

Popular destinations along the Black Sea Coast include Varna, Burgas, Nesebar, and Varvara, as well as Atanasovsko Lake, which is popular among birdwatchers. Popular vacation activities include cycling, mountain biking, hang gliding and paragliding. Recently, Bulgarians have been marketing their unique folk festivals, such as the Festival of Roses at Kazaniak and Karlovo, to tourists. Efforts to improve the country's infrastructure (such as a high-speed rail line); as well as develop the country's cultural tourism sector have been initiated by the government.

Despite the global economic downturn in 2009, Bulgaria's tourism industry has continued to expand. The Official Tourism Portal of Bulgaria reported that, between December 2012 and March 2013 alone, Bulgarian tourism accounted for 416 million euros, while 1,063,852 foreign visitors entered the country's borders in that three-month span, with 636,026 of them intent on enjoying leisure and recreation.

Evelyn Atkinson, Ann Parrish, &
Beverly Ballaro

DO YOU KNOW?

- The Bulgarian people follow an ancient tradition of exchanging, on the first day of March, small trinkets called martenitsas—typically tassels, pompoms, or human or animal figurines—fashioned out of twined red and white thread. According to popular lore, martenitsas convey health, prosperity, and longevity to their recipients. The *Guinness Book of World Records* lists Sofia as the home of the world's largest martenitsas ever made, 460 meters (1,509 feet) of which were wrapped around the Mall of Sofia building.

Bibliography

Donna Buchanan. *Performing Democracy: Bulgarian Music and Musicians in Transition*. Chicago, IL: University of Chicago Press, 2006.

Julian Perry. *Cicerone Guides: Walking in Bulgaria's National Parks*. Cumbria, UK: Cicerone Press, Ltd, 2010.

Linda Joyce Forristal. *Bulgarian Rhapsody: The Best of Balkan Cuisine*. Sunrise Pine Press, 2006.

Mark Baker, Chris Deliso, Richard Waters, & Richard Watkins. *Lonely Planet: Romania & Bulgaria*. Sixth ed. Melbourne, Australia: Lonely Planet, 2013.

Mary Neuberger. *The Orient Within: Muslim Minorities and the Negotiation of Nationhood in Modern Bulgaria*. Ithaca, NY: Cornell University Press, 2004.

R. J. Crampton. *A Concise History of Bulgaria*. Cambridge, UK: Cambridge University Press, 2006.

Rumen Daskalov. *The Making of a Nation in the Balkans: Historiography of the Bulgarian Revival*. Budapest: Central European UP, 2004.

Timothy Rice. *Music in Bulgaria: Experiencing Music, Expressing Culture*. Oxford, UK: Oxford UP, 2003.

Tzvetan Todorov. *Voices from the Gulag: Life and Death in Communist Bulgaria*. State College, PA: Pennsylvania State University Press, 1999.

Venelin Gane,. *Preying on the State: The Transformation of Bulgaria after 1989*. Ithaca, NY: Cornell UP, 2007.

Works Cited

_____. "U.S. Relations with Bulgaria." *Bureau of European and Eurasian Affairs: Fact Sheet*. U.S. Department of State, 28 Feb. 2014. Web. http://www.state.gov/r/pa/ei/bgn/3236.htm.

_____. "UNESCO Church in Sofia Reopens with New Frescoes." *Novinite.com: Sofia News Agency*. Novinite JSC, 4 Dec. 2006. Web. http://www.novinite.com/view_news.php?id=73564.

"About Us." Union of Bulgarian Composers. Union of Bulgarian Composers, 2009. http://www.ubc-bg.com/en/about_us.

"Bulgaria – Language, Culture, and Etiquette." *Kwintessential Cross-Cultural Solutions*. Kwintessential.co.uk, 2009. http://www.kwintessential.co.uk/resources/global-etiquette/bulgaria.html.

"Bulgaria Covered with Black Cloth on Czech Insulting Art Piece 'Entropa.'" *Novinite.com: Sofia News Agency*. Novinite JSC, 20 Jan. 2009. http://www.novinite.com/view_news.php?id=100578.

"Bulgaria." *International Helsinki Federation for Human Rights (IHF-HR)*. Report to the 61st Session of the U.N. Commission on Human Rights. IHF-HR, 2005. http://www.ihf-hr.org/documents/doc_summary.php?sec_id=58&d_id=4041.

"Bulgaria." *Map of Press Freedom*. Freedom House, 2014. https://freedomhouse.org/report/freedom-press/freedom-press-2014#.VY9HNtFRHIU.

"Bulgaria meets Lisbon criteria in women's employment." *Radio Bulgaria: Life in Bulgaria*. Radio Bulgaria, 12 Dec. 2008. http://www.bnr.bg/RadioBulgaria/Emission_English/News/en2212dkB9.htm.

"Bulgaria Travel Guide." *Virtual Tourist*. Virtual Tourist.com, Inc., 2015. Web. http://www.virtualtourist.com/travel/Europe/Bulgaria/Transportation-Bulgaria-BR-1.html.

"Bulgaria." *UNESCO World Heritage Site*. UNESCO World Heritage Centre, 2015. http://whc.unesco.org/en/statesparties/bg.

"Bulgaria—Amnesty International Report 2014/15." *Amnesty International, 2014*. https://www.amnesty.org/en/countries/europe-and-central-asia/bulgaria/.

"Bulgarian Cuisine and Recipes." *Recipes4us.co.uk*. Recipes4us.co.uk, March 2004. http://www.recipes4us.co.uk/Cooking%20by%20Country/Bulgaria%20Recipes%20Culinary%20History%20and%20Information.htm.

"Bulgarian Culture and Society." *About Bulgaria*. Embassy of Bulgaria in the United States, 1999. http://www.bulgaria-embassy.org/WebPage/About%20Bulgaria/Culture%20and%20Society.htm.

"Bulgaria: Human Rights Report." U.S. Department of State Bureau of Democracy, Human Rights, and Labor, 2013. www.state.gov/documents/organization/220473.pdf.

"Bulgarian Literature." *Art.bg*. Web Design Productions, 2003. Web. http://www.art.bg/lit.htm.

"Bulgarians." *Countries and Their Cultures*. Advameg, Inc. 2015. http://www.everyculture.com/wc/Brazil-to-Congo-Republic-of/Bulgarians.html.

"Christo and Jeanne-Claude." *Christo*, 2015. http://christojeanneclaude.net.

"Classic Bulgarian Meals." *Find Bulgarian Food*. Find Bulgarian Food LLC, 2015. Web. http://www.findbgfood.com/bgmeals.htm.

"Crisis Puts off Construction of Burgas-Alexandroupolis Oil Pipeline – Report." *Novinite.com: Sofia News Agency*. Novinite JSC, 12 Feb. 2009. Web. http://www.novinite.com/view_news.php?id=101195.

"Development of Opera in Bulgaria." University Center for International Studies, University of Pittsburgh, n.d. http://www.ucis.pitt.edu/opera/OFB/misc/develop.htm.

"Does the Government Care in Bulgaria?" *Violence Against against Women Fact Sheet*. Open Society Institute, 2006. http://www.stopvaw.org/sites/3f6d15f4-c12d-4515-8544-26b7a3a5a41e/uploads/BULGARIA_VAW_FACT_SHEET_2006_3.pdf.

"Every Other Prostitute in Brussels Is from Bulgaria's City of Sliven." *Novinite.com: Sofia News Agency*. Novinite JSC, 25 Nov. 2008. Web. http://www.novinite.com/view_news.php?id=99230.

"Good Manners in Bulgaria." *Travel Etiquette*. Travel Etiquette, 2009. Web. http://www.traveletiquette.co.uk/good-manners-bulgaria.html.

"Greg in Bulgaria." *Peace Corps Journals*. Blogger.com, 13 January 2009. Web. http://greginbulgaria.blogspot.com.

"Maps of the projects under Priority Axis I." *Organizational Programme on Transport, 2007–2013*. European Regional Development Cohesion Fund. European Union, 2013. http://www.optransport.bg/en/page.php?c=68.

"Monasteries." *Visit Bulgaria*. VisitBulgaria.com, 2015. Web. http://www.visitbulgaria.com/visitbg/index.php?cms=1&pID=10.

"Ms. W's Travels." *Peace Corps Journals*. Blogger.com, 20 May 2008. Web. http://mswstravels.blogspot.com.

"NGOs Encourage Bulgarian Parliament to Legislate to Provide Rights for People with Disabilities." *Mental Disability Advocacy Center*. Mental Disability Advocacy Center, 3 December 2008. Web. http://www.mdac.info/en/node/168.

"Office to Monitor and Combat Trafficking in Persons." *U.S. Department of State 2007 Trafficking in Persons Report – Bulgaria*. UN High Commissioner for Refugees, 12 June 2007. Web. http://www.unhcr.org/refworld/country,,USDOS,,BGR,4562d8b62,467be3a2c,0.html.

"Report on Progress under the Co-operation and Verification Mechanism in Bulgaria." *Novinite. com: Sofia News Agency*. Novinite JSC, 12 February 2009. Web. http://www.novinite.com/view_news.php?id=101191.

"Sightseeing: the Seven Rila Lakes." *Pictures of Bulgaria*. PicturesofBulgaria.com, 2005. Web. http://www.picturesofbulgaria.com/article/the_seven_rila_lakes.html.

"The Adventures of Richard and Shirley." *Peace Corps Journals*. Blogger.com, 25 September 2008. Web. http://bulgariafortwo.blogspot.com.

"The Nobel Prize in Literature, 1981 – Elias Canetti." *NobelPrize.org*. Nobel Media AB, 2015. Web. http://nobelprize.org/nobel_prizes/literature/laureates/1981/press.html.

"Total Goofs: Bulgaria Youth Hate Books, Best Versed in Pop Folk." *Novinite.com: Sofia News Agency*. Novinite JSC, 30 August 2007. http://www.novinite.com/view_news.php?id=84762.

"Traditional Wedding." *Bulgarian Travel Directory*. Journey.bg, 2009. http://en.journey.bg/bulgaria/bulgaria.php?guide=257.

"U.S. State Department: Bulgaria International Religious Freedom Report 2008." *Novinite.com: Sofia News Agency*. Novinite JSC, 23 September 2008. http://www.novinite.com/view_news.php?id=97221.

"United Nations Economic Commission for Europe." *Status of TEM Network*. United Nations Economic Commission for Europe, 2008. http://www.unece.org/trans/main/tem/temnet.html.

"Valya Balkanska." *Famous Bulgarians*. Veselin Lalev, 2008. http://www.investbulgaria.com/people/ValyaBalkanska.htm.

"Virtual Library of Bulgarian Literature Slovoto". *Slovoto*, 2015. http://www.slovo.bg/showlang.php3?ID=2.

"World Heritage Sites in Bulgaria." *World Heritage Site*, 2015. http://www.worldheritagesite.org/countries/bulgaria.html. Web. http://www.npr.org/sections/health-shots/2014/01/08/260747426/where-the-smokers-are-now-bulgaria-greece-and-macedonia.

Andrew Rettman, "EU raises alarm on Bulgaria corruption." *EUObserver*. 28 Jan. 2015. Web. https://euobserver.com/justice/127402.

Elka Agoston-Nikolova. "Post-Communist Bulgaria Challenges National Folklore Tradition." *Folklore: An electronic Journal of Folklore*. EKMFO, 19 Aug. 2008. Web. http://www.folklore.ee/Folklore/vol39/agoston.pdf.

Howard Friedman. "European Court Says Bulgaria Improperly Resolved Church Split." *Religion Clause*. Blogger.com, 13 Feb. 2009. http://religionclause.blogspot.com/2009/02/european-court-says-bulgaria-improperly.html.

Iva Dragostinova. *Politicised Culture, Identity and Nationalism in Post-Communist Bulgaria; the Chalga Discourse*. Scribd.com, 2009. http://www.scribd.com/doc/11307635/Politicised-Culture-Identity-and-Nationalism-in-PostCommunist-Bulgaria#document_metadata.

Ivan Dikov, Ivan. "Bulgaria 2008 Review: Foreign Policy." *Novinite.com: Sofia News Agency*. Novinite JSC, 2 Jan. 2009. http://www.novinite.com/view_news.php?id=100150.

Ivelina Puhaleva, Ivelina. "Charmed by UNESCO Frescos in Sofia." *Novinite.com: Sofia News Agency*. Novinite JSC, 1 Dec. 2006. http://www.novinite.com/view_news.php?id=73432.

Jeffrey Jensen Arnett, Jeffrey Jensen. *International Encyclopedia of Adolescence*. London, UK: Routledge, 2006.

Juliette Terzieff, Juliette. "Bulgarian Trafficking Victims Face Hard Homecoming." *Women's eNews.org*. Women's eNews, Inc., 26 Sept. 2004. Web. http://www.womensenews.org/article.cfm/dyn/aid/2003/context/archive.

Krassimir Martinov, . Krassimir. "Compromise between Work and Family Life." *Life in Bulgaria*. Radio Bulgaria, 10 Apr. 2006. Web. http://www.bnr.bg/RadioBulgaria/Emission_English/Theme_Lifestyle/Material/compromisewl.htm.

Liliya Sazonova, Liliya. "Bulgaria." *Stop Violence Against against Women*. The Advocates for Human Rights, 27 Oct. 2008. Web. http://www.stopvaw.org/Bulgaria2.html.

Maria Guineva, Maria. "Europe's Black Stain." *Novinite. com: Sofia News Agency*. Novinite JSC, 30 January

2009. Web. http://www.novinite.com/view_news. php?id=100854.

Milena Droumeva, Milena. "New Folk: The phenomenon of chalga in modern Bulgarian Folk." *Simon Fraser University*. Simon Fraser University, 2004. Web. http:// www.sfu.ca/~mvdroume/FPA341_term%20paper.pdf.

Olga Yoncheva. "10,000 Bulgarian Women Per per Year Victims of Human Trafficking." *News.bg*. Web Media Group News.bg, 5 Oct. 2007. Web. http://international. ibox.bg/news/id_867476283.

Peyman Nasehpour, Peyman. "The Many Names of the Doumbek – Bulgaria." *Rhythmweb*. Rhythmweb, 2002. Web. http://www.rhythmweb.com/doumbek/names.htm.

Rene Beekman. "Google search results link Bulgarian Government with failure, ruin, collapse." *The Sofia Echo*. 27 Jan. 2009. Web. http://www.sofiaecho. com/2009/01/27/666229_google-search-results-link-bulgarian-government-with-failure-ruin-collapse.

Roy Greenslade. "Why Bulgaria is the EU's lowest ranked country on press freedom index" *The Guardian*. Guardian News & Media Ltd., 23 Sept. 2014. http:// www.theguardian.com/media/greenslade/2014/sep/23/ press-freedom-bulgaria.

Rumyana Tzvetkova. "My Big Colorful Bulgarian Wedding." *Radio Bulgaria: Life in Bulgaria*. 7 Jan. 2008. http://www.bnr.bg/RadioBulgaria/Emission_ English/Theme_Lifestyle/Material/BFw.htm.

Scott Hensley. "Health Shots: Where The Smokers Are Now: Bulgaria, Greece And Macedonia." *NPR.org*. National Public Radio, 8 Jan. 2014.

Steven Ertelt. "Bulgaria Lawmakers Target High Abortion Rates, Underpopulation Problems." *Lifenews.com*. Lifenews.com, 17 Aug. 2006. http://www.lifenews.com/ nat2512.html.

Sue Bagust. "May It Fill Your Soul." *Central Europe Review*. 1.17 (18 Oct. 1999). http://www.ce-review. org/99/17/music17_bagust.html. 10 February 2009.

Bell Tower, St. Duje, Split, Croatia

CROATIA

Introduction

Croatia is located in the Balkan region of south-eastern Europe. It seceded from the Socialist Federal Republic of Yugoslavia in 1991 by a constitutional declaration of sovereignty and became The Republic of Croatia. Croatia's Mediterranean, Slavic, and European influences in governance, art, literature, and entertainment date to a time when the land was divided among three states: the Venetian Republic (an Italian state), the Austro-Hungarian Empire, and the Ottoman Empire.

Croatia's Dalmatian Coast is stunningly beautiful. Split and the coastal city of Dubrovnik, once described by poet Lord Byron (1788–1824) as "the pearl of the Adriatic," are recovering from the brutal political and ethnic conflict of the early 1990s.

Croatia's capital, Zagreb, is often referred to as a "city with a million hearts" due to its beauty and welcoming spirit. In 2005, *National Geographic* magazine named Croatia the most beautiful country in the world.

Croatia joined the European Union (EU) on July 1, 2013 to become the EU's 28th member, and on June 25, 2015, "statehood day," the country celebrated 24 years of independence. However, recent economic hardships and disillusionment with EU affiliation have begun to fuel a right-wing backlash characteristic of the fascist, ultranationalist Ustashe (or Ustaše) Croatian Revolutionary Movement of World War II.

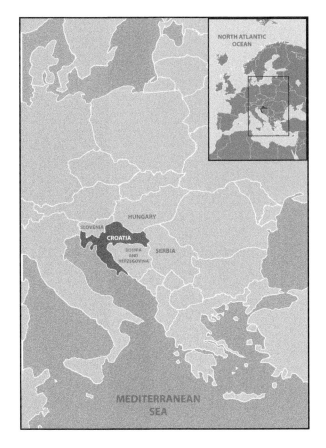

Official Language: Croatian
Population: 4,470,534 (2014 estimate)
Currency: Kuna
Coins: 100 lipa make a kuna; coins are issued in denominations of 1, 2, 5, 10, 20 and 50 lipa
Land Area: 55,974 square kilometers (21,611 square miles)
Water Area: 620 square kilometers (239 square miles)
National Motto: "Bog i Hrvati" (Croatian "God and Croats")
National Anthem: "Lijepa naša domovino" ("Our Beautiful Homeland")
Capital: Zagreb
Time Zone: GMT +1
Flag Description: Croatia's flag features three equally bold horizontal stripes of red (top), white (middle), and blue (bottom), with the Croatian coat of arms emblazoned in the center. The coat of arms is comprised of a larger shield of red and white checks, with a row of five smaller shields atop. The five smaller shields are the

---

GENERAL INFORMATION

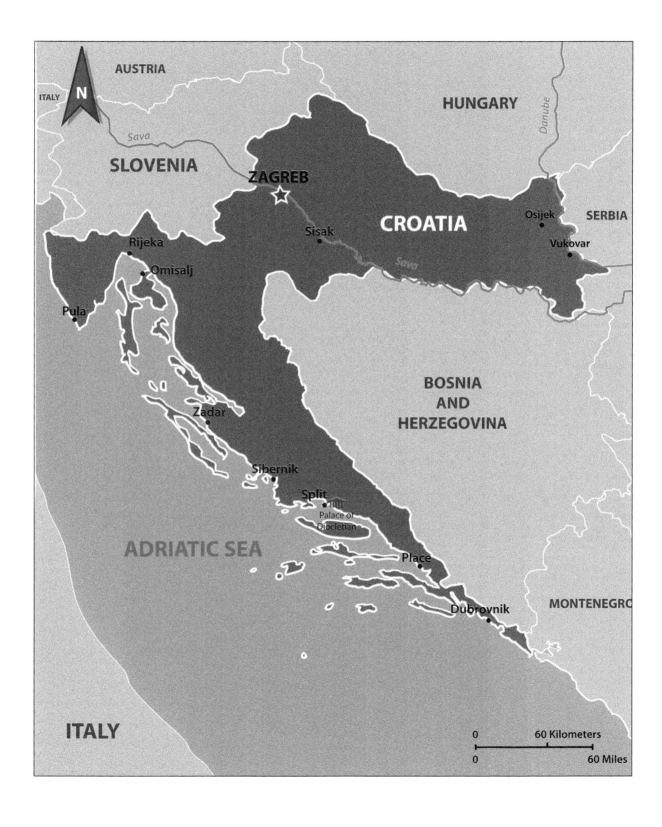

Principal Cities by Population (2011 estimates):

- Zagreb (688,163)
- Split (178,102)
- Rijecka (128,624)
- Osijek (108,048)
- Zadar (75,082)
- Sesvete (70,009)
- Slavonski Brod (53,131)
- Pula (57,460)
- Karlovac (55,705)
- Varaždin (46,946)

symbolic shields of the ancient regions of Croatia, Dubrovnik, Dalmatia, Istria, and Slavonia.

Population

Exactly 90.4 percent of those living in Croatia are ethnic Croats; a little over four percent of the population is ethnic Serbs, with the remaining population made up of Bosniaks, Hungarians, Slovenes, Czechs, and Romas.

Since the Croatian War of Independence or Homeland War (1991–1995), the Croat population has increased by over 10 percent. In 1989, 76 percent of the Croatian population self-identified as Catholic and 78 percent as ethnic Croats; 12 percent of the population self-identified as ethnic Serb and 11 percent as Orthodox Christian. Following the war for independence, the percentage of the Croatian population that self-identified as Catholic grew to 86.3 percent and the ethnic Croat population grew to just over 90 percent. The Serb population, in contrast, shrunk to 4.4 percent of the population, and 4.4 percent of the population self-identified as Orthodox Christian. This profound shift in demographics illustrates the displacement of a significant Serbian population, some killed in the conflict, some in exile, and some who have emigrated.

Croatia's population density is seventy-six people per square kilometer. Nearly 58.7 percent of Croatians live in urban areas, with most living in such large cities as Zagreb, Split, and Rijeka. Life expectancy for Croats is eighty years for women and seventy-two for men. The median age of Croats is approximately forty-two years. The infant mortality rate is 5.87 deaths per 1,000 live births.

Languages

The primary language is Croatian, a South-Slavic language that is also the official language of Vojvodina and Bosnia and Herzegovina. Croatian is spoken by around 95.6 percent of the population, but many Croats also speak or understand other languages, such as English, German, and Italian.

Native People & Ethnic Groups

Modern-day Croats trace their history back 13 centuries to a mass migration of Slavs into the region. People from Croatia are known as Croats or Croatians.

Croats comprise 90.4 percent of the population of Croatia. The next largest ethnic group are Serbs (or Serbians), who make up about 4.4 percent of the population, followed by much smaller populations of Bosniak, Hungarian, Slovene, Czech, Roma, Albanian, and Montenegrin peoples.

The main difference between ethnic Croats and ethnic Serbs is religious: Serbs are overwhelmingly members of Orthodox Christian religions (4.4 percent), while most Croats are Roman Catholics (86.3 percent).

Religions

Most Croats (86.3 percent) are Roman Catholic. Orthodox Christians, such as Serbian Orthodox and Greek Orthodox, comprise a much smaller segment of the population at 4.4 percent, followed by Muslims at 1.5 percent.

Climate

Inland northern Croatia has a continental climate, while the coastal, central, and mountainous regions are Mediterranean. Temperatures inland average 10° Celsius (50° Fahrenheit) to 15° Celsius (59° Fahrenheit) along the Adriatic coast. Warm summer temperatures along the coast, between 24° Celsius (75° Fahrenheit) and 26° Celsius (78° Fahrenheit), make this region an attractive destination for travelers.

ENVIRONMENT & GEOGRAPHY

Topography

Croatia is crescent-shaped. Within the crescent, Croatia straddles Bosnia and Herzegovina's northern and western borders. Croatia is bordered by Slovenia to the northwest, Hungary to the northeast, and Serbia to the west. The Adriatic Sea shapes Croatia's western border. On the extreme southern border, Croatian territory is interrupted by Bosnia Herzegovina's only access to the Adriatic. The city of Dubrovnik, which sits on the Adriatic, lies about 10 kilometers (6.2 miles) beyond that border and is bordered on the north and east by Bosnia Herzegovina and by Montenegro in the south.

Croatia has a diverse topography, with three main geographic regions. The eastern and northwestern regions sit among the Pannonian Alps; this area is mostly hilly and rocky. Between the Pannonian Basin and the coastal regions is a mountainous area. The Istrian and Dalmatian regions lie on the Adriatic Coast and are separated from the mainland by high mountains. Off the mainland of Croatia are 1,185 islands or islets. The highest point in Croatia is at Dinara (1,831meters/6,007 feet). Forty-six percent of Croatia is forested.

Notable rivers in Croatia include the Mirna, the Danube, and the Sava; the Lika region features several underground streams. Its two largest peninsulas are Istria and Pelješac. A vast amount of Croatia is karst, which is a type of landscape typified by sinkholes, caverns, and underground streams; within the karst, areas can be found many rare species of underground plants and animals.

Plants & Animals

Owing to its regional diversity, Croatia has a large number of native species of plants and animals. Grape vines and olive trees are abundant and economically valuable for some local industries.

The white truffle, which chefs worldwide consider one of the best tasting, is native to Istria. Black truffles also grow in that region. There are 260 indigenous species of tree in Croatia, more than are found in most of Eastern Europe. Trees commonly found in the wooded areas are beech and oak, as well as silver fir, ash, and Norway spruce. In the coastal region, there are meadows of *Posidonia oceanica*, also known as Neptune Grass.

In the lowlands region, common animals include the white-tailed eagle and the black stork, while in the coastal regions, dolphins, loggerhead turtles, and falcons are common. Endangered species native to Croatia include *canis lupus* (or common wolf), Monk seals, and marine turtles. The list of vulnerable species includes Bechstein's bat, the Eurasian otter, the garden dormouse, and others.

CUSTOMS & COURTESIES

Greetings

Formal greetings tend to vary according to the time of day and include "Dobro jutro" ("Good morning), "Dobar dan" ("Good afternoon" or "Good day"), "Dobra večer" ("Good evening"), or "Laku noć" ("Good night"). Greetings that are more general include "Zdravo" ("Hello"), "Kako ste?" ("How are you?"), and the informal "Ciao," one of coastal Croatia's many Italian borrowings. A less formal greeting, used mostly by young people, is "Bog," which literally means "God," and is used as both a greeting and farewell.

A firm handshake, with direct eye contact, is standard when first meeting someone and among acquaintances. Typically, a man should wait for a woman to extend her hand first. Close friends, and even acquaintances, will often embrace and kiss each other once on each cheek. (Unlike many cultures, the lips actually touch the cheek.) This is more common between women, or a man and a woman, than between two men.

Croats may introduce themselves by either their given names and surnames, or both. A person should be addressed in the same manner, with the addition of a professional or honorific title, if warranted. These include "Gospodin" ("Mr."), "Gospođa" ("Mrs."), and "Gospođica"

("Miss"). First names are commonly only used by close friends and family.

Gestures & Etiquette

Like many European languages, the Croatian language has two different words for "you": the informal "ti" and the formal "vi." Typically, the formal mode is used to address a person who is senior in age or status. Among near contemporaries or peers, two people will address each other formally, until the senior person suggests they use the informal mode of address. Grandparents, aunts, and cousins are typically addressed using "ti" without reference to age.

Croats use broader gestures than most Western cultures and have less sense of personal space. They touch each other frequently and stand very close while talking. They are often louder than would be polite in other cultures and swear more freely in casual conversation (with any profane language acting as an intensifier, rather than an expression of anger). Common gestures include bending down the middle and ring fingers while pointing with the index and pinkie finger, which expresses anger bordering on threat. Raising the thumb, index finger and middle finger together (as if counting three), is a gesture related to Serbian nationalism.

Hospitality is important in Croatia. When someone is offered something to eat or drink, it is considered impolite to refuse, specifically by stating "no thank you." If possible, one should accept the offer, and if it is necessary to refuse, the polite answer is "I cannot."

Eating/Meals

Croats typically eat three meals per day. The traditional breakfast is burek (or börek), a flaky pastry filled with cheese or meat and often served with freshly made yogurt. Most Croats eat a lighter meal of strong coffee, sweet pastries, yogurt, and fresh fruit. Lunch, or the midday meal, is typically the most important meal of the day, with Sunday lunch traditionally the most important weekly meal. Often eaten late, this meal is quite heavy. Because many Croats eat lunch late in the day, restaurants often serve a variety of marende (brunch-snacks) in the late morning and early afternoon. These are usually small servings of meat or fish dishes such as ćevapčići (spicy sausages made from ground beef, pork, or lamb), pljeskavica (a mixed meat patty similar to a hamburger), or ražnjići (pork shish kebab). Dinner is generally a light meal that eaten late.

Fresh bread is usually served with every meal, and meals often begin with a small glass of a local brandy or cognac. Wine is an important part of Croatian meals, though it is often diluted with water, soda, or even soft drinks. Meals typically end with small cups of coffee, either espresso in the coastal regions, or Turkish coffee in the areas once under Ottoman control. Croats use utensils in the European manner, keeping the fork in the left hand at all times and pushing food onto it with the knife.

Visiting

Because homes are small, coffee houses have traditionally provided a venue for people to entertain their friends. A meal together at a restaurant is generally limited to business settings or to show respect or gratitude, and the most common invitation is to join someone for a drink. In either case, the person extending the invitation will be expected to pay the bill, and it is typically considered impolite to split the check. However, there is a tacit understanding that if someone has been treated to dinner or drinks, he will return the favor.

Because most entertaining takes place in public venues, an invitation to someone's home is an honor. Guests customarily bring a small, wrapped gift even if the invitation is just for coffee. This practice is so common that most grocery stores offer wrapping services. Flowers are a common gift, with the exception of chrysanthemums, which are used only for funerals. The gift is given to the head of the household and is typically unwrapped later in private.

When invited to a Croatian home for dinner, guests are expected to arrive between 15 and 30 minutes later than the stated time. The meal typically includes several courses, ending with a liqueur and coffee. It is considered impolite not to finish the meal; at the very least, a guest should sample everything offered.

LIFESTYLE

Family

The traditional family unit in Croatia was patriarchal. In rural areas, clans or communities were centered on the zadruga, a patrimonial family property that was jointly owned and managed by a father and his sons. The patrilineal kin groups of the zadruga were largely dispersed during communist rule. It was generally replaced by a three-generation "stem family," typically made up of parents, children, and grandparents. The stem family remains common in rural areas, while fragmented families are the norm in urban areas. The Western-style nuclear family accounts for less than half of all households as a result of divorce, labor migration, a drop in the birth rate, and a decrease in the number of marriages.

Despite these changes in the structure of the family, family ties are still a central element of Croatian culture. For most Croats, the family circle, extended to include godparents and long-term friends, is the center of social life. Family members get together not only for major celebrations, such as holidays, christenings, and name days, but will often meet for short breaks during the workday.

Housing

During the communist period, Yugoslavians were encouraged to buy their homes. In Croatia today, housing is expensive in relation to incomes. As a result, larger homes are often shared by several generations of the same family, and young people often live with their parents for long periods, often past 30 years of age.

Traditional houses in the south are customarily built of stone. Along the coastal areas, which are typically more prosperous, homes usually have two stories. Inland, homes are commonly only one story, with reed, stone slab, or convex tile roofs. In other parts of the country, houses are typically one story high and built of oak logs, covered with wooden planks or clay mixed with chaff, and roofed with shingles, thatch, or flat tiles. In recent years, housing construction materials have shifted toward brick or concrete. In the cities, most people live in apartment buildings, ranging in style from 19th-century art nouveau buildings to high-rise apartment blocks dating from Croatia's communist period.

Food

Croatian cuisine draws on both Eastern European and Mediterranean cooking, with regional variations between the coastal and inland areas. Food in the coastal regions has been heavily influenced by Italian cooking and uses olive oil, fish, pasta, and rice. Inland, the food is heavier and is influenced by the cuisines of Hungary, Vienna, and Turkey. This type of Croatian food is often flavored with paprika and garlic. Croatian cuisine, in general, also relies on a seasoning called Vegeta, invented in 1958 by Croatian scientist Zlata Bartl (1920–2008) and added to most dishes. Sold in bulk at grocery stores, it is a compound made up of salt, sugar, cornstarch, dehydrated vegetables, and other spices.

Meat is the center of most meals, typically in the form of charcoal-grilled pork, veal chops or cutlets, or a mixed grill. Even dishes that appear to be vegetarian often include meat stock. Other popular ways to prepare meat include pašticada, a slow-cooked stew of beef and wine that is often served with Italian-style gnocchi (potato-based dumplings); turkey served with a type of pasta called mlinci; Hungarian-style goulash; and kulen, which is peppery salami from Slavonia and typically served with soft cheese, peppers, tomatoes, and pickled vegetables. Lamb is usually prepared whole on a spit roast in the sheep-rearing districts of Dalmatia and the islands.

Many traditional Croatian dishes feature sharp sheep's milk cheese, the most famous variety of which is paški sir. This is a hard cheese, similar to parmesan, from the island of Pag. Croatia is also renowned for its pršut, an air-dried Dalmatian ham similar to prosciutto. Another popular dish from the region near the Hungarian border is struckli, which consists of large pasta pockets similar to ravioli that are stuffed with cheese and baked. Mediterranean fruits (dates and figs) are also grown in season.

Croatia is known as a fine wine-producing region, with hundreds of different wines produced throughout the country. Popular types of wine-based beverages include bevanda, or red wine mixed with water, and gemischt (a German word actually meaning 'mixed'), which is wine—most often white—mixed with sparkling mineral water. Strong alcoholic drinks are popular, particularly fruit- and herb-flavored spirits, such as šljivovica (plum brandy) and maraskino (cherry-flavored liqueur). Many Croatians make flavored brandies at home.

Life's Milestones

Nearly 87 percent of Croats identify as Roman Catholic, and many rites of passage and milestones are rooted in the Catholic faith (the majority of the remaining population also identifies as Christian). This includes birth and adolescent rituals, such as baptism and communion, and marriage and funerary practices. The birth of a child is a cause for formal celebration. In addition to the rite of baptism, newborns and their families are often presented with money or a piece of gold jewelry by friends and relatives. Being asked to be a godparent to a new child is considered an honor, and often akin to becoming a member of the family.

Weddings traditionally have been the most important family and community event. They typically consist of an entire complex of ritual events in addition to the religious service. Other common traditions included the ceremonial transfer of the bride's trousseau (bridal attire and accessories) and symbolic acts by the bride on her arrival at her new home, such as holding a child in her lap, sweeping the floor, and starting a fire in the hearth. Weddings remain a lavish affair in contemporary Croatia. However, couples can choose to have either a civil or a religious ceremony, with a wedding feast the focus of the occasion. In addition, gift giving at weddings, traditionally, is competitive and reciprocal. Prior to the wedding of a child, parents will attend as many other weddings as possible to ensure a good return of gifts for their own child.

CULTURAL HISTORY

Art

For most of Croatia's history, its artists have studied in the various art capitals of Europe, most notably Venice, Vienna, and Paris. They also relied on the art patronage of Croatia's wealthy elite. Thus, few Croatian artists developed an international reputation or a distinctive style. One notable exception was the Croatian naïve art movement. Developed in the by 1930s by peasant painters Ivan Generalić (1914–1992), Ivan Rabuzin (1921–2008) and Ivan Lacković Croata (1932–2004), naïve art created socially-conscious images of peasant life using a folk-art style and techniques. The simple style and timeless themes of naïve paintings made Croatian art internationally famous in the 1950s.

Perhaps the best-known Croatian artist is the 20th century sculptor Ivan Meštrović (1883–1962). Mestrovic's style was marked by monumental, elongated figures and a taste for the heroic. His early work included bronze statues of Yugoslavian national heroes, most notably *The Kosovo Cycle* (1905). His studio is now a museum in Zagreb.

Architecture

For centuries, Croatia was an important center for architecture in the region. Its architectural heritage reflects a number of foreign influences, ranging from Romanesque and Gothic architecture from the 11th through the 15th centuries, to Baroque and Rococo architecture in the 17th and 18th centuries. The country is also known for its Roman architectural remains and its fortified medieval towns.

Croatia's architectural heritage is particularly varied because of its status during the 15th century, when the Renaissance flourished. During that time, Croatia was split between three states—the Venetian Republic (an Italian state), the Austrian Empire, and the Ottoman Empire. All of these states influenced public and religious architecture in what is now modern-day Croatia. During the 19th and 20th century, Croatian architecture was characterized by revivalist styles. The modern art nouveau movement was prominent during this period.

One distinctively Croatian architectural design form is the pleter (or troplet); a type of interwoven plait ornamentation similar to Celtic knot work that first appeared around 800 CE. It was an important element in medieval church portals and church furniture throughout Croatia. The earliest known example of the pleter appears on the baptismal font from the Holy Cross Church in Nin, the cradle of Croat settlement in the Balkans. The design has become such a pervasive national symbol that former President Franjo Tuđman (1922–1999) used it on his campaign posters to signify a return to traditional Croatian culture and a rejection of the failed ideal of Yugoslavia. Today it appears as a hatband on Croatian police uniforms.

Music
Croatian folk music, particularly from eastern Croatia, is dominated by the tamburica. This three- or five-stringed instrument is similar to a mandolin and is plucked or strummed. Beginning in the 19th century, tamburica orchestras played popular folk tunes throughout Croatia. In the 1980s, popular bands began to mix folk tunes with rock influences to create a tamburica-pop sound. This was a deliberate replacement for the folk-pop music of the former Yugoslavia. Traditional folk music remains a part of everyday life in rural Croatia, with local folklore societies dedicated to preserving songs and dances.

Croatia also enjoys a variety of regional choral traditions, derived from church choir singing. The mountain areas southwest of Zagreb are home to a dissonant form of polyphonic singing known as ojkanje or gange. A type of goatskin bagpipe and a nasal-sounding instrument similar to the oboe typically accompanies this style of singing. In the Međimurje region of northeastern Croatia, choirs of women sing unaccompanied

narrative songs of unrequited love. In coastal Dalmatia, almost every village has a polyphonic, a cappella male choir, or klapa, specializing in sentimental ballads about love, loss, and the sea.

Literature
Much of Croatia's national literature has been rooted in its history as a small nation contained within larger nation states. Despite Croatia's bloody struggle for independence from Yugoslavia throughout the 1990s, its poets and playwrights often expressed solidarity with other southern Slavs against the cultural and political domination of larger powers.

From the 15th through the 18th century, the struggle against the Ottoman Empire was a prevalent theme in narrative poems such as Marko Marulić's (1450–1524) *Judita* (written in 1501 and published in 1521), Ivan Gundulić's (1589–1638) epic poem *Osman* (1651), and Ivan Mažuranić's (1814–1890) *The Death of Smail-aga Čengić* (1846). In the 1830s, a young group of intellectuals and writers who called themselves the Illyrians created the ideal of a union of Southern Slavs within the Austro-Hungarian Empire. They saw this as a way to protect Croatian identity against the cultural imperialism of the dominant Germans and Hungarians.

Zagreb-born Miroslav Krleža (1893–1981) was the dominant figure in Croatian literature, from the creation of Yugoslavia at the end of World War I, until his death in 1981. Over his lifetime, Krleza wrote more than 40 volumes of short stories, novels, and poetry criticizing political and social injustice. His work exalted the struggles of the individual against the constraints of both bourgeois and socialist societies. His cultural criticism and his stance against socialist realism helped shape the course of Yugoslavian literature after World War II.

Under President Tuđman's regime, journalists and writers found themselves subjected to restrictions on what they could publish, similar to those suffered under communism. Possibly the most interesting literary resistance to President Tuđman's regime was the Festival of Alternative Literature. It was organized in the late 1990s by playwright and novelist Borivoj Radaković (1951–) as an alternative to the literary establishment of both the former Yugoslavia and the Republic of Croatia. It consists of a series of popular readings in cafés and discos in both Croatia and Serbia. Including writers from different generations and writing styles, the festival is held together by its rejection of both postmodern irony and nationalism.

Despite the limitations imposed by the government, writers began to explore the realities of life in the new republic. Numerous autobiographies and memoirs were published that captured images of life in the former Yugoslavia and the horrors of war. Slavenka Drakulić (1949–), in particular, built an international audience with her collections of observations on life after communism. Dubravka Ugrešić (1949–), who had already received attention in Yugoslavian literary circles in for her comic feminist novel *Fording the Stream of Consciousness* (1988), emerged as a major European writer with her explorations of change, loss, and exile in the novel *The Museum of Unconditional Surrender* (1996). Bosnian-born Croat Miljenko Jergović (1966–), author of the award-winning novel *Walnut Castles* (2003), is one of the most prominent of the younger generation of writers, and has had his work translated into over 20 languages.

CULTURE

Arts & Entertainment

In many ways, the arts in Croatia have changed drastically since the country achieved independence in the latter half of the 20th century. Though Croatian art continues to be influenced by the nation's historic crossroads, Croatian artists are re-examining their unique cultural and national heritage and exploring the realities of a country transitioning from communism, in which some artistic traditions were suppressed, toward democracy.

Croatian folk music first became an emblem of national identity in the 19th century, when members of the Illyrian movement championed

the tamburica as the symbol of a culture threatened by the Austro-Hungarian Empire. The tamburica symbolizes Croatian culture today. Tamburica musicians have since stretched the instrument's limits beyond traditional folk music to create orchestral music and tamburica-pop.

Croatia regularly hosts arts and cultural festivals, including the Music Biennale Zagreb, the Split Summer Festival—held in the ruins of the palace of Roman Emperor Diocletian, the International Folklore Festival, and the Dubrovnik Summer Festival, perhaps the country's most prestigious event.

Popular sports in Croatia include tennis, football (soccer), basketball, and handball. Among the most notable Croatian athletes in international sports are basketball players Dražen Petrović and Toni Kukoč, and football (soccer) player Davor Šuker. Croatian athletes have won Olympic medals in such sports as water polo, skiing, and basketball.

Cultural Sites & Landmarks

The United Nations Educational, Scientific, and Cultural Organization (UNESCO) recognizes seven sites in Croatia as requiring international recognition and preservation. These sites include the Historical Complex of Split (with the Palace of Diocletian), the Euphrasian Basilica in the town of Poreč, the historical cities of Trogir and Dubrovnik, the Cathedral of St. James in Šibenik, the town of Stari Grad (on the island of Hvar), and the Plitvice Lakes National Park.

The Roman Emperor Diocletian (244–311 BCE) ruled for 21 years. He took the first steps toward dividing the Roman Empire into two portions, ruled from both Rome and Constantinople. He retired to what is now the city of Split, where his palace remains. The Euphrasian Basilica at Poreč, built in the sixth century, is a good example of early Byzantine art. The basilica is known for the golden mosaics that decorate its apse (semi-circular recess, usually above the church's altar), which glitter with semi-precious stones and mother-of-pearl.

UNESCO recognized the historic center of the city of Trogir for its urban planning and its range of architecture, including Romanesque, Renaissance, and Baroque buildings.

The city of Dubrovnik was once described by poet Lord Byron (1788–1824) as "the pearl of the Adriatic." At its height during the Middle Ages, it had merchant colonies that reached from the Adriatic to the Black Sea and the third largest merchant fleet in the world. The city-state was dissolved by Napoleon in 1808, but it retained symbolic importance for 19th century Croats as a Croatian Athens. It was shelled during the Yugoslavian civil war in 1991. Today, the collection of Renaissance and Baroque churches, public buildings, and stone houses has been largely restored with the help of international funding.

The Plitvice Lakes National Park was inscribed as a World Heritage Site in 1979, though it remained endangered during the war. In fact, the national park is considered to be the place where the Croatian War of Independence (1991–1995) began. The park was recognized by UNESCO for its natural beauty, and it is home to a diverse range of flora and fauna. Since inscription, the park has been further expanded, most notably in 2000 when it was increased by another 102 square kilometers (39 square miles) in order to protect underground tributary streams. Each year, an estimated 1.1 million people visit, usually paying around 180 kuna ($32 USD) per adult admission.

Marija Bistrica is home to the largest and most important of the Catholic pilgrimage sites in Croatia, the Sanctuary of St Mary of the Snows. The church holds an early Gothic wooden statue known as the "Black Madonna with Child." According to tradition, the Madonna was bricked into the church walls in 1650 to protect it during a Turkish invasion. It was rediscovered 34 years later. The next day, the statue cured a paralyzed child, and pilgrims began to flock to the church. Today the statue is an object of veneration, attracting 600,000 visitors each year.

Libraries & Museums

Zagreb is known for its numerous museums and even claims to have more museums per square foot than any other city in the world. They include the Mimara museum, which once served as a middle school and has more than 3,750 works of art on display, including pieces by Goya and Rembrandt; the Croatian School Museum, which traces the history of education in Eastern Europe; and the Croatian History Museum. Other museums include the Zagreb City Museum, the Croatian Museum of Architecture, and museums focused on Croatian archaeology, ethnography, telecommunications, and natural history.

Holidays

Holidays in Croatia include Croatian Uprising Days and Croatian State Day (June 22 and 25), Croatian Independence Day (October 8), Christmas Day (December 25) and St. Stephen's Day (December 26).

Youth Culture

The violent upheaval of the 1990s left the country's economy in disarray, marked by high unemployment and stagnant wages. Young people are having difficulty finding jobs, forcing many to emigrate to Europe, Australia, and North America in search of work. Those who remain in Croatia often rely on the support of their family. The combined effects of the war and economic duress have also resulted in substantial differences in values and attitudes between the youth of the early 21st century and the previous generation, which came of age during the communist period. One of the biggest differences is the effect of privatization and free market principles. Youth in Croatia, now without the security provided by the communist system, are becoming more aggressively business oriented and independent.

In many regards, the youth culture of Croatia has rejected the Croatian culture that was extolled by previous generations. For example, Buddhist philosophy, particularly yoga and meditation, has become increasingly popular among young people as an alternative to the dogma and rituals of the Catholic Church. On the other hand, Serbian pop-folk music known as turbo-folk has enjoyed a renewed popularity among youth in Croatia, despite the genre's ties to Serbian nationalism in the recent past.

SOCIETY

Transportation

The most popular mode of public transportation in Croatia is the bus, and efficient bus systems exist in all major cities. Zagreb also has a tram and suburban rail system, and an inclined railway that connects the Lower and Upper Towns, though the latter operates mostly as a tourist attraction. Cabs are typically expensive and seen as a luxury. In certain cities, traffic congestion remains an ongoing problem and people prefer public transportation to driving.

Despite widespread congestion that often occurs in urban areas, private vehicle ownership continues to be perceived as a status symbol in the consumer society of post-communist Croatia. Drivers in Croatia drive on the right-hand side of the road; law requires seatbelt use, headlights are required both at night and during the day, and cell phone usage is illegal while driving (unless using a hands-free system). The U.S. Department of State claims that Croatian drivers have a reputation for driving fast, and on two-lane rural roads, this can be intimidating.

Transportation Infrastructure

There has been significant investment in road construction in the early 21st century. Various sections of the Rijeka-Zagreb Motorway (or Autocesta Rijeka–Zagreb) have been or are close to completion, and its connection with the European E65 roadway system (which starts in Sweden and ends in Greece) via the A1 is complete.

There is an extensive national railroad system (operated by Croatian Railways), but modernization of these lines has been an issue. Most Croats prefer to travel on the intercity and regional bus lines. These are considerably faster and reach towns and parts of the country that are not serviced by trains. Year-round ferries operate between the major cities along the Adriatic coast, from Rijecka to Dubrovnik, and connect the larger islands with the mainland and each other. Although Croatia has sixty-eight airports, five of which are international, Zagreb Airport is the country's main international airport.

Media & Communications

There are a limited number of national newspapers and magazines in Croatia. One company, Europapress Holding, the fastest-growing media company in southeast Europe, according to U.S.-based company, Media Monitors, publishes the two main daily newspapers, Večernji list and Jutarnji list, and most weekly and monthly periodicals. There are also several regional dailies and a popular daily tabloid, *24 Sata* (*24 Hours*). The US Department of State notes that 70 percent of local media outlets are partly or fully owned by local governments and 46 percent of local radio stations relied on funding from local governments

National commercial television and radio networks and dozens of independent local television stations successfully compete with the state-owned broadcasting system, Croatian Radio-Television (HRT), which is a member of the European Broadcasting Union. HRT1 is dedicated to news, educational programs, films, and documentaries. HRT2 concentrates on sports and foreign programs. In 2003, HRT assigned its third national network to the privately owned Nova-TV. Commercial television is largely aimed at a younger audience, with a focus on reality shows and celebrity coverage. Cable and satellite television has made significant inroads and many of the international media outlets such as HBO, Cinemax, and Fox have offerings for Croatian audiences.

Croatia has a strong cell phone network, with three primary providers—T-Mobile, Vipnet, and Tele2—and a number of smaller operators. Service is typically available nationwide, except in the mountainous regions. As of 2013, Internet users constituted an estimated 66.7 percent of the population. Internet access remains limited away from the main cities and in the southern part of the country.

SOCIAL DEVELOPMENT

Standard of Living
Croatia is ranked 47th out of 190 countries on the 2012 Human Development Index list.

Water Consumption
As in several other Eastern European nations, air and water pollution from industrial emissions is a major environmental problem for Croatia, resulting in acid rain and coastal water pollution.

Since the war of independence, Croatia has been modernizing and improving its water and sewer infrastructure, with financial assistance from the European Bank for Reconstruction and Development (EBRD). As of 2011, 98.5 percent of the population was connected to an improved water supply system, and 98.2 percent were connected to a sewage treatment plant.

Education
Croatians have a very high literacy rate: 98.9 percent for women and 99.7 percent for men. Croatian public education is typical of countries in the region, with primary and secondary education free and under the control of the Ministry of Education. The teacher-pupil ratio is 1:18. Education is compulsory for children, lasts eight years, and begins at six years of age. The net enrollment rate of primary school students is about 87 percent. Secondary education is not compulsory, although there are political initiatives to make it so.

University education is also largely free, and there are universities in the cities of Zagreb, Zadar, Split, Rijeka, and Osijek, several polytechnic universities throughout the country, and a Croatian Academy of Sciences and Arts in Zagreb.

While eight years of education are compulsory, on average in Croatia, males complete thirteen years of education, while females complete fourteen years. As a foreign language instruction begins in primary school, about half of the population speaks English and a third speaks German. Other languages include Italian, French, Russian, and Spanish.

Women's Rights
In 2006, the Croatian government adopted a national gender equality policy. It addressed questions of human rights protections, equal treatment in the labor market, gender sensitive education, actions against domestic violence, and increased participation of women in politics. The government also established the Office for Gender Equality, responsible for the fulfillment of gender equality laws and measures. However, gender equality remains a concern in the workforce, and issues such as domestic violence and human trafficking remain prevalent.

A popular Croatian proverb states, "The woman holds three corners of the house, the man just one." In practical terms, this means that a man is the legal head of the household, while women are responsible for all domestic duties and child rearing. As Croatia continues to emerge from its communist past in the early 21st century, most women expect to work outside the home, while retaining responsibility for traditional domestic duties. However, because women suffer disproportionately from Croatia's high unemployment rate, they make up only one third of the work force. Those that do find work primarily do so in the lower-paid industries, such as education or manufacturing, or in the hospitality sector.

In addition, though women tend to be better educated than men are, they are typically paid 20 to 40 percent less than their male colleagues for the same job. They seldom hold key corporate or managerial positions. They are also at a disadvantage in the job market due to Croatia's maternity leave benefit, which allow for a full salary up to six months and reduced pay thereafter. This is is often seen as an added cost by many employers. Women also continue to be underrepresented in politics, with only thirty-six women in the Croatian Parliament or 24 percent of available seats. Additionally, women continue to be the first targeted when layoffs occur.

Both domestic abuse and sexual harassment continue to be common problems in Croatian society, particularly in rural areas. In the former Yugoslavia, there were no laws to protect the victims of domestic abuse. Though laws have since been enacted to protect women against domestic violence and spousal rape, this behavior is often treated as a misdemeanor. The few cases that result in an indictment tend to receive lenient sentences. Croatia has taken steps to address this social ill, most notably by requiring authorities to maintain gender specific reports of violence. Enforcement remains sporadic at best. While the number of women who reported instances of domestic abuse has also increased, many non-governmental organizations (NGOs) estimate that more than three to one underreport instances of abuse. Human rights organizations are still struggling to protect women and children's rights, open safe houses, and provide legal services for court cases. The most recent plan to curb domestic violence is outlined in the 2008–2010 National Strategy for Protection against Domestic Violence, which calls for numerous measures to increase support to victims, provide treatment to those who commit abuse, and open shelters offering escape and refuge to abused women and children.

The trafficking of women, particularly for the commercial sex industry, also remains a problem in Croatia. Between 2002 and 2008, nearly 80 cases of human trafficking were reported, the majority of which involved young women, with estimates placing the actual number of incidents far higher. In 2013, the U.S. State Department labeled Croatia as a destination, source, and transit country for human trafficking and forced labor. In the same report, the U.S. State Department revealed that Croatia does meet the minimum requirements for the elimination of trafficking. The government also underreports cases and does not properly support victims, often making them provide difficult testimony multiple times. Prostitution is illegal in Croatia, but incidents have also been reported.

Health Care
Croatia has a universal health care system. Health care reform is a constant concern for Croatian government agencies. Health care is a guaranteed right of all Croatians, according to the country's 1990 constitution. In 1993, legislation was adopted that gave all Croats universal health care coverage, with benefits provided by a mix of state and private organizations. In 2012, 21 billion kuna was spent on health care.

Because of its history as part of a former Soviet republic, Croatia has remnants of the socialized health care system common throughout Eastern Europe. According to the World Health Organization (WHO), in 2012, Croatia's average total government spending on health care was 6.8 percent of the gross domestic product (GDP).

GOVERNMENT

Prior to the breakup of the Socialist Federal Republic of Yugoslavia, Croatia was part of a communist nation. Croatia declared its independence from Yugoslavia on June 25, 1991, and, since then, has been a presidential or parliamentary democracy.

Structure
Like the United States, Croatia has three branches of government: the executive, legislative, and judicial branches. The head of state is the President of the Republic, who appoints the Prime Minister; the Prime Minister is the head of the government. The Croatian legislature is the Hrvatski Sabor, made up of around 151 deputies who are elected by popular vote for four-year terms. Seventy-six seats are needed for a majority. Local government is comprised of 20 counties and their legislative bodies, or assemblies. The last parliamentary election was held on December 4, 2011, while the last local election occurred in 2013.

The ethnic and political conflicts that split Yugoslavia in the early 1990s, and the wars that followed, are essential to understanding modern-day Croatia. After the death of the longtime Yugoslav leader Marshal Josip Broz Tito in 1980, war erupted between the nationalist armies of Serbia, under President Milošević, and Croatia, under President Franjo Tuđman.

Major cities were shelled and attacked relentlessly by Serbian forces, leading to widespread ethnic cleansing (the violent displacement of people from a region) in such cities as Vukovar and Dubrovnik. Following ethnic cleansing (a term that originated in this conflict), Serb forces committed acts of startling atrocity against their recent compatriots, such as mass killings, rape, and torture. This became a central focus of international observers once the ethnic cleansing campaign became known worldwide.

Unfortunately, many efforts to stop these atrocities were bogged down in bureaucracy and indecision on the part of many important Croatian allies, including the United States.

Over the next few years, following successful international diplomatic and military efforts to end the conflict, an end to hostilities was reached, and the regional wars of the Balkans stopped. Nevertheless, the results of this tragedy will have repercussions for many decades to come.

Political Parties

Among the political parties operating in Croatia in the first decade of the 21st century are the Croatian Democratic Union (HDZ-center right), the Social Democratic Party of Croatia (SDP-center left), the Croatian People's Party-Liberal Democrats (HNS-center left, progressive), the Croatian Peasant Party (HSS-conservative coalition party of agricultural interests), the Istrian Democratic Assembly (IDS-left wing, socially liberal), and the Croatian Democratic Congress of Slavonia and Baranja (HDSSB-right wing nationalists). Most of these are young parties, only coming into existence following the end of the Croatian Communist Party in the early 1990s.

Parliamentary democracies often have a large number of political parties, which have a tendency to shift in terms of political platform and their alliance with other parties sharing common interests. Often, parliamentary systems are ruled by coalitions of two or more parties that unite to form a majority coalition. These coalitions differ in nature, with some coalitions having a lasting strength and others failing to govern at all. Additionally, it is not unusual for parties to dissolve because of personality conflicts within the organization.

As of the seventh parliamentary election since independence—held on December 4, 2011—the center-left Kukuriku coalition holds the majority in parliament, with 81 seats. The conservative Croatian Democratic Union (HDZ) holds 47 seats, six seats are held by the left-wing Labour Party, and six by the right-wing Croatian Democratic Alliance of Slavonia and Baranja (HDSSB).

Local Government

Local governments in Croatia are organized in two tiers. At one level, there are municipalities and communes (rural organizations that might be made up of several small towns) and counties at the second level. In general, local governments have autonomy on issues related to local affairs, such as planning and development, public utilities, infrastructure, social services, culture and sport, and environmental issues.

Judicial System

Croatia's judicial system is organized into three tiers. At the local level, there are 67 municipal courts, 21 county courts, and finally, the Supreme Court. A constitutional court is responsible for all matters related to the constitution. Croatian law reflects the shared values of its European Union neighbors. Judges are appointed by the State Judiciary Council and may remain on the bench until 70 years of age. The U.S. State Department has noted that local courts have been accused of discrimination (especially against ethnic Serbs), and others have accused the State Judiciary Council of discrimination in judicial appointments.

Taxation

Croatia employs a graduated, or progressive, tax system, meaning that income tax is based on what an individual earns; those earning more pay a higher percentage of their income towards taxes. The brackets are 12 percent on any income up to 26,400 kuna; 25 percent on income ranging from 26,400 to 105,600 kuna; and 40 percent for any income exceeding 105,600. Additionally, individuals pay a local income tax to their commune or municipality of residence. (Residents of Zagreb can pay up to 30 percent of their income towards this tax.)

Croatia also levies a value-added tax (VAT) as well as taxes on the purchase of cars, mineral oils (gasoline, heating oil), alcohol and beer, tobacco, coffee, and luxury items. A capital gains tax is levied and corporate income is subject to taxation.

Armed Forces

The Croatian Armed Forces were established in 1991, from National Guard forces. The armed forces now encompass the Croatian Army, the Croatian Navy, and the Croatian Air Force and Air Defense. In 2014, Croatian has 18,000 active personnel, some of which are participating in several United Nations peacekeeping missions. The effort in Afghanistan employs 350 Croatian servicepersons, while 15 are deployed to Chad, and seven to Pakistan. Military service has not been compulsory since 2008, and the government is working towards reducing the number of active service people.

Foreign Policy

Since Croatia declared independence in 1991, its foreign policy has focused on regional and trans-Atlantic integration and the establishment of economic ties and alliances with other democratic and transitioning nations. In particular, membership in the EU, which occurred on July 1, 2013, and the North Atlantic Treaty Organization (NATO), which occurred in April 2009, has important objectives. Croatia has also worked to normalize relations with neighboring transition countries in recent years, though some disputes are still ongoing, like border disputes with Bosnia and Herzegovina and maritime boundary disputes with Slovenia.

Before achieving membership, Croatia's main foreign policy goal had been acceptance into the EU, which the country first applied for in 2003. Accession talks had stalled in March 2005, when, among other disputes, Croatia failed to detain General Ante Gotovina (1955–). Indicted by the International Criminal Tribunal for the

Former Yugoslavia (ICTY) for his role in ethnic cleansing in the Krajina region during the military conflicts of the early 1990s, Gotovina was and is seen as a national hero by many Croats. Talks resumed in October 2005, after the chief prosecutor for the ICTY confirmed that Croatia was cooperating fully with the tribunal. Since 2005, Croatia has cooperated fully with the ICTY's investigations of allegations of war crimes committed by ethnic Croats in the Homeland War (1991–1995), including several controversial cases regarding high-ranking Croatian military officers.

In 1992, the United States recognized Croatia as an independent nation and opened an embassy in Zagreb. Croatia now has diplomatic relations with 174 countries. It maintains 51 embassies and 24 consulates abroad and has eight permanent diplomatic missions. Within Croatia, there are 52 foreign embassies and sixty-nine consulates. Many other foreign organizations, such as UNICEF, the World Bank, the International Criminal Tribunal for the former Yugoslavia, and the World Health Organization, maintain administrative offices within the country.

Between 1998 and 2008, the U.S. provided Croatia with an estimated $18 million (USD) (with a total of $52 million (USD) for the broader Balkans region as of 2014) for removing active land mines, as well as funding economic recovery through Southeastern Europe Economic Development (SEED) and U.S. Agency for International Development (USAID) programs. Croatia has also received financial assistance from the International Monetary Fund (IMF), the International Bank for Reconstruction and Development (IBRD), and the European Bank for Reconstruction and Development (EBRD).

Although trade relationships between the former Balkan countries are growing, Croatia's relationships with the other countries that made up the former Yugoslavia remain sensitive, particularly the relationship with Serbia. Conflicts regarding the status of several thousand people who are still missing from the Homeland War, and disputes with Bosnia and Herzegovina and

Slovenia over land and maritime borders, remain volatile. Croatia continues to build its regional and international profile, becoming a founding member of the Union for the Mediterranean and a non-permanent member of the UN Security Council (UNSC).

Human Rights Profile

International human rights law insists that states respect civil and political rights and promote an individual's economic, social, and cultural rights. The United Nations Universal Declaration on Human Rights (UDHR) is recognized as the standard for international human rights. Its authors sought the counsel of the world's great thinkers, philosophers, and religious leaders and were careful to create a document that reflects the core values shared by every world culture. (To read this document or view the articles relating to cultural human rights, go to http://www.ohchr.org/EN/UDHR/Pages/Introduction.aspx.)

The early years of the new Republic of Croatia, under the leadership of President Tuđman, were marred by systematic government attacks on individuals' civil and political rights. Since Tuđman's death in 1999 and Croatia's transition to a parliamentary government system in 2000 (the constitution was amended in 2001, reducing the power of the president), the country has made considerable progress in the observance of international human rights laws and standards.

The Croatian constitution prohibits discrimination based on gender, age, race, disability, language, or social status, as required by Article 2 of the UDHR. The constitution also guarantees eight seats in parliament for ethnic minorities, three for Serbs, and one each for several smaller minority populations. (The coalition government that came to power in the 2008 election was the first to include an ethnic Serb in its cabinet.) Nonetheless, discrimination against women and Croatia's ethnic and religious minorities remains a problem. Serbs make up the largest minority population in Croatia, and the one that suffers the most active discrimination. Much of the discrimination is a residual effect of the Homeland Wars, in which both the Serbian and Croatian forces were accused of widespread war crimes. It is also related to issues such as impunity and fair prosecution for war crimes, property restitution programs, and slow resolution of problems with permanent residency status. Serbs also continue to suffer from hate crimes and acts of violence, often directed at the Serbian Orthodox Church. Other ethnic minorities that have been subject to discrimination to a lesser degree include Jews, Italians, Austrians, Czechs, and Romani.

The Croatian constitution provides for freedom of religion, as called for in Article 18 of the declaration. While there is no legally established state religion, the Roman Catholic Church has considerable political influence. The Catholic religion is one of the primary ways in which Croats distinguish themselves from Serbs, and about 86.3 percent of the population identifies itself as Catholic. Religion classes are also part of the elementary school curriculum. Attendance is optional, but refusal to attend often results in social problems for students and their families.

The press was an official mouthpiece of the government in communist-run Yugoslavia. It continued to be deferential to the new Croatian government under the leadership of President Tuđman in the 1990s. Croatia's new constitution bans censorship and guarantees freedom of the press as outlined in article 19 of the UDHR. Largely, that ideal has been implemented. However, some officials sometimes continue to use libel laws to control the press, and both the national and local governments control large portions of the Croatia's broadcast media.

The Croatian government passed the Law on the Right of Access to Information in February 2013 in order to meet EU requirements. However, in 2014, the non-governmental watchdog organization Freedom House, still designated Croatia's press only "partly free," citing the country's criminalization of libel, its toleration of journalists' persecution, the five-year imprisonment that comes with hate speech, and the three-year sentence that accompanies any insult to Croatia itself, its flag, anthem, or coat of arms.

Migration

After the long period of military conflict with Serbia, many Serbs left Croatia, with the result that their population was severely diminished to around 4.4 percent.

Prior to the declaration of Croatian independence from Yugoslavia in 1991, 12 percent of Croats were ethnic Serbs. By 2001, there were nearly 400,000 fewer Serbians in Croatia than there had been in 1991, Many ethnic Serbs never returned to their homes in Croatia.

ECONOMY

Overview of the Economy

The U.S. Central Intelligence Agency estimates that the gross domestic product (GDP) for Croatia in 2014 was $87.67 billion (USD). Its GDP per capita was an estimated $20,400 for the same year, and the industrial production growth rate was 1.2 percent. The war in the 1990s nearly destroyed the economic stability of the region, and it has taken many years for recovery to begin. More recently, criticism has been leveled at government investment in failing industries, such as shipbuilding, as well as inadequate handling of corruption and organized crime. However, on July 1, 2013, Croatia became the 28th member of the European Union.

Zagreb is the economic center of Croatia, with numerous manufacturing and processing industries, including a prosperous chemical industry and the production of both petroleum and natural gas. It is also a major producer of machinery, electronics, pharmaceutical products, and several food products, while other industries include wood processing, leather and textiles, and printing. Zagreb's economy is considered relatively strong, with the average monthly salary for citizens being about 5,430 kuna (around $800 (USD) in 2015), which is higher than the national average. Overall, the economy of Zagreb, and Croatia as a whole, is relatively affluent compared to most other Eastern European nations and capitals.

The city is an important trade center in Croatia as well and hosts an annual International Trade Fair. Its position near the border of the Balkan Peninsula means Zagreb is a major trade hub between Central and Eastern Europe. Croatia's main trading partners include Italy, Germany, Bosnia and Herzegovina, Slovenia, Austria, and Serbia.

Industry

The Croatian economy rests on three major industries, the services sector, which accounts for almost 68.9 percent of the economy, industry (26.6 percent), and agriculture (4.5 percent). Many of Croatia's industries were forced to rebuild following the wars of the 1990s. Infrastructure expenditures, as well as restoration of some of Croatia's more popular tourist destinations, have helped to revitalize the tourist industry. Croatia's manufacturing sector produces such goods as chemicals and plastics, machine tools, electronics, and food and beverages. Croatia is also a major shipbuilder among European countries, although, in 2010, the shipping industry began experiencing a serious decline, and the EU cut the country's production capacity by half to meet fair competition standards. Because of these caps, Croatia's oldest shipyard, Kraljevica, went bankrupt. Several state-owned shipyards are currently for sale and faltering privatization efforts have resulted in Croatia pouring one billion euros of taxpayer money into restructuring capital, intended to entice ambivalent buyers.

Croatia is a major exporter of transport equipment, coke (by-product of coal), and refined products, textiles, and electrical and optical equipment. Its major export partners are Italy, Bosnia and Herzegovina, Germany, Slovenia, Austria, and Serbia.

Labor

In 2014, the US CIA estimates that the Croatian workforce numbered 1.725 million people. Of that number, more than 70.4 percent found work in the services industry, 27.6 percent in industry, and 1.9 percent in agriculture. As of 2014, Croatia had an estimated unemployment rate of around 19.7 percent of the workforce, which was higher than the EU rate of 11.5 percent in November 2014.

Energy/Power/Natural Resources

Natural resources in Croatia include petroleum and coal, hydropower. In 2005, Croatia, the EU, and several other Balkan nations signed the Energy Community Treaty, an effort to create an integrated EU energy (specifically electricity and gas) market. In force since its ratification by the European Parliament on May 29, 2006, the treaty has prompted energy infrastructure investment in the Balkan region. In October 2013, the Energy Community Ministerial Council chose to extend the treaty by ten years, to 2026.

Fishing

With over 5,600 kilometers of coastline and more than 1,000 islands, fishing in the Adriatic is both a key feature of the tourism industry, but also a viable industry, although one in decline. Croatia has found itself in several international conflicts with its Adriatic neighbors, namely the Italian government, over maritime borders. Incidents involving Italian fishing vessels in 2008 and 2010 highlight conflicts that Croatian officials have had regarding a protective zone off the coast, concerns of overfishing, and maritime borders. In 2013, commercial fishers also encountered financial hardship because of EU laws, imposed since Croatia's accession. These laws require anglers to purchase new nets and tools that fit EU specifications—at an expense that can run as much as $20,000 (USD)—and something for which the fishers were neither prepared nor compensated.

The fishing industry still accounts for about one percent of the nation's GDP. Despite having been in the country for nearly 20 years,

tuna farming is still a developing industry. Kali Tuna, founded in 1996 by Croatians returning from Australia with aquaculture experience, has since grown to be one of Croatia's largest Bluefin farms, with six farming sites near the Dalmatian Islands. However, in November 2014, Kali was sold to Japanese-based fish-farming giant Umami. Many other fish farms are family-owned and produce bass, bream, mussels, and oysters.

Forestry

Around 46 percent of Croatia is forested. Twenty-three percent of this forest is privately owned, while 77 percent is publicly owned and managed by either a state-owned forest company or other state agency. Over 40 percent of privately owned forests have management plans in place, in order to control tree-fellings. Around 97 percent of Croatian forests are natural, self-regenerating forests, while three percent are plantations. Broadleaf forests predominate at 75 percent, six percent are coniferous, and 19 percent are mixed. The most common species of tree are beech and oak.

Mining/Metals

Croatia's mined resources include bauxite, iron ore, china clay, calcium, natural asphalt, silica, mica, and salt.

Agriculture

Croatian agricultural products include wheat, corn, sugar beets, sunflower seeds, and fruits, such as grapes and citrus. However, despite this range of agricultural production, Croatia has had to import many products to meet the needs of all Croats.

In 2003, the Agriculture Competitiveness Enhancement program was started to help modernize Croatia's agricultural industry. In the first year alone, the agricultural economy grew nearly three percent. In 2010, the EU conducted a farm census, which it performs every 10 years. Croatia, which had undergone a similar farm survey in 2007 prior to accession, was part of this member reassessment. The country was determined to have 233,280 farms and 3.2 million agriculturally cultivated acres, or 23.3 percent of Croatia's total land area. Land worked by the owner was approximately 54 percent, while land worked by tenants was nearly 46 percent. Most Croatian farms are considered small, running an average of 13 acres.

Animal Husbandry

In Croatia, livestock generally includes pigs, cattle, chickens, goats, and sheep. Croatian slavonski kulen (salami) and dalmatinski pršut (ham) are valued meat products. Livestock is a major aspect of the agricultural sector, with many family farms and small producers dominating the industry.

Tourism

Like many other businesses, the tourist industry in Croatia was severely damaged by the wars of the 1990s. However, it underwent some improvement between 2001 and 2004: revenue from tourism increased from around $4 billion to more than $8 billion per year, and efforts have been underway since the 1990s to make Croatia a more popular tourist destination.

Croatia has always been renowned for its beaches with 1,773 kilometers (1,104 miles) of mainland coastline. Its entire western border is the Adriatic Sea. However, like many Eastern European nations, it also boasts many important historical and cultural attractions. Popular tourist destinations in Croatia include the coastal city of Dubrovnik, which is listed as a UNESCO World Heritage Site; the resort island of Mljet; the Istrian town of Pula, the site of the Croatia's Pula Film Festival; and the archaeological sites in the town of Krapina. Remains of medieval villages, castles, and other fortified towns are common throughout the country and can be found in places like the truffle-rich, Central Istria town known as Oprtalj; the art center Groznjan; Motovun, famous for its annual film festival; and the southern Dalmatian town of Korcula.

Considered one of central Europe's oldest cities, Zagreb is undergoing rapid development in the early 21st century, but maintains a reputation among tourists as a quiet, tranquil alternative to other modern European capitals.

Pamela Toler, Craig Belanger, &
Alex K. Rich

DO YOU KNOW?

- Croatia was the first country to recognize officially the fledgling United States after its independence from Great Britain in 1776. Zagreb began as two separate settlements called Kaptol and Gradec, situated on adjacent hills, and was established as early as the 11th century CE. The name Zagreb was first used to refer to this area in 1094, when a Roman Catholic bishop established a diocese under that name. Famous Croatians include racecar driver Mario Andretti (born in Montona, Kingdom of Italy; now Motovun, Croatia), tennis player Goran Ivanišević, and actor Goran Višnjić ("ER"). Others who can boast Croatian descent include former Nirvana bassist Krist Novoselic and political commentator Mary Matalin.

Bibliography

Celia Hawkesworth. *Zagreb: A Cultural History*. Oxford: Oxford University Press, 2008.

David Devos. *Magic Kingdom*. Smithsonian. January 2003.

Department of Defense. *Croatia in Perspective – Orientation Guide and Croatian Cultural Orientation: Zagreb, Dubrovnik. Split, Danube, Yugoslav, Slavic – Geography, History, Military, Religion, Catholicism, Traditions.* Progressive Management Publishing, 2015.

Dubravka Ugrešić, Dubravka. *The Museum of Unconditional Surrender*. Transl. Celia Hawkesworth. New York: New Directions, 2002.

Irina Ban. *Croatia – Culture Smart! The Essential Guide to Customs & Culture*. London: Kuperard, 2008.

Karen Evenden. *A Taste of Croatia*. Ojai, CA: New Oak Press, 2007.

Marcus Tanner. *Croatia: A Nation Forged in War*. Third ed. New Haven: Yale University Press, 2010.

Robert Kaplan. *Balkan Ghosts: A Journey Through History*. New York: Picador, 2005

Sharon Fisher. *Political Change in Post-Communist Slovakia and Croatia: From Nationalist to Europeanist*. New York: Palgrave Macmillan, 2006.

Slavenka Drakulic. *Café Europa: Life after Communism*. Zagreb: V.B.Z. Zagreb, 2014. The Best of Croatian Literature Ser.

Stephen Lavington and Francis Gooding, eds. *Croatia: Through Writers' Eyes*. London: Eland, 2006.

Tony Fabijancic. *Croatia: Travels in an Undiscovered Country*. Edmonton: University of Alberta Press, 2003.

Works Cited

_____. "Croatia." *Bureau of Democracy, Human Rights, and Labor*. U.S. Department of State, 11 Mar. 2008. Web.. http://www.state.gov/g/drl/rls/hrrpt/2007/100553.htm.

"Bureau of European and Eurasian Affairs: Fact Sheet." *U.S. Relations with Croatia*. U.S. Department of State, 29 Jul. 2014.

"Croatia Country Profile." BBC. *BBC News*. BBC, 23 Jan. 2012. http://news.bbc.co.uk/2/hi/europe/country_profiles/1097128.stm

"Croatia." *Croatian National Tourist Board, 2015*. Web. http://us.croatia.hr/Home/.

"Croatia." *2014 Freedom of Press Scores. Freedom House, 2015*. Web. https://freedomhouse.org/report/freedom-press/2014/croatia#.VY6HK9FRHIV.

"Croatia: Great Ecological Diversity." *Confédération Européenne des Propriétaires Forestiers*. *"Croatia: Great Ecological Diversity." CEPF.* Confédération Européenne des Propriétaires Forestiers, 2015. Web. http://www.cepf-eu.org/side.cfm?ID_kanal=96.

"Croatia." *The World Factbook*. Central Intelligence Agency, 2015. https://www.cia.gov/library/publications/the-world-factbook/geos/hr.html

"DK Publishing. DK Eyewitness Travel Guide: Croatia." New York: DK Publishing, Inc, 2015.

"Embassy of the Republic of Croatia in the USA." *Washington, DC. Republic of Croatia Ministry of Foreign and European Affairs, 2015.* Washington, DC. http://us.mvep.hr/en/.

"Republic of Croatia, 2015." Croatian Bureau of Statistics. Republic of Croatia, 2015. http://www.dzs.hr/default_e.htm

"Structure of agriculture in Croatia." *Eurostat: Statistics Explained*. Eurostat, 23 Feb. 2015. http://ec.europa.eu/eurostat/statistics-explained/index.php/Structure_of_agriculture_in_Croatia. http://www.state.gov/r/pa/ei/bgn/3166.htm.

Anja Mutic, Anja & Peter Dragicevich. *Lonely Planet Croatia*. London: Lonely Planet, 2015.

Irina Ban. *Croatia – Culture Smart! The Essential Guide to Customs & Culture*. London: Kuperard, 2008.

Celia Hawkesworth. *Zagreb: A Cultural History*. Oxford, UK: Oxford UP. 2008.

Dusan Stojanovic & Darko Bandic. "Far-Right Surges in Croatia as EU Disappointment Spreads." *ABC News*. ABC News Internet Ventures, 23 Jun. 2015. *ABC News*. http://abcnews.go.com/International/wireStory/surges-croatia-eu-disappointment-spreads-31959446?singlePage=true

James Stewart. *Croatia*. London, UK: Cadogan Guides, London, UK: 2009.

Jonathan Bousfield. *The Rough Guide to Croatia*. London: Rough Guides, 2013.

Josko Balamaric. *World Heritage Sites in Croatia: Exhibition Marking the 25th Anniversary of the 1st Croatian Heritage Sites on The World Heritage List*. Zagreb: Ministry of Culture of the Republic of Croatia, 2004.

Linda Bennett, ed. *Encyclopedia of World Cultures*. Vol 5. Europe. Boston: G. K. Hall & Company, 1991–96.

Michael Powell. *Behave Yourself! The Essential Guide to International Etiquette*. Guilford, Connecticut: The Globe Pequot Press, 2005.

Svanibor Pettan, ed. *Music, Politics, and War: Views from Croatia*. Zagreb: Institute of Ethnology and Folklore Research, 1998.

Traditional dancing costumes in Paphos, Cyprus

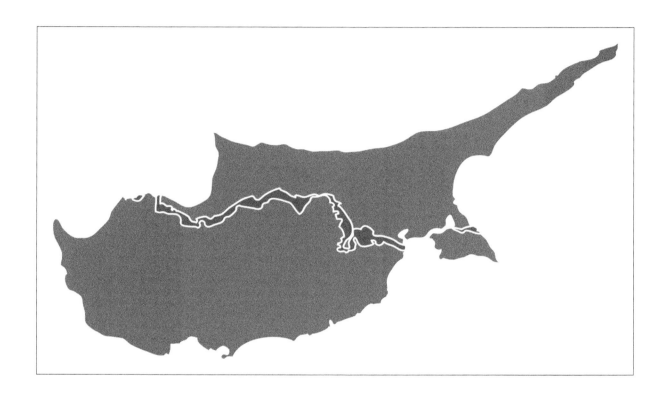

CYPRUS

Introduction

The Republic of Cyprus is an island nation in the eastern Mediterranean Sea. Situated between Europe and Asia, the island of Cyprus has been controlled by many peoples through the ages. During the late 14th and early 15th centuries, Cyprus was a cultural capital. During this period, many French musicians lived and worked in Nicosia, the capital, leaving their mark on Cypriot music. The culture of Cyprus also borrows heavily from both Greek and Turkish influences.

Today, the island is, in effect, two separate states. However, most of the world recognizes it as only one nation, the Republic of Cyprus (ROC). Only Turkey recognizes the Turkish Republic of Northern Cyprus (TRNC). The ROC is a member of the European Union, and Cypriots of both states are recognized as European citizens. Since 1974, a United Nations peacekeeping force has patrolled the Green Line, a buffer zone between the two areas.

Cyprus is heavily dependent on tourism, which makes the economy vulnerable to fluctuations in world financial conditions. On January 1, 2008, Cyprus joined the European Union (EU); the Turkish Republic of Northern Cyprus, dependent on and recognized only by Turkey, has yet to be recognized by both the EU and the United Nations (UN).

In 2012 and 2013, Cyprus experienced a financial crisis from which it is still recovering. After non-performing loans rose to high levels in 2011, the banking sector began to fail. Emergency loans from Russia, the European Central Bank, and the International Monetary Fund, among others, helped prop up the banking sector in Cyprus. ATMs rationed cash and citizens' money was seized by the Cypriot government to secure financial stability. For this reason and due to consistently high unemployment levels, Cypriots remain financially uneasy.

GENERAL INFORMATION

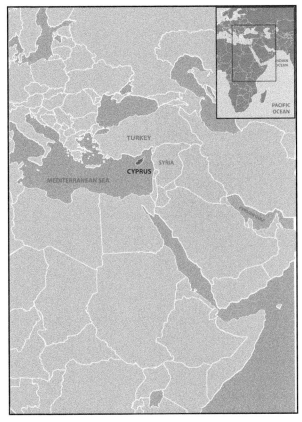

Official Language: Greek and Turkish
Population: 1,141,166 (2013 estimate)
Currency: Euro
Coins: The Euro is available in 1, 2, 5, 10, 20, and 50-cent coins. A 1 and 2 Euro coin is also available.

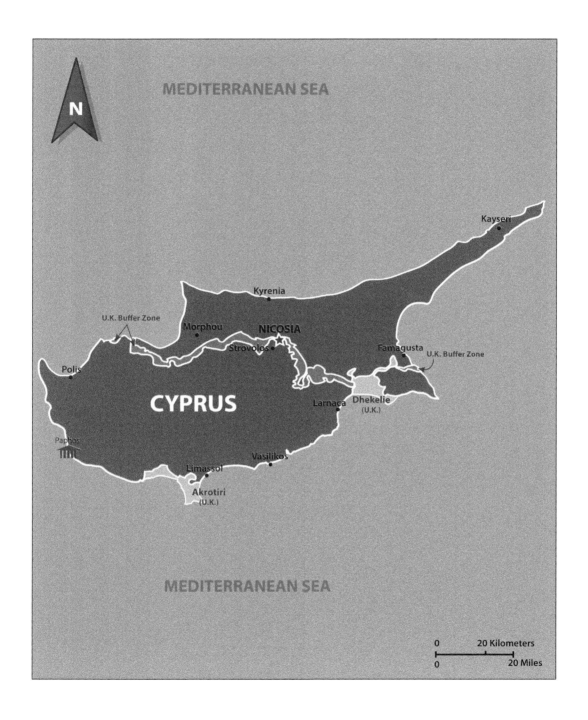

Principal Cities by Population (2011):

- Nicosia (239,277)
- Limassol (235,056)
- Lefkoşa (TRNC) (82,539)
- Gazimağusa (TRNC) (69,838)
- Larnaca (51,468)
- Paphos (32,892)
- Kyrenia (also Girne) (TRNC) (20,851)

Land Area: 9,241 square kilometers (3,567 square miles)
Water Area: 10 square kilometers (3 square miles)
National Anthem: The Greek national anthem, "Hymn to Freedom," is used.
Capital: Nicosia (Lefkoşa in Turkish)
Time Zone: GMT +2
Flag Description: The flag of the Republic of Cyprus depicts a copper-colored silhouette of the island nation suspended over two crossed green laurel leaves on a white background. The laurel leaves represent the country's hope for peace between its Turkish and Greek citizens.

Population

The Greek and Turkish components of Cyprus' population are divided mainly along the lines of language and religion. The ethnic composition of the island is about 77 percent Greek (mostly in the south) and 18 percent Turkish (mostly in the north). The remainder of the population is comprised of other minority groups. Greeks, Brits, and Russians are the largest ethnic immigrant groups, with small minorities of Palestinian, Armenian, Bulgarian, Filipino, Lebanese, and Kurdish communities. Since Cyprus joined the European Union (EU) in 2008, there has been an influx of immigrants from Poland and other Eastern European countries.

The largest city on the island is the capital, Nicosia (Lefkoşa in Turkish), with a total population of around 239,277 people (2011 estimate), not including close to 82,539 in the northern part. It is the considered the capital of both the ROC and the TRNC. Other large cities and towns include Limassol, Larnaca, and Paphos.

Famagusta (Gazimağusa) is the only major town in the TRNC. Roughly two-thirds of the population lives in urban areas.

The village of Pyla, in the eastern part of the ROC and one of only four villages in the UN Buffer Zone, is still populated by both its original Greek and Turkish Cypriot families, and boasts three churches and one mosque.

Language

In the ROC, 92 percent of the people are Greek Cypriot, and Greek is the dominant language. In the TRNC, 99 percent of the people are Turkish Cypriots, who primarily speak Turkish. English is commonly spoken in both sectors.

Native People & Ethnic Groups

Cyprus has been inhabited since prehistoric times, with the Greeks arriving around the 12th century BCE. Through the ages, the island has been conquered and controlled by the Phoenicians, the Egyptians, the Assyrians, the Persians, the Macedonians, the Romans, the Byzantines, the Venetians, the Ottoman Turks, and the British.

Modern Cyprus is composed mainly of descendants of the island's Greek and Turkish occupiers. The two groups are similar culturally. Both emphasize family honor and loyalty, but there are differences between urban and rural populations. City dwellers usually dress in Western clothing, but in the countryside, some men wear traditional highly decorated vests and baggy black trousers. The trousers are called brakas (or braccae) in Greek, and şalvar in Turkish. Some countrywomen wear short blouses and long sarkas, or skirts.

Religions

The majority of the Greek residents on the island are members of the Cypriot Orthodox Church (about 89.1 percent) and Nicosia is the spiritual center for many of the church's archbishops. The Cypriot Orthodox Greeks in Nicosia are considered some of the most devout Christians in Europe, with large percentages of the population regularly attending services. Most Turkish

Cypriots are Muslim, accounting for about 1.8 percent of the total population. Also in Cyprus, 2.9 percent identify themselves as Roman Catholic, two percent are Protestant or Anglican, and one percent is Buddhist.

Climate

Cyprus' Mediterranean climate means hot, dry summers, rainy winters, and high humidity. Autumn and spring are the shortest seasons. Nicosia, at the foot of the Kyrenia Mountains, experiences temperatures varying from 5° Celsius (41° Fahrenheit) in the winter to 36° Celsius (97° Fahrenheit) in the summer. Temperatures on the plains may reach 38° Celsius (100° Fahrenheit) during the summer.

The average annual rainfall amounts to about 100 centimeters (39.4 inches), but there is considerable variation from one year to the next. Elevation also affects rainfall. While the plains receive an average of 30 to 40 centimeters (12–16 inches) per year, some parts of the Troödos Mountains see up to 133 centimeters (52.3 inches). The Troödos also experience winter snow.

The summer months are hot and dry in Nicosia, and the city is entirely reliant on dams and irrigation for drinking water. Winter rains serve to fill the reservoirs, but the average annual rainfall on the entire island is a paltry 345 millimeters (13.6 inches). The climate of Nicosia is Mediterranean, with average temperatures in the summer months reaching 28° Celsius (82.8° Fahrenheit). Winter months are generally cooler, averaging a daily temperature of 10.5° Celsius (50.9° Fahrenheit).

ENVIRONMENT & GEOGRAPHY

Topography

The third largest island in the Mediterranean (after Sicily and Sardinia), Cyprus lies in the northeastern corner of the sea, 465 kilometers (40 miles) south of Turkey, 760 kilometers (470 miles) southeast of Greece, and 95 kilometers (60 miles) west of Syria. Cyprus is geographically part of Asia.

The Republic of Cyprus, in the southern part of the island, comprises 5,896 square kilometers (2,276 square miles) of the country's area. The Turkish Republic of Northern Cyprus, occupying the northern third of the island, accounts for 3,355 square kilometers (1,295 square miles).

The Kyrenia Mountains rise along the northern coast, and the rugged Troödos Mountains are in the south. In between the two mountain ranges lies the Mesaoria Plain. The plain provides the country's primary agricultural land, and the majority of the island's population lives in this area. In addition, several small plains lie along the southern coast.

The highest point in Cyprus is Mount Olympus, rising 1,952 meters (6,404 feet) above sea level in the Troödos Mountains. This should not be confused with the Mount Olympus of Greek mythology, which is located in Greece.

Nicosia is located in the center of Cyprus in an area known as the Mesaoria Plain. The Mesaoria is a flat and barren plain isolated from the rest of the island by the Troödos Mountains, the Kyrenia Mountains, and the Mediterranean Sea to the west. The plain is actually the ancient seabed that separated the Troödos and Kyrenia Mountains. Nicosia sits at an elevation of 220 meters (721 feet). A buffer zone, known as the Green Line, runs through the center of Cyprus, dividing the Turkish Cypriot and Greek Cypriot communities. Often referred to as the "Dead Zone," this UN-sanctioned barrier is only several meters wide in Nicosia, but fairly wide outside of the city and includes an abandoned international airport.

Plants & Animals

Despite its small size, Cyprus enjoys substantial biodiversity. Up to 1,800 flowering plant species are found on the island, 126 of which are endemic (growing naturally only there).

Tree species include cypress, oak, cedar, and forests of Aleppo pine. Although much of the island's forests have been destroyed, some have been replaced with "maquis," or herbal and evergreen shrub growths, which are often aromatic and thorny. Examples include Phoenician juniper, arbutus, and rockrose.

Cyprus is also home to more than 380 bird species and 298 fish species, as well as many species of reptiles, amphibians, and land mammals. Several species of mites, insects, crabs, and sponges are also found on the island.

The Cyprus mouflon, having existed in abundance since the Hellenistic and Roman periods, is the largest wild animal on the island. This rare wild sheep, endemic to Cyprus, is also the national symbol, appearing on the country's coins. Long endangered, the mouflon is a protected species today.

Its position in the Mediterranean makes Cyprus a natural stopover spot for migratory birds. Eleonora's falcon and the imperial eagle are birds of prey native to Cyprus. The green turtle and the loggerhead turtle, both of which breed on the beaches of the Akamas Peninsula, are found in the waters surrounding Cyprus. Monk seals also live in the waters, breeding in the caves along coast.

CUSTOMS & COURTESIES

Greetings

The island of Cyprus is divided between two main ethnic groups: Greek Cypriots in the southern two-thirds of the nation and Turkish Cypriots in the northern third. The country has operated as two separate entities since the Turks invaded in 1974. In the northern sector, Turkish language and customs and the Islamic religion are prevalent. Greek language, customs, and Eastern Orthodox Christianity characterize the southern sector. However, English is spoken widely, and most Cypriots are bi- or multi-lingual.

Despite linguistic differences, the customary greetings between Turkish and Greek Cypriots are similar. During a greeting, two parties generally shake hands and maintain direct eye contact. Turkish Cypriots may drop their eyes after the initial greeting as a sign of respect. In addition, it is important to recognize that Muslim men may not shake hands with a woman in accord with their faith. (It should also be noted that the left hand is not traditionally used in Muslim culture when greeting or interacting, as it is used for the cleansing of the body and thus considered impure.) In general, it is customary to shake hands with everyone when greeting them or leaving their company. The amount of familiarity shown when greeting depends on the relationship between parties and their relative age and social status.

Gestures & Etiquette

Overall, Cypriots are friendly, open people who maintain an easy approach to their interactions. This holds true in both Turkish and Greek communities, as both do not observe strict lines of personal space. As such, casual contact may be common when greeting or conversing. When meeting an unfamiliar person, one should wait for an invitation before using the person's first name. In addition, gift-giving is not a significant event, and people generally wait to open gifts rather than doing so on receipt.

Respect is customarily shown to those in positions of authority, and an extension of mutual trust, often shown through eye contact, is essential to communications. Also, Cypriots tend to avoid confrontation. Among Turkish Muslims, personal hygiene and orderliness of dress are taken quite seriously. In general, people engage in specific, but simple rituals of cleaning before prayers and meals, regardless of faith.

Eating/Meals

Meals are an important part of the day's activities and social interactions. Most Cypriots take a small breakfast in the morning, a midday lunch in the afternoon, and have their largest meal later in the evening. This final meal of the day can last for hours and is a time for appreciation and interaction. The appetizer, called meze, is often a crucial and central part of dinner.

Most Cypriot meals include fresh fruits and vegetables as well as grilled or stewed fish or meat. Cypriots often drink tea or coffee with their breakfast as well as after other meals. In Cyprus, coffee is served thick and sweet and often in the Turkish style, in which coffee beans are ground into a fine powder and mixed in a small pot with the desired amount of sugar and boiling water (and then boiled twice more). The latter is traditionally prepared right before serving and is served in small cups in one of three ways—sade (unsweetened), orta (somewhat sweet), and şekerli (very sweet). Cypriots also customarily serve and drink cold water with their coffee.

Cypriots eat in the continental style: the fork is held in the left hand and the knife in the right. Traditionally, if a person has not finished eating, he or she should cross the knife and fork on his or her plate, with the fork on top. Once finished, the knife and fork are placed next to each other along the side of the plate. Among Muslim persons, food and drink may only be handled with the right hand (due to the left hand's association with the cleansing of the body). Muslims are also restricted in the types of food they consume and refrain from pork and alcohol. Additionally, meat must come from animals that eat only plants and that have been slaughtered in an appropriate fashion. Such approved foods are called halal.

Visiting

When visiting a person's home, it is customary to bring a small gift, such as pastries. Lilies are not given as gifts because they are a funerary flower. Most home gatherings are somewhat casual, and guests are expected to dress neatly but informally. (Visitors at churches, monasteries, or official gathering are expected to dress more formally and may include the covering of a woman's arms.) Guests commonly compliment their hosts' home, and it is polite to offer to help with the preparation of a meal or the cleanup after a meal.

When gathering for dinner, one should stand until invited to sit. The oldest members of the group or guests of honor are served first. Individuals pass dishes with the right hand only, and it is expected that everyone will be offered second and even third helpings. Diners are also expected to finish the food on their plate.

LIFESTYLE

Family

Family forms the core of Cypriot society and has traditionally been considered the focal point of social structure and interaction. Strong familial ties and the value of extended family still characterize contemporary Cyprus, even though most modern homes are structured around the nuclear family (a couple and their children).

Family members are expected to respect their elders, and children are expected to care for their parents as they age or when they become ill. Likewise, extended family members are expected to help relatives in need. Though most Cypriot families no longer live as closely as they once did, parents and grandparents maintain close bonds with children and grandchildren.

Traditionally, matchmakers and parents arranged marriages. Though this is less common today, family members, especially in rural communities, still have a strong influence on the spousal choices of their children. In the past, families sought to give their children dowries upon marriage. While this is still practiced, contemporary provisions may be portions of family land, a house, furnishings, or money. Often, the families of both the bride and groom may sign a written dowry contract specifying what each family will provide the newlywed couple.

The divorce rate has almost doubled since the mid-20th century, but the number of extramarital births and single parents is still relatively low compared to other countries. Attitudes about marriage and family have relaxed somewhat and young adults are waiting longer to marry. This is also because more women are choosing to pursue higher education and professions. As Cypriot society has become urban and modern, the average size of families has also decreased, with more couples choosing to have no more than three children.

Housing

Historically, Cyprus has been a predominantly rural society, with most people settled in farms and villages. Homes were built from available resources, such as stone and sun-dried mud bricks. As people became more prosperous, their homes increased in size and were made from materials such as brick and concrete. The 20th century saw an increase in urbanization, with the majority of the population shifting to urban areas.

Following the Turkish invasion of 1974, Cyprus became divided. This division caused the displacement of thousands of families. Greeks in the north fled to the south and Turks fled north, all of them becoming refugees within their own country. A housing crisis resulted, and the governments of both sectors have been struggling to address this in the decades since. Cypriot government in the south has enacted programs to build low-cost housing for displaced persons in the cities or to temporarily house families in homes abandoned by the Turks. The government also provides aid in the form of rent subsidies for thousands of these internal refugees as well as for other low-income families.

Food

Cypriot cuisine and diet has evolved over the centuries as a result of the island's natural resources and its patterns of colonization. Notable culinary influences include Greek and Turkish cuisine, as well as other European and Asian traditions. Highly agricultural, Cyprus relies heavily on fresh fruits and vegetables, including grapes, citrus fruits, strawberries, melons, prickly pears, olives, tomatoes, and onions. The kolokas, a sweet root vegetable that has the texture of a potato when cooked, is also popular. Fruits and vegetables accompany most meals and are often prepared as main dishes, but Cypriots also consume fish and meat. Lamb is the most popular meat on the island, and Cypriots prefer goat and sheep to cattle (beef is rare). Most dishes are grilled or cooked in soups, stews, and casseroles. Fresh salads and yogurt are also common.

The most popular dish served in Cyprus is the meze, a collection of small appetizer-like items, including salads, vegetables, dips, and grilled meat or fish. The meze may be served as an appetizer or as the main dish. Other favorite dishes include halloumi cheese, pourgouri (boiled cracked wheat), hiromeri (a leg of pork pressed and smoked), kleftiko (lamb baked in an oven), sucuk or soutzoukos (a sweet made from grape juice and almonds). Additionally, avgholemono (an egg-lemon soup), moussaka (a mix of ground beef and spices baked and then layered between slices of eggplant), and tzatziki (a mix of yogurt and cucumber) are favorites. A common Turkish dish is yalanci dolma (grape vine leaves stuffed with onions; rice; herbs; and, sometimes, tomatoes).

Cypriots also enjoy a wide variety of desserts, especially pastries. Baklava, inherited from the island's Turkish roots, is a pastry made with thin, sweet filo dough, chopped nuts, and syrup or honey. Other traditional desserts include kataifi (another type of pastry made with a honeyed syrup), loukoumi, commonly called Turkish delight (a jelly-like or gum-like treat covered with powdered sugar). Loukoumades (or lokma in Turkish) are fried dough balls similar to doughnuts dipped in syrup or honey and cinnamon.

In addition to coffee and tea, wine is also a staple beverage among Greeks on Cyprus. The island has a long tradition of viniculture, or grape cultivation. Vineyards have been producing wines for thousands of years, and numerous local vineyards continue to operate.

Life's Milestones

Despite the divide between Turkish and Greek Cypriots and the presence of several minority groups, such as Armenians and Roma, Cypriot society is homogenous in terms of its life milestones. Education is crucial among all communities on the island, and the focus of a child's upbringing is to complete primary and secondary schooling. Generally, parents work to secure the best education possible for their children.

Following the completion of school around the age of seventeen, most young adults either advance into the workforce or pursue a higher education. Those who go on to college or university generally study abroad, most often in Greece or Turkey. Children are not considered independent of their parents until they have established their own households, most often through marriage. In this way, Cypriot society is conventional. In most cases, marriage is the defining line between childhood and adulthood.

Most Greek Cypriots align with Eastern Orthodox Christianity and observe the common practices of Western Christian faiths, such as baptism, communion, marriage, and funerary traditions. Children are baptized, or initiated into the Christian faith, soon after birth. Around 99 percent of Turkish Cypriots are Sunni Muslims. At birth, the Call to Prayer is whispered into a baby's ear to bring the infant to know Allah (God). A naming ceremony soon follows, often within the first week of life. For both Christian and Muslim Cypriots, marriage remains the major milestone.

CULTURAL HISTORY

Art

As with Cypriot architecture, the artistic heritage of Cyprus is a hybrid of European, Middle Eastern, and North African influences. Cyprus has a great wealth of ancient art in the form of pottery, sculpture, mosaics, and frescoes. Ancient Greeks, Romans, and other civilizations left traces of these artistic traditions among their ruins and numerous other folk arts. Archaeological museums in Cyprus highlight artifacts from Cyprus's distinct prehistoric and historic eras. The Lusignan, Venetian, and Byzantine periods also brought a variety of artistic influences. Much of this early and medieval art was religious in nature, such as icon paintings that honored Christian saints and other religious figures. The Ottoman influence is particularly evident at the Mevlevî ekke (also known as the Museum of the Whirling Dervishes or the Cyprus Turkish Museum) in northern Cyprus. The museum is a hallmark to Ottoman architecture and displays numerous Turkish artifacts, including Islamic calligraphy, weaponry, textiles, and musical instruments.

Architecture

The distinctive architecture of Cyprus reflects the Mediterranean island's diverse artistic heritage. Its style ranges from antiquity to modernism. Drawing on 10,000 years of history, the landscape of Cyprus is marked by the archaeological remains of many ancient civilizations. These include ancient Greece and Rome as well as the Byzantine and Persian empires. French Gothic, Turkish, and Islamic architectural styles are also evident.

The ancient Greeks brought rich mythological traditions with them to the island. They built grand temples to their deities, the remains of which can be found throughout the island (particularly in the region around Paphos, located on Cyprus' southwest coast). Many ruins on the island are also Persian and Roman in nature and include temples, tombs, theaters, and palaces. The influences of other ancient colonizers, such as the Phoenicians, the Assyrians, and the Egyptians, can also be seen. When the Roman Empire split in 395 CE, Cyprus passed under the rule of the eastern Byzantine Empire. Their architecture was a continuation of the Roman style, but was further defined by the erection of Christian churches and the use of architectural elements such as domes and ornate mosaics. Byzantine architecture also recycled many of the stonework and sites formerly occupied by ancient cultures. The region around Kyrenia bears many marks of Byzantine influence, including Kyrenia Castle, St. Hilarion Castle, and numerous chapels and monasteries.

In the 12th century, during the period of the Crusades, Cyprus came under the control of Christian Europe, most notably Guy of Lusignan (c. 1150–1194), a crusader who purchased the island in 1192. For three centuries, French Gothic cathedrals and military forts and castles that were constructed over older sites characterized the architecture of the island. Monuments from this era include Bellapais Monastery in Kyrenia, Kantara Castle, and Othello Castle near Famagusta. The Venetians ruled Cyprus for a short time during the 15th century. Many signs of their influence remain, including the great forts and stone walls built around many Cypriot towns. The Ottoman Turks ruled Cyprus for three centuries and brought with them a great deal of Islamic art, literature, and music, as well as an architectural style that blends Persian, Arab, and European influences.

Just as earlier peoples had done, the Turks rebuilt over existing sites, converting numerous ancient and medieval chapels and cathedrals into mosques. Among these, the Arab Ahmet Mosque in North Nicosia displays the hallmarks of classic Islamic architecture: dome, minarets, arched terraces, gardens, and fountain. The Selimiye Mosque, also in North Nicosia, reveals elements of both its French Gothic and Turkish Islamic influences. Other notable Ottoman structures include the Dervis Pasa Mansion and two caravanserai (inns especially built for traders and other travelers): the Gamblers' Inn (Kumarcılar Hanı) and the Great Inn (Büyük Han).

The Ottomans ceded control of Cyprus to Britain in 1878. From there, the modern era of building began, ushering in the use of new materials, such as steel, brick, and concrete. Given the nation's history of earthquake damage, many buildings are now designed with earthquake resistance in mind.

Music & Dance

Musical styles in Cyprus are grounded in the island's Greek heritage, but combine elements from other cultures as well. Cypriot melodies are less complex than many Western traditions and are based on a system of note scales called tropos, or modes. Like other Greek musical styles, most Cypriot music tends to follow and build upon established patterns. Musicians are commonly expected to improvise during their performances. During the Lusignan period (1191–1489), French musicians introduced the *ars subtilior* ("a more subtle art") style of music, which entailed a more complicated series of rhythms and notes. The Ottomans likewise brought Islamic traditions and the stylized music of the sultans' courts to the island. Turkish performers are also heavily improvisational.

Cypriot music has long served to enrich religious and other ceremonies, public gatherings, and festivities, such as weddings and the recitation of poems and stories. Cypriot music is commonly played on violins and traditional instruments, such as the laouto, the pidkiavli, and the tampoutsia. The laouto is a lute with four sets of double strings and is traditionally played with the quill of an eagle or vulture. The pidkiavli is a kind of flute made from reed and wood, played by shepherds in the field. The tampoutsia is a drum made from wood and goatskin, played with the hands or two sticks, and provides the rhythm of the music. Contemporary instruments include the guitar, accordion, and the bouzouki. Like the laouto, the bouzouki is a kind of lute that has a long neck and a pear-shaped body and sounds like a mandolin.

Cypriot music has been passed from generation to generation orally. Until recent times, the music has not been written down in scores. However, this is changing, and an effort is underway to document Cyprus's music traditions. Modern music blends the folk music of the past with Turkish and Greek pop music and international styles.

The dance traditions of Cyprus extend from the island's Greek roots and have evolved by drawing on the traditional dances and heritages of other occupying cultures. Traditionally, dance was performed to express high emotion and celebrate festivities, ceremonies, harvests, and other public events. Dancers were usually male, who performed at public events and ceremonies as well as other small gatherings; women were mostly limited to dancing at weddings.

Cypriot dances are performed in a sequence of movements by pairs of dancers, often two men, or two women, who face each other. They involve complicated footwork and include the stamping of feet and animated improvisation. Men performing solo dances will often do so with an object such as a sickle or knife in hand. Common dances performed in Cyprus include the kartzilamades, the tsamiko, the kalamatiano, the zeibekikos, the sousta, and the syrtos. The most popular dance, kartzilamas, features a sequence of male and female dancers who perform five movements, respectively. Each movement involves distinctive patterns of steps and music.

Literature & Drama

Cyprus not only plays a role in the classic literature of the ancient world, but also draws heavily on its own traditions. First settled by the Greeks of Peloponnesus (the southernmost peninsula of Greece), Cyprus and Cypriots earned a place in early Greek literature and drama. As the mythological birthplace of the deity Aphrodite, and as an island nestled between Greece and her trading partners in Asia and North Africa, Cyprus is referenced in Homer's epics, the *Iliad* and the *Odyssey*, as well as in Thucydides' *History of the Peloponnesian War.*

Early Cypriots carried on the epic traditions of their forebears. Cypriot literature began as an oral tradition, with bards singing epic and lyric poetry. Most lyric poetry was composed in the ionic meter, with four syllables (two short and two long) per metric foot, or line. Poets from mainland Greece and later native poets staged performances at temples across the island and in other public spaces. Over time, poets, philosophers, and other Greek Cypriots began writing down their verse and histories, including the *Kypria*, an epic poem attributed to Stasinos of Cyprus and written in the seventh century BCE. It relates the legendary origins of the island and the events of the Trojan War that predate the Homeric accounts. Cyprus is also the birthplace of the ancient philosopher Zeno of Citium (334–262 BCE), founder of the Stoic school of thought and whose philosophy emphasized the rule of reason over emotion.

Mainland Greek authors and playwrights were also widely read and performed on Cyprus. The plays of Sophocles (c. 496–406 BCE) and Euripides (c. 480–406 BCE) were popular and were enacted along with local plays at theaters erected in Salamis, Kourion, and Soloi.

Over time, each succeeding culture would bring its own literary traditions and influences. The Lusignans brought French literature, the Venetians brought Italian poetic traditions, including the works of Petrarch (1304–1374),

and the Ottomans introduced Turkish poetry and Islamic literature. Turkish poets called meddah frequented the courts and circles of the upper classes, reciting poems that blended Arabic and Persian traditions. In the late 19th century, British influence brought new literary and dramatic forms to the island. Shakespearean drama remains a prominent part of the Cypriot stage today.

CULTURE

Arts & Entertainment

Cypriot arts continue to hold aesthetic, functional, and spiritual roles in society. Moreover, while Cypriots continue to produce many fine works of visual art, literature, music, and theater, the island still has a strong tradition of folk arts. The people of Cyprus are especially renowned for lacemaking (particularly in the Lefkara region), silversmithing, and jewelry making. Other folk arts include weaving, pottery, copper, and brass works, woodworking, and silk works. The hallmarks of these particular handicrafts include Yemeni head scarves, which are hand made with fine cotton in patterns of flowers, leaves, and branches; silk works that feature detailed images woven into black and red fabric; pottery that includes hand-painted vessels and pitharia (giant earthenware jars); and hand-woven and embroidered rugs.

With a strong legacy of classical, Islamic, and European literature and drama, modern authors and playwrights in Cyprus continue to pursue traditional poetic, prose, and dramatic forms. Small presses and local literary journals endeavor to highlight Cypriot authors. The peace movement in Cyprus has worked to find common ground between Turkish and Greek Cypriots through poetry. Ancient theaters have been restored and new theaters built to continue the nation's dramatic traditions. The Cyprus Theater Organization, sponsored by the government, stages both classical and contemporary plays by Cypriot playwrights. Cyprus also has a lively and growing film industry in both its northern and southern regions. In 2006, the nation held its first international film festival, known as CYIFF or Cyprus Film Days. The country also held its first international short film festival (ISFFC), which will enter its fifth year in October 2015.

The favorite team sport in Cyprus is football (soccer); Cyprus has a national team that competes in the Olympics. Because of its mild climate, Cyprus often hosts northern and central European football and swim teams for winter training. Other common pastimes among Cypriots include hiking in the country, water sports, sailing, and winter sports in the Troödos Mountains.

Cultural Sites & Landmarks

The United Nations Educational, Scientific, and Cultural Organization (UNESCO) has recognized three World Heritage Sites in Cyprus, requiring international recognition and preservation efforts.

The first is the city of Paphos, which was included on the World Heritage List in 1980. Paphos is an ancient port replete with ruins, monuments, artwork, and numerous other features of past civilization. Believed to be inhabited as early as 10,000 years ago, Paphos is home to many ancient structures, including theaters, palaces, fortresses, tombs, and villas erected by the Mycenaeans of ancient Greece and other ancient peoples. The site also includes notable medieval churches and fortresses, including the Saranta Kolones, the Paphos Medieval Fort, the Agia Solomoni Church, the Church of Panagia Theoskepasti, and the Panagia Chrysopolitissa Church.

The second World Heritage Site is that of the Painted Churches in the Troödos Region. Situated in the Troödos Mountains in western Cyprus, this site actually comprises nine churches and one monastery from the Byzantine era of Cypriot history. These 10 structures all feature remarkable Byzantine frescoes and are notable for their humble exteriors, which contrast sharply with the remarkable paintings inside. Built from stone, wood, and thatch, they were designed to withstand the fierce elements of the mountainous climate.

The third World Heritage Site is Choirokoitia, also known as Khirokitia. Settlement at Choirokoitia dates back to Neolithic times (nearly 10,000 years ago), and the site has only been partially excavated and examined. Limited studies have revealed that early inhabitants at the archaeological site lived an agrarian lifestyle. They also buried their dead beneath the floors of the houses in which they lived, presumably to keep deceased family members close.

Several other historic and cultural sites in Cyprus have also been nominated as World Heritage Sites. These include three churches to be added to the existing Painted Churches site in the Troödos Region; three five-domed Byzantine churches located at Geroskipou and Peristerona; the rural settlement of Fikardou, Klirou Bridge, and Malounta Bridge; the villages of Kionia and Khandria (or Chandria); and Mount Olympus, the highest peak on the island at 1,952 meters (6,404 feet).

Libraries & Museums

Museums of note in the capital, Nicosia (Lefkoşa in Turkish), include the Cyprus Museum, the Byzantine Museum and Art Galleries, and the Cyprus Folk Art Museum. In North Cyprus, Nicosia is home to the National Struggle Museum, which opened its newest building in 2001 and presents documentary material from those who fought against imposed British imperialism.

The Cyprus Library, in Nicosia, serves as the national library of the island country. While the library's origin dates back to 1927, it was officially established in 1987. The State Archives of Cyprus, established in 1991, are also located in the capital.

Holidays

As with most everything else, holidays in Cyprus often vary between the Greek and Turkish sectors. Official holidays in the ROC include Greek Independence Day (March 25); the Anniversary of Cyprus Liberation Struggle, or Cyprus National Day (April 1); Cyprus Independence

Day (October 1); and Greek National Day (October 28).

Holidays specific to the TRNC include Peace and Freedom Day, or the anniversary of the 1974 Turkish invasion (July 20); Social Resistance Day (August 1); Turkish Republic Day (October 29); and Turkish Republic of Northern Cyprus Day (November 15).

Youth Culture

Family life and education form the primary components of youth culture in Cyprus. Cyprus has a thriving music and film industry that engages older youth, and dance clubs are common in major cities. The island offers numerous recreational opportunities, and youth may participate in numerous sports, notably football (soccer) and basketball. The Cyprus Sports Organization has built stadiums, pools, and other sports facilities and sponsors numerous sports teams and leagues. Among lower-class families and in rural areas, children are more likely to work on farms and in family businesses, but child labor in non-family industries is restricted.

Young people in the early 21st century have grown up in a relatively secure, peaceful environment, without the conflicts and struggles of earlier generations. This has enabled them to focus more on their educational and leisure pursuits. They have also been raised in an increasingly global world where modern technology, such as the Internet, exposes them to a wider breadth of culture and attitudes. As a result, Cypriot youth combine the traditions of their families, communities, and ethnic and religious heritages with the international influences of media and entertainment.

SOCIETY

Transportation

Buses are perhaps the most popular mode of public transportation, and run along most of the roadways. Generally, rural buses are operated locally and may only run once or twice a day. Regional bus companies also offer transportation, and buses within cities operate regularly. Bicycling

and foot traffic are also common. Traffic moves on the left side of the road.

Transportation Infrastructure

Transportation in Cyprus is conducted primarily along the island's vast network of roads, as there is no functioning railway system. In 1994, Cyprus completed a highway connecting Nicosia, Anthoupolis, and Kokkini Trimithia and has continued to expand on the highway system since that time. Sea and air transportation connects Cyprus to the rest of the world. Three international airports—at Larnaca and Paphos in the Greek sector and at Tymbou in the Turkish sector, called Ercan International Airport—carry passengers to and from Europe and other destinations. Sixteen regional airports and ten heliports operate within the country. Ship transport is largely foreign owned.

Media & Communications

Cyprus has nearly ten daily and nearly 30 weekly newspapers, mostly published in Greek, with *Phileleftheros* (meaning "The Liberal") the most widely read. There are two English dailies, *Cyprus Mail* and *Cyprus Reporter*, and over ten Turkish-language dailies, such as *Kıbrıs Postası*, in Northern Cyprus. Mainland Turkish dailies are also popular in Turkish areas. Periodicals, radio, and television programming are published and broadcasted in English and their native languages. The Cyprus Broadcasting Corporation (CyBC) is the island's public broadcaster, and there are a number of privatized entities. Generally, Cypriots have access to international television and radio broadcasts. Self-censorship has increased in recent years, and there are more allegations of censorship in the northern part of the country.

In the 1990s, the Greek sector installed fiber-optic cables under the sea and satellite linkup facilities, enabling expanded access to telecommunications; both sectors of the island are well connected in this regard. In 2013, 65.5 percent of the total population had a subscription to an Internet service provider or broadband service via an ADSL (asymmetrical digital subscriber line).

SOCIAL DEVELOPMENT

Standard of Living
Cyprus ranked fortieth out of 190 countries on the 2012 United Nations Human Development Index, which measures quality of life and standard of living indicators.

Water Consumption
According to UNICEF (United Nations International Children's Emergency Fund), 100 percent of Cyprus's residents enjoy improved access to clean water and adequate sanitation. Yet, Cyprus' main ecological problems involve water. There are no natural reservoirs on the island, and rainfall is irregular, even during the rainy season. In addition, seawater has entered the largest aquifer on the island, resulting in increased salination of the water in the north. Sewage and industrial wastes have polluted the island's water. As of 2010, the country reached what some are calling "peak water," when demand for water exceeds what natural resources are able to supply. Desalinization plants have been built, and a great deal of Cyprus' drinking water is now desalinated seawater. Other potential options to curb the crisis is water rationing and a proposed water pipeline from Turkey, but the latter cannot be separated from political issues.

Education
Both elementary and secondary education is free in Cyprus. In the ROC, elementary education is compulsory for children between the ages of six and 15 and children must attend school between seven and 15 years of age in the TRNC.

Secondary education lasts for six years. The first three years, at a gymnasium, are compulsory. The second three years are optional and are provided at lyceums or at technical schools. There are also a few comprehensive secondary schools, which offer all six years of secondary instruction.

In the Turkish section, students between the ages of 12 and 14 attend secondary-junior school. Lyceums and vocational schools provide secondary education for 15 to 17 year-olds.

The University of Cyprus in Nicosia, established in 1989 and admitting its first students in 1992, is the only university in the Greek part of the island. The largest of the four universities in the Turkish section is Eastern Mediterranean University in Famagusta.

The literacy rate in Greek Cyprus is 98.7 percent overall (99.3 percent among men, and 98.1 percent among women). Literacy rates are similarly high in the TRNC. Cyprus's educational success is attributed to the country's percent of GDP dedicated to educational spending, at seven percent, among the highest allocations in the European Union. Additionally, Cyprus boasts a working population of which more than 30 percent have attained higher education. Many Cypriots choose to pursue degrees outside of the country.

Women's Rights
Cyprus has traditionally been a patriarchal society in which the roles of men and women are clearly defined. Men dominate the public and professional sphere, and women operate largely in a domestic capacity. Though women have always worked alongside men, they have experienced limited educational and professional opportunities, suffered from discrimination in hiring and wage earning, and been subject to sexual harassment. In recent decades, as more women have entered a wider variety of fields in the workforce, women have made substantial gains in these areas.

Cypriot women now have greater access to education in Cyprus and abroad and hold more professional positions, though those positions are largely in the health and educational sectors. Under law, in both the republic and the TRNC, women have the same legal status as men and have the same rights under property and family law and in the judiciary. Still, women typically earn as much as 25 to 30 percent less than male counterparts. They also continued to suffer high levels of sexual harassment in the workplace and remain underrepresented in managerial positions. Women are still underrepresented politically as well. As of 2013, in the republic, only 11 women held seats in the 56-member parliament. In the TRNC, only four women held seats in the 50-member parliament that same year. In 2009, the mayor of Nicosia was one of only four women in Europe to lead an EU capital. Women held a few senior positions in the republic's executive and judicial branches, but none in the TRNC's.

Women in Cyprus continue to be the victims of human trafficking, sexual exploitation, and violence, including spousal abuse and rape. Despite laws and international agreements prohibiting human trafficking, Cyprus has become a destination country for women trafficked from Eastern and Central Europe, Asia, and Latin America. Many of these women were recruited to work as dancers or on artists' visas. However, once transported, they were often compelled to work in the sex industry. Efforts to combat trafficking in Cyprus have been minimal.

In both the republic and in the TRNC, laws prohibit spousal abuse and rape, but enforcement in both sectors is weak. Cultural and societal mores limit the number of cases reported, investigated, and prosecuted. In the TRNC, incidents of spousal abuse are considered family matters and rarely reported. In 2007, no cases of abuse were tried. In the republic, procedures exist for reporting and prosecuting abuse, but many victims are reluctant to report or to testify. However, medical and education professionals are required to report suspected cases of abuse.

In the republic, the National Mechanism for Women's Rights of the Ministry of Justice and Public Order is charged with advancing women's interests; in the TRNC, no government office exists to safeguard women's rights. Cyprus' feminist movement, which began in the 1990s, has been gaining ground, but is still widely regarded with derision—by both men and women. In general, women are still regarded as responsible for domestic duties and child rearing, even when working outside the home. As prosperity, technology, and urbanization increase, attitudes regarding women's status are relaxing.

Health Care

In 2014, life expectancy in Cyprus is roughly 75 years for men and 81 years for women, and slightly lower in the Turkish section. Through a focus on preventative medicine, diseases such as malaria, tuberculosis, and echinococcus have been nearly eliminated in Cyprus. Cypriot women receive free pap smears and mammograms.

In both the ROC and TRNC, there is roughly one doctor for every 500 people. Annual health expenditures in ROC as of 2013 are 7.4 percent of the GDP.

The National Social Security program provides a sixteen-week paid leave after childbirth, plus a birth allowance. While medical care is not free, costs are kept low through medical insurance funds. These funds are supported jointly by the government and private organizations.

GOVERNMENT

Structure

During World War I, Britain seized Cyprus from the Ottoman Empire, and in 1925, the island became a British crown colony. Britain deliberately fostered division between the Greek and Turkish Cypriots to keep them from uniting in a revolution. Nevertheless, Cyprus gained its independence from Britain in 1960.

Distrust between the two cultural groups led to violent clashes. A United Nations peacekeeping force landed in 1964, but violent outbreaks continued. In 1983, the Turkish Cypriots declared that the Turkish Republic of Northern Cyprus was an independent country. In 2015, an estimated 212,400 Cypriots, both Greek and Turkish, have been displaced by the conflict, some since 1974.

Cyprus is a republic with a unicameral legislative body. The president, elected to a five-year term, is the head of state and head of government.

The president appoints a Council of Ministers, or cabinet.

The House of Representatives has the potential to have 83 members, 56 elected by Greek Cypriots, 24 elected by Turkish Cypriots, and three observer members elected by minority populations. Since the separation of the TRNC, however, only the Greek Cypriot seats have been filled—the 24 Turkish seats have remained unfilled. Representatives are elected by popular vote to five-year terms.

In the TRNC, the legislative body is the unicameral Cumhuriyet Meclisi (Assembly of the Republic). Its 50 members are elected to five-year terms, as is the president. The president appoints the prime minister from the Assembly.

Political Parties

In the ROC, until the parliamentary elections of May 2011, the left wing, communist-oriented Progressive Party of Working People (AKEL) had been the dominant political party, holding the presidency and a majority in the legislature. In the 2009 presidential race, AKEL garnered 53 percent of the vote in a runoff. In 2010, along with Nepal, Cyprus had been one of only two nations in the world with a democratically elected communist leader. The tide began to turn with the 2011 parliamentary elections, during which the Democratic Rally (DISY), a center-right party, won twenty of the fifty-six seats, while AKEL took nineteen. Nine seats were taken by the centrist party Democratic Party (DIKO); five seats by the social-democratic Movement for Social Democracy (EDEK); three seats by the Greek-Cypriot nationalist-oriented European Party; and one seat by the environmentally oriented Greens.

Two years later, in ROC's runoff presidential election of February 2013, Nicos Anastasiades of DISY won the presidency with 57.48 of the popular vote. AKEL took just 42.52 percent of the vote.

Other parties involved in the 2013 election were the liberal-oriented United Democrats (EDI); the center-left Popular Socialist Movement (LASOK); the far-right National Popular Front (ELAM); and the social democratic Movement for Social Democracy (EDEK).

Local Government

The ROC is divided into six administrative districts: Famagusta, Kyrenia, Larnaca, Limassol, Nicosia, and Paphos. Kyrenia, as well as parts of Nicosia, Famgusta, and Larnaca, are considered TRNC territory. An appointed district officer leads districts.

Cyprus also has four exclaves (a territory politically or geographically attached to another territory, while not physically contiguous) under the control of the British Sovereign Base Area of Dhekelia—the villages of Ormidhia and Xylotympou, the Dhekelia power station, and the Paralimni area.

Within the ROC, local authorities are designated municipalities (largely urban) or communities (largely rural). Municipalities are led by democratically elected mayors for five-year terms. The mayor works with an elected municipal council and an administrative body. Municipalities are responsible for public services (such as waste management and public health), as well as human and social services, culture, and planning and development. Communities are largely responsible for the same government services, but they are administered by the president of the community and the community council.

Judicial System

The judicial system in Cyprus is comprised of courts for industrial disputes, rent control, family, military, district, and assize. The Courts of Justice Law established six civil courts, corresponding with the six districts of Cyprus: Nicosia, Larnaca, Limassol, Paphos, Famagusta, and Kyrenia. The Supreme Court of the Republic is the country's highest court, over which 13 judges preside.

Taxation

Cyprus's tax system is progressive, with a graduated income tax, meaning that those who earn more pay higher taxes. The government also levies value-added, corporate, capital gains (individual and corporate), and social security taxes, among others. In 2014, the highest personal income tax rate was 35 percent, while the corporate tax rate is a flat 12.5 percent. Any person making less than €19,500 pays no income taxes.

Armed Forces

The Cypriot National Guard, or the Greek Cypriot National Guard, constitute the armed forces of Cyprus and consist of air, naval, and land contingents. Conscription exists for Greek Cypriots and is in practice between the ages of 18 and 50, with a 25-month service obligation being the normal length of compulsory service. Foreign-based troops in Cyprus include the permanent Greek Hellenic Force in Cyprus. The Turkish Cypriot Security Force is the military for Northern Cyprus and is reinforced by the Turkish Military Forces in Northern Cyprus, maintained by Turkey.

Foreign Policy

In 1960, Cyprus won its independence from Britain, and the Republic of Cyprus was established with agreement from Britain, Greece, and Turkey. The resulting government provided for rule shared by executive, legislative, and judicial branches. The Turkish and Greek populations would both have representation in the executive and legislative branches, and Britain would maintain existing military bases on the island.

However, the Greek and Turkish leadership in Cyprus had difficulty coming together under the new independent government. In 1974, a Greek junta (military group) staged a coup and seized control of the Cypriot government. They declared unity with Greece despite protests by Turkish Cypriots and Turkey. Within a week, Turkey sent troops into Cyprus to restore order under the Cyprus constitution. International intervention quickly enacted a ceasefire before the conflict could erupt into war. The United Nations (UN) established a buffer zone and a demarcation or cease-fire line known as the Green Line, which separated the Greek sector in the south and the Turkish sector in the north. The

UN continued to sponsor attempts to reconcile the divided nation. In 1983, the Turkish leadership in the northern sector ceased participation in the talks and declared an independent Turkish Republic of Northern Cyprus (TRNC). However, the nationhood of this independent republic is only recognized by Turkey, although the TRNC has operated largely as its own nation since that time.

In the decades since 1974, the official Republic of Cyprus, comprising the two-thirds of the island that make up the Greek sector, and the TRNC have pursued separate foreign policies. Although the TRNC has been limited in its efforts because it has not been recognized as an autonomous nation by any international organizations, it has operated separately from the government of the southern republic. Overall, it has maintained close ties with Turkey and avoided most other international entanglements. The unofficial position of the TRNC has been that lack of international engagement would allow the continued de facto division of the nation.

Meanwhile, the Republic of Cyprus, dominated by Greek leadership, has actively sought to prevent international recognition of the TRNC. It has also worked to gain international support for a reunification agreement between the two parts of Cyprus that requires the withdrawal of Turkish troops. The republic wants to reunite the nation and enable the unrestricted movement of people and goods throughout the island.

The UN has maintained peacekeeping forces on Cyprus since before 1974. Britain still maintains its military bases, and Greece, Turkey, the United States, and other countries provide economic assistance to and have engaged in trade with both sides of the island. In 2013, almost 61 percent of the southern republic's imports come from Europe. The TRNC imports most of its goods from Turkey, but also engages in trade with European Union (EU) countries.

The Republic of Cyprus is a member of several major international bodies, including the UN, the Commonwealth of Nations, the Organization for Security and Cooperation in Europe (OSCE), the Council of Europe, and the EU. The TRNC, which is not considered a nation by these bodies, lacks membership in any such organizations. Similarly, the Republic of Cyprus has embassies and consulates around the world, while the TRNC maintains unofficial offices, often in the embassies of Turkey.

The TRNC has no international policy-making or treaty-signing power. The Republic of Cyprus, though not a major player on the world stage, tends to align itself with the positions of the EU. However, it also enjoys friendly relations with many non-EU nations, including Russia, China, Israel, Egypt, and Lebanon. Since the terrorist attacks on the US on September 11, 2001, the Republic of Cyprus has worked closely with the US government in the global "war on terrorism." The US and the republic also signed the Mutual Legal Assistance Treaty in September 2002, and Cyprus saw a hefty increase in American economic aid. Recently, the Republic of Cyprus has assisted the UN International Criminal Tribunal for the former Yugoslavia.

Since the split, negotiations between the Greek and Turkish leaderships have occurred sporadically, generally under the auspices of the UN. All such talks have failed to produce a binding agreement and reunification plan. Ongoing points of conflict include the resettlement of internal refugees, or displaced persons, the post-reunification governing structure and constitutional framework, and the role of Greece and Turkey and their respective military forces in the country. In 2008, when the two sides previously agreed to sit down to negotiations, Ledra Street in the capital of Nicosia, a major commercial district, was reopened to traffic from both sides of Cyprus for the first time since 1974. The last round of negotiations stalled in 2012, after the two sides reached an impasse over issues relating to power-sharing, Turkish settlers, and political boundaries. On February 11, 2014, both sides again agreed to resume the reunification talks. However, this effort at reconciliation was ended by the Greek Cypriots on October 7, 2014, following their discovery that Turkey had sent a ship to monitor oil and gas drilling efforts off the southern coast of Cyprus.

Human Rights Profile

International human rights law insists that states respect civil and political rights, and promote an individual's economic, social, and cultural rights. The United Nations Universal Declaration on Human Rights (UDHR) is recognized as the standard for international human rights. Its authors sought the counsel of the world's great thinkers, philosophers, and religious leaders and were careful to create a document that reflects the core values shared by every world culture. (To read this document or view the articles relating to cultural human rights, go to http://www.ohchr.org/EN/UDHR/Pages/Introduction.aspx.)

Overall, Cyprus, though divided between Turkish and Greek sectors, has maintained a system of government that acts largely in accordance with the UDHR. However, the US Department of State and international bodies and organizations such as the UN and Amnesty International (AI) have cited several problem areas. In the Greek-controlled republic, police abuse, the violation of asylum-seekers' rights, violence against women, and human trafficking remain concerns. In the Turkish-controlled TRNC, areas cited for improvement are police abuse, the arbitrary arrest and detention of citizens, restrictions on asylum-seekers, restrictions on citizens' privacy rights, and human trafficking.

Although both the southern republic and TRNC laws provide for the safety and equality of persons, violence directed against women, children, and minority groups occurred in both the Greek and Turkish sectors. In the Greek-controlled republic, Turkish Cypriots and Roma reportedly suffered discriminatory practices, and in the TRNC, Greek Cypriots and Maronites reported suffering discrimination. In both sectors, women and children were subject to abuse and exploitation. Women in particular were subject to human trafficking for the purposes of sexual exploitation, and the authorities were allegedly complicit in allowing the trafficking to occur undeterred. Enforcement and prosecution of existing laws was also lacking, and prison sentences for convictions were often shorter than the maximums allowed. In addition, facilities and protections for persons with disabilities were insufficient throughout the island.

In 2014, Freedom House, a non-governmental watchdog group, ranked Cyprus' press "free," a status that has not wavered since 2002. However, journalists and camerapersons reported in 2007 incidents of intimidation and assault by authorities. In that same year, in the Republic of Cyprus and the TRNC, suspects reported having been intimidated and beaten by police and that prisoners and detainees suffered abusive and inadequate conditions while in custody. In prisons in both sectors, overcrowding continued to be a significant problem. In the TRNC, authorities also failed to separate juvenile offenders from adult offenders, and in both sectors, nonviolent offenders were housed with violent offenders. TRNC authorities also reportedly failed to follow proper procedures in securing the rights of suspects and detainees. In some cases, suspects gave testimony without a lawyer present, and suspects who requested legal counsel were reportedly harassed and intimidated.

Cyprus law provides for the granting of asylum, and the Greek-controlled republic welcomed and provided for asylum-seekers, as required under the UDHR. However, reports indicated that many asylum-seekers were held in detention for six months or longer while awaiting decisions in their cases. In February 2013, the European Council on Refugees and Exiles reported that Cypriot authorities summarily closed Kokkinotrimithia, a temporary camp that held 300 Syrian and Palestinian refugees, leaving them with no means of shelter. Although the refugees had been granted three-month temporary residence permits, during which they could apply for asylum, many did not, as Cyprus' asylum laws often prevent family reunification. Nongovernmental organizations (NGOs), like Future Worlds Center, have also accused Cypriot police of conducting illegal arrests and deportations of asylum-seekers. As of April 2015, 2,700 persons were seeking asylum in the Republic of Cyprus. TRNC law, on the other hand, does not provide for the granting of asylum, and the TRNC government has failed to establish a system for taking in asylum-seekers. Reportedly, the TRNC refers asylum-seekers to the UN, but it is unclear what happens to the asylum-seekers after that.

Lastly, one significant area of concern to human rights advocates is the free movement of peoples within both territories and across the Green Line. Although the Republic of Cyprus did not restrict Greek Cypriots from traveling into the Turkish north, Republic authorities restrict Turkish Cypriots from crossing into Greek-controlled territory. Turkish Cypriots who were granted access were required to apply for temporary visas. Similarly, the TRNC required Greek Cypriots to apply for temporary visas to cross into the Turkish north and limited the movements of Greek Cypriots still living there. In addition, although the Republic and TRNC generally protected civil liberties, such as the freedom of speech and assembly, violations of these rights, particularly regarding journalists, were reported in both sectors. As of 2015, according to the Reporters without Borders' World Press Freedom Index, TRNC ranked seventy-sixth out of 180 countries in press freedom, while the Republic of Cyprus ranked much higher at twenty-fourth.

Migration

In 2014, the estimated number of migrants settling in Cyprus was 17,400, with 10,572 coming from EU countries and 6,632 hailing from non-EU countries, like the Philippines, the United States, Egypt, Ukraine, and Moldova, among others. Immigration has become a hot-button issue within the Cypriot government, as the government debates its ability to support the recent influx of asylum seekers from developing nations, as well as nations in conflict.

ECONOMY

Overview of the Economy

On January 1, 2008, Cyprus joined the European Union (EU) and adapted the Euro as the official currency for the island (the Turkish Lira is the currency of the north). (The Turkish Republic of Northern Cyprus, or TRNC, dependent on and recognized only by Turkey, has yet to be recognized by both the EU and the United Nations.) Despite being a politically divided island, the Cypriot per capita gross domestic product (GDP) is higher than the EU average, standing at $26,200 (USD) in 2015. However, even with these strong signs, economic policy is fragmented between the Greek and Turkish communities, and little coordination exists between the two sides. While it is the political capital of the island, Nicosia reflects this divided and fragmented economy.

Even with this division, Nicosia maintains a strong local economy despite the Nicosia International Airport being permanently shut down due to the civil strife of the mid-1970s (the chief ports of Larnaca and Limassol are both in ROC territory, as are the two international airports). Highly favorable laws on foreign direct investment have been essential to the local Nicosia economy, which the Greek-dominated Cypriot government passed to allow full foreign ownership of Cypriot companies. In addition, the government tax code encourages foreign companies to re-locate to Nicosia. These two policies have allowed Nicosia to become the headquarters for many foreign firms, especially companies involved in the maritime trade industries and shipping. The city also manufactures textiles, pottery, plastics, leather, and food and beverage products. Copper continues to be one of the important natural resources mined outside of the capital, although, since 2012, offshore natural gas drilling appears to be offering a promising future for the country.

With a highly educated population, Greek Nicosia has transformed into a service-based economy with just over 80 percent of its population involved in telecommunications, banking, or tourism. Tourism continues to be a large source of revenue for Nicosia, despite its lack of an international airport. Overall, nearly 87 percent of the Cypriot GDP derives from the service economy.

Turkish Nicosia does not have the same dynamic economy. Due to the political separation with the Cypriot government, the Turkish economy lacks foreign investment and is heavily subsidized by the Turkish government in Ankara. While the construction boom in Nicosia led to an impressive 11.4 percent GDP growth rate in 2004, economic growth rates have stalled slightly in recent years, amounting to just two percent in 2007.

Overall, the economy of the entire island depends heavily on tourism, especially the service industries associated with the tourist trade. The gross domestic product (GDP) is $25.04 billion (USD) (2014 estimate).

Industry

Industrial production in Cyprus has increased greatly since independence in 1960. Today, pharmaceuticals, textiles, footwear and clothing, and soap are all manufactured on the island. Although copper production has declined, gypsum, iron, chromium, and asbestos products are still produced. Ship repair is another large industry at the ports of Larnaca and Limassol.

Exports—primarily of citrus, pharmaceuticals, cigarettes, cement, clothing, and potatoes—represent 46.8% of the country's total GDP and bring in revenues of $1.916 billion (USD) (2014).

Labor

As of 2013, Cyprus has an estimated labor force of 356,700. Unemployment in the entire country stands at 16 percent in 2014. An estimated 80.1 percent of the workforce is employed in the services sector, followed by industry at 16 percent, and agriculture at nearly 3.9 percent.

Energy/Power/Natural Resources

Cyprus has few natural resources. In the past, copper was important to the economy, but the island's copper deposits have been mostly depleted, although deposits continue to be mined. Clay and gypsum are also mined, as are small amounts of salt, pyrites, marble, and asbestos. The island's timber is another valuable resource. However, the spread of urban areas is degrading the coast and destroying wildlife habitats.

In 2011, the U.S.-based firm, Noble Energy, located the first natural gas reserves in what is known as Block 12, or the Aphrodite Field, a site that involves deep-sea drilling. It is estimated to eventually yield between 3.6 and six trillion cubic feet of natural gas. In 2012, the Italian-South Korean energy consortium Eni/KOGAS signed an agreement to explore hydrocarbon resources in other blocks of the Cyprus Exclusive Economic Zone (EEZ). Exploratory drilling began in September 2014. Cyprus hopes to export its natural gas by 2022. In 2015, preliminary talks have begun with Egypt, whereby an undersea pipeline would allow Cyprus to export its reserves directly.

Fishing

The fishing industry in Cyprus has been operating under EU standards, which some claim is endangering the economic viability of the fishing industry, as the country abides by EU standards while other member nations do not. The country is engaged in talks within the EU to press its case, asking that other member nations abide by EU policies, as well as work with EU representatives to decide how many boats are allowed within designated fishing areas and how much fish they can catch. In the 21st century, the EU has supported the development of a fisheries policy in Cyprus, as well as funding initiatives to make the industry more competitive.

In response to the difficulties presented by commercial capture, aquaculture and fish farming has begun in earnest and happens primarily along Cyprus' southern coasts. The most popular method of culturing fish is open sea cages. The predominant cultivated species in Cyprus include gilthead seabream and European seabass, which are produced at an annual rate of 71 percent and 26.6 percent respectively. Other species include the common pandora and the Indian white prawn. In 2013, such aquaculture accounted for 81 percent of fish production in Cyprus.

Forestry

The forest industry, which is overseen by the Ministry of Agriculture, Natural Resources, and Environment, contributed less than one percent to the country's GDP. The industry is under threat by the country's lack of fresh water resources. Increasingly, finished goods are being imported to the country and the industry is failing to see growth.

Mining/Metals

The mining sector was valued at €79.5 million ($105.3 million USD) in 2001. In 2012, according to Statistical Survey for the Republic Cyprus, the mining and quarrying industry employed just 534 people. The country has deposits of asbestos, chromium, copper, gypsum, pyrite, and clay.

Agriculture

Following tourism in importance to the Cypriot economy is agriculture. According to the World Bank, in 2012, around than 13.5 percent of the island's land was arable. Agriculture also contributed 2.9 percent to the country's overall GDP. Crops grown in the ROC include barley, wheat, citrus fruits, grapes, olives, potatoes, and vegetables. Animal products include pork, lamb, poultry, and cheese. An estimated one in three farms specializes in fruits, particularly citrus fruits.

Principal crops in the TRNC are similar, with wheat, barley, potatoes, legumes (peas, beans, lentils), vegetables, citrus and other fruits, carobs (similar to chocolate), and olives predominating.

Animal Husbandry

Important livestock in Cyprus include dairy cattle, sheep, goats, pigs, and poultry. Turkish Cypriot farmers also produce mutton and lamb, goat meat, beef, poultry, wool and eggs, as well as sheep, goat, and cow milk. Each September, Northern Cyprus also holds the TRNC Agriculture, Animal Husbandry, Dairy Products & Farming Machinery Fair.

Tourism

According to Statistical Service of the Republic of Cyprus, in May 2015, approximately 307,449 million tourists visited the ROC, a 4.9 percent increase from the previous year. A majority of tourists hail from the United Kingdom, Sweden, Germany, Greece, and Russia. The TRNC hosts more than 425,000 tourists each year, and their tourism contributed to 9 percent of the GDP in 2014. Visitors from Turkey and the United Kingdom predominate in this part of the country.

The island's attractions include mountain and beach resorts and archaeological sites. Prominent historic sites include Kolossi Castle, dating from the Crusades in the third century; the painted church of Panagia tou Araka (Our Lady of the Pea), on the United Nations Educational, Scientific and Cultural Organization's (UNESCO) list of World Heritage Sites; and Choirokoitia (or Khirokitia), a Neolithic archaeological site.

Paphos has many points of interest, including its harbor, castle, and Roman mosaics found in excavated ancient houses. The town of Lefkara produces world-famous lace. Ayia Napa, a resort on the southeastern coast of the island, was once a family-oriented resort, but now has a vibrant club scene. The town also features a monastery, built around 1500 and located at the town's center. The town's name can be translated from Greek to mean "holy forest," a name that references the icon of St. Mary accidently discovered by a hunter passing through the wooded valley where the city now stands.

Christina Dendy, Ellen Bailey, &
Jeffrey Bowman

DO YOU KNOW?

- During the Crusades, England's King Richard I ("the Lionheart") captured Cyprus and sold it to the Knights Templar, a military religious order.

- Struck by the island's natural beauty, the ancient Greeks thought that Cyprus was the home of Aphrodite, the goddess of love.

Bibliography

_____. *View from the Bronze Age.* New York: E.P. Dutton & Co., Inc., 1976.

A. Bernard Knapp. *Prehistoric and Protohistoric Cyprus: Identity, Insularity, and Connectivity.* New York: Oxford University Press, 2008.

Andrew Borowiec. *Cyprus: A Troubled Island.* Westport, CT: Praeger Publishers, 2000.

Artemis Georgiou. *Cyprus: An Island Culture: Society and Social Relations from the Bronze Age to the Venetian Period.* Oxford, UK: Oxbow Books, 2012.

Cynthia Cockburn. *The Line: Women, Partition and the Gender Order in Cyprus.* London, UK: Zed Books, 2004.

James Ker-Lindsay. *The Cyprus Problem: What Everyone Needs to Know.* Oxford, UK: Oxford University Press, 2011.

Jos Simon. *The Rough Guide to Cyprus.* London, UK: Rough Guides, 2013.

Timothy Boatswain. *A Traveller's History of of Cyprus.* Northampton, UK: Interlink Books, 2005.

Vassos Karageorghis. *Early Cyprus: Crossroads of the Mediterranean.* Los Angeles, CA: Getty Publications, 2003.

William Mallinson. *Cyprus: A Modern History.* London, UK: I.B. Tauris, 2008.

Yiannis Papadakis, Nicos Peristianis, & Gisela Weiz, eds. *Divided Cyprus: Modernity, History, And an Island in Conflict.* Bloomington, IN: Indiana UP, 2006.

Works Cited

_____. "Food & Dining." *Cyprus.com.* Cyprus.com, 2015. http://www.cyprus.com/food---dining.html.

_____. "Foreign Operations Appropriated Assistance: Cyprus." *Bureau of European and Eurasian Affairs Fact Sheet.* U.S. Department of State, 20 Jan. 2009. Web. http://www.state.gov/p/eur/rls/fs/104020.htm.

_____. "Painted Churches in the Troödos Region." *World Heritage Site.* WHS, 2015. http://www.worldheritagesite.org/sites/troodosregion.html.

_____. "Paphos." *World Heritage Site.* WHS, 2015. http://www.worldheritagesite.org/sites/paphos.html.

_____. "U.S. Relations with Cyprus." *Bureau of European and Eurasian Affairs Fact Sheet.* U.S. Department of State, 27 Feb. 2014. http://www.state.gov/r/pa/ei/bgn/5376.htm.

_____. "World Heritage Sites in Cyprus." *World Heritage Site*. WHS, 2015. http://www.worldheritagesite. org/countries/cyprus.html.

"AIDA Update: Cyprus Continues to Detain Asylum Seekers Beyond Lawful Time-Limits." *Asylum Information Database*. European Council on Refugees and Exiles, 9 April 2015. Web. http://www. asylumineurope.org/news/09-04-2015/aida-update-cyprus-continues-detain-asylum-seekers-beyond-lawful-time-limits.

"Ancient Period." *Country Studies*. Country-Studies.com, n.d. Web. http://www.country-studies.com/cyprus/ancient-period.html

"Cyprus News Agency: News in English, 08-10-06." *HR-Net (Hellenistic Resources Network)*. Hellenistic Resources Institute, 6 Oct. 2008. http://www.hri.org/news/cyprus/cna/2008/08-10-06_2.cna.html.

"Cyprus." Amnesty International. "Cyprus" *Amnesty International Report 2014/15*. Amnesty International, 2015. https://www.amnesty.org/en/countries/europe-and-central-asia/cyprus/.

"Cyprus." *Bureau of European and Eurasian Affairs*. U.S, Department of State, n.d. http://www.state.gov/p/eur/ci/cy/.

"Cyprus—Culture, Customs and Etiquette." Kwintessential. Kwintessential, 2014. http://www.kwintessential.co.uk/resources/global-etiquette/cyprus-country-profile.html.

"Cyprus—in Pictures." Minneapolis, MN: *Lerner Publications Company*, 1992.

"Cyprus—Largest Cities." *GeoNames*. GeoNames.org, 2015. http://www.geonames.org/CY/largest-cities-in-cyprus.html.

"Eni, KOGAS to drill for gas in Cyprus." *OffShoreEnergyToday.com*. Offshore Energy Today, 31 July 2014. http://www.offshoreenergytoday.com/eni-kogas-to-drill-for-gas-in-cyprus/.

"Europe: Cyprus." CIA. "Europe: Cyprus." *The World Factbook*. Central Intelligence Agency, 2015. https://www.cia.gov/library/publications/the-world-factbook/geos/cy.html.

"Family and Marriage." *Country Studies*. Country-Studies. com, n.d. http://www.country-studies.com/cyprus/family-and-marriage.html.

"Featured Sites & Attractions." *Cyprus.com*. Cyprus. com, 2015. http://www.cyprus.com/cyprus-going-out-historical-places-famagusta.php.

"Featured Sports & Recreation Listings." *Cyprus.com*. Cyprus.com, 2015. http://www.cyprus.com/sports-recreation.html.

"Foreign Policy—the Republic of Cyprus." *Country Studies*. Country-Studies.com, n.d. http://www.country-studies.com/cyprus/foreign-policy---the-republic-of-cyprus.html.

"Latest Figures: Tourism Arrivals, May 2015." *Tourism*. Republic of Cyprus Statistical Service, 16 Jun. 2015. http://www.mof.gov.cy/mof/cystat/statistics.nsf/services_71main_en/services_71main_en?OpenForm&sub=1&sel=1.

"Mevlevi Tekke Museum of Whirling Dervishes." *Whatson-Northcyprus*. Whatson-Northcyprus, 2015. Web. http://www.whatson-northcyprus.com/interest/nicosia/north_nicosia/mevlevi_tekke.htm.

"Population." *Country Studies*. Country-Studies.com, n.d. Web. http://www.country-studies.com/cyprus/population.html.

"Society." *Country Studies*. Country-Studies.com, n.d. Web. http://www.country-studies.com/cyprus/society.html.

"Speak Greek." *Cyprus Travel Secrets*. Cyprus-Travel-Secrets.com, 2015. Web. http://www.cyprus-travel-secrets.com/speak-Greek.html.

"St. Barnabus' Monastery and Icon Museum." *Whatson-Northcyprus*. Whatson-Northcyprus, 2015. Web. http://www.whatson-northcyprus.com/interest/famagusta/salamis/barnabas.htm.

"Status of Women." *Country Studies*. Country-Studies.com, n.d. Web. http://www.country-studies.com/cyprus/status-of-women.html.

"The Foreign Policy of Internationalization, The." *Country Studies*. Country-Studies.com, n.d. Web. http://www.country-studies.com/cyprus/the-foreign-policy-of-internationalization.html.

"The Ruins of Soli." *Whatson-Northcyprus*. Whatson-Northcyprus, 2015. Web. http://www.whatson-northcyprus.com/interest/Lefke/soli.htm.

Blanca Garcia. "Cypriot People & Culture." *Cyprus.com*. Cyprus.com, 2015. http://www.cyprus.com/cypriot-people---culture.html.

Els Slots. "Choirokoitia." *World Heritage Site*. WHS, 2015. Web. http://www.worldheritagesite.org/sites/choirokoitia.html.

Jack Ewing. "As Cyprus Recovers from Baking Crisis, Deep Scars Remain." *New York Times*. The New York Times Company, 16 Mar. 2015. Web. http://www.nytimes.com/2015/03/17/business/international/as-cyprus-recovers-from-banking-crisis-deep-scars-remain.html?ref=topics.

Natasha Magruder. "Cyprus Facing Up to Life after after 'Peak Water'." *CNN.com*. Cable News Network/Turner Broadcasting Co., 22 Sept. 2010. Web. http://www.cnn.com/2010/WORLD/europe/09/20/cyprus.water/

Charles Bridge, Prague, Czech Republic

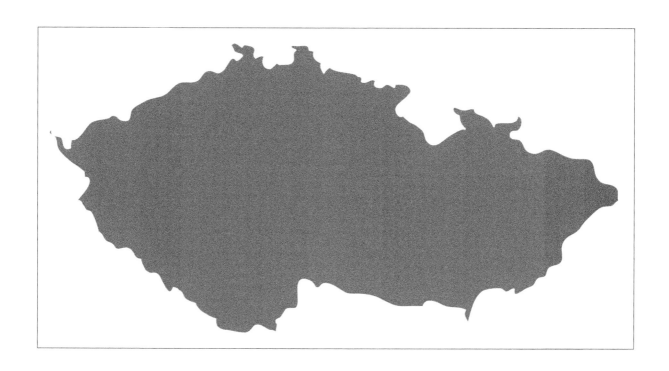

CZECH REPUBLIC

Introduction

The Czech Republic (Česká Republika) is located in Central Europe, bordered by Germany to the north and west, Poland to the northeast, Slovakia to the southeast, and Austria to the southwest. It was founded on January 1, 1993, when the former Czechoslovakia was divided into two separate nations, the Czech Republic and Slovakia, in a split known as the "Velvet Divorce."

Although the Czech Republic is one of the youngest nations in Europe, its history and culture date back hundreds of years. Czechs are known for their contributions to art, literature, music, and architecture. The Czech Republic is also famous for its beer production and its Bohemian glassware and crystal.

GENERAL INFORMATION

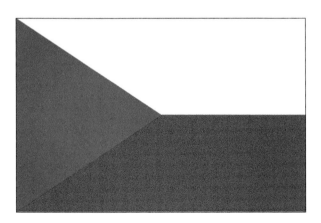

Official Language: Czech
Population: 10,627,448 (2014 estimate)
Currency: Czech koruna (or koruna česká)
Coins: Czech koruna coins are available in denominations of 10, 20 and 50 haléřů (100 of which are equal to one koruna), and 1, 2, 5, 10, 20, and 50 koruna.
Land Area: 77,247 square kilometers (29,825 square miles)
Water Area: 1,620 square kilometers (625 square miles)

National Motto: "Truth Prevails" (Pravda vítězí)
National Anthem: "Where is My Home?" ("Kde domov můj?")
Capital: Prague
Time Zone: GMT +1
Flag Description: The Czech flag features two bands of horizontal stripes, the top one white and the bottom red, and a blue isosceles triangle, the base of which rests on the left perimeter of the flag. The triangle's point reaches approximately halfway across the flag.

Population

About 73 percent of the population in the Czech Republic lives in cities and larger towns. In 2014, the median age of those living in the country was just under 41 years old, with 67.6 percent of the citizens falling between 15 and 64 years of age. Life expectancy is just over 78 years old.

Principal Cities by Population (2015 estimates):

- Prague (1,259,079)
- Brno (377,440)
- Ostrava (304,136)
- Plzeň (or Pilsen) (169,033)
- Liberec (102,562)
- Olomouc (99,809)
- Ústí nad Labem (93,409)
- České Budějovice (93,285)
- Hradec Králové (92,808)
- Havířov (75,049)

Languages

The majority of the population (95.4 percent) speaks Czech, which is the official language. Slovak speakers comprise 1.6 percent of the population. Czech is a Slavic language related to Russian and Bulgarian. It has a 42-letter alphabet.

Native People & Ethnic Groups

The Czechs are the native people of the Czech Republic, descended from Slavic tribes that arrived in the region around the 6th century. These people were concentrated in the historical regions of Bohemia and Moravia. The Boii, a Celtic tribe that arrived in what is now the Czech Republic circa 400 BCE, preceded the Czechs. Those Celts who remained at the time of the arrival of the Slavs were assimilated into the Slavic population.

Today, Czechs are the largest ethnic group in the Czech Republic, accounting for approximately 64.3 percent of the total population. Other significant ethnic groups are Moravians (5 percent of the population) and Slovaks (1.4 percent). While 27.5 percent of the population was of unspecified ethnicity in the 2011 census, minority groups within the Czech Republic include Poles, Hungarians, Germans, Silesians, and Roma (Gypsies).

Religions

According to the 2011 census, 10.4 percent identify as Roman Catholic, 1.1 percent identify as Protestant, and 88.5 percent either do not identify their religion or consider themselves unaffiliated with organized religion. Religious practices were suppressed in the former Czechoslovakia by the communist government, which remained in power for over 40 years, which may account for the number of citizens who do not practice any religion.

Other religions within the country include Judaism, Hinduism, and Islam. Before World War II, during the 1930s, approximately 360,000 Jews lived in the former Czechoslovakia, but by 2006, there were an estimated 4,000 Jews living in the country.

Climate

The Czech Republic has a temperate climate and experiences four seasons, with July being the hottest month and January the coldest. Summers tend to be cool, with average temperatures of about 20° Celsius (68° Fahrenheit), although in July temperatures can run above 30° Celsius (86° Fahrenheit). Winters are cold and humid, with temperatures averaging –5° Celsius (23° Fahrenheit).

Fog can develop in the lowlands during the winter. Precipitation varies depending on altitude, with higher elevations receiving an average of 165 centimeters (65 inches) per year, compared with 46 to 76 centimeters (18 to 30 inches) in low-lying areas.

ENVIRONMENT & GEOGRAPHY

Topography

The Czech Republic is a landlocked country surrounded by mountains. It consists of two major regions: the Bohemian Highlands in the west and the Moravian Lowlands to the east. The highlands account for two-thirds of the country's area.

The highlands are bordered by hills, valleys, and low mountains. The lowlands have large flat areas that are more suitable for farming. Silesia, a small section in northeastern Moravia, was once part of Poland and is regarded as a separate region from a historical and cultural perspective.

Mount Sněžka, the highest point in the Czech Republic at 1,603 meters (5,259 feet) above sea level, is located in northern Bohemia. It is part of the Krkonoše, a mountain range that separates the Czech Republic from Poland. The Jeseníky Mountains (or Hrubý Jeseník) are the highest mountain range in Moravia. The Bílé Kapaty (White Carpathian) Mountains separate Moravia from Slovakia.

Limestone formations called karst are found in central Bohemia. There are over 2,000 limestone caves in the Czech Republic. Sandstone formations are found in eastern Bohemia, including the Hrubá Skála, with rocks as tall as 365 meters (1,200 feet). Although the country has no active volcanoes, volcanic rock formations deep below the surface heat water to form hot springs. These natural hot springs are found throughout the country, but are most plentiful in western Bohemia. Karlovy Vary, or Karlsbad, (named after King of Bohemia and Holy Roman Emperor Charles IV) is one of the many spa towns that have been built around the springs.

The Vltava River is the country's longest river, stretching 430 kilometers (267 miles). The Vltava is a tributary of the Labe or Elbe River system and passes through Prague. The Morava River passes through Moravia and flows into the Danube River. The Odra (Oder) River flows northward to Szczecin Lagoon, shared by Germany and Poland, and eventually empties into the Baltic Sea.

The Czech Republic has 455 natural lakes, 350 of which are river lakes that developed in grasslands around the three major river systems in the country. Additionally, there are 21,800 artificial lakes and ponds. Many of the man-made lakes were created for fish farming. The largest of these artificial bodies of water are Lake Rožmberk and Lake Bezdrev.

Plants & Animals

Approximately one-third of the Czech Republic's area is covered by forests, despite widespread deforestation for logging. Beech, spruce, and oak trees grow at higher elevations, while maple and ash are found in the lowlands. Common softwood conifers include pine and fir trees.

Typical wildlife includes wolves, lynxes, foxes, chamois, wild boars, otters, minks, brown bears, European pine martens, golden jackals, and marmots. Eurasian badgers, European rabbits, and brown hares are found in the lowlands. Birds commonly spotted in the Czech Republic include owls, eagles, falcons, vultures, ducks, wild geese, and pheasants. Over 25 species of bat are also native to the Czech Republic, including the Barbastrelle, the Greater Noctule, Soprano Pipistrelle, and Greater Horseshoe Bat.

CUSTOMS & COURTESIES

Greetings

In the Czech culture, high respect is typically expressed for educational degrees or other formal titles. For example, Czechs often use double titles such as "Pane Doktor Kovař" that would translate to "Mr. Doctor Smith" in English. Czechs also use formal titles such as "Mr. Engineer," "Mrs. Professor" or "Mr. Director" and other such honorific addresses. This avoids any perception of rudeness or disrespect to the person greeted. Generally, initial greetings are formal and reserved, and Czechs do not address each other using first names unless they are well acquainted and usually of the same age. For instance, a thirty-year-old man will often permanently address even a sixty-year-old close friend with the honorific title of "Mr." as a sign of affectionate respect.

In addition, there is a formal level and informal level in Czech that must be closely observed. Using "ty" instead of "vy" in pronouns (thus creating the informal level of "you") and using the corresponding informal verb conjugations without invitation can easily be perceived as discourteous or even contemptuous. The offer to use informal Czech is generally offered by women and those of elder or higher status. When requesting assistance or otherwise interacting with strangers in society, one should first say "Dobrý deň" ("Good day") and then proceed to one's request.

Gestures & Etiquette

Good customer service was not part of socialist Czechoslovakia; rather, customers often curried favor with the sales and service personnel to get preferential treatment over the other customers. Although customer service has improved greatly since the Velvet Revolution and the collapse of communism, the remains of this system still linger, and there is still a tendency for service personnel to argue with or even offend customers. Therefore, when interacting in Czech society, one should show politeness and patience. One may or may not get good service in restaurants or elsewhere—especially outside of Prague, where personnel are not as well trained in dealing with tourists or foreigners.

Eating/Meals

In the past, most Czechs started their mornings with bread, butter, and jam, or bread and cheese. Today, the modern market economy has slowly introduced many varieties of international breakfast cereals to the table. Most children also have a "svačina" or mid-morning snack, and all schools take a break at about ten o'clock so that students can eat a sandwich and some fruit. All employers and other institutions also give Czechs a half-hour snack break around the same time.

Svačina is typically followed by lunch. The evening meal is usually taken at about six o'clock. Factories, large companies and all public schools have a cafeteria ("jídelna") for lunches—usually serving meat and potatoes or bread dumplings. If a company or institution does not have a cafeteria, it typically issues employees special lunch coupons for participating restaurants and fast-food establishments. Most people in larger towns eat in restaurants, which have dramatically increased in number in the early 21st century, and international cuisine has increased in availability. Additionally, in most towns, laborers often go to small cafeteria-style restaurants known as "bufets" that serve "hotová jídla" (ready-made meals) from a daily menu. These small cafeterias are quite popular among the working class because they are inexpensive and serve food quickly.

Visiting

There is a Czech saying that exemplifies their philosophy about visiting others: "Come and see us sometime—don't worry, we won't come and bother you either." Perhaps this sentiment is derived from the historic need to escape the prying eyes of totalitarian society and government for over 40 years. Nonetheless, Czechs generally prefer that their home lives are kept private, and they do not usually invite anyone except family or a few close friends to visit. Quite often, neighbors may formally greet each other on the street and may not know what the interior of each other's homes look like.

When they do invite someone to visit, Czechs are quite gracious hosts and will always offer something to drink. When visiting someone's home, the guest is expected to arrive on time and remove his or her shoes when first entering the home. Gifts, such as chocolates or a bottle of wine, are generally brought for dinner parties, and the guest usually brings some small gift for the children as well. As with most cultures, there is certain dining etiquette, and it is likely that guests and the elderly are seated and served first.

LIFESTYLE

Family

The fall of communism caused dramatic changes in Czech society, especially in its most basic institution, the Czech family. Under communist rule, couples married at a much younger age and had more children. Many factors contributed to this: young people faced difficulties developing a long-term single lifestyle; traveling was very limited or impossible; and the job market did not help people develop careers. There was also a housing shortage, and marriage—which enabled a couple to request a government-issued apartment—was the only way to begin a life independent from one's parents.

This all changed significantly after the revolution. Suddenly, young Czechs could travel and consider careers, and marriage was no longer a prerequisite to start a life. Consequently, young people began delaying married life, and cohabitation became increasingly common in contemporary Czech society. However, Czechs have one of the lowest birth rates in Europe (9.79 live births for every 1,000 people) in the early twenty-first century, and the average age for women's first baby is nearly 28 years old. Moreover, the country also has one of the highest divorce rates in all of Europe—50 percent of marriages end in divorce. These trends have become more of a concern to Czech society and government. Recently, the government has established initiatives to increase parental benefits and developed programs to encourage family-oriented policies in private companies.

Housing

In the past, at least two generations lived in most Czech houses, while many young families also lived in government-built project housing during communist rule. Today, an increasing number of married couples are building their own homes. This change in housing has been possible because the economic situation for Czechs has steadily improved since the inception of a market economy. In the mid-1990s, banks began to offer mortgage loans to a growing Czech middle class for the first time since the 1930s, and the number of homes built has grown every year in the Czech Republic since mortgages became available. For example, the number of homes built in 2007 was up by 38 percent from the previous year. Between January and May 2015, construction output also climbed by 11.9 percent and 5.5 percent more building permits were issued than during the same period in 2014. This reveals that the construction boom developing before the 2008 global financial crisis, which so heavily impacted U.S. housing markets, has not devastated the Czech building industry. Most of the abovementioned housing growth has occurred in regions just beyond large cities, in effect replacing large potato fields with new suburbs throughout the country. Prague and the entire Central Bohemian region have seen the most residential development thus far.

Food

Czech cuisine traditionally has strong Central European influences, and largely consists of meat (usually pork or beef) served with potatoes or dumplings with various sauces. Rice has also long been a Czech staple food and often replaces the potatoes or dumplings when accompanying meat and sauce. The traditional starter of Czech lunches and dinners is soup. The most traditional Czech food is roasted pork with bread dumplings and sauerkraut (vepřové maso, houskové knedlíky a zelí). For Christmas dinner, Czech families traditionally eat carp and potato salad.

Desserts (moučníky) are quite popular, and a love of desserts supports the local cake and sweet shop (cukrárna) in nearly every town or village in the country. Cookie baking is a popular activity during the Christmas season.

Czechs are also traditional brewers of beer (pivo) and are considered a nation of beer drinkers. Two world-renowned brands of Czech beer include Plzeňský Prazdroj (Pilsner Urquell) and Budějovický Budvar (Budweiser Budvar, or Czechvar). Beer is less expensive than a glass of soda or cup of coffee, and the per capita annual consumption of beer is about 148.6 liters, the equivalent of just under half a liter per day per person in the whole of the country.

Life's Milestones

Most Czech marriages are civil weddings and usually involve the gathering of friends and family at the town hall to witness the wedding, followed by a decorated motorcade through town. The wedding party often meets at a restaurant to continue the celebration.

In smaller towns, it has been tradition for the mayor to invite the parents of a newborn to sit in the front row of the town hall meeting, to welcome the new citizens of the town. Photographs are printed in the town bulletin.

In Bohemia, cremation is an increasingly common arrangement for the deceased, and an urn is traditionally placed in a glass case at the local cemetery. Czech cemeteries are often considered quite beautiful and are decorated with live flowers and trees that families of the deceased care for year round. Cemeteries are particularly beautiful for the Czech holiday Dušičky (All Soul's Day), dedicated to the memory of the dead and celebrated on November 2. Czech families gather at the tombs or urn cases of deceased relatives to tidy the site, lay wreaths and flowers there, and then light small candles that glow throughout the cemetery.

CULTURAL HISTORY

Art

During communist rule after World War II, literature was highly censored and could not contradict the principles of communism. As a result, some of the best Czech literature was produced as "samizdat" (or self-published) literature, government-suppressed literature that was illegally copied and distributed. Samizdat literature circulated among trusted friends, although doing so was an offense punishable by prison. Some great Czech writers emigrated to avoid censorship and persecution. Other writers such as Bohumil Hrabal (1914–1997) managed to write very colorful and rich prose that did not offend the Communist Party.

Censorship eased for several years during the Prague Spring of 1968, a period of political and artistic awakening under the leadership of Alexander Dubček (1921–1992), who had hoped to liberalize communism within Czechoslovakia. However, the Prague Spring was short-lived, lasting from January to August, when the Soviets removed Dubček from power and reasserted their control, and severe censorship returned. Dissident writers such as Václav Havel (1936–2011) were published abroad, but not domestically, except as samizdat literature, which is why samizdat hit a high point by the 1980s. Samizdat literature ended with the arrival of democracy in 1989, but remains in memory as the symbol for the freedom of expression in a time of oppression.

Theater also served the dissident movement. After World War II, all theaters were nationalized under communist rule, and theater largely became propaganda for the Communist Party. However, just as playwrights expressed dissidence under Nazi occupation, they eventually began expressing dissidence toward communist totalitarianism, and the concept of "samizdat" was then extended to theater performances. In the 1960s, playwrights such as Václav Havel, Milan Kundera (1929–) and others wrote controversial plays that were highly critical of the Communist Party and the one-party system of Czech socialism. Samizdat theaters, also known as "apartment theater" because they were held in residences, were unofficial theaters where controversial samizdat plays were performed. Samizdat playwrights, actors, and directors were often persecuted for expressing political dissidence in their art. Václav Havel, for example, was imprisoned for several years for dissident activities, including the writing of samizdat plays.

Film was less useful for expressing dissidence because of the nature of the medium. While books could be copied and passed between individuals, films were expensive to produce and had to be aired on television or projected with expensive theater equipment. However, in the 1960s, when totalitarian conditions eased, some directors took the opportunity to create films that were not influenced by socialist realism. This led to one of the best periods in Czech film known as Czech New Wave Cinema. Miloš Forman (1932–) directed several excellent Czech films before the invasion of Warsaw Pact troops in August 1968 (ending the "Prague Spring"). After the invasion, Forman immigrated to the United States and continued his film career, which included three Academy Award nominations.

The New Wave movement was made up of other quality directors such as Jiří Menzel (1938–), Věra Chytilová (1929–2014), Jan Němec (1936–), and other graduates from the Film and TV School of the Academy of Performing Arts (FAMU). During the Czech New Wave period, two films won Oscars in two consecutive years: *The Shop on Main Street* (1965) and *Closely Watched Trains* (1966). The latter is based on a novel by famed Czech writer Bohumil Hrabal (1914–1997). After the Prague Spring, the artistic quality of Czech film was destroyed by censorship once again, and the founders of the Czech New Wave cinema who had not emigrated were banned from making any more films. After the Velvet Revolution of 1989, Czech film slowly returned to its previous glory, and in 1996, the film *Kolya* won an Oscar in the category of Best Foreign Film.

One final art form important to the dissident movement was music, particularly rock and roll. In fact, in 1977, Václav Havel and other dissidents created and signed the famous Charter 77 civic initiative, which was central to the eventual overthrow of communism. It was created and signed in part because of the imprisonment of members of the underground rock band, The Plastic People of the Universe. Additionally, musicians—much like writers, painters, cartoonists, actors, and other artists—kept the spirit of the Czech nation alive during the country's long period of totalitarianism.

Architecture

Prague (Praha) and other cities in the Czech Republic are more than a thousand years old and historically connected to the rest of Europe. Because Czech cities developed through the same architectural periods—Romanesque, Gothic, Renaissance, baroque, rococo, and art nouveau—they share architectural history with the oldest and largest European cities. The Catholic Church and various royal dynasties were the two major powers that spread these distinct architectural styles. However, Czechs have incorporated their own unique elements into the larger architectural movements.

The earliest architectural style in Bohemia was Romanesque architecture. This early style of architecture was applied to the building of rotundas that are much more common in early Central Europe than in Western Europe. This leads historians to suggest that architects from the earliest Hungarian kingdom influenced the earliest period of architecture in the Czech lands. However, the first Czech royal dynasty, the Přemyslid dynasty (which reigned from the ninth to the 14th centuries), may have prevented

a continuing influence of Hungarian architects in Prague. At the beginning of the first millennium, the Magyars (Hungarians) took over the region that is today Slovakia, but could not take control of the Czech lands. This period likely caused a permanent social and cultural line to be drawn between Slovaks and Czechs, since Slovaks experienced centuries of Eastern influence, while the Czechs became more integrated into Western Europe.

During the 11th century, the Přemyslid dynasty continued to strengthen Bohemia by spreading Romanesque castles and fortresses throughout the land. At the same time, the Catholic Church spread Romanesque monasteries and churches. The Middle Ages in Bohemia saw a gradual evolution of Romanesque architecture into Gothic architecture. Fortifications were built around many towns and castles, while new churches were built in town centers. The Golden age of Bohemia was during the reign of Charles IV (1316–1378), who became the Holy Roman Emperor. He greatly expanded Czech cities during the high Gothic architectural period (1250–1500). The first Renaissance projects came at the end of the 15th century. A good example of this style in Prague is the Vladislav Hall (begun in 1493 and completed in 1502) at Prague Castle. Bohemia's most prominent medieval architect, Benedikt Rejt (c. 1450–c. 1536), built it.

By the end of the 16th century, Renaissance architecture faded as Baroque architecture spread. After Italy made its architectural impression on the Czech Republic during the Renaissance and baroque periods, the French followed suit with periods of rococo and neoclassicism. This is not surprising, since this was the period when Napoleon Bonaparte (1769–1821) conquered most of Europe. These styles became popular in Bohemia and Moravia from around the latter part of the 18th century to about the middle of the 19th century. Neoclassicism then gave way to a period of historical romanticism that mixed various elements from many architectural styles and periods.

At the beginning of the 20th century, art nouveau arrived in Prague through Vienna. The

Municipal House in Prague, begun in 1905 and completed in 1911, is a beautifully restored example of the art nouveau movement in Prague and is filled with allegorical and decorative works by Czech artists Karel Špillar (1871–1939), Alfons Mucha (1860–1939), Jan Preisler (1872-1918), and Max Švabinský (1873–1962). The Czechs also have a history of creating avant-garde buildings. At the end of art nouveau, some Czech architects developed a unique style of architecture that was based on principles of the cubist painting movement. Josef Gočár (1880–1945) was one of the founders of Czech cubist architecture and built the best-known example of Czech cubist architecture, the House of the Black Madonna. The building currently houses the Czech Museum of Cubism. Another more recent example of avant-garde architecture is the Tančící dům (or Dancing House, completed in 1996) on the bank of the Vltava River in the center of Prague. Designed by Croatian-Czech architect and Vlado Milunić (1941–) with help from Canadian architect Frank Gehry (1929–), the building resembles a woman and man dancing together and was originally named "Fred and Ginger" (after Fred Astaire and Ginger Rogers). The nickname persists.

Drama

Czech theater dates to the medieval period, when the Catholic Church staged religious plays to educate the illiterate population about the Bible. This influence was mixed with a later period, when traveling acting troupes from Italy, Hungary, and Germany performed in Bohemia. However, the modern theatrical tradition can be traced back to the Czech National Revival, which promoted Czech theater and, in fact, brought about the building of the Czech National Theatre.

The strongest period of growth for theater occurred after Czechoslovakia became an independent state in 1918. From 1918 to 1938, theater flourished thanks to the works of many playwrights. The most notable of these were František Langer (1888–1965), Karel Čapek (1890–1938), and his brother Josef Čapek (1887–1945). The country's independence—and

its uncensored theater—ended with the Nazi German occupation of 1938. Czech theater has a special place in Czech culture as an outlet for protest and dissidence. During Nazi occupation, Czech theater was suppressed and playwrights were persecuted.

Music

Because the Czech lands were part of several major kingdoms in Central Europe over the centuries, music was largely cultivated by the Catholic Church and the aristocracy. In fact, the capital of Prague remains to this day a major center for symphonic and operatic performances. The Czech lands have produced some of the world's greatest composers, including Bedřich Smetana (1824–1884) and Antonín Dvořák (1841–1904). All of the greatest Czech composers used folk melodies in their classical compositions. There are two main branches of Czech folk music from the nation's two main regions, Bohemia and Moravia. Essentially, this east-west cultural division occurred from about the 16th century onward and created two distinct styles of folk music. Bohemian folk music is called "instrumental folk," while the Moravian folk music is considered "vocal folk."

During the earliest period of Bohemian folk music, bagpipes were the only instruments that musicians played. Over the course of a few centuries, other wind instruments and drums joined the bagpipe. By the end of the 18th century, small country music bands (malá selská muzika) had become the standard form for Bohemian folk music. Compared to Slovak and Moravian folk music, Bohemian folk music has always been closer to Western musical styles and developments. The songs are usually in major keys, are strongly instrumental, and have a clear notation structure that is often symmetrical. Folk music was at the center of Czech births, weddings, funerals, village fairs, seasonal festivities, and various forms of folk dance.

Dance

In the 17th and 18th centuries, baroque instrumental music contributed to a period of many new folk dances in Bohemia—especially couple dances. Though there is little record of these dances, one rare folk dance catalog survived from the Litomyšl Estate (where composer Bedřich Smetana was born in 1824). The Litomyšl folk dance catalog outlines 23 popular Czech folk dances and was created to celebrate the 1836 coronation of Ferdinand V (1452–1516) in Prague. A few decades later, the Czech National Revival, a cultural movement that occurred during the 18th and 19th centuries, helped revive traditional folk dances, much in the same way it did with Czech folk music. During this period, some Czech folk dances came to be considered "national social dances" and were very popular among the wealthy and educated classes in Bohemia.

Although traditional folk music and dance went through some changes—especially once brass bands became popular—some of the older folk dances still continued as a tradition. This is particularly the case in Moravia (the most rural part of the Czech Republic), where couple dances, as well as an old tradition of male dances, still carry on today. For example, a military-inspired male saltation (involving jumps and rhythmic steps) dance, known as the Slovácký verbuňk of southeast Moravia, was designated as part of the country's Intangible Cultural Heritage (ICH) by the United Nations Educational, Scientific, and Cultural Organization (UNESCO) in 2005.

Literature

The earliest period of Czech literature dates back to the Christianization of Bohemia as a part of the Greater Moravian Empire during the ninth and 10th centuries. Two Byzantine missionaries, Cyril (826/7–869) and Methodius (815–885), Christianized the region and created a written language called Old Church Slavonic. They translated biblical texts, particularly from the New Testament; these texts are the oldest Czech literature. Old Church Slavonic was eventually replaced with Latin texts written in the Roman alphabet, which created a fundamental and enduring division between Slavic languages using the Roman alphabet and Slavic languages using variations of Cyrillic (based on the Greek alphabet).

Like most early literature, much of the earliest Czech literature is grounded in religion. However, a more secular tradition grew out of feudalism as tournaments, feasts, fairs, and legends of knighthood became part of Czech society. Later, some Czech literature was entirely focused on the adventures and heroic deeds of knights and was written in a Latin-based version of Czech.

Like many aspects of Czech society, Czech literature flourished under Charles IV (1346–1378), who was a cultivated and enlightened king. His founding of the first university in Central Europe in 1348, Charles University, did much to develop Czech literature. Jan Hus (c. 1369–1415) was the rector of Charles University and did much to create a literary language from Czech, including translating much of the Bible into vernacular Czech. (Hus was later burned at the stake for heresy and for his defiance of certain Catholic doctrines, making him an early pioneer of the Protestant movement and anticipating Martin Luther's *95 Theses* by a century). Because of his influence on Czech culture, Hus has been recognized with a national holiday, celebrated annually on July 6.

In 1468, the first book, the *Trojan Chronicle*, was printed in Plzeň, and over the next century, about 5,000 books were printed in the Czech lands. Czech books were about geography, medicine, history—and even cookbooks went into print. During the Czech National Revival literature flourished, and then experienced a golden age during the years 1918–1938, when the Czech lands were an independent modern nation.

CULTURE

Arts & Entertainment

In addition to its rich cultural past (as Czechoslovakia), the Czech Republic is home to a vibrant artistic community. The Czech film industry produces about thirty feature films and 1,200 documentaries and short films each year. However, finding distributors for Czech films remains difficult and securing adequate funds is consistently challenging. Many directors must produce commercials in order to make a living. Still, many Czech-born directors have met with commercial and critical success. Film director Miloš Forman, who won Academy Awards for *One Flew over the Cuckoo's Nest* (1975) and *Amadeus* (1984), was born in Czechoslovakia in 1932. Czech director Jiří Menzel, born in 1938, won the Academy Award for Best Foreign Language Film for *Closely Watched Trains* (1967). Jan Svěrák (1965–), whose film *Kolya* (*Kolja*) won the Academy Award for Best Foreign Language Film in 1996; Jan Hřebejk (1967–); Saša Gedeon (1970–); Petr Zelenka (1967–); and David Ondříček (1969–) are all part of the newest generation of prolific Czech filmmakers.

Of particular importance to both filmmakers and cinephiles is the Karlovy Vary International Film Festival, held each July in the spa town of western Bohemia. The film festival is one of the oldest of its kind and is Central and Eastern Europe's premier filmmaking event.

Puppetry and puppet theatre has long been a part of Czech culture. Black light theatre, in which actors or marionettes appear in fluorescent costumes under ultraviolet lights, is also popular.

The polka originated in eastern Bohemia in the 19th century. Popular modern musical genres include jazz, pop, rock, reggae, and folk. The Prague Spring International Music Festival is held annually between mid-May and early June.

Soccer, ice hockey, and tennis are the most popular sports in the Czech Republic. International tennis champions Martina Navratilova and Ivan Lendl are of Czech descent. Winter sports, including ice-skating, downhill and cross-country skiing, snowboarding and tobogganing, are also popular among Czechs. Many Czechs belong to a physical education organization called Sokol, which is an important part of their culture. Sokol clubs are also found in the United States and Canada.

Cultural Sites & Landmarks

The Czech Republic has twelve properties inscribed on the list of UNESCO World Heritage Sites, including much of the center of the

nation's capital, Prague. One look at this majestic city explains why Prague became one of the first locations in the former Czechoslovakia to join the World Heritage List (in 1992). Prague is an architectural gem that sits on both sides of a sweeping bend of the Vltava River. Czechs call it the city of a hundred spires (stověžatá Praha), but it is also known as the "Paris of the East" and the "Golden City." Its central areas are the Old Town (Staré Město), Lesser Town (or Menší Město pražské), and New Town (Nové Město), most of which was either significantly expanded or originally built during the reign of Charles IV in the 14th century. Throughout its long history, Prague was never significantly damaged in any wars or natural disasters, and it never went through any large-scale urban renewals. For these reasons, Prague is one of the few European cities that quite visibly demonstrates an entire history of development throughout the ages.

Next to Prague Castle stands St. Vitus Cathedral, which is an excellent example of Gothic architecture. This is the biggest and most important church in the country, and houses the tombs of several Bohemian kings. A walk down from the castle and cathedral hilltop leads to the Lesser Town, ending at the Charles Bridge, which began construction in 1357 and was completed in 1402. Just across the bridge is the Old Town Square, leading into the New Town, which Charles IV built as the "New Jerusalem." These areas were enlarged with urban growth during the high Gothic period, with more buildings and parks added during the high baroque period in the 17th century. Later historical periods are also blended into the city, so that touring Prague is necessarily touring the architectural history of Europe.

The Czech Republic also has other majestic locations on the World Heritage List. In the eastern region of the country, the city center of Olomouc has the Holy Trinity Column, an exceptional landmark designed in a unique Central European baroque style. The city of Telč in southern Moravia is known for its castle (also sometimes referred to as a chateau) and well-preserved Renaissance houses, which together form a long urban plaza that, to this day, is the town center. An hour east of Telč is the town Třebič, whose Jewish Quarter dates to the Middle Ages and is on the World Heritage List as a reminder to all of the peaceful co-existence of Jewish and Christian cultures from the Middle Ages to the 20th century.

Libraries & Museums

The Czech National Museum (or Národní muzeum) is located at the top of Prague's Wenceslas Square. The wide, tree-lined street is a center of business, transportation, and tourism for the city. Named after Saint Wenceslas, the patron saint of Bohemia, this large boulevard is often used for celebrations, festivals, and social demonstrations.

Other museums include Prague's Czech Museum of Fine Art, which focuses on the development of Czech 20th-century art; Prague's National Technical Museum (Národní technické muzeum), which focuses on the history of science and technology; and the Moravian Gallery in Brno (or Moravská galerie v Brně), which is the second largest museum in the Czech Republic. Other points of interest include the Prague Aviation Museum (or Letecké Muzeum Kbely) and the Museum of Decorative Arts (or Uměleckoprůmyslové muzeum v Praze), also in Prague. In the Old Town area of Prague is architect Josef Gočár's (1880–1945) House of the Black Madonna (or U Černé Matky Boží), which is both an example of cubist architecture and home to the Czech Museum of Cubism and the opulent Grand Café Orient restaurant, located on the museum's first floor.

Holidays

National holidays include Republic or Establishment Day (January 1), which marks the formation of the Czech Republic in 1993, and Czechoslovakian Statehood Day (October 28), marking the establishment of Czechoslovakia in 1918.

Freedom and Democracy Day (November 17) commemorates the anti-Nazi protests in 1939 and anti-communist demonstrations in 1989. Other official holidays include Labor Day, which is also called May Day (May 1), and Liberation Day (May 8), which celebrates the end of WWII in Europe. Religious holidays include Saint Wenceslas Day (September 28), honoring the patron saint of the Czech Republic, and Saints Cyril and Methodius Day (July 5). Jan Hus Day (July 6) celebrates the martyrdom of a Czech priest who attempted to initiate the first reforms within the Catholic Church and paved the way for the eventual Protestant movement.

Dušičky (also known as Památka zesnulých), or All Soul's Day, is not a national holiday, but it is widely observed on November 2 by cleaning the gravesites of loved ones and celebrating their memory.

Youth Culture

Czech youth in the early 21st century have been exposed to a greater breadth of mass and popular culture than previous generations. For example, films are often Czech-dubbed versions of Western cinema; American TV shows, such as *Friends*, continue to be popular; and reality TV shows are recreated from successful American versions for Czech consumption. In general, Czech youth are also becoming increasingly Internet-savvy, and many are avid computer gamers, who play online network games. Additionally, it has become less of an overstatement to suggest that nearly every Czech youth has a portable MP3 player (the standard used for transmitting digital music) and a cell phone.

There are, however, some distinct Czech traits within Czech youth, though these traits are elusive and difficult to define. Among young people, the two extremes are anarchists and skinheads, with the majority of youth somewhere in between. The skinheads generally come from uneducated industrial backgrounds, while anarchists often come from educated urban backgrounds. Additionally, some traditional aspects of Czech culture are still prevalent among youth. For example, their mothers tend to Czech boys until their girlfriends and future wives begin tending to them, and Czech girls are taught about homemaking and pass on the traditions of families more than men do.

SOCIETY

Transportation

According to the US State Department, driving conditions in the country are among the most dangerous in Europe. Side roads, country roads, and some roads within towns and cities are considered dangerous as they may feature uneven terrain, difficult-to-understand road signs, and unclear lane markings. Drivers should note that traffic lights in the Czech Republic are placed before the intersection, as opposed to after, as is the case in the United States. Drivers use the right side of the road in the Czech Republic.

Although cars are increasingly used for transportation throughout the Czech Republic, the country also has a long tradition of mass transportation systems. A thorough network of trains and buses connect every village to the rest of the nation, and the capital has one of the best public transportation systems in Europe.

The Czech Republic has 121 airports, with only 46 having paved runways. The largest airport in the country is Prague's Václav Havel Airport (or Letiště Václava Havla Praha), which is the hub for Czech Airlines and base for Travel Service Airlines. In 2014 alone, it saw 11,149,926 passengers and 50,897,792 kilograms (112,210,423 pounds) of cargo pass through it. Other major airports include the Brno-Tuřany Airport, which saw 486,134 passengers in 2014, and the Leoš Janáček Airport, which served 288,393 passengers in 2014.

Transportation Infrastructure

About two-thirds of Prague's inhabitants use the mass transportation system because parking, traffic jams, and accidents are an ever-increasing problem. In Prague, an interconnected system using the subway, streetcars, and buses allows commuters to get within a block of nearly any destination in the city.

Before the revolution, many people, including the aged, traveled by bicycle. For that reason, there is an intricate network of bike paths often running through beautiful forests that connect all the towns and villages. Today, these trails are color-coded tourist routes and are a rich network of bike paths that many Czechs use for leisure travel on weekends and holidays. Most Czechs now have modern mountain bikes for such trips, and biking is still quite popular in the Czech Republic.

Media & Communications

After the fall of communism in 1989, Czech media experienced a period of privatization. Additionally, when Czechoslovakia became the two nations of the Czech Republic and the Slovak Republic in 1992, some national media also split into two national media. For example, the Czech news agency (ČTK Česká tisková kancelář) split into a Czech and Slovak news service, as did public television. ČTK is a public service institution established by law and designed to provide objective and nonbiased information for citizens.

The major print media consists of *Lidové noviny* (*People's News*), a former dissident publication that today prints a daily newspaper; *Mladá fronta Dnes* (*Young Front Today*), a Prague-based national daily; *Právo* (meaning *Right* or *Law*), a left-leaning paper formerly called *Rudé Právo* (Czech for "The Red Right," which was the paper of the Communist Party); *Blesk* (*Flash*), a Prague-based tabloid daily that has the highest circulation in the country; and *The Prague Post*, the country's only English-language newspaper.

Public-owned television broadcast stations also split. In the Czech Republic, public television (ČT1 and ČT2) is still the largest broadcaster in the country, though two major private TV channels (TV Nova and TV Prima, which includes Prima Family and Prima Cool) now compete with national broadcasts, and there are many private radio stations. Recently, the country has begun digitizing television broadcasting and offering new Internet television systems. The nation shut down all analog broadcast signals on June 30, 2012 and was the first country in Central and Eastern Europe to do so. In 2013, 74.1 percent of the population was considered Internet users.

SOCIAL DEVELOPMENT

Standard of Living

The Czech Republic is ranked 28th on the 2012 United Nations Human Development Index, which measures quality of life indicators. The life expectancy at birth is 81 years for women and 75 years for men (2014 estimate).

Water Consumption

Both urban and rural populations have 100 percent access to improved water sources and sanitation facilities. In 2014, average daily water consumption dropped to 131.2 liters (35 gallons) per person, down 2.5 liters (0.7 gallons) from the previous year. The country's freshwater supply is replenished mainly through precipitation, and an annual average of 70 cm (27.5 inches) falls across highlands and lowlands.

Education

The Czech Republic has a high literacy rate, at 99 percent for both men and women. Education is compulsory and free for nine years, beginning at the age of six. After completing their basic education, students receive a Vysvědčení (or primary school leaving certificate). Secondary schools, or gymnasiums, are similar to American high schools and prepare students for college. Those who do not plan to attend college may enroll in technical or vocational schools.

As of 2015, the Czech Republic had 22 public, 2 state, and 44 private universities, of which Charles University is the oldest and most prestigious. Public and private universities fall under the purview of Ministry of Education, Youth, and Sports, while the Ministry of Defence and the Ministry of the Interior oversee state universities. The Academy of Fine Arts in Prague, the oldest art education institution in the Czech Republic, was established in 1799 by decree from Emperor Franz I. In 2004, 8.2 percent of women, and 11.8

percent of men had graduated from university. While in 2011, 59 percent of university graduates were women, up from 57 percent in 2002.

Women's Rights

Women in the Czech Republic first began organizing for rights during the period of the Czech National Revival in the 18th and 19th centuries, so that the women's movement and the movement for Czech independence were closely connected from the beginning. When Czechoslovakia first became a nation in 1918, women were already constitutionally guaranteed the right to vote and to run for public office. This can partly be attributed to the fact that the founder and first president of Czechoslovakia, Tomáš Garrigue Masaryk (1850–1937), held feminist views for his time and promoted the rights of women. At that time, women's rights were significantly advanced compared to other countries in the region. After World War II, communist philosophy—based on egalitarian principles—prevailed, and women enjoyed the same rights to education and work as their male counterparts. In fact, the Communist Party promoted feminist principles—even if the entire society lacked guaranteed rights to free speech.

After the Velvet Revolution, more women began working full time, though they also retained most of the responsibilities for homemaking and child rearing. By 1996, more Czech women were working outside the home—64 percent—than any other country of Eastern Europe. However, Czech men are better paid than Czech women are, and more men work in prestigious occupations and hold more high-level management positions. However, women are well represented in the healthcare field; for example, 50 percent of all physicians and 60 percent of all dentists are women. In addition, Czech society has a very strong social net for mothers, including an extended maternity leave and other related benefits.

In the early 21st century, human trafficking and domestic violence remain problems in the Czech Republic. As of 2004, a law was enacted that labeled domestic abuse as a distinct crime, which carries a sentence of up to eight years. The government administers programs for the awareness and prevention of both trafficking and domestic violence and rape.

Health Care

The Czech health care system is a blend of compulsory universal health care coverage and private care. The government, employers, and their employees contribute to health insurance costs. Some physicians enter into contracts with the insurance system and are reimbursed for their services.

Under the communist government, Czechoslovakia had a very good health care system, but the quality was affected somewhat by the shift to a free market economy. As of 2010, there were just under four physicians per 1,000 people and just under seven hospital beds per 1,000 people. Public funding for health care expenditures was 7.2 percent of the nation's GDP in 2013.

GOVERNMENT

Structure

The Czech Republic is a parliamentary representative democracy with three branches of government. The executive branch consists of the president, who is head of state; the prime minister, who is head of government; and the cabinet, whose members advise the other two supreme executive powers. The president is elected to a five-year term of office by the bicameral legislature. The president appoints the prime minister and the cabinet.

The bicameral legislature consists of a 200-member Chamber of Deputies (Poslanecká sněmovna) and an 81-member Senate (Senát). Members of the Senate are elected to six-year terms by popular vote. Members of the Chamber of Deputies, the lower house, are elected to four-year terms.

The country's highest court is the Constitutional Court, which is located in the city of Brno. Members of the Constitutional Court

are appointed by the president and serve unlimited terms. There is no death penalty in the Czech Republic.

The Czech Republic has thirteen administrative regions (kraje) plus the capital city, Prague. These regions are further divided into more than 6,000 municipalities. District bureaus have the right to levy local taxes, supervise the building and maintenance of roads, and administer the school system and public health and utilities.

Political Parties

In the 2013 Chamber of Deputies elections, the Czech Social Democratic Party (ČSSD) gained 50 seats, while the recently founded centrist party, ANO 2011, took 47 seats. The Communist Party of Bohemia and Moravia (KSČM) took 33, while fiscally conservative Tradition Responsibility Prosperity 09 (TOP 09) garnered 26 seats. The conservative Civic Democratic Party (ODS) held on to sixteen seats. The newly formed, right-wing populist Dawn of Direct Democracy (Dawn) took 14, as did the Christian and Democratic Union–Czechoslovak People's Party (KDU–ČSL).

The first direct presidential election, held on January 11, 2013, produced no clear vote majority, so a runoff election was held on January 25 between the two candidates most supported by the legislature: Miloš Zeman of the social-democratic Party of Civic Rights (SPOZ) and Karel Schwarzenberg of TOP 09. Zeman won 54.8 percent of the vote to become the new president of the Czech Republic. His opponent, Schwarzenberg, received 45.2 percent of the vote. Then presidential incumbent Václav Klaus of ODS was unable to seek reelection, as he had reached his term limit.

Local Government

There are 14 regional territories and over 6,000 municipalities in the Czech Republic. Each of these municipalities is a self-governing unit headed by a municipal council that is directly elected using a proportional electoral system. Citizens who are 18 years and older can both vote for and run for municipal office during elections that occur every four years. The democratically elected municipal councils ultimately appoint the region's mayor. The number of municipal council members is determined by the municipality's population.

Judicial System

The country's judicial system, defined in chapter four of the Czech Republic's constitution, is comprised of four tiers. The Constitutional Court occupies the highest tier. After this are so-called 'ordinary courts,' which are district or regional courts that handle civil and criminal cases. The country's Supreme Court rules on appeal cases from regional and district courts and is entirely separate from the Constitutional Court. Finally, there are Administrative Courts, which deal with cases related to elections, political parties, and governmental agencies.

Taxation

The Czech Republic imposes income taxes, corporate taxes, capital gains taxes, value-added taxes (VAT), real estate taxes, road taxes, inheritance taxes, and gift taxes. Personal income taxes are imposed at a flat rate of 15 percent, unless income is in excess of 1.2 million Czech koruna, at which point the rate graduates to 22 percent. Corporate tax is applied at 19 percent, while inheritance taxes range from one percent to 40 percent, based on the relationship of the inheritor to the deceased. Children inheriting property from their parents, for example, pay no inheritance tax.

Armed Forces

The military of the Czech Republic consists of three parts: General Staff of Czech Armed Forces (Praha), the Joint Forces (Olomouc), and the Support and Training Forces (Stara Boleslav). Conscription was abolished in 2004, but men ages 15 to 49 are eligible to serve. As of 2014, there were 21,100 soldiers and 7,530 civilian experts working on behalf of the Czech military in various locations throughout the world, including the Congo, Afghanistan, Kosovo, and Somalia. Reserve personnel numbered 1,300 in 2014.

Foreign Policy

Before the revolution of 1989, Czechoslovakia was a member of the Warsaw Pact, and Czech foreign policy was in complete alignment with the former Soviet Union. When Václav Havel (1936–2011) became president in 1989, he immediately began working toward integration with the West as his chief foreign policy objective.

Havel was president until 2003 (first over Czechoslovakia and then over the Czech Republic), and was highly influential in directing the new country's foreign policy for many years. In 1991, Havel gathered the leaders of countries from the former Soviet Union and officially dissolved the Warsaw Pact, which Havel considers one of his greatest accomplishments. This gave Havel time to gain membership into the North Atlantic Treaty Organization (NATO) and to oversee the nation's difficult transition into European Union (EU) membership, which became official on May 1, 2004. The Czech Republic is also a member of many other major Western international organizations, including the Organisation for Economic Co-operation and Development (OECD), the World Trade Organization (WTO), the International Monetary Fund (IMF), and the International Energy Agency (IEA).

A major obstacle to the formation of a clear and consistent foreign policy has been that no Czech elections have produced a clear majority. (For example, the 2006 elections yielded no majority victory, and therefore, a fragile government did not form until seven months after the general elections.) However, in looking at the Czech Republic's foreign policy over the two decades following the revolution, there has been an overall greater movement towards Western integration than other former Eastern bloc countries, including the Czech Republic's immediate neighbor, Slovakia.

In 2008, the Czech Foreign Minister Karel Schwarzenberg (1937–) outlined several of the most important foreign policy issues for the Czech Republic. One of these was whether the Czech Republic would ratify the Lisbon Treaty, which it did via the Constitutional Court on November 3, 2009. The Lisbon Treaty is the constitutional base for the European Union and, in turn, affects all EU member constitutions.

Another important foreign policy issue is the U.S anti-missile defense system that the Czech government agreed to base on its soil. In February 2007, the U.S. began negotiations with the Czech Republic and Poland to construct missile shield installations, called European Interceptor Sites, and accompanying radar tracking. The air defense radar would have been positioned in the Czech Republic. While the Czech government initially agreed, approximately two thirds of its citizens protested the potential military installation, and 130,000 people signed a petition calling for a referendum on the issue. The plan was eventually cancelled on September 17, 2009 and replaced AEGIS warships using a missile defense system that would not involve the Czech Republic.

In July 2015, the Czech Republic and Germany signed a joint declaration on strategic cooperation, vowing to meet annually and build greater cooperation and feedback on issues as diverse as foreign policy, defense, education, energy, transportation, and the battle against drug trafficking. The Czech Republic will also consult with Germany in its attempts to reconcile its ongoing human rights concerns with its aspirations to continued economic development. As of 2015, the Czech Republic has similarly close working relationships with the foreign ministers of France, Ireland, Poland, Slovakia, and the U.S.

Human Rights Profile

International human rights law insists that states respect civil and political rights and promote an individual's economic, social, and cultural rights. The United Nations Universal Declaration on Human Rights (UDHR) is recognized as the standard for international human rights. (To read this document or view the articles relating to cultural human rights, go to http://www.ohchr.org/EN/UDHR/Pages/Introduction.aspx.)

Article 19 of the UDHR protects the right to freedom of speech and expression. This is also a guaranteed right in the Czech national constitution. However, the Czech government has placed limitations on hate speech, and such laws

are supported and even promoted by the EU. For example, after several years of negotiating, 27 member countries of the EU agreed in April 2007 to a new set of rules and policies to combat racism and hate crimes. The new rules allow prison sentences up to three years for those convicted of denying or trivializing genocides, such as the Holocaust. Such crimes include speaking, writing, or behaving in such a way as to degrade, intimidate, or incite violence or prejudice against a person or a group of people based on their nationality, language, race, religion, or class. The Czech law concerning hate crimes specifically mentions groups using media, such as television, film, the printed press, and radio to spread racist messages, but the law does not specifically mention the Internet.

The Czech Republic has a significant Romani population, and both society and government have created a system of discrimination that denies Romani Czechs equal treatment and protection. The EU has applied pressure on the Czech government to end discriminatory practices and work on improving domestic conditions for the Romani population. In 2007, the European Court of Human Rights (ECtHR) ruled that the Czech Republic violated the rights of Romani children by unjustly forcing them to attend "special schools" for children with learning disabilities (Czech courts had previously rejected the case in the 1990s). That court ordered the Czech government to pay €4,000 to each of the 18 families that filed the suit, and the decision set an important precedent.

Other signs of social discrimination against the Romani population are quite apparent in Czech society. In November 2008, around 500 organized Czech neo-Nazis fought with police who blocked the group from marching into a Romani neighborhood in Litvínov in north Bohemia. A further indication of widespread Czech discrimination and racism could be seen from the very large crowd of local Czechs who openly sympathized with the neo-Nazi organization's march into the Romani ghetto. The Czech government has announced plans to ban the far-right Workers' Party of Social Justice (DSSS), which was behind the Litvínov march, though the party has announced it will simply form another organization in the event it is legally dissolved. Experts argue that the Czech government needs to take a more comprehensive approach in dealing with the issue of Romani ghettos and Czech social discrimination.

Romani organizations have warned the Czech government that if far-right extremism is not addressed, then there may be mass emigrations among the country's Romani population. Such emigrations from the Czech Republic have occurred in the recent past, and other governments, such as Canada and the United Kingdom (UK), have experienced large waves of Romani Czechs applying for asylum. For years, experts have been pointing out the growth of right-wing extremism in the Czech Republic, as evidenced by the development of anti-Romani Workers' Party of Social Justice (DSSS), which bills itself as a "defender of ordinary people" and promotes Czech isolationism. This growth potentially represents a political and social problem that could lead to major violations of international human rights laws.

ECONOMY

Overview of the Economy

The economy of the Czech Republic has fared better than most former members of the Central European Communist Bloc, but it still lags far behind those of its Western European neighbors. The gross domestic product (GDP) was estimated at $ 299.7 billion (USD) in 2014, with per capita GDP of $28,400 (USD). The Czech Republic joined the European Union on May 1, 2004.

Industry

The Czech Republic manufactures a variety of products, ranging from military equipment and armaments to precision microscopes and tractors. Brewing is also a major industry, with production volumes reaching 1,860,100 kiloliters (475,536,107 gallons) in 2013 alone.

After the fall of communism in 1989, the economy of Czechoslovakia underwent a transformation to become a market-driven free enterprise economy, a process that is still underway in the early 21st century. Businesses, factories, and

farms that used to be owned by the government were privatized, and foreign investors acquired some enterprises. Automotive production has accounted for nearly 40 percent of international investment. Škoda, an auto manufacturer established in 1895 and billing itself as the oldest automobile maker in the world, is a major exporter and employs thousands of workers. Many major American firms, like Bayer and Honeywell, have begun operating in the Czech Republic and often belong to what is known as "AmCham," or the American Chamber of Commerce in the Czech Republic. Germany is the Czech Republic's major trading partner, along with Slovakia, Austria, Poland, Russia, Italy, and the United Kingdom.

Labor

The labor force of the country in 2014 was an estimated 5.42 million people. As of 2012, 60 percent of the labor force worked in the services industries. About 37 percent of the work force was employed in the industries sector, and 2.6 percent worked in the agricultural sector. The Czech Republic's unemployment rate was 7.9 percent in 2014, with higher rates in northern Moravia and Bohemia, where steel is produced and coal is mined and processed.

Energy/Power/Natural Resources

Major natural resources are lignite (brown coal), anthracite (hard coal), graphite, clay, kaolin, gypsum, and natural gas. Metal ores include silver, lead, uranium, and zinc. However, the country must import iron ore products, generally from Russia and the Ukraine, as it has no economically exploitable deposits of its own. The Czech Republic's only domestic producer of uranium, Diamo, supplies one-third of the material needed to power the country's two nuclear energy plants. The rest of the uranium produced is exported to Russia, where it is further converted to fuel.

Due to its dependence on low-grade brown coal for heating and generating electrical power, the Czech Republic has experienced significant environmental problems, such as air pollution and acid rain.

Fishing

The Czech Republic has 455 natural lakes and 21,800 artificial lakes and ponds. Many of the artificial lakes were created for fish farming. Species of fish found in the area include carp, pike, European catfish, perch, and trout. Noted fisheries, among others, include Třeboň Fisheries (Rybářství Třeboň); Rybářský ráj, originally a gravel pit that was flooded and filled with carp, pike, pike-perch, and catfish; Lake Vrbenský (Vrbenské jezero), filled with carp, pike-perch, eel, and tench; and Lázně Bohdaneč, located in a spa town. Fish common to Czech waters include the chub (jelec tloušť), the brown trout (obecný pstruh), the pike (štíka), the pikeperch (candát obecný), and the catfish (sumec).

Forestry

Approximately one-third of the Czech Republic's area is covered by forests, despite widespread deforestation for logging. Beech, spruce, and oak trees grow at higher elevations, while maple and ash are found in the lowlands. Common softwood conifers include pine and fir trees.

Mining/Metals

Major natural resources are lignite (brown coal); anthracite (hard coal); graphite; clays, like bentonite and kaolin; gypsum; sand; and natural gas. Metals include silver, lead, uranium, and zinc. Because there are not enough iron deposits within the Czech Republic, iron ore products are imported, most often from Russia.

Agriculture

Agriculture accounts for 2.6 percent of the gross domestic product and employs 2.6 percent of the work force. Important crops include barley and hops (for the country's brewing industry), as well as sugar beets, wheat, rapeseed, and potatoes. Fruit crops include apples, plums, pears, cherries, strawberries, and currants.

Animal Husbandry

Farmers, contributing to agricultural products, raise livestock such as cattle, poultry, pigs, and sheep. In 2009, the sale of milk in the country totaled approximately $3.5 million (USD). That same year, almost 375,000 heads of cattle were sold for slaughter. However, these numbers have dropped in 2015, as domestic consumption of dairy products has declined by as much as 40 percent. Domestic demand for beef has similarly weakened, according The European Commission's recent Agriculture Report. Nevertheless, the country remains a net exporter of butter and skimmed milk powder.

Tourism

The Czech Republic is one of the most popular tourist destinations in Europe, and, accordingly, the country's travel and tourism industry is a significant contributor to its economy. In 2013, over 7.3 million tourists visited the Czech Republic, with over 1.4 million of them coming from neighboring Germany. Thanks to an 18-episode South Korean TV series, *Lovers in Prague*, which aired from September 2005 to November 2005, South Korean's interest in the Czech Republic has steadily climbed, and consequently, visitors from South Korea are up by 14 percent. In 2012, the Czech Tourist Authority supported the filming of the Norwegian movie *Reisen til julestjernen* (*Journey to the Christmas Star*) at Pernštejn castle, which has since boosted the number of Norwegian visitors by 16 percent.

The Czech Republic has a multitude of castles, cathedrals, museums, and other historic buildings. Prague is the top tourist destination, followed by the spa resort towns of Karlovy Vary (Karlsbad), Mariánské Lázně, and Františkovy Lázně in western Bohemia.

Some of the top tourist attractions in Prague are the Charles Bridge, Prague Castle, and the Old Town Square, with its medieval astronomical clock (or Pražský orloj). Dating to 1411, the Pražský orloj is the world's third oldest astronomical clock and the only one still functioning. Other attractions include the Cathedral of Saint Barbara in Kutná Hora, the sandstone labyrinths in Kokořín, and the Church of St. Bartholomew in Pilsen (Plzeň).

Sinclair Nicholas, Patricia Martin, &
Lynn-nore Chittom

DO YOU KNOW?

- The Czech Republic is believed to have one of the highest beer consumption per capita rates in the world. Pilsner beer originated in the town of Plzeň (also Pilsen) in 1842.

- The St. Vitus Cathedral in Prague, the largest church in the Czech Republic, took nearly 600 years to complete.

- The English word "robot" is derived from the Czech word "robota," meaning "serf labor," "hard work," or, figuratively, "drudgery."

- At 570 meters (1,870 feet) long, 130 meters (422 feet) wide and covering 7.28 hectares (17.98 acres), ninth-century Prague Castle is recorded in the *Guinness Book of World Records* as the largest ancient castle in the world.

Bibliography

"Country profile: Czech Republic." *BBC News*. BBC News Service, 26 Feb. 2015. Web. http://news.bbc.co.uk/1/hi/world/europe/country_profiles/1108489.stm.

Chris Jarrett, "Food, glorious food—Czech eating habits after 1989." *Radio Praha*. Český rozhlas, 30 Mar. 2006. http://www.radio.cz/en/article/77368.

Elizabeth A. Haas. "Czech Literature" *Expats.cz*. Expats.cz, 21 Jun. 2007. http://www.expats.cz/prague/article/czech-culture/czech-literature/.

Martin Mikule, "Czech family: few children, many divorces." *Radio Praha*. Český rozhlas, 17 Mar. 2005. Web. http://www.radio.cz/en/article/64472.

Sinclair Nicholas. *The AmeriCzech Dream: Cizinec v cizí zemi*. Prague: WD Publications, 2005.

"Historic Centre of Prague." *UNESCO World Heritage Web Site*. UNESCO World Heritage Centre, 2015. http://whc.unesco.org/en/list/616.

Works Cited

"2005 population estimates for cities in the Czech Republic." *Mongabay*. Mongabay.com, 2007. http://www.mongabay.com/igapo/2005_world_city_populations/Czech_Republic.html.

"Czech Republic and Germany sign agreement." *Prague Post*. PraguePost.com, 3 Jul. 2015. http://www.praguepost.com/eu-news/48657-czech-republic-and-germany-sign-agreement.

"Czech Republic Essentials." *My Czech Republic*. Local Lingo s.r.o., 2012. Web.

"Czech Republic." *Agricultural Situation and Perspectives in the Central and Eastern European Countries*. European Union, 2015. Web. http://ec.europa.eu/agriculture/publi/peco/czech/summary/sum_en.htm.

"Czech Republic: Mining, Minerals, and Fuel Resources." AZoMining Editors. *AZoMining.com*. AZoMining.com, 2015. http://www.azomining.com/Article.aspx?ArticleID=129.

"Czech Republic—Family." *Net Industries*. Net Industries, 2015. Web.

"Holašovice Historical Village Reservation." *UNESCO World Heritage Web Site*. UNESCO World Heritage Centre, 2015. http://whc.unesco.org/en/list/861.

"Number of tourists coming to the Czech Republic is constantly increasing" *Czech Republic: Land of Stories*. Czech Tourism, 2015. https://www.czechtourism.com/p/cn-tourist-to-czech-increase/.

"Population, Economy." *Jihočeský kraj*. Jihočeský kraj, 2011. Web.

"The history of architecture." *Hello Czech Republic*. Czech Ministry of Foreign Affairs, 2015. http://family.jrank.org/pages/333/Czech-Republic-Family.html.

http://www.czech.cz/en/culture/czech-arts/architecture/the-history-of-architecture/.

http://www.kraj-jihocesky.cz/foreign/eng/more2.php.

http://www.myczechrepublic.com/basics/facts.html.

Ian Willoughby, "Landmark ruling finds Czech state guilty of violating rights of Roma school children." *Radio Prague*. Český rozhlas, 14 Nov. 2008. Web. http://www.radio.cz/en/article/97560.

Jan Richter. "Romanies warn of mass emigration if government does not deal with far-right violence." *Radio Prague*. Český rozhlas, 4 Nov. 2008. Web. http://www.radio.cz/en/article/110612.

Marianne A. Ferber & Phyllis Hutton Raabe. "Women in the Czech Republic: Feminism, Czech Style." *International Journal of Politics, Culture & Society* 16.3 (Spring 2003): 407–430. *EBSCO Academic Search Complete*.

Petra Hejnova. "Women's Activism in the New Democracies: Uncovering Effects of Communist Policies on Czech Women" *Paper presented at the annual meeting of American Political Science Association*. Pennsylvania Convention Center, Philadelphia, PA, 31 Aug. 2006. Lecture.

Zdenek Vejvoda. "Folk music, song and dance in Bohemia and Moravia." *Czech Music*. July 2007: n.p. *Questia*. https://www.questia.com/magazine/1G1-171326425/folk-music-song-and-dance-in-bohemia-and-moravia.

Zoltán Dujisin, "Czech Republic: US Radar Provokes PR War." *Inter Press Service*. IPS-Interpress Service, 30 Nov. 2007. http://www.ipsnews.net/2007/11/czech-republic-us-radar-provokes-pr-war/.

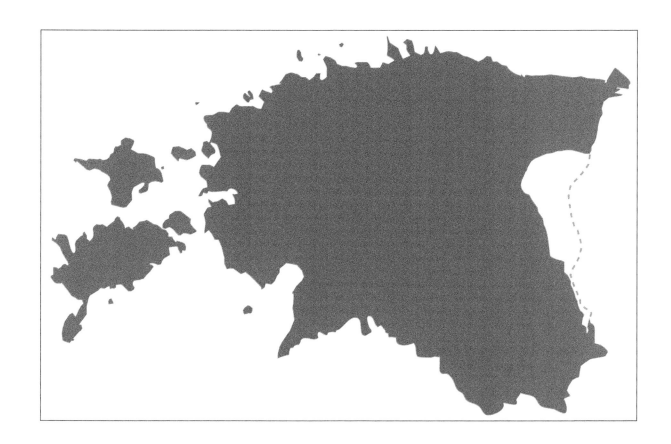

ESTONIA

Introduction

The Republic of Estonia is located in the eastern Baltic region of Europe. It is a low-lying country situated on the Baltic Sea and the Gulf of Finland. Throughout its history, Estonia has been deeply affected by European politics. Adolf Hitler's Nazi regime, Josef Stalin's communist Soviet Union, and the Cold War have all played a role in shaping the country during the 20th century.

Since it achieved independence in 1990, Estonia has sought to create an atmosphere of tolerance for ethnic and cultural minorities. It is known for its record of peaceful political neutrality in its quest for nationhood and for working to maintain stable relations between rival ethnic groups.

A number of Estonians have become famous for their contributions to science and the arts. Karl Ernst von Baer (1792–1876) was the first scientist to pursue modern embryology. The composers Eduard Tubin (1905–1982) and Arvo Pärt (1935–) are internationally celebrated.

GENERAL INFORMATION

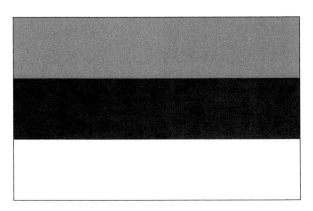

Official Language: Estonian
Population: 1,257,921 (2014 estimate)
Currency: Euro
Coins: The Euro is available in 1, 2, 5, 10, 20, and 50-cent coins. A 1 and 2 Euro coin is also available.
Land Area: 42,388 square kilometers (16,366 square miles)

Water Area: 2,840 square kilometers (1,096 square miles)
National Anthem: "Mu isamaa, mu õnn ja rõõm" ("My Fatherland, My Happiness and Joy")
Capital: Tallinn
Time Zone: GMT +2 (GMT +3 in summer)
Flag Description: The flag of Estonia features three horizontal bands of color: blue (top), black (middle), and white (bottom).

Population

The Estonians are a white, eastern European people that make up the majority of the population of Estonia. The largest minority groups in the country are Russians, Ukrainians, Belarusians, and a fractional percentage of Finns.

Most Estonians (67.6 percent in 2014) live in urban areas, particularly around the capital of Tallinn, which is the country's major industrial center. Rural areas tend to be less densely populated; approximately 32 percent of the population is rural.

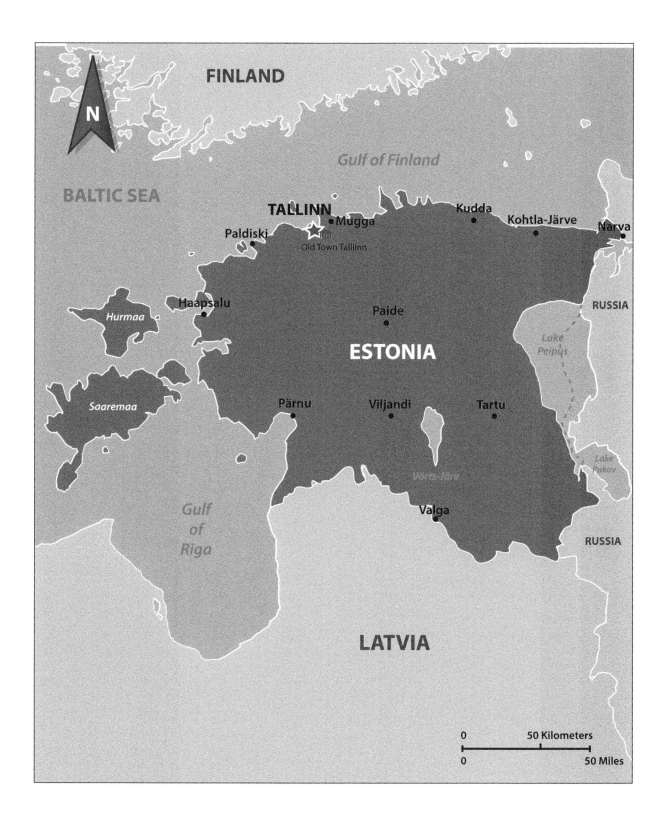

Principal Cities by Population (2014):

- Tallinn (435,245)
- Tartu (97,005)
- Narva (58,663)
- Pärnu (41,528)
- Kohtla-Järve (37,201)

The capital of Tallinn is home to 435,245 people and, of all the cities in the European Union, has the highest percentage of non-EU nationals living within its municipal limits. This demographic trend is due to the country's absorption into the Soviet Union when large numbers of Russian nationals were encouraged to immigrate to Tallinn and thereby diminish Estonian nationalism. Following independence from the Soviet Union, the Estonian government did not automatically grant these new arrivals Estonian citizenship. As it stands, 68.7 percent of the population is Estonian while almost 27 percent of the population is either Russian or Ukrainian.

Harju County, in the northwestern part of the country, has the highest population, with 572,103 residents in a 4,333 square-kilometer (1,673 square-mile) area. This represents 43.2 percent of the country's total population.

Languages

Estonian is what is known as a "Uralic" language, so called because it is related to languages that spread on either side of the Ural Mountains. It is related to Finnish and to the Samoyed language groups and is part of the Finno-Ugric linguistic groups. Modern Estonian culture is based in large part on this language, which has helped the Estonian people retain a sense of nationhood through the years.

Native People & Ethnic Groups

The modern people of Estonia are descended from a group known as the Finno-Ugrians. They are thought to have originated in the forests around the Ural Mountains.

The first inhabitants of the region were a migratory hunting and fishing people who arrived around 7500 BCE, after the glaciers

of the last ice age had receded. Because of the artifacts they left behind, the civilization of this early people is known as the Comb Ceramic culture (or Pit–Comb Ware culture). By 2000 BCE, Indo-European tribes known as the Baltic people had also settled in the area.

Between the 12th and 17th centuries, the native Estonian people found their lands occupied by Germans, Danes, and Swedes. However, the native language and culture persisted among the peasants, although much of the emerging Estonian elite had adopted the German culture and way of life.

Christianity arrived in the region in the 13th century when an order of crusading knights invaded from Germany. By the 16th century, the religion had become more firmly established after a succession of Christian countries, including Germany, Russia, Denmark, and Sweden, had ruled the area. During the Soviet period, religious freedom was taken away from the people and atheism was encouraged.

As of 2014, 68.7 percent of the country's population was Estonian, 24.8 percent was Russian, 1.7 percent was Ukrainian, one percent was Belarusian, and 0.6 percent was Finn.

Religions

Freedom of religion is granted by the country's constitution. Most Estonians—in fact 70.8 percent of them—do not formally associate themselves with any particular organized religion. However, the largest practicing religious population identifies as either the Estonian Apostolic Orthodox Church or the Eastern Orthodox Church, which together account for 16.2 percent of the population. Nearly 10 percent of the population belongs to the Estonian Evangelical Lutheran Church, while other major Christian religious groups within Estonia include the Seventh-Day Adventists, Roman Catholics, Methodists, and Pentecostals, which collectively claim 2.2 percent of the population.

Climate

Estonia has a temperate climate and four seasons. The Baltic Sea and the Gulf Stream keep the temperature and weather from becoming too extreme. The average annual precipitation in the country ranges from 56 to 71 centimeters (22 to 26 inches). The weather in Estonia is often cloudy, with the southeast region generally receiving the most precipitation.

The western coast and islands tend to have the warmest temperatures. Temperatures during July, generally the hottest month, average between 16.3° and 18.1° Celsius (61.3° and 64.6° Fahrenheit). In February, temperatures drop to around −5.7° Celsius (21.7° Fahrenheit). While the country does not see large amounts of snowfall, snow generally covers the ground throughout the winter because of the consistently low temperatures.

ENVIRONMENT & GEOGRAPHY

Topography

Estonia can be separated into two geographically distinct regions: Lower Estonia and Upper Estonia. Lower Estonia consists of the coastal regions in the west and the north, and over 1,500 islands. The largest island is Saaremaa (2,673 square kilometers/ 1,032 square miles). It is located in the West Estonian Archipelago.

Upper Estonia is an area that includes the central and southern parts of the country. This part of Estonia is urban and includes the cities of Rakvere, Paide, Viljandi, Tartu, and Võru. The farmland in Upper Estonia tends to be better suited for agriculture.

The capital, Tallinn, sits on the Gulf of Finland (or Soome laht) in the northeast corner of Estonia. The central part of the city is the Toompea Hill, a limestone hill that rises above the city some 30 meters (98 feet) and is part of Tallinn's Old Town, one of Estonia's UNESCO World Heritage Sites. Limestone cliffs and ridges characterize the city of Tallinn, and the highest point in the city is 64 meters (210 feet) above sea level. In addition to the many marshes and bogs, there are a large number of lakes and rivers in the country. The two largest bodies of water in Estonia are Lake Peipsi and Lake Võrtsjärv. The longest river is the Pärnu, which is 144 kilometers (89 miles) long.

There are no mountain ranges in Estonia, and much of the country lies at a low elevation. The average elevation is 100 meters (328 feet) above sea level. The highest point in the country is at Suur Munamägi in the north, which reaches a height of 318 meters (1,043 feet).

Plants & Animals

Estonia is a heavily forested country, with about half of the land area covered with trees such as pine, birch, and spruce. The western and coastal regions and the islands contain the largest variety of plant life, including rare species of orchids.

There are many large animal species in the country, including elk, roe deer, wild boar, beavers, lynxes, bears, and wolves. Fish are also plentiful, although coastal waters tend to be polluted. Some fish species include Atlantic salmon, both northern and common whitefish, brown trout, the Peipsi smelt, and the European chub, along with pike, perch, herring, sprat, and eel. Grey seals and ring seals may also be found off the coast.

The islands have a diverse bird population and are a good habitat for migratory birds and waterfowl. Species of bird commonly seen in Estonia include the barnacle goose, swans, eagles, storks, and the eider, as well as a number of protected species.

CUSTOMS & COURTESIES

Greetings

Greetings in Estonian culture are typically formal and reserved. When greeting someone, it is customary to stand (if seated) and shake hands while maintaining eye contact. If greeting a woman, one should wait until she extends her hand before taking it. However, men should initiate greetings with women, and younger people should initiate greetings with older people. One should always use a person's title when addressing them.

The most common phrases when greeting include "Tere" ("Hello"), "Tere hommikust"

("Good morning"), "Tere päevast" (Good afternoon), or "Tere õhtust" ("Good evening"). A common salutation between friends is "tšau" (loosely translated as both "Hi" and "Bye," like the informal Italian salutation, "Ciao"). Estonians tend to be reserved and take great pride in their culture. They are not effusive in regard to personal contact and typically only embrace to express very warm feelings or on special occasions.

Gestures & Etiquette

Compliments are rarely given in Estonian culture, are generally sincere, and offered sparingly. Similarly, criticism is seen as challenging a person's reputation and so should never be given publicly. Speaking in a soft voice and with a reserved manner is considered proper, while showing great emotion, speaking agitatedly, or using large hand gestures is considered impolite. It is also considered impolite to draw attention to oneself or to interrupt someone while they are speaking. Estonians are also known for a custom of silence and reticence that is thought to have evolved from the years spent under Soviet rule, when outspokenness was often met with imprisonment or worse. While this might contribute to the perception of Estonians as aloof or even unfriendly, their reserve is mostly due to the emphasis Estonian culture places on acting in a calm and dignified manner.

Since seniority, age, and experience are highly revered in Estonian society, using a person's title when addressing them, such as "Härra" ("Mr."), "Proua" ("Mrs.") and "Preili" ("Miss"), is very important. One should address someone by their first name only when the relationship is very friendly and then only when invited to do so. Similarly, the senior members of a group are expected to make decisions for the group as a whole.

Eating/Meals

The different groups that have ruled the region, including Swedes, Danes, Germans, and Russians, have influenced Estonian food and mealtime traditions variously. On a typical day, Estonians have a light breakfast before work or school, followed by a lunch in the mid- to late afternoon. Dinner is usually early in the evening. Lunch is the heaviest meal of the day and typically includes fish or a meat, along with potato porridge or salad.

Meals are eaten continental style, with the fork in the left hand and the knife in the right. Dining etiquette generally requires keeping one's elbows off the table. It is also considered impolite to begin eating before someone says, "Head isu" ("Good appetite"). In addition, one should try to finish everything on one's plate.

Visiting

Estonians are very hospitable and enjoy inviting guests over to celebrate occasions, such as birthdays, graduations, national holidays, and housewarmings. Visitors should be punctual and remove their shoes before entering a home. A tour of the house is typically not expected, since this would be considered an invasion of privacy. It is also considered polite to sit only when invited to do so. Before and after meals, visitors should offer to help the hostess with the preparation and cleanup, though this offer will probably be denied. It is also polite to compliment the hostess on the meal.

Flowers are the most common gift in Estonia, and it is a nice gesture to bring a gift of chocolate or flowers when visiting. However, there are many rules governing the giving of flowers in Estonian culture. For instance, the number of flowers should always be odd (unless there are more than ten flowers), since an even numbers of flower is given at funerals. Superstition also holds that yellow roses indicate the coming loss of a loved one, and should be avoided. The only white flowers that are acceptable are white roses, and red roses are only given on romantic occasions. Additionally, red carnations were often used to decorate Soviet memorials and are likewise avoided.

LIFESTYLE

Family

Families are very close in Estonia and serve as the core of social activities. In the cities, nuclear families are the most common, while extended families live together more often in the countryside.

The birth rate in Estonia is low, with just under eleven live births for every 1,000 people in 2014. Most families have only one or two children. Youth are relatively independent and often leave home to study or work. Elders receive a great deal of respect, and grandparents are likely to live with the family instead of a nursing home. Occasionally, young couples live with their parents until they have established their own homes.

Marriage is becoming less common in Estonia. Instead, many couples live together in common-law unions, or vabaabielu. Such common-law unions are generally registered after two years of cohabitation. In 2009, an estimated 40 percent of children were born in wedlock, with the average age of first-time mothers being twenty-six. Part of the reason for such low marriage rates might be cost, as traditional Estonian weddings are lavish affairs. Another deterrent might be Estonia's divorce rate, which is also quite high—in the early 21st century, nearly 70 percent of marriages end in divorce.

Housing

Barn-dwellings are a traditional style of Estonian farmhouse that have preserved the same shape and use for centuries. Built of round beams, barn-dwellings have low walls and a broad thatched roof. In addition to serving as a dwelling-place, they also include space for drying and threshing grain. Manor houses can also be seen dotting the Estonian countryside. They were originally built in the 18th and 19th centuries to house German noblemen. Manor houses are large and ornate, featuring architectural embellishments such as columns and turrets, as well as landscaped grounds. Many were modeled after the palaces and castles of Western Europe.

Today, many city-dwelling Estonians live in 19th-century wooden tenement houses, which used to be considered slums, but are now admired for their romantic charm. Bright red roofs and yellow or blue painted walls are common on city buildings. Many Estonians also live in garden suburbs just outside of the city. These private homes are usually low, bungalow-style buildings with a stone foundation and wooden walls.

Whatever their style or type, a majority of houses in Estonia include a sauna, or saun. The sauna is a central part of Estonian culture, and nearly all homes, apartment buildings, hotels, and even some restaurants have built-in saunas. Sauna rooms are generally wood-paneled with benches along the side. A brazier of coals sits in one corner, which is periodically doused with a ladleful of water to release steam into the air. During sauna parties, the tradition is to sit in the sauna for half an hour or so until one becomes quite overheated, then leave the sauna to take a quick cold shower and drink a glass of beer before returning. Some saunas provide salt, which occupants may rub onto their skin to induce the release of toxins. Some saunas also contain dampened birch branches (viht), which are rubbed against the skin for the same purpose.

Food

Traditional Estonian foods include fish, onions, potatoes, sausage, cabbage, and meat. Black rye bread is also a staple, and one of the most basic snacks is fried black bread rubbed with garlic (akin to American buttered toast). The Christmas feast is also a traditional meal and typically includes dishes such as roast pork, black pudding with cowberry (also known as lingonberry) jam, fried cabbage, and sauerkraut with roasted potatoes.

Estonian specialties include open-faced sandwiches with black bread, herring, and egg; rolls of ham filled with garlic, mayonnaise, and cheese; boiled potatoes served with herring or curds; and rhubarb cake. Porridges made from barley or potatoes are also popular. Traditional dishes include klimbisupp, a dumpling soup; kartulisalat or potato salad; porgandipirukas, a carrot-filled pie; frikadillisupp, meatballs in broth; and pirukas, pastry filled with savory ingredients, such as cabbage, carrots, meat, onions, and eggs. A traditional dessert is kompott, a cold fruit soup made with pears, gooseberries, or currants. A fun snack, considered a specialty food in Estonia, is kama, a flour made from roasted peas and grain. It is mixed with sour milk, kefir, or yogurt, and drunk during the summer as a refreshing treat. Salt or sugar can be added as well.

Traditional Russian tea is still served in villages along the Estonian side of Lake Peipsi (or Peipsi-Pihkva järv), which sits on Estonia's border with Russia. Many of these villages are home to "Old Believers," a Russian-speaking community that split from the Russian Orthodox Church in the late 18th century. Tea is served in a large samovar, or traditional Russian tea dispenser, with a teapot containing very strong tea on top. This tea is poured into a cup and then diluted with water from the samovar's tap. It is customarily served with pieces of rock sugar candy; after the candy is placed in the mouth, tea is sipped through the sugar so that the sugar dissolves.

Life's Milestones

Traditional Estonian culture placed great emphasis on marriage, although today this emphasis is declining. A common form of courtship was ehalkäimine, or bundling. When young women came of age, during the summer they would be allowed to sleep in the storehouse, where young men could visit at night. This allowed for young people to talk in private in an intimate setting. If a young man wished to propose to a woman, he or his relatives first had to make a symbolic offering, such as leaving a birch branch before the window of a girl's room or putting a knife in her pocket. If the gift was tossed away, the girl would not accept a proposal; if it was kept, the boy's relatives could visit the girl's family and propose. Proposals included bringing a cask of beer or sweet red alcohol to the girl's father; if he drank from it, he accepted the match.

Estonian weddings traditionally lasted for three days and included feasting and rituals of celebration. When a cap was placed on the bride's head, she was considered married. Then an apron would be tied around her waist, and guests would throw coins into the apron. Presents were also distributed to members of both families in various ways; for instance, belts and ribbons tied to the horns of a cow would belong to the bridegroom's mother.

Pregnancy and birth were also surrounded by custom and superstition. To predetermine the sex of a baby, parents would leave an ax or a needle under the bed in order to have a boy or girl, respectively. During pregnancy, a mother could not laugh, cry, or show strong emotion because it would affect the health of the child. When the child was born, a piece of silver was put on its chest to ward off evil spirits. Some superstitions are still common today, such as one, which warns that if a pregnant mother looks at a fire and touches a part of her body, when her child is born, it will have a mole on that spot.

CULTURAL HISTORY

Art

Due to the long period of oppression experienced by Estonians, few painters and artists came from Estonia prior to the 19th century. Instead, folk art is considered the repository of Estonian artistry. Estonians are renowned for their textile arts, such as weaving, embroidery, and knitting. Estonian embroidery often uses bright colors to create flowers, suns, stars, and traditional symbols or designs, like the eight-pointed star, a emblem of luck and rebirth. Estonians are especially known for their woven and embroidered blankets, called vaip. In traditional Estonian homes, decorated blankets were used as travel wraps, and these lap covers were considered a symbol of status. Another skill, knitting, is taught in schools and still practiced widely today. Additionally, there are more than a hundred traditional patterns for mittens, most of which have animal names like "pole-cat paws" or "elk-antlers." Some traditional knitting styles, such as complex lacework and multicolor patterns, have been in use continuously since the 16th century.

Two famous artists of the 15th century, Bernt Notke (c. 1435–1509), a painter and sculptor of sacred art, and Michel Sittow (1469–1525), who painted portraits of nobility in the Dutch tradition, both worked in Estonia. Ants Laikmaa (1866–1942) was an Estonian watercolor painter credited with bringing impressionism to Estonia. He established the Estonian Art Association in Tallinn in 1906 and was a founding member of the Estonian National Museum (Eesti rahva muuseum) in Tartu in 1909. Laikmaa was one of the few native artists who continued to work in Estonia instead of abroad.

Various groups have influenced contemporary Estonian visual arts during different periods. The artists of the World War I generation took inspiration from German expressionism, and during the 1930s, French post-impressionism was popular. In the mid-twentieth century, Estonian artists were compelled by the Soviet government to take on the style of socialist realism. In the 1960s, American pop art was hailed as an expression of freedom. Since then, Estonian visual art, like literature and music, has embraced questions of Estonian identity and attempted to find themes representative of Estonian culture. For instance, the graphic artist Günther Reindorff (1889–1974) depicted the unique granite boulders of Estonia's landscape as symbolic national monuments in his work. Similarly, artist and teacher Kaljo Põllu (1934–2010) uses themes from Estonian mythology and nature, translating ancient tradition into contemporary art.

Other notable contemporary Estonian visual artists include painter and collagist Mall Nukke (1964–), cartoonist and animator Priit Pärn (1946–), graphic artist Peeter Allik (1966–), painter Jüri Arrak (1936–), painter Evald Okas (1915–2011), video artist and painter Jaan Toomik (1961–), painter and writer Toomas Vint (1944–), and painter and architect Leonhard Lapin (1947–).

Estonian art in recent decades has been primarily focused on exploring and celebrating Estonian identity. It also addresses the country's relationships with Russia, as well as new trends of Western pop culture and globalization. Much of Estonian art is characterized by feelings of nationalism and an anxious desire to prove Estonia's cultural identity.

Architecture

Medieval Estonian architecture, some of which has survived into the modern era, includes strongholds, fortifications, churches, and monasteries, as well as a structure unique to the country: barn-dwellings, which were used during the Middle Ages to dry and thresh grain. Examples of medieval Estonian architecture include the Rakvere stronghold, located in Western Virumaa and constructed in the 12th century, and St. Jacob's, a fortified church constructed during the 13th century and located on Estonia's largest island, Saaremaa. Baltic nobility constructed manor houses beginning in the 1600s. These manor estates were vast, usually featuring a barn, stables, servant's lodgings, an icehouse, and an expansive lawn.

During WWII, many historic buildings and structures were destroyed, particularly in the city of Tartu. From the end of WWII until the mid-1950s, Stalinist architecture (or Soviet architecture) began to appear in Estonia. The city center of Pärnu was constructed in the Soviet style, as were many industrial towns in the northeastern region of the country.

Drama & Dance

Dancing does not have as strong a place in Estonian culture as singing. Folk dances such as the labajalavalss (a waltz), the kaera-jaan (a comedic quadrille, or square dance for four couples), and the tuljak (a courtship dance) are similar to Slavic dances. Performed collectively, these dances are stately and dignified, featuring patterns and repetitions instead of quick movements. Oral history and folklore have long been popular means of storytelling, but staged drama is a relatively recent phenomenon. The first play written in Estonian, *Saaremaa Onupoeg* (*The Cousin from Saaremaa*), by Lydia Koidula, was performed in 1870.

Music

Singing is often considered the backbone of Estonian culture and is rooted in the field songs of early agricultural laborers. Estonian folk music was passed on from generation to generation and was intimately tied to local folklore and tradition. Traditional Estonian folk songs are known as "runo songs," or regilaul, and are characterized by simple, repetitive melodies and meters. Runo songs often take the form of ballads, epic tales, work songs, or just narrations of daily life—a form of musical diary that can be passed on to future generations. During the period known as the Estonian National Awakening in the late 1800s, the Estonian author and folklorist Friedrich Reinhold Kreutzwald (1803–1882) collected and categorized hundreds of runo songs. He later used them as a basis for his national epic tale, *Kalevipoeg* (*Kalev's Son*). For his efforts, he is considered the father of Estonian national literature.

Estonia's first Folk Song Festival, called Üldlaulupidu, was held in 1869. Since then, a festival, which UNESCO has named one of the Masterpieces of the Oral and Intangible Heritage of Humanity, has been held every five years in Tallinn, Estonia's capital. Johann Voldemar Jannsen (1819–1890), a poet and journalist, is one of the key figures in Estonian music history. He led the choral group that organized the first festival, and he wrote the lyrics of the Estonian national anthem, "Mu isamaa, mu õnn ja rõõm" ("My Native Land, My Happiness and Joy"). Other important musicians include Rudolf Tobias (1873–1918), a composer and organist who composed the first Estonian instrumental pieces, and Miina Härma (1864–1941), the first female composer who wrote over 200 choral pieces.

Under Soviet rule (1944–1991), freedom of artistic expression was severely constrained. However, the Soviets allowed the Estonians to continue their tradition of holding the Üldlaulupidu every five years, in the belief that sharing cultural practices would promote solidarity between the different nations of the Soviet Union. Contrary to their expectations, however, the song festivals became a key method of keeping Estonian culture alive. Gustav Ernesaks (1908–1993), an Estonian composer who founded the Estonian National Male Choir, played an instrumental role in convincing the Soviet government to allow the festival to continue. He is honored throughout Estonia today with the title Laulutaat (Father of Song).

The Üldlaulupidu is held in Tallinn at Lauluväljak (Tallinn Song Festival Grounds), a venue able to accommodate 20,000 singers onstage and 300,000 people in the audience. During recent Song Festivals, however, the grounds have hosted up to 100,000 people. Historically, the festival provided the catalyst for throwing off Soviet rule, in what is known as the Singing Revolution. In 1988, during the Old Town Festival concert in Tallinn, 15,000 people began to march while singing. Although the repercussions for such a demonstration would have been severe, under Soviet Russia's policy of glasnost (a period of less censorship and greater transparency instituted by Mikhail Gorbachev in the late 1980s), the Russians were forbidden from intervening. The procession eventually numbered 150,000, and marched to the Singing Field, where they remained for six days. They also defiantly waved Estonian flags and sang the Estonian national anthem, both of which were prohibited by the Soviet government. This marked the beginning of Estonian resistance through song.

Under Soviet rule, rock music also became an expression of independence. The Estonian band Ruja, which released its first album in 1979, became an underground sensation. It brought progressive punk rock music to Estonia and often attracted the attention and wrath of Soviet authorities. Although its members faced harassment and some of its songs were banned, Ruja continued to advocate Estonian independence by setting to music nationalist poems like "Eile nägin ma Eestimaad" ("Yesterday, I Saw Estonia"), by Estonian poet Ott Arder (1950–2004).

Literature

Because Estonia was historically ruled by other countries, including Sweden, Germany, and Russia, literature written in the Estonian language was relatively rare before the Estonian National Awakening. Thus, early literature written about Estonia was primarily published in other languages. Early examples include *Heinrici Chronicon Livoniae* (*The Livonian Chronicle of Henry*), which contains Estonian folk poetry and was written in the 13th century, and the folk song anthology *Volkslieder* (1807) by German literary critic Johann Gottfried von Herder (1744–1803).

During the Protestant Reformation of the 16th and 17th centuries, increased printing in Estonia raised the national level of literacy. After the abolition of serfdom in 1816, and in stride with advancements in education, Estonian nationalist sentiments also arose. This period is known as the Estonian National Awakening. Nationalist literature written in the Estonian language became widely popular during this time, including the 1853 epic poem *Kalevipoeg* (*Kalev's Son*) by Friedrich Reinhold Kreutzwald (1803–1882). Based on a collection of oral folklore and runo songs, it is considered the Estonian national epic.

Jakob Hurt (1839–1907), an Estonian cultural leader and linguist, compiled the first systematic collection of Estonian folklore in the late 1800s. Hurt coined the phrase that has become a popular expression of the mentality of Estonians toward their culture: "If we cannot be great in number, we must be great in spirit." Other notable authors and poets include Kristjan Jaak Peterson (1801–1822) and Lydia Koidula (1843–1886). Although Peterson died young—at age twenty-one—he is considered the founder of Estonian poetry and a central contributor to the Estonian National Awakening. Koidula, one of the most prominent female Estonian poets, wrote poems that often dealt with patriotic themes. One example is "Mu isamaa on minu arm" ("My Country is My Love"), which was turned into a popular song and is considered Estonia's second national anthem. Other great Estonian literary figures include the poet Marie Under (1883–1980) and Anton Hansen Tammsaare (1878–1940), whose pentalogy, *Truth and Justice* (*Tõde ja õigus*) of 1926–1933, is considered a masterpiece of Estonian literature.

Modern Estonian writers, in particular, are quite prolific. They include the poet Hando Runnel (1938–), whose poems deal with themes such as the motherland, love, and satire. Many of his poems are full of allusions and puns, which helped them slip past the censors during Soviet rule. Other writers dealt with issues of Estonian history, politics, and identity in their work.

CULTURE

Arts & Entertainment

Estonian arts have flourished in the years following the country's independence from the Soviet Union and the lifting of state censorship. Theater is a popular form of entertainment. Along with museums and libraries, Estonian theaters enjoy government funding and support from the "Kultuurkapital" fund (Cultural Endowment of Estonia). The Estonian Ministry of Culture also founded the government-funded Estonian Film Foundation in 1997, and in 2007, the country made ten feature films. In 2011, that number fell to eight. One of the 2011 feature film productions was completely animated.

Estonia is home to a long tradition of folk culture. One form of traditional poetry is known as "regivärss," or rhythmic verse. There are also thousands of Estonian folk songs, and traditional music remains an important part of Estonian culture. In addition, quite a few Estonian musicians have become world famous. Among them are the conductor Tõnu Kaljuste (1953–) and composer Erkki-Sven Tüür (1959–).

Basketball is the most popular team sport in Estonia. Sports such as cross-country skiing, cycling, skating, and ice boating are also widely enjoyed in the country.

Cultural Sites & Landmarks

The capital of Tallinn, whose name comes from the phrase "taani linnus," meaning "Danish castle," was once one of the most fortified cities in the world and a vibrant trading center for much of the medieval period. Built in the 13th century, the city's historic center (called Old Town) is one of the best-preserved ancient cities in Northern Europe, kept almost entirely free of encroachment by modern architecture. In recognition of the city's medieval heritage, the Old Town of Tallinn was named a World Heritage Site in 1997 by the United Nations Educational, Scientific, and Cultural Organization (UNESCO).

Notable architecture within the Old Town includes the Dome Church (also called the Cathedral of Saint Mary the Virgin) on Toompea Hill. The Dome Church, completed in 1240, was reconstructed in 1686 after a devastating fire in 1684, which collapsed several vaults and damaged many stone carvings, particularly those in the chancel. Another notable landmark is St. Nicholas Church, which was also founded in the 13th century by German merchants. Inside the church is all that is left of the famous medieval painting Danse Macabre ("Dance of Death") by German painter Bernt Notke (c. 1435–1508), which originally measured 30 meters (98.4 feet) wide. The painting illustrates the inevitability of death for all men regardless of their station in life. Toompea Castle, which may have been in existence as early as the ninth century, is also located in Old Town. It is the home of Estonia's parliament, the Riigikogu.

One of the more recent additions to the Old Town is the Alexander Nevsky Cathedral, a Russian Orthodox church built between 1894 and 1900, when Estonia was under Russian rule. Though it stands as a reminder of Russian domination, the onion cupolas and mosaic designs of the cathedral are considered very beautiful. Legend states that the cathedral was built over the burial site of the legendary Estonian hero Kalev (from the national epic *Kalevipoeg*), whose curse made cracks appear in the foundation's walls.

The Lahemaa National Park, located in northern Estonia, was created in 1971, and was the first Soviet national park. The beautiful scenery of this park includes forests, coastal plains, limestone plateaus, waterfalls, and bogs. The Witch's Well in Tuhala is another cultural attraction that is associated with Estonian folk beliefs. Periodic eruptions of churning water in a field in Tuhala, which is situated over an underground river, are thought to be a sign that witches are taking a sauna underground. Estonians make pilgrimages to the water when it erupts, believing that it holds curative powers.

Estonia is also home to the Kihnu Cultural Space. This grouping of Baltic islands—the two primary islands being Kihnu and Manija—is home to a traditional people whose unique culture has persevered. Their unique cultural traditions include song, dance, ceremonies, and handicrafts. They are particularly known for their pre-Christian oral traditions of song and their woolen handicrafts. Their culture, coupled with the natural heritage of the islands, was proclaimed one of the Masterpieces of the Oral and Intangible Heritage of Humanity as maintained by UNESCO.

Libraries & Museums

The National Library of Estonia, established in 1918, is located in Tallinn. It has around 3.4 million books in its collection, as well as approximately 302,988 annual periodicals.

The Estonian National Museum, located in Tartu, houses over one million artifacts, including photographs, engravings, paintings, drawings, and ancient objects. The museum also has a collection of medieval folk costumes. The Art Museum of Estonia, founded in 1919, has several active branches: the Kumu Art Museum (or Kumu Kunstimuuseum); the Kadriorg Art Museum, located in Kadriorg Palace; the Niguliste Museum; and the Adamson-Eric Museum (or Adamson-Ericu Muuseum). Exhibitions include classic and contemporary Estonian art (at the Kumu Art Museum), Russian and European art (at the Kadriorg Art Museum), and the work of 20th-century painter Adamson-Eric (born Erich Karl Hugo Adamson, 1902–1968).

Holidays

Estonia celebrates a number of national holidays, many of which commemorate events of political importance. June 23 is Victory Day or "Võidupüha," which celebrates the victory of Estonia in the 1919 Battle of Võnnu.

St. John's Day, which is also known as Midsummer Day (or jaanipäev), is celebrated on June 24. St. John's Day is a holiday with pagan roots that is traditionally marked by special dinners and bonfires. Another major holiday is the Day of Restoration of Independence (or taasiseseisvumispäev), commemorated on August 20. This holiday celebrates the establishment of the Republic of Estonia in 1991.

Youth Culture

According to surveys on youth culture taken at the turn of the 21st century, Estonian youth are increasingly embracing globalization. As the country continues to push economic and social reform and break from its communist past, youth in Estonia are becoming more materialistic and status-oriented. They are also characteristically more secular than other Balkan or European youth.

Estonian youth culture has become increasingly influenced by Western culture, most notably in fashion, music, and even slang. For example, hip-hop culture has become popular, and English-language words have been adapted into the Estonian lexicon. Imported American films and restaurants have also become widespread in recent years. However, some feel that this influx of mass culture and foreign values is already threatening Estonia's national identity and traditional culture.

While recreational sports such as basketball and cross-country skiing are popular, one sport native to Estonia is ice cricket. This is a modified form of cricket played on the surface of a frozen lake. Ice cricket was invented in 2001 by the coach of Estonia's national cricket team, a British expatriate. Its popularity has already spread to England, Australia, New Zealand, and parts of Europe. Yearly from January to March, teams travel to Tallinn to compete against their Estonian rivals. Sailing is also a popular traditional pastime. Many Estonian children learn to sail at a young age, typically in small single-person sailboats. During the summer months, lessons are held where children practice tacking, racing, and maneuvering through the waves.

SOCIETY

Transportation
Within cities, travel by trolley, bus, and tram is common. Tickets can be purchased from newsstand kiosks at a discounted rate, or from the driver at a higher fare. Taxis are also available, but it is best to call a taxi service rather than rely on street taxis, since the fares charged by street drivers can be unreliable. Buses and trains are a good way to take day trips to the countryside. Some train lines also run internationally, though service is infrequent. During the warmer months, ferries are

a popular mode of transportation between Estonia and Finland, Sweden, Germany, and Russia.

The Lennart Meri Tallinn Airport in Tallinn, Estonia's capital, can be reached via direct flight from many other European cities, including London, Amsterdam, Helsinki, Moscow, and Copenhagen. The national airline is Estonian Air. Traffic moves on the right-hand side of the road.

Transportation Infrastructure
There are approximately 57,565 kilometers of roads in Estonia, and 16,489 kilometers of those roads are owned by the central government. Approximately 41,076 kilometers fall under the jurisdiction of local governments. Rural roads, as well as secondary roads, are not as well-maintained as the main motorways. As of 2015, only 12,926 kilometers are paved.

Estonia has 900 kilometers of common railway track and 1,200 kilometers of dedicated industrial lines for cargo transport. In the country's capital, public transport is well developed, and trams, trolleys, and buses are common modes of transport. The country has 13 airports, the largest of which is Lennart Meri Tallinn Airport.

The country also boasts 50 ships in the Merchant Marine, including three bulk carriers, 20 cargo ships, one combination bulk carrier, five container ships, two petroleum tankers, 13 roll-on/roll-off ships, and six short passenger boats. In 2015, there were 45 registered ports, most of them located along the Baltic. The largest of these ports are Muuga; Tallinn, which has several smaller ports around the city; Paldiski; Kunda; Pärnu; and Sillamäe.

Media & Communications
During the period of Soviet control, the Soviet government heavily regulated the Estonian media. During the 1970s and 1980s, publications had to pass through as many as five levels of censorship before they were permitted to be printed. From 1987 to 1993, however, this control became more relaxed, and the media began to engage with topics that had been formerly forbidden. After Estonia regained independence in 1991, the media began to operate free of political control.

Today, Estonians average four hours a day of television viewing and nearly five hours of radio listening. The national public television station is Eesti Televisioon (ETV), part of the Estonian Public Broadcasting service, Eesti Rahvusringhääling. The two other channels, both private, are Kanal 2 and TV3. According to the European Journalists Centre, 74.3 percent of Estonians regularly read newspapers and 58.9 percent regularly read magazines, although print media is generally on the decline. Seventy-four percent of Estonians watch the daily news, and all media is available in both Estonian and Russian. As of 2014, there were three daily newspapers in Estonian and one in Russian. The two main publications companies in the country are Eesti Meedia Group and Ekspress Group.

Online media resources continue to expand, as does Internet use. The Estonian government offers free Internet access and numerous wireless access points. As of 2012, there were 327,243 fixed broadband subscriptions, 924,699 wireless broadband subscriptions, and 865,494 hosts through which residents could gain Internet access. By 2013, Internet users made up about 80 percent of the population.

SOCIAL DEVELOPMENT

Standard of Living
Estonia ranked 33rd out of 190 countries on the 2012 United Nations Human Development Index, which measures quality of life indicators.

Water Consumption
The reserves of fresh water in Estonia are considered sufficient. Much of the water consumed comes from ground and surface water. The cities of Tallinn and Narva consume the most water in the country. Approximately 99.1 percent of the population has sustainable access to improved drinking water sources, with 99.8 percent access in urban areas and 97.6 percent in rural areas. Improved sanitation services are available to 95.8 percent of the urban population and 93.8 percent of the rural population.

Education
The basic educational system in Estonia is state-funded, and expenditures represent 5.2 percent of the GDP. The system itself consists of primary and secondary schools, as well as vocational schools. The number of private secondary schools, which must meet governmental education standards, is increasing. Three state examinations are required for a secondary education certificate.

Education is compulsory between seven and 17 years of age. While most children are educated in the Estonian language, some speak Russian at school. The country has a high rate of literacy, which stands at 99.8 percent for both males and females in 2015.

The number of students pursuing post-secondary education has been steadily increasing, with over 69,000 students enrolled in 2011. A standard begun with the founding of the University of Tartu in 1632, post-secondary institutions now number 33, with nine universities and 24 colleges and vocational schools. Fifteen of these institutions are privately funded. Among these are the Estonian Agriculture University at Tartu, Tallinn Technical University, and the Tallinn Pedagogical University.

The gender gap in education tends to favor female students in the early 21st century. In 2009, 86 percent of women between the ages of twenty and twenty-four had finished (at least) upper secondary school, compared to 78 percent of men in that same age bracket.

Women's Rights
According to traditional Estonian beliefs, "the woman is the neck that turns the man's head." This means that women play a significant role in family and communal life in Estonian culture. Although women toiled side-by-side in the fields with men as serfs, they were also traditionally expected to devote themselves to the home and child rearing.

Women achieved suffrage in 1918, when Estonia gained independence for the first time. Under Soviet rule, the percentage of women in the workplace was nearly 100 percent. In 2014, however, this number hovers around 57 percent.

Due to the communist policy of forced egalitarianism in the workplace under Soviet rule, feminism developed Soviet connotations, and many Estonian women are hesitant to bring up feminist issues. Social pressure still influences many women to go into fields that traditionally feminine, such as the education and social-assistance sectors. Interesting to note is that a common phrase in Estonian is "a wage worthy of a man." Cultural mores, such as the perception that it is shameful for a woman to support her husband, reveal the persistence of underlying prejudice about gender roles in Estonian society.

Upon the birth of a baby, one of the two parents—usually the mother, if she is employed—is granted 100 percent of his or her typical salary for 18 months following the birth. The new parent also receives a one-time grant of 320 Euros per child in the household during this period. After 18 months have elapsed, the parent has the right to return to his or her position. Such policies, in force since 2005, were enacted with an eye to boosting Estonia's flagging birthrate.

Today, although women tend to be better educated than men are, and female literacy stands at 100 percent, women receive lower wages for comparable work. Some estimates show that women's salaries are about 70 percent that of male counterparts. In addition, though sexual harassment in prohibited, it remains widespread. The number of women in government has been increasing slowly, although politics is still often viewed as a male-dominated profession, and political representation remains low for women. In 1990, Estonia's parliament was composed of 7 percent women; in 2008, the number had risen to 24 percent. By 2014, however, the number declined to 19 percent.

Domestic violence against women is an issue, and Estonia has neither specific laws prohibiting it nor services to aid those who seek to escape it, although several non-governmental organizations (NGOs) exist to address the issue. In 2006, 3,300 cases of domestic abuse were reported, but the number of actual cases is likely to be higher since women face social pressure to not report abuse. In 2006, there were also 73 reported rapes and 27 reported attempted rapes.

By 2013, the UN Committee against Torture advised Estonia to approve comprehensive legislation on violence against women, including legislation to combat domestic violence and marital rape. However, the Estonian government has been slow to respond. Moreover, as of 2015, Estonia has neither signed nor ratified the Council of Europe Convention on violence against women and domestic violence (known as the Istanbul Convention), which has been open for signatories since May 2011 and has been in force since August 1, 2014.

Abortion is legal. Prostitution in Estonia is legal, although organized prostitution is not. Human trafficking is a serious problem, with Estonia serving as a source, destination, and transit country for trafficking in women for sexual exploitation. The Estonian government declared trafficking a serious concern and adopted a national action plan in January 2006. It cooperates with the EU and the Nordic and Baltic Task Force on Trafficking in Persons.

Health Care

While Estonia was under the control of the Soviet Union, health care administration was centralized, and services were inadequate. The health structure suffered still more during Estonia's transition to an independent state.

After much reform, health care services are now under the purview of the Ministry of Social Affairs and funded by general taxation through the National Health Service. The Estonian Health Insurance Fund, created in 2001, provides health care coverage to citizens, and coverage is dependent on how much social tax is paid to the National Health Service by the individual seeking services. In 2013, nearly six percent of the GDP was spent on healthcare concerns, the country providing just over three doctors per 1,000 people and 5.3 hospital beds per 1,000 people.

Because Estonia experiences long periods of darkness and short days in the winter, mood disorders caused by lack of sunlight are a common health problem.

GOVERNMENT

Structure

After the Molotov-Ribbentrop Nonaggression Pact was signed by the Soviet Union and Germany in August 1939, the Soviet Union occupied Estonia, Latvia, Finland, and Lithuania, while Germany occupied Poland. When it was absorbed into the Soviet Union in 1940, the country became known as the Estonian Soviet Socialist Republic (ESSR). Under Josef Stalin's regime (1944–1953), the country saw the collectivization of farming and agriculture. Industry and manufacturing were also taken over by the government.

The ESSR was renamed the Republic of Estonia on May 8, 1990 and finally gained independence on August 20, 1991, when the first free elections were held. The Russian military officially withdrew from the country in 1994.

Today, Estonia is an independent nation, led by a freely elected president. The governing body consists of a parliamentary democracy directed by a prime minister. The legislative body is known as the Riigikogu, which works with the prime minister to propose and pass laws. The Supreme Court conducts matters of justice.

Political Parties

Political parties include the conservative Pro Patria Union (Isamaaliit), the liberal Reform Party (Eesti Reformierakond), the centrist and populist Centre Party (Eesti Keskerakond), and the center-left Constitution Party (Konstitutsioonierakond), which is concerned with Russian-minority interests. The People's Union (Eestimaa Rahvaliit) dropped from fourth to sixth place.

In the 2015 Riigikogu elections, of the 101 available seats, the Reform Party won thirty and 27.7 percent of the vote, the Centre Party won 27 and 24.8 percent of the vote, the Social Democratic Party won 15 seats and 15.2 percent of the vote, and Pro Patria/Res Publica won 14 seats and 13.7 percent of the vote. The Estonian Free Party (Eesti Vabaerakond), founded in 2014, secured eight seats and 8.7 percent of the vote,

while the Conservative People's Party (*Eesti Konservatiivne Rahvaerakond*) won seven seats and 8.1 percent of the vote.

Local Government

Local government comprises 15 counties, each of which is further subdivided into 227 municipalities, considered either parishes (vallad), if they are rural, or towns (linnad), if they are urban. Elections for municipal councils occur every four years, in October. The council elects a mayor, who oversees governance of the municipality.

Judicial System

The judicial system of Estonia comprises a three-tiered court system. The highest court is the Supreme Court, with 19 members and four separate chambers: civil, criminal, administrative, and constitutional. Under the Supreme Court, there are regional and appellate courts, as well as district and city courts.

Taxation

As of 2015, personal income tax is levied at a flat rate of 20 percent, payable for Estonian residents on worldwide income and, for non-residents, on income from Estonian sources. A corporate tax of 20 percent is also levied. Other taxes include a value-added tax (VAT), excise tax, land tax, social tax, commercial vehicle taxes, and taxes on both gambling winnings and tables owned by gambling establishments.

Armed Forces

The Estonian Defence Forces (Eesti Kaitsevägi) consist of a paramilitary defense league (Kaitseliit), ground force (Maavägi), air force (Eesti Õhuvägi), naval force (Merevägi). In 2015, there were approximately 17,500 active personnel and 218,886 reserves. Compulsory military service lasts between eight and eleven months for male citizens ages 18 to 28 years old.

According to the Ministry of Defense, an estimated 200 Estonian soldiers participated in foreign missions in 2011, including in Afghanistan, Iraq, Bosnia, and Kosovo.

Foreign Policy

Estonia has long identified itself as a Nordic country. It feels that it has more in common historically, linguistically, and cultural with the Nordic countries than with its Baltic or Eastern European neighbors. Throughout the late 1990s and early part of the 21st century, Estonia has orientated itself toward Western Europe and Scandinavia and striven to prevent itself from being seen as part of post-Soviet Eastern Europe. Additionally, Estonia has a high rate of technological and Internet development, as well as a relatively low level of corruption, compared to other post-Soviet countries and even some members of the European Union (EU).

Shortly after declaring independence in 1991, Estonia was admitted into the United Nations (UN). Estonia joined the North Atlantic Treaty Organization (NATO) in March 2004 and the EU in May of that same year. Estonia's relationship with Russia remains particularly tense. In 2005, after ten years of negotiations, Estonian and Russian foreign ministers signed a treaty regarding the disputed border between the two countries. However, Russia later pulled out of the agreement, citing clauses added by the Estonian parliament during ratification. In 2014 and 2015, Russia has continually violated Estonia's air space, which has intensified tensions existing between the two nations.

In April 2007, the removal of a Soviet-era war memorial from the main square in Tallinn provoked several days of rioting and looting by members of Estonia's ethnic Russian minority, who comprise nearly one-fourth of Estonia's population. Estonians viewed the memorial statue, known as the Bronze Soldier, as a symbol of Russian oppression, but Russians viewed it as a monument to the Russian soldiers who died in World War II. During the incident, 1,300 people were arrested and 100 were injured, including one fatality. In response to the statue's removal, Estonia experienced three weeks of cyber-attacks on Estonian websites. These attacks were suspected to have originated in Russia, and have been considered the world's first encounter with cyber warfare.

Estonia's relationship with the United States is close. Estonia has sent troops to Afghanistan since 2002, as part of the NATO-led coalition, and to Iraq since 2003, as part of the US-led coalition. It also participates in NATO training in Iraq. Additionally, it has sent peacekeeping troops to Bosnia and Kosovo and provided development assistance to Afghanistan, Georgia, Ukraine, Moldova, and other post-Soviet states. For the 2008–2010 period, Estonia's aid package to Afghanistan was set at $1.5 million (USD), and in 2008, the number of Estonian troops in the country totaled 140.

Human Rights Profile

International human rights law insists that states respect civil and political rights and also promote an individual's economic, social, and cultural rights. The United Nations Universal Declaration on Human Rights (UDHR) is recognized as the standard for international human rights. Its authors sought the counsel of the world's great thinkers, philosophers, and religious leaders and were careful to create a document that reflects the core values shared by every world culture. (To read this document or view the articles relating to cultural human rights, visit http://www.ohchr.org/EN/UDHR/Pages/Introduction.aspx.)

Estonia is believed to have a better human rights record than its Baltic neighbors. The constitution protects freedom of religion. The largest religions in the country are together Estonian Apostolic Orthodox and Eastern Orthodox, followed by Evangelical Lutheranism, although agnosticism is also very common. Traditional folk religious beliefs, including animism, are also widespread. Freedom of expression and assembly are also protected by the constitution and respected by the government, and recent elections have been deemed free and fair. (Estonia was also the first country to hold Internet voting during the 2005 municipal elections. The ease and popularity of this method has grown, and about 176,491 people voted online in the 2015 parliamentary elections.) Ultimately, there are still some ongoing human rights concerns, particularly regarding nationality and minority status, judiciary issues, and gender relations.

Russians who immigrated to Estonia during the Soviet occupation were considered noncitizens upon Estonia's independence in 1991. Since that period, Russian residents have had to apply for citizenship. This process includes demonstrating ability in the Estonian language. Estonian language ability is also mandatory in some government and public sector work environments. Amnesty International (AI) has criticized this policy as discriminatory against Russian-speaking Estonians. However, the Estonian government does subsidize Estonian language classes. Between 1992 and 2007, 147,000 people acquired Estonian citizenship. Another 10,719 became citizens between 2008 and 2014.

Estonia's judiciary is largely independent, and laws prohibiting arbitrary detention or arrest are mostly observed. However, the pretrial detention period has been criticized as being overly long, and there have been reports of police brutality, particularly in connection with the April 2007 riots in Tallinn. The situation with regard to Estonia's prison system is troubling; prisons and detention centers face overcrowding, lack of trained staff, and lack of funds.

Legally, women enjoy the same rights as men. However, women in Estonia in general receive lower wages than men do for equal work. Although unionization is legally protected, the Confederation of Estonian Trade Unions reported in 2007 and 2008 that unionized workers experienced discrimination in the private sector. Estonia also has problems with human trafficking, with Estonia functioning as an origin, transit, and destination country of women being transferred for the purposes of sexual exploitation. The Estonian government has been cooperating with the EU and the Nordic and Baltic Task Force on Trafficking in Persons to address this problem.

ECONOMY

Overview of the Economy

Historically, Estonia's economy was based on agriculture. The economy was completely transformed into a centralized, state-controlled structure under the communist Soviet Union. Small farms were collectivized and businesses were transferred to government ownership.

Since the late 20th century Estonia, along with its sister Baltic republics of Latvia and Lithuania, has become part of what economists call the "Baltic Tiger," in reference to the substantial economic growth rates that have characterized all three economies. Fuelled by the rapid growth of the IT and software development industries in Tallinn, Estonia has recorded the most impressive gains of all the "Baltic Tiger" republics. In recognition of these growth rates, the World Bank re-classified the Estonian economy from an upper-middle income economy to a high-income economy in 2007. Moreover, while its growth between 2000 and 2008 was recorded at roughly 109 percent by the International Monetary Fund (IMF), Estonia fell into recession in mid-2008 as a result of the real estate market crash and the ensuing global financial crisis, which significantly reduced export consumption rates.

Although Estonia rebounded well between 2009 and 2014, its growth rate still fell below 2 percent in 2014. The service industries are the most important sector of the economy, and few companies remain state-owned. The country's estimated gross domestic product (GDP) was $35.63 billion (USD) in 2014. The GDP per capita was approximately $26,600 (USD).

Estonia joined the European Union (EU) in 2004. The country has an open economy and receives most of its foreign investment from Sweden and Finland. Its major trade partners are Finland, Sweden, Russia, and Latvia, and to a lesser extent Germany and the United States. Estonia is also part of the World Trade Organization (WTO).

Industry

Although the manufacturing sector has declined, major industries in Estonia include engineering, electronics, wood, wood products, and textiles and accounts for 29.2 percent of the GDP. Traditional industries that remain important to the economy are fishing, timber, and shipbuilding. The largest and most important industry is the service industry; it includes transportation, information technology, telecommunications, banking, and food services and represents 67.2 percent of the GDP.

Because of its location on the Baltic Sea, Estonia has been a significant center of European trade and transportation. The Port of Muuga in Tallinn is one of best warm water harbors in Europe. Even though it is located in northern waters, the port does not become blocked by ice.

Government support has enabled Tallinn to expand in the computer and IT fields, and the city has become a hotspot for numerous technology start-ups, including Skype, which sold to eBay for $2.5 billion (USD) in 2005. Other important industries in the city include fish processing, textiles, and foodstuff production. In addition, nearly half of all registered companies in Estonia are located in the capital.

Labor

According to the CIA *World Factbook*, Estonia's labor force was estimated at approximately 669,800 in 2014. The majority of the workforce—an estimated 68 percent—works in the services industry. Just over 28 percent work in industry, while 3.9 percent work in the agriculture sector. The unemployment rate was 7.4 percent in 2014.

Energy/Power/Natural Resources

Estonia lacks any major natural resources. The most valuable minerals found in the country are oil shale and phosphorite. Oil shale provides the country with 90 percent of its energy. Wood, peat, and biomass also provide Estonia with alternative sources of energy.

There are also deposits of limestone, dolomite, and other crystalline building stone, which are useful to the construction industry. Additionally, Estonia's fisheries and forests are important to its economy.

Fishing

Common fish species harvested from the Baltic include cod, herring, perch, flounder, and rainbow smelt. Common catches from deep-sea fishing include redfish, shrimp, halibut, and ray. In April 2013, Estonia's Fisheries Council, part of the Ministry of Agriculture, developed a Fisheries Strategy for 2014–2020, which aims to enhance the country's fish stocks, coastal fishing, trawling, recreational fishing, processing, marketing, and research and development activities. The strategy is intended to encourage sustainability within the industry and improve economic returns, and to bring Estonia's fishing industry in line with the best practices endorsed by the European Maritime and Fisheries Fund (EMFF).

Forestry

An estimated 52 percent of the land in Estonia is forested. Birch, pine, and spruce are the most common tree species. Approximately 40 percent of the country's forests are state-owned, while the remainder is in the hands of private individuals or corporations. Estonia exports timber to countries such as Finland, Sweden, Germany, and the United Kingdom. Illegal logging (and illegal exporting) of timber products is an issue in the early 21st century. In addition, while Estonia requires the origin of timber products be legal, sustainable, and traceable, an estimated 40 percent of exported lumber is illegal. Estonia's lumber-related imports are subject to EU Timber Regulation laws.

Mining/Metals

According to Estonia's UN Report on mining, mineral resources for the country include clay, crystalline building stone, dolostone, lacustrine lime, limestone, oil shale, peat, and phosphorite.

Agriculture

In 2014, agriculture accounted for around 3.6 percent of the country's GDP, with around 14.9 percent of the land used for growing crops and raising livestock in 2011. Major agricultural products include livestock, milk, meat, eggs, cereals, legumes, potatoes, honey, and forage crops. Fruit orchards and berry farms are also common in the country.

Although Estonia has in the past had a strong agricultural industry, farming is less profitable today because of low prices, competition, and outdated farming practices. As a member of the EU, Estonia is working to bring its agricultural sector into compliance with EU standards.

Animal Husbandry

Primary livestock include chickens, pigs, cattle, and sheep. At the turn of the 21st century, pork was the main meat produced.

Tourism

Around 1.98 million foreign visitors cross Estonia's borders in 2014, generating more than €1.39 billion ($1.2 billion USD) in revenue for the country. Many tourists visit Tallinn, which offers a ferry link to Helsinki, Finland. While visitors regularly arrive from Finland and Sweden, visits by Germans, Latvians, U.S. Americans, and Japanese tourists sharply increased in 2014. According to Estonia's Official Tourism Bureau, foreign tourists were up two percent, and domestic tourists, which stood 1.1 million in 2014, increased by six percent.

Travelers to Estonia may participate in activities such as cycling, canoeing, and hiking in the country's four national parks or in nature preserves. Tallinn features museums, historical sites, theaters, and gardens of interest to tourists.

Evelyn Atkinson, Christina Healey, &
Jeffrey Bowman

DO YOU KNOW?

- The longest day of the year in Estonia lasts for slightly more than nineteen hours. The shortest day is only six hours long.
- The "Singing Revolution" in the late 1980s involved thousands of Estonians singing together to protest the communist government.

Bibliography

Anatol Lieven. *The Baltic Revolution: Estonia, Latvia, Lithuania and the Path to Independence.* Connecticut: Yale University Press, 1994.

Claire Thomson. *Estonia: Culture Smart! The Essential Guide to Customs and Culture.* London, UK: Kuperard, 2014.

David James Smith. *Estonia: Independence and European Integration.* London, UK: Routledge, 2002. Postcommunist States and Nations Ser.

Karin Annus Kärner, Karin Annus. *Estonian Tastes and Traditions.* New York: Hippocrene Books, 2015.

Marc Hyman. *Back on the Map: Adventures in Newly-Independent Estonia.* CreateSpace, 2009.

Mart Laar. *War in the Woods.* Michigan: Compass Press, 1992.

Neil Taylor. *Estonia.* Bucks, UK: Bradt Travel Guides, 2014.

Rein Taagepera. *Estonia: Return to Independence.* Boulder, CO: Westview Press, 1993. Westview Series on the Post-Soviet Republics Ser.

Toivo Miljan. *Historical Dictionary of Estonia.* Lanham, MD: Scarecrow Press, 2015.

Toivo U. Raun. *Estonia and the Estonians.* Stanford, CA: Hoover Institution Press, 2002.

Works Cited

_____ "Estonia." *U.S. Passports & International Travel.* Bureau of Consular Affairs, U.S. Department of State, n.d. http://travel.state.gov/content/passports/english/country/estonia.html.

_____ "U.S. Relations with Estonia." *Bureau of European and Eurasian Affairs Fact Sheet.* U.S. Department of State, 9 Jun. 2015. http://www.state.gov/r/pa/ei/bgn/5377.htm.

"About Ice Cricket." *Welcome to the World of Ice Cricket.* Tours 4 Sport, 2012. Web. http://www.icecricket.co.uk/about.html.

"Ants Laikmaa Museum." *Visit Estonia: Official Tourist Information Website.* Visitestonia.com, n.d. http://www.visitestonia.com/en/ants-laikmaas-home-museum.

"Back in the USSR." *Strolling in Estonia.* Blogger.com, 15 Dec. 2007. http://costabaker2007.blogspot.com.

"Estonia – Language, Culture, Customs, and Etiquette." *Kwintessential.* Kwintessential, 2014. http://www.kwintessential.co.uk/resources/global-etiquette/estonia.html.

"Estonia Blames Russia for Unrest." *BBC World News.* BBC, 29 Apr. 2007. http://news.bbc.co.uk/2/hi/europe/6604647.stm.

"Estonia Improves in CPI." *Transparency International.* MTÜ Korruptsioonivaba Eesti, 2015. http://www. transparency.ee/cm/en/.

"Estonia: Country Reports on Human Rights Practices—2013." *Bureau of Democracy, Human Rights, and Labor.* U.S. Department of State, 2013. http://www. state.gov/j/drl/rls/hrrpt/2013humanrightsreport/index.ht m?year=2013&dlid=220274#wrapper.

"Estonian Phrases." *Linguanaut.* Linguanaut.com, 2013. http://www.linguanaut.com/english_estonian.htm.

"Estonica." *Encyclopedia about Estonia.* Eesti Instituut, n.d. www.estonica.org.

"Getting Around, Tallinn Travel, Transport and Car Rental." *World Guides.* Travel Smart, Ltd, 2015. http://www.tallinn.world-guides.com/tallinn_travel.html.

"Historic Centre (Old Town) of Tallinn." *UNESCO World Heritage.* UNESCO World Heritage Centre, 2015. http://whc.unesco.org/en/list/822.

"Map of Freedom in the World." *Freedom House.* 2015. https://freedomhouse.org/report/freedom-world/ freedom-world-2015#.VZrFSdFRHIU.

"Nation in Transit—Estonia (2014)." *Freedom House.* 2014. https://freedomhouse.org/report/nations-transit/2014/estonia#.VZq-ddFRHIU.

"Parliament of Estonia." *Worldwide Guide to Women in Leadership.* Guide2womenleaders.com, 15 Apr. 2015. http://www.guide2womenleaders.com/ Estonia_Parliament.htm.

"Russia spurns Estonia border deal." *BBC World News.* BBC, 27 Jun. 2005. http://news.bbc.co.uk/2/hi/ europe/4626141.stm.

"The Castle of Alatskivi." *Sightseeing in Estonia.* Ìàêñèì Ñòàðîñòèí, 2007. http://travel.aviastar.org/estonia/ alatskivi.html.

"Toompea Castle." *Digital Tallinn.* Digital Tallinn, n.d. http://www.tallinn.info/toompea/.

"Tourism in Estonia in 2014." *VisitEstonia.com.* Enterprise Estonia, 13 Mar. 2015. Web. https://www.visitestonia. com/en/additional-navigation/press-room/eas-views-on-tourism/estonian-tourism-statistics.

Arne and Libby Kloostri. *Letters from Estonia.* Blogger. com, 2008. http://vesilind.blogspot.com/2008_04_01_ archive.html.

Ellen Barry. "A hole in the ground erupts, to Estonia's delight." *New York Times.* New York Times.com, 9 Dec. 2008. http://www.iht.com/articles/2008/12/09/ europe/09witches.php.

Els Slots. "Tallinn." *World Heritage Site.* WHS, 2015. http://www.worldheritagesite.org/sites/tallinn.html.

Ian Traynor. "Russia accused of unleashing cyberwar to disable Estonia." *The Guardian.* Guardian News and Media Limited, 17 May 2007. http://www.guardian. co.uk/world/2007/may/17/topstories3.russia.

James Tusty & Maureen Tusty. "The Music." *The Singing Revolution.* thesingingrevolution.com, 2015. http://www. singingrevolution.com/cgi-local/content.cgi?pg=2.

Marika Kristi Ets. "Marriage, Estonian Style." *The Baltic Times.* 23 Apr. 2008. Web. http://www.baltictimes.com/ news/articles/20298/.

Mel Huang. "Rock Estonian Style." *Central Europe Review* 1.19 (1 Nov. 1999). Web. http://www.ce-review. org/99/19/huang19.html.

Thomas Brinkhoff. "Estonia." *City Population.* Thomas Brinkhoff, 16 May 2015. http://www.citypopulation.de/ Estonia.html.

Tristan Priimägi. "On Runosong." 1976. *Estonian Culture.* 2.2 (February 2003). Web. http://www.einst.ee/culture/ II_MMIII/priimagi.html.

Vaike Reeman & Piret Ounapuu. *Crafts and Arts in Estonia Past and Present.* Estonian Institute Publications, n.d. http://www.einst.ee/publications/crafts_and_arts/index. html.

Fountain in Kutaisi Square, Georgia

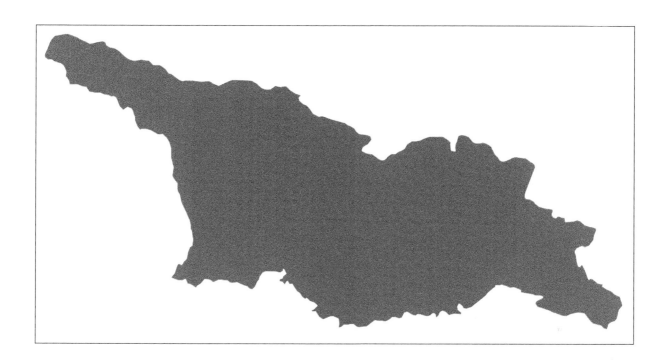

GEORGIA

Introduction

Georgia is a Central Asian republic bordered by Russia, Azerbaijan, Armenia, Turkey, and the Black Sea. For much of the last two centuries, the country has been in involved in a political conflict with Russia that has resulted, at times, in military skirmishes.

Georgians have fiercely preserved their ancient culture through centuries of onslaught and domination. The national poet is Shota Rustaveli, who wrote the medieval epic *The Knight in the Panther's Skin*. This work gave rise to a wealth of Georgian proverbs, and the main street in the capital, Tbilisi, is named for the author. Perhaps the most practiced artistic form in Georgia is music, which in its folk varieties is known for vocal polyphony, with three or four voices and complex harmonies. The Rustavi Choir is renowned for its renditions of traditional songs, while the Georgian State Dance Company has performed to acclaim around the world.

Since becoming an independent country in 1991, Georgia has struggled to forge a post-communist identity and has been beset by internal economic and ethnic tensions. A popular movement ousted the acting president in 2003. In the wake of the so-called "Rose Revolution," the new leadership aimed to stamp out corruption, bolster regional and international economic relations, and broker peace with separatists. Nonetheless, the country engaged in military conflict with Russia in August 2008 in what is now known as the Russo-Georgian War. Taking place in the strategically important Transcaucasia region, which borders the Middle East, this encounter is now considered the first European war of the 21st century.

GENERAL INFORMATION

Official Language: Georgian
Population: 4,935,880 (2014 estimate)
Currency: Georgian lari
Coins: The Georgian lari is subdivided into 100 tetri. Coins are available in denominations of 1, 2, 5, 10, 20, and 50 tetri, and 1 and 2 lari.

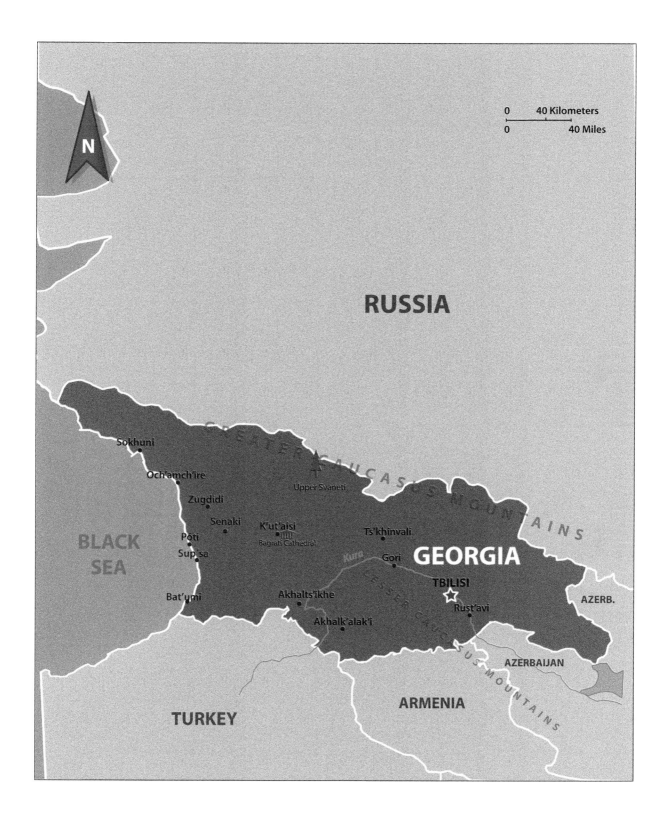

Principal Cities by Population (2014):

- Tblisi (1,118,035)
- Kutaisi (200,611)
- Batumi (154,100)
- Rustavi (122 900)
- Zugdidi (75,100)
- Gori (54,700)
- Poti (47,900)

Land Area: 69,700 square kilometers (26,916 square miles)

National Motto: Dzala ertobashia ("Strength is in Unity")

National Anthem: "Tavisupleba" ("Freedom")

Capital: Tbilisi

Time Zone: GMT +4

Flag Description: The flag of Georgia is the same flag that was once used for the medieval Georgian kingdom. The flag is white, with a red cross that divides the flag into four equal rectangles. In each white rectangle is a "bolnur-katskhuri" cross or small cross.

Population

The majority of Georgia's population is concentrated along the Black Sea coastline and in river basins. Over half of the population (53.5 percent) lives in urban centers. Tbilisi, in the Kura (also Mt'k'vari) River valley, is the largest city, with an estimated population of 1,485,293 in the wider metropolitan area. Kutaisi is the second largest city. Batumi, located on the Black Sea, is another important center. The country had a negative population growth rate of –0.11 percent in 2014.

Georgia has a diverse population, but ethnic Georgians comprise the majority at 83.8 percent of the total. Armenians, who generally live north of the Armenian border, make up about 5.7 percent. Russians, at about 1.5 percent, are scattered throughout the country. About 6.5 percent of the population is ethnic Azerbaijanis who live near the border with Azerbaijan.

Ossetians and Abkhaz (together at 2.5 percent) are special cases in the context of the Georgian population. Soviet leader Joseph Stalin incorporated both groups into Georgia in the early 20th century, despite their ethnic and cultural differences. Since the collapse of the Soviet Union, both the Ossetians and Abkhaz have sought independence from Georgia. Georgia's central government, however, is committed to maintaining the country's territorial integrity and recognizes limited autonomy within Georgia for both ethnic groups. South Ossetians live in north-central Georgia. Abkhazians are concentrated in the northwest part of the country along the Black Sea. Each ethnic group is supported by Russia in their aim to establish themselves as separate from Georgia.

Languages

Many languages are spoken in Georgia. Georgian is a South Caucasian language and does not belong to any major language family. It is written in a unique script that is distantly related to Greek. Armenian is an Indo-European language, Russian is a Slavic language, and Azerbaijani is a Turkic language. Ossetians and Abkhazians both speak their own languages, which belong to Indo-Iranian and Northwest Caucasian language families respectively. Minority ethnic groups are more apt to speak Russian as a second language than Georgian. Though Russian dominated official communications during the Soviet era, attempts to proscribe Georgian failed.

Native People & Ethnic Groups

Ethnic Georgian ancestry in the region extends back at least three millennia. Their stock was formed from a variety of Caucasian sub-groups. The political manipulations of regional populations, followed by the dissolution of the Soviet Union, have led to acute ethnic conflict between Georgians and minority ethnic groups who seek independence.

The Meskhetian Turks, comprised of several groups of Sunni Muslims, have a slightly different problem. Their traditional homeland was in southwest Georgia, but in 1944, they were deported from the territory by Stalin and dispersed across Central Asia. They have not yet been able to resettle in Georgia, though the new government is attempting to coordinate their return.

Georgians are the largest ethnic group in the country today, making up approximately 83.8 percent of the total population. Minority ethnic groups include Armenians (5.7 percent), Azerbaijanis (6.5 percent), Russians (1.5 percent), and Ossetians and Abkhazians (2.5 percent).

Religions

Georgia is one of the first Christian nations, having converted in the fourth century, and has long had a reputation for religious tolerance. Nearly 84 percent of the population identifies with the Georgian Orthodox church. Minority religions include Islam (9.9 percent), Russian Orthodox, Armenian Orthodox (3.9 percent), and Catholic (0.8 percent). Islam is the religion of both Azerbaijanis and Adjarians, an ethnic Georgian group that became Muslim in the 17th century. They are concentrated in southern Georgia near the Turkish border.

Climate

Georgia's climate is as varied as its terrain. Along the Black Sea, a sub-tropical climate prevails. The region has high humidity and precipitation, with annual rainfall averaging between 1,000 and 2,000 millimeters (between 39 and 78 inches). Average temperatures for this region are 5° Celsius (41° Fahrenheit) in January and between 22° and 24° Celsius (72° and 75° Fahrenheit) in July. In contrast, average temperatures for Tbilisi, in the southeast, are 2° and 4° Celsius (36° and 39° Fahrenheit) in January and 25° Celsius (77° Fahrenheit) in July. However, temperatures can climb as high as 31° Celsius (88° Fahrenheit).

The Greater Caucasus protect colder weather coming from the north, except at higher elevations, where snow and ice last year-round above 3,600 meters (11,811 feet). Otherwise, the summers are cool, and the winters cold and rainy in typical lower Alpine patterns. The central Surami Range prevents the influence of the Black Sea climate from reaching Georgia's eastern plain, where the summers are hot, the winters cold, and precipitation low.

Rockslides, mudslides, and avalanches occur frequently in the mountains, and the region is prone to earthquakes.

ENVIRONMENT & GEOGRAPHY

Topography

The Georgian terrain is highly varied, though 85 percent of it is classified as mountainous. The exceptions are the Kartaliniya Plain in the east and the Kolkhida Lowland along the Black Sea coast, which forms Georgia's western border.

The Greater Caucasus dominates most of the country's northern border with Russia. Deep gorges, sharp escarpments, and meadows characterize these mountains. From this range the country's highest peaks rise, including Gora Shkhara (5,193 m/17,040 ft), Jangi-Tau (or Dzhangi-Tau [5,051 m/16,572 ft]), and Mount Kazbek (5,047 meters/16,558 feet). The Lesser Caucasus Mountains, which border Azerbaijan and Armenia in the south, are much lower. The Surami (or Likhi) is a mountain range running northeast to southwest and joining the Greater and Lesser Caucasus.

As many as 25,000 rivers flow through Georgia. The longest, the Mtkvari (formerly known as the Kura), extends 351 kilometers (218 miles) across Georgia and empties into the Caspian Sea. The Rioni (327 kilometers; 203 miles) flows from the Greater Caucasus and empties into the Black Sea. The country's few lakes are generally small and are located at high elevations.

Tbilisi is located in eastern Georgia at an altitude of 380 meters (1,246 feet). The city occupies the depression of a gorge that was formed by the Mtkvari (Kura) River and has grown up on both embankments. It is surrounded by low mountains of the Trialeti and Kartliysky ranges on three sides. The route between western and eastern Transcaucasia follows the gorge.

Plants & Animals

The largest variety of plants and animals is found in the alpine regions of Georgia, since the lowlands are heavily cultivated, and the eastern plain is hot and dry. The country has about 4,400 species of plants, of which 1,200 (27 percent) are endangered or extinct.

Forests, which cover around 37 percent of the country, and meadows are concentrated in the mountain regions. Among the common trees are oak, pine, boxwood, and manna (also known as tamarisk). Few trees grow on the plain, which supports mostly grasses and shrubs.

Animal life follows a similar distribution pattern. Georgia has over 500 different animal and bird species, many of them endemic to the Caucasus region. Foxes, deer, wolves, boar, martens, hedgehogs, rodents, and pheasants are among the animals found in the forests. Other indigenous carnivore species include the Eurasian lynx and the striped hyena, while herbivores include moose, gazelle, and wild goats are native to the country.

CUSTOMS & COURTESIES

Greetings

The typical greeting in Georgia is "Gamarjoba" ("Hello"). The response is to say the same, or, more informally, to respond with "Gagimarjos." When meeting for the first time, men typically shake hands. Women will also shake hands, but more often in a business situation. Friends (both men and women) use the European-style greeting of a light kiss on each cheek, but the practice is more common among women. Touching while speaking is common and generally acceptable among friends or acquaintances.

While colleagues of roughly the same rank will use each other's first names, it is common to address a person of a higher rank with their title and last name. In interactions with service people, such as at restaurants or stores, clerks typically address adult customers as "Sir" ("Batoni") or "Madam" ("kalbat'oni").

Gestures & Etiquette

Georgians are expressive people and frequently use their hands for emphasis while speaking. While the "thumbs up" expression is sometimes used, the "OK" sign, as it is used in North American culture, is considered a rude gesture in Georgia. When beckoning someone, Georgians use the palm down instead of palm up, which is also considered impolite.

Georgians are a hospitable people, and hospitality is expected to be received graciously. For example, the splitting of the bill while dining is not customary and can be considered disrespectful to the party that issued the invitation. Likewise, it is generally considered rude to refuse a drink when offered. Additionally, Georgians generally refrain from drinking wine without first making a toast. However, toasts are not customarily made when drinking other beverages. It is considered acceptable to leave food on one's plate, though most food offerings, including drinks, should at least be tasted before being refused.

Other areas of etiquette include attire and punctuality. In rural areas, women dress more conservatively than in the cities. However, women in both urban and rural areas typically wear clothing that covers their knees, shoulders, arms, chests and heads when entering church. Georgians are generally punctual.

Eating/Meals

Georgians generally follow European-dining times, with three meals per day. Lunch is the main meal of the day, and people usually return home to eat a hot lunch at this time. Georgians rarely snack or eat junk food. They are also traditionally known for singing at meal times, and there are many familiar Georgian "table songs."

The "Georgian table," or supra, is a unique and traditional feast held for special occasions and when hosting visitors. More than a meal, a supra is more like a ceremony, which has its roots in ancient times, and can last until well past midnight. One person is appointed the tamada, or 'toastmaster,' of the ceremony. The tamada sets the tone for the feast with an opening toast, and, if it is a large celebration, appoints assistants called tolumbashis. They will speak when called upon, but only to support the themes initiated by the tamada.

There are very strict rules for a supra. No one must interrupt when the tamada is speaking and if someone who is not a tolumbashi wants to make a toast, he or she must first ask the tamada's permission. Permission must also be asked to leave the table. There are certain toasts that are obligatory such as blessings for the health, happiness, and prosperity of the family, and thanks and wishes for protection of the participants at the end of the feast. The tamada should make sure the toasts are done in correct order, as well as monitoring the festive tone of the dinner. A wine-filled horn called a kantsi is also traditionally passed around, and everyone drinks from it. Lastly, food for the supra is brought to the table continuously, rather than in courses. Table songs are sung, and supras often involve dance competitions.

Visiting

Georgia is famous for its hospitality, and Georgians are known to open their doors even to strangers. In Georgian poetry and folktales, hospitality is a quality that is praised more highly than any other quality. A traditional Georgian saying is that "a guest is a gift from God." Any visitor is welcomed warmly, and although visitors typically call before stopping by, it is not necessary to give a lot of advance notice.

Generally, visitors never go to another home as a guest without something in hand. When visiting a Georgian home, it is customary to bring a gift (something non-consumable) on the first visit. On subsequent visits, flowers or chocolate are considered polite. Because guests are so esteemed, they are offered whatever they want in the host's home. If, for example, a guest admires a small piece of artwork or a book, the host will offer it to the guest and may be offended if the guest refuses to take it. Be it food, drink, or anything else, visitors are expected to accept all offers made to them.

LIFESTYLE

Family

In Georgian culture, the extended family is the norm and many Georgians live in multigenerational homes. When a couple gets married, the woman typically moves in with the husband's family. In the family hierarchy, the eldest man is considered to be the head of the household, while the eldest woman is in charge of the domestic duties and child rearing. If both parents work, the grandmother or aunts are often responsible for childcare. Extended families often get together for events such as weddings or baptisms and frequently live in the same neighborhood. In recent years, divorce has become common in Georgia, as it no longer holds the social stigma it once did.

Housing

A traditional Georgian house is a two-story structure with a balcony on the second floor. Many houses are built around a courtyard, and even in the cities, families usually have a garden for growing grapes or other fruit. In urban areas, many apartment houses that date to the turn of the 20th century, feature spacious apartments and balconies. Soviet-era high-rise apartment buildings still exist in the larger cities, but many are now in disrepair and often uninhabited. Many urban Georgians have dachas, or country houses, outside of the city.

Food

Traditional Georgian cuisine has a wealth of culinary influences, ranging from Middle Eastern flavors to cross-blended Asian and European tastes and techniques. A priority is often placed on meat dishes, and the use of sauces, cheeses, spices, and nuts is prominent. During the Soviet era, Georgian food was known as the best cuisine in all of the republics, noted for its variety and flavor, which stood out from the bland diets of other confederate cultures. Food continues to be an important part of Georgian culture—meant to be shared and enjoyed—and Georgians would be more likely to say, they "live to eat" rather than "eat to live."

While different dishes are found in different areas, there are a few that can be commonly found throughout the country. Khachapuri, a boat-shaped cheese and egg bread sometimes cooked in a clay oven, is found everywhere and can be eaten any time during the day. Some of the most popular meat dishes are khinkali (a spicy meat dumpling) and mtsvadi (lamb skewers). Common vegetable dishes include badradzhani (eggplant covered in walnut sauce and pomegranate seeds) and lobio (a bean salad with coriander, walnuts, garlic, and onions). In areas near the Black Sea, the skewered sturgeon dish shamtsuari is typical. Sauces made of plums, crushed walnuts, pomegranate seeds, figs, or berries accompany dishes of all types.

Georgians often call their country the "birthplace of wine." In fact, ancient documents show that as far back as the ninth century BCE, the people who lived in what is now Georgia used wine as currency in their trade with the Assyrians. Georgian wine, made from regional red and white grape varieties, is still made according to age-old methods. These include, in some areas, the underground storage of the wine in clay jars. Georgian semi-sweet white wines are considered the most popular type.

Life's Milestones
The majority of people in Georgia are Orthodox Christians, and many Georgian milestones are rooted in the Christian faith, including weddings, baptisms, and funerary practices. Of particular note are the large and festive baptism parties held after the customary religious ceremony.

At a Georgian wedding, the bride and groom traditionally don crowns for the ceremony. The groom dips the ring into a glass of wine and passes the glass to the bride, who drinks from it. The groom then retrieves the ring to place it upon the bride. Members of the wedding party accompany the couple to their new home, where they break a plate for good luck. It is custom for unmarried guests to take pieces of the broken plate to place under their pillows in order to dream of future spouses.

When someone dies in Georgia, the body is traditionally kept at the home for seven days. According to Georgian Orthodox tradition, mourning extends for 40 days after the death.

CULTURAL HISTORY

Art
The people of the early tribes and kingdoms of what is now Georgia were known throughout the ancient world for their production of jewelry and other objects in gold and other precious metals. Christianity has remained the state religion since the early fourth century. This has resulted in ornamentation of architecture, such as church frescoes and icons (often encrusted with jewels or gilded), illuminated manuscripts (whose ornate bindings are also frequently encrusted with jewels), and traditional crafts such as embroidery. Sculpture, painting, and other applied arts developed from the 19th century onward. Art during the Soviet period was largely communist-influenced, ideologically themed, and politically-repressed.

Architecture
The ancient kingdoms that made up what is now Georgia were situated between two significant ancient civilizations—the Persians to the south and east and the Greek to the west. They borrowed architectural elements from many different cultures and adapted them to materials available in their region. A distinctly Georgian style developed around the time the region adopted Christianity in the early fourth century CE. Early Georgian churches, many of which are still standing, are based on the Roman basilica style (which is the primary style for medieval Christian churches). Georgians added pitched roofs, domes, and towers that had been part of the local building tradition.

Medieval Georgian architecture is characterized by castles and defensive towers as well as monasteries and other dwellings built in caves in Georgia's rocky mountains. Through the years, Georgia fell under Persian, Mongol, Arab, and Ottoman rule, and the influence of these cultures can be seen in Georgian architecture as well. From the 19th century onward, Georgian architecture was strongly influenced by Russia, which annexed the country in 1801. The neoclassical and baroque styles popular in Russia during this period were adopted for public buildings. Later, after Georgia became part of the Soviet Union, architecture emphasized function over aesthetics.

Drama
The history of Georgian theater may be traced back to the third century BCE. Early theater was

characterized by the reenactment of epic stories, often with the use of masks, singing, and dancing. Georgia's centuries of foreign rule inspired many plays of protest and satire, a genre which is still strong in contemporary Georgian theater.

The Rustaveli National Theatre in Tbilisi, which has been operating since 1879, hosts some of the country's most prestigious theatrical productions. New plays are written and produced in Georgia each year, but Georgians also flock to see performances of Shakespearean plays, either in Georgian or in English, with simultaneous translators. Interpretations of Georgian legends are popular with Georgians and tourists alike.

Georgia has a history of filmmaking dating back to 1908. The industry continued even through years of communist rule, but almost came to a standstill after independence due to lack of funds. Several Georgian directors, such as the award-winning Otar Iosseliani (1934–), have relocated to France for financial reasons, but continue to make movies about Georgia in the Georgian language. The Tbilisi International Film Festival, which started in 2000, brings international films to Georgia and helps highlight Georgian movies. In 2006, the Batumi International Art-House Film Festival (known as BIAFF) was launched, featuring independent films from around the world.

Music & Dance
Georgia's music is rooted in the traditions of the ancient tribes that once lived within its borders. Reports from the Greeks and Assyrians indicate that these ancient people often went into battle singing, and archeologists have unearthed centuries-old pipes and string instruments. Many of these archaic instruments were the precursors to instruments still popular in modern-day Georgia. They include the salamuri (a kind of flute resembling a recorder), the panduri (a three-string fretted instrument similar to a lute), and the chonguri (a three-stringed, unfretted instrument).

Once Georgia adopted Christianity, a unique tradition of sacred music developed in churches and monasteries, known as polyphonic choral music. This music was characterized by chanting and singing designed for three or more voices instead of one. This style of music was later adapted for secular use. In 2001, the United Nations Educational, Scientific, and Cultural Organization (UNESCO) recognized Georgia's ancient tradition of polyphonic singing as a Masterpiece of the Oral and Intangible Heritage of Humanity.

Georgian folk songs were developed to accompany all kinds of events and activities, from everyday work songs (milking songs, harvesting songs, lullabies) to songs for special occasions (weddings, holidays, feasts). In keeping with the polyphonic tradition, almost all of these songs were mostly based on three-part harmony rather than melody or singing in unison. A special part for a single male voice, called a krimanchuli (which is similar to a yodel) was sometimes incorporated. Men and women traditionally never sang together, but rather in choral groups of a single gender.

Georgian dance traditions date back to pagan times and include sacred dances that imitated the movements of celestial bodies. These were used to mark occasions, such as hunting and harvesting. Different regions of the country eventually developed their own dances. In general, male parts in Georgian folk dance are athletic and energetic, including leaps and squats. Graceful, fluid movements characterize female parts. The khevsurulia is a well-known sword dance from the mountainous north, in which dancers break out into solos or duets, showing off their prowess with the weapon. The kartuli, a dance known throughout Georgia, is a romantic dance between a single man and woman. The acharuli is a male-female line dance, which features energetic footwork by men and graceful spinning and hand movements by women. Costume is an important part of Georgian dance and varies according to region.

Literature
Georgia has a long written tradition and its own distinct alphabet, which is not used by any other language. The earliest existing Georgian manuscripts date back to the early Christian period

and are mostly translations of Greek Orthodox psalms and hymns. Georgia's oldest surviving manuscript is the story of a martyred saint written by a fifth-century priest.

During the country's "Golden Age" (around the 11th to 13th centuries), epic poetry that was strongly influenced by the Persian tradition began to develop in Georgia. *The Knight in the Panther's Skin* (also transliterated as *The Knight in the Tiger Skin*), considered to be Georgia's national epic, was written during this period by Shota Rustaveli (c.1172–c.1216). He is still recognized as one of Georgia's greatest poets. Other epic works of this period were written to praise the kings and queens of past, preserve local legends and folklore, or promote the courtly ideals of the time, such as chivalry and honor.

Poetry continued to be a popular form of written expression throughout the centuries in Georgia. Its forms and subject matter often closely mirrored developments in Europe, such as the Romantic period, which impacted Georgian literature from roughly 1830 to 1905. The late 19th and 20th centuries saw more politically driven writing. Georgian fiction is often historical or political in nature, and during Soviet rule, many Georgian writers were censored or jailed for their views.

CULTURE

Arts & Entertainment

Georgians are a very educated and cultured people, and they place a high value on the arts. There are numerous museums, theaters, and concert halls in Tbilisi (and to a lesser extent, in other big cities), and attendance at cultural events is generally high. Traditional music, dance, and literature are cherished, and many efforts have been made to keep them alive. However, Georgians are also very open to new forms of expression and embrace foreign art and culture.

Dance is one of the most popular forms of expression in Georgia. Georgian dancers are the most widely recognized Georgian artists internationally. Georgians are particularly proud of

George Balanchine (born Giorgi Melitonovitch Balanchivadze, 1904–1983), the legendary 20th-century choreographer and co-founder of the New York Ballet City who was Georgian (although born in Russia). The Georgian National Ballet was founded in 1945 in order to help preserve the many traditional cultural dances that were being lost to younger generation. The group has a busy international performance schedule that takes them all over the world, but they are based at the Tbilisi State Opera and Ballet Theatre, an opulent, Moorish Revival-style building that was opened in 1851 and renovated in 1896 following a fire. The Georgian State Dance Company performs their modern interpretations of traditional Georgian dances all over the world.

Georgians love to hear live music, and in Tbilisi, they have many options. Jazz is a favorite with Georgians. The Black Sea Jazz Festival in Batumi has been held annually since 1988 and has a counterpart in the capital, called the Tbilisi Jazz Festival. In Tblisi, there are many European-style clubs (with DJs), as well as clubs featuring local artists performing folk, pop, or rock music. Opera remains popular in Georgia and the Tbilisi State Opera and Ballet Theatre puts on a full schedule of performances each year. Georgians also enjoy classical music, and the concerts are often held at the Tbilisi State Conservatoire, a musical academy founded in 1917.

Poetry is a beloved art form in Georgia. Many historical Georgian poets enjoy national hero status. The main street in Tbilisi is named after the medieval poet Shota Rustaveli, and another major thoroughfare is named after 19th century writer and poet Ilia Chavchavadze (1837–1907). The Tbilisi International Book Festival, held each year, features books published in Georgian, awards for Georgian writers, and readings by Georgian and foreign writers. Live performances of poetry and other writing take place in cafés and bookshops in Tbilisi and other major cities. Many Georgian writers are also known for their translation of foreign works of literature into Georgian.

Visual arts have played an important part in Georgian history and remained strong even under

Soviet rule. In Tbilisi, the Georgian Museum of Arts features the work of Georgian artists and craftspeople, from the Bronze Age to the 20th century. The Center of Contemporary Art, also in Tbilisi, features the work of contemporary artists from both Georgia and the greater Caucasus territories. The museum also highlights late modernist work that was repressed under Soviet government. Georgia has an active contemporary visual arts scene with many photographers and painters, like Alexander Berdysheff (1964–), Eka Abuladze (1964–), and Zura Apkhazi (1968–), who show their work internationally. Tbilisi's Art Gene Festival is an annual two-week festival founded by artists and musicians in 2003. It includes creative explorations of indigenous folk cultures—including contemporary and traditional music, dance, film, and visual arts and crafts—from different regions of the country and by Georgians living abroad.

Cultural Sites & Landmarks

The best view of Tbilisi is from atop the hill that overlooks Georgia's capital city and most important cultural center. The central feature of this area is the fortress of Narikala, which was built in the fourth century CE by the ruling Persians. Through the years, the various foreign powers that occupied Georgia expanded its fortifications. The Arabs built a palace inside the walls and an observatory nearby (now in ruins). The Church of St. Nicholas, originally built on the site in the 12th century, was destroyed when munitions stored there by Russian troops exploded in the early 19th century. The church was rebuilt in 1996. Also in the vicinity is a tall aluminum statue known as Kartvlis Deda, or Mother of the Georgians, who is depicted with a bowl of wine in one hand and a sword in the other. The main entrance to the Tbilisi Botanical Gardens is located at the base of the hill upon which the fortress sits. Several historic churches, as well as a synagogue, mosque, and Zoroastrian temple, are located nearby.

Not far from Tbilisi is Mtskheta (also spelled Meskheta), which was the capital of Iberia, one of the two kingdoms that made up early Georgia.

It is considered the spiritual center of Georgia. Designated a UNESCO World Heritage Site in 1994 because of its historical significance and monuments, Mtskheta was the first area in Georgia to adopt Christianity. Georgians call it "the Second Jerusalem." One of the major attractions in Mtskheta is Svetiskhoveli Cathedral, an 11th-century church built by the Georgian architect Arsukisdze atop the remains of Georgia's first Christian church. It is now a UNESCO World Heritage Site. Also in Mtskheta is the Jvari Church and monastery, which dates from the sixth century and is said to be Georgia's oldest standing church. The Samtavro Monastery dates from the fourth century. Just outside of Mtskheta is the sixth-century monastery of Shio-Mgvime. Once home to over 2,000 monks, the monastery complex includes a church and monastic cells carved into the nearby limestone rocks.

The cave monasteries of David Gareja (Davit'garejis samonastro komplek'si), located near the border with Azerbaijan, are built into rock caves high up on cliffs overlooking a semi-desert area. Monks who had traveled to Syria and returned to Georgia to copy and translate Christian manuscripts into Georgian founded the monasteries in the sixth century. A school of fresco painting developed here, and some remnants of early frescoes still survive. The monasteries were ransacked by various invaders through the years and fell into disrepair, but some restoration has recently been undertaken. Two of the monasteries are still occupied. The nearby 17th-century Church of St. Nicolas, built near one of the functioning monasteries, also houses impressive frescoes.

The Upper Svaneti Region, a province in northwest Georgia near the border with Russia, has also been recognized as a UNESCO World Heritage Site. Considered the highest inhabited area of Europe, this mountainous location features villages with intact medieval defensive towers and dwellings, which have been continuously occupied for hundreds of years. The Svans who live there speak a language that is related to, but distinct from, Georgian. Their isolation has helped keep their unique cultural traditions intact.

Libraries & Museums

Tbilisi's museums display the history and development of Georgian culture. At the National Museum and the Georgian State Art Museum, displays of pre-Christian and Christian archaeology and art demonstrate the fineness of Georgian artistry, especially as it pertains to metalwork. Other museums of note in the capital include the Museum of Soviet Occupation and the Open Air Museum of Ethnography, both administered as part of the Georgian National Museum, as well as the Animated Puppet Museum and the Georgian National Center of Manuscripts.

The National Parliamentary Library of Georgia serves as the country's primary depository for books and dates back to the mid-19th century. In all, the library houses a collection of 3,641,456 million books, including the private collections of past nobility and the first printed Georgian books. Other libraries of note include Kutaisi State Scientific-Universal Library and the National Science Library, which largely serves the employees of the Academy of Science. As of 2004, there were roughly 5,000 working libraries in the country, half of which were public libraries.

Holidays

In addition to the holidays associated with the Orthodox tradition, Georgians celebrate St. George's Day (November 23) in recognition of the country's patron saint. Secular holidays include Independence Day (May 26), marking the 1918 declaration of independence from the Russian Empire, and Constitution Day (August 24), marking the approval of the new 1995 constitution.

Youth Culture

In urban areas, Georgian youth are generally considered technologically savvy and have similar tastes and behaviors to the youth cultures of neighboring European countries. (In their tastes in music and fashion, young Georgians are mostly influenced by the US, Russia, and both Eastern and Western Europe.) Most own cell phones and other electronic devices, and many homes have cable or satellite TV, exposing Georgian youth to international broadcasts and programming.

Generally, most Georgian youth are open-minded about trying new things and are keenly interested in current events. By the age of sixteen, most Georgians can speak at least two, and sometimes three different languages. Today, however, many young Georgians are choosing not to learn or correctly speak Russian for political reasons.

SOCIETY

Transportation

In the cities, a popular mode of transportation is by marshutka, a van that typically holds around 15 people and follows flexible routes. Tbilisi also has city buses and a subway system. Owning a family car is common in urban areas, but families rarely have more than one. The same is true in rural areas, where there is little access to public transportation. Traffic moves on the right-hand side of the road.

Transportation Infrastructure

Since Georgia gained independence from Russia, there has been a lack of adequate investment in infrastructure. It is possible to travel overland to Turkey, Azerbaijan, and Armenia from Georgia. There are numerous customs checkpoints along the major roads, which also make travel by car time-consuming. Georgia is connected to Russia, Azerbaijan, and Armenia by rail, and there is rail service between the major cities within Georgia. Ferry service to and from Turkey, Bulgaria, and Ukraine is available out of the port cities on the Black Sea.

Shota Rustaveli Tbilisi International Airport has service to international locations including Russia, Western Europe, and Central Asia. There is a smaller airport in Batumi, with flights to neighboring countries, and David the Builder Kutaisi International Airport, just outside the second largest city in Georgia offers flights to nine destinations in Central and Eastern Europe, including Budapest and Istanbul.

Media & Communications

Since achieving independence, Georgia has moved to privatize the media and telecommunications industries in the country. Georgia maintains publicly funded radio and TV stations, known as First Channel and Second Channel, which are purportedly independent of government control. There are also several other private and cable TV stations in Georgia, as well as access to international satellite TV, which broadcasts programs from US television, including the reality show *The O. C.* and the NBC drama *Las Vegas*. Georgian Radio broadcasts in Georgian and five other languages, while Tbilisi Television broadcasts in Georgian and Russian. The international shortwave radio broadcasts of Radio Georgia ceased transmission in 2005.

Georgia has several daily and weekly newspapers, published in Georgian, Russian, and English. There are also a number of online newspapers published in English and Georgian and several news agencies based in Georgia.

Internet access in Georgia is widespread in urban areas. The cost is high for individual accounts, and many people get access through public institutions, business offices, or Internet cafés. In 2014, there were an estimated 2,188,311 million Internet users in Georgia— representing nearly 44.4 percent of the population. This is up from just 7.6 percent of the population in 2006.

The Georgian constitution guarantees freedom of the press, but in recent years international observers have expressed concern about freedoms that have been taken away from journalists. Freedom House, an independent civil liberties watchdog group, declared Georgia to be only "partly free" in 2015. Beginning in 2014, the news outlets *Batumelebi*, *Netgazeti*, *Guria News*, Livepress.ge, Studio Monitor, Information Center Kakheti, and TV-25 each reported that the Georgia Ministry of Internal Affairs has withheld information and that some news outlets have received preferential treatment, while others have had their access to officials strictly limited.

SOCIAL DEVELOPMENT

Standard of Living

Georgia ranked 80th out of 190 countries on the 2012 United Nations Human Development Index, which measures quality of life and standard of living indicators.

Water Consumption

According to 2012 statistics from the World Health Organization (WHO), approximately 98.7 percent of the population had access to improved sources of drinking water, while an estimated 93.3 percent had access to improved sanitation. Water is abundant in the country, and foreign aid has helped to rebuild water and sanitation infrastructure damaged because of the 2008 conflict in South Ossetia.

Education

The Georgian state provides a free and compulsory education from the first to the eleventh grades. The adult literacy rate stands at 99.8 percent. Since 1991, lack of adequate funding has lowered the formerly high standard of education.

Georgians have traditionally attained a high level of university or college education. Some of the country's institutes of higher learning include the Ivane Javakhishvili Tbilisi State University, the Tbilisi State Medical University, The Tbilisi Academy of Arts, Grigol Robakidze University, Caucasus University, the International Black Sea University, the Georgian Academy of Sciences, and the Georgian Technical University, all of which are located in the nation's capital. The now twenty-year-old Sukhishvili University and the much older Gori University are both in the Gori district, part of central Georgia, while the city of Kutaisi, second only to Tbilisi in size, is home to Akaki Tsereteli State University. The Abkhazian State University, founded in 1979, is located in the Abkhaz capital of Sukhumi.

Women's Rights

Georgia has traditionally had a patriarchal society, with decision-making power resting primarily with male family members. One of the positive outcomes of Soviet rule in Georgia was that the country reached nearly 100 percent literacy and women were given equal access to education. As a result, Georgian women were able to enter professional fields, such as medicine, law, education, and business. Some women have been able to rise to high positions in government. As of 2012, there were 12 women holding seats in the Georgian parliament, up from seven in 2011. Women also hold many positions in healthcare and education, but the majority still holds lower-level positions. Women are also frequently paid less than male counterparts are, and it is still rare to find women in positions of leadership in business.

Women in Georgia report that sexist attitudes are still prevalent in the workplace, and men continue to discount women's contributions. At home, women are still expected to complete virtually all household duties, such as cooking and cleaning. Georgian women report that gender stereotyping is rampant in Georgia, and that there is little public acknowledgement that it is a problem. Additionally, while it is common in urban areas for women to pursue careers, in rural areas, many women are prevented from working outside the home because their husbands will not permit it. Those who do work outside the home are often engaged in the agricultural or informal sector, where they receive low pay and no benefits. Georgia ratified the UN's Convention on the Elimination of All Forms of Discrimination against Women (CEDAW) in 2002. However, the parliament has made little progress toward creating laws that ensure that women's rights are actually guaranteed in Georgia.

Domestic violence has long been an unreported and unpunished crime in Georgia. Because of the social stigma associated with it, women have kept quiet about abuse and police have regarded it as a personal matter. In 2006, the Georgian parliament passed its first law on the issue. The law gives victims the ability to file for immediate protective orders if they have been abused, and it gives police the authority to issue restraining orders against abusers. Human trafficking, particularly for the purposes of sexual exploitation, also remains a growing problem in Georgia. Young girls, often from rural areas, are lured in by offers of employment abroad. Once they have left the country, they essentially become the property of their abductors and are held as slaves. Until recently, there has been no legislation to protect women from this practice, and laws are still pending.

The age-old tradition of "bride kidnapping," in which a man can forcibly take a woman from her home for the purpose of marriage, has reportedly been on the rise in parts of southern Georgia. After a woman has been abducted and held for a night, she has no choice but to marry her abductor in order to save her honor. While the kidnapping used to be considered only a minor offense, it now has greater consequences, although few women pursue legal action because of family pressure.

Health Care

During much of the Soviet era, Georgia had a socialized health care system of high quality. Throughout the 1990s, that quality declined drastically as the system struggled to cope with lack of funding, inadequate supplies, and an overwhelming number of refugees from war-torn regions. The health care system is only just beginning to recover from these difficulties, though it has had to convert from socialized to privatized medicine. As of 2013, the country spent 9.4 percent of its GDP on healthcare-related issues. In addition, for every 1,000 people in Georgia, there are 4.3 doctors and 2.6 hospital beds.

GOVERNMENT

Structure

Like other countries that were once part of the Soviet Union, Georgia has had little experience with democratic institutions and free market practices. The process of building such institutions and implementing the economic reforms has caused numerous setbacks since independence. The current government, however, has made great strides towards creating a stable, prosperous country.

Georgia is a democratic republic. According to the 1995 constitution, it is headed by a president elected by popular vote to a five-year term, with a two-term limit. The Council of Ministers, overseen by the Minister of State, is appointed by the president, as are three of the nine Constitutional Court justices and the prefects who oversee local administrations.

The legislature is a unicameral body with 150 members elected to four-year terms. The seats are filled by two methods: proportional representation, based on votes received by each political party and by territorial unit. Three of the nine Constitutional Court justices and all of the Supreme Court justices are appointed by the legislature.

Political Parties

Political parties in Georgia cross the political spectrum. Until the 2013 presidential elections, the center-right United National Movement wielded the most political power in the country. In October 2013, however, Giorgi Margvelashvili of the Georgian Dream Party, which was established in 2012 and embraces multiple political ideologies, won by an enormous margin, garnering 1,012,569 votes and 62.12 percent of the popular vote.

Other political parties include the conservative Democratic Movement-United Georgia, The Georgian Way, the center-left Georgian Labour Party, the National Forum, the United Communist Party of Georgia, Our Georgia-Free Democrats, the conservative Industry Will Save Georgia, and the Greens.

Local Government

Georgia is divided into nine administrative regions, nine cities, and three autonomous republics. Administrative regions are subdivided into villages, communes, towns, and cities, each of which is administered by a publicly elected governing body. Georgia's capital, Tbilisi, has a local council that is elected by proportional voting.

The autonomous republics of Abkhazia and South Ossetia, in their drive to secede, each have local governments that the central government does not recognize. The autonomous republic of Adjara has a local government that works closely with the Georgian central government.

Judicial System

Georgia's judicial branch is comprised of a Supreme Court, a Constitutional Court, and Courts of Appeal. The chair of Georgia's Constitutional Court is nominated by the president and appointed by parliament. Circuit courts, regional courts, and city courts adjudicate at the local level. Common law judges are nominated by the Ministry of Justice and appointed by the president. The disputed territory of Abkhazia and the autonomous republic of Adjara have supreme courts that operate separately from the Georgian Supreme Court.

The enforcement of decisions handed down by Georgia's courts remains a significant challenge to the country's judicial system. In addition, a large number of cases continue to be affected by political influence.

Taxation

Georgia's tax system has been significantly simplified in recent years. In addition, instances of corruption related to the payment and collection of taxes have been reduced. As of 2010, Georgians pay a flat income tax of 20 percent, and, since 2008, corporations operating in Georgia pay a flat income tax of 15 percent. A value-added tax (VAT, similar to a consumption tax) is also levied at a rate of 18 percent, in addition to taxes on dividends and interest.

Armed Forces

The armed forces of Georgia, officially the Georgian Armed Forces (sakartvelos sheiaraghebuli dzalebi), consist of several service branches, including land forces, an air force (part of the land forces as of 2010), an elite Special Forces branch, and a coast guard. A small national guard, numbering 554 personnel, is also maintained. Conscription exists, and consists of an 18en-month service obligation for males between the ages of eighteen and thirty-five. As of 2013, there were 37,825 active military personnel and 140,000 reserves.

Georgian troops have participated in peace-keeping missions in countries such as Kosovo, Iraq, and Afghanistan. Following the country's conflict with Russia in 2008, Georgia prioritized the rebuilding of its armed forces, including the implementation of more modernized weaponry and air-defense systems. In 2010, defense funding for the military represented and estimated 4 percent of the country's gross domestic product (GDP). However, by 2013, expenditures were reduced to 1.2 percent of the GDP.

Foreign Policy

For hundreds of years, Georgia's foreign policy has been dominated by its relationship with Russia (which annexed Georgia in 1801). Apart from a brief period of independence in 1917—and a protectoral period under the British from 1918 to 1920—Georgia continued to be ruled by Russia (through the Soviet Union) until it became an independent country in 1990. Post-independence, Russia's relationship with Georgia has not been smooth. Russia saw Georgia as being too "pro-Western" and was displeased with Georgia's strengthening ties to the U.S., NATO, and the EU. When Russia entered into a conflict with the breakaway province of Chechnya, Russia accused Georgia of supporting the Chechens.

The relationship between Russia and Georgia declined in August 2008 when an armed conflict broke out in South Ossetia. The region had been in dispute since the end of the Georgian civil war in 1993. Russia was one of the only two nations (the other being Nicaragua) that recognized the independence of South Ossetia, a province that broke away from Georgia during the war. Russia sent troops when fighting broke out, claiming to defend the many ethnic Russians in the area. Later, the Russian troops entered Georgian territory. The conflict continued until a cease-fire was negotiated. In the conflict, Georgia received strong support from the U.S. and the EU, which both condemned Russia's actions, but stopped short of issuing sanctions. The leaders of six former Soviet states also sided with Georgia in the conflict, with then president of the Ukraine, Viktor Yushchenko, actually raising the rent

on the Russian naval base at Sevastopol in the Crimea. Poland, Hungary, and the United Kingdom similarly spoke out in support of Georgia. However, Italy and Belarus sided with Russia.

Relations between Georgia and its neighbors Armenia, Azerbaijan, and Turkey have also been complicated. When Armenia and Azerbaijan fought over the breakaway province of Nagorno-Karabakh in the late 1980s and early 1990s, Georgia assisted to Armenia. This strained relations with Azerbaijan and Turkey, which supported Azerbaijan. However, aside from a few border disputes, Georgia's relations with Azerbaijan are generally positive, and Georgia has had positive relations with Turkey, which has become a net importer of Georgia's hydroelectric power. Georgia's closest international ally, however, is the US. Georgia was the third largest contributor of troops to the Coalition Forces in Iraq, but pulled out after the conflict with Russia started in August 2008.

Georgia is a member of the UN (United Nations), Organization for Security and Cooperation in Europe (OSCE), the World Bank, the World Trade Organization (WTO), the International Monetary Fund (IMF), and other international economic organizations. Because of the events of August 2008, Georgia left the Commonwealth of Independent States, effective August 2009, because Georgia felt that the members did not do enough to avoid the conflict, which had such devastating humanitarian and economic consequences for Georgia.

Human Rights Profile

International human rights law insists that states respect civil and political rights and promote an individual's economic, social, and cultural rights. The United Nations Universal Declaration on Human Rights (UDHR) is recognized as the standard for international human rights. Its authors sought the counsel of the world's great thinkers, philosophers, and religious leaders and were careful to create a document that reflects the core values shared by every world culture. (To read this document or view the articles relating to cultural human rights, go to http://www.ohchr.org/EN/UDHR/Pages/Introduction.aspx.)

When Georgia became an independent republic in 1990, the country established a new constitution that aimed to promote democracy and protect human rights after decades of repressive Soviet rule. In reality, making the transition to democracy was neither quick nor easy. The newly elected government was soon overthrown by the party of former communist leader Eduard Shevardnadze (1928–2014). Corruption in Shevardnadze's government quickly became a problem and had a very harmful effect on human rights.

Shevardnadze's executive office pressured judges to make certain rulings, and judges were frequently found to be accepting bribes, so individuals were not ensured fair trials. Police corruption and brutality was widespread, and there were many reports of police using torture during interrogation. Furthermore, there were widespread reports of people being arrested and held without due process. Despite pledges of reform by Mikheil Saakashvili (1967–), who took over after the resignation of Shevardnadze in 2004, many human rights issues remained unaddressed. For example, prisoners in Georgia continued to be held in overcrowded detention centers for long periods without trial, experiencing unhygienic conditions, and lack of sufficient food or access to medical care. The conditions lead to prison riots that resulted in the deaths of prisoners. Police brutality and corruption continues to be a problem.

While Georgia has a long tradition of religious tolerance, members of religious minorities, such as evangelical Christians, were subject to persecution during the Shevardnadze era, though the situation is said to have improved since then. While Georgia made great strides toward more free expression and assembly and freedom of the press, some backsliding has occurred, and media outlets complain of favoritism and limited access to officials, particularly since 2012. Before this, in 2007, police also attacked peaceful protesters, which called into question Saakashvili's commitment to democratic reforms. At the time state of emergency was declared, during which the government suspended all news broadcast except by state-run media. This was seen as a huge blow to freedom of the press. Giorgi Margvelashvili (1969–) of the Georgian Dream coalition, which has enacted positive reforms, replaced Saakashvili in November 2013.

Several provinces in Georgia are seeking independence, and armed violence has flared up in these areas periodically since the civil war ended in 1993. Protecting citizens has become a major human rights issue in Georgia. In these conflicts, many civilians have been driven from their homes, injured, or killed. Most significantly, in 2008, Russian forces entered the Georgian province of South Ossetia, leading to a five-day war. While a cease-fire agreement was reached, during the conflict, houses were burned or looted, causing citizens to flee. The government has been unable to ensure the safety of those wishing to return to the area, leaving thousands of people displaced. International bodies such as the EU have called upon Georgia to provide basic safety for the citizens of this area.

Georgia also has an ongoing child labor issue and has an estimated 121,659 children, ages five to 14, engaged in some type of agricultural or industrial employment.

ECONOMY

Overview of the Economy

The transition from a command economy, combined with civil unrest, shattered the Georgian economy in the early 1990s. Unemployment stood at over 54 percent and inflation was rampant. Meanwhile, a local underground economy flourished. The situation has greatly improved since then, because of new leadership, austerity measures, International Monetary Fund (IMF) loans, and foreign investment. In 2014, the gross domestic product (GDP) was $34.27 billion and the per capita GDP was $7,700 (USD).

At the end of 2006, the Baku–Tbilisi–Ceyhan (BTC) pipeline—an oil pipeline originating in Baku, Azerbaijan, and crossing Georgia to Turkey—began full operation. Georgia itself does not have oil reserves, but the projected economic benefits that it will derive from transit fees are great and are anticipated to reach $62.5 million (USD) annually. The pipeline will pass through Tbilisi, where Georgia's share in the project will mainly be administered.

Industry

The industrial sector accounts for 21.8 percent of the GDP and employs 8.9 percent of the work force. Mining, steel production, silk production, and tool making are important industries, but food processing is the most important and relies on the country's extensive agricultural wealth.

Tbilisi is a national and regional economic hub. Both crime and corruption have decreased since the change of government in 2003, and international investment has increased. Circumstances have improved further with the 2012 parliamentary election of the Georgian Dream Party, which took a majority of legislative seats and has subsequently pushed for additional reforms. Local industries produce textiles, alcoholic beverages, foodstuffs, tools, farming equipment, and electrical equipment. Tbilisi is also the country's center for education and scientific research.

Labor

Georgia's labor force was estimated at roughly 1.959 million in 2011. The majority of the labor force—nearly half at 55.6 percent—worked in agriculture, while 35.5 percent were employed in the services sector and 8.9 percent were employed in the industrial sector. The country's unemployment rate was 14.9 percent in 2014, an increase from 14.6 percent in 2013.

Energy/Power/Natural Resources

Manganese, copper, gold, and coal are Georgia's primary minerals, but there are also significant deposits of iron ore as well as alabaster, marble, and slate. The lowlands and river basins have been heavily cultivated for agricultural production and, therefore, do not have tree growth. Dense mountain forests provide wood for both timber and pulp.

Since 2010, Georgia has become a hydropowered nation. An estimated 85 percent of the country's energy now comes from hydroelectric power plants, stationed along the 300 hydro-capable rivers in Georgia. Moreover, the country has been able to export the energy it produces to its neighbors, Russia, Azerbaijan, Armenia, and Turkey. Turkey, for example, has become a net importer of Georgia's electricity. With funding from European Bank for Reconstruction and Development, Germay's KfW Bankengruppe, and the European Investment Bank, Georgia is now constructing a 500/400 kV high-voltage transmission line and converter station on the border with Turkey to ease and increase conduction capacity.

The Soviet Union, with its emphasis on maximizing production with little concern for the effects, left a legacy of environmental problems. Since independence, Georgia has lacked the funding and technology to counteract them. The problems are acute in and around the industrial center of Rustavi, and many cities have polluted air. Soil also suffers from an overuse of fertilizers and pesticides as well as erosion. Moreover, the Black Sea has been severely polluted by untreated wastewater.

Fishing

Much of the fishing in the Black Sea waters off the Georgian coast has been licensed to other nations in recent years. However, the country has begun efforts to reestablish its domestic fishing industry. In 2009, a new fishing and anchovy processing company was opened in the coastal city of Poti.

Forestry

The World Bank's International Development Agency has helped Georgia to reestablish its forestry industry in the years following the collapse of the Soviet Union, and wood products remain one of the country's main export products. An estimated 45 percent of Georgia's land is forested and includes oak, ash, elm, and chestnut trees. Fir trees have become very rare. In 2011, forestry contributed $61.4 million (USD) to the nation's economy, which represents 0.5 percent of its GDP in that fiscal year.

Challenges related to reforestation programs and enforcement of existing logging regulations remain. Noteworthy is that he Caucasus has been chosen as one of the 200 World Wildlife Fund ego-regions for its indigenous plants, variety of species, and rare biomes, among other criteria.

Mining/Metals

Georgia produces manganese, copper, and gold. The country continues to work toward attracting foreign investment in its mineral resources. There are still more than 100 quarries and mines that extract arsenic, lead, zinc, iron, and silver, along with barite, andesite, bentonite clay, diatomite, talc, calcite, and basalt.

Copper represented an estimated 8 percent of Georgia's total exports in 2005, but just 5.2 percent in 2014. Gold represented 5.4 percent of exports in 2014, while refined petroleum accounted for 11 percent and ferroalloys 8.1 percent. Industry, including the production of steel, employs approximately nine percent of the country's work force and represents an estimated 26 percent of its overall gross domestic product. The country remains a significant political player in Europe's natural gas and oil market because major supply pipelines pass through its territory.

Agriculture

Georgia is blessed with rich soil and a wide range of microclimates. Agriculture accounts for 21 percent of the GDP. Over 50 percent of the labor force is engaged in a wide variety of agricultural activities, most of which are very labor-intensive.

Major cash crops include tea and citrus fruits—both cultivated in the warm lowlands—and grains, hazelnuts, grapes, and sugar beets. The wine-making industry counts upwards of forty wineries, some of the most active of which are Teliani Valley, Gevelli, Giuaani, Telavis Marani, Tbilvino, Kindzmarauli Marani, Badagoni, and Mukhrani. In 2010, Georgia exported the greatest number of bottles to the Ukraine, Kazakhstan, Belarus, Poland, and Latvia. Extremely popular Georgian wine varieties include 17 whites, like the semi-sweet Alaznis Veli; 20, like the dry Mukuzani; and seven fortified versions, including the port-style Marabda. The five major viniculture regions in Georgia are Kakheti, which produces 70 percent of Georgian grapes,

Kartli, Imereti, Ajara, and Racha-Lechkhumi and Kvemo Svaneti in northwest Georgia.

Animal Husbandry

Sheep, cattle, and pigs are the most commonly kept livestock in Georgia. Although agriculture is the country's largest economic sector, animal husbandry represents only an estimated 25 percent of the country's total agriculture production.

Tourism

Georgia was once the favored vacation spot among Soviet citizens. In fact, before 1991, Tbilisi enjoyed a high level of tourism from Soviet visitors, but the instability following the USSR's collapse caused the industry to falter. The civil unrest, crime, and movement of refugees marking the post-independence period scared away all but the most stalwart tourists and damaged much of the country's infrastructure. Since the security situation has stabilized somewhat, Georgia is attempting to improve its image abroad and realize its potential as a tourist hotspot. Currently, an estimated 3 million tourists visit each year, thanks in part to the country's wine culture and historical destinations. Tourists from Russia rose by 72 percent in 2012 alone, thanks to the abolishment of visa requirements.

The majority of tourists use Tbilisi as their point of entry and spend time in the city. Tbilisi was chosen as the site for the Youth Olympic Festival of 2015. The event is expected to attract 4,000 athletes from forty-nine European countries, along with thousands of spectators. Similarly, in 2015, Georgia will host the Union of European Football Associations Super Cup, which is expected to boost foreign visitor numbers as well.

Outside the capital, the mountains, vineyards, and the cave city of Vardzia attract the greatest number of visitors. The so-called Georgian Military Road, which leads north into Russia, is a popular route for viewing mountain scenery and visiting remote conical-topped churches that typify the Georgian style.

Joanne O'Sullivan, Michael Aliprandini, &
Savannah Schroll Guz

DO YOU KNOW?

• Modern historians consider Georgia to be the place where Jason and the Argonauts sought the mythical Golden Fleece.

• Legend has it that Prometheus, the mythological figure who stole fire from the gods and gave it to humans, was chained to the top of Mount Kazbegi (also Kazbek) as a punishment. This mountain is the third highest in Georgia.

• Marco Polo began his travels along the Silk Road from Tbilisi.

Bibliography

"A Country Study: Georgia." *Country Studies*. The Library of Congress, 27 Jul. 2010. Web. http://lcweb2.loc.gov/frd/cs/getoc.html.

"EU: Focus on Civilian Protection in Georgia-Russia Talks." *Human Rights Watch*. Human Rights Watch, 14 Oct. 2008. Web. http://www.hrw.org/news/2008/10/14/eu-focus-civilian-protection-georgia-russia-talks

"Georgia: Communication Styles." *Centre for Intercultural Learning, Foreign Trade and International Trade Canada*. Foreign Affairs and International Trade Canada, 15 Dec. 2011. Web. http://www.intercultures.ca/cil-cai/overview-apercu-eng.asp?iso=ge.

David Gorji. *Georgian Gorgeous or Gorgeous Georgians?: ?: Country of Georgia in the Caucasus*. Creative Angel Publishing, LLC, 2014.

Glenn E. Curtis. *Armenia, Azerbaijan, and Georgia: Country Studies*. 1995. 2nd ed. Seattle, WA: CreateSpace, 2013.

John Noble, Michael Kohn, & Danielle Systermans. *Lonely Planet: Georgia, Armenia, and Azerbaijan*. 4th ed. Hawthorne: Lonely Planet, 2012.

Natia Abramia. *Georgia—Culture Smart!: !: The Essential Guide to Customs & Culture*. London, UK: Kuperard, 2012.

T. P. Sulakvelidze. *Georgian Cuisine*. Transl. Boris Ushumirskiy. Seattle, WA: CreateSpace, 2014.

Tara Booth. "Tomb Treasures of Ancient Georgia at the Fitzwilliam Museum." *24-Hour Museum*. Arts Council England, 21 Oct. 2008. Web. http://www.culture24.org.uk/history-and-heritage/art61826.

Works Cited

"Ancient Georgian traditional Qvevri wine-making method." *UNESCO Intangible Cultural Heritage*. UNESCO, 2013. http://www.unesco.org/culture/ich/RL/00870.

"City of Kutaisi Website." Kutaisi government, 2015. http://kutaisi.gov.ge

"Freedom in the World 2015: Georgia." *Freedom House*. Freedom House, 2015. https://freedomhouse.org/report/freedom-world/2015/georgia#.VZsHs9FRHIU.

"Georgia country profile—Overview." *BBC News*. BBC, 15 Apr. 2015. Web. http://www.bbc.com/news/world-europe-17301647.

"Georgia." *Families for Russian and Ukrainian Adoption*. FRUA, Inc., 2015. Web. http://www.frua.org/countriesandculture/georgia.

"Georgia." Global Forest Watch. "Georgia." *GlobalForestWatch.org*. Global Forest Watch, 2013. http://www.globalforestwatch.org/country/GEO.

Central Intelligence Agency. "Georgia." *The World Factbook*. Central Intelligence Agency, 2015. https://www.cia.gov/library/publications/the-world-factbook/geos/gg.html.

"Georgia." *UNESCO*. UNESCO World Heritage Centre, 2015. http://whc.unesco.org/en/statesparties/ge.

"Georgia/Russia conflict: Counting the cost of war: Return, security, and truth still a long way off." *Amnesty International*. Amnesty International, 18 Nov. 2008. https://www.amnesty.org/press-releases/2008/11/georgiarussia-conflict-counting-cost-war-return-security-and-truth-still/.

"Georgia: Police Beat Peaceful Protesters for Second Day." *Human Rights Watch*. Human Rights Watch, 7 Nov. 2007. http://www.hrw.org/news/2007/11/07/georgia-police-beat-peaceful-protesters-second-day.

"Georgian Folklore." *Song and Dance National Ensemble*. Song and Dance National Ensemble, 2015. http://ensemble.tsmu.edu

"Georgian Polyphonic Singing." *UNESCO Intangible Cultural Heritage*. UNESCO, 2008. Web. http://www.unesco.org/culture/ich/RL/00008.

"Human Trafficking Is Still Urgent Problem." *HumanRights.ge: Web Portal on Human Rights in Georgia*. HRIDC, 21 January 2008. http://humanrights.ge/index.php?a=main&pid=6971&lang=eng.

"Parliament of Georgia Website." Parliament of Georgia, 2015. http://www.parliament.ge/en/.

"Q & A: Conflict in Georgia." *BBC News*. BBC, 11 Nov. 2008. http://news.bbc.co.uk/2/hi/europe/7549736.stm.

Violence Against Women in Georgia." *Stop Violence against Women*. The Advocates for Human Rights, June 2011. Web. http://www.stopvaw.org/georgia.

Daisy Sindelar. "World: Women in Government Still a Rarity in Many Countries." *Radio Free Europe/Radio Liberty*. RFE/RL, 8 Mar. 2007. Web. http://www.rferl.org/content/article/1075134.html.

David Mchedlishvili. *About Georgia*. David A. Mchedlishvili, 2010. Web. http://members.tripod.com/ggdavid/georgia.

Eka Mchedlidze. "Every Fifth Woman Suffers from Domestic Violence." *HumanRights.ge: Web Portal on Human Rights in Georgia*. HRIDC, 26 Mar. 2008. Web. http://humanrights.ge/index.php?a=main&pid=7072&lang=eng.

Jacqueline Carambat. "Georgian Folk Dancers Awe Crowd with Smoke, Swords." *The Orion*. California State University, 19 Sept. 2007.

Karl Idsoog. "Journalism Rises and Stumbles in The Republic of Georgia." *IIP Digital*. U.S. Department of State, 16 Apr. 2008. http://iipdigital.usembassy.gov/st/english/publication/2008/05/20080518193617wrybakcuh0.8979303.html#axzz3fA2X4r9Z.

Lawrence Sheets. "Kidnapping custom makes a comeback in Georgia." *National Public Radio*. NPR, 14 May 2006. http://www.npr.org/templates/story/story.php?storyId=5403695.

Liza Tavdumadze. "Georgian Hydropower Turns River Flow into Cash Flow." *HydroWorld.com*. PennWell Corporation, 2014. Web. http://www.hydroworld.com/articles/print/volume-21/issue-01/articles/russia---central-asia/georgian-hydropower-turns-river.html.

Marcel Theroux. "Discovering Wine in Georgia." *BBC Travel*. BBC, 23 Oct. 2012. http://www.bbc.com/travel/story/20121012-discovering-wine-in-georgia.

Matt Gross. "Frugal Traveler: Dodging Traffic and Pitfalls in Gourmet Georgia." *New York Times*. The New York Times Company, 19 Jul. 2006. Web. http://www.nytimes.com/2006/07/19/travel/19frugaltraveler.html.

Oliver Bernier. "The Treasures of Tbilisi." *New York Times*. The New York Times Company, 30 Sept. 1990. Web. http://www.nytimes.com/1990/09/30/travel/the-treasures-of-tbilisi.html.

Tamta Khelaia. "Art Gene Celebrates Music and Cultural Diversity." *The Georgian Times*. Georgian Times Media Holding, 28 Jul. 2008. Web. http://www.times.ge/archive/index.php?m=home&newsid=11716&lang=eng.

Tom Porteous. "Georgia: A Challenge for Europe." *Human Rights Watch*. Human Rights Watch, 23 Aug. 2008. Web. http://www.hrw.org/news/2008/08/23/georgia-challenge-europe.

The Hungarian Parliament Building, Budapest, Hungary

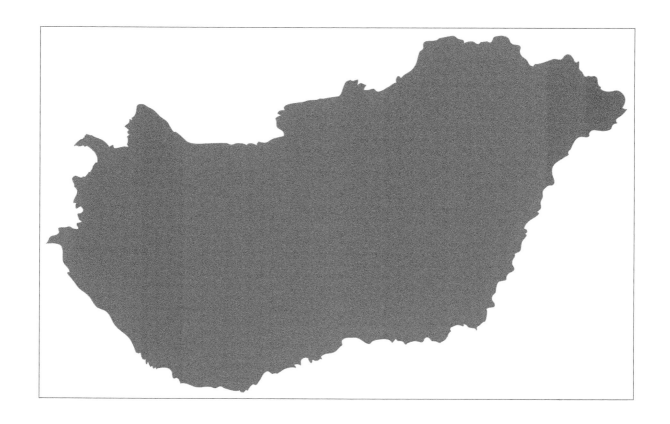

HUNGARY

INTRODUCTION

Hungary is a landlocked country in Central Europe that borders Austria and Slovenia to the west, Croatia and Serbia to the south, the Ukraine and Romania to the east, and Slovakia to the north. In 1989, Hungary shifted to a market-driven economy from a centrally planned communist model. Hungary became a member of the European Union on May 1, 2004.

Budapest is the capital of Hungary and that nation's cultural, economic, and industrial center. Originally separate cities, Buda and Pest merged in 1873 to form the river-straddling metropolis often referred to as the "Queen of the Danube." Considered one of Central Europe's loveliest cities, Budapest has evoked comparisons to Prague and Vienna. In a new climate of freedom, Budapest enjoyed a cultural and economic revival during the 1990s. Today it has re-emerged not only as the vibrant capital of a free and independent Hungary, but also as one of Central Europe's fastest-growing cities.

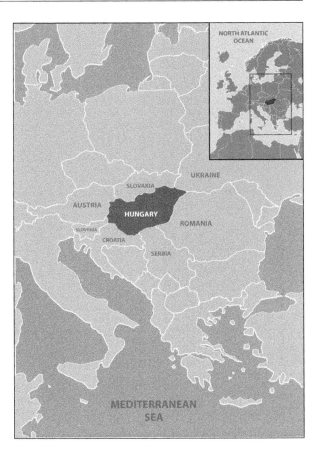

GENERAL INFORMATION

Official Language: Hungarian
Population: 9,919,128 (2014 estimate)
Currency: Hungarian forint
Coins: The Hungarian forint is available in coin denominations of 5, 10, 20, 50, 100, and 200 forint.
Land Area: 89,608 square kilometers (34,597 square miles)
Water Area: 3,420 square kilometers (1,230 square miles)

National Motto: "Cum Deo pro Patria et Libertate!" ("With the help of God for Homeland and Freedom")
National Anthem: "Isten, áldd meg a magyart" ("God Bless the Hungarians")
Capital: Budapest
Time Zone: GMT +1
Flag Description: The flag of Hungary features a tricolor design, with three equal horizontal bands of red (top), attributed to strength and the spilled blood of nationals; white (middle), attributed to faithfulness and freedom; and green (bottom; attributed to hope and the fertility of the country's pastures. A "de facto" version of the flag features the Hungarian coat of arms centered in the tricolor design.

Population

Magyars are the major ethnic group living in Hungary and their settlement can be traced

Principal Cities by Population (2014):

- Budapest (1,744,665)
- Debrecen (204,333)
- Szeged (161,921)
- Miskolc (161,265)
- Pécs (156,801)
- Győr (128,567)
- Nyíregyháza (117,852)
- Kecskemét (114,226)
- Székesfehérvár (100,570)
- Szombathely (79,590)

back to the ninth century. They descended from the Ugrian people, who may have come from either Europe or Asia and are believed to have descended from nine original tribes. The word "Magyar" stems from the name of the most renowned of the Hungarian tribes, the Megyer. Ethnic Hungarians now make up the majority of the population—an estimated 85.6 percent as of the 2011 official census—while Romani represent 3.2 percent of the country's population and 1.9 percent are German.

Approximately 70.8 percent of the population lives in urban areas (2014). Budapest, the capital and largest city, is home to approximately 1.7 million people, or approximately 20 percent of Hungary's total population. The population growth rate was –0.21 in 2014.

Languages

Magyar, or Hungarian, is the official language of Hungary. Spoken by 99.6 percent of people in the country, the Hungarian language is unique in Europe. It is part of the Finno-Ugric language group, but has Roman characters. The language also has some common traits with Finnish and Estonian. Other languages spoken in Hungary include Armenian, Bulgarian, Greek, Macedonian, Polish, Romanian, Ukrainian, and Eastern and Western Yiddish. German and English are also widely spoken.

Native People & Ethnic Groups

Historians speculate that a primarily Slavic population originally inhabited Hungary, though their numbers in the area were probably small before the Magyars arrived at the end of the ninth century. Many other ethnic groups including German, Slavic, and Turkic peoples influenced the region of the Danube. Today, ethnic groups in the country include Roma, Germans, Slovaks, Croats, Serbs, and Romanians. Hungarians are the dominant ethnicity, at approximately 85.6 percent of the population as of the 2011 census.

Religions

Catholicism is the predominant religion in Hungary, observed by 37.2 percent of the population, though Calvinists are a sizable religious minority at 11.6 percent. Approximately 2 percent of the population is Lutheran. In addition, 18.2 percent of the population identify themselves as atheists or are not affiliated with any church. Hungary is also home to more Jewish people (between 35,000 and 120,000, according to the World Jewish Congress) than any other country in Central and Eastern Europe; as of 2014, a large percentage lived in Budapest, where there are twenty active synagogues.

Climate

Located in the center of Europe, Hungary has a continental climate. The coldest weather is in January, and the hottest weather is in August. Autumn and spring are very short seasons. Rain primarily falls during the growing season, and the entire country's average annual precipitation is around 57.7 centimeters (23 inches). Hungary has approximately 74 sunny days per year.

Budapest, the capital, has a temperate climate marked by hot, humid summers and short winters, although the city does see significant snowfall on occasion. The city experiences approximately 56.3 centimeters (22.2 inches) of rainfall annually. Summer temperatures average around 22° Celsius (72° Fahrenheit) and winter temperatures around –2° Celsius (29° Fahrenheit).

ENVIRONMENT & GEOGRAPHY

Topography

Hungary is a completely landlocked country in the Carpathian Basin. It is primarily flat, though there are some hills and mountains, especially on the Slovakian border. Hungary can be divided into three major regions, which are the Great Plain, the Transdanube, and the Northern Hills.

The highest point in Hungary is Kékes in the Mátra Mountains, at 1,014 meters (3,327 feet). The lowest point is in the south, on the Tisza River, at 77.6 meters (255 feet) above sea level. The two main rivers that run north to south through Hungary are the Danube and the Tisza. The largest freshwater lake in Europe, Lake Balaton (592 square kilometers/229 square miles), is located in Hungary. Hungarians often refer to this vast lake as "the Hungarian Sea." Other smaller lakes include Lake Velence and Lake Ferto.

Budapest is located in northern Hungary and consists of three urban centers: Buda and Obuda (generally referred to as one entity under the name of Buda) occupy the hilly western bank of the Danube River, while Pest lies opposite on the flat plains flanking the river's eastern side. Buda comprises about one-third of the city's 525 square kilometers (203 square miles) while Pest makes up the remainder. Nine bridges span the Danube to link Buda and Pest.

Plants & Animals

Hungary is famous for its bird watching, and the Hortobágy National Park is one of the best birding venues in Europe. Included in the many species that can be seen there are the endangered great bustard (also known as the Hungarian Ostrich), white-winged black terns, sweet-singing aquatic warblers, spoonbills, ibises, and purple- and black-crowned night herons. In addition, white storks are often seen nesting on houses throughout the country. Of the nearly 350 bird species found in Hungary, ten have been considered threatened since 2013, according to World Bank statistics.

Though most of Hungary's mammals are also found in the rest of Europe, some rare species include wildcat, lake bat, and Pannonian lizard. Among Hungary's ten national parks are Kiskunság National Park, Körös-Maros National Park (where twelve different snail species can be found), Fertő-Hanság Nemzeti Park (on the Austrian border), and Zemplén Forest Reserve.

CUSTOMS & COURTESIES

Greetings

In general, Hungarians tend to be aggressive and open in their communication. This openness manifests itself in the fabric of daily conversation, in which Hungarians consider it normal to discuss personal details. Furthermore, Hungarians may commonly consider those unwilling to share intimate details as untrustworthy. Generally, greeting phrases can be either formal or informal, and each phrase is different depending on whether the speaker is addressing one person or a group. For example, the word "Szia," an informal way of saying "hello," becomes "Sziasztok" when addressing a group. In addition, Hungarians use special honorific phrases when speaking to persons who are older or of higher social status.

Hungarians also use different greetings depending on the time of day. The word "jó," (good) may be combined with the time of day—"reggelt" (morning), "napot" (afternoon), "estét" (evening), and éjszakát (night)—to phrase greetings such as "Good morning" or "Good afternoon." The saying "Vigyázz" ("Take care") is often used to bid farewell. While the question "Hogy van" ("How are you") is interchangeable with the word "hello" in the United States and parts of Europe, Hungarians don't ask this question, unless they are genuinely asking for the details of someone's life and well-being.

Gestures & Etiquette

Most greetings begin with a handshake, accompanied by direct eye contact. Kissing the cheeks as a greeting is common, even among acquaintances. This usually begins with the kissing of the right cheek, followed by the left. When greeting a woman, a man should wait for the woman to offer her hand and/or cheek in greeting. In formal greeting, a man may bow to a woman slightly while taking her hand. Though less common in modern society, the kissing of the hand was seen as a symbol of reverence and respect, and men may also kiss a woman's hand as a form of greeting. This honorific greeting, often referred to as "csókolom" ("I kiss it"—meaning the hand), is also traditionally a sign of respect to elders.

Generally, business meetings are more formal than social meetings and require different etiquette. Punctuality and convention are important, but most Hungarians also like to create a relaxed atmosphere where business is handled in conjunction with friendly conversation, stories, and jokes and often dining and drinking. In addition, Hungarians may commonly list their surnames before their given names. It is also important to refrain from using a person's first name unless given permission.

Eating/Meals

Hungarians generally begin the day with a substantial meal of hot dishes, such as ham, eggs, grains, and sometimes fruit. Sweets are not common in the traditional morning meal. The largest meal is eaten at midday, generally followed by a short period of rest. Roasted meats, stew, and other main courses are generally eaten at midday and not in the evening. Instead, the evening meal is generally small, and usually consists of cold dishes or leftovers from the midday meal. Food is a major part of Hungarian culture and most celebrations are accompanied by a communal meal.

Hungarians drink casually in a variety of social situations. For decades after the Hapsburgs, a European ruling house that held power from the late 13th to the early 20th centuries, were overthrown in Hungary, it was considered unlucky to toast glasses when drinking beer. This is because the Hapsburgs often toasted with beer over the bodies of dead Hungarians. In modern Hungarian culture, toasting with beer no longer holds the same significance, though older Hungarians still practice the custom. As in many cultures, Hungarians always make direct eye contact when toasting.

Visiting

Punctuality is important to Hungarians in both social and business situations. Arriving slightly early is acceptable, but guests should always inform their hosts if they will be arriving late. Guests generally bring a gift (of candy, alcohol, or flowers perhaps) for their hosts. Flowers, in particular, are given in odd numbers due to the use of even numbers of flowers in funeral traditions.

Hosts will generally offer a drink to an arriving guest, and it may be considered impolite to refuse. Politeness is a virtue in Hungarian culture and use of the terms "köszönöm" ("thank you") and "kérem" ("please") are helpful in any social situation. Compliments are appreciated in social circumstances and should be used liberally when visiting a Hungarian home. In some homes, hosts might ask guests to remove their footwear before entering the house.

When invited to a meal, guests should dress formally. It is expected that guests will compliment the hosts and chef repeatedly on the quality of the food and the condition of the house. Empty plates and glasses are filled repeatedly until the guest is no longer able to consume. Leaving food on the plate and liquid in the glass can signal to the hosts that no more food or drink is required.

LIFESTYLE

Family

The structure of the family has changed significantly throughout Hungarian history. In modern times, the extended family groups of traditional Hungarian society eventually gave way to smaller, nuclear family units (consisting of a mother, father, and typically two children), especially in urban areas. In some rural communities, individuals continue living with their families even after marriage. However, it is more common for both males and females to remain in the home until marriage and then move with their spouse to a new home.

Poverty and unemployment are significant problems in Hungary. Approximately 14 percent of the population lives below the nationally established poverty line. The percentage of women working outside the home has increased by more than 40 percent since the 1980s and continues to be a major factor in determining family culture. During the 1950s and 1960s, as birthrates fell below replacement levels, the Hungarian government began a program to encourage larger families. This program included financial incentives for parents. The trend has continued and it was estimated in 2014 that the population was decreasing at a rate of 0.21 percent annually.

Though marriage is important in popular culture, Hungarians are accepting of non-traditional families and cohabitation. For example, in a 1997 national poll, more than 80 percent of Hungarians responded that it was acceptable for couples to have children out of wedlock. Childrearing, however, has remained a major source of fulfillment for Hungarians. More than 90 percent of Hungarians in the poll listed having a child as "necessary for fulfillment."

Housing

Typical Hungarian houses are simple and are similar to Finnish or Swedish architectural traditions. Concrete, brick, and synthetic materials are typically used for both urban and suburban housing. In cities such as Budapest, a larger number of residents live in apartments, generally in the one- or two-bedroom style. Approximately 20 percent of Hungarians, most of whom fall into the middle or lower-middle class income categories, live in large housing estates at the periphery of the cities. In 1998, the Hungarian office of statistics estimated that 91 percent of the houses in Hungary were privately owned. On Lake

Balaton, it is estimated that 1,000 summer and holiday homes are owned by British citizens.

Data collected by the Hungarian Central Statistics Office in 2011 indicated that the size of private homes in Hungary has continued to increase and that persons purchasing new homes were more likely to purchase property in semi-rural areas near towns with populations under 50,000. The number of renters in both privately owned and government-subsidized housing in Budapest alone fell slightly between 2001 and 2011, dropping from 101,790 to 95,976. While the number of renters fell, the average size of rental apartments increased from 81 to 94 square meters (871 to 1,011 square feet).

Food

Hungarian food has its roots in the Magyar culture, in which wild game and domestic livestock formed the basis of most meals. Generally, most sauces and seasonings are simple in Hungarian dishes. Hungarians prefer spicy fare, and paprika, pepper, and sour cream feature prominently in many main courses. Pork is the most common meat in Hungarian cuisine, followed by beef, chicken, and other types of poultry. Goose fat is a component of many Hungarians dishes. In fact, Hungary exports goose fat to other countries.

The best-known Hungarian dish is gulyás (goulash), a soup that has its origins in Magyar culture. The preparation generally involves cooking fresh meat with onions and spices and then drying the meat so that it can be boiled later to make a thick soup. As goulash spread to other countries, cooks began preparing it as a stew rather than a soup. However, the dish is often still prepared in the traditional manner in Hungary.

A typical main course in Hungary may involve a type of pecsenye, which can refer to any type of pan-fried meat seasoned with onion, paprika, pepper, and salt. Vegetables, such as cabbage and other greens, may be served with the meat. Cabbage is a popular vegetable in Hungary, and stuffed cabbage rolls, called töltött káposzta, is a traditional Hungarian dish consisting of meat, vegetables, and sauce wrapped in cabbage leaves and then boiled. Sour cream or tejföl, which is a thickened cream common in Eastern European cuisine, is often served with stuffed cabbage.

The palacsinta is a thin, stuffed pancake, similar to a crêpe, and often served as a dessert in Hungary. Common in many types of European cuisine, such pancakes can be combined with fruit, cream, and chocolate, or can be used with meat and savory sauce for a main dish. Sometimes wheat flour is used to give the palacsinta a hearty flavor.

Historically, Hungary is renowned for producing some of the finest wines and liquors in Europe, and its red wines are well established in the international wine market. Wine makers in the Tokaji region produce a variety of sweet wines that are highly prized as dessert delicacies. Hungary also produces several famous fruit brandies, including pear and apricot flavors. The apricot brandy, called "barackpálinka," has gained worldwide acclaim from liqueur aficionados.

Life's Milestones

A majority of Hungarians are Christian, and the rites of passage are similar to those in other Christian cultures, including baptism, communion, confirmation, and marriage. In addition, an individual's birth is usually celebrated by a small, family-oriented celebration, similar to birthday traditions in other countries.

Hungary is one of a number of European countries that maintain the Catholic tradition of celebrating "name days." These are nationally recognized celebrations for all people bearing the same given name. For example, February 10 is set aside to celebrate persons named Elvira, while October 1 is set aside for the name Malvin. In Hungary, the celebration of name days is usually more elaborate than the celebration of an individual's birthday and is accompanied by parties or family feasts.

Graduation from secondary school is seen as an important event and is marked by several unique traditions, including the ribbon-pinning ceremony known as szalagavató. This ceremony is conducted shortly before students graduate from secondary school. Students also participate in the ballagás (marching), where the students march from classroom to classroom, singing songs of appreciation to their teachers and fellow students.

As in many cultures, marriage marks the transition to adulthood. However, an increasing number of Hungarians are choosing to postpone or forgo marriage. In addition, married women have options concerning naming conventions. While some women choose to keep their maiden name, others take their husband's surname. It is also common for women to take both their husband's surname and given name followed by a suffix to indicate "wife of." If the woman chooses to take her husband's full name, friends and family may generally call her by her former given name.

CULTURAL HISTORY

Art

The art of the Magyar people—the largest ethnic group in Hungary—reflects the traditional nomadic lifestyle of the tribes that first occupied the Carpathian Basin in Central Europe, which was first settled as far back as 5000 BCE. Paintings and artifacts have revealed a strongly equestrian culture (pertaining to horseback riding), and equine images dominate early paintings, sculptures, and funerary artifacts. After 900 CE, Magyar art begins to show distinct foreign influences, such as ornamental decorative patterns that bear a strong resemblance to similar traditions in the Middle East.

By the medieval period, beginning in the 11th century CE, Hungarian art was similar to that of many European nations. In the Lower Church of Feldebrő, a Roman Catholic Church located in the village of Feldebrő, art historians have found Renaissance-style frescos and wall paintings clearly related to Italian and Byzantine traditions. Between the 13th and 16th centuries, Renaissance art and architecture gave way to the Gothic style. The painter Master M.S., largely believed to have lived in the town of Banská

Štiavnica in the 16th century, and whose true name is unknown, is considered one of the greatest Hungarian late Gothic/early Renaissance painters.

A secular artistic movement also arose in the 17th century, led by artists such as German painter and engraver Georg Philipp Rugendas (1665–1742), who often traveled across Europe and brought new techniques to Hungary. Another important tradition was the sculpting of elaborate burial tombs for wealthy families and public figures, which emerged in the 16th century. These funerary monuments were often covered with decorative images carved into marble and featured ornate inscription. The Austrian Hapsburg Dynasty took control of Hungary in 1718, and there was a subsequent rise in anti-Hapsburg art across the country. From the 18th to the late 19th century, Hungarian art was similar to Austrian and German art. For example, renowned Hungarian painter Ádám Mányoki (1673–1757), known for his portraits and baroque style, learned his trade in Hamburg, Germany.

Tivadar Csontváry Kosztka (1853–1919), often called the father of post-impressionist art in Hungary, was one of the first great artists of the 20th century and a pioneer of the modern art movement. Csontváry Kosztka and his contemporaries encouraged a new generation of artists to break free of traditional influences and explore modernism, cubism, impressionism, and a variety of other styles.

Architecture

While the nomadic Magyar did not often use permanent buildings and therefore left few architectural remnants, European culture brought new architectural themes to Hungary. The first important structures built in Hungary were stone castles and monasteries in the late 13th and early 14th centuries. During this period, Hungarian architecture was influenced by Romanesque and Gothic styles. The evolution of Hungarian architecture is next witnessed in the construction of numerous churches and cathedrals, which also shifted from classical Romanesque to Gothic

in the 15th century. Stylistic elements of the Renaissance period would then replace Gothic architecture. Baroque architecture, which figured strongly in the construction of several palaces, became popular in the 17th and 18th centuries. In addition, during Hungary's occupation by the Turkish Ottoman Empire in the 16th and 17th centuries, Islamic architecture arose in some areas, as evident in the construction and style of mosques.

The early 20th century also saw the end of centuries of baroque and Gothic architecture. From 1910 to 1920, a group of young architects known as the "Fiatalok," emerged as the pioneers of the modern architectural movement. From this early modern period, Hungarian architecture began to resemble the modern building styles of Finland and Denmark.

Budapest is famous for its religious architecture. Catholic landmarks include Castle Hill's Matthias Church as well as Saint Stephen's Basilica, which, with a seating capacity of 8,500, is Budapest's largest church. The church's massive dome is visible from all points in the city. Budapest is also home to Europe's largest synagogue, a reflection of its origins in the 19th century, an era in which one-quarter of the population of Budapest was Jewish. The synagogue grounds feature a memorial sculpture of a willow tree; its leaves are engraved with the names of Jewish Holocaust victims, of which there were more than half a million in Hungary.

Drama

From 1900 until the start of World War I in 1914, the Hungarian film industry grew at a rapid rate. By 1910, Hungary had more than 270 theaters, most of which were in Budapest. The first Hungarian film to win national attention during this early period was *Sárga csikó* (*Yellow Foal*), which was produced in 1912 and distributed worldwide. However, a number of prominent directors and actors would leave Hungary during World War I. Among them was Mihály Kertész (1886–1962), who shot footage of soldiers during World War I and later moved to the United States. Working under the name Michael

Curtiz, he directed more than 100 films, including *Casablanca*, one of the most beloved films in American movie history.

In 1919, following the communist revolution in Hungary, the government nationalized the film industry. A new Nationalist School of filmmakers developed and the film industry again flourished. However, the government began censoring film and many prominent directors and writers either stopped producing films or left the country. Even the advent of talking films in the 1930s did little to invigorate the industry.

In 1944, during the Second World War, Soviet forces occupied Budapest after an extended battle that destroyed most of the city. In the wake of World War II, the film industry was forced to rebuild from the ground up. From 1945 to the 1960s, the socialist government continued to place strict censorship guidelines on the film industry. As the government relaxed censorship restriction in the 1960s, a new generation of young directors, including visionaries like Ferenc Kardos (1937–1999), began using film to explore the political and social history of the nation. This was the beginning of modern and independent cinema in Hungary. The shift to a democratic system in the 1980s inspired further developments in film, including the growth of "art house" cinema in Budapest and other cities.

Music

Historically, the church has also influenced Hungarian music. Under communist rule, musicians in Hungary were held to rigid guidelines that required music to adhere to folk traditions. In recent years, musicians have regained their artistic freedom. Two major musical institutions in Budapest are the Academy of Music and the Philharmonic Society. Recently, there has been a revival of Hungarian folk music and country dances especially among the younger crowds.

Two types of Gypsy music originated in Hungary, including the music of the Romani (Roma) people, an ethnic minority with ties to India and the Middle East. Roma music was traditionally performed without instruments, using only percussion and vocals to create melodies. Another type of Gypsy music, related to Spanish and Russian Gypsy traditions, produces music using the fiddle (violin), bass, and a Hungarian instrument known as the cymbalom, which is similar to a large dulcimer (stringed instrument). Gypsy music is considered the native music of Hungary and is celebrated across the country at festivals, fairs, and traditional gatherings.

In addition to folk music, Hungary also has a rich tradition of classical and chamber music, including the works of well-known composers Zoltán Kodály (1882–1967) and Béla Bartók (1881–1945). The 19th century was a cultural peak for Hungarian composers, who blended the popular European baroque style with traditional Hungarian forms. Other famous composers include Ferenc Erkel (1810–1893) and Franz Liszt, (1811–1886). The Hungarian government takes a stake in preserving classical music through funding and other incentives given to those wishing to perform and study orchestral music. In recent years, the government has also begun to offer support for artists seeking to preserve traditional folk music.

Literature

The earliest Hungarian literature was heavily dominated by European Christian influences. The traditional culture of the tribes living in and around the Carpathian Basin was largely denounced and, in some cases, destroyed after Hungary came under Christian control. The earliest known example of Hungarian writing is a funeral text known as the Halotti beszéd és könyörgés (Funeral Sermon and Prayer), which was translated from Latin into the Magyar language in the early 13th century.

During the Reformation period, works of religious significance, including translations of the Bible, became common. György Bessenyei (1747–1811) is an important figure in the movement to break away from traditional, religious literature and create a nationalist literary tradition. Working as both a playwright and a novelist, Bessenyei's works, such as the play *The Philosopher,* from 1777, borrowed from revolutionary literary movements in France and elsewhere in Europe. The foundation of the Hungarian Academy of Science in 1825 was a major milestone as the organization produced and supported numerous writers and playwrights. The academy also maintained one of the first catalogs of Hungarian-language literature. In the early 20th century, poetry gained prominence as the most innovative literary style, with poets like Sándor Weöres (1913– 1989).

Nationalist literature was heavily curtailed during the political turmoil of the early 20th century. During this period, any poets and writers worked outside of Hungary, publishing literature critical of the communist regime. After the 1960s, with censorship restrictions relaxed, new generations of poets, playwrights, and novelists brought new life to Hungarian literature. Modern writers such as Péter Esterházy (b. 1950–) and János Háy (b. 1960–) helped to initiate a postmodernist trend and brought Hungarian literature to international attention.

CULTURE

Arts & Entertainment

During the Hungary's socialist period, which lasted from 1944 until the 1980s, Hungarian art and music was sponsored by the state. As such, state restrictions significantly curtailed artistic freedom. Restrictions on the types of music and art that could be imported created an isolated and underground artistic community. Even after the transition to a democratic system, the underground art and music scene in Budapest remained vibrant, helping to highlight artists and musicians who, for a variety of reasons, are unaccepted by the mainstream.

Beginning in the 1960s, the arts scene in Hungary diversified rapidly, driven by the music and underground arts of Budapest. Rock and roll music was the first to arrive in Budapest, followed rapidly by other genres, both from native artists, and imported from abroad. However, modern Hungary enjoys a rich artistic community, the traditional folk art and music of the

Hungarian people has remained an important source of national unity.

In the 21st century, Hungarian art reflects the entire range of Hungarian history and the dominating effect of cultural globalization. In an effort to retain elements of their native culture, some modern artists began exploring the folk traditions of the Magyar, using modern materials and methods to bring new life to ancient themes.

Art and music are part of the basic curriculum in elementary and secondary schools. Hungary maintains a law stating that every child has the right to develop his or her talents in music and art and state sponsorship is granted to musical training institutions. All music schools eligible for state funding are members of the Association of Hungarian Music and Art Schools. While music schools charge tuition, the government has systems in place to provide grants for qualifying students wishing to attend art or music school at the secondary or higher educational levels.

Sports are very popular in Hungary, particularly football (soccer). Football games are often covered and followed widely on the television and radio. Water polo and volleyball are also very popular. The country also takes pride in its performance at the Olympic Games, and has won more than 167 Olympic gold medals (and more than 482 medals overall).

Cultural Sites & Landmarks

The "Castle District" of Budapest, Hungary's capital, contains numerous buildings of cultural and historic significance. In fact, many of the city's sites, including the Castle District, Andrássy Avenue (Andrássy út), and the banks of the Danube River, are designated as United Nations Educational, Scientific and Cultural Organization (UNESCO) World Heritage Sites. The historic district's Mátyás-templom (Matthias Church), which was named for King Matthias I (1443–1490) and provides an example of neo-Gothic architecture, is one of the most prominent features of the Castle District. The church was founded in 1255, but gained fame under the reign of Matthias, who ruled from 1458–1490 and was married twice in the church. The church was transformed into a mosque under the rule of the Ottoman Turks. Hungarian architect Frigyes Schulek (1841–1919) eventually restored it in the 19th century.

The Királyi Palota (Buda Palace) was first constructed after the Mongolian invasion of the 13th century. The palace was destroyed during the Turkish invasion and was rebuilt after the Hapsburg conquest of Hungary, becoming a smaller, baroque-style palace as a result. The palace was damaged again during World War II, when German soldiers used the palace to defend against a Russian invasion. Today, Buda Palace, which retains architectural elements from all of its various reconstructions, is considered a cross section of Hungarian architectural history.

Visitors to Budapest can also visit Szoborpark (Memento Park), which contains dozens of sculptures of famous figures from the nation's communist period. The Városliget (City Park) of Budapest is another popular destination for tourists. Established as a public green space in the 13th century, the park contains the Municipal Zoological Park and Botanical Gardens, in addition to the Museum of Fine Arts and the Budapest Amusement Park, a popular playground for children.

The Esztergomi bazilika (Esztergom Basilica) in the city of Esztergom is the seat of the Catholic Church in Hungary. It is also the largest church in Hungary and the third largest in Europe. Visited by tourists for its architectural beauty and picturesque location along the Danube River, the Esztergom has long served as one of the most important tourist attractions for the small city.

Lake Balaton in western Hungary is one of the nation's most popular ecological attractions and is the largest freshwater lake in Eastern Europe. The lake, which is roughly 592 square kilometers (229 square miles), is sometimes colloquially referred to as the "Hungarian Sea." Other tourists seeking naturalistic settings may visit the Western Carpathian Mountains, which

are one of the most ecologically vibrant areas in Hungary and are popular with hikers, campers, and birdwatchers.

In addition to the numerous Budapest sites, Hungary is home to seven other World Heritage Sites, as designated by UNESCO. They include the historic village of Hollókő; the Caves of Aggtelek Karst and Slovak Karst, located in northern Hungary on the country's boundary with Slovakia; the territorial Millenary Benedictine Abbey of Pannonhalma, founded in the 10th century; Hortobágy National Park, the first national park in the nation's history; the Christian Necropolis of Pécs (a large burial site); the cultural environment of Lake Neusiedl; and the historic wine region of Tokaj-Hegyalja.

Libraries & Museums

Budapest is home to dozens of museums. Some of the most noteworthy include the Budapest History Museum, which houses the main collection of Budapest's archaeological finds from ancient Roman times through the 13th century; the Hungarian National Gallery, which traces Hungarian history from the Magyar Conquest to the present; the Hungarian National Museum; and the Hungarian Natural History Museum.

Two museums dedicated to exploring modern chapters in Hungarian history are the Memento (or Statue) Park and the House of Terror. Located in the former headquarters of the Nazi Party and, later, the communist secret police (KGB), the House of Terror documents the brutal repression practiced in Hungary by these two regimes. Memento (or Statue) Park, an open-air museum, displays relics of Hungary's communist past in the form of huge political statues and monuments removed from their original pedestals following the 1991 departure of the last occupying Soviet troops from Hungary.

The Royal Castle in Budapest houses the country's largest library, the National Széchényi Library, which has a permanent display about Hungarian librarians and readers. Along with the University of Debrecen Library, the National

Széchényi Library serves as one of Hungary's two national libraries.

Holidays

There are many public holidays in Hungary, including New Year's Day (January 1), Easter Monday (variable), Labor Day (May 1), Whit Monday (variable), National Day (August 20 & 21), 1956 Revolution Memorial Day (October 23), and All Saint's Day (November 1). The anniversary of the 1848 uprising against Austrian rule is celebrated each year on March 15.

Youth Culture

Social interaction is a major facet of youth culture, and Hungarian youth have a wealth of options, including cafés, bars, discotheques (nightclubs), and public theaters. Dancing is a popular activity for adolescents and young adults, and clubs in the major cities often offer all-ages dancing events. One of the most popular recent trends has been the development of emo culture in Hungary, typically characterized by gothic (or 'goth') fashion trends and certain styles of music.

There is no minimum age for alcohol consumption in Hungary. However, individuals must be at least 18 years of age to purchase alcohol (the minimum age for purchase was raised from 14 in 2002). Despite more relaxed restrictions on drinking and purchasing alcohol, there is a lower incidence of teen alcoholism than in the US.

Modern Hungarian youth are exposed to greater international influences than any previous generation. Bilingual and English education are more common, and English words are sometimes commonly used in Hungarian slang. Children in Hungary sometimes use the English phrase "hello," for example, when saying goodbye to each other.

Since the 1980s, Hungarians have been eagerly accepting of music with electronic elements, such as hip-hop, house, trance, techno, and drum and base. Hip-hop, in particular, has become increasingly popular in Hungary, especially among youth of the Romani minority. Hungarian hip-hop can be divided into distinct genres, with bands such as DSP and rappers, like Sub Bass Monster, standing out as contemporary leaders. In addition, the artist Gansta Zolee and his group, who perform in a gansta rap style in which street life is glorified, are one of the best-selling examples in recent years. There is also a variety of local rock, indie rock, and pop bands that are popular with young Hungarians. Musical groups, such as the popular Mizantrop, who blend elements of several genres, including electronica, pop, and rock, similarly create a unique sub-genre of popular music.

SOCIETY

Transportation

The capital of Budapest has the most extensive public transportation system in Hungary, including a subway system (metro), above ground trams, trolleys, busses, and taxi service. Except for taxis, the public transport in Budapest is operated by Budapesti Közlekedési Vállalat Zrt (BKV), a state-owned company that accounts for more than half of the city's passenger traffic. Passengers can recognize the different options by their colors, with blue buses, yellow trams, and red trolleys. In addition, each metro line is painted a different color to aid in identification.

BKV buses, trolleys, and trams typically run from 4:30 am to 11 pm, with supplemental "night buses" traveling the major throughways and streets throughout the night. BKV buses also have routes that extend to the suburbs and nearby towns and cities. Tickets are generally purchased at vending machines near metro or bus stations, or at newspaper stands and retail stores. Passengers are required to validate their ticket, usually at an automated kiosk, before boarding the vehicle. Although BKV operates on the honor system, ticket agents make periodic checks of their vehicles and will charge a cash penalty to anyone without a validated ticket. Customers also have the option of purchasing a monthly or annual pass. Hungarian citizens over the age of 65 are granted free travel on all BKV vehicles.

In other cities, passengers may only have bus and taxi options for public transportation. Taxis are expensive in Hungary and will frequently overcharge visitors from outside the country. There is also a domestic train system, operating from a hub in Budapest, which travels to most of the nation's cities and has stops in rural areas. Though many Hungarians own automobiles, traffic congestion in major cities often makes public transportation the more attractive option. Traffic moves on the right-hand side of the road.

Transportation Infrastructure
Because of Hungary's central location, the country is an important transportation corridor for Europe. In fact, the country is home to four important transport corridors, and the country maintains an extensive network of roads, including international roads (or European transit roads), which comprise a road system that is considered among the best of all EU members. The railway network is similarly well developed, and, as of 2014, approximately 20 percent of all freight is transported via rail within the country. Through the Danube, Hungary has access to both the North and Black Seas. The country's primary international airport is the Budapest Airport, in Budapest.

Media & Communications
Hungary has both state- and privately-owned media companies. The privatization of the media began after the collapse of communism and has accelerated since the transition to democracy in the 1980s. There are more than 40 daily newspapers in Hungary and a variety of magazines and weekly papers. The most popular print publications are the left-leaning *Népszabadság* (*The Free People*), which boasted circulation of 46,000 in 2013, and *Metro*, a free, ad-dependent broadsheet distributed by the Swedish-owned, Luxembourg-based media company Metro International.

Political bias in the media has been a constant issue in Hungary, with newspapers such as *Népszabadság* perceived as supporting a primarily liberal political stance, while others, such as *Magyar Nemzet* (*Hungarian Nation*), are seen as conservative news outlets. The *Budapest Sun*, once the nation's largest English-language daily with articles geared towards tourists and expatriates living in the city, closed in late January 2009. *Budapest Times*, another English-language newspaper, is published weekly by the German-owned, Budapest-based company Budapest-Zeitung Kft. Foreign media organizations, including Germany's Axel Springer Group and the Austrian company Westdeutsche Allgemeine Zeitungsgruppe own many of Hungary's newspapers.

Television in Hungary is also divided between public and private organizations. The company Magyar Televízió (Hungarian Television) operates the nation's oldest public television stations, known as M1 and M2. The abolishment of television license fees in 2002 greatly reduced the funds available for public television. In 1992, the state opened a second public network, Duna TV (Danube Television), which is separate from M1 and M2, but provides some of the same programming. In addition to public television, Hungarians now have access to hundreds of programming options through cable and satellite television.

Though there is no government censorship in Hungary, observers have often accused newspapers and television of being politically biased, especially in the case of state-funded outlets. Internet coverage is common in Hungarian cities and is not subject to censorship or restrictions. In 2013, Internet usage had penetrated 72.6 percent of the population.

SOCIAL DEVELOPMENT

Standard of Living
Hungary ranked 43rd out of 190 countries on the 2012 United Nations Human Development Index, which measures quality of life and standard of living indicators.

Water Consumption

According to 2014 statistics from the World Health Organization (WHO), Hungary's population has universal coverage to improved drinking water sources and sanitation. Hungary sources its water supply mostly from subsurface water sources.

Education

Hungarian children begin school at the age of six and usually finish by the age of eighteen. Upon finishing, students receive a secondary leaving certificate, though the type of degree they receive is based on what type of school they attended.

The sequence of study runs from Basic First Stage (ages six to ten) to Basic Second Stage (ages ten to fourteen) and then to Comprehensive (ages fourteen to eighteen) and/or General Secondary (age ten to eighteen). Academic secondary schools are called gymnasiums, while vocational schools are called vocational secondary schools, or szakközépiskola. Vocational schools also offer differing levels of leaving certificates.

Although colleges and universities in Hungary often work closely with one another (many college faculty also teach in a university), they offer different types of degrees. Colleges require three to four years of training, after which a college level degree, or Főiskolai oklevél, is awarded. Universities usually demand four to five years of study and grant university level degrees, or Egyetemi oklevél. In Hungary, there are seventeen state universities, one private university, thirteen state-funded colleges, 26 church-affiliated universities and colleges, and nine foundation-run colleges.

The literacy rate in Hungary is 99 percent, with males at 99.1 percent and females as a solid 99 percent.

Women's Rights

According to the penal code, women are guaranteed equal rights and protection under the law. Despite preventative laws, domestic violence continues to be a serious issue in Hungary. There are no current laws directly prohibiting domestic violence except for those that prohibit assault in all forms. NGOs (non-governmental organizations) estimate that nearly 20 percent of Hungarian women have been victims of domestic abuse. Investigations by Amnesty International revealed that a majority of spousal abuse cases go unreported and that the failure to report crimes is because of a prevailing attitude that the judicial system cannot, or will not, aid victims.

Hungarian law prohibits rape in all forms and imposes a penalty of between two and 15 years in prison for convicted rapists. However, Amnesty International reported in 2007 that a majority of rapes are unreported. As such, many victims commonly have little faith in the legal system. Some NGOs have also objected to the definition of "rape" in the Hungarian Penal Code, which requires a victim to prove that he or she resisted her assailant or that his or her life was in jeopardy.

The Hungarian government legalized prostitution in 1999 and enacted laws to govern the behavior of prostitutes and clients. Under current laws, local authorities must designate an area for legal prostitution if the population demonstrates the desire to patronize prostitutes. The Magyarországi Prostituáltak Érdekvédelmi Egyesülete (MPEE), or the Sex Worker's Advocacy Association, is an organization, formed in 2000, to protect and lobby for prostitutes' rights. The organization arranges for periodic health checks, as required by law, and acts as an activist for sex workers. The MPEE routinely charges that the police do not properly protect prostitutes from harassment and/or violence.

Abortion is legal in Hungary and the state has a strong record of protecting women's reproductive rights as established under the UDHR convention. The government revised abortion law in 1992 and added several conservative statues, including a law that requires women to submit to counseling and wait at least three days before obtaining an abortion. State law explicitly states that abortions should be considered only in "crisis" conditions. The country's new constitution, adopted in April 2011, protects the fetus from the point of conception and will perhaps eventually pave the way for stricter abortion laws. However, as of 2015, no such alteration to existing laws has been made. Still, there has been some concern, on the part of NGOs, that state-funded healthcare programs do not support contraceptive measures, representing a failure of the government to encourage effective family planning.

Health Care

The health care system in Hungary is publicly funded and promises its citizens universal coverage regardless of employment status. It is controlled by the National Health Insurance Fund (HIF), which, along with the Ministry of Health, makes contracts with care providers. Much of the funding for health care comes from employer and employee taxes, with deficits covered by the central budget. However, most medical facilities are owned and operated at the state and local levels. Supplemental private insurance is also made available, but it is somewhat limited due to the prominence of public health care.

GOVERNMENT

Structure

After World War II, Hungary fell under communist rule. The people revolted against the communist government in 1956, but the effort failed. The country had its first multiparty elections in 1990, which also began the move towards a free market.

Hungary is a parliamentary democracy with a unicameral legislative system. The National Assembly, or Országgyűlés, now consists of 199 members, who are elected every four years. Between 1990 and 2014, however, the number of members was 398. This body has the highest legislative authority. All citizens of Hungary are eligible to vote after reaching 18 years of age, and voter participation is usually high. Only citizens who are serving jail sentences are barred from voting or running for election.

The president of Hungary is elected for five-year terms, with a maximum of two terms, by the National Assembly. The prime minister is elected by the National Assembly after presidential consultation.

Political Parties

The country's major political parties include the Federation of Young Democrats (Fidesz) and the Hungarian Socialist Party (MSVP). The Fidesz–Hungarian Civic Alliance, a national conservative party, represents the supermajority. As of the April 6, 2014 parliamentary elections, Fidesz gained 133 total seats, followed by the Unity (Összefogás) party, which achieved 38 seats. Jobbik, or Movement for a Better Hungary (Jobbik Magyarországért Mozgalom), gained 23 seats, while the Politics Can Be Different (Lehet Más a Politika!) party added five seats. As in 2009, these are the only four parties to win seats in the National Assembly, although there are various other minor parties.

Local Government

Local government operates on the local and regional level in Hungary, with the difference lying in the administrative tasks and duties accountable to each level of governance. Hungary is split into 19 counties, 23 urban counties, and one capital city (Budapest). Local government also operates at the local level in cities and villages, and at one time, there were 175 "subregions," or governmental levels within counties. However, in 2013, this system was abolished and replaced with 198 districts. Local governance involves a two-tiered system, comprised of a subordinate, bureaucratic framework and an autonomous framework.

Judicial System

Hungary maintains a four-tiered judicial system, consisting of the Curia, which is Hungary's highest judicial body, and followed by twenty regional courts, which correspond to the nineteen counties and the city of Budapest. Thereafter, there are five regional courts of appeal and 111 district courts. These lower courts operate as courts of first instance, and hear commercial, civil, and criminal cases (with county courts also acting as local courts of second instance and hear administrative and criminal matters of a more serious matter). Special tribunes, acting as a labor court, can be enacted to hear labor disputes.

Taxation

Hungary's income tax is now levied at a flat rate of 16 percent. Other taxes levied include a social security, dividend income, interest income, and a value-added tax (or VAT, similar to a consumption tax, which was raised to 27 percent—the highest in the EU—in January 2012, although some medicines are sold with only five percent VAT). A 2011 tax bill reduced the country's capital gains tax to 16 percent, and, for qualifying corporations, lowered the corporate tax rate to 10 percent. In 2014, the corporate tax rate stood at 19 percent, with only 10 percent levied on those corporations generating less than 500 million Hungarian Forints.

Armed Forces

The armed forces of Hungary, officially the Hungarian Home Defence Force, consist of two branches—the Hungarian Ground Force and the Hungarian Air Force. Active military personnel numbered roughly 29,700 in 2013, with 17,000 reserves. There is currently no conscription, as it was abolished in November 2004. However, voluntary military service entails a six-month obligation and is open to citizens between 18 and 40 years of age.

Foreign Policy

Since 1989, Hungary's primary foreign policy goals have been to join international financial and defense organizations. These goals were largely fulfilled when Hungary joined the North Atlantic Treaty Organization (NATO) defense alliance in 1999 and the European Union (EU) in 2004. Hungary was admitted into the United Nations (UN) in 1955. In the early 21st century, Hungary's primary foreign policy has been to strengthen its economic position within the EU. Hungary marks the eastern border of the EU and in 2003 began implementing the Schengen Agreement, which opens its national borders and removing border checkpoints, allowing free travel between EU member nations. Despite this move towards greater openness, in 2015, Hungary's Prime Minister, Viktor Orbán, expressed a hard line against asylum-seekers, and opposed the welcoming of immigrants. In July 2015, Orbán even discussed the erection of a thirteen-foot, 109-mile fence that would run along the border it shares with Serbia in order to stop the flow of illegal immigrants passing into Hungary, which, between January and July of 2015, numbered roughly 67,000.

Hungary is also a member of the Visegrádi Együttműködés (Visegrád Group, or Visegrád Four), a Central European economic and political alliance between Hungary, the Czech Republic, Poland, and Slovakia. The group formed in 1991 as all four countries were lobbying for inclusion into the EU. Among the group's major projects was the establishment of a scholarship fund in 1992, open to visiting professors and students studying issues common to member countries, and the creation of a special commission on energy in 2002 to fund and collect research on energy supply and distribution issues.

One of Hungary's major foreign relations issues concerns a dispute with Slovakia. This occurred after the Hungarian government withdrew from its agreement to complete part of the Gabčíkovo–Nagymaros hydroelectric dam along the Danube River. The dam project began in 1991, but stalled in 1992 as the Hungarian government cited economic concerns. Slovakia turned to international courts in 1996 in an attempt to force Hungary to complete the Gabčíkovo portion of the dam. However, Hungary maintained that is was not in its interest to resume construction, and dispute remains unresolved as of 2011.

Human Rights Profile

International human rights law insists that states respect civil and political rights and promote and individual's economic, social, and cultural rights. The United Nations Universal Declaration on Human Rights (UDHR) is recognized as the standard for international human rights. Its authors sought the counsel of the world's greatest thinkers, philosophers, and religious leaders and were careful to create a document that reflects the core values shared by every world culture. (To read this document or view the articles relating to cultural human rights, visit http://www.ohchr.org/EN/UDHR/Pages/Introduction.aspx.)

Hungary has an excellent record of maintaining human rights as defined by the UDHR. Some non-governmental organizations (NGOs) have issued reports suggesting that police persecution of Romani and other Gypsy groups continued in some areas, which is a violation of Article 7 of the UDHR guaranteeing equal treatment under the law. In some cases, treatment of Romani may also constitute a violation of Article 9, prohibiting arbitrary detention and arrest. However, accusations by NGOs have been unsubstantiated, and Hungarian law prohibits arbitrary arrest and prosecution.

The treatment of Romani citizens is Hungary's most pressing human rights issue. In addition to police treatment, some NGOs have also accused Hungarian police of failing to provide equal protection, according to Article 7, to Romani citizens. Surveys conducted by Amnesty International indicate the Romani are more often the target of racial violence and property damage by militant youth groups. Human Rights Watch reports that police have not adequately investigated or prosecuted instances of abuse against Romani individuals.

Hungary generally respects the rights of citizens to assemble, as stated in Article 20, and the right of expression, as expressed in Article 19. In 2005, protests in Budapest against the government became violent and more than 300 people were arrested after police used tear gas and water cannons to disperse crowds. The motivation behind the protest was government corruption and a legacy of leaders still connected to the communist regime. After the incident, participants filed more than 150 cases of police abuse. Eighteen officers involved in the incident were eventually charged with abuse.

In early July 2015, Hungary's parliamentary body passed legislation calling for tighter immigration controls, including lengthier camp detentions and the erection of a fence along the Hungarian-Serbian border to prevent the surge of asylum seekers and other émigrés. The Hungarian government estimates that 72,000 refugees had crossed Hungary's border by July 2015 alone, up from 43,000 in all of 2014. The United Nations and human rights groups have criticized all extended temporary camp detentions, the ponderous red tape associated with asylum application, and the new border fence.

ECONOMY

Overview of the Economy

In 2014, the estimated gross domestic product (GDP) of Hungary was $239.9 billion USD. Industry accounts for 31.1 percent of this total. The service sector leads all other sectors at 65.5 percent of the GDP. The GDP per capita is an estimated $24,300 (USD) for 2014. Germany, Romania, Austria, Slovakia, Italy, France, the United Kingdom, Poland, and Russia are Hungary's major trading partners.

Budapest has historically been responsible for the largest share of the Hungarian economy. More than half of all foreign investment in Hungary goes to Budapest, whose commercial endeavors provide more than a third of the country's gross domestic product (GDP). The capital is the seat of half of the nation's food processing industry and two-thirds of its agricultural trade.

Budapest's economy has undergone a dramatic transformation since the introduction of free-market reforms in the 1990s. Subsequent foreign investment spurred an ongoing business and construction boom. It also helped fuel a surge in the tourism industry in Budapest, which attracted 3,106,430 visitors in 2013 alone. Today, the Budapest Stock Exchange is among the most profitable in Central Europe, and the capital has emerged as one of the region's premier economic centers.

In 2013, Hungary was successful in reducing its global debt to under 3 percent of its GDP, leading the European Commission to release the country from the Excessive Deficit Procedure, a protocol under which Hungary's government operated since its 2004 entry into the EU.

Industry

In recent years, industry has contributed an increasing amount to the overall development of the Hungarian economy, and in 2014, its growth rate stood at 3.1 percent. Mining, metallurgy, construction materials, processed foods, textiles, pharmaceuticals, and motor vehicles dominate manufacturing. Machinery and equipment are the most important exports in Hungary, accounting for more than half of all exports. Comparatively, food products, raw materials, and fuels and electricity are less significant exports.

The many large factories that dominate Pest's outlying districts have historically constituted the bulk of Hungary's industrial base. Budapest leads the nation in the manufacture of electronics, farm machines, pharmaceuticals, textiles, chemicals, railway equipment, buses, boats, and computer components.

Labor

Hungary's work force was an estimated 4.388 million in 2014. As of 2014, the unemployment rate improved, standing at just over seven percent, down from 9.1 percent in 2013. The majority of the labor force—an estimated 63.2 percent—is concentrated in the services sector, while 29.7 percent is employed in the industrial sector. Agriculture accounts for just over 7.1 percent of the work force.

Energy/Power/Natural Resources

Much of the Hungarian land is fertile, so arable land and abundant water are valuable natural resources. Other important natural resources are bauxite, coal, and natural gas. Moreover, almost one-fifth of Hungary is forested.

In the Matra and Bukk Mountains, there are large amounts of lignite, which can be used to generate electricity. Some of the non-ferrous metal ores found in Hungary are copper, lead, zinc, silver, and gold. Gold prospecting takes place in the Tokaj Mountains of northeast Hungary, as well as in the area of Füzérradvány and Telkibánya.

Geothermal energy is another important resource in Hungary. It is estimated that the country has 2,500 cubic kilometers of geothermal wells, which store a considerable amount of heat energy. There are over 1400 registered wells throughout Hungary, 950 of which are in use. This energy is in demand in order to heat greenhouses and buildings, as well as the water supply.

The conservation of natural resources is an important issue in Hungary. Substantial investments have been made to improve Hungary's standards of waste management, increase energy efficiency, and decrease air, soil, and water pollution. These improvements are necessary in order to comply with the strict environmental requirements of the European Union.

Fishing

As a landlocked nation, the consumption of fish is mostly supported through imports. Lakes and rivers provide a minor source of fish. Pollution resulting from a toxic sludge disaster in 2010 affected the fisheries of the Danube River, harming and depleting fish stock. The industry is still recovering.

Forestry

Forests and woodland make up about one-fifth of the Hungarian landscape and are a combination of broadleaf varieties and evergreens. The production of hardwood products is a primary facet of the forestry industry, and a good percentage of harvested wood is used for the production of energy.

Mining/Metals

Minor makes up a small fraction of Hungary's economy, and the country is a minor producer of mineral commodities. Industrial metal and mineral production was concentrated in metals, such as aluminum and manganese ore, and industrial minerals, such as bauxite, cement, clays, sand and gravel, and stone. Raw materials form a large percentage of Hungary's imports. Mining accounts for just under three percent of the country's labor force.

Agriculture

Agriculture continues to account for approximately 3.4 percent of Hungary's GDP. Wheat, corn, sunflower seed, potatoes, sugar beets, pigs, cattle, poultry, and dairy products are some of the most valuable agricultural commodities. The annual production of wheat, Hungary's leading crop, is 5.1 metric tons, while the country's overall grain production stands at 16.1 metric tons.

The land in Hungary is extremely fertile. More than half the country's land is arable, and nearly two-thirds of that farmland is under cultivation. For the most part, Hungary produces all of the food it needs to feed its population within its own borders.

Animal Husbandry

Important livestock raised in Hungary includes cattle, goats, horses, pigs, poultry, and sheep.

Tourism

With the largest freshwater lake in Europe (Lake Balaton) and plenty of spas, thermal baths, and springs, Hungary is one of the world's most popular tourist destinations. There are many castles still standing in Hungary, which also attract tourists. Some of the most famous castles are the Royal Palace in Budapest; Nagyvázsony and Szigliget on Lake Balaton; and Sümeg, one of the best-preserved medieval castles in Hungary, which is located in the town Sümeg. Spa tourism is also a large facet of the country's tourism industry.

In 2014, 9.5 million foreign visitors crossed Hungary's borders, while domestic tourism and their accompanying overnight stay increased by 10 percent, according to Hungary's Deputy Secretary for Tourism. In December 2014 alone, thanks to Hungary's restorative baths and holiday culture, all major hotels were booked full throughout the country.

Most tourists who visit Hungary are European, and in 2014, they primarily hailed from Germany, Austria, and Russia. In 2013 and 2014, the Hungarian National Tourist Office specifically targeted these countries with marketing campaigns, leading to the rise in this tourist demographic.

Micah Issitt, Kim Nagy, Beverly Ballaro, &
Savannah Schroll Guz

DO YOU KNOW?

- The capital is famous for its prized thermal bath complexes, which have provided area residents and visitors with therapeutic benefits for centuries. Fed by more than 100 natural thermal springs, the baths have earned Budapest an international reputation as the "City of Spas."

- Budapest's Basilica of Saint Stephen houses one of Catholic Hungary's most treasured relics: what most Hungarians believe to be the mummified so-called Holy Right Hand of Hungary's first Christian king, Stephen I.

- Puppetry is a popular form of street and theater entertainment in Hungary. There are three puppet theaters in Budapest, including the largest in Central Europe: the Budapest Puppet Theatre, or Budapest Bábszínház.

Bibliography

_____. *Hungary: Between Democracy and Authoritarianism*. Oxford, UK: Oxford UP, 2012.

Anikó Gergely. *Culinaria Hungary: A Celebration of Food and Tradition*. 2nd ed. Potsdam, Germany: H. F. Ullmann Publishing, GmbH., 2015.

Attila Kovacs & Eva Szacsvay. *Folk Culture of the Hungarians*. Budapest, Hungary: Museum of Ethnography Press, 2003.

Brian Mclean. *Hungary—Culture Smart!: A Quick Guide to Customs and Etiquette*. London, UK: Kuperard Press, 2006.

Bryan Cartledge. *The Will to Survive: A History of Hungary*. 3rd ed. New York: Hurst & Co., 2011.

Istvan Bori, ed. *The Essential Guide to Being Hungarian: 50 Facts and Facets of Nationhood*. Williamstown, MA: New Europe Books, 2012.

John S. Glaser. *Living Within the Truth: 1989 and the Rise of Civil Society in the Czech Republic, Hungary and Poland*. Philadelphia, PA: Xlibris Corp., 2005.

Miklós Molnár. *A Concise History of Hungary*. Trans. Anna Magyar. New York: Cambridge University Press, 2001. Cambridge Concise Histories Ser.

Norm Longley. *The Rough Guide to Hungary,* 6th ed. London, UK: Rough Guides, 2005.

Paul Lendvai. *The Hungarians: A Thousand Years of Victory in Defeat*. Transl. Ann Major. Princeton, NJ: Princeton University Press, 2004.

Peter F. Sugar, Péter Hanák, & Frank Tibor. *A History of Hungary*. Evansville, IN: Indiana University Press, 1990.

Sabrina P. Ramet, ed. *Eastern Europe: Politics, Culture and Society Since 1939*. Evansville, IN: Indiana University Press, 1999.

Stephen Sisa. *The Spirit of Hungary: A Panorama of Hungarian History and Culture*. 3rd ed. Morristown, NJ: Vista Court Books, 1995.

Steve Fallon, Anna Kaminski, & Caroline Sieg . *Lonely Planet Hungary.* 7th ed. Oakland, CA: Lonely Planet Press, 2013.

Works Cited

"2014 Figures Reveal Tourism Boom in Hungary." *WeLoveBudapest*. We Love Publishing Kft., 2015. http://welovebudapest.com/culture/2014.figures.reveal. tourism.boom.in.hungary.

"Amnesty International Report 2014/15." *Amnesty International Online*. Amnesty International, 25 Feb. 2015. https://www.amnesty.org/en/documents/pol10/0001/2015/en/.

"Country Profile: Hungary." *BBC News*. 14 Feb. 2012. http://news.bbc.co.uk/2/hi/europe/country_profiles/1049641.stm.

"Gazetteer of Hungary." *Hungarian Central Statistics Office Online*. Hungarian Central Statistics Office, 2011.

"Home Page." *Szexmunkások Érdekvédelmi Egyesülete* (Sex Workers Advocacy Association). Szexmunkások Érdekvédelmi Egyesülete, 7 July 2015.

"Hungary." *Bureau of European and Eurasian Affairs: Countries and Other Areas*. U.S. Department of State, n.d. http://www.state.gov/p/eur/ci/hu/.

"Hungary MPs approve border fence and anti-migrant law." *BBC News*. BBC, 7 Jul. 2015. http://www.bbc.com/news/world-europe-33421093.

"Hungary." *The World Bank*. The World Bank Group, 2015. http://data.worldbank.org/country/hungary.

"Hungary." *The World Factbook*. Central Intelligence Agency, 24 June 2015. https://www.cia.gov/library/publications/the-world-factbook/geos/hu.html.

"Hungary." *WorldJewishCongress.org*. World Jewish Congress, 2014. http://www.worldjewishcongress.org/en/about/communities/HU.

"Introducing Hungary." *Lonely Planet Online*. Lonely Planet, 2015. http://www.lonelyplanet.com/worldguide/hungary/.

"Regional Data—Budapest." *Population Census 2011*. Hungarian Central Statistics Office, 2011. http://www.ksh.hu/nepszamlalas/tables_regional_01. http://www.nepszamlalas.hu/eng/other/hnk2007/tartalom.html. http://www.prostitualtak.hu/.

Pablo Gorondi. "Hungary: Fence on Serbia Border Forced Step to Stop Migrants." *ABC News*. Yahoo!-ABC News Network, 1 Jul. 2015. http://abcnews.go.com/International/wireStory/hungary-serbia-meet-debate-hungarian-border-fence-plan-32146599.

Antal Kampis. *The History of Art in Hungary*. Trans. Lili Halapy. Budapest: Corvina Press, 1966.

Emil Krén & Dániel Marx. "History of Painting and Sculpture in Hungary." *Fine Arts in Hungary Online*. T-Systems Hungary Ltd., n.d. http://www.hung-art.hu/tours/index.html.

Richard Webber. "Home in on Hungary: The living is easy, the housing is cheap and it's only a two hour flight from the UK – Eastern Europe awaits." *Daily Mail Online*. Assoc. Newspapers Ltd, 2 Mar. 2011. http://www.dailymail.co.uk/property/article-1362277/Home-Hungary-The-living-easy-housing-cheap-s-hour-flight-UK--Eastern-Europe-awaits.html

Fifteenth century Mbretit Mosque, Pristina, Kosovo

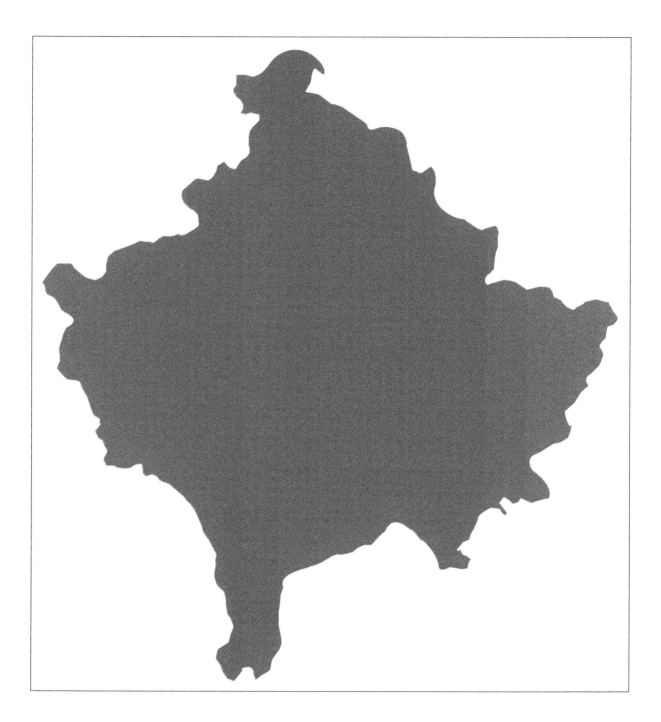

Kosovo

Introduction

The Republic of Kosovo was founded on February 17, 2008, when it declared its independence from Serbia. Kosovo is a landlocked territory located to the east of the Adriatic Sea. It is bordered on the south by Macedonia and Albania. To the north lies Serbia, and to the west is Montenegro. Although Kosovo declared independence once before in 1990, the declaration was not widely recognized. Kosovo's recent declaration was seen as legitimate by Western powers, including the United States. However, the Provisional Institutions of Self-Government Assembly of Kosovo, adopted in 2008, caused controversy in Eastern Europe. Since then over one hundred countries have recognized Kosovo; and even Serbia, from which it split in 2008, has agreed to open a dialogue regarding the normalization of relations between the two countries.

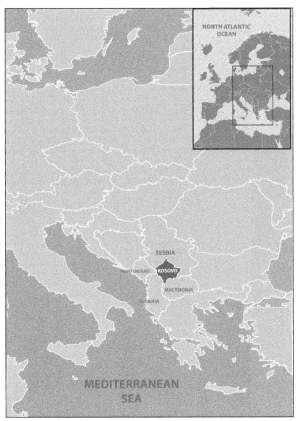

GENERAL INFORMATION

Official Language(s): Albanian, Serbian
Population: 1,859,203 (2014 estimate)
Currency: Euro
Coins: The Euro is available in 1, 2, 5, 10, 20, and 50-cent coins. A 1 and 2 Euro coin is also available.
Land Area: 10,887 square kilometers (4,203 square miles)
National Anthem: "Europe" by Mendi Mengjiqi

Capital: Pristina
Time Zone: GMT +1
Flag Description: The flag of Kosovo consists of a golden map of the country itself, centered in a dark blue field (background). A slight arc of six five-pointed white stars sits above the geographical map, each representing one of the country's six major ethnicities: Albanians, Serbs, Turks, Gorani, Roma, and Bosniaks.

Population

Kosovo, which is divided into 30 municipalities, is home to a variety of ethnic groups. Albanians make up the dominant ethnic group, accounting for approximately 92.9 percent of the total population. Bosniaks make up 1.6 percent; Serbs make up about 1.5 percent of the population, and Turks 1.1 percent. Other minority groups in Kosovo include Roma, Ashkali, Egyptian and Gorani. Approximately 58 percent of the population lives in rural areas. A large majority of the

Principal Cities by Population (2012):

- Pristina (172,033)
- Prizren (102,117)
- Urosevac (81,988)
- Peje (170,000) (2008)
- Pec (75,411)
- Ferizaj (170,000) (2008)
- Gjakove (150,000)
- Mitrovica (71,162)
- Dakovica (65,282)
- Gjilan (130,000) (2008)
- Gnjilane (57,432)
- Podujevo (130,000)
- Vucitrn (102,600)
- Rrahovec (73,700)

population lives in rural regions outside of the capital of Pristina; unofficially, the metropolitan population of the city was estimated at over 200,000 in 2012. The capital's Serbian population decreased substantially since 2004 due to ethnic conflict and cleansing; as early as 1991, the Serbian minority was listed at over 13 percent in an official census.

As of 2014, approximately 44 percent of the population was under the age of 25, giving Kosovo one of the youngest populations of all European countries.

Languages

Albanian is the prominent language at 94.5 percent, though the Serbian (1.6 percent) and Bosnian (1.7 percent) languages are commonly used; English is also becoming more widely spoken since the UN Interim Administration was established in 1999. For example, English is widely spoken and considered by many to be the official language for the entire city center of Pristina, the capital.

Native People & Ethnic Groups

The Balkan Peninsula was first populated by the Illyrians. As early as the fifth century, the Slavs made the Balkan Peninsula their home and, led by the "Unknown Archont," established

the Serbian Empire. "Unknown Archont" is a term given by historians to the Serbian leader that helped establish this early regime. Albanian speakers followed the Slavs from the Adriatic region in the eighth century. Beginning in nine CE, the Romans inhabited the area.

Religions

Islam is the major religion of Kosovo (95.6 percent), while the Serb population is Serbian Orthodox (1.5 percent) and Roman Catholic (2.2 percent). A portion of Serbs in Kosovo are also Protestant.

Climate

Kosovo has a continental climate, influenced by prevalent Mediterranean and alpine conditions. Autumn and spring seasons are relatively cool with seasonal rainfall, while the average summer temperature is 22° Celsius (72° Fahrenheit). Winters are snowy, with average temperatures of –2° Celsius (32° Fahrenheit). Kosovo's average high temperatures vary between 25 and 38° Celsius (77 and 100° Fahrenheit). The heaviest rainfall occurs between the months of October and December, with little rainfall during the summer months.

ENVIRONMENT & GEOGRAPHY

Topography

Kosovo is located in the center of the Balkan Peninsula and features a mostly mountainous and rugged terrain, with various hillocks and river valleys. It occupies an area of 10,887 square kilometers (4,211 square miles). A landlocked nation, Kosovo's major rivers are the White Drim, or Beli Drim, located in southern Kosovo, and which ultimately empties into the Adriatic Sea. The Ibar, located in the northwestern region of Kosovo, ultimately flows into the Danube and Morava rivers, the Lepenac, which runs in the southeast, and ultimately flows into the Aegean Sea via the Vardar river; and the Sitnica, which is a major tributary of the Ibar.

Kosovo's highest peak is Gjeravica, which reaches an elevation of 2,656 meters (8,714 feet) above sea level. The Šars Mountain range, bordering Macedonia, is a popular region for skiing and tourism. The country's main lakes lie in the northern region.

Pristina is located on the northeast edge of the Kosovo Plain in northwestern Kosovo, a region in southeastern Europe that existed mainly as an autonomous state within Serbia and the former Yugoslavia for much of the 20th century. The city is surrounded by plateaus to the south and north, and sits adjacent to the Kopaonik Mountain range, or the Silver Mountains. It occupies an area of 572 square kilometers (220 square miles).

Plants & Animals

Kosovo's variable climate has a significant influence on the diversity of the country's plants and animals. Fruit, mulberry, black oak, and Canadian poplar trees are prevalent in lower lands, while deciduous trees such as the beech are popular in areas that are more mountainous. Fir, chestnut, and pine trees are found in higher altitudes.

In addition to widespread populations of rabbit, deer, and boar, Kosovo is also home to wild hens, wolves, and chamois; bears are common in the mountainous regions. Marine animals include salmon trout, catfish, and carp, while the region's many bird species include the raven, magpie, field sparrow, and pheasants and quails. Rare and endangered animal species in Kosovo include the Eurasian lynx (Lynx lynx), the golden eagle (Aquila chrysaetos), the emperor eagle (Aquila heliaca), and the white stork (Ciconia ciconia).

Hawks are common birds of prey in Kosovo.

CUSTOMS & COURTESIES

Greetings

Handshakes are a common greeting and parting gesture in Kosovo. In some situations, friendly handholding may persist well into the initial exchange of verbal greetings. Many Kosovar men will combine a handshake with the placement of one hand on their heart. They may also incline their body slightly forward in a shallow bow when meeting an especially beloved or respected person. Alternate kissing on each cheek, either twice or three times, is another common form of greeting between both men and women. This intimate gesture is more common when people are greeting or leaving family members or others to whom they are close. Lastly, it is considered polite for everyone in a room to stand when someone new enters.

Polite Kosovan greetings involve the asking of several ritual questions, including inquiries into one's family and well-being. Common greetings include "Tungjatjeta," or simply "Tung" ("Hello," or literally "May you have a long life"), and several variations of the phrase "How are you," including "A jeni lodhë" ("Are you tired"), "A je mërzitë" ("Are you upset"), and "A po plakesh" ("Are you getting old").

Gestures & Etiquette

Islam is the predominant religion in Kosovo and a strong influence on the nation's generally conservative etiquette. However, Kosovo is characterized as a secular nation with little strict interpretation of Muslim law and customs—a self-described laid back version of Islam. (In fact, Kosovo is known for its religious pluralism.) For example, dress codes for women are generally unrestrictive, and shorts and bare legs are not considered taboo. Nevertheless, visitors to mosques or the homes of pious Muslims should dress accordingly.

Kosovars may be characterized as an inquisitive people. For instance, it is generally not considered ill mannered for Kosovars to make immediate inquiries about the marital status of new acquaintances, as well as to ask whether or not they have children. Such questions, which may seem overly personal to Western observers, are an indication of the great importance placed on family ties in Kosovan life among both Albanians and Serbs. On the other hand, the subject of politics is more often a taboo subject.

Like many other cultures, nonverbal gestures are often important to communication in Kosovo. In addition to raising and lowering their heads in a nod to demonstrate agreement, Kosovars occasionally also use an upward jerk of the chin to indicate disagreement. Other nonverbal signs of skepticism include soft tongue clicking and a slow side-to-side shake of the head—but the latter, confusingly, can mean, "Yes, I am listening."

Eating/Meals

People in Kosovo generally eat in the continental style: fork in the left hand and knife held in the right. Three meals per day are common, and breakfast consists of light fare such as eggs, bread, and meat. Lunch is traditionally the main meal of the day and generally occurs later in the afternoon. Supper is traditionally a light affair and may occur in the later evening hours, generally around 8:00 pm.

Coffee in Kosovo, and the Balkan region at large, serves as a social lubricant. Its consumption may be prevalent in social interactions of every kind, including friendly conversations, romantic overtures, business negotiations, or political dealings. Coffee is generally served extremely sweet and typically accompanied by cigarettes. Though no clear estimations exist, Kosovo is generally regarded as having a heavily smoking population.

Visiting

Hosting visitors is an honorable occasion in traditional Kosovar society. Visits typically occur frequently and are an important facet of establishing and maintaining the close familial ties that define Kosovar and Albanian society. When visiting, it is customary for people to remove their footwear upon entering. In some households, a pair of simple slippers designed to be worn indoors may be offered by the host. Traditionally, shoes that

are kept clean and neat in spite of the dusty conditions of many of the country's roads are a sign of good breeding in Kosovar culture.

Guests will customarily be offered tea or Turkish coffee, and food is generally spread on the table as well; to decline refreshments may be perceived as disrespectful. In addition, guests and hosts might often exchange small gifts. These may consist of sweets or other snacks, but are also likely to be useful household objects, such as towels or even small items of clothing. It is somewhat more common for the host(s) to offer their guest a gift upon parting.

LIFESTYLE

Family

Until fairly recently, family life for both Serbians and Albanians in most rural areas reflected a traditional patriarchal structure that dated back centuries in the Balkan region. Under this structure, a village was composed of a small number of households, and each household might include ten or more members from multiple, but related, families. Within a household, every immediate family group was headed by a working husband, whose overall position in the hierarchy of the extended family depended on age. Brothers, their wives, and their children shared the same property and acted as a small, relatively self-sufficient social and financial collective.

Traditional family life in Kosovo since the end of the 20th century has been disrupted by three factors: ethnic violence and Serbian control during the late 1980s and 1990s; conflict between Serbian forces and the Albanian Kosovo Liberation Army (KLA); and NATO air strikes that drove Yugoslav troops from Kosovo in 1999. Most observers agree, however, that the most devastating cause of the breakdown of both individual families and the fabric of society as a whole in Kosovo was the campaign of forced displacement and ethnic cleansing undertook by Serbian soldiers and police in 1999. A vast number of ethnic Albanian Kosovars were violently expelled from their homes. Many fled to surrounding countries, and not all have returned to Kosovo in the intervening years. Those who have returned have often relocated to cities.

Generally, while the traditional multi-family household structure in Kosovo has been greatly eroded by years of flux and migration, it has not completely disappeared from rural areas. In urban areas, family units are often much smaller and consist of just the immediate family members.

Housing

The most characteristic Albanian Kosovan dwelling is the traditional kulla, a multistory house that rises into a tower at its peak (thus enabling it to serve as a kind of fortress against attacks). The design of the kulla dates back to the end of the 18th century, when in-fighting frequently occurred between rival Albanian clans. Kullas are generally characterized by their sturdy outer walls, made of thick stone or brick, and wooden walls that form room divisions in the building's interior. The lower floors of a kulla were generally used for working, cooking, and housing livestock; while the top floor consisted of sleeping quarters for the men of the family and their guests, (women and children traditionally lived in a separate wing). While kullas continued to be constructed into the early years of the 20th century, most of them were partially or completely destroyed by the fires that raged across Kosovo during the 1999 war.

Following the 1999 conflict, housing in Kosovo was in turmoil; the public administration of housing was either nonexistent or rife with discrimination, and a substantial amount (one-third to one-half) of housing infrastructure was damaged or destroyed. Illegal housing also became rampant. Today, a large number of Kosovars live in prefabricated concrete apartment buildings, many of which have been constructed since the conflict to accommodate the influx of residents from the countryside into the cities. The restoration of property rights also remains a contentious issue in postwar Kosovo in the early 21st century.

Food

The cuisine of Albanian Kosovars, like that of Albania itself, has a Mediterranean influence and exhibits Turkish, Greek, and Italian culinary traditions. Commonly used vegetables include peppers, eggplants, tomatoes, cucumbers, and various beans, while beef, lamb, and poultry, often served in the form of kebabs, are the most popular meats. Trout is also often served in Kosovo, and olives, yogurt, feta, lemon, and garlic are prominently featured. Dairy products are also important staples.

The quintessential Albanian-Kosovar dish is perhaps flija, a buttery, flaky pie made by stacking thin layers of pastry one on top of another, with each layer baked individually. Mantija, or meat-filled pastries, are another characteristic Albanian delicacy, similar to the burek served throughout the Mediterranean and the Balkans. Both flija and ćevapčići, a dish consisting of minced meat, are considered national dishes.

The food eaten by Serbian Kosovars arises out of many of the same cultural influences, but also contains more European flavors, especially tastes from Austria and Hungary. Popular traditional dishes include pljeskavica, grilled patties of seasoned ground meat; sarma, cabbage stuffed with meat and rice; and proja, cheesy corn bread served with yogurt. Sljivovica, the Serbian liquor made from plums, is strong and sweet smelling, but the most popular liquor in Kosovo, made by Albanians and Serbs alike, is a clear alcohol distilled from grape juice known as raki.

Life's Milestones

Because of the central role of the family in both Serbian and Albanian society, wedding rituals are extremely important to all Kosovars. Traditionally, the rituals and celebrations associated with a wedding last an entire week, and are largely orchestrated and paid for by the groom's family. (The custom is for a bride to be chosen for the groom by his female relatives, based not on beauty or wealth, but on various factors relating to her family background.) Serbian and Albanian weddings also share a custom in which the bride and her family are expected to put on a display of mournfulness. Female relatives sing sad songs and there may be weeping as the young woman leaves for the groom's house. These gestures are intended to indicate the bride and her family's grief over the fact that she is being "given up" from her own household to become a member of the groom's family.

Of course, each culture retains its own idiosyncratic set of marriage traditions and symbols. In a Serbian wedding, the bride's brother-in-law lets a stream of candies rain down over the bride's head from a shoe, to bring good luck. Before an Albanian couple weds, the matchmaker (often an uncle of the groom) leaves one shoe untied as he walks to the bride's house, a custom that is supposed to ensure a smooth path toward marriage.

CULTURAL HISTORY

Art

The contemporary arts scene in Kosovo since the war has been dominated by an emerging group of bold young artists whose works serve as a vehicle for direct commentary on the country's history of ethnic violence and repression and the struggle to define national identity. These artists, the vast majority of whom are Albanian, often work in several different media, including installation art, photography, and other visual arts such as performance and video art. Among Kosovo's preeminent 21st-century artists are Albert Heta (1974–) and Sokol Beqiri (1964–).

Heta's work tends to use extremely simple gestures to create dramatic or shocking effects. In 2001, for instance, he created "Happiness – Independence Day: 1 Minute," a faux news broadcast inserted into an actual national news program. In it, an announcement was made that Kosovo's declaration of independence had been formally recognized by the United Nations Security Council (UNSC) and the United States, something that was not true at the time. Beqiri's 2001 installation piece "End of Expressionism (Painted by a Madman)" does not shy away from depicting the brutality suffered by many Kosovars during the conflict. The installation combines documentary photographs of human corpses and a video showing an execution with ornate paintings of images from the Bible.

Traditional handicrafts, such as woodcarvings and engravings, have a lengthy history in Kosovo; copper, brass, silver, and magnesium are typical materials used in such crafts.

Architecture

Despite Kosovo's deeply Albanian identity, the country's true architectural masterpieces are its many Serbian Orthodox churches and monasteries. These particular churches and monasteries represent a distinct blend of eastern Byzantine and Romanesque religious architecture and sacred art. Churches built in this style tend to have one or more dome-shaped structures and are typically constructed out of layers of red bricks, mortar, and gray stones. On the inside, they are often decorated with ornate frescoes. In 2004, the United Nations Educational, Scientific and Cultural Organization (UNESCO) designated four particular Serbian Orthodox churches and monasteries—Dečani Monastery, Patriarchate of Peć Monastery, Our Lady of Ljeviš, and the Gračanica Monastery—as a collective World Heritage Site (Medieval Monuments in Kosovo).

The region of Kosovo is also known for its European Muslim heritage and Islamic architecture, including kullas (traditional stone mansions) and over 600 mosques. However, the Serbs targeted a substantial number of these mosques and other Ottoman and Islamic buildings in 1998 and 1999. It is estimated that 90 percent of kullas and one third of Islamic mosques—207 of 609—were destroyed or damaged. Similarly, dozens of Serbian churches, parish houses, and monasteries were damaged or destroyed in the early years of the 21st century by Albanian rioters frustrated by Serbian subjugation, and fell under the jurisdiction of the North Atlantic Treaty Organization (NATO).

Film

The history of cinema in Kosovo dates back to the late 1960s, when an organization known as Kosovafilm was founded by the Yugoslavian government to produce and distribute short films and documentaries, and later feature-length films. While Kosovafilm was technically an independent entity, it was hampered by the state through various indirect means, such as censorship and heavy post-production editing. As a result, most Kosovan films of this era tend to be characterized by socialist idealism that does not reflect the harsh social realities that existed within the country. After being shut down by the Serbian government in 1990, Kosovafilm was reestablished at the end of the war in 1999. In 2005, it released *Kukumi* (or *The Kukum*), its first feature film in more than a decade. Directed by Isa Qosja (1947–), the film chronicles the postwar experiences of three patients who are released from a mental institution by NATO forces.

Music

The most distinctive genre of music popularly produced in Kosovo in recent decades is more closely associated with the Serbian population than with the Albanian. Known as tallava, or turbo-folk, this is an exuberant and somewhat forceful style of recording that also has a presence in other Balkan countries. Tallava is marked by the surprising melding of traditional Roma folk songs (the Roma are an ethnic group within Serbia) with techno rhythms. During the 1990s, Serbian tallava recordings often contained lyrics promoting nationalist sentiments.

Literature

Beginning in the 14th century, Ottoman rulers of Kosovo banned creative literature published in the Albanian language (as well as schools teaching in Albanian). When the country was taken over by Serbia, a similar ban was enforced. Nevertheless, the literary journal *Jeta e Re* (A New Life), which was founded in 1949, served as a modest vehicle for many young Albanian writers during this period. In 1974, a change in the Yugoslavian constitution awarded Kosovo broad autonomy within the Republic of Serbia, ushering in a renewed era of creative energy. Writers and poets such as Esad Mekuli (1916–1995), Eqrem Basha (1948–), and Azem Shkreli (1938–1997) are among those who have helped shape the character of modern Albanian literature in Kosovo.

Kosovo is also the source of a large body of Serbian-language literature dating back to the 13th century. In addition, the land of Kosovo itself holds a special place in the tradition of Serbian epic poetry. The most famous of these is the so-called *Kosovo Cycle*—a collection of heroic ballads and fragments of other folk poems collected and published by the Serbian scholar Vuk Stefanovic Karadzic (1787–1864). The poems honor and bear witness to the Turkish takeover of the Serbian empire in the late 14th century, especially the 1389 Battle of Kosovo.

CULTURE

Arts & Entertainment

Kosovo also has a rather undeveloped music industry as compared to the rest of Europe. The music scene is often more democratic and dynamic for youth in Kosovo, who have more opportunities to record and promote their music. Popular music among young people includes folk, modern rock, and hip-hop music, and notable performers include Troja, Gjurmët, and Diadema. Ilir Bajri is a well-known jazz and electronic performer on the Kosovar music scene.

Football (soccer), basketball, and handball are all popular sports in Kosovo. Beginning in 2003, several formal sports federations were established, including the Basketball Federation of Kosovo, the Handball Federation of Kosovo, and the Table Tennis Federation of Kosovo (TTFK).

Annual festivals include the Dokufest, an international documentary and short film festival held in the city of Prizren, and the Pristina Jazz Festival, held in the capital since 2005.

Cultural Sites & Landmarks

Kosovo's most famous landmarks are its medieval monuments—the four Serbian Orthodox churches recognized as a collective World Heritage Site by UNESCO. First is the modest Visoko Dečani Monastery, a 14th-century monastery located in the western part of the country. It was constructed out of alternating slabs of yellow onyx and pale purple marble and is capped by a pillared cupola. Inside, the walls are completely covered by a stunning array of colorful frescoes depicting various biblical scenes and stories. The Patriarchate of Peć Monastery is a collection of four churches, three of which are linked by a common chapel and antechamber. The remaining sites, Our Lady of Ljeviš, and the Gračanica Monastery, are known for their 14th-century and 13th-century frescoes, respectively. The paintings in the Church of the Virgin of Levisa are particularly significant because they show traces of two distinct artistic traditions: the eastern Orthodox Byzantine and the Italian Romanesque style.

The country's capital, Pristina, is home to numerous cultural sites and landmarks, including the Kosovo Museum. Pristina also houses the Mbretit Mosque, built by Sultan Mehmet II al-Fatih (1432–1481) in the 15th century—from 1460 to 1461. It once boasted the largest cupola in the area. Other mosques of interest in the city include the Pirinaz Mosque, Bazaar Mosque, and Jashar Pasha Mosque. Other attractions include the National Library, the National Theatre, and the Dodona Puppet Theatre.

The historic city of Prizren, settled at the foot of the Sar Mountains, was once the capital of Serbia and an important center of trade and commerce. Today, the region is notable for its large collection of ancient mosques, churches, and houses, as well as for a few surviving Turkish baths dating back to the Ottoman era. The two most significant monuments in Prizren are the Sinan Pasa Mosque, built in the 17th century out of marble that was taken from an even older monastery, and Bogorodica Ljeviska, a 14th-century church that was among those that sustained extensive damage in 2004's ethnically motivated violence.

In 1977, the Law on the Protection of Cultural Monuments was passed, which identified 426 cultural institutions and monuments in Kosovo that required protection, including twenty-one in Pristina. As of 2006, many of those sites had disappeared, while those that remained were in poor condition. The archive for Pristina's Institute for the Protection of Cultural Monuments also remains under the control of the government of neighboring Serbia, which retreated from the city following the Kosovo War. Monuments such as the National Martyr's Monument and the Kosovo Heroes Monument were erected to honor those who fought for Kosovo's independence and liberation throughout the Balkan Peninsula's long history.

Libraries & Museums

Pristina is home to the Kosovo Museum, which houses a wide collection of ethnological displays and archaeological artifacts. The building, constructed in the Austro-Hungarian style, originally served as an administrative site during Kosovo's period of Ottoman rule (1455–1912). It was later the command post of the Yugoslavian army before being turned into an archeological and cultural museum. Other museums of note in the capital include the Ethnographic Museum, the Independence Museum, and the one-room Kosovo Railways Museum.

Pristina is also home to the national library, officially the National University Library of Kosovo, inaugurated in 1982. Over 50 percent of the library's collection consists of Albanian language titles. It was estimated that half of all books in Kosovo's libraries—and 175 libraries themselves—were burned due to ethnic cleansing between 1998 and 1999.

Holidays

The Muslim holidays of Ramadan (the nine month of the Muslim calendar), Eid al-Fitr (the festival of fast breaking), and Eid al-Adha (the festival of sacrifice) are widely observed in Kosovo; in the Orthodox faith, Orthodox Christmas and Orthodox Assumption are celebrated. In addition to religious holidays, national observances include Independence Day, designated as February 17, and Flag Day, observed in November in honor of Albanian unity.

Youth Culture

Kosovo is one of the youngest countries in Europe. At the close of the first decade of the

21st century, more than half of the population was younger than 35 years of age. However, one of the key challenges faced by Kosovar youth is employment, which was staggeringly high since after the turn of the century. In fact, an increase in drug and alcohol abuse and participation and association with radical nationalist organizations, Albanian and Serbian alike, have been attributed to this rise in unemployment. Nevertheless, there has recently been a blossoming of creative energy among young Kosovars.

Kosovo has a rather undeveloped music industry in the early 21st century, as compared to the rest of Europe. The local scene is often more democratic and dynamic for youth in Kosovo, who have more opportunities to record and promote their music themselves. The recording of homemade music, namely the genres of rap, rock, and pop, has been boosted by efforts like the opening of the Mitrovica Rock School, which held its first session in 2008. The school is working to train dozens of enthusiastic young Kosovars each year in all aspects of pop and rock music performance.

Due to a lack of cultural spaces, such as cinemas, resulting from Kosovo's socialist history and recent conflicts, social contact between people is an important part of youth culture. Going to the theater has become a more common activity, and young people often socialize in bars or cybercafés, and congregate to watch television or DVDs. In addition, many older youth are channeling their energies into producing their own literary and cultural magazines, and becoming increasingly involved in art and theater.

SOCIETY

Transportation

Public transportation within and between Kosovo's urban areas is managed by a combination of state-owned companies that predate the war, plus a growing number of private van and bus companies. Together, they service a wide-ranging network of transportation routes that is inexpensive, quick, and reasonably efficient.

However, since most of the vehicles that travel this network are relatively old, they are a major contributing factor to Kosovo's current air pollution problem. Another reason air pollution has increased dramatically in the past decade is the sharp rise in private car ownership that has taken place since the war. Most of these cars are bought secondhand from Germany and other European countries, and many do not meet current emissions standards. Traffic moves on the right-hand side of the road.

One particularly notable change in Kosovo's transportation system since 1999 has been the introduction of special "minority bus shuttles" designed to carry safely Serbian Kosovars— these days, a vulnerable minority population— back and forth. The United Nations Mission in Kosovo (UNMIK) first implemented the shuttle services, in response to several violent bomb attacks against buses carrying Serbian passengers. They have since been taken over by the Kosovo government.

Transportation Infrastructure

The transportation infrastructure in Kosovo has suffered from both the ravages of war and from a dire lack of funding for maintenance. As a result, the majority of the country's roads are aging and in poor condition. They have deteriorated even further since the conflict, having been driven over by a great number of heavy military vehicles and large trucks carrying food and other supplies.

Pristina, the capital and commercial center of the country, is connected by rail to Skopje in Macedonia, and to Durrës in the Republic of Albania by the Durrës-Pristina highway. The Pristina International Airport is the major airport for Kosovo.

Media & Communications

The proliferation of a free and private media industry in Kosovo is a relatively recent development. Prior to 1989, the media was owned and run by the socialist Yugoslavian state, and for the 10 years following that, Serbian-language media outlets were prevalent. Independent journalists were few in number and many who continued to report in Kosovo were harassed, arrested, or even attacked. Since the end of the war in 1999, the number of privately operated media outlets in Kosovo, including newspaper, radio, and television stations, has flourished. However, many media outlets are struggling to survive with limited revenue and funding. Competition from Western European cable television stations is an especially significant obstacle for Kosovo's broadcasting media.

The vast majority of print and broadcast media companies in Kosovo today are Albanian-run organizations offering Albanian-language news. RTK, the public broadcaster, runs one television station, and there are an additional two private television stations that broadcast programming around the country. RTK also runs two national radio stations: Radio Kosova and Blue Sky. The three major daily newspapers are all privately owned and include Koha Ditore, Zeri, and Bota So. Besides the national media, according to a 2004 report commissioned by the USAID, there are 85 radio stations and 20 television stations presenting local news reporting in various cities across Kosovo.

Since the end of the 199 conflict, the telecommunications market and infrastructure of Kosovo was described as "chaotic." Post and Telecom of Kosovo, now PTK J.S.C., is the nation's public telecommunications authority, and in 2006, Kosovo was the only country in the region with only one mobile telephone operator. As of 2007, there were 562,000 mobile phones in use. As of December 2008, there were an estimated 377,000 Internet users in Kosovo, representing just over 20 percent of the population.

SOCIAL DEVELOPMENT

Standard of Living
As a non-United Nations member, Kosovo is not calculated to be ranked on the United Nations Human Development Index, which measures quality of life and standard of living indicators. However, the country would be ranked as having medium human development.

Water Consumption
In 2007, only about half of the population of Kosovo had access to municipal water supply systems, and nearly 60 percent of the population was using untreated water sources. Systems to monitor the quality of drinking water are not universally in place, and there is little to no monitoring of wastewater from municipal sewage systems. The government's objective is to have water supply and sanitation systems in place in 95 percent of households by 2015. As of 2014, roughly 61 percent of Kosovo had access to clean water.

Education
Beginning in the early 21st century, Kosovo implemented a reformed educational system. This consisted of pre-school, elementary, lower secondary, higher secondary, secondary professional, and university levels. Higher secondary is classified by a general, or "gymnasium," curriculum, and is pursued by students with collegiate aspirations. The secondary professional level emphasizes a vocational education and is classified by Artisans, which constitutes two years of study, and Technica, which constitutes four years of study. This type of education is pursued by those interested in industries such as textile manufacturing and tourism.

The educational system in Kosovo faces problems ranging from a lack of funding and textbooks to inconsistent training of teachers. Traineeships, or internships, are an underdeveloped aspect of the school curriculum. Other educational issues include a lack of access for students with special needs and inadequate preschool facilities. The literacy rate among women in Kosovo is 89.8 percent, compared to 97.7 percent among men (2007 UNESCO).

Women's Rights
Kosovo continues to struggle with the issue of women's rights, most notably the problem of widespread domestic abuse and human trafficking. In 2000, a study commissioned by the UN found that 25 percent of Kosovar women had been the victims of some form of abuse, either

physical or psychological. In 2007, there were more than 1,000 reported cases of domestic violence against women; however, human rights activists estimate the actual number of victims may in fact be many times higher. The human trafficking of woman for prostitution or slavery has a long history throughout the Balkan region. Kosovo is considered a transit point and both a source and destination country for human traffickers. Since the conclusion of the Kosovo War, numerous laws have been enacted to protect victims of domestic violence and human trafficking. According to organizations like Kosova Women's Network (KWN), however, the legal mechanisms designed to safeguard women's rights need to be implemented far more strenuously.

The gender gap in education is another pressing issue facing Kosovo's female population. Early 21st-century estimates by the United Nations Children's Fund (UNICEF) indicate that nearly 15 percent of Kosovo's rural female population is illiterate. In addition, it is estimated that almost 50 percent of Albanian girls never finish ninth grade, and that a mere 43 percent of all enrolled secondary school students are girls. One reason for this imbalance is the sheer lack of schools in the country, meaning transportation and safety concerns become a factor in attendance. In addition, the struggling postwar economy has left schools themselves severely underfunded. Community partnerships between families and schools have helped to channel donations, most notably providing textbooks and uniforms for rural girls. Women's adult-education programs are helping to improve the basic literacy and general knowledge skills of older girls and women who have already entered the workforce, or are unable to attend school fulltime.

Health Care

Kosovo's transition from a former socialist nation, coupled with violent ethnic conflict during the 1990s, have adversely affected the nation's health care system; insufficient investment in medical staff training and the maintenance or destruction of infrastructure and equipment have created public health challenges. In addition, ethnic segregation became a concern as Roma and Serbian minorities were often prevented from accessing health care following the war of 1998–99.

Kosovo has attempted to reform its health care system in the early 21st century. The reformed system is based on a "family practice" approach, in which doctors, nurses, and other health care professionals work in teams. Prenatal and early childhood care is also an area of focus; Kosovo had one of the highest infant mortality rates in all of Europe in the early 21st century. Tuberculosis and mental health issues are also major health concerns.

According to a UN report in 2007, 37 percent of the population lived in poverty, and 15.2 percent were in absolute poverty. Although 95 percent of births take place in medical facilities, due to a lack of proper equipment and education, Kosovo has the highest maternal mortality rate in Europe.

GOVERNMENT

Structure

After the Second World War, Kosovo was as an autonomous region in Serbia under the Socialist Federal Republic of Yugoslavia (SFRY), which existed from 1945 until 1992, and was ruled by Josip Broz Tito (1892–1980) for the majority of that time. This republic was a communist state that included modern day Bosnia and Herzegovina, Croatia, Macedonia, Montenegro, Serbia, and Slovenia. Under Tito's leadership, Yugoslavia remained a neutral actor in the Cold War and helped to form the Non-Aligned States. During this time, the Albanian population in Kosovo grew, and Albanian nationalism intensified.

Following Tito's death in 1980, the SFRY held together but was not recognized by the international community. Communist leaderships were established in each republic, and ethnic conflict would eventually lead to the dismantling of the republics.

Slobodan Milosevic, president of the state of Serbia from 1989 to 1997, and president of the SFRY from 1997 to 2000, is one of the more widely known figures of this period in the history of the Balkans. Milosevic, a Serb, believed that Serbian majorities had the right to remain a part of Yugoslavia. However, critics accused him of being corrupt and interested only in shoring up more power for himself. In 1989, Milosevic stripped Kosovo of its autonomy, allowing the government of Serbia to have direct control over the region.

The Kosovo War, which occurred between 1996 and 1999, was fought between Serbian and Yugoslav forces and the Kosovo Liberation Army (KLA). The KLA, an Albanian guerilla organization, supported an independent Kosovo. A fourth player in the conflict was the North Atlantic Treaty Organization (NATO), which became involved in late March 1999. NATO forces aimed to end the violence in the region, which had resulted in the displacement of hundreds of thousands of people.

By the end of 1999, major military conflict had ended. Milosevic and several of his colleagues were tried at The Hague for human rights abuses and crimes against humanity for the persecution of and military action against ethnic Albanians.

When the war concluded, governance of Kosovo was transferred to the United Nations (UN). The UN Interim Administration Mission in Kosovo (UNMIK) was established on June 10, 1999. In February 2008, the Assembly of the Republic of Kosovo, an institution within the Provisional Institutions of Self-Government (PISG) established by UNMIK, adopted a declaration of independence for Kosovo. The Republic of Serbia is one of many countries that has yet to recognize Kosovo's independence, asserting that Kosovo remains an autonomous province.

The head of government is the prime minister, while the chief of state is the acting president, elected to a five-year term by the unicameral Kosovo Assembly, who also elects the prime minister. The assembly consists of 120 seats, 100 of which are directly elected. Ministers in the assembly serve four-year terms, and 10 seats are reserved for Serbians.

Political Parties

Kosovo has a multi-party system, and parties must form coalition governments. Major parties include the Democratic Party of Kosovo (PDK),

which together with a group of smaller coalition partners won 37 seats in the assembly in the 2014 legislative election; the Democratic League of Kosovo (LDK), which won 30 seats; the Movement for Self-Determination (VV), which won 16 seats; and the Alliance for the Future of Kosovo, which took 11 seats. Several other parties were represented by under 10 seats each.

Local Government

Kosovo is administratively divided into 38 municipalities, and the majority of government services are provided through municipalities, which are largely self-regulated. Kosovo is working towards a more decentralized system of government. New municipalities with predominate minority communities were also created following independence.

Judicial System

Kosovo's fledgling justice system is still in the process of being rebuilt. It initiated a new judicial system in January 2013. The Supreme Court is the highest judiciary body. Courts operate at the district and municipal levels. At least 15 percent of Supreme Court and district judges must be from ethnic minority communities or backgrounds.

Taxation

Taxes levied in Kosovo include personal income tax, corporate tax, value-added tax (VAT, a form of consumption tax, typically levied at 16 percent in Kosovo), custom duties, excise tax, and municipal property tax. The personal income tax rate varies up to 10 percent.

Armed Forces

Following independence, the new Kosovo government started the process of creating the civilian-controlled Kosovo Security Force. Initially, the force was planned to consist of 2,500 active military personnel and 800 reservists, and is to focus on civil emergencies. The security force, armed only with light weaponry, was officially launched in 2009, after having been NATO-trained. NATO reduced their troop presence in Kosovo from 10,000 to 4,000 in 2011.

Foreign Policy

Kosovo is a self-declared independent country in the region of southeastern Europe known as the Balkans. In the late 1990s, Kosovo underwent a massive internal conflict when an ethnic Albanian rebel movement pushed for the country's secession from Serbia. After Kosovo became a self-declared independent nation in February 2008, it was formally recognized by 56 of the 192 member nations of the UN, and 22 nations of the European Union (EU). Among the notable countries that have recognized Kosovo as an independent nation are the U.S., the United Kingdom (UK), France, and Germany, which welcome what they see as the beginnings of democracy in a region with a history of totalitarian rule.

Among the nations that continue to reject Kosovo's unilateral assertion of independence are Serbia and Russia. Serbia contends that Kosovo is an indivisible province of the Serbian republic, and continues to have a contentious relationship with Kosovo. In March 2009, Kosovo accused Serbia of influencing crime in its northern region, while Serbia implicated organized crime within Kosovo in widespread human trafficking and arms and drug smuggling. Russia supports Serbia's position and does not want to see other Eastern European states break away from its sphere of influence. In addition, Spain, Cyprus, Greece, Romania, and Slovakia have opposed recognizing Kosovo – either because they intend to show support for Serbia, or because they do not wish to set a pattern that may be followed by separatist movements in their own countries.

Kosovo also maintains a unique relationship with Albania. Although it is certain that most Albanian Kosovars connect very deeply with their Albanian roots, there has been little to no political movement in Kosovo since the end of the war toward a union with Albania. This is something that many Serbs, both inside Kosovo and outside it, believe ethnic Albanian Kosovars want. In fact, less than 10 percent of Kosovars supported such a union in a 2005 poll, suggesting that the country's residents have made significant headway towards developing a unique, coherent identity of their own.

Human Rights Profile

International human rights law insists that states respect civil and political rights, and promote an individual's economic, social, and cultural rights. The United Nations Universal Declaration on Human Rights (UDHR) is recognized as the standard for international human rights. Its authors sought the counsel of the world's great thinkers, philosophers, and religious leaders, and were careful to create a document that reflects the core values shared by every world culture. (To read this document or view the articles relating to cultural human rights, visit http://www.un.org/en/documents/udhr/.)

Kosovo's constitution incorporates the principles set forth in international human rights conventions and treaties. However, various areas of concern still exist. According to the 2008 report prepared by the U.S. Department of State, some of the most pressing human rights issues facing Kosovars today include deaths and injuries from landmines and ammunition left over from the recent war. Violence that is motivated by ethnic tension, persistent antagonism and discrimination against minority Serbs and Roma, corruption within the government; and violence and discrimination against women and girls, especially with regard to domestic abuse and human trafficking face Kosovars.

Article 2 of the UDHR calls for the equality of all citizens before the law, regardless of race, religion, or gender. Generally, the government is respectful of the human rights of its residents, but societal discrimination against minorities is a persistent problem. In particular, relations between Kosovo's ethnic communities continue to be strained. This has resulted in various violent incidents in recent years, including rock throwing and other physical attacks on Kosovo Serbs, especially Serbian Orthodox clergy and worshippers traveling to and from sacred buildings. Kosovo police have even installed security devices and hired guards to protect a number of Serbian Orthodox religious sites.

Kosovo's Ministry of Justice is working to reduce obstacles faced by minorities who find themselves caught up in the country's justice system. For example, a group of court liaison officers has been appointed to assist minorities with court appearances and documentation. In addition, after several complaints arose regarding unfair treatment for ethnic minorities in criminal trials, many cases in which Kosovo Serbs are involved are now tried by foreign judges and prosecutors, rather than local Albanians. Despite a target of 16 percent minority employment, the number of ethnic minorities—including Kosovo Serbs, Romas, Ashkalis, and Egyptians—represented in the government and other public institutions continues to be just over 10 percent.

Article 19 of the UDHR protects the universal rights to freedom of opinion and expression, and these rights are generally well respected in contemporary Kosovo. There are no government restrictions on access to the Internet or attempts to censor the information available to residents on the World Wide Web. Citizens and organizations are free to express their political, cultural, and personal views through various online media. Freedom of assembly and association, outlined in Article 20, are not proscribed by law. Given sufficient advance notice (48 hours), public protests, and demonstrations are free to occur. It is worth noting, however, that in recent years the police through forceful means have occasionally broken up demonstrations that have turned violent.

ECONOMY

Overview of the Economy

Kosovo's economy has made significant strides in the early 21st century as the country shifts to a market-based system. However, Kosovo is still dependent on foreign aid and assistance, and remittances from dispersed citizens account for roughly 30 percent of the nation's gross domestic product (GDP). Privatization has been the most significant driver of economic growth in recent years, though the country has had difficulty privatizing businesses that had been state-owned, or socially owned, during communist rule.

Nonetheless, Kosovo's citizens remain among the poorest in Europe, if not globally, earning only an average annual income of roughly $8,000 per capita in 2014. Just over 40 percent of the population was unemployed during the same period. In addition, nearly 45 percent of the population lives below the poverty line, with 15 percent living in extreme poverty. The country's GDP was roughly $5.9 billion in 2014. The Euro is the official currency of Kosovo, though the Serbian dinar is commonly accepted in areas heavily populated by Serbians.

Industry

The country's industries are still recovering from the breakup of Yugoslavia, which had a widespread negative effect on the population. Kosovo's unresolved international status also contributed to corruption related to the dispersal of financial relief, and to the growth of a thriving informal sector. In addition, Kosovo's mining and metal industries have stalled since the latter half of the 20th century due to outdated equipment and a lack of investment, while technical issues and insufficient investments have also slowed down industrial development in the nation as a whole.

Construction materials, wood, and plastic are key imports, while scrap metals, machinery, and leather continue to be produced domestically.

While Pristina is historically known as a trade and mining center (lead, silver, and zinc are mined in the nearby Kopaonik Mountains), it has also developed as a modern commercial center featuring diverse industries such as textile manufacturing, woodworking, food production, and the manufacture of jewelry, metal goods, and pharmaceuticals.

Labor

Unemployment affects approximately 31 percent of the labor force in 2014, and the country has the highest unemployment rate in Europe. Labor costs in Kosovo are the lowest in the region. The estimated labor force as of 2013 was 483,200. Agriculture accounts for 5.9 percent, industry 16.8 percent, and services 77.3 percent.

Energy/Power/Natural Resources

Kosovo is one of the richest countries in Eastern Europe in terms of natural resources, including substantial quantities of nickel, lead, zinc, magnesium, lignite (one of the world's largest reserves, in fact), kaolin, chrome, bauxite, and silver.

Kosovo also has extensive coal reserves, in addition to oil reserves. Due to the country's strategic position in the center of the Balkan Peninsula, its rivers are important for trade, transportation, and irrigation. Unchecked industrial pollution has been a major concern, however, and there is no system to monitor air pollution in the country.

Forestry

Roughly, one-third of Kosovo's land is forested, and the forestry industry provides employment for an estimated one out of every 10 citizens, or nearly 10 percent of the population. The harvesting of public forests provides steady revenue for the government, and accounts for between roughly two and three percent of the gross domestic product, but mismanagement, lack of infrastructure, and illegal logging remain concerns. The majority of wood harvested is used for firewood. The predominant commercial species are beech and oak.

Mining/Metals

Kosovo has significant mineral deposits, and Kosovo's mineral industry has produced silica sand, gravel, lead, zinc ore, nickel, bentonite, and limestone. However, production of minerals decreased significantly in 2009. The fifth-largest reserve of lignite is also in Kosovo, and the country is a primary regional producer of the mineral.

Agriculture

Despite a mostly rugged terrain rich in mineral resources, agriculture is an important economic activity in Kosovo, mainly due to the fertile plains in the center of the country. In 2014, agriculture accounted for roughly 13 percent of the nation's GDP. Cereal crops such as maize, wheat, and barley are important agricultural products, as are sunflowers, tomatoes, tobacco, sugar beets, and oilseeds, though the production of the latter products has declined in the early 21st century due to price fluctuations and factory closures. In recent years, grape production has also declined due to a saturated international wine industry. Approximately 80 percent of agricultural land is under private ownership.

Animal Husbandry

Animal husbandry, particularly dairy farming, and remains a mainstay of the Kosovar economy and the country is geographically suited for livestock farming. Overall, Kosovo is not self-sufficient in terms of food production, however, and most food is imported. Poultry is the primary Kosovo livestock, followed by cattle, sheep, pigs, and goat, as well as buffalo to a much lesser extent.

Tourism

Kosovo has yet to firmly establish itself as a tourist destination; interest in visiting the country particularly waned in the latter 20th and early 21st centuries due to violence, a tumultuous political climate, and poor preservation of the environment and historic sites. The tourism industry has seen a resurgence, however, and tourism has accounted for roughly 10 percent of the nation's GDP in recent years. Tourism in Pristina is a fledgling industry in the early 21st century, and accommodations are limited but growing.

Popular tourist attractions include the Old Town district in the historical city of Prizren, known for its Islamic architecture, the scenic Rugova Gorge, the Pec Patriachy monastery, and the Gjakova Old Bazaar, which dates back to the 17th century. Skiing, hunting, and trout fishing are popular activities among visitors.

M. Lee and Bill Rickards

DO YOU KNOW?

- A large image of former United States President Bill Clinton can be seen overlooking Bill Clinton Boulevard in Pristina. Former British Prime Minister Tony Blair and Mother Teresa, of Albanian descent, also have streets named after them in the capital.

Bibliography

Gail Warrander and Verena Knaus. *Kosovo.* Guilford, CT: The Globe Pequot Press, 2007.

Gojiko Subotic. *Art of Kosovo: The Sacred Land.* New York: Monacelli Press, 1998.

Greg Campbell. *The Road to Kosovo: A Balkan Diary.* Boulder, CO: Westview Press, 2000.

Harold B. Sege. *The Columbia Guide to the Literatures of Eastern Europe since 1945.* New York: Columbia University Press, 2003.

Robert Elsie. *Historical Dictionary of Kosova.* Lanham, MD: Scarecrow Press, 2004.

Tim Judah. *Kosovo: What Everyone Needs to Know.* New York: Oxford University Press, 2008.

Victoria Clark. *Why Angels Fall: A Portrait of Orthodox Europe from Byzantium to Kosovo.* New York: St. Martin's Press, 2000.

William G. O'Neill. *Kosovo: An Unfinished Peace.* Boulder, CO: Lynne Rienner Publishers, 2002.

Works Cited

"2008 Human Rights Report: Kosovo." *Released by the Bureau of Democracy, Human Rights, and Labor.* U.S. Department of State. February 25, 2009. Online. http://www.state.gov/g/drl/rls/hrrpt/2008/eur/119462.htm

"Kosovo Media Assessment: Final Report." March 2004. *U.S. Agency for International Development (USAID).* http://www.usaid.gov/kosovo/pdf/Kosovo_Media_Assessment.pdf

"Minority Bus Shuttle Project in Kosovo." *United Nations Refugee Agency (UNHCR).* 28 February , 2001. Online. http://portal.unesco.org/en/files/20060/108264820 41Pages_97-113_KOSOVO_report_distilled.pdf/ Pages%2B97-113%2BKOSOVO_report_distilled.pdf

"Regions and Territories: Kosovo." *BBC News Channel.* March 30. 2009. Online. http://news.bbc.co.uk/2/hi/ europe/country_profiles/3524092.stm

"Serbian Cuisine." *Embassy of the Republic of Serbia in the U.S.A.* http://www.serbiaembusa.org/upfiles/hrana.pdf

"Sokol Beqiri." *The International Artist Database.* "Sokol Beqiri." http://www.culturebase.net/artist.php?1455

"The World Factbook: Kosovo." Online. *Central Intelligence Agency.* https://www.cia.gov/library/ publications/the-world-factbook/geos/kv.html

"Vernacular Architecture and Various Sites." *United Nations Educational, Scientific, and Cultural Organization (UNESCO).* 2006. http://portal.unesco.org/ en/files/20060/10826482041Pages_97-113_KOSOVO_ report_distilled.pdf/Pages%2B97-113%2BKOSOVO_ report_distilled.pdf

Anthony Barilla. "Mitrovica Rock School brings back town's former glory." 10 February, 2009. http://www. newkosovareport.com/200902091605/Culture-and-Sports/Mitrovica-Rock-School-brings-back-town-s-former-glory.html

"Human Rights & Visual Culture eBook." *European Network of Young Cinema Online.* http://issuu.com/ emiliep/docs/hrvc_book_final_web_0616/12

Frank D'hondt. "Re-Creating Kosovo Cities." *International Society of City and Regional Planners.* http://www. isocarp.net/Data/case_studies/912.pdf

Gail Warrander and Verena Knaus. "Kosovo." Guilford, CT: *The Globe Pequot Press*, 2007.

Gojiko Subotic. "Art of Kosovo: The Sacred Land." New York: *Monacelli Press*, 1998. http://articles.latimes.com/2008/mar/10/world/fg-women10?s=g&n=n&m=Broad&rd=www.google.com &tnid=1&sessid=ceeb2104ad5e13290bdf5ced0fa4ede9 8b79c09d&uuid=ceeb2104ad5e13290bdf5ced0fa4ede98 b79c09d&pg=2&pgtp=article&eagi=&cat=news+%26+ current+events&page_type=article&exci=2008_03_10_ world_fg-women10 http://hdr.undp.org/en/reports/global/hdr2005/

Ivor Hansen. "The World: Learning to Fly; Kosovo's Young Get By With a Little Help From the West." *The New York Times*, 11 February 2001. http://www.nytimes. com/2001/02/11/weekinreview/the-world-learning-to-fly-kosovo-s-young-get-by-with-a-little-help-from-the-west.html?n=Top/Reference/Times%20Topics/ Subjects/F/Foreign%20Aid

Nora Hasani and Zana Limani. "Sharp Rise in Postwar Suicides Alarms Kosovo." *Focus Information Agency*, 7 June, 2007. http://www.focus-fen.net/?id=l8402

Regional and Environmental Center for Central and Eastern Europe. "Strategic Environmental Analysis of Kosovo," *Regional and Environmental Center for Central and Eastern Europe.* July 2000. http://www.rec.org/REC/ publications/CountryReports/Kosovo.pdf

Robert Elsie. Historical Dictionary of Kosova. Lanham, MD: *Scarecrow Press*, 2004.

Sana Limani and Driton Maliqi. "Kosovo: Girls face pressure to stop 'wasting time' in school." *Institute for War and Peace Reporting (IWPR)*, 29 April 2004. http://www.reliefweb.int/rw/rwb.nsf/db900sid/ACOS-64C7R8?OpenDocument

Tracy Wilkinson. "Kosovo''s Women Suffer." *The Los Angeles Times*, 10 March 2008.

United Nations Children's Fund (UNICEF). "CEE/CIS: Hidden Crises." http://www.ungei.org/gap/reportEurope. php

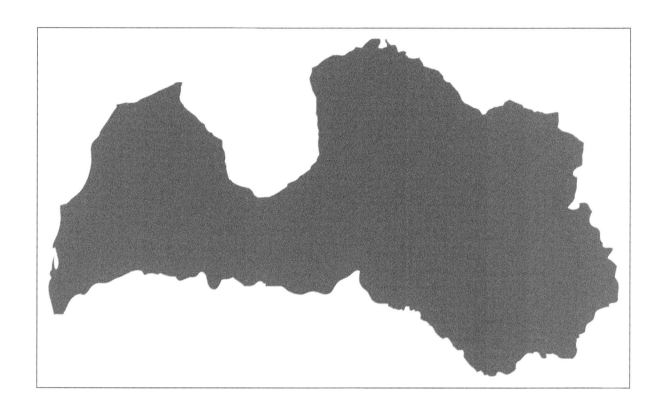

LATVIA

Introduction

The Republic of Latvia is located in Eastern Europe, on the Baltic Sea. It is bordered by Russia to the east, Estonia to the north, Belarus to the southeast, and Lithuania to the south. Latvia regained its independence in 1991, following the dissolution of the Soviet Union. Except for a short independence between World War I and World War II, Latvia had been under German or Russian rule since the 12th century. It is now a full member of both the European Union and NATO.

Riga is the capital of Latvia and the largest capital of the three Baltic states (Estonia, Latvia, and Lithuania). Often called the "Paris of the East" due to its rich art nouveau architecture, Riga is a prominent European tourist destination. Historically, the capital was an important trading post between Northern Europe and Russia, and by 1900, Riga had the third largest industrial population in the Russian Empire.

Since independence from the Soviet Union in 1991, Riga has seen enormous economic growth, and with Latvian membership in the EU granted in 2004, the city of Riga hopes to expand its economic stability in the 21st century. Latvia joined the euro zone in 2014.

GENERAL INFORMATION

Official Language: Latvian
Population: 2,165,165 (2014 estimate)
Currency: Euro (2014)
Coins: The euro coins are divided into eight denominations: 1, 2, 5, 10, 20 and 50 cent, 1 and 2
Land Area: 62,249 square kilometers (24,034 square miles)

Water Area: 2,340 square kilometers (903 square miles)
National Anthem: "Dievs, sveti Latviju" ("God Bless Latvia")
Capital: Riga
Time Zone: GMT +2
Flag Description: The flag of Latvia features a brownish-red field, or background, with a single white horizontal band running through the center. The colors of the flag have been attributed to a Latvian legend, in which a wounded Latvian leader is wrapped in a white sheet later used as a rallying flag, but the colors have also been attributed to the blood shed for freedom and nationalism, as well as righteousness and truth. The Latvian flag is one of the oldest flags in the world.

Population

The population of Latvia is made up of native Latvians, Russians, and other Slavs. The country was nearly three-quarters Latvian before the Soviet occupation began in 1940. Now, after

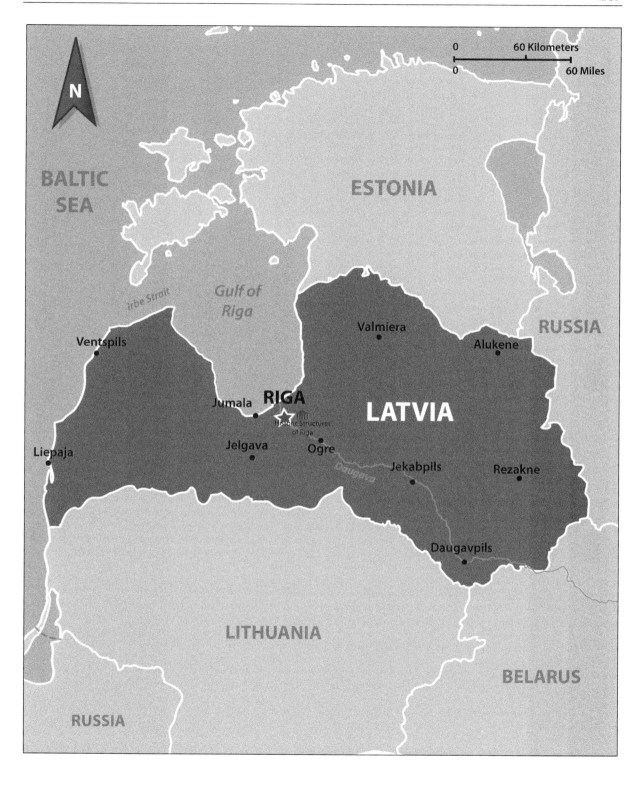

Principal Cities by Population (2012):

- Riga (693,919)
- Daugavpils (102,338)
- Liepaja (82,790)
- Jelgava (66,880)
- Jurmala (54,715)
- Ventspils (42,715)
- Rezekne (34,460)

independence, roughly 60 percent of the population is Latvian, while 27 percent is Russian (2011 estimate). The remaining population is made up of Belarusians, Ukrainians, Poles, and Lithuanians.

Since World War II, the population has practically abandoned the rural countryside in favor of urban areas; in fact, about 68 percent of the population is urban (2010 estimate). The three biggest cities are Riga, the capital, Daugavpils, known for its Church of St. Peter, and Liepaja. Independence in the late 20th century, however, brought relaxed emigration restrictions and the urban population of Riga has declined from an all-time high of 909,135 in 1990. This demographic shift is also explained by the fact that during the Soviet period the government encouraged ethnic Russian and Belarusian emigrants to settle in Riga. Following independence, the Latvian government refused to automatically grant citizenship to these new arrivals.

Overall, Latvia's population is drastically declining; as of 2010, the population growth rate was –0.8 percent, while the net migration rate was –2.32. According to an early 21st-century United Nations projection, Latvia will lose up to 44 percent of its current population by 2050.

Languages

Latvian remains the official language. Many inhabitants of Riga, the capital, also speak Russian or German, and English is becoming increasingly common in the capital region.

Native People & Ethnic Groups

Latvia's native people are called Letts, a Baltic people who speak Lettish, which is similar to Lithuanian. The Lettish people first appeared in the area in the ninth century. They were converted to Christianity in the 12th century during the Saxon Crusades.

The Baltic people are first noted in historical accounts of the amber trade with the Roman Empire in the first century. During the 10th and 11th centuries, the Swedish and the Slavs began encroaching upon the area from the west the east. When the Saxon crusades began in the 12th century, the area was taken over by German missionaries. It was named Livonia and became a subject, feudal nation forced to pay tithes and taxes. This Livonian Confederation lasted for 300 years.

Since the last decade of the 20th century, Latvia has asserted its national identity, first through a successful Latvian Popular Front election while still under Soviet rule in 1990, and then with its official independence a year later. As a result, there is still tension between the country's Latvian population and its Russian population. For instance, until Latvia was pressured by the United Nations and the United States, the newly independent Latvia made it difficult for Russians living there to obtain citizenship.

Minority ethnic groups in Latvia include Poles, Lithuanians, Germans, and Estonians.

Religions

Latvia is primarily Christian, with the largest denominations as of 2006 being Lutheran (19.6 percent) and Russian Orthodox (15.3 percent). In Riga, the capital, a city famous for its medieval and Renaissance churches, the population is relatively secular; it was estimated in 2004 that only 7 percent of the city's population regularly attends religious services.

Climate

The skies over Latvia are mostly cloudy, with 150 to 180 overcast days each year. Because of the air coming in from the Atlantic Ocean, the country is mostly cloudy and humid, with cool and rainy summers. There are only about thirty to forty days of complete sunshine per year. Latvia receives an average of 600 millimeters (24 inches) of rain annually.

The average temperature during summer is 17° Celsius (63° Fahrenheit), but can rise as high as 34° Celsius (93° Fahrenheit). From December to March, the temperature drops to between –2° and –7° Celsius (28° and 19° Fahrenheit). At times, the temperature drops much lower.

The climate of Riga is mild and temperate during the summer months but severely cold in the winter. The average summer temperature is a mild 21° Celsius (70° Fahrenheit) but winter temperatures plunge to an average of –7.3° Celsius (19° Fahrenheit). Winter snowfall and autumn rain make up for a majority of the precipitation in Riga and the climate is wet with an average annual precipitation of 636 millimeters (25 inches).

ENVIRONMENT & GEOGRAPHY

Topography

Latvia is mostly one large plain made up of a mixture of hills and lowlands. It has 531 kilometers (330 miles) of coastline. On the eastern side of the country, the elevation tends to be higher. The Central Vidzeme Uplands reach a height of 311 meters (1,020 feet). In the west, the Venta River cuts through the Kurzeme Upland.

The country is filled with peat bogs, which are created when organic material collects and decomposes because of poor drainage. There are also swamps and marshes, in addition to lakes and streams. The main rivers are the Amata River, which runs through the Gauja National Park; the Western Dvina, which is called the Daugava by locals; the Venta, in western Latvia; and the Lielupe River, located in central Latvia.

Riga is located on the Gulf of Riga, which is a natural protected harbor on the Baltic Sea. The city itself is located in a basin where several rivers, the largest of which is the Daugava River, drain into the gulf. The mouth of the Daugava River forms the harbor of the city and centuries of silt accumulation have created numerous islands and peninsulas in the harbor. The port of Riga is also a major shipping center, and the site of a modernization project that began in

2006. Like the rest of Latvia, Riga is flat, with the highest elevation being a mere nine meters (27 feet) above sea level.

Plants & Animals

Latvia supports a number of different bird species. Its numerous marshes are home to herons and storks. Other birds include orioles, owls, partridges, grouse, and larks. Apart from these, the usual forest wildlife is found throughout Latvia: foxes, rabbits, and squirrels, as well as more exotic animals such as badgers and weasels. Conservationists have been mindful of the elk and deer populations, which have been on the rise.

More than 40 percent of the country is forested with a combination of birch and aspen. The coast has many sandy beaches, and the fish include cod and herring.

CUSTOMS & COURTESIES

Greetings

Although Latvians are generally quite friendly, they are also reserved and value politeness. Handshakes are the common form of greeting, and are typically firm and quick. Friends, family, and acquaintances may also embrace or exchange kisses on the cheek. Honorific or formal titles, such as "Kung" ("Sir") or "Kundze" ("Madam"), are also usually expected when addressing people. It is also advisable to use a person's first name only if invited to do so.

A casual greeting is "Sveiks" ("Hi"), with "Labdien" ("Hello") the more formal version. The casual phrase "Kā tev klājas?" ("How's it going?") is also commonly used. For a more formal situation, "Kā jums iet?" ("How are you?") is appropriate. Lastly, most Latvians speak Russian, but maintain a great deal of pride in their culture and heritage.

Gestures & Etiquette

Latvians do not outwardly express much emotion, and they use minimal gesturing during conversation. Excessive use of the hands or exaggerated movements in an argument or discussion would likely be frowned upon. It is thought rude to completely avoid eye contact, but also unacceptable to constantly maintain eye contact with a person.

Latvians take business seriously and prefer formality. Business attire, such as suits, is still preferred, although business casual is beginning to be accepted. Latvians generally also tend to be quiet and thoughtful. Talking loudly in public, especially on buses or trains, is usually considered impolite. However, this etiquette is becoming less disapproved of amongst the younger generation. Additionally, formal table manners are expected when dining. Latvians also dine in the continental style while eating: fork held in the left hand, knife held in the right hand.

Eating/Meals

Breakfast in Latvia, or brokastis, is traditionally sandwiches, usually with cheese or cold meat. Pancakes, cereal, or eggs may also be served. Tea, coffee, milk, and yogurt-based drinks are also common. Midday meals can range from one to three courses. Soup may be a first course, or served as the entire meal. A typical main course includes fried meat or fish, along with a starch, such as potatoes, rice, or buckwheat, and then a salad. Desserts can be anything from fruit to pudding to ice cream. Latvians will drink tea, coffee, milk, fruit juices, or kefir, a cultured-milk drink, at lunch.

In the evening, Latvians usually have a second meal that is similar to the midday meal. However, as workers have become busier and international influences become stronger, particularly in urban areas, Latvians increasingly are dining out or eating fast or prepared foods. Latvian mealtimes have also become more flexible, especially in cities—people have dinner in restaurants as late as 10 or 11 o'clock at night.

Visiting

In Latvia, it is considered polite to bring a small gift for the host when visiting. Flowers are an important part of Latvian culture, so they are a fine gift for both sexes. However, bouquets should always contain an odd number of flowers, as even-numbered bunches are traditionally placed on graves. Red roses are also associated with funerals and mourning, and should be avoided. Candy and wine or liquor are also appropriate gifts. Gifts are typically opened when first received. In addition, Latvians generally appreciate punctuality. It is also common practice to remove one's shoes before entering the host's home. Formal attire, particularly for a dinner engagement, is typically the rule of thumb.

LIFESTYLE

Family

Traditionally, Latvian culture has been defined by strong familial ties and traditions. It remains commonplace for three generations to reside under the same roof, often with the grandparents caring for any children as both parents enter the workforce. Latvian families are also typically small, and since the turn of the 20th century, Latvian couples on average are having fewer children. Latvian families are also traditionally hierarchical; elder family members are treated with respect and adult children are expected to care for their elderly parents.

Housing

Traditional houses in rural Latvia often consisted of wooden farmhouses with thatched roofs. Many of these homesteads were complexes that included a detached bathhouse, smokehouse, and barn.

During the Soviet era, many Latvians migrated to urban areas. To accommodate this, high-rise apartment blocks that were designed for functionality rather than aesthetics were built. Since independence, modern apartment complexes have continued to fill the cityscapes of Latvia, though without the socialist style of architecture that defined their predecessors. Apartments generally are quite small, and many families own weekend homes in the country.

Since Latvia achieved independence in 1991, housing has transitioned from government subsidization to a free-market system and privatization.

However, a lack of adequate housing and investment, particularly in urban areas, has hindered reform in the housing sector. This is particularly apparent in the capital of Riga, where roughly one-third of the Latvian population resides. In recent years, social policy programs have been enacted, such as the provision of rental housing for low-income residents and maintenance programs to improve housing that has fallen into disrepair.

Food

The cuisine of Latvia shares many similarities with the cuisines of neighboring Baltic cultures, and is influenced by German, Russian, and Swedish cuisine. Due to Latvia's proximity to the Baltic Sea, fish is common, and native products such as pork, potatoes, cabbages, beans, peas, and barley are all staples. While exotic spices have not featured prominently in traditional Latvian food, common ingredients include caraway seeds, onion, garlic, and white mustard. Honey is a more common sweetener than sugar, though fresh berries, a popular dessert, are often sweet enough on their own. Dairy products such as eggs and milk are part of everyday life in Latvia, and Latvians even drink a curdled form of milk called rūgušpiens or kefīrs.

Bread in all shapes and forms is popular in Latvia, with different regions having their own specialties. As in other northern countries, such as Sweden, Norway, and Russia, dark rye bread is popular. Potatoes in all forms (including potato salad and pancakes), beets, cabbage, smoked fish, sour cream, and berries are other common Latvian foods that are also found in Scandinavia and Russia. Pīrāgis are small pastries stuffed with bacon and onion that are similar to the Russian and Polish pirozhki, and are traditionally filled with cabbage, meat, or potatoes.

Pelēki spirņi ar speķi, a thick stew of gray peas boiled with bacon and fried meat is a traditional Latvian dish. Skabā putra is a cold soup that combines cracked barley, sour cream, buttermilk, and milk. Kliņģeris is often served on birthdays and other holidays; a sweet bread rather than a cake, it is filled with raisins and flavored with orange, lemon, and cardamom (a popular spice in northern Europe), while saffron adds yellow color. The dough is shaped like a pretzel and is topped with almonds and sugar.

Life's Milestones

Birthday celebrations in Latvia still include many ancient traditions. The birthday honoree might be awakened with songs, and is traditionally presented with flowers and other gifts, as well as a party. During the celebration, the guest of honor is presented with a specially decorated chair that is traditionally lifted once for each year of the person's age. Name days are treated like a second birthday. A name day is the feast day of the Christian saint after whom a person is named. While birthday parties are usually for invited guests only, name day parties are generally open to anyone.

Weddings also retain some of the old traditions. Oak trees are revered in Latvia, so oak leaves may be used to decorate the entrance of the church where the wedding will be held. Latvian brides wear white, a highly regarded color in Latvia, as they do in other Western cultures. Singing is an important part of weddings and wedding banquets include many courses. The "New Wife's Torte," a cake, is eaten by guests after midnight. Large banquets, singing, and dancing are also part of funerals. Graves in Latvia are visited often by families of the dead, and gatherings at cemeteries can be a way to bring even family members who live abroad together.

CULTURAL HISTORY

Art

Throughout most of the country's history, the development of the arts in Latvia mirrored the history of Western art. Located on the Baltic Sea, Latvia has long been the target of other nations, particularly landlocked countries seeking maritime trade routes. These nations brought with them foreign influences and their own native artistic traditions. The earliest examples of art in Latvia are small prehistoric sculptures, mostly depicting human and animal forms. Indo-European settlers who inhabited the area around 2500 BCE made jewelry and decorated other objects with symbols such as the sun and the moon.

Germanic tribes arrived in the 12th century CE, marking the advent of trade and Christianity in the region. Religion began to influence art and architecture, and churches were first built in Western architectural styles such as Romanesque and Gothic. One such example is the Dome Cathedral in Riga, which, along with St. Peter's Church and St. Simon's Church in Cesis, is an example of the Gothic style of architecture popular in Western Europe at the time. Sculpture and architecture remained the most popular art forms in Latvia, and most stone and wood sculptures were made for churches. The Latvians also became renowned for their ornate, complicated woodcarvings. The Northern Renaissance came to Latvia in the 16th and 17th centuries, with new artistic ideas brought by artists traveling from other parts of Europe to find work. Wood sculptures and religious themes were still common, but painting also began to develop. Wealthy citizens commissioned portraits, and landscape paintings and other secular art appeared.

After Russia gained control of Latvia in the late 18th century, Latvian artists traveled to Russia and other parts of Europe to train. In the latter half of the 19th century, Latvian national identity emerged as an important artistic theme. Painters such as Jānis Rozentāls (1866–1916), Vilhelms Purvītis (1872–1945), and Jānis Valters (1869–1932) began to include nationalist themes in their paintings. They depicted the lives of ordinary Latvians, native landscapes, and Latvian folklore elements. In the early 20th century, modern trends and Western artistic movements, such as cubism, were also incorporated into Latvian art. New technology helped make graphic arts, or prints, popular.

Art nouveau, an art movement from the late 19th and early 20th centuries, had a tremendous influence in Latvia. The movement sprung from the idea that an artistic style should affect all types of art, especially painting, architecture, furniture, and even fashion. Curved lines, flower and animal motifs, and folkloric themes are all characteristic of the art nouveau style. In Riga, the largest city in the Baltic states, a number of buildings feature art nouveau designs, and the city is considered one of the great centers of art nouveau architecture.

After World War I, when Latvia briefly achieved independence, Latvian artists and architects reacted to the ornate art nouveau style by experimenting with sleek modernism and abstract forms. After Soviet occupation in 1940, functionalism rather than beauty was emphasized, particularly in architecture, and artists were forced to produce art that promoted Soviet beliefs. Perhaps the most famous Latvian-born artist of the 20th century was Mark Rothko (1903–1970), a painter classified as an abstract expressionist. As part of a widespread Latvian diaspora, he became a leading voice in American art.

In the 1990s, after Latvia regained independence, artists began to experiment with new and emerging art trends. Exhibitions that focused on installations or site specific art began to appear, taking place in theaters, train stations, and other places outside of galleries and museums. Even artists who worked in traditional styles began to produce massive pieces on material or structures beyond canvas. As Latvia moves into its third decade of independence, art is alive and well, and the nation is again becoming an international center for the visual arts.

Architecture

Latvia's architectural heritage is perhaps best exemplified by the capital, Riga. Famous for its narrow winding streets, the Old Town of Riga, or the Vercriga, is the historic medieval center of the city that was declared a United Nations Educational, Scientific and Cultural Organization (UNESCO) World Heritage Site in 1997. While much of the medieval character of the Old Town remains, the architecture in the area is predominantly art nouveau, from the late 19th century period when the prosperous city renovated the quarter with a distinctly Latvian style. Inspired by Austrian, Finnish, and German architects, this style combines natural Latvian building materials of stone and wood with the folk customs and cultures of Latvia. Characterized by steep roofs, heavy walls, and unique ornamental motifs, the art nouveau buildings helped transform Riga into the "Paris of the East." Also in the Old City is the medieval Town Hall Square, where the city government was located during the initial settlement of the city. Part of the Latvian government is located in the nearby Riga Castle, which was built in the 14th century and serves as the residence and offices for the president of Latvia. Heavily redesigned in the 17th century, the Riga Castle is a classic example of the Northern European baroque architectural style.

Dance & Drama

Folk dances have long been part of Latvian tradition. Like other folk art forms, traditional Latvian dances were passed on from generation to generation, and originated as part of local festivals or celebrations such as weddings. Formal dance emerged in 1870 through the Riga Latvian Theater. Different theaters then began teaching actors their own styles of dance, or used imported professional dancers from Moscow or other Russian cities. In 1918, the Latvian Opera was founded and included ballet in its musical productions. In 1913, the Riga Ballet School was established, and featured famed ballet choreographers from Russia, particularly from the famed Mariinsky Ballet, a classical ballet company based in Saint Petersburg.

Theater has also been part of Latvian life for centuries. As in most of Europe, the earliest plays were religious or morality tales. During the 18th and 19th centuries, theater in Latvia was generally performed for the German aristocracy. By the late 1800s, the Riga Russian Theatre had opened (followed by the Latvian National Theater in 1919) and plays written by native Latvians were being produced. Theatre also played a very important part in maintaining a national Latvian identity during the period of Soviet occupation. Though plays had to conform to Soviet political ideals, they were performed in Latvian, which helped keep the language alive.

Music

Latvia's rich musical history begins with the dainas, four-line folk songs that were part of the Latvian oral tradition. Many of these dainas feature folkloric themes and deities, and were traditionally accompanied by instruments such as the zither (stringed instrument). In the 19th century, many of these folk songs were compiled and systemized by Krišjānis Barons (1835–1923), who is often referred to as the "father of the dainas." Barons was also associated with the Young Latvians, or Latvian National Awakening movement.

Jāzeps Vītols (1863–1948) was one of the most important composers in the development of Latvian classical music. He taught for many years at Russia's St. Petersburg Conservatory and founded the Latvian Conservatory of Music in 1920. That same year, the first Latvian opera, *Baņuta*, composed by Alfrēd Kalniņš (1879–1951), was performed. Pēteris Vasks (1946–) and Mariss Jansons (1943–) are two of the more famous contemporary conductors. Following classical music, Western musical styles began to influence Latvian music, particularly after independence. Modern styles such as rock and roll and hip-hop are increasingly gaining popularity in the early 21st century.

Literature

Latvia's literary heritage is rooted in the strong oral traditions of the country's native peoples. For centuries, stories were told rather than written. In the 12th century, during Germanic rule, German became the primary written language, particularly since Latvian was seen as a peasant tongue. The earliest literature printed was religious material, and a full Latvian translation of the Bible appeared in the late 17th century. However, poets such as Svante Gustav Dietz (1670–1723) and Vilis Steineks (c. 1681–c. 1735) dealt with topics such as war and territorial conflict. In the 18th century, Gotthard Friedrich Stender (1714–1796) was credited with founding Latvian secular literature, and published poetry, a dictionary, and a Latvian grammar book.

During the 19th century, Latvians became increasingly interested in their own national identity. A number of writers, notably Krišjānis Barons, began to collect and transcribe Latvian folklore. Latvians writers such as Andrejs Pumpurs (1841–1902) and Rainis, the pseudonym of Jānis Pliekšāns (1865–1929), began to write novels, poems, and plays in the Latvian language. Many novels focused on peasant and rural life, as did the poetry of Rūdolf Blaumanis (1863–1908). Pumpurs, associated with the Latvian National Awakening movement of the 1850s to 1880s, wrote the Latvian epic *Lāčplēsis*, adapted from folklore into an epic poem. The poem is said to symbolize Latvia's own struggle against foreign invasion. Rainis, a poet and editor imprisoned for his radical politics, wrote a play, *Fire and Night* (1905), based on *Lāčplēsis* about a worker struggling against the foreign aristocracy.

When the Soviet Union occupied Latvia during World War II, many Latvian writers were deported or fled the country, and their exile experiences became a major part of their work. The writers who remained had to work within the rules of Soviet literature, which required that they promote Soviet political beliefs and socialist realism. Artists who remained include Arvids Grigulis (1906–1989) and Albert Bels (1938–), a novelist who became successful while experimenting with genres and modernist techniques.

CULTURE

Arts & Entertainment

Since independence, Latvia has firmly established in its own artistic voice. Latvian artists are becoming internationally known, and the various arts festivals hosted by the nation attract people from around the world.

Latvia has a long history of filmmaking. Even during the long period of Soviet occupation, filmmakers managed to produce notable work while staying within the political guidelines of communist Russia. However, when Latvia became independent, it lost the funding and support of the Soviet filmmaking industry. The country established a national film school in 1990, and Latvian filmmakers have since been working to regain a foothold on the international film scene. Animated Latvian films, short films, and documentaries have received prizes at various film festivals around the world, and in 2007 alone, Latvian films won thirty-six prizes. Latvia also has its own film festivals: Riga holds the International Film Festival "Arsenals" each year; Bimini, the International Festival of Animation Films, also takes place in Riga; and the Riga International Fantasy Film Festival is a competition in the genres of science fiction, fantasy, and horror.

Notable Latvian films in recent years include *The Shoe* (1998), directed by Laila Pakalniņa (1962–), and *Rigas sargi* (Defenders of Riga, 2007), directed by Aigars Grauba (1965–). *The Shoe* is a comedy about life in a Latvian village under the Soviet occupation, in which Latvian villagers must outwit the Soviet troops, and was screened at the 1998 Cannes Film Festival. (Pakalniņa's film *Python*, another absurdist story of an investigation gone wrong, was shown at the 2003 Venice Film Festival.) Grauba's film, *Rigas sargi*, was the most expensive film ever produced in Latvia, but also became its biggest success at the box office. The movie tells the story of the Latvians fight for independence against the Russians and Germans in 1919. *Rigas sargi* (*Defenders of Riga*) was Latvia's official entry in the foreign language film category of the 2009 Academy Awards, but was not nominated. For the 2010 Academy Awards, Latvia submitted the comedy-drama *Amaya*, by Latvian director Maris Martinsons (1960–), for the Academy Award for Best Foreign Language Film.

Folk songs and choir competitions remain an important aspect of contemporary Latvian culture, and Latvians have maintained a strong tradition of classical music and dance. The Latvian National Opera puts on operas and ballets each year and tours internationally. It also presents the Riga Opera Festival each year. The International Baltic Ballet Festival, which draws competition worldwide, includes all types of dance—ballet, modern, and even tango. It traditionally opens with a performance that is free for the public.

Latvian music began to break out of the Soviet restrictions in the late 1980s. Perkōns was a typical 1980s hard rock band that won a following in Latvia, but was occasionally banned by the Soviets for its wild concerts. A rock opera based on the national epic, *Lāčplēsis*, premiered in 1988 and is still performed today. In 1999, Latvia made its presence known on the European music scene when the Latvian band Brainstorm came in second in the influential Eurovision Song Contest. In 2002, the Latvian pop singer Marie N, the stage name of Marija Naumova (1973–), won the contest. Riga was also chosen as a host site for the Eurovision Song Contest in 2003.

Cultural Sites & Landmarks

During the 19th century, the city of Riga was often referred to as the "Paris of the East" because of its beauty and culture. Removed from much of the world during Soviet occupation in the 20th century, it has since become a modern, vibrant metropolis with a glorious history. The city is home to numerous landmarks, including the 13th-century St. Peter's and Doma cathedrals (though both structures have been rebuilt due to fire and the effects of war). St. George's Cathedral, or the White Stone Castle, is a remnant of a larger castle that was constructed in 1207 (now home to the Museum of Applied Arts). The city is also known for its art nouveau architecture, and there are an estimated 800 buildings in that style. In 1997, the United Nations Educational, Scientific, and Cultural Organization (UNESCO) added the Historic Centre of Riga to its World Heritage List for its architectural and cultural significance.

Outside of Riga, Rundāle Palace, in southern Latvia, is a well-known example of baroque and rococo architecture. It was built in the 18th century by the Italian architect Francisco Rastrelli (1700–1771), who also designed Russia's famous Winter Palace. Rastrelli also designed Jelgava Palace, found in the same region. In western Latvia, the city of Ventspils has the Livonian Order Castle, which dates from 1290; it is now the Ventspils Museum. Ludzu, founded in the 12th century, is probably Latvia's oldest town.

It is located in eastern Latvia, and still has some surviving examples of medieval buildings.

Libraries & Museums

Latvia's national museums include the Latvian Museum of National History, located in Riga and established in the late 19th century, and the Latvian National Museum of Art, which houses a collection of more than 50,000 artistic works. The National History Museum contains the largest collection of Latvian cultural artifacts.

Secondary museums include the Museum of the History of Riga and Navigation, considered the oldest museum of the Baltic states; the Museum of Latvian Railroad History; the Latvian Photography Museum; and the Latvian Nature Museum, also considered one of the Baltic states' oldest museum institutions. The Museum of the Occupation of Latvia, in Riga, focuses on the country's history between 1940 and 1991. Other museums are dedicated to a range of special niches and national heritages, including ceramics, film, and antique vehicles.

The National Library of Latvia, located in Riga, serves as the country's legal depository. Founded in the early 20th century, it houses a collection of over 4 million books and other resources. The library began the mass digitalization of its collection in 2010. In all, the country is home to over 1,000 school libraries and nearly 50 university-based research libraries.

Holidays

Aside from Christian holidays, Latvia celebrates the Proclamation of the Republic of Latvia on November 18. It was on this day in 1918 that the country initially declared its independence from Soviet Russia. It actually regained that independence on May 4, 1990, which it celebrates as Independence Day. This independence was further solidified by the breakup of the Soviet bloc in 1991.

Another important holiday for the country is Midsummer's Eve and Day, also known as St. John's Eve, on June 23 and 24. The country celebrates with a traditional festival on this day. National holidays also include Labor Day on May 1.

Youth Culture

With the advent of the Internet and satellite TV, Latvian youth culture has become increasingly exposed and influenced by Western trends and culture. While Latvian youth have their own music, they also listen to musicians popular in the rest of Europe. Also, films popular in the United States reach a large audience in Latvia, and Latvian teens, who are not required to wear school uniforms, can easily find the foreign fashions they see in magazines, films, and on TV.

Generally, the social lives of Latvian youth revolve around school and their families. At school, they participate in many activities, such as choir and sports teams (ice hockey is Latvia's most popular sport).

SOCIETY

Transportation

Riga has a strong public transportation system for travel within the city that features buses, trams, and trolleybuses. Taxis also are available, and can be found in other Latvian cities as well. Trains run regularly between Riga and a few major cities, including Jelgava and Jūrmala. Buses, however, are a quicker and often cheaper option for getting to other parts of the country, and remain the popular mode of public transportation. Traffic moves along the right-hand side of the road.

Most major European airlines fly into Riga International Airport, and there is train service to Latvia from Moscow and Saint Petersburg, as well as bus service from a number of European cities. Ferries from Lübeck in Germany leave four times a week for Riga.

Transportation Infrastructure

Latvia has an extensive rail network, totaling over 2,303 kilometers (1,431 miles). The country has 73,202 kilometers (45,486 miles) of highways, although more than half are not paved. The country has two ports along its sandy coastline, at Riga and Ventspils. Riga was once called the

"Paris of the North," and remains the cosmopolitan hub of the Baltic region. Latvia formed its own airline after declaring its independence. Until that time, all of the country's air traffic operated out of Moscow.

Media & Communications

In general, the mass media in Latvia is considered diverse. LETA is the national news agency in Latvia, and there are state-owned radio and television stations, as well as commercial ones. Latvia has many newspapers types—serious broadsheets, gossipy tabloids, and financial news—and language media is available in both Russian and Latvian. Some of the more popular national newspapers include *Diena* (an estimated circulation of 55,000) and *Vesti segodnja* (Today's News, estimated circulation of 35,000), which focuses more on Russian interests. Radio remains a viable and popular medium, and an estimated 85 percent of Latvians listen to the radio at least once per week.

There are few restrictions on speech in Latvia; however, libel and hate speech are punishable by imprisonment. Additionally, the Latvian government has made it illegal to discuss the country's financial system. In 2008, both a prominent journalist and a pop singer were detained by the government for voicing their opinions of Latvia's economic crisis and its central bank policy.

Cell phones are more common in Latvia than landline phones. In 2012, there were an estimated 2.31 million cell phones in use in Latvia. Internet use is also widespread, with 1.177 million subscribers in 2007. Additionally, as of 2010, there were an estimated 1.5 million Internet users in Latvia, representing approximately 67 percent of the total population.

SOCIAL DEVELOPMENT

Standard of Living

Latvia ranked 48th out of 187 countries on the 2013 United Nations Human Development Index, which measures quality of life and standard of living indicators.

Water Consumption

According to 2012 statistics from the World Health Organization (WHO), Latvia has nearly universal access to improved drinking water, an estimated 98 percent. Approximately the same percentage of the population has access to improved sanitation.

Education

Latvia has had a near-100 percent literacy rate since the 1890s, following the tide of industrialization. Instruction is conducted in Latvian, and the country is home to the University of Latvia, Riga Technical University, and the Latvian Academy of Sciences. Education in Latvia generally begins at the age of seven, and is free (at the primary and secondary level) and mandatory until age fifteen. Basic education lasts nine years. Following basic education, a third of students opt for vocational training. As of 2007, Latvia was home to approximately sixty institutes of higher education, the majority of which were funded by the state. In 2015, Latvia's literacy rate reached an estimated 100 percent.

Women's Rights

Latvian women have the same rights as men under the law, including family law, property law, and in the courts. Latvian labor laws also protect women from discrimination in hiring and states that employers must grant equal pay for equal work. Nevertheless, women still suffer discriminatory treatment when it comes to employment and equal wages. In 2010, the income difference between men and women was 17.6 percent. Although women hold 42 percent of the management positions in Latvia, they are rarely found in upper management or decision-making positions. Sexual harassment is against the law in Latvia, but it is severely underreported, and enforcement is ineffective. This is largely due to a culture in which women are reluctant to file complaints about sexual harassment due to social stigma. Additionally, women often don't feel that reporting problems are worth risking their jobs.

Abuse against women, particularly domestic abuse, is also illegal, but similarly underreported.

Many abused women are unaware of their rights, or receive inadequate support from authorities and the court system. Shelters for battered women haven't been established, and while family centers handle women with children who are in crisis, they are rarely an option for women without children. There are no hotlines specifically for women who have been assaulted; some general crisis hotlines provided by nongovernmental organizations (NGOs) are the only resource for women in trouble. In addition, while rape was criminalized, spousal rape is not, and human trafficking continues to be a serious issue.

Women received the right to vote when Latvia first became independent in 1918. However, they remain underrepresented in the government. Vaira Vike-Freiberga (1937–) was elected as the first woman president of Latvia in 1999 and served two terms. However, in 2007 and 2008, women only represented 19 percent of the seats in Latvia's parliament, and 23.5 percent of the government positions at the ministerial level. By 2015, only 16 percent of the seats in parliament were held by women—a decline. Despite this underrepresentation, women continue to improve their opportunities in Latvia. In 2005, women made up 40.5 percent of the students enrolled in vocational schools and 63.2 percent of the students at colleges and universities. Lastly, out of the 43,176 people who used a government job counseling service, 64.5 percent were women.

Health Care

In the years since independence, Latvia has modernized its system of health care and citizen welfare. During the period of the Cold War, the quality of Latvia's general health care declined along with the Soviet Union. Nevertheless, conditions have improved since the late 20th century. Latvia's infant mortality rate is an estimated 13.6 deaths per every 1,000 live births (2014 estimate). In addition, life expectancy for men is 68 years; while life expectancy for women is 78 years, (2014 estimate). The Ministry of Welfare administers all health care, social security, pensions, and welfare, which is in charge of maintaining and improving the social welfare of Latvians.

GOVERNMENT

Structure

Latvia began to regain its national identity in the 1980s, as Russia moved toward glasnost ("openness") and perestroika ("restructuring"). The Latvian Popular Front emerged in 1988 and went on to win national elections in 1990. After independence in 1991, the newly formed democratic government restored the 1922 constitution. In the June 1993 elections, only people who were citizens prior to the 1940 invasion were allowed to vote. This strict definition of Latvian citizenship was later altered after diplomatic pressure from the European Union and the World Trade Organization.

The current government of the Republic of Latvia is a parliamentary democracy with three branches. The executive branch is made up of a chief of state (president), and the head of the government (prime minister). The cabinet, called the Council of Ministers, is nominated by the prime minister, and later appointed by the Parliament. The president, elected by Parliament, serves a four-year term and appoints the prime minister.

The Parliament, also called the Saeima, is comprised of 100 seats. Its members are elected by popular vote every four years. The Supreme Court of Latvia makes up the judicial branch. Its judges are appointed by Parliament. Citizens must be eighteen years old to vote. The right to vote is universal for Latvian citizens.

The last election was held on June 3, 2015. Raimonds Vejonis was elected president with 55 out of 100 votes. The next election will be held in 2019.

Political Parties

Latvia has a multi-party system. Multiple parties with differing political philosophies form coalition governments. These parties include the Social Democratic Party (SC), Unity, the Union of Greens and Farmers (ZZS), and the National Alliance. Individual parties will occasionally merge to form political unions. In the legislative elections in 2014, the results, by seats, were as follows: SC, 24; Unity, 23; ZZS, 21; National Alliance, 17; all others, 15.

Local Government

Latvia's government is organized into three parts: the central government, the immediate tier, and local governments. The immediate tier is organized into 33 territorial units. Local government in Latvia consists of 453 rural municipalities and is administrated by the Latvian Association of Local and Regional Governments.

Judicial System

Latvia's judicial system is comprised of the Supreme Court, regional courts, and district courts. Judges are appointed by parliament. The country's courts continue to be plagued by corruption. Few investigations into incidents of corruption occur and political influence within the judicial system remains widespread.

Taxation

As a sum, Latvia has low to moderate tax rates, including a flat personal income tax rate of 26 percent and a corporate tax rate of 15 percent. Other taxes levied include a value-added tax (or VAT, similar to a consumption tax, or a tax on the sale of goods and services), excise taxes, a natural resources tax, and a real estate tax.

Armed Forces

The armed forces of Latvia, officially the National Armed Forces, is made up of several service branches, including land, air, and sea forces, and a national guard. There is no conscription, and the minimum age for service is eighteen. Latvian forces have participated in several international affairs, including operations in Afghanistan. The country has participated in the International Security Assistance Force, or ISAF, led by NATO, since 2003. The Latvian armed forces have also previously participated in peacekeeping missions in the Balkan region.

Foreign Policy

With its long history of foreign occupation, Latvia's foreign policy has long been dictated and influenced by other governments. Since achieving independence in 1991, however, Latvia has been able to establish its own identity in the European and international community. Latvia joined the UN in 1991 and both the North Atlantic Treaty Organization (NATO) and the European Union (EU) in 2004. Since that time, the country's foreign policy priorities have focused on national and regional security, the strengthening of democracy, the promotion of economic development and investment, and the support of the Latvian diaspora, and the promotion of Latvian culture on the world stage.

Latvia has developed a particularly close relationship with the United States. The US was among a number of nations that never recognized the Soviet takeover of Latvia in 1940, and the embassy in the U.S. continued to operate throughout the Soviet occupation. In 1991, the U.S. re-established full diplomacy with Latvia. Today Latvia shares many of the goals of other UN member states, including a commitment to ending poverty, maintaining democracies, halting the spread of disease, and promoting gender equality and education for everyone. Latvian troops have been part of NATO and EU military missions in Macedonia, Bosnia-Herzegovina, Kosovo, and Afghanistan. Latvia has also sent troops to Iraq.

Latvia also works closely with the other Baltic states to manage issues that are important to the region, including energy security, terrorism, pollution, and illegal immigration. Latvia's foreign policy is also rooted in the idea that helping Latvians first—including those who live outside Latvia—will make the nation a strong member of the international community. Of particular note are Latvia's relations with Russia. Latvia has a significant population of Russian-speaking citizens—estimated at around 30 percent of the population—and Russia has expressed concern over Latvia's naturalization and language laws. The two countries also signed a border agreement in 2007.

Human Rights Profile

International human rights law insists that states respect civil and political rights, and promote an individual's economic, social, and cultural rights. The United Nations Universal Declaration on Human Rights (UDHR) is recognized as the standard for international human rights. Its authors sought the counsel of the world's great thinkers, philosophers, and religious leaders, and were careful to create a document that reflects the core values shared by every world culture. (To read this document or view the articles relating to cultural human rights, go to http://www.un.org/en/documents/udhr/.)

Latvia has long supported human rights. In fact, thirty years before the adoption of the UDHR, Latvia included its own declaration of human rights in the Act of Proclamation of the Republic of Latvia in 1918. During the long Soviet occupation, however, human rights violations were not uncommon. Thousands of Latvians were deported and many were executed during this period of "Russification," which attempted to firmly implant Soviet ideals in Latvia. Since returning to independence, Latvia has tried to uphold its belief in human rights.

The Satversme, the Latvian constitution, was adopted in 1922 and provides protection for a number of human rights. It guarantees equality for all human beings in Latvia, and the right to defend those rights in a court of law. Everyone in Latvia has the right to liberty, security, and privacy. In Latvia, the church is separate from the state, and there is complete freedom of religion. Latvians have freedom of expression and freedom of association. Workers have the right to collectively bargain and strike, and senior citizens and those unable to work have the right to social security. The state also provides for disabled, parentless, and abused children, and provides free primary and secondary education. Ethnic minorities also have the right to maintain their culture and language.

Despite the guarantees provided by the constitution, Latvia, like many European nations, has struggled with hate crimes, usually against ethnic minorities. The Roma, an Eastern

European people once known as gypsies, have been discriminated against in Latvia. There also have been problems with anti-Semitism. Conflicts also have been reported between native Latvians and the Russians who were brought into the country during the Soviet occupation. Russians who came to Latvia after 1940 are required to take a naturalization test in order to become full citizens. The test requires them to take an oath of loyalty, show some knowledge of Latvia's history, and speak Latvian. Without the exam, they forfeit their right to vote and lose other rights guaranteed to them as natural citizens. Meanwhile, Latvians resent Russians who they feel are taking their jobs and are refusing to integrate into society.

In 1993, the Latvian Centre for Human Rights (LCHR) was created. The LCHR monitors and reports human rights violations, and provides aid and legal assistance for people who have suffered discrimination. The LCHR works both domestically and internationally to provide expert opinions about rights issues, and to advocate for legislative change. It also attempts to heighten public awareness of discrimination and to improve tolerance. Latvian laws have been created to try to combat discrimination, including hate speech and racism as a motivation for a crime. However, the challenge remains enforcement of the laws, as well as educating the people in order to prevent the crimes before they happen.

ECONOMY

Overview of the Economy

Since declaring its independence, Latvia has worked to free itself from economic dependence on Russia. By privatizing public industries and encouraging foreign investment, the Latvian government has helped integrate the economy with the more developed economies of Western Europe and the United States. However, Latvia still must import much of its energy and raw materials to continue its rate of production. A member of the World Trade Organization, Latvia's biggest export partners are Great Britain, Germany, and Sweden.

Riga underwent an economic boom in recent years that coincided with skyrocketing growth rates throughout the Baltic States. Economists referred to this boom as the "Baltic Tiger." In all three countries, gross domestic product (GDP) rates grew between five and 12 percent during 2000–2007. In 2014, however, Latvia's GDP grew by 2.7 percent.

Riga continues to provide a special economic boost for the country by being a major transit point for goods from Latvia, Russia, and Asia. Along with finished goods, Riga serves as a port for Russian oil; Russia exports nearly 13 percent of its heavy crude through the city, and larger port facilities are planned. Due to the strained capacity of U.S. ports, several American companies have expressed interest in utilizing Riga as a transit point on a "New Silk Road," which would bring Chinese goods across Asia and to American ports on the East Coast.

In 2014, the estimated gross domestic product (GDP) of Latvia was $32.82 billion. The estimated per capita GDP is approximately $23,900.

Industry

Latvia is the most industrialized of the Baltic states. Its industry is based on machine building and metal engineering. The country produces large products such as refrigerators, washing machines, and motorcycles, as well as radios and other smaller consumer electronic devices. Other products produced in Latvia include street and railroad cars, agricultural machinery, and processed foods.

Much like Estonia to the north, Latvia has tried to develop an information technology industry in Riga. Estonian dominance of these industries in the Baltic states, however, has limited Riga to more traditional industries such as chemical processing, textiles, papermaking, and communication equipment. However, the significant economic strides have helped make the financial services sector a major part of the economy, a transition helped by the presence of the Bank of Latvia, which is headquartered in the city.

Labor

The Latvian labor force was estimated at 1.014 million in 2014. The services sector accounts for more than half of the work force—approximately 67 percent as of 2010—while industry and agriculture account for 24 and 8.8 percent, respectively. The unemployment rate in 2014 was roughly 9.5 percent, a slow decrease from 9.9 percent in 2013.

Energy/Power/Natural Resources

There is a variety of minerals found in Latvia, including limestone, peat (which can be burned like charcoal), dolomite, sand, and amber. Hydroelectric and thermoelectric stations are located along the Daugava River. All of the country's power stations remain on a single power grid, a remnant of Soviet occupation.

Despite the use of hydropower, less than half of Latvia's energy comes from domestic sources. The rest comes from imported fuel and power systems in northwest Russia. A few oil sources have been found in the Kurzeme Peninsula.

Fishing

Latvia's fishing industry contributes 1.7 percent of the country's total GDP. Approximately 1.2 percent of employed Latvians work in the fisheries trade. The country's fishing fleet has about 400 vessels, catching cod, herring, and sprat. Latvia also has seven state-owned fish farms that produce canned fish products.

Forestry

Forestry, particularly sales of timber, accounts for approximately one-third of Latvia's income. Wood products represent an estimated 19 percent of Latvia's manufacturing sector. Overall, forestry makes up approximately four percent of the country's overall GDP. The Latvian Forest Industry Federation oversees lumber regulations. Other tree species in Latvia include birch, ash, and alder.

Mining/Metals

Although Latvia does not have significant mineral reserves, it does have deposits of industrial minerals including limestone, gravel, and sand.

Latvia also produces iron, steel, and cement. These materials represented an estimated nine percent of the country's exports in 2009.

Agriculture

Latvia's agricultural production is based mainly on meat and dairy. Two-thirds of farmland is reserved for crops, with the rest serving as pastures. Important crops include rye grain, sugar beets, potatoes, and flax. Meat production concentrates on beef and pork. The country also harvests fish, mainly cod and herring, from the Baltic Sea.

Between 1947 and 1950, Latvia's farms were collectivized under Soviet control. At the time of independence, there were approximately 374 collective farms and 237 state farms. After independence, Latvia began to privatize its farming industry.

Animal Husbandry

Livestock animals in Latvia include cattle, pigs, sheep, and goats. Latvia also produces large quantities of milk and eggs. An estimated 681 million eggs were produced in the country in 2009. Although the country remains a significant producer of dairy products, the number of dairy cows in the country has decreased in recent years.

Tourism

Tourists often make trips out of the cities to the countryside where they can visit castles. The architecture in cities such as Riga is a mixture of the dramatic, decorative Old European Jugendstil (or art nouveau) architecture, and the more practical, industrial-looking concrete structures of the Soviet period.

The Latvian government has also invested substantially into modernizing and expanding the Riga International Airport, the largest airport of the Baltic countries. The city has already benefited from this expansion by the large number of tourists visiting Riga during the spring and summer months, and a large seasonal service economy has developed.

Kirsten Anderson, Barrett Hathcock, Jeffrey Bowman

DO YOU KNOW?

- In a 1989 demonstration of independence from the former Soviet Union, citizens of Estonia, Latvia and Lithuania joined hands in a large chain that stretched from Riga to Tallinn and Vilnius, the three capitals of the newly independent Baltic States.

- The oldest factory in Latvia is the Laima Chocolate factory, which has been operating for 125 years.

- Visitors as well as natives place flowers at the base of the Freedom Monument in Riga, which was built to commemorate Latvian independence.

Bibliography

Alan Palmer. *The Baltic: A New History of the Region and Its People*. New York: The Overlook Press, 2006.

Aldis Purs. *Baltic Facades: Estonia, Latvia, and Lithuania since 1945*. London: Reaktion Books, 2012.

Daina Stukuls Eglitis. *Imagining the Nation: History, Modernity, and Revolution in Latvia*. University Park: Pennsylvania State University Press, 2002.

Kevin O'Connor. *Culture and Customs of the Baltic States*. Westport: Greenwood Press, 2006.

Maria Kalnins. *Latvia: A Shorth History*. London: Hurst, 2015.

Modris Eksteins. *Walking Since Daybreak*. Boston: Houghton Mifflin, 1999.

Works Cited

http://ec.europa.eu/employment_social/publications/2005/ke6705977_en.pdf

http://globaledge.msu.edu/countryinsights/links.asp?countryID=60&regionID=2)

http://hdrstats.undp.org/countries/data_sheets/cty_ds_LVA.html

http://latviansonline.com/news/article/1659/

http://latvianstuff.com/Kringel.html

http://news.bbc.co.uk/1/hi/world/europe/country_profiles/1106666.stm

http://query.nytimes.com/gst/fullpage.html?res=9B0CE4DD1F38F93BA35755C0A964948260

http://theenvelope.latimes.com/news/env-et-eichhorn-2008dec23,0,6815594.story

http://www.afs.fi/chapter_images/981_Latvia.pdf

http://www.am.gov.lv/en/news/speeches/2008/September/24-1/

http://www.am.gov.lv/en/policy/4641/4642/Muznieks/

http://www.am.gov.lv/en/policy/guidlines/

http://www.ballet-festival.lv/par_fest_en.html

http://www.classical-composers.org/comp/wihtol

http://www.codefusion.com/latvian/greetings/greetings.html

http://www.cosmopolis.ch/english/music/72/latvian_national_opera_lno.htm

http://www.culturecrossing.net/basics_business_student.php?id=114

http://www.eurofound.europa.eu/eiro/studies/tn0612019s/lv0612019q.htm

http://www.humanrights.org.lv/upload_file/IHF_2006.pdf

http://www.iht.com/articles/2006/11/15/news/latvia.php

http://www.imdb.com/title/tt0471359/

http://www.kultura.lv/en/heritage/20/

http://www.kultura.lv/en/heritage/21/

http://www.kultura.lv/en/heritage/24/

http://www.kultura.lv/en/heritage/30/

http://www.kwintessential.co.uk/etiquette/doing-business-latvia.html

http://www.kwintessential.co.uk/resources/global-etiquette/latvia.html

http://www.languagehelpers.com/words/latvian/addressing.html

http://www.latfilma.lv/index.html

http://www.latfilma.lv/index.html

http://www.latfilma.lv/s/251/index.html

http://www.latvia-newyork.org/english/facts.php

http://www.latvians.com/en/Music/music.php

http://www.li.lv/index.php?Itemid=488&id=38&option=com_content&task=view

http://www.li.lv/index.php?option=com_content&task=view&id=103&Itemid=1136

http://www.li.lv/index.php?option=com_content&task=view&id=41&Itemid=1130

http://www.li.lv/index.php?option=com_content&task=view&id=76&Itemid=42

http://www.li.lv/index.php?option=com_content&task=view&id=76&Itemid=42

http://www.li.lv/index.php?option=com_content&task=view&id=79&Itemid=1133

http://www.li.lv/index.php?option=com_content&task=view&id=79&Itemid=1133

http://www.li.lv/index.php?option=content&task=view&id
=84&Itemid=433

http://www.music.lv/vitols/vitolsENG.htm

http://www.riga.lv/EN/Channels/About_Riga/Riga_
architecture/Art_nouveau/default.htm

http://www.riga.lv/EN/Channels/About_Riga/Riga_
architecture/Old_Riga/default.htm

http://www.riga-life.com/riga/arsenals-film-festival

http://www.riga-life.com/riga/art-nouveau

http://www.riga-life.com/riga/art-nouveau

http://www.state.gov/g/drl/rls/hrrpt/2007/100567.htm

http://www.tageo.com/index-e-lg-cities-LV.htm

http://www.worldheritagesite.org/sites/riga.html

http://www.yfu.lv/yfu/en/page.php?id=latvia

Nicola Williams, Cathryn Kemp, and Debra Herrman,
Lonely Planet Estonia, Latvia, & Lithuania. Victoria:
Lonely Planet Publications. Pequot Press.

Stephen Baister and Chris Patrick. *Latvia (Bradt Travel
Guide)*. Guilford: The Globe

Trakai Castle, Vilnius, Lithuania

LITHUANIA

Introduction

Located on the shore of the Baltic Sea in central Europe, Lithuania traces its history back to the first Indo-European tribes, which settled the area in 2000 BCE and intermarried to become the Balts. The Balts, mentioned in Roman documents of the first century, were early traders in the amber that washes up on the Curonian Spit. Baltic longevity, though, has been tempered by a long history of conflict. Lithuania's strategic location on the Baltic Sea at the geographical center of Europe's great trading and military routes has made the country a temptation for 2,000 years worth of empires.

In 1990, Lithuania became the first of the three Baltic Republics to declare its independence from the Soviet Union. Since 1990, the small republic has restructured itself for integration into Western Europe. Lithuania joined the United Nations in 1991, and joined both the North Atlantic Treaty Organization (NATO) and the European Union in 2004. In 2015, it joined the euro zone.

Since 1990, when it declared independence for the second time, Lithuania has transformed itself into a vibrant economy and a cultural haven. Lithuanian folk art is famous for its carved wooden crosses, suns, weathercocks, and saints that mark village centers, churchyards, and other significant locations. Although banned during Soviet occupation in the 20th century, the carvings remain a characteristic part of the Lithuanian landscape.

GENERAL INFORMATION

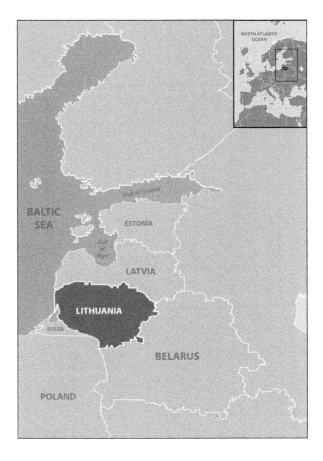

Official Language: Lithuanian
Population: 3,505,738 (2014 estimate)
Currency: Euro (2015)
Coins: The euro coins are divided into eight denominations: 1, 2, 5, 10, 20 and 50 cent, 1 and 2 euro.
Land Area: 62,680 square kilometers (24,200 square miles)
Water Area: 2,620 square kilometers (1,011 square miles)
National Anthem: "Tautiska Giesme" ("The National Song")
Capital: Vilnius
Time Zone: GMT +2
Flag Description: The flag of Lithuania depicts three horizontal bands of color that are equal in size: one yellow, one green, and one red. Each color represents either a national virtue or a physical element related to Lithuania's people and history. Red represents both courage and the blood shed during the nation's struggle for

Principal Cities by Population (2012):

- Vilnius (540,608)
- Kaunas (340,316)
- Klaipeda (179,063)
- Šiauliai (124,534)
- Panevežis (110,901)
- Alytus (65,151)

independence; yellow, the country's wheat fields and the sun; and green represents the ideal of hope and Lithuania's forests.

Population

Lithuania's population is 84.1 percent ethnic Lithuanian, 6.6 percent Polish, 5.8 percent Russian, and 1.2 percent Belarusian. Another 3.5 percent of the population descends from other, mostly European backgrounds. (These numbers are based on a 2011 estimate.)

The capital, Vilnius, is home to about 540,000 people. The city's population density is one of the highest in the country. The Lithuanian urban population consists of 66.5 percent of the total (2014 estimate).

With a low birth rate and ongoing migration from the country, the nation's population is not expected to grow. The cities of Vilnius and Marijampole, in the southern region of Lithuania, retain the country's highest population densities.

Languages

The Lithuanian language, spoken by the majority of the population, has an ancient heritage; it belongs to the same family as Sanskrit, and is of particular interest to comparative linguists because it has changed so little over the centuries. In addition to Lithuanian, which is the country's official language, Polish and Russian are also commonly spoken.

Native People & Ethnic Groups

Ethnic Lithuanians are descended from the Balts, a people who migrated to the shores of the Baltic Sea around 2000 BCE. During the 12th century,

the primary Baltic tribes living in the area that is now Lithuania were the Samogitians in the west and the Aukstaitiai in the east. United under the Catholic King Jogaila during the 14th century, the two tribes found themselves linked to the Polish by the marriage of King Jogaila to the Polish Crown Princess. The royal marriage was the prelude to formal union in the 1569 Treaty of Lublin.

As a result of the longstanding ties to Poland, Lithuania's Baltic culture had a strong Polish influence, particularly among Lithuania's upper classes. After an invasion by Russia's Ivan the Terrible in 1558, however, Lithuania and its Polish counterpart entered into a 450-year course of fighting off Russian, German, and Swedish territorial expansion and cultural influence.

In spite of its troubled political history, or perhaps because of it, Lithuanians are some of the most ethnically homogeneous people in Europe. An estimated 84 percent of the country's current population is native Lithuanian. Minority groups include Poles, Russians, Belarusians, and Ukrainians. Most of the country speaks High Lithuanian, though speakers in the west speak a dialect called Low Lithuanian. The language itself is one of only two surviving branches of the early Baltic languages. A written mention of Lithuanian dating back to 1009 makes it one of the earliest European languages, as well.

The breakdown of languages spoken in the country is 82 percent Lithuanian, 8 percent Russian, 5.6 percent Polish, and 4.4 percent unspecified or other (2011 estimate).

Religions

Lithuania is predominantly Roman Catholic, although the country also has members of Lutheran, Russian Orthodox, Protestant, Evangelical Christian Baptist, Muslim, and Jewish religious faiths. The Romuva movement, based in Vilnius and Kraunas, practices a pagan religion based on current interpretations of early Baltic folk myth and practices.

Climate

Temperatures in Lithuania's moderate climate range from highs of 14° to 22° Celsius (57°

to 72° Fahrenheit) during the late spring and summer months, but rarely rise above 4° Celsius (39° Fahrenheit) between March and November.

Annual precipitation (rain, ice, and snow) is a modest 66 centimeters (26 inches), although averages increase to 90 centimeters (35 inches) in some areas of the uplands and decrease to 52 centimeters (21 inches) in the northern part of the country.

ENVIRONMENT & GEOGRAPHY

Topography
Lithuania is predominantly flat. The Baltic coastline rises to 66 meters (216 feet) along the thin 98-kilometer (61-mile) long Curonian Spit, but otherwise sits just above sea level. Running parallel to the coastline, the Spit creates a sheltered waterway along the Lithuanian shore.

Lithuania's interior includes uplands dotted with small lakes. The hilly uplands are also at relatively low elevations. Lithuania reaches its highest point at Kruopine Hill, which rises to a modest 294 meters (964 feet). The soil is rich and fertile throughout Lithuania. The Neris and the Nemunas Rivers weave their way through the southern portion of the country, meeting at Kaunas.

Nearly one-third of Lithuania is covered in woodlands, although just under a third of that area is young forests.

Plants & Animals
Approximately 30 percent of Lithuania is forested, mostly by pine trees, fir trees, and birch trees. Other tree species include oak, maple, and asp. In 2009, the Kamanos Nature Reserve celebrated the thirtieth anniversary of its founding. The reserve is home to a variety of bird species, including eagles, cranes, wood sandpipers, and golden plovers. Lithuania is also home to a variety of lakes that provide an active ecosystem for wildlife.

Examples of animal species found throughout Lithuania include boar, mink, deer, and beaver. Lithuania is home to a variety of endangered species, including the lynx and over fifteen bird species. All game animals in Lithuania are considered state-owned.

CUSTOMS & COURTESIES

Greetings
In Lithuania, business associates and friends greet one another with a handshake and direct eye contact. Family and young people may greet each other with an embrace. Lithuanians tend to maintain eye contact during greetings despite being physically reserved. Customarily, business associates and acquaintances address one another with title and last name. Lithuanians generally revert to the usage of first names once the relationship has reached a comfortable level of familiarity and trust. Common Lithuanian greetings and phrases include "Labas" ("Hi"), "Labas rytas" ("Good morning"), "Labas vakaras" ("Good evening"), "Sveiki atvyke" ("Welcome"), and "Kaip sekasi?" ("How are you?").

Lithuania has four distinct ethnic subgroups, including the Aukstaiciai (known as the highlanders), who live in the southern and eastern areas of Lithuania; the Dzukai, who live in southeast Lithuania; the Suvalkieciai, who live in south-

Traditional Lithuanian peasant costume.

west Lithuania; and the Zemaiciai (known as lowlanders), who live in western Lithuania. Each of these groups has different social customs and norms that influence greetings and social life in general. For instance, the Dzukai are believed to be the most physically and emotionally expressive Lithuanians, while the Zemaiciai are felt to be the most reserved and traditional. Lithuania's four ethnic groups have distinct accents and dialects that mark and identify their members.

Gestures & Etiquette

Lithuanians tend to be physically reserved and use gestures sparingly. Gestures tend to be culturally specific, and Lithuanians generally limit hand gestures and large physical gestures. Lithuanians tend to believe in folk stories and hold numerous superstitions. The gestures that are used in Lithuania tend to be linked to superstitions. For example, Lithuanians may hold off bad luck by spitting over their shoulder or knocking on a wood surface. In addition, Lithuanian tradition holds that it is unlucky to shake hands in a doorway or eat a meal while sitting at the corner of a table. Lastly, Lithuanians say "no" physically by crossing their forearms into an "X" formation rather than shaking their heads. Taboo gestures include pointing at a person, touching a person while talking, and talking with both hands in pockets.

In Lithuania, etiquette dictates that guests bring a gift of wine, flowers, or sweets when visiting business associates, friends, or family. Chrysanthemum flowers and white flowers are never given as social gifts as they are associated respectively with funerals and weddings. Hosts open and partake of gifts during social occasions.

Eating/Meals

In Lithuania, the social aspects of dining tend to be ritualized and orderly. During family meals, the father generally sits at the head of the table and the eldest son sits to his right. During dinner parties, hosts or heads of household assign seats at the table. In Lithuania, social custom dictates that bread is placed on the dining table before any other food. The father cuts and passes the bread to signal that the meal has begun. Different pieces of the bread (such as the ends and the middle piece) are given to family members based on their age and marital status.

Lithuanians generally eat three meals a day including breakfast, lunch, and dinner. Lithuanians who work on farms or engage in other hard labor may add additional snacks to their daily meals. Breakfast and lunch tend to be the largest meals of the day. Traditional Lithuanian breakfasts include porridge and pancakes, while traditional Lithuanian lunches include soup, meat, and potatoes. Lithuanians generally eat a small evening meal.

Table manners are relaxed and rarely judged. Traditionally, Lithuanians hold their utensils in a continental style with the fork in the left hand and knife in the right hand. Hands are kept above the table throughout the meal. The host or head of household generally offers the first toast. Napkins may be kept on the table. Lithuanians turn their spoons upside down to signal that they are full.

Lithuanians are very welcoming to guests and value hospitality. When a person arrives at a Lithuanian household during a meal, the head of the household usually invites the guest to join the meal. When guests leave a party or social gatherings, hosts generally send a small gift of food home with each guest. Dinner invitations should be reciprocated whenever possible.

Visiting

In Lithuania, guests and visitors are warmly welcomed. Hosts offer their adult guests food and drink, and guests are expected to accept. Guests usually bring a small gift of flowers, sweets, or alcohol. A typical party guest might bring a gift of krupnika (Lithuania's traditional honey liquor). Hosts usually offer their guests a drink of krupnika and toast by saying "I sveikata" ("You're welcome here" or "Cheers").

Traditional occasions for visiting include Kuèios (Christmas Eve) and Velykos (Easter). Family and friends gather on Christmas Eve to eat a special meal called kucia. Traditionally, Lithuanians make a feast table from bales of hay and white tablecloth. The hay represents Jesus' time in the manger and serves as symbolic place for the souls of dead family members to rest during the celebration. Twelve meatless dishes, such as porridge, biscuits with sweet poppy seeds (kučiukai), beet soup, fish, pickled mushrooms, apples, and nuts, are prepared to symbolize the hope for the twelve bountiful months ahead. Holy wafers (dievo pyragai) and Christmas bread are also traditionally always present. Family and friends gather around the abundant meal to light candles. The head of the household will direct each person to a seat. The head of the household will leave one seat empty to symbolize respect for all who died that year.

Families and friend visit one another during the Easter holiday to celebrate rebirth and the promise of a bountiful harvest year. Traditionally, children visit their godparents and neighbors during the afternoon on Easter and receive dyed eggs as gifts. In the late afternoon, family and friends share a traditional Easter feast of baked pig, pig's head, veal, sausage, cheese, and beer. Visitors bring baskets of eggs to dye and eat. The head of the household begins the Easter feast by hitting two eggs together, and the unbroken egg remains uneaten throughout the meal.

LIFESTYLE

Family

Lithuanians value their families and prioritize family obligations above other obligations and responsibilities. More often, Lithuanians look to their family and church for leadership and role models. Lithuanian families tend to include married adults, children, and extended family. Women, including those who work within and outside of the home, are generally responsible for cooking and cleaning chores. Older relatives are traditionally involved in childrearing responsibilities. Lithuanians who live abroad usually send money, clothing, and other forms of support to help struggling Lithuanian family members.

Marriages in Lithuania involve legal registration and elaborate religious ceremonies.

However, marriage rates have been declining in Lithuania following the end of Soviet occupation and the rise in educational opportunities for women.

Housing

Lithuanian architecture reflects the country's political and religious history. For instance, concrete apartment building built for function rather than aesthetics exist in great number, and are a reminder of Soviet-era occupation. Sixteenth-century castles and forts, once the homes of nobility, also remain intact. Traditional wood churches and houses, built by Lithuanians during the 18th and 19th centuries, cover the countryside. Lithuanians who live in urban areas generally keep a small garden outside of the city to grow vegetables to can and pickle for winter consumption. Lithuanians who can afford the option tend to live in rural cottages during the summer months.

Since independence in 1991, Lithuanian housing has undergone vast privatization. At the turn of the century, over 90 percent of Lithuanians owned their own homes and apartments. Modern housing market elements, such as homeowners associations, homeowners insurance, and mortgage programs, are also growing increasingly common in Lithuania.

Food

The cuisine of Lithuania is similar to the cuisines of Eastern Europe, notably Russian, Polish and Ukrainian cuisines. Lithuania has a strong tradition of regional foods and the Lithuanian diet is generally filled with foods that are inexpensive and locally available. The cold weather in Lithuania for much of the year creates shortages of fresh produce, as well as a strong desire for warm and nourishing foods. Staple foods include grains, pork, smoked meats, cabbage, beets, and potatoes. While most Lithuanians eat their meals at home, restaurants are growing increasingly common in Lithuania's major cities.

Lithuania's distinct ethnic groups, including the Aukstaiciai, Zemaiciai, Dzukai, and Suvalkieciai, have distinct food preferences and food options.

For instance, the Aukstaiciai live in an area that is easy to farm. As a result of the bounty produced on grain and dairy farms, the Aukstaiciai favor grain and cheese dishes. The Zemaiciai are known for their sour butter, porridges, and gruels. The Dzukai live in a sandy and forested area of Lithuania. As a result, the Dzukai favor shade-growing foods such as buckwheat, mushrooms, and potatoes. The Suvalkieciai favor long lasting foods such as smoked meats and sausages.

Traditional Lithuanian dishes include kanapiø koðë, šaltibarščiai, cepelinai, kiaulës kojos troðkintos su kopûstais, and pyragas su aguonomis. Kanapiř koďë is hemp porridge prepared with hemp seed, chopped onion, flour, water, and salt. Saltibarščiai is cold beet soup with buttermilk; cepelinai are boiled potato dumplings filled with meat served with fried pork or sour cream. Kiaulës kojos troðkintos su kopûstais are pork feet braised with sauerkraut, and the meal is prepared with pork feet, sauerkraut, potatoes, lard, bay leaves, and sat. Pyragas su aguonomis is poppy seed cake made with flour, milk, eggs, yeast, sugar, poppy seeds, nuts, vanilla, and candied orange peel.

Life's Milestones

As of 2005, nearly 80 percent of Lithuanians identified with Roman Catholicism. As such, the most important Lithuanian life milestones include birth, marriage, and death. There are many rites and rituals surrounding these events. For instance, ceremonial eating and drinking is common at all births, weddings and funerals.

When a baby is born in Lithuania, friends and family traditionally hang a garland of flowers around the doorway of the baby's home. (Garland decorations are also common at birthdays.) Babies are then celebrated and named during a christening ceremony. In addition to birthdays, Lithuanians celebrate name days. Name days are a tradition in much of Europe and Latin America in which people celebrate a day associated with their given name. Name days are typically celebrated with cake, presents, and congratulations.

In Lithuania, marriage marks the beginning of the adult life as well as the union of families.

Matchmakers help families make advantageous marriage matches. At a wedding, guests generally bring pastries, cakes, and drinks as offerings for the bride and groom. After the ceremony, the bride and groom are traditionally offered bread, salt, and drink, and wedding guests are given a piece of the wedding cake to take home.

Lithuanians follow ancient funeral traditions, such as cremation, dating from the 11th century. Most Lithuanian families cremate their dead and bury the ashes. Lithuanians do not generally dread death; instead, death is believed to be a path to a serene and happy afterlife. Lithuanians celebrate their dead family members and the dead are never forgotten. For instance, during celebratory meals, families traditionally put out special plates of food to honor dead family members.

CULTURAL HISTORY

Art

In Lithuania, folk art is made for a variety of purposes, most notably for religious rituals, international sale, and for functional or domestic use. Both fine folk art and applied folk art are a ubiquitous part of Lithuanian culture and daily life. For instance, fine folk art, which includes paintings, graphics, sculptures, small shrines and crosses, adorn and decorate churches and family homes. Lithuanians use applied folk art on a daily basis for cooking, repairs, and religious celebrations. This includes decorative tools and carvings made from wood, metal, clay, and amber. Lithuanian folk art, which is perceived as a symbol of Lithuanian national identity, began to be exhibited internationally during the 19th century.

Lithuania's folk painting tradition dates back to the 18th century. When traditional painting canvases are not available, Lithuanian folk artists paint on boards, tin plates, and linen. Most Lithuanian folk artists are self-taught. Common painting subjects and themes include religious stories, figures, landscapes, and village scenes. Lithuanian folk paintings, many of which depict intricate details of Lithuanian clothing styles or rituals, serve as a record of Lithuania's ethnic culture. Celebrated Lithuanian painters include Monika Bičiunienė (1910–2009) and Elena Kniuškaitė (1950–), among others. Perhaps the most famous Lithuanian painter is modernist Mikalojus Konstantinas Čiurlionis (1875–1911), who painted nearly 300 paintings and had a significant impact on the culture of Lithuania.

The art of etching and fretwork, a type of low relief carving on paper, wood, and metal sheets, dates to ancient times. Religious portraiture is the most common subject for etchings and fretwork. The tradition of wooden sculpture, both religious and secular in theme, dates to the 19th century. Religious subjects include saints and romanticized depictions of Jesus Christ. Secular subjects include folktales, chores, holidays, and battles. Wooden sculptures, which usually stand between 17 and 38 centimeters (7 and 15 inches) high, are common in Lithuanian churches and households. Other folk art traditions include applied woodcarvings (such as spindles and towel holders), religious props (such as carved masks, Easter eggs, and palms) and religious shrines and crosses for home and church. In fact, Lithuanian cross crafting, which is the making of crosses and altars, was recognized by the United Nations Educational, Scientific, and Cultural Organization (UNESCO) as a Masterpiece of the Oral and Intangible Heritage of Humanity.

The Russian occupation changed Lithuania's folk art tradition. During the decades of Soviet occupation, Lithuanians viewed folk art as a reflection and symbol of the truest and best parts of Lithuanian identity and society. During years of Soviet rule, Lithuanian museums and cultural centers collected Lithuanian folk art (particularly textiles such as traditional sashes and weavings, production spinning tool and graphics, and small architectural monuments and paintings) and researched traditional folk practices as a means of preserving Lithuanian traditions.

Throughout the 20th century, folk art, including weaving, woodwork, and sculpture, was sent on exhibit to foreign countries as a means of representing Lithuanian culture as something separate and distinct from Soviet culture. During the decades of Soviet occupation, Lithuanian

artists came together in the planning of exhibits as well as seminars at creativity camps and contests. Under the Soviets, the Lithuanian government offered regional art awards or prizes. The Lithuanian Ministry of Culture offered the most prestigious award for folk artists.

Architecture

The oldest architecture in Lithuania dates back to the 14th century. The country is also home to Gothic-style churches from the 15th century. Lithuania is renowned for its castles, such as Biržai Castle, which was originally constructed in 1589. The Vilnius Cathedral, built in the 18th century, is considered one of the best examples of baroque architecture in Europe. Although several castles in Lithuania exist only in the form of ruins today, others have seen extensive restoration work. Restored castles include Raudone Castle and the Trakai Island Castle.

The years of Soviet control in Lithuania saw the construction of residential structures and state buildings of Stalinist design. Modern Lithuanian architecture has been influenced by Finnish, French, and German designs. Today, Lithuania's capital of Vilnius celebrates the country's architectural traditions; particularly in the section of the city known as the "old town." Vilnius and other Lithuanian cities are also home to contemporary office and residential buildings.

Drama

Theater is an important part of the lives of most Lithuanians. In the 16th century, Lithuanians began attending formal theatrical productions (often performed in French or Polish) at the Rulers' Palace of the Lower Castle. In the early 20th century, plays began to be performed for the first time in the Lithuanian language. Professional theaters, traveling drama troops, and drama schools grew in great number during the 20th century. The theater is credited with helping to maintain Lithuanian national identity during years of Soviet occupation. The cities of Vilnius, Kaunas, Klaipėda, and Panevėžys are the center of Lithuania's theater community. The Lithuanian government sponsors numerous theater companies.

Lithuanians' enjoyment of theater and drama is not limited only to formal productions. Lithuania has a long history of folk dance. Folk dances accompany nearly every religious and secular celebration, including births, weddings, funerals, and harvests. Lithuanian folk dances reflect the nation's history, aesthetics, and morals, and tend to be emotionally restrained. Often performed to simple songs rather than instrumental music, folk dances generally belong to one of four categories: polyphonic singing dances, circle dances, game dances, and paired dances.

Polyphonic singing dances (sutartinių šokiai) are simple dances performed by three or four singing women; an unlimited number of dancers performs circle dances (rateliai); games dances (žaidimai), traditionally performed by youth, involve the completion of a task and are performed to a rhyme; paired dances (šokiai) are performed to instrumental music and improvisation is uncommon.

Music

Lithuania's musical history includes strong folk and classical traditions. Lithuanian folk music includes songs and instrumental pieces, and is traditionally performed during music festivals, celebrations, rituals, and work. Common types of Lithuanian folk song include ritual songs, sutartinės, and raudos (laments or sad songs), as well as marital and war songs. Lithuanians also have songs for different work chores, such as herding, ploughing, hay production, harvesting, milling, washing clothes, and hunting. Instrumental folk music is usually performed to accompany dancing. Common instruments used in Lithuanian folk music include self-sounding instruments such as the dzingulis (bell), terkšlė, and kleketas (rattles), and skrabalai (wooden bells). Drums such as the būgnas and būgnelis, string instruments such as the kanklės (similar to a zither) and puslinė (played with a bow), and wind instruments such as the skudučiai (multi-pipe whistles) and various forms of pipes and flutes are common.

Lithuania's classical music tradition, which dates to the 14th century, is rooted in the church,

and early classical Lithuanian music was written for church organs. During the 20th century, Lithuania's classical music scene grew as Lithuanians worked to develop their own cultural identity distinct from Russia. Well-known Lithuanian composers include the painter Čiurlionis, Juozas Naujalis (1869–1934), and Kazimieras V. Banaitis (1896–1963). Lithuanian classical composers are celebrated for their ability to combine Lithuanian folk elements and Western musical traditions. Jurgis Karnavičius (1884–1941) and Mikas Petrauskas (1873–1937) are credited with developing Lithuanian opera.

Literature

Lithuania's literary history dates to the Middle Ages when Lithuanian scholars wrote religious and historical chronicles in Latin and Polish. Beginning in the 16th century, Lithuanians began to write poetry, fiction, and religious texts in the Lithuanian language. During this period, the Bible was translated into Lithuanian and the first Lithuanian language dictionary appeared. In the 18th century, secular literature, including *Ezopo Pasakecios* (Aesop's Fables), grew in popularity.

Lithuania's modern literary tradition is strongly associated with the nation's political struggles during World Wars I and II and years of Soviet occupation. Lithuanian writers explored the country's experiences in genres such as national romanticism, symbolism, and existentialism. Writers faced tough political choices regarding whether to continue with their art or change their art to accommodate the political climate of the day. As a result, many Lithuanian writers left Lithuania during the 20th century to escape the environment created by Soviet occupation.

Popular Lithuanian writers include Balys Sruoga (1896–1947), Marius Katiliskis (1914–1980) and Bronius Radzevicius (1940–1980). Lithuanian poetry, with its many descriptions of Lithuanian traditions, character, and culture, is also credited with preserving Lithuania's national culture. Famous Lithuanian poets include Adam Mickiewicz (1798–1855), Juliusz Słowacki (1809–1849), Oscar Milosz (1877–1939), and Jurgis Baltrušaitis (1873–1944).

CULTURE

Arts & Entertainment

Lithuania only recently became a sovereign nation. The Soviet Union occupied and controlled Lithuania off and on from 1940 to 1991, and the arts have played a large role in reshaping and forging Lithuania's sovereign identity. In particular, the arts in Lithuania have been used widely as a vehicle for keeping Lithuanian culture alive during times of oppression and occupation. The arts also spurred the Lithuanian national identity and independence movement. Thus, the role of the contemporary arts (particularly folk art) is a reflection of the country's 21st-century culture, traditions, collective experience, and social consciousness.

However, the role of the arts is changing in newly independent and sovereign Lithuania. The arts do not have to carry the responsibility of keeping Lithuanian culture alive as they did during times of Soviet oppression. Lithuanian artists are now free to explore new artistic techniques, sensibilities, and aesthetics. The Lithuanian People's Art Society and the Union of Lithuanian Folk Artists (ULFA) have worked to unite Lithuanian folk artists. ULFA has six regional offices that offer opportunities for exhibiting and training in weaving, sculpture, woodworking, graphics, painting, ceramics, metalwork, jewelry, and other traditional arts. The arts in Lithuania receive limiting funding from the government, and the majority of artists are self-supporting. Lithuanian artists often travel to foreign countries for artistic study or opportunities such as fellowships or residencies.

Folk music has become an essential part of Lithuanian ethnic identity. Every four years, choirs and folk dance groups gather from all over the globe for the World Lithuanian Song Festival, held in July. Folk music is broken into groupings that indicate a song's purpose, including songs for mourning, celebration, work, or religious occasions. Traditional instruments include the daudyté, a wooden trumpet, the stringed kanklés, the skrabalai, small wooden bells, and wooden panpipes called the skuduèiai. Women usually perform the folk dances, although polkas and waltzes include both men and women.

Lithuania's troubled history has produced a tradition of emigrants, who have sent back cultural traditions and styles from throughout the world. Modern jazz has found its way into the heart of Lithuanian culture, producing world-renowned artists and the International Jazz Festival in Kaunas every April.

An anomaly amongst its European neighbors, Lithuania is famous for its basketball players. Lithuanian legend Steponas Darius (1896–1933) introduced the game after a trip to the United States in the 1920s. Since then, the game has become a focal point in the government's efforts to promote athletics and physical activity for the health of its population. Basketball clubs thrive throughout the country along with football (soccer), bodybuilding, track and field, boxing, weightlifting, judo, volleyball, rowing, wrestling, cycling, sailing, swimming, and tennis.

Cultural Sites & Landmarks

In 2009, the capital of Vilnius was named the European Capital of Culture. The city is home to many of Lithuania's cultural sites and features a diverse range of architecture—including Gothic, Renaissance, baroque, and classical. Popular landmarks include the Presidential Palace, the Vilnius Castle Complex, and numerous museums and religious monuments and churches that date back to the early Middle Ages. Originally constructed as a medieval town, the capital's historic section, Vilnius Old Town, was designated as a World Heritage Site by UNESCO. Three other sites in Lithuania are included on the World Heritage List as requiring international recognition and preservation efforts. They are the Curonian Spit, the Kernavè Archaeological Site (Cultural Reserve of Kernavè), and the Struve Geodetic Arc.

The Curonian Spit is natural landscape of sand dunes. (A spit is a coastal land formation.) Humans have occupied the Curonian Spit since prehistoric times. Lithuanians have been working to stabilize and restore the sandy dunes since the 19th century. The dunes and pine forests are home to elk, deer, and wild boar. The Kernavė Archaeological Site (Cultural Reserve of Kernavė), located in Eastern Lithuania, is a collection of important early human archaeological sites, including the town of Kernavė, forts, unfortified settlements, and burial sites dating from the late Paleolithic period to the Middle Ages. Researchers and tourists alike visit the archaeological site to learn about ancient land use, fortification strategies (such as hill forts), and Pagan and Christian funeral traditions.

The Struve Geodetic Arc is part of a 19th-century land survey project that stretches through ten countries. The survey, which reflects the first accurate measurement of a meridian or line or longitude, is an important early achievement in the field of earth science. The Struve Geodetic Arc helped 19th-century scientists collaborate and establish the exact size and shape of the earth. The Lithuanian station point, one of thirty-four in the whole survey, is marked with a commemorative statue.

Libraries & Museums

Lithuania is home to a large number of museums, ranging from large national museums to local historical museums and art galleries. The Ministry of Culture oversees national museums, including the Vilnius Picture Gallery, the Museum of Applied Art, and Radvila Palace. Lithuania's National Gallery of Art in Vilnius houses the world's largest collection of native Lithuanian works from the 20th and 21st centuries. The museum was renovated and expanded in 2009.

The Martynas Mažvydas National Library of Lithuania (NLL), originally built in 1919, is located in Vilnius. In 2006, the library was home to a collection of nearly 7 million items. In 2009, the NLL marked its 90th anniversary by renovating its main building. The library has published a monthly periodical, entitled *In the World of Books*, since 1949.

Holidays

Lithuania celebrates New Year's Day, Christmas, Christmas Eve, Easter, and All Saints Day. On Defenders of Freedom Day (January 13), Lithuanians honor the demonstrators killed by Soviet troops in 1991 when Lithuania declared its independence from the Soviet Union. The country's troubled history is further reflected in its two independence days. Independence Day (February 16) commemorates the 1918 Declaration of Independence. March 11 marks the restoration of Lithuania's statehood in 1990.

On the Day of Mourning and Hope (June 14), Lithuanians remember the first mass deportation to Siberia under Stalin in 1941. Mindaugus, first King of Lithuania, is honored on the Day of Statehood (July 6). Black Ribbon Day commemorates the 1939 Russian-Nazi pact that prompted the invasion of Lithuania at the beginning of World War II, and the Day of Nation honors Vytautus the Great, the 15th-century king who ruled during Lithuania's golden age.

Youth Culture

Lithuanians value high levels of education and the country's high literacy rate—99.7 percent in 2008—reflects Lithuania's commitment to education. The majority of Lithuanians complete twelve years of education and then attend university or vocational schools. Lithuanian youth are also encouraged to pursue music or art lessons and more teenagers and young adults are studying abroad in increasingly large numbers. In general, young Lithuanian women tend to study education while young Lithuanian men study computing and technology and business.

Lithuanian youth typically follow the popular fashion and music trends of Europe, though for many, personal or unique clothing styles are not generally encouraged. While most films are foreign releases, Lithuanian cinema is growing in scope and popularity, and attending the cinema is a popular pastime for Lithuanian youth. Basketball is Lithuania's most popular sport and a popular recreational activity for teens and adults alike. When not engaged in sports, art lessons or schooling, Lithuanian youth are expected to stay close to home and help with younger siblings and household chores.

SOCIETY

Transportation

After Lithuania achieved independence in 1991, the number of privately owned cars in the country grew exponentially—from an estimated 510,000 to over three million by 2003. The capital of Vilnius and many other major cities have well-developed systems of public transportation, including what is considered one of the most extensive trolleybus network in Europe in Vilnius. Rail, bus, and taxi service are common modes of transportation domestically, and hitchhiking is allowed. Traffic moves on the right-hand side of the road.

Transportation Infrastructure

As of 2013, Lithuania's transportation system included nearly sixty airports, 1,767 kilometers (1,100 miles) of railway, 441 kilometers (274 miles) of waterway, and 84,166 kilometers (52,195 miles) of roadway. The majority of roads and airports are paved. There are major domestic airports in the cities of Palanga and Vilnius. Two international airlines, Lithuanian Airlines and Lietuva, fly in and out of the Kaunas International Airport in Kaunas. Commercial air travel flies through the one commercial airport in Siauliai. Klaipeda, with ferry connections to Sweden and Germany, is Lithuania's only seaport and terminal. The port town of Klaipeda has maritime connections to over 200 foreign ports and major cities such as Vilnius and Kaunas have rail access to the Baltic Sea.

Media & Communications

Lithuania's media and communication systems have grown significantly since Soviet occupation ended in 1991. This new era of political independence has created technological and creative opportunities, allowing the free press to grow in number and quality. Daily newspapers include *Lietuvos Rytas* (Lithuania's Morning), *Respubliká*, *Lietuvos Aidas* (The Echo of Lithuania) and *Kauno Diena* (Kaunas Daily). The Lithuanian constitution guarantees and protects free speech and press.

Lithuania's telephone system, which included 667,300 landlines and five million mobile phones in 2012, is considered adequate by international standards. The Lithuanian government, along with private companies, is working to improve international and residential coverage. Radio, television, and Internet are popular sources of entertainment and connection. In 2010, there were and estimated 2.1 million Internet users. The Lithuanian National Radio and Television (LRT) controls most broadcasting.

SOCIAL DEVELOPMENT

Standard of Living

Lithuania ranks 35th out of 187 countries on the 2013 United Nations Human Development Index, which measures quality of life and standard of living indicators.

Life expectancy in Lithuania is about 76 years at birth—71.2 for men and 82.02 for women (2014 estimate). Infant mortality is low at approximately six deaths per 1,000 live births.

Water Consumption

Clean drinking water is sufficiently available throughout Lithuania, the majority of which is obtained from groundwater sources. However, Lithuania faces challenges related to updating its water treatment and delivery infrastructure. In 2004, an estimated one million Lithuanians received water from wells instead of the country's public drinking water system—though that situation has improved since then. As of 2012, 95.9 percent of the population received clean drinking water from improved sources. As for unimproved, 4.1 percent obtained their water from these sources.

Education

Lithuania's educational system requires all students to attend school from ages six to 16 years of age. Kindergarten programs for four and five year olds are available. Under the national system, elementary school lasts for four years, until age 10, followed by basic (middle) school until age 14, and senior secondary school until 18 years old.

During secondary school, students may study either at traditional academic institutions (gimnajiza) or at one of the technical, vocational, or training institutes. An estimated 40 percent of students who receive their Secondary School Certificates continue on to higher education.

Lithuania has fifteen universities and twenty-nine research institutions. Vilnius Saint Joseph Seminary is the country's only Catholic institution. Private programs, usually run through the universities, offer adult education classes.

Public education in Lithuania is free through the secondary programs. University students must pay fees, but scholarships and bursaries are available. The government subsidizes the universities.

Almost all education in Lithuania is conducted in the Lithuanian language. However, a select number of schools also teach in Polish or Russian. Lithuania's 2000 census estimated the country's literacy rate to be over 99 percent among both males and females; a 2015 estimate rated literacy at 99.8 percent.

Women's Rights

The role and treatment of women in Lithuanian society, culture, and political life has changed significantly since Lithuania declared independence in 1991. The transition to a market economy has begun to change perceptions of gender roles, family structures, and opportunities for women in the workplace. The Division for the Advancement of Women by the Government developed the following objectives to advance the place of women in Lithuanian society: achieve the society's comprehension that rights of women are universal human rights, develop laws that guarantee equal rights and opportunities for men and women, and achieve equal rights for women and men in the society and family.

Women's rights have remained a national concern and focus in Lithuania since that time. For example, the Lithuanian government's 1996 "Action Plan of Advancement of Women of Lithuania" initiated a national discussion on women's rights. The document made the fol-

lowing assertions about the place of women in Lithuanian society in the mid 1990s: Lithuanian society does not perceive women's rights as human rights; a gap exists between opportunities for men and women to participate in economic activities; the Lithuanian society is indifferent to the health problems of women and children; enrollment discrimination in higher education schools persists; and women's participation in politics and public administration is low.

Despite gains in status and opportunity for women since the introduction of the 1996 initiative, Lithuanian women continue to experience widespread domestic violence. Lithuanian law does not criminalize domestic violence and few domestic violence complaints reach the courts. Prostitution and trafficking in women for the purpose of sexual exploitation are also growing problems in Lithuania. They country is designated as a source, transit, and destination for the trafficking of women and girls. Approximately 39 abuse shelters operate in Lithuania and assist victims of domestic violence, forced prostitution, and human trafficking.

Sexual harassment is illegal under Lithuanian law. However, a fear of reprisal or publicity prevents many women from filing harassment claims. Additionally, while Lithuanian women have the same legal rights as men as described under family and property law, women are usually paid less than male counterparts are. On average, women receive 84 percent of the wages that men earn and experience unequal working conditions. There are a number of women's rights groups and non-governmental organizations (NGOs) working to improve the status of women in Lithuania. Ultimately, the role and treatment of Lithuanian women in society, culture, and political life is changing and improving in Lithuania because of new government equal-rights policy, advocacy by women's rights organizations, and a growing number of women elected to parliament.

Observers estimate that 40 percent of identified Lithuanian trafficking victims are women and girls subjected to sex trafficking within the country. Although the government had no official interagency anti-trafficking working group in 2013, the General Prosecutor's office launched its own interagency working group in February 2014.

Health Care

Until Lithuania attained its independence in 1990, health care was provided through the Soviet Union's centralized health system. In the years immediately following independence, illness and disease rates rose in the country as government officials strove to replace the old Soviet system.

At present, Lithuania has a mandatory health insurance system, which provides care for most medical and some psychological and psychiatric conditions. Lithuania's Ministry of Health has also prioritized preventative programs, including educational programs targeting the spread of HIV/AIDS through sexual contact, and policies promoting physical activity and nutrition to fight heart disease, obesity, and depression. The government has also been working to reduce tobacco and alcohol consumption in the country.

In addition to these health concerns, Lithuania is contending with the increased costs of an aging population—Lithuania's median age is almost 38—and the long term health effects of the 1986 Chernobyl nuclear disaster in neighboring Belarus.

GOVERNMENT

Structure

Although Lithuania has been a distinct political state since at least the 14th century, the modern Lithuanian nation first gained its independence on November 11, 1918, when its German occupiers surrendered at the end of World War I. The Lithuanian Republic that was established on that day immediately came under attack. Polish troops invaded Vilnius in 1919, taking the capital. In 1920, the Russian government recognized Lithuanian independence for the first time, but a military coup in 1926 left the country under a fascist-style military rule.

On August 23, 1939, the Russian government signed a non-aggression treaty known as the Molotov-Ribbentrop Pact, in which Lithuania was parceled out to Nazi Germany. Lithuania's refusal to participate in the invasion of Poland prompted Nazi and Soviet leaders to move Lithuania to the Soviet sphere of influence. Lithuania became a Soviet republic soon afterward, but was invaded by the Nazis a year later. Almost all of Lithuania's native Jewish population was murdered between 1941 and 1944, when the Soviet Red Army invaded again.

Lithuania remained part of the Soviet Union until 1990. Defying a Soviet government under Mikhail Gorbachev, Lithuania became the first Eastern European country to legalize non-communist political parties. Thirteen Lithuanian protestors died when the Soviet military stormed key public buildings in Vilnius. With the August 1991 coup against Gorbachev, Lithuania seized its independence. The Soviet government formally recognized the independent Lithuanian Republic one month later. Ten days after that, Lithuania became a member of the United Nations.

The Republic of Lithuania is run as a parliamentary democracy. Lithuanians elect their president by popular vote for a five-year term in office. The president chooses a premier with approval from Parliament.

The Parliament, or Seimas, has 141 members, 71 of whom are elected by direct popular vote and seven of whom are elected by proportional representation. All Seimas members serve four-year terms.

Political Parties

Lithuania has a multi-party, coalition government. The country's major parties include the Social Democratic Party (LSDP), the Homeland Union-Lithuanian Christian Democrats (TS-LKD), and the Labor Party (DP). In legislative elections held in 2012, the results, by number of parliamentary seats won, were as follows: LSDP, 38; TS-LKD, 33; DP, 29; Order and Justice Party (TT): 11; all others, 19.

Local Government

Lithuania is divided into ten districts (known as "apskritys"), urban settlements, and district towns. The country's 10 districts are subdivided into 60 municipal councils known as "savivaldybes." Individuals are elected to municipal councils by the public via secret ballot for two terms of two years. The Association of Local Authorities in Lithuania is a non-profit, non-governmental group that represents the interests of local government at the federal level.

Judicial System

Lithuania's judicial system consists of four levels of courts. A fifth court, the Constitutional Court of the Republic of Lithuania, can overturn or nullify legal decisions made by other courts. However, it is not considered part of Lithuania's general judicial system. Judges who sit on the Constitutional Court are appointed to nine-year terms by Parliament, which chooses from a selection of nine nominees named by the president, the chairperson of Parliament, and the chairperson of the Supreme Court. The Supreme Court and the Court of Appeal are the two main federal courts in Lithuania. County courts and district courts adjudicate at the municipal level.

Taxation

Lithuanians pay a flat income tax, which in 2009 was set at 15 percent. Individual taxpayers in Lithuania pay a variable tax for health insurance coverage. Businesses in the country also play a standard corporate income tax rate. Other taxes collected include capital gains taxes, taxes on interest, and taxes on patent royalties.

Armed Forces

The Lithuanian Armed Forces consists of five branches, including a land force, naval force, and air force, as well as a volunteers forces and a special operations force. The Ministry of Defence has established bilateral military cooperation with most European Union and NATO members. As of 2010, career military personnel in the armed forces numbered 7,800.

Foreign Policy

Throughout the 20th century, Lithuania struggled to protect its citizens and become a sovereign nation. For the most part, the Soviet Union occupied and controlled Lithuania from 1940 to 1991. In particular, German and Soviet occupations killed over 780,000 Lithuanians between 1940 and 1954. In 1991, Lithuania declared its national independence and joined the United Nations (UN). In 2004, Lithuania joined the North Atlantic Treaty Organization (NATO) and the European Union (EU). In addition, Lithuania is also a member of the Organization for Security and Cooperation in Europe (OSCE), and the Council of Europe (which works for European integration). The EU and the United States are committed to helping Lithuania restructure and transition to a market economy.

Today, Lithuania is a strong ally to European nations (particularly Poland) and the U.S., and is a strong supporter of democracy worldwide. A U.S.-Lithuanian diplomatic relationship was established in 1922. Despite pressure from Russia from 1940 through 1991, the U.S. refused to recognize Russia's occupation and seizure of Lithuania. In 2008, Lithuania joined a visa waiver program allowing Lithuanians to travel to the US for short visits without a visa. Lithuania also contributes military support to NATO's International Security Assistance Force (ISAF) in Afghanistan and Iraq, and contributes support to peacekeeping efforts in Bosnia and Kosovo. In addition, Lithuania provides development aid and democratic council to the Ukraine, Moldova, and Georgia.

Lithuania's government pursues economic reform to strengthen Lithuania's slow-growing economy. Lithuania is engaged in active trade relationships with most of its Central and Eastern European neighbors. Lithuania's main trading partners include Russia, Latvia, Germany, Poland, Estonia, the United Kingdom (UK), Denmark, Belarus, and the Netherlands. Lithuania, along with other small European countries, also actively works to protect Eastern Europe from Russian expansion. Lithuania encourages the EU to admit Eastern European states, and promotes Eastern Europe's political and economic engagement worldwide.

Lithuania is party to international environmental agreements on air pollution, air pollution-nitrogen oxides, air pollution-persistent organic pollutants, biodiversity, climate change, climate change, endangered species, hazardous wastes, law of the sea, ozone layer protection, ship pollution, and wetlands. The Lithuanian government is also working to end Lithuania's reputation for being a destination point for drugs from Asia, Latin America, Western Europe, and the Baltic countries.

Human Rights Profile

International human rights law insists that states respect civil and political rights, and promote an individual's economic, social, and cultural rights. The United Nations Universal Declaration on Human Rights (UDHR) is recognized as the standard for international human rights. Its authors sought the counsel of the world's great thinkers, philosophers, and religious leaders, and were careful to create a document that reflects the core values shared by every world culture. (To read this document or view the articles relating to cultural human rights, visit http://www.un.org/en/documents/udhr/.)

Lithuania's constitution protects many of the same human rights guaranteed under the UDHR. For instance, Article 2, which states that everyone is entitled to legal rights and freedoms without distinction of race, color, sex, language, religion, political or other opinion, national or social origin, property, birth or other status, is supported by the Lithuanian constitution. Lithuanian law also prohibits discrimination based on age, disability, race, ethnicity, and religious belief. However, discrimination against women and minorities is widespread. Additionally, acts of anti-Semitism, including vandalism of Jewish graves and monuments, displays of neo-Nazi sentiment, and public anti-Semitic comments have been common.

Other human rights abuses and concerns occur to a lesser degree, including the requirement that at least one individual in an official marriage have Lithuanian citizenship, residency or ancestry. Moreover, while the Lithuanian constitution guarantees the right to the free practice of religion, the Lithuanian government grants special benefits and exemptions to state-recognized traditional religious communities. In addition, though individuals are allowed to criticize the government without reprisal, libel is punishable by fine or imprisonment. Prison conditions also remain a concern, as does the mistreatment of convicted and detained persons. Nonetheless, the Lithuanian human rights policy is based on the notion that social, moral, economic, and cultural rights are interrelated and equally important, and in general, Lithuanians value social, moral, economic, and cultural equality, opportunity, and openness for their own citizens and those abroad.

ECONOMY

Overview of the Economy

In the aftermath of the 1998 Russian economic crisis, Lithuania joined the World Trade Organization and the European Union, and the economy has shown promising signs of growth. In 2014, Lithuania's gross domestic product (GDP) was estimated at nearly $79 billion (USD). The per capita GDP was estimated at $26,700 (USD).

After Lithuania declared its independence, the capital of Vilnius experienced a period of economic decline, but is now one of the region's most vital and modern economies. About one third of the country's GDP is generated in Vilnius County. The fastest growing part of Vilnius's economy is the service sector, which encompasses industries such as food, tourism, transportation, information technology and communications, health care, and real estate.

Industry

Lithuania's largest industries include petroleum refining, shipbuilding, furniture production, textile manufacturing, and food processing. Important manufactured products include agricultural machinery, electronic components, electric motors, television sets, refrigerators and freezers, and fertilizers.

Labor

In 2012, an estimated 72.5 percent of Lithuanian's were employed by the country's service sector. Just over 19 percent were employed by the country's industrial sector and less than 8 percent were employed in agriculture. Unemployment has gone down from 11.8 percent in 2013 to 11.1 percent in 2014. The Lithuanian Labour Exchange, overseen by the Ministry of Social Security and Labour, operates employment offices throughout the country. Although Lithuania struggled with widespread unemployment throughout the 1990s, its move to a free-market economy and acceptance into the European Union in 2004 resulted in an improved labor market.

Energy/Power/Natural Resources

Although modestly sized oil reserves have been found in western Lithuania, they remain relatively underdeveloped. The country's largest supplier of electricity in Lithuania through out the 1980s and 1990s was the Ignalina Nuclear Power Plant. However, the plant was decommissioned and shut down in 2009. Following the closing of the Ignalina plant, there have been discussions between Lithuanian officials and officials from Poland, Latvia, and Estonia about constructing a new nuclear power facility.

Lithuania has extensive sources of geothermal energy, particularly near its border with the Baltic Sea. Further development of the country's geothermal energy sources is a significant part of its National Energy Strategy. Approximately five percent of the country's energy comes from hydroelectricity generated from the Nemunas and Neris rivers.

Fishing

In 2005, there were 271 registered vessels in Lithuania's fishing industry. Lithuanian fishing companies harvest mackerel, cod, herring, redfish, and shrimp from the Baltic Sea. The Ministry of Agriculture regulates the country's fishing industry. The European Union provided 12 million Euros of funding in 2004 to help modernize Lithuania's fishing industry.

Forestry

Lithuania's forestry sector, which operates on approximately 35 percent of the country's total forest area, is privately owned. Forest products include logs, pulpwood, board wood, and firewood. Beginning in 2007, efforts to increase revenues from recreational opportunities and non-timber forest products, such as mushrooms and berries, have been initiated by forest owners.

Mining/Metals

Lithuania is home to moderate supplies of clay, limestone, sand, and dolomite. Large supplies of iron ore have been uncovered in southern Lithuania. Efforts to further investigate and develop the country's mineral resources in ways that can be economically beneficial while remaining safe for the environment and regional ecosystems continue. By 2008, mining and quarrying represented about a half a percent of Lithuania's gross economic activity.

Agriculture

Agriculture accounts for about six percent of Lithuania's gross domestic product (GDP), employing about 20 percent of the workforce. The mineral rich soil of the Baltic lowlands provides fertile ground for the harvesting of grain, potatoes, sugar beets, flax, and vegetables. Lithuanian farms also produce significant quantities of beef, milk, and eggs. In coastal waters of the Baltic, fishing remains an important industry.

Animal Husbandry

Small livestock farms are more common in Lithuania. Common livestock breed include poultry, cattle, and pigs, and to a lesser extent, sheep.

Tourism

Lithuania's tourist industry remains small and generally limited to visitors from neighboring countries. Government proposals to boost tourism through the improvement of transportation to and within the country are underway. Since 2010, the amount of tourists visiting Lithuania has increased from approximately 1.5 to just over 2 million people.

Simone Isadora Flynn, Amy Witherbee, M. Lee

DO YOU KNOW?

- Founded by Jesuits in 1579, Vilnius University is the oldest higher learning institution in the Baltic region, and was at the center of Europe's counter-reformation movement.

- Women attained full political rights in Lithuania in 1918, two years before women in the United States won the right to vote. A woman served as the chair of the first Lithuanian Parliament in 1920.

- The geographic center of Europe is located in Lithuania at a spot on the road between Vilnius and Moletai.

- Lithuania is home to the Hill of Crosses, a pilgrimage site that, as of 2006, had over 100,000 crosses placed upon it. The hill was also a symbolic venue of peaceful resistance during Soviet occupation.

Bibliography

Aldis Purs. *Baltic Facades: Estonia, Latvia, and Lithuania since 1945.* London: Reaktion Books, 2012.

GediminasLankauskas. *The Land of Weddings and Rain: Nation and Modernity in Post-Socialist Lithuania.* Toronto: University of Toronto Press, 2015.

Gordon McLachlan. *Lithuania.* London: Bradt Travel Guides, 2008.

Ida Harboe Knudsen. *New Lithuania in Old Hands: Effects and Outcomes of Europeanization in Rural Lithuania.* London: Anthem Press, 2012.

Lonely Planet and Brandon Presser. *Estonia, Latvia, and Lithuania.* Oakland, CA: Lonely Planet, 2012.

Works Cited

"A Country Study: Lithuania." *Library of Congress Country Studies.* http://lcweb2.loc.gov/frd/cs/lttoc.html.

"About Us." *Lithuanian Folk Artists' Society* (n.d.). http://www.lietuvostautodaile.lt/index.php?option=com_content&task=view&id=103&Itemid=50.

"Action Plan of Advancement of Women of Lithuania." *Division for the Advancement of Women by the Lithuanian Government, Resolution No. 1299* (1996). http://www.un.org/esa/gopher-data/conf/fwcw/natrep/NatActPlans/lithuani/lithua1.

"Lithuania." *CIA World Fact Book.* https://www.cia.gov/library/publications/the-world-factbook/print/lh.html.

"Lithuania." *U.S. Department of State.* http://www.state.gov/r/pa/ei/bgn/5379.htm.

"Lithuania." *UNESCO World Heritage List.* http://whc.unesco.org/en/statesparties/lt.

"Lithuania." World Atlas. http://www.worldatlas.com/webimage/countrys/europe/lt.htm.

"Lithuania: Country Reports on Human Rights Practices." *U.S. Department of State.* http://www.state.gov/g/drl/rls/hrrpt/2006/78824.htm.

"Lithuania: Language, Culture, Customs, and Etiquette." *Kwintessential Cross Cultural Solutions.* http://www.kwintessential.co.uk/resources/global-etiquette/lithuania.html.

"Lithuania: The Country and the Nation." *Randburg.* http://www.randburg.com/li/general/index.asp.

"Lithuanian Phrases." *Linguanaut.* http://www.linguanaut.com/english_lithuanian.htm.

"Population Estimates for Cities in Lithuania." *Mongabay.* http://www.mongabay.com/igapo/2005_world_city_populations/Lithuania.html.

"Universal Declaration of Human Rights." *United Nations.* http://www.un.org/en/documents/udhr/.

Birutë Imbrasienë. "Lithuanian Traditional Foods." *Vilnius, Lithuania: Baltos Lankos Publishers* (1998). http://ausis.gf.vu.lt/eka/food/fcont.html.

Elena Počiulpaitė, "Fine Arts" (n.d.). http://ausis.gf.vu.lt/eka/art/art_c.html.

Eugenija Venskauskaitė, "Dances" (n.d.). http://ausis.gf.vu.lt/eka/dances/dancec.html.

Vytas Nakas. "The Music of Lithuania — A Historical Sketch." *Lituanus: Lithuanian Quarterly Journal Of Arts And Sciences* 20.4 (1974). http://Www.Lituanus.Org/1974/74_4_06.Htm.

MACEDONIA

Introduction

Cradled in the Balkan Mountains between the countries of the Adriatic Sea and the Aegean, modern Macedonia owes its existence to the volatile histories of its neighbors. Though Macedonia did not emerge as a nation-state until 1991, Macedonians trace their history as far back as the ninth century BCE. Since that era, the legend of Macedonia has survived primarily as a region, absorbed, fought over, and divided up among neighboring empires and nations. Macedonia declared its independence from Yugoslavia on September 8, 1991.

Although Macedonia became an EU candidate in 2005, the country still faces challenges, including fully implementing an agreement regarding its ethnic Albanian population, resolving a name dispute with Greece, improving relations with Bulgaria, stimulating economic growth and development, bolstering the independence of the judiciary, and supporting media freedom. Macedonia's membership in NATO was blocked by Greece at the Alliance's Summit of Bucharest in 2008.

Traditional art in Macedonia comes from the Slavic cultures that settled in the area centuries ago. Most of this tradition remains in the form of metalwork, literature, religious music, woodcarving, frescoes, and imagery that came out of Macedonia's Byzantine culture during the medieval era. Macedonians also trace their language and literary tradition to the ninth-century saints Cyril and Methodius who, according to medieval church records, developed the written Cyrillic alphabet used by modern Macedonians from their monastery in Ohrid. Today, Macedonian nationalism relies heavily on its literary tradition. During a cultural rebirth in the 1940s, a modern Macedonian written tradition began based on a break from the work of older authors.

GENERAL INFORMATION

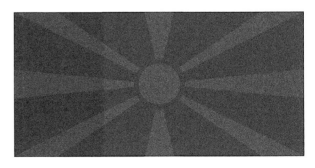

Official Language: Macedonian
Population: 2,091,719 (2014 estimate)
Currency: Macedonian denar
Coins: The Macedonian denar is divided into 100 deni; coins are available in denominations of 50 deni and 1, 2, 5, 10, and 50 denari.
Land Area: 25,433 square kilometers (9,819 square miles)

Principal Cities by Population (2012):

- Skopje (486,596)
- Kumanovo (118,750)
- Bitola (84,867)
- Tetovo (76,895)
- Prilep (73,743)
- Veles (57,615)
- Ohrid (55,258)
- Gostivar (53,675)

Water Area: 280 square kilometers (108 square miles)

National Anthem: "Desnes nad Makedonija se ragja" ("Today over Macedonia")

Capital: Skopje

Time Zone: GMT +1

Flag Description: The flag of Macedonia features a yellow sun against a red background. The sun, known as "the new sun of liberty," is located in the center of the flag, with eight stylized rays emitting from it.

Population

The Republic of Macedonia is carved out of a region known for its diversity of cultures, ethnicities, and histories. Modern Macedonians generally claim a Slavic ancestry.

Today, a little more than 64 percent of the population in the Republic consider themselves to be Macedonian. Almost two percent call themselves Serbian, a related Slavic-based ethnic group that is associated with the adjacent country of Serbia. About four percent of the population identifies as Turkish, three percent as Roma (formerly called Gypsies), and a variety of other minority cultures reflect the area's historic association with the Ottoman Empire and Europe-Asia trading. However, the second most important ethnic group in contemporary Macedonia is Albanian, estimated at a little more than 25 percent of the Republic's current population.

During the late 1990s, the federation of Slavic states known as Yugoslavia crumbled amid multiple outbreaks of civil and ethnic violence. Macedonia peacefully withdrew from the Yugoslav Federation in 1991, but the massacre of Albanian citizens in neighboring Serbia created a wave of refugees into surrounding countries, including the newly independent Macedonia.

With careful policy realignments and cooperation from the United Nations, Macedonia has managed thus far to avoid the civil violence that plagues its neighbors. The rapid immigration into Macedonia, however, strained government infrastructure in the young republic.

Skopje is the capital and largest city of Macedonia; of the roughly 501,000 (2014) people who live in Skopje in the early 21st century, nearly 70 percent are Macedonian; Albanians are the next largest group, accounting for 20 percent of the population. Other ethnic groups include Roma, Serbs and, to a lesser extent, Turks, Bosniaks, and Aromanians. Approximately 67 percent of the population resides in urban areas. As of 2014, the country had a positive population growth rate of 0.21 percent.

Languages

The official language of Macedonia is Macedonian (64.2 percent), unique to the country, though the Albanian (25.2 percent) and Serb-Croatian languages (about 9.5 percent) are also spoken.

Native People & Ethnic Groups

Archeologists trace civilization in Macedonia back to the Paleolithic era, around 6000 BCE. However, the area has never been isolated. Operating as a crossroads between Western, Central, and Southern Europe, Macedonia is characterized by the constant modification of its culture.

In the sixth and seventh century, tribes of Slavic peoples migrating from the Carpathian Mountains and the Danube River Basin invaded Macedonia and other Balkan lands of the Byzantine Empire. As the invaders settled in the area, many integrated their Slavic identities with existing Macedonian culture. Combining Slavic traditions, language, alphabet, and religious structures with those of the Macedonians, the offspring of these invaders eventually recreated the culture of the Macedonian region while retaining the old Macedonian legends and history.

Modern ethnic Macedonians consider themselves to be the natural inheritors of the area's rich blend of traditions, but Albanians, Serbs, Bulgarians, and others also lay claim to the area.

Religions

The country's ethnic Macedonian population traditionally practices Macedonian Orthodox Christianity, and nearly 65 percent of the population adheres to the Macedonian Orthodox faith; other religions represented include Islam, and, to a lesser extent, Catholicism. Unlike their Serbian and Macedonian neighbors, Albanian residents and citizens trace their ancestry to a non-Slavic people in ancient Macedonia. The prevalence of Albanian citizens and refugees accounts for the fact that 33.3. percent of people in Macedonia are Muslim.

Climate

Despite its small size, Macedonia has three regions with different climates. Most of the country experiences a mild continental climate, characterized by cold winters and dry, hot summers. Temperatures reach their extremes in the country's basins and valleys, and precipitation can come in the form of rain, snow, or hail.

In the most mountainous areas of the country, as along the northern part of the Albanian border, Macedonia has a mountainous climate characterized by high snowfall amounts in the winter and cooler temperatures year round.

Along the Vardar River south of Skopje and in the Gevgelija-Valandovo, Dojran, and Strumica-Radovis ravines, Macedonia has a Mediterranean climate. Moderated by warm winds off the Aegean Sea, this southernmost part of Macedonia has warmer temperatures and drier weather throughout the year.

During July, the area's hottest month, temperatures reach a daily average of 25° Celsius (77° Fahrenheit), although temperatures in the town of Demir Kapija can climb as high as 40° Celsius (104° Fahrenheit). Winter temperatures are relatively mild, with a January average of 3° Celsius (38° Fahrenheit).

The climate in the capital of Skopje is temperate, and is characterized by a mixture of Mediterranean, continental and mountainous conditions. Temperatures during the winter are often mild, with an average temperature of 3° Celsius (41° Fahrenheit) during the coldest months of January and February. Summers are typically long and dry, and characterized by medium heat and humidity; the average temperature from May through September is 30° Celsius (86° Fahrenheit). Spring is typically colder than the fall.

ENVIRONMENT & GEOGRAPHY

Topography

Modern day Macedonia lies in the southern part of the Balkan Peninsula, bounded by Bulgaria to the east, Yugoslavia to the north, Albania to the west, and Greece to the south. The country is covered with mountainous, rugged terrain, with deep valleys and basins.

The River Vardar runs through the center of Macedonia, coming from northern Albania and winding its way through Greece toward the Aegean. Macedonia also has three lakes: Lake Ohrid, which it shares with Albania; Lake Prespa, shared with Albania and Greece; and Lake Dojran on the easternmost part of the border with Greece. Macedonia's mountains soar to a maximum height of 2,764 meters (9,068 feet), at the peak of Mount Korab.

Skopje, the capital, is located on the Balkan Peninsula at a highly elevated point of the Vardar River; two major trade routes connect the city to Belgrade and Athens. In addition, Skopje is the geographical mid-point between Triana and Safia, the capitals of Macedonia's neighboring nations, Albania and Bulgaria. The city occupies an area of 1,818 square kilometers (1,129 square miles). The central district itself is 225 square kilometers (87 square miles), and sits 240 meters (787 feet) above sea level. The city is surrounded by the Balkan Mountain range and connected to suburbs and other cities by the Vardar River.

Plants & Animals

Macedonia's high elevations and deep basins support a wide variety of plant and animal life. Bear, deer, and boar roam the country's national parks. Shrubs and forest growth cover the mountainsides, with steppe meadows above 2,000 meters (6,562 feet).

The Mavorovo National Park in western Macedonian is said to contain six life zones, sustaining 22 forest and 16 grass ecosystems, with more than 1,300 plant species and 145 species of trees.

CUSTOMS & COURTESIES

Greetings

The vast majority of Macedonians are ethnic Slavs who speak Macedonian. Minority groups include Albanians, Turks, Serbs, and Roma. These minorities each have their own language and customs. In Macedonian, the most common greetings are "Dobro utro" ("Good morning"), "Dobar den" ("Good day"), "Dobra vecher" ("Good evening"), and "Zdravo" ("Hello").

When exchanging greetings in Macedonia, two people who do not know each other generally shake hands. Friends and family may instead greet each other with two or three kisses on the cheek or with an embrace. Among Muslim people, men and women often do not shake hands, embrace, or kiss on greeting because of their religious rules. Muslims also use only the right hand when shaking as the left hand is used for washing and is considered unclean. During a greeting, it is important to maintain direct eye contact. This is a sign of trust and respect. Macedonian society values rank and status, so appropriate titles are customarily used.

Gestures & Etiquette

Macedonia has a somewhat formal but friendly and open society. Personal space is respected but may be closer than among many Americans. Generally, people keep about an arm's length between them. Family and friends may stand closer and may touch each other lightly on the

hand, arm, or back when talking. Female friends often hold hands or walk arm in arm. People who do not know one another keep slightly more space between themselves and do not touch other than to shake hands.

Macedonians are very conscious of age and status. Younger individuals are expected to show deference, or respect, to their elders. People of lower rank are likewise expected to show respect for people of higher professional, educational, or official status. Macedonians are polite but open people who tend to speak directly about most matters and indirectly about serious matters that might cause offense. They speak quickly, and freely ask about one another's families, jobs and businesses, and other aspects of their lives.

Macedonians also gesture a great deal when talking and communicating. They may wave their finger back and forth when saying "no," or they may simply shake their head and click their tongue instead of saying "no." In contrast, people in eastern Macedonia, near Bulgaria, shake their heads to say "yes" rather than "no." In addition, Macedonians generally beckon with their entire hand, not a finger, and may motion for a person to come to them by gesturing with their hand palm down rather than palm up.

Eating/Meals

Macedonians generally eat three meals a day. Office workers take a light breakfast around nine o'clock in the morning before going to work, while field and factory workers tend to eat earlier in the morning. Most Macedonians eat supper after an afternoon break or rest period. Dinner is the main meal and usually eaten later at night. In Macedonia, people prepare meals right before they are eaten. If food has been left over from a previous meal, they typically incorporate that food into the new meal.

Table manners similar to those of neighboring Slavic countries are generally observed. People should wait to be seated and should wait for the hostess or head of household to signal the start of the meal before eating. It is impolite to put one's elbows on the table, and hands should be visible during a meal. It is also considered rude to refuse food and to make noises while eating.

Each year, Muslim Macedonians celebrate the month of Ramadan. During this time, most people fast during the hours between sunrise and sunset. This means that they do not eat, drink, or smoke from morning to night. In the evening, after dark, family and friends gather to break their fast.

Visiting

Macedonians place great value on their hospitality. During a visit, the guest is considered the most important person in the house, and people make every effort to welcome and tend to the guest. Guests should not try to clean, wash dishes, or find something for themselves. If a guest needs something, he or she should ask. In addition, when food and drink are offered, it is considered impolite or offensive to refuse.

Small gifts are appreciated, but not required, and homemade items, such as food or drink, are customarily appreciated. Extravagant or expensive gifts are considered offensive. When offered a gift, it is rude not to accept. Traditionally, Macedonians remove their shoes at the door when entering a home; however, this practice is less common today.

LIFESTYLE

Family

Family is the center of social life in Macedonia. Traditionally, large extended families comprising parents, their unmarried daughters, and their sons and their sons' spouses and children live together. Today, smaller nuclear families are more common, especially in urban areas with smaller living spaces. Marriage is the binding tie among Macedonian families. In the past, parents have arranged marriages among their children, but today, individuals choose their partners. Marriage is still the norm, however, and divorce and remarriage are uncommon.

In general, Macedonian families have maintained a patriarchal way of life. Family roles have long been clearly defined by sex, with men serving as the head of the family. Today, women and men are both likely to work outside the home, and women play a significant part in professional society. However, women are still expected to manage the home and children. Generally, children are expected to help in the home and tend to stay with their families until they marry and start their own family.

Minority ethnic groups have their own family patterns and lifestyles. The Roma are still largely nomadic and live in tribes organized by clan. Clans are extended family groups. These clans generally live, work, and travel together. The Roma are very family-oriented, and marriages are often arranged to form alliances between families or clans.

Housing

Macedonia was once a primarily rural, agricultural society. Today, 57.1 percent of the population is urban (as of 2015). Nearly a quarter of the population lives in the capital, Skopje. In cities, most people live in high-rise apartment buildings. Most apartments have balconies, which residents often use for storage and clothes drying. Historic neighborhoods offer older houses, which are often one-story homes that open on central courtyards; wealthier homes may be one or two stories. Houses and other buildings in the cities reflect various architectural traditions, including European Mediterranean and Ottoman influences. In rural villages, homes are traditionally made from stone, red brick, or concrete brick. The Roma move from place to place, living in temporary shelters, or settle in poor communities similar to shantytowns (informal settlements) on the outskirts of towns and cities.

Food

Macedonian cuisine is strongly influenced by the region's combined European and Middle Eastern heritage. The Macedonian diet is largely comprised of meat, fruit, vegetables, and dairy products. Breads and roasted meats are quite common, and fresh fruits and vegetables accompany most meals. Favorite dishes among Macedonians include bean casserole (called tavche-gravche), stuffed grape leaves (sarma), cold cucumber and garlic soup, various types of grilled kebabs, and sataras, a dish made from pork, veal, onion, and peppers. Macedonia is known for the quality of its peppers. Macedonians also eat a great deal of fish, particularly trout from Lake Ohrid.

Macedonians usually eat a small breakfast of bread and cheese. Sometimes, they have eggs. Dinners begin with the meze (appetizer), which among non-Muslims is accompanied with a fruit brandy called rakia. The most popular rakia is a plum brandy. Ajvar is a common appetizer or side dish made from paprika, eggplant, tomato, and sometimes string beans. Pastries are the most common dessert. Baklava is a dessert made mostly in winter, though pastry shops serve it year-round.

As in other Mediterranean countries, Turkish coffee is popular in Macedonia. Turkish coffee is a strong, sweet coffee prepared in a certain way. In Macedonia, it is usually served with a cup of ice water. Hosts often serve Turkish coffee to visitors. In fact, guests may be served three cups of coffee: the ozguldum, or welcome coffee; the muabet, or conversational coffee; and the sikter, or farewell coffee. Reading the leftover coffee grounds to tell fortunes has become a popular pastime among Macedonian women.

Life's Milestones

Education, family, and religion influence the major milestones of a Macedonian's life. At the age of seven, children begin attending public schools, which is compulsory until the age of fourteen. At that time, some students go on to institutions of higher learning, while others return to their families and work. The main cultural milestone is marriage, and most children live with their families until they marry.

Other important milestones are defined by a person's religious practices. Most Macedonians are Eastern Orthodox Christians—64.8 percent—and follow a set of seven mysteries similar to the sacraments in Western Christianity. Infants undergo baptism and chrismation (or confirmation), rituals meant to bring them into

Eastern Orthodoxy and unite them with the Holy Spirit. Marriage is another of the great mysteries. Other religious groups, such as Roman Catholics and Muslims, follow their own faith's practices.

CULTURAL HISTORY

Art

Early Macedonian art is rooted in the ancient art of the Greeks, and includes sculpture, functional handicrafts such as urns and pottery, and other folk arts. The visual arts also flourished during the Roman Empire, and included ornate frescoes and mosaics, such as those found in the ruins at Stobi. Much of Macedonia's historic artwork comprises the sacred icons, frescoes, and other sculptures and paintings of the Byzantine period. Strumica Church of the Fifteen Holy Martyrs of Tiberiopolis is home to the oldest frescoes in the nation. Other medieval frescoes may be found at the Church of St. Nicholas in Varos, the Church of St. Sophia in Ohrid, and at other churches and monasteries throughout Macedonia.

During the medieval period, portraiture and icon painting were also popular. Religious icons are found in most of the medieval Christian churches and basilicas. An especially remarkable collection of fifty terracotta icons was unearthed at the town of Vinica. These icons feature numerous religious figures and Christian saints, as well as depictions of famous biblical stories.

Macedonia is also known for the woodcarvings and sculptures of its Slavic people. The Church of St. Sophia in Ohrid features the oldest examples of Macedonian woodcarving in its altar screen. Other carvings, generally made with floral and animal designs, can be found in the monasteries of Slepce, Treskavec, Zrze, and Varos, as well as in the Monastery of the Holy Immaculate Virgin of Kičevo. Similarly, much of the Ottoman and Islamic artwork that remains in the country is in the form of decorative painting and carving in historic mosques, caravanserai (roadside inns on trade routes), baths, and palaces.

Architecture

The ancient and modern architecture of the Republic of Macedonia reflects the region's diverse history. Neolithic peoples first settled in the region that is now Macedonia more than 8,000 years ago. They left behind great megaliths but few other structures. The first great Macedonian kingdoms in the ninth century BCE grew into an empire under Alexander the Great in the fourth century BCE. Traces still survive in Ohrid in the ruins of temples and public basilicas, a gymnasium, and a columned agora (market). Ancient Rome left behind monumental architecture throughout Macedonia as well. Roman sites including a third-century amphitheater in Ohrid, the ruins of Pertenius palace containing Roman mosaics, marble work, and ornamental tiles in Stobi, and the monumental remains of a Roman fortress, aqueduct, and theater in the capital of Skopje.

During the medieval era, Byzantine and Slavic architecture was predominant. Sacred architecture in the form of churches and monasteries mark Byzantium's influence. Characterized by ornate domes, naves (central part of a church), and sacred frescoes and icons, these religious structures are hallmarks of Macedonia's architectural landscape. Secular structures, such as King Samuel's Fortress in Ohrid, are testaments to the Slavs' growing power. In the 14th century CE, the Ottomans brought Turkish and Islamic styles to the region. They converted many churches and chapels to mosques, building tall minarets, arches, terraces, and covered porches. The Ottomans also opened up the tightly fortified urban spaces to make room for gardens, fountains, and grand bazaars, palaces, and public buildings. Skopje and Tetovo contain the most notable remnants of Ottoman architecture, including Turkish baths, a bezisten (covered bazaar), mosques, and travelers' inns called caravanserai. In the late 19th century, as the Ottoman Empire dissolved, European influence reasserted itself, making living and working space more suited to city spaces and functional use.

Music & Dance

Macedonia has strong traditions of music and dance that are rooted in folk culture and in religion. Many of the lasting musical styles of Macedonia grew from the Byzantine Church through instrumental music and sacred hymns. John Koukouzeles (1280–1360), a 14th-century composer, was perhaps the best-known Byzantine musician known for his impact on the orthodox chants of the period.

Under the Ottomans, more folk and regional music developed, especially among Slavic peoples. Macedonians clung to their folk traditions as a way of preserving their culture and heritage and easing their livelihoods. In the 19th century, music reached a professional tier again, with the emergence of classical and other uniquely Macedonian styles. Atanas Badev (1860–1908), a student of the Moscow Academy of Music, has been considered the first modern Macedonian musician. He produced his works in the mid-1800s, but only one of those works, "Liturgy for a Mixed Choir," has survived. Other respected 19th- and 20th-century composers and students of music include Stefan Gajdov (1905–1992), Trajko Prokopijev (1909–1979), and Todor Skalovski (1909–2004). By the end of the 19th century, orchestras and choirs were performing throughout Macedonia, as were smaller folk bands and independent musicians.

As with Macedonian music, many of the country's dance traditions emerged over time through folk celebrations and communal events. Many early folk dances, such as the dodolari and the rusalii, emerged from popular traditions meant to bring rain, encourage a good harvest, or celebrate special occasions. Other traditional dances grew out of religious rituals and ceremonies. Among these are the dances of dervishes, meant to express and celebrate their spirituality. Among the ethnic minorities in Macedonia, the Romani people have long been known for their music and dance, full of colorful costumes, vibrant melodies and rhythms, and instrumental variations and intonations. Popular Slavic folk dances include the kopacka, the kostursko oro, and the raspukala šar planina. In the 19th and 20th centuries, new dance and music forms such as ballet and opera were introduced to Macedonia from Europe.

Literature & Drama

Early Macedonian languages were among the first literary languages in Europe. Though early Macedonians had strong oral traditions, they also inherited many Greek and Roman epics, plays, philosophies, and histories. The brothers Cyril (827–869) and Methodius (826–885)—also known as Kiril and Metodija—of Thessaloniki composed the first truly Macedonian texts in the ninth century. Together, they helped establish Macedonian literature through their translations of Hebrew, Greek, and Latin religious texts, as well as through books of sermons, hymns, and prayers. During the same century, Clement (Kliment) of Ohrid (c. 840–916) founded the Ohrid literary school and translated many church texts while writing his own book of prayers and sermons.

Byzantines and Ottomans brought other languages and literary forms and styles to Macedonia during the medieval and later centuries. However, Macedonians largely continued to develop their own literary traditions. Under the Ottomans, Macedonian authors branched away from strictly religious material and began producing more secular, literary works. Nineteenth-century writers such as Kuzman Sapkarev (1834–1909), Marko Cepenkov (1829–1920), and the brothers Dimitar (1810–1862) and Konstantin Miladinov (1830–1862) worked to gather and record traditional folk tales, songs, and oral literature. During this century, Macedonian dramatic literature and theater was also established with the works of Jordan Hadzi Konstantinov-Dzinot (1821–1882) and Vojdan Cernodrinski (1875–1951). Early 19th-century Macedonian authors, such as Kiril Peychinovich (1771–1845), whose works are all devoted to religion, were also influential in Bulgaria as well.

During the 20th century, Macedonian authors branched further into the creative realm, producing large numbers of poetry volumes, short story collections, novels, and plays. Cernodrinski, Nikola Kirov-Majski (1880–1962), and Atanas Razdolov (1872–1931) are among the best-known early 20th-century Macedonian writers. The poet Kočo Racin (1908–1943) helped establish the modern era of Macedonian literature, which was carried on by a new generation of Macedonian novelists, poets, and playwrights following the first and second world wars. These authors included poets Blaže Koneski (1921–1993), Aco Sopov (1923–1982), Slavko Janevski (1920–2000), and Kole Nedelkovski (1912–1941), novelists Vlado Maleski (1919–1984) and Stale Popov (1902–1965), and playwright Anton Panov (1906–1967).

CULTURE

Arts & Entertainment

The arts have held a cherished place in Macedonian society for centuries. Today, the Macedonian Academy of Arts and Sciences and numerous galleries, museums, universities, archaeological sites, and theaters continue to support and highlight the work of Macedonian artists. In Skopje, both the Museum of Contemporary Art and the Daut Pasha Baths offer the best collection of visual art by both Macedonian and international artists. Other galleries and museums around the nation supplement its selection with exhibits of ancient and modern art. The World Cartoon Gallery, the only international gallery of cartoon art, is also located in Skopje.

Today, most Macedonian artists train at the Skopje Art Academy. Each year, local and global artists of all ages also have the opportunity to participate in numerous workshops and artists' colonies around the country. Among these is the International Children's Artistic Colony, or the Young Bitola Monmartr, held in Bitola. Young artists produce paintings based on Macedonian architecture, and their work is displayed in cities around the nation. Macedonians are also well known for their folk arts and handicrafts, including the weaving of colorful rugs and blankets. Many Macedonians are expert gold- and silversmiths and urn-makers, called stomnari. Their urns and other ceramics are largely made from terracotta. Ethnic minorities each have their own traditional crafts. The Roma are particularly well known for their metalwork, basket weaving, and woodcarving.

For a small country, Macedonia has a remarkable number of novelists, playwrights, essayists, and poets. The poet Koco Racin (1908–1943) ushered in the modern era of Macedonian literature. He is particularly well known for his poetry collection entitled *Beli Mugri* (White Dawns, 1939). Other celebrated Macedonian authors include children's author Boris Bojadjiski (1915–1959), narrator and playwright Kole Casule (1921–2009), novelist and storywriter Tasko Georgievski (1935–), poet Ante Popovski (1931–2003), and novelist Koce Solunski (1922–). Many remarkable female authors have also influenced Macedonian literature, including poet Vladislava Spiroska (1978–), novelist, storywriter and poet Elizabeta Bakovska (1969–), and poet and essayist Katica Kulavkova (1951–).

Theater and dramatic performance continue to be mainstays of Macedonian society. Thirteen professional theater troupes put on more than 1,600 performances each year. These theater companies include the Drama Company of the Macedonian National Theatre; the Drama Theatre; the Theatre of the Nationalities with the Albanian and Turkish Drama Companies; and the Children's Theatre. They perform historic and modern, local and international productions. Dramatic performances are also a major part of the Ohrid Summer Music and Theatre Festival held each year, and the Festival of the Amateur Theatres in Kocani offers up-and-coming performers an opportunity to show off their talent.

Music is a major part of public life in Macedonia. The nation has one philharmonic orchestra, six chamber groups, and numerous independent bands and musicians in a variety of genres. Each year, Macedonian cities and institutions also host a variety of music and dance festivals, including the Balkan Festival of Folk Songs and Dances held every year in Ohrid, the Festival of Folk Instruments and Songs in Dolneni, and the Ohrid Summer Music and Theatre Festival. Folk music and dance traditions in Macedonian draw heavily on Slavic, Turkish, and other ethnic styles. The Romani people are especially well known for their vibrant dances and music. In the 19th and 20th centuries, classical music, ballet,

and opera grew in popularity and maintain a large following and selection of artists. Each year, the Opera Company and the Ballet Company of the Macedonian National Theatre in Skopje both put on several acclaimed performances. In addition, each year Skopje hosts the May Opera Evenings, an international event that draws opera singers from more than 50 countries.

Cultural Sites & Landmarks

Macedonia has a unique, largely mountainous landscape as well as a diverse cultural heritage shaped by Greek, Roman, Slavic, and Ottoman influences. The United Nations Educational, Scientific and Cultural Organization (UNESCO) has recognized one ecological and cultural site as a World Heritage Site, and is considering three other sites as candidates for protection.

The Lake Ohrid region was the only official World Heritage Site in Macedonia as of early 2009. The site consists of an early town once known as Lichnidos, which was settled more than 2,500 years ago, and includes many remnants of ancient Greek, Roman, and Slavic culture. The area also features more than 40 religious buildings, including churches, monasteries, and mosques. For example, the St. Pantelejmon, the oldest Slavic monastery in Macedonia, dates from the 11th century and is home to a collection of more than 800 Byzantine religious icons. In addition, the 10th century Samuel's Fortress, a remnant of Slavic rule, is also part of the site.

Beyond its historical and cultural significance, the Lake Ohrid site has also been preserved for its ecological importance. Lake Ohrid is the largest freshwater lake in Macedonia and has a diverse selection of flora and fauna, including many endemic species. The lake itself is known for its large trout population and its mysterious eels, which travel thousands of miles from the Sargasso Sea in the Americas. The eels live at the bottom of Lake Ohrid for ten years before returning to the Sargasso Sea to mate and reproduce.

The three sites that UNESCO is considering as World Heritage Site status are Cave Slatinski Izvor, Markovi Kuli, and the archaeo-astronomical site at Kokino. The site of Cave Slatinski Izvor is valued for its natural features and has the longest known cave in Macedonia. Known for the great diversity of its stalagmites and stalactites, the cave system also features an underground river, natural chasms, ponds, cascades, a dry riverbed, and a natural spring. Markovi Kuli is a rocky landscape on the slopes of the hill of Cardak. The site contains various ruins ranging from those of a prehistoric Iron Age settlement, to ancient Greek, Roman, and medieval Slavic settlements. One of the largest towers in Macedonia, dating from the third century, stands atop the hill, and a great necropolis and stone throne from the ninth and 10th centuries remains.

The archaeo-astronomical site at Kokino is actually an ancient megalithic observatory. Atop the rocky hill of Tatichev Kamen, about 1,013 meters (3,323 feet) above sea level, prehistoric peoples once moved and erected monumental stones to build this observatory. The site served a dual purpose—its builders gathered to observe the movements of heavenly bodies, as well as to perform important religious rituals. Two large platforms form the base of the observatory. On the bottom platform, four stone seats, or thrones, stand. Other giant stones serve as markers for the ancient peoples' observations. At the bottom of Tatichev Kamen, archaeologists have found artifacts and remains of ancient settlements. Among these are ceramic vessels, or containers, and moulds for making axes and pendants. Studies of the site indicate that people lived there between the 19th and the 7th century BCE.

Macedonia offers many other remarkable cultural and natural sites. Like Lake Ohrid, Lakes Prespa and Dojran are known for their unique species of flora and fauna, as well as for their natural beauty. Four national parks—Pelister, Mavrovo, Mount Galichica, and Jansen Forest Reserve—feature glacial lakes, stone rivers, caves, waterfalls, gorges, and other stunning land- and waterscapes. At Konopiste, unique natural earth pillars take the shape of pyramids. Unlike the pyramids of Egypt, erosion shaped these landforms.

Libraries & Museums

Macedonia has several libraries and museums. The National and University Library St. Kliment Ohridski in Skopje was opened in 1944 and houses Macedonia's largest collection of historical documents and ancient artifacts. The Museum of Macedonia is home to a large collection of folk art and ancient relics, including examples of pottery from the Neolithic Age, the Bronze Age, and the Iron Ages. Other museums include the Rock Arte Centre of Kravato and the University St. Kiril and Metodij Botanical Gardens.

Holidays

Macedonia celebrates public holidays on New Year's Eve (January 1), Orthodox Christmas Eve and Christmas Day (January 6 and 7), Women's Day (March 8), Labor Day/May Day (May 1), St. Cyrilus and St. Methodius Day (May 24), and Independence Day (September 8). Llinden (also called St. Elijah's Day), in honor of the Macedonian uprising, is celebrated with a folk music festival held in August.

Youth Culture

Education is compulsory for children between seven and 15 years of age. However, fewer than half of male students and only half of female students attend secondary school, and fewer still pursue higher educations. The vast majority of those youth who pursue secondary and higher education are ethnic Macedonian Slavs. Minorities, particularly the Roma, are greatly underrepresented in secondary and higher education. In fact, it is estimated that nearly half of Romani children leave school by the fifth grade, with many becoming street children at an early age. The government estimates that between 500 and 1,000 children are living on the streets of Macedonia's cities.

National law prohibits children from working until the age of 15, but many children continue to work in unofficial capacities, selling wares on the street, or working with their families. In general, Macedonian children live with their families until they have reached adulthood or have married. During this time, they are expected to help with household chores and obligations. Older siblings are also expected to help care for younger children.

Among more affluent communities, young adults tend to socialize by frequenting coffee shops, discos, and bars. Dating is more formal in Macedonia, and a young couple does not usually go on dates before beginning an official relationship. Early dating usually entails a young couple frequenting coffee shops and discos together. Traditionally, young men have been expected to ask young women out, but it is now more common for young women to initiate a courtship.

SOCIETY

Transportation

Inner-city public transportation is well maintained and bus service is a common mode of travel and transportation. There are two bus services operating in the capital of Skopje, one state-owned. Taxis also operate in major cities, but are considered expensive for long-term domestic travel. Traffic moves on the right-hand side of the road.

Transportation Infrastructure

Macedonia has a fairly reliable and basic transportation system, with some areas in disrepair. Paved roads connect the major cities while the railroads, characterized as quaint and inexpensive, connect Macedonia to Serbia, Greece, and other European nations. There are nearly 170 railroad stations and approximately 699 kilometers (434 miles) of railway lines. Macedonia has two major airports, at Skopje and Ohrid, and eight other airports as of 2013, most of which are regional airports. Eight of the total 10 airports are paved and two are not.

Media & Communications

Macedonia has modern and accessible media and communications networks. Though the government owns the broadcasting stations, all print media is independently owned and broadcast stations generally operate independently. Macedonians also have access to numerous international broadcast and print media outlets. In 2007, fifty-two television stations operated in Macedonia, and by 2008, more than sixty radio stations were broadcasting. As of 2012, there were three national channels and one satellite network, and five privately owned national channels. There are also about 75 local commercial TV stations with a large number of cable operators offering domestic and international programs. The nation offers 10 major daily newspapers as well as numerous weekly and monthly publications. Publications are available in Macedonian, Albanian, English, and other languages. As of 2012, there were three privately owned radio stations broadcasting nationally, and about 70 local commercial radio stations.

As in other countries, cellular phone use has overtaken landline phone use. In 2007, nearly 500,000 people had mainline telephones and more than 1.5 million had cell phones. By 2012, the number of landlines had decreased to 407,900, and cellular phones had increased to about 2.2 million. In recent years, the government has undertaken efforts to build Internet cafés in major cities and several operate in Skopje alone. The government estimates that over one million people were using the Internet in 2010, more than 51 percent of the population.

SOCIAL DEVELOPMENT

Standard of Living

Macedonia ranked 78th out of 187 countries on the 2013 United Nations Human Development Index, which measures quality of life and standard of living indicators.

Infant mortality is high by European standards, at just under eight deaths per 1,000 live births (2014 estimate). Average life expectancy is almost 76 years—73.2 for men and 78.5 for women (2014 estimate).

Water Consumption

Macedonia is home to over 30 rivers and over 50 natural and artificial lakes. Although water is widely considered safe to drink, water quality can be poor in some rural areas. In addition, some areas of Macedonia still make use of antique water infrastructure that can jeopardize water safety.

Education

The Republic of Macedonia requires all children to attend primary school from seven to 15 years of age. After completing eight years of elementary education, Macedonian students may obtain a Secondary School Leaving Certificate from one of the country's "gimnazija" schools by completing a four-year program. Alternatively, students may attend a technical, vocational, or art school to receive the Leaving Certificate.

Classes may be taught in Macedonian, Albanian, or Turkish, depending on the student population, but all students must take classes in Macedonian if it is not the primary language of instruction.

Macedonia offers professional degrees, such as law, business, or teaching, in its institutions of higher education. There is no tuition for Macedonian residents and the length of programs varies by institution and by program.

In 2015, the country's literacy rate was estimated at 97.8 percent. 98.8 percent of men and 96.8 percent of women are literate.

Women's Rights

Macedonia has traditionally been a patriarchal society. Male family members have held most decision-making power and men have occupied most positions of professional and political leadership in the country. However, the role of women in Macedonian society has changed greatly in recent years, and women have made significant strides in the public realm. Today, more women hold dominant positions in the workforce, are better represented politically, and are gaining more ground in traditionally male-dominated areas such as law, science, and engineering.

However, home life is still somewhat imbalanced. Though women and men are considered equal in principle, most household and child-rearing responsibilities still fall to the female members of a family. Men have largely professional obligations while women have professional and domestic roles. In that sense, discriminatory practices against women in the workplace are still present. They continue to earn less than their male counterparts do, and many women face discriminatory practices due to pregnancy. Sexual harassment has also continued to be a problem, and there are no laws prohibiting such behavior.

Spousal abuse and rape and other forms of violence against women have continued to go unaddressed in Macedonia. Many victims do not report abuse or rape for fear of bringing shame on their families and because requirements for conviction place a heavy burden on the victim to prove the violation. The government operates at least six crisis centers to help victims of abuse and rape, and many nonprofit groups have also begun programs to provide counseling, medical help and shelter and to assist women in other ways. Macedonia is also considered an origin, transit, and destination for human trafficking, particularly for the purpose of sexual and labor exploitation. The government's anti-trafficking laws and efforts have shown positive results since 2006, but the issue of human trafficking and forced prostitution and slavery remain serious concerns. In a 2014 Trafficking in Persons Report by the US Department of State, "The government identified 15 victims of trafficking in 2013, an increase from eight in 2012. Of these, nine were minors; five minors were victims of sex trafficking; and one victim was awaiting repatriation from Croatia."

Health Care

Macedonia proved free and accessible health care to every citizen. There are public medical centers, specialized hospitals, and hundreds of village medical units in operation throughout the country. There are more than 800 private health organizations in Macedonia, and care is also provided at the University of Sts. Cyrilus and Methodius School of Medicine.

GOVERNMENT

Structure

Macedonia declared its independence from Yugoslavia on September 8, 1991. Prior to its inclusion in Yugoslavia (originally created as the Kingdom of Serbs, Croats, and Slovenes following the Treaty of Versailles); Macedonia had been under the sovereignty of Serbia. Prior to this, the entire region was ruled by the Ottoman Empire. Other portions of the original Macedonian region are still included within the boundaries of Greece and Bulgaria.

Largely because of competing claims to the territory once held by the ancient Macedon Empire, the term "Macedonia" provokes debate within the region. For this reason, Greece objected to United Nations, NATO, and European Union recognition of the new Republic's name and national symbols. These international bodies therefore refer to Macedonia as the Former Yugoslav Republic of Macedonia (FYROM), until the matter is fully resolved with Greece. Macedonia is currently awaiting a decision on its application for EU membership.

Macedonia's government is a parliamentary democracy. There is universal suffrage with a voting age of eighteen. A popular election determines which political parties will fill 120 seats in the Sobranie (Assembly), Macedonia's legislative body. The Sobranie elects a prime minister.

The president is elected to a five-year term by popular vote. The current president, Gjorge Ivanov was reelected in 2014 with a 55.3 percent vote. The judicial system is structured under the Supreme Court, the Constitutional Court, and the Republican Judicial Council. The Sobranie appoints all higher court judges.

Political Parties

Macedonia's government operates using a multiparty system, where a large group of political parties form coalition governments. Major political parties include the Social Democratic Union of Macedonia (SDSM), the Internal Macedonian Revolutionary Organization-Democratic Party for Macedonian National Unity (VMRO-DPMNE) and the Democratic Union for Integration (DUI). The number of seats held by these parties in the Sobranie following elections in 2014 were as follows: VMRO-DPMNE, 61; SDSM, 34; DUI, 19; all others, nine.

Local Government

Macedonia is organized into 84 municipalities. Skopjie is divided into 10 distinct municipalities. Municipalities are further divided into communities, which are administered by elected local councils. All levels of local government follow legal regulations stipulated by Macedonia's national government.

Judicial System

Macedonia's judicial system is organized into the Supreme Court, the Republican Judicial Council, and the Constitutional Court. The country's legal system is based on civil law. Macedonia's Constitutional Court, which is comprised of nine judges, adjudicates legal conflicts between branches of government. Judges who are members of the Constitutional Court are appointed by parliament. In addition, parliament appoints a public prosecutor to a six-year term. Corruption remains a significant problem in Macedonia's court system.

Taxation

Macedonia has relatively low taxes compared to other European countries and is widely considered a regional tax shelter. A corporate tax of 10 percent is collected, but no tax is charged on reinvested corporate profits. Other taxes include property taxes, a value added tax and excise duties on some goods. Taxes consist of an estimated 26.5 percent of the GDP in 2014.

Armed Forces

The armed forces of Macedonia, officially the Army of the Republic of Macedonia, are a security force that maintains an army and air force, as well as a Special Forces branch (known as the Wolves). Conscription was abolished in 2008, and 18 is the minimum age for voluntary service. Macedonian soldiers have participated in several international peacekeeping missions, including in Afghanistan, Kosovo, and Iraq.

Foreign Policy

Since splitting from the former Yugoslavia and gaining its independence in 1991, the Republic of Macedonia has been active in world political and economic affairs. Its primary interests are in maintaining trade relations, encouraging foreign investment in the nation, maintaining regional security, and supporting the formation of world democracies and peaceful resolutions to conflicts. A key priority among Macedonian officials is also gaining membership in major international bodies and organizations.

Macedonia is a member of the United Nations (UN), the International Monetary Fund (IMF), the World Bank, and the International Atomic Energy Agency (IAEA). It is also a member of important regional bodies, such as the Central European Free Trade Agreement (CEFTA). However, Macedonia has been blocked from full membership in the European Union (EU) and in the North Atlantic Treaty Organization (NATO) by an ongoing dispute with Greece over its name. Greek officials object to Macedonia using either "Macedonia" or "the Republic of Macedonia" as its official name. They considered this an infringement on their cultural and historic heritage, as more than two-thirds of the lands that once belonged to the historic Macedonian empire are part of Greece. Though Macedonia qualifies and has been approved for membership in the EU and in NATO, it cannot officially be admitted until the conflict with Greece, which is already a member of these bodies, is resolved.

In general, Macedonia has strong and friendly relations with most of its neighbors and even maintains a reliable trade relationship with Greece. Its major trading partners are European and include Serbia, Montenegro, Spain, Germany, Belgium, Bulgaria, Greece, Italy, Turkey, Croatia, and Slovenia. Trade with the United States accounts for less than two percent of its imports and exports. However, Macedonia does rely on the U.S., as well as other countries, for a great deal of economic assistance.

Despite its small size, Macedonia has provided troops and support for various international efforts, including NATO-led peacekeeping efforts in Kosovo, the US-led coalition military efforts in Afghanistan, and the U.S.-led war in Iraq. Macedonia is particularly concerned about prevention and elimination of global terrorism and the protection of human rights, and supports efforts to rebuild and secure democratic governments in Afghanistan and Iraq. It has also supported efforts to prevent Iran and North Korea from obtaining or using nuclear weapons, and encourages ongoing diplomatic discussions with these countries.

Human Rights Profile

International human rights law insists that states respect civil and political rights, and promote an individual's economic, social, and cultural rights. The United Nations Universal Declaration on Human Rights (UDHR) is recognized as the standard for international human rights. Its authors sought the counsel of the world's great thinkers, philosophers, and religious leaders, and were careful to create a document that reflects the core values shared by every world culture. (To read this document or view the articles relating to cultural human rights, visit http://www.un.org/en/documents/udhr/).

In general, Macedonia has worked hard to ensure the human rights of a vast majority of its citizens. However, some rights are not protected to the extent that they should be, particularly among minorities. The U.S. Department of State and international bodies and organizations such as Amnesty International (AI) have cited several key problem areas.

Allegations of police violence and discrimination, particularly toward the Roma, continue. Critics have charged that officials have done little to reprimand or correct officers or to determine the actual causes of death of Romani individuals in custody. Local nonprofit groups alleged that the police have committed more than 100 incidents of excessive force and abuse against ethnic Macedonians, Albanians, and Roma in 2007 alone. In addition, prison conditions were generally poor and did not meet international standards.

The judiciary system itself is legally independent of the executive and the legislative branches. However, in practice, many officials are corrupt and subject to pressure from other politicians, as well as from interests and individuals in society. Other government officials have been accused of using their budget-making power to exert control over judges' processes and decisions. Corruption throughout various levels and branches of government has been rampant, and citizens and groups have lodged hundreds of complaints. In recent years, the government has increased efforts to investigate and root out corrupt officials.

The constitution protects freedom of speech and of the press, but laws do prohibit any forms of hate speech intended to provoke religious or ethnic conflict. Freedom of religion and freedom of assembly are also guaranteed, though the government does require religious groups to register in order to hold public worship ceremonies and gatherings. Similarly, the law also prohibits discrimination against women and ethnic minorities. However, such practices have continued, particularly in the workplace and in the allocation of services. Ethnic Albanians, Turks, and Roma have accused the government of keeping them in a position of second-class citizenship without the same rights or access to opportunities as ethnic Macedonians. Each group has demanded recognition of their language and cultural practices, greater representation in political spheres, and better social services and access to housing, jobs, and education. People with disabilities have also charged that the government has not upheld its legal obligations in protecting their rights to equal access to employment, education, healthcare, and public spaces.

ECONOMY

Overview of the Economy

Once the most undeveloped of the former Yugoslav states, Macedonia successfully built an industrial economy in the wake of the Yugoslavian break up. However, a dispute with Greece over the Macedonian name and national symbols, combined with heavy trade sanctions against Macedonia's former Yugoslav trade partners, nearly crippled the growing economy until 1996. Since that time, Macedonia's industries have been recovering at a quick pace, but instability in Serbia and Albania remain a constant threat to financial growth in the region. In 2014, Macedonia's estimated per capita GDP was $ 13,200.

Skopje's location along the Belgrade-Athens highway, and halfway between Triana and Safia, makes it a major trading and transportation center. The cotton, tobacco, grains, and livestock produced in rural areas of Macedonia are all traded in Skopje. In addition, over half of the country's exports are to the European Union (EU), particularly Bulgaria, Serbia, Greece, Russia, and Ukraine.

Industry

Macedonia mines, manufactures, and processes coal, metallic chromium, lead, zinc, ferronickel, textiles, tobacco, timber products, and steel. The country also has developed food processing plants and bus manufacturing plants. Skopje is a center for the production of iron and steel, chemicals, timber, clothing and textiles, leather, electrical machinery, office supplies and foodstuffs. Although some of these industries have closed or declined since Macedonia declared itself a republic in 1991, new industries have taken their place; for example, trade and banking industries have become important to the economy, as have tourism and sports.

Labor

The labor force in Macedonia was estimated at 961,400 in 2014. Over half of the work force—an estimated 52.6 percent—is employed in the services industry, while 29.1 percent are employed in industry; the agricultural sector accounts for approximately 18.3 percent of the work force. The unemployment rate in Macedonia was reported as high as 32 percent in

2009. Since then, it has gone down to 28 percent in 2014.

Energy/Power/Natural Resources

Despite its mountainous terrain, over 20 percent of Macedonia's land mass is arable. Forested areas provide timber, and mining in the country yields low-grade iron ore, copper, lead, zinc, chromite, manganese, nickel, tungsten, gold, silver, asbestos, and gypsum.

Fishing

Macedonia's fishing industry is based in the western part of the country. Large amounts of cormorant, carp, and lake trout are caught at Lake Ohrid and Doyran Lake. The majority of freshwater fish caught in Macedonia are used for domestic consumption.

Forestry

Macedonia does not produce wood products and does not have an economically significant forestry industry.

Mining/Metals

The production of iron, steel, and cement are major industries in Macedonia. Industry employed an estimated 29.5 percent of the country's workforce in 2014. The country also produces copper. Mining makes up an estimated 1 percent of Macedonia's GDP.

Agriculture

Macedonia's agriculture accounts for about 9 percent of the country's total gross domestic product (GDP). Major crops include rice, tobacco, wheat, corn, millet, cotton, sesame, mulberry leaves, citrus, and vegetables. The agricultural sector also raises cattle, pigs, fowl, and lamb for food consumption.

Animal Husbandry

Although livestock not a leading agriculture sector in Macedonia, the country does produce cattle and poultry for domestic consumption. Other livestock animals raised in the country include pigs and goats. Eggs, sheep milk, and cow milk are also produced in Macedonia.

Tourism

Though regional violence and fears of political instability seem to have died down somewhat since 2002, Macedonia has not been able to attract tourists. For those who do venture to Macedonia, the 2,400-year-old town of Ohrid is the most popular attraction. Aside from the scenic beauty of Lake Ohrid, the town boasts an accumulation of ruins and archeological treasures from its thousands of years as a center of trade and of Eastern European Christianity. The United Nations Educational, Scientific, and Cultural Organization (UNESCO) has named Ohrid a World Heritage Site.

Christina Dendy, Amy Witherbee,
Anne Whittaker

DO YOU KNOW?

- After the earthquake in 1963, 87 nations from all over the world dispatched teams of rescue volunteers to help the victims of the earthquake; as a result, Skopje was nicknamed "City of Solidarity." The clock that hung in the railway station prior to 1963 remains preserved in the ruins stopped at the precise time of 5:17, the moment when the earthquake hit Skopje.

- Lake Ohrid, on the Albanian border, is one of the deepest lakes in Europe and one of the oldest in the world.

- Mother Teresa, a Catholic nun who earned international recognition for her lifetime of charity work in India, was born in Skopje, Macedonia.

Bibliography

Andrew Rossos. "Macedonia and the Macedonians." Stanford: *Hoover Institution Press*, 2007.

Christopher Deliso. "Hidden Macedonia." London: *Haus Publishers Ltd.*, 2007.

Harvey Pekar. "Macedonia." New York: *Villard*, 2007.

Hugh Poulton. "Who Are the Macedonians?" Bloomington: *Indiana University Press*, 2000.

Ian F. Hancock. "We Are the Romani People." Hertfordshire: *University Of Hertfordshire Press*, 2002.

Jan Yoors. "The Heroic Present: Life among the Gypsies." New York: *Monacelli*, 2004.

Keith Brown. "The Past in Question: Modern Macedonia and the Uncertainties of Nation." Princeton, NJ: *Princeton University Press*, 2003.

Thammy Evans. "Macedonia." London: *Bradt Travel Guide*, 2012.

Works Cited

"Archaeo-Astronomical Site Kokino." UNESCO. http://whc.unesco.org/en/tentativelists/5413/

"Cave Slatinski Izvor." *UNESCO.* http://whc.unesco.org/en/tentativelists/1917/.

"Country Profiles: FYR Macedonia." *UNIFEM.* http://www.unifem.sk/index.cfm?module=project&page=country&CountryISO=MK

"Kopacka (Lesnoto/Pravoto) [Macedonia] Dance History & Background." *Folk with Dunav.* http://www.dunav.org.il/dance_histories/macedonia_kopacka.html

"Kostursko [Macedonian from Northern Greece] Dance History & Background." *Folk with Dunav.* http://www.dunav.org.il/dance_histories/macedonia_kostursko.html

"Macedonia (FYROM) Internet Usage and Marketing Report." *Internet World Stats.* http://www.internetworldstats.com/eu/mk.htm

"Macedonia (Tier 1)." *Trafficking on Human Persons Report, June 2008. U.S. Department of State.* http://gvnet.com/humantrafficking/Macedonia-2.htm

"Macedonia Women's Rights Centre—Shelter Centre." http://humanrightshouse.org/Articles/5160.html

"Macedonia." Au Pair in America. http://www.aupairinamerica.com/resources/culture_quests/macedonia.asp

"Macedonia." Culture Crossing. http://guide.culturecrossing.net/basics_business_student.php?id=122

"Macedonia." *The World Factbook.* https://www.cia.gov/library/publications/the-world-factbook/geos/mk.html

"Macedonia." *U.S. Department of State.* http://www.state.gov/r/pa/ei/bgn/26759.htm

"Macedonia." *World Book.* http://www.worldbookonline.com.oh0063.oplin.org/advanced/article?id=ar336170&st=macedonia

"Macedonia: Country Reports on Human Rights Practices." *U.S. Department of State* http://www.state.gov/g/drl/rls/hrrpt/2006/78826.htm

"Macedonia: Etiquette When Doing Business." *Kwintessential.com.* http://www.kwintessential.co.uk/cross-cultural/intercultural-communication-translation-news/2008/05/09/macedonia-etiquette-when-doing-business/

"Macedonian Cultural and Historical Resource Center." http://faq.macedonia.org

"Macedonian Cultural and Information Center." http://www.macedonia.co.uk

"Macedonian Food & Dining." *Iexplore.com.* http://www.iexplore.com/dmap/Macedonia/Dining

"Markovi Kuli." *UNESCO.* http://whc.unesco.org/en/tentativelists/1918/

"Natural and Cultural Heritage of the Ohrid Region." *UNESCO.* http://whc.unesco.org/en/list/99

"Overcoming Stereotypes Through Romani Music in Macedonia." *Amala School.* http://www.galbeno.com/overcoming-stereotypes-through-romani-music-in-macedonia/

"Raspukala Sar Planina (Lesnoto/Pravoto) [Macedonia] Dance History & Background." *Folk with Dunav.* http://www.dunav.org.il/dance_histories/macedonia_raspukala_sar_planina.html

"Roma." *World Book.* http://www.worldbookonline.com.oh0063.oplin.org/advanced/article?id=ar241070&st=roma

"Slavs." *World Book.* http://www.worldbookonline.com.oh0063.oplin.org/advanced/article?id=ar514060&st=slavs

"The Former Yugoslav Republic of Macedonia." *Tageo.com* http://www.tageo.com/index-e-mk-cities-MK.htm

"The Former Yugoslav Republic of Macedonia." *UNESCO.* http://whc.unesco.org/en/statesparties/mk

Connie Emerson. "Lake Ohrid, Macedonia Offers History and Beauty." *Suite101.com.* http://eeuroperussiatravel.suite101.com/article.cfm/ohrid_and_its_lake

Cyber Macedonia. http://www.cybermacedonia.com/

Dennis Boxell. "An Introduction to Macedonian Folk Dances." http://www.dunav.org.il/dance_regions/macedonia.html

Republic of Macedonia Ministry of Foreign Affairs. http://www.mfa.gov.mk/

Park fountain in Chisinau, Moldova

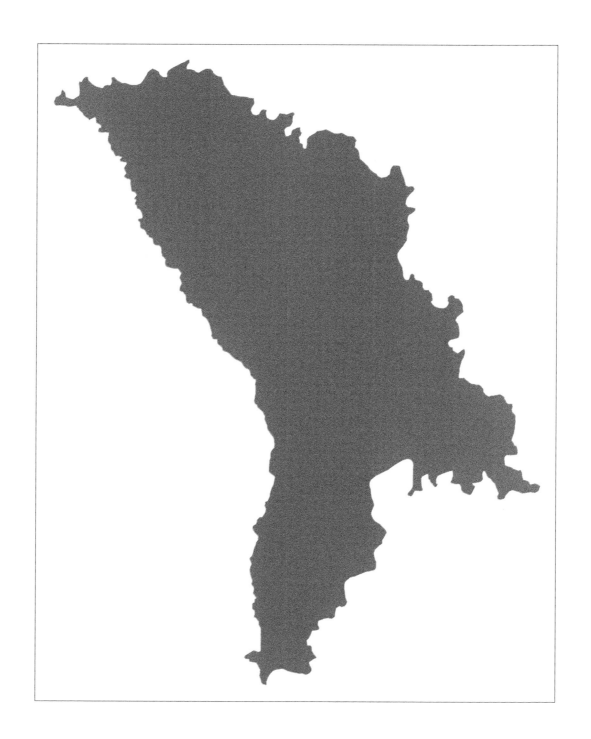

MOLDOVA

Introduction

In ancient times, Moldova was known as the gateway between Europe and Asia. The country experienced repeated invasions and many wars. For decades, the territory was exploited, stripped of its resources, and environmentally damaged by the Soviet Union. Now a multiethnic, independent republic with an agrarian-based economy, the Republic of Moldova is one of the poorest countries in Europe.

Since the dissolution of the Soviet Union and the establishment of an independent nation, the people of Moldova have begun to break free from the oppression that characterized the region for so long. Since Moldovan artists were trained for decades in the Soviet tradition, native art tended to be conservative; however, with this independence, Moldavians are beginning to explore new possibilities for their futures, particularly in education and the arts. Folk art remains a strong tradition in Moldova, resulting in brightly colored pottery and ceramics, carpets, and fabrics. Stone- and wood-carving are other traditional art forms that are still practiced.

GENERAL INFORMATION

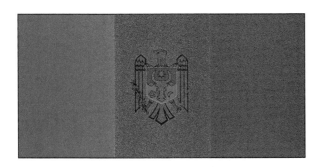

Official Language: Moldovan
Population: 3,583,288 (2014 estimate)
Currency: Moldovan leu
Coins: The Moldovan leu is divided into 100 bani; coins circulate in values of 1, 5, 10, 25, and 50 bani.
Land Area: 32,891 square kilometers (12,699 square miles)

Water Area: 960 square kilometers (370 square miles)
National Anthem: "Limba Noastra" ("Our Tongue")
Capital: Chişinău (Kishinev)
Time Zone: GMT +2
Flag Description: The flag of Moldova consists of three equal vertical bars of blue (left), gold (middle), and red (right). Centered in the golden middle stripe is the coat of arms of Moldova, which features an eagle gripping a shield that displays the head of an aurochs, an extinct wild cattle.

Population

Moldova is densely populated, with as many as 150 people per square kilometer (388 people per square mile). Just over half of the population lives in rural areas, while an estimated 45 percent of the population is urban (2014 estimate).

Principal Cities by Population (2012):

- Chişinău (554,585)
- Tiraspol (132,105)
- Bălţi (97,237)
- Tighina (90,627)
- Rîbniţa (46,997)
- Cahul (39,400) (2010)
- Ungheni (38,000) (2010)

In fact, only five cities have an estimated population of 50,000 or more, with the capital, Chişinău, the largest by far. In the countryside, there are many villages of between 1,000 and 5,000 inhabitants.

The majority of the population is Moldovan (75.8 percent), a non-Slavic ethnic group. Other ethnic groups include Ukrainian (8.4 percent), Russian (5.9 percent), Gagauz (4.4 percent), Romanian (2.2 percent), Bulgarian (1.9 percent), and other (one percent). Ethnic Moldovans tend to live in rural areas, particularly in the northern and central part of the country. Russians and Ukrainians congregate in urban areas, particularly in Transdniestria (Transnistria). The Gagauz live in several communities in southern Moldova.

The population of Moldova was estimated as 3,583,288 in 2014, but that estimate does not include the territories under the control of Transnistria, a breakaway territory on Moldova's eastern border with Ukraine. In the 2004 census, the population was estimated at 3,383,332. The country had a population growth rate of -0.07 in 2010, however.

Languages

While the national language of Moldova is Moldovan (58.9 percent)—the Moldovan language is a dialect of Romanian (16.4 percent)—it is common to also hear Russian (16 percent), Ukrainian (3.8), Gagauz (3.1 percent), and Bulgarian (1.1 percent). Russian and Ukrainian, along with the Gagauz language, a Turkic language spoken by the Gagauz, are recognized as regional languages.

Native People & Ethnic Groups

According to the 2004 census, an estimated 78 percent of the population is either Moldovan or Romanian. Ukrainians and Russians account for just under 15 percent, and the Gagauz are one of the largest minority ethnic groups. The Gagauz are a Turkic people who live in communities in several nations, but most Gagauz, however, live in Moldova. After years of struggle and threats of civil war, they won recognition of the autonomous region of Gagauz Yeri (Gagauzland) or Gagauzia, in southern Moldova.

Relations are also tense with the Slavic (Ukrainian and Russian) majority in Transnistria, along Moldova's eastern border with Ukraine. This group proclaimed the Trans-Dniestr Republic (Transdniestria) in 1990, and has been supported by the Russian Army in several violent clashes during the early 1990s. In 1997, the Moldovan government agreed to a peace accord, giving the region greater autonomy.

Religions

Approximately 93.3 percent of the population of Moldova belongs to the Eastern Orthodox Church. Other major religions include Roman Catholic, Jewish, Armenian Apostolic, Seventh-day Adventist, Baptist, Pentecostal, and Molokan. Most Gagauz are Eastern Orthodox Christians. Freedom of religion is fully guaranteed by the constitution of the Republic of Moldova.

Climate

Moldova's climate, with its long, warm summers and mild winters, favors agriculture. The average temperature in Chişinău in July is 21° Celsius (70° Fahrenheit); the average January temperature is –4° Celsius (24° Fahrenheit). Moldova enjoys plenty of sunshine (up to 45 percent of the year).

Rainfall is light, ranging from 60 centimeters (24 inches) in the north to 40 centimeters (16 inches) in the south. Most rainfall occurs in early summer and in October. Rain is often heavy and accompanied by thunderstorms.

Chişinău has a moderate climate with four distinct seasons. During the winter months, temperatures may drop as low as -20° Celsius (–4° Fahrenheit), but generally remain around –4° Celsius (25° Fahrenheit). Summer temperatures can range from 20° Celsius (68° Fahrenheit) to 40° Celsius (104° Fahrenheit), and droughts are common in the region.

ENVIRONMENT & GEOGRAPHY

Topography

Moldova, one of the smallest of the former Soviet Republics, is a landlocked country in southeastern Europe. The republic is nearly surrounded by Ukraine, which bounds it on the north, east, and south. Romania lies on the western border.

The northern part of the country consists of the Moldovan plateau, characterized by limestone outcroppings and deposits of sand, gravel, and gypsum. Steep hills roll through central Moldova, where landslides are a natural hazard. The south is another steppe area, with black, fertile soil. Most of this area is cultivated.

The highest point in the country is at the peak of Dealul Balanesti (430 meters/1,411 feet), in the west-central part of the country. The country's major rivers are the Nistru and the Prut. The Nistru is 1,402 kilometers (871 miles) long. It rises in the Carpathian Mountains of Ukraine and flows generally southeast through much of eastern Moldova. It empties into the Black Sea in Ukraine. The 970-kilometer (603-mile) Prut rises in western Ukraine, also in the Carpathian Mountains. It also flows generally southeast and forms the border with Romania. It empties into the Danube at the southern tip of Moldova.

The country's largest natural lake is Beleu, in the lower Prut valley, which covers 6.26 square kilometers (2.4 square miles). Other large lakes include Bik (3.72 square kilometers/1.43 square miles), and Drachele (2.65 square kilometers/1.02 square miles). Lacul ("Lake") Ghidighici, a reservoir 12 kilometers (7.4 miles) north of Chişinău, is Moldova's largest artificial lake.

Chişinău is located near the center of Moldova. The city is situated along seven hills and is crossed by both the Bîc and Isnovat Rivers. Chişinău covers an area of 120 square kilometers (46 square miles) which is divided into five sectors: Buiucani, Rîşcani, Ciocana, Botanica, and Centre.

Plants & Animals

Moldova supports approximately 1,900 species of vegetation, mostly in the forests or on the steppes. The cordrji, or old oak forests, are home to many beautiful trees. The oldest oak tree is more than 600 years old.

Destruction of habitat through lumbering operations has resulted in the disappearance of more than 45 species of wildlife. Remaining forest animals include rabbits, ground squirrels, roebucks, foxes, deer, wild boar, and birds.

Freshwater fish are of great economic importance in Moldova. Both natural and artificial lakes are used in fish farming. The most important species are crucian, carp, perch, bream, and soodak (a kind of pike).

CUSTOMS & COURTESIES

Greetings

Greetings in Moldova customarily include the traditional nod of the head or a handshake. When formal introductions are expected, reserved demeanor is the norm, and includes a firm handshake and direct eye contact. In addition, older Moldovans may traditionally kiss a woman's hand when meeting them, but this may seem forward for foreign men to do so. Close friends may typically embrace, which can include a small kiss (peck) on each cheek, beginning with the left cheek. In the urban areas of Moldova, people usually only shake hands when they greet each other, but a man should wait for the woman to first offer her hand. When in mixed company, a man should always shake a woman's hand before shaking another man's hand.

Common greetings in Moldovan include "Buna Ziua" ("Good Day") and "Noroc" ("Hi"). In Russian, the greeter may say "Zdravstrvuite" ("Hello") or "Privet" ("Hi").

Gestures & Etiquette

Children and teenagers always use first names when addressing each other, but formal and honorific titles are expected when addressing adults and elders. Unless adults are close friends or relatives, they also will use formal and honorific titles when speaking to each other; this includes titles such as "doctor" and "professor." As with most cultures, strangers and people who are not close speak formally with one another, as this behavior does not match the formal style and level of the language being used. (Overall, the formal and informal levels with the Moldovan language naturally create a more formal and psychologically distant style of social interaction.) In addition, Moldovans, with the exception of family and childhood friends, generally refer to a person using the person's title and last name until invited to speak on a first-name basis.

Moldovans generally stand close together when speaking, but customarily refrain from contact. Women may traditionally refrain from eye contact when speaking with men, as this may be interpreted as flirtation. (Traditionally, men perceived strong eye contact from women as a sign of romantic interest.) In a professional or business setting, direct eye contact between men and women is expected and is not considered too forward.

The elderly hold a position of high respect in Moldovan culture, and are customarily treated with deference by young to middle-aged Moldovans. This includes courteous public acts such as offering one's seat on public transportation or offering to carry heavy baggage or other bulky items.

Eating/Meals

Urban Moldovans usually consume a quick, light breakfast, often consisting of bread with sausage, cheese, or rolls with butter and fruit preserves. Breakfast is typically accompanied by coffee or tea. Rural Moldovans generally eat larger breakfasts, which may include hot porridge, potatoes, bread, and sheep cheese. For rural Moldovans, breakfast is usually the main meal of the day, except on weekends when they prepare a multi-course lunch eaten by the entire family.

In urban areas, lunch is generally eaten as the day's main meal, and might consist of soup, salad, and a main course of meat, most often chicken or pork. Afternoon snacks may precede lunch, and include a sandwich or roll with butter and cheese, and drink juice or tea. (Coffee, tea, milk, juice, or stewed fruit are the most common nonalcoholic beverages in Moldova, while most adult Moldovans drink wine with their lunches and dinners.) At dinner, both rural and urban Moldovans usually eat something simpler, much like the urban breakfast.

When eating at home, the main meal (lunch) is customarily placed in serving dishes in the center of the table and served communally, with each person taking their own portion. While eating, Moldovans keep their hands and forearms above the table. Moldovans also traditionally eat in the continental style: a knife in the right hand and fork in the left hand.

Visiting

It is a matter of honor for Moldovans to show great hospitality and generosity to guests. When invited to a meal, guests are expected to arrive on time, though informal affairs are afforded more leeway. A guest typically dresses in semiformal, if not formal attire, and is treated with great honor. It is customary to remove one's shoes, and the host may offer a pair of slippers for the guest to wear in the home. Foreign visitors are always considered highly honored guests, and are always treated in the best way a family can afford. Most Moldovan homes have a casa mare (big room), which is specifically for holding celebrations and feasts.

At formal meals, it is considered polite to wait until everyone is served—or, traditionally, until the host says "Pofta buna" ("Good appetite")—to begin eating. The guest usually sits at the right side of the host, who occupies the head of the table. A guest might insistently be offered a second helping, and compliments to the host are appreciated.

LIFESTYLE

Family

The family is quite important in Moldovan society. In the urban parts of Moldova, most families include two children, while rural Moldovan families often consist of three or four children. An important part of Moldovan socialization centers on respect for the elderly and care for the aged. There are very few nursing homes for the elderly or the disabled since these people are nearly always cared for within the homes of extended family. Children remain quite close to parents and grandparents throughout life, and the Moldovan sense of immediate family extends over two or three generations.

Recent economic hardship has caused significant disruption to the traditional Moldovan family; according to estimates in the early 21st century, about 25 percent of working-age Moldovans have left the country to find employment. In fact, more than a third of the entire country's gross domestic product (GDP) comes from remittances (money sent by migrant workers to their families). Over 50 percent of these migrant workers are Moldovan women who have been forced to leave their children behind. Consequently, approximately one-third of all Moldovan children are currently being raised without one or both parents.

Housing

Quite often, families of two or three generations share one home, an arrangement derived partly from poverty and a scarcity of housing, and from the central role of family in society. Young couples in urban areas often have difficulty obtaining their own home, and typically move in with the bride's parents. In the cities, two or three generations of a family usually live in a small apartment, while extended families in rural areas typically share a house. However, houses in rural Moldova often lack running water or other modern conveniences. In the countryside, nearly all Moldovans maintain a garden, a trend that is noticeable even in urban areas and cities. In fact, growing food was a common activity as part of the Soviet Union since the markets were inadequate, a situation that has not changed drastically since Moldova achieved independence (Moldova is the poorest country in Europe).

Food

Moldovan cuisine typically includes soups, stews, and various meat and fish dishes usually accompanied by vegetables and salads. However, Moldovan cuisine varies somewhat according to regions of the country. In eastern and northern Moldova, Ukrainian and Russian cuisine is common. For example, borscht (a soup using beetroot as the primary ingredient) is the most common soup in eastern Moldova. Another common Moldovan dish of Russian origin is pelmeni, which is a kind of dumpling usually stuffed with pork, beef, lamb, or mushrooms.

Romania runs along the entire western border of Moldova, so traditional Romanian cuisine is standard in western Moldova. For example, mamaliga, a kind of mushy dumpling made from cornmeal, is one of the most common dishes throughout Romania and Moldova. Mamaliga is often used as a substitute for bread in many Romanian and Moldovan dishes, and quite a few traditional meals in Moldova include mamaliga (or mamalyga), either as a main ingredient or as a side dish. A quite popular Moldovan dish is stuffed cabbage leaves served with mamaliga. Mamaliga is also served with meat, cheese, or cream.

In southern Moldova, there is a stronger Bulgarian culinary influence. Mangea, a special chicken sauce that originated in Bulgaria, is common in southern Moldova. Also, because of the significant Gaguaz minority, who are historically of Turkish origin, Turkish cuisine is also quite common in Moldova. Gagauz culture offers such traditional meals as sorpa, a highly seasoned soup made of lamb. Other standard Moldovan dishes are mititei, which are grilled sausage rolls; placinte, a flaky, stuffed pastry; and fried onions with sour cream.

Finally, making wine is a centuries-old tradition in Moldova, and drinking wine is common everywhere in Moldova. Wine is also one of the country's biggest exports. Other popular alcoholic drinks include brandy, especially tuica, a plum brandy.

Life's Milestones

Marriage is the most celebrated milestone for Moldovans. Many Moldovan couples first perform an Orthodox wedding ceremony—approximately 98.5 percent of the Moldovan population belongs to the Eastern Orthodox Church—and then perform the official civil ceremony afterward. At the close of the wedding ceremony, the bride traditionally trades her veil for a scarf to indicate she has transitioned from a girl to a mature woman and wife. She then gives the veil to the maid of honor, who is expected to marry next. Wedding guests customarily celebrate with feasting and dancing, sometimes for several days. In villages, the entire population might attend a lengthy feast held throughout the night.

The center of the wedding feast is always held in the casa mare, which is the most important room and family center in Moldovan homes. The walls of this room are traditionally filled with photographs of extended family and embroidered homespun towels that help create the family memorial. At dawn, after the first night of celebrating, everyone sits while the bride is given an infant to hold in her arms. Tradition holds that this will assure the bride that she will soon bear children. The casa mare is also the central meeting place after the couple's newborn child is christened. Guests are invited to celebrate with food and other refreshments in the casa mare of the parent's home. Also, when a member of the family dies, there is a funeral gathering in the casa mare.

CULTURAL HISTORY

Art

In the 1800s, Russia was the main influence and cultivator of fine arts in Moldova. At the time, Chişinău had one small elementary school for teaching children the fine arts. Most Moldovans who were serious about furthering their art studies went to the St. Petersburg Academy of Fine Arts in Russia, or to various Romanian fine arts academies. Shortly following World War II, a high school dedicated to fine arts opened in Chişinău, but again many Moldovan artists who graduated from this school went to Russia to earn higher arts degrees. Thus, Russia, with its long-standing relations with the French royal court and other Western European high societies, has been the primary influence for fine arts development in Moldova.

However, the 19th-century Russian influence on Moldovan art was short-lived, as the Russian influence eventually corrupted the Moldovan artistic aesthetic. Once Russia transformed into the Soviet Union, it began censoring all the Moldovan fine arts. This period of censorship lasted from the 1940s up to 1991, when the country declared independence following the dissolution of the Soviet Union. For about half a century, Moldovan art was forced to include and promote communist ideology, so nearly all paintings, drawings, sculptures, and monuments were created to celebrate heroes such as Karl Marx (1818–1883), a revolutionary communist and prominent socialist thinker, and Josef Stalin (1878–1953), former leader of the Soviet Union, as well as other Soviet and Moldovan communists.

The same can be said of the other Moldovan arts such as theater or literature, except that these arts also created a modern sort of myth out of the proletariat (working or lower classes). In order for Moldovan artists to be produced, published, or exhibited, they had to use a specific style known as socialist realism. Socialist realism portrayed figures as nearly mythological or larger than life, and the style always carried propagandist idealism and optimism about communism and socialism, and the perfect society these theories espoused. Thus, there are various historical factors that have caused Moldova to remain underdeveloped in its national tradition of fine arts. Rather, as a people Moldovans have for many centuries invested their creative energies into folk art, making the Moldovan folk arts exquisite and quite intricate.

The most renowned Moldovan folk arts, which have centuries of development behind them, are pottery, carpet-making, weaving, stonemasonry, and woodworking. Traditional Moldovan pottery is always created on a potter's wheel, and Moldovan craftsmen make a wide variety of items, from pots and plates to toys and tiles. Moldovan pottery is burned using two different methods — the oxygenated and non-oxygenated techniques. The two techniques create two standard base colors, red and black. Red pottery is often painted various natural colors or it may be etched and then covered with clear enamel. Plates, bowls, jugs, water pitchers, or other large containers are usually decorated in a uniquely Moldovan style that is brightly colored original art. Black pottery is decorated more simply, using the "rock polish" method, and black pottery is not enameled.

Moldovans also have a long and distinguished tradition in carpet making. Carpet making developed alongside embroidery, and both crafts tend to use designs that resemble plants or various geometrical motifs. The traditional colors most used in Moldovan carpets are bright and rich, with red and green most commonly used. Moldovan carpets are smooth, without pile, and are of the same type of weave as linen.

Architecture

Ancient Roman fortifications were the earliest permanent architecture in Moldova. According to legend, the Roman Emperor Trajan (52–117 CE) built these earliest defenses, known as Trajan's Wall, when the ancient Romans conquered Dacia (which mainly corresponds to modern-day Moldova and Romania). The fortifications extant in Moldova consist of earthen walls and palisades, and are known as the Lower Trajan's Wall and Upper Trajan's Wall. It is now believed that these defensive structures were built not by Romans, but in the third and fourth centuries, respectively, centuries after Trajan's death. Centuries later, Romanesque architecture was used to build some of the earliest fortresses.

Byzantine architecture was the most influential style to shape Moldova. Byzantine architecture, which reached Moldova early in its development, was a continuation of Roman architecture and was heavily influenced by Eastern Orthodox Christianity. (This architectural style was further ingrained during Russian domination in Moldova since Eastern Orthodox became the primary religion of the Russian and Balkan kingdoms.) In the earliest phase, Stephen III of Moldavia (c. 1432–1504), also known as Stephen the Great, fought to ensure the Moldovan region remained free from various neighboring nations and the Ottoman Empire (1299–1923). Though Stephen's medieval reign was a period of continual war, it also became one of the most significant periods of early cultural and architectural development. According to legend, Stephen constructed a religious building after each of his many military victories. One of the most significant constructions was the Putna Monastery, which contains the monarch's tomb. The monastery is considered a primary example of early Moldavian art.

Russia began dominating Moldovan territory in the 18th century. This cultural and architectural influence lasted for several centuries, and can be strongly felt today. Russia first occupied Moldova in 1739, and came into stable possession of Moldova in 1812. As a condition to end the Russo-Turkish War of 1806–1812, the Ottoman Empire signed the Bucharest Treaty, which ceded the territory known as Bessarabia, a historical region encompassing present-day Moldova, to Russia. It was during this part of Moldova's history that most of the nation's capital, Chişinău (Kishinev in Russian), was constructed in a neo-Byzantine architectural style. Russia would further exert its influence over the region during the Stalinist period of the Soviet Union, which significantly shaped Moldova's architecture. Soviet architecture was mostly functional, rather than aesthetic, and this can be seen in the prefabricated concrete buildings, such as the ubiquitous multi-storey apartment projects, erected during Moldova's Soviet period.

Drama

The Moldovan theater tradition has its roots in the medieval period when Orthodox rituals and mysteries were transformed into religious dramas. By the late 18th century, folk traditions and traveling carnivals had evolved into a specific style of folk theater. During its early years under Russian occupation, Moldovan arts, including theater, were harshly suppressed. The Russian language was legally pronounced the national language, and Moldovan language was forbidden in public. Thus, plays or other performances were not allowed in Romanian or Moldavian.

The first state theater, the Chişinău National Theater, opened in 1921 during a very brief period of Moldovan national independence after World War I. The national theater only survived a few decades of artistic freedom before the newly formed Soviet Union, which gained control of Moldova, began using theater to promote social realism and communist ideals. At that time, in the late 1940s, Moldova's national theater was renamed the Pushkin State Theater, after the Russian poet Alexander Pushkin (1799–1837).

Soviet cultural policies became slightly relaxed in the mid-20th century, which allowed the staging of Romanian plays. These exchanges of theatrical tours between Romania and Moldova had a positive effect on Moldovan theater. Theaters began performing the plays of poet and playwright Vasile Alecsandri (1821–1890), who had encouraged Moldovan nationalism in the previous century, and had co-authored a manifesto of the revolutionary movement in Moldova.

Music

The folk music of southeastern Europe is quite different from other music traditions in Europe. This is probably because the Ottoman Empire significantly influenced Moldovan music, giving it a distinctly Eastern sound that is quite different from Western music. Moldovan folk music is characteristically played at a fast tempo, has very complex and often syncopated rhythms, and uses improvisation and melodic embellishments.

During Moldova's Soviet period, the communist government promoted folk culture. However, the government also promoted social realism, the state-sanctioned style of art, and injected Russian culture into Moldovan traditions and performances. The Soviet Union also attempted to change some aspects of Moldovan folk music, dance, and costume traditions in order to make Moldova seem more distinct from Romania's folk traditions. This was because the Soviet Union believed that building a more distinct national Moldovan culture would diminish the possibility that Moldova would want to join with Romania. Nevertheless, Moldovan music and many of its other folk traditions are quite closely related to Romanian traditions.

Literature

The Moldovan (or Moldavian) language is a central symbol of nationhood and cultural heritage for Moldovans. The language was largely suppressed during the many years of Soviet dominance and became an important political issue as the Soviet Union collapsed. The Moldovan and Romanian languages are extremely similar, and it is argued that the Moldovan language is merely a dialect of Romanian. In fact, Moldavian as a language, is identical to Romanian, differing only in phonetics and vocabulary. Likewise, the literary development of Moldova is inextricably tied to Romania.

The first Moldovan books were Orthodox religious texts printed in the mid-17th century. Centuries later, writers such as Ion Creangă (1839–1889) and Mihai Eminescu (1850–1889)—the two held a lasting friendship—represented an emerging literary movement in

Moldova. About a century later, when the Soviet Union annexed Moldova, the Soviet government attempted to end Moldova's close cultural ties with Romania. Many ethnic Romanian writers, artists, and intellectuals were either executed or deported, usually to Siberia to work in gulags (prison slave camps). Romanian literature was officially banned and books were printed in Russian. At that time, the Soviet Union used socialist realism to transform Moldovan art and literature into tools for communist propaganda.

In March 1989, a magazine called *Glasul* ("The Voice") was printed in Latvia, and was smuggled into and distributed throughout Moldova. *Glasul* was the first magazine published in the Roman alphabet, and it had an enormous effect on the Moldovan population. Public opinion and protests forced the government to pass the Language Law in August 1989, which made Moldovan the official language of Moldova, and returned Moldovan to the Latin alphabet.

CULTURE

Arts & Entertainment
Moldova celebrates many artistic and cultural festivals throughout the year. October 14, City Day, is marked by theatrical performances and street exhibitions. During Martsishor, the March spring festival, people give each other flowers and martsishors, small red-and-white tokens that symbolize hope.

Chișinău is the home of the National Opera, established in the mid-1940s, and the National Ballet, established in 1957. The country's most famous opera singer is Maria Bieșu (1935–2012). Maria Bieșu Invites is an annual international festival of opera and ballet named in honor of the singer. Famous ballet dancers include the duo of Alexei and Cristina Terentiev.

Since Moldovan artists were trained for decades in the Soviet tradition, art tends to be conservative. Artists leading a more contemporary movement include graphic artists Marc Verlan (1963–) and illustrator Violeta

Zabulica-Diordiev (1966–). Folk art is a strong tradition in Moldova, resulting in brightly colored pottery and ceramics, carpets, and fabrics. Stone- and wood-carving are other traditional art forms that are still practiced.

Carpet making in contemporary Moldova exists at various levels: many rural women make carpets for their households, and the craft has been handed down through many generations. In addition, while there are professional artists who specialize in carpet making, Moldovan carpets are also produced industrially. Moldovans have also developed certain techniques and motifs in woodworking. Common designs carved into the wood include the rosette (foliage or floral design), a wolf's tooth, or a rhombus. The skill in carving these traditional designs have been passed down through many generations, and modern artisans continue to earn handsome wages for their work detailing the interiors of houses, public buildings, and churches.

Cultural Sites & Landmarks
Because the Republic of Moldova is located at the crossroads between Asia and Europe, it has been shaped by many diverse cultures. Moldova's architecture served as a primary example of this, but centuries of conflict and destruction have greatly reduced the country's architectural heritage. (During World War II, for example, the capital of Chișinău lost about 75 percent of its residential housing.) Nonetheless, some of Moldova's architectural heritage is still extant, including a series of historic churches surrounding Chișinău. The Mazarache (Mazarakievskaya) Church (1752), St. Konstantine and Helena (1777), and the Annunciation Church (1807) are all on hills overlooking the capital, and have architectural styles that date back to the Middle Ages.

Other landmarks in the capital include the Triumphal Arch (or Victory Arch), built in 1840, and the famous Gates of Chișinău. The capital is also home to numerous museums, including the National History Museum, the Fine Arts Museum, and the Pushkin House Museum (the Russian poet lived in the city from 1820–1823).

One of the most interesting cultural sites in Moldova is Orheiul Vechi, located northeast of Chișinău. Archaeologists have uncovered many thousands of years of human history at this site, dating back to the Stone Age. The site is probably best known for its monastery complex that is carved into the cliffs overlooking the Raut River. In the 13th century CE, Orthodox monks dug the cave monastery (Manastire in Pestera), and dwelled there for the next 500 years. The Soviet government closed down the monastery and its aboveground church in the 1940s, but several years after the Moldovan revolution, in 1996, Orthodox monks returned and began restoring the site. The large bluff at Orheiul Vechi has six complexes of interlocking caves that were dug and expanded over the course of thousands of years.

Another significant cultural site is the Soroca fortress, a well-preserved fortress built in the Middle Ages. The site was originally built in wood, but was completely rebuilt in stone during the 16th century. In fact, the Soroca fortress is Moldova's only medieval structure that has survived intact to the present. The Soroca fortress is also famous as the exact site where, in 1711, the Russian army and the Moldovan army met to combine their forces to battle the Turkish hordes.

Libraries & Museums

The National Museum of Ethnography and Natural History of the Republic of Moldova is located in the capital, Chișinău. This museum is the largest, oldest, and most visited museum in Moldova; it annually attracts over 50,000 visitors, and houses a collection of more than 165,000 artifacts. Most of the museum's collections relate to the natural and anthropological history of the Moldovan region and include zoological, botanical, paleontological, archeological, and ethnographical specimens. In all, the country boasts a network of more than sixty-five museums, with the majority, such as the Fine Arts Museum and the Pushkin House Museum, concentrated in Chișinău.

The National Library of Moldova is located in the capital. Established in the early 19th century, it holds more that 2.1 million books and serials as of 2009. The country is home to nearly 1,400 public libraries and nearly 1,500 school libraries.

Holidays

Eastern Orthodox Christians in Moldova celebrate Christmas on January 7 and 8, and Easter in April. The spring festival of Martsishor is celebrated on March 1.

Other official holidays in Moldova include Memorial Day (April 27), Labor Day (May 1), Victory and Commemoration Day (May 9), and Independence Day (August 27). The Gagauz celebrate December 23 as the day they gained autonomous status in 1994.

Youth Culture

A large generation gap currently exists between Moldovan youth and older generations. Previous generations were educated and socialized under the Soviet Union and the banner of communism, when corruption, powerlessness, and poor living conditions were accepted features of life. Moldovan youth, however, are much less patient with corruption and the lack of improvement in the Moldovan standard of living. This gap can be seen in the April 2009 elections. Mostly students and the younger generation comprised the protests and riots against the government and election results. The gathering was well over 10,000 people, and most of them were Moldovan youth who felt disillusioned with the Moldovan system. A significant number of them believed that "none of the above" should be an option on election ballots since they do not believe in any of the current parties or candidates. Young people are also the most mobile, as they are the largest percentage willing to leave the country to find work elsewhere. Many youth may emigrate for better conditions, which will ultimately have a negative effect on the country.

SOCIETY

Transportation

Moldovans most frequently use buses for transportation, which serve as the main transport system domestically and abroad. The bus system in Moldova is quite inexpensive. In Chişinău and its suburbs, there are also privately operated minibuses called marshrutkas that follow the major bus and trolleybus routes in smaller time intervals. Another common means of transportation in Moldova are its railroads. The country's only major airport is in Chişinău. As of 2013, Moldova had five airports and 1,190 kilometers of railway. Traffic moves on the right-hand side of the road in Moldova.

Transportation Infrastructure

The nation of Moldova is connected to the major cities of Europe and the Middle East through the Chişinău International Airport. Although the airport is physically small, with just four terminal gates, it is capable of handling an annual capacity of over 5 million travelers. The railroad from Chişinău connects to most of Moldova's largest cities, and trains regularly run to Odessa (in Ukraine) on the Black Sea. Highways also link Moldova's main cities, but many roads are in need of repair. Within the city of Chişinău, public transportation is available through buses, minibuses, and taxis.

Media & Communications

Television is the dominant medium. For decades, Moldovans have had access to three main state television channels; after the revolution, one private channel began broadcasting. The Moldovan government owns one of the channels (Radioteleviziunea Nationala), the Romanian government owns another (Televiziunea Romana), and the Russian government owns one channel (Ostankino Kanal 1). In 1995, one independent television station began in Chişinău. There are also about fifty national and local radio stations. Moldovan newspapers are generally pro-government or opposition leaning in their coverage of Moldovan politics and current events. Political parties also publish their own titles. Moldovan editions of Russian newspapers are among the best-selling publications.

As part of the Soviet Union, telephone service in Moldova was poor and inadequate. Since independence, a German company has upgraded about 10,000 digital lines in Chişinău, and a new telecommunications company, backed by Greek and Italian telecommunications partners, has been making infrastructure improvements. Moldova also has several cell phone operators, and the number of cell phone users is growing tremendously since the turn of the 21st century. According to the CIA *World Factbook*, in 2012 there were 1.21 million people using landlines and 4.08 million with cell phones. Additionally, as of 2010, there were approximately 1.3 million Internet users, though usage was primarily concentrated in Moldova's largest cities.

SOCIAL DEVELOPMENT

Standard of Living

Moldova ranked 114th out of 187 countries on the 2014 United Nations Human Development Index, which measures quality of life and standard of living indicators.

Water Consumption

Groundwater is the source of drinking water for approximately two-thirds of the Moldovan population. As of 2008, an estimated 47 percent of the population lacked access to clean and safe drinking water, and more than half of the population lacked piped water in their households (a number that climbs to over 80 percent in rural areas).

Education

Education is compulsory in Moldova for children between seven and 16 years of age. Primary school last for four years, and age eleven begins secondary education. Secondary school is completed in two cycles of five years and two years.

Several of the country's 45 universities are in Chişinău. Of these, the Technical University of Moldova, founded in 1964, is the only technical university that is accredited by the government. The Academy of Economic Studies of Moldova was founded in 1991.

Moldova does not have a long history of higher education. The oldest university in the country is the State Medical and Pharmaceutical University in Chişinău, founded in 1946.

The Comrat State University, in Comrat, is Gagauzia's only university.

Moldova's literacy rate is 99 percent (99.7 percent among men, and 99.1 percent among women). In the early 21st century, the net enrolment ratios for male and female students in preschool, primary school, and secondary school were nearly even.

Women's Rights

Gender roles in Moldova are quite traditional. For example, women are always responsible for meal preparations and all domestic housework, while men are considered the "breadwinners" for the family. However, typically both spouses work outside of the home, but women have been finding it harder to find jobs because men are usually given precedence whenever unemployment figures rise.

Another problem Moldovan women face is domestic violence. Approximately 25 percent of all Moldovan women have experienced sexual or physical violence at some time in their lives, and the legal and social framework to protect and support women is quite limited. The lack of support is partly from national poverty, but also from a general social mentality that violence against wives is acceptable. This particular problem also feeds into commercial sex trafficking. If a Moldovan woman wants to escape from a violent spouse she must start over, including changing where she lives and works. This is why some women risk responding to ads for jobs in other countries that they suspect are jobs as prostitutes. Some of these women are desperate to escape domestic violence and do not have battered women's shelters or other support systems domestically.

Women in Moldova who become pregnant outside of marriage, as well as those who have abortions, are socially stigmatized. Thus, women who have abortions may face abuse. Even though Moldovan law does not have criminal penalties against women who have illegal abortions, women may nevertheless be charged with intentional and premeditated murder. The European Court of Human Rights (ECtHR) heard a lawsuit against the Moldovan government for prosecuting abortion as a case of premeditated murder. The suit charged that, by sentencing a woman to twenty years in prison for having an abortion, the Moldovan government violated a number of rights guaranteed by the European Convention on Human Rights (ECHR). The suit also served as an attempt to make post-abortion care a basic part of women's healthcare in Moldova, and to ensure that such care is provided in all settings, including prisons.

Health Care

Per capita annual health expenditure is approximately $100 USD. The country has 3.5 doctors for every 1,000 people. Average life expectancy is seventy years—approximately 66 years for men and 74 years for women (2014 estimate).

Health care is provided primarily by the government. It is supported by taxes, but even so, many of the poor cannot afford care. The government is working to institute a system of mandatory insurance coverage. Recently, the World Bank and the Dutch government have established the $10 million Moldova Health Investment Fund to provide health centers and doctors for many rural villages.

GOVERNMENT

Structure

Moldova declared independence from Russia in 1990. It was officially recognized as an independent republic on August 27, 1991.

Crowning of bride and groom is part of a traditional wedding ceremony in Moldova.

The president is the head of state and is elected by popular vote to a four-year term. The prime minister (usually the head of the majority party) is elected by Parliament as the head of government and governs with a Council of Ministers. In case of a "no confidence" vote by Parliament, the Council of Ministers must resign. The Moldovan Parliament is a unicameral legislature. Its 101 members are elected directly to four-year terms.

Political Parties

As of the 2014 parliamentary elections, Moldova's multiparty system is mostly dominated by three political parties, the Party of Socialists (PSRM), the Liberal Democratic Party (PLDM), and the Communist Party (PCRM), which hold twenty-five, 23, and 21 seats, respectively, in parliament. Two other parties, the Democratic Party and the Liberal Party, hold 19 and 13 parliamentary seats, respectively. There are numerous minor parties in the country, none of which gained or maintained any representation in the 2014 parliamentary elections, held in November.

In the summer of 2014, the Moldovan government signed and ratified an Association Agreement with the European Union (EU), advancing the government's policy priority of EU integration. Following the country's most recent legislative election in November 2014, the three pro-European parties that entered Parliament won 55 of the body's 101 seats, enough for a majority coalition. After negotiations among the three broke down, however, two of the parties—the Liberal Democratic Party (PLDM) and the Democratic Party (PD)—agreed to form the Alliance for a European Moldova (AEM) and a minority government with their combined 42 seats. In February 2015, the PLDM and the PD secured Communist Party (PCRM) support to win parliamentary approval with 60 votes for their minority government.

Local Government

The country is divided into 32 raions (administrative divisions), three municipalities, and one autonomous special administrative district, Gagauzia; the breakaway region of Transnistria remains disputed. The country has two levels of local governance, with the first operating at the village, city (of which there are 51), and municipal levels, and the second level comprised of districts, called judets. Councils and mayors are the authoritative representatives of government at the local level.

Judicial System

The Supreme Court of Justice represents the judicial branch of government. Jurisdiction then extends to the Court of Appeals, most concentrated at the district and municipal level, and ordinary courts. The Constitutional Court oversees constitutional administrations of justice, and is not hierarchically ranked in the system of courts.

Taxation

Moldova maintains a relatively moderate income tax rate, with a top rate of 18 percent. There is no corporate tax. Other national taxes levied include a value-added tax (or VAT), excise taxes, road taxes, and a privatization tax. Local taxes include land and real estate taxes, natural resources taxes, and territory development tax.

Armed Forces

The armed forces of landlocked Moldova consist of the Moldovan Ground Forces and the Moldovan Air Force. Conscription exists, and 18 is the minimum age for compulsory service, which lasts one year. The armed forces remain relatively small and ill equipped though modernization has become more of a priority in recent years.

Foreign Policy

Historically, Moldova has been aligned with Russia, and the government has fluctuated between establishing close ties with Russia and the European Union (EU) in recent years. However, Russian relations probably reached their lowest point shortly after the Moldovan revolution when the Transnistria (or Transdniestria) region of Moldova (in the east) broke away from Moldova, resulting in a five-month war. Afterward, Moldova accused Russia of assisting the separatists in the region, and the Russian military continues to maintain a presence in the breakaway region. The dispute remains unresolved and is the most central foreign policy issue for Moldova. Moldova and Ukraine operate border patrols that monitor the movement of people and commodities through the breakaway region. The entire region is under the supervisory auspices of the Organization for Security and Cooperation in Europe (OSCE).

Moldova is a member of the United Nations (UN), the Commonwealth of Independent States (CIS), the OSCE, the Partnership for Peace program of the North Atlantic Treaty Organization (NATO), and the Council of Europe. Communist rule of the country has severely slowed privatization, and has created a trend toward re-nationalization of companies in Moldova. The Moldovan government's non-communist economic and finance ministers have resigned from office, and the International Monetary Fund (IMF) and World Bank have both restricted and placed many stipulations to their lending programs that would strengthen the Moldovan market economy. Lastly, integration with Europe continues to be a central issue and debate of Moldova's foreign relations.

Human Rights Profile

International human rights law insists that states respect civil and political rights, and promote an individual's economic, social, and cultural rights. The United Nations Universal Declaration on Human Rights is (UDHR) recognized as the standard for international human rights. (To read this document or view the articles relating to cultural human rights, visit http://www.un.org/en/documents/udhr/.)

Moldova has achieved a credible human rights record considering its status as the poorest nation in Europe. Nevertheless, various relevant UN committees have expressed concern with Moldova's human rights record in their respective areas. Moldova submitted its first report to the Committee

for Economic, Social and Cultural Rights six years past the agreed upon deadline. During that time, various non-governmental organizations (NGOs) such as Amnesty International have reported widespread ill treatment and torture of suspects and prisoners by Moldovan police officers. According to such country reports, there is also concern with the high level of corruption within the Moldovan police force and other government institutions.

When human rights lawyers and advocates within Moldova have raised violations issues, they have been harassed by police and government. When they published information about human rights violations, the Moldovan government threatened to prosecute these lawyers on the grounds of "misuse of official position." Reports have also been filed that some opposition politicians have been harassed and intimidated for expressing political views contrary to the government line.

According to international human rights monitoring agencies, Moldova's biggest human rights issues are human trafficking violations, particularly in the trafficking of women and girls for commercial sexual exploitation. In the last decade, a network of Eastern European criminal organizations has been trafficking Moldovan women to other countries in Eastern Europe, Western Europe, and the Middle East. Girls and young women are also trafficked domestically from Moldova's rural areas to Chişinău, and children are trafficked to neighboring countries for forced labor. Further exacerbating the issue is corruption within the government and among police and customs authorities. In short, officials accept bribes to permit the trafficking. When international organizations have informed the Moldovan government of the problem, the government has done little to stop the trafficking. Moldova does not fully comply even with the minimum standards for the elimination of trafficking, and has not been making significant efforts to do so. The Moldovan government failed to look into any allegations of officials being complicit in trafficking, which was cited in a 2007 report, and the government did not demonstrate any effort to identify trafficking victims in 2008, a year in which the country was targeted as the main European source for human trafficking.

ECONOMY

Overview of the Economy

Although it is the poorest country in Europe, Moldova has made progress in improving its economy. The government has supported privatization of land, reduced interest rates, and removed many governmental controls and preferential treatment policies. As a result, the economy has shown steady growth. Continued progress is expected to be threatened by political factions that are resisting the reforms. Moldova's per capita gross domestic product (GDP) is estimated at $4,800 (USD) in 2014.

Industry

Consumer goods are the focus of Moldovan industry. Major industrial activity includes the production of food products, beverages, cigarettes, carpets, footwear, textiles, appliances, and farm equipment. The chemical industry produces a small amount of synthetic fibers, plastics, paint, and varnish. The construction industry produces cement and prefabricated concrete structures. Moldova earns approximately $2.6 billion (USD) each year exporting food, textiles, and machinery.

Chişinău is Moldova's industrial center. The city contributes to the country's light engineering needs through the manufacturing of measuring equipment, machine tools, tractors, pumps, refrigerators, washing machines, and insulated wiring. Chişinău is particularly important to the winemaking industries of Moldova; it is the nation's export outlet. Moldova is placed seventh among the world's top wine exporters. Wine exports account for nearly half of the nation's export earnings and

one quarter of the nation's gross domestic product (GDP).

Almost all of Moldova's energy is imported from Russia, and energy shortages following the breakup of the Soviet Union impeded industrial production.

Labor

Moldova's labor force was estimated at 1.23 million in 2014. As of 2012, the services sector accounted for nearly 60 percent of the work force, while agriculture employed roughly 26 percent. Industry accounted for only 13 percent of the labor force. The unemployment rate was reported as 6.2 in 2014.

Energy/Power/Natural Resources

There are protected natural zones throughout Moldova, containing caves, toltry (coral formations), and evidence of prehistoric civilization. The largest and most beautiful cave, Cinderella, also known as Emil Racovitza, is in the northern part of the country. With a length of 89 kilometers (55 miles), it is the world's third-longest gypsum cave.

Current environmental issues arise largely from Soviet exploitation, including poor agricultural methods and the heavy use of agricultural chemicals (including pesticides such as DDT). Contamination of soil and groundwater is a major concern. Soil erosion and river silting result from heavy rains and floods.

Forestry

Moldova's forests once covered 40 percent of the country, but are now limited to less than 10 percent of the land, mostly in the hilly central area. Most of the forests are comprised of old oak trees. The oak is the emblem of the country. More valuable economically, however, are the country's beech trees, which are rare.

Mining/Metals

Moldova's mineral resources include lignite, phosphorites, gypsum, sand and gravel, and limestone. Many of these resources are used to make construction materials, and are often found on the surface instead of in mines. Oil and brown coal have been discovered in the south. Mining operations recover gypsum and peat.

Agriculture

Moldova's agriculture and food industry is the most important part of the country's economy. Nearly 56 percent of the land is arable, and almost all of this is under cultivation. Agriculture accounts for more than half of the country's GDP, and employs two-thirds of the labor force.

More than 72 percent of the arable soil is fertile black soil (called cernoziom), created by the forests which once covered Moldova. Even the eroded soil does not seriously inhibit agriculture, because vineyards flourish in eroded soils. Vineyards in the southern part of the country produce fine, internationally popular wines.

Principal crops include cereals, vegetables and fruits, and tobacco. Livestock and animal products are varied. Forestry produces wood for both industry and fuel.

Problems facing Moldova's agriculture business include weather variations, flooding, erosion, and fluctuating world prices.

Animal Husbandry

Sheep and goats, cattle, pigs, poultry, and horses are the primary livestock in Moldova.

Tourism

Nearly 93,000 tourists visit Moldova annually, accounting for approximately $1.3 billion (USD) in spending. The Federation of Sport and Tourism of the Republic of Moldova and Moldova-Tur SA, both based in Chişinău, promote tourism in Moldova.

Moldova's picturesque rolling green hills, river valleys, orchards, and whitewashed villages attract many visitors. The country operates more than 40 national parks, the largest of which is Tzaul (46 hectares/113 acres). Moldova's wine country is another popular tourist attraction. Tours and tastings are given at wineries such as Cricova, Cojusna, Milestii, and Mici, not far from Chişinău.

Near the village of Rudi, in the north, are more than 250 archaeological sites, dating as far back as the Iron Age. The ancient Greek historian Herodotus mentions one of these, the ancient town of Methonium. The area has been called the "Museum under the Open Sky." Other historic sites in Moldova include 10th-century cave monasteries, 15th-century Orthodox monasteries, old wooden churches, and ancient and medieval fortresses.

Sinclair Nicholas, Ellen Bailey,
Lynn-nore Chittom

DO YOU KNOW?

- One of the largest underground wine cellars in the world is located just 15 kilometers (9 miles) north of Chişinău at a location known as the Cricova Mines. The limestone from the mines has been used to build the impressive white buildings of Chişinău and the surrounding towns, and the open tunnels of the former mine are now used to house the nation's wines. Some Moldovan health resorts, in fact, use wine therapy to treat people who have been exposed to radiation.

- The earliest references to the city of Chişinău date from 1466, when the city functioned as a small Christian monastic community within a province known as Bessarabia.

Bibliography

Charles King. "The Moldovans: Romania, Russia, and the Politics of Culture." Stanford, CA: *Hoover Institution Press*, 1999.

Donald L. Dyer, ed. "Studies in Moldovan: The History, Culture, Language, and Contemporary Politics of the People of Moldova." New York: *Columbia University Press*, 1996.

Robert Reid and Leiff Pettersen. "Romania and Moldova." Oakland, CA: *Lonely Planet*, 2007.

Stephen Henighan. "Lost Province: Adventures in a Moldovian Family." Vancouver: *Beach Holme*, 2002.

William H. Hill. Russia, the Near Abroad, and the West: Lessons from the Moldova-Transdniestra Conflict." Washington, D.C.: *Woodrow Wilson Center Press*, 2012.

Works Cited

"Country Profile: Moldova." *BBC News*.

"Moldova." *Business Eastern Europe*. EBSCO Business Source Complete database.

"Foreign Relations." *Republic of Moldova Official Website*. http://news.bbc.co.uk/2/hi/europe/country_profiles/3038982.stm
http://romania-on-line.net/general/moldova.htm
http://search.ebscohost.com/login.aspx?direct=true&db=bth&AN=33160069&site=ehost-live
http://search.ebscohost.com/login.aspx?direct=true&db=bth&AN=36097288&site=ehost-live

Michael Wines, "History Course Ignites a Volatile Tug of War in Moldova." *New York Times*. (February 25, 2002). April 2, 2009.

"Moldova: Risk Summary." *Emerging Europe Monitor: Russia & CIS*. EBSCO Business Source Complete database.

Republic of Moldova. http://www.moldova.md/en/relatile/

D. Rubin, P. Nagy, and P. Rouyer. *The World Encyclopedia of Contemporary Theatre: Europe – Moldova*.

Medieval town of Budva, Montenegro

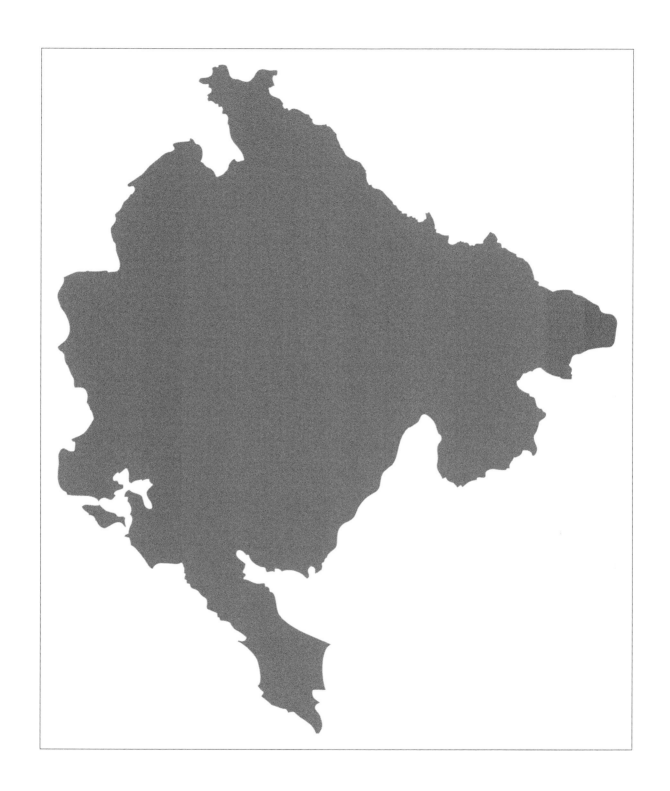

MONTENEGRO

Introduction

Montenegro is a country in Southeastern Europe. It is bordered in the east by Serbia, Kosovo, and Albania, and on the west by Bosnia-Herzegovina and the Adriatic Sea. The country once formed one half of the State Union of Serbia and Montenegro. However, Montenegro and Serbia each declared independence in June 2006.

GENERAL INFORMATION

Official Language: Montenegrin
Population: 650,036 (July 2014 estimate)
Currency: Euro
Coins: The Euro is available in 1, 2, 5, 10, 20, and 50-cent coins. A 1 and 2 Euro coin are also available.
Land Area: 13,452 square kilometers (5,193 square miles)
Water Area: 360 square kilometers (138 square miles)
National Anthem: "Oh, the Bright Dawn of May"
Capital: Podgorica
Time Zone: GMT +1
Flag Description: The flag of Montenegro features a golden-bordered red field with the country's coat of arms (a golden double-headed eagle with a lion on its chest) centered in the middle.

Population

Montenegro is a country of many ethnic groups. The majority of Montenegro's Serb population lives in the northern municipalities and along the Adriatic Sea. Montenegrins occupy the center of the country, and are largely concentrated in the capital of Podgorica. According to official statistics dating to 2011, Montenegrins made up 45 percent of the total population, followed by Serbians at approximately 28 percent. Other ethnic groups include Bosnian Muslims, Albanians, Croats, and Roma (subgroup of the Romani). As of 2014, 63.8 percent of the total population is urban.

Languages

While Montenegrin is the official language, Serbian is spoken widely followed by Bosnians and Albanians. According to the 2011 census, Serbian speakers accounted for nearly 43 percent of the population, followed by Montenegrin (37 percent), Bosnian, and Albanian (just over five percent each). Roughly, four percent of the population spoke an unspecified language.

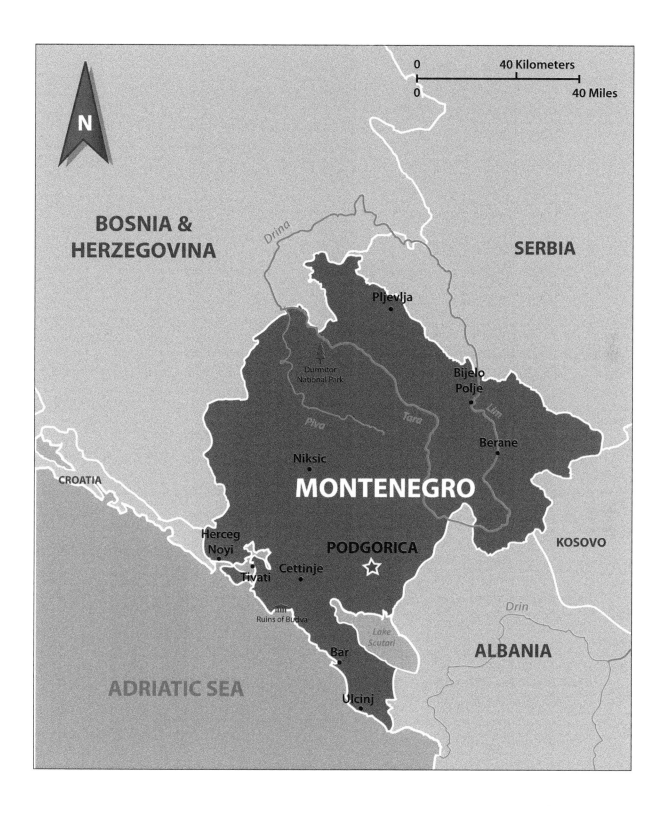

Principal Cities by Population (2012):

- Podgorica (149,228)
- Nikšić (58,644)
- Pljevlja (20,979)
- Bar (15, 861)
- Bijelo Polje (15,084)

Native People & Ethnic Groups

First populated by Illyrians, the region now known as Montenegro was inhabited by Romans beginning in nine CE. Slavs colonized the area in the fifth century. In the seventh century, the "Unknown Archont" established what became known as an early Serbian Empire in the Balkans. "Unknown Archont" is the term given by historians to the Serbian leader that helped to establish this early regime.

Religions

Orthodox Christian is the predominant religion; according to 2011 data from *The World Factbook*, over 72 percent of the population identified as belonging to the Serbian Orthodox Church. However, all religions in Montenegro have established rights and are considered separate entities from the state. Other religions present in the country include Sunni Islam and Roman Catholicism, among others.

Climate

Montenegro has a seasonal continental climate, with cold winters and warm summers. The weather tends to be cooler and drier in the mountains, while the plains and valleys experience warmer and more humid conditions. In the southern regions, the average summer temperature reaches 22° Celsius (71° Fahrenheit), while the mountainous north has an average temperature of 18° Celsius (64° Fahrenheit).

Parts of Montenegro, especially in the southern regions, have a Mediterranean climate; summers are dry and winters mild. Temperatures tend to be warmer in these areas than in the rest of the country, and can average 27° Celsius (81° Fahrenheit). Winter temperatures in the south average 8° Celsius (46° Fahrenheit), and typically remain around −3° Celsius (27° Fahrenheit) at higher altitudes in the north.

During the winter, the country experiences an average of forty days of snow in the lowlands; the mountains can receive three times as much snow. Montenegro averages five meters (around 200 inches) of precipitation per year. Much of this rain falls in the mountains during the colder parts of the year.

ENVIRONMENT & GEOGRAPHY

Topography

Montenegro is divided into 21 municipalities and occupies an area of 13,812 square kilometers (5,019 square miles). It is mountainous, with a small section of coastal plain along the Adriatic Sea. The Zeta is Montenegro's major river, and is used to generate hydroelectric power. Montenegro's highest mountains include Bobotov Kuk peak in the Durmitor Mountains. Bobotov Kuk measures 2,523 meters (8,277 feet) in height.

Most of Montenegro's land consists of flat farmland, which is used for vineyards, growing grain, and for livestock. The eastern and northernmost section of the country is forest. The land in southwester Montenegro, bordering the Adriatic Sea, is used to grow olives, grapes, and citrus fruits.

Podgorica is located in the southern part of Montenegro on the Zeta plain, and surrounded by several important trade routes and waterways. The city lies at the convergence of the Ribnica and Morača Rivers, with the Zeta, Cijevna, and Sitnica Rivers in close proximity. In addition, Podgorica is situated near Lake Scudari (Skadar), and is just 65 kilometers (40 miles) north of the Adriatic Sea. To the north of the city is a series of hills, the largest of which is Gorica Hill at 107 meters (351 feet).

The capital occupies 1,441 square kilometers (556 square miles), and is divided into three municipalities: Podgorica City, Golubvoci, and Tuzi. Podgorica is also close to some of Montenegro's ski resorts in the north of the country, including Zlatar, Zlatibor, Brezovica, Jahorina, and Popova Shapka in Macedonia.

Plants & Animals

Montenegro has extensive forests of oak and beech trees. Cyprus forests can also be found in parts of southern Montenegro. While there is evidence that the region was once heavily forested, erosion, and agriculture have destroyed many of the trees. Most of the mountain country is covered with forest, although areas within southern Montenegro do not have enough soil cover to support the trees. Instead, Mediterranean vegetation known as maquis has grown in their place.

Animals that are commonly found in Montenegro include bears, deer, martens, and wild pigs. The region is also home to predators like wolves and foxes. The region's many bird species include the pygmy cormorant (*Phalacrocorax pygmeus*), the ferruginous duck (*Aythya nyroca*), the long-legged buzzard (*Buteo rufinus*), and the saker falcon (*Falco cherrug*).

CUSTOMS & COURTESIES

Greetings

Montenegrins typically shake hands when first greeting friends and family, but they occasionally embrace and kiss each other on the cheek three times. They use formal verbal greetings when meeting a new acquaintance, but are generally more informal after becoming better acquainted. Montenegrins are comfortable, in most cases, with making direct eye contact, especially for greetings. As a rule, they are direct with each other when communicating. It is also not unusual for there to be personal contact when conversing. As such, personal space is not extremely restricted or formal. However, though a person might touch another on the shoulder, people of the opposite sex rarely touch when talking.

Gestures & Etiquette

Montenegrins value courage, honor, and loyalty most among a person's attributes. They also value

making a good impression, including pronouncing names and words correctly. When talking to each other, it is not uncommon for Montenegrins to be physically demonstrative. It is also common to see people embrace one another in public. The hospitable nature of Montenegrins is evident in their practice at waving to children and police officers—but not to other adults—when driving by in a car, as pedestrians are common even in rural areas.

When visiting monasteries and shrines, people dress respectfully, and not in beach clothes. When leaving chapels, Montenegrins traditionally walk out backwards and they kiss the relics of the Orthodox Church. Common practice in all religious buildings in Montenegro, Christian and Muslim alike, is to remove shoes before walking inside.

Eating/Meals

Montenegrins eat their meals in typical European fashion, except for breakfast, which is large and might consist of eggs, bread, a meat, and a dip that is made of sour cream, called kajmak. The main meal of the day in Montenegro is lunch. It is not eaten until later in the afternoon, which is different from most other European countries. A Montenegrin's lunch varies according to whether they reside along the coast or in the highland. For example, lunch usually consists of seafood, a salad, and bread along the coast, as is typical in Mediterranean cuisines. In the highland region or farther inland, the food is more influenced by surrounding countries, such as Turkish lamb kebabs or musakka, which is made with layers of minced lamb, eggplant, tomato, and white sauce. Hungarian goulash, a stew or soup with beef and vegetables, is another common inland meal. As the main meal, lunch often includes a dessert. Montenegrins have adapted the baklava to their own tastes by adding raisins and chopped walnuts. Along the coast, Montenegrins enjoy continental-influenced desserts, such as crêpes.

The last meal of the day is generally the lightest, which Montenegrins typically eat at around eight o'clock in the evening. While they eat more seafood along the coast, they also consume cured meats, as are typical in Mediterranean cultures. Inland meals often include potatoes and some form of meat, whether lamb, beef, or pork. Montenegrins enjoy sauerkraut rolls, called sarma, served with mashed potatoes. Bread commonly accompanies most meals in Montenegro.

Visiting

Visiting friends is an important part of Montenegrin culture. As close family ties are important, Montenegrins value frequent visits in their friends' homes. When invited to a Montenegrin's home, visitors usually bring a gift as a token of gratitude. A bottle of wine or coffee used for making Turkish coffee is appreciated, as are imported gifts. When special occasions arise, such as birthdays, visitors bring gifts that are opened after the visitors leave, as it is considered impolite to open gifts in front of guests.

It is customary to offer visitors a glass of fruit brandy called rakija and make a toast. When toasting, visitors make eye contact with the one who is making the toast. Eating dinner at a Montenegrin's home could easily become a feast. It is considered rude not to eat whatever is offered, and Montenegrins enjoy lavishing their guests with traditional dishes.

LIFESTYLE

Family

Family and kinship is very important to Montenegrins. After years of political and ethnic strife, people have generally become somewhat

Traditional folk costumes in Montenegro.

suspicious of outsiders, preferring to be self-reliant. Because of the importance of the family, Montenegrins maintain tight bonds, in part for reliance and strength.

A typical Montenegrin household might house several generations. Only until recently, as more people move to cities, have Montenegrins stopped living in clans. The typical nuclear family includes one or two children. However, extended families still live together, with grandparents helping to care for young children, and adults often assist aging parents who require care.

More recently, younger Montenegrins are moving into their own apartments, and while parents used to arrange marriages for their children, this is no longer traditionally practiced. Though Montenegrins once married younger, adults now choose their own marriage partners typically during their late twenties. The family's social order remains patriarchal, though women are increasingly working outside of the home.

Housing

Montenegrin housing ranges from old rural estates to modern detached family homes. Generally, these dwellings are built out of wood, stone, or brick and are fairly modest. Rural housing is situated close together, rather than spread out, and groups of older houses might be surrounded by an old mud or stone wall for protection (in some cases, older homes also include a watchtower). Courtyards and fences add to the privacy of individual rural Montenegrin homes. Low-rise apartment buildings are common in Montenegrin cities. Newer or remodeled buildings include modern European designs and materials, including wood floors and ceramic-tile bathrooms. The structures themselves are made out of stone, wood, or brick, with modern buildings made out of slab concrete.

The mix of traditional and modern homes along the Adriatic Sea might include traditional features such as terracotta tile roofs and stone masonry. Their sizes can range from bungalows to larger three- and four-bedroom homes. Modern homes, like many apartments, might be a mix of concrete and steel with windows that have aluminum shutters to help insulate against the hot coastal sun. Homes on the coast often have terraces and large windows for viewing the scenery.

Food

Montenegrin cuisine is hearty, and its influences extend back hundreds of years and vary according to either the northern highland or coastal regions. The highland region is especially known for hearty cuisine. The national meatball-like dish cevapcici, which is made with pork and beef, resembles sausage and includes onions and chili pepper. A few Montenegrin highland dishes include some form of milk and bread, such as the highland dish kacamak. Kacamak is made with a wheat, corn, or barley flour and stirred with cheese until the mixture reaches a thick consistency. Kacamak is used an added ingredient in many Montenegrin dishes, and is also eaten alone. Another popular food is a cicvara, a thick, energy-rich stew that most often includes potatoes, flour, and cheese similar to new cottage cheese or clotted cream. Popara mixes bread and cheese, and is a Montenegrin take on pizza.

Mediterranean cultures, especially Italy, heavily influence coastal cuisine in Montenegro. Breads, cheeses, and cured meats are Italian-influenced staples that are included in nearly every meal. Bread is made with barley, wheat, rye, or corn flour, and whether served alone or in a dish with cheese or milk, it is served with Montenegrin food. Special cheeses include skorup, which is like cottage cheese, and those that are unpasteurized (not boiled), as well as fresh cheeses kept in oil. Strong cured meats include sausages and a smoked ham called prsuta, which is considered a worthy rival to Italian cured hams such as prosciutto. Lamb is traditionally made with the process called "under sac." This method involves cooking lamb in an iron pan under embers and ash to seal in the flavor.

The distinctive pita bread, known to many Middle Eastern cultures, comes in multiple varieties in Montenegro. These breads are typically made with wheat and sometimes include green herbs. Montenegrins drink handmade buttermilk or use it to make a dish similar to yogurt. They also make sour cream, which is used with all kinds of dishes, from meats to savory pancakes to desserts.

Life's Milestones

The wedding is an important ceremony in Montenegro and can last for days. Marriages are not arranged and are decided between the man and the woman. To bless a marriage with children, the bride lifts a young or baby boy three times at the doorway of her new home. A godmother or godfather, known as the kuma or kum, are not related by blood but are integral in raising children. The kuma or kum helps name the baby and honored at the child's baptism.

One of the most important milestones in Montenegro is the attendance of the funeral. Missing a funeral is considered more disrespectful than missing a person's wedding. Montenegrins hold special ceremonies for the deceased. They present food that includes meats and salads at the cemetery during the burial and on the one-year anniversary of the death.

CULTURAL HISTORY

Art

Early Montenegrin painting was mostly religious in nature. It was concentrated in monasteries and chapels where frescoes generally depicted religious figures, saints, and biblical scenes. Beginning in the 20th century, landscape painting, portraitures, and still life, mostly in the European impressionist style, became popular. Many Montenegrin artists also moved to surrounding European countries where they found financial support. One of the best-known early 20th-century Montenegrin painters was Pero Pocek (1878–1963), who studied painting in Italy. Pocek is known for his impressionist works, as well as his series of paintings inspired by *The Mountain Wreath*, a well-known work of Montenegrin literature. Other significant

Montenegrin painters include Milo Milunovic (1897–1967), who studied the impressionist Paul Cézanne (1839–1906) and painted primarily impressionist works. Petar Lubarda (1905–1974) used a restrained palette to paint landscapes and subjects from Montenegrin history.

After World War I, many artists such as Milunovic and Lubarda returned to their country (which had become Yugoslavia) after the fall of the Kingdom of Montenegro. During this period, which preceded World War II, artists demonstrated an increasing spirit of nationalism. While a great deal of Montenegrin art was destroyed during World War II, artists again focused on traditional folk, landscape, or nationalistic themes through the remainder of the 20th century. Painters and sculptors also employed various modern techniques that were popular throughout Europe, such as surrealism and abstract expressionism.

Architecture

Montenegro's architecture reflects the country's diverse mix of Mediterranean and Central and Eastern European traditions. Religious buildings and monuments especially reveal the Romanesque, Gothic, and baroque influences in the Mediterranean region. After the Russian Revolution in 1917, Byzantine architects created hundreds of buildings in Montenegro's interior region. The hemispherical domes and exposed, striped masonry are evident in many buildings, particularly monasteries, throughout continental Montenegro.

Montenegro's architectural heritage is perhaps best reflected in the preserved medieval town of Kotor. As part of the collective site designated as the Natural and Culturo-Historical Region of Kotor, it was recognized as a World Heritage Site by the United Nations Educational, Scientific, and Cultural Organization (UNESCO). This includes the city's fortifications, the old town itself, and the surrounding region. Of note is the Romanesque Cathedral of Saint Tryphon, built in 12th-century Kotor in honor of the fortified town's patron saint. It features a towering size, rounded arches, vaulted supports, and large towers. Fourteenth-century frescoes and silver and gold reliefs adorn the cathedral that resembles the basilicas (large church) of southern Italy. The basilica of Saint Luke in Kotor was also built in the Romanesque style, but at the end of the 12th century.

The surrounding region includes the old town of Perast, located along the Bay of Kotor (Boka Kotorska). The town is home to approximately sixteen baroque palaces, and a unique baroque chapel, Our Lady of the Rock (Gospa od Škrpjela). It was built in 1632 on a small man-made island in the Bay of Kotor. After sailors from the nearby town of Perast noticed a picture of the Virgin Mary sitting atop a rock sticking out of the water, sailors continued to add rocks to the site, eventually constructing a tiny island. The chapel also contains sixty-eight baroque paintings from the 17th century.

Drama

The Montenegrin National Theatre, in Podgorica, has its roots in the Titograd Town Theatre, a local institution founded in the early 1950s. In 1969, it was officially designated as the national theater. The theater grew, both in terms of success and in terms of artistic development, under the direction of Vladimir Popović (1935–1981) in the 1970s; in the 1980s, a fire left the national theater structureless, both physically and figuratively. However, after re-establishing in a new home, the national theater staged more than forty productions between 1997 and 2007. As of 2009, Montenegro is home to nine theaters. The early 21st century also witnessed the founding of the Montenegrin Theatre Festival.

Music

Though music has not been a prominent feature of Montenegrin arts, a long history of vocal music has often been partnered with the gusle (the national instrument). The gusle is a Baltic stringed instrument that is often used in Slavic music and resembles the rebab played in the Ottoman Empire. From the tenth through the 19th century, compositions were primarily religious. Archbishop Jovan of Duklja is credited with composing the earliest religious chants during the tenth and 11th centuries. The chants were written using medieval musical notes called neumes, which predated standard, modern musical notation. During the late 12th century, secular military music was recorded in the *Ljetopis Popa Dukljanina* (Chronicle of the Priest of Duklja), and traveling musicians were popular.

Military music composition remained influential in Montenegrin society, as defense against surrounding invading armies gained importance throughout the centuries. In fact, the first known classical compositions were not created until the late 19th century. Jovan Ivanisevic (1860–1889), Montenegro's first notable and educated composer, created orchestral, chorus and piano pieces. He is considered the most important Montenegrin composer of his time, and laid the foundation for symphonic and music art in the Balkan nation.

Montenegrin music in the 20th century turned toward folk themes, as in the music of Borislav Taminjzic (1933–1992). His poetic texts and fixed rhythms gained him a wide following. Montenegrin music began to flourish in during the early part of the century as more music schools were established (the first music school was founded in 1934). Late 20th-century musicians began to incorporate Western styles of music, such as electronica in the 1980s and hip-hop in the 1990s. By the end of the century, however, hip-hop music was published less frequently because of the lack of record label support.

Literature

One of the earliest known works of Montenegrin literature is *Kraljevstvo Slavena* (Kingdom of Slavs) or *Ljetopis Popa Kukljanina* (Chronicle of Father Doclean), written in the 12th century by an unknown Benedictine priest. During that same century, a Montenegrin tale of romance involving the iconic Jovan Vladimir (975–1016), ruler of the medieval state of Duklja, was first transcribed from the oral tradition. In addition, numerous 13th-century manuscripts are kept in Montenegrin monasteries. In the late 15th century (when Montenegro was called Zeta), the first state-owned printing press published two

volumes of the book *Oktoih* (Book of Psalms), complete with woodcut illustrations.

The famous 19th-century Montenegrin poet Petar II Petrović-Njegoš (1813–1851) is considered the country's first notable writer. His works include *Gorski vijenac* (The Mountain Wreath), written in 1847. This oral folk epic about ethnic conflict between Christians and Muslims influenced Serbian nationalism. In general, Njegoš's work is known throughout Montenegro for influencing a nationalistic sentiment. In fact, most of the subjects of 19th-century epic and lyric poetry were nationalistic, reflecting the increasing desire of Montenegrins to develop a sovereign nation. Through the 20th century, authors such as Mihailo Lalić (1914–1992), Milovan Djilas (1911–1995), and Radovan Zogović (1907–1986) focused on world wars and partisan battles in the Slavic region.

CULTURE

Arts & Entertainment

The drive for Montenegrin identity and ethnic strife are common themes among the country's contemporary arts, and literature is no exception. Montenegrin writers have recently focused on recent political issues that include the country's independence. Contemporary writers and journalists such as Andrej Nikolaidis (1974–) and Ognjen Spahić (1977–) write critically on political and cultural issues in Montenegro. Both have written for the pro-independence daily newspaper *Vijesti*. Some of Nikolaidis's essays in other papers about ethnic cleansing and the independence movement have actually provoked death threats. The writer and poet Balša Brković (1966–) is an editor at *Vijesti* and uses historical settings for settings of contemporary cultural issues.

Film and theatre in Montenegro have made a considerable impact both within and outside the country, especially considering the size of the population of about 6,00,000 people. As with literature, 21st-century film and theatre focuses on identity and cultural conflict. The film *Pogled sa*

Ajfelovog tornja (*The View from the Eiffel Tower,* 2005), which centers on a woman, explores themes of migration and cultural conflict that were endemic to Montenegro's culture during previous decades. The film *Opet Pakujemo Majmune* (*We Pack the Monkeys Again*, 2004) was directed by Montenegro's first woman director, Marija Perović (1972–), and is about the conflict between contemporary and traditional Montenegrin culture. Every August, the Herceg Novi Film Festival is an international film festival that highlights new Montenegrin films.

Theater in Montenegro is based in the Montenegrin National Theatre, which is in Podgorica and creates contemporary productions. The Faculty of Drama develops productions for the theater around the country, and since independence has developed more than forty new productions. Many of the productions are performed in surrounding countries and throughout Europe, giving Montenegrin theater international status and recognition.

Along with Podgorica, Cetinje is an important Montenegrin center of arts and culture. The Art Gallery in Cetinje has maintained the work of important Montenegrin artists since it was founded in 1950. It continues to highlight contemporary Montenegrin and international painters, sculptors, and artists who create installations and other modern works. Through the Faculty of Fine Arts in Cetinje, contemporary artists gain international exposure by exhibiting their work in other countries. Contemporary Montenegrin painter Boris Dragojevic (1956–) paints technical landscape scenes of the Mediterranean. More recently, Dragojevic and other Montenegrin painters have painted surreal and fantasy worlds, often of Montenegrin scenery to evoke a sense of home.

Twenty-first century Montenegrin gatherings frequently involve the country's traditional circle dance called the oro, which means, "circle." The dance involves people dancing in a circle, arms on each other's shoulders, with two people in the middle taking turns singing. Such traditional dancing has held sway during the country's recent turbulent history and well into the 21st century, as Montenegrins not only try to maintain cultural traditions, but also find strength as a new nation. The dance, as well as singing, serves as an emotional outlet for Montenegrins.

One of the more recent trends in Montenegrin music is that of turbo-folk music. This style, which musicians began playing in the early 1990s, transforms urban Serbian music by adding soul, rock and roll, and garage-band styles. The music is characterized by quick and aggressive instrumentation and vocals. Some of the more well-known turbo-folk bands are Ceca, Nino, and Sneki. While the musician Ceca used her music to support former Yugoslav president Slobodan Milošević (1941–2006), many other musicians used their music to oppose his rule. Still other musicians, especially before Montenegrin independence, used their music to evoke nationalist sentiment.

Cultural Sites & Landmarks

Montenegro's memorable landmarks range from its numerous historical sites, such as the cultural landscape of the Kotor region, to its beautiful landscapes, including inland mountainous and coastal beaches. The town of Budva, considered one of the oldest settlements on the Adriatic coast (and in the Balkan region), was settled in the fifth century BCE, and contains remnants of Greek, Roman, and Venetian ruins. Budva's beaches and nightlife attract tourists to the town that burned nearly to the ground in 1979 but was rebuilt and restored. The town contains numerous notable churches, one of which dates back to the 15th century.

Dramatic scenery along the southern coastal area can be found in the town of Ulcinj, which is a mix of old battlements, an active nightlife, and the 12,000-meter (7.5-mile) Velika Plaza beach. Europe's largest resting spot for migratory birds is at the nearby national park, Lake Scutari, at Ulcinj's Salt Flats. Nearby, the artificial island Ada Bojana is the country's most southern town and contains a large number of fish and seafood restaurants. Because Montenegro still lacks an infrastructure with adequate roads and electric supplies to many coastal towns, the government is developing a system to handle tourism to many towns.

Just inland, the historical town of Cetinje was the center of Montenegrin culture and the previous capital of Montenegro. Cetinje was founded in the 15th century, when the Cetinje Monastery, which is Serb Orthodox, and Vlaška church were built. Libraries are a very important cultural aspect of Cetinje. The oldest libraries in the country are preserved at the Library of Cetinje Monastery.

For nature and sports, tourists and Montenegrins alike enjoy the mountainous northern area's ski resorts. Zablijak, the town on Mount Durmitor, is the most famous ski and snowboarding resort in the country. Durmitor National Park is listed as a UNESCO World Heritage Site, which contains seventeen glacier lakes and hundreds of different plants and animals. The highest town in the Balkan region, Zablijak, is 1,456 meters (4,778 feet) above sea level.

Along with the high mountains are deep gorges in Montenegro's interior. The Tara River Gorge's canyon is the longest in Europe and the second deepest in the world at 1,300 meters (4,266 feet). Rafters float down the Tara River during the summer. The 17th-century Monastery of Ostrog, in central Montenegro, is dramatically positioned against a large vertical slope. From there, pilgrims and visitors can view the stretch of the Bjelopavlici plain. One of the churches at the monastery sits in a cave with frescoes placed directly on the rock's face.

Libraries & Museums

As Montenegro's cultural hub, Podgorica is home to numerous museums and cultural institutions. Podgorica City Museum has a collection detailing the area's Roman heritage. The Museum of Marko Miljanov, a Montenegrin cultural figure, is in nearby Medun. The Natural History Museum contains information about wildlife and plant life in the Balkan region. There is also the Petrovic Palace, a gallery-museum that houses art from as early as the seventh century, and the Contemporary Gallery, which is an important center for Podgorica's contemporary art scene. Several other museums are located in the city of Cetinje.

The Central National Library of Montenegro, "Djurdje Crnojevic" in Cetinje, serves as the country's legal depository. The library is also considered the nation's preeminent scientific library. Between 2009 and 2011, the library underwent a National Program of Library Digitization to further integrate its catalog and services with other European national libraries.

Holidays

Holidays recognized in Montenegro include Independence Day (May 21), Statehood Day (July 13), and New Years Day. Orthodox Christmas—a majority of the population is Orthodox Christian—is celebrated on January 7. In keeping with the Orthodox tradition, Good Friday and Easter are also widely recognized holidays, as is May Day.

Youth Culture

Free and compulsory education in Montenegro begins at the elementary level, and includes children between six and 14 years of age. This is followed by secondary education, which allows students to embark on a professional, vocational (trade), or broad educational tract. This level of education typically lasts four years (between the ages of fifteen and eighteen) and is followed by tertiary education, or higher learning. Between 2005 and 2009, the Montenegrin government implemented a series of educational reforms, which included the printing of all textbooks in Montenegrin beginning in 2009.

Youth culture in Montenegro is similar to Western youth culture, and is generally centered on socializing, whether through school, church, or family gatherings. Teenagers are typically afforded more freedom, and often congregate at cafés or the cinema. Young Montenegrins also enjoy playing sports, such as football (soccer), basketball, and water polo. In fact, water polo has gained such a following in Montenegro that the country sent a team to compete in the 2008 Olympics in Beijing.

Because of the country's recent independence, the government has sponsored various programs to engage young Montenegrins in issues to develop a strong and healthy society. For example, the Youth Council of Montenegro developed a public information campaign that engaged teenagers through roundtable discussions about the prevention of corruption in society. The judiciary, the police, and the economy were three of the target areas for developing this awareness.

SOCIETY

Transportation

Montenegrins get around the country by either railway or by car, (traffic moves on the right-hand side). Roads in Montenegro have no more than two lanes, and some are in the process of being redesigned for safety. Public buses connect Montenegro with Croatia and Serbia and other neighboring countries, as well as all Montenegrin cities. Railways of Montenegro is the national railway carrier, responsible for both passengers and freight. The country only has passenger railway links with Serbia.

Transportation Infrastructure

New roads and bridges are being planned to make travel quicker throughout parts of Montenegro and to Albania. (Neglect during the Yugoslav wars and economic crises of the 1990s left roadways in disrepair and below European standards.) Montenegro's railways also suffered serious deterioration due to lack of funding in the 1990s. As such, the government is working to upgrade certain railways as well, specifically the Belgrade-Bar railways that are used for passengers. Though railways mainly carry freight in Montenegro, the Podgorica-Schodër railway runs into Albania and will be upgraded to carry passengers as well as freight. Passengers also travel to the two international airports, but Podgorica Airport has been modernized and tends to handle more flights.

In June 2008, the Ministry of Transport, Maritime Affairs, and Telecommunications signed a deal with the International Finance Corporation (IFC) to further improve the country's transportation. Since then, a number of highway projects have got underway.

Media & Communications

After years of fighting in the 1990s, journalism in Montenegro developed independent perspectives, as the media was controlled by various political viewpoints. After the regime of Slobodan Milošević, who ruled the Federal Republic of Yugoslavia (FRY) as president from 1997 until 2000, political tensions and control over journalism became relaxed. Montenegro began to develop a more independent media that expresses a wide perspective of views. Both state-owned and private newspapers exist in the country. (The state-owned *Pobjeda* was put up for public sale in 2007, but its debt burden put off potential buyers.)

An independent governing board is supposed to ensure the independence of public broadcasting media in Montenegro, but the government continues to compromise this independence. Public media includes national public radio and a public television broadcaster. Montenegro is home to three public television stations and fourteen public radio stations. There are nineteen private television stations and forty-one private radio stations. Foreign media also broadcast in Montenegro through local stations.

In 2004, the United States assisted the development of the country's telecommunications infrastructure and policy through a grant from the US Trade and Development Agency (USTDA). As of 2006, there were an estimated 50,000 Internet users, representing nearly 8 percent of the population. (That figure had purportedly risen to just over 290,000 by 2010.) As of December 2012, Montenegro also had one of Europe's highest mobile phone penetration rates.

SOCIAL DEVELOPMENT

Standard of Living

Montenegrin ranked 51 out of 182 countries on the 2013 United Nations Human Development Index, which measures quality of life and standard of living indicators.

Water Consumption

Groundwater is the primary source of drinking water in Montenegro; springs provide approximately 70 percent. The majority of the population—over 98 percent (2012)—has access to piped water. Access to improved sanitation and drinking water sources is nearly universal. Water supply and wastewater overhauls, launched in 2009 through foreign aid, have helped to reduce the strain tourism puts on the local infrastructure, particularly in coastal towns and cities.

Education

Elementary education in Montenegro is mandatory and provided by the government. Children attain their elementary education between six and 15 years of age. The next level of education, known as secondary education, is based upon how students fair in the elementary level.

There are three types of secondary education in Montenegro. Gimnazija ("Gymnasium") is widely considered to be the type of secondary education pursued by those interested in later attending college. Students take general courses and receive a broad education. The other two levels of secondary education are comprised of Strŭna škola ("Professional schools") and Zanatska škola ("Vocational schools"). These are focused more on specific occupational pursuits.

College level education, known as Visoko obrazovanje ("High education") and Više obrazovanje ("Higher education"), typically lasts four to six years.

Women's Rights

Montenegro's constitution prohibits discrimination against women at work, but no other gender protections are listed in the document. However, the country has not prevented discrimination, and has had an uneven record in prosecuting suspects for crimes against women. Additionally, women often do not receive equal pay as their male counterparts, and relatively few women hold high-level positions in commerce or government. Overall, the patriarchal nature of Montenegrin society favors men's dominant roles in society and at home, including the control of property.

The country passed the Law on Gender Equality in 2007 to regulate gender discrimination as well as encourage equal opportunities for women in business and politics. As of 2007, nine women sat on the eighty-one-seat assembly, and one woman sat in the cabinet. As a member of the Convention of Elimination of all Forms of Discrimination against Women (CEDAW), Montenegro has committed its government to increasing gender equality. However, international organizations and observers agree that much work lies ahead for gender equality in the country.

Of particular concern is the treatment of Romani women in Montenegro, who confront layers of discrimination within their own culture and in the larger Montenegro society; Roma culture is largely patriarchal, placing traditional expectations on women's family and society roles.

Montenegro is on a Tier 2 Watch List for its lack of increased efforts to reduce the trafficking of women and girls. Though human trafficking is illegal in Montenegro, women and young girls are transferred from Eastern Europe and the Balkans to Western Europe. They are brought from Bosnia and Herzegovina, Serbia, Kosovo, Romania, Ukraine, and Russia, and the children typically must resort to begging for food. Government authorities have consistently reported few incidences of trafficking, but international organizations document repeated violations of the crime. Montenegro has not yet ratified the Convention on Action against Trafficking in Human Beings.

Domestic violence is a crime in Montenegro, and though it occurs at alarming rates, victims rarely report complaints. As of 2007, it is estimated that one in every five women experiences some type of violence, and though more domestic violence cases are being reported, there is a disproportionate number of cases being prosecuted. Rape also continues to be a significant issue (including spousal rape), and rape victims tend to be stigmatized due to engrained societal attitudes. International organizations also report the inadequate number of social welfare facilities to support abuse victims.

Health Care

Montenegro has attempted to reform its health system following years of internal and regional strife in the 1990s. The disorder and economic collapse of that decade, coupled with an outdated socialist health care system, has created public health challenges. One area of focus is the health of children and women, including the need for better vaccination programs and early childhood care. The country has successfully eradicated polio.

GOVERNMENT

Structure

The Socialist Federal Republic of Yugoslavia (SFRY) existed from 1945 until 1992, led by Josip Broz Tito for the majority of that time. This republic was a communist state that included modern day Bosnia and Herzegovina, Croatia, Macedonia, Montenegro, Serbia, and Slovenia.

Following Tito's death in 1980, ethic conflicts would eventually lead to the dismantling of the republics. The wrenching apart of the former Yugoslav provinces, including Serbia and Montenegro and Croatia, was not peaceful. Various ethnic groups that at one time comprised the federation expressed their dissent in both widespread demonstrations and all out warfare. Brutal periods of war ensued. The country would gain independence in 2006, and the country's constitution was officially proclaimed the following year.

Montenegro is a parliamentary republic with the president as head of state. The government's executive branch is headed by a prime minister, and is composed of a deputy prime minister and a cabinet of ministers. Montenegro's parliament is a unicameral (one-chamber) body consisting of 81 publically elected members. Members of parliament serve a four-year term. The Parliament of Montenegro is responsible for appointing the presidentially nominated position of prime minister.

Political Parties

Montenegro is a multi-party state and political parties form coalitions in parliament. Elections were last held on October 14, 2012 (next to be held by 2016). Seats by party/coalition as of May 2015 include the Coalition for European Montenegro (with thirty-nine seats), the Democratic Front (20 seats), the SNP (nine seats), Positive Montenegro (five seats), the Bosniak Party (three seats), Albanian and Croatian minority parties (three seats), Independent (two seats).

Local Government

Local government consists of twenty-one municipalities (divided into three regions, though there is no governance at the regional level) and two municipal administrative units in the capital of Podgorica. Within the capital, neighborhoods or local communities have limited self-governance for municipal matters. Bodies of self-government include local assemblies, as well as a directly elected municipal president or mayor.

Judicial System

Within Montenegro's court system, first instance or basic courts handle minor criminal cases and civil disputes while commercial courts operate as courts of first instance for commercial matters. Higher courts try more serious criminal matters, and an Appellate Court hears appeals from the higher courts and commercial courts. Other courts include the Administrative Court, Constitutional Court, and Supreme Court, the highest judicial body in the Montenegrin court system.

Taxation

Montenegro levies flat tax rates, including a flat income tax rate of nine percent and a flat and competitive corporate tax rate of 9 percent. Other taxes levied include an inheritance tax, a value-added tax (or VAT, similar to a consumption tax), and a property tax.

Armed Forces

The Montenegrin armed forces consist of three service branches: the Montenegrin Ground Army, the Montenegrin Navy, and the Montenegrin Air Force. There is no conscription (it was abolished in 2006 after independence) and 18 is the minimum military age. Following Montenegro's declaration of independence, it announced a planned reduction to 2,500 active military personnel.

Foreign Policy

The country's foreign policy in the early 21st century is one marked by integration into several European economic and political organizations aimed at strengthening the region. Montenegro's foreign policy also focuses on strong bilateral relations and strong relations with neighboring states. Montenegro became a new republic in June 2006 after people in the State Union of Serbia and Montenegro voted in a May 2006 referendum to declare Montenegrin independence. After drafting a constitution, the newly elected parliament then adopted the referendum on October 19, 2007. In its declaration of independence, it cited the specific foreign policy goals of attaining membership in the European Union (EU), of the United Nations (UN), and of the North Atlantic Treaty Organization (NATO).

Montenegro is developing national and international policies in line with the European community. Following Montenegro's declaration of independence, the EU, the five permanent UN Security Council (UNSC) members, and the Republic of Serbia have recognized the country as a nation. Montenegro joined the Organization for Security and Cooperation in Europe (OSCE) on June 22, 2006, which will support Montenegro's domestic reforms, and it was admitted to the UN General Assembly (UNGA) as the 192nd member state on June 28, 2006. Nearly one year later, on May 11, 2007, Montenegro joined the Council of Europe. Furthering its early initiatives to work with the EU, Montenegro signed a Stabilization and Association Agreement (SAA) in October 2007 and a World Trade Organization (WTO) bilateral agreement in April 2008. Montenegro has also joined the World Bank and the International Money Fund (IMF). By December of 2008, Montenegro had applied to be an official member of the EU.

Montenegro's focus on developing strong ties with neighboring countries is due to its interest in joining the EU. The new republic borders Croatia, Bosnia and Herzegovina, Serbia, Kosovo, and Albania, all of which Montenegro views as sharing similar policy goals for developing a strong southeastern Europe. Montenegro is also building ties with the Russian Federation, the Peoples' Republic of China, Turkey, and Egypt. It is likewise building relationships with Australia and Argentina, two countries to which former Montenegrins have emigrated over past decades.

Montenegro had been united in 1992 with Serbia and Belgrade in the Federal Republic of Yugoslavia. Tensions arose between Montenegro's government and Yugoslavian President Milošević's campaign of ethnic cleansing in Kosovo in 1998 to 1999, eventually ending his rule. By 2003, Montenegro had entered into a union with Serbia. However, while Montenegrins reaffirmed their national identity by separating from Serbia in 2006, maintaining strong ties with the country continues to be important to Montenegro. To help Montenegro establish diplomatic ties in countries around the world, Serbia agreed to provide diplomatic services where Montenegro has yet to establish its own embassy. Both countries also signed an agreement in which Serbia gives Montenegrins protection abroad at Serbian consular embassies.

Since August 2008, the U.S. has had a diplomatic and assistance-based relationship with Montenegro. The U.S. maintains an embassy in Podgorica and has contributed to strengthening the country's democratic institutions, as well as its business climate and economic growth. In fact, an American Chamber of Commerce (AmCham Montenegro) began operating in Montenegro in November 2008 to help grow local business and help attract foreign investment.

Human Rights Profile

International human rights law insists that states respect civil and political rights, and promote an individual's economic, social, and cultural rights. The United Nations Universal Declaration on Human Rights (UDHR) is recognized as the standard for international human rights. Its authors sought the counsel of the world's great thinkers, philosophers, and religious leaders, and were careful to create a document that reflects the core values shared by every world culture. (To read this document or view the articles relating to cultural human rights, visit http://www.un.org/en/documents/udhr/).

Montenegro has not been in full compliance with Article 2 of the UDHR. The country's constitution does not provide minorities protection against discrimination. For example, a large Roma population—more than 16,000—exists in Montenegro as refuges from Kosovo. However, 87 percent of the Roma population in Montenegro is mostly illiterate and is not afforded the right to education. The country also ranked last among nine countries surveyed for its inclusion of the Roma population. At the end of 2008, nearly half as many refugees from Croatia, Bosnia and Herzegovina were also denied access to the basic political, social, and economic rights as Montenegrin citizens, in conflict with several articles of the UDHR. Even refugee children born in Montenegro are denied these basic rights. (However, education is free and compulsory for others through the 8th grade.)

Montenegro's penal code prohibits torture as described in Article 5 of the UDHR, but monitoring agencies reported police beatings of detained suspects in 2007. Additionally, in 2006, seventeen ethnic Albanian men reported being tortured during arrest, and their trials did not follow international standards. In conflict with Article 9 in the UDHR, Montenegro has not resolved certain war crimes and suspected extrajudicial killings from the war in Kosovo in the 1990s. For example, there has been no progress regarding the investigations of former police officers indicted in 2006 for the disappearance of eighty-three Bosniak (Bosnian Muslim) civilians in 1992. Certain extrajudicial killings between 2004 and 2007 also remain unsolved.

Though Montenegro's constitution requires an independent judiciary, the many instances of poor cooperation between police and prosecutors, judicial corruption, and judges allowing the fear of reprisals affect their decisions complicate the issue. Further, the executive branch of government controls the court's finances, creating an inappropriate measure of influence over judicial decision-making. In accordance with Article 10 of the UDHR, those accused of a crime in Montenegro have the right to be present at his or her own trial. However, the impaired decisions of judges in trials are in conflict with the article.

The National Security Agency (NSA) committed arbitrary interferences in privacy, which conflict with Article 12 of the UDHR. The organization is reported to have practiced surveillance without court approval against different political groups. Regarding other freedoms, Montenegro follows Article 18 in the UDHR by protecting the freedom of religion. However, some tensions between religious and ethnic groups remain.

Though the Montenegro constitution provides for freedom of speech and the press, the court can ban violent, hateful, or intolerant media content, in conflict with Article 19 of the UDHR. In 2007, there were reports of individual attacks against journalists. Although no reports of government censorship of the media have been made, some government officials have threatened media organizations that criticize their actions. The government also does not adhere to national laws that prevent government control of former state-owned media.

ECONOMY

Overview of the Economy
The region faced serious economic problems beginning in 1998. These problems were due in part to high inflation, economic sanctions, and widespread military conflict. The country also faced difficulties in privatizing companies that had been socially owned during the years of communist rule when it was part of the former Yugoslavia.

Podgorica is the main economic and administrative center of Montenegro, and the government and financial industry occupies the bulk of the city's work force. The city is home to two financial exchanges, the Montenegro Stock Exchange (MNSE) and the New Securities Exchange of Montenegro (NEX).

Light industries in the city include the manufacture of textiles, vehicles, and aluminum and the processing of tobacco. Other industries in the city include telecommunications and construction, both of which have experienced rapid growth in recent years. The two largest companies in Podgorica are Kombinat aluminijuma Podgorica, maker of aluminum, and AD Plantaže, an important winery in the region.

Foreign investment in Montenegro continues slowly in the early 21st century, although economic reforms have helped to stabilize the country's markets. Foreign investment in the capital has increased since Montenegro declared itself an independent state in 2006. The country's gross domestic product (GDP) was an estimated $9.499 billion (2014 estimate). The GDP per capita was $15,200 (2014 estimate).

Industry

Montenegro's industry is still recovering from the effects of the break up of Yugoslavia. Sanctions by the United Nations (UN) combined with the disparity with which financial relief efforts were dispersed throughout the former Yugoslavia, had a widespread negative impact on the population of Montenegro.

Economic reform laws and privatization efforts have helped to stabilize the country's economy in the early 21st century. Montenegro has also made the Euro its legal currency. Iron, steel and various textiles continue to be produced in Montenegro.

Labor

As of 2014, Montenegro's labor force was estimated at 263,200, with an unemployment rate of 18.5 percent (2014 estimate). The majority of the labor force—an estimated 76.8 percent in 2014 — is employed in the services sector.

Energy/Power/Natural Resources

Montenegro has large resources of coal and aluminum. Montenegro is also known for its bauxite and lignite. Montenegro also has large quantities of antimony, a metal that is used in an alloy for casting purposes, as a flame retardant, and in automobile parts. The country's navigable rivers have been important for trade and transportation, and for hydroelectric power generation.

Fishing

Montenegro's coastal area along the Adriatic is home to the country's small fishing industry. As of 2010, the small fleet numbered under 20 vessels; four years, earlier, in 2006, only 52 workers were registered as full-time anglers. Trout farming is a productive sector and mussels and sea bass have shown commercial potential. In Lake Skadar, carp and eel are caught for commercial use.

Forestry

Forestry and wood processing are important economic sectors in the country. Montenegro's forest cover is one of the largest in Europe—woodland and forests cover over half of the country—and the country adopted a National Forest Policy in 2008 to balance commercial and environmental concerns and issues. The main commercial species are conifers, including spruce and pine. Illegal cutting remains a concern. In 2010, wood burning accounted for about 6 percent of the country's total energy consumption.

Mining/Metals

The production of bauxite and aluminum and alumina are primary sectors of Montenegro's mineral industry. Other commercial commodities include crude steel, coal, gravel, salt, lime, and stone.

Agriculture

Agriculture, particularly livestock, is a mainstay of the Montenegrin economy. Some of the major agricultural products of Montenegro include cereal crops such as maize and wheat, in addition to sugar beets, sunflowers, and potatoes.

Animal Husbandry

Cattle (including dairy cows), sheep, goats, pigs, and poultry are the common livestock raised in Montenegro.

Tourism

In spite of the political turmoil and violence of the 1990s, tourism has been a growing industry in Montenegro. In fact, Montenegro has one of the fastest growing tourism economies in Europe. The travel and tourism sector employs over 160,000 people in the country, representing 4.3 percent of the total workforce. It is estimated that more than 600,000 visit Montenegro during the summer season each year. Tourist attractions in Montenegro include beach resorts along the Adriatic Coast and the historic city of Ulcinj.

Kathryn Bundy, Joshua Pritchard, Ian Paul

DO YOU KNOW?

- One of the first global recognitions of Montenegro's independence occurred when Ivana Knežvić of Bar, Montenegro, won the 2006 Miss World pageant.

- Podgorica was previously known as Titograd from 1944 through 1992, when the country was a republic incorporated in the Socialist Federal Republic of Yugoslavia (SFRY). When the SFRY dissolved in 1992, the name was restored. A Serbian name, Podgorica means "under the little mountain," a reference to Gorica Hill, which overlooks the center of the capital.

- The 2008 Summer Olympics in Beijing, China, mark the debut of Montenegro as an independent country after membership was granted in July 2007 by the International Olympic Committee (IOC). Football (soccer) and basketball remain the country's two most popular sports.

Bibliography

"Montenegro." *The Montenegrin Association of America.* http://www.montenegro.org.

Annalisa Rellie. "Montenegro." Bucks, England: *Bradt Travel Guides*, 2008.

Christopher Deliso. "Culture and Customs of Serbia and Montenegro." Abingdon, England: *Greenwood Press*, 2008.

David C. King. "Serbia and Montenegro." New York, New York: *Benchmark Press*, 2005.

Elizabeth Roberts. "Realm of the Black Mountains." Ithaca, New York: *Cornell University Press*, 2007.

Kenneth Morrison. "Montenegro: A Modern History." London, England: *I.B. Tauris*, 2009.

Peter Dragicevich. "Montenegro." Oakland, CA: *Lonely Planet*, 2015.

Rudolph Abraham. "The Mountains of Montenegro." Cumbria, England: *Cicerone Press*, 2007.

Sabrina P. Ramet. "Eastern Europe: Politics, Culture, and Society Since 1939." Indiana: *Indiana University Press*, 1999.

Works Cited

"A Short History of Montenegrin Music." http://www.montenegro.org/music.html. Montenegro.org.

"Foreign Policy Priorities of Montenegro." http://74.125.47.132/search?q=cache:8k748ZqNXCAJ:www.gom.cg.yu/files/1196434702.pdf+montenegro+foreign+policy+relations&hl=en&ct=clnk&cd=1&gl=us. *Ministry of Foreign Affairs of Montenegro.*

"Montenegrin Youth Council Leads Public Information Campaign about Corruption." http://www.ortmap.org/htms/akcija/akcija_success_stories_2.htm.

"Montenegro." *Central Intelligence Agency: The World Factbook.* https://www.cia.gov/library/publications/the-world-factbook/geos/mj.html.

"Montenegro." http://www.culturecrossing.net/basics_business_student.php?id=233. *Culture Crossing.*

"Montenegro." http://www.montenegro.org. *The Montenegrin Association of America.*

"Montenegro." http://www.montenegro.travel/.

"Montenegro." http://www.state.gov/g/drl/rls/hrrpt/2007/100575.htm. U.S. Department of State.

"Montenegro." *Microsoft Encarta Online Encyclopedia* 2008. http://encarta.msn.com/encyclopedia_761555558/montenegro.html. *Microsoft Corporation.*

"Montenegro: A Round Table on Domestic Violence in Montenegro: current status and future activities." http://www.undp.org.me/unct/16rt.html. *United Nations Development Programme.*

"Montenegro: Amnesty International Report 2007." http://www.amnesty.org/en/region/montenegro/report-2007. *Amnesty International.*

"Montenegro: Amnesty International Report 2008." http://www.amnesty.org/en/region/montenegro/report-2008. *Amnesty International.*

"Montenegro: Food and Drink." http://www.visit-montenegro.com/montenegro-food.htm.

"Montenegro—Largest Cities." http://www.geonames.org/ME/largest-cities-in-montenegro.html. *GeoNames.*

"Montenet: Culture of Montenegro." http://www.montenet.org/culture/culture.htm.

"Olga Perovic: Contemporary Montenegrin Figurative Arts." http://www.montenegrina.net/pages/pages_e/painting/conteporary_montenegrin_figurative_arts.htm. *Montenegrina Painting.*

"Panorama of Contemporary Montenegrin Literature." http://www.okf-cetinje.org/OKF-Panorama-of-Contemporary-Montenegrin-Literature_59_1. *Otvoreni Kulturni Forum Cetinje.*

"Television Across Europe: Regulation, Policy and Independence." http://www.mediapolicy.org/tv-across-europe/television-across-europe-regulation-policy-and-2/television-across-europe-regulation-policy-and/montenegro-from-warmongering-to-liberal-reform. *Media Policy.*

"Trafficking in Persons Report." http://podgorica.usembassy.gov/trafficking_in_persons_report_2007.html. Embassy of the United States; Podgorica, Montenegro.

"Women's Action." http://www.wa.cg.yu/Women%E2%80%99s_Action.htm.

Annalisa Rellie. "Montenegro." Bucks, England: *Bradt Travel Guides*, 2008.

Ulf Brunnbauer, ed. "(Re)Writing History. Historiography in Southeast Europe after Socialism." Münster: *Lit Verlag*, 2004.

Polish folk dancers in traditional costumes

POLAND

Introduction

The Republic of Poland (Polish, "Polska") is a country in north-central Europe whose strategic geographical position and lack of natural barriers have often made the site of European power struggles. A great power during the 17th century, Poland lost all its territory during the wars of the 18th century, and ceased to exist as a sovereign nation until after World War I.

Poland threw off communist rule in 1989 and has become a member of the European Union and the North Atlantic Treaty Organization (NATO). The country is renowned for the beauty of its mountains, lakes, and seacoast, as well as for its arts festivals, which draw millions of visitors from around the world.

GENERAL INFORMATION

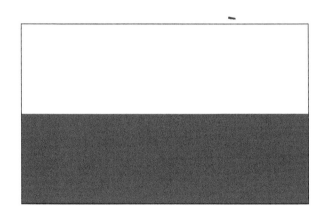

Official Language: Polish
Population: 38,346,279 (July 2014 estimated)
Currency: Zloty
Coins: Coins come in denominations of 1, 2, and 5 zloty. The zloty is subdivided into 100 groszy, which come in denominations of 1, 2, 5, 10, 20, and 50.
Land Area: 304,255 square kilometers (117,473 square miles)
Water Area: 8,430 square kilometers (3,254 square miles)
National Anthem: "Mazurek Dabrowskiego" ("Dabrowski's Mazurka")
Capital: Warsaw

Time Zone: GMT + 1
Flag Description: The flag of Poland features a horizontal bicolor design, with a white horizontal band above an equally sized red horizontal band.

Population

Poland's population is mostly urban, with 60.6 percent of its citizens living in or near urban areas in 2014. Warsaw, the capital, is the largest city. In 2012, its population was estimated at 1.7 million. Of the country's 16 regions, those with the highest populations in 2009 were the Lower Silesian region, the Kuyavian-Pomeranian region, the Lublin region, the Lubusz region, and the Lodz region.

Poland's population today is comprised largely of ethnic Poles, who make over 96 percent (2011 est.) of the population. World War II, the Holocaust atrocities, the forced removal of ethnic minorities, and post-war changes in

Principal Cities by Population (2012):

- Warsaw (1.7 million in 2012)
- Kraków (754,095)
- Łódź (725,658)
- Wrocław (627,562)
- Poznań (549,403)
- Gdańsk (449,794)
- Szczecin (401,343)
- Bydgoszcz (351,345)
- Lublin (347,159)

Poland's national boundaries have all played a role in creating that reality.

Languages

Polish belongs to the West Slavic family of languages, which includes Czech and Slovak, and is the primary tongue of almost all Poles. Around 6 million speakers live outside of Poland, including in other Central European countries and the United States. Polish has complex grammar, including five genders, and French, Latin, German, and Russian have heavily influenced the vocabulary.

Native People & Ethnic Groups

The Poles are a Slavic or Eastern European people, but are linked to the West through Roman Catholicism and the Latin alphabet. Poland's original inhabitants were largely a loose collection of Slavic tribes, including the Poles.

Ethnic Poles make up the largest ethnic population in the country, and the Polish government today officially recognizes a number of ethnic minorities in Poland; Germans, Ukrainians, Lithuanians, Belarusians, and Roma. According to the CIA *World Factbook*, as of 2011, 0.2 percent of the country's population is made up of Germans and 0.1 percent is Ukrainian, while the other aforementioned ethnic minorities comprise fewer than two percent of the country's total population.

Religions

Religion plays a crucial role in Polish life. The Roman Catholic Church dominates; nearly 87 percent of the population identifies as Roman Catholic. The other main Christian groups are the Eastern Orthodox Church and small numbers of Protestants. Jewish people have slowly begun to return to Poland and reestablish communities.

Climate

Poland's climate is continental and temperate. Summers are usually warm, rather than hot, and not overly humid. The average summer temperature is around 24° Celsius (75° Fahrenheit). Winters are cold, with average temperatures slightly below 18° Celsius (0° Fahrenheit), and with considerable amounts of snow.

Maritime air currents from the Atlantic bring a mix of Arctic and subtropical air, depending on which predominates at the time, Poland can experience mild or cold weather. Precipitation is dependable, supporting Poland's rich agriculture.

ENVIRONMENT & GEOGRAPHY

Topography

Poland has five main geographical regions: the central lowlands, the lesser Poland uplands, the southern mountains, the lake district, and the Baltic coast. The central lowlands include the vast plain across which invaders have traveled. To the south are the lesser Poland uplands, a series of foothills rising to the southern mountains. The southern mountains include the Carpathian and Sudeten ranges. The Carpathians include the Tatra Range, which rise in places to alpine heights. The country's highest point is at the peak of Mount Rysy, 2,499 meters (8,199 feet) above sea level. The highest point in the Sudetens is Mount Sniezka (1,602 meters/5,256 feet above sea level).

There are over 9,000 lakes in Poland, many of them in the northern lake district. This region is heavily wooded but also has extensive marshlands. The sandy Baltic Coast, a popular tourist destination, is home to the major port cities Gdansk, Gdynia, and Szczecin.

Poland has a number of major rivers, all of which flow into the Baltic Sea. Though these bodies of water have not generally kept out invaders, they have served as important commercial routes. In the west are the Oder and Neisse, which form the boundary with Germany. The Vistula, which flows through Warsaw, is the country's largest river.

Plants & Animals

Poland is home to many wild animal species, particularly in the forested regions and in the northern lakes and marshlands. In Poland's primeval forests one can find endangered species such as wolves and Eurasian beavers, as well as small numbers of the European bison.

Around one-fourth of Poland's area is covered with forest, mostly in the northeast. Northern Poland and the mountainous areas are covered largely with pine and other coniferous species. Deciduous species such as oak and beech grow in the other parts of the country.

CUSTOMS & COURTESIES

Greetings

Polish people generally shake hands when greeting. In the event of a large gathering, each person will typically shake hands with everyone else, and go through formal introductions with any strangers. At parties and other social occasions, the hosts will introduce people to others, usually starting with the oldest then youngest women, and then the oldest then youngest men. Social introductions in Poland are generally reserved but courteous. When meeting for the first time, the person should offer a firm handshake, and offer a polite smile and firm eye contact while saying "Dzien dobry" ("Good day"). In the evening, one may say "Dobry wieczor" ("Good evening").

An age-old custom that still thrives in Poland, particularly among women, is the offering of three symbolic air kisses on the cheek. The correct procedure is to start by kissing the left cheek, then the right, then the left cheek again. Men may also offer three symbolic kisses to other men, but this is customarily done among

close friends or relatives when they meet for special occasions. Work colleagues may also kiss when they meet socially, but rarely do so at work.

Eye contact during conversation is quite important, and speaking to someone while looking elsewhere might be interpreted as disrespectful. In most situations, one should also address people by their honorific titles—either "Pan" (Mr.) or "Pani" (Mrs.)—and their last name. Titles are considered prestigious and are quite important to use during conversation. Academic or professional titles are also used with any honorific titles. One should never speak on a first name basis unless one is invited to do so; this transition from using formal to informal names is an important social step for which the Polish have a centuries-old protocol. The shift from using formal to informal greetings (and also speech in general) is a ritual that indicates that a person's status has changed to a trusted and more private standing with a person or group. Generally, first names are only used after mutual consent between adult friends. However, Polish teenagers and children are always called by their first names.

Gestures & Etiquette

Bruderszaft is akin to a fraternal toast and indicates the transition from a formal relationship to a closer, informal relationship. In a bruderszaft toast, two people simultaneously raise a toast to each other, then interlock arms and down their drinks. Afterward, they exchange cheek kisses and tell the other person "From now on, please call me (the person's first name)." After this ceremonial toast, relations between the two people change from official to personal. If an elder person, or someone of higher social standing (for example, a director to his employee) invites a person to a bruderszaft toast, then under no circumstances may the invited person decline the invitation, as this would be highly insulting.

After a bruderszaft toast, the two people always call each other by first names. Related to this, an elder or person of higher position may say "Możemy przejść na 'ty'" ("May we use informal Polish"). "Ty" is the informal form of "you," and indicates transitioning to an informal, first-name basis. Moving to the informal "ty" is considered an honor in personal relations. However, it also means the other person must be remembered on all special occasions, such as Christmas, birthdays, or name days. Similar to a birthday, Polish "Name Day" is the day that everyone of a certain first name is honored. Name days are written on most Polish calendars, so that each day of the year has a specific first name that is to be celebrated. This anniversary is important to Poles, and is celebrated much more than in Poland than in other cultures where name days are observed. Though it is enough to offer best wishes to someone on his or her name day, many offer a small gift, such as flowers or chocolates, especially if it is the name day of a close friend or relative.

Eating/Meals

Poles traditionally eat four times a day. Since the workday begins early in Poland, usually between five and seven o'clock, Poles have pierwsze sniadanie (first breakfast), which they eat just before going to work or school. This early meal is a quick, light breakfast, usually of bread, butter and jam, or bread, butter and some cold meat such as ham. At around 10 or 11 o'clock, Poles have drugie sniadanie (second breakfast). The second breakfast, which is most often a small snack, allows Poles to delay having lunch until at least two o'clock. During the week, Poles traditionally eat lunch after finishing work at around four o'clock, while on weekends they have lunch a few hours earlier. Lunch is the main course of the day. Dinner comes later in the evening, traditionally eaten anywhere from seven to nine o'clock, and is a lighter meal similar to the first breakfast.

In the past few decades, this eating pattern has been changing. Poles have begun having earlier lunches as a break from work, which results in earlier dinners. This shift is happening because of the market economy that was introduced after 1989. The Polish have customarily preferred cooking and eating at home, and in the past they rarely ate in restaurants. This is still the case with Poland's older generations, but the younger generation has shown an increasing tendency to eat at restaurants. Regardless of where they eat, Poles generally use continental table manners: hold the fork with the left hand and the knife with the right hand. It is also considered good manners to keep both hands above the table during the meal (though without the elbows resting on the table) and to refrain from eating until everyone has been served, or until the host or head of the family begins eating.

Visiting

Poles enjoy having formal parties on special occasions, and they often invite friends for dinner, or simply for after-dinner visits. Poles are gracious hosts who offer many plates of various snack foods and drinks for their guests. If invited to dinner in someone's home, it is customary to take one's shoes off before entering the home. It is also customary to offer a small gift to the hosts and their children. For the adults, typical gifts include wine, flowers (by tradition, always an odd number of flowers should be given) and pastries. Gifts for children include candies, chocolates, or small toys. When visiting, Poles usually dress semi-formally, if not formally, depending on whether it is a short visit or a dinner party.

If invited for dinner, the guest should offer to help prepare things for the dinner and assist with clearing the table and cleaning up afterward. This is more a gesture of politeness, and the hostess will most likely refuse any offer of help—also out of politeness. Whether it is an informal visit or a dinner invitation, the offering of a toast is quite traditional and may be frequent. The host offers the first toast, and such toasts are usually made with vodka (the most common Polish drink) in a small glass containing one swallow. The guest should reciprocate with a toast later in the meal.

LIFESTYLE

Family

Poles consider family life to be highly important, and Poland has one of the lowest divorce rates in Europe. The pervasiveness of Catholicism in

Polish society is certainly part of the reason for the low divorce rate and emphasis on family life. Approximately 90 percent of the Polish population identifies as Roman Catholic, and a high percentage regularly attends church services. The family is the most important social structure, and Poles feel strong obligations to their families. Extended families are commonplace in Poland, and are the foundation of the individual's social network. Although families are generally larger in rural Poland (where parents may have three or four children), in urban Poland the most common family unit is the nuclear family (two parents with two children).

The economic situation of most Polish families in the early 21st century necessitates that both parents work outside the home. Though the majority of women have jobs outside the home, they continue to bear a large part of domestic responsibilities and child rearing. Nonetheless, it has become more common for older children to bear certain responsibilities, such as helping with household upkeep and caring for younger siblings. Senior citizens are usually cared for by their adult children.

Housing

After World War II, the Soviet Union heavily influenced a period of mass construction in Polish cities. During this period, large public housing projects were built of prefabricated concrete, though these buildings were generally of low quality. The public housing projects throughout the country are usually between five and seven stories tall, and usually have two or three rooms plus a kitchen and a bathroom. The vast majority of urban Polish citizens currently live in these older apartments built during Poland's forty years of communist socialism. However, these buildings are deteriorating and most need renovations.

Near the end of the communist era, and thereafter, lack of housing became a major social problem. After the fall of communism, state construction ceased while private construction faced many complications. Also, many Poles living in state-owned apartments needed to somehow transition to private ownership. In 1990, Poland was estimated to need about 2 million additional homes for Polish citizens. The problem has since increased rather than decreased, and various studies show that as many as 6.5 million citizens in Poland live in substandard homes, many of which were built during the socialist period and have deteriorated. The Polish housing shortage has been difficult for Polish government and society to resolve, and is expected to endure for some decades.

Food

Polish cuisine shares many of the same characteristics as neighboring cultures, namely the cuisines of Germany, Hungary, Russia, and the Czech and Slovak republics. Polish meals are traditionally quite hearty, and pork, sausage, and poultry are the most commonly eaten meats. Meat is usually eaten with potatoes or bread dumplings, with many traditional dishes incorporating beetroot, celery root, cucumbers, mushrooms, and sauerkraut. Cabbage is also used in many dishes, such as salads, soups and stews, and sour cream is often used in various sauces or soups. Pickled vegetables and pickled fish are also common to the Polish diet, and vodka is often consumed particularly with pickled foods such as herring. The typical herbs and spices used to flavor Polish cuisine are caraway seeds, dill, marjoram, parsley, and pepper.

Traditionally, the main meal is lunch, and is composed of three courses. The meal starts with soup, after which the main course is served. Salads, which are a common part of lunch, are eaten with the main course. Dessert, sometimes served with tea or coffee, is served shortly after the main course. Popular Polish desserts include cheesecake, crepes, doughnuts, honey cake, poppy seed cake, and various types of strudel.

More for reasons of economy than health, Poles also traditionally serve quite a few vegetarian dishes. For example, pierogi is a national dish made of small bread dumplings that are filled with sauerkraut and mushrooms, or cheese and potatoes. Also, dumplings filled with fruit, most commonly plums, are a traditional meal that is served with powdered sugar and melted butter on top. Poles also prepare other sweet dishes such as pancakes topped with jam or fruit, and rice baked with apples or other fruit.

Life's Milestones

When a girl reaches womanhood, she celebrates "Andrzejki" on November 30. Andrzejki offers predictions to young ladies about love and marriage. This ritual is ancient and of uncertain origin, and is still popular today, though it is more a form of amusement and entertainment than a solemn ritual. Married women and males are traditionally not allowed to attend the Andrzejki ritual. The most common way to obtain the prediction is to pour heated wax onto water through the opening of an old key, and then to hold the cooled piece of flat wax against light and observe the silhouettes that are cast onto a wall. This supposedly creates ghostly images of what the future holds for the girl. If nothing else, this ritual indicates the importance of marriage to young Polish girls.

During communist Poland, most Poles married before age twenty, and unmarried women in their mid-20s were considered spinsters (or past the common age for marrying). While Poles are increasingly marrying later than the traditional age in the early 21st century, marriage remains the most important milestone for the Polish people. An old and popular marriage tradition is that of the "Bread and Salt Blessing." When the wedding reception begins, the parents of the bride and groom offer the newly married couple bread sprinkled with salt on a plate and a goblet of wine. This is followed by a traditional saying: "According to the old Polish custom, we welcome your marriage with bread and salt, that your home will always have plenty." Afterwards, the bride and groom smash the plate and the glass for good luck, and the lengthy wedding reception begins. The first toast and song during the reception is called "Sto lat" ("One hundred years"), which is sung by all the guests to wish 100 years of good health to the bride and groom.

CULTURAL HISTORY

Art

The Polish-Lithuanian Commonwealth collapsed in 1795, and over a period of years Prussia, Russia and Austria annexed various regions of Poland into their own territories. However, because the Polish people lived as a single nation for many centuries, and because they held a common language, culture, and traditions, they considered themselves a divided nation struggling to regain its rightful statehood. The arts were central to this struggle by keeping a sense of Polish national identity alive. This crucial role of the Polish arts can be seen quite strongly during the years that Poland was without nationhood.

In the 19th century, Polish culture went through a period of strong artistic movements and dynamic growth. During this period, important painters such as Jan Matejko (1838–1893), Józef Chełmoński (1849–1914), and Henryk Siemiradzki (1843–1902) kept the Polish painting scene thriving. Jan Matejko was particularly important as a painter because he created internationally renowned oils, many of which depicted historical scenes of Polish history. His paintings such as *Polonia* ("Poland") embodied the idea of lost nationhood to remind the Poles of their history and national identity. Some of the artists in this period were also part of the Młoda Polska (Young Poland) artistic movement. This transborder movement became well known throughout the regions of partitioned Poland and helped give the Poles a sense of national identity.

Immediately after World War I in 1918, Poland re-established its independence as the II Rzeczpospolita Polska (Second Polish Republic). Its revived nationhood was short-lived, however, after Germany occupied Poland in 1939. The Nazi occupation (1939–1945) represented a concerted effort to destroy Polish cultural life. Many Polish scholars and artists were sent to concentration camps, and the arts were entirely suppressed. Many Polish artists and scholars died in concentration camps, and many cultural artifacts were either deliberately destroyed or stolen by the Third Reich. Nevertheless, art became an important expression of Poland's national identity, and represented national resistance to foreign occupation.

Much of what is of national cultural value in Poland today was hidden and preserved by various individuals and organizations that worked in a loose underground network to maintain Polish heritage and nationhood. This network, known as the Polskie Państwo Podziemne (Polish Underground State), remained loyal to the Polish government in exile (based in London) throughout World War II. Among its responsibilities, the Polish Underground State gathered and preserved many paintings and other Polish cultural artifacts. Thus, Nazi Germany's attempt to destroy Polish culture ultimately had the effect of strengthening the Poles' sense of national culture and identity.

Architecture

The Polans (meaning "people of the fields") were an agrarian Slavic tribe that settled in the region of modern-day Poland from around the seventh century CE. In the earliest period of Polish settlement, the only architectural structures to be found were mostly primitive wooden cottages and gords (meaning "fenced areas"). A gord had a high fortress wall, built up from earth and wood, which enclosed a group of small wooden houses. The first enlarged settlements, called podgrodzie (meaning "below the fenced area"), developed near the most important gords, such as a gord surrounding a ruler's home, or located at a major trade junction. In this way, some gords, like Kraków, became Poland's first major cities. From the 11th through the 13th centuries, many of these gords were reinforced and expanded to become the first castles and citadels of the early Polish state.

Most historians contend that the Polish state formally came into being in the year 965 CE. It was during this time that the ruling Piast dynasty converted to Christianity. During the dynasty's 400-year reign, Poland became a strong kingdom in Central Europe and was tightly connected to the Catholic Church. Throughout this medieval period, castles, cathedrals and other buildings were built in the Romanesque and Gothic styles of architecture.

Later, during the Polish Renaissance, which lasted from the late 15th to the late 16th century, Renaissance architecture prevailed. It emphasized the harmony and beauty in nature. Three distinct sub-styles developed in three regions of Poland during this period. The southern part of Poland was influenced by the architecture of the Italian Renaissance; Pommerania, along the southern coast of the Baltic Sea, was influenced by the Dutch Renaissance (or the Renaissance in the Low Countries); and the predominant architectural style in central Poland came to be known as the Lublin Renaissance, or "Kalisz-Lublin" style. This latter style was marked by rich ornamentation, barrel-vaulted and aisle-less churches, and the use of stucco. Unlike other kingdoms in Central Europe, Polish Renaissance architecture continued until the end of the 16th century.

The Polish baroque period occurred during the Polish-Lithuanian Commonwealth, from the mid-16th to the late 18th century. The baroque style of architecture contrasted with earlier Renaissance architecture in that is was often dramatic and disharmonious. Some prominent examples of secular baroque architecture include Wilanów Palace, in the capital of Warsaw, and the Royal Castle of Warsaw. The Polish nobility also popularized the cultural trend of Sarmatism during this period. Sarmatism combined Asian philosophy and dress styles with Polish traditions, and was unique to Polish culture.

Drama

Although Polish cinema dates back to the early 20th century, it did not gain international attention until after World War II when the National Film School in Łódź was founded in 1948. Poland's greatest directors, including Roman Polański (1933–), Krzysztof Kieślowski (1941–1996), and Andrzej Wajda (1926–), all studied at the Łódź Film School. The communist government eased its censorship of Polish film during the years 1956–1981, and the Polish film industry flourished. During this period, two of Polish cinema's most important artistic movements developed: the "Polish School" (from 1956–1961), and the "Cinema of Moral Anxiety" (from 1975–1981).

After the fall of communism in 1989, Polish cinema began collaborating with other countries on large film productions. Some of the more famous co-productions include *Schindler's List* (1993). Animated film, which has had a long and distinguished tradition in Poland, has also been created through co-productions with other countries. In 2008, a Polish film company co-produced *Peter and the Wolf* (2006) with a British film production company, which won the Academy Award for best animated short film. The same year, another Polish co-production, *Madame Tutli Putli* (2007), was nominated for the same award, indicating the Polish film industry's new trend to co-produce world-class animated films.

Music

Polish music first evolved from Poland's close association with the Catholic Church. This was because some of the oldest Polish music had to be translated from Latin—the official language of the church—to Polish so that it could be recited by the masses. This included the earliest Polish national hymn, "Bogurodzica" ("Mother of God"). The Catholic Church was the most significant influence on early Polish composers. Mikołaj of Radom (circa 1390–1440) created Poland's first polyphonic compositions. During the Polish Renaissance, Wacław of Szamotuły (1520–1560) wrote poetry in Latin and Polish, and wrote musical compositions in both Latin and Polish. Marcin Leopolita (1530–1589) and Mikołaj Gomółka (1535–1609) were also great Renaissance composers whose compositions expressed religious contemplation.

A few centuries later, Poland saw its traditions and folklore enter the world stage through the music of Frédéric Chopin (1810–1849). Chopin wrote piano compositions that borrowed melodies of Polish folk dances such as the mazurka. Again, many of these folk dance melodies evolved from early Church modes such as Ludian or Dorian. The Polish folk dances were mainly accompanied by the shepherd's reed flute, violin, and a type of bagpipe known as the duda.

Dance

Folk dances are popular in Poland and date back as far as the 16th century. There are five major Polish folk dances. They include the polonaise, a processional formal dance generally accompanied by the music of Chopin; the oberek (stemming from the Polish verb "to spin"), a rhythmic couple's dance; the mazurka, a lively dance done in triple time; the kujawiak, a slow couple's dance that originated in Central Poland; and the krakowiak, a fast dance inspired by the movement horses, a beloved animal in Polish culture. While the polka is a popular dance in 20th century Poland, it did not originate there, but rather in Bohemia, which is now the Czech Republic.

Literature

In the 19th century, Polish culture went through a period of strong artistic movements and dynamic growth. This period witnessed a wealth of Polish literature from writers such as Bolesław Prus (1847–1912), Eliza Orzeszkowa (1841–1910), Stefan Żeromski (1864–1925), and Henryk Sienkiewicz (1846–1916). In 1905, Sienkiewicz was the first Pole to receive the Nobel Prize in Literature.

However, the Nazi occupation (1939–1945) represented a concerted effort to destroy Polish cultural life. Many Polish scholars and artists were sent to concentration camps, and the arts were entirely suppressed. Some of the underground literature written during World War II was not actually recognized until a few decades after the war. For example, Bruno Schulz (1892–1942), who died during Nazi occupation, posthumously gained international attention for his short stories. Many Polish artists and scholars died in concentration camps, and many cultural artifacts were either deliberately destroyed or stolen by the Third Reich. Nevertheless, art became an important expression of Poland's national identity, and represented national resistance to foreign occupation.

Much of what is of national cultural value in Poland today was hidden and preserved by various individuals and organizations that worked in a loose underground network to maintain Polish heritage and nationhood. This network, known as the Polskie Państwo Podziemne (Polish Underground State), remained loyal to the Polish government in exile (based in London) throughout World War II. Among its responsibilities, the Polish Underground State gathered and preserved many paintings and other Polish cultural artifacts. Thus, Nazi Germany's attempt to destroy Polish culture ultimately had the effect of strengthening the Poles' sense of national culture and identity.

After World War II, Polish communists working with the Soviet Union crushed all Polish opposition parties. Many members of the former Polish Underground State, who had fought against Nazi occupation, were branded as traitors and sent to Russian prisons and labor camps. Polish opposition leaders were imprisoned in Moscow and tried in a showcase trial. Many Polish writers were forced into exile, where again their writing came to represent a free and independent Poland. Many writers defected to France and published their works through Jerzy Giedroyc's (1906–2000) Paris-based publishing house. Great writers such as Witold Gombrowicz (1904–1969), Gustaw Herling-Grudziński (1919–2000), Czesław Miłosz (1911–2004), and Sławomir Mrożek (1930–2013) left Poland and published abroad where the Polish communist government could not censor them. In 1980, Miłosz received the Nobel Prize in Literature, which was symbolically important for the growing Polish dissident movement.

CULTURE

Arts & Entertainment

The arts have always been central to the struggle to keep a sense of Polish national identity alive. This crucial role of the arts and literature in particular, can be seen quite strongly during the years that Poland was without nationhood. Many books were also published underground in Poland during the communist years. Between 1976 and 1990, about 6,000 different titles were published and distributed through a Polish underground literary movement. During communist rule, Polish film, literature, visual arts, and music effectively expressed resistance to Polish communism. In this way, the Polish arts played an important role in overthrowing totalitarianism.

Polish jazz, which was officially suppressed during many years of communist rule, and was later tolerated disapprovingly by the Polish communists, earned a deserving international reputation for innovation and excellence. Krzysztof Komeda (1931–1969), Tomasz Stanko (1942–), Michał Urbaniak (1943–), and Leszek Możdżer (1971–) are a few of the internationally renowned Polish jazz artists who have significantly contributed to the Polish jazz scene.

Folk culture is strong in Poland, and Poles enjoy taking part in folk festivals that include dancing and instrumental music. Folk dance troupes are particularly popular in modern-day Poland. Dancers tend to wear traditional customs according to the specific dances. Female dancers generally wear their hair in two braids and may also wear flowers in their hair or scarves. Their costumes may include a bodice or jacket, a full skirt, and lace-up books. Male folk dancers wear traditional coats and trousers.

Cultural Sites & Landmarks

Poland has 14 sites inscribed on the World Heritage List administered by the United Nations Educational, Scientific, and Cultural Organization (UNESCO), as well as five sites that have tentative status. The historic center of Kraków was the first to be entered onto the list in 1978. Kraków was originally the capital of Poland. However, in 1609, King Zygmunt III Vasa (1587–1632) relocated the capital to Warsaw, where it remains to this day. The historic center of Kraków is located just below the Wawel Castle, which Casimir III the Great (1310–1370) ordered built during the period of gothic architecture. In the 14th century, the king and queen of Poland, Jogaila (1348–1434) and Jadwiga (Hedwig, 1373–1399), significantly expanded the castle. In the early 16th century, King Sigismund I the Old (Zygmunt I in Polish, 1467–1548) commissioned many international elite architects, sculptors and decorators to convert the castle into a Renaissance palace. Kraków is among the best-preserved Gothic and Renaissance historical centers in Europe.

However, many Polish buildings incurred substantial damage during World War II and were extensively repaired, including the Royal Wawel Castle. The cities of Gdańsk, Szczeczin, and Wroclaw also saw serious architectural destruction, and the Germans razed a large part of Warsaw. After the war, the communist Polish government restored or completely rebuilt historical sites to emphasize Poland's determination to maintain its heritage. Thus, many of the buildings and sites that seem centuries old are actually post-World War II reconstructions. For example, the Warsaw's Old Town, including the Royal Castle, added as a World Heritage Site in 1980, was entirely reconstructed after being decimated. The historic centers of Gdańsk and Wrocław were also reconstructed. Other renowned structures in Poland that are inscribed on the World Heritage List include the Churches of Peace in Jawor and Swidnica; the Castle of the Teutonic Order in Malbork; the Wooden Churches of Southern Little Poland; the Medieval Town of Toruń; and the Old City of Zamość.

One of the most important UNESCO sites in Poland is Auschwitz-Birkenau, which served as Nazi concentration and extermination camps from 1940–1945. The two camps, built adjacent to each other during Nazi Germany's occupation of Poland, were the largest concentration camps in the Third Reich. The camps were originally concentration camps for Poles and Soviet prisoners of war. From 1942 to 1944, they became the main mass extermination camps for Jews. It is estimated that about 1.5 million men, women, and children were systematically starved, tortured, and then murdered in the gas chambers. Other victims included tens of thousands of Poles and thousands of Roma and Sinti prisoners. The camps' fortified walls, barbed wire, gallows, gas chambers and cremation ovens are important historical reminders of the horrifying conditions under which the Nazi genocide took place, and thus comprise an important Holocaust museum.

Libraries & Museums

The National Library of Poland, established in 1928, is located in Warsaw and is the national book depository for all Polish publications. Its collection includes two million books and 26,000 manuscripts. In the late 20th century, there were over 10,300 public libraries in Poland. The oldest academic library in the country is that of Jagiellonian University, which was established in 1364.

The National Museum in Warsaw houses collections of ancient art as well as 16th-century Polish art. The Auschwitz-Birkenau State Museum was established in 1947 on the grounds of two World War II concentration camps, Auschwitz I and Auschwitz II-Birkenau. The museum campus features many camp buildings, including a crematorium and gas chamber, as well as an extensive collection of objects owned by prisoners of the camps. These objects include over 80,000 shoes, 3,800 suitcases, and 570 camp garments. The Historical Museum, founded in Krakow in 1899, focuses on the history of that city; its collections include artwork such as paintings and drawings, as well as historical documents.

Holidays

Many Polish holidays have religious significance, and are related to the Roman Catholic faith. These include the Assumption of the Blessed Virgin Mary (August 15) and Pentecost Sunday (the seventh Sunday after Easter). Easter Monday is known as "Wet Monday" or Dyngus Day ("Wet Monday"), and is celebrated with courtship rituals involving dousing members of the opposite sex with buckets of water.

Two important political holidays occur in May. May 1 is the official State Holiday, which is purposely not called "Labor Day" in order to avoid connections with the communist past. Constitution Day (May 3) honors the 1791 passage of Poland's first written constitution. The

Picnic (May 2) is not an official holiday but is used by many Poles to make a long weekend between the other two days.

Independence Day (November 11) commemorates November 11, 1918, the day on which World War I ended and on which the Polish Republic was reestablished.

Youth Culture

The majority of Polish youth, particularly adolescents and teenagers, are becoming increasingly Internet-savvy, and frequently use communication technologies such as chat rooms and email. Online gaming sites have also become popular. In fact, recent research studies estimate that over 80 percent of Polish high school students use the Internet on a daily basis. However, those same studies suggest that Polish parents are generally uninformed about their children's Internet activity. Like youth around the world, Polish teenagers enjoy watching television, particularly MTV Poland, and eating at international fast-food restaurants. (As of 2009, there were over 200 McDonald's fast food restaurants in Poland.) Polish youth also embrace Western fashions and styles. For example, the techno music culture that rose to popularity in Britain in the early 1990s appeared in Poland several years later in the mid 1990s.

After Poland joined the EU in 2004, many member states extended an open door policy on foreign workers. As a result, there was an enormous migration of Polish youth to countries such as England and Ireland. As many as 2 million Poles migrated to the British Isles because of higher wages and the fact that the English language is easier to learn in its early stages. However, the economic downturn of 2008 caused a mass migration back to Poland, where the economy remained stable.

SOCIETY

Transportation

Poles in the largest cities greatly rely on mass transportation that is generally effective and reliable. Nearly all towns have a public bus system that connects to nearby towns and cities, and more than thirty of the largest cities have extensive streetcar systems, including Gdańsk, Katowice, Kraków, Łódź, Poznań, Szczecin, Warsaw and Wrocław. Warsaw is Poland's only city with a subway system, though the Warsaw subway is by no means an extensive underground network like those of London, Paris, or Prague.

The most extensive public transportation network in Poland is the railway system. In most cities, the main railway station is located near or in the city center, and is highly integrated with the local bus and streetcar transportation systems. The railway network of Poland is an estimated 23,420 kilometers (14,553 miles) in total length, and 11,626 kilometers (7,224 miles) of this system have overhead wires that power electric trains. Polish State Railways (PKP) is the third largest railway in Europe, but its equipment and service is of lower quality than other European Union (EU) countries. In 2000, the Polish government began to privatize PKP, which should lead to equipment and infrastructure modernization. Traffic moves on the right-hand side of the road in Poland.

Transportation Infrastructure

Poland has a thorough road network, but road improvements and repairs have not kept up with the country's increasing road usage. In 2006, from a total of 423,997 kilometers (263,460 miles) of roadways, 295,356 kilometers (183,526 miles) were paved roads.

In the early 21st century, road construction began on several major highways spanning Poland; by 2012, it is estimated that eight of the 10 major Polish cities will be connected by major highways. Improvements to the country's transportation infrastructure have been funded in part by the European Union.

Media & Communications

During communism, the entire Polish media was centralized under one-party rule. The Central Press and Entertainment Board of Inspection censured and controlled all print media content, while the Radio and Television Committee censured and controlled all electronic media content. After 1989, these government organizations quickly came to an end, and Polish society created a free press. Opposition journalists who had worked for an underground press connected to the main dissidence organization, Solidarity, began legally publishing various journals and newspapers, and the daily newspaper *Gazeta Wyborcza* (Voters Daily) quickly became Poland's largest newspaper. *Fakt* is also a popular publication in Poland.

Prior to the fall of communism, Poland's television network Telewizja Polska (TVP) was a monopoly run by the government. The network is still in existence with three public television stations, TVP1, TVP2, and TVP3, a regional network station. Although TVP still has a large audience and advertising revenue, it has experienced a decline in its income and has been losing an important segment of the market. The Radio and Television Act of 1992 created the National Broadcasting Council (KRRiT), which is Poland's main broadcast media regulator that issues broadcast licenses. Private TV stations that have received licensing have successfully launched new channels in recent years. Private media companies are prepared for the complete digitalization of Polish television, scheduled for 2012; Poland completed its analogue switch-off on 23 July 2013.

Under communism, Poland also had an underdeveloped and outmoded telecommunications infrastructure. Since that time, however, France Telecom bought the largest share of the former state-owned Polish telephone monopoly, and invested into modernizing the national landline system. In December 2005, the last analog exchange was shut down, and all telephone lines now operate through fully computerized exchanges. In 2012, there were about 6.1 million landline phones in Poland, while over 50 million Poles had acquired a cell phone. There are three competing cell phone networks in Poland with similar market shares: Era, Orange Polska, and Plus GSM. A fourth network, Play Mobile, began offering network services in early 2007. Additionally, as of 2009, an estimated 22.452 million Poles were regular Internet users.

SOCIAL DEVELOPMENT

Standard of Living

In 2013, Poland ranked 35 out of 182 countries on the United Nations Human Development Index, which measures quality of life indicators.

Water Consumption

Access to water is relatively high in Poland, with 100 percent of the country's urban population and 87.8 percent of its rural population having access to improved water sources.

Education

Poland enjoys a 99.8 percent literacy rate, and has an extensive public education system. The Roman Catholic Church plays an important role, and all students must receive religious instruction. Primary school attendance, between the ages of seven and 13 is mandatory.

Secondary education has two levels. The lower level (the "gymnasium") is roughly equivalent to junior high school in the United States. Several types of upper secondary schooling exist. The three-year lyceum is roughly equivalent to U.S. high school, and prepares a student for university or technical studies.

Many universities in Poland date from the Middle Ages. One of the oldest and most prestigious is the Jagiellonian University in Krakow, established in 1364; alumni include astronomer Nicolaus Copernicus (1473–1543) and Pope John Paul II (1920–2005). Other major university towns are Warsaw, Krakow, Gdansk, and Lublin. During the communist era, the Catholic University of Lublin (founded 1918) was notable as the only independent university in Eastern Europe.

According to the World Bank, 64 percent of the female labor force had attained secondary education and 27 percent had attained tertiary education; in comparison, 72 percent of the male labor force had attained secondary education and 17 percent had attained tertiary education.

Women's Rights

Women in Poland enjoy a high degree of equality; they comprise around one-third of all administrators and managers, and 60 percent of all professional/technical workers. They also hold 20 percent of the seats in the lower house of parliament.

In 1995, the governmental policy on women's issues became the responsibility of the office of Governmental Plenipotentiary for Women and Family. However, in 2005 the Polish government abolished that office. The UN Committee on the Elimination of Discrimination against Women (CEDAW), as well as many relevant European NGOs, has expressed concern about this abolition. However, as of 2011, the Polish government had refused to re-establish the office. The same UN committee also expressed concern over the Polish parliament's repeated rejection of a comprehensive law on gender equality. Thus, although the Polish constitution guarantees women equal rights, there is no other legislation to ensure those equal rights, particularly in the workplace, are protected in Poland. Furthermore, women's representation in the Polish government has always been quite low, which has caused some women's groups to argue that not enough women are involved in these decisions at the governmental level. In 2011, however, a gender quota system was adopted for parliamentary and local elections.

Women are further marginalized when it comes to the workforce, particularly in terms of equal pay and rights. One grievous example involves the establishment of a 1999 retirement law that required women to retire at age 60 and at age 65 for men. The unequal retirement age for women means that women will get a smaller government retirement pension than men. A proposal to amend this system, such that women would have the option to choose retiring anywhere from 60 to 65 years of age, was rejected by the Polish senate. Additionally, older women from age 55 upward are often pushed into early retirement due to the prevailing cultural notion that older women should retire to help with their grandchildren. The Poland's civil rights commissioner intervened to stop the forced early retirement of women civil servants during government reforms in 1997.

Women constitute the majority of domestic violence victims in Poland. According to the recent surveys commissioned by the Ministry of Labour and Social Policy and which were conducted at the end of 2010, 45 percent of respondents (40 percent of men and 49 percent of women) live or lived in households where domestic violence took place. However, the Polish courts usually consider domestic violence a minor crime, and judges often either dismiss cases or issue suspended sentences.

The Act on Counteracting Family Violence was subsequently changed: the amendments from 2010 included more effective measures for the isolation of the perpetrator of violence (such as eviction) as well as more extensive involvement of public prosecutor's offices and courts on behalf of the victim. The number of shelters for battered women is also inadequate in Poland. As of 2011, there were approximately 10 shelters that provide psychological, medical and legal aid for women victims of violence. Forced prostitution, particularly as it relates to human trafficking, is also a serious issue that is exacerbated by the fact that prostitution is legal. Poland is often regarded as a country of origin, transit and destination in regards to human trafficking and, as of 2008, the county has been linked to an estimated 15,000 victims. In May 2013, the government adopted a 2013–2015 national action plan for combating trafficking. The plan was developed in coordination with NGOs and prioritizes enhanced care for child victims, more training for those likely to encounter victims, and information campaigns targeting the most vulnerable populations.

Health Care

The central government completely controlled health care during the communist era. Although it was free, medical care was often of poor quality. In the post-communist era, Poland is working to improve public health through privatization and decentralization.

Private medical care has been available since 1989, but is expensive. Public health was increasingly decentralized during the 1990s, with power given to local medical facilities and regional boards known as "Health Funds." Poles' health has also suffered due to poor lifestyle habits including a fatty diet, heavy alcohol use, and smoking.

GOVERNMENT

Structure

The current Third Polish Republic, a parliamentary democracy, was established in 1989. The current constitution dates from 1997.

Poland's executive branch includes the president and the Council of Ministers, the latter headed by the prime minister. The president, the head of state, is popularly elected every five years. The Council of Ministers, or cabinet, is appointed on the advice of the prime minister. Ministers are usually selected from the majority party or ruling coalition of the lower house of Parliament.

Poland has a two-house parliament. When the houses are meeting in joint session, the parliament is known as the National Assembly. The 100-member upper house is the Senate, and the 460-member lower house is the Sejm, whose members are known as deputies. The Council of Ministers is responsible to the Sejm, which may call for a vote of no confidence if it dislikes the government's policies. The Sejm's presiding officers are known as the Presidium.

Members of both houses are elected to four-year terms, in direct popular elections. Senators are elected by majority vote, to represent the sixteen provinces. A political party generally must receive at least five percent of the total vote in order to have deputies in the Sejm.

On April 10, 2010, Poland's President Lech Kaczynski was killed in a plane crash near Smolensk, Russia. Also on board was First Lady Maria Kaczynska, the general staff of the Polish army, several parliament members, the governor of the central bank, and the deputy minister of foreign affairs. The crash killed 96 people in all. The group on the plane was en route to a ceremony honoring 20,000 Poles killed in Russia's Katyn Forest during World War II. Leaders worldwide expressed sympathy and solidarity with Poland in the days after the incident.

Political Parties

The largest political parties in Poland in the early 21st century include the Citizens' Platform (PO), which supports a free-market economy; the Law and Justice Party (PiS), a right-wing party that also favors a free-market economy; the Democratic Left Alliance (SLD), a social democratic party; and the Polish Peoples Party (PSL), a labor-friendly, left-leaning party.

Local Government

Poland is divided into sixteen provinces, which are overseen by a governor, regional assembly, and executive, who handles budgeting and development planning. Members of the regional assembly are elected to four-year terms, and the governors are appointed by the prime minister.

Judicial System

The court system of Poland comprises a Supreme Court, which oversees the military, administrative, and general courts. Supreme Court judges are appointed by the president. Other courts include the Constitutional Tribunal and State Tribunal.

Taxation

As of 2010, the top income tax levied in Poland is 32 percent, while the corporate tax rate is a flat 19 percent. Other taxes include inheritance taxes, value-added taxes (VAT), and transfer taxes.

Armed Forces

The Polish Armed Forces comprise the Polish Air Force, Polish Land Forces, Polish Navy, and Polish Special Forces. As of 2010, there were approximately 100,000 active military personnel in Poland.

Foreign Policy

The failure of communist governance led to the annulment of the Warsaw Pact (the Soviet-sponsored military-treaty organization which was in direct opposition to the North Atlantic Treaty Organization, or NATO). As a result, Poland and other former Soviet republics and Eastern European member countries were suddenly faced with an unstable military and economic vacuum. Because of this, the first foreign policy issues that the new democratic Polish government faced in the early 1990s were those of re-establishing security and economic relations with nearby countries of the former Eastern Bloc (member states of the Warsaw Pact). Poland was quite active in its work to re-establish ties and promote bilateral and multilateral agreements. Additionally, after communism fell in the Baltic republics of Lithuania, Latvia, and Estonia, Poland was the first Eastern European country to extend diplomatic recognition to those countries.

In 1991, Poland also joined the Visegrád Group, now called the Visegrád Four (V4). The V4 (the Czech Republic, Hungary, Poland and the Slovak Republic) created a declaration on cooperation for European integration. The Visegrád agreement committed Poland to eliminate all traces of totalitarianism, to build democracy, to ensure human rights, and to integrate into Western Europe. It seems likely that their private talks were also about joining NATO since, by late 1991, all Visegrád participants had entered into agreements with NATO.

Thus, Poland set its foreign policy course for joining NATO and the EU. Poland became a full member of NATO in 1999, which meant the country made a clear shift from Eastern Bloc alliance to the United States and Western European alliance. NATO membership is certainly one of the most important events in Poland's post-communist history, though Poland's entrance into the EU in 2004 was equally important. Gaining EU membership meant Poland would be assured that its alliance with Western Europe would remain a central and permanent part of its foreign policy.

Since the fall of communism, Poland continues to build very close ties with the U.S. This is particularly evident in the recent transitions in Polish government, which witnessed the appointment of numerous politicians who supported pro-American and EU agendas. These ties were further solidified on August 20, 2008, when the minister of foreign affairs signed a missile defense agreement with the US that would allow American missile bases to be built in Poland. Poland was also one of the largest military contributors to the US-led 2003 Iraq War—behind the United Kingdom (UK), the U.S., and Australia.

Human Rights Profile

International human rights law insists that states respect civil and political rights, and promote an individual's economic, social, and cultural rights. The United Nations Universal Declaration on Human Rights (UDHR) is recognized as the standard for international human rights. Its authors sought the counsel of the world's great thinkers, philosophers, and religious leaders, and were careful to create a document that reflects the core values shared by every world culture. (To read this document or view the articles relating to cultural human rights, visit http://www.un.org/en/documents/udhr/.)

Since the democratization of the country, beginning with the fall of communism in 1989, Poland has standardized its approach to human rights abuses and drastically improved its human rights record. However, some key areas of concern remain, particularly as they relate to the U.S.-led "war on terror." For example, the EU has been investigating Poland's involvement with the US Central Intelligence Agency's (CIA) program of secret detention facilities and renditions flights. The European Parliament (EP) demanded that Poland investigate its involvement in those facilities that are in Polish territory. The EU concluded that Poland failed to investigate properly the claims of secret rendition camps within its borders.

Following a parliamentary investigation, the UN urged Poland to release its findings into the presence of secret CIA detention centers. However, Poland's prime minister at the time, and current leader of Poland's main opposition party Law and Justice (PiS), Jarosław Kaczyński (1949–), informed the UN that the Polish government considered the allegations a closed issue.

The Parliamentary Assembly of the Council of Europe (PACE) released additional new evidence showing that the CIA was operating secret detention centers in Poland from 2002 to 2005. PACE called for democratic oversight of military intelligence services and foreign intelligence services operating in Poland, and for transparent investigations. Poland denied any involvement in hosting secret detention centers. In 2009, the secret detention centers were still a central and unresolved human rights issue for Poland. In July 2014, *The New York Times* reported, "The existence of a C.I.A. "black site" prison in Poland has been widely reported for years, but the United States government considers the list of countries that hosted the prisons to be highly classified .... Poland has never publicly acknowledged hosting a C.I.A. prison, and, as a young democracy that experienced state-sanctioned repression during decades of Communist rule, it had a fierce public debate about its alleged complicity in the program."

The Polish government has also been accused of intolerant attitudes and using discriminatory policies against homosexuals in Poland. Human rights non-governmental organizations (NGOs) have been concerned over Polish government proposals that seek to stop the "promotion of homosexuality and other deviance" in Polish schools, and to punish those who promote such behavior. In a related event, Poland has been accused of violating the right to freedom of peaceful assembly and association. In 2005, the then-mayor of Warsaw Lech Kaczyński (President of Poland from 2005) banned gay rights activists from holding an Equality Parade in Warsaw. The activists then successfully challenged this

Polish government ban in the European Court of Human Rights (ECtHR). The court reached a unanimous decision that the ban was illegal and discriminatory.

ECONOMY

Overview of the Economy

Since the downfall of communism, Poland has worked to move its economy toward a free-market system. This has often been difficult, due to the aging infrastructure inherited from the communist era, and lack of investment. Poland was forced to make drastic economic and monetary reforms in order to qualify for membership in the European Union. The EU provided Poland $17 billion (USD) in economic assistance between 2004 and 2006.

Poland in the early 1990s faced immense inflation and unemployment. As of 2008, unemployment was around 9.7 percent of a total workforce of more than 17 million. The workforce is divided evenly among industry/construction, agriculture, services, and public sectors.

As of 2014, the overall gross domestic product (GDP) was $941.4 billion USD. Per capita GDP was estimated at $24,400 (USD).

Industry

Poland's industry is mostly heavy, focusing on the manufacture of iron and steel, coal, and ships. Poland's shipbuilding industry came into world prominence in the 1980s, through the rise of the labor union Solidarity. Other major industries are chemicals and textiles.

Industry is trying to restructure itself in the face of new technology. Polish industry faces problems because of its reliance on domestic coal for power; although cheap, coal has furthered Poland's environmental problems.

Many of Poland's most important trading partners are EU members, including France, Italy, and Germany. Other important trading partners are Eastern European neighbors Russia and the Czech Republic.

Labor

The labor force of Poland was estimated to be 18.26 million in 2014. In 2014, the unemployment rate was estimated at 8.2 percent.

Energy/Power/Natural Resources

Poland is rich in natural resources, particularly coal, natural gas, petroleum, and industrial metals such as silver, lead, and copper. There are large amounts of arable land, as well as large forests. More than one-quarter of the country is forested, with both evergreens and deciduous species.

Post-communist Poland suffers severe environmental problems, relating to the country's rapid industrialization during the Cold War. A particular problem is air pollution from the country's coal-fired power plants, and water pollution from industrial runoff.

Fishing

The fishing industry is most prevalent along the nation's Baltic Sea shoreline, and much of the fish caught in Poland is used for domestic consumption; however, the industry contributes little to the country's GDP and employs relatively few workers. In 2007, approximately 145,000 tons of fish were caught in the country. Common coastal fish species include herring and cod, while inland fisheries tend to produce carp and trout.

Forestry

In 2007, approximately 92,450 square kilometers (35,695 square miles) of Poland were covered by forests. Over three-quarters of the country's forests are owned by the government. Common tree species include conifers, such as pine, fir, and spruce, as well as oak, maple, and ash. Poland exports wood products such as paper, lumber, and furniture.

Mining/Metals

According to the United Nations, the mining and manufacturing industries contributed 25 percent to the nation's GDP in 2007. Commonly mined materials include copper, coal, lignite, natural gas, sulfur, and salt.

Agriculture

Agriculture is a major employer, involving about 17 percent of Poland's total workforce. Yet agriculture productivity is low in terms of contribution to GDP, accounting for less than five percent of the total. This is largely because Poland's farms are usually small and family-owned.

The country produces most of its own food. The major crops include potatoes, rye, sugar beets, wheat, and oats.

Animal Husbandry

Poultry, pork, and dairy are important agricultural sectors.

Tourism

Poland has become increasingly popular as a tourist destination in the post-communist era. This trend is likely to continue, since the country's entry into the European Union. In the mid-1990s, Poland received around 18 million tourists per year.

Winter sports, especially skiing, are popular in the mountains. Other popular destinations are the country's centuries-old health spas and the Baltic Sea resorts. The Bialowieza Forest, home of the European bison, is a United Nations Educational, Scientific, and Cultural Organization (UNESCO) World Heritage Site. The natural beauty of the Mazury Lake District in the northeast also attracts visitors.

Though many landmarks have been destroyed by centuries of war, Poland offers many historic sites. Among the most historic are the ancient cities of Warsaw, Krakow, Lublin, and Wroclaw.

Sinclair Nicholas, Eric Badertscher,
Beverly Ballaro

DO YOU KNOW?

- The Polish national anthem "Mazurek Dabrowskiego" ("Dabrowski's Mazurka") is named in honor of General Jan Henryk Dabrowski (1755–1818), a Pole who commanded Napoleon's Polish Legions in Italy. The anthem was originally the unit's battle song.

- The Polish-Lithuanian Commonwealth was noted for its innovative political system, including a written constitution and elective monarchy, and extensive political and religious liberty. Its constitution of May 3, 1791, was one of the world's first written constitutions.

- Pope John Paul II, was born Karol Wojtyla in 1920 in Wadowice, Poland. In his youth, he was deeply involved in preserving Poland's cultural life as a writer, poet, and actor, often doing so underground in resistance to Nazi policies in his country.

- In order to recreate sections of Warsaw's main thoroughfare, the Royal Way, the engineers and architects charged with rebuilding Warsaw after its destruction during World War II relied on the paintings of the Venetian-born artist Bernardo Bellotto (1721–1780), professionally known as Canaletto. Canelleto had served as a painter at the court of Poland's last king and his canvases provided 20th-century urban planners with accurate models to replicate.

- Warsaw's somber 1948 Monument to the Heroes of the Ghetto, honoring the Jewish heroes of the Warsaw Ghetto uprising, is crafted of bronze and granite that were set aside by Hitler for a monument celebrating the Third Reich.

Bibliography

Adam Zamoyski. "The Polish Way: A Thousand-Year History of Poles and Their Culture." New York: *Hippocrene Books*, 1993.

Christopher Garbowski. "Religious Life in Poland: History, Diversity, and Modern Issues." Jefferson, NC: *McFarland*, 2014.

Greg Allen. "Poland – Culture Smart! The Essential Guide to Customs and Culture." London: *Kuperard*, 2010.

Jerzy Lukowski and Hubert Zawadzki. "A Concise History of Poland, 2d ed." New York: *Cambridge University Press*, 2006.

Jonathan Bousefield and Mark Salter. "Rough Guide to Poland." London: *Rough Guides*, 2009.

Mark Baker and Tim Richards. "Poland." Oakland, CA: *Lonely Planet*, 2012.

Sophie Hodorowicz Knab. "Polish Customs, Traditions, and Folklore." New York: *Hippocrene Books*, 1996.

Works Cited

"Council of Europe: Secret CIA Prisons Confirmed." *Human Rights Watch*. http://www.hrw.org/en/news/2007/06/07/council-europe-secret-cia-prisons-confirmed.

"Cultural Information: Poland - Communication Styles." *CountryInsights*. http://www.intercultures.ca/cil-cai/intercultural_issues-en.asp?lvl=8&ISO=pl&SubjectID=2.

"Facts and Myths about Poland." *Translation Management Europe*. http://www.tm-europe.org/index.php?q=node/attractions

"Foreign Policy." *Polish Ministry of Foreign Affairs Website*. http://www.poland.gov.pl/Foreign,policy,371.html

"Lifestyle." *Polish Ministry of Foreign Affairs Website*. http://www.poland.gov.pl/Lifestyle,414.html.

Poland." Central Intelligence Agency *World Factbook*: https://www.cia.gov/library/publications/the-world-factbook/geos/pl.html.

"Poland: The Role of Women." *U.S. Library of Congress*. http://countrystudies.us/poland/36.htm.

"Poland: Largest cities and towns and statistics of their population." http://www.world-gazetteer.com/wg.php?x=&men=gcis&lng=en&des=wg&srt=npan&col=abcdefghinoq&msz=1500&geo=-173.

"Report on implementation of women's rights in Poland." http://www.feministki.org.pl/pl/raport.html

"The History of Wawel Castle and Cathedral." http://www.valsworld.org/holocaust/wawelhill.pdf.

Anna Mulrine. "As the Americans Move On, Polish Troops Take Over a Fight." *U.S. News & World Report*. EBSCO Academic Search Complete. http://search.ebscohost.com/login.aspx?direct=true&db=a9h&AN=35407406&site=ehost-live

Jeffrey Stinson. "Polish immigrants go home as work dries up in Britain." *USA Today*. (Dec. 2008). EBSCO Academic Search Complete. http://search.ebscohost.com/login.aspx?direct=true&db=a9h&AN=J0E371596340108&site=ehost-live

Maciej Golubiewski. "Poland Pressured on Abortion and Sexual Orientation by UN Human Rights Committee." http://www.lifesitenews.com/ldn/2008/apr/08042501.html

ROMANIA

Introduction

Romania is located in Southeastern Europe. Both the country and culture experienced a revolution in December 1989 that resulted in the execution of brutal communist leader Nicolae Ceausescu. Today, Romania is a democratic nation with a free-market economy, and mostly privatized industrial and agricultural sectors.

Since the end of brutal communist rule in 1989, Romanian society and the arts have also grown. The arts are now used as vehicles for rebuilding Romanian national identity. Romania's artists and ethnic groups, particularly Roma, are free to share their vision, traditions, and cultural sensibility without censorship or persecution.

While there is no longer much direct government support available for the arts, traditional Romanian art forms are being taught and exhibited around the world. These include pottery, music, wood carving, and sculpture, painted eggs, textiles, masks, and glasswork.

The Romanian Language has its roots in Latin, but also incorporates words from Slavic languages.

GENERAL INFORMATION

Official Language: Romanian
Population: 21,729,871 (July 2014 estimate.)
Currency: New leu
Coins: One hundred bani equal one leu. Coins are issued in denominations of 1, 5, 10, and 50 bani.

Land Area: 229,891 square kilometers (88,761 square miles)
Water Area: 8,500 square kilometers (3,281 square miles)
National Anthem: Desteapta-te, Romane" ("Wake Up, O, Romanian!")
Capital: Bucharest
Time Zone: GMT +5
Flag Description: The Romanian flag is a vertical tricolor featuring stripes of blue (hoist, or left, side), yellow (center), and red (right) representing liberty, justice, and fraternity respectively.

Population

Romania is divided into six informal regions: Moldavia in the northeast, Walachia in the south, Transylvania in the center and northwest, Banat in the west, Bucinova in the north, and Dobruja in the southeast.

Central and southwest Walachia and central and northwest Transylvania are the most

Principal Cities by Population (2012):

- Bucharest (1.9 million)
- Timişoara (306,462)
- Cluj-Napoca (303,047)
- Craiova (293,567)
- Galaţi (286,530)
- Constanţa (297,503)
- Iaşi (290,422)
- Braşov (275,514)
- Ploieşti (224,406)
- Brăila (206,599)

heavily populated areas in Romania. Average population density is roughly 90 people per square kilometer (233 people per square mile), and roughly 54 percent of the population live in urban areas.

Bucharest is Romania's largest city, with an estimated population of 1.872 million as of 2014. It is located in Walachia in the southeast. The second largest city is Timişoara (population 306,462), located in Banat in the western region.

Languages
Romanian, a romance language similar to classical Latin, is Romania's official language. Its origin dates back to the Roman occupation of Dacia in the second century. Modern Romanian incorporates many words from Slavic languages.

Native People & Ethnic Groups
The majority of Romanians (about 91 percent) are descendents of Dacians who lived in early Romania in the second century. Hungarians constitute just over six percent of the population (2011 estimate.). The Roma, a nomadic people commonly called gypsies, account for 3.1 percent (2011 est.) of the population. Other ethnic minority groups include Germans, Ukrainians, Russians, and Turkish people, each accounting for less than 1 percent of the population. Transylvania and Banat have the

highest percentage of minorities and Walachia and Moldavia the smallest.

Historically, between 2000 and 700 BCE, a people of Indo-European origin called the Thracians lived in the area that would eventually become Romania. In 700 BCE, they mingled with Greeks who arrived via the Black Sea, and their land became known as Dacia. The Dacians were conquered by the Roman Empire in 106.

The Romans withdrew in 271, and despite their short occupation, they had a long-lasting effect on the Dacians, who adopted the Roman religion and language.

Until Romania gained independence in 1878, it was invaded and occupied by Huns, Goths, Slavs, Magyars (Hungarians), Saxons (Germanic people), and Ottoman Turks. There are still minority Hungarian and German populations in Romania today.

Religions
Nearly 82 percent of Romanians belong to the Romanian Orthodox Church. The remainder of the population is Roman Catholic, Protestant, Pentecostal, or Greek Orthodox.

Climate
Romania experiences four separate seasons: winter is typically cold and foggy with heavy snowfall, spring is mild and rainy, summer is hot and sunny, and autumn is cool and rainy.

In Bucharest, the average summer temperature is 16° to 30° Celsius (61° to 86° Fahrenheit). In winter, the temperature may drop as low as −7° Celsius (19° Fahrenheit). The temperature is higher in the south and east than in the Carpathian Mountains. Average annual rainfall is between 60 and 70 centimeters (24 and 26 inches), most of which falls between April and June. The Carpathian Mountains receive twice as much rain as the plains because the mountains restrict air masses from the Atlantic, preventing them from reaching the southern and eastern parts of the country. Dobruja in the east is the country's driest region.

ENVIRONMENT & GEOGRAPHY

Topography

Romania borders Ukraine in the north, Moldova on the northeast, Hungary on the northwest, Serbia on the southwest, Bulgaria on the south, and the Black Sea on the southeast. The Carpathian Mountains, which cover one-third of Romania, run the length of the country from the north to the southwest. The mountain range is U-shaped, and partially surrounds the Transylvania plateau in its center. The Carpathians are divided into the Eastern Carpathians, the Western Carpathians, and the Southern Carpathians (Transylvania Alps). The Southern Carpathians contain Romania's highest peak, Mount Moldoveanu, at 2,544 meters (8,346 feet) above sea level.

Elevated plateaus account for another third of Romania's area, while lowland plains, such as the Walachian plain in the south, make up the remainder.

Throughout the entire Carpathian range are over 3,000 mineral and thermal springs, and near the Eastern Carpathians are small volcano-like cones 5 to 6 meters (16 to 20 feet) high that spew sulfur and methane-laced mud. Another unique geological feature, found predominantly in the Southern Carpathians, is a cave system of over 12,000 caves.

The Danube River is the longest river in Romania, and Europe's second-longest, extending for a total of 2,850 kilometers (1,771 miles) through several countries (1,075 kilometers/668 miles of its length are in Romania). The Danube winds along Romania's southern border, sprouting numerous tributaries, and empties by way of the Danube Delta in eastern Romania into the Black Sea.

Romania has over 2,300 lakes. The largest, Lake Razelm in the Danube Delta, measures 415 square kilometers (160 square miles).

Plants & Animals

The plains are predominantly steppe grassland, the majority of which has been cultivated for agricultural use. The plateaus are a combination of grassland and broad-leaved forests. Nearly 30 percent of Romania is covered by forest.

In the Carpathian Mountains, deciduous forests of oak, sycamore, maple, and poplar grow at the higher altitudes. Coniferous forests of pine, spruce, fir, juniper, little willow, and barberry dot the landscape and other alpine and sub-alpine shrubs and grasses grow at lower altitudes. Over 1,350 species of flowers grow in the Carpathians, among them Transylvanian columbine, yellow poppy, and saxifrage at higher elevations, and crocuses, narcissi, anemones, daffodils, and lilacs in the foothills.

Deer, bears, wolves, lynx, foxes, and badgers live in the lower forests of the Carpathian Mountains, while chamois (a type of antelope) live in the rocky outcrops in higher elevations. The Carpathians are also home to many different species of birds including eagles, falcons, green woodpeckers, jays, and grey owls.

The Danube Delta is roughly 87 percent wetland and contains expansive reed marshes. These marshes are home to over 300 birds, both migratory and indigenous. Approximately 60 percent of the world's pygmy cormorant population lives in the Danube Delta, as does half the world's red-breasted goose population (in winter). Also present are Dalmatian pelicans, flamingoes, night herons, swans, ducks, bee-eaters, white-tailed eagles, and egrets. Sturgeon, carp, and many other species of fish populate the tributaries of the delta.

On the dry portions of the Danube Delta, woody vines and softwood forests grow, and snakes, mink, muskrat, foxes, and wild cats are found.

CUSTOMS & COURTESIES

Greetings

Romanians greet one another in a formal and reserved manner. Handshakes, direct eye contact, and the use of formal titles are common. Greetings are generally exchanged in a quiet voice. Romanians use an honorific title—such as "Domnul" ("Mr.") and "Doamna" ("Mrs. or

Ms.")—along with last name to demonstrate respect and acknowledge age or social status. Romanians of equal social status or age may greet one another with first names. Romanian friends or family may kiss each other on both cheeks in greeting. In business settings, Romanians value formality, courtesy, punctuality, predictability, and politeness.

Common Romanian greetings and phrases include "Bună" ("Hello"), "Bună ziua" ("Good day"), "Bună dimineața" ("Good morning"), "Bună seara" ("Good evening"), and "Ce mai faceți?" ("How are you?").

Gestures & Etiquette

Gesturing is common in Romania. While Romanians generally speak quietly and value formality, they are also physically expressive. Romanian culture includes many gestures that will be familiar to visitors from throughout Europe and North America. For instance, Romanians convey non-verbal agreement through by nodding the head forward or making a thumbs-up sign. However, Romanians have subtle variations to their gesturing and etiquette that characterizes their own special form of non-verbal communication. For instance, Romanians maintain unbroken eye contact as a means of conveying sincerity and trust. Romanians also tend to stand two to three feet apart when speaking to one another.

Romanians have culturally specific taboo gestures. For example, Romanians consider the American OK gesture (circle formed by joined thumb and index finger) to be an obscene gesture. In addition, breaking eye contact or maintaining only intermittent eye contact with Romanians may create a lack of trust.

In Romania, proper etiquette dictates the exchange of handshakes when meeting a friend or business associate. Proper etiquette also requires that friends, family and business associates arrive on time and spontaneous social events are uncommon. Romanians are customarily generous and polite, and young people and men are expected offer their seats to elders and women on buses or in cafés. Romanians are wary but polite

with strangers, an attribute that carries over from communist rule.

Eating/Meals

In Romania, the social aspects of dining tend to be fixed and formal and vary between urban and rural areas. Romanians tend to have formal table manners and keep their hands above the table throughout the meal. Romanians eat in the continental style: the fork in the left hand and the knife in their right. Additionally, the head of a household or host may say the traditional phrase "Pofta buna" ("Good appetite") to signal the beginning of a meal.

Romanians living in urban areas generally eat three meals, including breakfast, lunch, and dinner. Breakfast is typically a modest meal of bread, butter, or coffee and tea. Lunch, which is eaten in the early afternoon, is traditionally the largest meal of the day. Popular lunch foods include mititei (grilled sausage), borsch (cabbage soup), sarmale (cabbage rolls), and ciorba (lamb soup). Dinner is generally a small meal of salad, soup, and bread. In Romanian cities, lunch and dinner often include local wines or tuica (plum brandy). Urban Romanians may finish lunch and dinner with a small dessert such as placinte (fruit pie) and baklava (sweet pastry of nuts and honey).

Romanians living in rural areas will plan their meals around their farm work. Romanians working on farms will usually have a heartier breakfast than those living in the city. Farm workers usually eat a small midday snack and a large dinner once the day's labors are over.

Celebratory meals include wedding feasts and the annual sheep feast called Simbra Oilor. Wedding feasts involve generous amounts of wine and tuica. The annual sheep feast celebrates the seasonal movement of sheep herds to high pastures. The annual sheep feast is a community-wide meal of wine, tuica, meat, and cheese.

Visiting

When visiting someone's home in Romania, guests generally keep proper etiquette in mind. First and foremost, guests may be expected to take off their shoes once entering the house. It is also customary to bring flowers, sweets, or liquor for their hosts. Even numbers of flowers are preferred. Hosts open their gifts during the social visit and share the contents of the gift when appropriate. Guests are also expected to greet children in a household with the same enthusiasm and courtesy as they greet their adult hosts.

Romanians are very welcoming and friendly to guests. Hosts traditionally offer their visitors a glass of palinca (Romanian brandy) and a snack or meal, and guests are expected to accept these offers of food and drink. Guests are also expected to show their appreciation to the host by eating, drinking, and engaging all the family and friends who are present.

Popular occasions for visiting friends and family include New Year's Day, Labor Day, Independence Day, and the National Day of Romania. Romanians also visit friends and family during annual spring and summer festivals. For example, friends and family living in the city of Brașov celebrate the Pageant of the Juni with parades and feast meals with friends and family.

LIFESTYLE

Family

Romanian families provide stability for individuals and society as a whole, and offer social, emotional, and financial support. Due to housing shortages in Romania, many generations of a family may live together in one home. The absence of modern household amenities and conveniences, such as refrigerators, freezers, and washing machines, in many Romanian households make household chores labor intensive and time consuming. Thus, the presence of a larger extended family eases the individual work burden. Romanian families tend to be hierarchical and patriarchal. Fathers are traditionally in charge and inheritance law favors men. While women may legally inherit property and assets, the oldest son in a family usually inherits the family's estate or holdings.

Historically, matchmakers arranged marriages and the bride's family provided a dowry of textiles. In addition, rural marriages were social and political unions that joined farms and villages. In contemporary Romania, people are free to choose a husband or wife based on love or shared interests. Under Soviet rule, the government required civil ceremonies and heavily discouraged church weddings. Divorce is legal in Romania.

Housing

Romania is suffering from a housing shortage in the early 21st century. Reasons for the housing shortage include earthquake damage, war damage, delayed maintenance, urban growth, and Soviet housing policies. Under Soviet rule, there was a decline in new construction and waiting lists for apartments and houses often spanned years. Bribes for housing placements were common during the Soviet-era.

In contemporary Romania, home ownership tends to be too expensive for most Romanians. Multi-generational families tend to live together due to the shortage and expense of housing, and overcrowding and unsanitary living conditions are common. In addition, many dwellings in Romania lack adequate sewer and water utilities. Traditional rural housing is characterized by its wooden shingles and red tiled roofs. Urban housing options include high-rise apartments and detached houses. Romanians increasingly choose to live in urban centers for the access to jobs, services, and transportation.

Food

Romania's national cuisine is simple and flavorful and influenced by neighboring cultures, particularly the Balkan cuisine and those of Germany, Russia, Poland, and Hungary. The staple foods and ingredients that make up Romania's cuisine include pork, beef, lamb, fish, vegetables, and dairy foods. Romanians raise pigs for wintertime and celebratory meals. Traditionally, Romanians cook their food in clay vessels and cast-iron kettles. Traditional Romanians dishes include drob de miel, sarmale, and cozonac.

Drob de miel is a form of haggis eaten at Easter time. Drob de miel includes liver from a lamb, heart from a lamb, lungs from a lamb, green onions, garlic, green parsley, green dill, raw egg, boiled eggs, sour cream, oil, salt and pepper. The organs are boiled and mixed with fresh ingredients. Drob de miel can be eaten warm or cold. Sarmale are cabbage rolls that are prepared with cabbage leaves, sauerkraut, ground pork, onions, rice, lard, tomato sauce, sour cream, salt, and pepper. The ingredients are baked and the dish is served hot. Cozonac is a holiday sweet bread that is usually baked by the older women in a family. Romanians believe that the mood and spirit of the baker will influence the taste and texture of the cozonac. Ingredients include flour, eggs, sugar, butter, oil, milk, yeast, salt, rum, vanilla, and lemon peel. Cozonac is traditionally baked in large batches in an outside clay oven.

Romanians living in rural areas often make their own cheese and wine. Homemade Romanian cheeses are made from the milk of sheep, cows, buffalo, and goat. Romania is the 10th largest producer of wine in the world.

Life's Milestones

In Romania, marriage is the most important life milestone and marks a couple's transition into adulthood. The majority of Romanians adhere to the Romanian Orthodox faith (a branch of Eastern Christianity dating to 1054) and marriage is customarily conducted as apart of a ritualized church ceremony. Under communist rule, government officials discouraged church weddings as a means of undermining the church's influence and control. The communist government required that people marry in a civil ceremony. In the early 1990s, as communist influence ended in Romania, church weddings became hugely popular again.

Romanians no longer depend on matchmakers or elders in the family to find a spouse. Instead, they choose a spouse based on love and compatibility. In the traditional Romanian wedding ceremony, most common in rural Romania, brides wear their hair braided with flowers, feathers, and jewels. Grooms wear white leather vests and hats adorned with flowers, leaves, and feathers. The groom may shave his beard on the wedding day as a way of symbolizing the change that is taking place in his life. As part of the traditional ceremony, the marrying couple apologizes to their families for leaving the family home and setting off on their own.

CULTURAL HISTORY

Art

Romanian folk art is collected and exhibited throughout Romania and the world. Many Romanian folk artists are originally from Maramureş in northwest Romania. Traditional Romanian art forms include pottery, woodcarving and sculpture, painted eggs, textiles, masks, and glasswork.

Romanian pottery is traditionally made by hand or on a kick wheel. Popular designs include geometric lines, floral patterns, and animal figures. Pottery centers or towns throughout Romania are associated with distinct styles and techniques. Prominent Romanian pottery towns include Horezu, Rădăuţi, Corund, and Marginea. Romanian folk artists carve intricate designs onto wooden doorways, window frames, gates, hope chests, and musical instruments, as well as functional items such as walking sticks and ladles. Common designs include the tree of life, ropes, angels, and floral and animal motifs. A family's social status is reflected in the level of intricacy involved in the carvings that adorn the family's belongings.

Traditionally, Romanian artisans and local women paint hollowed-out or carved wooden eggs (which symbolized renewal) as part of the Easter celebrations. Traditional designs include geometric etchings on a red or blue background. Romanian textiles include rugs and costumes, and Romanian rugs, much like pottery, reflect the regions in which they are made. Rugs are traditionally hand woven and dyed using the plant dyes available by region. Common rug designs include the tree of life, flowers, birds, and geometric patterns. Romanian folk costumes, with embroidery and glass beading, are also considered works of folk art. Romanian masks, made of animal hide and fabric, are worn during festivals and collected by folk museums. The Romanian glass-blowing tradition continues to thrive in the towns of Avrig, Turda, and Buzău.

Romania also celebrates many internationally known fine artists, including Nicolae Grigorescu (1838–1907), Theodor Aman (1831–1891), and Constantin Brâncuşi (1876–1957). Grigorescu was a prominent landscape artist, while Aman was a celebrated portrait artist. Brâncuşi was a modern artist known for his wood and metal sculptures.

Architecture

The oldest style of architecture in Romania is evident in the wooden churches that are still being constructed in areas such as the Maramureş region and northern Transylvania. Built in the 17th and 18th centuries, these tall churches feature thick log construction, tall spires, shingled roofs, and detailed carvings on windows and doorframes. Wooden structures were built because the Hungarians had banned the construction of stone churches in Romania.

Gothic churches and castles, such as the Biserica Neagră and Bran Castle (commonly referred to as Dracula's Castle) in and near Brasov, reflected the style of the 14th century. In the 14th and 15th centuries, fortified cities were developed in places such as Sibiu and Sighişoara in Transylvania, German cities that became important European centers for trade. In the 15th and 16th centuries, monasteries were constructed in Moldavia under the direction of Stephen the Great (1457–1504) and Prince Petru Rares (1487–1546). The structures are said to reflect a blending of Gothic and Byzantine architecture and some, particularly Putna and Voronet, were adorned with interior and exterior paintings.

In the 17th and 18th centuries, the Brancovenesc style emerged in Wallachia under the reign of Constantin Brancoveanu. The Brancovenesc style is said to be a mix of Byzantine and Baroque styles and came to be considered distinctly Romanian, with stone carvings and ornate decoration. In the 19th and 20th centuries, what is now called a neo-classical style arose, blending the country's architectural past with Western concepts, evidenced in buildings like the Romanian Athenaeum in Bucharest and the Baroque Palace in Oradea.

In 1892, The Romanian Society of Architects, made up primarily of architects trained at the Ecole des Beaux-Arts in Paris, established the National School of Architecture. One of the founding fathers and a prominent architect of the time was Ion Mincu (1852–1912). Mincu, while heavily influenced by the beaux arts movement, sought a unique, neo-Romanian style for his country.

Most rural homes were simple structures with thatched or shingled roofs. Some homes featured an intricately carved wooden gate at the front of the property. These wooden gates are now considered a treasure, as many were removed or destroyed during the country's communist period.

Drama

Romanian theater saw its start in the homes of the wealthy and social elite. Between 1817 and 1819, three theaters were established in Bucharest: the Oravita Theatre, the Arad Theatre, and the Red Fountain, featuring works in the Romanian language. The Literary Society, formed in 1827, promoted the establishment of the School of Dramatic Art, which began to offer performances of Western plays in translation.

In the middle of the 19th century, a new literary movement sought to establish a vibrant Romanian cultural revival. Among the playwrights of the time were Vasile Alecsandri (1821–1890) and Bogdan Petriceicu Hasdeu (1838–1907). Later playwrights developed a unique Romanian body of work after the country declared independence in 1877. I.L. Caragiale (1852–1912) is considered one of Romania's preeminent literary figures; his plays, many comedies, often criticized Romanian society. In the late 19th and early 20th century, theater in Romania thrived, with a great number of playwrights who had not only local recognition, but had ties with others in the European arts community.

The theater community in Romania suffered during the first and second world wars, but in the period between those conflicts, saw a resurgence in the works of authors such as Lucian Blaga (1895–1961) and Gib I. Mihăescu (1894–1935), who often dealt with issues of identity and the human condition. After the wars and with the onset of the communist regime, theater in Romania reflected the state's focus on social realism.

After the fall of the communists, theater in Romania once again began to thrive. The *New York Times*, in an article about several exchanges between Romanian- and US-based theater companies, noted that a shift is visible in the Romanian theater community. Where once dramatic productions were director led and social criticism was hidden in metaphor, Romanian playwrights are now choosing a more forthright and realistic style. What results is a conflict between generations that is being played out on Romanian theatrical stages. These cultural exchanges, though, have given both American and Romanian dramatists insight into their current practices and viewpoints.

Music

Folk music is Romania's oldest musical tradition. It is often performed by lăutari (Roma musicians) and tarafs (Roma bands). Communist rule suppressed Roma, or gypsy performers throughout the 20th century. The end of communist rule in 1989 allowed Roma musicians, and folk musicians in general, to perform in more venues throughout Romania. Today, lăutari and tarafs play in cafés, festivals, and orchestra halls. Popular instruments used in Romanian folk music include the nai (panpipes), the tembal (dulcimer), the bucium (woodwind instrument), the gorduna (double bass), and violin.

Regional folk musical traditions persist to this day, in part, as a result of the communist government's policy of regional isolationism. Areas of Romania known for distinct forms of Romanian folk music include Banat, Bukovina, Crişana, Dobruja, Maramureş, and Oaş, and the historical regions of Moldavia, Transylvania, and Greater Wallachia. Different regions are associated with different instruments, rhythms, and types of ensembles. The doina, with many regional variations, is Romania's most popular type of lyrical folk song. Other types of Romanian folk music include the bocet (a lament), cantec batranesc (ballad) and cand ciobanu si-a pierdut oile (sorrowful songs).

Romanian folk music has influenced Romanian dance music as well as Romanian classical music. For example, Dinu Lipatti (1917–1950), a classical pianist and composer, and Georges Enesco (1881–1955), a classical violinist and composer, created folk music inspired compositions.

Dance

Romania's many rural villages remained isolated from one another and larger urban areas until late in the 20th century. Because of this government-orchestrated isolation, peasant farm culture flourished and Romania's regional folk dance traditions remain strong and regionally distinct. Romania's folk dance traditions involve village dances and ensemble dances. Amateur and professional dance troops or ensembles are common throughout Romania. Romanian folk dance arrangements include chain dances, men's dances, and couple's dances.

The hora is Romania's national dance. The hora varies by geographic region and festive occasion. Romanian folk dances tend to be associated with particular geographic regions of Romania or particular festivities such as weddings. Popular folk dances include the arcanul, a traditional dance from Romania's Moldavian area; asa beau oamnii buni, a simple dance and hymn from Transylvania; and baitaneasca, a country-dance from Romania's Moldavia region. Batuta is a group of different dance steps and rhythms from southern Moldavia and Dobrogea. Ca la nunta la artari is a Romanian wedding dance and tune from Muntenia, and calusari is a traditional dance from Oltennia. Perinita is a popular wedding dance involving handkerchiefs and dancers arranged in a circle. Alunelu uses either single or double crossing steps and stamping, and is danced throughout southern Romania.

Romania's dance and drama communities changed following the end of communist rule in 1989. Over the last two decades in Romania, the growth in political and artistic freedom has allowed for new theater, playwriting, and cinema traditions to slowly emerge.

Literature

Romanian literature has its roots in early forms of ballads and folktales. As early as the 16th century, Romanians were spreading popular folktales from village to village. Early folktales were often accompanied by music. Written works began to appear during the period from the 16th to 18th century.

Romania's national literary tradition began during the early 19th century. Romanian writers work in multiple genres, including poetry, plays, fiction, essay, literary criticism, and memoir. Historically, Romanian writers, particularly those writing during the period of communist rule, often used their writing as vehicles for political criticism and protest. The decades of communist rule (1948–1989) were a time of isolation and frustration for Romanian writers. The communist government censored writing and controlled publishing opportunities.

Well-known Romanian writers include Ion Creangă (1839–1889), Mihai Eminescu (1850–1889), and Ion Luca Caragiale (1852–1912). Creangă used traditional storytelling strategies to enliven his fiction and autobiography; Eminescu incorporated national history and current politics into his poetry; Caragiale incorporated politics into his comic plays. Romanian writers who have reached high-levels of international popularity include Tristan Tzara (1896–1963) and Eugène Ionesco (1912–1994). Works by both Tzara and Ionesco have been translated into many different foreign languages.

CULTURE

Arts & Entertainment

In Romania, the role of the arts reflects the country's 21st century culture, traditions, collective experience, and social consciousness. During the communist years (1948–1989), Romania's traditional arts and crafts (such as painted eggs, rugs, pottery, wood sculpture, textiles, masks, and glass) went underground as a means to keep Romanian culture alive in times of oppression. Under communism, the arts were strictly controlled and artists were required to join artist unions and collectives. Artistic censorship was common and the communist government directed and required that artists produce work in the social realist genre. In particular, the communist government wanted Romanian artists to create pieces that celebrated and glorified industrial workers and communist leaders.

Since the end of brutal communist rule in 1989, the arts have grown and thrived in Romania. While there is no longer much direct government support available for the arts, there is a new sense of artistic freedom. Government censorship has, for the most part, ended. Artists are newly free to express their artistic vision and sensibility without censorship and control. The arts are now used as vehicles for rebuilding Romanian national identity in the post-communist years. Traditional Romanian art forms are being taught and exhibited around the world. For example, the Romanian Folk Art Museum in Philadelphia and the Romanian Cultural Institute in New York offers traveling exhibits and educational programs of Romanian arts and culture in the United States and Romania.

In addition to the international growth of Romanian folk art, Romanian musicians, actors and writers are working to promote their individual talents and build Romania's arts identity. Romanian musicians, including Romanian opera singers, jazz musicians, composers, and folk singers, are involved in international collaborations and performances that blend Romanian music with other musical forms and styles. Romanian actors highlight their talents in Romania's annual National Theater Festival. The Medieval Arts Festival in Sighisoara, Romania, is an annual event highlighting medieval works of art, music, and drama. The American-Romanian Theatre Exchange (ARTE), began in 2006, works to promote the role of theater in international diplomacy. The Romanian Writers' Guild organizes literary festivals, translation fellowships and literary prizes. For instance, Romania's Ovidius Grand Prize is awarded annually in recognition of the value of literary works that affirm freedom of expression and inter-ethnic tolerance.

Spectator sports, especially soccer, are popular forms of entertainment in *Romania*. Romanians play soccer, tennis, table tennis, chess, card games, and a native sport called oinya, which is similar to baseball and cricket. They also take advantage of outdoor recreation areas and enjoy hiking, running, skiing, sailing, swimming, and kayaking.

Cultural Sites & Landmarks

Romania is considered one of the more beautiful countries in southeastern Europe and has a wealth of cultural sites and landmarks, ranging from medieval castles and towns and painted monasteries, to the rugged nature of the Carpathian Mountains and the haunting legacy of Transylvania, the historic province that inspired the Dracula legend. In fact, the United Nations Educational, Scientific, and Cultural Organization (UNESCO) recognizes seven sites as World Heritage Sites in Romania for their cultural and natural importance. They are the churches of Moldavia; the Dacian fortresses of the Orastie Mountains; the Danube Delta; the historic center of Sighişoara; the monastery of Horezu; a collective series of villages with fortified churches in Transylvania; and the wooden churches of Maramureş.

The churches of northern Moldavia include seven churches built as early as the 15th century. The exterior of the churches are decorated with Byzantine-era frescoes. These frescoes, which depict elaborate religious stories, are considered to be masterpieces. The Dacian fortresses of the Orastie Mountains were built by the Dacian kingdom as early as the first century BCE and include six fortress buildings. The Dacian fortresses, which were innovative for their time, combine military and religious techniques, styles, and imagery. The Romans conquered the Dacian Kingdom fortresses in the

second century CE. UNESCO recognizes the fortresses as being characteristic of the defensive architecture common to the Late Iron Age in Europe.

The Danube Delta is the largest and best-preserved delta in Europe. (A delta is a triangular area of low watery land located at the mouth of a river.) The delta, with multiple lakes and marshes, is a protected area of 300 species of bird and 45 species of freshwater fish. The historic center of Sighişoara is a preserved medieval town nearly 850 years old. Sighişoara was a small-fortified town established by the Saxons of Transylvania (a group of German merchants and craftspeople). Sighişoara is an example of the Transylvanian Saxons' culture. Sighişoara keeps the architectural techniques and sensibilities alive, even while the culture and traditions of the Transylvanian Saxons, as a whole, is waning due to emigration and social change.

The monastery of Horezu, established by Prince Constantine Brancovan (1654–1714) in 1690, was built in the Brancovan style, characterized by architectural balance, religious elements, sculptural detail, portraits, and decorative elements. The monastery of Horezu, located in Walachia, was a famous school of mural and icon painting during the 18th century. The seven villages with fortified churches in Transylvania, built from the 13th to the 16th centuries, are located in Southern Transylvania. These seven villages, founded by Transylvanian Saxons, reflect the cultural life of Transylvania. These seven villages are unified by their land-use patterns, settlement patterns, and family farmstead organization.

Lastly, the wooden churches of Maramureş in Northern Romania include eight churches built to incorporate different architectural styles and solutions. The churches, built into mountain landscape, are tall narrow buildings with clock towers ad shingled roofs. The wooden churches of Maramureş preserve a period in Romanian history when craftspeople and artists worked to combine Orthodox religious traditions and the Gothic style.

Libraries & Museums

Romania has a number of museums, among which is the National Museum of Art of Romania, containing an impressive medieval art collection, much of which was recovered from monasteries that were destroyed during Ceausescu's communist regime. It also boasts the work of Romanian sculpturist Constantin Brancusi (1876–1957) and painters Nicolae Grigorescu (1838–1907) and Theodor Pallady (1871–1956). Another museum of note is the National Village Museum, an open-air museum that features a number of homes and villages procured from villages throughout Romania. The museum is highly respected and has over 270 structures. Other museums within Bucharest include the Natural History Museum and the National Geologic Museum, among many other museums and cultural sites.

Romania's National Library, established in 1859, owes its earliest volumes to the library at St. Sava College. The St Sava collection included almost 1,000 French publications. The national library now houses a collection in excess of 8 million items.

Holidays

A public holiday unique to Romania is Union Day, celebrated on December 1. Union Day commemorates the formation of Romania from the 1918 union of Transylvania, Bucovina, Basarabia, and Cadrilater. The holiday was celebrated on August 23 prior to the fall of communism.

Other official holidays include Flag Day (June 26), National Anthem Day (July 29), and Constitution Day (December 8).

Youth Culture

The attitudes and culture of Romanian youth in the post-communist era are often described as being worlds apart from previous generations. While the traditional family and familial ties remain an important part of Romanian society, Romanian youth in the early 21st century are becoming more outspoken and independent. They are generally responsible for themselves, their studies, their household chores, and their

siblings. While much of this cultural change can be traced politically—particularly the fall of the Iron Curtain and Romania's integration into the European community—the advent of the Internet has also ushered in Western influences and a heightened awareness of globalization.

Due to the economic uncertainty that occurred during Romania's transition to independence and a free market economy, many Romanian youth struggle with planning their futures and unemployment rates for young adults are high. Options for Romanian youth include higher education, working in a foreign country, or competing for a local job. Many young people choose to continue their studies at vocational schools, technical institutes, or teacher-training programs. Young Romanians are also generally politically minded and aware of Romania's complex history and current events. Historically, it was the youth of Romania that helped spur the 1989 Romania Revolution which marked the end of the authoritarianism of President Nicolae Ceausescu (1918–1989) and the beginning of a new culture of autonomy.

Romanian youth participate in a variety of sports, with football (soccer) the most popular. Other popular sports based on registered participants include tennis, rugby, wrestling, and handball. Youth fashion in Romania tends to reflect individual means and style. The Romanian cinema is popular, and socialization generally occurs among family, in school, or within public groups or sports for children. Young adults frequent nightclubs, bars, Internet cafés, and similar venues. Romanian youth are also becoming more active in terms of travel and sports tourism.

SOCIETY

Transportation

Romania is located at an important geographical point between Europe and Asia. This location results in significant movement of people and goods through Romanian ports and cities.

Domestically, Romanians travel by car, bus, state and privately owned taxis, and train, as well as ferry service and subway service where applicable, and bicycling in both inner cities and rural areas. Trains and highways connect all the major cities in Romania. The Bucharest metro (subway system), first planned in the 1930s but not built until the 1980s, offers a modern and convenient transportations system for Romanians and tourists alike. In fact, the Bucharest public transport network is considered one of the largest public transportation networks in Europe.

Romanians drive on the right side of the road and steering wheels are placed on the left-hand side. Seatbelts are required by law.

Transportation Infrastructure

As of 2013, Romania had forty-five airports, two heliports, and an estimated 10,77kilometers of railway. As of 2013, there were 84,185kilometers of roadway. The majority of airports and secondary roadways are unpaved. Romanian ports and sea terminals include Brăila, Constanţa, Galaţi, Mancanului, and Tulcea.

Media & Communications

Television is the most popular medium in Romania and the state television service offers six channels nationally and cable stations are available. As of 2006, Romania had 698 radio stations and 623 television broadcast stations. Popular daily newspapers include *Evenimentul Zilei* (Events of the Day), *Adevarul de Cluj* (Truth of Cluj), *Romania Libera* (Free Romania), *Adevarul* (Truth), and *Libertatea* (Liberty).

While Romania's media changed drastically after the fall of communism, freedom of the press remains a serious human rights issue for Romania. Under Soviet rule, the Romanian government used the media to spread government propaganda and disinformation. While the Romanian constitution forbids censorship and guarantees freedom of expression, the specifics of the law forbid journalists from defaming the country. The Romanian government is also known to fine, intimidate, physically brutalize, and imprison journalists. (However, as of 2007, journalists can no longer be incarcerated

for defamation.) International attention on and scrutiny of the Romanian media is slowly improving the situation for journalists in Romania.

Romania's communication systems also began to change radically after Soviet control ended in 1989. Romanians are increasingly use technology to stay connected to friends and family domestically and abroad, and the Internet is growing in scope and popularity. In 2009, there were an estimated 7.787 million Internet users and 2.667 million Internet hosts as of 2012. Romania's telephone system is also improving its domestic and international service. In 2012, Romania had 4.68 million telephone lines and 22.7 mobile phones in use.

SOCIAL DEVELOPMENT

Standard of Living

In 2013, Romania was ranked 54 out of 182 countries on the United Nations Human Development Index, a comparative index that measures a country's quality of life.

Water Consumption

According to the World Health Organization (WHO), seven million people in Romania get their water from wells, many of which are compromised because of pollution that includes nitrates, bacteria, and pesticides. The government has focused its water management efforts on urban populations, where 80 percent of the population is connected to the water supply. Rural communities, which can reach as low as 30 percent connection, are trying alternate methods such as filters to clean their water for consumption.

In its 2010 report on World Water Day, the Romania government noted that despite a 10 percent decrease between 2005 and 2008, the country's percentage of untreated or insufficiently treated wastewater was 70 percent. Almost 43 percent of the population is connected to a sewage treatment facility, but none of the major sewage plants met European standards.

Education

The Romanian educational system consists of primary school (for children between the ages of seven and 10), lower secondary school (ages 11 to 14), and upper secondary school (ages 15 to 18). Primary school and lower secondary school attendance is compulsory, but many children forgo school to work on their families' farms. Public education is free up to the university level. Although severely under-funded, public schools teach well-rounded curriculums. On average, students in Romania spend fourteen years in school.

Today, approximately one-third of Romanian students attend private schools (including universities). There are dozens of universities in the country, both public and private, including the University of Bucharest, the Alexandru Ioan Cuza University of Iaşi, and the Babeş-Bolyai University in Cluj. According to a report from the World Bank, "One of Romania's key priorities continues to be upgrading the skills of its population to meet Europe 2020 targets and bring the level of achievement of Romanian children in key subjects to current levels found in most European countries. A National Education Law in force since early 2011 promotes changes in virtually all areas of education."

As of 2015, the average literacy rate in Romania was 98.8 percent, 99.1 percent for men, and 98.5 percent for women.

Women's Rights

In Romania's largely patriarchal society, men and women are treated quite differently. This is a stigma of inferiority attached to women and they are discouraged from entering into the workforce and the political arena. While the role of women is changing in the post-communist era, they still face numerous significant disadvantages and challenges. Additionally, while Romanian law affords women equal rights in family and property law and under the legal system, the government does not adequately enforce or protect these rights.

Romanian women also experience significant amounts of domestic violence and rape, despite the fact that both are against the law. Seventy-five percent of victims are female and 25 percent are male, according to 2012 data. The Romanian government has no programs in place to address the problem of domestic violence and does not recognize the special problem of spousal abuse. Few domestic violence cases are prosecuted or go to trial, and Romanian law does not specify sentencing rules for domestic violence cases. Prostitution, which is illegal in Romania, is also a growing social problem. Romania's large cities, such as Bucharest, are known as destinations for sex tourism. Further exacerbating the issue is the fact that while prostitutes are punished with fines and imprisonment, sex customers risk no legal penalty. Romania is also considered an origin, transit, and destination country for human trafficking, particularly for the purposes of sexual and labor exploitation.

Romanian men and families often discourage women from seeking employment outside the family home. Romanian women have few role models of successfully employed women, and job training and opportunities for women are few. Romanian women tend to pursue low paying professions and hold few private sector management positions. Women also earn significantly less than their male counterparts do. Sexual harassment, while illegal, is prevalent and often unreported.

The Romanian Ministry of Labor, Social Solidarity, and Family is the government agency responsible for advancing women's rights and opportunities. While the agency is charged with organizing programs for women, proposing new laws that advance women's rights, monitoring new laws for sexual bias, and training women for skilled professions, the agency is slow to act and accomplish its stated goals. However, the agency has managed to secure female workers in Romania the right to return to their jobs after maternity leave. The Asociatia Femeilor Din Romania (Women's Association of Romania, or AFR) is the main women's rights organization in Romania and the leader in the Romanian women's rights movement. The AFR, with twenty offices throughout Romania, is a NGO dedicated to furthering the place of women in Romanian society. The AFR's areas of special interest include Romanian women's reproductive health, education, economic empowerment, violence against women and women's rights.

Health Care

The Romanian health care system is unable to meet the needs of the population. There are only 49,000 doctors in Romania, and most of them are underpaid and ill-equipped to deal with increasing numbers of tuberculosis, hepatitis A, and AIDS patients. Many doctors require bribes in exchange for medical services.

Unsanitary conditions and contaminated drinking water have led to a general state of poor health in Romania. Combined with the increase in prices of medical goods and services since the revolution in 1989, the decline in public health has severely burdened Romania's public welfare system. The state is unable to provide sufficient health insurance coverage for everyone.

Access to health care in Romania is skewed towards the wealthy. Roughly, half of the poor do not seek care as needed, and much of the public funding allocated to health care is wasted on inefficient and unnecessary services or treatments. The current health system is biased toward inpatient hospital care. Recent government health reforms seek to promote cost-effective outpatient and primary care services and make other necessary changes.

In 2014, Romanians have an average life expectancy of seventy-four years, and an infant mortality rate of 10 deaths per 1,000 live births.

GOVERNMENT

Structure

Romania is a republic with a central government that consists of an executive branch, a legislative branch, and a judicial branch, all of which operate independently. The country's current constitution was written in 1991.

The president is the chief of state, supreme commander of the armed forces, and the chairperson of the Supreme Defense Council. The executive branch also includes the prime minister, who is the head of government, and the cabinet, a council of ministers. The president is elected to a five-year term by popular vote (there is universal suffrage for citizens over 18 years of age) and cannot serve more than two terms. The president selects the prime minister, and the prime minister selects the cabinet.

The legislature is a bicameral parliament made up of the Chamber of Deputies and the Senate, members of which are elected by popular vote to four-year terms.

Political Parties

Romania is a parliamentary democracy with a large number of political parties, not all holding seats in government. Parliamentary democracies often have a large number of political parties, which have a tendency to shift in terms of political platform and their alliance with other parties sharing common interests. Often, parliamentary systems are ruled by coalitions of two or more parties that unite to form a majority coalition. These coalitions differ in nature, with some coalitions having a lasting strength and others failing to govern at all. Additionally, it is not unusual for parties to dissolve because of personality conflicts within the organization.

In 2012, Romanian politics was dominated by the Social Liberal Union (USL), which won 273 seats. The Right Romania Alliance (ARD) won 56 seats; the People's Party (PP-DD) won 47, followed by the Democratic Union of Hungarians in Romania (UDMR) and ethnic minorities, which both won 18 seats.

Local Government

Romania's local administration is divided into 41 counties and the city of Bucharest. The central government selects local county prefects; prefects act on the directions of central government administrations. Voters elect county and local councils, as well as council presidents and mayors. Local governments are responsible for developing budgets (with revenues coming from central government and local taxation).

Judicial System

Since Romania's entry into the European Union (and prior to that event) judicial reform has been a high priority concern. In 2014, Transparency International ranked Romania's corruption at 69 out of 175; Scores range from zero (highly corrupt) to 100 (very clean). Transparency International Romania formed a working group in 2009 with other Transparency International in the region to identify regional challenges in fighting high-level corruption, improve regional law-enforcement capacities, and align national and international standards.

The High Court of Cassation and Justice is Romania's highest court, on which judges, selected by the president, serve six-year terms, and cannot be removed from the bench before the end of their terms. Local and county courts handle civil and criminal matters, and a court of appeals handles the appeal process.

Taxation

The Romanian government levies personal income, corporate, and capital gains taxes. Additionally, Romanians pay into the social security system that includes social security, heath care, and unemployment. There is also a value-added tax (VAT) and building and land taxes.

Armed Forces

The Romanian Armed Forces are made up of an army, a navy, special operations and an air force. A voluntary force, Romanian troops have served previously in Iraq and with NATO (North Atlantic Treaty Organization) forces in Afghanistan.

Foreign Policy

Romania was under strict communist control from 1948 through 1989 and isolated from much of the world. Once this era ended, Romania's foreign policy focused on European integration, and forging Western alliances. The country joined several notable international organizations and alliances, including the NATO in 2004 and the European Union (EU) in 2007. Romania is also a member of the Organization for Security and Cooperation in Europe (OSCE), the Southeast Europe Cooperation Initiative (SECI), the Black Sea Economic Cooperation (BSEC), and the World Bank, among others. Romania continues to integrate itself into Western markets and alliances, and foreign countries and organizations are working with Romania to address its communist legacy of economic underdevelopment, bureaucratic red tape, and government corruption.

Romania's communist years, with its isolationist approach, left the nation without an adequate industrial base for production and export. Foreign aid is helping Romania cope with its currency depreciation and rising energy costs. Romania's main trading partners include Italy, Germany, France, Turkey, Hungary, the United Kingdom (UK), Russia, and Austria. Romania is also party to international environmental agreements concerning air pollution, biodiversity, climate change, desertification, endangered species, environmental modification, and hazardous wastes.

Romania has had international disputes over ownership of the Zmiyinyy Island with Ukraine. The International Court of Justice (ICJ) decided that Zmiyinyy was an island and drew the maritime borders between the two countries. At stake within the conflict over Zmiyinyy Island were the oil and gas deposits that lay offshore and which country owned the rights to those deposits. Additionally, Romania has joined the European Union in protesting Ukraine's plans to dredge the Bystroye Channel, a channel that leads into the Danube Delta (which is largely within Romanian borders) to the Black Sea. As the Danube Delta is a UNESCO World Heritage Site and a fragile ecosystem, Romania is joined by several interested parties who contend that the Ukrainian plan is detrimental to the delta. This matter rests with the ICJ for resolution despite Ukraine's plans to proceed. the ICJ ruled largely in favor of Romania in its dispute submitted in 2004 over Ukrainian-administered Zmiyinyy/Serpilor (Snake) Island and Black Sea maritime boundary delimitation; Romania opposes Ukraine's reopening of a navigation canal from the Danube border through Ukraine to the Black Sea

Human Rights Profile

International human rights law insists that states respect civil and political rights, and promote an individual's economic, social, and cultural rights. The United Nations Universal Declaration on Human Rights (UDHR) is recognized as the standard for international human rights. Its authors sought the counsel of the world's great thinkers, philosophers, and religious leaders, and were careful to create a document that reflects the core values shared by every world culture. (To read this document or view the articles relating to cultural human rights visit http://www.un.org/en/documents/udhr/.)

Article 2 of the UDHR, which states that everyone is entitled to legal rights and freedoms without distinction of race, color, sex, language, religion, political or other opinion, national or social origin, property, birth or other status, is supported by the Romanian constitution but not always in the actions of the government. The Romanian government does not generally protect the rights of women, children, and minorities. As a result, women, children and minorities, particularly ethnic Hungarians called Roma, experience comparatively high levels of discrimination and violence. The Roma, for example, experience high levels of police harassment and arrest.

Article 16 of the UDHR, which states that men and women of any race, nationality, or religion have the right to marry and establish a family, is currently supported by the Romanian constitution. The body of Romanian law that defines the entire Romanian civil law system is codified under the title of Codul Civil Român (The Romanian Civil Code), initially published in July 2009, but enacted on October 1, 2011. The new Code clarifies key principles of Romanian law and crystallizes certain legal concepts that have been long recognized in legal literature and practice.

Article 18 of the UDHR, which supports the right to freedom of thought, conscience and religion, so long as the practice of religion does not violate public morality, decency, or the public order, is protected by the Romanian constitution. While the Romanian government generally respects religious freedoms, recent laws infringe on the rights of those committed to smaller minority or fringe religions. For example, the government requires religious groups to register officially for recognition and financial support, but does not adequately publicize the registration procedure. In addition, the Romanian government enacted a law in 2007 requiring that religious groups have a membership that equals 0.1 percent of the total population before they are recognized by the government. As a result, many religious organizations are unable to receive official government status due to small membership. Religious groups must also receive official recognition before they are allowed to establish churches or schools, hire and pay clergy, or receive tax exemptions.

Article 19 of the UDHR, which guarantees the right to freedom of opinion and expression, is protected by Romanian law. The Romanian government is working with the Romanian media to decriminalize libel, insult, and defamation of Romania. Despite legal protections, the Romanian media and international non-governmental organizations (NGOs) charge the Romanian government with intimidation, censorship, and violence against the press.

Articles 27–29 of the UDHR in part invoke the need for national and international social, moral, economic, and cultural support for the rights and freedoms set forth in the declaration. This is supported by Romanian law, but not Romanian officials nor Romanian society. Romanian society, despite being free of communist control for approximately two decades, continues to experience social hierarchy, classicism, and inequality.

Migration

In the early 21st century, those leaving Romania largely did so for economic and employment reasons, seeking work in other European nations such as Italy, Spain, Portugal and the United Kingdom. Entering the EU in 2007 has opened other countries to Romanians looking for employment. Immigrants to Romania tend to come from Turkey and China, largely seeking work. An increase in foreign workers is anticipated due to the need for labor and the country's aging population.

ECONOMY

Overview of the Economy

After experiencing a recession after the transition from a communist economy, Romania has stabilized its economy in recent years. The country's extensive natural resources, fertile farmland, and skilled workforce all provide potential for economic growth. Romania joined the European Union in 2007.

In 2014, Romania's gross domestic product (GDP) was estimated at $388 billion (USD), with a per capita GDP of $19,400 (USD). The unemployment rate was 6.4 percent of a workforce of more than 9.172 million. In 2011 just over 22 percent of the population was living below the poverty line.

Industry

Industry is partially privatized and the bulk of manufacturing has, since 1989, shifted from iron, steel, and heavy machinery manufacturing to textile, footwear, auto assembly, and light machinery manufacturing. Oil production, mining, and timber processing are all still major industries, though timber processing is on the decline.

Romania imports fuel, machinery, chemicals, minerals, textile products, metals, and agricultural products, and exports metal products, footwear, light machinery, minerals, fuels, chemicals, and agricultural products.

Labor

Of Romania's labor force, which numbers 9.172 million people, 43.9 percent work in the service sector, more than 27 percent in agriculture, and 28 percent in industry.

Energy/Power/Natural Resources

Oil, coal, and natural gas are Romania's most abundant natural resources, although oil reserves are shrinking. Romania does not need to import oil or coal, because its reserves are ample enough for the entire country. Methane and other natural gases are present in the Transylvanian Plateau and are used in conjunction with industry.

Fishing

The fishing industry in Romania has been in decline after joining the EU and falling under European fisheries policies that aim at curbing overfishing in the Baltic Sea. Inland waters are a good source for sturgeon, carp, catfish, pike, perch, and bream. Aquaculture is developing in Romania, with silver carp, bighead carp, and grass carp introduced to those waters and common and crucian carp, as well as trout, indigenous to those waters.

Forestry

Twenty-six percent of Romania is forested, with 96 percent of that forest publicly owned. Hardwoods prevail, including beech and oak, and softwoods cover 31 percent of forests.

Mining/Metals

Romania's mineral resources include salt, copper, manganese, iron, molybdenum, bauxite, lead, and zinc.

Agriculture

Approximately 40 percent of the land in Romania is cultivated; most of the country's farmland is located in the fertile plains of the Walachia region in the south.

Important crops include wheat, rye, barley, corn, potatoes, sugar beets, and sunflower seeds, grapes for wine production, tomatoes, and cabbage. Fisheries provide fresh fish.

Cereal grain (wheat, rye, and barley) is the number one crop in terms of volume, accounting for about 20 percent of Romania's total agricultural yield, and requiring the use of 57 percent of total farmable land for its production.

The agricultural industry has become increasingly privatized since the revolution in 1989. Over 80 percent of farms are privately owned.

Animal Husbandry

Livestock products include lamb, chicken, and eggs.

Tourism

Romania's tourism industry has benefited greatly from the fall of communism, and is now a sizeable component of the country's service industry. In 2013, just over eight million tourists visited Romania.

Tourists enjoy Romania's thermal and mineral springs and visit spa resorts in areas such as Covasna and the Black Sea coast (which has many popular public beaches as well).

Architecture in Bucharest attracts much tourist attention; a popular destination is the Palace of Parliament.

Other popular tourist attractions are the Saxon towns Brasov and Sighisoara in the Transylvania region, which contain well-preserved buildings from the medieval period, and Bran Castle, also known as "Dracula's Castle."

Tourists also enjoy bird watching in the Danube Delta and hiking in the Carpathian Mountains.

Simone Isadora Flynn, PhD

DO YOU KNOW?

- The character of Count Dracula in Bram Stoker's 1898 novel *Dracula* is thought to have been inspired by Vlad Tepes, the ruler of Walachia (which would eventually become part of Romania) in the 15th century. Vlad was known for impaling tens of thousands of criminals and dissidents on stakes.

- During the 1976 Summer Olympics, Romanian gymnast Nadia Comaneci recorded the first perfect score in Olympic gymnastics competition.

- In 2000, cyanide from a gold smelting plant near Baia Mare leaked into the Somes River, eventually reaching the Tisza and Danube rivers, killing a large number of fish, and earning the designation of Europe's worst environmental disaster since the Chernobyl nuclear disaster in 1986.

- Petrache Poenaru (1799–1875) invented and received the patent for the first fountain pen with a replaceable cartridge in 1827. He also designed the Romanian tricolor flag.

Bibliography

Charles King. "The Moldovans: Romania, Russia, and the Politics of Culture." *Stanford: Hoover Institution*, 1999.

Darren Longley and Tim Burford. "Rough Guide to Romania." London: *Rough Guides*, 2011.

Debbie Stowe. "Romania—Culture Smart! The Essential Guide to Customs and Culture." London: Kuperard, 2008.

Denise Roman. "Fragmented Identities: Popular Culture, Sex, and Everyday Life in Postcommunist Romania." Lanham, MD: *Lexington Books*, 2007.

Keith Hitchins. "A Concise History of Romania." New York: *Cambridge University Press*, 2014.

Mark Baker. "Romania and Bulgaria." Oakland, CA: *Lonely Planet*, 2013.

Works Cited

"About Us." *Women's Association of Romania*. http://www.afr.ro/english/indexen.htm.

"A Country Study: Romania." *Library of Congress Country Studies*. http://lcweb2.loc.gov/frd/cs/rotoc.html.

"Balkan Folk Dance Music." *Folk with Dunav*. http://www.dunav.org.il/balkan_music_romanian.html.

"Crafts of Romania." *Romania Tourism*. http://www.romaniatourism.com/crafts.html.

"Cultural Aspects." *National Institute For Research & Development In Informatics*. http://www.ici.ro/romania/en/cultura/index.html.

"Culture of Romania." *Countries and Their Cultures*. http://www.everyculture.com/No-Sa/Romania.html.

"Days and Nights of Literature Festival at Neptun." *Embassy of Romania*. http://oslo.mae.ro/index. php?lang=en&id=31&s=33445.

"Food & Wine." *Romania Tourism*. http://www. romaniatourism.com/foodwine.html.

"Greeting." *Learn the Romanian Language*. http://www. rapido.org.uk/greetings.html.

"Letter to the Romanian Government Urging Protection of All Families without Discrimination." *Human Rights Watch* (Feb. 2008). http://www.hrw.org/en/ news/2008/02/06/letter-romanian-government-urging-protection-all-families-without-discrimination.

"Literature." *Info Romania*. http://www.ici.ro/romania/en/ cultura/literatura.html.

"Romania: Background Notes." *U.S. Department of State*. http://www.state.gov/r/pa/ei/bgn/35722.htm.

"Romania." CIA World Fact Book. https://www.cia.gov/ library/publications/the-world-factbook/print/ro.html

"Romania: Country Reports on Human Rights Practices." *U.S. Department of State*. http://www.state.gov/g/drl/rls/ hrrpt/2006/78834.htm.

"Romania." *Encyclopedia of the Nations*. http://www. nationsencyclopedia.com/Europe/Romania.html.

"Romania." *Info Romania*. http://www.ici.ro/romania/en/ romania.html.

"Romania: Language, Culture, Customs, and Etiquette." *Kwintessential Cross Cultural Solutions*. http://www. kwintessential.co.uk/resources/global-etiquette/romania. html "Romania." *UNESCO World Heritage List*. http:// whc.unesco.org/en/statesparties/ro.

"Romania." *World Atlas* (n.d.). http://www.worldatlas.com/ webimage/countrys/europe/ro.htm.

"Romanian Cuisine." *Nation Master*. http://www. nationmaster.com/encyclopedia/Romanian-cuisine.

"Romanian Folk Art Museum." *Romanian Museum*. http:// www.romanianculture.us/museum.html.

"Romanian Folk Dance Music." *Folk with Dunav*. http:// www.dunav.org.il/balkan_music_romanian.html.

"Romanian Food." *Exploring Romania*. http://www. exploringromania.com/romanian-food.html.

"Romanian Meals, Customs, and Foods." *Food and Culture Resources*. http://www.food-links.com/countries/ romania/foods-commonly-used-romania.php.

"Romanian Traditional Dance Contexts." *Traditional Dance in Romania*. http://www.eliznik.org.uk/ RomaniaDance/.

"Romanian Traditions." *Ciao Romania*. http://www. ciaoromania.com/traditions.html.

"Universal Declaration of Human Rights." *United Nations*. http://www.udhr.org/UDHR/default.htm.

Saint Basil's Cathedral, Red Square, Moscow, Russia

RUSSIA

Introduction

Even after a large loss of territory following the collapse of the Soviet Union in 1991, the Russian Federation, or Russia, remains the largest country in the world, stretching over two continents in the northern hemisphere. Throughout history, Russia's influence in international affairs has been significant, particularly during the 20th century. Russians have also made profound contributions in culture and technology, in particular literature and space exploration. Between 1922 and 1991, the relations of Western powers with the Soviet Union defined much of the world's political order. In recent years, conflicts with its neighbors, including Georgia and Ukraine, have strained relations in the region and across the international diplomatic scene.

GENERAL INFORMATION

Official Language: Russian
Population: 142,423,773 (July 2015 estimated)
Currency: Ruble
Coins: The ruble is available in 1, 5, 10 and 50 kopek coins. In addition, 1, 2, 5 and 10 ruble coins are also available.
Land Area: 16,376,870.0 (2014 estimated) (excluding Crimea)
Water Area: 720,500 sq km
National Anthem: "Hymn of the Russian Federation"
Capital: Moscow
Time Zone(s): Russia spans eleven time zones: GMT +2 to +12 (In the summer: GMT +3 to +13)

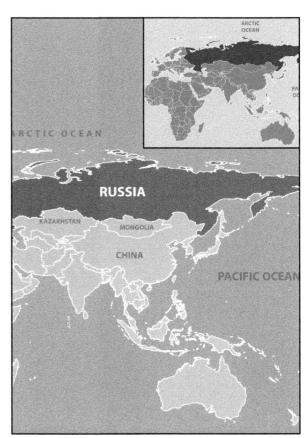

Population

Russia has the 10th largest population in the world (July 2014 estimate). Approximately 80 percent of its population lives in one quarter of the country's land, on the European side of the Ural Mountains.

Russia's major cities and industrial centers are located in its western region, near Europe. At an estimated 11,918,057, Moscow has the largest population. St. Petersburg follows with nearly 5 million. Other major cities include Novosibirsk and Nizhniy Novgorod. The population is predominantly urban, with about 26 percent living in rural areas.

Average life expectancy has risen from sixty-six in 2008 to 70.47 in 2015. Life expectancy for males, at nearly 65 years, is significantly lower than females at 76.5 years (2015 estimated). Infant mortality is nearly seven deaths per 1,000 live births (2015 estimated). These demographic trends have been exacerbated by the deterioration

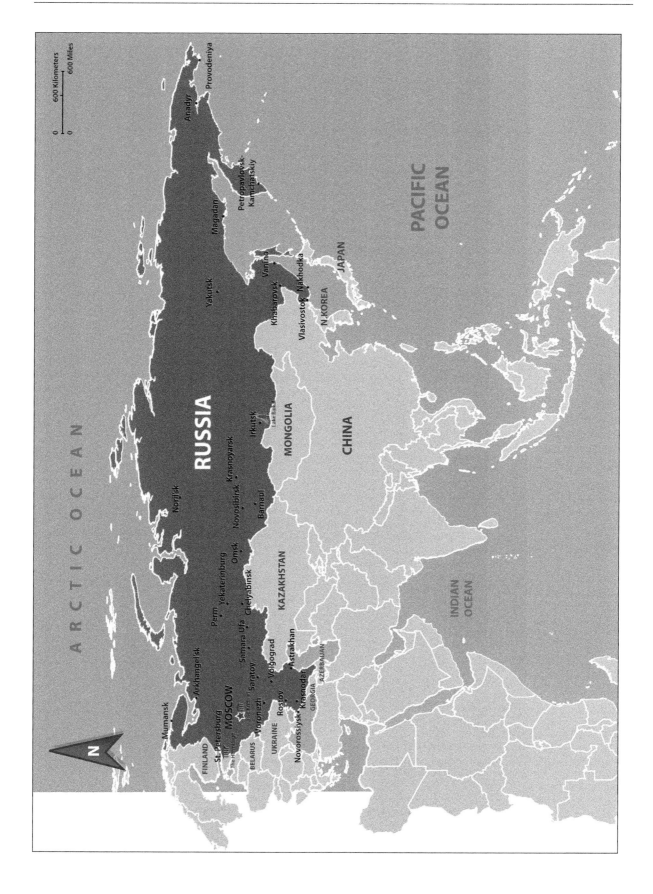

**Principal Cities by Population
(2012 estimate, unless noted):**

- Moscow (11,918,057)
- St. Petersburg (4,990,602
- Novosibirsk (1,511,369)
- Nizhni Novgorod (1,257,260)
- Yekaterinburg (1.3m)
- Samara (1,170,381)
- Omsk (1,158,627)
- Kazan (1,168,745)
- Krasnoyarsk (1,006,856)
- Perm (1,007,272)

of Russia's health care system. A 2015 report from The Moscow Times states that, "According to the State Statistics Service, from 2005 to 2013 the number of health facilities in rural areas fell by 75 percent, from 8,249 to 2,085. That number includes a 95 percent drop in the number of district hospitals, from 2,631 to only 124, and a 65 percent decline in the number of local health clinics, from 7,404 to 2,561."

Moreover, significant portions of the population suffer health-related problems attributable to heavy drug and alcohol consumption, environmental hazards, and poor nutrition. Men are more affected by these problems more than women, as evident in the life expectancy gap.

Languages
Despite the more than 100 languages spoken in the country, Russian dominates in nearly every public sphere, reflecting the Soviet policy of designating Russian as the language of education. Russian is a Slavic language and is written in the Cyrillic alphabet.

Native People & Ethnic Groups
Ethnic Russia's make up nearly 78 percent of the country's total population. More than 100 ethnic groups of Asian and European stock form the restimated Ethnic Russians derive from the Eastern Slavic group, which split off from other Slavs before the 17th century and migrated north and east into modern-day Russia.

The Tatars (nearly 4 percent of the population) and Ukrainians (1.4 percent), also of Slavic stock, are the largest minorities in Russia. The three other main ethnic groups are the Altaic, the Uralic, and the Caucasus. With very few exceptions, even in autonomous regions defined by ethnicity, ethnic Russians are dominant. Small populations of Tatars, Belarusians, Ukrainians, Georgians, Armenians, and Central Asian ethnic groups generally speak their own language in addition to Russian.

Russia has a history of xenophobia and many ethnic minorities in the country have faced discrimination and violence, both from security forces and from gangs.

A host of undocumented migrant workers, many of them from Central Asian republics, have appeared in Moscow in recent years, despite an internal permit system which attempts to restrict illegal settlement. They are estimated to number more than one million.

Though minorities now have broader rights than they did during the Soviet era, they still struggle to preserve their cultures and limited autonomy. One Caucasus group, the Chechens, engaged in two devastating wars for independence from Russia. The first war lasted from 1994 to 1996. The second occurred from 1999 to 2009 and ended in the defeat of the Chechen rebel movement. According to the BBC, "Many accuse the pro-Moscow Chechen leader, Ramzan Kadyrov, of treating Chechnya as a personal fiefdom. His government faces accusations—which it denies—of suppressing media and other freedoms, as well as human rights violations, including kidnappings and torture. There is concern that Chechnya effectively remains outside the ambit of Russian law, fanned by the arrest in 2015 of five Chechens—one with ties to Mr Kadyrov's security forces— in connection with the murder of Russian opposition politician Boris Nemtsov."

Religions
Orthodox Christianity has been a dominant force in both public and private affairs since it

became the state religion in the year 988 CE. During Soviet times, religious institutions had to conform to an atheistic state. Not only was religious practice discouraged, but many churches and monasteries were closed or destroyed. Freedom of worship was relaxed in the 1980s and fully restored after the collapse of the Soviet Union. Approximately half of the population now professes the Orthodox faith. Moscow is the seat of the patriarchate of the Russian Orthodox Church, which enjoys an important role in the cultural life of the city after decades of proscription under communism.

Islam is the second most practiced religion in Russia. According to a 2011 report, the number of Muslims in Europe grew from 29.6 million in 1990 to 44.1 million in 2010. The Russian government also guarantees broad rights to practitioners of Judaism and Buddhism, the other two religions considered part of Russia's heritage.

Climate

The Russian climate ranges from the sub-arctic to the subtropical, but is predominantly northern continental. Moderating influences from warmer seas and oceans do not reach Russia, either because of the distance from these bodies of water or because a mountain range blocks them.

Russia is, however, subject to influence from the colder Arctic and North Atlantic Oceans, contributing to European Russia's and Northern Siberia's long, cold winters and short summers. Winter light is brief in the northern zones, whereas white nights prevail during the summer.

Precipitation is moderate to low; even the wetter agricultural areas are sometimes prone to drought. Heavy snowfall is typical. In European Russia, annual snow cover ranges from forty to 200 days. In Siberia the annual range is between 120 and 250 days. The northernmost regions have permanently frozen ground that can reach depths of several hundred feet.

European Russia experiences warm summers and average winter temperatures below

freezing. Moscow's temperatures fall between −13° to -6° Celsius (9° to 21° Fahrenheit) in January and between 13° to 24° Celsius (56° to 75° Fahrenheit) in July. Average winter temperatures for Siberia are freezing or below. Vladivostok, for example, experiences temperatures from -17° to -9° Celsius (1° to 16° Fahrenheit) in January and from 15° to 20° Celsius (59° to 69° Fahrenheit) in July.

Moscow has a continental climate that is moderated by Atlantic winds. Winters are snowy and cold, with January temperatures averaging -10.3° Celsius (13.5° Fahrenheit) and short hours of daylight. Summers are warm, with long hours of daylight. Annual precipitation, which falls as snow in winter and as rain in summer, averages 610 millimeters (24 inches).

ENVIRONMENT & GEOGRAPHY

Topography

Russia can be divided into broad natural zones that cross the country in east-west belts. The taiga, or forest zone, covers approximately 45 percent of the country's area. It is found in the middle latitudes, and is home to about 33 percent of the population.

The steppe consists of treeless, grassy plains. Two of these, the East European Plain and the West Siberian Plain, divided by the Ural Mountains, account for large portions of Russia. The largest plains in the world, together they cover 2.5 million square kilometers (965,255 square miles). Where it is not swampland, the steppe is the most successful agricultural area in Russia.

The treeless, marshy tundra makes up about 10 percent of the land, in a band across Russia's northern reaches. Permafrost allows only patches of moss and lichens to grow there.

Russia has several mountain ranges, mostly in the eastern portion of the country. The low mineral-rich Urals form the continental divide between Europe and Asia. Mount Elbrus, rising from the Caucasus Mountains along the southwestern border, is Europe's highest point at 5,642 meters (18,510 feet).

Among Russia's many rivers is the longest in Europe, the Volga, stretching 3,510 kilometers (2,181 miles). It supports four major cities and is an important inland waterway. Even longer rivers are located east of the Urals. The Ob and Irtysh are part of the same river system, which is the longest in Russia and the fourth longest in the world. These rivers, which empty into the Arctic Ocean, stretch 5,410 kilometers (3,362 miles).

The country's most important lake is located in southern Siberia. Lake Baikal is the largest and deepest freshwater lake in the world, reaching a maximum depth of 1,713 meters (5,620 feet). It is estimated to contain 20 percent of the world's total fresh water. Moscow, the country's capital, is located in European Russia, a broad, heavily forested plain west of the Ural Mountains. Its metropolitan area occupies 1,081 square kilometers (417 square miles). Ranging in elevation from 130 to 253 meters (from 427 to 830 feet), it is in a river basin that is flat except for the slight rise of the Sparrow Hills.

The center of modern Moscow follows its original layout, with concentric circles radiating out from the central fortification, the Kremlin. Roads now encircle Moscow and continue to expand into the surrounding tracts of forest as private car use becomes increasingly common. Beyond the modern city center are numerous high rise apartment buildings, most of them constructed during the Soviet period. Separate from the living areas but also outside the center are numerous industrial sites.

The Moscow River flows through the city and connects it to five seas. The headwaters of the largest river in Europe, the Volga, rise west of Moscow; a canal links the Moscow River to the Volga, giving the city access to major shipping ways.

Plants & Animals

Except for tropical rainforest, every major vegetation zone is represented in Russia. The taiga has the largest coniferous forest in the world, though deciduous trees grow there as well. The trees are small and widely dispersed, and species include larch, pine, birch, poplar, fir, oak, and beech. In swampy areas of the taiga, bushes and grasses grow instead of trees. Steppe land, where it is not under cultivation, supports a variety of grasses.

Russia's natural zones are home to a variety of animal life. Among the animals that live in the forests are elks, lynx, and brown bears (considered to be the national symbol). On the steppe, wolves, deer, and rodents flourish, as do birds and reptiles. The tundra supports reindeers, arctic foxes, walruses, seals, and polar bears.

The largest cat in the world, the Siberian tiger, is found in the far east of the country. An estimated 300 Siberian tigers live in the wild, probably all in Russia. Its status is considered critical.

Many other animals in Russia are listed as critically endangered, some of them endemic species like the Evorsk vole and the Wrangel lemming. Endangered species include the blue whale, the snow leopard, and the European mink.

CUSTOMS & COURTESIES

Greetings

When Russian men meet, they exchange firm handshakes. The handshake is usually accompanied with a verbal greeting, such as "Zdrastvut" ("Hello"), "Dobrae utra" ("Good morning"), "Dobry den" ("Good afternoon"), or "Dobry vechir" ("Good evening") and continuous eye contact. Men also shake hands with women, but they generally use a softer handshake. Male friends may greet each other by embracing, and when female friends meet, they may kiss each other on the cheek three times.

A standard way of addressing someone is by using their first name followed by their patronymic: their father's first name with "ich" added to the end for men and "ovna" added to the end for women. Members of the Communist Party may still address each other as "comrade," although this form of address is no longer used by the general population. Using a more old-fashioned form of address, one may use "Gospodin" ("Sir") for men and "Gospozha" ("Madam") for women.

Gestures & Etiquette

Russians tend to be less outgoing and demonstrative with strangers than many Europeans. It has been observed that many Russians can even be chilly or surly with strangers. The same Russians are likely to be warm and affectionate with family and friends. This may be a vestige of life during the upheaval of Stalinist reform, when Russians were encouraged to denounce their neighbors and millions of Russians disappeared into gulags (forced labor camps), were deported, or killed. Even under more moderate Soviet leaders, denunciations and police control taught Russians to distrust strangers.

Russians share with other Europeans a comfort with physical contact. Russians do not require as much distance from the people they are speaking with as Americans do, and will often stand within a foot of each other when talking. They are also more likely to touch the people with whom they are speaking.

Many Russian gestures resemble American gestures. Russians may point to their temple and twirl their finger to indicate that something is crazy. A thumbs-up means the same thing for Russians as it does for Americans. However, the American "OK" sign is considered vulgar in Russia. Moreover, pointing is considered more offensive by Russians than it is by Americans.

Gift giving is an important part of Russian etiquette. Russians exchange gifts on many occasions, and visitors will typically bring gifts with them. Russians will even bring a small gift, often flowers, to dinner parties. Flowers, in fact, are important in Russian culture, and Russians give them to friends and to family. The number and color of flowers given are significant. Russians bring an even number of flowers to funerals; for all other occasions, they bring an odd number. As in many cultures, red flowers are associated with

love and white with innocence. Yellow is associated with betrayal.

Russian etiquette also generally dictates traditional roles for men and women. Men are usually expected to open doors for women, pay the bill at restaurants, and pour drinks for women at the table.

Eating/Meals

Russians today typically have three meals a day. The first meal is called zavtrak, and it is eaten at the beginning of the day. This meal is usually accompanied by tea. The second, eaten at midday, is called obed. Obed is often translated as "dinner," because it is the main meal for most Russian families. It may consist of several courses, including dessert, and it is often accompanied by vodka or beer. Most Russians eat the midday meal at home, though some Russians eat at their workplaces. The third meal is eaten in the evening, and is called uzhin, or "supper." It is generally smaller than the midday meal. Restaurants, however, serve multi-course evening meals.

Visiting

Russians are known for their generosity, and a visitor to a Russian home can expect to be treated with great generosity. Regardless of their means, Russians often prepare lavish meals for their guests. These may include large spreads of appetizers, followed by several courses. Russian guests also often show generosity by bringing gifts for their hosts. They may bring flowers (always in odd numbers) or some other small item. Visitors may also be expected to remove their shoes at the door. Some Russian families will have slippers for their guests to wear in the house. At formal events, however, guests will wear their own shoes.

A Russian meal will typically be accompanied by vodka or some other alcoholic drink, such as cognac, champagne, or wine. Generally, guests will be expected to drink with their hosts. They will also be expected to toast. Russian toasts are often elaborate, and guests will be expected to say a few words when they toast. Typically, a guest will toast the host and the women in the room, as well as the meal.

LIFESTYLE

Family

In Russia, several generations of a family often live together. Young couples in particular often live with their parents. This is partly due to the expense of housing in Russia, but it may also be due in part to Russians' tendency to stay close their families. Even when Russians do not share apartments with their families, they often choose apartments in the same apartment complexes.

In the city apartments are small and the cost of living is high. This causes many couples in the city to have fewer children. In the countryside, homes are often larger, and couples tend to have more children.

Housing

Most Russians in the city live in high-rise apartment complexes, most of which were built in the Soviet era. They are typically made of pre-fabricated concrete blocks, and they have a minimalist, uniform appearance. Apartments in these complexes are small. Since the fall of the Soviet Union, however, developers have begun building new apartment complexes with roomier apartments.

Communal apartments are still common in Russia. In a communal apartment, the kitchen and bathroom may be shared by several families, and each family will be confined to a single room. However, communal apartments are becoming less common.

Food

Historically, the Russian diet has consisted of fairly simple foods, including boiled meats, fish, radishes, beetroot, and potatoes. These are still important foods in the Russian diet. More lavish meals also have a place in Russian tradition. With the rise of the aristocracy in the 18th century, Western European foods were brought to Russia.

These included such basic foods as butter, pastries and ice cream. It also included hors-d'oeuvres, which became an important part of feasting for Russians. Known as zakuski in Russian, hors-d'oeuvres often include caviar, mushrooms with sour cream, and vodka, wine, or liqueur.

Bread and porridge (or kasha) are also traditional foods in Russia, and are still often eaten for breakfast. They have both been staple foods for some families, and may be eaten at any meal. Other breakfast foods may include pancakes and omelets. Lunch in Russia is a large meal, and may include zakuski, salads, and soups. Lunch often includes borscht, a soup made from beets or cabbage. Dinner is much smaller and may consist only of zakuski.

Life's Milestones

Under Soviet rule, all weddings were required to take place in a secular "wedding palace." While couples are still required to marry in such venues, they may also have a separate wedding ceremony in a church. Historically, Russian women have tended to marry at a younger age than women in many other European countries do. While Russian society remains in flux, this appears to be true today.

When a person dies in Russia, a funeral is held on the third day after death, according to Russian Orthodox tradition. Those who come are expected to bring flowers (in an even number). Often a paper band is put across the forehead of the deceased, and mourners kiss the band as they pass the casket. If there is a burial, mourners attend the burial ceremony. Nearly half of the deceased in Moscow today are cremated instead of buried, partly due to the expense of burial. The deceased is also usually given a memorial dinner, where family and friends gather.

CULTURAL HISTORY

Art & Architecture

The Slavic ancestors of the Russians celebrated their conversion to Christianity through the beauty of their churches and artwork. The association between beauty and faith may have contributed to the special character of Russian art. Foreign observers often note the gravity and exalted themes of Russian art, from the early Christian art of the 11th century to the psychological novels of the 19th century.

Before they converted to Christianity, the Eastern Slavs had a tradition of wooden architecture, as well as carved idols. There was also a tradition of animal motifs in decoration. With their conversion to Christianity, they imported architectural and artistic styles from the Byzantine Empire (330–1453). They began building churches followed the standard ground plans of Byzantine architecture, and they began painting frescoes using the Byzantine iconography and techniques. Over time, the shapes used for the domes of churches evolved into Russia's famous onion, or candle flame, shape. Like much of Russian culture, onion domes have become associated for with Eastern culture, specifically Islam. It is likely that any similarity between Russian and Islamic architecture is due to the common influence of Byzantine architecture.

Frescoes became less common in churches as wood was more widely used as a construction material. Icons painted on pieces of wood or other materials became much more common and important in church rituals. Russian icon painters gradually moved further away from naturalism. Where classical art had used perspective to draw the viewer into a space within the picture, Russian icon painters favored an inverse perspective, which pushed the viewer out. While there were strict guidelines for the composition and content of icons, Russian iconographers developed distinct personal styles. Two of the most famous iconographers were Theophanes the Greek (c. 1340–1410), an immigrant, and Andrei Rublev (c. 1360s-1437). Theophanes was known for the intensity and dynamism of his paintings. Rublev was known for the gracefulness of his paintings and is considered Russia's greatest medieval painter of frescoes and Orthodox icons.

Some of Russia's great building projects began with the rise of Moscow in the 15th century. The oldest existing church in the Moscow Kremlin was built in the late 14th century. The church was built by Italian architects, although they were required by Tsar Ivan III (1440–1505) to emulate earlier Russian architecture. Later Italian architects introduced some Italian Renaissance innovations to Kremlin architecture. Shortly after, Russian architects made some of their most famous innovations. The Church of the Ascension was built with its all-masonry "tent roof," and Saint Basil's Cathedral with its colorful onion domes.

In the 17th and 18th centuries, Westernizing tsars brought in a flood of Western culture. Western theater was introduced from England, and the first opera, orchestra and ballet were established. Naturalism was allowed in iconography, encouraging the development of Western styles. Under Peter the Great (1672–1725), Saint Petersburg was founded on the coast of the Baltic Sea and became a showcase of Western European architecture and culture. Russian artists also were sent to Western Europe for training, and easel painting took root in Russia.

By the 19th century, the highly educated Russian aristocracy had absorbed much of Western Europe's artistic traditions and the philosophies of many of its great thinkers. They were deeply engaged in finding Russia's place in these artistic traditions and applying these philosophies to spiritual questions. As a result, the 19th century is considered the culture's golden age, producing astonishing literature, music and painting. By the beginning of the 20th century, Russian artists were making remarkable strides in abstract painting. Two schools in particular explored different directions in abstraction: constructivism, which emphasized design, production, and material, and suprematism, which focused on geometric forms as exemplified by Kazimir Malevich's (1878–1935) painting Black Square (which was, in fact, a black square).

For much of the 20th century, Russian art was preoccupied with themes dictated by the Soviet government. Most Russian art aimed either to support Soviet ideology or to critique or subvert it. The fall of the Soviet Union left artists with the difficult task of interpreting the legacy of Soviet art and finding new directions.

Some artists began this task even before the final collapse of the Soviet Union. They initiated a movement in Russian art that became important in post-Soviet art. The movement, called Sots art (socialist art or socialist pop art), combines the social realist style of art that was sanctioned by the Soviet government with the ironic sensibility of Western pop art.

Even outside of the Sots Art movement, much contemporary Russian art is preoccupied with the Soviet past. While most Russian artists reject the Soviet ideology, their art often seems to express nostalgia for Soviet life. It often depicts everyday life in the Soviet Union, or objects that were common in the Soviet Union. Some artists have returned to the neo-classical style that was popular in the 19th century, while abstraction, which was associated with capitalism, has become acceptable.

Music

The composer Modest Mussorgsky (1839–1881) strived to develop a purely Russian music. He believed that Russian music must be true to the Russian people, and must be based on the sounds of their speech. Other composers of the 19th century displayed more Western influences. Pyotr Tchaikovsky (1840–1893), in particular, faithfully followed the conventions of Western symphonic music. Other important Russian composers of the century were Alexander Borodin (1833–1887), who was also dedicated to a distinct Russian style of music, and Nikolai Rimsky-Korsakov (1844–1908), who is known for his operas and folk influences.

Literature

Classical French poetry, and the novels and poetry of England provided models for Alexander Pushkin (1799–1837), Russia's literary icon, who is credited with establishing Russian literature. One of his more famous works, *Eugene Onegin*, which he called "a novel in verse," achieved a kind of realistic portraiture and narrative that

would be important in the work of later novelists. Nikolai Gogol (1809–1852), on the other hand, turned against the conventions of classicism, writing stories and novels populated with lowly, vulgar characters.

The most famous works of Russian literature internationally were the realist novels of the mid to late 19th century. Fyodor Dostoevsky (1821–1881) was one of the earliest novels working in this school. His novels are famed for their deep penetration into the psychologies of their characters. His characters struggle with moral and spiritual dilemmas that have resonated with many readers worldwide. Leo Tolstoy (1828–1910) was also famed for his treatment of character, and is often considered unmatched in his physical and psychological character portrayals.

Literature, music, and film have also seen greater freedom since the fall of the Soviet Union in 1991. The thaw started before the fall under the reforms of Gorbachev. As part of Gorbachev's policy of allowing greater openness in Soviet society, he lifted bans on many books, musical compositions, and film. One of the most famous writers, Alexander Solzhenitsyn (1918–2008), had written famous accounts of life in Soviet forced labor camps. His books were widely read in the West but strictly banned in the Soviet Union. Gorbachev lifted the ban on Solzhenitsyn's books and Solzhenitsyn, along with other exiled writers, was invited to return to the Soviet Union; he returned in 1994. Since then a number of poets and novelists have made their mark, including Lyudmila Petruschevskaya (1938–), Vladimir Sorokin (1955–), and Victor Peleven (1962–).

CULTURE

Arts & Entertainment

Russians have contributed to most major Western art movements. Their achievements in literature and classical music are particularly renowned.

Numerous Russian cultural and scientific luminaries were born in Moscow or have ties to it, including Leo Tolstoy, Alexander

Pushkin, Vladimir Mayakovsky, and Andrei Sakharov. The city's main rival for cultural standing, particularly in performing arts, plastic arts, and literature, is the former capital, St. Petersburg.

Several of the world's premier art museums and theaters are located in Moscow. The opera and ballet companies of the Bolshoi Theater enjoy one of the highest international reputations in the performing arts. Moscow is also well served by urban parks. Gorky Park, Neskuchniy Garden, and Izmaylovsky Park are three such areas offering natural settings and amusements for the city's population

Western music, including rock, heavy metal, and pop, is extremely popular among Russians, particularly younger Russians. Russian rock, alternative rock, and progressive rock is also popular. Moscow holds a variety of rock festivals each year.

In addition to the popularity of Western-made movies, there exists a hugely successful Russian film industry. Although the industry struggled financially during the 1990s, it has rebounded in recent decades, creating popular movies for Russian audiences ranging from science fiction to historical dramas. Recent popular and critically notable movies include *House of Fools* (2002), *Night Watch* (2004), *The Island* (2006), *12* (2007), *How I Ended This Summer* (2010), and *Leviathan* (2014).

Cultural Sites & Landmarks

Russia has long been known for distinctive and striking architecture. Although many of Russia's great structures have been demolished or destroyed, many of the most famous remain. Many of these historic structures have been designated as World Heritage Sites by the United Nations Educational, Scientific, and Cultural Organization (UNESCO). There are twenty-three such sites throughout Russia. These include the Architectural Ensemble of the Trinity Sergius Lavra, a significant Russian Orthodox monastery; the historic center and monuments of Saint Petersburg; the Church of the Ascension in Kolomenskoy; and the Citadel, Ancient City and Fortress Buildings of Derbent, the southernmost city in Russia which dates back to the eighth century BCE, and is considered the oldest Russian city.

The Moscow Kremlin is a fortress surrounded by walls and square red towers with pyramidal roofs. The Kremlin took shape as Moscow grew in importance. In the 14th century, when Moscow first became politically important, the old wooden fences surrounding it were replaced with walls. Later, as Moscow became the powerful center of the Russian Empire (1721–1917), the tsars built magnificent palaces and cathedrals in the Kremlin. This history is reflected in the evolution of architectural styles seen in the Kremlin. Some of the cathedrals have drum-shaped towers topped with golden cupolas, following one of the earliest styles of Russian architecture. However, the dominant building in the Kremlin, the Grand Kremlin Palace, was designed in the baroque style common in Western Europe.

In 1990, the Moscow Kremlin, and Red Square, the city's famous city square, were designated as a collective United Nations World Heritage Site for their history and architecture. Saint Basil's Cathedral stands in Red Square, and has long impressed the world with its fanciful onion domes and spires with colored swirls and stripes.

Some of the most interesting cultural landmarks lie outside of the major cities. The Abramtsevo Artists' Colony is secluded in the woods northeast of Moscow. It is distinguished from other country estates by several remarkable structures and by a remarkable history. The estate was owned by two patrons of the arts successively. The first, Sergei Aksakov (1791–1859), was often host to writers who would become famous in the 19th century, such as Gogol. (Gogol is said to have written much of his most famous work at Abramtsevo.) The second, Savva Mamontov (1841–1918), was closely associated with artists in the populist movement, which took folk art and traditional Russian art as inspirations. Mamontov decided to make Abramtsevo a workshop for populist art. Soon, some of the most important artists of the day were living and working there, including Ilya Repin (1844–1930) and Mikhail Vrubel (1856–1910).

While UNESCO has recognized Russia for its architectural importance to humanity, the country also has made numerous natural contributions to the World Heritage List. These include the Western Caucasus, which includes the Caucasus Mountains and the Caucasian State Nature Biosphere Reserve; Central Sikhote-Alin, a mountain range known for its temperate zones; Virgin Komi Forests, the largest virgin forest in Europe; and the Golden Mountains of Altai, which is known for its vegetation and endangered inhabitants such as the snow leopard.

Libraries & Museums

In Moscow, the Pushkin Museum showcases art from around the world, while the Tretyakov Gallery showcases Russian art. One of the world's premier art gallery and museum is the State Hermitage Museum in St. Petersburg. It holds of millions of treasured works of arts and artifacts, and is also the site of the famous and stunning Winter Palace, once a residence for the Russian monarchs. Hundreds of museums are located in St. Petersburg alone. National repositories include the Russian State Library, in Moscow, and the National Library of Russia, in St. Petersburg.

Holidays

Russians celebrate a host of secular and religious holidays, with Orthodox Easter being of special importance in the church calendar. Both the anniversary of the 1917 revolution (November 7) and independence from the communist system which the revolution ushered in (June 12) are celebrated. Victory Day (May 9) commemorates the millions of Russians who died in World War II and the service of Russia's veterans.

Youth Culture

Since the fall of communism in the 1990s, Russian culture has become more accepting of Western influences. Coupled with increasing access to Western popular culture through the Internet, Russian youth trends are now similar to, or the same as, those in United States and the United Kingdom. Urban areas have their own popular club or dance scene—in which some affluent youth have achieved a sort of celebrity status. Western fashions are widely popular. Additionally, as Russia puts more distance between its communist past, Russian youth are increasingly embracing globalization.

Nonetheless, the lives of young people in Russia in the early 21st century continue to reflect the larger realities of Russian society. It remains a society in which there is a large gap between the wealthy and the impoverished. It is also an unstable society in which the rich are not secure in their wealth. Although Russian youth have long been characterized or critiqued as being apolitical, there has been a growing segment of politically active youth in recent years, though many contend that this active segment is dominated by extremism.

SOCIETY

Transportation

Russians drive on the right-hand side of the road. The majority of roads in Russia are paved, but the country does have high road accident death numbers. Outside of cities, bus transportation remains the most common mode of public transportation. Traditional trams (streetcars or trolleys), minibuses, and taxis are also common. In recent years, private car ownership has increased.

Transportation Infrastructure

Moscow is known for a subway system that features stations with elaborate decorations. Some of these stations have sculptures in the old social realist style sanctioned by the Soviets, while others have chandeliers. The system serves between six and eight million passengers per day. Five other Russian cities have similar subway systems. In 2015, the city of Moscow marked the first anniversary of the July 15, 2014 metro crash—the worst accident ever to hit the Russian capital's subway system.

Rail transport is also a popular mode of transportation in Russia. One of the most famous railroads in the world extends from Moscow to the Pacific: the Trans-Siberian Railroad. It is primarily used for freight trains, which carry minerals and produce, among other things. However, it is also a regular route for passenger coaches, and many people travel the Trans-Siberian Railroad to see the steppes and the forests of Siberia.

As a major transportation hub, encompassing nine railway stations and extensive river and sea access, Moscow serves as a transit point for many imports and exports. The Moscow region also has one of the country's most developed road systems.

There are several hundred airports located throughout Russia, including three international airports in Moscow. Russian airports handle millions of business travelers and tourists annually.

Media & Communications

Under Soviet rule, the media was controlled by the state. The Soviet government dictated what was said on the news. When the Soviet Union fell, newspapers and radio and television stations, like other state assets, were privatized. This brought in a greater degree of freedom of speech. In addition, many new newspapers and television and radio broadcasts were created. However, most media assets fell into the hands of Russia's emerging business tycoons, many of whom had close links with the government. Many people saw this as a limitation on the freedom and diversity of the media.

When Vladimir Putin (1952–) became president and began expanding state control over the countries assets again, Russia's newspapers and television and radio stations were gradually brought under state control again. While there is still a greater diversity of media in Russia than there had been under the Soviets, and most Russians can access foreign news media, many people see signs of state intervention in the reporting of the prominent news programs

Infrastructure problems continue to hamper telecommunications development in Russia.

Due to the poor conditions of landlines, and the expansive nature of the country itself, satellite communications are in high demand. As of 2012, there were an estimated 42.9 million landlines in use, and 261.9 million mobile phones in use. As of 2009, there were an estimated 40.853 million Internet users.

SOCIAL DEVELOPMENT

Standard of Living

The 2013 Human Development Index, which is compiled by the United Nations, ranked Russia at 57 in the world (out of a total of 187). Foreign investment and high oil prices have helped to improve the standard of living in Russia in recent years. This follows several years of negative growth in demographic numbers such as life span and literacy after the fall of the Soviet Union. Nonetheless, medical care in Russia remains below Western standards. It was estimated that 11 percent of Russians were living under the poverty line in 2013. This number was estimated at 40 percent in 1999.

Water Consumption

Russia faces serious challenges related to seawater and groundwater pollution. In some areas of Russia, citizens routinely boil water prior to using it in order to kill bacteria and disease. Many other regions of the country import water. Untreated sewage and industrial pollution continue to affect a large number of rivers and lakes throughout the country. This has impacted not only the availability of drinking water, but fish and wildlife.

Numerous government initiatives have been introduced in recent years aimed at helping to improve issues of water availability and water pollution in Russia, though these have had little real-world impact. About 70 percent of the population obtains drinking water from surface water sources, 40 percent of which do not comply with international hygienic norms. More than 25 percent of water pipelines from surface reservoirs are not equipped with purification systems.

Education

Education from the first through the ninth grades is free and compulsory. By choice, students can then continue into higher levels or attend a vocational program. Russians in general receive a sound education—the literacy rate in Russia approaches 100 percent.

The country has over 500 post-secondary educational institutions, most of which specialize in individual fields. The country's more than forty universities generally instruct students in the arts and sciences. Moscow State University is the country's largest and most prestigious, followed by St. Petersburg State University.

Literacy rates in Russia are very high. In 2015, it was estimated that 99.7 percent of the population could read and write—99.7 percent of males and 99.6 percent of females.

Women's Rights

Women have often been a powerful force in Russian politics. In medieval Russia, women were the major drivers of a fundamentalist movement that caused a great upheaval in the Russian Orthodox Church and led to increasing power for the tsar. Women were also active in the St. Petersburg terrorist networks that destabilized the Russian monarchy in the early 20th century. And during the collectivization of the early Soviet days, peasant families discovered that women could lead the most effective resistance to the reforms.

While Russian culture typically encouraged traditional virtues in women, it exalted those virtues in icons and stories. The traditional virtues of women were often raised to the level of heroism, as in Maxim Gorky's (1868–1936) *The Mother* (1907), a novel about the mother of a revolutionary. Outside of these traditional roles, women have often directly wielded power in Russia. In the 18th century, Catherine the Great (1729–1796) made significant territorial gains for Russia and helped to determine the direction Russia would take in the next century. A groundbreaking feminist movement took root in Russia in the 19th century. Inspired in part by the writings of Western feminists, Russian feminists established women's communes throughout the country and called for political and social reform. They opened higher education and some professions to women. When the Provisional Government took leadership in 1917, it gave women the full right to vote.

Soviet rule brought some significant gains in women's rights. With the support of a prominent feminist in the Communist Party, Alexandra Kollontai (1872–1952), liberalized divorce laws were passed in the early days of the Soviet Union. In the later decades of the Soviet Union, women overtook men in higher education. They began to dominate some professions, such as medicine and law. During the Soviet era there were also many high-profile women scientists and writers. Up until the reforms of the late 20th century, Soviet law even set quotas for the number of women in official positions.

During these reforms, quotas for women in government were lifted, and the number of women in government plummeted. Since the fall of the Soviet Union, political representation of women has remained weak, while economic power has largely eluded them. During the capitalization that followed the fall of the Soviet Union, the assets that were newly privatized mostly fell in the hands of men. Women also faced discriminatory hiring practices, and some recent studies suggest that Russian women earn as much as 30 percent less than their male counterparts. However, women are still better represented among the highly educated, and have been better able to fill new professional positions.

Prostitution has been on the rise in Russia, and, as in many parts of the world, prostitutes in Russia are often forced into the work. Some of them were kidnapped in Russia or abroad, while others were sold by relatives. The Russian police have been fighting the sex trade, but the criminal gangs who traffic women are not often prosecuted, and Russian authorities in certain areas have been accused of being lax in following up on reported disappearances. Human trafficking continues to be a serious problem in Russia, which is classified as a source, transit and destination country for the trafficking of women for commercial sex or forced labor. It has been contended by international monitoring agencies and non-governmental organizations (NGOs) that human trafficking and prostitution within Russia has, at times, been facilitated by corrupt government officials.

Violence against women continues to be a serious issue in Russia, and a legal definition of domestic violence does not exist in the country. Because of the obscurity associated with domestic and spousal abuse, victims are often discouraged from prosecuting, and authorities are often accused of discouraging victims from coming forward or of inadequately investigating cases of domestic violence. Social stigma also prevents women from reporting spousal rape, and there are no concrete laws prohibiting sexual harassment. As recently as 2007, Russia's Ministry of Internal Affairs believes that an estimated 14,000 women were killed by significant others or family members, and Amnesty International (AI) contends that 36,000 women were the victims of domestic abuse on a daily basis. In 2013, domestic abuse was still not recognized as a crime in Russia, making it difficult for victims to seek shelter. There are no national statistics for domestic abuse in Russia, but according to a 2013 report from the BBC, an estimated 600,000 women in Russia face physical and verbal abuse at home every year. Of that number, 14,000 die from injuries inflicted by husbands or partners. In the same year, it was noted that the capital of Moscow only has one state-funded refuge.

Health Care

Russia has a socialized health care system. Once well developed, it has declined in quality over the last several decades, due to meager funds. As a result, it struggles to cope with the needs of the population.

GOVERNMENT

Structure

Russia is a federation divided into executive, legislative, and judicial branches, as set out in the 1993 constitution. The national government presides over a variety of administrative units: 21 republics, 49 provinces, six territories, 10 regions, and one autonomous oblast. Moscow and St. Petersburg have federal status. Local governments are under tight control of the central government.

A president, elected by popular vote to a six year term (the term length was extended from four to six years in late 2008, effective after the 2012 election), heads the executive branch and is limited to two consecutive terms. The president is vested with broad powers as commander-in-chief of the armed forces and head of the Security Council; he also appoints the judges of the highest judicial body. A prime minister, appointed by the president, serves beneath the president. Presidential appointments are subject to approval by the legislative branch.

This branch, called the Federal Assembly, is bicameral. It is composed of the Council of the Federation, the upper house, and the State Duma, the lower house. Two representatives from each administrative unit are elected to serve in the upper house. The State Duma has 450 elected seats.

The judicial branch consists of three branches: the Constitutional Court is the highest, followed by the Supreme Court and the Supreme Arbitration Court. Each has separate spheres of jurisdiction.

Political Parties

Before 1991, the Communist Party of the Soviet Union presided over every aspect of Russian politics. As of January 2014, 78 political parties are registered with Russia's Ministry of Justice, but only four parties maintain representation in Russia's national legislature. These include A Just Russia, the Communist Party of the Russian Federation (CPRF), the Liberal Democratic Party of Russia (LDPR) and United Russia.

Local Government

The Russian Federation is divided into federal subjects. There are six existing types of federal subjects, each of which has representation in the Federal Assembly, despite operating with differing degrees of autonomy. The types of federal subjects are known as republics, krais, oblasts, federal cities, autonomous oblasts, and autonomous okrugs.

The Russian Federation consists of twenty-one republics, nine krais, forty-six oblasts, two federal cities, one autonomous oblast, and four autonomous okrugs. Areas of non-Russian ethnicity are republics and have the right to establish their own official language. The krais and oblasts are essentially the same in everything but name; each are administrative divisions of the larger federation. Russia's two federal cities are Moscow and Saint Petersburg and its only autonomous oblast is the Jewish Autonomous Oblast (JAO) in the southeast corner of the country. The area's religiously affiliated namesake is a remnant of an earlier nationalist policy and today the majority of the JAO population is Russian, not Jewish.

Russian elections have come under criticism by several international organizations in recent years, who claimed that their outcomes are influenced by the government and that the government also actively prevents the participation of some parties in the political process.

Judicial System

The highest level of Russia's judicial system is divided into three separate courts: the Supreme Court, the High Court of Arbitration, and the Constitutional Court. One segment of the arbitration court system handles matters related to business and economics while another hears civil and domestic matters for city and rural districts. The Constitutional Court is a stand-alone entity that addresses constitutional law and has no judiciary bodies beneath it. Cases are tried by either a panel of judges or a single judge, although Russia has in recent decades begun to implement a trial by jury in some instances.

Critics of the Russian judicial system state that it is too large and in need of consolidation. Additionally, critics continue to question the impartiality of judges when it comes to cases involving political dissent or involving those who are seen as a potential threat to the existing order.

Taxation

The system of taxation in Russia, known as the Russian Tax Code, imposes a system of federal, regional, and local taxes. The country's oil and natural gas industry is heavily taxed and the government generates vast stores of revenue from this sector of the economy. Other industries such as telecommunications, construction, and agriculture are also taxed by the federal government but at a lower rate.

Among the regional and local taxes are included a property tax, vehicle tax, and land tax. Small business taxes for local businesses are also imposed. Individuals pay an income tax annually.

Armed Forces

The Armed Forces of the Russian Federation is overseen by the Ministry of Defense and commanded by the president of the Russian Federation. It consists of the Russian Air Force, Ground Forces, and Navy. The army also has several specialized divisions. Russia's defense budget was estimated to be $33 billion (USD) in 2009, with an estimated 35 million enlisted service members. In October 2014. *The Moscow Times* reported that the Russian defense budget would hit a record $81 billion in 2015. According 2015 report from Reuters, "Russia has an order book worth $40 billion dollars for weapons over the next three to four years, with the biggest buyers coming from India, China, the Middle East, and Latin America."

The Russian army holds one of the world's largest stockpiles of nuclear weapons and reports differ as to whether or not it holds more than the United States. Following the fall of the Soviet Union, the Russian government came under criticism from its allies, who argue that more should be done to account for such weapons to prevent their procurement by terrorist organizations.

Foreign Policy

Since the days of the tsars, Russia has been a global power and has profoundly influenced its neighbors and the world. Many of the Baltic and Eastern European nations have, over the course of history, been parts of the Russian Empire, as have vast tracts of land stretching through Mongolia to the Pacific Ocean.

In the Soviet era, Russia's domestic agenda influenced the technological and ideological development of the United States. The Soviet Union launched the first satellite and put the first man in space, spurring the U.S. to increase its development of space technology. The arms race between the U.S. and the Soviet Union accelerated the development of military technology in both countries. In addition, the Soviet Union's promotion of atheism led the U.S. to take an explicitly pro-religious stance, adding "under God" to the Pledge of Allegiance at the height of the Cold War. Lastly, as the world's first communist country, the Soviet Union became a model for China and other communist nations.

The Russian Federation that formed after the fall of the Soviet Union does not contain all of the non-Russian regions that belonged to the Soviet Union. However, many of the regions that were formerly part of the Soviet Union and the Tsarist Empire are still important to Russia's sense of national identity. Ukraine, for instance, is viewed by many Russians as a part of Russia. Historically Ukraine, a country on the western border of SRussia, was important in the development of Russia. Ukraine was later the birthplace of many of Russia's great leaders and artists. However, Ukraine has evolved a distinct language and sense of national identity, and when the Soviet Union fell, Ukraine declared independence.

Since then, Russian leaders have been antagonistic toward Western-leaning leaders in Ukraine and have been accused of tampering in Ukraine's elections. When Viktor Yuschenko (1954–2010), a Western-leaning liberal, ran against a pro-Russia candidate for president, many people believed Russia was involved in attempts to ensure his defeat. Suspicion especially circled around the poisoning of Yuschenko with dioxin, which endangered his life and disfigured his face. When independent observers claimed that the election had been rigged in favor of Yuschenko's opponent, Russia staunchly defended the results, and accused Western powers (in particular, the US) of meddling in Ukraine's affairs. Yuschenko was eventually brought to power by massive popular protests in his support, an event known as the "Orange Revolution."

Georgia was also a part of the Soviet Union and the Russian Empire. Like Ukraine, it contributed great leaders and thinkers to Russian culture. Joseph Stalin (1878–1953), perhaps the most important Soviet leader, was from Georgia. Georgia declared independence when the Soviet Union fell. However, Russia has intervened in Georgia's civil strife, supporting the breakaway provinces South Ossetia and Abkhazia. This led to war between Russia and Georgia in 2008. The conflict ended with a settlement negotiated by the European Union (EU). The settlement called for the withdrawal of Russian troops, but some Russian forces remained in South Ossetia and Abkhazia, and Russia retains control of their borders. Russia extended its control by signing a treaty with South Ossetia in March 2015. Under the agreement, South Ossetia's military and economy will be incorporated into Russia's. The treaty also promises to make it easier for South Ossetians to get Russian citizenship, and to raise salaries for civil servants and state pensions. The previous year, a similar treaty was signed with Abkhazia.

Against opposition from abroad, Russia annexed Ukraine's Crimean Peninsula in March 2014, after Ukraine's pro-Moscow President Viktor Yanukovych was ousted following street protests that turned bloody. Russia called Yanukovych's ouster a coup by radical Ukrainian nationalists and said it entered the region to stabilize it. A referendum on secession from Ukraine was held in Crimea on March 16, 2014, even as Russian troops and militant separatists were gathering. The results of the referendum were presented as supporting Crimea's becoming part of Russia.

Russia's foreign policy is shaped by its influential role in the global economy, the establishment of strategic regional security and economic agreements, the promotion of Russian culture (particularly in former Soviet republics), and its handling of its natural resources, particularly oil and natural gas. Relations with the US have grown somewhat contentious in recent years.

Russia is against the expansion of the North Atlantic Treaty Organization (NATO) into territories and the proposed establishment of a U.S. missile defense outpost in neighboring Poland. In addition, the US-led war in Iraq in 2003, as well as opposite stances regarding the civil war in Syria and fighting in Ukraine, have caused rifts between the countries. The country maintains membership in several notable international organizations such as the Commonwealth of Independent States (CIS), Organization for Security and Cooperation in Europe (OSCE), and the UN Security Council. Russia also strengthened its ties with NATO and the EU.

Human Rights Profile

International human rights law insists that states respect civil and political rights, and also promote an individual's economic, social and cultural rights. The United Nations Universal Declaration on Human Rights (UDHR) is recognized as the standard for international human rights. Its authors sought the counsel of the world's great thinkers, philosophers, and religious leaders, and were careful to create a document that reflects the core values shared by every world culture. (To read this document or view the articles relating to cultural human rights, visit http://www.un.org/en/documents/udhr/.)

With Gorbachev's reforms in the 1980s and with the fall of the Soviet Union, Russians enjoyed greater freedom of opinion and expression than they had for decades. Through most of the Soviet Union's history, the freedom of opinion and expression was systematically suppressed and all news media were state-run. All publications were rigorously censored by the state and foreign and domestic books were banned. Artists were regularly denounced for works that did not adhere to state ideology.

Since the fall of the Soviet Union, the government of the Russian Federation has taken control of most media, including television. The government appears to exercise some control over the content of the news reporting and other broadcasts, violating Article 19 of the UDHR. However, the current government allows more freedom of speech than the Soviet government did. The Soviet government also strictly regulated religious activity, violating Article 18 of the UDHR under Stalin, the Communist Party denounced Christians as enemies of the people, and many Christians were sent to labor camps or executed when they resisted reforms. Teaching religion to children was also forbidden. In the 1960s, the Soviet government set up committees to oversee churches, and unauthorized religious activities could be punished by up to five years in labor camps.

With Gorbachev's reforms, religion has been practiced more openly in Russia. The constitution of the Russian Federation guarantees freedom of religion and the separation of church and state. However, Russian Orthodoxy enjoys a privileged status, and is legally recognized for its contributions to the country's history. Recent laws have made it possible for the government to curtail the activities of certain religious groups. In 2007, Russian police arrested Baptists attending a religious event. The police told them that the Baptist community was a "harmful sect."

Some of the most severe human rights violations of the Soviet Union have left scars on communities in Russia, Ukraine, and elsewhere. During the collectivization of the late 1920s and early 1930s, landowners and peasants were forced to give up much of their property and work on communal farms. Many were not able to produce as much grain under the new arrangement. In addition, government troops took vast portions of their crops to supply the cities. The result was a massive famine that wiped out entire villages. In order to keep the peasants from fleeing their land, the government issued passports to city-dwellers, but not to rural peasants, reducing them to serfs. This, along with the vast complex of forced-labor camps that grew under Stalin, violated numerous articles of the UDHR.

Migration

In the years following the fall of the Soviet Union, an estimated 2.5 million Russians have migrated from former Soviet states to Russia proper. Included in this number are internal migrants from Tajikistan, Azerbaijan, Uzbekistan, and

Kazakhstan. During the country's two wars with Chechnya, a number of Chechens fled the fighting and resettled in other regions of Russia. Russia also sees a small number of immigrants from North Africa and the Middle East.

ECONOMY

Overview of the Economy

Russia's domestic economy is fueled by the sale of its exploitable natural resources. These natural resources account for more than 40 percent of the national budget. In 2004 they together generated $103 billion (USD) in sales.

Economic activity is concentrated in the western portion of the country. The per capita GDP was estimated at $24,800 (USD) in 2014. The total GDP was an estimated $2.057 trillion (USD).

Russia's transition to a market economy, beginning in 1991, has been nowhere as obvious or successful as in Moscow. Moscow is an economic powerhouse, and it attracts investors from around the world despite a sometimes uncertain business climate. Textile production, construction, trade, and administration of the country's vast natural resources are also important sectors of the local economy.

An explosion in small business ownership has been one of the most significant features of privatization in the economy. Another feature has been the development of a small middle class as well as an extreme range between rich and poor.

Industry

Engineering and metalworking, two important Russian industries, produce a range of goods, from vehicles and precision tools to helicopters and defense equipment.

Labor

In 2014, Russia's unemployment rate was estimated at 4.9 percent. As of 2012 Russia's labor force was 27.8 percent in industry, 9.7 percent in agriculture, and the majority 62.5 percent in services.

Energy/Power/Natural Resource

Russia is rich in natural resources, many of which have been exploited in the western portion of the country. However, vast reserves remain, often in remote areas where the climate and distances make exploitation difficult and expensive. The most prevalent include petroleum, natural gas, coal, timber, and precious and nonferrous metals.

Russia produces the most natural gas in the world and ranks third in oil production. Its pipelines measure 140,000 kilometers (86,991 miles) for natural gas and 63,000 kilometers (54,745 miles) for crude oil and other petroleum products. Russia is estimated to have 35 percent of the world's total reserves of natural gas and oil reserves measuring eight to 11 billion tons.

Exploitation of these resources has come at a high cost. During the Soviet era, the government pursued a program of rapid industrialization that gave little regard to the environment. Many areas have thus suffered extreme ecological degradation. Soil, air and water pollution are all serious problems. Some areas have been contaminated by nuclear waste, others by chemical dumping or poor wastewater management. It is estimated that about 40 percent of Russia faces varying degrees of pollution.

Fishing

Russia has one of the largest fishing industries in the world, and its fleet works nearly every major ocean. About 25 percent of the annual catch is taken from the Atlantic and Arctic Oceans.

Forestry

The timber industry is also important for the Russian economy. Pine, larch, fir and birch are the trees most commonly processed. It is estimated that the industry has the potential to rival the oil and gas industry in terms of revenue.

Mining/Metals

Russia's vast territory contains a wide variety of minerals and metals. The country is one of the world's leading producers and exporters of mineral commodities including aluminum, coal, copper, diamond, gold, nickel, and tin.

Agriculture

Only about 10 percent of Russia's land is cultivated. Crops are grown on approximately 60 percent of this land. Various types of wheat have the highest yield, followed by barley. Potatoes are also important, both for the Russian diet and for making vodka.

Cabbages, beets, carrots, apples and tomatoes are commonly cultivated fruits and vegetables. It is also very common for Russians to grow vegetables in small kitchen gardens.

Animal Husbandry

The Russian agriculture industry underwent a prolonged period of reorganization following the decline of the Soviet Union and the dissolution of state-run collective farms. The transition to a market system negatively impacted livestock production numbers. As a result, the government has begun to make efforts to subsidize the production of cattle. In the meantime, Russia continues to import billions of dollars of dairy, meat, and livestock products.

Tourism

Russia has a vast but as yet unrealized potential for tourism. During the Soviet area, comparatively few tourists were allowed to visit Russia. In the mid-1990s, however, the industry started gaining significant ground and is growing, even though the tourist infrastructure is less developed than that of other European countries.

Tourists now number over 18.5 million annually, visiting mostly during the summer. In general they confine themselves to Western Russia. Major attractions include historic cities, towns and villages, cultural events like the ballet, and museums such as the Hermitage in St. Petersburg and the Pushkin Museum in Moscow.

Jake Gillis, Michael Aliprandini

DO YOU KNOW?

- The Russian word for "quickly" has given the word "bistro" to the French and English languages.

- The Soviet space program launched the first man into space, on April 12, 1961. The astronaut, Yuri Gagarin, made a single orbit of the earth in two hours.

- Moscow now competes with New York and London for the greatest number of resident billionaires.

Bibliography

"Insight Guides: Russia, Belarus, and Ukraine." *APA Publications*, 2009.

D. S. Mirsky. "A History of Russian Literature." New York: *Alfred A. Knopf*, 1960.

James H. Billington. "The Icon and the Axe: an Interpretive History of Russian Culture." New York: *Vintage*, 1970.

Orlando Figes. "Natasha's Dance." New York: *Metropolitan Books*, 2002.

Tamara Talbot Rice. "A Concise History of Russian Art." London: *Thames and Hudson*, 1963.

Vladimir Andrle. "A Social History of Twentieth-Century Russia." New York: *Edward Arnold*, 1994.

Works Cited

"Alexander Solzhenitsyn dies at 89." *BBC*. http://news.bbc.co.uk/2/hi/europe/7540038.stm

"Combating and Prevention of Human Trafficking." *Angel Coalition*. http://www.angelcoalition.org/epjs/e_trafficking.html

"Customs of Russia." *MSN Encarta*. http://encarta.msn.com/sidebar_631522251/Customs_of_Russia.html

"Discovering the Kremlin." *President of Russia*. http://www.kremlin.ru/eng/articles/history_04.shtml

"Khrennikov." *Classical Net*. http://www.classical.net/music/comp.lst/acc/khrennikov.php

"Moscow's Abramtsevo Artists Colony." *Moscow Info*. http://www.moscow.info/suburbs/abramtsevo.aspx

"Oleg Kulik." *Tate Modern: Live Culture*. http://www.tate.org.uk/modern/exhibitions/liveculture/olegkulik.htm

"Pledge of Allegiance and Its 'under God' Phrase." *Religious Tolerance*. http://www.religioustolerance.org/nat_pled1.htm

"Russia - Language, Culture, Customs, and Etiquette." *Kwintessential*: http://www.kwintessential.co.uk/resources/global-etiquette/russia-country-profile.html

"Russia." *MSN Encarta*. http://encarta.msn.com/encyclopedia_761569000_7/russia.html

"Russia." *U.S. Department of State*. http://www.state.gov/g/drl/rls/irf/2007/90196.htm

"Russian Law Allows Marriage at 14." *BBC*. http://news.bbc.co.uk/2/hi/europe/2378347.stm

"Six Months after Caucasus War: South Ossetia Becomes Thorn in Russia's Side." Spiegel. http://www.spiegel.de/international/world/0,1518,598311-2,00.html

"U.S. and Russia clash over Ukraine 'vote rigging,'" *Sydney Morning Herald* http://www.smh.com.au/news/World/US-and-Russia-clash-over-Ukraine-vote-rigging/2004/11/24/1101219605803.html

"Art Crime." *Suprematisme*. 1920–1927. http://web.archive.org/web/20070314055854/http://www.renewal.org.au/artcrime/pages/malevich1.html

"The State Hermitage Museum."

Alla Efimova. "Idea against Materia: On the Consumption of Post-Soviet Art." http://www.artmargins.com/content/feature/efimova1.html

Antonio Lupher. "Artists' Retreat." http://context.themoscowtimes.com/stories/2005/08/19/109.html

Brian Smith. "Common Meals in Russia." http://asiancuisine.suite101.com/article.cfm/common_meals_in_russia

Erin E. Arvedlund. "Russian TV Turns away from Crisis." *New York Times*. http://www.nytimes.com/2004/09/04/international/europe/04media.html?_r=1&scp=3&sq=russia%20media&st=cse

Grace Glueck. "Nyet to Passe Soviet Realism, Yes to Lenin as Mickey Mouse." http://query.nytimes.com/gst/fullpage.html?res=9A02E7D8173DF936A35751C1A9659C8B63&sec=&spon=&pagewanted=all

http://mnweekly.ru/local/20080724/55338788.html

http://www.bbc.com/news/world-europe-18188085

http://www.bbc.com/news/world-europe-21474931

http://www.cnn.com/2015/03/16/europe/russia-putin-crimea-nuclear/

http://www.hermitagemuseum.org/html_En/index.html

http://www.reuters.com/article/2015/02/23/us-russia-crisis-arms-rostec-idUSKBN0LR10P20150223

http://www.themoscowtimes.com/business/article/russian-defense-budget-to-hit-record-81bln-in-2015/509536.html

http://www.themoscowtimes.com/opinion/article/russian-health-care-is-dying-a-slow-death/519253.html

James Oestreich. "Suddenly Seeing More in Rachmaninoff." http://query.nytimes.com/gst/fullpage.html?res=9D02E5DD1730F931A3575AC0A9679C8B63&sec=&spon=&pagewanted=3

Matthew Chance. "Russia's Sex Slave Industry Thrives, Rights Groups Say." *CNN* http://www.cnn.com/2008/WORLD/europe/07/18/russia.prostitution/index.html

Michael R. Gordon. "Russian Media, Free of One Master, Greet Another." *New York Times*. http://query.nytimes.com/gst/fullpage.html?res=9F06E2DE1438F935A25750C0A961958260&sec=&spon=&pagewanted=1

Michael Wines. "Russia's Media Variety Survives Network's Travail." *New York Times*. http://query.nytimes.com/gst/fullpage.html?res=980DE6D91039F93BA15757C0A9679C8B63&&scp=7&sq=russia%20media&st=cse

Poebe Taplin. "Abramtsevo - Where Beauty Is Everywhere." http://mnweekly.ru/local/20081114/55356864.html

Robert Auty and Dimitri Obolensky, eds. *"An Introduction to Russian Art and Architecture."* Cambridge: *Cambridge University Press*, 1980.

Sabrina Tavernise. "Young, Russian, and Rich -- for Now at Least." *New York Times*. http://query.nytimes.com/gst/fullpage.html?res=9902E2D81F3FF93AA15754C0A9659C8B63&sec=&spon=&pagewanted=1

Seth Mydans. "SOVIET TURMOIL; Exiled Russian Writers, Free to Return, Find Visiting Is Enough." http://query.nytimes.com/gst/fullpage.html?res=9D0CE2DD123DF935A3575AC0A967958260&n=Top/Reference/Times%20Topics/Subjects/I/Immigration%20and%20Refugees

Simon Karlinsky. "The Menshivik, Bolshevik, Stalinist Feminist." 4 January 1981. *New York Times* http://query.nytimes.com/gst/fullpage.html?res=9E00E6D6163BF937A35752C0A967948260&sec=&spon=&pagewanted=1

Tom Redwood. "The Cross-Currents of New Russian Film." *Real Time Arts*. http://www.realtimearts.net/article.php?id=9174

Traditional Serbian meal – kajmak cheese, bread and meat

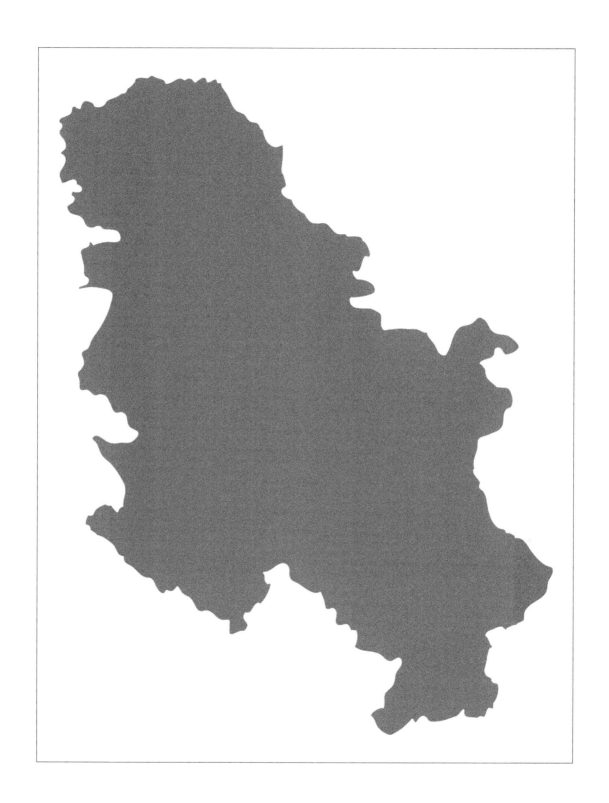

SERBIA

Introduction

The Republika Srbija, or the Republic of Serbia, is nation the landscape and people of which have experienced decades of political and cultural upheaval, often on a terrifying scale. The region was battered by war throughout the 1990s. The economic and social collapse that resulted from the conflicts caused a large-scale exodus of young Serbs to Europe, Australia and North America. This continues to have an enormous impact on the lives of people in Serbia in the early 21st century.

After years of conflict, Serbia's artistic community has become vibrant once again, and continues to contribute to art, literature, music, and film. Much of Serbia's social life takes place in public places. Coffee houses are a traditional place where Serbs entertain their friends.

Serbia's most distinctive architectural achievement is the series of small, richly decorated, medieval churches. Strategically built in remote areas, the churches are distinguished by multiple cupolas (domelike structures) and facades (exterior walls).

The national capital is Belgrade. It is called the "Gate to the Balkans" and has served as an important port on Europe's most important trade route, from the Black Sea in the east, to the North Sea and the Atlantic in the west.

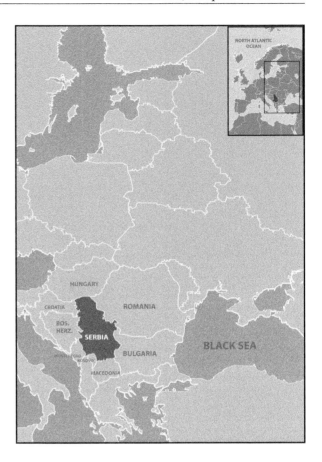

GENERAL INFORMATION

Official Language: Serbian
Population: 7,209,764 (July 2014 est.)
Currency: Dinar
Coins: One hundred dinara equal one dinar. Coins come in denominations of 1, 2, 5, 10, and 20 dinar.
Land Area: 77,474 square kilometers (29,912 square miles)
National Anthem: "Bože pravde" ("God of Justice")
Capital: Belgrade (Beograd)
Time Zone: GMT +1
Flag Description: Serbia's flag features a tricolor of Pan-Slavic colors—red (top), blue (middle), and white (bottom), emblazoned with the coat of arms of Serbia slightly left of center.

Principal Cities by Population (2012):

- Belgrade (1,350,987)
- Novi Sad (252,459)
- Niš (187,415)
- Kragujevac (150,841)
- Subotica (105,329)
- Zrenjanin (76,180)
- Čačak (73,100)
- Leskovac (64,958)
- Smederevo (64,025)

Population

Most of the population (just over 83 percent) of Serbia is of ethnic Serbian descent. Hungarians, Romany, Yugoslavs, Bosniaks, and Montenegrins are all minorities within the country. Because Serbia was rapidly industrialized during the second half of the 20th century, much of its population is urban (55.5 percent as of 2014).

Refugees make up a percentage of the nation's population, as of December 2014 there were an estimated 43,751 refugees residing in Serbia. Many refugees are from Croatia, as well as Bosnia-Herzegovina and Kosovo. Serbia has also suffered from a brain drain, with many college-educated citizens leaving the country in the 1990s. Serbia's population is aging and the country is experiencing a negative growth rate.

Languages

Serbian is the country's official language and is spoken by the majority of its citizens (88 percent). Other languages spoken in the country include Hungarian, Bosniak, and Romany.

Native People & Ethnic Groups

A majority of Serbia's native people are ethnic Serbians, making up just over 83 percent of the population. Minority groups include Hungarians (3.5 percent), Romany (2.1 percent), Bosniaks (2 percent), The refugee population is largely ethnic Serbian, while their countries of origin range from Croatia to Bosnia-Herzegovina and Kosovo.

Religions

A majority of citizens belong to the Serbian Orthodox Church (nearly 85 percent). A small number, about 5 percent, are Roman Catholic; 3.1 percent are Muslim, and 1 percent identify as Protestant.

Climate

Serbia experiences a seasonal continental climate, with cold winters and warm summers. The weather tends to be cooler and drier in the mountains, while the plains and valleys experience warmer and more humid conditions. In the southern regions, the average summer temperature reaches 22° Celsius (71° Fahrenheit), while the mountainous north has an average temperature of 18° Celsius (64° Fahrenheit).

Each year, Serbia receives 56 to 190 centimeters (22 to 75 inches) of precipitation. The late spring and autumn tend to be the rainiest times of year. During the winter, the country experiences an average of forty days of snow in the lowlands; the mountains can receive three times as much snow.

ENVIRONMENT & GEOGRAPHY

Topography

Serbia is a landlocked country in southeastern Europe. It is bordered by Bosnia-Herzegovina and Croatia in the west, Hungary in the north, Romania in the northeast, Bulgaria in the southeast, and Macedonia, Kosovo, and Montenegro in the south. Serbia is mountainous and prone to earthquakes.

Much of Serbia is mountainous, particularly in the western and central regions. Its two largest rivers are the Danube and the Sava. The highest hills in Serbia are the Fruska Gora Hills in the west, which reach an altitude of 540 meters (1,765 feet). The highest peak is in the Kopaonik Mountains, measuring 2,017 meters (6,617 feet) above sea level. Serbia's mountains fall within the Dinaric Alps and the Carpathian and Rhodope ranges. In the northeast, the Iron Gate Gorge reaches depths of 30 meters (90 feet), and is 100 kilometers (60 miles) long.

Belgrade (or Beograd, as it is called locally) is the capital of Serbia. The city is situated on the Danube River where it is joined by one of its major tributaries, the Sava.

Plants & Animals

Serbia has extensive forests of oak and beech trees. Cyprus forests can also be found in the south. While there is evidence that the region was once heavily forested, erosion, and agriculture have destroyed many of the trees.

Animals that are commonly found in Serbia include bears, deer, martens, and wild pigs. The region is also home to predators like wolves and foxes. The region's many bird species include the pygmy cormorant (Phalacrocorax pygmeus), the ferruginous duck (Aythya nyroca), the long-legged buzzard (Buteo rufinus), and the saker falcon (Falco cherrug).

Traditional female dress from central Serbia.

CUSTOMS & COURTESIES

Greetings

Formal greetings in Serbia tend to vary according to the time of day. For example, "Dobro jutro" ("Good morning"), "Dobar dan" ("Good day"), and "Dobro vece" ("Good evening") are all common phrases. Young people often use the less formal greetings of "Chao" ("Hello") and "Zdravo" ("Goodbye"). When meeting someone for the first time, people might say "Drago me je" ("I am pleased"). Greetings are often followed by asking "kako ste" ("How are you?").

A handshake, with direct eye contact, is the usual greeting between strangers and acquaintances in Serbia. Avoiding eye contact is seen as disrespectful, and men typically wait for a woman to offer her hand. If there are several people already in the room, a newcomer will shake everyone's hand, beginning with the women. If a woman or an older person comes into the room, it is polite to stand up to greet them. Introductions are typically made using honorific titles and surnames, such as "Gospodin" ("Mr"). Usually, only family or close friends use someone's first name.

Close friends and family members may kiss each other three times on alternating cheeks in greeting. (Threes are important in Serbian culture.) Unlike other cultures, where the kiss is appropriate between women, or men and women, the greeting kiss is also commonly offered between two men. However, younger generations are beginning to abandon the three-kiss greeting in favor of a single kiss on the cheek.

Gestures & Etiquette

Like many European languages, Serbian has both a formal and informal form of "you": "vi" and "ti." An individual uses the formal mode of address when speaking to anyone to whom he or she owes respect, typically an older person or a superior. A Serb would also use the formal mode when speaking to someone that she had just met or has known for a long time, but does not know well.

The Serbian three-fingered salute, or tri prsta, is made by raising the thumb, index finger, and middle finger together, as if ordering three glasses of water. While people disagree about the origin of the salute, one popular explanation is that the salute comes from the Orthodox way of making the sign of the cross with three fingers, and was used as a covert gesture of defiance during the Ottoman period. The gesture is also attributed to Prince Milos Obrenovic (1780–1860), who is said to have begun the Second Serbian Uprising against the Ottomans in 1815 by saluting a crowd of Serbian dissidents and saying "Here am I and here are you. War to the Turks." Both versions root the gesture in Serbia's long resistance against Ottoman rule.

Whatever its roots, by the 20th century, the tri prsta had become a popular, and often provocative, symbol of Serbian nationalism. During the Yugoslavian wars of the 1990s, Serbian soldiers often flashed the salute during military operations in response to the "V" gesture used by Croats, Bosniaks, and Albanians. Today, the gesture is used most often by Serbian sports fans and athletes when celebrating victory, particularly in international competitions. Serbian politicians also make the gesture at political rallies.

Eating/Meals

Serbs typically have a light breakfast, often no more than a cup of Turkish coffee. Serbs eat the main meal of the day in the afternoon at the end of the workday (which typically runs from 8:00 am to 2:00 pm with no lunch break). A meal will usually include a first course of fresh bread and smoked meat, cheese, or a savory spread, followed by a meat dish and a salad of pickled vegetables. Meals may traditionally begin with a glass of slivovica (plum brandy) or another strong liqueur, and are generally accompanied by a local wine. Dinner is usually a lighter meal eaten in the evening.

Turkish coffee is an important part of everyday life in Serbia. Not only is it served at the end of most meals, but a stop at local coffee house for a Turkska kafa with a friend or co-worker is often considered a common part of the workday. Each cup of coffee is brewed individually by boiling coffee, water and sugar together in a special pot with a long handle. The final result is very strong, with a thick layer of grounds in the bottom of the cup.

Visiting

Much of Serbia's social life takes place in public places. Coffee houses are a traditional place where Serbs entertain their friends. In addition, many Serbs enjoy the custom of public socializing known as korzo, named after the pedestrian street that runs through the center of most Serbian towns. After dinner in the warm weather, the main street of a town is traditionally closed to traffic and people stroll along the street, greeting friends and neighbors.

In Serbia, hospitality is taken seriously. When invited to a Serbian home for the first time, it is customary to bring a small gift, such as flowers, chocolates, or a bottle of wine. The host generally opens such gifts right away. A guest in a Serbian home will always be offered something to drink. When offered something to eat or drink, one should always accept. In more traditional homes, a guest will be offered slatko, literarily "something sweet." The host will bring out a tray with a small glass of water and a spoon for each guest and a bowl of homemade fruit preserves or honey. When each guest is offered the bowl, he eats a spoonful of the sweet, drinks some of the water, and then puts the used spoon in the glass.

Additionally, it is a special honor to be invited to join a family for its annual celebration of the family's patron saint, known as the slava. When dining out, the host expects to pay the bill and will often do so away from the table to avoid protests. Dividing a bill so that each person can pay his own share is unheard of.

LIFESTYLE

Family

Family ties in Serbia are traditionally very close. In fact, the Serbian language has no word for cousin, and these family members are traditionally referred to as sisters and brothers. The traditional family unit in Serbia was the zadruga, an extended family made up of a man, his wife, and the families of their married sons. When the father died, the household would be divided. In some cases, this meant disassembling the house and dividing the building materials among the sons. Today, most rural Serbs still live in extended family households. Even in cities, it is common to find parents, their adult children, and grandchildren living in one household. Retired grandparents often take care of their grandchildren while their parents work.

Each extended family also has its own patron saint, passed down from father to son. Families come together each year to celebrate the patron saint's day in a ritual called slava, which means "praise." The entire family returns to the home of the male head of the family for a time of feasting and thanksgiving, centered on a ritual in which a priest lights a candle and breaks special bread called kolac. The family then says prayers over a dish of koljvo, a preparation of sweetened cracked wheat that is served in memory of the dead.

Housing

In Serbia's cities, most people live in older single-family brick homes or small apartments in high-rise buildings. Children typically share a bedroom and kitchens are too small to eat in. In smaller towns and rural areas, people build and own their own homes. Homes often take many years to complete because they are generally built in stages. Traditionally, homes were built of brick and stucco with tile roofs and wooden balconies. Today, concrete and brick are the preferred building materials. People in rural areas still use coal and wood stoves to heat their homes, though electric heaters are becoming more common.

Housing in the early 21st century is a major issue in Serbia, especially for young people in urban areas. Between 350,000 and 800,000 refugees arrived in Serbia as a result of the military conflicts with Croatia and Bosnia-Herzegovina between 1991 and 1995 and the Kosovo War in 1999. During the same period, Serbian cities were damaged by North American Treaty Organization (NATO) bombing in 1999, leaving thousands homeless. After the conflicts ended, many of the Serbian refugees from other regions chose to stay in Serbia, putting additional pressure on an already tight housing market.

Food

Serbian cuisine combines the dishes and flavors of Central Europe with those of Turkey. A typical meal will start with fresh bread and kajmak, a fresh cheese that tastes like a blend of butter and cream cheese. Other popular first courses include smoked meats such as ham or uzicki prsut, a hard smoked beef similar to beef jerky; pihtije, jellied pork or duck flavored with garlic; and ajvar, a spread made from eggplant and peppers.

Most meals center around meat, often grilled pork, lamb or veal. Some popular meat dishes include spicy grilled patties made from a combination of beef, pork and lamb (pljeskavica), pork or veal shish kebobs with peppers and onions, and stews similar to Hungarian goulash. Serbs also make a number of dishes that combine meat with vegetables, including stuffed cabbage rolls, roast meat with sauerkraut, zucchini stuffed with meat and rice, and moussaka, a baked dish of ground meat, eggplant and potatoes.

Freshwater fish, particularly trout and carp, are popular in the northern part of Serbia. One common dish is a fish stew made with a great deal of paprika. Both sweet and hot peppers are used in many dishes in Serbia. They are stuffed, roasted, pickled, or sliced fresh into a salad with tomatoes and onions. Dried peppers are ground into paprika, a spice that is widely used in Serbian cooking.

Other Serbian specialties include proja, a cornbread stuffed with kajmak cheese and ham; gibanica, an egg and cheese strudel; djuvec, a tomato based vegetable stew; burek, a flaky pastry filled with cheese, spinach, or meat and often served with freshly made yogurt; and zito, a sweet creamed wheat porridge flavored with nuts and raisins and served with whipped cream as a dessert.

Life's Milestones

In Serbia, godparents (kumovi) play an important role in both baptisms and weddings and become valuable members of the family. Families are often linked by relationships between godparents and godchildren over several generations. In addition to sponsoring a child at his baptism, godparents are traditionally responsible for choosing the child's name, cutting the umbilical cord, and giving a child their first haircut. They are also responsible for the child if something happens to the parents and often provide childcare if no member of the extended family is available. In an Orthodox wedding, kumovi traditionally guaranteed that there were no impediments to the marriage. Today, they serve as the two witnesses required by law and sign the marriage certificate.

Funerals are traditionally held the day after someone dies. Tables are set up at the burial site and a lavish meal of salads and roasted meats is served to the mourners. Similar feasts are held forty days, six months and one year later. The gravestone, which typically includes photographs as well as an inscription, is placed on the grave at the one-year anniversary feast.

CULTURAL HISTORY

Art

Early Serbian art was mostly religious in nature. Medieval Serbian artists decorated the interior surfaces of their monasteries and churches with frescoes (paintings made directly on fresh plaster) that combined Byzantine and Romanesque elements to create a uniquely Serbian style. The Serbian frescoes used the iconography of earlier Byzantine mosaics, but the human figures in the paintings are more physical and their faces are individual enough to suggest character. The paintings also portray a wider choice of subject matter, including lives of the saints and Serbian royalty and biblical stories.

During the Ottoman period, Western-style painting diminished. With the creation of an independent Serbian kingdom in the 19th century, Serbian painting was strongly influenced by European artistic movements, as filtered first through Germany and Austria, and later through the Soviet Union. The Yugoslavian naïve art movement, which used a folk-art style and techniques, gained an international reputation in the 20th century. Begun in the 1930s by a colony of Croatian peasant-painters, the style was adopted by artists throughout Yugoslavia and remained popular through the 1960s. Serbian artists such as Janko Brasic (1906–1994), Miloslav Jovanovic (1935–), and Dusan Jevtovic (1925–2011) became known for their paintings of Serbian life and folklore.

Architecture

Serbia's most distinctive architectural achievement is the series of small, richly decorated, monastic churches built during the reign of the Nemanjic kings. These kings ruled medieval Serbia from the late 12th through the early 15th century. Strategically built in remote areas by a dynasty that was constantly threatened by Hungary, the Hapsburgs and the Ottoman Empire, the churches are distinguished by multiple cupolas (domelike structures) and facades (exterior walls) striped with alternating rows of colored brickwork and polished stone.

Like most churches in the Orthodox tradition, Serbian churches are built around a central worship area called a naos, generally topped by a dome symbolizing heaven. The central part of the church is separated from the area where the clergy perform the service by the iconostasis, a tall wooden screen decorated with elaborate carving and icons. With the arrival of the Ottomans in the 15th century, many of these monasteries were destroyed or converted into mosques. The Patrijarsija Monastery in Pec remained an active Serbian Orthodox church under the Ottomans, becoming a focus point for Serbian ethnic identity.

Drama

Serbian films began to attract an international audience in the 1980s, just as Yugoslavia was beginning to dissolve. A number of younger directors produced award-winning films that explored the impact of war on ordinary people and the possibility of friendship across ethnic lines. Some, such as Zoran Masirevic's *Granica* ("The Border," 1990,) directed by Zoran Maŝirević (1960–), used events from the Nazi occupation of Yugoslavia during World War II to illustrate contemporary issues. Others, such as Srdjan Dragojevic's (1963–) *Pretty Villages, Pretty Flames* (1996), dealt directly with questions raised by the Yugoslavian wars of the 1990s.

The most influential of this generation of Serbian film directors is Bosnian-born Emir Kusturica (1954–), whose work draws comparisons to both surrealism and absurdist humor. He is best known for *The Time of the Gypsies* (1989), a film about Serbia's Roma peoples, and the controversial *Underground* (1995), a black-comedy history of Yugoslavia from the beginning of World War II to the conflicts of the 1990s.

Music

Serbia enjoys a diverse folk music tradition that combines influences from Hungary, Turkey, and Serbia's Roma population with the music of other regions of the former Yugoslavia. The music uses a variety of instruments, including the accordion, a one-stringed fiddle known as the gusle, a wooden shepherd's flute, and the gadje and the caraba (bagpipes made from goatskin). During the Yugoslavian period, Serbs also adopted the tamburica, a Croatian instrument similar to the mandolin. Unlike Croatians, who often group the instrument into tamburica orchestras, the Serbs combine the instrument with a violin and an accordion to play fast-paced Roma-style music.

Possibly the most typically Serbian form of folk music is blehmuzika, brass trumpet music with roots in Ottoman military bands and Roma folk music. Even the smallest town has a three- or four-piece band of amateur musicians that plays at weddings and other celebrations. Blehmuzika gained an international audience when the Boban Markovic Orkestar provided the soundtrack to Serbian director Emir Kusturica's (1954–) award-winning films *Time of the Gypsies* (1988) and *Underground* (1995).

In the 1990s, during the regime of President Slobodan Milošević (1941–2006), popular music became a political battleground. The fight was between the officially sanctioned alternative folk music known as "turbo-folk" and the international rock popularized by the independent radio station Radio B92. Popular Serbian singer Rambo Amadeus (1963–) coined the term "turbo-folk" in the late 1980s to describe a style of music that combined electronic rock instrumentation with traditional folk music. In the 1990s, turbo-folk's driving rhythms and nationalist lyrics became associated with the gangster culture that pervaded Serbia under Milosevic. The best-known turbo-folk artist was Svetlana Ražnatović (1973–), known to her fans simply as Ceca. Ceca came to symbolize the relationship between turbo-folk and aggressive Serbian nationalism when she married the Serbian paramilitary leader Jeljko "Arkan" Raznjatovic (1952–2000) in 1995 in a ceremony that was broadcast live on Serbian national television.

The nationalist rhetoric of turbo-folk was challenged by the international mix of grunge, punk, and techno rock played by Radio B92. The Serbian Communist Party opened B92 in May 1989 as a temporary student radio station. After its officially sanctioned two weeks of operation were over, Radio B92 stayed on the air, broadcasting an unusual mix of music, radical talk radio, and independent news reporting. The station's motto was "Don't trust anyone, not even us." In 1993, B92 formed the Association of Independent Electronic Media (ANEM) with seven other Serbian radio stations and began to expand its operations to include publishing and CD production. The station opened Belgrade's first Internet service provider, Opennet, and an indie cultural center, Cinema Rex.

Literature

Serbia has a long-standing oral tradition of epic poetry, celebrating events beginning with the Serbian defeat by the Ottomans at the famous Field of Blackbirds (Kosovo Field) in 1389 and continuing through the resistance movement in World War II. The poems were traditionally recited to the accompaniment of the one-stringed fiddle called the gusle. Performers called guslari still recited these poems in rural Serbia as late as the 1960s. The poems are generally heroic in nature, dealing with historic battles, Serbian kings, uprisings against the Ottomans, and questions of Serbian nationality. The most famous are the so-called "Kosovo cycle," a series of poems centered on the defeat at Kosovo, which became a defining element in Serbia's political mythology.

In the early 19th century, Serbian philologist Vuk Stefanovic Karadzic (1787–1864) collected many of these poems and published them. (Karadzic also wrote the first Serbian dictionary and created the modern Serbian alphabet.) The popularity of Karadzic's collection inspired the development of a Serbian literary tradition and the appearance of a new generation of poets. The most notable of these were Bishop Petar Petrovic Njegos (1813–1851) and Jovan Jovanovic Zmaj (1833–1904).

After World War II, Serbian novelists and poets began to draw on the themes, images, and poetic style found in the traditional Serbian folk epics. The first of these writers to reach an international audience was Bosnian-born novelist Ivo Andric (1892–1975). He won the Nobel Prize in Literature in 1961, the first Yugoslavian to win a Nobel Prize. It is generally agreed that his most important novel is *Bridge Over the River Drina* (1945), in which he portrayed four centuries of Bosnian history by interweaving stories, historical events, and folk tales connected to a famous bridge built by the Ottomans in the city of Visegrad. In recent years, Milorad Pavić (1929–2009), creator of the post-modern masterpiece *Dictionary of the Khazars* (1984), has become the best-known Serbian writer in international circles.

CULTURE

Arts & Entertainment

Serbia has made some important contributions to art, literature, music, and film, and boasts a vibrant artistic community. Music known as turbofolk is popular in the country's clubs; it is a mixture of traditional folk music and modern rock. Western-style rock, punk, and hip-hop music have made great inroads in Serbian culture. One well-known rock group is called Fish Soup, and Svetlana Ceca is a favorite turbofolk singer.

Serbian writers of note include Nobel Prize-winning author Ivo Andrić (1892–1975), who wrote the 1945 novel *The Bridge on the Drina*. Other recognized authors include Dobrica Ćosić (1921–2014) and Mileta Prodanovic (1959–). Famous Serbian poets include Vasko Popa (1922–1991), Jovan Ducic (1871–1943), and Desanka Maksimovic (1898–1993). Theater is also very popular in Serbia, and Serbian filmmaker Emir Kusturica has been recognized at the international Cannes Film Festival.

Favorite sports in the country include soccer, basketball, and gymnastics. Hunting and fishing are popular outdoor pastimes.

Cultural Sites & Landmarks

The archeological site at Lepenski Vir, located on the Danube in Djerdap National Park, is the oldest known Neolithic settlement in Europe, dating from between 7000 and 4600 BCE. A settled community existed at the site at a time when most people in Europe were still nomadic hunters. The site is famous for its distinctive life-size stone sculptures that appear to be fish-headed men, possibly representing a river deity or fish totem. The ruins of the Golubac Fortress stand at the entrance to Djerdap National Park. Built in the 14th century, on the same site as an earlier Roman settlement, the fortress is made up of three linked compounds guarded by nine square towers. Its position on the embankment where the Danube River narrows to form the Iron Gate Gorge allowed whoever held the fortress to control traffic on the river. Golubac was captured by the Turks in 1391 and changed hands several times before Prince Mihailo Obrenovic (1823–1868) reclaimed it for the Principality of Serbia, a newly autonomous province of the Ottoman Empire in 1867.

The Studenica Monastery complex is a magnificent example of Serbian church architecture, and one of the holiest places in the Serbian Orthodox religion. It was begun in the late 12th century by King Stefan Nemanja (1109–1199), the founder of the Nemanjic dynasty, who was later canonized as St. Simeon, the first Serbian saint. The largest and richest of the Serbian Orthodox monasteries, Studenica was originally made up of nine churches within an oval walled complex, and three remain today. The exterior is built of polished marble quarried from the surrounding hills with intricately carved windows and doorways. The interior includes some of the finest examples of medieval Serbian frescoes. The complex includes the tomb of St. Simeon, and many Serbs make a pilgrimage to the monastery each year on his feast day. The monastery complex was listed as a protected World Heritage Site by the United Nations Educational, Scientific and Cultural Organization (UNESCO) in 1986.

Kalemegdan Fortress was the original center of the city of Belgrade. Strategically located above the surrounding plain, the site was first fortified by the Celts in the third century BCE, and later by the Romans. It was consistently a border post, marking the frontier in turn between Rome and the Central European barbarians, Byzantium, and finally Hapsburg Austria and Ottoman Turkey. The fortress was held at various times by both the Hapsburgs and the Ottomans. Rebuilt many times, most recently by the Austrians in the 18th century, the most impressive portions of the fortifications date from the 15th century rule of the Hungarian prince Stefan Lazarevic (1402–1427).

Libraries & Museums

The National Museum of Serbia, in Belgrade, is the nation's oldest and largest. Established in 1844, the museum houses a collection of over 400,000 archeological, numismatic (related to currency), artistic, and historic objects from Serbia and other nations. Additionally, the Museum of Natural History, established in 1895, is also in Belgrade.

The National Library of Serbia, located in Belgrade, was established in 1832 and houses a collection of 5.6 million items, including Cyrillic manuscripts, maps and prints, journals, Turkish documents, and other historical and cultural artifacts.

Holidays

In addition to celebrating Orthodox Christian holidays like Christmas and Easter, Serbia observes several national holidays. Serbia National Day is held on February 15. Constitution Day is observed throughout the nation on April 27.

May Day, a spring festival that occurs at the beginning of May and lasts for two days, often involves political rallies and speeches alongside the festivities. The holiday has also become associated with the labor movement, and labor demonstrations have taken place in Belgrade.

Youth Culture

The destruction of the Serbian economy by the conflicts of the 1990s continues to have an enormous impact on the lives of young people in Serbia. The years during and immediately following the wars saw a large-scale exodus of young Serbs to Europe, Australia and North America. Unemployment is high, with the Statistical Office of the Republic of Serbia reporting a 2010 unemployment rate of 19.2 percent—18.3 percent for men and 20.4 percent for women.

Serbian youth are treated as adults at an earlier age than is typical in North America, and enjoy a great deal of freedom at an early age. If they are not on the university track, they often enter the job market at 15 or 16 years of age. An employed 16-year-old is a legal adult, able to vote and buy tobacco and alcohol. At 18, unemployed youths become legal adults.

Youth culture in the towns and cities includes an active nightlife, sometimes fueled by a very high average consumption of coffee, tobacco, and alcohol. Smaller towns host dances at local youth cultural centers that are a holdover from the youth organizations of the communist period. There is an active club culture in the cities. Belgrade, in particular, is known for the floating raft nightclubs called splavovi and underground clubs that move frequently and operate solely by word of mouth.

SOCIETY

Transporation

Historically, the Danube and its tributaries made Serbia a transportation hub between Eastern and Western Europe. However, the country's role in European trade has declined since the 1990s.

Intercity buses are the most common means of travel within Serbia. Buses run frequently between towns, and Belgrade is a travel hub for buses to most parts of the country. Trains are an alternative for some locations, but the railway network has deteriorated over the last two decades, in large part as a result of damage caused by NATO bombings. Trains run less often than buses and, with the exception of international express services, take two to three times longer than buses on similar routes.

Car ownership remains a luxury, but public transportation is good in urban areas. Most cities have extensive local bus lines, with additional tram and trolley bus service in Belgrade. Taxis are commonly available and inexpensive. Traffic in Serbia travels on the right side of the road.

Transportation Infrastructure

Serbia enjoys a unique advantage in terms of location, as the Morava Valley stands at the crossroads of Europe and Greece and the Anatolian peninsula, avoiding cross-mountain transport.

Much of Serbia's transportation infrastructure, including major highways and river ports, was damaged during war and is still being rebuilt. In addition, Serbia lost its ports on the Adriatic when Montenegro invoked its constitutional right to secede from the Federal Republic of Yugoslavia (FRY) in 2006.

In 2010, the Serbian government announced that the proceeds from the government's sale of Telekom Srbija would be directed towards infrastructure spending, specifically, in the construction of main thoroughfares and transversal roads across the country.

Media & Communications

Like other parts of the infrastructure, the country's telecommunication system was damaged by the NATO bombing and has been slow to rebuild. Fewer people have telephones in Serbia than in surrounding countries, though the number of wireless users is growing rapidly. However, good quality service is limited to urban areas. As of 2013, an estimated 51.5 of the population were Internet users.

Due to an active program of privatization, much of Serbia's media is now privately owned or operated jointly by the government and private investors. The largest and most influential daily newspapers in Serbia are *Politika*, *Danas*, and *Vecernje Novosti*, all of which are privately owned. *Blic* is another popular English-language daily.

Independent radio and television networks and stations successfully compete with Serbia's state-owned broadcasting service, RTS and RTS-Radio. The owners of the two most widely watched independent television stations, TV Pink and the former BKTV, had ties to the Milošević regime. Both stations were accused of broadcasting programs that promoted a culture of intolerance. TVB92 is an offshoot of the radio station Radio B92, which earned a reputation for journalistic integrity for its opposition to the Milošević regime.

The Serbian Communist Party opened B92 in May 1989 as a temporary student radio station. After its officially sanctioned two weeks of operation were over, Radio B92 stayed on the air, broadcasting an unusual mix of music, radical talk radio, and independent news reporting. The station's motto was "Don't trust anyone, not even us." In 1993, B92 formed the Association of Independent Electronic Media (ANEM) with seven other Serbian radio stations and began to expand its operations to include publishing and CD production. The station opened Belgrade's first Internet service provider, Opennet, and an indie cultural center, Cinema Rex.

Radio B92 was shut down four times between 1991 and 2000 for encouraging demonstrations against the Milošević regime. When the station was shut down for the third time in April 1999, Radio B92 switched its news broadcasts to the Internet, attracting over one million hits to its website every day. Shut down for the fourth time in May 2000, the station went underground, moving its premises daily and transmitting its radio and television broadcasts from other ANEM stations, as well as stations over the border in Bosnia and Romania. Other stations downloaded Radio B92's broadcasts from the Internet and re-broadcast them worldwide. During this period, the station also promoted two concert tours in Serbia that encouraged people to vote in the 2000 elections.

Today, Radio B92 is the most prominent member of ANEM, which includes 37 radio stations, 19 television stations, and 60 affiliate members. The organization's primary purpose is to advocate for independent media in Serbia. One of its most high-profile programs was the "Truth, Responsibility, and Reconciliation Project," which used radio and television to acknowledge the horrors of the war years and move toward reconciliation with Serbia's neighbors. ANEM members and other independent media organizations occasionally suffer vandalism, bomb threats, and other forms of intimidation from extreme nationalist groups who are displeased with their coverage of subjects such as the status of Kosovo independence or Serbia's actions in the wars of the 1990s.

SOCIAL DEVELOPMENT

Standard of Living
Serbia ranked 77 on the 2013 United Nations Human Development Index, which measures quality of life and standard of living indicators.

Water Consumption
UNICEF (the United Nations International Children's Emergency Fund) has no statistics for access to clean water and sanitation for Serbia, but in 2010, news reports from Serbia claimed that only 35 percent of the population was connected to the sewage network. It is the government's intention to increase that percentage to 65 percent by 2019 through enacting the Law on Waters. The government indicated that local authorities would be responsible for ensuring a plan for an access to clean water and sanitation vision and strategy.

Education
Serbia has a literacy rate of about 96 percent, and students attend school for an average of ten years. Men have a higher literacy rate than women; the literacy rate is 99.1 percent among men, and 97.2 percent among women. Trends, though, indicate that females are staying in school longer—an average of 15 years in comparison to male students, who average fourteen years of education.

Instruction is carried out in the Serbian language. Ethnic groups like the Roma have been underserved in education, while refugees, children with disabilities, and displaced persons are often excluded from the educational system.

Primary education in Serbia is compulsory for children between seven and 15 years of age. Secondary education lasts for four years and can take place at a grammar, vocational, or art school. Students generally attend secondary school between the ages of fifteen and nineteen, and receive a certificate upon graduation. The Ministers of Education supervise school curricula in conjunction with the country's Education Councils.

Students may continue on to higher education, and pursue either a university or non-university program. There are more than six universities in Serbia, including the University of Belgrade and the University in Nis.

Women's Rights
The Serbian constitution guarantees women equal rights under the law, but the laws regarding equality are seldom enforced. Groups that monitor women's rights feel that Serbian women have actually lost ground in terms of equality since the dissolution of the former Yugoslavia, largely

because of the effects of the economic disruptions of the war years. Roma women, who face both ethnic and gender discrimination, are particularly vulnerable.

The traditional division of labor in Serbia was "men on the outside and women on the inside." As the country grew more urbanized in the 20th century, women began to take over the agricultural work as the men in the family found more lucrative factory jobs. Today, women continue to be responsible for traditional household tasks and childcare even though they make up 43.79 (2013 estimate) percent of the work force.

Discrimination in the job market is almost universal. Although Serbian law requires equal pay for equal work, in practice women earn between 28 and 40 percent less than their male counterparts. More than half the university graduates in Serbia are women, but they do not have the same job opportunities as men and seldom hold senior management positions in a company. In addition, women are legally forbidden to do work that is physically demanding or dangerous. For the most part, women work in civil service, primary education, social welfare, and industries that can be seen as an extension of their traditional domestic roles, such as the textile and food industries. A growing number of women are nurses, but few are doctors. Due to high unemployment rates, many women work in the informal economy as maids, housekeepers and childcare workers. However, women are represented in the Serbian parliament, as well as in the legal profession.

Domestic abuse is common in Serbia. Women's rights groups estimate that roughly, one-third of Serbia women are victims of physical violence and half suffer psychological abuse. The World Health Organization (WHO) reports that in many cases women do not report abuse because they view it as normal behavior. Cases of domestic violence are also not reported because women remain financially dependent on their husbands and cannot count on support from their families. Both public and private support services for women who are victims

of domestic abuse are very limited. Reports of domestic violence, a crime in Serbia only since 2002, have climbed considerably in recent years. Figures compiled by a network of social care centers showed that reported cases stood at 9,325 in 2012, as compared to 3,441 in 2006. Police records showed criminal complaints at 2,730 in the first nine months of 2013, compared to 317 for all of 2002.

Serbia also remains a source, transit, and destination country for human trafficking. In 2013, the government initiated prosecutions in 51 trafficking cases under Article 388 (compared with 45 cases in 2012).

Health Care

Since gaining independence, Serbia has attempted to reform its health system. The disorder and economic collapse of the 1990s, coupled with an outdated socialist health care system, created public health challenges. One area of focus is the health of children and women, including the need for better vaccination programs and early childhood care. The country has successfully eradicated polio.

In the early 21st century, breast and cervical cancer were identified as the first and second leading causes of death among women in Serbia. (Contrast this with the U.S. where cervical cancer is the seventh leading cause of death among women.) Early detection has been highlighted as the underlying problem. The Save a Life program, established through USAID, is an effort to raise awareness among Serbian women about medical screening for these conditions. In 2010, the Serbian government developed a national action plan aimed at women's health. Among the government's initiatives was a plan to increase the acquisition of the appropriate medical screening equipment and target funds for the accompanying medical training.

In addition to improving primary care, the nation is also striving to restructure its hospitals and human resources system. In Serbia, the Ministry of Health oversees public health and administers the Serbian Health Insurance Fund.

GOVERNMENT

Structure

The Republic of Serbia (since 2006) has been a nation in transition. It moved from the Socialist Federal Republic of Yugoslavia (1990–1992) to the Federal Republic of Yugoslavia (1992–2003) to the State union of Serbia and Montenegro (2003–2006), to its current status as an independent republic. Along the way, it endured the Yugoslav and Kosovo Wars, the brutal leadership of former President Slobodan Milošević, the declaration of independence of Montenegro, and the declaration of Kosovo's independence in 2008. As of 2010, Serbia does not recognize Kosovo's independence; instead, Kosovo is regarded as a United Nations-governed entity within the borders of the Serbian republic.

The Republic of Serbia established its constitution in 2006. Among its provisions, it grants autonomy to northern province of Vojvodina, which has its own parliament, government, and economy.

The country's president is chief of state, while the prime minister is head of government and is elected by the National Assembly. The Republican Ministries act as the cabinet. Serbia's legislative branch consists of a National Assembly of 250 members, elected every four years.

Political Parties

Parliamentary democracies often have a large number of political parties, which have a tendency to shift in terms of political platform and their alliance with other parties sharing common interests. Often, parliamentary systems are ruled by coalitions of two or more parties that unite to form a majority coalition. These coalitions differ in nature, with some coalitions having a lasting strength and others failing to govern at all. Additionally, it is not unusual for parties to dissolve because of personality conflicts within the organization. One coalition/party dominated the 2014 general election: the SNS-led Coalition with 48.4 percent of the vote. The SNS-led Coalition includes the Serbian Progressive Party or SNS,

Social Democratic Party of Serbia (SDPS), New Serbia (NS), Movement of Socialists (PS), and Serbian Renewal Movement (SPO).

Local Government

Local government in Serbia is complicated by the status of two provinces—Vojvodina and Kosovo. Vojvodina is autonomous—politically and economically; Kosovo is autonomous by its own declaration, and because of its UN administration. While the Republic of Serbia has sanctioned Vojvodina's status, it does not acknowledge Kosovo's independence. Nevertheless, official government units have been established for the entire nation (including Vojvodina and Kosovo)—with 150 municipalities and 24 cities as the local forms of self-government. Some cities and municipalities are joined as districts, but there is no district level government, only administration. There are two districts in the republic.

Judicial System

Two systems, the courts of general jurisdiction, which include municipal, district, appellate courts, as well as the Supreme Court of Cassation and the courts of special jurisdiction, including commercial courts, the High Commercial Court, the High Magistrates Court, and the Administrative Court, characterize the Republic of Serbia's judicial system.

Taxation

The Serbian government levies personal and corporate income, capital gains, royalties, and property taxes, as well as payroll contributions towards social security.

Armed Forces

The Serbian Armed Forces comprises the Land Forces Command (with a river force on the Danube), Air, and Defense Forces.

Foreign Policy

Serbia's most pressing foreign policy issue in the early 21st century is resolution of the status of the province of Kosovo, which many

Serbians consider the historic and symbolic heart of Serbia. In 1997, the Kosovo Liberation Army (KLA), supported by most of the ethnic Albanian majority, rebelled against Serbian rule. Milošević sent in Serbian troops to quell the uprising, and an estimated 880,000 ethnic Albanian refugees fled to nearby nations with reports of atrocities and forced expulsions by the Serbs. After failing to bring Serbia to peace talks with the KLA, NATO began air strikes against Serbia in March 1999. A United Nations (UN) sponsored peace agreement was signed in June 1999. Since then, the region has been administered by the UN.

In February 2008, the Kosovo parliament declared independence from Serbia. The United States (U.S.) government recognized Kosovo an independent nation the following day. By the end of 2008, more than fifty nations recognized Kosovo's independence. Serbia, backed by Russia and China, continues to denounce the declaration as illegal. At Serbia's request, the UN passed a resolution in October 2008, requesting the International Court of Justice (ICJ) to review the question of whether Kosovo's declaration of independence is legitimate. In July of 2010, the ICJ ruled that Kosovo's declaration of independence did not violate international law. Serbian president Boris Tadić stated that Serbia would never acknowledge Kosovo's declaration and the republic continues to seek talks within the UN over Kosovo's status.

The Yugoslavian wars of the 1990s and the status of Kosovo have shaped Serbia's relationships with other countries. Serbia, then the dominant member of FRY, lost its seat in the UN in 1992 as a result of its attempts to consolidate ethnic Serbs throughout the Balkan area by means of force. When the International Criminal Tribunal for the Former Yugoslavia (ICTY) was formed in 1993, Serbia initially refused to cooperate in the arrest of indicted war criminals, further damaging its relationships with the international community. In 1999, the US and most European countries broke off relations with Serbia and withdrew their embassies just before the NATO bombing campaign began.

After the fall of Milošević in October 2000, most foreign countries, including the US, re-opened their embassies in Belgrade. Serbia regained its seat in the UN and became an active participant in international organizations such as the International Monetary Fund (IMF), the Organization for Security and Cooperation in Europe (OSCE), and the World Bank. In 2002, Serbia began to cooperate in a sporadic way with the ICTY, extraditing a number of indicted war criminals for trial, including Milošević.

In 2005, the EU began talks with Serbia regarding a stabilization and association agreement with Serbia. The talks have been suspended and resumed several times due to Serbia's repeated failure to cooperate with ICTY. (The ICTY wants the extradition of Serbian war criminals.) In 2009, Serbia officially applied for membership with the EU, with the goal of accession in 2015. Serbia has asked that its relationship with Kosovo be kept out of EU accession talks.

Human Rights Profile

International human rights law insists that states respect civil and political rights, and promote an individual's economic, social, and cultural rights. The United Nations Universal Declaration on Human Rights (UDHR) is recognized as the standard for international human rights. Its authors sought the counsel of the world's great thinkers, philosophers, and religious leaders, and were careful to create a document that reflects the core values shared by every world culture. (To read this document or view the articles relating to cultural human rights visit http://www.un.org/en/documents/udhr/.)

The Serbian constitution generally upholds Article 2 of the UDHR, guaranteeing equal rights regardless of race, gender, disability, language or social status. Nonetheless, Serbia has a history of discrimination and violence against its ethnic minorities. Reports of ethnic cleansing and genocide directed against the Albanian majority in Kosovo led to the NATO bombing of Serbia in 1999. According to the CIA *World Factbook* (2011 estimate), 83.3 percent of the population, excluding Kosovo, is Serbian. Minority populations continue to experience degrees of discrimination by the Serbian state and occasional abuse at the hands of nationalist Serbs. The Roma, in particular, are the targets of police violence, physical and verbal abuse, and economic discrimination.

The Serbian government generally recognizes the right to freedom of religion, as defined in Article 18 of the DHR. However, the Serbian Orthodox Church does receive some preferential treatment, and religious minorities suffer occasional hate crimes, mostly in the form of vandalism. The 2006 law on religions has raised concerns about religious and ethnic discrimination among minority groups. There is no established church in Serbia, but the 2006 law identified seven traditional Serbian religious communities: Serbian Orthodoxy, Islam, Roman Catholicism, the Slovak Evangelical Church, Judaism, the Reform Christian Church, and the Evangelical Christian Church. Other religious groups, many of which were previously recognized, are required to register for recognition as a practicing religious group. Registration has proved difficult and confusing and non-recognition threatens the ability of a group to openly practice its religion through discriminatory tax and property laws.

The freedom of opinion and expression called for in Article 19 of the UDHR is a relatively new concept in Serbia. The press was an official mouthpiece of the government in both the former Yugoslavia and under the Milošević regime. Since the fall of Milošević in the 2000 elections, the Serbian government has relaxed its control on the media, though it retains the power to revoke broadcasting licenses without notice or appeal. The state-run news agency, Tanjug, is still in place, but the media is mostly independent and privately owned. State-funded radio and television broadcasters are being privatized at the national, regional and local levels.

Migration

Serbia's migration rate stands at zero per 1,000 residents in 2014. In a *Bloomberg Businessweek* article of 2010, the magazine reported that many of the nation's young people planned to leave the country for opportunities elsewhere. The loss of younger populations has a direct impact on government revenues, pension systems, and other social development issues.

ECONOMY

Overview of the Economy

Serbia faced serious economic problems beginning in 1998. These problems were due in part to high inflation, economic sanctions, and war. The country also faced difficulties in privatizing companies that had been socially owned during the years of communism. Because of the global financial crisis that began in 2008, Serbia experienced a reduction in both manufacturing and exports to Western Europe; in 2009, the economy contracted by 3 percent. The country's gross domestic product (GDP) was $89.59 billion (USD) in 2014. The GDP per capita was $12,500 (USD).

Industry

Serbia is a highly industrialized country. Industry brings in 15.6 percent of Serbia's GDP, while services account for almost a third of GDP. Belgrade is the largest industrial center in Serbia.

Goods that are manufactured in the country include automobiles, automobile parts, and electronic equipment. Iron and steel, as well as textiles, are also produced in the country.

Serbia's most important trading partners are Russia, Italy, and Germany.

Labor

Serbia's labor force numbers 2.818 million people as of 2014. Unemployment in 2014 was high, measuring 17.6 percent. The majority of the country's workers are employed in the services sector (almost 56 percent), 21.9 percent of working Serbians are employed in agriculture and 215.6 percent are involved in industry, while the majority (62.5 percent) work in the services sector.

Energy/Power/Natural Resources

Among Serbia's resources are coal, lead, zinc, nickel, gold, pyrite, and chrome. Copper and iron ore are found there in great quantities. Coal and hydroelectric dams are the country's primary energy sources. Oil and natural gas have been discovered in the country, but that industry is in the development phase. In 2008, Gazprom, the world's (and Russia's) largest gas extractor, bought Serbia's largest oil and gas producer, NIS. Gazprom agreed to construct the South Stream gas pipeline through Serbia, giving the government of Serbia a 49 percent ownership stake and revenues from transit fees. **Serbia** has extensive air and water pollution in urban areas.

Forestry

Twenty-nine percent of the area of Serbia is covered by forests, with the state controlling almost 40 percent of those forests. Because of Serbia's geographic position, it is in a position to avail itself of the transport corridors to Western Europe and Asia Minor. The lowlands of Vojvodina and the mountains in central Serbia have been identified as major forestry areas and the country's has been identified as a source of both coniferous and deciduous species. Sawn wood and furniture products are primarily made from beech, poplar, and conifers.

Local markets have been continually strong, and the furniture industry in Serbia is well respected. Forestry makes up about 1.4 percent of the country's GDP and contributes to about 3.63 percent of its industrial output.

Mining/Metals

Serbia's mineral deposits are not abundant, but the country does produce copper ore, refined copper, pig iron, crude steel, and petroleum. In 2008, mining and quarrying contributed to 1.3 percent of the nation's GDP, with 77 percent of that number attributable to coal and peat mining.

The outlook for the mining industry is modest, with increased private investment the industry's greatest hope for growth.

Agriculture

Serbia has a long tradition of farming. Agriculture accounts for 13 percent of the country's GDP. It employs less than one-fourth of the population in Serbia. Some of the major agricultural products of Serbia include cereal crops like maize and wheat, sugar beets, sunflowers, and potatoes.

Animal Husbandry

Livestock is an undeveloped industry in Serbia, contributing about 32 percent to the country's agricultural output (compared to 70 percent in other EU countries). Swine production dominated the industry, at 32 percent, followed by cattle (six percent), dairy (five percent), poultry (four percent), eggs (three percent), and sheep (1.5 percent). The heaviest decline in the livestock industry occurred between 1985 and 2005. Growth is anticipated in this sector, as the economy and infrastructure improves.

Tourism

In spite of the political turmoil and violence of the 1990s, tourism has been a growing industry in Serbia. In 2013, 922,000 tourists visited Serbia. The government has announced that it will open Lepenski Vir, a Mesolithic archeological site in the Danube River Basin, to tourists. Additional private investment, as well as global economic recovery, is expected to increase tourist traffic to the country.

Tourists frequent mountain spas such as Zlatibor and Kopaonik, cities such as Belgrade and Novi Sad, and many cruise the Danube.

Pamela Toler, Christina Healey, Sabrina
Baskey-East

DO YOU KNOW?

- Serbia is the largest exporter of raspberries in the world, accounting for one-third of world production.

- Legend has it that Attila the Hun, who died in 453, was buried under the Kalemegdan Fortress in Belgrade.

- Belgrade was the center of the worst hyperinflation in history. Between October 1993 and January 1995, prices increased by five quadrillion percent.

- In the 7,000 years since Belgrade was first inhabited, it has been conquered by forty armies and rebuilt 38 times.

Bibliography

Asne Seierstad. *With Their Backs to the World: Portraits from Serbia.* Translated by Sindre Kartvedt. London: *Virago Press*, 2005.

Branimir Anzulovic. *Heavenly Serbia: From Myth to Genocide.* New York: *New York University Press*, 1999.

Lara Zumkic. *Serbia—Culture Smart! The Essential Guide to Customs and Culture.* Lawrence Mitchell. *Serbia.* Buckinghamshire, UK: *Bradt Travel Guides*, 2013.

Robert D. Kaplan. *Balkan Ghosts: A Journey Through History.* New York: Picador, 2000 London: *Kuperard*, 2012.

Tim Judah. *The Serbs: History, Myth and the Destruction of Yugoslavia,* 3d ed. New Haven, CT: *Yale University Press*, 2010.

Vasa Mihailovich and Mikasinovich Branko, eds. *An Anthology of Serbian Literature.* Bloomington, IN: *Slavica Publishers*, 2007.

Works Cited

Andrew Baruch Wachtel. "Making A Nation, Breaking A Nation: Literature and Cultural Politics in Yugoslavia." Stanford, California. *Stanford University Press.* 1998.

"Background Notes. Serbia." *United States State Department.* http://www.state.gov/r/pa/ei/bgn/5388.htm

"BBC News Country Profile—Serbia." http://news.bbc.co.uk/2/hi/europe/country_profiles/5050584.stm

"BBC News: Timeline—Kosovo." http://news.bbc.co.uk/2/hi/europe/country_profiles/3550401.stm

"CIA World Factbook." https://www.cia.gov/library/publications/the-world-factbook/geos/ri.html

"Country Report on Human Rights Practices in Serbia." *United States State Department.* http://www.state.gov/g/drl/rls/hrrpt/2007/100583.htm

J. A. Cuddon. "The Companion guide to Yugoslavia." Englewood Cliffs, N.J. *Prentice Hall.* 1984.

Jovana Gec, "Serbia in Domestic Violence Crisis." Dec. 2013. http://news.yahoo.com/ap-enterprise-serbia-domestic-violence-crisis-111210065.html

Linda A. Bennett, ed. Encyclopedia of World Culture. Vol. 4. Europe. Boston. G.K. Hall. 1991–96

Martin Dunford. "The Rough Guide to Yugoslavia." London. Routledge & Kegan Paul. 1985.

"Serbia." 2009. *Encyclopædia Britannica Online.* 3 2009 http://search.eb.com/eb/article-255483

"Official Website of the Serbian Government." *http://www.srbija.gov.rs*

Michael A. Schuman, Nations in Transition: Serbia and Montenegro. New York. *Facts on File.* 2004.

"Serbia—Society and Culture." Petaluma, California. *World Trade Press.* 2008.

"The Statesman's Year Book Online." Ed. Barry Turner. *Palgrave.* 2008. www.statesmansyearbook.com

Saint Martin's Cathedral, Bratislaug, Slovakia

SLOVAKIA

Introduction

Slovakia (known in Slovak as Slovensko) is a country in Central Europe that was once part of the former nation of Czechoslovakia. During much of the twentieth century, the region was part of the Soviet-controlled Eastern Bloc. In 1993, Czechoslovakia was peacefully dissolved into the independent nations of Slovakia and the Czech Republic. Since independence, the country has moved toward a free-market economy and has joined the European Union (EU).

Slovakia is one of the more prosperous countries of Central Europe, with a reasonably well developed infrastructure. Since the fall of communism, tourism has increased, with visitors enjoying the scenic Carpathian Mountains and River Danube, and well-preserved historic cities such as Bratislava.

GENERAL INFORMATION

Official Language: Slovak
Population: 5,443,583 (July 2014 estimate)
Currency: Euro
Coins: Slovak Euro coins come in denominations of .01, .02, .05, .10, .20, .50, 1, and 2 Euro.
Land Area: 48,105 square kilometers (18,573 square miles)
Water Area: 930 square kilometers (359 square miles)
National Anthem: "Slovak Hymn" ("Slovenská hymna")
Capital: Bratislava
Time Zone: GMT +2

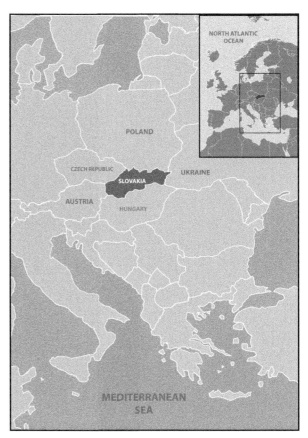

Flag Description: The flag of Slovakia features three equally sized horizontal bands of white, blue, and red, which are the pan-Slavic colors. In the vertical center (and off to the left, or hoist, horizontally) is a Slovakian coat of arms.

Population

In 2014, it was estimated that the population of Slovakia was 5.4 million. The population is largely comprised of ethnic Slovaks (approximately 80 percent of the population). Since the mid-1990s, Slovak has been the official language. There is a large Hungarian minority, representing around 8.5 percent of the population. Other sizeable minorities include Czechs, Ruthenians, Ukrainians, Russians, Germans, and Poles.

The Roma (once referred to as "Gypsies") are another minority. According to census figures, they represent two percent of population, though there are indications from local governments that the number may be higher, between

Principal Cities by Population (2012):

- Bratislava (421/218)
- Košice (233,346)
- Prešov (90,597)
- Žilina (85,528)
- Nitra (82,752)
- Banská Bystrica (79,265)
- Trnava (67,190)
- Martin (58,430)

five and six percent. The Roma face a certain amount of discrimination, and have even suffered violent attacks from far-right white supremacist groups.

Languages

The Slovak language is part of the Slavic family, and is closely related to the Czech and Polish spoken in neighboring countries. It is derived from the "Old Slavonic" language, the ancestor of all the Slavic tongues, and is written using Latin letters. The three main dialects are bounded by geography, the western, central, and eastern parts of the country. Approximately 78 (2011 est.) percent of the population, speaks Slovakian as their first language.

Native People & Ethnic Groups

During Roman times, what is now Slovakia was known as Pannonia, and was inhabited by Celtic tribes. In the fifth century, as Rome declined, Slavs began settling the region. During the ninth and tenth centuries, Slovakia was part of the Slavic realm known as known as Great Moravia.

The Hungarians or Magyars conquered the Slovaks in the 10th century and dominated the region until the establishment of Czechoslovakia after World War I. From the late 19th century until the fall of the Austro-Hungarian Empire, the Hungarians sought to "Magyarize" the Slovaks and make them speak Hungarian. During this period, the Slovaks began developing their language as a way to preserve their national identity

within the empire. The Jewish and German communities in Slovakia also date from the Middle Ages.

There are many dialects of the Romani language, but in 2008, a standardized Romani dialect was established as the language of the Slovakian Romas. Almost 10 percent of the country's population is Hungarian; Hungarians in Slovakia tend to live in the southern region of the country, along the border it shares with Hungary.

Religions

Slovakia has been largely Christian since the ninth century. Around 85 percent of the population belongs to one of the various branches of Christianity, mostly Roman Catholic (around 62 percent of the population). The once-large Jewish community suffered heavy losses in World War II; only a few thousand remain of the 100,000 Jews who once lived in Slovakia.

Climate

Slovakia has a temperate, continental climate. The country receives between 63 and 100 centimeters (24 to 40 inches) of precipitation per year, though much of this falls in the western mountains as heavy snowfall during the winter months. In much of the country, however, including the Carpathian foothills, snow rarely accumulates more than 1 meter (approximately 3 feet).

Winters are relatively mild, with average temperatures of around 3° Celsius (27° Fahrenheit). Summers are cool, though the southern and eastern parts of the country can receive temperatures as high as 20° Celsius (68° Fahrenheit).

ENVIRONMENT & GEOGRAPHY

Topography

Slovakia borders the Czech Republic to the northwest, Austria to the southwest, Hungary to the south, Ukraine to the east, and Poland to the north. Slovakia's geography is largely mountainous in the northern and central parts of the country, while the southern part is covered by lowlands, home to most of the country's farms.

The Carpathian Mountain range covers much of the western part of the country. The Tatras range, part of this chain, includes the country's highest point, the Gerlachovsky Stit, which rises 2,655 meters (8,711 feet) above sea level. Several large rivers flow through the Slovakian lowlands, including the Vah, the Hornad, and the famous Danube.

Plants & Animals

Slovakia's mountain regions are heavily forested, and are home to many large wild species, including large game such as bear. Common animal species include sizeable populations of brown bear, lynx, and wolves.

The forests are a mixture of coniferous and deciduous species. Evergreens include Norway spruce and silver fir. Deciduous varieties include maple and pine. In the lowlands, one finds mixed forests containing beech and many varieties of oak.

The country has nine national parks; many of them, such as Tatra National Park, protect mountainous areas.

CUSTOMS & COURTESIES

Greetings

As in many other languages, formal and informal levels of speech are an important part of Slovak culture. The formal greeting in Slovak is "Dobry Den" ("Good Day"), typically used when greeting business contacts and other professional colleagues. Generally, a formal greeting is also offered when meeting another person for the first time, since an informal greeting such as "Ahoj" ("Hi") would seem too forward and familiar. In addition, a formal greeting is typically used to show respect for seniority or as a general sign of courtesy.

When walking into a shop or approaching a shop attendant, Slovaks typically offer a formal greeting first, and then make their request. Failing to do so might be interpreted as rude. Eventually, a Slovak speaker may transition from formal to the informal speech with another Slovak speaker. However, it is customary that the older person first offers to "tykat" (use informal Slovak), which rarely happens. If the communication is between a man and a woman, the woman must be the one to make this offer of using informal speech.

In the countryside, it is acceptable to smile and offer a formal greeting to a passing stranger. In the city, Slovaks have a tendency to avoid direct eye contact with strangers. Additionally, strangers receive no greeting because they are neither a formal acquaintance, nor a friendly acquaintance. In addition, the sense of friendliness in Slovakia is more subdued than in other Western cultures. For example, an American who smiles a lot and seems openly friendly is often perceived as disingenuous within the context of Slovak culture.

Gestures & Etiquette

Slovak society is sensitive to obeying formalities and displaying good manners. For example, on trains or in other public settings where a Slovak wishes to sit, he or she will typically ask the person sitting in the adjoining seat whether or not the empty seat is taken, even when the answer is obvious. Further, when an elderly person boards a train, bus or other form of public transportation, it is expected that any younger Slovak offer his or her seat if no other seats are available. Additionally, Slovaks also never rest their feet in an opposite seat, as this would be considered rude. Lastly, showing good manners also entails being helpful with disabled people, pregnant women and small children.

Slovaks tend to speak softly in public, so as not to disturb others. As such, complete silence on a train or bus is quite common, and Slovaks can become somewhat annoyed by foreigners who conduct themselves in a loud manner. However, this soft-spoken tendency among Slovaks is not typically evident in restaurants and pubs, where it is acceptable to become quite animated and loud. Furthermore, there is little social stigma attached to the consumption of alcohol in Slovakia. In fact, serving alcohol is common in most eateries. This national custom is even respected by international chains such as McDonald's, which serves beer to its customers.

Eating/Meals

On weekdays, many of Slovakia's workers rise early—typically at five or six o'clock—to eat a quick, light breakfast. This often consists of bread, butter and jam, and a cup of coffee or tea. A break to eat a quick snack, typically a roll with butter or cheese, an apple or some other fruit, is commonly taken around 10 o'clock in the morning. Slovaks then have lunch sometime between twelve and two o'clock, and most small shops in Slovak towns are closed during those hours. However, with the advent of globalization, this has been gradually changing. For example, large supermarkets have replaced many of the traditional small grocers, and these new international supermarket chains are open continually.

Lunch is the largest meal of the day in Slovakia. On weekends, the entire family customarily gathers for an extended period at lunchtime. Before beginning the meal, the head of the home may say "Dobrú chuť" ("Enjoy your meal"), with the same given as a reply by everyone seated at the table. Typically, lunches start with soup, and are concluded by a dessert, such as sweet rolls or cake, and coffee. Additionally, Slovaks typically eat using a knife and a fork in the continental style (knife in the right hand, fork in the left hand), mostly because the knife is not only an instrument for cutting meat, but it is equally important for pushing the food onto the fork. Dinner is usually lighter than lunch, and often features cold meals such as open-faced sandwiches with butter, cheese, liver paste, salami or other smoked sausages.

Visiting

Slovaks are generally guarded about their private lives, and do not readily or quickly invite new acquaintances into their homes. If a guest is invited to a Slovak's home, the Slovak is certainly extending a sense of trust and friendship. However, the guest should not use informal Slovak, especially if the use of formal Slovak has been established.

When visiting someone's home, it is quite common that the visitor offers a small gift. Most often, this consists of a good bottle of wine, flowers, or perhaps some chocolates. If the host has children, the guest should bring some candy or individual small gifts. Slovaks customarily take off their shoes when they enter the home. The host might then offer a pair of slippers or house shoes to wear. Usually, the host will also offer the guest something to drink. This may include coffee, tea, mineral water, or alcoholic beverages such as beer or wine. Additionally, a shot of hard liquor such as slivovica (plum brandy), jablkovica (apple brandy), or borovička (a national specialty made from juniper berries) might be offered.

LIFESTYLE

Family

Slovak families often go back many generations in a specific town or area, and there is little migration. Under communist rule, this centuries-old tendency to remain in the same location changed somewhat. The communist government often arranged for permanent housing—usually in public housing apartments—if a person was willing to relocate to some town that needed certain occupations filled, such as teachers or factory workers. Thus, there was an increase in family migrations during the communist era.

In traditional Slovak families, men are generally less involved with child rearing, while women are expected to manage the children as well as the household. Traditionally, women did not become involved in public affairs or any form of politics, and they rarely developed personal careers. This changed significantly during the years of communism, and many women began working outside the home, though they were still expected to manage the children and household. Today, women with professional careers are quite common, and this is on the rise since the development of the market economy.

Housing

Quite often, several generations may live in the same house. The most common arrangement is that the parents live on one floor of a two-story house, while one of the children and their immediate family will reside on the second floor. However, this tradition is probably due to economic necessity rather than cultural tradition. In recent years, particularly since the promotion of the Slovak market economy, there has been an increase in housing construction in Slovakia, and many young families have been moving into their own homes.

After 40 years of communist rule as part of Czechoslovakia, most Slovak towns—including relatively small towns with populations of only several thousand inhabitants—have large areas of public housing. These areas typically surround the historical centers of larger cities, and feature a type of building known as "panelový dom," a large square apartment building made of pre-fabricated, pre-stressed concrete, but the colloquial term for these buildings, "paneláky," is much more frequently used. While these public housing projects are an unpleasant reminder of Slovakia's communist era, many middle-class Slovak families still reside in giant paneláky neighborhoods.

Food

Hungarian, Austrian, German, and Slavic cooking traditions have all influenced Slovakian cuisine, helping to create some unique Slovak dishes. The Slovaks commonly cook Hungarian dishes such as goulash. The Austrian and Germanic tradition of using large amounts of sauerkraut with pork is also well represented in Slovak cooking. For example, one national dish called zelňačka, also known as kapustnica, is a thick soup consisting of sauerkraut with paprika, pieces of Hungarian smoked sausage and sour cream. This particular soup is also called the Slovak Christmas soup, though it is prepared throughout the year.

Another favorite Slovak food is "halušky." Halušky are thick, soft noodles that are commonly added to the main meat dish, and are a standard part of the diet in other Eastern European countries such as Hungary, Poland and the Ukraine. Halušky are generally made with wheat flour that is mixed with potatoes, though the noodles may be made entirely of wheat flour or entirely of potatoes. Bryndzové halušky is a dish made of these noodles, covered with a soft cheese sauce made from sheep's milk, and topped with small pieces of fried bacon. It is considered a national dish in Slovakia.

In autumn, Slovaks have a tradition in which they feast upon baked goose. A particular type of potato pancake, called a lokša, traditionally accompanies this meal. Additionally, pečená husa a lokše (baked goose and potato cakes) is eaten at the beginning of Slovak wine season, when grapes are harvested and new wines are produced. At that time, Slovaks like to drink burciak, an early wine that is similar to a fermented cider. Burciak is yellowish-brown in color, bubbly, and actually tastes quite different from traditional wine. Every fall, Slovak villagers sell their homemade burciak from temporary roadside tables and stands.

Life's Milestones

Roman Catholicism is the dominant religion in Slovakia, and has largely influenced the culture's traditions, customs, and milestones. However, there are traditions that are unique to the Slovak culture and way of life. For example, Slovaks do not have typical "baby showers." When a Slovak mother brings her child home from the hospital, various friends and relatives visit her over the first few weeks and bring a gift for the new child. For the first few weeks following the infant's birth, it is common for the new mother to be attended to by her own mother, who runs the household and helps with the infant's care. On the day the child is born, the father traditionally gathers with all his friends for an extended celebration, commonly in a pub, where the new father buys drinks for everyone.

Slovak weddings are often civil ceremonies at the local town hall, though many couples have church weddings. After the wedding, the newly married couple traditionally has a reception for their guests at a restaurant or at their home, where they customarily receive wedding gifts. Often, the celebration lasts until morning, though many Slovak families celebrate with relatives for as long as three days. Additionally, many Slovaks are musicians, while nearly all enjoy singing traditional folk songs and dancing, so wedding parties are warm and lively events that might require some physical endurance.

CULTURAL HISTORY

Art

Folk arts and crafts have long been an important part of Slovakia's cultural heritage, and remain a popular tradition in contemporary Slovakia. While folk art includes intangible arts such as music, singing, and dance, it also includes tangible arts such as woodcarving, fabric weaving, ceramics and decorative glass making and painting, all of which are widely practiced today. All of these folk arts have been evolving throughout Slovakia's history, and have even influenced the formal arts in Slovakia.

The most widespread and popular folk art is music. Music in Slovakia has always been quite organic, arising naturally from the experiences of rural Slovakia. In addition, integral to Slovakian folk culture is dance, and each region of the country features different dances. In the Low Orava region, for example, the cepovy is an energetic dance in which the dancers' movements mimic the threshing of wheat.

Architecture

Though Slavic tribes migrated to the region of Slovakia between 400 and 500 CE, Slovakia—or the Slovak Republic as it is formally known— did not come into existence until 1993, when the country split with the Czech Republic and became an independent and sovereign nation. Historically, the Slovak tribes that settled in the region were part of various larger kingdoms and empires. As part of these larger kingdoms, the Slovaks enjoyed both political stability and an influx of cultural diversity. This diversity

influenced the architectural styles that helped build the beautiful cities of present-day Slovakia.

Architecturally, Slovakia is a crossroads between ancient cultures and empires, most notably the Byzantine and Roman empires in the east. This makes for a complicated and intertwined history. From the 11th through the 14th centuries, what is now Slovakia was part of the Kingdom of Hungary. The Ottoman Empire (which lasted until the 20th century) expanded into Hungary in the early 16th century, resulting in the partitioning of the country and the establishment of Royal Hungary. This small territory in the northwestern part of Hungary, where the Hapsburgs (the royal house of Hungary) maintained their kingdom, corresponds to what is now Slovakia. Thus, Hungarian society and history affected the architectural development of Slovakia for centuries. The prevalence of Hungarian culture in Slovakian history creates a clear difference between the Slovak and Czech traditions. The oldest buildings in larger Slovakian cities such as Bratislava look more like those found in Budapest (the capital of Hungary) than Prague (the capital of the Czech Republic).

Outside of the general Hungarian influence, there are also architectural differences according to the country's specific regions. For example, the buildings in the western part of Slovakia are more strongly influenced by the Germanic and Roman Catholic traditions of the former Austria-Hungary alliance. As a result, there are more Catholic churches in the western part of Slovakia, while the traditions of Russian Orthodoxy are more prevalent in the east. This can be seen in the ornate onion domes of orthodox churches and other large buildings.

Generally, elements of Gothic, Romanesque and Baroque architecture are widespread in Slovakia, from the medieval towns of its countryside to the urban centers, where these various architectural styles often overlap within the same building. For example, Slovakia's numerous cathedrals typically have distinct elements of Renaissance, Baroque or Art Nouveau (a decorative style prevalent at the end of the 19th century) architecture. Additionally, Slovak folk architecture—prevalent in villages, where local materials such as wood, clay, and hay were used—is uniquely superimposed upon the architecture of these periods.

Drama

Though dramatic traditions in Slovakia date back several centuries, drama has been less influential than music and dance in Slovak folk culture. Prior to Christianization, which was largely ushered in by the work of two missionary brothers (Cyril and Methodius), the earliest Slovak theatrical tradition was mostly the enactment of pagan myths. After the institutionalization of Christianity in the ninth century, the Slovak pagan dramas were transformed into religious dramas that typically related biblical stories.

Beginning in the 17th century, various theatrical troupes toured through Slovakia. German- and Italian-speaking troupes were followed by Hungarian acting companies in the 19th century. However, Czech theatre was perhaps the most influential in developing a formal Slovak or national theatre. The Slovak National Theatre opened its doors in 1920. The Slovak National Theatre supported the first professional theatre group in Slovakia, though for several years some of these actors were Czech because there was a shortage of trained Slovak actors.

Slovak film emerged in the 1920s, and was influenced by Slovak folk tradition. The best-known film from this period of Slovak cinema is a silent film called *Jánošík*, released in 1921. Juraj Jánošík was an outlaw who was sentenced to death in 1713, and is considered Slovakia's most famous folk hero, essentially equivalent to the legend of Robin Hood. The film, based on Slovak legends about his life, was the first Slovakian full-length feature film, and made Slovakia the tenth country in the world to produce a full-length film. The film's director, Slovak-American Jaroslav Siakel (1896–1997), was financed by Slovak-Americans in Chicago, while another Slovak-American wrote the screenplay.

However, the Slovak film tradition has been more influenced by Czech film. The best Slovak directors have always worked side-by-side with the best Czech directors—often in Prague, where there was a stronger film and studio industry. A good example of this is the directing duo of Ján Kadár (1918–1979), a Slovak, and Elmar Klos (1910–1993), a Czech. Kadár and Klos co-directed *The Shop on Main Street* (1965), the first Czechoslovak film to win an Academy Award (for best foreign-language film). Kadár was also a professor at the Film and TV School of the Academy of Performing Arts in Prague (FAMU), and he trained many of the directors who were behind the Czechoslovak/Czech New Wave Cinema of the 1960s. Juraj Jakubisko (1938–), an internationally recognized Slovak film director, first became known for his part in this cinematic movement of Czechoslovakia, with many other Slovak directors also strongly influenced by the movement. The modern era of cinema in Slovakia was ushered in by the establishment of the Slovak Film Institute (SFI) in 1963.

Music

The centuries-old traditions of music and dance are important parts of Slovak folk culture. In fact, before the Slavic tribes settled in what is present-day Slovakia, wandering Celtic tribes had already introduced ancient instruments and music to the region. Thus, even in contemporary society, there is a clear similarity between Celtic folk music and both Slovak and Czech folk music.

The other historical influence on Slovakian music was the church. The oldest written forms of music in Slovakia are church songs in Old Slavonic (also known as Old Church Slavonic), considered the first literary Slavic language. These religious songs, largely from the empire of Great Moravia during the ninth and early 10th centuries, evolved over time into more complex, sacred music. Moravian folk music traditions were also influential in the development of folk traditions in the Czech Republic, as well. However, the Slovak folk tradition has always been the more popular form of music throughout the centuries.

Folk music has been one of the strongest influences on the more formal or higher music forms in Slovakia. For example, in classical music, some of Slovakia's most well-known composers have incorporated folk melodies into their symphonies or other musical compositions. This is related to the emergence of an independent national classical music tradition unique to Slovakia. Classical composers began developing a Slovak classical music tradition in the 19th century. By the early 20th century, the nation had some world-class composers creating a unique Slovak style of classical music that borrowed heavily from Slovak folk music.

The tradition came to the national forefront with composers such as Frico Kafenda (1883–1963), who transcribed many folk songs into piano compositions. Other 20th-century composers who carried on this tradition include Ján Cikker (1911–1989), Gejza Dusík (1907–1988), Alexander Moyzes (1906–1984), Andrej Očenáš (1911–1995), and Eugen Suchoň (1908–1993).

Today, classical music is a permanent formal tradition in Slovakia. The country supports some world-class orchestras such as the Philharmonic Orchestra of Bratislava and Košice, the Symphonic Orchestra of Bratislava Broadcast, and the Slovak Chamber Orchestra. Although classical music still plays an important role in the national life of Slovakia, it has gradually declined as other music forms, such as jazz, rock and roll and, most recently, rap and hip-hop, have become popular among Slovak youth.

In 2005, the United Nations Educational, Scientific, and Cultural Organization (UNESCO) added a unique Slovak folk instrument called the fujara, along with its associated music, to its list of Masterpieces of the Oral and Intangible Heritage of Humanity. The fujara is also known as a "fipple flute," and was a woodwind instrument that Slovak shepherds played for centuries. Typically over five feet in length and with three finger holes, the instrument produces very low tones that imitate gurgling streams or other natural sounds.

Dance

Slovak dance has always remained closely related to Slovak folk music, with certain traditions and styles dating back centuries. Unique regional folk dances have always accompanied the various folk music traditions in various regions of Slovakia. Every year, Slovakia continues to hold hundreds of festivals where various ethnic folk ensembles perform their music and dance traditions. These traditions have also remained a popular part of youth culture. Many young Slovaks, particularly those living in rural Slovakia, are quite enthusiastic about Slovak folk music and dance traditions. Additionally, Slovak ballet has also borrowed pieces of traditional folk dance and integrated these dances into the more formal artistic ballet and modern dance forms. In fact, polka dance music has its origins in the traditions of Slovakian folk music, despite being commonly associated with the folk music traditions of neighboring Poland.

Literature

Throughout their history, the Slovak people have struggled with their sense of national identity. Their earliest literary efforts either argued for national identity and rights, or tried to establish the Slovak language as a legitimate, separate language in which to write and publish. Thus, early Slovak literature was an important part of the country's political development.

Near the end of the 17th century, Slovak writers pointed out the predominance of the Czech language (largely the norm due to its usage in the widespread Protestant Kralická Bible, the first complete version of the Bible in the Czech language). "Slovakized Czech" was used by Slovak academics for their writing, and the Slovak language was simply the vernacular or common speech, with no literary tradition. Some Slovak intellectuals began making the case for Slovak language education, and for publishing linguistic textbooks based entirely on the Slovak language. Until the early 18th century, Slovak writers were mainly concerned with transforming Slovak into a respectable, publishable language.

In 1787, Anton Bernolák (1762–1813) helped establish the West Slovak dialect as an independent literary language by codifying its vocabulary and grammatical methods. Bernolák and many other writers of his generation were members of the Societas Excolendae Linguae Slavicae (Society for the Cultivation of the Slavic Language). They created the linguistic textbook necessary to lend the language formal legitimacy. Following this standardization, a few Slovak writers began using West Slovak as a written language. An increasing number of educated Slovaks began reading the works of writers such as Juraj Fándly (1750–1811), who composed the first major literary work in the new standard, or celebrated Slovak poets such as Ján Hollý (1785–1849).

Poetry remained a dominant literary form in Slovakian culture well into the 20th century, with themes of Slovak nationalism and the realism of war and daily life prevalent. Prominent modern Slovakian writers include the poets Pavol Országh Hviezdoslav (1849–1921) and Ivan Krasko (1876–1958), and the prose writer Martin Kukučín (1860–1928), considered Slovakia's best representative of realism. In the decades following World War II, until the fall of communism in Eastern Europe in the 1990s, socialist and politically influenced literature was prevalent.

CULTURE

Cultural Sites & Landmarks

The cultural and natural significance of Slovakia is apparent in its medieval and folk architecture—prevalent in the country's castles, cathedrals and historic villages—and renowned mountainscapes. Slovakia is also home to nine national parks and seven UNESCO World Heritage Sites. Two of these sites—the Caves of Aggtelek Karst and Slovak Karst and the Primeval Beech Forests of the Carpathians—are considered trans-boundary sites since they are shared with Hungary and Ukraine, respectively. Additionally, the capital, Bratislava, is home to numerous landmarks and historic sites.

Slovaks developed some interesting techniques for using wood as the primary building material, which is at the center of Slovak folk architecture. In 2008, UNESCO listed the wooden churches of Slovakia as a collective World Heritage Site (officially designated as the Wooden Churches of the Slovak part of the Carpathian Mountain Area). The list includes two Roman Catholic churches and three Protestant and Greek Orthodox churches, all constructed between the sixteenth and eighteenth centuries. These churches were built of wood by necessity—at that time, there was a law that Greek Catholic churches could not be built of stone. They originally made no use of nails, and featured decorative wood carving techniques. Additionally, many of these wooden churches still managed to make use of traditional onion domes, albeit wooden ones. In fact, of all the countries of Europe, Slovakia has the highest density and greatest diversity of wooden churches.

Slovak folk architecture also includes the mud-brick homes of western and central Slovakia, and the wooden and log houses built in northern and eastern Slovakia. In 1993, UNESCO inscribed the village of Vlkolínec as a World Heritage Site for its traditional log houses and its preserved architecture that is characteristic of a historic central European village. Additionally, the towns of Banská Štiavnica and Bardejov were also added as World Heritage Sites for their preserved medieval and folk architecture. Banská Štiavnica was also recognized for the cultural importance of its technical monuments, namely those related to metallurgy and mining.

Slovakia is home to numerous ancient and medieval castles, though most of them now exist as ruins. One of the best-known castles is Spiš Castle, one of the largest fortified castles in Europe. The castle ruins and its surrounding villages, officially listed as Spiš Castle and its Associated Cultural Monuments, was placed on the UNESCO World Heritage List in 1993. Spiš Castle is also a good example of architectural periods and styles overlapping and blending over time. The earliest Romanesque gates and other structures of Spiš were incorporated into a later

Gothic building period. The late Gothic chapel of St. Elizabeth replaced an earlier Romanesque chapel that was destroyed at Spiš. In the sixteenth century, the Thurzo family who owned Spiš castle continued expanding the estate with a Renaissance-styled palace. After the Czaky family came into possession of the grounds in the next century, they continued expanding Spiš, and completed the east palaces in the 17th century.

Slovakia's capital, Bratislava, is home to a wealth of cultural sites and landmarks, many of which chronicle Slovak's history and path towards sovereignty. St. Martin's Cathedral, built in 1452, was the site of the coronation of Hungary's royalty. The eighteenth-century Grassalkovich Palace is now home to the president. Bratislava Castle is perhaps the most recognizable landmark in the capital. The site upon which the ancient castle sits is believed to have been inhabited as early as the Stone Age. Additionally, the capital is home to the Slovak National Museum and National Theater, as well as museums dedicated to Slovakia's Jewish, Carpathian and Hungarian culture.

Libraries & Museums

The Slovak National Museum, established in 1961, is headquartered in Bratislava and comprises eighteen museums, some of which are located in other regions of the country, such as the Ethnographic Museum in Martin. The Bojnice Museum, established in 1950, is located in a 12th-century fortress and houses collections of art, ranging from ancient to contemporary. The Balneological Museum in Piestany, established in 1931, specializes in anthropology, archeology, and balneology (science of thermal baths and spas) collections.

The Slovak National Library was established in 1975 and is based in Martin. It houses almost four million resources, approximately 9,000 of which date back to the 16th century. It also serves as the country's copyright and legal deposit.

Holidays

Slovaks celebrate the Day of the Establishment of the Slovak Republic, which commemorates the separation of Czechoslovakia into the Czech Republic and Slovakia, on January 1, which is also celebrated as New Year's Day. The Anniversary of Slovak National Uprising, which commemorates the Slovak insurgency during WWII against the Nazis, is celebrated on August 29, and Slovak Constitution Day is celebrated on September 1st. Christian holidays such as Christmas (December 25) and Easter (spring) are also celebrated in Slovakia.

Youth Culture

Slovakian youth in the early 21st century are growing up in an era of globalization that is markedly different from the experience of previous Slovak generations. Nearly all Slovak youth in cities are frequent users of the Internet. Young Slovaks are, like much of the globalized youth around the world, engaged in online gaming, chat sessions, discussion forums, and social network sites (SNS). A large number of young Slovaks regularly use these new Internet technologies for entertainment and communication, and this is causing a shift in the profile of Slovakian youth. In fact, recent studies show that there is a definite shift away from television viewing and toward interactive Internet content.

There is also a dramatic increase in the number of Slovakian youth who choose to go abroad for either employment or adventure, or both. Slovakia's membership in the EU has opened its borders and caused travel that is much more international and employment opportunities. Today, it is fairly common to meet a young Slovaks in cities such as London, where they may work for a year or two, often while studying the English language. There is also a significant increase in the number of Slovak youth who communicate well in English, and this relates to the other two trends.

SOCIETY

Transportation

The public transportation system in Slovakia is well developed, particularly when compared to the United States. Slovakia has a solid network of mass transportation in every large town, and train or bus systems run frequently between most cities and urban areas, often with regular arrival and departure times separated by an hour or less. In addition, the capital and all large cities have a thorough network of streetcar lines or trolleybuses (electric buses that are powered by overhead power lines), but no subways are used in Slovakia. However, there are plans to build a subway system in Bratislava.

The most common mode of transportation for Slovaks is by train, and nearly every town has a very active train station, usually located in the town center. Since the fall of communism, many more Slovaks have begun using cars. However, because the private ownership of cars remains expensive, ownership remains low among the majority of the population. In addition, Slovakia's rail network has direct connections to many of the main cities throughout Europe, including Berlin, Hamburg, Warsaw, Copenhagen, Rome, Moscow, Athens, Barcelona, Paris and many other European cities. Traffic moves on the right-hand side of the road in Slovakia.

Transportation Infrastructure

There are approximately 43,916 (2010 estimate) kilometers (27,719 miles) of roadways in Slovakia. Highways include motorways, which are generally two-laned, and expressways, which are generally four-laned. In 2006, there were an estimated 3,658 km (2,273 m) of railroad track in Slovakia, and its neighboring countries of Austria, Hungary, Poland, Czech Republic, and Ukraine are all accessible by rail. International airports in Slovakia include the Kosice International Airport, the M. R. Stefanik Airport, the Poprad-Tatry Airport, and the Zilina Airport.

Media & Communications

Slovak Television (Slovenská televízia or STV) is a state-owned public television network that came into existence in 1991. It split from the former Czechoslovak Television that existed prior to the toppling of communism in the 1989 Velvet Revolution. A mix of government funding, mandatory television fees and advertising revenue funds STV. However, the network has declined since several commercial stations, such TV Markiza, TA3 and TV Joj, began competing with it. Many Slovaks also have access to cable and satellite TV, and programming is often dependent on their location in the country. For example, many Slovaks watch regional broadcasts coming from neighboring countries such as the Czech Republic, Hungary, Poland, and Austria. Popular newspapers include the *Nový Čas* and *SME*, with the *Slovak Spectator* the only English-language paper.

The market economy in Slovakia has largely modernized telecommunications and media, and the growth of cellular telephone service has dwarfed the traditional landline services. In 2012, there were 975,000 Slovaks using landline connections, while there were 6.095 million who were using cell phone service. Additionally, while the number of Internet users in the rural areas is low because of lower income and computer literacy, a growing number of urban youth are regularly using the Internet. Internet service is available through several different technologies. As of 2009, an estimated 65.3 percent of the population was using the Internet on a regular basis.

SOCIAL DEVELOPMENT

Standard of Living

Despite the problems of the communist era, Slovakia entered the 21st century with a relatively well-developed infrastructure and a well-educated workforce. The country ranked thirty-seven out of 187 countries on the 2013 United Nations Human Development Index (HDI), which measures quality of life indicators.

Water Consumption

Access to water and sanitation services is very high in Slovakia. In 2012, 100 percent of the population was connected to the public water supply, and 100 percent of rural and urban households were connected to improved water supplies. In 2012, nearly 100 percent of the population had access to sanitation services.

Education

Slovakia has a generally well-educated population, as well as a highly skilled work force. Almost the entire population is literate. Slovak is the language of instruction, although students from the leading minority groups can take classes in their own languages. School is compulsory for children between the ages of six and sixteen.

As in many other European countries, secondary education provides separate tracks for vocational education and university preparatory studies; the preparatory schools are known as "gymnasiums." Slovakia has private and parochial schools in addition to the state-run system.

Major universities include the Comenius University of Bratislava (founded 1919), named for Renaissance scholar Jan Comenius (1592–1670), and the Slovak Technical University in Bratislava (founded 1938).

The World Economic Forum publishes an annual Global Gender Gap Report that analyzes the economic and social disparities between women and men and ranks them according to country. In 2014, Slovakia ranked ninetieth out of 134 countries. In 2014, the literacy rate was over 99 percent.

Women's Rights

The recent efforts to shift the Slovak Republic toward regional and global integration and into the EU caused significant legal changes for Slovak women. The Slovak government established a department of equal opportunities within its Ministry of Labour, Social Affairs, and Family in 1999, in an attempt to harmonize Slovak legislation with EU laws. Thus, EU membership brought some immediate changes in outlook as well as legislation for Slovak women, particularly in the area of employment equality.

Additionally, the Slovak government made substantial amendments to the Slovak Labor Code in 2002. The new amendments mainly dealt with improved employment conditions for pregnant women, or single women with children. This was important since nearly half of Slovak women work full time. In addition, the Slovak government's labor code reforms follow the EU principles of ensuring equal treatment for men and women in the workplace, and offering equal opportunities in vocational training and job promotion.

The level of education afforded women in Slovakia is similar or, in some fields, higher than men. This has been the case for several decades, and the ratio of university graduates is nearly the same for men as it is for women. Slovak men and women see no gender inequality in access to education, although this is not the case in the labor market. For example, there are fewer Slovak women in higher positions at universities or in top management positions. In addition, Slovakia still has a large pay difference along gender lines. In 1999, Slovak women made 24 percent less than Slovak men. A 2013 report found that the percentage remained nearly the same (women made a reported 20 percent less than men). Additionally, the representation of women in politics is relatively low—19 percent in 2014—and some social services and networks for Slovak women are inadequate or altogether absent. For example, there are very few help lines, battered women refuges, or rape crisis centers.

However, maternity leave for Slovak women is quite good: they receive six months leave with 90 percent of their full salary. Immediately after maternity leave expires, Slovak women can then go on "parental leave" for up to three years. This is one of the longest allowed parental leave periods in the EU. During paternal leave, the Slovak government pays the parent a flat-rate monthly payment that is around 25 percent of a typical Slovak salary. In October 2008, legislation was introduced that proposed extending women's maternity leave to one full year with full salary.

Health Care

Slovakia's health-care system is well developed, and moving toward a more market-based system.

There are many private hospitals and physicians in addition to the state-run system inherited from the communist era. The infant mortality rate is low, at 5.35 deaths per 1,000 live births (2014 estimate). Life expectancy at birth is around 73 years for men and over 73 years for women (2014 estimate).

Many health problems in Slovakia are related to environmental problems (particularly air pollution) created during the country's Cold War-era industrialization. Conditions have improved somewhat as the government has shut down old factories. Other problems are related to lifestyle. Many Slovakian citizens are heavy smokers and drinkers, and have a diet heavy in cholesterol. Spas, many of them based at mineral springs or hot springs, are a popular means of improving health. Slovaks are also fond of sports, which helps promote better health.

GOVERNMENT

Structure

Slovakia is a parliamentary republic. The president, elected directly by popular vote, serves a five-year term as head of state. Duties include serving as commander-in-chief of the armed forces, and vetoing legislation. The prime minister is the head of government, and holds most of the actual power; he or she is appointed by the president from the majority party or ruling coalition. The president appoints the cabinet officers based on the prime minister's recommendations.

Slovakia has a single-house legislature of 150 members, known as the Narodna Rada Slovenskej Republiky (National Council of the Slovak Republic). Members are elected to four-year terms, under a system of proportional representation.

Political Parties

There are many political parties in Slovakia. The Christian Democratic Movement (KDH) was established in 1990. In the March 2012

parliamentary elections, the KDH won 8.8 percent of the vote and sixteen seats in the National Council. The Direction-Social Democracy (SMER-SD), founded in 1999, won 44.4 percent of the vote in the 2012 parliamentary elections and 83 seats in the National Council. The Ordinary People and Independent Personalities (OLaNO) won 8.6 percent of the vote, earning 16 seats on National Council.

The Most-Hid (or Bridge) won 6.9 percent of the vote and thirteen seats in the National Council in the 2012 parliamentary elections. Slovak Democratic and Christian Union-Democratic Party (SDKU-DS) won 6.1 percent of the vote and eleven seats in the National Council. The Freedom and Solidarity Party (SaS) won 5.9 percent of the vote in the 2012 elections and 11 seats in the National Council.

Local Government

Slovakia has 79 okresy (administrative districts), which are grouped into eight kraje, or counties. Municipalities elect their own governments directly. Since the beginning of the 21st century, Slovakia has made efforts to give local governments more authority.

Judicial System

Slovakia's highest court is the thirteen-member Constitutional Court, the function of which is to rule on cases of constitutional law. The president from nominees selected by the legislature appoints members. The Supreme Court is the highest appellate court; its members are appointed by the president from nominations provided by the Judicial Council, a body comprised of top legal experts.

Taxation

Both income tax and corporate tax are levied at a rate of 19 percent. Other taxes levied include property taxes and value-added taxes (VAT).

Armed Forces

The Armed Forces of the Slovak Republic comprises ground forces, air forces, and special forces.

Foreign Policy

At the turn of the 21st century, foreign policy in Slovakia shifted from international isolation and toward global responsibility and economic integration, particularly within the European community. This shift was emphasized by the Slovak Republic's bid for membership in the European Union (EU), which it joined in 2004. It joined the North Atlantic Treaty Organization (NATO) the same year, largely for the purposes of military integration. The Slovak government also worked on new security treaties with three neighboring countries that had already joined NATO: Poland, Hungary, and the Czech Republic. Slovakia also became a member state of the Organization for Economic Cooperation and Development (OECD), the World Trade Organization (WTO) and the Organization for Security and Co-operation in Europe (OSCE). Additionally, Slovakia has been a member of the UN since 1993, and served on the UN Security Council (UNSC).

This shift in foreign policy also dictated how Slovakia dealt with the internal conditions of its various ethnicities. For example, the EU stated that membership was largely contingent on how Slovakia moved forward in protecting its various ethnic minorities. As a result, the Slovak Parliament passed legislation that was aimed at ensuring fair and respectful conditions for minority groups Also, to improve its status to gain EU membership, the Slovak government improved its foreign relations with neighboring countries such as the Czech Republic and Hungary.

In 2012, Robert Fico, the leader of the Direction-Social Democracy (SMER) party, resumed power as the prime minister. The SMER is a breakaway party of the Party of the Democratic Left (SDL), which was essentially the successor of the Communist Party of Slovakia. (Fico was a member of the Communist Party of Czechoslovakia.) This initial change in leadership in 2006 also brought about a change in the direction of Slovak foreign policy. Fico began to roll back some of the goals and reforms of the previous administration, and he strengthened relations with countries that are at odds with US foreign policy. Particularly, Fico developed stronger relations with Russia, and expressed his opinion that it was a mistake for the previous administration to concentrate Slovakia's foreign policy on the U.S. Fico has also developed stronger ties to Cuba, Libya, China, and Venezuela, and some analysts argue that this further demonstrates a significant shift in Slovak foreign policy.

Human Rights Profile

International human rights law insists that states respect civil and political rights, and promote an individual's economic, social, and cultural rights. The United Nations Universal Declaration on Human Rights (UDHR) is recognized as the standard for international human rights. Its authors sought the counsel of the world's great thinkers, philosophers, and religious leaders, and were careful to create a document that reflects the core values shared by every world culture. (To read this document or view the articles relating to cultural human rights visit http://www.un.org/en/documents/udhr/.)

Article 19, which protects the right to freedom of speech and expression, is respected in the Slovak constitution, but the Slovak government has placed limitations on hate speech. The law is intended to prevent extremist groups, particularly neo-Nazi groups, from publishing and speaking hatefully about other races in public. Slovak law states that defaming nationalities or races carries a maximum sentence of three years in prison. Additionally, denying that the Holocaust occurred carries a minimum sentence of six months, and a maximum sentence of three years. The EU promotes such legislation to control far right nationalist sentiments in its member states.

In 2008, the Slovak government passed legislation that many journalists and publishers believe will produce a chilling effect on the free press. One provision of the bill allowed the government to prosecute editors for publishing articles that promote any of sixteen different classifications of hate. The application of this clause, being open to the government's interpretation, is problematic to a free press. The second provision gives individuals a broad "right of reply" to any articles published in the Slovak print media. Journalists believe this allows politicians to force unfair access to the reading public. In short, the Slovak government now gets the last word.

Article 4, which states, "No one shall be held in slavery or servitude; slavery and the slave trade shall be prohibited in all their forms," covers human trafficking. This has become a major concern for Slovakia. Women and girls from countries to the east are often trafficked through Slovakia. In addition, Vietnamese men are trafficked to Slovakia as forced laborers, and Romani (Gypsy) women and girls are trafficked domestically for sexual exploitation.

Articles 2 and 7 are intended to protect people from discrimination based on race, sex, language, religion, political or other opinion, national or social origin, property, birth or other status. Slovakia has a large Romani population, and it appears that Articles 2 and 7 are not adequately applied to Romani Slovaks in several ways. According to the census of 2011 there are 105,738 Roma living in Slovakia. Romani communities, concentrated in southern and eastern Slovakia, are essentially segregated. In Slovak society, Romani Slovaks experience higher rates of discrimination and poverty. Hate crimes against Romani Slovaks have been increasing rather than decreasing, and many more hate crimes likely go unreported because police are resistant to reporting crimes as racially motivated.

In 2003, a human rights report was released demonstrating that there was a quiet sterilization program targeting Romani women in state hospitals. The Slovak government's reaction was to file a criminal complaint against the authors of the report for publishing false information. That way, if the government's investigation failed to substantiate their claims, the authors of the report could be prosecuted. The government then stated that if the investigation did support their allegations, then the authors

of the report could be prosecuted for failing to file a report with the Slovak police. Many critics felt that this was a government tactic to "kill the messenger."

According to the *Washington Post* in 2011, the head of a U.S. human rights watchdog called on Slovakia's government "to finally acknowledge clearly and unequivocally that Romani women in Slovakia were, at one time, targeted for sterilization."

Another human rights issue has been Slovakia's arms sales to countries with poor human rights records, such as Liberia and Angola.

ECONOMY

Overview of the Economy

Slovakia's economy is growing rapidly in the post-communist era, although the 1990s were somewhat rocky due to political corruption and excessive government spending. The economy stabilized toward the end of the decade, and in 2004 Slovakia was accepted for membership in the European Union.

In 2014, the gross domestic product (GDP) was estimated at $149.5 billion (USD). The per capita GDP was estimated at $27,600 (USD).

Industry

In the 21st century, Slovakia has become a major site for foreign investment, particularly in manufacturing. The automobile industry has grown thanks to the presence of skilled workers but relatively low wages. The unemployment rate was 13.2 percent as of 2014.

Other major industries include heavy manufacturing, energy industries, ceramics, chemicals, and textiles. Mining has been a major industry since the Middle Ages, when Slovakia was a major producer of gold and silver.

Slovakia's main trading partners are European, particularly the countries of Central and Eastern Europe. Entry into the European Union offers the prospect of improved trade, but raises questions about Slovakia's ability to compete against EU countries with even lower wages.

Labor

In 2014, the labor force of Slovakia was estimated to be 2.363 million, and the unemployment rate was estimated to be 13.2 percent. Just under 4 percent of the labor force works in agriculture, nearly 26 percent works in the industrial sector, and just over 70 percent works in the services industry.

Energy/Power/Natural Resources

In 2013, Slovakia produced 5,200 barrels of crude oil a day.

Fishing

In the early 21st century, 2,158 hectares (5,332 acres) of land in Slovakia are used for fish farming. The two most commonly farmed fish species are carp and rainbow trout. Fish production does not meet domestic demand, so the country relies on fish imports.

Forestry

Approximately six million cubic meters of timber are produced in Slovakia annually, underpinning the country's furniture and timber industries. Much of Slovak's timber is exported to the Czech Republic, Austria, and Germany.

Mining/Metals

Minerals produced in Slovakia include antimony, mercury, iron, copper, lead, zinc, magnesite, and limestone.

Agriculture

Although manufacturing has become a major part of the Slovakia economy, agriculture remains important. The southern part of Slovakia, in particular, is heavily agricultural in comparison to the more industrialized north. Around 30 percent of the land is arable.

The main food crops include wheat, potatoes, barley, and sugar beets. Grape-growing is another important farm activity, to support the country's wine industry.

Animal Husbandry

Livestock include sheep, cattle, pigs, and poultry.

Tourism

Slovakia's tourist trade has grown steadily since the fall of communism. Tourists come to enjoy the beautiful landscape, as well as the historic sites in cities such as Bratislava, which boasts the medieval Bratislava Castle, two palaces (the Primate's Palace and the Mirbach Palace), and numerous museums and universities.

Sinclair Nicholas, Eric Badertscher

DO YOU KNOW?

- The Slovakian capital of Bratislava was once the capital of the Kingdom of Hungary.
- During the era of Hungarian rule, Bratislava was known as Pressburg. The division of Czechoslovakia into the separate Czech Republic and Slovak Republic became known as the "Velvet Divorce" (a reference to the non-violent "Velvet Revolution" of 1989, which overthrew Czechoslovakia's communist government).

Bibliography

Brendan Edwards. "Slovakia—Culture Smart! The Essential Guide to Customs and Culture." London: *Kuperard*, 2011.

Karen Henderson. "Slovakia: The Escape from Invisibility." New York: *Routledge*, 2002.

Lonely Planet and Lisa Dunford. "Czech and Slovak Republics." Oakland, CA: *Lonely Planet*, 2010.

Stanislav J. Kirschbaum. "A History of Slovakia: The Struggle for Survival." New York: *St. Martin's*, 2005.

Works Cited

Anna Kisselgoff. "Dance Review; Slovak Folk Troupe in Its New York Debut." New York Times. (23 Nov. 1994). http://query.nytimes.com/gst/fullpage.html?res= 9C01E6DC1630F930A15752C1A962958260Jana Balaova. "Chapter IX: Slovaks on the Road to National Self-Determination." From Cultural Heritage and Contemporary Change, Series IVA. Eastern and Central Europe, Vol. 5, eds. Tibor Pichler and Jana Gaparkova. Council for Research in Values Philosophy. http://www.crvp.org/book/Series04/IVA-5/chapter_ix.htm

"Coerced Sterilizations in the Czech Republic and Slovakia." Commission on Security and Cooperation in Europe, United States Helsinki Commission. Vol. 151. No. 154. (18 Nov. 2005) http://csce.gov/index.cfm?FuseAction=ContentRecords.ViewDetail&ContentRecord_id=264&Region_id=84&Issue_id=0&ContentType=S&ContentRecordType=S&CFID=6578421&CFTOKEN=87159563

"Comments to the Fourth Periodic Report of the Slovak Republic on Performance of the Obligations Arising from the Convention on the Elimination of All Forms of Discrimination Against Women." Committee on the Elimination of Discrimination against Women, 41st Session in June – July 2008. Centre for Civil and Human Rights http://www2.ohchr.org/english/bodies/cedaw/docs/ngos/CFIDH_Slovakia_41.pdf

"Hate Crime Report Card-Slovak Republic." Human Rights First. (June 23, 2008) http://www.humanrightsfirst.org/discrimination/pages.aspx?id=137 http://www.mongabay.com/igapo/2005_world_city_populations/Slovakia.html http://www.washingtonpost.com/wp-dyn/content/article/2011/03/22/AR2011032202551.html

"Labour Code 2002 (Act No. 311/2001) – Slovakia." International Labour Organization Web Site. http://www.ilo.org/public/english/employment/gems/eeo/law/Slovakia/act1.htm

Ladislav Macháček. "Regional and Local Youth Policy in Slovakia (2007)." http://www.youth-partnership.net/youth-partnership/news/news_56.html

Lucia Kubošova,. "EU to highlight gender pay gap ahead of Women's Day." (23 Feb. 2007). http://euobserver.com/9/23565

Marianna Oravcova. "Chapter I: The Ethnic and Cultural Dimension of National Emancipation: The Evocation of the Slovak Nation. From Cultural Heritage and Contemporary Change, Series IVA." Eastern and Central Europe, Vol. 5, eds. Tibor Pichler and Jana Gaparkova. http://www.crvp.org/book/Series04/IVA-5/chapter_i.htm

Norbert Brazda. "Country Report—Slovak Republic." The APC European Internet Rights Project. http://europe.rights.apc.org/c_rpt/slovak_r.html

Peter Magvaši. "Women 2000: Gender Equality, Development, and Peace in the Twenty-First Century." (6 June, 2000) http://un.org/womenwatch/daw/followup/beijing+5stat/statments/Slovakia6.htm

"Proclamation 2005: 'The Fujara and its Music.'" UNESCO World Heritage Web Site. UNESCO Intangible Cultural Heritage – ICH. http://www.unesco.org/culture/ich/index.php Path: Country; Slovakia.

Sonya Lee. "Overcoming Fear to Fight Sterilizations." Los Angeles Times. (3 March, 2003). http://articles.latimes.com/2003/mar/03/world/fg-roma3

"Slovak Republic: Country Reports on Human Rights Practices-2007." U.S. Department of State. (11 March, 2008). http://www.state.gov/g/drl/rls/hrrpt/2007/100584.htm

"Slovakia urged to curb arm sales." BBC News. (10 Feb., 2004) http://news.bbc.co.uk/2/hi/europe/3475973.stm

"Trafficking in Persons Report." U.S. Department of State. 4 June, 2008. http://www.state.gov/g/tip/rls/tiprpt/2008/105389.htm

"Spišský Hrad and its Associated Cultural Monuments." 1 Nov. 2008. UNESCO World Heritage Web Site. http://whc.unesco.org/en/list/620

Zuzana Vranova. "Women's representation in public sphere in Slovakia." http://alda-europe.eu/alda/upload/Working_Groups/women_in_politics_-_Slovakia-Profesionalne_zeny.pdf

Statue on the Dragon Bridge in Ljubljana, Slovenia

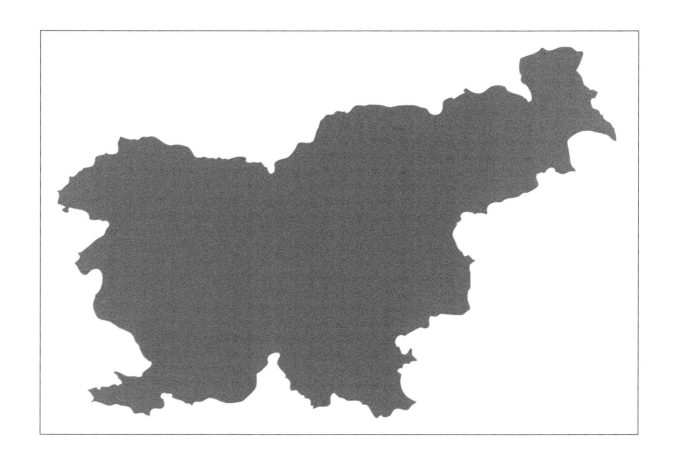

SLOVENIA

Introduction

The Republic of Slovenia is a Central European nation formed in 1991 after the breakup of the former Yugoslavia. Located on the Adriatic Sea, Slovenia is bordered on the south and east by Croatia (another former Yugoslav republic), on the west by Italy, and by Hungary and Austria on the north.

The Slovenes are a southern Slavic people with historically close ties to Western Europe, partly from centuries of Austrian rule. Since independence, Slovenia has joined the North Atlantic Treaty Organization (NATO) and the European Union (EU). Tourists visit Slovenia to enjoy Adriatic coast resorts, winter sports in the country's mountains, and more cosmopolitan attractions in Ljubljana, the capital.

GENERAL INFORMATION

Official Language: Slovenian (Italian and Hungarian have official status in areas of mixed population)
Population: 1,988,292 (July 2014 estimate)
Currency: Euro
Coins: One hundred cents equal one Euro. Coins are issued in 1, 2, 5, 10, 20, and 50 cents and 1- and 2-euro denominations.
Land Area: 20,151 square kilometers (7,780 square miles)
Water Area: 122 square kilometers (47 square miles)
National Anthem: "Zdravljica" ("A Toast")
Capital: Ljubljana
Time Zone: GMT +2

Flag Description: The Slovenian flag features three equal and horizontal stripes of white (top), blue (middle), and red (bottom). The Slovenian coat of arms is emblazoned on the upper hoist (left) side of the white and blue stripe. The coat of arms features Mt. Triglav, with blue waves in the foreground symbolizing the Adriatic Sea and Slovenian rivers. Three stars arranged in an inverted triangle hang above Mt. Triglav.

Population

Slovenia is a heavily Westernized country with a well-developed infrastructure. The population is distributed evenly between rural and urban areas. Over 249,000 of the country's total inhabitants live in the capital, Ljubljana and nearly 50 percent of the population lives in urban areas. Besides Ljubljana, Maribor and Celje are the main cities.

Many Slovenes live in the surrounding countries. Italy in particular has a substantial

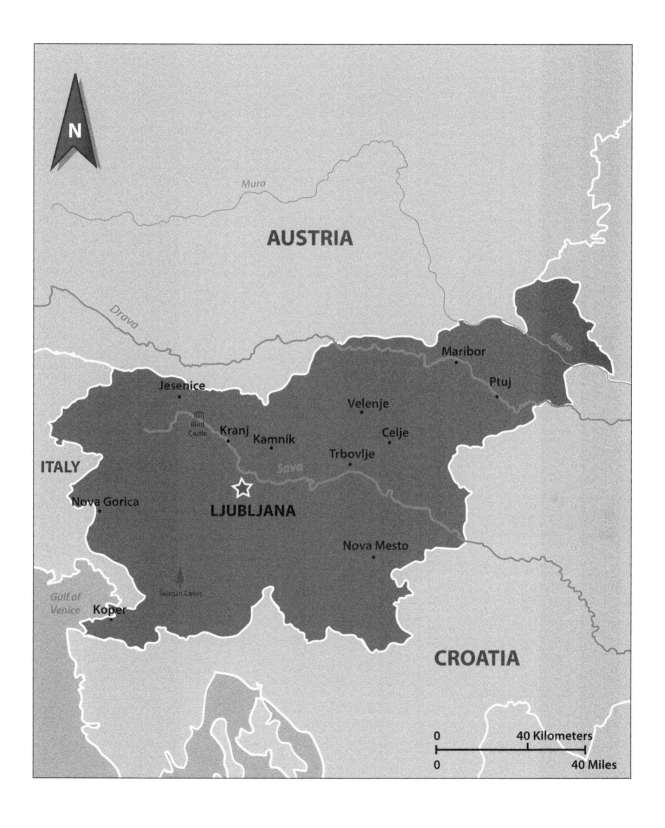

Principal Cities by Population (2012):

- Ljubljana (249,700)
- Maribor (87,234)
- Celje (35,458)
- Kranj (33,704)
- Velenje (26,305)
- Koper (26,305)
- Novo Mesto (23,142)

Slovene population, numbering around 100,000. Southwestern Austria, Croatia, and Hungary also have sizeable numbers of Slovene inhabitants. All four nations recognize the Slovenes as a protected minority, with additional rights. Many Slovenes have also immigrated to the Americas.

Languages

Slovenian (or Slovene), is a South Slavic language spoken by approximately two million people around the world. There are numerous dialects, including the German-influenced "Windisch" dialect of southwestern Austria. Besides German, Serbo-Croatian has influenced the Slovenian language. The 19th century nationalist movement helped strengthen the use of Slovenian as a national language. In the 20th century, Slovenian served as one of Yugoslavia's official languages.

Native People & Ethnic Groups

Illyrian and Celtic peoples were the earliest settlers of what is now Slovenia. In the first century BCE, the Romans conquered the region and named it "Illyricum." The Slovenes settled there during the sixth century, following the fall of Rome. Though they established small states of their own, they came under German domination, and from the 14th century onward, were ruled by the Austrian Hapsburgs.

The Slovenes are a Slavic people whose culture reflects both Alpine and Mediterranean influences. They speak Slovenian, a language that is related to Croatian, Serbian, and Bulgarian.

Slovenia's population is largely Slovene (around 83 percent), but there are sizeable Italian and Hungarian minorities; these groups enjoy extensive rights under the constitution, including the right to use their own language for official business and education in areas of mixed population. The Roma, or Gypsies, have more limited protection. There are no special protections for the Izbrisani ("erased"), immigrants from the other former Yugoslav republics who essentially became stateless after the breakup of Yugoslavia. Under a 2003 ruling by the Constitutional Court, Slovenia must offer citizenship to all such persons who were living in Slovenia when the country declared independence. As of 2010, though, the Slovenian government has still not acted on the court's decision and the matter has been elevated to the European Court of Human Rights in Strasbourg, France,

Religions

The Slovenes are largely Roman Catholic, though the Protestant Reformation made strong inroads during the 16th century and the Bible was translated into Slovenian. The 2002 census listed 58 percent of the population as Roman Catholic, with sizeable minorities of Eastern Orthodox (two percent) and other Christian groups (less than one percent). There is also a substantial Muslim population (two percent). Around 10 percent of the population is atheistic, or has no declared religion.

Climate

Slovenia's climate is generally moderate. There are three main climatic regions: "Alpine" in the northern mountains, "Mediterranean" along the coast, and "Continental" in the eastern part of the country. In the Alpine regions, summers are pleasant and winters are cold. The coastal regions are warm in summer and generally mild in winter. The eastern "Continental" region has the most noticeable seasonal changes, with hot summers and cold winters.

In general, winter temperatures range from −2° to 0° Celsius (28° to 32° Fahrenheit), with an average summer temperature of 19° Celsius (66° Fahrenheit).

ENVIRONMENT & GEOGRAPHY

Topography

Slovenia is largely a country of hills and mountains, particularly in the north, where mountain chains include the Julian Alps, the Dinarides, Kamnik-Savinja Alps, the Pohorje, and Karavanke Mountains. The highest point is at the peak of Mount Triglav, which rises 2,864 meters (9,396 feet) above sea level.

Ljubljana is located in the center of Slovenia, situated in a wide basin of land surrounded by the Julian Alps mountain range. The city covers an area of about 273 square kilometers (105 square miles) and is within easy driving distance of the Adriatic Sea. The Ljubljanica River, a tributary of the Sava River, which is Slovenia's main river, bisects the city; on the left bank are most of Ljubljana's modern buildings and commercial enterprises, while on the right bank are the Old Town section and Ljubljana Castle, a famous medieval castle that is more than eight hundred years old. The city's two major suburbs are the Krakovo and Trnovo districts, which are divided by a wide canal.

The eastern part of the country is covered by the Pannonian plain. There is also a vast plain known as the Kras Plateau, located between Ljubljana and the Italian border. This region includes limestone caves and underground rivers. Much of the country is covered by forests.

The country has a small (47 kilometers, or 29 miles) coastline along the Adriatic Sea, running from Italy to Croatia. The longest river is the Sava, which runs for 221 kilometers (137 miles) and drains into the Danube. Other rivers are the Drava (another Danube tributary) and the Kolpa (on the Croatian border).

Plants & Animals

Slovenia has rich and diverse flora and fauna, especially in the mountains and forests. Around half of Slovenia is forested. Species in lower-lying regions include beech, linden, and oak. The linden, or lime tree, is particularly beloved as a national symbol. Mountain forests typically consist of pine, fir, and spruce. Many beautiful wildflowers grow in the mountain regions, including gentians such as the edelweiss.

Slovenia is home to many large game animals, such as deer and boar, as well as medium-sized carnivores such as the fox, lynx, and European wild cat. Large carnivores are somewhat rare, though several hundred brown bears live in Slovenia. Among the country's most famous domesticated species are the Lippizaner trained horses, raised in the town of Lipica.

CUSTOMS & COURTESIES

Greetings

Slovenians tend to be reserved when meeting new people. A handshake is a common way to greet someone new, accompanied by a friendly smile and direct eye contact. Handshakes should be firm and last for a few seconds. When greeting people, "Dober dan" ("Good day") is widely used, as are "Dobro jutro" ("Good morning") and "Dober večer" ("Good evening"). Among close friends and family, kissing twice (once on each cheek) or hugging is also common when greeting. When approaching a group, it is typical to shake hands and greet each person individually. If someone approaches, it is appropriate to stand and greet him or her properly. Nodding is also a common greeting in informal situations.

It is respectful to use professional or academic titles when greeting someone, including "Gospa" ("Madam"), "Gospodièna" ("Miss"), or "Gospod" ("Sir"). These are customarily used until individuals are on a first-name basis. As first names tend to indicate intimacy and are only used among close friends and family, it is considered presumptuous to use someone's first name without an invitation. When saying goodbye, it is common to shake hands again. The phrase "Nasvidenje" is a formal farewell, and "Zdravo," which can be used to mean both "hello" or "goodbye."

Gestures & Etiquette

When talking, Slovenians typically expect about an arm's length of personal space between people; friends and family tend to be physically closer. Physical contact is not common with strangers. While touching someone's arm or shoulder will probably not offend most people, some Slovenians might feel it is too forward or overly intimate. When conversing, direct eye contact is the norm, and staring is considered rude. Pointing is considered slightly rude, and it is customary to gesture with the entire hand. In general, Slovenians also tend to be punctual in both professional and social situations, with few exceptions.

Slovenians are generally very polite and soft-spoken, and it is expected that one will listen to what someone has to say without interruption. Slovenians also appreciate humility and might be put off by those who brag about their accomplishments. Slovenians are known for having a good sense of humor, though self-deprecating humor is less common.

Eating/Meals

Slovenians tend to have a quick breakfast, consisting of coffee (kava, usually espresso or Turkish coffee) or tea (čaj) and bread (kruh) or a variety of pastries. Occasionally, a leisurely breakfast can also include eggs and meat or yogurt. Lunch or dinner often starts with a soup (juha), usually a chicken or beef broth with egg noodles. Main dishes are generally centered on meat (meso), commonly pork, or beef, and customarily served with potatoes (krompir). Veal (telečje) and cutlets (zrezek) are also popular, and seafood is more common along the Adriatic coast. Salad (solata) is usually seasoned with oil and vinegar and eaten alongside the main dish. The Italians have also influenced Slovenian cuisine, and one can find pasta, pizza, ravioli, and risotto in many Slovenian restaurants. Slovenians traditionally eat in the continental style: fork held in the left hand, knife held in the right hand.

When going out for a drink or a small snack, Slovenians do not customarily split the bill. One person will treat, and the other should try to reciprocate the next time. Another common option for lunch would be that one person pays for the food, and one person pays for the wine.

Dining etiquette also dictates refraining from placing one's elbows on the table and properly resting one's wrists on the table instead.

Visiting

When visiting a Slovenian's home, guests will customarily remove their shoes. Traditionally, the host might offer slippers for the guests to wear. It is not expected, but guests usually bring a small gift for their host, such as flowers or a bottle of wine. When presenting a gift, it should be wrapped nicely. Bright and cheerful colors are encouraged, as there are no taboo colors, and the gift recipient will likely open the gift as soon as it is received.

Slovenians are open to discussing most topics of conversation, including earlier communist rule and the former Yugoslavia. The one sensitive topic that should be broached carefully is the Slovenian civil war that took place during World War II. Also, Slovenians do not like being considered part of Eastern Europe and identify with either Central Europe or Western Europe. As one of the most prosperous countries in the region, they feel they have more in common with wealthier European nations. When a guest leaves a Slovenian's home, it is common for the host to walk their guest out to see them off.

LIFESTYLE

Family

In the 1990s, it was common to see several generations of family members living together. As urban life became increasingly popular, many young people migrated to the cities. While multigenerational living is no longer as common in urban areas, the family unit still plays a central role in Slovenian life. Marriage is encouraged and common, and divorce rates are low in Slovenia.

Domestic life is important, and Slovenians are known for their private gardens, even in urban settings. Many grow their own vegetables and/or have cut flowers from their own gardens on display in their homes. Slovenians also believe their homes and neighborhoods are extensions of themselves, so they tend to prioritize cleanliness.

Housing

Most Slovenians in both rural and urban areas live in houses or apartments (typically rubble-stone masonry or brick masonry). These tend to be small, and children often share a bedroom. Many families who live in the cities also own a small vacation home in the mountains, by a body of water or near a spa for weekend getaways.

Land ownership in Slovenia was historically determined by primogeniture, a tradition by which the oldest son inherits the family land. Forty-three percent of Slovenian land is used for agriculture, which makes it one of the "greenest" countries in Europe, despite a decrease in the number of people choosing to become farmers.

Almost half of the Slovenian population lives in urban centers, and this number is growing as more young people choose to leave rural settings and migrate toward cities. As a result, cities have become increasingly crowded. To alleviate this, the government has also built apartment housing projects that are aesthetically appealing, modern, and ecological, such as the Honeycomb complex in Izola or the Tetris apartments in Ljubljana.

Food

Slovenian food is often described as simple and plain, with traditional cuisine characterized as heavy (or caloric) and seasoned. However, there is a range of distinct influences and regional cuisines, many of which are similar to those found in neighboring countries. Influences include Austrian (sausage, strudel, and schnitzels), German (meats and starches), Italian (pasta-based dishes such as ravioli or potato dumplings), Hungarian (goulash and stews) and Balkan cuisine (grilled meat and meat pastries). Popular dishes are often characterized by common or traditional ingredients, including potatoes, turnips, cabbage, beans, olives, grapes and grilled meats (particularly pork), as well as flour-based meals (such as buckwheat dishes), stews and cheese and bread. The region is also known for its high quality wines and for seafood from the Adriatic Sea.

Slovenia has many national dishes, including štruklji, rolled dumplings made of yeast dough that have a variety of fillings, including cottage cheese, or other ingredients such as potatoes, walnuts or beans. Gibanica is a traditional pastry that can be rolled or layered with ingredients such as raisins, cottage cheese, poppy seeds, nuts, or apples. Žganci is a dish made with buckwheat, salt, water, and cracklings (pork rind). Pražen krompir are sautéed potatoes, and kmecka pojedina, is considered a "peasant's feast" that contains sauerkraut and smoked meats.

The most popular Slovenian sweets include potica, a traditional pastry made from rolled dough, often filled with raisins or walnuts, and palačinke, a thin pancake usually topped with fruit jam, nuts, or chocolate. The Slovenians have also incorporated the Austrian strudel into their desserts, and because Albanians run many bakeries, sweets like baklava have become popular.

In recent years, there has been a slow food movement in Slovenia. This often involves up to eight courses and an emphasis on local produce, traditional dishes, and a relaxed atmosphere in which to connect with friends and family. Sometimes, a different wine may be paired with each course.

Life's Milestones

The majority of Slovenians are Roman Catholic, and most milestones are practiced in the Christian faith. The most common rites of passage are baptism, first communion, and confirmation. Marriage is very common and, along with starting a family, remains a significant milestone. Family plays a central role in Slovenian social life, and family events are often the most meaningful moments in a young Slovenian's life.

There are also many milestones that are less ceremonial. For example, climbing Mount Triglav, the highest point in Slovenia's Julian Alps, is considered a Slovenian rite of passage. First-timers reaching the summit of Triglav are often surprised to find they are greeted with an old-fashioned spanking. Adults and youngsters alike are draped over a Triglav veteran's knees, and they get swatted on the bottom with climbing rope. Other mountain climbers have been known to burst into folk song and cheer for the new Triglav climbers.

Some claim Slovenian national pride is a prerequisite of being a proper Slovenian and that military service is a rite of passage. Education is free and compulsory until age fifteen, at which point higher educational or vocational training are available as options.

CULTURAL HISTORY

Art

Slovenian artists have historically combined neighboring European influences with the country's rich folk heritage to create a unique Slovenian artistic tradition. Slovenian church frescoes from as early as the 12th and 13th centuries have been documented. Slovenian art mostly followed European trends until the end of the 19th century, when Anton Ažbe (1862–1905) opened an art school in Munich. Ažbe became one of the first Slovenian artists recognized internationally. His students, Ivan Grohar (1867–1911), Rihard Jakopic (1869–1943), Matija Jama (1872–1947), and Matej Sternen (1870–1949), garnered even more acclaim as artists.

At the beginning of the 20th century, Gvidon Birolla (1881–1963), Maksim Gaspari (1883–1980), and Hinko Smrekar (1883–1943), collectively referred to as the group Vesna (Spring), became known for incorporating Slovenian folk motifs into their artwork. Other notable 20th-century artists include expressionist France Kralj (1985–1960); modern graphic artist Božidar Jakac (1899–1989); expressionist painter, graphic artist and photographer Veno Pilon (1896–1970), and constructivist Avgust Černigoj (1898–1985).

Architecture

Throughout its history, Slovenia's architecture has been influenced by the traditions of neighboring European countries. Its architecture includes Romanesque castles and churches, fortified medieval towns, and mansions and palaces built in the post-medieval Renaissance style. Many of Slovenia's urban buildings have been influenced by modern architectural movements, such as art nouveau. While Slovenia has absorbed numerous mainstream architectural styles over time, it has also carved out its own interpretations, often with folk or nationalist themes.

Slovenia's most famous architect is Jože Plečnik (1872–1957), considered both the last classical architect and the first post-modern architect. He designed the majority of notable buildings, bridges and public spaces in Slovenia's capital, Ljubljana. One of his most famous works is the National and University Library (1936–1941), the exterior of which is covered in red brick and a variety of stones, ranging in both size and texture. The interior reading room features large windows on both the east and west walls, creating a bright space that serves as a metaphor for the enlightenment of learning. Aside from his many buildings, Plečnik is also known for his design of the renowned Triple Bridge (Tromstovje most, 1929–1932), which features white stone balustrades (row of ornate supports) on three bridges, and his open Market (1939–1944) in Ljubljana, with stone pillars and graceful arches lining the Ljubljanica River.

Drama

Slovenia's vibrant artistic culture is perhaps best experienced through the performing arts, which include theater, street theater, dance, music, and puppetry. With a population of approximately two million people, Slovenia is home to 12 professional theaters, nine professional theater companies, two opera and ballet houses and two professional puppet theaters. Over one million theater tickets are sold each year, and theaters often organize or participate in city festivals.

After World War II, several theaters were opened in Slovenia, and experimental pieces with themes related to existentialism, nihilism and the absurd were often featured. In the 1960s and 1970s, plays became more politically charged. In the 1980s, a physical, non-verbal theater movement began that continues today. The 1990s broke media lines, as architects and visual artists experimented with performance art and visual and audio media converged. Andrej Rozman Roza (1955–) is a contemporary artist who embodies this emerging art form. Roza has helped create hundreds of theater productions and films as both an actor and songwriter. He creates everything from street performances and children's pieces to sophisticated drama for adults, and has received numerous awards for his work.

Street theater began in 1982 with the Ana Monró Theatre and has been steadily growing in popularity since. Slovenians celebrate the Ana Desetnica International Street Theatre Festival annually, and circus art troupes and improvisation theater groups have also become increasingly popular. Other troupes, such as the Little Flying Circus, Buffetto Mini Circus, and Saltimbanko Magic World, add to Slovenia's lively street theatre scene. Commercial theater, focused mainly on comedies and often located on the outskirts of town, became popular in the 1990s. Amateur theaters have also been steadily growing.

Puppetry is a respected art in Slovenia, and aside from the two professional puppetry theaters, there are several puppetry festivals. Slovenia is also home to over 20 puppetry theater groups who perform sophisticated productions for children and adults alike, and almost 200 amateur puppetry theater groups.

Music

Slovenian music is diverse in its offering as well as its popularity. According to the Slovenian Institute for Civilization and Culture, folk music is the most popular musical form in the country, followed by pop music, classical, and rock and roll. The music scene in Slovenia is extremely active, and crossover with countries such as Italy, Croatia, Austria, and Germany has historical roots and is common in the present day.

Folk music in Slovenia is most often characterized by the polka, and Slovenia shares that tradition with other Alpine cultures such as Austria and Germany. Oberkrainer music is polka band music popularized by Slavko Avsenik (1929–2015), who leads one of the world's most popular polka and waltz bands, Ansambel bratov Avsenik. Avsenik has inspired other musicians in the Midwestern United States (known as Cleveland-style bands) to both play and record his music.

Velike Goslarije (big bands) is another type of folk music played with cimbaloms (a kind of hammered or plucked dulcimer), strings, and wood instruments. Harmonized singing was once popular, and still remains so in smaller villages, as do traditional instruments such as the bowed zither, panpipes, the mih (double bagpipe), and sopile (Istrian oboe).

Classical music in Slovenia derives from the area's history as part of the Austrian Empire and is largely influenced by the West. In the 16th and 17th centuries, both religious and secular music forms developed, and Italian works became an influential factor in Slovenian music. In 1701, an Academia Philharmonicorum was established in Ljubljana and Italian operas were often performed in the city.

In the late 18th century, after an economic crisis, German music came to have more influence in the country. Some attribute its success to the fact that German was a popular second language to many in Slovenia. In 1794, the Philharmonische Gesellschaft was formed, beginning a wave of orchestral formations in central Europe. The 19th century saw a development of nationalistic music that met resistance from a German minority. Later developments were influenced by both impressionists and the avant-garde movements. Today, the Slovenian Philharmonic, based in Ljubljana, carries on the strong tradition of classical music and is joined with four other professional orchestras in the country.

Popular and rock music in Slovenia are heavily influenced by the West. Musicians such as Magnifico, Peter Lovšin, Zoran Predin, and Vlado Kreslin play within Slovenia and throughout Europe.

Literature

Slovenian literature dates back to the 10th century. The Freising Manuscript, a series of three religious texts, is considered the oldest Slavic document written in the Latin alphabet. Most early literature was religious in nature. The Protestant Reformation of the 16th century having a large impact on Slovene writers, including Primož Trubar (1508–1586). He was excommunicated from the Catholic Church for his radical ideas and moved to Germany in 1547. He wrote the first two books in Slovene, *Catechismus* (which includes Slovenia's first printed musical manuscripts) and *Abecedarium*. Trubar addresses his readers as Slovenes, which many credit as the first sign of Slovenian nationalism. Even today, Trubar's early work is considered by many to be the beginning of Slovene poetry, prose, and intellectual debate.

Poetry was popular in the 17th and 18th centuries, and Slovene drama became increasingly popular as well. The French Revolution inspired both the poet Valentin Vodnik (1758–1819) and the playwright Anton Tomaž Linhart (1756–1795). Their work expressed the desire for personal freedom while advocating limited governmental power. In the 19th century, with the rise of romanticism, France Prešeren (1800–1849) led what some consider the "Slovenian Renaissance." His poetry is revered and his musical composition "Zdravljica" (A Toast, 1844) became the Slovenian national anthem in 1994. Since 1947, Slovenia observes Prešeren Day on February 9, an annual holiday honoring the poet. The Prešeren Award and Prešeren Foundation Awards are also presented on this day. These prestigious awards are the highest honor given to artists in Slovenia.

The 19th century also gave rise to Slovene literary criticism, and is considered the "golden age" of the novel in Slovenia. Josip Jurčič (1844–1881), Fran Levstik (1831–1887), Janko Kersnik (1852–1897), and Ivan Tavčar (1851–1923) were considered the forerunners of this era, often creating works that dealt with rural life and class stratification.

CULTURE

Arts & Entertainment

Slovenian literature has tended to reflect the sentiment of the people. At the turn of the 20th century, the "moderna" generation, also referred to as the "damn poets movement," led by poets Josip Murn Aleksandrov (1879–1901) and Dragotin Kette (1876–1899), rose to the forefront. Ivan Cankar (1876–1918), a writer, poet, playwright, and political activist, was considered one of the leading forces of the era. His work often criticized the rise of industrialism and softening values in the face of greed. Along with poet and playwright Oton Župančič (1878–1949), Cankar pushed political boundaries by arguing for a Yugoslavian nation state.

During World War II, writers Edvard Kocbek (1904–1981), Jože Udovič (1912–1986), and Ivan Minatti (1924–) encouraged national resistance against Nazism and fascism. Vladimir Bartol's (1903–1967) novel *Alamut* (1938) was translated into at least 19 languages, and remains one of the world's most popular Slovenian novels. Bartol based his story of a manipulative Islamic ruler on real historic events, but the characters were understood to represent the European dictators.

Poet Srečko Kosovel (1904–1926) became a posthumous national icon when he was rediscovered in the mid-20th century. Disenchanted young intellectuals, artists, and poets of the time embraced his work. Like Cankar, he felt Europe had become too materialistic and that Slovenia needed to rise above oppression from external powers. Though his poetry is complex and difficult to categorize, some have divided his work into impressionist, expressionist and constructionist eras. Kosovel was known for his innovative approach to poetry, which often included mathematical symbols and lacked traditional grammar and syntax. He also incorporated elements of Dadaism, surrealism and futurism into his work.

Poet Milan Jesih (1950–) and writer Lojze Kovačič (1928–2004) rose to prominence in the 1970s and 1980s as they addressed existential questions. The next generation of writers, including Marko Švabić (1949–1993), Berta Bojetu (1946–1997), Branko Gradišnik (1951–), Milan Kleč (1954–), Uroš Kalčič (1951–), and Boris Jukić, wanted to explore a lighter, more playful fiction. They included elements of magical realism or metafiction in their work. The 1980s saw even less brooding and more of an acceptance of the increasing diversity in both culture and art. Writers like Alojz Ihan (1961–), Aleš Debeljak (1961–) and Uroš Zupan (1963–) were influenced by multiculturalism. A newer movement called Young Slovenian Prose emphasizes short pieces of prose and a return to existential questioning.

In visual arts, the 1950s heralded an open exchange between Slovenian artists and artists from abroad. Slovenian artists studied art in other countries, and foreign artists felt more liberated to express themselves outside of their home countries. Slovenian artists experimented with realism, then with modernism and pop art. While the Yugoslavian government formulated its own version of socialism, artists were allowed free creative rein as long as it did not involve overt political criticism.

In the late 1960s, a new group called OHO emerged and started what they called the reism movement, which derived from the Latin word "es," meaning "thing." Rather than perceive the world as controlled by humans, they wanted to portray a world in which people and things were equal. What began as an artistic movement became a way of life. Just as OHO was beginning to be recognized internationally, its members decided to leave art as a career and started a community on an abandoned farm.

Neue Slowenische Kunst (New Slovenian Art in German, often simply referred to as NSK) was formed in 1984 as an art collective. Its work often incorporates images of totalitarian regimes as a form of political statement. There are several branches of NSK, including the rock band, Laibach (Ljubljana in German). Irwin is a group of visual artists that only take credit collectively; the theater and performance art group Noordung, named in honor of Slovenian space scientist Herman Potočnik Noordung (1892–1929); Novi

kolektivizem (New Collectivism in Slovene, often referred to as NK), specializing in graphic design; and the NSK Department of Pure and Applied Philosophy, which delves into questions regarding religion, good and evil, sexuality and other philosophical quandaries.

In 1990, the Autonomous Cultural Centre Metelkova mesto (often referred to as Metelkova) was formed. Originally led by the Movement for the Culture of Peace and Non Violence and the Student Cultural Centre Association, Metelkova now has over two hundred partner organizations and has become the largest alternative culture center in Slovenia. Located in Ljubljana, Metelkova is a thriving community of philosophizing artists that fosters discussion and art production. It hosts festivals and events for everything from jazz to punk to electronica, is home to gay and lesbian clubs, and was registered as a national cultural heritage site in 2005.

Cultural Sites & Landmarks

Slovenia's sole World Heritage Site, as designated by the United Nations Educational, Scientific and Cultural Organization (UNESCO), are the Škocjan Caves, a series of limestone caves. The caves have a depth of over 200 meters and six kilometers of tunnels, and contain many waterfalls (the Reka River flows through the caves). The caves are also home to one of the largest underground caverns in the world. The largest, Martel's Chamber, has a cross-section of 12,000 square meters and a volume of 2.2 million cubic meters.

Near the Škocjan Caves, in Mušja jama, archeologists have found over 600 metal objects in fifty-meter deep ravines dating back to the 12th through eighth century BCE. Remnants of weapons and animal bones date back to the Bronze Age and suggest that the area around the caves was considered a significant religious site. People would travel for hundreds of kilometers, from Italy, the Alps, the Balkans and even from Greece, to make animal sacrifices to the gods. Burial sites dating to the first century BCE attest to the area's continued significance. Because of its unique character, blending Mediterranean, sub-Mediterranean, Central European, Illyrian and Alpine climates, one can find several rare and endangered species of birds and bats, as well as Alpine and Mediterranean flora flourishing near the caves.

Slovenia is home to many castles, and the most famous ones include Predjama Castle, which is built into the 123-meter-high cave entrance of a limestone cliff and integrates the stone into its interior. Bled Castle is located on a cliff overlooking Lake Bled and Slovenia's only island, Bled Island, in the middle of the lake. Ljubljana Castle overlooks the capital and serves as a museum, performance venue, and the only place in the city where couples can be wed in common-law marriage.

The capital, Ljubljana, is organized in a compact and dense fashion, laid out in a grid that is easy to navigate. As such, walking and bicycling are both excellent ways to get around. The city has many squares, around which the various forms of its bustling street life are centered. There are three main squares in the Old Town: Stari, Mestni, and Gornji. The busiest square in Ljubljana's modern quarter is Preseren Square, also called Presernov Square, which takes its name from France Prešeren, Slovenia's most famous poet. It is considered the city's central square and was closed to automobile traffic in 2007.

Libraries & Museums

With over two hundred museums, even Slovenians are hard-pressed to say which are the most important. The most popular include the National Museum of Slovenia, located in Ljubljana, which houses many of the nation's most precious historical artifacts, and the War Museum in Kobarid, which won the 1993 European Museum of the Year Award for its objective and sensitive portrayal of war. Other museums include the National Gallery and the Museum of Modern Art.

Slovenia's National and University Library in Ljubljana, designed by renowned architect Joze Plecnik, is adding a new wing that will open in 2011. Its collection, which includes

many works of national significance, includes medieval manuscripts and an extensive music collection. Many monasteries and private church libraries house older, more valuable manuscripts. For instance, the first two Slovenian translations of the Bible are held by the Franciscan order libraries.

Holidays

Slovenia's national holiday is Statehood Day (June 25). Independence Day is celebrated on December 26. Preseren Day (February 8) is a cultural holiday honoring poet France Preseren. The Day of Uprising against Occupation (April 27) commemorates the Slovenian fight against the Nazi occupation of World War II.

Reflecting the nation's religious heritage, several Christian holidays are on the official calendar. These include Assumption Day (August 15), Reformation Day (October 31), and All Souls' Day (November 1), in addition to holidays such as Christmas and Easter.

Youth Culture

Slovenian youth are very active. Their social lives often revolve around attending the cinema and sporting events, as well as frequenting discos and bars. Drinking and smoking are widely acceptable, and are alluring to many youth. Dating is common and customs surrounding dating have changed; females, once traditionally asked out by males, are now more open to taking the initiative.

The quality of education in Slovenia is very high, and the student-to-teacher ratio is less than 11:1. There is usually no dress code in school or university, and students enjoy expressing themselves through fashion. The university academic calendar begins in October and concludes in July.

In 2001, the Urska Dance School in Ljubljana started a tradition of mass quadrille dancing in the streets to celebrate the last day of school. In 2007, this tradition expanded to include 42,060 high school students from forty-five cities in Slovenia, Serbia, Bosnia-Herzegovina, Macedonia, and Croatia. They simultaneously took to the streets and broke a Guinness World

Record for public dancing (they danced to a quadrille from *Die Fledermaus* by Johann Strauss); 11,000 students danced in the streets of Ljubljana alone.

SOCIETY

Transportation

Highways and railroads connect Slovenia easily with its neighbors, Hungary, Austria, Italy, and Croatia, and service is generally reliable and punctual. There are also trains from Ljubljana to various European Union (EU) member nations, including Italy, Switzerland, Germany, Czech Republic, Bulgaria, Greece, Macedonia, Serbia, Hungary, Austria, and Croatia. Most local travel is done by car in Slovenia and most Slovenians drive to their destinations. Bikes are popular for short distances, and buses offer many options both between and within cities.

Roads in Slovenia are generally well maintained and cars travel on the right side of the road. Law, as are daytime headlights requires Seatbelt use; cell phone usage is prohibited while driving. Highway vignettes, or toll stickers, are required for driving on expressways and motorways. They may be purchased at gas stations and newsstands and are available in weekly, monthly, or yearly denominations.

Transportation Infrastructure

Slovenia has a well-developed transportation system. There are fourteen airports, six of which have paved runways, and three of which are international. Ljubljana is the busiest airport in the nation. There was a small celebration when the annual number of passengers surpassed one million in 2004. Koper is Slovenia's main port, and over 15 million tons of cargo passed through in 2007.

Media & Communications

There is a variety of broadcasting available in Slovenia, with numerous FM and AM radio stations and a great variety of television stations, both publicly and privately owned. The *Slovenia*

Times is the English newspaper in Slovenia, and the most popular dailies are the *Delo, Slovenske novice, Dnevnik* and *Vecer*. Freedom of speech is guaranteed by the Slovenian constitution and is generally observed. However, journalists have also been known to self-censor when commenting on domestic politics to avoid indirect political pressure.

Slovenia has a well-developed communications network, with 2.246 million mobile phone subscribers in 2012; many people have both landlines and mobile phones. In 2009, there were an estimated 1.298 million Internet users.

SOCIAL DEVELOPMENT

Standard of Living

Slovenia ranked 25th out of 187 countries on the 2013 United Nations Human Development Index.

Water Consumption

Slovenia enjoys being one of Europe's water-rich nations, as it enjoys Alpine and sub-Alpine runoff, rivers, streams, springs, lakes, and the Adriatic Sea. According to the government statistical office, Slovenia has four times the European average of water per capita. Ninety-seven percent of the running water in Slovenia comes from underground sources, as surface waters are becoming increasingly polluted.

Slovenia's wastewater treatment is in development, as many households are not connected to a wastewater treatment plant, but use cesspools. About 73 percent of wastewater is treated, but most treated and untreated wastewater is released into surface waters.

Education

Slovenia has a well-developed educational system and high literacy rate (99.7 percent as of 2015). During the 1990s, Slovenia began reforming the communist-era system to increase flexibility and choice. Nine years of schooling ("basic education") are compulsory, from the ages of six to fifteen. Pre-school is available but is not required, but statistics show that Slovenians have an average school life expectancy of 16 years (17 for women and 16 for men).

After completing early secondary education at age 15, students have several options. They can attend a four-year general secondary school known as gimnazije ("gymnasiums") to prepare for further studies at a university; they can attend a four-year technical school; or they can attend a vocational program for two and a half to three years leading up to further education or entry into their field of specialty. The final secondary school examination, which also serves as a university entrance examination, is known as the Matura.

The residents of Ljubljana are considered a well-educated group; the literacy rate is near 100 percent and talents for language, literature, and the arts are highly valued. Of the city's residents, more than 50,000 are university students in attendance at the city's university, making the population of Ljubljana an exceptionally youthful one.

Higher education is either academic or professional. Post-communist Slovenia has both private and public institutions of higher learning. The University of Ljubljana, the country's oldest, was founded in 1919 but traces its history back to academies established in the 16th century. The University of Maribor was founded during the communist era. The University of Primorska is the country's newest, established in 2003. Students who complete their undergraduate studies obtain a diploma leading to the first post-graduate degree of "specialist." This is followed by the master's degree and the doctorate.

Women's Rights

Slovenian women have held civil rights equal to men since World War II. In general, Slovenian women are well educated, are well represented in the workforce, and are not subject to gender discrimination. On average, Slovenian women complete seventeen years of education while Slovenian men only average sixteen years. Additionally, Slovenian women also hold the same literacy rate—99.7 percent for men and 99.7 percent for women (2015 estimate). In

2007, it was estimated that Slovenian women earned eight percent less than their male counterparts, which was almost half of the EU average of 15 percent. Slovenian women have also increased their political representation: under Prime Minister Borut Pahor (1963–), who held the office of the prime ministry from 2008 through 2012, five of the 18 ministers selected were women (two more than his predecessor).

To promote women in the workforce, the Slovenian government has taken measures to give both parents the option to rear their children. Mothers are given 105 days of maternal leave, and fathers are offered 90 days of paternal leave (of which 15 days are fully paid). Parental leave, lasting 260 days, begins immediately after maternal leave and may be shared between parents. Certain Slovenian corporations such as Lek, a large pharmaceutical company, have implemented family-friendly proposals for both men and women. The Office for Equal Opportunities of Slovenia also created a campaign entitled "Daddy, Activate Yourself," in which they promoted active fatherhood.

According to a 2013 human development report (HDR) from the UN, Slovenia was ranked 25 (out of 182 nations) in the gender-related development index (GDI). This ranking was based on their human development index (HDI), which measures life expectancy, purchasing power and income (standard of living), and adult literacy and educational enrolment at the primary, secondary, and tertiary levels, while also accounting for gender differences.

Traditional thinking still pervades the culture, however, and few fathers take advantage of their paternity leave. In 2011, 78 percent of fathers took up to 15 days of paternity leave; however, only 21 percent of fathers took additional paternity leave and only 7 percent of fathers took any part of the available shared parental leave., leaving most of the child-rearing responsibilities to women. Further, according to the UN Development Fund for Women (UNIFEM), domestic violence against women is an underreported problem in Slovenia, and Amnesty International (AI) claimed that one in seven Slovenian women had been raped, but only 5 percent sought help. According to the US Department of State, while Slovenian authorities seem to comply with complaints, human trafficking, particularly for the purpose of sexual exploitation, continues to be an issue. However, not a frequent source or destination country, Slovenia is often used as a transit country for women from Eastern Europe and the Balkan region.

Health Care

Slovenia's health care system is administered by the Ministry of Health. As of 2014, the average life expectancy at birth was about 77 years. All citizens are required to have a certain amount of health insurance. In Slovenia, compulsory health insurance is mandatory for all Slovenian residents, but not all costs (except for children and certain illnesses) are covered under the compulsory system. A non-profit organization, the Mutual Health Insurance Company, was established in 1999 to provide voluntary health insurance to cover additional medical costs. In 2010, there were approximately 2.54 doctors per 1,000 inhabitants.

GOVERNMENT

Structure

From the Middle Ages until World War I, the Slovenes were ruled by the Austrian Hapsburg dynasty. After the Austro-Hungarian Empire fell in 1918, the Slovenes joined with the Serbs and Croats to form an independent state, known from 1929 onward as the Kingdom of Yugoslavia. The kingdom collapsed during World War II, as the result of the Nazi occupation (1941–1945). The royal government-in-exile lost power to the communists after the war.

During the communist era, Slovenia was part of the Socialist Federal Republic of Yugoslavia, but the Slovenes found themselves increasingly unhappy in what they saw as a federation dominated by Serbs and Croats. A secession movement grew during the late 1980s, and Slovenia declared its independence on June 25, 1991; a

10-day war with Yugoslavia was almost without casualties, as Yugoslavia withdrew its military forces quickly after resistance from Slovenia. The country received recognition from the European Community in 1992, and joined the EU and NATO in 2004.

Slovenia's head of state is the popularly-elected president, who serves a five-year term. The president has little actual power, but serves as a symbol of national unity by exercising moral authority. The prime minister and cabinet officers, who are elected by Parliament, carry out most of the business of government. The president appoints the prime minister from the majority party.

The Slovenian parliament, known as the Skupšcina Slovenije (Slovenian Assembly) has two houses. The larger body, the National Assembly (Drzavni zbor), has ninety members who are elected every four years. Representation is ensured for the country's ethnic minorities; the Italians and Hungarians each receive one seat. The National Assembly is responsible for all legislation. The National Council (Drzavni Svet) has forty members and serves as an advisory body. It represents various interest groups and professional organizations.

Political Parties

From the beginning of the Republic, Slovenian politics was dominated by the liberal party, the Liberal Democracy of Slovenia (LDS). They lost the majority in 2004 to the Slovenian Democratic Party (SDS), a center-right party. While the SDS held power from 2004, the Social Democrats (SD), a center-left party, were in opposition. In the late 1990s and early 2000s, the SD party platform adopted policies that are more moderate and gained several prominent former LDS politicians, which put it in a strong position going into the 2008 election. In 2008, they secured a slight majority, 30.45 percent of the electorate, to the 29.26 garnered by the SDS. Parties and political coalitions continued to evolve in subsequent years.

In the 2014 election, the Modern Center Party (SMC) won 34.6 percent of the vote and

36 seats; the Slovenian Democratic Party (SDS) won 20.7 percent of the vote and 21 seats; the Democratic party of Pensioners of Slovenia (DeSUS) won 10.2 percent of the vote and 10 seats; the United Left (ZL) won six percent of the vote and six seats, followed by the New Slovenia (NSi) at 5.6 percent, the Alliance of Alenka Bratusek (ZaAB) at 4.3 percent, and minority parties taking the remaining 12.6 percent of the vote.

Local Government

Slovenia has no regional governments, and administration beneath the national level is handled entirely by municipalities, of which there are 210 (eleven classified as urban). Municipal governments (mayors and councilors) are elected every four years by popular vote and are responsible for budgets, managing municipal property, planning and development, zoning, providing local services, pre-school and primary education, and transportation infrastructure. Funding is generated locally, through taxes and asset revenue, except in those municipalities that require aid from the central government.

Judicial System

Slovenia's highest court is the nine-member Constitutional Court. Judges are nominated by the president and appointed by the National Assembly, for one nine-year term. The country's eleven-member Judicial Council recommends candidates to Parliament, who them appoints them to indefinite terms of office.

There are forty-four district, eleven regional, and four higher courts. Specialized courts handle labor, social insurance, and administrative issues.

Taxation

Slovenia levies a progressive tax on income and profit for businesses and individuals, as well as payroll and property taxes, value-added and excise taxes on goods and services, social security taxes, and other taxes and fees.

Armed Forces

The volunteer Slovenian Armed Forces consist of an army, navy, and air force. Slovenian forces have assisted in North Atlantic Treaty Organization (NATO) operations in Bosnia and Herzegovina, Kosovo, Afghanistan, Iraq, Chad, and Lebanon. The U.S. lends bilateral military assistance to Slovenia, which largely consists of training opportunities.

Foreign Policy

When Slovenia declared its independence from the former Yugoslavian states in 1991, a 10-day war ensued. There were minimal casualties before Slovenia emerged victorious, and the newly independent nation granted citizenship to all residents, regardless of ethnicity or origin. Since then, Slovenia has accepted over 100,000 Bosnian refugees and has been at the forefront in stabilizing the region. In 1992, Slovenia joined the UN and has since demonstrated a commitment to positive relations with other members of the international community. Slovenia also joined NATO. In 2004, it attained membership in the EU, even maintaining the organization's rotating presidency in 2008. In 2009, the prime ministers of Croatia and Slovenia signed a deal to settle a long-running border dispute (helping to remove a key obstacle to Croatia's prospects of securing European Union membership).

Slovenia makes an effort to participate in international aid both in providing monetary assistance to victims of natural disasters, and in deploying troops to conflict zones through NATO, the EU, and the UN. Slovenia has taken in refugees from Kosovo and supported refugees from Darfur. Slovenians play an active role in the Organization for Security and Co-operation (OSCE), for which Slovenia served as chairman-in-office in 2005. Slovenia also holds membership in numerous international organizations and economic associations, including the World Trade Organization (WTO), of which Slovenia was a founding member, the European Bank for Reconstruction and Development (EBRD), the Central European Free Trade Agreement

(CEFTA), and the European Free Trade Association (EFTA). Slovenia also served as chairperson of the International Atomic Energy Agency's (IAEA) board of governors from 2006 to 2007.

Part of Slovenia's willingness to cooperate with the international community is economically based. Two-thirds of its trade is with other members of the EU (primarily Germany, Italy, Austria, and France). Slovenia maintains bilateral military agreements with twenty-nine countries, most notably with the United States, and it participates in five major multinational regional peacekeeping bodies. Slovenia created the International Trust Fund for Demining and Mine Victims Assistance (ITF) and developed a demining device now used in Bosnia and Herzegovina, throughout the Balkans, and even in Central Asia and Cyprus. Slovenia has ratified all 13 anti-terrorism conventions and is a member of the Southeast European Defense Ministerial (SEDM) and the Proliferation Security Initiative (PSI), whose aim is to halt the proliferation of weapons of mass destruction (WMD).

Human Rights Profile

International human rights law insists that states respect civil and political rights, and promote an individual's economic, social, and cultural rights. The United Nations Universal Declaration on Human Rights (UDHR) is recognized as the standard for international human rights. Its authors sought the counsel of the world's great thinkers, philosophers, and religious leaders, and were careful to create a document that reflects the core values shared by every world culture. (To read this document or view the articles relating to cultural human rights, visit http://www.un.org/en/documents/udhr/.)

Slovenia generally has an excellent human rights record, and the Slovenian constitution protects civil liberties such as freedom of speech, freedom of religion, and the freedom to assemble. However, Slovenia has been criticized by international human rights watch groups for its treatment of "erased" citizens and discrimination against ethnic minorities, particularly the Romani.

Amnesty International (AI) has accused Slovenia of failing to restore citizenship to thousands of people who had been living in Slovenia, but failed to apply for citizenship, resulting in unemployment and a lack of health coverage for that segment of society. The Slovenian government has responded to this claim by stating that citizenship was offered to all those residing in the country when independence was declared on June 25, 1991. In particular, the government stated that all people, regardless of race, religion, or former citizenship, were allowed to apply for Slovenian citizenship by December 26, 1991. However, on February 26, 1992, the government "erased" from record all who did not register by the deadline and maintains that it does not discriminate. While AI still condemned Slovenia for this act, in 2008 the international community voted overwhelmingly for Slovenia to take a seat on the UN Human Rights Council (UNHRC).

Autochthonous (indigenous) Italian and Hungarian minorities in Slovenia are protected by law and allowed to use their national symbols and provide bilingual education for their youth. In addition, each group maintains a representative in parliament. As of 2009, the Romani, however, are not protected in the same manner, but the Slovenian government is taking steps to remedy the situation. Approximately 3,000 Romani are registered in Slovenia, but AI estimates the actual number to be somewhere between 7,000 and 12,000. The goal is to better integrate the Roma into the Slovenian community, legalize Roma settlements, and provide both employment and educational infrastructure. In education, the Slovenian government's stated aims are to teach both Slovene and Romani languages and Slovene and Romani history, culture and identity.

Migration

Slovenia's net migration rate in 2014 is 0.37 per 1,000 people. In the first decade of the 21st century, Slovenia saw an increase in immigration from Balkan nations seeking employment and most immigrants were men. Immigration to Slovenia has stabilized in the wake of the global economic crisis begun in 2008. Many foreign workers have left the country since the economic downturn.

ECONOMY

Overview of the Economy
Slovenia is one of the most prosperous parts of the former Yugoslavia and the former Eastern Bloc. In spite of its socialist history, and its transition from socialism in the late 20th century, Slovenia boasts a thriving market economy that is both stable and growing. Since the end of communism, the Slovenian government has worked to privatize the economy and promote foreign investment.

Unlike several of its neighbors, the country has not been plagued by soaring inflation rates and until the global economic crisis that began in 2008, had managed to keep unemployment at a manageable level. The country's two biggest industries are manufacturing (steel, textiles, and machinery) and mining (stone, coal, lime, and aluminum). The impact of the economic crisis in Slovenia has tightened access to credit for the country's business sector, and some have pointed out that Slovenia has avoided foreign direct investment. In 2010, Slovenia joined the Organization for Economic Cooperation and Development (OECD). According to Slovenia's minister of finance, participation in this organization will increase Slovenia's reputation in international capital markets.

The capital Ljubljana, which is responsible for about one quarter of the country's gross domestic product (GDP), has a rich and varied economy. The city manufactures petrochemicals, processed food, electronics, and pharmaceutical products, and its retail, financial, and service industries contribute significant earnings. In addition, it is an important center for the wine trade--one out of every three farms in Slovenia grows wine grapes.

In 2004, Slovenia joined the European Union (EU), a move which required extensive economic and monetary reforms. In 2014, the gross domestic product (GDP) was estimated at $ $61.24 billion (USD), with a per capita GDP of $29,400 (USD).

Industry
Slovenia has moved toward an industrial and service-based economy. In 2014, industry accounted for about 28 percent of GDP, and services for nearly 70 percent. Major industries include heavy manufacturing, metallurgy and smelting, electronics manufacturing, chemicals processing, and tourism.

Slovenia trades mainly with its neighbors in Central Europe, particularly Italy, Croatia, and Germany. There are three ports (Izola, Koper, Piran), all located on the Adriatic Sea.

Labor
Slovenia is recovering from the global economic crisis that began in 2008. The unemployment rate in 2014 was 13 percent. Among the labor force, the bulk of workers are employed in the services sector (62.8 percent), followed by 35 percent in the manufacturing sector, only an estimated 2.2 percent of the population finds employment in agriculture.

Energy/Power/Natural Resources
Slovenia has many rich resources, including extensive mineral deposits, timber forests, and fertile land. Minerals include energy resources such as lignite coal and oil, precious metals such as silver, as well as other important industrial materials such as uranium. The country's rivers provide extensive hydropower.

The country's rapid industrialization during the communist era caused extensive environmental damage to the country, including acid rain.

Fishing
Slovenia's fishing industry is characterized by marine and freshwater sectors. Up until 2008, the Slovenian government was in conflict with the Croatian government over fishing territories in

the Adriatic. In 2008 though, the Croatian government decided to suspend the controversial Ecological and Fisheries Protection Zone, which had put a significant portion of the Adriatic under Croatian control, limiting fishing by other EU countries. The 2008 decision suspended the zone for other EU members.

According to Slovenia's Statistical Office, 118 people were employed in the marine fishing industry, 53 percent of which were self-employed. Of the number of registered vessels, less than half were used for fishing, while the rest were used for aquaculture or fish farming.

Forestry

Slovenia's land area is covered by almost 60 percent of forest, dominated by beech, fir-beech, and beech-oak. Seventy-two percent of forest areas are privately owned, while the state owns 28 percent. Forestry contributes about 0.2 percent to the country's GDP. Analysts claim that the forestry industry is not organized and is not producing at capacity.

Mining/Metals

The focus of the Slovenian mining industry is in coal, natural gas, petroleum, and a variety of industrial minerals. In 2010, the mining industry saw a drop in production.

Agriculture

Agriculture remains important to the Slovenian economy, despite industrialization. Around two percent of workers are employed in agriculture and agriculture provides only 2 percent of GDP (2014 estimate). Crops such as potatoes, grapes, grains such as wheat, and sugar beets are grown.

Animal Husbandry

The main agricultural activity in Slovenia is raising livestock (cattle, sheep, and poultry).

Tourism

Slovenia has actively promoted tourism since the downfall of communism, though the Balkan War has hurt business to some degree. Tourism is a major part of the economy, valued at over $2 billion USD. Many visitors come from other parts of the former Yugoslavia, as well as from neighboring countries such as Italy.

Ljubljana, an ancient city with Roman origins, offers historic sites as well as cosmopolitan entertainment. A popular attraction is the Lippizaner Stallion stud farm in Lipica, where the famous Lippizaner trained horses are bred.

Jennifer Kan Martinez,
Eric Badertscher, M. Lee

DO YOU KNOW?

- The name of Mount Triglav, the country's tallest mountain, means "three heads."

- Before the Euro, Slovenia's currency was the tolar. The word 'tolar' has the same origin as the United States 'dollar.' Both derive from the thaler, a historic European silver coin first minted during the Renaissance.

- According to local myth, the ancient Greek hero Jason, who was fleeing from King Aites, from whom he had stolen the Golden Fleece, founded Ljubljana. According to the legend, Jason sailed up a river and came upon the city of Ljublana. The dragon that Jason is said to have killed there is represented on the Ljubljana coat of arms.

- There is no definitive theory about the true origin of the city's name, which may derive from the name of an ancient Slavic god named Laburus. The name "Ljubljana" has also been linked to the Latin words for "a flooding river," or to the Slavic word for "beloved."

Bibliography

Ivan Cankar. "Martin Kacur: The Biography of an Idealist." Budapest: *Central European Press*, 2009.

John Corsellis. "Slovenia 1945: Memories of Death and Survival after World War II." New York: *I.B. Tauris*, 2005.

John K. Cox. "Slovenia: Evolving Loyalties." New York: *Routledge*, 2005.

Lonely Planet and Mark Baker. "Slovenia." Oakland, CA: *Lonely Planet*, 2013.

Oto Luthar, et al. "The Land Between: A History of Slovenia." Frankurt am Main: *Peter Lange*, 2013.

Rick Steves. "Rick Steves' Croatia and Slovenia." Berkeley, CA: Avalon, 2014.

Works Cited

"2008 Statistical Report: Slovenia." *United Nations Human Development Reports*. http://hdrstats.undp.org/2008/countries/country_fact_sheets/cty_fs_SVN.html.

"About OECD." Organisation for Economic Co-operation and Development. http://www.oecd.org/.

Alex Steger. "Literary perspectives: Slovenia." *Eurozine*, 27 June 2007. http://www.eurozine.com/pdf/2007-06-27-steger-en.pdf

Barica Razpotnik. "Rapid Reports: Population." *Statistical Office of the Republic of Slovenia*. http://www.stat.si/doc/statinf/05-si-007-0803.pdf.

"Candidature of Slovenia for Human Rights Council." *United Nations*, 1 May 2006. http://www.un.org/ga/60/elect/hrc/slovenia.pdf.

Carol Kaufman. "A River's Gifts." *National Geographic*, Jan. 2007. http://ngm.nationalgeographic.com/print/2007/01/slovenia-river-excavation/kaufmann-text

"Country Reports on Human Rights Practices: Slovenia." *U.S. Department of State*. http://www.state.gov/g/drl/rls/hrrpt/2006/78839.htm#.

"Culture of Slovenia." *Countries and Their Cultures*. http://www.everyculture.com/Sa-Th/Slovenia.html.

"Facts and Figures on Gender Equality: Slovenia." *International Labour Organisation*. http://www.ilo.org/public/english/region/eurpro/budapest/download/gender/slovenia.pdf.

"Highest Proportion of Women in New Slovenian Government." *Wien International*, 19 Nov. 2008. http://www.wieninternational.at/en/node/11309.

Joanna Walters. "Reach for the top and a birching." *The Observer*, 12 Nov. 2000. http://www.guardian.co.uk/travel/2000/nov/12/climbingholidays.slovenia.observerescapesection

"Kobariski Musej." *Kobariski Musej*. http://www.kobariski-muzej.si/

"Lek among first companies in Slovenia to receive family-friendly company certificate." *Lek*, 14 May 2007. http://www.lek.si/eng/media-room/press-releases/3873/.

Mike Chino. "Slovenia's Gorgeous Honeycomb Housing Complex." *Inhabitat*, 23 June 2008http://www.inhabitat.com/2008/06/23/slovenias-gorgeous-honeycomb-housing-complex/.

"NSK State." *The State of NSK*. http://www.nskstate.com.

"Office for Equal Opportunities of Slovenia." *European Fatherhood*. http://fatherhood.social.dk/projetcs/SI.html.

"One Million Passengers Annually for the First Time." *Aerodrom Ljubljana*, 8 Dec. 2004. http://www.lju-airport.si/eng/novica.asp?IDn=501&IDM=86.

Polona Prešeren. "Slovenia.si." Slovenia.si: Your Gateway to Information on Slovenia, 2009. http://www.slovenia.si/

Regina Hackett. "Slovenian art collective is adept at working politics and art." *Seattle Post-Intelligencer*, 19 Nov. 2004 http://seattlepi.nwsource.com/visualart/200214_visual19.html

"Republic of Slovenia." *United Nations Development Fund for Women*. http://www.unifem.sk/index.cfm?module=project&page=country&CountryISO=SI#_ftn2.

"Rights under insurance for parental protection." The Government of the Republic of Slovenia, Ministry of Labour, Family, and Social Affairs, 2008. http://www.mddsz.gov.si/en/areas_of_work/family/rights_under_insurance_for_parental_protection/#c16906

"Škocjan Caves." UNESCO World Heritage Center. http://whc.unesco.org/en/list/390/.

"Škocjan Caves Park." Park Škocjanske Jame, *Slovenia*, 2006. http://www.park-skocjanske-jame.si/eng/.

"Slovenia." *Central Intelligence Agency*. https://www.cia.gov/library/publications/the-world-factbook/geos/si.html#Comm

"Slovenia." *Culture Crossing: World guide to cross-cultural etiquette*. http://www.culturecrossing.net/basics_business_student.php?id=184.

"Slovenia." *Passport to Trade*. http://www.businessculture.org/

"Slovenia." *U.S. Department of State*. http://www.state.gov/r/pa/ei/bgn/3407.htm.

"Slovenia." *World Housing Encyclopedia*, 2002. http://www.world-housing.net/

"Slovenia: Amnesty International's Briefing to the UN Committee on Economic, Social and Cultural Rights." *Amnesty International, USA*. http://www.amnestyusa.org/document.php?id=ENGEUR680022005&lang=e.

"Slovenia–Language, Culture, Customs and Etiquette." *Kwintessential Cross Cultural Solutions*. http://www.kwintessential.co.uk/resources/global-etiquette/slovenia.html.

"Slovenia-Official Travel Guide." *Slovenian Tourist Board*. http://www.slovenia.info/

"Slovenia Respects Human Rights." *Government of the Republic of Slovenia, Ministry of the Interior*. http://www.mnz.gov.si/nc/en/splosno/cns/news/article/12027/5783/.

"Srečko Kosovel." *Poetry International Web.* http:// slovenia.poetryinternationalweb.org/piw_cms/cms/ cms_module/index.php?obj_id=5043.

Stephen Holden. "Facing the Menace of Totalitarianism." *New York Times*, 2 Oct. http://query.nytimes.com/gst/ fullpage.html?res=9C06E0DA1F3CF931A35753C 1A960958260.

Tim Doling and Helena Pivec. "Slovenia Cultural Profile." *Visiting Arts, Ministry of Culture of Slovenia and British Council Slovenia*. http://www.culturalprofiles.net/ Slovenia/Directories/Slovenia_Cultural_Profile/-1.html

"Tetris Apartments." Ofiz, Oct. 2007. http://www.ofis a.si/ default.cfm?Kat=0309&ProdID=65.

"The State of the World's Human Rights: Slovenia." *Amnesty International Report*. http://thereport.amnesty. org/eng/regions/europe-and-central-asia/slovenia.

"Traffic Conditions." *Traffic Information Centre*, 10 Feb. 2009 http://www.promet.si/?lang=2

Zoran Triglav, Aljoša Ocepek, and Miran Hladnik, "Eating Out." *Slovenian for Travelers*. http://www.ff.uni-lj.si/ publikacije/sft/eating.htm

"Works." *Jože Plečnik Virtual Museum*. http://www. plecnik.net/.

"World Cultures: Slovenes." *Every Culture*. http:// www.everyculture.com/wc/Rwanda-to-Syria/ Slovenes.html

"Writers Residence in Slovenia." *Center for Slovenian Literature*. http://www.ljudmila.org/litcenter/key/1.htm

Saint Michael's Cathedral in Kiev, Ukraine

Ukraine

Introduction

The name Ukraine means "borderland." It is an apt name for the country, as it shares boundaries with a number of other countries in southeastern Europe. Ukraine became independent from the Soviet Union in 1991. It boasts a unique culture and ethnic heritage, and has been called the "breadbasket" of the Eastern European region.

In the early 21st century, Ukraine finds itself at a crossroads as it embraces its new connection with the West. Relations with Russia grew tense in March 2014, when Russia's parliament endorsed President Vladimir Putin's request to send military forces into Crimea, an autonomous region of southern Ukraine with strong Russian loyalties. Shortly thereafter, Russia completed its annexation of Crimea following a referendum that was considered illegitimate by Ukraine and much of the rest of the world.

GENERAL INFORMATION

Official Language: Ukrainian
Population: 44,429,471 (July 2015 estimate)
Currency: Hryvnia
Coins: 100 kopiykas equal one hryvnia. Kopiykas come in denominations of 1, 2, 5, 10, 25, and 50. There is also a one hryvnia coin.
Land Area: 579,330 square kilometers (223,680 square miles) (including Crimea)
Water Area: 24,220 square kilometers (9,351 square miles)

National Anthem: "Shche ne vmerla Ukraina" ("Ukraine Still Lives")
Capital: Kyiv/Kiev
Time Zone: GMT +2
Flag Description: The Ukrainian flag features two equal and horizontal stripes: blue (azure) on the top and golden yellow on the bottom. The blue represents the sky; the yellow represents fields of grain.

Population

Ukrainians make up the majority of the population of Ukraine, numbering about 78 percent in 2014. There are a variety of other ethnic groups living there, including Russians, the largest minority group at 17 percent of the population. Other groups include Belarusians, Moldovans, Hungarians, Bulgarians, Jews, Poles, and Crimean Tartars. Native minority groups include the Boiky, the Hutsuly, and the Dolyniany, which are descended from ancient Slavic tribes.

Principal Cities by Population (2012):

- Kyiv (2,803,716)
- Kharkiv (1,431,461)
- Dnipropetrovs'k (987,629)
- Odesa (997,189)
- Donets'k (944,552)
- Zaporizhzhia (766,736)
- L'viv (723,605)
- Kryvyi Rih (654,964)
- Mykolaiv (491,693)
- Mariupol' (458,415)

[NOTE: All Ukrainian place names are given with their Ukrainian transliteration. Some may be more familiar in Russian: for example, Kyiv (Ukrainian) versus Kiev (Russian).]

Ukraine has a higher population of women to men, with 0.86 males to each female (2009 estimate). Some attribute that disparity to economic migration to other areas of Europe. The larger cities tend to be in the industrialized eastern portion of the country (a 2015 estimate from the CIA *World Factbook* states that nearly 70 percent of the population lives in urban areas), with the west of country largely rural in nature, although the city of L'viv is there, with a population of over 700,000.

Languages

While Ukrainian, a Slavic language, is the official language of Ukraine, Russian is also frequently used. A 2012 legislation enables a language spoken by at least 10 percent of an oblast's population to be given the status of "regional language," allowing for its use in courts, schools, and other government institutions; Ukrainian remains the country's only official language nationwide.

Native People & Ethnic Groups

Modern Ukrainians are a white eastern European people of Slavic heritage. Like Russians and Belarusians, Ukrainians are known as Eastern Slavs.

There has been some debate over the origins of the Ukrainian people. One theory states that Ukrainians, Russians, and Belarusians are descended from a single group of ancient Slavic people called the Rus. However, Ukrainians have worked toward distinguishing themselves as a separate ethnic group from Russians and Belarusians. The Ukrainian language is distinct from Russian, and Ukrainian literature and culture are unique.

The region of Crimea, a peninsula within the Black Sea, in the south of the country, has a special status in the constitution. Russians make up the majority of Crimea's population, and most did not wish to remain part of Ukraine. In 1992, Crimea seceded from Ukraine and created its own constitution as an autonomous region within the country. Jews first settled in the region in the fourth century BCE, primarily in Crimea and along the coast near the Black Sea. Most of the country's Muslims also live in Crimea.

Religions

Ukraine is primarily a Christian country. Tradition asserts that the first Christians were baptized in Ukraine in 988. Religious groups faced persecution under Soviet rule, when many clerics were forced to flee the country or were imprisoned. Today, there are a number of Christian denominations in the country, including the Ukrainian Orthodox Church, the Ukrainian Greek Orthodox Church, and the Roman Catholic Church. Other religions practiced in Ukraine include Judaism and Islam.

Climate

Ukraine experiences a moderate climate that varies according to region. Typically, the south and west are warmer, while the north and east are cooler. The country has four seasons and an annual winter snowfall, although most precipitation occurs during summer. Ukraine receives over 48 centimeters (19 inches) of precipitation per year.

The country's mountain regions have a mountain climate, while areas in southern Crimea are Mediterranean. Summer temperatures average 18° to 20° Celsius (65° to 69° Fahrenheit); winter temperatures are regularly below freezing.

ENVIRONMENT & GEOGRAPHY

Topography

Ukraine is bordered by Belarus on the north and Russia on the north and east. The Black Sea forms a natural border in the south, with Moldova and Romania located to the southwest. Hungary, Slovakia, and Poland share boundaries with Ukraine in the west.

Ukraine consists primarily of four vegetative zones: forest, forest-steppe, steppe, and Mediterranean. There are vast plains and plateaus. Much of the land has an average elevation of around 300 meters above sea level. There are two major mountain ranges in the country: the Carpathian Mountains are located in the southwest, and the Crimean Mountains on the Crimean peninsula. The Crimean Riviera has a number of beaches and bays with tourist resorts.

The country's largest rivers are the Dnieper, Dniester, and the Boh. The Dnieper is the largest river in Ukraine, measuring 2,285 kilometers (1,419 miles) long. There are a few shallow lakes in the northwest and in south.

Ukraine is known for its many springs. There are healthful mineral springs throughout the country, as well as carbon dioxide springs in the Carpathians and Caucasus. Radioactive springs can be found on the shores of the Black Sea.

The capital, Kyiv, sits on the western and eastern banks of the Dnieper River in the lowlands of northern Ukraine, midway between the start of the Dnieper in northwest Russia and its mouth at the Black Sea.

Plants & Animals

Ukraine has over 16,000 species of plants in its various vegetation zones. The forests consist primarily of oak, beech, and hornbeam. Evergreen trees such as juniper, silver fir, and pine are common in the mountain regions. In addition to large expanses of pastureland, Ukraine also contains high mountain meadows. Plants like fig, olive, orange, and lemon trees grow in the country's Mediterranean zone.

There are over 28,000 animal species in Ukraine, although the country has few native species. Among the larger mammals are elk, lynx, brown bear, and white hare. Bird species such as the capercaillie, black grouse, and hazel hens are also common. Ukraine is home to several bat species, such as the lesser mouse-eared bat and the long-winged bat.

In 1986, the nuclear power plant in Chernobyl (in the north of the country) experienced a meltdown. This disaster contaminated nearby soil and vegetation with radiation, and the city itself was evacuated and relocated to Slavutych, a city developed to house the survivors of the Chernobyl disaster. Ukraine is still working to repair the environmental damage caused by the meltdown.

The Ukrainian government has also plans to expand nature preserves such as the Askania Nova state park.

CUSTOMS & COURTESIES

Greetings

When meeting someone in Ukraine for the first time, it is appropriate to say "Vitayu" ("Hello") and to offer a firm handshake with direct eye contact, while repeating one's name. Gloves should always be removed before shaking hands. Ukrainians, like Russians, often introduce themselves by their first name and their middle name, which is based on their father's first name. Close male friends may add a hug or a pat on the back. Women often greet friends, family and other women with a series of three alternating kisses on the cheek. Generally, greetings are never offered over the threshold of the entrance to a house or building, as this is considered bad luck. Such greetings and farewells should take place entirely inside or outside the doorway.

In corporate environments, when business associates meet for the first time, they generally introduce themselves with their full name (first, middle, and last), as well as any academic or professional titles they hold. Business cards are customarily exchanged, and foreign visitors should take the time to have cards printed in Ukrainian (or to obtain double-sided cards).

After initial formalities are over, Ukrainian business etiquette tends to be more informal than in other countries.

Gestures & Etiquette

Typically, Ukrainians tend to be reserved in public. They refrain from loud conversation and frown on public displays of emotion or self-promotion. In addition, Ukrainians value simplicity and directness in conversation, which can sometimes be perceived as being impolite or rude. However, once a personal connection is made, Ukrainians are generally considered warm, welcoming and generous.

Traditional Western rules of etiquette are important in Ukraine. For example, men are expected to hold doors for women, assist them with heavy packages, and help them into and out of their overcoats. When riding public transportation, men and healthy young women should give up their seats for the elderly, disabled, and mothers with small children. In addition, speaking with crossed arms or with hands thrust into pockets is considered extremely rude, particularly in front of older people. Sitting with legs spread wide or with one crossed over the other is also generally considered inappropriate.

The most complex Ukrainian rules of etiquette address behavior at group dinners and celebrations. Guests should not begin eating until the host has welcomed everyone and formally started the meal. Ukrainians pride themselves on their generosity at the table, so it can be considered rude to refuse servings of food. Guests should also try to serve themselves a small portion of each dish offered.

Furthermore, the offering of toasts is an important part of Ukrainian social gatherings. It is customary for each adult or head of each household at the table to offer a toast, so guests should be prepared for their turn. The host of the party is responsible for making sure that everyone's glass is full. Empty bottles are often removed from the table immediately. In addition, bread is typically never thrown away, as it is an important religious and cultural symbol of life and prosperity.

Eating/Meals

Ukrainians typically eat three meals a day. Breakfast is commonly a light meal, usually consisting of bread or a cereal such as kasha (buckwheat). Often, breakfast is accompanied by tea. Lunch is eaten in the early afternoon, and is usually the main meal of the day. It is often served in two courses, including a soup (such as borscht) and a dish with meat or poultry (often leftovers from the previous dinner). The evening dinner is usually a family meal, and is most often prepared and eaten at home. Ukrainian families rarely eat out, due to the cost and the inconvenience of getting to and from restaurants, especially in the evening.

In rural areas, it is common for Ukrainian families to cultivate their own gardens and make pickles and preserves to be consumed during the winter. In addition, many Ukrainian houses have an unheated basement, shed or cottage that serves as a walk-in cooler when the weather gets colder. Food is brought inside to the table for dinner and afterward, leftovers are simply carried back to the cooler.

Generally, Ukrainians use utensils in the continental manner, which constitutes holding the knife in the right hand while using the fork in the left (not switching hands to bring food to the mouth). Hands are always kept on the table, with wrists (not elbows) resting on the table edge.

Visiting

When visiting someone's home for the first time, it is customary to bring a small gift. These may include chocolates, a bottle of vodka, or a small souvenir from the guest's hometown. Flowers are also welcome, but only in odd numbers (even numbers are for funerals). Carnations and yellow blooms should be avoided, as the former are used for funerals and the latter are associated with false intentions. Gifts are generally opened after the guests have departed, and not immediately after they are received. In many homes, visitors are asked to remove their shoes in the entryway. They also may be temporary provided with slippers to wear during their stay.

After dinner, it is common for the hosts to bring out photo albums and share memories of family members or recent holidays and trips. Popular social activities may also include chess, which is almost as popular as football (soccer) in Ukraine, and singing. Ukrainians love to sing, and some households may even own karaoke machines. Generally, most evenings end relatively early, so that guests can make their way safely home before it gets too late.

LIFESTYLE

Family

Traditionally, domestic life Ukraine was built around large extended families living together in one village, and often under one roof. Although this structure still exists in some rural areas (especially in the west), today most Ukrainian households are based on the single family unit. However, in most families, elderly parents live with the child that will inherit their property. Often, they help in the raising of children and in maintaining the house.

The poor economic conditions of the late Soviet and post-independence eras have forced many young couples to live with their parents, often in cramped quarters. These pressures have contributed to high rates of divorce and low birth rates. In addition, many younger Ukrainians are also seeking educational and career opportunities abroad. These factors have led to an overall decline in the Ukrainian population in the late-20th and early-21st centuries, and have altered the traditional family structure in many households.

Housing

In major cities, most inhabitants live in large Soviet-era apartment blocks, which are generally solid in construction, but vary widely in terms of appearance and cleanliness. Apartment tenants sometimes divide long hallways into smaller sections in order to create more private spaces.

Most Ukrainians prefer to live in single-family houses. A typical Ukrainian home is walled and gated, often with a private yard and a garden. Older houses are typically one story structures, constructed from stone or stucco. Cold winters and seeping moisture during the spring thaw make upkeep difficult, so the exteriors often appear weathered and run-down. Some newer homes are constructed with modern materials, including plastics and composites. Wealthier Ukrainians tend to build robust, multi-story homes out of stone or concrete, decorated with ornate detailing or metalwork.

In addition, many Ukrainians, especially city dwellers, own summer cottages in the country, called dachas. Often, these are little more than one-room sheds on tiny plots of land. Nevertheless, they provide a welcome escape from cramped city living and a place to cultivate gardens and enjoy the outdoors.

Food

Generally, Ukrainian cuisine is similar to Russian and Polish cuisine, with Turkish and German influences. Due to the country's rich soil and productive farmland, a wide range of local produce and meats is typically available as ingredients. For these reasons, Ukraine was once referred to as the "breadbasket" of the Soviet Union.

Bread is the most important part of the Ukrainian diet. It serves not only as a staple, but also has deep religious and cultural significance. In addition to the dense rye bread used for daily consumption, Ukrainians prepare specialty breads for nearly every holiday or celebration. Kolach is a braided bread served with Sunday meals and on family holidays. Korovai, lezhen and dyven are prepared for weddings to represent different aspects of marriage. Paska, a cake-like bread filled with nuts and dried fruits, is ritually prepared once a year for Easter.

Pork is another Ukrainian favorite, and pork fat is a commonly used ingredient. In addition to being used for cooking, pork fat is also fried or smoked and eaten by itself. Kovbasa sausage, in particular, is popular (it is better known in the West by its Polish name, kielbasa). Every region and household has its own signature recipes for varenyky dumplings, made from dough stuffed with potatoes, mushrooms, meat, vegetables or fruits. Ukrainians also make their own version of borscht, the Russian beet soup. The Ukrainian version is sweeter, richer, and usually pinker in color. The Ukrainian version also contains more beets and meat, with less cabbage as filler. In the summer, Ukrainians enjoy outdoor grilling, especially shashlik – lamb kabobs served on skewers and marinated with Mediterranean flavors.

Life's Milestones

Over time, many ancient Ukrainian rituals have simply been absorbed into Christian celebrations and traditions. In addition, many practices, which were discouraged under Soviet rule, are being rediscovered and adapted for modern times.

One important tradition is the selection of godparents (kumy) to watch over the child. The kumy play a key role in the postryzhennya, the child's first haircut, which takes place several months after the birth. In addition, a child's birth is a time of feasting and celebration.

Modern weddings are set in motion when the groom-to-be brings his family and friends to ask his future bride's parents for her hand in marriage. A few months after consent is granted, the couple is often married in a civil ceremony while standing together on an embroidered cloth. They then proceed to a church ceremony, where the union is blessed by a priest. Afterwards, the wedding party typically celebrates the union at a boisterous reception, featuring feasting, toasts, dancing and practical jokes. Instead of (or in addition to) a wedding cake, Ukrainian weddings feature a korovai, a special bread prepared with flour contributed by both families.

Ukrainian funerals are often repeated nine days after the person's death, again after forty days, and then annually. Many Ukrainians also observe Zeleni sviata, a festival of remembrance which takes place fifty days after Easter. In addition, when visiting a grave, it is a common custom for Ukrainians to bring vodka or other spirits as well as some of the departed's favorite foods. They will often place a portion of food and drink on the gravestone, and share the rest amongst themselves while reminiscing about their lost loved one.

CULTURAL HISTORY

Art

Ukraine's history dates back to circa 4500 BCE. Since that time, the area has experienced dozens of major and minor migrations and invasions from Europe, Asia and the Middle East. This pattern continued into the modern era. Foreign domination in Ukraine ended with a declaration of independence in 1991 following the dissolution of the Soviet Union. Consequently, Ukrainian culture reflects a wide range of influences, based on language and heritage as opposed to ethnicity.

The modern Ukrainian nation traces its roots to the medieval state of Kyivan Rus'. This Slavic kingdom, founded in the ninth century, encompassed present-day northern Ukraine, Belarus and Western Russia. Eastern Christianity became the official religion of the kingdom in the 10th century under the reign of Vladimir I (c. 958–1015). This period of Christianization also witnessed the cultural influence of the Byzantine Empire, one of the most culturally and commercially dominant empires in European history. After the decline of Kyivan Rus' in the 13th century, much of Ukraine came under Polish rule. This period saw the rise of the Cossacks, tribe-like martial societies existing almost as independent states within Ukraine's borders. Cossack culture would become largely influential in providing the basis of much of Ukraine's modern national identity.

In the 18th century, Ukraine was largely dominated by Russia. As a result, Ukrainian culture was suppressed by the Russian tsars, or emperors. However, Russian culture of the time was strongly influenced by Ukrainians, as many of the Russian Empire's leading composers, artists and thinkers were Ukrainian. The Bolshevik Revolution in 1917 transformed the Russian Empire into the Union of Soviet Socialist Republics (USSR), or Soviet Union, the world's first communist state. During the period of Soviet control, Ukrainian traditions were occasionally used to promote pro-Soviet propaganda. However, for the most part, Ukrainian cultural traditions were suppressed by the Soviet state, especially during a series of genocidal purges and forced relocations during the 1930s.

The collapse of the Soviet Union in 1991 led to a resurgence in Ukrainian language and nationalism. After the peaceful Orange Revolution of 2004 swept away a pro-Russian government, the Ukrainian people were free to fully express their unique cultural heritage. Yet, Ukrainians had similar concerns after the pro-Russian Viktor Yanukovych was elected president in 2010. Protests were triggered in 2013 by Yanukovych's decision not to sign an association agreement with the European Union, because of pressure from Russia. By 2014, protesters insisted on Yanukovych's removal. His security forces withdrew from the city center, and Yanukovych soon fled the capital, eventually going into exile in Russia. After Yanukovych left, Russia—which strongly opposed the protests and ties between Ukraine and Europe—invaded the country. Using a combination of Russian troops (from its naval base in Sevastopol), Special Forces, Cossacks, and local separatists, the Kremlin quickly captured the Crimean Peninsula and annexed it to the Russian Federation in mid-March.

Architecture

Ukraine's architectural tradition begins with the introduction of the Byzantine style after the country adopted Eastern Christianity in the 10th century. Byzantine architecture was largely a continuation of Roman architecture. One particular feature of Byzantine architecture is the use of domes, as well as mosaics and vaults. The Saint Sophia Cathedral in Kiev and the nearby Holy Trinity Church provide examples of this style, while Romanesque half-columns and simple arches appear in later churches. Gothic architecture is rare, due in part to the constant warfare of this period (roughly the 12th to 16th centuries), which made it difficult to invest decades in building such complex structures.

During the late Renaissance, the Cossack aristocracy, led by the 17th century leader Ivan Mazepa (1639–1709), adopted grand, ornate Baroque forms and added Byzantine elements. This style, which is called Ukrainian Baroque (or Cossack Baroque) is simpler and less decorative than the Western European version. Baroque style, which developed during the 17th and 18th centuries, is characterized by harmony in both visual and spatial relationships. Examples can be found throughout Ukraine, such as the St. George Cathedral at Vydubychi. In addition, many overseas Ukrainian communities have built churches in this style, reflecting its prominent place in Ukraine's cultural identity.

Unfortunately, much of Ukraine's architectural heritage has been lost. Many structures were destroyed during World War II. Furthermore, throughout the Soviet era, official government atheism led to the neglect or misuse of churches. Some architectural treasures have even been the victims of social progress or modernization, as local citizens seek to modernize their communities.

Drama

Ukraine enjoys a rich theatrical past, ranging from one-act folk dramas to private plays enacted in 19th-century estates by travelling dramatists. Two theatrical traditions developed, an urban theater tradition featuring Russian and Ukrainian productions in the Russian language, and a more amateur, rural tradition in the Ukrainian language, which was banned in the mid-19th century. These Ukrainian-language productions were largely the work of travelling troupes of actors based in western Ukraine; the Ukrainska Besida Theater was a popular troupe in the late-19th and early 20th century. At the same time, cities under Russian control were extremely limited in their choice of production, with social and historical themes forbidden under censorship laws.

These censorship restrictions lightened somewhat in the early 20th century, and a more creative and progressive theater scene developed after 1917. The development of the Berezil Theatre by Les Kurbas (1887–1937) in 1922 ushered in a new era of theater, with more avant-garde themes and productions, and providing a venue for the production of Ukrainian plays by native writers, particularly Mykola Kulish (1892–1937). Kulish wrote several plays that met the fate of the censors when put into production. Censors were carefully tailoring literature and drama to confirm with the Soviet Party message, and many of Kulish's plays were revised. Kulish began his career by writing about the post-Soviet life in Ukraine, but turned to comedies in the late 1920s. In 1933, he was removed and later arrested, and most of his manuscripts were taken by authorities and destroyed.

Meanwhile, in western Ukraine, a Theater of the Western Ukrainian National Republic was established. It was short-lived, as all theaters eventually came under the control of the Soviet Union, which established national theaters and enacted a policy in all the arts centered on "socialist realism." Socialist realism required that writers depict the Soviet "reality," but really became a vehicle for authorities to re-educate citizens about how good their lives really were—in spite of what they really thought—and glorified the new order and bureaucracies created in this new social structure.

It wasn't until the 1990s that the Ukrainian theater began to rise once again. In the early 21st century, the Ukrainian theater scene is alive and well, boasting more than 100 theatres that include the National Opera of Ukraine, the National Academic Drama Theater of I. Franko, and the National Academic Theater of Russian Drama of Lesya Ukrainka.

Music

Traditional Ukrainian music is an essential element of the nation's culture, reflecting both the hardships and the joys of rural life. Ukrainian folk music is largely based on minor keys, which have different harmonies and sounds than music based on major keys. Often, music based on minor keys is described as sad or melancholy. Ukrainian folk music is typically performed on a plucked or strummed stringed instrument, including traditional instruments such as the four-stringed kobza and the bandura, both similar to the lute.

In addition, Ukrainian folk songs often feature colorful or melancholy vocals. This style traces its roots to the wandering kobzars of the Cossack era, who sang and performed epic songs on the kobza. Similarly, bandurists performed their music on banduras. Kobzars, bandurists and other folk musicians were persecuted throughout Ukrainian history, particularly during Polish rule and under the rule of the Russian tsars.

During the Soviet era, the Communist Party suppressed Ukrainian music. However, it was sometimes used for political purposes, such as to promote ties between Ukrainian peasants and Russian workers. Despite this repression, Ukrainian composers and performers continued to create music reflecting their musical heritage, often in exile. One of the most renowned Ukrainian composers during this period was Mykola Lysenko (1842–1912). Lysenko was a strong promoter of Ukrainian folk music and the founder of the Ukrainian national school of music.

Independence in 1991 led to a resurgence in Ukrainian language and culture, including the adoption of a traditional 19th century hymn, "Shche ne vmerla Ukrainy" ("Ukraine's [glory] has not perished"), as the national anthem. However, Russian language music continued to receive official preference until the peaceful Orange Revolution of 2004. Ukrainian musicians played an important role in these protests, entertaining and inspiring the crowds who had gathered outside in freezing temperatures. The unofficial anthem of the movement, "Razom Nas Bahato" ("Together We Are Many"), combined traditional tones with elements of rock and hip-hop music. This is a reflection of modern Ukrainian music in general, which draws from a wide range of influences, but maintains strong ties to tradition.

Literature

Ukrainian literature, as with most Slavic languages, has its roots in works written in Church Slavonic during the period of Kyivan Rus.' The 16th century witnessed the rise of folk epics depicting the stories of Cossack adventures. This in turn led to Ivan Kotlyarevsky's (1768–1838) satirical version of Virgil's *Aeneid* in the late 18th century, the first major work to be written in the Ukrainian vernacular (spoken style).

The most important figure in Ukrainian literature is the 19th century poet Taras Shevchenko (1814–1861). In works such as *Kobzar* (1840), a collection of poems, and *Zapovit* (Testament), Shevchenko highlighted Cossack and agrarian village life while criticizing the imperial rule of Tsarist Russia. Through his work, Shevchenko not only established modern Ukrainian literature, he also laid the foundation for the modern written Ukrainian language. His work helped develop the Ukrainian sense of national identity, and its influence continues to be felt throughout Ukrainian society. Kyiv's National University bears his name, and monuments in his honor can be found throughout the country, as well as Ukrainian communities around the world.

During the Soviet era, many Ukrainian writers chose to live in exile, rather than submit to Soviet censorship and repression. Bohdan Krawciw (1904–1975), Evhen Malaniuk (1897–1968) and Teodosii Osmachka (1895–1962), who avoided execution by pretending to be insane, were among those who explored Ukrainian themes and nationalism from abroad. Those who remained in Ukraine and continued to express themselves, often paid for their defiance with imprisonment or death, as in the case of poet Vasyl' Stus (1938–1985), who perished in a forced labor camp. After independence, Ukrainian literature has gradually experienced a renaissance. Ukrainians are now free to explore literature from throughout their history and to add to this heritage.

CULTURE

Arts & Entertainment

Favorite sports in Ukraine include soccer, volleyball, basketball, and ping-pong. Ukrainians also enjoy chess. Hiking and mountaineering remain popular outdoor activities. Ukrainian athletes have been successful participants in the Olympic Games, particularly in events such as gymnastics and figure skating.

The dominant trend in contemporary Ukrainian art is a movement to embrace Ukrainian traditions and to shift from the Russian-dominated influences of past centuries. This movement is reflected in the widespread use of blue and yellow (the national colors) on official government graphic design, artwork and architecture – even buses. Red (associated with Russia) is notably underutilized.

Many previously unknown or underappreciated Ukrainian artists are now recognized as leaders in their fields, such as Anatol Petritsky (1895–1964), known for his graphic arts and set design; avant-garde artist Vasili Yermilov (1894–1967), who helped popularize constructivism in art in the 1920s (constructivism artists focus on concrete or practical links or uses in art); and painter Alexander Bogomazov (1880–1930), who incorporated cubism and futurist interests in his work.

However, despite the government's public promotion of Ukrainian arts and its support of key national institutions, it provides little direct funding to the arts community in Ukraine. This is largely due to its focus on other political and economic priorities. The government does provide some incentives, such as low-rent studios and other working spaces, and tax breaks for companies that donate profits to the national film industry. Non-governmental organizations (NGOs) also fill this gap to a certain extent. Many of these groups survive on support from foreign foundations and corporate sponsorship.

However, government efforts to encourage Ukrainian culture at the expense of Russian culture have led to unintended consequences. For example, a law passed in 2007 required that all foreign films be dubbed into Ukrainian, instead of Russian. This led not only to legal challenges, but to a decline in box office revenues, partly due to a lack of facilities for creating Ukrainian-dubbed versions. Furthermore, it alienated Ukraine's leading director, Kira Muratova, who produces her films in Russian, often in partnership with Russian studios. Issues such as this illustrate the unforeseen challenges Ukraine faces in promoting its national arts.

Cultural Sites & Landmarks

With its rich history and wide range of cultural influences, Ukraine offers a wealth of cultural sites and landmarks. These include five sites designated as World Heritage Sites by the United Nations Educational, Scientific and Cultural Organization (UNESCO). In addition, in July 2007, the Ukrainian people voted on the "Seven Wonders of Ukraine." The contest, conducted in two parts, allowed Internet users and experts residing in Ukraine to vote on the sites that highlighted important aspects of Ukrainian culture and history. Internet users voted on twenty-one candidate sites as narrowed down by an expert council.

The two highest ranked sites in the contest were Sofiyivsky Park in central Ukraine and Kiev Pechersk Lavra, or Kiev Monastery of the Caves. The national park in Sofiyivka, created by a Polish noble for his wife, provides a peaceful sprawl of landscaped gardens and marble classical statues. The nearby Pechersk Lavra Monastery was founded shortly afterward, growing from hillside caves occupied by a pair of monks into a major religious center.

Following these two sites are the island of Khortystsya and the impressive fortress of Kam'yanets-Podilsky. Khortystsya, or the Great Khortystsya Island, is on the Dnipro River and shows evidence of human settlements dating back to 30,000 BCE. It was also an important center of Cossack society between the 16th and 18th centuries. The fortress of Kam'yanets-Podilsky, overlooking the River Smotrych, preserves the essence of a fortified 14th century medieval town. Another fortress, at Khotyn, was an important crossroads between East and West during the Middle Ages. It was also the site of a historical battle in 1691, in which the Cossacks prevented the Turks from invading Western Europe.

Rounding out the "Seven Wonders of Ukraine" are the ruins at Chersonesus and the Saint Sophia Cathedral in Kiev. The ancient Greek ruins at Chersonesus, in the Crimea, an autonomous republic of Ukraine, date from the sixth century BCE. The Saint Sophia

Cathedral—which derives its name from the famous Hagia Sophia cathedral in Istanbul, Turkey—was built early in the 11th century CE, shortly after the adoption of Christianity. Its towering gold-tipped minarets (spires) and rich collection of mosaics and frescoes are a magnificent example of Byzantine architecture.

Of these seven locations, the Saint Sophia Cathedral and Pechersk Lavra Monastery are also listed as a UNESCO World Heritage Site. Other UNESCO sites include the historical center of the city of Lviv, called Old Town, and the ancient Primeval Beech Forests of the Carpathians, which Ukraine shares with Slovakia. Ukraine also hosts a section of the Struve Geodetic Arc, a system of 19th-century survey stations that helped scientifically measure the actual shape and size of the earth. The chain was designated as a World Heritage Site in 2005.

In the summer months, many Ukrainians and tourists head for the Crimean peninsula on the Black Sea. Privileged members of the Communist Party had their vacation homes there during the Soviet era. The resort town of Yalta, on the south of peninsula, is famous as the site of a key meeting between United States President Franklin Roosevelt, British Prime Minister Winston Churchill and Soviet Premier Josef Stalin near the end of the Second World War. The week-long meeting, known as the Yalta Conference, was the second of three meetings in which the order of Europe following World War II and the surrender of Germany was prioritized and established.

In addition, sites dedicated to World War II can be found throughout Ukraine. These include the vast Museum of the Patriotic War in Kyiv to smaller monuments erected in the centers of most cities and towns. One unusual example is the memorial to the men of FC Start – a Kyiv football (soccer) club who defied the Nazi invaders by refusing to deliberately lose a match to a German team. They won their last game, and most were sent to concentration camps to perish. However, their courage became a symbol of resistance to oppression – an important theme for the Ukrainian people.

Libraries & Museum

Ukraine's National Art Museum has emerged as the centerpiece of Ukrainian cultural history. Founded in 1898 as the Kyiv City Museum of Antiquities and Art, the museum initially housed examples of Ukrainian art, ranging from medieval religious icons to Cossack portraits to the paintings of the multi-talented national poet Taras Shevchenko. The museum's history parallels the overall experience of Ukrainian arts over the last century, as well as its post-independence re-emergence. It reflects key themes: exploration of Ukrainian national identity, repression under Russian and Soviet rule, defiance through underground activity and work in exile, and finally, homecoming and triumphant re-emergence.

Holidays

Christian holidays are very important in Ukrainian culture, including Christmas Eve, Lent, and Holy Week. During the Easter season, special masses are celebrated and Easter eggs, or "pysanky," are painted with intricate designs. Ukrainian Independence Day is commemorated on August 24.

Youth Culture

Like much of modern Ukrainian society, the nation's youth culture is moving away from Russian trends toward native Ukrainian influences and those imported from the West. For example, on a typical week, the Ukrainian top 40 pop charts may include equal parts Russian/Ukrainian groups and American artists, with a scattering of other European or international artists. Western movie imports are popular, although Ukrainian tastes can be somewhat unusual.

While Western fashions are growing increasingly popular, one fashion trend involves the wearing of sports jerseys, mostly from Ukrainian and other European club teams, but National Basketball Association (NBA) teams as well. Also, young women commonly strive to emulate the glamorous style of their older sisters and mothers from an early age. Lastly, many of the current generation of Ukrainian youth are looking outside their country for career opportunities. Ambitious young Ukrainians are learning English, which they see as a valuable tool for their future, instead of Russian, which is tied to the Soviet past. This phenomenon has contributed to Ukraine's overall decline in population.

SOCIETY

Transportation

Ukraine's transportation system fell into neglect after the collapse of the Soviet Union. However, the government is gradually making improvements, particularly in and around the major cities. Traveling around the rest of rural Ukraine can be difficult, particularly during the winter months.

For in-town transportation, the larger cities provide subway or trolley service. Outside the city centers, and in most smaller cities and towns, Ukrainians rely on small marshutka buses, or minivans, to get around. Taxis are available, but generally expensive. In rural villages, cars are rare and public transportation services are usually non-existent. Often, horse-drawn carts are still being used. For the average Ukrainian, these challenges often make running even simple errands into a day-long chore.

Cars in Ukraine travel on the right-hand side of the road. The steering wheel is on the left-hand side of the vehicle and seat belt use is required by law.

Transportation Infrastructure

Most of the larger cities are served by trains, which are fairly reliable, though many buses and facilities are over forty years old. Buses reach most of the rest of the country, as well, although roads are poorly maintained in many areas. Automobile travel in Ukraine can be dangerous due to the unkempt roads and low driving standards. In addition, air travel within Ukraine is limited, since many regional airports are closed or reduced to handling only a few regular flights.

Media & Communications

The transition from state-controlled media toward a free and open media market is one area in which Ukraine has made significant progress in recent years. As of 2006, the country listed over 1,200 radio and television outlets and roughly 25,000 newspapers and magazines. Of these, only about 4 percent were owned by the government. Actual censorship is rare, and the government does not restrict access to international news or entertainment sources. As of 2009, there were 7.77 million Internet users. Wireless service is available in and around most cities. Another recent trend is the government's promotion of Ukrainian language media. This effort reflects a desire to distance the country from Russian influence and to move closer to the West.

However, Ukraine still faces challenges in establishing a truly open media. The government continues to use the media as a tool to influence the public. Paid political messages and editorials are often misrepresented as actual news items, and journalists are still subject to intimidation and violence. Also, although government officials are legally required to provide access to information, they are rarely held accountable for failing to do so. Another issue is copyright infringement. Piracy of both locally and internationally produced material has been widespread.

SOCIAL DEVELOPMENT

Standard of Living

Ukraine ranked 83 in a field of 187 countries in the 2013 United Nations Human Development Index.

Water Consumption

According to the CIA *World Factbook*, as of 2012, 98.1 percent of Ukraine's population has access to improved water drinking water sources and 96.5 percent have access to improved sanitation. Ukraine is dealing with a number of infrastructure issues related to its history as a Soviet bloc country. Water in some areas, particularly the Dnipro Basin, suffers from untreated sewage, industrial waste, radiation (from Chernobyl), and agricultural runoff and animal waste. In the early 21st century, a strategic program was implemented to clean up the water resources in that area, address sustainable development, and implement a resource management program.

Education

The educational system in Ukraine consists of primary, secondary, and vocational education. Basic primary and secondary education takes approximately twelve years to complete. Ukraine's Ministry of Education emphasizes civic and cultural values in education. Citizens have the right to pursue learning to the level they choose and women usually experience fifteen years of education, while men pursue fourteen years, on average.

There are over 27,000 schools in the country, which also has 149 universities, colleges, and post-graduate institutions. Ukraine's universities include Bila Cerkva State Agrarian University, Chernivci State University, East Ukrainian State University, and the Odessa State Maritime Academy. The literacy rate in Ukraine is nearly 100 percent.

Typically, Ukrainian public schools are co-educational; however, most elite private schools support single-sex education. The country is seeing an increasing number of private secondary schools. Private schools tend to emphasize Ukrainian culture, aesthetics, and folklore more than public schools do. Public schools are more likely than private to have inadequate textbooks and outdated curricula.

Women's Rights

Before Soviet rule, Ukrainian women traditionally held a prominent place in their social structure and had greater rights and freedoms, especially when compared to other male-dominated societies. Mothers, sisters and wives were given high status. In some regions, Ukrainian women even took the lead in pursuing marriage, and it was common for inheritances to be equally divided without regard to gender. Although men were the primary providers, women were responsible for running the household.

The role and status of women changed during the Soviet era. As part of the communist system and philosophy, Ukrainian women were encouraged to contribute to the economy by working. Soviet propaganda emphasized the equality of the sexes, and promoted the image of the women and men working side by side in the fields and factories. However, women faced significant discrimination in the workplace. Even highly educated women were directed toward "technical" fields such as education and medicine, and were excluded from careers requiring management and leadership skills. In addition, women were not only expected to work, but to take responsibility for caring for the children and maintaining the home. These trends have carried over into the post-Soviet era. Women continue to be excluded from higher paying jobs and management positions. In general, they receive less pay then men for the same type of work. In addition, the vast majority of unemployed are women. As a result, many women seek opportunities outside Ukraine and become victims of human trafficking for forced labor or sex work.

Domestic violence is also common. Legally, divorce can be initiated by either spouse, and assets are supposed to be divided equally. In reality, women suffer financially through divorce, although they are more often awarded custody of children. Furthermore, abuse and divorce are over twice as common in the eastern areas of the country. The western regions, which are more distant from Russian influence, have maintained stronger ties to traditional roles and attitudes. For example, men are more likely to assist in maintaining the home and raising children.

Ukraine's recent moves to embrace its traditions suggest that the situation of women may improve. Entrepreneurial women are establishing their own successful businesses, and in some cases supporting their households. The elevation of Yulia Timoschenko, a widely popular politician, to the post of prime minister in 2007 (she served until 2010) illustrated the willingness of the Ukrainian people to once more embrace female leadership.

Health Care

Health care is a social service provided by the Ukrainian government. State and local budgets provide most of the funding for health services. However, the quality of the health care system in Ukraine is inconsistent, even though the country has many hospitals and medical clinics and a high doctor-patient ratio. The best medical care is found in urban areas.

The Ukrainian government is attempting to improve the health care system, and to guarantee fairness and equality in health care distribution. One strategy is to train more primary care and family practice physicians and health care providers.

Ukraine faces several public health issues related to poor health, evident by the high infant mortality rate (almost 9 deaths per 1,000 live births) and the low life expectancy, particularly for men, which is nearly 67 years as compared to women, at seventy-six years. Experts attribute the low life expectancy for men to the high number of smokers, as well as widespread alcohol abuse. Poverty and environmental pollution also play a large role in general poor health.

GOVERNMENT

Structure

In December 1992, a referendum was held in which the Ukrainian people voted overwhelmingly in support of national independence. While subsequent elections in Ukraine have taken place successfully, there have been instances of illegal activity, such as coercion of voters, candidates and abuse of absentee ballots. Most glaring among these was the 2004 assassination attempt on the life of then-candidate Viktor Yushchenko. He survived poisoning and became the country's president.

Ukraine is a parliamentary democracy. The president is the chief of state and has the power to nominate the prime minister, who heads the parliament. Ukraine's parliament is known as the Supreme Rada; it has 450 elected members who serve four-year terms. Suffrage in Ukraine is universal at 18 years of age.

The country's constitution, which was created in 1996, guarantees freedom of speech, religion, and the press. However, the state has been known to try to control media outlets through intimidation. While the constitution does not deny rights to ethnic minorities, it prioritizes the social and political development of the Ukrainian culture.

Political Parties

In 2009, more than 150 political parties were registered with the Ukrainian Ministry of Justice. This large number of political parties forces them to form coalitions with other political parties in order to gain or exercise power. Further, these alliances have a tendency to shift in terms of political platform and some have characterized political alliances in Ukraine as largely personality driven, rather than platform driven.

In the 2014 elections, the People's Front party (NF) took 22.1 percent of the vote and 82 seats, while Petro Poroshenko Bloc (BBP) took 21.8 percent of the vote and 132 seats. Samopomich took 11 percent of the vote and 33 seats; the Opposition Bloc (OB) took 9.4 percent and 29 seats, and Radical took 7.4 percent and 22 seats. Other parties represented in the 2014 election include Batkivshchnya ("Fatherland"), Svoboda ("Freedom") and the Communist Party of Ukraine (CPU).

Local Government

Kyiv is the administrative center of the Kyiv Oblast, one of twenty-four oblasts, or provinces, in Ukraine. The Kyiv Oblast has an area of 28,400 square kilometers (10,965 square miles) and encompasses 25 districts and 25. Kyiv is a self-governing municipality, so it is not under the jurisdiction of the oblast governing body.

Municipalities within Ukraine are administered by a council and an executive committee, at the oblast level, councils are representative and work with local administrators which are appointed by the president and the Cabinet of Ministers, to whom they are accountable.

Judicial System

Local courts within Ukraine handle criminal and civil issues. Appeals courts are next in the hierarchy, handling appeals. High courts, one for administrative matters and another for economic and commercial issues, follow. The Supreme Court is the highest court in the country.

The court system in Ukraine does not enjoy public support or confidence, and are not considered particularly independent; between 2005 and 2008, courts averaged a 99.5 percent conviction rate. This record does not deviate substantially from that under the Soviet era, leading many to lack faith in an independent judiciary.

Taxation

Taxes levied in Ukraine include an income tax (the standard rate at 15 percent), corporate taxes (at 25 percent in 2010), as well as a value-added tax (VAT). Other fees and taxes are levied accordingly.

Armed Forces

Ukraine boasts the second largest military in Europe. Made up of Ground Forces, National Guard, Navy, Air Force, and Air Defense Force, the Ukrainian military was inherited by the newly independent state in 1991—along with its impressive arsenal. Since that time, the military has complied with the Strategic Arms Reduction Treaty (START) and is moving towards nuclear non-proliferation. Additionally, the military has come to be civilian controlled and is expected to be a volunteer force going into the second decade of the 21st century.

Ukraine is an active member of several UN Peacekeeping efforts, has declared neutrality, and has entertained the idea of joining the North Atlantic Treaty Organization (NATO), a move that is not favored in neighboring Russia.

Foreign Policy

Ukraine's strategic location, large population, emerging economy, and sizeable military make it a potentially economic and political powerhouse. However, the country is still establishing its presence in international affairs, independent from the influence of Russia.

As part of the USSR, Ukraine had no separate foreign policy. International relations were dictated and led by the Soviet leadership in Moscow. After the collapse of the Soviet Union, Ukraine declared its independence and its neutrality. It was a founding member of the Commonwealth of Independent States (CIS), a coalition of eleven former republics of the USSR, including Russia. Although the members of CIS were sovereign states, during the 1990s they followed Russia's lead on issues of foreign policy.

Since the turn of the 21st century, Ukraine has become more independent from Russia. Although it is neutral, Ukraine contributed troops and material to the US-led invasion of Iraq in 2003 (which was opposed in the UN by Russia). In 2005, Ukraine eliminated visa requirements for visitors from countries in the European Union (EU) and the US. Business and leisure travelers from these nations can now enter the country with only a passport. It has also strengthened ties to its neighbors, Poland, Slovakia, Hungary and Romania – all former communist states that have also embraced the West. In addition, Ukraine and Poland co-hosted the UEFA European Football championships in 2012, marking the first time that the tournament was held in Eastern Europe since 1976.

Ukraine has especially increased its efforts to join Western international organizations – especially the EU and the North Atlantic Treaty Organization (NATO) defense alliance (it applied for membership in 2008, but that decision was shelved due to influence from neighboring Russia). The existing members of both these organizations are split on whether Ukraine has made enough progress in economic and political reforms to be eligible for membership. In addition, they do not wish to directly confront Russia, which is strongly opposed to Ukraine joining NATO. The West is trying to maintain a balancing act by promising Ukraine that it will eventually be able to join these organizations, while delaying any immediate action that might increase tensions with Russia.

Another area in which Ukraine finds itself caught is in energy policy, where it seeks a positive relationship with its Western and European neighbors. Key natural gas pipelines from Russia to Western Europe run through Ukraine. Since 2000, Russia has twice suspended the gas supply, claiming Ukraine has failed to live up to financial agreements. These disruptions not only have an impact on Ukraine, but also cause energy prices in Western Europe to rise, affecting the global economy. Many observers believe that Russia's actions have been politically motivated, to punish Ukraine for moves toward the West, or to undermine the pro-Western government before key elections.

In 2010, the Ukrainian government announced that it was seeking funds from the European Bank for Reconstruction and Development and the World Bank to modernize its gas transportation system. During the Tymoshenko administration (2007–2010), the government had announced plans for gas infrastructure development, but implied that it would be doing so without the cooperation of the Russian government. In 2010, with a government under Prime Minister Azarov that was sympathetic and cooperative with the Russian government, the Ukrainian government declared its interest in seeking Russian cooperation.

Despite some of the government's efforts to move away from Russian influence, the country still contains a large Russian minority. The Russian language is still widely used, and the two nations share many other deep cultural and economic ties. In March 2014, Russia completed its annexation of Crimea—against the preferences of many in the international community. In August of the same year, Putin dispatched regular Russian troops into eastern Ukraine while publicly denying their presence. An on-again, off-again state of war over separation of the eastern region has existed since.

At the end of December 2014, Poroshenko signed a law dropping the country's nonaligned status, raising the possibility of joining NATO in the future.

Human Rights Profile

International human rights law insists that states respect civil and political rights, and promote an individual's economic, social, and cultural rights.

The United Nations Universal Declaration on Human Rights (UDHR) is recognized as the standard for international human rights. Its authors sought the counsel of the world's great thinkers, philosophers, and religious leaders, and were careful to create a document that reflects the core values shared by every world culture. (To read this document or view the articles relating to cultural human rights, visit http://www.un.org/en/documents/udhr/.)

Human rights in Ukraine have improved since the country's independence, and particularly since the Orange Revolution of 2004. However, serious problems still exist, particularly in the areas of discrimination, police abuse and government corruption. And relations with Russia have weakened, owing to the annexation of Crimea. When measured against this document, Ukraine's s performance is mixed. Article 2 of the UDHR, which rejects discrimination of any kind, is particularly relevant in Ukraine, due to the significant presence of minority groups within the country. Officially, the government supports such initiatives as preserving the culture of the Roma (gypsies) and helping the displaced Tatar peoples return to their Crimean homeland. However, racism and anti-Semitism is widespread in society, and minority groups are often targets of police abuse.

Ukraine performs poorly with regard to Articles 9 through 11, which address legal protections from unjust arrest and imprisonment. Police violence and coercion in general remains a serious problem. Jails and prisons are overcrowded and unsanitary, and accused individuals often wait months before trial. In many ways, the criminal justice system has not changed since the Soviet era.

Men and women are free to enter into marriage by their own choice and to obtain divorces, as stated by Article 16. However, women often receive fewer financial and legal protections in the divorce process. Freedom of religion, as laid out in Article 18, is widely accepted. Orthodox Christianity is the dominant faith, but does not overtly influence government policy. Freedom of expression, as defined in Article 19, has greatly improved since the Soviet era. The government generally does not practice censorship, although it does manipulate the press for its own purposes.

The additional rights of expression and cultural participation described in Article 27 generally hold true, except for the mentally ill, who can be kept in psychiatric hospitals without their consent. However, protection of intellectual and artistic rights (copyrights) is weak and piracy has become a serious problem. Ukraine does support international efforts to promote basic human rights, as outlined in Article 28, as an active participant in UN peacekeeping missions and humanitarian efforts. Finally, with regards to Article 29, no individuals or groups officially receive any special preference or freedom from social obligations, although certain persons (politicians and the wealthy) are able to manipulate the system for their own advancement and benefit.

As Ukraine progresses in its transition from a Soviet republic to a sovereign nation, the Ukrainian government may be positively influenced by its desire to bring the country into international economic and political bodies, especially the EU. Since these organizations have basic human rights requirements, Ukraine's leadership will have to improve the situation in their country in order to be considered for membership.

Migration

In 2015, Ukraine's estimated migration rate is 2.25 per 1,000 persons, meaning that it is losing citizens. This is a reversal from its situation in the early 1990s, after independence, when many Ukrainians returned to Ukraine, often from other Soviet states. Even then, almost as many Ukrainians emigrated from Ukraine as entered. In the early 21st century, economic hardship is the greatest driver of Ukrainian emigration.

ECONOMY

Overview of the Economy

Ukraine has been a member of the International Monetary Fund (IMF) and the World Bank since 1992. While widespread poverty and economic decline occurred in the 1990s, the economy has been growing. However, obstacles to widespread successful economic growth, including bureaucracy and corruption, remain a problem.

The country has begun to trade more extensively with Western European countries, and remains a steady trading partner with Russia. Some of the country's exports include ferrous and nonferrous metals, mineral products, chemicals, and machinery such as tractors. Ukraine also exports grain, transport equipment, and textiles.

In 2014, the gross domestic product (GDP) was an estimated $ 373.1 billion (USD). The per capita GDP was $ $8,200 (USD).

Industry

Roughly, one-third of the Ukrainian economy is based on industry and construction. Major industries include the manufacture of ferrous metals and products, coke, oil and gas transport, and fertilizer. Machinery that is manufactured in the country includes airplanes, turbines, metallurgical equipment, diesel locomotives, and tractors.

Labor

The labor force in Ukraine numbers more than 22 million people. In 2014, the unemployment rate was 8.8 percent. 68.4 percent of the workforce finds employment in the services sector, 26 percent are employed in industry, and almost six percent work in the agricultural sector.

Energy/Power/Natural Resources

One of Ukraine's most visible resources is its expanse of fertile agricultural land. Beneath the surface are deposits of coal, iron ore, natural gas, and petroleum.

Fishing

While not a major sector of the national economy, fisheries and fish canning are important to local economies. Ukraine is known for fish such as sturgeon, herring, carp, pike, and anchovies, found in the country's rivers, the Black Sea, and the Sea of Azov.

Forestry

Timber is harvested in Ukraine, and the lumber industry supports a number of paper manufacturers.

Mining/Metals

Ukraine is rich in minerals: rock salt, limestone, marl, and dolomite are all extracted from the land, as are coal and iron ore. The country is also the largest source of manganese in the world. Precious stones found in Ukraine include topaz, quartz, agate, opal, and garnet.

Agriculture

Agriculture accounts for 24 percent of Ukraine's economy. During the Soviet regime, farming was collectivized and controlled by the state. Today, the country is trying to update farming practices and identify environmentally friendly methods of farming.

Ukraine has fertile soil, and has historically been an important source of food in the Eastern European region. Major crops include wheat, corn, sugar beets, and sunflower seeds. Farmers in Ukraine also grow soybeans, tobacco, and flax.

Animal Husbandry

Ukraine has been a major producer of beef in the region.

Tourism

Tourism in Ukraine is a growing economic sector, accounting for roughly 13 percent of the country's GDP. Visitors contribute nearly $800 million (USD) to the economy per year. About 10 percent of the population is employed in the travel and tourism industries.

There are a number of beaches, spas, and resorts in the country, especially near the Black Sea and the Sea of Azov. Increasing numbers of tourists are coming from Western Europe, often to go skiing in the Carpathian Mountains, or to cycle through the scenic countryside.

Ryan Hegg, Christina Healey,
Jamie Aronson

DO YOU KNOW?

- The United States recently changed its English-language spelling of Kiev to "Kyiv" to match Ukraine's official Latin-alphabet spelling of the name.

- Instead of exchanging gifts on Christmas, Ukrainian families give gifts on New Year's Day.

- In 1240, Mongolian tribes led by Batu Khan, who was Genghis Khan's grandson, captured the city of Kiyiv/Kiev and ruled there for a century.

- The Golden Gates of Kiev are the country's oldest historical monument. The city of Kiyiv was founded more than 1,500 years ago.

Bibliography

Andrew Wilson. *The Ukrainians: Unexpected Nation*. New Haven: Yale University Press, 2009.

Andrew Wilson. *Ukraine Crisis: What It Means for the West*. New Haven: Yale University Press, 2014.

Anna Reid. *Borderland: A Journey through the History of Ukraine*. New York: Basic Books, 2015.

Anna Shevchenko. *Ukraine—Culture Smart! The Essential Guide to Customs and Culture*. London: Kuperard, 2012.

Lonely Planet and Marc DiDuca. *Ukraine*. Oakland, CA: Lonely Planet, 2014.

Rajan Menan, and Eugene B. Rumer. *Conflict in Ukraine: The Unwinding of the Post-Cold War Order*. Cambridge, MA: MIT Press, 2015.

Yael Ohana, comp. *Culture and Change in Ukraine*. Bratislava: East European Reflection Group, 2007.

Works Cited

Adrian Karatnycky. "Ukraine's Orange Revolution." Foreign Affairs. Mar/Apr. 2005. http://www. foreignaffairs.org/20050301faessay84205/adrian-karatnycky/ukraine-s-orange-revolution.html

All Ukrainian Population Census. *Census State Statistics Committee of Ukraine*. http://www.ukrcensus.gov.ua/eng/.

Anna Bernadska. "Ukraine." *LabforCulture*. September 2005. *European Cultural Foundation*. 21 July 2008. http://www.labforculture.org/en/Directory/Region-in-focus/Previous-Regions-in-Focus/Ukraine.

"Country Briefings: Ukraine." 31May 2008. *Economist*. 12 July 2008. http://www.economist.com/countries/Ukraine/.

Culture of the New Independent States (NIS): Selected Aspects of the New Independent

States Religion/Culture; Volume I: Country Area Studies--Ukraine, Belarus,

Georgia, Armenia. Monterey: *Defense Language Institute*, 1999: 1-59.

Encyclopedia of Ukraine. 2001. *Canadian Institute of Ukrainian Studies – University of Alberta/*

University of Toronto. 12 July 2008. http://www. encyclopediaofukraine.com.

Government Portal: Web Portal of Ukrainian Government. *The Office of Development Strategy of Information Resources and Technology, Government of Ukraine*. 15 June 2008. http://www.kmu.gov.ua/control/en http://www.cnn.com/2015/02/10/europe/ukraine-war-how-we-got-here/ http://data.un.org/Data. aspx?d=POP&f=tableCode%3A240 https://freedomhouse.org/report/freedom-world/2015/ ukraine#.Va5W8_lViko https://www.cia.gov/library/publications/the-world-factbook/geos/up.html

"Human Rights Watch – Ukraine." County Reports on Human Rights Practices. Mar. 2006. *U.S. Department of State - Bureau of Democracy, Human Rights, and Labor* http://www.state.gov/g/drl/rls/hrrpt/2005/61682.htm.

International Research and Exchanges Board. Media Sustainability Index : The Development of Sustainable Media in Europe and Eurasia. Washington: IREX, 2007: 172-183

Kateryna Khinkulova. "Ukraine cherishes orange sounds." BBC News. 21 Nov. 2005. http://news.bbc.co.uk/2/hi/ europe/4456858.stm

Nicklaus Laverty. "The Problem of Lasting Change: Civil Society and the Colored Revolutions in Georgia and Ukraine." *Demokratizatsiya*.

"Ukraine.com." *Paley Media*. http://www.ukraine.com.

"Ukrainian Government undertake moves to make patronage of art economically profitable" *Ukrainian Radio*. 8 Oct. 2004. National Radio Company of Ukraine. http://nrcu.gov.ua/index.php/index.php/index. php?id=148&listid=4180

"Ukrainian Weddings." *University of Alberta Museums and Collections Services*. http://www.museums.ualberta.ca/ exhibits/ukrnwedding/index.html.

"Ukraine." *Encyclopædia Britannica Online*. 2008 http:// www.britannica.com/eb/article-9108710.

"With allies like these." *Economist*.

Appendix One:
World Governments

Commonwealth

Guiding Premise

A commonwealth is an organization or alliance of nations connected for the purposes of satisfying a common interest. The participating states may retain their own governments, some of which are often considerably different from one another. Although commonwealth members tend to retain their own sovereign government institutions, they collaborate with other members to create mutually agreeable policies that meet their collective interests. Some nations join commonwealths to enhance their visibility and political power on the international stage. Others join commonwealths for security or economic reasons. Commonwealth members frequently engage in trade agreements, security pacts, and other programs. Some commonwealths are regional, while others are global.

Typical Structure

A commonwealth's structure depends largely on the nature of the organization and the interests it serves. Some commonwealths are relatively informal in nature, with members meeting on a periodic basis and participating voluntarily. This informality does not undermine the effectiveness of the organization, however—members still enjoy a closer relationship than that which exists among unaffiliated states. Commonwealths typically have a president, secretary general, or, in the case of the Commonwealth of Nations (a commonwealth that developed out of the British Empire), a monarch acting as the leader of the organization. Members appoint delegates to serve at summits, committee meetings, and other commonwealth events and programs.

Other commonwealths are more formal in structure and procedures. They operate based on mission statements with very specific goals and member participation requirements. These organizations have legislative bodies that meet regularly. There are even joint security operations involving members. The African Union, for example, operates according to a constitution and collectively addresses issues facing the entire African continent, such as HIV/AIDS, regional security, environmental protection, and economic cooperation.

One of the best-known commonwealths in modern history was the Soviet Union. This collective of communist states was similar to other commonwealths, but the members of the Soviet Union, although they retained their own sovereign government institutions, largely deferred to the organization's central leadership in Moscow, which in turn deferred to the Communist Party leadership. After the collapse of the Soviet Union, a dozen former Soviet states, including Russia, reconnected as the Commonwealth of Independent States. This organization features a central council in Minsk, Belarus. This council consists of the heads of state and heads of government for each member nation, along with their cabinet ministers for defense and foreign affairs.

Commonwealth structures and agendas vary. Some focus on trade and economic development, as well as using their respective members' collective power to address human rights, global climate change, and other issues. Others are focused on regional stability and mutual defense, including prevention of nuclear weapons proliferation. The diversity of issues for which commonwealths are formed contributes to the frequency of member meetings as well as the actions carried out by the organization.

Role of the Citizen

Most commonwealths are voluntary in nature, which means that the member states must choose to join with the approval of their respective governments. A nation with a democratic government, therefore, would need the sanction of its popularly elected legislative and executive bodies in order to proceed. Thus, the role of the private citizen with regard to a commonwealth is indirect—the people may have the power to vote for or against a legislative or executive candidate based on his or her position concerning membership in a commonwealth.

Some members of commonwealths, however, do not feature a democratic government, or their respective governmental infrastructures are not yet in place. Rwanda, for instance, is a developing nation whose 2009 decision to join the Commonwealth of Nations likely came from the political leadership with very little input from its citizens, as Rwandans have very limited political freedom.

While citizens may not directly influence the actions of a commonwealth, they may work closely with its representatives. Many volunteer nonprofit organizations—having direct experience with, for example, HIV/AIDS, certain minority groups, or environmental issues—work in partnership with the various branches of a commonwealth's central council. In fact, such organizations are frequently called upon in this regard to implement the policies of a commonwealth, receiving financial and logistical support when working in impoverished and/or war-torn regions. Those working for such organizations may therefore prove invaluable to the effectiveness of a commonwealth's programs.

Michael Auerbach
Marblehead, Massachusetts

Examples

African Union
Commonwealth of Independent States
Commonwealth of Nations
Northern Mariana Islands (and the United States)
Puerto Rico (and the United States)

Bibliography

"About Commonwealth of Independent States." *Commonwealth of Independent States.* CIS, n.d. Web. 17 Jan. 2013.

"AU in a Nutshell." *African Union.* African Union Commission, n.d. Web. 17 Jan. 2013.

"The Commonwealth." *Commonwealth of Nations.* Nexus Strategic Partnerships Limited, 2013. Web. 17 Jan. 2013.

Communist

Guiding Premise

Communism is a political and economic system that seeks to eliminate private property and spread the benefits of labor equally throughout the populace. Communism is generally considered an outgrowth of socialism, a political and economic philosophy that advocates "socialized" or centralized ownership of the economy and the means of production.

Communism developed largely from the theories of Karl Marx (1818–83), who believed that a revolution led by the working class must occur before the state could achieve the even distribution of wealth and property and eliminate the class-based socioeconomic system of capitalist society. Marx believed that a truly equitable society required centralized control of credit, transportation, education, communication, agriculture, and industry, along with eliminating the rights of individuals to inherit or to own land.

Russia (formerly the Soviet Union) and China are the two largest countries to have been led by communist governments during the twentieth and twenty-first centuries. In both cases, the attempt to bring about a communist government came by way of violent revolutions in which members of the former government and ruling party were executed. Under Russian leader Vladimir Lenin (1870–1924) and Chinese leader Mao Zedong (1893–1976), strict dictatorships were instituted, curtailing individual rights in favor of state control. Lenin sought to expand communism into developing nations to counter the global spread of capitalism. Mao, in his form of communism, considered ongoing revolution within China a necessary aspect of communism. Both gave their names to their respective versions of communism, but neither Leninism nor Maoism managed to achieve the idealized utopia envisioned by Marx and other communist philosophers.

The primary difference between modern socialism and communism is that communist groups believe that a social revolution is necessary to create the idealized state without class structure, where socialists believe that the inequities of class structure can be addressed and eliminated through gradual change.

Typical Structure

Most modern communist governments define themselves as "socialist," though a national communist party exerts control over all branches of government. The designation of a "communist state" is primarily an external definition for a situation in which a communist party controls the government.

Among the examples of modern socialist states operating under the communist model are the People's Republic of China, the Republic of Cuba, and the Socialist Republic of Vietnam. However, each of these governments in fact operates through a mixed system of socialist and capitalist economic policies, allowing private ownership in some situations and sharply enforcing state control in others.

Typically, a communist state is led by the national communist party, a political group with voluntary membership and members in all sectors of the populace. While many individuals may join the communist party, the leadership of the party is generally selected by a smaller number of respected or venerated leaders from within the party. These leaders select a ruling committee that develops the political initiatives of the party, which are thereafter distributed throughout the government.

In China, the Communist Party elects both a chairperson, who serves as executive of the party, and a politburo, a standing committee that makes executive decisions on behalf of the party. In Cuba, the Communist Party selects individuals who sit for election to the National Assembly of People's Power, which then serves directly as the state's sole legislative body.

In the cases of China, Cuba, and Vietnam, the committees and leaders chosen by the communist party then participate directly in electing leaders to serve in the state judiciary. In addition, the central committees typically appoint individuals to serve as heads of the military and to lower-level, provincial, or municipal government positions. In China, the populace elects individuals to local, regional, and provincial councils that in turn elect representatives to sit on a legislative body known as the National People's Congress (NPC), though the NPC is generally considered a largely ceremonial institution without any substantial power to enact independent legislation.

In effect, most modern communist states are controlled by the leadership of the national communist party, though this leadership is achieved by direct and indirect control of lesser legislative, executive, and judicial bodies. In some cases, ceremonial and symbolic offices created under the communist party can evolve to take a larger role in state politics. In China, for instance, the NPC has come to play a more important role in developing legislation in the twenty-first century.

Role of the Citizen

In modern communist societies, citizens have little voice in selecting the leadership of the government. In many communist states, popular elections are held at local and national levels, but candidates are chosen by communist party leadership and citizens are not given the option to vote for representatives of opposing political parties.

In most cases, the state adopts policies that give the appearance of popular control over the government, while in actuality, governmental policies are influenced by a small number of leaders chosen from within the upper echelons of the party. Popularly elected leaders who oppose party policy are generally removed from office.

All existing communist states have been criticized for human rights violations in terms of curtailing the freedoms available to citizens and of enacting dictatorial and authoritarian policies. Cuba, Vietnam, and China, for instance, all have laws preventing citizens from opposing party policy or supporting a political movement that opposes the communist party. Communist governments have also been accused of using propaganda and misinformation to control the opinion of the populace regarding party leadership and therefore reducing the potential for popular resistance to communist policies.

Micah Issitt
Philadelphia, Pennsylvania

Examples

China

Cuba

Laos

North Korea

Vietnam

Bibliography

Caramani, Daniele. *Comparative Politics*. New York: Oxford UP, 2008. Print.

Priestland, David. *The Red Flag: A History of Communism.* New York: Grove, 2009. Print.

Service, Robert. *Comrades! A History of World Communism*. Cambridge: Harvard UP, 2007. Print.

Confederation/Confederacy

Guiding Premise

A confederation or confederacy is a loose alliance between political units, such as states or cantons, within a broader federal government. Confederations allow a central, federal government to create laws and regulations of broad national interest, but the sovereign units are granted the ultimate authority to carry out those laws and to create, implement, and enforce their own laws as well. Confederate governments are built on the notion that a single, central government should not have ultimate authority over sovereign states and populations. Some confederate governments were born due to the rise of European monarchies and empires that threatened to govern states from afar. Others were created out of respect for the diverse ideologies, cultures, and ideals of their respective regions. Confederations and confederacies may be hybrids, giving comparatively more power to a federal government while retaining respect for the sovereignty of their members. True confederate governments are rare in the twenty-first century.

Typical Structure

Confederate governments are typically characterized by the presence of both a central government and a set of regional, similarly organized, and sovereign (independent) governments. For example, a confederate government might have as its central government structure a system that features executive, legislative, and judicial branches. Each region that serves as members of the confederation would have in place a similar system, enabling the efficient flow of lawmaking and government services.

In some confederations, the executive branch of the central government is headed by a president or prime minister, who serves as the government's chief administrative officer, overseeing the military and other government operations. Meanwhile, at the regional level, another chief executive, such as a governor, is charged with the administration of that government's operations.

Legislative branches are also similarly designed. Confederations use parliaments or congresses that, in most cases, have two distinct chambers. One chamber consists of legislators who each represent an entire state, canton, or region. The other chamber consists of legislators representing certain populations of voters within that region. Legislatures at the regional level not only have the power to create and enforce their own laws, but also have the power to refuse to enact or enforce any laws handed down by the national government.

A confederation's judiciary is charged with ensuring that federal and regional laws are applied uniformly and within the limits of the confederation's constitutional framework. Central and regional governments both have such judicial institutions, with the latter addressing those legal matters administered in the state or canton and the former addressing legal issues of interest to the entire country.

Political parties also typically play a role in a confederate government. Political leadership is achieved by a party's majority status in either the executive or the legislative branches. Parties also play a role in forging a compromise on certain matters at both the regional and national levels. Some confederations take the diversity of political parties and their ideologies seriously enough to create coalition governments that can help avoid political stalemates.

Role of the Citizen

The political role of the citizen within a confederate political system depends largely on the constitution of the country. In some confederacies, for example, the people directly elect their legislative and executive leaders by popular vote. Some legislators are elected to open terms—they may technically be reelected, but this election is merely a formality, as they are allowed to stay in office until they decide to leave or they die—while others may be subject to term limits or other reelection rules. Popularly elected legislators and executives in turn draft, file, and pass new laws and regulations that ideally are favorable to the voters. Some confederate systems give popularly elected legislators the ability to elect a party leader to serve as prime minister or president.

Confederations are designed to empower the regional government and avoid the dominance of a distant national government. In this manner, citizens of a confederate government, in some cases, may enjoy the ability to put forth new legislative initiatives. Although the lawmaking process is expected to be administered by the legislators and executives, in such cases the people are allowed and even encouraged to connect and interact with their political representatives to ensure that the government remains open and accessible.

Michael Auerbach
Marblehead, Massachusetts

Examples

European Union
Switzerland
United States under the Articles of Confederation (1781–89)

Bibliography

"Government Type." *The World Factbook*. Central Intelligence Agency, n.d. Web. 17 Jan. 2013.

"Swiss Politics." *SwissWorld.org*. Federal Department of Foreign Affairs Presence Switzerland, n.d. Web. 17 Jan. 2013.

Constitutional Monarchy

Guiding Premise

A constitutional monarchy is a form of government in which the head of state is a monarch (a king or queen) with limited powers. The monarch has official duties, but those responsibilities are defined in the nation's constitution and not by the monarch. Meanwhile, the power to create and rescind laws is given to a legislative body. Constitutional monarchies retain the ceremony and traditions associated with nations that have long operated under a king or queen. However, the constitution prevents the monarch from becoming a tyrant. Additionally, the monarchy, which is typically a lifetime position, preserves a sense of stability and continuity in the government, as the legislative body undergoes periodic change associated with the election cycle.

Typical Structure

The structure of a constitutional monarchy varies from nation to nation. In some countries, the monarchy is predominantly ceremonial. In such cases, the monarch provides a largely symbolic role, reminding the people of their heritage and giving them comfort in times of difficulty. Such is the case in Japan, for example; the emperor of that country was stripped of any significant power after World War II but was allowed to continue his legacy in the interest of ensuring that the Japanese people would remain peaceful. Today, that nation still holds its monarchical family in the highest regard, but the government is controlled by the Diet (the legislature), with the prime minister serving in the executive role.

In other countries, the sovereign plays a more significant role. In the United Kingdom, the king or queen does have some power, including the powers to appoint the prime minister, to open or dissolve Parliament, to approve bills that have been passed by Parliament, and to declare war and make peace. However, the monarch largely defers to the government on these acts. In Bahrain, the king (or, until 2002, emir or

hereditary ruler) was far more involved in government in the late twentieth and early twenty-first centuries than many other constitutional monarchs. In 1975, the emir of Bahrain dissolved the parliament, supposedly to run the government more effectively. His son would later implement a number of significant constitutional reforms that made the government more democratic in nature.

The key to the structure of this type of political system is the constitution. As is the case in the United States (a federal republic), a constitutional monarchy is carefully defined by the government's founding document. In Canada, for example, the king or queen of England is still recognized as the head of state, but that country's constitution gives the monarch no power other than ceremonial responsibilities. India, South Africa, and many other members of the Commonwealth of Nations (the English monarch's sphere of influence, spanning most of the former British colonies) have, since gaining their independence, created constitutions that grant no power to the English monarch; instead, they give all powers to their respective government institutions and, in some cases, recognize their own monarchs.

A defining feature of a constitutional monarchy is the fact that the monarch gives full respect to the limitations set forth by the constitution (and rarely seeks to alter such a document in his or her favor). Even in the United Kingdom itself—which does not have a written constitution, but rather a series of foundational documents—the king or queen does not step beyond the bounds set by customary rules. One interesting exception is in Bahrain, where Hamad bin Isa Al-Khalifa assumed the throne in 1999 and immediately implemented a series of reforms to the constitution in order to give greater definition to that country's democratic institutions, including resuming parliamentary elections in 2001. During the 2011 Arab Spring uprisings, Bahraini protesters called for further democratic reforms to be enacted, and tensions between the ruler and his opposition continue.

Role of the Citizen

In the past, monarchies ruled nations with absolute power; the only power the people had was the ability to unify and overthrow the ruling sovereign. Although the notion of an absolute monarchy has largely disappeared from the modern political landscape, many nations have retained their respective kings, queens, emperors, and other monarchs for the sake of ceremony and cultural heritage. In the modern constitutional monarchy, the people are empowered by their nation's foundational documents, which not only define the rights of the people but the limitations of their governments and sovereign as well. The people, through their legislators and through the democratic voting process, can modify their constitutions to expand or shrink the political involvement of the monarchy.

For example, the individual members of the Commonwealth of Nations, including Canada and Australia, have different constitutional parameters for the king or queen of England. In England, the monarch holds a number of powers, while in Canada, he or she is merely a ceremonial head of state (with all government power centered in the capital of Ottawa). In fact, in 1999, Australia held a referendum (a general vote) on whether to abolish its constitutional monarchy altogether and replace it with a presidential republic. In that case, the people voted to retain the monarchy, but the proposal was only narrowly defeated. These examples demonstrate the tremendous power the citizens of a constitutional monarchy may possess through the legislative process and the vote under the constitution.

Michael Auerbach
Marblehead, Massachusetts

Examples

Bahrain
Cambodia
Denmark
Japan
Lesotho
Malaysia
Morocco
Netherlands
Norway
Spain
Sweden
Thailand
United Kingdom

Bibliography

Bowman, John. "Constitutional Monarchies." *CBC News*. CBC, 4 Oct. 2002. Web. 17 Jan. 2013.
"The Role of the Monarchy." *Royal.gov.uk*. Royal Household, n.d. Web. 17 Jan. 2013.

Constitutional Republic

Guiding Premise

A constitutional republic is a governmental system in which citizens are involved in electing or appointing leaders who serve according to rules formulated in an official state constitution. In essence, the constitutional republic combines the political structure of a republic or republican governmental system with constitutional principles.

A republic is a government in which the head of state is empowered to hold office through law, not inheritance (as in a monarchy). A constitutional republic is a type of republic based on a constitution, a written body of fundamental precedents and principles from which the laws of the nation are developed.

Most constitutional republics in the modern world use a universal suffrage system, in which all citizens of the nation are empowered to vote for or against individuals who attempt to achieve public office. Universal suffrage is not required for a nation to qualify as a constitutional republic, and some nations may only allow certain categories of citizens to vote for elected leaders.

A constitutional republic differs from other forms of democratic systems in the roles assigned to both the leaders and the citizenry. In a pure democratic system, the government is formed by pure majority rule, and this system therefore ignores the opinions of any minority group. A republic, by contrast, is a form of government in which the government's role is limited by a written constitution aimed at promoting the welfare of all individuals, whether members of the majority or a minority.

Typical Structure

To qualify as a constitutional republic, a nation must choose a head of state (most often a president) through elections, according to constitutional law. In some nations, an elected president may serve alongside an appointed or elected individual who serves as leader of the legislature, such as a prime minister, often called the "head of government." When the president also serves as head of government, the republic is said to operate under a presidential system.

Typically, the executive branch consists of the head of state and the executive offices, which are responsible for enforcing the laws and overseeing relations with other nations. The legislative branch makes laws and has overlapping duties with the executive office in terms of economic and military developments. The judicial branch, consisting of the courts, interprets the law and the constitution and enforces adherence to the law.

In a constitutional republic, the constitution describes the powers allotted to each branch of government and the means by which the governmental bodies are to be established. The constitution also describes the ways in which governmental branches interact in creating, interpreting, and enforcing laws. For instance, in the United States, the executive and legislative branches both have roles in determining the budget for the nation, and neither body is free to make budgetary legislation without the approval of the other branch.

Role of the Citizen

In a constitutional republic, the citizens have the power to control the evolution of the nation through the choice of representatives who serve on the government. These representatives can, generally through complicated means, create or abolish laws and even change the constitution itself through reinterpretations of constitutional principles or direct amendments.

Citizens in a republic are empowered, but generally not required, to play a role in electing leaders. In the United States, both state governments and the federal government function according to a republican system, and citizens are therefore allowed to take part in the election of leaders to both local and national offices. In addition, constitutional systems generally allow individuals to join political interest groups to further common political goals.

In a constitutional democratic republic such as Guatemala and Honduras, the president, who serves as chief of state and head of government, is elected directly by popular vote. In the United States, a constitutional federal republic, the president is elected by the Electoral College, whose members are selected according to the popular vote within each district. The Electoral College is intended to provide more weight to smaller states, thereby balancing the disproportionate voting power of states with larger populations. In all constitutional republics, the citizens elect leaders either directly or indirectly through other representatives chosen by popular vote. Therefore, the power to control the government is granted to the citizens of the constitutional republic.

Micah Issitt
Philadelphia, Pennsylvania

Examples

Guatemala

Honduras

Iceland

Paraguay

Peru

United States

Uruguay

Bibliography

Baylis, John, Steve Smith, and Patricia Owens. *The Globalization of World Politics: An Introduction to International Relations*. New York: Oxford UP, 2010. Print.

Caramani, Daniele. *Comparative Politics*. New York: Oxford UP, 2008. Print.

Garner, Robert, Peter Ferdinand, and Stephanie Lawson. *Introduction to Politics*. 2nd ed. Oxford: Oxford UP, 2009. Print.

Hague, Rod, and Martin Harrop. *Comparative Government and Politics: An Introduction*. New York: Palgrave, 2007. Print.

Democracy

Guiding Premise

Democracy is a political system based on majority rule, in which all citizens are guaranteed participatory rights to influence the evolution of government. There are many different types of democracy, based on the degree to which citizens participate in the formation and operation of the government. In a direct democratic system, citizens vote directly on proposed changes to law and public policy. In a representative democracy, individuals vote to elect representatives who then serve to create and negotiate public policy.

The democratic system of government first developed in Ancient Greece and has existed in many forms throughout history. While democratic systems always involve some type of majority rule component, most modern democracies have systems in place designed to equalize representation for minority groups or to promote the development of governmental policies that prevent oppression of minorities by members of the majority.

In modern democracies, one of the central principles is the idea that citizens must be allowed to participate in free elections to select leaders who serve in the government. In addition, voters in democratic systems elect political leaders for a limited period of time, thus ensuring that the leadership of the political system can change along with the changing views of the populace. Political theorists have defined democracy as a system in which the people are sovereign and the political power flows upward from the people to their elected leaders.

Typical Structure

In a typical democracy, the government is usually divided into executive, legislative, and judicial branches. Citizens participate in electing individuals to serve in one or more of these branches, and elected leaders appoint additional leaders to serve in other political offices. The democratic system, therefore, involves a combination of elected and appointed leadership.

Democratic systems may follow a presidential model, as in the United States, where citizens elect a president to serve as both head of state and head of government. In a presidential model, citizens may also participate in elections to fill other governmental bodies, including the legislature and judicial branch. In a parliamentary democracy, citizens elect individuals to a parliament, whose members in turn form a committee to appoint a leader, often called the prime minister, who serves as head of government.

In most democratic systems, the executive and legislative branches cooperate in the formation of laws, while the judicial branch enforces and interprets the laws produced by the government. Most democratic systems have developed a system of checks and balances designed to prevent any single branch of government from exerting a dominant influence over the development of governmental policy. These checks and balances may be instituted in a variety of ways, including the ability to block governmental initiatives and the ability to appoint members to various governmental agencies.

Democratic governments generally operate on the principle of political parties, which are organizations formed to influence political development. Candidates for office have the option of joining a political party, which can provide funding and other campaign assistance. In some democratic systems—called dominant party or one-party dominant systems—there is effectively a single political party. Dominant party systems allow for competition in democratic elections, but existing power structures often prevent opposing parties from competing successfully. In multiparty democratic systems, there are two or more political parties with the ability to compete for office, and citizens are able to choose among political parties during elections. Some countries only allow political parties to be active at the national level, while other countries allow political parties to play a role in local and regional elections.

Role of the Citizen

The citizens in a democratic society are seen as the ultimate source of political authority. Members of the government, by contrast, are seen as servants of the people, and are selected and elected to serve the people's interests. Democratic systems developed to protect and enhance the freedom of the people; however, for the system to function properly, citizens must engage in a number of civic duties.

In democratic nations, voting is a right that comes with citizenship. Though some democracies—Australia, for example—require citizens to vote by law, compulsory participation in elections is not common in democratic societies. Citizens are nonetheless encouraged to fulfill their voting rights and to stay informed regarding political issues. In addition, individuals are responsible for contributing to the well-being of society as a whole, usually through a system of taxation whereby part of an individual's earnings is used to pay for governmental services.

In many cases, complex governmental and legal issues must be simplified to ease understanding among the citizenry. This goal is partially met by having citizens elect leaders who must then explain to their constituents how they are shaping legislation and other government initiatives to reflect constituents' wants and needs. In the United States, citizens may participate in the election of local leaders within individual cities or counties, and also in the election of leaders who serve in the national legislature and executive offices.

Citizens in democratic societies are also empowered with the right to join political interest groups and political parties in an effort to further a broader political agenda. However, democratic societies oppose making group membership a requirement and have laws forbidding forcing an individual to join any group. Freedom of choice, especially with regard to political affiliation and preference, is one of the cornerstones of all democratic systems.

Micah Issitt
Philadelphia, Pennsylvania

Examples

Denmark
Sweden
Spain
Japan
Australia
Costa Rica
Uruguay
United States

Bibliography

Barington, Lowell. *Comparative Politics: Structures and Choices*. Boston: Wadsworth, 2012. Print.

Caramani, Daniele. *Comparative Politics*. New York: Oxford UP, 2008. Print.

Przeworski, Adam. *Democracy and the Limits of Self Government*, New York: Cambridge UP, 2010. Print.

Dictatorship/Military Dictatorship

Guiding Premise

Dictatorships and military dictatorships are political systems in which absolute power is held by an individual or military organization. Dictatorships are led by a single individual, under whom all political control is consolidated. Military dictatorships are similar in purpose, but place the system under the control of a military organization comprised of a single senior officer, or small group of officers. Often, dictatorships and military dictatorships are imposed as the result of a coup d'état in which the regime in question directly removes the incumbent regime, or after a power vacuum creates chaos in the nation. In both situations, the consolidation of absolute power is designed to establish a state of strict law and order.

Typical Structure

Dictatorships and military dictatorships vary in structure and nature. Some come about through the overthrow of other regimes, while others are installed through the democratic process, and then become a dictatorship as democratic rights are withdrawn. Still others are installed following a complete breakdown of government, often with the promise of establishing order.

Many examples of dictatorships can be found in the twentieth century, including Nazi Germany, Joseph Stalin's Soviet Union, and China under Mao Tse-tung. A number of dictatorships existed in Africa, such as the regimes of Idi Amin in Uganda, Charles Taylor in Liberia, and Mu'ammar Gadhafi in Libya. Dictatorships such as these consolidated power in the hands of an individual leader. A dictator serves as the sole decision-maker in the government, frequently using the military, secret police, or other security agencies to enforce the leader's will. Dictators also have control over state institutions like legislatures. A legislature may have the ability to develop and pass laws, but if its actions run counter to the dictator's will, the latter can—and frequently does—dissolve the body, replacing its members with those more loyal to the dictator's agenda.

Military dictatorships consolidate power not in the hands of a civilian but in an individual or small group of military officers—the latter of which are often called "juntas." Because military dictatorships are frequently installed following a period of civil war and/or a coup d'état, the primary focus of the dictatorship is to achieve strict order through the application of military force. Military dictatorships are often installed with the promise of an eventual return to civilian and/or democratic control once the nation has regained stability. In the case of North Korea, one-party communist rule turned into a communist military dictatorship as its leader, Kim Il-Sung, assumed control of the military and brought its leadership into the government.

In the late twentieth and early twenty-first centuries, dictatorships and military dictatorships are most commonly found in developing nations, where poverty rates are high and regional stability is tenuous at best. Many are former European colonies, where charismatic leaders who boast of their national heritage have stepped in to replace colonial governments. National resources are typically directed toward military and security organizations in an attempt to ensure security and internal stability, keeping the regime in power and containing rivals. Human rights records in such political systems are typically heavily criticized by the international community.

Role of the Citizen

Dictatorships and military dictatorships are frequently installed because of the absence of viable democratic governments. There is often a disconnect, therefore, between the people and their leaders in a dictatorship. Of course, many dictatorships are identified as such by external entities and not by their own people. For example, the government of Zimbabwe is technically identified as a parliamentary democracy, with Robert Mugabe—who has been the elected leader of the country since 1980—as its president. However, the international community has long complained that Mugabe "won" his positions through political corruption, including alleged ballot stuffing. In 2008, Mugabe lost his first reelection campaign, but demanded a recount. While the recount continued, his supporters attacked opposition voters, utilizing violence and intimidation until his opponent, Morgan Tsvangirai, withdrew his candidacy, and Mugabe was restored as president.

By definition, citizens do not have a role in changing the course of a dictatorship's agenda. The people are usually called upon to join the military in support of the regime, or cast their vote consistently in favor of the ruling regime. Freedom of speech, the press, and assembly are virtually nonexistent, as those who speak out against the ruling regime are commonly jailed, tortured, or killed.

Michael Auerbach
Marblehead, Massachusetts

Examples

Belarus (dictatorship)
Fiji (military dictatorship)
North Korea (military dictatorship)
Zimbabwe (dictatorship)

Bibliography

Clayton, Jonathan. "China Aims to Bring Peace through Deals with Dictators and Warlords." *Times* [London]. Times Newspapers, 31 Jan. 2007. Web. 6 Feb. 2013.

"Robert Mugabe—Biography." *Biography.com.* A+E Television Networks, 2013. Web. 6 Feb. 2013.

Ecclesiastical

Guiding Premise

An ecclesiastical government is one in which the laws of the state are guided by and derived from religious law. Ecclesiastical governments can take a variety of forms and can be based on many different types of religious traditions. In some traditions, a deity or group of deities are considered to take a direct role in the formation of government, while other traditions utilize religious laws or principles indirectly to craft laws used to manage the state.

In many cultures, religious laws and tenets play a major role in determining the formation of national laws. Historically, the moral and ethical principles derived from Judeo-Christian tradition inspired many laws in Europe and North America. Few modern governments operate according to an ecclesiastical system, but Vatican City, which is commonly classified as a city-state, utilizes a modernized version of the ecclesiastical government model. All states utilizing an ecclesiastical or semi-ecclesiastical system have adopted a single state religion that is officially recognized by the government.

In some predominantly Islamic nations, including the Sudan, Oman, Iran, and Nigeria, Islamic law, known as sharia, is the basis for most national laws, and government leaders often must obtain approval by the leaders of the religious community before being allowed to serve in office. Most modern ecclesiastical or semi-ecclesiastical governments have adopted a mixed theocratic republic system in which individuals approved by religious authorities are elected by citizens to hold public office.

Typical Structure

In an ecclesiastical government, the church or recognized religious authority is the source of all state law. In a theocracy, which is one of the most common types of ecclesiastical governments, a deity or group of deities occupies a symbolic position as head of state, while representatives are chosen to lead the government based on their approval by the prevailing religious authority. In other types of ecclesiastical governments, the chief of state may be the leading figure in the church, such as in Vatican City, where the Catholic Pope is also considered the chief of state.

There are no modern nations that operate on a purely ecclesiastical system, though some Islamic countries, like Iran, have adopted a semi-ecclesiastical form of republican government. In Iran, the popularly elected Assembly of Experts—comprised of Islamic scholars called mujtahids—appoints an individual to serve as supreme leader of the nation for life, and this individual has veto power over all other governmental offices. Iranian religious leaders also approve other individuals to run as candidates for positions in the state legislature. In many cases, the citizens will elect an individual to serve as head of government, though this individual must conform to religious laws.

In an ecclesiastical government, those eligible to serve in the state legislature are generally members of the church hierarchy or have been approved for office by church leaders. In Tibet, which functioned as an ecclesiastical government until the Chinese takeover of 1951, executive and legislative duties were consolidated under a few religious leaders, called lamas, and influential citizens who maintained the country under a theocratic system. Most modern nations separate governmental functions between distinct but interrelated executive, legislative, and judicial branches.

Many modern semi-ecclesiastical nations have adopted a set of state principles in the form of a constitution to guide the operation of government and the establishment of laws. In mixed constitutional/theocratic systems, the constitution may be used to legitimize religious authority by codifying a set of laws and procedures that have been developed from religious scripture.

In addition, the existence of a constitution facilitates the process of altering laws and governmental procedures as religious authorities reinterpret religious scriptures and texts.

Role of the Citizen

Citizens in modern ecclesiastical and semi-ecclesiastical governments play a role in formulating the government though national and local elections. In some cases, religious authorities may approve more than one candidate for a certain position and citizens are then able to exercise legitimate choice in the electoral process. In other cases, popular support for one or more candidates may influence religious authorities when it comes time to nominate or appoint an individual to office.

In ecclesiastical governments, the freedoms and rights afforded to citizens may depend on their religious affiliation. Christians living in a Christian ecclesiastical government, for instance, may be allowed to run for and hold government office, while representatives of other religions may be denied this right. In addition, ecclesiastical governments may not recognize religious rights and rituals of other traditions and may not offer protection for those practicing religions other than the official state religion.

Though religious authority dominates politics and legislative development, popular influence is still an important part of the ecclesiastical system. Popular support for or against certain laws may convince the government to alter official policies. In addition, the populace may join local and regional religious bodies that can significantly affect national political developments. As local and regional religious groups grow in numbers and influence, they may promote candidates to political office, thereby helping to influence the evolution of government.

Micah Issitt
Philadelphia, Pennsylvania

Examples

Afghanistan
Iran
Nigeria
Oman
Vatican City

Bibliography

Barrington, Lowell. *Comparative Politics*: *Structures and Choices*. Boston: Wadsworth, 2012. Print.

Hallaq, Wael B. *An Introduction to Islamic Law*. New York: Cambridge UP, 2009. Print.

Hirschl, Ran. *Constitutional Theocracy*. Cambridge, MA: Harvard UP, 2010. Print.

Failed State

Guiding Premise

A failed state is a political unit that at one point had a stable government that provided basic services and security to its citizens, but then entered a period marked by devastating conflict, extreme poverty, overwhelming political corruption, and/or unlivable environmental conditions. Often, a group takes hold of a failed state's government through military means, staving off rivals to fill in a power vacuum. The nominal leadership of a failed state frequently uses its power to combat rival factions, implement extreme religious law, or protect and advance illicit activities (such as drug production or piracy). Failed states frequently retain their external borders, but within those borders are regions that may be dominated by a particular faction, effectively carving the state into disparate subunits, with some areas even attaining relative stability and security—a kind of de facto independence.

Typical Structure

Failed states vary in appearance based on a number of factors. One such factor is the type of government that existed prior to the state's collapse. For example, a failed state might have originally existed as a parliamentary democracy, with an active legislature and executive system that developed a functioning legal code and administered to the needs of the people. However, that state may not have adequately addressed the needs of certain groups, fostering a violent backlash and hastening the country's destabilization. An ineffectual legislature might have been dissolved by the executive (a prime minister or president), and in the absence of leadership, the government as a whole ceased to operate effectively.

Another major factor is demographics. Many states are comprised of two or more distinct ethnic, social, or religious groups. When the ruling party fails to effectively govern and/or serve the interests of a certain segment of the population, it may be ousted or simply ignored by the marginalized faction within the state. If the government falls, it creates a power vacuum that rival groups compete to fill. If one faction gains power, it must remain in a constant state of vigilance against its rivals, focusing more on keeping enemies in check than on rebuilding crippled government infrastructure. Some also seek to create theocracies based on extreme interpretations of a particular religious doctrine. Frequently, these regimes are themselves ousted by rivals within a few years, leaving no lasting government and keeping the state in chaos.

Failed states are also characterized by extreme poverty and a lack of modern technology. Potable water, electricity, food, and medicine are scarce among average citizens. In some cases, these conditions are worsened by natural events. Haiti, for example, was a failed state for many years before the devastating 2010 earthquake that razed the capitol city of Port au Prince, deepening the country's poverty and instability. Afghanistan and Ethiopia—with their harsh, arid climates—are also examples of failed states whose physical environments and lack of resources exacerbated an already extreme state of impoverishment.

Most failed states' conditions are also worsened by the presence of foreigners. Because their governments are either unable or unwilling to repel terrorists, for example, failed states frequently become havens for international terrorism. Somalia, Afghanistan, and Iraq are all examples of states that failed, enabling terrorist organizations to set up camp within their borders. As such groups pose a threat to other nations, those nations often send troops and weapons into the failed states to engage the terrorists. In recent years, NATO, the United Nations, and the African Union have all entered failed states to both combat terrorists and help rebuild government.

Role of the Citizen

Citizens of a failed state have very little say in the direction of their country. In most cases, when a faction assumes control over the government, it installs strict controls that limit the rights of citizens, particularly such rights as freedom of speech, freedom of assembly, and freedom of religion. Some regimes allow for "democratic" elections, but a continued lack of infrastructure and widespread corruption often negates the legitimacy of these elections.

Citizens of failed states are often called upon by the ruling regime (or a regional faction) to serve in its militia, helping it combat other factions within the state. In fact, many militias within failed states are comprised of people who were forced to join (under penalty of death) at a young age. Those who do not join militias are often drawn into criminal activity such as piracy and the drug trade.

Some citizens are able to make a difference by joining interest groups. Many citizens are able to achieve a limited amount of success sharing information about women's rights, HIV/AIDS and other issues. In some situations, these groups are able to gain international assistance from organizations that were unable to work with the failed government.

Michael Auerbach
Marblehead, Massachusetts

Examples

Chad

Democratic Republic of the Congo

Somalia

Sudan

Zimbabwe

Bibliography

"Failed States: Fixing a Broken World." *Economist*, 29 Jan. 2009. Web. 6 Feb. 2012.

"Failed States." Global Policy Forum, 2013. Web. 6 Feb. 2012.

"Somalia Tops Failed States Index for Fifth Year." *CNN.com*. Turner Broadcasting System, 18 June 2012. Web. 6 Feb. 2012.

Thürer, Daniel. (1999). "The 'Failed State' and International Law." *International Review of the Red Cross*. International Committee of the Red Cross, 31 Dec. 1999. Web. 6 Feb. 2012.

Federal Republic

Guiding Premise

A federal republic is a political system that features a central government as well as a set of regional subunits such as states or provinces. Federal republics are designed to limit the power of the central government, paring its focus to only matters of national interest. Typically, a greater degree of power is granted to the regional governments, which retain the ability to create their own laws of local relevance. The degree to which the federal and regional governments each enjoy authority varies from nation to nation, based on the country's interpretation of this republican form of government. By distributing authority to these separate but connected government institutions, federal republics give the greatest power to the people themselves, who typically vote directly for both their regional and national political representation.

Typical Structure

A federal republic's structure varies from nation to nation. However, most federal republics feature two distinct governing entities. The first is a central, federal government, usually based in the nation's capital city. The federal government's task is to address issues of national importance. These issues include defense and foreign relations, but also encompass matters of domestic interest that must be addressed in uniform fashion, such as social assistance programs, infrastructure, and certain taxes.

A federal republic is comprised of executive, legislative, and judicial branches. The executive is typically a president or prime minister—the former selected by popular vote, the latter selected by members of the legislature—and is charged with the administration of the federal government's programs and regulations. The legislature—such as the US Congress, the Austrian Parliament, or the German Bundestag—is charged with developing laws and managing government spending. The judiciary is charged

with ensuring that federal and state laws are enforced and that they are consistent with the country's constitution.

The federal government is limited in terms of its ability to assert authority over the regions. Instead, federal republics grant a degree of sovereignty to the different states, provinces, or regions that comprise the entire nation. These regions have their own governments, similar in structure and procedure to those of the federal government. They too have executives, legislatures, and judiciaries whose foci are limited to the regional government's respective jurisdictions.

The federal and regional segments of a republic are not completely independent of one another, however. Although the systems are intended to distribute power evenly, federal and regional governments are closely linked. This connectivity ensures the efficient collection of taxes, the regional distribution of federal funds, and a rapid response to issues of national importance. A federal republic's greatest strength, therefore, is the series of connections it maintains between the federal, regional, and local governments it contains.

Role of the Citizen

A federal republic is distinguished by the limitations of power it places on the national government. The primary goal of such a design was to place the power of government in the hands of the people. One of the ways the citizens' power is demonstrated is by participating in the electoral process. In a federal republic, the people elect their legislators. In some republics, the legislators in turn elect a prime minister, while in others, the people directly elect a president. The electoral process is an important way for citizens to influence the course of their government, both at the regional and federal levels. They do so by placing people who truly represent their diverse interests in the federal government.

The citizen is also empowered by participating in government as opposed to being subjected to it. In addition to taking part in the electoral process, the people are free to join and become active in a political party. A political party serves as a proxy for its members, representing their viewpoint and interests on a local and national level. In federal republics like Germany, a wide range of political parties are active in the legislature, advancing the political agendas of those they represent.

Michael Auerbach
Marblehead, Massachusetts

Examples
Austria
Brazil
Germany
India
Mexico
Nigeria
United States

Bibliography
"The Federal Principle." *Republik Österreich Parlament.* Republik Österreich Parlament, 8 Oct. 2010. Web. 6 Feb. 2013.

"The Federal Republic of Germany." *Deutscher Bundestag.* German Bundestag, 2013. Web. 6 Feb. 2013.

Collin, Nicholas. "An Essay on the Means of Promoting Federal Sentiments in the United States." *Friends of the Constitution: Writings of the "Other" Federalists, 1787–1788.* Ed. Colleen A. Sheehan and Gary L. McDowell. Online Library of Liberty, 2013. Web. 6 Feb. 2013.

Federation

Guiding Premise

A federation is a nation formed from the unification of smaller political entities. Federations feature federal governments that oversee nationwide issues. However, they also grant a degree of autonomy to the regional, state, or other local governments within the system. Federations are often formed because a collective of diverse regions find a common interest in unification. While the federal government is installed to address those needs, regions with their own distinct ethnic, socioeconomic, or political characteristics remain intact. This "separate but united" structure allows federations to avoid conflict and instability among their regions.

Typical Structure

The primary goal of a federation is to unify a country's political subunits within a national framework. The federal government, therefore, features institutions comprised of representatives from the states or regions. The representatives are typically elected by the residents of these regions, and some federal systems give the power to elect certain national leaders to these representatives. The regions themselves can vary considerably in size. The Russian Federation, for example, includes forty-six geographically large provinces as well as two more-concentrated cities as part of its eighty-three constituent federation members.

There are two institutions in which individuals from the constituent parts of a federation serve. The first institution is the legislature. Legislatures vary in appearance from nation to nation. For example, the US Congress is comprised of two chambers—the House of Representatives and the Senate—whose directly elected members act on behalf of their respective states. The German Parliament, on the other hand, consists of the directly elected Bundestag—which is tasked with electing the German federal chancellor, among other things—and the state-appointed Bundesrat, which works on behalf of the country's sixteen states.

The second institution is the executive. Here, the affairs of the nation are administered by a president or similar leader. Again, the structure and powers of a federal government's executive institutions varies from nation to nation according to their constitutional framework. Federal executive institutions are charged with management of state affairs, including oversight of the military, foreign relations, health care, and education. Similarly diverse is the power of the executive in relation to the legislative branch. Some prime ministers, for example, enjoy considerably greater power than the president. In fact, some presidents share power with other leaders, or councils thereof within the executive branch, serving as the diplomatic face of the nation but not playing a major role in lawmaking. In India, for example, the president is the chief executive of the federal government, but shares power with the prime minister and the Council of Ministers, headed by the prime minister.

In order to promote continuity between the federal government and the states, regions, or other political subunits in the federation, those subunits typically feature governments that largely mirror that of the central government. Some of these regional governments are modified according to their respective constitutions. For example, whereas the bicameral US Congress consists of the Senate and House of Representatives, Nebraska's state legislature only has one chamber. Such distinctive characteristics of state/regional governments reflect the geographic and cultural interests of the region in question. It also underscores the degree of autonomy given to such states under a federation government system.

Role of the Citizen

Federations vary in terms of both structure and distribution of power within government institutions. However, federal systems are typically democratic in nature, relying heavily on the participation of the electorate for installing representatives in those institutions. At the regional level, the people vote for their respective legislators and executives either directly or through political parties. The executive in turn appoints cabinet officials, while the legislators select a chamber leader. In US state governments, for example, such a leader might be a Senate president or speaker of the House of Representatives.

The people also play an important role in federal government. As residents of a given state or region, registered voters—again, through either a direct vote or through political parties—choose their legislators and national executives. In federations that utilize a parliamentary system, however, prime ministers are typically selected by the legislators and/or their political parties and not through a direct, national vote. Many constitutions limit the length of political leaders' respective terms of service and/or the number of times they may seek reelection, fostering an environment in which the democratic voting process is a frequent occurrence.

Michael Auerbach
Marblehead, Massachusetts

Examples

Australia
Germany
India
Mexico
Russia
United States

Bibliography

"Federal System of India." *Maps of India*. MapsOfIndia. com, 22 Sep. 2011. Web. 7 Feb. 2013.

"Political System." *Facts about Germany*. Frankfurter Societäts-Medien, 2011. Web. 7 Feb. 2013.

"Russia." *CIA World Factbook*. Central Intelligence Agency, 5 Feb. 2013. Web. 7 Feb. 2013.

Monarchy

Guiding Premise

A monarchy is a political system based on the sovereignty of a single individual who holds actual or symbolic authority over all governmental functions. The monarchy is one of the oldest forms of government in human history and was the most common type of government until the nineteenth century. In a monarchy, authority is inherited, usually through primogeniture, or inheritance by the eldest son.

In an absolute monarchy, the monarch holds authority over the government and functions as both head of state and head of government. In a constitutional monarchy, the role of the monarch is codified in the state constitution, and the powers afforded to the monarch are limited by constitutional law. Constitutional monarchies generally blend the inherited authority of the monarchy with popular control in the form of democratic elections. The monarch may continue to hold significant power over some aspects of government or may be relegated to a largely ceremonial or symbolic role.

In most ancient monarchies, the monarch was generally believed to have been chosen for his or her role by divine authority, and many monarchs in history have claimed to represent the will of a god or gods in their ascendancy to the position. In constitutional monarchies, the monarch may be seen as representing spiritual authority or may represent a link to the country's national heritage.

Typical Structure

In an absolute monarchy, a single monarch is empowered to head the government, including the formulation of all laws and leadership of the nation's armed forces. Oman is one example of a type of absolute monarchy called a sultanate, in which a family of leaders, called "sultans," inherits authority and leads the nation under an authoritarian system. Power in the Omani sultanate remains within the royal family. In the event of the sultan's death or incapacitation, the Royal Family Council selects a successor by consensus from within the family line. Beneath the sultan is a council of ministers, appointed by the sultan, to create and disseminate official government policy. The sultan's council serves alongside an elected body of leaders who enforce and represent Islamic law and work with the sultan's ministers to create national laws.

In Japan, which is a constitutional monarchy, the Japanese emperor serves as the chief of state and symbolic representative of Japan's culture and history. The emperor officiates national ceremonies, meets with world leaders for diplomatic purposes, and symbolically appoints leaders to certain governmental posts. Governmental authority in Japan rests with the Diet, a legislative body of elected officials who serve limited terms of office and are elected through popular vote. A prime minister is also chosen to lead the Diet, and the prime minister is considered the official head of government.

The Kingdom of Norway is another example of a constitutional monarchy wherein the monarch serves a role that has been codified in the state constitution. The king of Norway is designated as the country's chief of state, serving as head of the nation's executive branch. Unlike Japan, where the monarch's role is largely symbolic, the monarch of Norway has considerable authority under the constitution, including the ability to veto and approve all laws and the power to declare war. Norway utilizes a parliamentary system, with a prime minister, chosen from individuals elected to the state parliament, serving as head of government. Though the monarch has authority over the executive functions of government, the legislature and prime minister are permitted the ability to override monarchical decisions with sufficient support, thereby providing a system of control to prevent the monarch from exerting a dominant influence over the government.

Role of the Citizen

The role of the citizen in a monarchy varies depending on whether the government is a constitutional or absolute monarchy. In an absolute monarchy, citizens have only those rights given to them by the monarch, and the monarch has the power to extend and retract freedoms and rights at will. In ancient monarchies, citizens accepted the authoritarian role of the monarch, because it was widely believed that the monarch's powers were derived from divine authority. In addition, in many absolute monarchies, the monarch has the power to arrest, detain, and imprison individuals without due process, thereby providing a strong disincentive for citizens to oppose the monarchy.

In a constitutional monarchy, citizens are generally given greater freedom to participate in the development of governmental policies. In Japan, Belgium, and Spain, for instance, citizens elect governmental leaders, and the elected legislature largely controls the creation and enforcement of laws. In some countries, like the Kingdom of Norway, the monarch may exert significant authority, but this authority is balanced by that of the legislature, which represents the sovereignty of the citizens and is chosen to promote and protect the interests of the public.

The absolute monarchies of medieval Europe, Asia, and Africa held power for centuries, but many eventually collapsed due to popular uprisings as citizens demanded representation within the government. The development of constitutional monarchies may be seen as a balanced system in which the citizens retain significant control over the development of their government while the history and traditions of the nation are represented by the continuation of the monarch's lineage. In the United Kingdom, the governments of Great Britain and Northern Ireland are entirely controlled by elected individuals, but the continuation of the monarchy is seen by many as an important link to the nation's historic identity.

Micah Issitt
Philadelphia, Pennsylvania

Examples

Belgium
Bhutan
Japan
Norway
Oman
United Kingdom

Bibliography

Barrington, Lowell. *Comparative Politics*: *Structures and Choices*. Boston: Wadsworth, 2012. Print.

Dresch, Paul, and James Piscatori, eds. *Monarchies and Nations: Globalisation and Identity in the Arab States of the Gulf*. London: Tauris, 2005. Print.

Kesselman, Mark, et al. *European Politics in Transition*. New York: Houghton, 2009. Print.

Parliamentary Monarchy

Guiding Premise

A parliamentary monarchy is a political system in which leadership of the government is shared between a monarchy, such as a king or queen, and the members of a democratically elected legislative body. In such governments, the monarch's role as head of state is limited by the country's constitution or other founding document, preventing the monarch from assuming too much control over the nation. As head of state, the monarch may provide input during the lawmaking process and other operations of government. Furthermore, the monarch, whose role is generally lifelong, acts as a stabilizing element for the government, while the legislative body is subject to the periodic changes that occur with each election cycle.

Typical Structure

Parliamentary monarchies vary in structure and distribution of power from nation to nation, based on the parameters established by each respective country's constitution or other founding document. In general, however, parliamentary monarchies feature a king, queen, or other sovereign who acts as head of state. In that capacity, the monarch's responsibilities may be little more than ceremonial in nature, allowing him or her to offer input during the lawmaking process, to approve the installation of government officials, and to act as the country's international representative. However, these responsibilities may be subject to the approval of the country's legislative body. For example, the king of Spain approves laws and regulations that have already been passed by the legislative branch; formally appoints the prime minister; and approves other ministers appointed by the prime minister. Yet, the king's responsibilities in those capacities are subject to the approval of the Cortes Generales, Spain's parliament.

In general, parliamentary monarchies help a country preserve its cultural heritage through their respective royal families, but grant the majority of government management and lawmaking responsibilities to the country's legislative branch and its various administrative ministries, such as education and defense. In most parliamentary monarchies, the ministers of government are appointed by the legislative body and usually by the prime minister. Although government ministries have the authority to carry out the country's laws and programs, they are also subject to criticism and removal by the legislative body if they fail to perform to expectations.

The legislative body itself consists of members elected through a democratic, constitutionally defined process. Term length, term limit, and the manner by which legislators may be elected are usually outlined in the country's founding documents. For example, in the Dutch parliament, members of the House of Representatives are elected every four years through a direct vote, while the members of the Senate are elected by provincial government councils every four years. By contrast, three-quarters of the members of Thailand's House of Representatives are elected in single-seat constituencies (smaller districts), while the remaining members are elected in larger, proportional representation districts; all members of the House are elected for four-year terms. A bare majority of Thailand's senators are elected by direct vote, with the remainder appointed by other members of the government.

Role of the Citizen

While the kings and queens of parliamentary monarchies are the nominal heads of state, these political systems are designed to be democratic governments. As such, they rely heavily on the input and involvement of the citizens. Participating in legislative elections is one of the most direct ways in which the citizen is empowered. Because the governments of such systems are subject to legislative oversight, the people—through their respective votes for members of parliament—have influence over their government.

Political parties and organizations such as local and municipal councils also play an important role in parliamentary monarchies. Citizens' participation in those organizations can help shape parliamentary agendas and build links between government and the public. In Norway, for example, nearly 70 percent of citizens are involved in at least one such organization, and consequently Norway's Storting (parliament) has a number of committees that are tied to those organizations at the regional and local levels. Thus, through voting and active political involvement at the local level, the citizens of a parliamentary monarchy help direct the political course of their nation.

Michael Auerbach
Marblehead, Massachusetts

Examples
Netherlands
Norway
Spain
Sweden
Thailand
United Kingdom

Bibliography
"Form of Government." *Norway.org.* Norway–The Official Site in the United States, n.d. Web. 17 Jan. 2013.
"Issues: Parliament." *Governmentl.nl.* Government of the Netherlands, n.d. Web. 17 Jan. 2013.
"King, Prime Minister, and Council of Ministers." *Country Studies: Spain.* Lib. of Congress, 2012. Web. 17 Jan. 2013.
"Thailand." *International Foundation for Electoral Systems.* IFES, 2013. Web. 17 Jan. 2013.

Parliamentary Republic

Guiding Premise

A parliamentary republic is a system wherein both executive and legislative powers are centralized in the legislature. In such a system, voters elect their national representatives to the parliamentary body, which in turn appoints the executive. In such an environment, legislation is passed more quickly than in a presidential system, which requires a consensus between the executive and legislature. It also enables the legislature to remove the executive in the event the latter does not perform to the satisfaction of the people. Parliamentary republics can also prevent the consolidation of power in a single leader, as even a prime minister must defer some authority to fellow legislative leaders.

Typical Structure

Parliamentary republics vary in structure from nation to nation, according to the respective country's constitution or other governing document. In general, such a system entails the merger of the legislature and head of state such as a president or other executive. The state may retain the executive, however. However, the executive's role may be largely ceremonial, as is the case in Greece, where the president has very little political authority. This "outsider" status has in fact enabled the Greek president to act as a diplomatic intermediary among sparring parliamentary leaders.

While many countries with such a system operate with an executive—who may or may not be directly elected, and who typically has limited powers—the bulk of a parliamentary republic's political authority rests with the legislature. The national government is comprised of democratically elected legislators and their appointees. The length of these representatives' respective terms, as well as the manner by which the legislators are elected, depend on the frameworks established by each individual nation. Some parliamentary republics utilize a constitution for this

purpose, while others use a set of common laws or other legal precepts. In South Africa, members of the parliament's two chambers, the National Assembly and the National Council of Provinces, are elected differently. The former's members are elected directly by the citizens in each province, while the latter's members are installed by the provincial legislatures.

Once elected to parliament, legislators are often charged with more than just lawmaking. In many cases, members of parliament oversee the administration of state affairs as well. Legislative bodies in parliamentary republics are responsible for nominating an executive—typically a prime minister—to manage the government's various administrative responsibilities. Should the executive not adequately perform its duties, parliament has the power to remove the executive from office. In Ireland, for example, the Dail Eireann (the House of Representatives) is charged with forming the country's executive branch by nominating the Taoiseach (prime minister) and approving the prime minister's cabinet selections.

Role of the Citizen

A parliamentary republic is a democratic political system that relies on the involvement of an active electorate. This civic engagement includes a direct or indirect vote for representatives to parliament. While the people do not vote for an executive as well, by way of their vote for parliament, the citizenry indirectly influences the selection of the chief executive and the policies he or she follows. In many countries, the people also indirectly influence the national government by their votes in provincial government. As noted earlier, some countries' parliaments include chambers whose members are appointed by provincial leaders.

Citizens may also influence the political system through involvement in political parties. Such organizations help shape the platforms of parliamentary majorities as well as selecting candidates for prime minister and other government positions. The significance of political parties varies from nation to nation, but such organizations require the input and involvement of citizens.

Michael Auerbach
Marblehead, Massachusetts

Examples
Austria
Greece
Iceland
Ireland
Poland
South Africa

Bibliography

"About the Oireachtas." *Oireachtas.ie.* Houses of the Oireachtas, n.d. Web. 7 Feb. 2013.

"Our Parliament." *Parliament.gov.* Parliament of the Republic of South Africa, n.d. Web. 7 Feb. 2013.

Tagaris, Karolina, and Ingrid Melander. "Greek President Makes Last Push to Avert Elections." *Reuters.* Thomson Reuters, 12 May 2012. Web. 7 Feb. 2013.

Presidential

Guiding Premise

A presidential system is a type of democratic government in which the populace elects a single leader—a president—to serve as both head of state and the head of government. The presidential system developed from the monarchic governments of medieval and early modern Europe, in which a royal monarch, holder of an inherited office, served as both head of state and government. In the presidential system, the president does not inherit the office, but is chosen by either direct or indirect popular vote.

Presidential systems differ from parliamentary systems in that the president is both the chief executive and head of state, whereas in a parliamentary system another individual, usually called the "prime minister," serves as head of government and leader of the legislature. The presidential system evolved out of an effort to create an executive office that balances the influence of the legislature and the judiciary. The United States is the most prominent example of a democratic presidential system.

Some governments have adopted a semi-presidential system, which blends elements of the presidential system with the parliamentary system, and generally features a president who serves only as head of state. In constitutional governments, like the United States, Mexico, and Honduras, the role of the president is described in the nation's constitution, which also provides for the president's powers in relation to the other branches of government.

Typical Structure

In most modern presidential governments, power to create and enforce laws and international agreements is divided among three branches: the executive, legislative, and judicial. The executive office consists of the president and a number of presidential advisers—often called the cabinet—who typically serve at the president's discretion and are not elected to office. The terms of office for the president are codified in the state constitution and, in most cases, the president may serve a limited number of terms before he or she becomes ineligible for reelection.

The president serves as head of state and is therefore charged with negotiating and administering international treaties and agreements. In addition, the president serves as head of government and is therefore charged with overseeing the function of the government as a whole. The president is also empowered, in most presidential governments, with the ability to deploy the nation's armed forces. In some governments, including the United States, the approval of the legislature is needed for the country to officially declare war.

The legislative branch of the government proposes new laws, in the form of bills, but must cooperate with the executive office to pass these bills into law. The legislature and the executive branch also cooperate in determining the government budget. Unlike prime ministers under the parliamentary system, the president is not considered a member of the legislature and therefore acts independently as the chief executive, though a variety of governmental functions require action from both branches of government. A unique feature of the presidential system is that the election of the president is separate from the election of the legislature.

In presidential systems, members of the legislature are often less likely to vote according to the goals of their political party and may support legislation that is not supported by their chosen political party. In parliamentary systems, like the government of Great Britain, legislators are more likely to vote according to party policy. Presidential systems are also often marked by a relatively small number of political parties, which often allows one party to achieve a majority in the legislature. If this majority coincides with the election of a president from the same party, that party's platform or agenda becomes dominant until the next election cycle.

The judicial branch in a presidential system serves to enforce the laws among the populace. In most modern presidential democracies, the president appoints judges to federal posts, though in some governments, the legislature appoints judges. In some cases, the president may need the approval of the legislature to make judicial appointments.

Role of the Citizen

In a democratic presidential system, citizens are empowered with the ability to vote for president and therefore have ultimate control over who serves as head of government and head of state. Some presidential governments elect individuals to the presidency based on the result of a popular vote, while other governments use an indirect system, in which citizens vote for a party or for individuals who then serve as their representatives in electing the president. The United States utilizes an indirect system called the Electoral College.

Citizens in presidential systems are also typically allowed, though not required, to join political parties in an effort to promote a political agenda. Some governmental systems that are modeled on the presidential system allow the president to exert a dominant influence over the legislature and other branches of the government. In some cases, this can lead to a presidential dictatorship, in which the president may curtail the political rights of citizens. In most presidential systems, however, the roles and powers of the legislative and executive branches are balanced to protect the rights of the people to influence their government.

In a presidential system, citizens are permitted to vote for a president representing one political party, while simultaneously voting for legislators from other political parties. In this way, the presidential system allows citizens to determine the degree to which any single political party is permitted to have influence on political development.

Micah Issitt
Philadelphia, Pennsylvania

Examples

Benin
Costa Rica
Dominican Republic
Guatemala
Honduras
Mexico
United States
Venezuela

Bibliography

Barington, Lowell. *Comparative Politics*: *Structures and Choices*. Boston: Wadsworth, 2012. Print.

Caramani, Daniele. *Comparative Politics*. New York: Oxford UP, 2008. Print.

Garner, Robert, Peter Ferdinand, and Stephanie Lawson. *Introduction to Politics*. 2nd ed. Oxford: Oxford UP, 2009. Print.

Republic

Guiding Premise

A republic is a type of government based on the idea of popular or public sovereignty. The word "republic" is derived from Latin terms meaning "matters" and "the public." In essence, a republic is a government in which leaders are chosen by the public rather than by inheritance or by force. The republic or republican governmental system emerged in response to absolute monarchy, in which hereditary leaders retained all the power. In contrast, the republican system is intended to create a government that is responsive to the people's will.

Most modern republics operate based on a democratic system in which citizens elect leaders by popular vote. The United States and Mexico are examples of countries that use a democratic republican system to appoint leaders to office. However, universal suffrage (voting for all) is not required for a government to qualify as a republic, and it is possible for a country to have a republican government in which only certain categories of citizens, such as the wealthy, are allowed to vote in elections.

In addition to popular vote, most modern republics are further classified as constitutional republics, because the laws and rules for appointing leaders have been codified in a set of principles and guidelines known as a "constitution." When combined with universal suffrage and constitutional law, the republican system is intended to form a government that is based on the will of the majority while protecting the rights of minority groups.

Typical Structure

Republican governments are typically led by an elected head of state, generally a president. In cases where the president also serves as the head of government, the government is called a "presidential republic." In some republics, the head of state serves alongside an appointed or elected head of government, usually a prime minister.

This mixed form of government blends elements of the republic system with the parliamentary system found in countries such as the United Kingdom or India.

The president is part of the executive branch of government, which represents the country internationally and heads efforts to make and amend international agreements and treaties. The laws of a nation are typically created by the legislative branch, which may also be composed of elected leaders. Typically, the legislative and executive branches must cooperate on key initiatives, such as determining the national budget.

In addition to legislative and executive functions, most republics have a judiciary charged with enforcing and interpreting laws. The judicial branch may be composed of elected leaders, but in many cases, judicial officers are appointed by the president and/or the legislature. In the United States (a federal republic), the president, who leads the executive branch, appoints members to the federal judiciary, but these choices must be approved by the legislature before they take effect.

The duties and powers allotted to each branch of the republican government are interconnected with those of the other branches in a system of checks and balances. For instance, in Mexico (a federal republic), the legislature is empowered to create new tax guidelines for the public, but before legislative tax bills become law, they must first achieve majority support within the two branches of the Mexican legislature and receive the approval of the president. By creating a system of separate but balanced powers, the republican system seeks to prevent any one branch from exerting a dominant influence over the government.

Role of the Citizen

The role of the citizen in a republic depends largely on the type of republican system that the country has adopted. In democratic republics, popular elections and constitutional law give the public significant influence over governmental development and establish the people as the primary source of political power. Citizens in democratic republics are empowered to join political groups and to influence the development of laws and policies through the election of public leaders.

In many republican nations, a powerful political party or other political group can dominate the government, preventing competition from opposing political groups and curtailing the public's role in selecting and approving leaders. For instance, in the late twentieth century, a dominant political party maintained control of the Gambian presidency and legislature for more than thirty years, thereby significantly limiting the role of the citizenry in influencing the development of government policy.

In general, the republican system was intended to reverse the power structure typical of the monarchy system, in which inherited leaders possess all of the political power. In the republican system, leaders are chosen to represent the people's interests with terms of office created in such a way that new leaders must be chosen at regular intervals, thereby preventing a single leader or political entity from dominating the populace. In practice, popular power in a republic depends on preventing a political monopoly from becoming powerful enough to alter the laws of the country to suit the needs of a certain group rather than the whole.

Micah Issitt
Philadelphia, Pennsylvania

Examples
Algeria
Argentina
Armenia
France
Gambia
Mexico
San Marino
South Sudan
Tanzania
United States

Bibliography
Caramani, Daniele. *Comparative Politics*. New York: Oxford UP, 2008. Print.
Przeworski, Adam. *Democracy and the Limits of Self-Government*. New York: Cambridge UP, 2010. Print.

Socialist

Guiding Premise

Socialism is a political and economic system that seeks to elevate the common good of the citizenry by allowing the government to own all property and means of production. In the most basic model, citizens cooperatively elect members to government, and the government then acts on behalf of the people to manage the state's property, industry, production, and services.

In a socialist system, communal or government ownership of property and industry is intended to eliminate the formation of economic classes and to ensure an even distribution of wealth. Most modern socialists also believe that basic services, including medical and legal care, should be provided at the same level to all citizens and not depend on the individual citizen's ability to pay for better services. The origins of socialism can be traced to theorists such as Thomas More (1478–1535), who believed that private wealth and ownership led to the formation of a wealthy elite class that protected its own wealth while oppressing members of lower classes.

There are many different forms of socialist philosophy, some of which focus on economic systems, while others extend socialist ideas to other aspects of society. Communism may be considered a form of socialism, based on the idea that a working-class revolution is needed to initiate the ideal socialist society.

Typical Structure

Socialism exists in many forms around the world, and many governments use a socialist model for the distribution of key services, most often medical and legal aid. A socialist state is a government whose constitution explicitly gives the government powers to facilitate the creation of a socialist society.

The idealized model of the socialist state is one in which the populace elects leaders to head the government, and the government then oversees the distribution of wealth and goods among the populace, enforces the laws, and provides for the well-being of citizens. Many modern socialist governments follow a communist model, in which a national communist political party has ultimate control over governmental legislation and appointments.

There are many different models of socialist states, integrating elements of democratic or parliamentary systems. In these cases, democratic elections may be held to elect the head of state and the body of legislators. The primary difference between a socialist democracy and a capitalist democracy can be found in the state's role in the ownership of key industries. Most modern noncommunist socialist states provide state regulation and control over key industries but allow some free-market competition as well.

In a socialist system, government officials appoint leaders to oversee various industries and to regulate prices based on public welfare. For instance, if the government retains sole ownership over agricultural production, the government must appoint individuals to manage and oversee that industry, organize agricultural labor, and oversee the distribution of food products among the populace. Some countries, such as Sweden, have adopted a mixed model in which socialist industry management is blended with free-market competition.

Role of the Citizen

All citizens in a socialist system are considered workers, and thus all exist in the same economic class. While some citizens may receive higher pay than others—those who work in supervisory roles, for instance—limited ownership of private property and standardized access to services places all individuals on a level field with regard to basic welfare and economic prosperity.

The degree to which personal liberties are curtailed within a socialist system depends upon the type of socialist philosophy adopted and the degree to which corruption and authoritarianism play a role in government. In most modern communist governments, for instance, individuals are often prohibited from engaging in any activity seen as contrary to the overall goals of the state or to the policies of the dominant political party. While regulations of this kind are common in communist societies, social control over citizens is not necessary for a government to follow a socialist model.

Under democratic socialism, individuals are also expected to play a role in the formation of their government by electing leaders to serve in key positions. In Sri Lanka, for instance, citizens elect members to serve in the parliament and a president to serve as head of the executive branch. In Portugal, citizens vote in multiparty elections to elect a president who serves as head of state, and the president appoints a prime minister to serve as head of government. In both Portugal and Sri Lanka, the government is constitutionally bound to promote a socialist society, though both governments allow private ownership and control of certain industries.

Citizens in a socialist society are also expected to provide for one another by contributing to labor and by forfeiting some ownership rights to provide for the greater good. In the Kingdom of Sweden, a mixed parliamentary system, all citizens pay a higher tax rate to contribute to funds that provide for national health care, child care, education, and worker support systems. Citizens who have no children and require only minimal health care benefits pay the same tax rate as those who have greater need for the nation's socialized benefits.

Micah Issitt
Philadelphia, Pennsylvania

Examples

China
Cuba
Portugal
Sri Lanka
Venezuela
Zambia

Bibliography

Caramani, Daniele. *Comparative Politics*. New York: Oxford UP, 2008. Print.

Heilbroner, Robert. "Socialism." *Library of Economics and Liberty*. Liberty Fund, 2008. Web. 17 Jan. 2013.

Howard, Michael Wayne. *Socialism*. Amherst, NY: Humanity, 2001. Print.

Sultanate/Emirate

Guiding Premise

A sultanate or emirate form of government is a political system in which a hereditary ruler—a monarch, chieftain, or military leader—acts as the head of state. Emirates and sultanates are most commonly found in Islamic nations in the Middle East, although others are found in Southeast Asia as well. Sultans and emirs frequently assume titles such as president or prime minister in addition to their royal designations, meshing the traditional ideal of a monarch with the administrative capacities of a constitutional political system.

Typical Structure

A sultanate or emirate combines the administrative duties of the executive with the powers of a monarch. The emir or sultan acts as the head of government, appointing all cabinet ministers and officials. In Brunei, a sultanate, the government was established according to the constitution (set up after the country declared autonomy from Britain in 1959). The sultan did assemble a legislative council in order to facilitate the lawmaking process, but this council has consistently remained subject to the authority of the sultan and not to a democratic process. In 2004, there was some movement toward the election of at least some of the members of this council. In the meantime, the sultan maintains a ministerial system by appointment and also serves as the nation's chief religious leader.

In some cases, an emirate or sultanate appears similar to a federal system. In the United Arab Emirates (UAE), for example, the nation consists of not one but seven emirates. This system came into being after the seven small regions achieved independence from Great Britain. Each emirate developed its own government system under the leadership of an emir. However, in 1971, the individual emirates agreed to join as a federation, drafting a constitution that identified the areas of common interest to the entire group of emirates. Like Brunei, the UAE's initial government structure focused on the authority of the emirs and the various councils and ministries formed at the UAE's capital of Abu Dhabi. However, beginning in the early twenty-first century, the UAE's legislative body, the Federal National Council, has been elected by electoral colleges from the seven emirates, thus further engaging various local areas and reflecting their interests.

Sultanates and emirates are at times part of a larger nation, with the sultans or emirs answering to the authority of another government. This is the case in Malaysia, where the country is governed by a constitutional monarchy. However, most of Malaysia's western political units are governed by sultans, who act as regional governors and, in many cases, religious leaders, but remain subject to the king's authority in Malaysia's capital of Kuala Lumpur.

Role of the Citizen

Sultanates and emirates are traditionally nondemocratic governments. Like those of other monarchs, the seats of emirs and sultans are hereditary. Any votes for these leaders to serve as prime minister or other head of government are cast by ministers selected by the emirs and sultans. Political parties may exist in these countries as well, but these parties are strictly managed by the sultan or emir; opposition parties are virtually nonexistent in such systems, and some emirates have no political parties at all.

As shown in the UAE and Malaysia, however, there are signs that the traditional sultanate or emirate is increasingly willing to engage their respective citizens. For example, the UAE, between 2006 and 2013, launched a series of reforms designed to strengthen the role of local governments and relations with the people they serve. Malaysia may allow sultans to continue their regional controls, but at the same time, the country continues to evolve its federal system, facilitating multiparty democratic elections for its national legislature.

Michael Auerbach
Marblehead, Massachusetts

Examples

Brunei
Kuwait
Malaysia
Qatar
United Arab Emirates

Bibliography

"Brunei." *The World Factbook*. Central Intelligence Agency, 2 Jan. 2013. Web. 17 Jan. 2013.

"Malaysia." *The World Factbook*. Central Intelligence Agency, 7 Jan. 2013. Web. 17 Jan. 2013.

"Political System." *UAE Interact*. UAE National Media Council, n.d. Web. 17 Jan. 2013.

Prime Minister's Office, Brunei Darussalam. Prime Minister's Office, Brunei Darussalam, 2013. Web. 17 Jan. 2013.

Theocratic Republic

Guiding Premise

A theocratic republic is a type of government blending popular and religious influence to determine the laws and governmental principles. A republic is a governmental system based on the concept of popular rule and takes its name from the Latin words for "public matter." The defining characteristic of a republic is that civic leaders hold elected, rather than inherited, offices. A theocracy is a governmental system in which a supreme deity is considered the ultimate authority guiding civil matters.

No modern nations can be classified as pure theocratic republics, but some nations, such as Iran, maintain a political system largely dominated by religious law. The Buddhist nation of Tibet operated under a theocratic system until it was taken over by Communist China in the early 1950s.

In general, a theocratic republic forms in a nation or other governmental system dominated by a single religious group. The laws of the government are formed in reference to a set of religious laws, either taken directly from sacred texts or formulated by religious scholars and authority figures. Most theocratic governments depend on a body of religious scholars who interpret religious scripture, advise all branches of government, and oversee the electoral process.

Typical Structure

In a typical republic, the government is divided into executive, legislative, and judicial branches, and citizens vote to elect leaders to one or more of the branches of government. In most modern republics, voters elect a head of state, usually a president, to lead the executive branch. In many republics, voters also elect individuals to serve as legislators. Members of the judiciary may be elected by voters or may be appointed to office by other elected leaders. In nontheocratic republics, the citizens are considered the ultimate source of authority in the government.

In a theocratic republic, however, one or more deities are considered to represent the ultimate governmental authority. In some cases, the government may designate a deity as the ultimate head of state. Typically, any individual serving as the functional head of state is believed to have been chosen by that deity, and candidates for the position must be approved by the prevailing religious authority.

In some cases, the religious authority supports popular elections to fill certain governmental posts. In Iran, for instance, citizens vote to elect members to the national parliament and a single individual to serve as president. The Iranian government is ultimately led by a supreme leader, who is appointed to office by the Assembly of Experts, the leaders of the country's Islamic community. Though the populace chooses the president and leaders to serve in the legislature, the supreme leader of Iran can overrule decisions made in any other branch of the government.

In a theocratic republic, the power to propose new laws may be given to the legislature, which works on legislation in conjunction with the executive branch. However, all laws must conform to religious law, and any legislation produced within the government is likely to be abolished if it is deemed by the religious authorities to violate religious principles. In addition, religious leaders typically decide which candidates are qualified to run for specific offices, thereby ensuring that the citizens will not elect individuals who are likely to oppose religious doctrine.

In addition, many modern nations that operate on a partially theocratic system may adopt a set of governmental principles in the form of a constitution, blended with religious law. This mixed constitutional theocratic system has been adopted by an increasing number of Islamic nations, including Iraq, Afghanistan, Mauritania, and some parts of Nigeria.

Role of the Citizen

Citizens in a theocratic republic are expected to play a role in forming the government through elections, but they are constrained in their choices by the prevailing religious authority. Citizens are also guaranteed certain freedoms, typically codified in a constitution, that have been formulated with reference to religious law. All citizens must adhere to religious laws, regardless of their personal religious beliefs or membership within any existing religious group.

In many Middle Eastern and African nations that operate on the basis of an Islamic theocracy, citizens elect leaders from groups of candidates chosen by the prevailing religious authority. While the choices presented to the citizens are more limited than in a democratic, multiparty republic, the citizens nevertheless play a role in determining the evolution of the government through their voting choices.

The freedoms and rights afforded to citizens in a theocratic republic may depend, in part, on the individual's religious affiliation. For instance, Muslims living in Islamic theocracies may be permitted to hold political office or to aspire to other influential political positions, while members of minority religious groups may find their rights and freedoms limited. Religious minorities living in Islamic republics may not be permitted to run for certain offices, such as president, and must follow laws that adhere to Islamic principles but may violate their own religious principles. Depending on the country and the adherents' religion, the practice of their faith may itself be considered criminal.

Micah Issitt
Philadelphia, Pennsylvania

Examples

Afghanistan
Iran
Iraq
Pakistan
Mauritania
Nigeria

Bibliography

Cooper, William W., and Piyu Yue. *Challenges of the Muslim World: Present, Future and Past*. Boston: Elsevier, 2008. Print.

Hirschl, Ran. *Constitutional Theocracy*. Cambridge: Harvard UP, 2010. Print.

Totalitarian

Guiding Premise

A totalitarian government is one in which a single political party maintains absolute control over the state and is responsible for creating all legislation without popular referendum. In general, totalitarianism is considered a type of authoritarian government where the laws and principles used to govern the country are based on the authority of the leading political group or dictator. Citizens under totalitarian regimes have limited freedoms and are subject to social controls dictated by the state.

The concept of totalitarianism evolved in fascist Italy in the 1920s, and was first used to describe the Italian government under dictator Benito Mussolini. The term became popular among critics of the authoritarian governments of Fascist Italy and Nazi Germany in the 1930s. Supporters of the totalitarian philosophy believed that a strong central government, with absolute control over all aspects of society, could achieve progress by avoiding political debate and power struggles between interest groups.

In theory, totalitarian regimes—like that of Nazi Germany and modern North Korea—can more effectively mobilize resources and direct a nation toward a set of overarching goals. Adolf Hitler was able to achieve vast increases in military power during a short period of time by controlling all procedural steps involved in promoting military development. In practice, however, pure totalitarianism has never been achieved, as citizens and political groups generally find ways to subvert complete government control.

Totalitarianism differs from authoritarianism in that a totalitarian government is based on the idea that the highest leader takes total control in order to create a flourishing society for the benefit of the people. By contrast, authoritarian regimes are based on the authority of a single, charismatic individual who develops policies designed to maintain personal power, rather than promote public interest.

Typical Structure

In a fully realized totalitarian system, a single leader or group of leaders controls all governmental functions, appointing individuals to serve in various posts to facilitate the development of legislation and oversee the enforcement of laws. In Nazi Germany, for instance, Adolf Hitler created a small group of executives to oversee the operation of the government. Governmental authority was then further disseminated through a complex network of departments, called ministries, with leaders appointed directly by Hitler.

Some totalitarian nations may adopt a state constitution in an effort to create the appearance of democratic popular control. In North Korea, the country officially operates under a multiparty democratic system, with citizens guaranteed the right to elect leaders to both the executive and legislative branches of government. In practice, the Workers' Party of North Korea is the only viable political party, as it actively controls competing parties and suppresses any attempt to mount political opposition. Under Supreme Leader Kim Il-sung, the Workers' Party amended the constitution to allow Kim to serve as the sole executive leader for life, without the possibility of being removed from office by any governmental action.

In some cases, totalitarian regimes may favor a presidential system, with the dictator serving officially as president, while other totalitarian governments may adopt a parliamentary system, with a prime minister as head of government. Though a single dictator generally heads the nation with widespread powers over a variety of governmental functions, a cabinet or group of high-ranking ministers may also play a prominent role in disseminating power throughout the various branches of government.

Role of the Citizen

Citizens in totalitarian regimes are often subject to strict social controls exerted by the leading political party. In many cases, totalitarian governments restrict the freedom of the press, expression, and speech in an effort to limit opposition to the government. In addition, totalitarian governments may use the threat of police or military action to prevent protest movements against the leading party. Totalitarian governments maintain absolute control over the courts and any security agency, and the legal/judicial system therefore exists only as an extension of the leading political party.

Totalitarian governments like North Korea also attempt to restrict citizens' access to information considered subversive. For instance, North Korean citizens are not allowed to freely utilize the Internet or any other informational source, but are instead only allowed access to government-approved websites and publications. In many cases, the attempt to control access to information creates a black market for publications and other forms of information banned by government policy.

In some cases, government propaganda and restricted access to information creates a situation in which citizens actively support the ruling regime. Citizens may honestly believe that the social and political restrictions imposed by the ruling party are necessary for the advancement of society. In other cases, citizens may accept governmental control to avoid reprisal from the military and police forces. Most totalitarian regimes have established severe penalties, including imprisonment, corporal punishment, and death, for criticizing the government or refusing to adhere to government policy.

Micah Issitt
Philadelphia, Pennsylvania

Examples

Fascist Italy (1922–1943)
Nazi Germany (1933–1945)
North Korea
Stalinist Russia (1924–1953)

Bibliography

Barrington, Lowell. *Comparative Politics*: *Structures and Choices*. Boston: Wadsworth, 2012. Print.

Gleason, Abbot. *Totalitarianism: The Inner History of the Cold War*. New York: Oxford UP, 1995. Print.

McEachern, Patrick. *Inside the Red Box: North Korea's Post-Totalitarian Regime*. New York: Columbia UP, 2010. Print.

Treaty System

Guiding Premise

A treaty system is a framework within which participating governments agree to collect and share scientific information gathered in a certain geographic region, or otherwise establish mutually agreeable standards for the use of that region. The participants establish rules and parameters by which researchers may establish research facilities and travel throughout the region, ensuring that there are no conflicts, that the environment is protected, and that the region is not used for illicit purposes. This system is particularly useful when the region in question is undeveloped and unpopulated, but could serve a number of strategic and scientific purposes.

Typical Structure

A treaty system of government is an agreement between certain governments that share a common interest in the use of a certain region to which no state or country has yet laid internationally recognized claim. Participating parties negotiate treaty systems that, upon agreement, form a framework by which the system will operate. Should the involved parties be United Nations member states, the treaty is then submitted to the UN Secretariat for registration and publication.

The agreement's founding ideals generally characterize the framework of a treaty. For example, the most prominent treaty system in operation today is the Antarctic Treaty System, which currently includes fifty nations whose scientists are studying Antarctica. This system, which entered into force in 1961, focuses on several topics, including environmental protection, tourism, scientific operations, and the peaceful use of that region. Within these topics, the treaty system enables participants to meet, cooperate, and share data on a wide range of subjects. Such cooperative activities include regional meetings, seminars, and large-scale conferences.

A treaty system is not a political institution in the same manner as state governments. Rather, it is an agreement administered by delegates from the involved entities. Scientists seeking to perform their research in Antarctica, for example, must apply through the scientific and/or government institutions of their respective nations. In the case of the United States, scientists may apply for grants from the National Science Foundation. These institutions then examine the study in question for its relevance to the treaty's ideals.

Central to the treaty system is the organization's governing body. In the case of the Antarctic Treaty, that body is the Antarctic Treaty Secretariat, which is based in Buenos Aires, Argentina. The Secretariat oversees all activities taking place under the treaty, welcomes new members, and addresses any conflicts or issues between participants. It also reviews any activities to ensure that they are in line with the parameters of the treaty. A treaty system is not a sovereign organization, however. Each participating government retains autonomy, facilitating its own scientific expeditions, sending delegates to the treaty system's main governing body, and reviewing the treaty to ensure that it coincides with its national interests.

Role of the Citizen

Although treaty systems are not sovereign government institutions, private citizens can and frequently do play an important role in their function and success. For example, the Antarctic Treaty System frequently conducts large-scale planning conferences, to which each participating government sends delegates. These teams are comprised of qualified scientists who are nominated and supported by their peers during the government's review process. In the United States, for example, the State Department oversees American participation in the Antarctic

Treaty System's events and programs, including delegate appointments.

Another area in which citizens are involved in a treaty system is in the ratification process. Every nation's government—usually through its legislative branch—must formally approve any treaty before the country can honor the agreement. This ratification is necessary for new treaties as well as treaties that must be reapproved every few years. Citizens, through their elected officials, may voice their support or disapproval of a new or updated treaty.

While participating governments administer treaty systems and their secretariats, those who conduct research or otherwise take part in activities in the region in question are not usually government employees. In Antarctica, for example, university professors, engineers, and other private professionals—supported by a combination of private and government funding—operate research stations.

Michael Auerbach
Marblehead, Massachusetts

Example
Antarctic Treaty System

Bibliography
"Antarctic." *Ocean and Polar Affairs.* US Department of State, 22 Mar. 2007. Web. 8 Feb. 2013.
"About Us." *Antarctic Treaty System.* Secretariat of the Antarctic Treaty, n.d. Web. 8 Feb. 2013.
"United Nations Treaty Series." *United Nations Treaty Collection.* United Nations, 2013. Web. 8 Feb. 2013.
"Educational Opportunities and Resources." *United States Antarctic Program.* National Science Foundation, 2013. Web. 8 Feb. 2013.

Appendix Two: World Religions

African Religious Traditions

General Description

The religious traditions of Africa can be studied both religiously and ethnographically. Animism, or the belief that everything has a soul, is practiced in most tribal societies, including the Dogon (people of the cliffs), an ethnic group living primarily in Mali's central plateau region and in Burkina Faso. Many traditional faiths have extensive mythologies, rites, and histories, such as the Yoruba religion practiced by the Yoruba, an ethnic group of West Africa. In South Africa, the traditional religion of the Zulu people is based on a creator god, ancestor worship, and the existence of sorcerers and witches. Lastly, the Ethiopian or Abyssinian Church (formally the Ethiopian Orthodox Union Church) is a branch of Christianity unique to the east African nations of Ethiopia and Eritrea.

Number of Adherents Worldwide

Some 63 million Africans adhere to traditional religions such as animism. One of the largest groups practicing animism is the Dogon, who number about six hundred thousand. However, it is impossible to know how many practice traditional religion. In fact, many people practice animism alongside other religions, particularly Islam. Other religions have spread their adherence and influence through the African diaspora. In Africa, the Yoruba number between thirty-five and forty million and are located primarily in Benin, Togo and southwest Nigeria. The Zulu, the largest ethnic group in South Africa, total over eleven million. Like Islam, Christianity has affected the number of people who still hold traditional beliefs, making accurate predictions virtually impossible. The Ethiopian or Abyssinian Church has over thirty-nine million adherents in Ethiopia alone.

Basic Tenets

Animism holds that many spiritual beings have the power to help or hurt humans. The traditional faith is thus more concerned with appropriate rituals rather than worship of a deity, and focuses on day-to-day practicalities such as food, water supplies, and disease. Ancestors, particularly those most recently dead, are invoked for their aid. Those who practice animism believe in life after death; some adherents may attempt to contact the spirits of the dead. Animists acknowledge the existence of tribal gods. (However, African people traditionally do not make images of God, who is thought of as Spirit.)

The Dogon divide into two caste-like groups: the inneomo (pure) and innepuru (impure). The hogon leads the inneomo, who may not sacrifice animals and whose leaders are forbidden to hunt. The inneomo also cannot prepare or bury the dead. While the innepuru can do all of the above tasks, they cannot take part in the rituals for agricultural fertility. Selected young males called the olubaru lead the innepuru. The status of "pure" or "impure" is inherited. The Dogon have many gods. The chief god is called Amma, a creator god who is responsible for creating other gods and the earth.

The Dogon have a three-part concept of death. First the soul is sent to the realm of the dead to join the ancestors. Rites are then performed to remove any ritual polluting. Finally, when several members of the village have died, a rite known as dama occurs. In the ritual, a sacrifice is made to the Great Mask (which depicts a large wooden serpent and which is never actually worn) and dancers perform on the housetops where someone has died to scare off any lingering souls. Often, figures of Nommo (a worshipped ancestral spirit) are put near funeral pottery on the family shrine.

The Yoruba believe in predestination. Before birth, the ori (soul) kneels before Olorun, the wisest and most powerful deity, and selects a destiny. Rituals may assist the person in achieving his or her destiny, but it cannot be altered. The Yoruba, therefore, acknowledge a need for ritual and sacrifice, properly done according to the oracles.

Among the Yoruba, the shaman is known as the babalawo. He or she is able to communicate with ancestors, spirits and deities. Training for this work, which may include responsibility as a doctor, often requires three years. The shaman is consulted before major life decisions. During these consultations, the shaman dictates the right rituals and sacrifices, and to which gods they are to be offered for maximum benefit. In addition, the Yoruba poetry covers right conduct. Good character is at the heart of Yoruba ethics.

The Yoruba are polytheistic. The major god is Olorun, the sky god, considered all-powerful and holy, and a father to 401 children, also gods. He gave the task of creating human beings to the deity Obatala (though Olorun breathed life into them). Olorun also determines the destiny of each person. Onlie, the Great Mother Goddess, is in some ways the opposite of Olorun. Olorun is the one who judges a soul following death. For example, if the soul is accounted worthy, it will be reincarnated, while the unworthy go to the place of punishment. Ogun, the god of hunters, iron, and war, is another important god. He is also the patron of blacksmiths. The Yoruba have some 1,700 gods, collectively known as the Orisa.

The Yoruba believe in an afterlife. There are two heavens: one is a hot, dry place with potsherds, reserved for those who have done evil, while the other is a pleasant heaven for persons who have led a good life. There the ori (soul) may choose to "turn to be a child" on the earth once more.

In the Zulu tradition, the king was responsible for rainmaking and magic for the benefit of the nation. Rainmakers were also known as "shepherds of heaven." They performed rites during times of famine, drought or war, as well as during planting season, invoking royal ancestors for aid. Storms were considered a manifestation of God.

The Zulu are also polytheistic. They refer to a wise creator god who lives in heaven. This Supreme Being has complete control of everything in the universe, and is known as Unkulunkulu, the Great Oldest One. The Queen of heaven is a virgin who taught women useful arts; light surrounds her, and her glory is seen in rain, mist, and rainbows.

The Ethiopian Church incorporates not only Orthodox Christian beliefs, but also aspects of Judaism. The adherents distinguish between clean and unclean meats, practice circumcision, and observe the seventh-day Sabbath. The Ethiopian (or Abyssinian) Church is monotheistic and believes in the Christian God.

Sacred Text

Traditional religions such as animism generally have no written sacred texts. Instead, creation stories and other tales are passed down orally. The Yoruba do have some sacred poetry, in 256 chapters, known as odus. The text covers both right action in worship and ethical conduct. The Ethiopian Church has scriptures written in the ancient Ge'ez language, which is no longer used, except in church liturgy.

Major Figures

A spiritual leader, or hogon, oversees each district among the Dogon. There is a supreme hogon for the entire country. Among the Yoruba, the king, or oba, rules each town. He is also considered sacred and is responsible for performing rituals. Isaiah Shembe is a prophet or messiah among the Zulu. He founded the Nazareth Baptist Church (also called the amaNazaretha Church or Shembe Church), an independent Zulu Christian denomination. His son, Johannes Shembe, took the title Shembe II. In the Ethiopian Church, now fully independent, the head of the church is the Patriarch. Saint Frumentius, the first bishop of Axum in northern Ethiopia, is credited with beginning the Christian tradition during the fourth century. King Lalibela, noted for authorizing construction of monolithic churches carved underground, was a major figure in the twelfth century.

Major Holy Sites

Every spot in nature is sacred in animistic thinking. There is no division between sacred and profane—all of life is sacred, and Earth is Mother. Sky and mountains are often regarded as sacred space.

For the Yoruba of West Africa, Osogbo in Nigeria is a forest shrine. The main goddess is Oshun, goddess of the river. Until she arrived, the work done by male gods was not succeeding. People seeking to be protected from illness and women wishing to become pregnant seek Osun's help. Ilé-Ifè, an ancient Yoruba city in Nigeria, is another important site, and considered the spiritual hub of the Yoruba. According to the Yoruba creation myth, Olorun, god of the sky, set down Odudua, the founder of the Yoruba, in Ilé-Ifè. Shrines within the city include one to Ogun. The shrine is made of stones and wooden stumps.

Mount Nhlangakazi (Holy Mountain) is considered sacred to the Zulu Nazareth Baptist Church (amaNazaretha). There Isaiah Shembe built a High Place to serve as his headquarters. It is a twice-yearly site of pilgrimage for amaNazarites.

Sacred sites of the Ethiopian Church include the Church of St. Mary of Zion in Axum, considered the most sacred Ethiopian shrine. According to legend, the church stands adjacent to a guarded chapel which purportedly houses the Ark of the Covenant, a powerful biblical relic. The Ethiopian Church also considers sacred the eleven monolithic (rock-hewn) churches, still places of pilgrimage and devotion, that were recognized as a collective World Heritage Site by the United Nations Educational, Scientific and Cultural Organization.

Major Rites & Celebrations

Most African religions involve some sacrifice to appease or please the gods. Among the Yoruba, for example, dogs, which are helpful in both hunting and war, are sacrificed to Ogun. In many tribes, including the Yoruba, rites of passage for youth exist. The typical pattern is three-fold: removal from the tribe, instruction, and return to the tribe ready to assume adult responsibilities. In this initiation, the person may be marked bodily through scarification or circumcision. The Yoruba also have a yearly festival re-enacting

the story of Obatala and Oduduwa (generally perceived as the ancestor of the Yorubas). A second festival, which resembles a passion play, re-enacts the conflict between the grandsons of these two legendary figures. A third festival celebrates the heroine Moremi, who led the Yoruba to victory over the enemy Igbo, an ethnicity from southeastern Nigeria, and who ultimately reconciled the two tribes.

Yoruba death rites include a masked dancer who comes to the family following a death, assuring them of the ancestor's ongoing care for the family. If the person was important in the village, a mask will be carved and named for them. In yearly festivals, the deceased individual will then appear with other ancestors.

Masks are also used in a Dogon funeral ritual, the dama ceremony, which is led by the Awa, a secret society comprised of all adult Dogon males of the innepuru group. During ceremonial times, the hogon relinquishes control and the Awa control the community. At the end of the mourning period the dama ceremony begins when the Awa leave the village and return with both the front and back of their heads masked. Through rituals and dances, they lead the spirit of the deceased to the next world. Control of the village reverts to the hogon at that point. The Wagem rites govern contact with the ancestors. Following the dama ceremony, the eldest male descendant, called the ginna bana, adds a vessel to the family shrine in the name of the deceased. The spirit of the ancestor is persuaded to return to the descendents through magic and sacrificial offerings, creating a link from the living to the first ancestors.

Ethiopian Christians observe and mark most typical Christian rites, though some occur on different dates because of the difference in the Ethiopian and Western calendars. For example, Christmas in Ethiopia is celebrated on January 7.

ORIGINS

History & Geography

The Dogon live along the Bandiagara Cliffs, a rocky and mountainous region. (The Cliffs of Bandiagara, also called the Bandiagara Escarpment, were recognized as a UNESCO World Heritage Site due to the cultural landscape, including the ancient traditions of the Dogon and their architecture.) This area is south of the Sahara in a region called the Sahel, another region prone to drought (though not a desert). The population of the villages in the region is typically a thousand people or less. The cliffs of the Bandiagara have kept the Dogon separate from other people.

Myths of origin regarding the Dogon differ. One suggestion is that the Dogon came from Egypt, and then lived in Libya before entering the the region of what is now Burkina Faso, Mauritania, or Guinea. Near the close of the fifteenth century, they arrived in Mali.

Among the Yoruba, multiple myths regarding their origin exist. One traces their beginnings to Uruk in Mesopotamia or to Babylon, the site of present-day Iraq. Another story has the Yoruba in West Africa by 10,000 BCE.

After the death of the Zulu messiah Isaiah Shembe in 1935, his son Johannes became the leader of the Nazareth Baptist Church. He lacked the charisma of his father, but did hold the church together. His brother, Amos, became regent in 1976 when Johannes died. Johannes's son Londa split the church in 1979 when Amos refused to give up power. Tangled in South African politics, Londa was killed in 1989.

The Ethiopian Orthodox Church is the nation's official church. A legend states that Menelik, supposed to have been the son of the Queen of Sheba and King Solomon, founded the royal line. When Jesuits arrived in the seventeenth century, they failed to change the church, and the nation closed to missionary efforts for several hundred years. By retaining independence theologically and not being conquered politically, Ethiopia is sometimes considered a model for the new religious movements in Africa.

Founder or Major Prophet

The origins of most African traditional religions or faiths are accounted for through the actions of deities in creation stories rather than a particular founder. One exception, however, is Isaiah Shembe, who founded the Nazareth Baptist Church, also known as the Shembe Church or amaNazarite Church, in 1910 after receiving a number of revelations during a thunderstorm. Shembe was an itinerant Zulu preacher and healer. Through his influence and leadership, amaNazarites follow more Old Testament regulations than most Christians, including celebrating the Sabbath on Saturday rather than Sunday. They also refer to God as Jehovah, the Hebrew name for God. Shembe was regarded as the new Jesus Christ for his people, adapting Christianity to Zulu practice. He adopted the title Nkosi, which means king or chief.

The Ethiopian Orthodox church was founded, according to legend, by preaching from one of two New Testament figures—the disciple Matthew or the unnamed eunuch mentioned in Acts 8. According to historical evidence, the church began when Frumentius arrived at the royal court. Athanasius of Alexandria later consecrated Frumentius as patriarch of the church, linking it to the Christian church in Egypt.

Creation Stories

The Dogon believe that Amma, the sky god, was also the creator of the universe. Amma created two sets of twins, male and female. One of the males rebelled. To restore order, Amma sacrificed the other male, Nommo, strangling and scattering him to the four directions, then restoring him to life after five days. Nommo then became ruler of the universe and the children of his spirits became the Dogon. Thus the world continually moves between chaos and order, and the task of the Dogon is to keep the world in balance through rituals. In a five-year cycle, the aspects of this creation myth are re-enacted at altars throughout the Dogon land.

According to the Yoruba, after one botched attempt at creating the world, Olorun sent his son Obatala to create earth upon the waters. Obatala tossed some soil on the water and released a five-toed hen to spread it out. Next, Olorun told Obatala to make people from clay. Obatala grew bored with the work and drank too much wine. Thereafter, the people he made were misshapen or defective (handicapped). In anger, Olorun relieved him of the job and gave it to Odudua to complete. It was Odudua who made the Yoruba and founded a kingdom at Ilé-Ifè.

The word *Zulu* means "heaven or sky." The Zulu people believe they originated in heaven. They also believe in phansi, the place where spirits live and which is below the earth's surface.

Holy Places

Osun-Osogbo is a forest shrine in Nigeria dedicated to the Yoruba river goddess, Osun. It may be the last such sacred grove remaining among the Yoruba. Shrines, art, sculpture, and sanctuaries are part of the grove, which became a UNESCO World Heritage site in 2005.

Ilé-Ifè, regarded as the equivalent of Eden, is thought to be the site where the first Yoruba was placed. It was probably named for Ifa, the god associated with divination. The palace (Afin) of the spiritual head of the Yoruba, the oni, is located there. The oni has the responsibility to care for the staff of Oranmiyan, a Benin king. The staff, which is eighteen feet tall, is made of granite and shaped like an elephant's tusk.

Axum, the seat of the Ethiopian Christian Church, is a sacred site. The eleven rock-hewn churches of King Lalibela, especially that of Saint George, are a pilgrimage site. According to tradition, angels helped to carve the churches. More than 50,000 pilgrims come to the town of Lalibela at Christmas. After the Muslims captured Jerusalem in 1187, King Lalibela proclaimed his city the "New Jerusalem" because Christians could no longer go on pilgrimage to the Holy Land.

AFRICAN RELIGIONS IN DEPTH

Sacred Symbols

Because all of life is infused with religious meaning, any object or location may be considered or become sacred in traditional African religions. Masks, in particular, have special meaning and may be worn during ceremonies. The mask often represents a god, whose power is passed to the one wearing the mask.

Sacred Practices & Gestures

The Yoruba practice divination in a form that is originally Arabic. There are sixteen basic figures—combined, they deliver a prophecy that the diviner is not to interpret. Instead, he or she recites verses from a classic source. Images may be made to prevent or cure illness. For example, the Yoruba have a smallpox spirit god that can be prayed to for healing. Daily prayer, both morning and evening, is part of life for most Yoruba.

In the amaNazarite Church, which Zulu Isaiah Shembe founded, singing is a key part of the faith. Shembe himself was a gifted composer of hymns. This sacred music was combined with dancing, during which the Zulu wear their traditional dress.

Rites, Celebrations & Services

The Dogon have three major cults. The Awa are associated with dances, featuring ornately carved masks, at funerals and on the anniversaries of deaths. The cult of the Earth god, Lebe, concerns itself with the agricultural cycles and fertility of the land; the hogon of the village guards the soil's purity and presides at ceremonies related to farming. The third cult, the Binu, is involved with communication with spirits, ancestor worship, and sacrifices. Binu shrines are in many locations. The Binu priest makes sacrifices of porridge made from millet and blood at planting time and also when the help of an ancestor is needed. Each clan within the Dogon community has a totem animal spirit—an ancestor spirit wishing to communicate with descendents may do so by taking the form of the animal.

The Dogon also have a celebration every fifty years at the appearing of the star Sirius B between two mountains. (Sirius is often the brightest star in the nighttime sky.) Young males leaving for three months prior to the sigui, as it is called, for a time of seclusion and speaking in private language. This celebration is rooted in the Dogon belief that amphibious creatures, the Nommo, visited their land about three thousand years ago.

The Yoruba offer Esu, the trickster god, palm wine and animal sacrifices. Because he is a trickster, he is considered a cheater, and being on his good side is important. The priests in Yoruba traditional religion are responsible for installing tribal chiefs and kings.

Among the Zulu, families determine the lobola, or bride price. They believe that a groom will respect his wife more if he must pay for her. Further gifts are then exchanged, and the bride's family traditionally gives the groom a goat or sheep to signify their acceptance of him. The groom's family provides meat for the wedding feast, slaughtering a cow on the morning of the wedding. The families assemble in a circle and the men, in costume, dance. The bride gives presents, usually mats or blankets, to members of her new family, who dance or sing their thanks. The final gift, to the groom, is a blanket, which is tossed over his head. Friends of the bride playfully beat him, demonstrating how they will respond if he mistreats his new wife. After the two families eat together, the couple is considered one.

In the traditional Zulu religion, ancestors three generations back are regarded as not yet settled in the afterlife. To help them settle, offerings of goats or other animals are made and rituals to help them settle into the community of ancestors are performed.

Christmas is a major celebration in Ethiopian Christianity. Priests rattle an instrument derived from biblical times, called the sistra, and chant to begin the mass. The festivities include drumming and a dance known as King David's dance.

Judy A. Johnson, MTS

Bibliography

A, Oladosu Olusegun. "Ethics and Judgement: A Panacea for Human Transformation in Yoruba Multireligious Society." *Asia Journal of Theology* 26.1 (2012): 88–104. Print.

Barnes, Trevor. *The Kingfisher Book of Religions*. New York: Kingfisher, 1999. Print.

Dawson, Allan Charles, ed. *Shrines in Africa: history, politics, and society*. Calgary: U of Calgary P, 2009. Print.

Doumbia, Adama, and Naomi Doumbia. *The Way of the Elders: West African Spirituality*. St. Paul: Llewellyn, 2004. Print.

Douny, Laurence. "The Role of Earth Shrines in the Socio-Symbolic Construction of the Dogon Territory: Towards a Philosophy of Containment." *Anthropology & Medicine* 18.2 (2011): 167–79. Print.

Friedenthal, Lora, and Dorothy Kavanaugh. *Religions of Africa*. Philadelphia: Mason Crest, 2007. Print.

Hayes, Stephen. "Orthodox Ecclesiology in Africa: A Study of the 'Ethiopian' Churches of South Africa." *International Journal for the Study of the Christian Church* 8.4 (2008): 337–54. Print.

Lugira, Aloysius M. *African Religion*. New York: Facts on File, 2004. Print.

Mbiti, John S. *African Religions and Philosophy*. 2nd ed. Oxford: Heinemann, 1991. Print.

Monteiro-Ferreira, Ana Maria. "Reevaluating Zulu Religion." *Journal of Black Studies* 35.3 (2005): 347–63. Print.

Peel, J. D. Y. "Yoruba Religion as a Global Phenomenon." *Journal of African History* 5.1 (2010): 107–8. Print.

Ray, Benjamin C. *African Religions*. 2nd ed. Upper Saddle River: Prentice, 2000. Print.

Thomas, Douglas E. *African Traditional Religion in the Modern World*. Jefferson: McFarland, 2005. Print.

Bahá'í Faith

General Description

The Bahá'í faith is the youngest of the world's religions. It began in the mid-nineteenth century, offering scholars the opportunity to observe a religion in the making. While some of the acts of religious founders such as Buddha or Jesus cannot be substantiated, the modern founders of Bahá'í were more contemporary figures.

Number of Adherents Worldwide

An estimated 5 to 7 million people follow the Bahá'í faith. Although strong in Middle Eastern nations such as Iran, where the faith originated, Bahá'í has reached people in many countries, particularly the United States and Canada.

Basic Tenets

The Bahá'í faith has three major doctrines. The first doctrine is that there is one transcendent God, and all religions worship that God, regardless of the name given to the deity. Adherents believe that religious figures such as Jesus Christ, the Buddha, and the Prophet Muhammad were different revelations of God unique to their time and place. The second doctrine is that there is only one religion, though each world faith is valid and was founded by a ""manifestation of God" who is part of a divine plan for educating humanity. The third doctrine is a belief in the unity of all humankind. In light of this underlying unity, those of the Bahá'í faith work for social justice. They believe that seeking consensus among various groups diffuses typical power struggles and to this end, they employ a method called consultation, which is a nonadversarial decision-making process.

The Bahá'í believe that the human soul is immortal, and that after death the soul moves nearer or farther away from God. The idea of an afterlife comprised of a literal "heaven" or "hell" is not part of the faith.

Sacred Text

The Most Holy Book, or the Tablets, written by Baha'u'llah, form the basis of Bahá'í teachings. Though not considered binding, scriptures from other faiths are regarded as "Divine Revelation."

Major Figures

The Bab (The Gate of God) Siyyad 'Ali Mohammad (1819–50), founder of the Bábí movement that broke from Islam, spoke of a coming new messenger of God. Mirza Hoseyn 'Ali Nuri (1817–92), who realized that he was that prophet, was given the title Baha'u'llah (Glory of God). From a member of Persia's landed gentry, he was part of the ruling class, and is considered the founder of the Bahá'í faith. His son, 'Abdu'l-Bahá (Servant of the Glory of God), who lived from 1844 until 1921, became the leader of the group after his father's death in 1892. The oldest son of his eldest daughter, Shogi Effendi Rabbani (1899–1957), oversaw a rapid expansion, visiting Egypt, America, and nations in Europe. Tahirih (the Pure One) was a woman poet who challenged stereotypes by appearing unveiled at meetings.

Major Holy Sites

The Bahá'í World Center is located near Haifa, Israel. The burial shrine of the Bab, a pilgrimage site, is there. The Shrine of Baha'u'llah near Acre, Israel, is another pilgrimage site. The American headquarters are in Wilmette, Illinois. Carmel in Israel is regarded as the world center of the faith.

Major Rites & Celebrations

Each year, the Bahá'í celebrate Ridvan Festival, a twelve-day feast from sunset on April 20 to sunset on May 2. The festival marks Baha'u'llah's declaration of prophethood, as prophesized by the Bab, at a Baghdad garden. (Ridvan means Paradise.) The holy days within that feast are the first (Baha'u'llah's garden arrival), ninth (the arrival of his family), and twelfth (his departure from Ridvan Garden)—on these days, the Bahá'í do not work. During this feast, people attend social events and meet for devotions. Baha'u'llah referred to it as the King of Festivals and Most Great Festival. The Bahá'í celebrate several other events, including World Religion Day and Race Unity Day, both founded by Bahá'í, as well as days connected with significant events in the life of the founder. Elections to the Spiritual Assemblies, and the national and local administrations; international elections are held every five years.

ORIGINS

History & Geography

Siyyad 'Ali Muhammad was born into a merchant family of Shiraz in 1819. Both his parents were descendents of the Prophet Muhammad, Islam's central figure. Like the Prophet, the man who became the Bab lost his father at an early age and was raised by an uncle. A devout child, he entered his uncle's business by age fifteen. After visiting Muslim holy cities, he returned to Shiraz, where he married a distant relative named Khadijih.

While on pilgrimage in 1844 to the black stone of Ka'bah, a sacred site in Islam, the Bab stood with his hand on that holy object and declared that he was the prophet for whom they had been waiting. The Sunni did not give credence to these claims. The Bab went to Persia, where the Shia sect was the majority. However, because Muhammad had been regarded as the "Seal of the Prophets," and the one who spoke the final revelation, Shia clergy viewed his claims as threatening, As such, nothing further would be revealed until the Day of Judgment. The authority of the clergy was in danger from this new movement.

The Bab was placed under house arrest, and then confined to a fortress on the Russian frontier. That move to a more remote area only increased the number of converts, as did a subsequent move to another Kurdish fortress. He was eventually taken to Tabriz in Iran and tried before the Muslim clergy in 1848. Condemned, he was caned on the soles of his feet and treated by a British doctor who was impressed by him.

Despite his treatment and the persecution of his followers—many of the Bab's eighteen disciples, termed the "Letters of the Living," were persistently tortured and executed—the Bab refused to articulate a doctrine of jihad. The Babis could defend themselves, but were forbidden to use holy war as a means of religious conquest. In three major confrontations sparked by the Shia clergy, Babis were defeated. The Bab was sentenced as a heretic and shot by a firing squad in 1850. Lacking leadership and grief-stricken, in 1852 two young Babis fired on the shah in 1852, unleashing greater persecutions and cruelty against those of the Bahá'í faith.

A follower of the Bab, Mirza Hoseyn 'Ali Nuri, announced in 1863 that he was the one who was to come (the twelfth imam of Islam), the "Glory of God," or Baha'u'llah. Considered the founder of the Bahá'í Faith, he was a tireless writer who anointed his son, 'Abdu'l-Bahá, as the next leader. Despite deprivations and imprisonments, Baha'u'llah lived to be seventy-five years old, relinquishing control of the organization to 'Abdu'l-Bahá before the time of his death.

'Abdu'l-Bahá, whom his father had called "the Master," expanded the faith to the nations of Europe and North America. In 1893, at the Parliament of Religions at the Chicago World's Fair, the faith was first mentioned in the United States. Within a few years, communities of faith were established in Chicago and Wisconsin. In 1911, 'Abdu'l-Bahá began a twenty-eight month tour of Europe and North America to promote the Bahá'í faith. Administratively, he established the spiritual assemblies that were the forerunner of the Houses of Justice that his father had envisioned.

During World War I, 'Abdu'l-Bahá engaged in humanitarian work among the Palestinians in the Holy Land, where he lived. In recognition of his efforts, he was granted knighthood by the British government. Thousands of people, including many political and religious dignitaries, attended his funeral in 1921.

'Abdu'l-Bahá conferred the role of Guardian, or sole interpreter of Bahá'í teaching, to his eldest grandson, Shoghi Effendi Rabbani. To him, all questions regarding the faith were to be addressed. Shoghi Effendi Rabbani was a descendent of Baha'u'llah through both parents. He headed the Bahá'í faith from 1921 to 1963, achieving four major projects: he oversaw the physical development of the World Centre and expanded the administrative order; he carried out the plan his father had set in motion; and he provided for the translating and interpreting of Bahá'í teachings, as the writings of both the Bab and those of Baha'u'llah and 'Abdu'l-Bahá have been translated and published in more than eight hundred languages.

Beginning in 1937, Shoghi Effendi Rabbani began a series of specific plans with goals tied to deadlines. In 1953, during the second seven-year plan, the house of worship in Wilmette, Illinois, was completed and dedicated.

Although the beliefs originated in Shi'ite Islam, the Bahá'í Faith has been declared a new religion without connections to Islam. To followers of Islam, it is a heretical sect. During the reign of the Ayatollah Khomeini, a time when Iran was especially noted as intolerant of diverse views, the Bahá'í faced widespread persecution.

Founder or Major Prophet

Mirza Husayn Ali Nuri, known as Baha'u'llah, was born into privilege in 1817 in what was then Persia, now present-day Iran. At twenty-two, he declined a government post offered at his father's death. Although a member of a politically prestigious family, he did not follow the career path of several generations of his ancestors. Instead, he managed the family estates and devoted himself to charities, earning the title "Father of the Poor."

At twenty-seven, he followed the Babis's movement within Shia Islam, corresponding with the Bab and traveling to further the faith. He also provided financial support. In 1848, he organized and helped to direct a conference that explained the Bab's teaching. At the conference, he gave

symbolic names to the eighty-one followers who had attended, based on the spiritual qualities he had observed.

Although he managed to escape death during the persecutions before and after the Bab's death, a fact largely attributed to his upbringing, Baha'u'llah was imprisoned several times. During a four-month stay in an underground dungeon in Tehran, he realized from a dream that he was the one of whom the Bab had prophesied. After being released, he was banished from Persia and had his property confiscated by the shah. He went to Baghdad, refusing the offer of refuge that had come from Russia. Over the following three years a small band of followers joined him, including members of his family. When his younger brother attempted to take over the leadership of the Babis, Baha'u'llah spent two years in a self-imposed exile in the Kurdistan wilderness. In 1856, with the community near anarchy as a result of his brother's failure of leadership, Baha'u'llah returned to the community and restored its position over the next seven years.

Concerned by the growing popularity of the new faith, the shah demanded that the Babis move further away from Persia. They went to Constantinople where, in 1863, Baha'u'llah revealed to the whole group that he was "He Whom God Will Make Manifest." From there the Bahá'í were sent to Adrianople in Turkey, and at last, in 1868, to the town of Acre in the Holy Land. Baha'u'llah was imprisoned in Acre and survived severe prison conditions. In 1877, he moved from prison to a country estate, then to a mansion. He died in 1892 after a fever.

Philosophical Basis

The thinking of Shia Muslims contributed to the development of Bahá'í. The writings incorporate language and concepts from the Qur'an (Islam's holy book). Like Muslims, the Bahá'í believe that God is one. God sends messengers, the Manifestations of God, to instruct people and benefit society. These have included Jesus Christ, the Buddha, the Prophet Muhammad, Krishna, and the Bab. Bahá'í also goes further than Islam in accepting all religions—not just Judaism, Christianity, and Islam—as being part of a divinely inspired plan.

Shia Muslims believe that Muhammad's descendents should lead the faithful community. The leaders, known as imams, were considered infallible. The Sunni Muslims believed that following the way (sunna) of Muhammad was sufficient qualification for leadership. Sunni dynasties regarded the imams as a threat and executed them, starting with two of Muhammad's grandsons, who became Shia martyrs.

In Persia, a state with a long tradition of divinely appointed rulers, the Shia sect was strong. When the Safavids, a Shia dynasty, came to power in the sixteenth century, the custom of the imamate was victorious. One tradition states that in 873, the last appointed imam, who was still a child, went into hiding to avoid being killed. For the following sixty-nine years, this twelfth imam communicated through his deputies to the faithful. Each of the deputies was called bab, or gate, because they led to the "Hidden Imam." Four babs existed through 941, and the last one died without naming the next bab. The Hidden Imam is thought to emerge at the end of time to bring in a worldwide reign of justice. From this tradition came the expectation of a Mahdi (Guided One) to lead the people.

During the early nineteenth century, many followers of both the Christian and Islamic faiths expected their respective messiahs to return. Shia teachers believed that the return of the Mahdi imam was near. In 1843, one teacher, Siyyid Kázim, noted that the Hidden Imam had disappeared one thousand lunar years earlier. He urged the faithful to look for the Mahdi imam.

The following year in Shiraz, Siyyad 'Ali Mohammad announced that he was the Mahdi. (*Siyyad* is a term meaning descended from Muhammad.) He referred to himself as the Bab, though he expanded the term's meaning. Eighteen men, impressed with his ability to expound the Qur'an, believed him. They became the Letters of the Living, and were sent throughout Persia (present-day Iran) to announce the dawning of the Day of God.

In 1853, Mirza Husayn Ali Nuri experienced a revelation that he was "He Whom God Shall Make Manifest," the one of whom the Bab prophesied. Accepted as such, he began writing the words that became the Bahá'í scriptures. Much of what is known of the early days of the faith comes from a Cambridge academic, Edward Granville Browne, who first visited Baha'u'llah in the 1890. Browne wrote of his meeting, introducing this faith to the West.

The emphasis of the Bahá'í faith is on personal development and the breaking down of barriers between people. Service to humanity is important and encouraged. Marriage, with a belief in the equality of both men and women, is also encouraged. Consent of both sets of parents is required prior to marrying.

Holy Places

The shrine of the Bab near Haifa and that of Baha'u'llah near Acre, in Israel, are the two most revered sites for those of the Bahá'í faith. In 2008, the United Nations Educational, Scientific, and Cultural Organization (UNESCO) recognized both as World Heritage Sites. They are the first such sites from a modern religious tradition to be added to the list of sites. Both sites are appreciated for the formal gardens surrounding them that blend design elements from different cultures. For the Bahá'í, Baha'u'llah's shrine is the focus of prayer, comparable to the significance given to the Ka'bah in Mecca for Muslims or to the Western Wall for Jews.

As of 2013, there are seven Bahá'í temples in the world; an eighth temple is under construction in Chile. All temples are built with a center dome and nine sides, symbolizing both diversity and world unity. The North American temple is located in Wilmette, Illinois. There, daily prayer services take place as well as a Sunday service.

THE BAHÁ'Í FAITH IN DEPTH

Governance

Elected members of lay councils at international, national, and local levels administer the work of the faith. The Universal House of Justice in Haifa, Israel, is the location of the international nine-member body. Elections for all of these lay councils are by secret ballot, and do not include nominating, candidates, or campaigns. Those twenty-one and older are permitted to vote. The councils make decisions according to a process of collective decision-making called consultation. They strive to serve as a model for governing a united global society.

Personal Conduct

In addition to private prayer and acts of social justice, those of the Bahá'í faith are encouraged to have a profession, craft, or trade. They are also asked to shun and refrain from slander and partisan politics. Homosexuality and sexual activity outside marriage are forbidden, as is gambling.

The Bahá'í faith does not have professional clergy, nor does it engage in missionary work. However, Bahá'í may share their faith with others and may move to another country as a "pioneer." Pioneers are unlike traditional missionaries, and are expected to support themselves through a career and as a member of the community.

Avenues of Service

Those of the Bahá'í Faith place a high value on service to humanity, considering it an act of worship. This can be done through caring for one's own family or through one's choice of vocation. Within the local community, people may teach classes for children, mentor youth groups, host devotional programs, or teach adult study circles. Many are engaged in economic or social development programs as well. Although not mandated, a year or two of service is often undertaken following high school or during college.

United Nations Involvement

Beginning in 1947, just one year after the United Nations (UN) first met, the Bahá'í Faith was represented at that body. In 1948, the Bahá'í International Community was accredited by the UN as an international nongovernmental organization (NGO). In 1970, the faith received special consultative status with the UN Economic and Social Council (ECOSOC). Following World War I, a Bahá'í office opened in Geneva, Switzerland, where the League of Nations was headquartered. Thus the Bahá'í Faith has a long tradition of supporting global institutions.

Money Matters

The International Bahá'í Fund exists to develop and support the growth of the faith, and the Universal House of Justice oversees the distribution of the money. Contributions are also used to maintain the Bahá'í World Center. No money is accepted from non-Bahá'í sources. National and local funds, administered by National or Local Spiritual Assemblies, are used in supporting service projects, publishing endeavors, schools, and Bahá'í centers. For the Bahá'í, the size of the donation is less important than regular contributions and the spirit of sacrifice behind them.

Food Restrictions

Bahá'í between fifteen and seventy years of age **fast** nineteen days a year, abstaining from food and drink from sunrise to sunset. Fasting occurs the first day of each month of the Bahá'í calendar, which divides the year into nineteen months of nineteen days each. The Bahá'í faithful do not drink alcohol or use narcotics, because these will deaden the mind with repeated use.

Rites, Celebrations & Services

Daily prayer and meditation is recommended in the Bahá'í faith. During services there are mediations and prayers, along with the reading of Bahá'í scriptures and other world faith traditions. There is no set ritual, no offerings, and no sermons. Unaccompanied by musical instruments, choirs also sing. Light refreshments may be served afterwards.

Bahá'í place great stress on marriage, the only state in which sex is permitted. Referred to as "a fortress for well-being and salvation," a monogamous, heterosexual marriage is the ideal. To express the oneness of humanity, interracial marriages are encouraged. After obtaining the consent of their parents, the couple takes the following vow: "We will all, verily, abide by the will of God." The remainder of the service may be individually crafted and may also include dance, music, feasting, and ceremony. Should a couple choose to end a marriage, they must first complete a year of living apart while trying to reconcile differences. Divorce is discouraged, but permitted after that initial year.

Judy A. Johnson, MTS

Bibliography
Albertson, Lorelei. *All about Bahá'í Faith*. University Pub., 2012. E-book.
Bowers, Kenneth E. *God Speaks Again: an Introduction to the Bahá'í Faith*. Wilmette: Bahá'í, 2004. Print.
Buck, Christopher. "The Interracial 'Bahá'í Movement' and the Black Intelligentsia: The Case of W. E. B. Du Bois." *Journal of Religious History* 36.4 (2012): 542–62. Print.
Cederquist, Druzelle. *The Story of Baha'u'llah*. Wilmette: Bahá'í, 2005. Print.
Echevarria, L. *Life Stories of Bahá'í Women in Canada: Constructing Religious Identity in the Twentieth Century*. Lang, 2011. E-book.
Garlington, William. *The Bahá'í Faith in America*. Lanham: Rowman, 2008. Print.
Hartz, Paula R. *Bahá'í Faith*. New York: Facts on File, 2006. Print.
Hatcher, William S. and J. Douglas Martin. *The Bahá'í Faith: The Emerging Global Religion*. Wilmette: Bahá'í, 2002. Print.
Karlberg, Michael. "Constructive Resilience: The Bahá'í Response to Oppression." *Peace & Change* 35.2 (2010): 222–57. Print.
Lee, Anthony A. *The Bahá'í Faith in Africa: Establishing a New Religious Movement, 1952–1962*. Brill NV, E-book.
Momen, Moojan. "Bahá'í Religious History." *Journal of Religious History* 36.4 (2012): 463–70. Print.
Momen, Moojan. *The Bahá'í Faith: A Beginner's Guide*. Oxford: Oneworld, 2007. Print.
Smith, Peter. *The Bahá'í Faith*. Cambridge: Cambridge UP, 2008. Print.
Wilkinson, Philip. *Religions*. New York: DK, 2008. Print.

Buddhism

General Description

Buddhism has three main branches: Theravada (Way of the Elders), also referred to as Hinayana (Lesser Vehicle); Mahayana (Greater Vehicle); and Vajrayana (Diamond Vehicle), also referred to as Tantric Buddhism. Vajrayana is sometimes thought of as an extension of Mahayana Buddhism. These can be further divided into many sects and schools, many of which are geographically based. In Buddhism, these different divisions or schools are regarded as alternative paths to enlightenment (Wilkinson 2008).

Number of Adherents Worldwide

An estimated 474 million people around the world are Buddhists. Of the major sects, Theravada Buddhism is the oldest, developed in the sixth century BCE. Its adherents include those of the Theravada Forest Tradition. From Mahayana Buddhism, which developed in the third to second centuries BCE, came several offshoots based on location. In what is now China, Pure Land Buddhism and Tibetan Buddhism developed in the seventh century. In Japan, Zen Buddhism developed in the twelfth century, Nichiren Buddhism developed a century later, and Soka Gakkai was founded in 1937. In California during the 1970s, the Serene Reflection Meditation began as a subset of Sōtō Zen. In Buddhism, these different divisions or schools are regarded as alternative paths to enlightenment.

Basic Tenets

Buddhists hold to the Three Universal Truths: impermanence, the lack of self, and suffering. These truths encompass the ideas that everything is impermanent and changing and that life is not satisfying because of its impermanence and the temporary nature of all things, including contentment. Buddhism also teaches the Four Noble Truths: All life is suffering (Dukkha). Desire and attachment cause suffering (Samudaya). Ceasing to desire or crave conceptual attachment

ends suffering and leads to release (Nirodha). This release comes through following the Noble Eightfold Path—right understanding (or view), right intention, right speech, right conduct, right occupation, right effort, right mindfulness, and right concentration (Magga).

Although Buddhists do not believe in an afterlife as such, the soul undergoes a cycle of death and rebirth. Following the Noble Eightfold Path leads to the accumulation of good karma, allowing one to be reborn at a higher level. Karma is the Buddhist belief in cause-effect relationships; actions taken in one life have consequences in the next. Ultimately, many refer to the cessation or elimination of suffering as the primary goal of Buddhism.

Buddhists do not believe in gods. Salvation is to be found in following the teachings of Buddha, which are called the Dharma (law or truth). Buddhism does have saint-like bodhisattvas (enlightened beings) who reject ultimate enlightenment (Nirvana) for themselves to aid others.

Sacred Text

Buddhism has nothing comparable to the Qur'an (Islam's holy book) or the Bible. For Theravada Buddhists, an important text is the Pāli Canon, the collection of Buddha's teachings. Mahayana Buddhists recorded their version of these as sutras, many of them in verse. The Lotus Sutra is among the most important. The Buddhist scriptures are written in two languages of ancient India, Pali and Sanskrit, depending on the tradition in which they were developed. Some of these words, such as karma, have been transliterated into English and gained common usage.

Major Figures

Siddhartha Gautama (ca. 563 to 483 BCE) is the founder of Buddhism and regarded as the Buddha or Supreme Buddha. He is the most highly regarded historical figure in Buddhism.

He had two principle disciples: Sariputta and Mahamoggallana (or Maudgalyayana). In contemporary Buddhism, the fourteenth Dalai Lama, Tenzin Gyatso, is a significant person. Both he and Aung San Suu Kyi, a Buddhist of Myanmar who was held as a political prisoner for her stand against the oppressive regime of that nation, have been awarded the Nobel Peace Prize.

Major Holy Sites

Buddhist holy sites are located in several places in Asia. All of those directly related to the life of Siddhartha Gautama are located in the northern part of India near Nepal. Lumbini Grove is noted as the birthplace of the Buddha. He received enlightenment at Bodh Gaya and first began to teach in Sarnath. Kusinara is the city where he died.

In other Asian nations, some holy sites were once dedicated to other religions. Angkor Wat in Cambodia, for example, was constructed for the Hindu god Vishnu in the twelfth century CE. It became a Buddhist temple three hundred years later. It was once the largest religious monument in the world and still attracts visitors. In Java's central highlands sits Borobudur, the world's largest Buddhist shrine. The name means "Temple of Countless Buddhas." Its five terraces represent what must be overcome to reach enlightenment: worldly desires, evil intent, malicious joy, laziness, and doubt. It was built in the eighth and ninth centuries CE, only to fall into neglect at about the turn of the millennium; it was rediscovered in 1815. The complex has three miles of carvings illustrating the life and teachings of the Buddha. In Sri Lanka, the Temple of the Tooth, which houses what is believed to be one of the Buddha's teeth, is a popular pilgrimage site.

Some of the holy sites incorporate gifts of nature. China has four sacred Buddhist mountains, symbolizing the four corners of the universe. These mountains—Wǔtái Shān, Éméi Shān, Jiǔhuá Shān, and Pǔtuó Shān—are believed to be the homes of bodhisattvas. In central India outside Fardapur, there are twenty-nine caves carved into the granite, most of them with frescoes based on the Buddha's life. Ajanta, as the site is known, was created between 200 BCE and the fifth century CE. Five of the caves house temples.

The Buddha's birthday, his day of death, and the day of his enlightenment are all celebrated, either as one day or several. Different traditions and countries have their own additional celebrations, including Sri Lanka's Festival of the Tooth. Buddhists have a lunar calendar, and four days of each month are regarded as holy days.

ORIGINS

History & Geography

Buddhism began in what is now southern Nepal and northern India with the enlightenment of the Buddha. Following his death, members of the sangha, or community, spread the teachings across northern India. The First Buddhist Council took place in 486 BCE at Rajagaha. This council settled the Buddhist canon, the Tipitaka. In 386 BCE, a little more than a century after the Buddha died, a second Buddhist Council was held at Vesali. It was at this meeting that the two major schools of Buddhist thought—Theravada and Mahayana—began to differ.

Emperor Asoka, who ruled most of the Indian subcontinent from around 268 to 232 BCE, converted to Buddhism. He sent missionaries across India and into central parts of Asia. He also set up pillars with Buddhist messages in his own efforts to establish "true dharma" in the kingdom, although he did not create a state church. His desire for his subjects to live contently in this life led to promoting trade, maintaining canals and reservoirs, and the founding a system of medical care for both humans and animals. Asoka's son Mahinda went to southern Indian and to Sri Lanka with the message of Buddhism.

Asoka's empire fell shortly after his death. Under the following dynasties, evidence suggests Buddhists in India experienced persecution. The religion continued to grow, however, and during the first centuries CE, monasteries and monuments were constructed with support from local rulers. Some additional support came from women within the royal courts. Monastic centers also grew in number. By the fourth century CE, Buddhism had become one of the chief religious traditions in India.

During the Gupta dynasty, which lasted from about 320 to 600 CE, Buddhists and Hindus began enriching each other's traditions. Some Hindus felt that the Buddha was an incarnation of Vishnu, a Hindu god. Some Buddhists showed respect for Hindu deities.

Also during this era, Mahavihara, the concept of the "Great Monastery," came to be. These institutions served as universities for the study and development of Buddhist thinking. Some of them also included cultural and scientific study in the curriculum.

Traders and missionaries took the ideas of Buddhism to China. By the first century CE, Buddhism was established in that country. The religion died out or was absorbed into Hinduism in India. By the seventh century, a visiting Chinese monk found that Huns had invaded India from Central Asia and destroyed many Buddhist monasteries. The religion revived and flourished in the northeast part of India for several centuries.

Muslim invaders reached India in the twelfth and thirteenth centuries. They sacked the monasteries, some of which had grown very wealthy. Some even paid workers to care for both the land they owned and the monks, while some had indentured slaves. Because Buddhism had become monastic rather than a religion of the laity, there was no groundswell for renewal following the Muslim invasion.

Prominent in eastern and Southeast Asia, Buddhism is the national religion in some countries. For example, in Thailand, everyone learns about Buddhism in school. Buddhism did not begin to reach Western culture until the nineteenth century, when the Lotus Sutra was translated into German. The first Buddhist temple in the United States was built in 1853 in San Francisco's Chinatown.

Chinese Communists took control of Tibet in 1950. Nine years later, the fourteenth Dalai Lama left for India, fearing persecution. The Dalai Lama is considered a living teacher (lama) who is to instruct others. (The term *dalai* means "great as the ocean.") In 1989, he received the Nobel Peace Prize.

Buddhism experienced a revival in India during the twentieth century. Although some of this new beginning was due in part to Tibetan immigrants seeking safety, a mass conversion in 1956 was the major factor. The year was chosen to honor the 2,500th anniversary of the Buddha's death year. Buddhism was chosen as an alternative to the strict caste structure of Hinduism, and hundreds of thousands of people of the Dalit caste, once known as untouchables, converted in a ceremony held in Nagpur.

Founder or Major Prophet

Siddhartha Gautama, who became known as the "Enlightened One," or Buddha, was a prince in what is now southern Nepal, but was then northern India during the sixth century BCE. The name Siddhartha means "he who achieves his aim." He was a member of the Sakya tribe of Nepal, belonging to the warrior caste. Many legends have grown around his birth and early childhood. One states that he was born in a grove in the woods, emerging from his mother's side able to walk and completely clean.

During Siddhartha's childhood, a Brahmin, or wise man, prophesied that he would grow to be a prince or a religious teacher who would help others overcome suffering. Because the life of a sage involved itinerant begging, the king did not want this life for his child. He kept Siddhartha in the palace and provided him with all the luxuries of his position, including a wife, Yashodhara. They had a son, Rahula.

Escaping from the palace at about the age of thirty, Gautama first encountered suffering in the form of an old man with a walking stick. The following day, he saw a man who was ill. On the third day, he witnessed a funeral procession. Finally he met a monk, who had nothing, but who radiated happiness. He determined to leave his privileged life, an act called the Great Renunciation. Because hair was a sign of vanity in his time, he shaved his head. He looked for enlightenment via an ascetic life of little food or sleep. He followed this path for six years, nearly starving to death. Eventually, he determined on a Middle Way, a path neither luxurious as he had known in the palace, nor ascetic as he had attempted.

After three days and nights of meditating under a tree at Bodh Gaya, Siddhartha achieved his goal of enlightenment, or Nirvana. He escaped fear of suffering and death.

The Buddha began his preaching career, which spanned some forty years, following his enlightenment. He gave his first sermon in northeast India at Sarnath in a deer park. The first five followers became the first community, or sangha. Buddha died around age eighty, in 483 BCE after he had eaten poisoned food. After warning his followers not to eat the food, he meditated until he died.

Buddhists believe in many enlightened ones. Siddhartha is in one tradition regarded as the fourth buddha, while other traditions hold him to have been the seventh or twenty-fifth buddha.

His disciples, who took the ideas throughout India, repeated his teachings. When the later Buddhists determined to write down the teachings of the Buddha, they met to discuss the ideas and agreed that a second meeting should occur in a century. At the third council, which was held at Pataliputta, divisions occurred. The two major divisions—Theravada and Mahayana—differ over the texts to be used and the interpretation of the teachings. Theravada can be translated as "the Teachings of the Elders," while Mahayana means "Great Vehicle."

Theravada Buddhists believe that only monks can achieve enlightenment through the teachings of another buddha, or enlightened being. Thus they try to spend some part of their lives in a monastery. Buddhists in the Mahayana tradition, on the other hand, feel that all people can achieve enlightenment, without being in a monastery. Mahayanans also regard some as bodhisattvas, people who have achieved the enlightened state but renounce Nirvana to help others achieve it.

Philosophical Basis

During Siddhartha's lifetime, Hinduism was the predominant religion in India. Many people, especially in northern India, were dissatisfied with the rituals and sacrifices of that religion. In addition, as many small kingdoms expanded and the unity of the tribes began to break down, many people were in religious turmoil and doubt. A number of sects within Hinduism developed.

The Hindu belief in the cycle of death and rebirth led some people to despair because they could not escape from suffering in their lives. Siddhartha was trying to resolve the suffering he saw in the world, but many of his ideas came from the Brahmin sect of Hinduism, although he reinterpreted them. Reincarnation, dharma, and reverence for cows are three of the ideas that carried over into Buddhism.

In northeast India at Bodh Gaya, he rested under a bodhi tree, sometimes called a bo tree. He meditated there until he achieved Nirvana, or complete enlightenment, derived from the freedom of fear that attached to suffering and death. As a result of his being enlightened, he was known as Buddha, a Sanskrit word meaning "awakened one." Wanting to help others, he began teaching his Four Noble Truths, along with the Noble Eightfold Path that would lead people to freedom from desire and suffering. He encouraged his followers to take Triple Refuge in the Three Precious Jewels: the Buddha, the teachings, and the sangha, or monastic community. Although at first Buddha was uncertain about including women in a sangha, his mother-in-law begged for the privilege.

Greed, hatred, and ignorance were three traits that Buddha felt people needed to conquer. All three create craving, the root of suffering. Greed and ignorance lead to a desire for things that are not needed, while hatred leads to a craving to destroy the hated object or person.

To the Four Noble Truths and Eightfold Path, early devotees of Buddhism added the Five Moral Precepts. These are to avoid taking drugs and alcohol, engaging in sexual misconduct, harming others, stealing, and lying.

The precepts of the Buddha were not written down for centuries. The first text did not appear for more than 350 years after the precepts were first spoken. One collection from Sri Lanka written in Pāli during the first century BCE is known as Three Baskets, or Tipitaka. The three baskets include Buddha's teaching (the Basket of Discourse), commentary on the sayings (the Basket of Special Doctrine), and the rules for monks to follow (the Basket of Discipline). The name Three Baskets refers to the fact that the sayings were first written on leaves from a palm tree that were then collected in baskets.

Holy Places

Buddhists make pilgrimages to places that relate to important events in Siddhartha's life. While Lumbini Grove, the place of Siddhartha's birth, is a prominent pilgrimage site, the primary site for pilgrimage is Bodh Gaya, the location where Buddha received enlightenment. Other pilgrimage sites include Sarnath, the deer park located in what is now Varanasi (Benares) where the Buddha first began to teach, and Kusinara, the city where he died. All of these are in the northern part of India near Nepal.

Other sites in Asia that honor various bodhisattvas have also become pilgrimage destinations. Mountains are often chosen; there are four in China, each with monasteries and temples built on them. In Japan, the Shikoku pilgrimage covers more than 700 miles and involves visits to eighty-eight temples along the route.

BUDDHISM IN DEPTH

Sacred Symbols

Many stylized statue poses of the Buddha exist, each with a different significance. One, in which the Buddha has both hands raised, palms facing outward, commemorates the calming of an elephant about to attack the Buddha. If only the right hand is raised, the hand symbolizes friendship and being unafraid. The teaching gesture is that of a hand with the thumb and first finger touching.

In Tibetan Buddhism, the teachings of Buddha regarding the cycle of rebirth are symbolized in the six-spoke wheel of life. One may be reborn into any of the six realms of life: hell, hungry spirits, warlike demons called Asuras, animals, humans, or gods. Another version of the wheel has eight spokes rather than six, to represent the Noble Eightfold Path. Still another wheel has twelve spokes, signifying both the Four Noble Truths and the Noble Eightfold Path.

Tibetan Buddhists have prayer beads similar to a rosary, with 108 beads representing the number of desires to be overcome prior to reaching enlightenment. The worshipper repeats the Triple Refuge—Buddha, dharma, and sangha—or a mantra.

The prayer wheel is another device that Tibetan Buddhists use. Inside the wheel is a roll of paper on which the sacred mantra—Hail to the jewel in the lotus—is written many times. The lotus is a symbol of growing spiritually; it grows in muddied waters, but with the stems and flowers, it reaches toward the sun. By turning the wheel and spinning the mantra, the practitioner spreads blessings. Bells may be rung to wake the hearer out of ignorance.

In Tantric Buddhism, the mandala, or circle, serves as a map of the entire cosmos. Mandalas may be made of colored grains of sand, carved or painted. They are used to help in meditation and are thought to have a spiritual energy.

Buddhism recognizes Eight Auspicious Symbols, including the banner, conch shell, fish, knot, lotus, treasure vase, umbrella, and wheel. Each has a particular significance. A conch shell, for example, is often blown to call worshippers to meetings. Because its sound travels far, it signifies the voice of Buddha traveling throughout the world. Fish are fertility symbols because they have thousands of offspring. In Buddhist imagery, they are often in facing pairs and fashioned of gold. The lotus represents spiritual growth, rooted in muddy water but flowering toward the sun. The umbrella symbolizes protection, because servants once used them to protect royalty from both sun and rain.

Sacred Practices & Gestures

Two major practices characterize Buddhism: gift-giving and showing respect to images and relics of the Buddha. The first is the transaction between laity and monks in which laypersons present sacrificial offerings to the monks, who in return share their higher state of spiritual being with the laity. Although Buddhist monks are permitted to own very little, they each have a begging bowl, which is often filled with rice.

Buddhists venerate statues of the Buddha, bodhisattvas, and saints; they also show respect to his relics, housed in stupas. When in the presence of a statue of the Buddha, worshippers have a series of movements they repeat three times, thus dedicating their movements to the Triple Refuge. It begins with a dedicated body: placing hands together with the palms cupped slightly and fingers touching, the devotee raises the hands to the forehead. The second step symbolizes right speech by lowering the hands to just below the mouth. In the third movement, the hands are lowered to the front of the chest, indicating that heart—and by extension, mind—are also dedicated to the Triple Refuge. The final movement is prostration. The devotee first gets on all fours, then lowers either the entire body to the floor or lowers the head, so that there are five points of contact with the floor.

Statues of the Buddha give a clue to the gestures held important to his followers. The gesture of turning the hand towards the ground indicates that one is observing Earth. Devotees assume a lotus position, with legs crossed, when in meditation.

Allowing the left hand to rest in the lap and the right hand to point down to Earth is a gesture used in meditation. Another common gesture is to touch thumb and fingertips together while the palms of both hands face up, thus forming a flat triangular shape. The triangle signifies the Three Jewels of Buddhism.

Food Restrictions

Buddhism does not require one to be a vegetarian. Many followers do not eat meat, however, because to do so involves killing other creatures. Both monks and laypersons may choose not to eat after noontime during the holy days of each month.

Rites, Celebrations, & Services

Ancient Buddhism recognized four holy days each month, known as *uposatha*. These days included the full moon and new moon days of each lunar month, as well as the eighth day after each of these moons appeared. Both monks and members of the laity have special religious duties during these four days. A special service takes place in which flowers are offered to images of the Buddha, precepts are repeated, and a sermon is preached. On these four days, an additional three precepts may be undertaken along with the five regularly observed. The three extra duties are to refrain from sleeping on a luxurious bed, eating any food after noon, and adorning the body or going to entertainments.

In Theravada nations, three major life events of the Buddha—birth, enlightenment, and entering nirvana—are celebrated on Vesak, or Buddha Day. In temples, statues of Buddha as a child are ceremonially cleaned. Worshippers may offer incense and flowers. To symbolize the Buddha's enlightenment, lights may be illuminated in trees and temples. Because it is a day of special kindness, some people in Thailand refrain from farm work that could harm living creatures. They may also seek special merit by freeing captive animals.

Other Buddhist nations that follow Mahayana Buddhism commemorate these events on three different days. In Japan, Hana Matsuri is the celebration of Buddha's birth. On that day, people create paper flower gardens to recall the gardens of Lumbini, Siddhartha's birthplace. Worshippers also pour perfumed tea over statues of Buddha; this is because, according to tradition, the gods provided scented water for Siddhartha's first bath.

Poson is celebrated in Sri Lanka to honor the coming of Buddhism during the reign of Emperor Asoka. Other holy persons are also celebrated in the countries where they had the greatest influence. In Tibet, for instance, the arrival of

Padmasambhava, who brought Buddhism to that nation, is observed.

Buddhists also integrate their own special celebrations into regular harvest festivals and New Year activities. These festivities may include a performance of an event in the life of any buddha or bodhisattva. For example, troupes of actors in Tibet specialize in enacting Buddhist legends. The festival of the Sacred Tooth is held in Kandy, Sri Lanka. According to one legend, a tooth of Buddha has been recovered, and it is paraded through the streets on this day. The tooth has been placed in a miniature stupa, or sealed mound, which is carried on an elephant's back.

Protection rituals have been common in Buddhism from earliest days. They may be public rituals meant to avoid a collective danger, such as those held in Sri Lanka and other Southeast Asia nations. Or they may be designed for private use. The role of these rituals is greater in Mahayana tradition, especially in Tibet. Mantras are chanted for this reason.

Customs surrounding death and burial differ between traditions and nations. A common factor, however, is the belief that the thoughts of a person at death are significant. This period may be extended for three days following death, due to a belief in consciousness for that amount of time after death. To prepare the mind of the dying, another person may read sacred texts aloud.

Judy A. Johnson, MTS

Bibliography

Armstrong, Karen. *Buddha*. New York: Penguin, 2001. Print.

Barnes, Trevor. *The Kingfisher Book of Religions*. New York: Kingfisher, 1999. Print.

Chodron, Thubten. *Buddhism for Beginners*. Ithaca: Snow Lion, 2001. Print.

Eckel, Malcolm David. *Buddhism*. Oxford: Oxford UP, 2002. Print.

Epstein, Ron. "Application of Buddhist Teachings in Modern Life." *Religion East & West* Oct. 2012: 52–61. Print.

Harding, John S. *Studying Buddhism in Practice*. Routledge, 2012. E-book. Studying Religions in Practice.

Harvey, Peter. *An Introduction to Buddhism: Teachings, History and Practices*. 2nd ed. Cambridge UP, 2013. E-book.

Heirman, Ann. "Buddhist Nuns: Between Past and Present." *International Review for the History of Religions* 58.5/6 (2011): 603–31. Print.

Langley, Myrtle. *Religion*. New York: Knopf, 1996. Print.

Low, Kim Cheng Patrick. "Three Treasures of Buddhism & Leadership Insights." *Culture & Religion Review Journal* 2012.3 (2012): 66–72. Print.

Low, Patrick Kim Cheng. "Leading Change, the Buddhist Perspective." *Culture & Religion Review Journal* 2012.1 (2012): 127–45. Print.

McMahan, David L. *Buddhism in the Modern World*. Routledge, 2012. E-book.

Meredith, Susan. *The Usborne Book of World Religions*. London: Usborne, 1995. Print.

Morgan, Diane. *Essential Buddhism: A Comprehensive Guide to Belief and Practice*. Praeger, 2010. E-book.

Wilkinson, Philip. *Buddhism*. New York: DK, 2003.Print.

Wilkinson, Philip. *Religions*. New York: DK, 2008. Print.

Christianity

General Description

Christianity is one of the world's major religions. It is based on the life and teachings of Jesus of Nazareth, called the Christ, or anointed one. It is believed that there are over thirty thousand denominations or sects of Christianity worldwide. Generally, most of these sects fall under the denominational families of Catholicism, Protestant, and Orthodox. (Anglican and Oriental Orthodox are sometimes added as separate branches.) Most denominations have developed since the seventeenth-century Protestant Reformation.

Number of Adherents Worldwide

Over 2.3 billion people around the world claim allegiance to Christianity in one of its many forms. The three major divisions are Roman Catholicism, Eastern Orthodox, and Protestant. Within each group are multiple denominations. Roman Catholics number more than 1.1 billion followers, while the Eastern Orthodox Church has between 260 and 278 million adherents. An estimated 800 million adherents follow one of the various Protestant denominations, including Anglican, Baptist, Lutheran, Presbyterian, and Methodist. Approximately 1 percent of Christians, or 28 million adherents, do not belong to one of the three major divisions

There are a number of other groups, such as the Amish, with an estimated 249,000 members, and the Quakers, numbering approximately 377,000. Both of these churches—along with Mennonites, who number 1.7 million—are in the peace tradition (their members are conscientious objectors). Pentecostals have 600 million adherents worldwide. Other groups that are not always considered Christian by more conservative groups include Jehovah's Witnesses (7.6 million) and Mormons (13 million) (Wilkinson, p. 104-121).

Basic Tenets

The summaries of the Christian faith are found in the Apostles Creed and Nicene Creed.

In addition, some churches have developed their own confessions of faith, such as Lutheranism's Augsburg Confession. Christianity is a monotheistic tradition, although most Christians believe in the Trinity, defined as one God in three separate but equal persons—Father, Son, and Holy Spirit. More modern, gender-neutral versions of the Trinitarian formula may refer to Creator, Redeemer, and Sanctifier. Many believe in the doctrine of original sin, which means that the disobedience of Adam and Eve in the Garden of Eden has been passed down through all people; because of this sin, humankind is in need of redemption. Jesus Christ was born, lived a sinless life, and then was crucified and resurrected as a substitute for humankind. Those who accept this sacrifice for sin will receive eternal life in a place of bliss after death. Many Christians believe that a Second Coming of Jesus will inaugurate a millennial kingdom and a final judgment (in which people will be judged according to their deeds and their eternal souls consigned to heaven or hell), as well as a resurrected physical body.

Sacred Text

The Bible is the sacred text of Christianity, which places more stress on the New Testament. The canon of the twenty-six books of the New Testament was finally determined in the latter half of the fourth century CE.

Major Figures

Christianity is based on the life and teachings of Jesus of Nazareth. His mother, Mary, is especially revered in Roman Catholicism and the Eastern Orthodox tradition, where she is known as Theotokos (God-bearer). Jesus spread his teachings through the twelve apostles, or disciples, who he himself chose and named. Paul (Saint Paul or Paul the Apostle), who became the first missionary to the Gentiles—and whose writings comprise a bulk of the New Testament—is a key figure for the theological treatises embedded in his letters to early churches. His conversion occurred after Jesus' crucifixion. All of these figures are biblically represented.

Under the Emperor Constantine, Christianity went from a persecuted religion to the state religion. Constantine also convened the Council of Nicea in 325 CE, which expressed the formula defining Jesus as fully God and fully human. Saint Augustine (354–430) was a key thinker of the early church who became the Bishop of Hippo in North Africa. He outlined the principles of just war and expressed the ideas of original sin. He also suggested what later became the Catholic doctrine of purgatory.

In the sixth century, Saint Benedict inscribed a rule for monks that became a basis for monastic life. Martin Luther, the monk who stood against the excesses of the Roman Catholic Church, ignited the seventeenth-century Protestant Reformation. He proclaimed that salvation came by grace alone, not through works. In the twentieth century, Pope John XXIII convened the Vatican II Council, or Second Vatican Council, which made sweeping changes to the liturgy and daily practice for Roman Catholics.

Major Holy Sites

The key events in the life of Jesus Christ occurred in the region of Palestine. Bethlehem is honored as the site of Jesus's birth; Jerusalem is especially revered as the site of Jesus's crucifixion. The capital of the empire, Rome, also became the center of Christianity until the Emperor Constantine shifted the focus to Constantinople. Rome today is the seat of the Vatican, an independent city-state that houses the government of the Roman Catholic Church. Canterbury, the site of the martyrdom of Saint Thomas Becket and seat of the archbishop of the Anglican Communion, is a pilgrimage site for Anglicans. There are also many pilgrimage sites, such as Compostela and Lourdes, for other branches of Christianity. In Ethiopia, Lalibela is the site of eleven churches carved from stone during the twelfth century. The site serves as a profound testimony to the vibrancy of the Christian faith in Africa.

Major Rites & Celebrations

The first rite of the church is baptism, a water-related ritual that is traditionally administered to infants or adults alike through some variant of sprinkling or immersion. Marriage is another rite of the church. Confession is a major part of life for Roman Catholics, although the idea is also present in other branches of Christianity.

The celebration of the Eucharist, or Holy Communion, is a key part of weekly worship for the liturgical churches such as those in the Roman Catholic or Anglican traditions. Nearly all Christians worship weekly on Sunday; services include readings of scripture, a sermon, singing of hymns, and may include Eucharist. Christians honor the birth of Jesus at Christmas and his death and resurrection at Easter. Easter is often considered the most significant liturgical feast, particularly in Orthodox branches.

Many Christians follow a calendar of liturgical seasons. Of these seasons, perhaps the best known is Lent, which is immediately preceded by Shrove Tuesday, also known as Mardi Gras. Lent is traditionally a time of fasting and self-examination in preparation for the Easter feast. Historically, Christians gave up rich foods. The day before Lent was a time for pancakes—to use up the butter and eggs—from which the term Mardi Gras (Fat Tuesday) derives. Lent begins with Ash Wednesday, when Christians are marked with the sign of the cross on their foreheads using ashes, a reminder that they are dust and will return to dust.

ORIGINS

History & Geography

Christianity was shaped in the desert and mountainous landscapes of Palestine, known as the Holy Land. Jesus was driven into the wilderness following his baptism, where he remained for forty days of fasting and temptation. The Gospels record that he often went to the mountains for solitude and prayer. The geography of the deserts and mountains also shaped early Christian spirituality, as men and women went into solitude to pray, eventually founding small communities of the so-called desert fathers and mothers.

Christianity at first was regarded as a sect within Judaism, though it differentiated itself early in the first century CE by breaking with the code of laws that defined Judaism, including the need for circumcision and ritual purity. Early Christianity then grew through the missionary work of the apostles, particularly Paul the Apostle, who traveled throughout the Mediterranean world and beyond the Roman Empire to preach the gospel (good news) of Jesus. (This is often called the Apostolic Age.)

Persecution under various Roman emperors only served to strengthen the emerging religion. In the early fourth century, the Emperor Constantine (ca. 272-337) made Christianity the official religion of the Roman Empire. He also convened the Council of Nicea in 325 CE to quell the religious controversies threatening the Pax Romana (Roman Peace), a time of stability and peace throughout the empire in the first and second centuries.

In 1054 the Great Schism, which involved differences over theology and practice, split the church into Eastern Orthodox and Roman Catholic branches. As Islam grew stronger, the Roman Catholic nations of Europe entered a period of Crusades—there were six Crusades in approximately 175 years, from 1095-1271—that attempted to take the Holy Land out of Muslim control.

A number of theologians became unhappy with the excesses of the Roman church and papal authority during the fifteenth and sixteenth centuries. The Protestant Reformation, originally an attempt to purify the church, was led by several men, most notably Martin Luther (1483-1546), whose ninety-five theses against the Catholic Church sparked the Reformation movement. Other leaders of the Protestant Reformation include John Knox (ca. 1510-1572), attributed as the founder of the Presbyterian denomination, John Calvin (1509-1564), a principle early developer of Calvinism, and Ulrich Zwingli (1484-1531), who initially spurred the Reformation in Switzerland. This period of

turmoil resulted in the founding of a number of church denominations: Lutherans, Presbyterians, and Anglicans. These groups were later joined by the Methodists and the Religious Society of Friends (Quakers).

During the sixteenth and seventeenth centuries, the Roman Catholic Church attempted to stem this wave of protest and schism with the Counter-Reformation. Concurrently, the Inquisition, an effort to root out heresy and control the rebellion, took place. There were various inquisitions, including the Spanish Inquisition, which was led by Ferdinand II of Aragon and Isabella I of Castile in mid-fifteenth century and sought to "guard" the orthodoxy of Catholicism in Spain. There was also the Portuguese Inquisition, which began in 1536 in Portugal under King John III, and the Roman Inquisition, which took place in the late fifteenth century in Rome under the Holy See.

During the modern age, some groups became concerned with the perceived conflicts between history (revealed through recent archaeological findings) and the sciences (as described by Charles Darwin and Sigmund Freud) and the literal interpretation of some biblical texts. Fundamentalist Christianity began at an 1895 meeting in Niagara Falls, New York, with an attempt to define the basics (fundamentals) of Christianity. These were given as the inerrant nature of the Bible, the divine nature of Jesus, his literal virgin birth, his substitutionary death and literal physical resurrection, and his soon return. Liberal Christians, on the other hand, focused more on what became known as the Social Gospel, an attempt to relieve human misery.

Controversies in the twenty-first century throughout Christendom focused on issues such as abortion, homosexuality, the ordination of women and gays, and the authority of the scriptures. An additional feature is the growth of Christianity in the Southern Hemisphere. In Africa, for example, the number of Christians grew from 10 million in 1900 to over 506 million a century later. Initially the result of empire-building and colonialism, the conversions in these nations have resulted in a unique blend of native religions and Christianity. Latin America has won renown for its liberation theology, which was first articulated in 1968 as God's call for justice and God's preference for the poor, demonstrated in the ministry and teachings of Jesus Christ. Africa, Asia, and South America are regions that are considered more morally and theologically conservative. Some suggest that by 2050, non-Latino white persons will comprise only 20 percent of Christians.

Founder or Major Prophet

Jesus of Nazareth was born into a peasant family. The date of his birth, determined by accounts in the Gospels of Matthew and Luke, could be as early as 4 or 5 BCE or as late as 6 CE. Mary, his mother, was regarded as a virgin; thus, Jesus' birth was a miracle, engendered by the Holy Spirit. His earthly father, Joseph, was a carpenter.

At about age thirty, Jesus began an itinerant ministry of preaching and healing following his baptism in the Jordan River by his cousin, John the Baptist. He selected twelve followers, known as apostles (sent-ones), and a larger circle of disciples (followers). Within a short time, Jesus' ministry and popularity attracted the negative attention of both the Jewish and Roman rulers. He offended the Jewish leaders with his emphasis on personal relationship with God rather than obedience to rules, as well as his claim to be coequal with God the Father.

For a period of one to three years (Gospel accounts vary in the chronology), Jesus taught and worked miracles, as recorded in the first four books of the New Testament, the Gospels of Matthew, Mark, Luke, and John. On what has become known as Palm Sunday, he rode triumphantly into Jerusalem on the back of a donkey while crowds threw palm branches at his feet. Knowing that his end was near, at a final meal with his disciples, known now to Christians as the Last Supper, Jesus gave final instructions to his followers.

He was subsequently captured, having been betrayed by Judas Iscariot, one of his own twelve apostles. A trial before the Jewish legislative body, the Sanhedrin, led to his being condemned for blasphemy. However, under Roman law, the Jews did not have the power to put anyone to death. A later trial under the Roman governor, Pontius Pilate, resulted in Jesus being crucified, although Pilate tried to prevent this action, declaring Jesus innocent.

According to Christian doctrine, following the crucifixion, Jesus rose from the dead three days later. He appeared before many over a span of forty days and instructed the remaining eleven apostles to continue spreading his teachings. He then ascended into heaven. Ultimately, his followers believed that he was the Messiah, the savior who was to come to the Jewish people and deliver them. Rather than offering political salvation, however, Jesus offered spiritual liberty.

Philosophical Basis

Jesus was a Jew who observed the rituals and festivals of his religion. The Gospels reveal that he attended synagogue worship and went to Jerusalem for celebrations such as Passover. His teachings both grew out of and challenged the religion of his birth.

The Jews of Jesus' time, ruled by the Roman Empire, hoped for a return to political power. This power would be concentrated in a Messiah, whose coming had been prophesied centuries before. There were frequent insurrections in Judea, led in Jesus' time by a group called the Zealots. Indeed, it is believed that one of the twelve apostles was part of this movement. Jesus, with his message of a kingdom of heaven, was viewed as perhaps the one who would usher in a return to political ascendancy.

When challenged to name the greatest commandment, Jesus answered that it was to love God with all the heart, soul, mind, and strength. He added that the second was to love one's neighbor as one's self, saying that these two commands summarized all the laws that the Jewish religion outlined.

Jewish society was concerned with ritual purity and with following the law. Jesus repeatedly flouted those laws by eating with prostitutes and tax collectors, by touching those deemed unclean, such as lepers, and by including

Gentiles in his mission. Women were part of his ministry, with some of them providing for him and his disciples from their own purses, others offering him a home and a meal, and still others among those listening to him teach.

Jesus's most famous sermon is called the Sermon on the Mount. In it, he offers blessings on those on the outskirts of power, such as the poor, the meek, and those who hunger and thirst for righteousness. While not abolishing the law that the Jews followed, he pointed out its inadequacies and the folly of parading one's faith publicly. Embedded in the sermon is what has become known as the Lord's Prayer, the repetition of which is often part of regular Sunday worship. Much of Jesus' teaching was offered in the form of parables, or short stories involving vignettes of everyday life: a woman adding yeast to dough or a farmer planting seeds. Many of these parables were attempts to explain the kingdom of heaven, a quality of life that was both present and to come.

Holy Places

The Christian church has many pilgrimage sites, some of them dating back to the Middle Ages. Saint James is thought to have been buried in Compostela, Spain, which was a destination for those who could not make the trip to the Holy Land. Lourdes, France, is one of the spots associated with healing miracles. Celtic Christians revere places such as the small Scottish isle of Iona, an early Christian mission. Assisi, Italy, is a destination for those who are attracted to Saint Francis (1181-1226), founder of the Franciscans. The Chartres Cathedral in France is another pilgrimage destination from the medieval period.

Jerusalem, Rome, and Canterbury are considered holy for their associations with the early church and Catholicism, as well as with Anglicanism. Within the Old City of Jerusalem is the Church of the Holy Sepulchre, an important pilgrimage site believed to house the burial place of Jesus. Another important pilgrimage site is the Church of the Nativity in Bethlehem. It is built on a cave believed to be the birthplace of Jesus, and is one of the oldest operating churches in existence.

CHRISTIANITY IN DEPTH

Sacred Symbols

The central symbol of Christianity is the cross, of which there are many variant designs. Some of them, such as Celtic crosses, are related to regions of the world. Others, such as the Crusader's cross, honor historic events. The dove is the symbol for the Holy Spirit, which descended in that shape on the gathered disciples at Pentecost after Jesus's ascension.

Various symbols represent Jesus. Candles allude to his reference to himself as the Light of the World, while the lamb stands for his being the perfect sacrifice, the Lamb of God. The fish symbol that is associated with Christianity has a number of meanings, both historic and symbolic. A fish shape stands for the Greek letters beginning the words Jesus Christ, Son of God, Savior; these letters form the word *ichthus*, the Greek word for "fish." Fish also featured prominently in the scriptures, and the early apostles were known as "fishers of man." The crucifixion symbol is also a popular Catholic Christian symbol.

All of these symbols may be expressed in stained glass. Used in medieval times, stained glass often depicted stories from the Bible as an aid to those who were illiterate.

Sacred Practices & Gestures

Roman Catholics honor seven sacraments, defined as outward signs of inward grace. These include the Eucharist, baptism, confirmation, marriage, ordination of priests, anointing the sick or dying with oil, and penance. The Eastern Orthodox Church refers to these seven as mysteries rather than sacraments.

Priests in the Roman Catholic Church must remain unmarried. In the Eastern Orthodox, Anglican, and Protestant denominations, they may marry. Both Roman Catholic and Eastern Orthodox refuse to ordain women to the priesthood.

The Orthodox Church practices a rite known as chrismation, anointing a child with oil following its baptism. The "oil of gladness," as it is known, is placed on the infant's head, eyes, ears, and mouth. This is similar to the practice of confirmation in some other denominations. Many Christian denominations practice anointing the sick or dying with oil, as well as using the oil to seal those who have been baptized.

Many Christians, especially Roman Catholics, use a rosary, or prayer beads, when praying. Orthodox believers may have icons, such as small paintings of God, saints or biblical events, as part of their worship. There may be a font of water that has been blessed as one enters some churches, which the worshippers use to make the sign of the cross, touching fingers to their forehead, heart, right chest, and left chest. Some Christians make the sign of the cross on the forehead, mouth, and heart to signify their desire for God to be in their minds, on their lips, and in their hearts.

Christians may genuflect, or kneel, as they enter or leave a pew in church. In some churches, particularly the Catholic and Orthodox, incense is burned during the service as a sweet smell to God.

In some traditions, praying to or for the dead is encouraged. The rationale for this is known as the communion of saints—the recognition that those who are gone are still a part of the community of faith.

Catholic, Orthodox, and some branches of other churches have monastic orders for both men and women. Monks and nuns may live in a cloister or be engaged in work in the wider world. They generally commit to a rule of life and to the work of prayer. Even those Christians who are not part of religious orders sometimes go on retreats, seeking quiet and perhaps some spiritual guidance from those associated with the monastery or convent.

Food Restrictions
Historically, Christians fasted during Lent as preparation for the Easter celebration. Prior to the Second Vatican Council in 1962,

Roman Catholics did not eat meat on Fridays. Conservative Christians in the Evangelical tradition tend to eliminate the use of alcohol, tobacco, and drugs.

Rites, Celebrations & Services
For churches in the liturgical tradition, the weekly celebration of the Eucharist is paramount. While many churches celebrate this ritual feast with wine and a wafer, many Protestant churches prefer to use grape juice and crackers or bread.

Church services vary widely. Quakers sit silently waiting for a word from God, while in many African American churches, hymns are sung for perhaps an hour before the lengthy sermon is delivered. Some churches have a prescribed order of worship that varies little from week to week. Most services, however, include prayer, a sermon, and singing, with or without musical accompaniment.

A church's architecture often gives clues as to the type of worship one will experience. A church with the pulpit in the center at the front generally is a Protestant church with an emphasis on the Word of God being preached. If the center of the front area is an altar, the worship's focus will be on the Eucharist.

Christmas and Easter are the two major Christian celebrations. In liturgical churches, Christmas is preceded by Advent, a time of preparation and quiet to ready the heart for the coming of Christ. Christmas has twelve days, from the birth date of December 25 to the Epiphany on January 6. Epiphany (to show) is the celebration of the arrival of the Magi (wise men) from the East who came to worship the young Jesus after having seen his star. Their arrival is believed to have been foretold by the Old Testament prophet Isaiah, who said "And the Gentiles shall come to thy light, and kings to the brightness of thy rising" (Isaiah 60:3). Epiphany is the revealing of the Messiah to the Gentiles.

In the early church, Easter was preceded by a solemn period of fasting and examination, especially for candidates for baptism and penitent sinners wishing to be reconciled. In Western churches, Lent begins with Ash Wednesday, which is six and half weeks prior to Easter. By excluding Sundays from the fast, Lent thus gives a forty-day fast, imitating that of Jesus in the wilderness. Historically forbidden foods during the fast included eggs, butter, meat, and fish. In the Eastern Church, dairy products, oil, and wine are also forbidden.

The week before Easter is known as Holy Week. It may include extra services such as Maundy Thursday, a time to remember Jesus's new commandment (*maundy* is etymologically related to *mandate*) to love one another. In some Catholic areas, the crucifixion is reenacted in a Passion play (depicting the passion—trial, suffering, and death—of Christ). Some churches will have an Easter vigil the Saturday night before or a sunrise service on Easter morning.

Judy A. Johnson, MTS

Bibliography

Bakker, Janel Kragt. "The Sister Church Phenomenon: A Case Study of the Restructuring of American Christianity against the Backdrop of Globalization." *International Bulletin of Missionary Research* 36.3 (2012): 129–34. Print.

Bandak, Andreas and Jonas Adelin Jørgensen. "Foregrounds and Backgrounds—Ventures in the Anthropology of Christianity." *Ethos: Journal of Anthropology* 77.4 (2012): 447–58. Print.

Barnes, Trevor. *The Kingfisher Book of Religions*. New York: Kingfisher, 1999. Print.

Chandler, Daniel Ross. "Christianity in Cross-Cultural Perspective: A Review of Recent Literature." *Asia Journal of Theology* 26.2 (2012): 44–57. Print.

Daughrity, Dyron B. "Christianity Is Moving from North to South—So What about the East?" *International Bulletin of Missionary Research* 35.1 (2011): 18–22. Print.

Kaatz, Kevin. *Voices of Early Christianity: Documents from the Origins of Christianity*. Santa Barbara: Greenwood, 2013. E-book.

Langley, Myrtle. *Religion*. New York: Alfred A. Knopf, 1996.

Lewis, Clive Staples. *Mere Christianity*. New York: Harper, 2001. Print.

McGrath, Alistair. *Christianity: An Introduction*. Hoboken, New Jersey: Wiley, 2006. Print.

Meredith, Susan. *The Usborne Book of World Religions*. London: Usborne, 1995. Print.

Ripley, Jennifer S. "Integration of Psychology and Christianity: 2022." *Journal of Psychology & Theology* 40.2 (2012): 150–54. Print.

Stefon, Matt. *Christianity: History, Belief, and Practice*. New York: Britannica Educational, 2012. E-book.

Wilkinson, Philip. *Christianity*. New York: DK, 2003. Print.

Wilkinson, Philip. *Religions*. New York: DK, 2008. Print.

Zoba, Wendy Murray. *The Beliefnet Guide to Evangelical Christianity*. New York: Three Leaves, 2005. Print.

East Asian Religions

General Description

East Asian religious and philosophical traditions include, among others, Confucianism, Taoism, and Shintoism. Confucianism is a philosophy introduced by the Chinese philosopher Confucius (Kongzi; 551–479 BCE) in the sixth century BCE, during the Zhou dynasty. Taoism, which centers on Tao, or "the way," is a religious and philosophical tradition that originated in China about two thousand years ago. Shinto, "the way of the spirits," is a Japanese tradition of devotion to spirits and rituals.

Number of Adherents Worldwide

Between 5 and 6 million people, the majority of them in China, practice Confucianism, once the state religion of China. About 20 million people identify as Taoists. Most of the Taoist practitioners are in China as well. In Japan, approximately 107 million people practice Shintoism, though many practitioners also practice Buddhism. Sects of Shinto include Tenrikyo (heavenly truth), founded in 1838, with nearly 2 million devotees. Shukyo Mahikari (divine light) is another, smaller sect founded in the 1960s. Like other sects, it is a blend of different religious traditions (Wilkinson 332–34).

Basic Tenets

Confucianism is a philosophy of life and does concerns itself not with theology but with life conduct. Chief among the aspects of life that must be tended are five key relationships, with particular focus on honoring ancestors and showing filial piety. Confucianism does not take a stand on the existence of God, though the founder, Confucius, referred to "heaven." Except for this reference, Confucianism does not address the question of life after death.

Taoists believe that Tao (the way or the flow) is in everything. Taoism teaches that qi, or life energy, needs to be balanced between yin and yang, which are the female and male principles

of life, respectively. With its doctrine of the evil of violence, Taoism borders on pacifism, and it also preaches simplicity and naturalness. Taoists believe in five elements—wood, earth, air, fire and water—that need to be in harmony. The five elements lie at the heart of Chinese medicine, particularly acupuncture. In Taoism, it is believed that the soul returns to a state of nonbeing after death.

Shinto emphasizes nature and harmony, with a focus on lived experience rather than doctrine. Shinto, which means "the way of the gods," is a polytheistic religion; Amaterasu, the sun goddess, is the chief god. At one point in Japan's history, the emperor was believed to be a descendant of Amaterasu and therefore divine. In Tenrikyo Shinto, God is manifested most often as Oyakami, meaning "God the parent."

Shinto teaches that some souls can become kami, a spirit, following death. Each traditional home has a god-shelf, which honors family members believed to have become kami. An older family member tends to the god-shelf, placing a bit of food and some sake (rice wine) on the shelf. To do their work, kami must be nourished. The Tenrikyo sect includes concepts from Pure Land Buddhism, such as an afterlife and the idea of salvation.

Sacred Texts

Five classic texts are sacred to the Confucians. These include the I Ching, or Book of Changes; the Book of Odes; the Book of History; the Book of Rites; and the Annals of Spring and Autumn. The Analects, a collection of Confucius's sayings, is another revered classic. The Tao Te Ching (The Way of Power) is the most sacred book of the Taoists. Those who practice Shinto hold sacred two works: the Kojiki (Record of Ancient Matters) and the Nihon-gi (Chronicles of Japan). Both texts, which contain legends and creation myths, were written during the eighth century.

Major Figures

Confucius, who lived during the sixth century, was the first great philosopher of China. Mengzi (Meng-tzu; 371–289 BCE), known in the West as Mencius, developed Confucius's teachings about the higher power guiding human life. Another ancient Chinese philosopher, Laozi(or Lao-tzu), is the founder of Taoism. He is believed to have been a contemporary of Confucius's in the central region of China. Modern scholars are not certain he ever existed, though one account includes the story of Confucius visiting Laozi. Chuang Tzu wrote of Laozi and his ideas during the fourth and third centuries BCE. Shinto's major figures include Ō no Yasumaro (d. 723), the compiler of the Kokiji who acted under the orders of Empress Gemmei and consulted a bard known to have an infallible memory; the scholar Motoori Norinaga (1730–1800), whose work led to a revived interest in ancient Shinto texts; and Nakayama Miki (1798–1887), the farmer's wife who founded Tenrikyo.

Major Holy Sites

Most Confucian sacred places are located within private homes, where an ancestral shrine and an altar to gods and spirits are maintained. In China's Shandong Province is Qufu, the site of Confucius's family mansion, temple, and cemetery. The temple was built in 478 BCE, only a year after Confucius's death, and has been maintained and enlarged. In addition to its status as a holy site, the United Nations Educational, Scientific, and Cultural Organization (UNESCO) has placed it on their World Heritage List.

Taoists regard mountains as a way to communicate with Earth's primeval powers and with those who are immortal. Five of the nine sacred mountains in China are associated with Taoism: Hengshan in both the north and the south, Songshan in the south, Taishan in the east, and Huashan in the west. The holiest of the five is Taishan, which symbolizes stability, prevents natural disasters, and ensures fertility.

Shintoism has a high regard for natural beauty. As such, Shinto shrines are everywhere, particularly in mountains or near waterfalls.

Mountains in particular are regarded as homes of the gods. Mount Fuji is the holiest Shinto mountain, and climbing it to reach the shrine on its peak is an act of worship. More than forty thousand shrines are dedicated to Inari, the rice god.

Shinto was formalized during the Yamato period (the name for ancient Japan), and because the emperor of the imperial dynasty was from the Yamato area and was considered divine, the whole region is revered. At Ise, located near the coast in Mie Prefecture, southeast of Nara, the shrine has been rebuilt every twenty years for at least fourteen centuries. This rebuilding ensures that Toyouke-Ōmikami (the harvest goddess) and Amaterasu (the sun goddess) are renewed in vigor, which in turn invigorates both the rice crop and the imperial line. Those who have died in war are revered as kami in Japan. In Tokyo, a shrine called Yasukuni is dedicated to them. However, there is controversy surrounding the place because of its association with Japan's extreme nationalism prior to World War II.

Sacred Texts

Five classic texts are sacred to the Confucians. These include the I Ching, or Book of Changes; the Book of Odes; the Book of History; the Book of Rites; and the Annals of Spring and Autumn. The Analects, a collection of Confucius's sayings, is another revered classic. The Tao te Ching (The Way of Power) is the most sacred book of the Taoists. Those who practice Shinto hold sacred two works: the Kojiki (Record of Ancient Matters) and the Nihon-gi (Chronicles of Japan). Both texts, which contain legends and creation myths, were written during the eighth century.

Major Figures

Confucius, who lived during the sixth century, was the first great philosopher of China. Mengzi (Meng-tzu; 371–289 BCE), known in the West as Mencius, developed Confucius's teachings about the higher power guiding human life. Another ancient Chinese philosopher, Laozi,(or Lao-tzu) is the founder of Taoism. He is believed to have been a contemporary of Confucius in the central region of China. Modern scholars are not certain he ever existed, though one account includes the story of Confucius visiting Laozi. Chuang Tzu wrote of Laozi and his ideas during the fourth and third centuries BCE. Shinto's major figures include Ō no Yasumaro, the compiler of the Kokiji who acted under the orders of Empress Gemmei and consulted a bard known to have an infallible memory; the scholar Motoori Norinaga (1730–1800), whose work led to a revived interest in ancient Shinto texts; and Nakayama Miki (1798–1887), the farmer's wife who founded Tenrikyo.

Major Holy Sites

Most Confucian sacred places are located within private homes, where an ancestral shrine and an altar to gods and spirits are maintained. In China's Shandong Province is Qufu, the site of Confucius's family mansion, temple and cemetery. The temple was built in 478 BCE, only a year after Confucius's death, and has been maintained and enlarged. In addition to being a holy site, the United Nations Educational, Scientific, and Cultural Organization (UNESCO) has placed it on their World Heritage List.

Taoists consider mountains as a way to communicate with Earth's primeval powers and with those who are immortal. Five of the nine sacred mountains in China are associated with Taoism. They are Hengshan in both the north and south, Songshan in the south, Taishan in the east, and Huashan in the west. The holiest of the five is Taishan, which symbolizes stability, prevents natural disasters, and ensures fertility.

Shintoism has a high regard for natural beauty. As such, Shinto shrines are everywhere, particularly in mountains or near waterfalls. Mountains in particular are regarded as homes of the gods. Mount Fuji is the holiest Shinto mountain, and climbing it to reach the shrine on its peak is an act of worship. More than forty thousand shrines are dedicated to Inari, the rice god.

Shinto was formalized during the Yamato period (the name for ancient Japan), and because the emperor of the imperial dynasty is from the Yamato area, and was considered divine, the whole region is revered. At Ise, located near the coast in the Mie prefecture southeast of Nara, the shrine has been rebuilt every twenty years for at least fourteen centuries. This rebuilding ensures that Toyouke-Ōmikami (the harvest goddess) and Amaterasu (the sun goddess) are renewed in vigor, which in turn invigorates both the rice crop and the imperial line. Those who have died in war are revered as kami in Japan. In Tokyo, a shrine called Yasukuni is dedicated to them. However, there is controversy surrounding the place because of its association with Japan's extreme nationalism prior to World War II.

Major Rites & Celebrations

Confucian celebrations have to do with honoring people rather than gods. At Confucian temples, the philosopher's birthday is celebrated each September. In Taiwan, this day is called "Teacher's Day." Sacrifices, music and dance are part of the event.

Taoism has a jiao (offering) festival near the winter solstice. It celebrates the renewal of the yang force at this turning of the year. During the festival priests, who have been ritually purified, wear lavish clothing. The festival includes music and dancing, along with large effigies of the gods which are designed to frighten away the evil spirits. Yang's renewal is also the focus of New Year celebrations, which is a time for settling debts and cleaning house. Decorations in the yang warm colors of gold, orange and red abound.

Many of the Shinto festivals overlap with Buddhist ones. There are many local festivals and rituals, and each community has an annual festival at the shrine dedicated to the kami of the region. Japanese New Year, which is celebrated for three days, is a major feast. Since the sixteenth century, the Gion Festival has taken place in Kyoto, Japan. Decorated floats are part of the celebration of the shrine.

ORIGINS

History & Geography

During the Zhou dynasty (1050–256 BCE) in China, the idea of heaven as a force that controlled events came to the fore. Zhou rulers believed that they ruled as a result of the "Mandate of Heaven," viewing themselves as morally superior to those of the previous dynasty, the Shang dynasty (1600-1046 BCE). They linked virtue and power as the root of the state.

By the sixth century the Zhou rulers had lost much of their authority. Many schools of thought developed to restore harmony, and were collectively known as the "Hundred Schools." Confucius set forth his ideas within this historical context. He traveled China for thirteen years, urging rulers to put his ideas into practice and failing to achieve his goals. He returned home to teach for the rest of his life and his ideas were not adopted until the Han dynasty (206 BCE–220 CE). During the Han period, a university for the nation was established, as well as the bureaucratic civil service that continued until the twentieth century. When the Chinese Empire fell in 1911, the Confucian way became less important.

Confucianism had influenced not only early Chinese culture, but also the cultures of Japan, Korea, and Vietnam. The latter two nations also adopted the bureaucratic system. In Japan, Confucianism reached its height during the Tokugawa age (1600–1868 CE). Confucian scholars continue to interpret the philosophy for the modern period. Some regard the ideas of Confucius as key to the recent economic booms in the so-called "tiger" economies of East Asia (Hong Kong, Singapore, South Korea, Taiwan, and Thailand). Confucianism continues to be a major influence on East Asian nations and culture.

Taoism's power (te) manifests itself as a philosophy, a way of life, and a religion. Philosophically, Taoism is a sort of self-help regimen, concerned with expending power efficiently by avoiding conflicts and friction, rather than fighting against the flow of life. In China, it is known as School Taoism. As a way of life, Taoism is concerned with increasing the amount of qi available through what is eaten and through meditation, yoga, and tai chi (an ancient Chinese martial art form). Acupuncture and the use of medicinal herbs are outgrowths of this way of

life. Church Taoism, influenced by Buddhism and Tao Chiao (religious Taoism), developed during the second century. This church looked for ways to use power for societal and individual benefit.

By the time of the Han dynasty (206–220 CE), Laozi had been elevated to the status of divine. Taoism found favor at court during the Tang dynasty (618–917 CE), during which the state underwrote temples. By adapting and encouraging people to study the writings of all three major faiths in China, Taoism remained relevant into the early twentieth century. During the 1960s and 1970s, Taoist books were burned and their temples were destroyed in the name of the Cultural Revolution (the Great Proletarian Cultural Revolution). Taoism remains popular and vital in Taiwan.

Shinto is an ancient religion, and some of its characteristics appeared during the Yayoi culture (ca. 300 BCE–300 CE). The focus was on local geographic features and the ancestry of local clan leaders. At first, women were permitted to be priests, but that equality was lost due to the influence of Confucian paternalism. The religion declined, but was revived in 1871 following the Meiji Restoration of the emperor. Shoguns (warlords) had ruled Japan for more than 250 years, and Shinto was the state religion until 1945. It was associated with the emperor cult and contributed to Japan's militarism. After the nation's defeat in World War II, the 1947 constitution forbade government involvement in any religion. In contemporary Shinto, women are permitted to become priests and girls, in some places, are allowed to carry the portable shrines during festivals.

Founder or Major Prophet
Confucius, or Kongzi ("Master Kong"), was a teacher whose early life may have included service in the government. He began traveling throughout the country around age fifty, attempting and failing to interest rulers in his ideas for creating a harmonious state. He returned to his home state after thirteen years, teaching a group of disciples who spread his ideas posthumously.

According to legend, Taoism's founder, Laozi, lived during the sixth century. Laozi may be translated as "Grand Old Master," and may be simply a term of endearment. He maintained the archives and lived simply in a western state of China. Weary of people who were uninterested in natural goodness and perhaps wanting greater solitude in his advanced years, he determined to leave China, heading for Tibet on a water buffalo. At the border, a gatekeeper wanted to persuade him to stay, but could not do so. He asked Laozi to leave behind his teachings. For three days Laozi transcribed his teachings, producing the five-thousand-word Tao Te Ching. He then rode off and was never heard of again. Unlike most founders of religions, he neither preached nor promoted his beliefs. Still, he was held with such regard that some emperors claimed descent from him.

No one is certain of the origin of Shinto, which did not have a founder or major prophet. Shinto—derived from two Chinese words, *shen* (spirit) and *dao* (way)—has been influenced by other religions, notably Confucianism and Buddhism.

Philosophical Basis

Confucianism sought to bring harmony to the state and society as a whole. This harmony was to be rooted in the Five Constant Relationships: between parents and children; husbands and wives; older and younger siblings; older and younger friends; and rulers and subjects. Each of these societal relationships existed to demonstrate mutual respect, service, honor, and love, resulting in a healthy society. The fact that three of the five relationships exist within the family highlights the importance of honoring family. Ritual maintains the li, or rightness, of everything, and is a way to guarantee that a person performed the correct action in any situation in life.

Taoism teaches that two basic components—yin and yang—are in all things, including health, the state, and relationships. Yin is the feminine principle, associated with soft, cold, dark, and moist things. Yang is the masculine principle,

and is associated with hard, warm, light, and dry things. By keeping these two aspects of life balanced, harmony will be achieved. Another concept is that of wu-wei, action that is in harmony with nature, while qi is the life force in all beings. The Tao is always in harmony with the universe. Conflict is to be avoided, and soldiers are to go as if attending a funeral, solemnly and with compassion. Taoism also teaches the virtues of humility and selflessness.

Shinto is rooted in reverence for ancestors and for the spirits known as kami, which may be good or evil. By correctly worshipping the kami, Shintoists believe that they are assisting in purifying the world and aiding in its functioning.

Holy Places

Confucianism does not always distinguish between sacred and profane space. So much of nature is considered a holy place, as is each home's private shrine. In addition, some Confucian temples have decayed while others have been restored. Temples do not have statues or images. Instead, the names of Confucius and his noted followers are written on tablets. Like the emperor's palace, temples have the most important halls placed on the north-south axis of the building. Temples are also internally symmetrical, as might be expected of a system that honors order. In Beijing, the Temple of Heaven, just south of the emperor's palace, was one of the holiest places in imperial China.

Taoism's holy places are often in nature, particularly mountains. The holiest of the five sacred mountains in China is Taishan, located in the east. Taoism also reveres grottoes, which are caves thought to be illuminated by the light of heaven.

In the Shinto religion, nature is often the focus of holy sites. Mount Fuji is the most sacred mountain. Near Kyoto the largest shrine of Inari, the rice god, is located. The Grand Shrines at Ise are dedicated to two divinities, and for more than one thousand years, pilgrims have come to it. The Inner Shrine (Naiku) is dedicated to Amaterasu, the sun goddess, and is Shinto's most holy location. The Outer Shrine (Geku) is dedicated to

Toyouke, the goddess of the harvest. Every twenty years, Ise is torn down and rebuilt, thus renewing the gods. Shinto shrines all have torii, the sacred gateway. The most famous of these is built in the sea near the island of Miyajima. Those going to the shrine on this island go by boat through the torii.

EAST ASIAN RELIGIONS IN DEPTH

Sacred Symbols

Water is regarded as the source of life in Confucianism. The water symbol has thus become an unofficial symbol of Confucianism, represented by the Japanese ideogram or character for water, the Mizu, which somewhat resembles a stick figure with an extra leg. Other sacred symbols include the ancestor tablets in shrines of private homes, which are symbolic of the presence of the ancestor to whom offerings are made in hopes of aid.

While not a sacred symbol as the term is generally used, the black and white symbol of yin and yang is a common Taoist emblem. Peaches are also of a symbolic nature in Taoism, and often appear in Asian art. They are based on the four peaches that grew every three thousand years and which the mother of the fairies gave to the Han emperor Wu Ti (140–87 BCE). They are often symbolic of the Immortals.

The Shinto stylized sun, which appears on the Japanese flag, is associated with Amaterasu, the sun goddess. The torii, the gateway forming an entrance to sacred space, is another symbol associated with Shinto.

Sacred Practices & Gestures

Confucian rulers traditionally offered sacrifices honoring Confucius at the spring and autumnal equinoxes. Most of the Confucian practices take place at home shrines honoring the ancestors.

Taoists believe that one can reach Tao (the way) through physical movements, chanting, or meditation. Because mountains, caves, and springs are often regarded as sacred sites, pilgrimages are important to Taoists. At a Taoist

funeral, a paper fairy crane is part of the procession. After the funeral, the crane, which symbolizes a heavenly messenger, is burned. The soul of the deceased person is then thought to ride to heaven on the back of the crane.

Many Shinto shrines exist throughout Japan. Most of them have a sacred arch, known as a torii. At the shrine's entrance, worshippers rinse their mouths and wash their hands to be purified before entering the prayer hall. Before praying, a worshipper will clap twice and ring a bell to let the kami know they are there. Only priests may enter the inner hall, which is where the kami live. During a festival, however, the image of the kami is placed in a portable shrine and carried in a procession through town, so that all may receive a blessing.

Rites, Celebrations & Services

Early Confucianism had no priests, and bureaucrats performed any rituals that were necessary. When the Chinese Empire fell in 1911, imperial ceremonies ended as well. Rituals have become less important in modern times. In contemporary times the most important rite is marriage, the beginning of a new family for creating harmony. There is a correct protocol for each aspect of marriage, from the proposal and engagement to exchanging vows. During the ceremony, the groom takes the bride to his family's ancestor tablets to "introduce" her to them and receive a blessing. The couple bows to the ancestors during the ceremony.

After a death occurs, mourners wear coarse material and bring gifts of incense and money to help defray the costs. Added to the coffin holding are food offerings and significant possessions. A willow branch symbolizing the deceased's soul is carried with the coffin to the place of burial. After the burial, family members take the willow branch to their home altar and perform a ritual to add the deceased to the souls at the family's shrine.

Confucians and Taoists celebrate many of the same Chinese festivals, some of which originated before either Confucianism or Taoism began and reflect aspects of both traditions. While some festivals are not necessarily Taoist, they may be led by Taoist priests. During the Lantern Festival, which occurs on the first full moon of the New Year, offerings are made to the gods. Many of the festivals are tied to calendar events. Qingming (Clear and Bright) celebrates the coming of spring and is a time to remember the dead. During this time, families often go to the family gravesite for a picnic. The Double Fifth is the midsummer festival that occurs on the fifth day of the fifth month, and coincides with the peak of yang power. To protect themselves from too much of the male force, people don garments of the five colors—black, blue, red, white, and yellow—and with the five "poisons"—centipede, lizard, scorpion, snake, and toad—in the pattern of their clothes and on amulets. The gates of hell open at the Feast of the Hungry Ghosts. Priests have ceremonies that encourage the escaped evil spirits to repent or return to hell.

Marriage is an important rite in China, and thus in Taoism as well. Astrologers look at horoscopes to ensure that the bride and groom are well matched and to find the best day for the ceremony. The groom's family is always placed at the east (yang) and the bride's family to the west (yin) to bring harmony. When a person dies, the mourners again sit in the correct locations, while the head of the deceased points south. White is the color of mourning and of yin. At the home of the deceased, white cloths cover the family altar. Mourners may ease the soul's journey with symbolic artifacts or money. They may also go after the funeral to underground chambers beneath the temples to offer a sacrifice on behalf of the dead.

In the Shinto religion, rites exist for many life events. For example, pregnant women ask at a shrine for their children to be born safely, and the mother or grandmother brings a child who is thirty-two or thirty-three-days-old to a shrine for the first visit and blessing. A special festival also exists for children aged three, five or seven, who go to the shrine for purifying. In addition, a bride and groom are purified before the wedding, usually conducted by Shinto priests. Shinto priests may also offer blessings for a new car or building. The New Year and the Spring Festival are among the most important festivals, and shrine virgins, known as miko girls, may dance to celebrate life's renewal. Other festivals include the Feast of the Puppets, Boys' Day, the Water Kami Festival, the Star Feast, the Festival of the Dead, and the autumnal equinox.

Judy A. Johnson, MTS

Bibliography

Barnes, Trevor. *The Kingfisher Book of Religions*. New York: Kingfisher, 1999. Print.

Bell, Daniel A. "Reconciling Socialism and Confucianism? Reviving Tradition in China." *Dissent* 57.1 (2010): 91–99. Print.

Chang, Chung-yuan. *Creativity and Taoism: A Study of Chinese Philosophy, Art and Poetry*. London: Kingsley, 2011. E-book.

Coogan, Michael D., ed. *Eastern Religions*. New York: Oxford UP, 2005. Print.

Eliade, Mircea, and Ioan P. Couliano. *The Eliade Guide to World Religions*. New York: Harper, 1991. Print.

Lao Tzu. *Tao Te Ching*. Trans. Stephen Mitchell. New York: Harper, 1999. Print.

Li, Yingzhang. *Lao-tzu's Treatise on the Response of the Tao*. Trans. Eva Wong. New Haven: Yale UP, 2011. Print.

Littlejohn, Ronnie. *Confucianism: An Introduction*. New York: Tauris, 2011. E-book.

Littleton, C. Scott. *Shinto*. Oxford: Oxford UP, 2002. Print.

Mcvay, Kera. *All about Shinto*. Delhi: University, 2012. Ebook.

Merton, Thomas. *The Way of Chuang Tzu*. New York: New Directions, 1965. Print.

Oldstone-Moore, Jennifer. *Confucianism*. Oxford: Oxford UP, 2002. Print.

Poceski, Mario. *Chinese Religions: The EBook*. Providence, UT: Journal of Buddhist Ethics Online Books, 2009. E-book.

Van Norden, Bryan W. *Introduction to Classical Chinese Philosophy*. Indianapolis: Hackett, 2011. Print.

Wilkinson, Philip. *Religions*. New York: DK, 2008. Print.

Hinduism

General Description

Hinduism; modern Hinduism is comprised of the devotional sects of Vaishnavism, Shaivism, and Shaktism (though Smartism is sometimes listed as the fourth division). Hinduism is often used as umbrella term, since many point to Hinduism as a family of different religions.

Number of Adherents Worldwide

Between 13.8 and 15 percent of the world's population, or about one billion people, are adherents of Hinduism, making it the world's third largest religion after Christianity and Islam. The predominant sect is the Vaishnavite sect (Wilkinson, p. 333).

Basic Tenets

Hinduism is a way of life rather than a body of beliefs. Hindus believe in karma, the cosmic law of cause and effect that determines one's state in the next life. Additional beliefs include dharma, one's religious duty.

Hinduism has no true belief in an afterlife. Rather, it teaches a belief in reincarnation, known as samsara, and in moksha, the end of the cycle of rebirths. Different sects have different paths to moksha.

Hinduism is considered a polytheist religion. However, it is also accurate to say that Hinduism professes a belief in one God or Supreme Truth that is beyond comprehension (an absolute reality, called Brahman) and which manifests itself in many forms and names. These include Brahma, the creator; Vishnu, the protector; and Shiva, the re-creator or destroyer. Many sects are defined by their belief in multiple gods, but also by their worship of one ultimate manifestation. For example, Shaivism and Vaishnavism are based upon the recognition of Shiva and Vishnu, respectively, as the manifestation. In comparison, Shaktism recognizes the Divine Mother (Shakti) as the Supreme Being, while followers of Smartism worship a particular deity of their own choosing.

Major Deities

The Hindu trinity (Trimurti) is comprised of Brahma, the impersonal and absolute creator; Vishnu, the great preserver; and Shiva, the destroyer and re-creator. The goddesses corresponding to each god are Sarasvati, Lakshimi, and Parvati. Thousands of other gods (devas) and goddesses (devis) are worshipped, including Ganesha, Surya, and Kali. Each is believed to represent another aspect of the Supreme Being.

Sacred Texts

Hindus revere ancient texts such as the four Vedas, the 108 Upanishads, and others. No single text has the binding authority of the Qur'an (Islam's holy book) or Bible. Hindu literature is also defined by Sruti (revealed truth), which is heard, and Smriti (realized truth), which is remembered. The former is canonical, while the latter can be changing. For example, the Vedas and the Upanishads constitute Sruti texts, while epics, history, and law books constitute the latter. The Bhagavad Gita (The Song of God) is also considered a sacred scripture of Hinduism, and consists of a philosophical dialogue.

Major Figures

Major figures include: Shankara (788–820 CE), who defined the unity of the soul (atman) and absolute reality (Brahman); Ramanuja (1077–1157 CE), who emphasized bhakti, or love of God; Madhva (1199–1278 CE), scholar and writer, a proponent of dualism; Ramprahsad Sen (1718–1775 CE), composer of Hindu songs of devotion, poet, and mystic who influenced goddess worship in the; Raja Rammohun Roy (1772–1833 CE), abolished the custom of suttee, in which widows were burned on the funeral pyres of their dead husbands, and decried polygamy, rigid caste systems, and dowries; Rabindranath Tagore (1861–1941 CE), first Asian to win the Nobel Prize in Literature; Dr. Babasaheb R. Ambedkar (1891–1956 CE), writer of India's constitution and leader of a mass conversion to Buddhism; Mohandas K. Gandhi (1869–1948 CE), the "great soul" who left a legacy of effective use of nonviolence.

Major Holy Sites

The major holy sites of Hinduism are located within India. They include the Ganges River, in whose waters pilgrims come to bathe away their sins, as well as thousands of tirthas (places of pilgrimage), many of which are associated with particular deities. For example, the Char Dham pilgrimage centers, of which there are four—Badrinath (north), Puri (east), Dwarka (west) and Rameshwaram (south)—are considered the holy abodes or sacred temples of Vishnu. There are also seven ancient holy cities in India, including Ayodhya, believed to be the birthplace of Rama; Varanasi (Benares), known as the City of Light; Dwarka; Ujjian; Kanchipuram; Mathura; and Hardwar.

Major Rites & Celebrations

Diwali, the Festival of Lights, is a five-day festival that is considered a national holiday in India. Holi, the Festival of Colors, is the spring festival. Krishna Janmashtmi is Krishna's birthday. Shivaratri is Shiva's main festival. Navaratri, also known as the Durga festival or Dasserah, celebrates one of the stories of the gods and the victory of good over evil. Ganesh Chaturthi is the elephant-headed god Ganesha's birthday. Rathayatra, celebrated at Puri, India, is a festival for Jagannath, another word for Vishnu.

ORIGINS

History & Geography

Hinduism, which many people consider to be the oldest world religion, is unique in that it has no recorded origin or founder. Generally, it developed in the Indus Valley civilization several thousand years before the Common Era. The faith blends the Vedic traditions of the Indus Valley civilization and the invading nomadic tribes of the Aryans (prehistoric Indo-Europeans). Most of what is known of the Indus Valley

civilization comes from archaeological excavations at Mohenjo-Daro (Mound of the Dead) and Harappa. (Because Harappa was a chief city of the period, the Indus Valley civilization is also referred to as the Harappan civilization.) The Vedas, a collection of ancient hymns, provides information about the Aryan culture.

The ancient Persian word *hind* means Indian, and for centuries, to be Indian was to be Hindu. Even now, about 80 percent of India's people consider themselves Hindu. The root word alludes to flowing, as a river flows. It is also etymologically related to the Indus River. At first, the term Hindu was used as an ethnic or cultural term, and travelers from Persia and Greece in the sixteenth century referred to those in the Indus Valley by that name. British writers coined the term *Hinduism* during the early part of the nineteenth century to describe the culture of India. The Hindus themselves often use the term Sanatana Dharma, meaning eternal law.

The Rigveda, a collection of hymns to various gods and goddesses written around 1500 BCE, is the first literary source for understanding Hinduism's history. The Vedas were chanted aloud for centuries before being written down around 1400 CE. The Rigveda is one of four major collections of Vedas, or wisdom: Rigveda, Yajurveda, Samaveda, and Atharvaveda. Together these four are called Samhitas.

Additionally, Hinduism relies on three other Vedic works: the Aranyakas, the Brahamans, and the Upanishads. The Upanishads is a philosophical work, possibly written down between 800 and 450 BCE, that attempts to answer life's big questions. Written in the form of a dialogue between a teacher (guru) and student (chela), the text's name means "to sit near," which describes the relationship between the two. Along with the Samhitas, these four are called Sruti (heard), a reference to their nature as revealed truth. The words in these texts cannot be altered.

Remaining works are called Smriti, meaning "remembered," to indicate that they were composed by human writers. The longer of the Smriti epics is the Mahabharata, the Great Story of the Bharatas. Written between 300 and 100 BCE, the epic is a classic tale of two rival, related families, including teaching as well as story. It is considered the longest single poem in existence, with about 200,000 lines. (A film made of it lasts for twelve hours.)

The Bhagavad Gita, or Song of the Lord, is the sixth section of the Mahabharata, but is often read as a stand-alone narrative of battle and acceptance of one's dharma. The Ramayana is the second, shorter epic of the Mahabharata, with about fifty thousand lines. Rama was the seventh incarnation, or avatar, of Vishnu. The narrative relates the abduction of his wife, Sita, and her rescue, accomplished with the help of the monkey god, Hanuman. Some have regarded the Mahabharata as an encyclopedia, and the Bhagavad Gita as the Bible within it.

Although many of the practices in the Vedas have been modified or discontinued, sections of it are memorized and repeated. Some of the hymns are recited at traditional ceremonies for the dead and at weddings.

Hinduism has affected American life and culture for many years. For example, the nineteenth-century transcendental writers Margaret Fuller and Ralph Waldo Emerson were both influenced by Hindu and Buddhist literature, while musician George Harrison, a member of the Beatles, adopted Hinduism and explored his new faith through his music, both with and without the Beatles. In 1965, the International Society for Krishna Consciousness (ISKCON), or the Hare Krishna movement, came to the Western world. In addition, many people have been drawn to yoga, which is associated with Hinduism's meditative practices.

Founder or Major Prophet

Hinduism has no founder or major prophet. It is a religion that has developed over many centuries and from many sources, many of which are unknown in their origins.

Philosophical Basis

Hinduism recognizes multiple ways to achieve salvation and escape the endless cycle of rebirth. The way of devotion is the most popular. Through worship of a single deity, the worshipper hopes to attain union with the divine. A second path is the way of knowledge, involving the use of meditation and reason. The third way is via action, or correctly performing religious observances in hope of receiving a blessing from the gods by accomplishing these duties.

Hinduism is considered the world's oldest religion, but Hindus maintain that it is also a way of living, not just a religion. There is great diversity as well as great tolerance in Hinduism. While Hinduism does not have a set of dogmatic formulations, it does blend the elements of devotion, doctrine, practice, society, and story as separate strands in a braid.

During the second century BCE, a sage named Patanjali outlined four life stages, and the fulfilled responsibilities inherent in each one placed one in harmony with dharma, or right conduct. Although these life stages are no longer observed strictly, their ideas still carry weight. Traditionally, these codes applied to men, and only to those in the Brahman caste; members of the warrior and merchant classes could follow them, but were not obligated. The Shudra and Dalit castes, along with women, were not part of the system. Historically, women were thought of as protected by fathers in their childhood, by husbands in their youth and adulthood, and by sons in old age. Only recently have women in India been educated beyond the skills of domestic responsibility and child rearing.

The earliest life stage is the student stage, or brahmacharya, a word that means "to conduct oneself in accord with Brahman." From ages twelve to twenty-four, young men were expected to undertake learning with a guru, or guide. During these twelve years of studying the Veda they were also expected to remain celibate.

The second stage, grihastha, is that of householder. A Hindu man married the bride that his parents had chosen, sired children, and created a livelihood on which the other three stages depended.

Vanaprastha is the third stage, involving retirement to solitude. Historically, this involved leaving the house and entering a forest dwelling.

A man's wife had the option to go with him or to remain. This stage also involved giving counsel to others and further study.

At the final stage of life, sannyasis, the Hindu renounces material goods, including a home of any sort. He may live in a forest or join an ashram, or community. He renounces even making a fire, and lives on fruit and roots that can be foraged. Many contemporary Hindus do not move to this stage, but remain at vanaprastha.

Yoga is another Hindu practice, more than three millennia old, which Patanjali codified. The four forms of yoga corresponded to the Hindu avenues of salvation. Hatha yoga is the posture yoga seeking union with god through action. Jnana yoga is the path to god through knowledge. Bhakti yoga is the way of love to god. Karma yoga is the method of finding god through work. By uniting the self, the practitioner unites with God. Yoga is related etymologically to the English word *yoke*—it attempts to yoke the individual with Brahman. All forms of yoga include meditation and the acceptance of other moral disciplines, such as self-discipline, truthfulness, nonviolence, and contentment.

Aryan society was stratified, and at the top of the social scale were the priests. This system was the basis for the caste system that had long dominated Hinduism. Caste, which was determined by birth, affected a person's occupation, diet, neighborhood, and marriage partner. Vedic hymns allude to four varnas, or occupations: Brahmins (priests), Kshatriyas (warriors), Vaishyas (merchants and common people), and Shudras (servants). A fifth class, the Untouchables, later known as Dalit (oppressed), referred to those who were regarded as a polluting force because they handled waste and dead bodies. The belief was that society would function properly if each group carried out its duties. These varnas later became wrongly blended with castes, or jatis, which were smaller groups also concerned with a person's place in society.

The practice of Hinduism concerns itself with ritual purity; even household chores can be done in a ritualistic way. Some traditions demand ritual purity before one can worship. Brahmin priests, for example, may not accept water or food from non-Brahmins. Refusal to do so is not viewed as classism, but an attempt to please the gods in maintaining ritual purity.

Mohandas Gandhi was one of those who refused to use the term *Untouchable*, using the term *harijan*(children of God), instead. Dr. Babasaheb R. Ambedkar, who wrote India's constitution, was a member of this class. Ambedkar and many of his supporters became Buddhists in an attempt to dispel the power of caste. In 1947, following India's independence from Britain, the caste system was officially banned, though it has continued to influence Indian society.

Ahimsa, or dynamic harmlessness, is another deeply rooted principle of Hinduism. It involves six pillars: refraining from eating all animal products; revering all of life; having integrity in thoughts, words, and deeds; exercising self-control; serving creation, nature, and humanity; and advancing truth and understanding.

Holy Places

In Hinduism, all water is considered holy, symbolizing the flow of life. For a Hindu, the Ganges River is perhaps the most holy of all bodies of water. It was named for the goddess of purification, Ganga. The waters of the Ganges are said to flow through Shiva's hair and have the ability to cleanse sin. Devout Hindus make pilgrimages to bathe in the Ganges. They may also visit fords in the rivers to symbolize the journey from one life to another.

Pilgrimages are also made to sites associated with the life of a god. For example, Lord Rama was said to have been born in Ayodhya, one of the seven holy cities in India. Other holy sites are Dwarka, Ujjian, Kanchipuram, Mathura, Hardwar, and Varanasi, the City of Light.

After leaving his mountain home, Lord Shiva was thought to have lived in Varanasi, or Benares, considered the holiest city. Before the sixth century, it became a center of education for Hindus. It has four miles of palaces and temples along the river. One of the many pilgrimage circuits covers thirty-five miles, lasts for five days, and includes prayer at 108 different shrines. Because of the river's sacred nature, Hindus come to bathe from its many stone steps, called ghats, and to drink the water. It is also the place where Hindus desire to be at their death or to have their ashes scattered. Because Varanasi is regarded as a place of crossing between earth and heaven, dying there is thought to free one from the cycle of rebirth.

The thirty-four Ellora Caves at Maharashtra, India, are known for their sculptures. Built between 600 and 1000 CE, they were cut into a tufa rock hillside on a curve shaped like a horseshoe, so that the caves go deeply into the rock face. Although the one-mile site includes temples for Buddhist, Jain, and Hindu faiths, the major figure of the caves is Shiva, and the largest temple is dedicated to Shiva.

Lastly, Hindu temples, or mandirs, are regarded as the gods' earthly homes. The buildings themselves are therefore holy, and Hindus remove their shoes before entering.

HINDUISM IN DEPTH

Sacred Symbols

The wheel of life represents samsara, the cycle of life, death and rebirth. Karma is what keeps the wheel spinning. Another circle is the hoop of flames in which Shiva, also known as the Lord of the Dance, or Natraja, is shown dancing creation into being. The flames signify the universe's energy and Shiva's power of both destruction and creation. Shiva balances on his right foot, which rests on a defeated demon that stands for ignorance.

The lotus is the symbol of creation, fertility, and purity. This flower is associated with Vishnu because as he slept, a lotus flower bloomed from his navel. From this lotus Brahma came forth to create the world. Yoga practitioners commonly assume the lotus position for meditation.

Murtis are the statues of gods that are found in both temples and private homes. They are often washed with milk and water, anointed with oil, dressed, and offered gifts of food or flowers. Incense may also be burned to make the air around the murti sweet and pure.

One of Krishna's symbols is the conch shell, a symbol of a demon he defeated. A conch shell is blown at temples to announce the beginning of the worship service. It is a visual reminder for followers of Krishna to overcome ignorance and evil in their lives.

For many years, the Hindus used the swastika as a holy symbol. (*Swastika* is a Sanskrit word for good fortune and well-being.) The four arms meet at a central point, demonstrating that the universe comes from one source. Each arm of the symbol represents a path to God and is bent to show that all paths are difficult. It is used at a time of new beginnings, such as at a wedding, where it is traditionally painted on a coconut using a red paste called kum kum. The symbol appears as a vertical gash across the horizontal layers on the southern face of Mount Kailas, one of the Himalayas's highest peaks, thought to have been the home of Shiva. The mountain is also near the source of the Ganges and the Indus Rivers. The use of the swastika as a symbol for Nazi Germany is abhorrent to Hindus.

Some Hindus use a mala, or rosary, of 108 wooden beads when they pray. As they worship, they repeat the names of God.

Sacred Practices & Gestures

Many homes have private altars or shrines to favorite gods. Statues or pictures of these deities are offered incense, flowers and food, as well as prayers. This daily devotion, known as puja, is generally the responsibility of women, many of whom are devoted to goddesses such as Kali or Sita. A rich family may devote an entire room of their house to the shrine.

Om, or Aum, a sacred syllable recorded first in the Upanishads, is made up of three Sanskrit letters. Writing the letter involves a symbol resembling the Arabic number three. Thus, it is a visual reminder of the Trimurti, the three major Hindu gods. The word is repeated at the beginning of all mantras or prayers.

Each day the Gayatri, which is perhaps the world's oldest recorded prayer, is chanted during the fire ritual. The prayer expresses gratitude to the sun for its shining and invokes blessings of prosperity on all. The ritual, typically done at large consecrated fire pits, may be done using burning candles instead.

Holy Hindu men are known as sadhus. They lead ascetic lives, wandering, begging, and living in caves in the mountains. Regarded as having greater spiritual power and wisdom, they are often consulted for advice.

Food Restrictions

Many Hindus are vegetarians because they embrace ahimsa (reverence for and protection of all life) and oppose killing. In fact, Hindus comprise about 70 percent of the world's vegetarians. They are generally lacto-vegetarians, meaning that they include dairy products in their diets. However, Hindus residing in the cold climate of Nepal and Tibet consume meat to increase their caloric intake.

Whether a culture practices vegetarianism or not, cows are thought to be sacred because Krishna acted as a cowherd as a young god. Thus cows are never eaten. Pigs are also forbidden, as are red foods, such as tomatoes or red lentils. In addition, garlic and onions are also not permitted. Alcohol is strictly forbidden.

Purity rituals before eating include cleaning the area where the food is to be eaten and reciting mantras or praying while sprinkling water around the food. Other rituals include Annaprasana, which celebrates a child's eating of solid food—traditionally rice—for the first time. In addition, at funerals departed souls are offered food, which Hindus believe will strengthen the soul for the journey to the ancestors' world.

Serving food to those in need also generates good karma. Food is offered during religious ceremonies and may later be shared with visiting devotees of the god.

To show their devotion to Shiva, many Hindus fast on Mondays. There is also a regular fast, known as agiaras, which occurs on the eleventh day of each two-week period. On that day, only one meal is eaten. During the month of Shravan, which many consider a holy month, people may eat only one meal, generally following sunset.

Rites, Celebrations & Services

Many Hindu celebrations are connected to the annual cycle of nature and can last for many days. In addition, celebrations that honor the gods are common. Shiva, one of the three major gods, is honored at Shivaratri in February or March. In August or September, Lord Krishna is honored at Krishnajanmashtmi. Prayer and fasting are part of this holiday.

During the spring equinox and just prior to the Hindu New Year, Holi is celebrated. It is a time to resolve disputes and forgive or pay debts. During this festival, people often have bonfires and throw objects that represent past impurity or disease into the fire.

Another festival occurs in July or August, marking the beginning of the agricultural year in northern India. Raksha Bandhan (the bond of protection) is a festival which celebrates sibling relationships. During the festivities, Hindus bind a bauble with silk thread to the wrists of family members and friends.

To reenact Rama's defeat of the demon Ravana, as narrated in the Ramayana, people make and burn effigies. This festival is called Navaratri in western India, also known as the Durgapuja in Bengal, and Dasserah in northern India. It occurs in September or October each year as a festival celebrating the victory of good over evil. September is also time to celebrate the elephant-headed god Ganesha's birthday at the festival of Ganesh Chaturthi.

Diwali, a five-day festival honoring Lakshmi (the goddess of good fortune and wealth), occurs in October or November. This Festival of Lights is the time when people light oil lamps and set off fireworks to help Rama find his way home after exile. Homes are cleaned in hopes that Lakshmi will come in the night to bless it. People may use colored rice flour to make patterns on their doorstep. Competitions for designs of these patterns, which are meant to welcome God to the house, frequently take place.

Jagannath, or Vishnu, is celebrated during the festival Rathayatra. A large image of Jagannath rides in a chariot pulled through the city of Puri.

The temple for Hindus is the home of the god. Only Brahmin priests may supervise worship there. The inner sanctuary of the building is called the garbhagriha, or womb-house; there the god resides. Worshippers must be ritually pure before the worship starts. The priest recites the mantras and reads sacred texts. Small lamps are lit, and everyone shares specially prepared and blessed food after the service ends.

Judy A. Johnson, MTS

Bibliography

Barnes, Trevor. *The Kingfisher Book of Religions*. New York: Kingfisher, 1999. Print.

Harley, Gail M. *Hindu and Sikh Faiths in America*. New York: Facts on File, 2003. Print.

Iyengar, B. K. S. and Noelle Perez-Christiaens. *Sparks of Divinity: The Teachings of B. K. S. Iyengar from 1959 to 1975*. Berkeley: Rodmell, 2012. E-book.

"The Joys of Hinduism." *Hinduism Today* Oct./Dec. 2006: 40–53. Print.

Langley, Myrtle. *Religion*. New York: Knopf, 1996. Print.

Meredith, Susan. *The Usborne Book of World Religions*. London: Usborne, 1995. Print.

Rajan, Rajewswari. "The Politics of Hindu 'Tolerance.'" *Boundary 2* 38.3 (2011): 67–86. Print.

Raman, Varadaraja V. "Hinduism and Science: Some Reflections." *Journal of Religion & Science* 47.3 (2012): 549–74. Print.

Renard, John. *Responses to 101 Questions on Hinduism*. Mahwah: Paulist, 1999. Print.

Siddhartha. "Open-Source Hinduism." *Religion & the Arts* 12.1–3 (2008): 34–41. Print.

Shouler, Kenneth and Susai Anthony. *The Everything Hinduism Book*. Avon: Adams, 2009. Print.

Soherwordi, Syed Hussain Shaheed. " 'Hinduism'—A Western Construction or an Influence?" *South Asian Studies* 26.1 (2011): 203–14. Print.

Theodor, Ithamar. *Exploring the Bhagavad Gita: Philosophy, Structure, and Meaning*. Farnham and Burlington: Ashgate, 2010. E-book.

Whaling, Frank. *Understanding Hinduism*. Edinburgh: Dunedin, 2010. E-book.

Wilkinson, Philip. *Religions*. New York: DK, 2008. Print.

Islam

General Description

The word *Islam* derives from a word meaning "submission," particularly submission to the will of Allah. Muslims, those who practice Islam, fall into two major groups, Sunni and Shia (or Shi'i,) based on political rather than theological differences. Sunni Muslims follow the four Rightly Guided Caliphs, or Rashidun and believe that caliphs should be elected. Shia Muslims believe that the Prophet's nearest male relative, Ali ibn Abi Talib, should have ruled following Muhammad's death, and venerate the imams (prayer leaders) who are directly descended from Ali and the Prophet's daughter Fatima.

Number of Adherents Worldwide

Approximately 1.6 billion people, or 23 percent of the world's population, are Muslims. Of that total, between 87 and 90 percent of all Muslims are Sunni Muslims and between 10 and 13 percent of all Muslims are Shia. Followers of the Sufi sect, noted for its experiential, ecstatic focus, may be either Sunni or Shia.

Basic Tenets

Islam is a monotheistic faith; Muslims worship only one God, Allah. They also believe in an afterlife and that people are consigned to heaven or hell following the last judgment.

The Islamic faith rests on Five Pillars. The first pillar, Shahadah is the declaration of faith in the original Arabic, translated as: "I bear witness that there is no god but God and Muhammad is his Messenger." The second pillar, Salah, are prayers adherents say while facing Mecca five times daily at regular hours and also at the main service held each Friday at a mosque. Zakat, "the giving of a tax," is the third pillar and entails giving an income-based percentage of one's wealth to help the poor without attracting notice. The fourth pillar is fasting, or Sawm, during Ramadan, the ninth month of the Islamic calendar. Certain groups of people are excused from the fast, however. The final pillar is the Hajj, the pilgrimage to Mecca required of every able-bodied Muslim at least once in his or her lifetime.

Sacred Text

The Qur'an (Koran), meaning "recitation," is the holy book of Islam.

Major Figures

Muhammad, regarded as the Prophet to the Arabs—as Moses was to the Jews—is considered the exemplar of what it means to be a Muslim. His successors—Abu Bakr, Umar, Uthman, and Ali—were known as the four Rightly Guided Caliphs.

Major Holy Sites

Islam recognizes three major holy sites: Mecca, home of the Prophet; Medina, the city to which Muslims relocated when forced from Mecca due to persecution; and the Dome of the Rock in Jerusalem, believed to be the oldest Islamic building in existence. Muslims believe that in 621 CE Muhammad ascended to heaven (called the Night Journey) from a sacred stone upon which the Dome was constructed. Once in heaven, God instructed Muhammad concerning the need to pray at regular times daily...

There are also several mosques which are considered primary holy sites. These include the al-Aqsa Mosque in the Old City of Jerusalem, believed by many to be the third holiest site in Islam. The mosque, along with the Dome of the Rock, is located on Judaism's holiest site, the Temple Mount, where the Temple of Jerusalem is believed to have stood. Muslims also revere the Mosque of the Prophet (Al-Masjid al-Nabawi) in Medina, considered the resting place of the Prophet Muhammad and the second largest mosque in the world; and the Mosque of the Haram (Masjid al-Haram or the Sacred or Grand Mosque) in Mecca, thought to be the largest mosque in the world and site of the Ka'bah, "the sacred house," also known as "the Noble Cube," Islam's holiest structure.

Major Rites & Celebrations

Two major celebrations mark the Islamic calendar. 'Id al-Adha, the feast of sacrifice—including animal sacrifice—held communally at the close of the Hajj (annual pilgrimage), commemorates the account of God providing a ram instead of the son Abraham had been asked to sacrifice. The second festival, 'Id al-Fitr, denotes the end of Ramadan and is a time of feasting and gift giving.

ORIGINS

History & Geography

In 610 CE, a forty-year-old businessman from Mecca named Muhammad ibn Abdullah, from the powerful Arab tribe Quraysh, went to Mount Hira to meditate, as he regularly did for the month of Ramadan. During that month, an entire group of men, the hanif, retreated to caves. The pagan worship practiced in the region, as well as the cruelty and lack of care for the poor, distressed Muhammad. As the tribe to which he belonged had become wealthy through trade, it had begun disregarding traditions prescribed by the nomadic code.

The archangel Jibra'il (Gabriel) appeared in Muhammad's cave and commanded him to read the words of God contained in the scroll that the angel showed him. Like most people of his time, Muhammad was illiterate, but repeated the words Jibra'il said. Some followers of Islam believe that this cave at Jebel Nur, in what is now Saudi Arabia, is where Adam, the first human Allah created, lived.

A frightened Muhammad told only his wife, Khadija, about his experience. For two years, Muhammad received further revelations, sharing them only with family and close friends. Like other prophets, he was reluctant about his calling, fearing that he was—or would be accused of being—possessed by evil spirits or insane. At one point, he tried to commit suicide, but was stopped by the voice of Jibra'il affirming his status as God's messenger.

Muhammad recalled the words spoken to him, which were eventually written down. The Qur'an is noted for being a book of beautiful language, and Muhammad's message reached many. The Prophet thus broke the old pattern of allegiance to tribe and forged a new community based on shared practice.

Muhammad considered himself one who was to warn the others of a coming judgment. His call for social justice and denunciation of the wealthy disturbed the powerful Arab tribe members in Mecca. These men stood to lose the status and income derived from the annual festival to the Ka'bah. The Prophet and his followers were persecuted and were the subject of boycotts and death threats. In 622 CE, Muslim families began a migration (hijrah) to Yathrib, later known as Medina. Two years earlier, the city had sent envoys seeking Muhammad's leadership for their own troubled society. The hijrah marks the beginning of the Islamic calendar.

The persecutions eventually led to outright tribal warfare, linking Islam with political prowess through the victories of the faithful. The Muslims moved from being an oppressed minority to being a political force. In 630 CE, Muhammad and ten thousand of his followers marched to Mecca, taking the city without bloodshed. He destroyed the pagan idols that were housed and worshipped at the Ka'bah, instead associating the hajj with the story of Abraham sending his concubine Hagar and their son Ishmael (Ismail in Arabic) out into the wilderness. With this victory, Muhammad ended centuries of intertribal warfare.

Muhammad died in 632, without designating a successor. Some of the Muslims believed that his nearest male relative should rule, following the custom of the tribes. Ali ibn Abi Talib, although a pious Muslim, was still young. Therefore, Abu Bakr, the Prophet's father-in-law, took the title khalifah, or caliph, which means successor or deputy. Within two years Abu Bakr had stabilized Islam. He was followed by three additional men whom Muhammad had known. Collectively, the four are known as the Four Rightly Guided Caliphs, or the Rashidun. Their rule extended from 632 until 661. Each of the final three met a violent death.

Umar, the second caliph, increased the number of raids on adjacent lands during his ten-year rule, which began in 634. This not only increased wealth, but also gave Umar the authority he needed, since Arabs objected to the idea of a monarchy. Umar was known as the commander of the faithful. Under his leadership, the Islamic community marched into present-day Iraq, Syria, and Egypt and achieved victory over the Persians in 637.

Muslims elected Uthman ibn Affan as the third caliph after Umar was stabbed by a Persian prisoner of war. He extended Muslim conquests into North Africa as well as into Iran, Afghanistan, and parts of India. A group of soldiers mutinied in 656, assassinating Uthman.

Ali, Muhammad's son-in-law, was elected caliph of a greatly enlarged empire. Conflict developed between Ali and the ruler in Damascus whom Uthman had appointed governor of Syria. The fact that the governor came from a rival tribe led to further tensions. Increasingly, Damascus rather than Medina was viewed as the key Muslim locale. Ali was murdered in 661 during the internal struggles.

Within a century after Muhammad's death, Muslims had created an empire that stretched from Spain across Asia to India and facilitated the spread of Islam. The conquerors followed a policy of relative, though not perfect, tolerance toward adherents of other religions. Christians and Jews received special status as fellow "People of the Book," though they were still required to pay a special poll tax in exchange for military protection. Pagans, however, were required to convert to Islam or face death. Later, Hindus, Zoroastrians, and other peoples were also permitted to pay the tax rather than submit to conversion. Following the twelfth century, Sufi mystics made further converts in Central Asia, India, sub-Saharan Africa, and Turkey. Muslim traders also were responsible for the growth of Islam, particularly in China, Indonesia, and Malaya.

The Muslim empire continued to grow until it weakened in the fourteenth century, when it was replaced as a major world power by European states. The age of Muslim domination ended with the 1683 failure of the Ottoman Empire to capture Vienna, Austria.

Although lacking in political power until recent years, a majority of nations in Indonesia, the Middle East, and East and North Africa are predominately Islamic. The rise of Islamic fundamentalists who interpret the Qur'an literally and seek victory through acts of terrorism began in the late twentieth century. Such extremists do not represent the majority of the Muslim community, however.

Like Judaism and Christianity, Islam has been influenced by its development in a desert climate. Arabia, a region three times the size of France, is a land of steppe and desert whose unwelcoming climate kept it from being mapped with any precision until the 1950s. Because Yemen received monsoon rains, it could sustain agriculture and became a center for civilization as early as the second millennium BCE. In the seventh century CE, nomads roamed the area, guarding precious wells and oases. Raiding caravans and other tribes were common ways to obtain necessities.

Mecca was a pagan center of worship, but it was located not far from a Christian kingdom, Ethiopia, across the Red Sea. Further north, followers of both Judaism and Christianity had influenced members of Arab tribes. Jewish tribes inhabited Yathrib, the city later known as Medina. Neither Judaism nor Christianity was especially kind to those they considered pagans. According to an Arabian tradition, in 570 the Ethiopians attacked Yemen and attempted an attack on Mecca. Mecca was caught between two enemy empires—Christian Byzantine and Zoroastrian Persia—that fought a lengthy war during Muhammad's lifetime.

The contemporary clashes between Jews and Muslims are in part a result of the dispersion of Muslims who had lived in Palestine for centuries. More Jews began moving into the area under the British Mandate; in 1948, the state of Israel was proclaimed. Historically, Jews had been respected as a People of the Book.

Founder or Major Prophet

Muslims hold Allah to be the founder of their religion and Abraham to have been the first Muslim. Muhammad is God's prophet to the Arabs. The instructions that God gave Muhammad through the archangel Jibra'il and through direct revelation are the basis for the Islamic religion. These revelations were given over a period of twenty-one years. Because Muhammad and most of the Muslims were illiterate, the teachings were read publicly in chapters, or suras.

Muhammad did not believe he was founding a new religion. Rather, he was considered God's final Prophet, as Moses and Jesus had been prophets. His task was to call people to repent and to return to the straight path of God's law, called Sharia. God finally was sending a direct revelation to the Arab peoples, who had sometimes been taunted by the other civilizations as being left out of God's plan.

Muhammad, who had been orphaned by age six, was raised by an uncle. He became a successful businessman of an important tribe and married Khadija, for whom he worked. His integrity was such that he was known as al-Amin, the trusted one. He and Khadija had six children; four daughters survived. After Khadija's death, Muhammad married several women, as was the custom for a great chief. Several of the marriages were political in nature.

Muhammad is regarded as the living Qur'an. He is sometimes referred to as the perfect man, one who is an example of how a Muslim should live. He was ahead of his time in his attitudes toward women, listening to their counsel and granting them rights not enjoyed by women in other societies, including the right to inherit property and to divorce. (It should be noted that the Qur'an does not require the seclusion or veiling of all women.)

Islam has no religious leaders, especially those comparable to other religions. Each mosque has an imam to preach and preside over prayer at the Friday services. Although granted a moral authority, the imam is not a religious leader with a role comparable to that of rabbis or priests.

Philosophical Basis

Prior to Muhammad's receiving the Qur'an, the polytheistic tribes believed in Allah, "the god." Allah was far away and not part of worship rituals, although he had created the world and sustained it. He had three daughters who were goddesses.

Islam began pragmatically—the old tribal ways were not working—as a call for social justice, rooted in Muhammad's dissatisfaction with the increasing emphasis on accumulating wealth and an accompanying neglect of those in need. The struggle (jihad) to live according to God's desire for humans was to take place within the community, or the ummah. This effort was more important than dogmatic statements or beliefs about God. When the community prospered, this was a sign of God's blessing.

In addition, the revelation of the Qur'an gave Arab nations an official religion. The Persians around them had Zoroastrianism, the Romans and Byzantines had Christianity, and the Jews of the Diaspora had Judaism. With the establishment of Islam, Arabs finally could believe that they were part of God's plan for the world.

Four principles direct Islam's practice and doctrine. These include the Qur'an; the traditions, or sunnah; consensus, or ijma'; and individual thought, or ijtihad. The term sunnah, "well-trodden path," had been used by Arabs before Islam to refer to their tribal law.

A fifth important source for Islam is the Hadith, or report, a collection of the Prophet's words and actions, intended to serve as an example. Sunni Muslims refer to six collections made in the ninth century, while Shia Muslims have a separate Hadith of four collections.

Holy Places

Mecca was located just west of the Incense Road, a major trade route from southern Arabia to Palestine and Syria. Mecca was the Prophet's home and the site where he received his revelations. It is also the city where Islam's holiest structure, the Ka'bah, "the sacred house," was located. The Ka'bah was regarded as having been built by Abraham and his son Ishmael. This forty-three-foot gray stone cube was a center for pagan idols in the time of Muhammad. In 628 the Prophet removed 360 pagan idols—one for each day of the Arabic lunar year—from inside the Ka'bah.

When the followers of Muhammad experienced persecution for their beliefs, they fled to the city of Medina, formerly called Yathrib. When his uncle Abu Talib died, Muhammad lost the protection from persecution that his uncle had provided. He left for Ta'if in the mountains, but it was also a center for pagan cults, and he was driven out. After a group of men from Yathrib promised him protection, Muhammad sent seventy of his followers to the city, built around an oasis about 215 miles north. This migration, called the hijra, occurred in 622, the first year of the Muslim calendar. From this point on, Islam became an organized religion rather than a persecuted and minority cult. The Prophet was buried in Medina in 632, and his mosque in that city is deeply revered.

Islam's third holiest site is the Dome of the Rock in Jerusalem. Muslims believe that the Prophet Muhammad ascended to heaven in 621 from the rock located at the center of this mosque. During this so-called night journey, Allah gave him instructions about prayer. In the shrine at the Dome of the Rock is a strand of hair that Muslims believe was Muhammad's.

Shia Muslims also revere the place in present-day Iraq where Ali's son, Husayn, was martyred. They regard the burial place of Imam Ali ar-Rida in Meshed, Iran, as a site of pilgrimage as well.

ISLAM IN DEPTH

Sacred Symbols

Muslims revere the Black Stone, a possible meteorite that is considered a link to heaven. It is set inside the Ka'bah shrine's eastern corner. The Ka'bah is kept covered by the kiswa, a black velvet cloth decorated with embroidered calligraphy in gold. At the hajj, Muslims walk around it counterclockwise seven times as they recite prayers to Allah.

Muslim nations have long used the crescent moon and a star on their flags. The crescent moon, which the Ottomans first adopted as a symbol during the fifteenth century, is often placed on the dome of a mosque, pointing toward Mecca. For Muhammad, the waxing and waning of the moon signified the unchanging and eternal purpose of God. Upon seeing a new moon, the Prophet confessed his faith in God. Muslims rely on a lunar calendar and the Qur'an states that God created the stars to guide people to their destinations.

Islam forbids the making of graven images of animals or people, although not all Islamic cultures follow this rule strictly. The decorative arts of Islam have placed great emphasis on architecture and calligraphy to beautify mosques and other buildings. In addition, calligraphy, floral motifs, and geometric forms decorate some editions of the Qur'an's pages, much as Christian monks once decorated hand-copied scrolls of the Bible. These elaborate designs can also be seen on some prayer rugs, and are characteristic of Islamic art in general.

Sacred Practices & Gestures

When Muslims pray, they must do so facing Mecca, a decision Muhammad made in January 624 CE. Prior to that time, Jerusalem—a holy city for both Jews and Christians—had been the geographic focus. Prayer involves a series of movements that embody submission to Allah.

Muslims sometimes use a strand of prayer beads, known as subhah, to pray the names of God. The beads can be made of bone, precious stones, or wood. Strings may have twenty-five, thirty-three or 100 beads.

Food Restrictions

Those who are physically able to do so fast from both food and drink during the daylight hours of the month Ramadan. Although fasting is not required of the sick, the aged, menstruating or pregnant women, or children, some children attempt to fast, imitating their parents' devotion. Those who cannot fast are encouraged to do so the following Ramadan. This fast is intended to concentrate the mind on Allah. Muslims recite from the Qur'an during the month.

All meat must be prepared in a particular way so that it is halal, or permitted. While slaughtering the animal, the person must mention the name of Allah. Blood, considered unclean, must be allowed to drain. Because pigs were fed garbage, their meat was considered unclean. Thus Muslims eat no pork, even though in modern times, pigs are often raised on grain.

In three different revelations, Muslims are also forbidden to consume fermented beverages. Losing self-control because of drunkenness violates the Islamic desire for self-mastery.

Rites, Celebrations, and Services

The **mosque** is the spiritual center of the Muslim community. From the minaret (a tower outside the mosque), the call to worship occurs five times daily—at dawn, just past noon, at midafternoon, at sunset, and in the evening. In earliest times, a muezzin, the official responsible for this duty, gave the cry. In many modern countries, the call now comes over a speaker system. Also located outside are fountains to provide the necessary water for ritual washing before prayer. Muslims wash their face, hands, forearms, and feet, as well as remove their shoes before beginning their prayers. In the absence of water, ritual cleansing may occur using sand or a stone.

Praying involves a series of movements known as rak'ah. From a standing position, the worshipper recites the opening sura of the Qur'an, as well as a second sura. After bowing to demonstrate respect, the person again stands, then prostrates himself or herself to signal humility. Next, the person assumes a sitting posture in silent prayer before again prostrating. The last movement is a greeting of "Peace be with you and the mercy of Allah." The worshipper looks both left and right before saying these words, which are intended for all persons, present and not.

Although Muslims stop to pray during each day when the call is given, Friday is the time for communal prayer and worship at the mosque. The prayer hall is the largest space within the mosque. At one end is a niche known as the mihrab, indicating the direction of Mecca, toward which Muslims face when they pray. At first, Muhammad instructed his followers to pray facing Jerusalem, as the Jewish people did. This early orientation was also a way to renounce the pagan associations of Mecca. Some mosques serve as community centers, with additional rooms for study.

The hajj, an important annual celebration, was a custom before the founding of Islam. Pagan worship centered in Mecca at the Ka'bah, where devotees circled the cube and kissed the Black Stone that was embedded in it. All warfare was forbidden during the hajj, as was argument, speaking crossly, or killing even an insect.

Muslims celebrate the lives of saints and their death anniversaries, a time when the saints are thought to reach the height of their spiritual life. Mawlid an-Nabi refers to "the birth of the Prophet." Although it is cultural and not rooted in the Qur'an, in some Muslim countries this is a public holiday on which people recite the Burdah, a poem that praises Muhammad. Muslims also celebrate the night that the Prophet ascended to heaven, Lailat ul-Miraj. The Night of Power is held to be the night on which Allah decides the destiny of people individually and the world at large.

Like Jews, Muslims practice circumcision, a ceremony known as khitan. Unlike Jews, however, Muslims do not remove the foreskin when the male is a baby. This is often done when a boy is about seven, and must be done before the boy reaches the age of twelve.

Healthy adult Muslims fast between sunrise and sunset during the month of Ramadan. This commemorates the first of Muhammad's revelations. In some Muslim countries, cannons are fired before the beginning of the month, as well as at the beginning and end of each day of the month. Some Muslims read a portion of the Qur'an each day during the month.

Judy A. Johnson, MTS

Bibliography

Al-Saud, Laith, Scott W. Hibbard, and Aminah Beverly. *An Introduction to Islam in the 21st Century*. Wiley, 2013. E-book.

Armstrong, Lyall. "The Rise of Islam: Traditional and Revisionist Theories." *Theological Review* 33.2 (2012): 87–106. Print.

Armstrong, Karen. *Islam: A Short History*. New York: Mod. Lib., 2000. Print.

Aslan, Reza. *No god but God: The Origins, Evolution, and Future of Islam*. New York: Random, 2005. Print.

Badawi, Emran El-. "'For All Times and Places': A Humanistic Reception of the Qur'an." *English Language Notes* 50.2 (2012): 99–112. Print.

Barnes, Trevor. *The Kingfisher Book of Religions*. New York: Kingfisher, 1999. Print.

Ben Jelloun, Tahar. *Islam Explained*. Trans. Franklin Philip. New York: New, 2002. Print.

Esposito, John L. *Islam: the Straight Path*. New York: Oxford UP, 1988. Print.

Glady, Pearl. *Criticism of Islam*.Library, 2012. E-book.

Holland, Tom. "Where Mystery Meets History." *History Today* 62.5 (2012): 19–24. Print.

Langley, Myrtle. *Religion*. New York: Knopf, 1996. Print.

Lunde, Paul. *Islam: Faith, Culture, History*. London: DK, 2002. Print.

Nasr, Seyyed Hossein. *Islam: Religion, History, and Civilization*. New York: Harper, 2002. Print.

Pasha, Mustapha Kamal. "Islam and the Postsecular." *Review of International Studies* 38.5 (2012): 1041–56. Print.

Sayers, Destini and Simone Peebles. *Essence of Islam and Sufism*. College, 2012. E-book.

Schirmacher, Christine. "They Are Not All Martyrs: Islam on the Topics of Dying, Death, and Salvation in the Afterlife." *Evangelical Review of Theology* 36.3 (2012): 250–65. Print.

Wilkinson, Philip. *Islam*. New York: DK, 2002. Print.

Wilkinson, Philip. *Religions*. New York: DK, 2008. Print.

Jainism

General Description

Jainism is one of the major religions of India. The name of the religion itself is believed to be based on the Sanskrit word *ji*, which means "to conquer or triumph," or *jina*, which means "victor or conqueror." The earliest name of the group was Nirgrantha, meaning bondless, but it applied to monks and nuns only. There are two sects: the Svetambaras (the white clad), which are the more numerous and wear white clothing, and the Digambaras (the sky clad), the most stringent group; their holy men or monks do not wear clothing at all.

Number of Adherents Worldwide

Jainism has about five million adherents, most of them in India (in some estimates, the religion represents approximately 1 percent of India's population). Because the religion is demanding in nature, few beyond the Indian subcontinent have embraced it. Jainism has spread to Africa, the United States, and nations in the Commonwealth (nations once under British rule) by virtue of Indian migration to these countries.

Basic Tenets

The principle of nonviolence (ahimsa) is a defining feature of Jainism. This results in a pacifist religion that influenced Mohandas Gandhi's ideas on nonviolent resistance. Jains believe that because all living creatures have souls, harming any of those creatures is wrong. They therefore follow a strict vegetarian diet, and often wear masks so as to not inhale living organisms. The most important aspect of Jainism is perhaps the five abstinences: ahimsa, satya (truthfulness), asteya (refrain from stealing), brahmacarya (chaste living), and aparigraha (refrain from greed).

A religion without priests, Jainism emphasizes the importance of the adherents' actions. Like Buddhists and Hindus, Jainists believe in karma and reincarnation. Unlike the Buddhist and Hindu idea of karma, Jainists regard karma as tiny particles that cling to the soul as mud clings to shoes, gradually weighing down the soul. Good deeds wash away these particles. Jainists also believe in moksha, the possibility of being freed from the cycle of death and rebirth. Like many Indian religions, Jainism does not believe in an afterlife, but in a cycle of death and rebirth. Once freed from this cycle, the soul will remain in infinite bliss.

While Jains do not necessarily believe in and worship God or gods, they believe in divine beings. Those who have achieved moksha are often regarded by Jains in the same manner in which other religions regard deities. These include the twenty-four Tirthankaras (ford makers) or jinas (victors), those who have escaped the cycle of death and rebirth, and the Siddhas, the liberated souls without physical form. The idea of a judging, ruling, or creator God is not present in Jainism.

Jainists believe that happiness is not found in material possessions and seek to have few of them. They also stress the importance of environmentalism. Jainists follow the Three Jewels: Right Belief, Right Knowledge, and Right Conduct. To be completely achieved, these three must be practiced together. Jainists also agree to six daily obligations (avashyaka), which include confession, praising the twenty-four Tirthankaras (the spiritual leaders), and calm meditation.

Sacred Text

The words of Mahavira were passed down orally, but lost over a few centuries. During a famine in the mid-fourth century BCE, many monks died. The texts were finally written down, although the Jain sects do not agree as to whether they are Mahavira's actual words. There are forty-five sacred texts (Agamas), which make up the Agam Sutras, Jainism's canonical literature. They were probably written down no earlier than 300 BCE. Two of the primary texts are the Akaranga

Sutra, which outlines the rule of conduct for Jain monks, and the Kalpa Sutra, which contains biographies of the last two Tirthankara. The Digambaras, who believe that the Agamas were lost around 350 BCE, have two main texts and four compendia written between 100 and 800 CE by various scholars.

Major Figures

Jainism has no single founder. However, Mahavira (Great Hero) is one of the Tirthankaras or jinas (pathfinders). He is considered the most recent spiritual teacher in a line of twenty-four. Modern-day Jainism derives from Mahavira, and his words are the foundation of Jain scriptures. He was a contemporary of Siddhartha Gautama, who was revered as the Buddha. Both Mahavira and Rishabha (or Adinatha), the first of the twenty-four Tirthankaras, are attributed as the founder of Jainism, though each Tirthankara maintains founding attributes.

Major Holy Sites

The Jain temple at Ranakpur is located in the village of Rajasthan. Carved from amber stone with marble interiors, the temple was constructed in the fifteenth century CE. It is dedicated to the first Tirthankara. The temple has twenty-nine large halls and each of the temple's 1,444 columns has a unique design with carvings.

Sravanabegola in Karnataka state is the site of Gomateshwara, Lord Bahubali's fifty-seven-foot statue. It was constructed in 981 CE from a single chunk of gneiss. Bahubali is considered the son of the first Tirthankara. The Digambara sect believes him to have been the first human to be free from the world.

Other pilgrimage sites include the Palitana temples in Gujarat and the Dilwara temples in Rajasthan. Sometimes regarded as the most sacred of the many Jain temples, the Palitana temples include 863 marble-engraved temples. The Jain temples at Dilwara were constructed of marble during the eleventh and thirteenth centuries CE. These five temples are often considered the most beautiful Jain temples in existence.

Major Rites & Celebrations

Every twelve years, the festival of Mahamastak-abhisheka (anointing of the head) occurs at a statue of one of Jain's holy men, Bahubali, the second son of the first Tirthankara. The statue is anointed with milk, curd, and ghee, a clarified butter. Nearly a million people attend this rite. Jainists also observe Diwali, the Hindu festival of lights, as it symbolizes Mahavira's enlightenment.

The solemn festival of Paryusana marks the end of the Jain year for the Svetambaras (also spelled Shvetambaras). During this eight-day festival, all Jains are asked to live as an ascetic (monk or nun) would for one day. Das Laxana, a ten-day festival similar to that of Paryusana, immediately follows for the Digambara sect. During these special religious holidays, worshippers are involved in praying, meditating, fasting, forgiveness, and acts of penance. These holy days are celebrated during August and September, which is monsoon season in India. During the monsoons, monks prefer to remain in one place so as to avoid killing the smallest insects that appear during the rainy season. The Kalpa Sutra, one of the Jain scriptures, is read in the morning during Paryusana.

The feast of Kartaki Purnima follows the four months of the rainy season. It is held in the first month (Kartik) according to one calendar, and marked by a pilgrimage to the Palitana temples. Doing so with a pure heart is said to remove all sins of both the present and past life. Those who do so are thought to receive the final salvation in the third or fifth birth.

ORIGINS

History & Geography

In the eastern basin of the Ganges River during the seventh century BCE, a teacher named Parshvanatha (or Parshva) gathered a community founded on abandoning earthly concerns. He is considered to be the twenty-third Tirthankara (ford-maker), the one who makes a path for salvation. During the following century, Vardhamana, called Mahavira (Great Hero), who was considered the twenty-fourth and final spiritual teacher of the age, formulated most Jain doctrine and practice. By the time of Mahavira's death, Jains numbered around 36,000 nuns and 14,000 monks.

A division occurred within Jainism during the fourth century CE. The most extreme ascetics, the Digambaras (the sky-clad), argued that even clothing showed too great an attachment to the world, and that laundering them in the river risked harming creatures. This argument applied only to men, as the Digambaras denied that a soul could be freed from a woman's body. The other group, the Svetambaras (the white-clad), believed that purity resided in the mind.

In 453 or 456 CE, a council of the Svetambara sect at Saurashtra in western India codified the canon still used. The split between the Digambaras, who did not take part in the meeting, and Svetambaras thus became permanent. Despite the split, Jainism's greatest flowering occurred during the early medieval age. After that time, Hindu sects devoted to the Hindu gods of Vishnu and Shiva flourished under the Gupta Empire (often referred to as India's golden age), slowing the spread of Jainism. Followers migrated to western and central India and the community became stronger.

The Digambaras were involved in politics through several medieval dynasties, and some Jain monks served as spiritual advisers. Royalty and high-ranking officials contributed to the building and maintenance of temples. Both branches of Jainism contributed a substantial literature. In the late medieval age, Jain monks ceased to live as ascetic wanders. They chose instead to don orange robes and to live at temples and other holy places.

The Muslims invaded India in the twelfth century. The Jains lost power and fractured over the next centuries into subgroups, some of which repudiated the worship of images. The poet and Digambara layman Banarsidas (1586-1643) played a significant role in a reform movement during the early 1600s. These reforms focused on the mystical side of Jainism, such as spiritual exploration of the inner self (meditation),

and denounced the formalized temple ritual. The movement, known as the Adhyatma movement, resulted in the Digambara Terapanth, a small Digambara sect.

The Jainists were well positioned in society following the departure of the British from India. Having long been associated with the artisan and merchant classes, they found new opportunities. As traditional Indian studies grew, spurred by Western interest, proponents of Jainism began to found publications and places of study (In fact, Jain libraries are believed to be the oldest in India.) The first Jain temple outside India was consecrated in Britain during the 1960s after Jains had gone there in the wake of political turmoil.

The Jains follow their typical profession as merchants. They publish English-language periodicals to spread their ideas on vegetarianism, environmentalism, and nonviolence (ahimsa). The ideas of ahimsa were formative for Mohandas Gandhi, born a Hindu. Gandhi used nonviolence as a wedge against the British Empire in India. Eventually, the British granted independence to India in 1947.

Virchand Gandhi (1864–1901) is believed to be the first Jain to arrive in America when he came over in 1893. He attended the first Parliament of World Religions, held in Chicago. Today North America has more than ninety Jain temples and centers. Jains in the West often follow professions such as banking and business to avoid destroying animal or plant life.

Founder or Major Prophet

Mahavira was born in India's Ganges Basin region. By tradition, he was born around 599 BCE, although some scholars think he may have lived a century later. His story bears a resemblance to that of the Buddha, with whom he was believed to have been a contemporary. His family was also of the Kshatriya (warrior) caste, and his father was a ruler of his clan. One tradition states that Mahavira's mother was of the Brahman (priestly) caste, although another places her in the Kshatriya.

Because he was not the eldest son, Mahavira was not in line for leadership of the clan.

He married a woman of his own caste and they had a daughter. Mahavira chose the life of a monk, with one garment. Later, he gave up wearing even that. He became a wandering ascetic around age thirty, with some legends stating that he tore out his hair before leaving home. He sought shelter in burial grounds and cremation sites, as well as at the base of trees. During the rainy season, however, he lived in towns and villages.

He followed a path of preaching and self-denial, after which he was enlightened (kevala). He spent the next thirty years teaching. Eleven disciples, all of whom were of the Brahman caste, gathered around him. At the end of his life, Mahavira committed Santhara, or ritual suicide through fasting.

Philosophical Basis

Like Buddhists and the Brahmin priests, the Jains believe in human incarnations of God, known as avatars. These avatars appear at the end of a time of decline to reinstate proper thinking and acting. Such a person was Mahavira. At the time of Mahavira's birth, India was experiencing great societal upheaval. Members of the warrior caste opposed the priestly caste, which exercised authority based on its supposed greater moral purity. Many people also opposed the slaughter of animals for the Vedic sacrifices.

Jainists share some beliefs with both Hinduism and Buddhism. The Hindu hero Rama, for example, is co-opted as a nonviolent Jain, while the deity Krishna is considered a cousin of Arishtanemi, the twenty-second Tirthankara. Like Buddhism, Jainism uses a wheel with twelve spokes; however, Jainism uses the wheel to explain time. The first half of the circle is the ascending stage, in which human happiness, prosperity, and life span increase. The latter half of the circle is the descending stage, involving a decrease of life span, prosperity, and happiness. The wheel of time is always in motion.

For Jainists, the universe is without beginning or ending, and contains layers of both heaven and hell. These layers include space beyond, which

is without time, matter, or soul. The cosmos is depicted in art as a large human. The cloud layers surrounding the upper world are called universe space. Above them is the base, Nigoda, where lowest life forms live. The netherworld contains seven hells, each with a different stage of punishment and misery. The middle world contains the earth and remainder of the universe—mankind is located near the waist. There are thirty heavens in the upper world, where heavenly beings reside. In the supreme abode at the apex of the universe, liberated souls (siddha) live.

Jainism teaches that there are six universal entities. Only consciousness or soul is a living substance, while the remaining five are non-living. They include matter, medium of rest, medium of motion, time, and space. Jainism also does not believe in a God who can create, destroy, or protect. Worshipping goddesses and gods to achieve personal gain or material benefit is deemed useless.

Mahavira outlined five basic principles (often referred to as abstinences) for Jainist life, based on the teachings of the previous Tirthankara. They are detachment (aparigraha); the conduct of soul, primarily in sexual morality (brahmacharya); abstinence from stealing (asteya); abstinence from lying (satya); and nonviolence in every realm of the person (ahimsa).

Like other Indian religions, Jainism perceives life as four stages. The life of a student is brahmacharya-ashrama; the stage of family life is gruhasth-ashrama; in vanaprasth-ashrama, the Jainist concentrates on both family and aiding others through social services; and the final stage is sanyast-ashrama, a time of renouncing the world and becoming a monk.

Like many religions, Jainism has a bias toward males and toward the rigorous life of monks and nuns. A layperson cannot work off bad karma, but merely keeps new bad karma from accruing. By following a path of asceticism, however, monks and nuns can destroy karma. Even members of the laity follow eight rules of behavior and take twelve vows. Physical austerity is a key concept in Jainism, as a saint's highest ideal is to starve to death.

Holy Places

There are four major Jain pilgrimage sites: the Dilwara temples near Rajasthan; the Palitana temples; the Ranakpur temple; and Shravan Begola, the site of the statue of Lord Bahubali. In addition, Jains may make pilgrimages to the caves of Khandagiri and Udayagiri, which were cells for Jain monks carved from rock. The spaces carved are too short for a man to stand upright. They were essentially designed for prayer and meditation. Udayagiri has eighteen caves and Khandagiri has fifteen. The caves are decorated with elaborate carvings.

JAINISM IN DEPTH

Sacred Symbols

The open palm (Jain Hand) with a centered wheel, sometimes with the word *ahimsa* written on it, is a prominent Jain symbol. Seen as an icon of peace, the open palm symbol can be interpreted as a call to stop violence, and also means "assurance." It appears on the walls of Jain temples and in their publications. Jainism also employs a simple swastika symbol, considered to be the holiest symbol. It represents the four forms of worldly existence, and three dots above the swastika represent the Three Jewels. The Jain emblem, adopted in 1975, features both the Jain Hand (the open palm symbol with an inset wheel) and a swastika. This year was regarded as the 2,500th anniversary of Mahavira being enlightened.

Sacred Practices & Gestures

Jains may worship daily in their homes at private shrines. The Five Supreme Beings stand for stages in the path to enlightenment. Rising before daybreak, worshippers invoke these five. In addition, devout Jainists set aside forty-eight minutes daily to meditate.

To demonstrate faithfulness to the five vows that Jains undertake, there are four virtuous qualities that must be cultivated. They are compassion (karuna), respect and joy (pramoda), love and friendship (maitri), and indifference toward and noninvolvement with those who are arrogant (madhyastha). Mahavira stressed that Jains must be friends to all living beings. Compassion goes beyond mere feeling; it involves offering both material and spiritual aid. Pramoda carries with it the idea of rejoicing enthusiastically over the virtues of others. There are contemplations associated with these virtues, and daily practice is suggested to attain mastery.

Some Jainists, both men and women, wear a dot on the forehead. This practice comes from Hinduism. During festivals, Jains may pray, chant, fast, or keep silent. These actions are seen as removing bad karma from the soul and moving the person toward ultimate happiness.

Food Restrictions

Jainists practice a strict vegetarian way of life (called Jain vegetarianism) to avoid harming any creature. They refuse to eat root vegetables, because by uprooting them, the entire plant dies. They prefer to wait for fruit to drop from trees rather than taking it from the branches. Starving to death, when ready, is seen as an ideal.

Rites, Celebrations & Services

Some festivals are held annually and their observances are based on a lunar calendar. Mahavir Jayanti is an example, as it celebrates Mahavira's birthday.

Jains may worship, bathe, and make offerings to images of the Tirthankaras in their home or in a temple. Svetambaras Jains also clothe and decorate the images. Because the Tirthankaras have been liberated, they cannot respond as a deity granting favors might. Although Jainism rejects belief in gods in favor of worshipping Tirthankaras, in actual practice, some Jainists pray to Hindu gods.

When Svetambara monks are initiated, they are given three pieces of clothing, including a small piece of white cloth to place over the mouth. The cloth, called a mukhavastrika, is designed to prevent the monk from accidentally eating insects.

Monks take great vows (mahavratas) at initiation. These include abstaining from lying, stealing, sexual activity, injury to any living thing, and personal possessions. Monks own a broom to sweep in front of where they are going to walk so that no small creatures are injured, along with an alms bowl and a robe. The Digambara monks practice a more stringent lifestyle, eating one meal a day, for which they beg.

Nuns in the Svetambaras are three times more common than are monks, even though they receive less honor, and are required to defer to the monks. In Digambara Jainism, the nuns wear robes and accept that they must be reborn as men before progressing upward.

The observance of Santhara, which is religious fasting until death, is a voluntary fasting undertaken with full knowledge. The ritual is also known as Sallekhana, and is not perceived as suicide by Jains, particularly as the prolonged nature of the ritual provides ample time for reflection. It is believed that at least one hundred people die every year from observing Santhara.

Judy A. Johnson, MTS

Bibliography

Aristarkhova, Irina. "Thou Shall Not Harm All Living Beings: Feminism, Jainism, and Animals." *Hypatia* 27.3 (2012): 636–50. Print.

Aukland, Knut. "Understanding Possession in Jainism: A Study of Oracular Possession in Nakoda." *Modern Asian Studies* 47.1 (2013): 103–34. Print.

Barnes, Trevor. *The Kingfisher Book of Religions*. New York: Kingfisher, 1999. Print.

Langley, Myrtle. *Religion*. New York: Knopf, 1996. Print.

Long, Jeffery. *Jainism: An Introduction*. London: I. B. Tauris, 2009. Print.

Long, Jeffrey. "Jainism: Key Themes." *Religion Compass* 5.9 (2011): 501–10. Print.

Rankin, Aidan. *The Jain Path*. Berkeley: O Books, 2006. Print.

Shah, Bharat S. *An Introduction to Jainism*. Great Neck: Setubandh, 2002. Print.

Titze, Kurt. *Jainism: A Pictorial Guide to the Religion of Non-Violence*. Delhi: Motilal Banarsidass, 2001. Print.

Tobias, Michael. *Life Force: the World of Jainism*. Berkeley:Asian Humanities, 1991. E-book, print.

Wiley, Kristi L. *The A to Z of Jainism*. Lanham: Scarecrow, 2009. Print.

Wiley, Kristi L. *Historical Dictionary of Jainism*. Lanham: Scarecrow, 2004. Print.

Wilkinson, Philip. *Religions*. New York: DK, 2008. Print.

Judaism

General Description

In modern Judaism, the main denominations (referred to as movements) are Orthodox Judaism (including Haredi and Hasidic Judaism); Conservative Judaism; Reform (Liberal) Judaism; Reconstructionist Judaism; and to a lesser extent, Humanistic Judaism. In addition, the Jewry of Ethiopia and Yemen are known for having distinct or alternative traditions. Classical Judaism is often organized by two branches: Ashkenazic (Northern Europe) and Sephardic Jews (Spain, Portugal, and North Africa).

Number of Adherents Worldwide

Judaism has an estimated 15 million adherents worldwide, with roughly 41 percent living in Israel and about 41 percent living in the United States. Ashkenazi Jews represent roughly 75 percent, while Sephardic Jews represent roughly 25 percent, with the remaining 5 percent split among alternative communities. Within the United States, a 2000-01 survey stated that 10 percent of American Jews identified as Orthodox (with that number increasing), 35 percent as Reform, 26 percent as Conservative, leaving the remainder with an alternative or no affiliation. [Source: Wilkinson, 2008]

Orthodox Judaism, which was founded around the thirteenth century BCE, has 3 million followers. Members of Reform Judaism, with roots in nineteenth-century Germany, wanted to live peacefully with non-Jews. Therefore, they left the laws that prevented this vision of peace and downplayed the idea of a Jewish state. Reform Judaism, also known as Progressive or Liberal Judaism, allows women rabbis and does not require its adherents to keep kosher. About 1.1 million Jews are Reform; they live primarily in the United States. When nonkosher food was served at the first graduation ceremony for Hebrew Union College, some felt that the Reform movement had gone too far. Thus the Conservative movement began in 1887. A group

of rabbis founded the Jewish Theological Seminary in New York City, wanting to emphasize biblical authority above moral choice, as the Reform tradition stressed. Currently about 900,000 Jews practice this type of Judaism, which is theologically midway between Orthodox and Reform. The Hasidim, an ultra-conservative group, began in present-day Ukraine around 1740. There are 4.5 million Hasidic Jews.

Basic Tenets

Though there is no formal creed (statement of faith or belief), Jews value all life, social justice, education, generous giving, and the importance of living based on the principles and values espoused in the Torah (Jewish holy book). They believe in one all-powerful and creator God, Jehovah or Yaweh, a word derived from the Hebrew letters "YHWH," the unpronounceable name of God. The word is held to be sacred; copyists were required to bathe both before and after writing the word. Jews also believe in a coming Messiah who will initiate a Kingdom of Righteousness. They follow a complex law, composed of 613 commandments or mitzvot. Jews believe that they are God's Chosen People with a unique covenant relationship. They have a responsibility to practice hospitality and to improve the world.

The belief in the afterlife is a part of the Jewish faith. Similar to Christianity, this spiritual world is granted to those who abide by the Jewish faith and live a good life. Righteous Jews are rewarded in the afterlife by being able to discuss the Torah with Moses, who first received the law from God. Furthermore, certain Orthodox sects believe that wicked souls are destroyed or tormented after death.

Sacred Text

The complete Hebrew Bible is called the Tanakh. It includes the prophetic texts, called the Navi'im, the poetic writings, the Ketubim, and the Torah, meaning teaching, law, or guidance. Torah may refer to the entire body of Jewish law or to the first five books of the Hebrew Bible, known as the Pentateuch (it is the Old Testament in the Christian Bible). Also esteemed is the Talmud, made up of the Mishnah, a written collection of oral traditions, and Gemara, a commentary on the Mishnah. The Talmud covers many different subjects, such as law, stories and legends, medicine, and rituals.

Major Figures

The patriarchs are held to be the fathers of the faith. Abraham, the first patriarch, was called to leave his home in the Fertile Crescent for a land God would give him, and promised descendents as numerous as the stars. His son Isaac was followed by Jacob, whom God renamed Israel, and whose twelve sons became the heads of the twelve tribes of Israel. Moses was the man who, along with his brother Aaron, the founder of a priestly line, and their sister Miriam led the chosen people out of slavery in Egypt, where they had gone to escape famine. The Hebrew Bible also details the careers of a group of men and women known as judges, who were really tribal rulers, as well as of the prophets, who called the people to holy lives. Chief among the prophets was Elijah, who confronted wicked kings and performed many miracles. Several kings were key to the biblical narrative, among them David, who killed the giant Goliath, and Solomon, known for his wisdom and for the construction of a beautiful temple.

Major Holy Sites

Most of Judaism's holy sites are within Israel, the Holy Land, including Jerusalem, which was the capital of the United Kingdom of Israel under kings David and Solomon; David captured it from a Canaanite tribe around 1000 BCE. Within the Old City of Jerusalem is the Temple Mount (where the Temple of Jerusalem was built), often considered the religion's holiest site, the Foundation Stone (from which Judaism claims the world was created), and the Western (or Wailing) Wall. Other sites include Mount Sinai

in Egypt, the mountain upon which God gave Moses his laws.

Major Rites & Celebrations

The Jewish calendar recognizes several important holidays. Rosh Hashanah, literally "first of the year," is known as the Jewish New Year and inaugurates a season of self-examination and repentance that culminates in Yom Kippur, the Day of Atonement. Each spring, Passover commemorates the deliverance of the Hebrew people from Egypt. Shavuot celebrates the giving of the Torah to Moses, while Sukkot is the harvest festival. Festivals celebrating deliverance from enemies include Purim and Hanukkah. Young adolescents become members of the community at a bar or bat mitzvah, held near the twelfth or thirteenth birthday. The Sabbath, a cessation from work from Friday at sundown until Saturday when the first star appears, gives each week a rhythm.

ORIGINS

History & Geography

Called by God perhaps four thousand years ago, Abraham left from Ur of the Chaldees, or the Fertile Crescent in Mesopotamia in present-day Iraq, to go the eastern Mediterranean, the land of Canaan. Several generations later, the tribe went to Egypt to escape famine. They were later enslaved by a pharaoh, sometimes believed to have been Ramses II (ca. 1279–1213 BCE), who was noted for his many building projects. The Israelites returned to Canaan under Moses several hundred years after their arrival in Egypt. He was given the law, the Ten Commandments, plus the rest of the laws governing all aspects of life, on Mount Sinai about the thirteenth century BCE. This marked the beginning of a special covenant relationship between the new nation, known as Israel, and God.

Following a period of rule by judges, kings governed the nation. Major kings included David, son-in-law to the first king, Saul, and David's son, Solomon. The kingdom split at the beginning of the reign of Solomon's son

Rehoboam, who began ruling about 930 BCE. Rehoboam retained the ten northern tribes, while the two southern tribes followed a military commander rather than the Davidic line.

Rehoboam's kingdom was known as Israel, after the name Jehovah gave to Jacob. Judah was the name of the southern kingdom—one of Jacob's sons was named Judah. Prophets to both nations warned of coming judgment unless the people repented of mistreating the poor and other sins, such as idolatry. Unheeding, Israel was taken into captivity by the Assyrians in 722 BCE. and the Israelites assimilated into the nations around them.

The Babylonians captured Judah in 586 BCE. After Babylon had been captured in turn by Persians, the Jewish people were allowed to return to the land in 538 BCE. There they began reconstructing the temple and the walls of the city. In the second century BCE, Judas Maccabeus led a rebellion against the heavy taxes and oppression of the Greek conquerors, after they had levied high taxes and appointed priests who were not Jewish. Judas Maccabeus founded a new ruling dynasty, the Hasmoneans, which existed briefly before the region came under the control of Rome.

The Jewish people revolted against Roman rule in 70 CE, leading to the destruction of the second temple. The final destruction of Jerusalem occurred in 135 under the Roman Emperor Hadrian. He changed the city's name to Aelia Capitolina and the name of the country to Palaestina. With the cultic center of their religion gone, the religious leaders developed new methods of worship that centered in religious academies and in synagogues.

After Christianity became the official state religion of the Roman Empire in the early fourth century, Jews experienced persecution. They became known for their scholarship, trade, and banking over the next centuries, with periods of brutal persecution in Europe. Christians held Jews responsible for the death of Jesus, based on a passage in the New Testament. The Blood Libel, begun in England in 1144, falsely accused Jews of killing a Christian child to bake unleavened bread for Passover. This rumor persisted for centuries, and was repeated by Martin Luther during the Protestant Reformation. England expelled all Jews in 1290; they were not readmitted until 1656 under Oliver Cromwell, and not given citizenship until 1829. Jews were also held responsible for other catastrophes—namely poisoning wells and rivers to cause the Black Death in 1348—and were often made to wear special clothing, such as pointed hats, or badges with the Star of David or stone tablets on them.

The relationship between Muslims and Jews was more harmonious. During the Muslim Arab dominance, there was a "golden age" in Spain due to the contributions of Jews and Muslims, known as Moors in Spain. This ideal and harmonious period ended in 1492, when both Moors and Jews were expelled from Spain or forced to convert to Christianity.

Jews in Russia suffered as well. An estimated two million Jews fled the country to escape the pogroms (a Russian word meaning devastation) between 1881 and 1917. The twentieth-century Holocaust, in which an estimated six million Jews perished at the hands of Nazi Germany, was but the culmination of these centuries of persecution. The Nazis also destroyed more than six hundred synagogues.

The Holocaust gave impetus to the creation of the independent state of Israel. The Zionist movement, which called for the founding or reestablishment of a Jewish homeland, was started by Austrian Jew Theodor Herzl in the late nineteenth century, and succeeded in 1948. The British government, which had ruled the region under a mandate, left the area, and Israel was thus established. This ended the Diaspora, or dispersion, of the Jewish people that had begun nearly two millennia before when the Romans forced the Jews to leave their homeland.

Arab neighbors, some of whom had been removed forcibly from the land to create the nation of Israel, were displeased with the new political reality. Several wars have been fought, including the War of Independence in 1948, the Six-Day War in 1967, and the Yom Kippur War in 1973. In addition, tension between Israel and its neighboring Arab states is almost constant.

When the Jewish people were dispersed from Israel, two traditions began. The Ashkenazi Jews settled in Germany and central Europe. They spoke a mixture of the Hebrew dialect and German called Yiddish. Sephardic Jews lived in the Mediterranean countries, including Spain; their language, Ladino, mixed Hebrew and old Spanish.

Founder or Major Prophet

Judaism refers to three major patriarchs: Abraham, his son Isaac, and Isaac's son Jacob. Abraham is considered the first Jew and worshipper in Judaism, as the religion began through his covenant with God. As the forefather of the religion, he is often associated as the founder, though the founder technically is God, or Yahweh (YHWH). Additionally, the twelve sons of Jacob, who was also named Israel, became the founders of the twelve tribes of Israel.

Moses is regarded as a major prophet and as the Lawgiver. God revealed to Moses the complete law during the forty days that the Jewish leader spent on Mount Sinai during the wilderness journey from Egypt to Canaan. Thus, many attribute Moses as the founder of Judaism as a religion.

Philosophical Basis

Judaism began with Abraham's dissatisfaction with the polytheistic worship of his culture. Hearing the command of God to go to a land that would be shown to him, Abraham and his household obeyed. Abraham practiced circumcision and hospitality, cornerstones of the Jewish faith to this day. He and his descendents practiced a nomadic life, much like that of contemporary Bedouins. They migrated from one oasis or well to another, seeking pasture and water for the sheep and goats they herded.

The further development of Judaism came under the leadership of Moses. A Jewish child adopted by Pharaoh's daughter, he was raised and educated in the palace. As a man, he identified with the Jewish people, killing one of the Egyptians who was oppressing a Jew. He subsequently fled for his life, becoming a shepherd in the wilderness, where he remained for forty years. Called by God from a bush that burned but was not destroyed, he was commissioned to lead the people out of slavery in Egypt back to the Promised Land. That forty-year pilgrimage in the wilderness and desert of Arabia shaped the new nation.

Holy Places

The city of Jerusalem was first known as Salem. When King David overcame the Jebusites who lived there, the city, already some two thousand years old, became the capital of Israel. It is built on Mount Zion, which is still considered a sacred place. David's son Solomon built the First Temple in Jerusalem, centering the nation's spiritual as well as political life in the city. The Babylonians captured the city in 597 BCE and destroyed the Temple. For the next sixty years, the Jews remained in exile, until Cyrus the Persian conqueror of Babylon allowed them to return. They rebuilt the temple, but it was desecrated by Antiochus IV of Syria in 167 BCE. In 18 BCE, during a period of Roman occupation, Herod the Great began rebuilding and expanding the Temple. The Romans under the general Titus destroyed the Temple in 70 CE, just seven years after its completion.

The city eventually came under the rule of Persia, the Muslim Empire, and the Crusaders before coming under control of Britain. In 1948 an independent state of Israel was created. The following year, Jerusalem was divided between Israel, which made the western part the national capital, and Jordan, which ruled the eastern part of the city. The Western or Wailing Wall, a retaining wall built during Herod's time, is all that remains of the Second Temple. Devout Jews still come to the Wailing Wall to pray, sometimes placing their petitions on paper and folding the paper into the Wall's crevices. The Wall is known as a place where prayers are answered and a reminder of the perseverance of the Jewish people and faith. According to tradition, the Temple will be rebuilt when Messiah comes to inaugurate God's Kingdom.

The Temple Mount, located just outside Jerusalem on a natural acropolis, includes the Dome of the Rock. This shrine houses a rock held sacred by both Judaism and Islam. Jewish tradition states that it is the spot from which the world was created and the spot on which Abraham was asked to sacrifice his son Isaac. Muslims believe that from this rock Muhammad ascended for his night journey to heaven. Much of Jerusalem, including this holy site, has been and continues to be fought over by people of three faiths: Judaism, Islam, and Christianity.

Moses received the law from God on Mount Sinai. It is still regarded as a holy place.

JUDAISM IN DEPTH

Sacred Symbols

Observant Jewish men pray three times daily at home or in a synagogue, a center of worship, from the word meaning "meeting place." They wear a tallis, or a prayer shawl with tassles, during their morning prayer and on Yom Kippur, the Day of Atonement. They may also cover their heads as a sign of respect during prayer, wearing a skullcap known as a kippah or yarmulka. They find their prayers and blessings in a siddur, which literally means "order," because the prayers appear in the order in which they are recited for services. Jewish daily life also includes blessings for many things, including food.

Tefillin or phylacteries are the small black boxes made of leather from kosher animals that Jewish men wear on their foreheads and their left upper arms during prayer. They contain passages from the Torah. Placing the tefillin on the head reminds them to think about the Torah, while placing the box on the arm puts the Torah close to the heart.

The Law of Moses commands the people to remember the words of the law and to teach them to the children. A mezuzah helps to fulfill that command. A small box with some of the words of the law written on a scroll inside, a mezuzah is hung on the doorframes of every door in the house. Most often, the words of the Shema,

the Jewish recitation of faith, are written on the scroll. The Shema is repeated daily. "Hear, O Israel: the Lord your God, the Lord is one. . . . Love the Lord your God with all your heart, and with all your soul, and with all your might."

Jews adopted the Star of David, composed of two intersecting triangles, during the eighteenth century. There are several interpretations of the design. One is that it is the shape of King David's shield. Another idea is that it stands for daleth, the first letter of David's name. A third interpretation is that the six points refer to the days of the work week, and the inner, larger space represented the day of rest, the Sabbath, or Shabot. The Star of David appears on the flag of Israel. The flag itself is white, symbolizing peace and purity, and blue, symbolizing heaven and reminding all of God's activity.

The menorah is a seven-branch candlestick representing the light of the Torah. For Hanukkah, however, an eight-branched menorah is used. The extra candle is the servant candle, and is the one from which all others are lit.

Because the Torah is the crowning glory of life for Jewish people, a crown is sometimes used on coverings for the Torah. The scrolls of Torah are stored in a container, called an ark, which generally is covered with an ornate cloth called a mantle. The ark and mantle are often elaborately decorated with symbols, such as the lion of Judah. Because the Torah scroll, made of parchment from a kosher animal, is sacred and its pages are not to be touched, readers use a pointed stick called a yad. Even today, Torahs are written by hand in specially prepared ink and using a quill from a kosher bird. Scribes are trained for seven years.

A shofar is a ram's horn, blown as a call to repentance on Rosh Hashanah, the Jewish New Year. This holiday is the beginning of a ten-day preparation for the Day of Atonement, which is the most holy day in the Jewish calendar and a time of both fasting and repentance.

Sacred Practices & Gestures

Sacred practices can apply daily, weekly, annually, or over a lifetime's events. Reciting the Shema, the monotheistic creed taken from the

Torah, is a daily event. Keeping the Sabbath occurs weekly. Each year the festivals described above take place. Circumcision and bar or bat mitzvah are once-in-a-lifetime events. Each time someone dies, the mourners recite the Kaddish for seven days following death, and grieve for a year.

Food Restrictions

Kosher foods are those that can be eaten based on Jewish law. Animals that chew the cud and have cloven hooves, such as cows and lamb, and domestic poultry are considered kosher. Shellfish, pork, and birds of prey are forbidden. Keeping kosher also includes the method of preparing and storing the food. This includes animals which are slaughtered in a way to bring the least amount of pain and from which all blood is drained. In addition, dairy and meat products are to be kept separate, requiring separate refrigerators in the homes of the Orthodox.

Rites, Celebrations & Services

Sabbath is the weekly celebration honoring one of the Ten Commandments, which commands the people to honor the Sabbath by doing no work that day. The practice is rooted in the Genesis account that God rested on the seventh day after creating the world in six days. Because the Jewish day begins at sundown, the Sabbath lasts from Friday night to Saturday night. Special candles are lit and special food—included the braided egg bread called challah—for the evening meal is served. This day is filled with feasting, visiting, and worship.

Boys are circumcised at eight days of age. This rite, B'rit Milah, meaning "seal of the covenant," was first given to Abraham as a sign of the covenant. A trained circumciser, or mohel, may be a doctor or rabbi. The boy's name is officially announced at the ceremony. A girl's name is given at a special baby-naming ceremony or in the synagogue on the first Sabbath after she is born.

A boy becomes a "son of the commandment," or bar mitzvah, at age thirteen. At a special ceremony, the young man reads a portion of

Torah that he has prepared ahead of time. Most boys also give a speech at the service. Girls become bat mitzvah at age twelve. This ceremony developed in the twentieth century. Not all Orthodox communities will allow this rite. Girls may also read from the Torah and give a sermon in the synagogue, just as boys do.

When a Jewish person dies, mourners begin shiva, a seven-day mourning period. People usually gather at the home of the deceased, where mirrors are covered. In the home, the Kaddish, a collection of prayers that praise God and celebrate life, is recited. Traditionally, family members mourn for a full year, avoiding parties and festive occasions.

The Jewish calendar offers a series of feasts and festivals, beginning with Rosh Hashanah, the Jewish New Year. At this time, Jews recall the creation. They may also eat apples that have been dipped into honey and offer each other wishes for a sweet New Year. The next ten days are a time of reflection on the past year, preparing for Yom Kippur.

This Day of Atonement once included animal sacrifice at the Temple. Now it includes an all-day service at the synagogue and a twenty-five-hour fast. A ram's horn, called a shofar, is blown as a call to awaken to lead a holier life. The shofar reminds Jewish people of the ram that Abraham sacrificed in the place of his son, Isaac.

Passover, or Pesach, is the spring remembrance of God's deliverance of the people from slavery in Egypt. In the night that the Jewish people left Egypt, they were commanded to sacrifice a lamb for each household and sprinkle the blood on the lintels and doorposts. A destroying angel from God would "pass over" the homes with blood sprinkled. During the first two nights of Passover, a special meal is served known as a Seder, meaning order. The foods symbolize different aspects of the story of deliverance, which is told during the meal by the head of the family.

Shavuot has its origins as a harvest festival. This celebration of Moses receiving the Torah on Mount Sinai occurs fifty days after the second day of Passover. To welcome the first fruits of the season, the synagogue may be decorated with fruit and flowers. Traditionally, the Ten Commandments are read aloud in the synagogue.

Purim, which occurs in February or March, celebrates the deliverance of the Jews during their captivity in Persia in the fifth century BCE. The events of that experience are recorded in the Book of Esther in the Hebrew Bible (Tanakh). The book is read aloud during Purim.

Sukkot, the feast celebrating the end of the harvest, occurs in September or October. Jews recall God's provision for them in the wilderness when they left Egypt to return to Canaan. Traditionally, huts are made and decorated with flowers and fruits. The conclusion of Sukkot is marked by a synagogue service known as Simchat Torah, or Rejoicing in the Law. People sing and dance as the Torah scrolls are carried and passed from person to person.

Hanukkah, known as the Festival of Lights, takes place over eight days in December. It celebrates the rededicating of the Temple under the leader Judas Maccabeus, who led the people in recapturing the structure from Syria in 164 BCE. According to the story, the Jews had only enough oil in the Temple lamp to last one day, but the oil miraculously lasted for eight days, after which Judas Maccabeus re-dedicated the Temple. On each day of Hanukkah, one of the eight candles is lit until all are burning. The gift-giving custom associated with Hanukkah is relatively new, and may derive from traditional small gifts of candy or money. The practice may also have been encouraged among those integrated with communities that exchange gifts during the Christmas season.

Judy A. Johnson, MTS

Bibliography

Barnes, Trevor. *The Kingfisher Book of Religions*. New York: Kingfisher, 1999. Print.

"A Buffet to Suit All Tastes." *Economist* 28 Jul. 2012: Spec. section 4–6. Print.

Charing, Douglas. *Judaism*. London: DK, 2003. Print.

Coenen Snyder, Saskia. *Building a Public Judaism: Synagogues and Jewish Identity in Nineteenth-Century Europe*. Cambridge: Harvard UP, 2013. E-book.

Diamant, Anita. *Living a Jewish Life*. New York: Collins, 1996. Print.

Exler, Lisa and Rabbi Jill Jacobs. "A Judaism That Matters." *Journal of Jewish Communal Service* 87.1/2 (2012): 66–76. Print.

Gelernter, David Hillel. *Judaism: A Way of Being*. New Haven: Yale UP, 2009. E-book.

Kessler, Edward. *What Do Jews Believe?* New York: Walker, 2007. Print.

Krieger, Aliza Y. "The Role of Judaism in Family Relationships." *Journal of Multicultural Counseling & Development* 38.3 (2010): 154–65. Print.

Langley, Myrtle. *Religion*. New York: Knopf, 1996. Print.

Madsen, Catherine. "A Heart of Flesh: Beyond 'Creative Liturgy.'" *Cross Currents* 62.1 (2012): 11–20. Print.

Meredith, Susan. *The Usborne Book of World Religions*. London: Usborne, 1995. Print.

Schoen, Robert. *What I Wish My Christian Friends Knew About Judaism*. Chicago: Loyola, 2004. Print.

Stefnon, Matt. *Judaism: History, Belief, and Practice*. New York: Britannica Educational, 2012. E-book.

Wertheimer, Jack. "The Perplexities of Conservative Judaism." *Commentary* Sept. 2007: 38–44. Print.

Wilkinson, Philip. *Religions*. New York: DK, 2008. Print.

Sikhism

General Description

The youngest of the world religions, Sikhism has existed for only about five hundred years. Sikhism derives from the Sanskrit word *sishyas*, which means "disciple"; in the Punjabi language, it also means "disciple."

Number of Adherents Worldwide

An estimated 24.5 million people follow the Sikh religion. Most of the devotees live in Asia, particularly in the Punjab region of India (Wilkinson, p. 335).

Basic Tenets

Sikhism is a monotheistic religion. The deity is God, known as Nam, or Name. Other synonyms include the Divine, Ultimate, Ultimate Reality, Infinity, the Formless, Truth, and other attributes of God.

Sikhs adhere to three basic principles. These are hard work (kirt kao), worshipping the Divine Name (nam japo), and sharing what one has (vand cauko). Meditating on the Divine Name is seen as a method of moving toward a life totally devoted to God. In addition, Sikhs believe in karma, or moral cause and effect. They value hospitality to all, regardless of religion, and oppose caste distinctions. Sikhs delineate a series of five stages that move upward to gurmukh, total devotion to God. This service is called Seva. Sahaj, or tranquility, is practiced as a means of being united with God as well as of generating external good will. Sikhs are not in favor of external routines of religion; they may stop in their temple whenever it is convenient during the day.

Sikhism does not include a belief in the afterlife. Instead, the soul is believed to be reincarnated in successive lives and deaths, a belief borrowed from Hinduism. The goal is then to break this karmic cycle, and to merge the human spirit with that of God.

Sacred Text

The Guru Granth Sahib (also referred to as the Aad Guru Granth Sahib, or AGGS), composed of Adi Granth, meaning First Book, is the holy scripture of Sikhism. It is a collection of religious poetry that is meant to be sung. Called shabads, they were composed by the first five gurus, the ninth guru, and thirty-six additional holy men of northern India. Sikhs always show honor to the Guru Granth Sahib by carrying it above the head when in a procession.

A second major text is the Dasam Granth, or Tenth Book, created by followers of Guru Gobind Singh, the tenth guru. Much of it is devoted to retelling the Hindu stories of Krishna and Rama. Those who are allowed to read and care for the Granth Sahib are known as granthi. Granthi may also look after the gurdwara, or temple. In the gurdwara, the book rests on a throne with a wooden base and cushions covered in cloths placed in a prescribed order. If the book is not in use, it is covered with a cloth known as a rumala. When the book is read, a fan called a chauri is fanned over it as a sign of respect, just as followers of the gurus fanned them with chauris. At Amritsar, a city in northwestern India that houses the Golden Temple, the Guru Granth Sahib is carried on a palanquin (a covered, carried bed). If it is carried in the city, a kettle drum is struck and people welcome it by tossing rose petals.

Major Figures

Guru Nanak (1469–1539) is the founder of Sikhism. He was followed by nine other teachers, and collectively they are known as the Ten Gurus. Each of them was chosen by his predecessor and was thought to share the same spirit of that previous guru. Guru Arjan (1581–1606), the fifth guru, oversaw completion of the Golden Temple in Amritsar, India. Guru Gobind Singh (1675–1708) was the tenth and last human guru. He decreed that the True Guru henceforth would be the Granth Sahib, the scripture of the Sikhs. He also founded the Khalsa, originally a military order of male Sikhs willing to die for the faith; the term is now used to refer to all baptized Sikhs.

Major Holy Sites

Amritsar, India, is the holy city of Sikhism. Construction of the city began under Guru Ram Das (1574–1581), the fourth guru, during the 1570s. One legend says that the Muslim ruler, Emperor Akbar, gave the land to the third guru, Guru Amar Das (1552–74). Whether or not that is true, Amar Das did establish the location of Amritsar. He chose a site near a pool believed to hold healing water.

When construction of the Golden Temple began, only a small town existed. One legend says that a Muslim saint from Lahore, India, named Mian Mir laid the foundation stone of the first temple. It has been demolished and rebuilt three times. Although pilgrimage is not required of Sikhs, many come to see the shrines and the Golden Temple. They call it Harmandir Sahib, God's Temple, or Darbar Sahib, the Lord's Court. When the temple was completed during the tenure of the fifth guru, Arjan, he placed the first copy of the Guru Granth Sahib inside.

Every Sikh temple has a free kitchen attached to it, called a langar. After services, all people, regardless of caste or standing within the community, sit on the floor in a straight line and eat a simple vegetarian meal together. As a pilgrimage site, the langar serves 30,000–40,000 people daily, with more coming on Sundays and festival days. About forty volunteers work in the kitchen each day.

Major Rites & Celebrations

In addition to the community feasts at temple langars, Sikhs honor four rites of passage in a person's life: naming, marriage, initiation in Khalsa (pure) through the Amrit ceremony, and death.

There are eight major celebrations and several other minor ones in Sikhism. Half of them commemorate events in the lives of the ten gurus.

The others are Baisakhi, the new year festival; Diwali, the festival of light, which Hindus also celebrate; Hola Mahalla, which Gobind Singh created as an alternative to the Hindu festival of Holi, and which involves military parades; and the installing of the Guru Granth Sahib.

ORIGINS

History & Geography

The founder of Sikhism, Nanak, was born in 1469 CE in the Punjab region of northeast India, where both Hinduism and Islam were practiced. Both of these religions wanted control of the region. Nanak wanted the fighting between followers of these two traditions to end and looked for solutions to the violence.

Nanak blended elements of both religions and also combined the traditional apparel of both faiths to construct his clothing style. The Guru Granth Sahib further explains the division between Sikhs and the Islamic and Muslim faiths:

Nanak would become the first guru of the Sikh religion, known as Guru Nanak Dev. A Muslim musician named Bhai Mardana, considered the first follower, accompanied Nanak in his travels around India and Asia. Guru Nanak often sang, and singing remains an important part of worship for Sikhs. Before his death, Nanak renamed one of his disciples Angad, a word meaning "a part of his own self." He became Guru Angad Dev, the second guru, thus beginning the tradition of designating a successor and passing on the light to that person.

Guru Baba Ram Das, the fourth guru, who lived in the sixteenth century, began constructing Amritsar's Golden Temple. The structure was completed by his successor, Guru Arjan Dev, who also collected poems and songs written by the first four gurus and added his own. He included the work of Kabir and other Hindu and Muslim holy men as well. This became the Adi Granth, which he placed in the Golden Temple.

Guru Arjan was martyred in 1606 by Jehangir, the Muslim emperor. His son Hargobind became the sixth guru and introduced several important practices and changes. He wore two swords, representing both spiritual and worldly authority. Near the Golden Temple he had a building known as Akal Takht, or Throne of the Almighty, erected. In it was a court of justice as well as a group of administrators. Even today, orders and decisions enter the community from Akal Takht. Guru Hargobind was the last of the gurus with a direct link to Amritsar. Because of conflict with the Muslim rulers, he and all subsequent gurus moved from the city.

The tenth guru, Gobind Singh, created the Khalsa, the Community of the Pure, in 1699. The members of the Khalsa were to be known by five distinctive elements, all beginning with the letter *k*. These include kes, the refusal to cut the hair or trim the beard; kangha, the comb used to keep the long hair neatly combed in contrast to the Hindu ascetics who had matted hair; kaccha, shorts that would allow soldiers quick movement; kara, a thin steel bracelet worn to symbolize restraint; and kirpan, a short sword not to be used except in self-defense. Among other duties, members of this elite group were to defend the faith. Until the middle of the nineteenth century, when the British created an empire in India, the Khalsa remained largely undefeated.

In 1708, Guru Gobind Singh announced that he would be the final human guru. All subsequent leadership would come from the Guru Granth Sahib, now considered a living guru, the holy text Arjan had begun compiling more than a century earlier.

Muslim persecution under the Mughals led to the defeat of the Sikhs in 1716. The remaining Sikhs headed for the hills, re-emerging after decline of Mughal power. They were united under Ranjit Singh's kingdom from 1820 to 1839. They then came under the control of the British.

The British annexed the Punjab region, making it part of their Indian empire in 1849, and recruited Sikhs to serve in the army. The Sikhs remained loyal to the British during the Indian Mutiny of 1857–1858. As a result, they were given many privileges and land grants, and with

peace and prosperity, the first Singh Sabha was founded in 1873. This was an educational and religious reform movement.

During the early twentieth century, Sikhism was shaped in its more modern form. A group known as the Tat Khalsa, which was more progressive, became the dominant way of understanding the faith.

In 1897, a group of Sikh musicians within the British Army was invited to attend the Diamond Jubilee of Queen Victoria in England. They also traveled to Canada and were attracted by the nation's prairies, which were perfect for farming. The first group of Sikhs came to Canada soon after. By 1904, more than two hundred Sikhs had settled in British Columbia. Some of them later headed south to Washington, Oregon, and California in the United States. The first Sikh gurdwara in the United States was constructed in Stockton, California, in 1912. Sikhs became farmers, worked in lumber mills, and helped to construct the Western Pacific railroad. Yuba City, California, has one of the world's largest Sikh temples, built in 1968.

Sikh troops fought for Britain in World War I, achieving distinction. Following the war, in 1919, however, the British denied the Sikhs the right to gather for their New Year festival. When the Sikhs disobeyed, the British troops fired without warning on 10,000 Sikhs, 400 of whom were killed. This became known as the first Amritsar Massacre.

The British government in 1925 did give the Sikhs the right to help manage their own shrines. A fragile peace ensued between the British and the Sikhs, who again fought for the British Empire during World War II.

After the war ended, the Sikh hope for an independent state was dashed by the partition of India and Pakistan in 1947. Pakistan was in the Punjab region; thus, 2.5 million Sikhs lived in a Muslim country where they were not welcome. Many of them became part of the mass internal migration that followed Indian independence.

In 1966, a state with a Sikh majority came into existence after Punjab boundaries were redrawn. Strife continued throughout second half of twentieth century, however, as a result of continuing demands for Punjab autonomy. A second massacre at Amritsar occurred in 1984, resulting in the death of 450 Sikhs (though some estimates of the death toll are higher). Indian troops, under orders from Indian Prime Minister Indira Gandhi, fired on militant leaders of Sikhs, who had gone to the Golden Temple for refuge. This attack was considered a desecration of a sacred place, and the prime minister was later assassinated by her Sikh bodyguards in response. Restoration of the Akal Takht, the administrative headquarters, took fifteen years. The Sikh library was also burned, consuming ancient manuscripts.

In 1999, Sikhs celebrated the three-hundredth anniversary of the founding of Khalsa. There has been relative peace in India since that event. In the United States, however, Sikhs became the object of slander and physical attack following the acts of terrorism on September 11, 2001, as some Americans could not differentiate between Arab head coverings and Sikh turbans.

Founder or Major Prophet

Guru Nanak Dev was born into a Hindu family on April 15, 1469. His family belonged to the merchant caste, Khatri. His father worked as an accountant for a Muslim, who was also a local landlord. Nanak was educated in both the Hindu and Islamic traditions. According to legends, his teachers soon realized they had nothing further to teach him. After a direct revelation from Ultimate Reality that he received as a young man, Nanak proclaimed that there was neither Muslim nor Hindu. God had told Nanak "Rejoice in my Name," which became a central doctrine of Sikhism.

Nanak began to preach, leaving his wife and two sons behind. According to tradition, he traveled not only throughout India, but also eventually to Iraq, Saudi Arabia, and Mecca. This tradition and others were collected in a volume known as Janamsakhis. A Muslim servant of the family, Mardana, who also played a three-stringed musical instrument called the rebec, accompanied him, as did a Hindu poet, Bala Sandhu, who had been a friend from childhood

(though the extent of his importance or existence is often considered controversial).

Nanak traveled as an itinerant preacher for a quarter century and then founded a village, Kartarpur, on the bank of Punjab's Ravi River. Before his death he chose his successor, beginning a tradition that was followed until the tenth and final human guru.

Philosophical Basis

When Guru Nanak Dev, the first guru, began preaching in 1499 at about age thirty, he incorporated aspects of both Hinduism and Islam. From Hinduism, he took the ideas of karma and reincarnation. From Islam, he borrowed the Ultimate as the name of God. Some scholars see the influence of the religious reformer and poet Kabir, who lived from 1440 until 1518. Kabir merged the Bhakti (devotional) side of Hinduism with the Islamic Sufis, who were mystics.

Within the Hindu tradition in northern India was a branch called the Sants. The Sants believed that God was both with form and without form, unable to be represented concretely. Most of the Sants were illiterate and poor, but created poems that spoke of the divine being experienced in all things. This idea also rooted itself in Sikhism.

Guru Nanak Dev, who was raised as a Hindu, rejected the caste system in favor of equality of all persons. He also upheld the value of women, rejecting the burning of widows and female infanticide. When eating a communal meal, first begun as a protest against caste, everyone sits in a straight line and shares karah prasad (a pudding), which is provided by those of all castes. However, Sikhs are expected to marry within their caste. In some cases, especially in the United Kingdom, gurdwaras (places of worship) for a particular caste exist.

Holy Places

Amritsar, especially the Golden Temple, which was built in the sixteenth century under the supervision of the fifth guru, Guru Arjan, is the most sacred city.

Ram Das, the fourth guru, first began constructing a pool on the site in 1577. He called it

Amritsar, the pool of nectar. This sacred reflecting pool is a pilgrimage destination. Steps on the southern side of the pool allow visitors to gather water in bottles, to drink it, to bathe in it, or to sprinkle it on themselves.

SIKHISM IN DEPTH

Sacred Symbols

The khanda is the major symbol of Sikhism. It features a two-edged sword, representing justice and freedom, in the center. It is surrounded by a circle, a symbol of both balance and of the unity of God and humankind. A pair of curved swords (kirpans) surrounds the circle. One sword stands for religious concerns, the other for secular concerns. The khanda appears on Sikh flags, which are flown over every temple.

Members of the Khalsa have five symbols. They do not cut their hair, and men do not trim their beards. This symbol, kes, is to indicate a harmony with the ways of nature. To keep the long hair neat, a comb called a kangha is used. The third symbol is the kara, a bracelet usually made of steel to represent continuity and strength. When the Khalsa was first formed, soldiers wore loose-fitting shorts called kaccha. They were worn to symbolize moral restraint and purity. The final symbol is a short sword known as a kirpan, to be used only in self-defense. When bathing in sacred waters, the kirpan is tucked into the turban, which is worn to cover the long hair. The turban, which may be one of many colors, is wound from nearly five yards of cloth.

Sacred Practices & Gestures

Sikhs use Sat Sri Akal (truth is timeless) as a greeting, putting hands together and bowing toward the other person. To show respect, Sikhs keep their heads covered with a turban or veil. Before entering a temple, they remove their shoes. Some Sikhs may choose to wear a bindhi, the dot on the forehead usually associated with Hinduism.

When Guru Gobind Singh initiated the first men into the Khalsa, he put water in a steel bowl and added sugar, stirring the mixture with his sword and reciting verses from the Guru Granth as he did so. He thus created amrit (immortal), a holy water also used in baptism, or the Amrit ceremony. The water represents mental clarity, while sugar stands for sweetness. The sword invokes military courage, and the chanting of verses brings a poetic spirituality.

The Sikh ideal of bringing Ultimate Reality into every aspect of the day is expressed in prayers throughout the day. Daily morning prayer (Bani) consists of five different verses, most of them the work of one of the ten gurus; there are also two sets of evening prayers. Throughout the day, Sikhs repeat the Mul Mantra, "Ikk Oan Kar" (There is one Being). This is the first line of a brief creedal statement about Ultimate Reality.

Food Restrictions

Sikhs are not to eat halal meat, which is the Muslim equivalent of kosher. Both tobacco and alcohol are forbidden. Many Sikhs are vegetarians, although this is not commanded. Members of the Khalsa are not permitted to eat meat slaughtered according to Islamic or Hindu methods, because they believe these means cause pain to the animal.

Rites, Celebrations, & Services

The Sikhs observe four rite of passage rituals, with each emphasizing their distinction from the Hindu traditions. After a new mother is able to get up and bathe, the new baby is given a birth and naming ceremony in the gurdwara. The child is given a name based on the first letter of hymn from the Guru Granth Sahib at random. All males are additionally given the name Singh (lion); all females also receive the name Kaur (princess).

The marriage ceremony (anand karaj) is the second rite of passage. Rather than circle a sacred fire as the Hindus do, the Sikh couple walks four times around a copy of the Guru Granth Sahib, accompanied by singing. The bride often wears red, a traditional color for the Punjabi.

The amrit initiation into the Khalsa is considered the most important rite. It need not take place in a temple, but does require that five

Sikhs who are already Khalsa members conduct the ceremony. Amrit initiation may occur any time after a child is old enough to read the Guru Granth and understand the tenets of the faith. Some people, however, wait until their own children are grown before accepting this rite.

The funeral rite is the fourth and final rite of passage. A section of the Guru Granth is read. The body, dressed in the Five "K's," is cremated soon after death.

Initiation into the Khalsa is now open to both men and women. The earliest gurus opposed the Hindu custom of sati, which required a widow to be burned on her husband's funeral pyre. They were also against the Islamic custom of purdah, which required women to be veiled and covered in public. Women who are menstruating are not excluded from worship, as they are in some religions. Women as well as men can be leaders of the congregation and are permitted to read from the Guru Granth and recite sacred hymns.

The Sikh houses of worship are known as gurdwaras and include a langar, the communal dining area. People remove their shoes and cover their heads before entering. They touch their foreheads to the floor in front of the scripture to show respect. The service itself is in three parts. The first segment is Kirtan, singing hymns (kirtans) accompanied by musical instruments, which can last for several hours. It is followed by a set prayer called the Ardas, which has three parts. The first and final sections cannot be altered. In the first, the virtues of the gurus are extolled. In the last, the divine name is honored. In the center of the Ardas is a list of the Khalsa's troubles and victories, which a prayer leader recites in segments and to which the congregation responds with Vahiguru, considered a word for God. At the end of the service, members eat karah prasad, sacred food made of raw sugar, clarified butter, and coarse wheat flour. They then adjourn for a communal meal, Langar, the third section of worship.

Sikhism does not have a set day for worship similar to the Jewish Sabbath or Christian Sunday worship. However, the first day of the month on the Indian lunar calendar, sangrand,

and the darkest night of the month, masia, are considered special days. Sangrand is a time for praying for the entire month. Masia is often considered an auspicious time for bathing in the holy pool at the temple.

Four of the major festivals that Sikhs observe surround important events in the lives of the gurus. These are known as gurpurabs, or anniversaries. Guru Nanak's birthday, Guru Gobind Singh's birthday, and the martyrdoms of the Gurus Arjan and Tegh Bahadur comprise the four main gurpurabs. Sikhs congregate in the gurudwaras to hear readings of the Guru Granth and lectures by Sikh scholars.

Baisakhi is the Indian New Year, the final day before the harvest begins. On this day in 1699, Guru Gobind Singh formed the first Khalsa, adding even more importance to the day for Sikhs. Each year, a new Sikh flag is placed at all temples.

Diwali, based on a word meaning string of lights, is a Hindu festival. For Sikhs, it is a time to remember the return of the sixth guru, Hargobind, to Amritsar after the emperor had imprisoned him. It is celebrated for three days at the Golden Temple. Sikhs paint and whitewash their houses and decorate them with candles and earthenware lamps.

Hola Mohalla, meaning attack and place of attack, is the Sikh spring festival, which corresponds to the Hindu festival Holi. It is also a three-day celebration and a time for training Sikhs as soldiers. Originally, it involved military exercises and mock battles, as well as competitions in archery, horsemanship, and wrestling. In contemporary times, the festival includes athletic contests, discussion, and singing.

Judy A. Johnson, MTS

Bibliography

Barnes, Trevor. *The Kingfisher Book of Religions*. New York: Kingfisher, 1999. Print.

Dhanjal, Beryl. *Amritsar*. New York: Dillon, 1993. Print.

Dhavan, Purnima. *When Sparrows Became Hawks: The Making of the Sikh Warrior Tradition, 1699–1799*. Oxford: Oxford UP, 2011. Print.

Eraly, Abraham, et. al. *India*. New York: DK, 2008. Print.

Harley, Gail M. *Hindu and Sikh Faiths in America*. New York: Facts on File, 2003. Print.

Jakobsh, Doris R. *Sikhism and Women: History, Texts, and Experience*. Oxford, New York: Oxford UP, 2010. Print.

Jhutti-Johal, Jagbir. *Sikhism Today*. London, New York: Continuum, 2011. Print.

Langley, Myrtle. *Religion*. New York: Knopf, 1996. Print.

Mann, Gurinder Singh. *Sikhism*. Upper Saddle River: Prentice, 2004. Print.

Meredith, Susan. *The Usborne Book of World Religions*. London: Usborne, 1995. Print.

Sidhu, Dawinder S. and Neha Singh Gohil. *Civil Rights in Wartime: The Post-9/11 Sikh Experience*. Ashgate, 2009. E-book.

Singh, Nikky-Guninder Kaur. *Sikhism*. New York: Facts on File, 1993. Print.

Singh, Nikky-Guninder Kaur. *Sikhism: An Introduction*. Tauris, 2011. E-book.

Singh, Surinder. *Introduction to Sikhism and Great Sikhs of the World*. Gurgaon: Shubhi, 2012. Print.

Wilkinson, Philip. *Religions*. New York: DK, 2008. Print.

Index